World Civilizations

Adam Hall
Fall 2002

WORLD CIVILIZATIONS

The Global Experience

Volume 2

❖❖

THIRD EDITION

PETER N. STEARNS
George Mason University

MICHAEL ADAS
Rutgers University

STUART B. SCHWARTZ
Yale University

MARC J. GILBERT
North Georgia College & State University

New York San Francisco Boston
London Toronto Sydney Tokyo Singapore Madrid
Mexico City Munich Paris Cape Town Hong Kong Montreal

Publisher: Priscilla McGeehon
Developmental Director: Lisa Pinto
Marketing Manager: Sue Westmoreland
Supplements Editor: Jennifer Ackerman
Senior Production Manager: Eric Jorgensen
Project Coordination, Text Design, and Electronic Page Makeup: Electronic Publishing Services Inc., NYC
Cover Designer/Manager: Nancy Danahy
Cover Photo: © PhotoSpin. Detail of a woven bag from Africa.
Photo Researcher: PhotoSearch, Inc.
Senior Manufacturing Buyer: Dennis J. Para
Printer and Binder: Quebecor World—Versailles
Cover Printer: Coral Graphic Services

Library of Congress Cataloging-in-Publication Data

Stearns, Peter N.
   World civilizations: the global experience / Peter N. Stearns, Michael Adas, Stuart B.
Schwartz, Marc J. Gilbert.—3rd ed.
      p.cm.
   includes bibliographical references and index.
      ISBN 0-321-03812-6 -- ISBN 0-321-04479-7--ISBN 0-321-03813-4
      1. Civilization--History. 2. Civilization--History--Sources. I. Adas, Michael, II.
Schwartz, Stuart B. III. Title.

CB69 .S84 2001
909--dc21   00-041203

Please visit our website at http://www.awl.com/stearns

ISBN 0-321-04479-7 (SVE version)/ 0-321-03812-6 (Volume 1)/0-321-03813-4 (Volume 2)

2 3 4 5 6 7 8 9 10—RNV—03 02 01

Brief Contents

Detailed Contents

⬙

PART 4

The World Shrinks,
1450–1750   514

PART 5

Industrialization and Western Global Hegemony, 1750–1914 690

Chapter 29

The Industrialization of the West, 1760–1914 696

Chapter 30

Industrialization and Imperialism: The Making of the European Global Order 726

Chapter 31

The Consolidation of Latin America, 1830–1920 754

Chapter 32

Civilizations in Crisis: The Ottoman Empire, the Islamic Heartlands, and Qing China 780

PART 6

The 20th Century in World History   828

List of Maps

Preface

When we began to work on the first edition of *World Civilizations: The Global Experience* in the early 1990s, we did so out of the conviction that it was time for a world history textbook truly global in its approach and coverage and yet manageable and accessible for today's college students. Our commitment to that goal continues with this third edition. We seek to present a truly global history—one that discusses the evolution and development of the world's leading civilizations—and balances that coverage with examination of the major stages in the nature and degree of interactions among different peoples and societies around the globe. We view world history not as a parade of facts to be memorized or a collection of the individual histories of various societies. Rather, world history is the study of historical events in a global context. It combines meaningful synthesis of independent development within societies with comparative analysis of the results of contacts between societies.

Several decades of scholarship in world history and in area studies by historians and other social scientists have yielded a wealth of information and interpretive generalizations. The challenge is to create a coherent and comprehensible framework for organizing all this information. Our commitment to world history stems from our conviction that students will understand and appreciate the present world by studying the myriad forces that have shaped that world and created our place within it. Furthermore, study of the past in order to make sense of the present will help them prepare to meet the challenges of the future.

APPROACH

The two principal distinguishing characteristics of this book are its global orientation and its analytical emphasis. This is a true *world* history textbook. It deals seriously with the Western tradition but does not award it pride of place or a preeminence that diminishes other areas of the world. *World Civilizations: The Global Experience* examines the histories of all areas of the world and all peoples according to their growing or waning importance. It also considers what happened across regions by examining cross-civilizational developments such as migration, trade, the spread of religion, disease, plant exchange, and cultural interchange. Civilizations or societies sometimes slighted in world history textbooks—such as the nomadic societies of Asia, Latin American societies, the nations of the Pacific Rim, and the societies of nonurban sedentary peoples—receive attention here.

Many world history textbooks function as factual compendia, leaving analytical challenge to the classroom. Our goal throughout this book has been to relate fact to interpretation while still allowing ample opportunity for classroom exploration. Our analytical emphasis focuses on how key aspects of the past and present have been shaped by global forces such as the exchange of technology and ideas. By encouraging students to learn how to assess continuity and change, we seek to help them relate the past to the present. Through analysis and interpretation students become active, engaged learners, rather than passive readers of the facts of historical events.

PERIODIZATION

This text pays a great deal of attention to periodization, an essential requirement for coherent presentation. *World Civilizations: The Global Experience* identifies six periods in world history, each period determined by three basic criteria: a geographical rebalancing among major civilizational areas, an increase in the intensity and extent of contact across civilizations, (or, in the case of the earliest period, cross-regional contact), and the emergence of new and roughly parallel developments in most, if not, all of these major civilizations. The book is divided into six parts corresponding to these six major periods of world history. In each part, basic characteristics of each period are referred to in chapters that discuss the major civilizations in the Middle East, Africa, Asia, Europe and the Americas, and in several cross-cutting chapters that address larger world trends. Part intro-

ductions identify the fundamental new characteristics of parallel or comparable developments and regional or international exchange that define each period.

After sketching the hunting and gathering phase of human existence, Part I, "The Origins of Civilization," focuses on the rise of agriculture and the emergence of civilization in parts of Asia, Africa, Central America, and southeastern Europe—the sequence of developments that set world history in motion from the origin of the human species until about 3000 years ago.

Part II, "The Classical Period in World History," deals with the growing complexity of major civilizations in several areas of the world. During the classical period, civilizations developed a new capacity to integrate large regions and diverse groups of people through overarching cultural and political systems. Yet many regions and societies remained unconnected to the increasingly complex centers of civilization. Coverage of the classical period of world history, then, must consider both types of societies.

"The Postclassical Era," the period covered in Part III of the book, saw the emergence of new commercial and cultural linkages that brought most civilizations into contact with one another and with nomadic groups. The decline of the great classical empires, the rise of new civilizational centers, and the emergence of a network of world contacts, including the spread of major religions, are characteristics of the postclassical era.

Developments in world history over the three centuries from 1450 to 1750 mark a fourth period in world history—the period covered in Part IV, "The World Shrinks." The rise of the West, the intensification of global contacts, the growth of trade, and the formation of new empires define this period and separate it from the preceding postclassical period.

Part V, "Industrialization and Western Global Hegemony, 1750–1914," covers the period of world history dominated by the advent of industrialization in Western Europe and growing European imperialism. The increase and intensification of commercial interchange, technological innovations, and cultural contacts all reflected the growth of Western power and the spread of Western influence.

"The 20th Century in World History," the focus of Part VI, defines the characteristics of this period as the retreat of Western imperialism, the rise of new political systems such as communism, the surge of the United States and the Soviet Union, and a variety of economic innovations including the achievements of Japan and the Pacific Rim. Part VI deals with this most recent period of world history and some of its portents for the future.

THEMES

We have tried to make world history accessible to today's students by using several themes as filters for the vast body of information that constitutes the subject. These themes provide a perspective and a framework for understanding where we have come from, where we are now, and where we might be headed.

Commonalities Among Societies

World Civilizations: The Global Experience traces several key features of all societies. It looks at the technologies people have developed—for humans were tool-making animals from an early date—and at the impact of technology on the physical environment. It examines social organization, including the inequalities between the two genders and different social classes. And it discusses the role of human agency: how individuals have shaped historical forces. These three areas—technology and the environment, inequalities and reactions to inequalities, and human agency—are three filters through which to examine any human society.

Contacts Between Civilizations

Large regional units that defined aspects of economic exchange, political institutions, and cultural values began to spring up more than 5000 years ago. These civilizations—that is, societies that generate and use an economic surplus beyond basic survival needs—created a general framework for the lives of most people ever since. But different regions had a variety of contacts, involving migration, trade, religious missionaries, exchanges of diseases and plants, and wars. Formal relations between societies—what we now call international relations—also were organized. Many aspects of world history can be viewed in terms of whether societies had regular connections, haphazard interchange, or some mix of the two.

FEATURES

The features in *World Civilizations: The Global Experience* have been carefully constructed and honed over the course of three editions. Our aim has been to provide students with tools to help them learn how to analyze change and continuity.

New Full-Color Design

The most immediately visible change to *World Civilizations: The Global Experience* is that this edition is published in full color and a larger format. Full-color maps, specially developed to provide a global orientation, help students easily recognize and distinguish geographical features and areas. Maps in the part and chapter introductions highlight major developments during each period and familiarize students with all areas of the world. Full-color photos help bring history to life.

Part Introductions

Part introductions define the characteristics of the period of world history covered in that part, examine parallel or comparable developments that occurred among different societies as well as the new kinds of global contacts that arose, and identify key themes to be explored in the chapters that follow. Part introductions give students a context for analyzing the content of each chapter as well as a framework for seeing how the chapters within a part relate to one another. Timelines summarize the events of the chronological period covered.

Chapter Introductions

Introductions to each chapter identify the key themes and analytical issues that will be examined in the chapter. Chapter 10, for example, on the spread of civilization, examines how cultures in four dramatically different areas of the world were influenced by developments in the centers of civilization. The chapter introduction begins with discussion of the basic issues debated over the spread of civilizations, such as whether early breakthroughs like agriculture were repeatedly reinvented or spread through contact and migration. Then it goes on to consider different processes of cultural expansion, such as conquest, trade, and missionary activity. This introduction gives the reader a context for understanding the similarities and differences in the diverse civilizations discussed in the chapter: sub-Saharan Africa, northern Europe, Japan, and the Pacific islands.

Timelines

The timelines have been newly designed for this edition. Each part begins with an extensive timeline that outlines the period under consideration. The timeline includes events in all the societies involved. Each chapter begins with a timeline that orients the student to the period, countries, and key events of the chapter.

Section-Opening Focal Points

Focal point sections after each main chapter head give students a focus with which to understand the topic. In Chapter 30, on industrialism and imperialism, the first section of the chapter discusses how imperialism in Asia drew the European powers of the time. The focal point in that section introduces the contrasts between powers that were willing to adopt the lifestyles of the people they sought to rule, such as the Dutch in Java, and those that imposed Westernization from early on, such as the British in India. This focus gives the reader a point of view with which to evaluate colonization during a particular era, not just a set of places, dates, and events to memorize.

Visualizing the Past

New to this edition and appearing in selected chapters, *Visualizing the Past* asks students to deal with pictorial evidence, maps, or tables to interpret historical patterns. Text accompanying the illustrations provides a level of analysis, and a series of questions draws the students into providing their own analyses. In Chapter 1, for example, this feature presents and analyzes various figures of women in early art.

Documents

Excerpts from original documents are included in *Document* boxes to give the reader contact with diverse voices of the past. We share a firm commitment to include social history involving women, the nonelite, and experiences and events outside the spheres of politics and high culture. Each document is preceded by a brief, scene-setting narration and followed by probing questions to guide the reader through an analysis of the document. In Chapter 22, on the transformation of the West, the *Document* box presents two essays with different points of view from the early 17th century that show the tensions between the genders about the role of women. The notes preceding the essay lay out the changing conditions and the resulting debate. After the essays, the reader is prompted to compare the two in various ways and consider which represents a break with Western gender tradition.

In Depth Sections

Each chapter contains an analytical essay on a topic of broad application. The essay is followed by questions intended to probe student appreciation of the topic and suggest questions or interpretive issues for further thought. The *In Depth* section in Chapter 15, which covers the Byzantine Empire, steps aside slightly from the discussion of Byzantium and Orthodox Europe to look at the question of where one civilization ends and another begins—a question still relevant today. How does one define states that sit between clearly defined civilizations and share some characteristics of each culture? The analytical argument in this section encompasses contested borders, mainstream culture, religion, language, and patterns of trade and looks more specifically at Poland, Hungary, and Lithuania, with elements of both western Europe and Russia in their cultures. The questions after the analysis prompt the reader to think about these difficult-to-define civilization border areas.

Conclusions

Each chapter ends with a conclusion that goes beyond a mere summary of events. Conclusions reiterate the key themes and issues raised in the chapter and offer additional insights into the chapter. In Chapter 14, on African civilizations and the spread of Islam, the Conclusion points out that the chapter focused on the Sudanic states and the Swahili coast, but goes on to give perspective on the effect of Islam on sub-Saharan Africa. Other examples can be found in the chapters covering the 20th century, in which Conclusions highlight events of which students have had first-hand experience.

Further Readings

Each chapter includes several annotated paragraphs of suggested readings. The reader receives reliable guidance on a variety of books: source materials, standards in the field, encyclopedic coverage, more readable general interest titles, and the like.

On The Web

New to this edition are annotated website lists. Every effort has been made to find reliable, stable websites that are likely to endure. Even if some disappear, however, the annotations give the reader the key words necessary to search for similar sites.

Glossary

At the back of the book, preceding the index, is a comprehensive glossary, another feature that sets this book apart. It includes conceptual terms, frequently used foreign terms, and names of important geographic regions and key characters on the world stage. Much of world history will be new to most students, and this glossary will help them develop a global vocabulary.

ACKNOWLEDGMENTS

Grateful acknowledgment is made to the following colleagues and reviewers, who made many useful suggestions during the development of this edition.

Norman R. Bennett
Boston University

Houri Berberian
California State University

Martin Berger
Youngstown State University

Kenneth J. Bindas
Kent State University

Suzanne Cahill
University of California at San Diego

Daniel Castro
Southwestern University

John W. Cell
Duke University

Mark W. Chavalas
University of Wisconsin—La Crosse

Joan L. Coffey
Sam Houston State University

Steven C. Davidson
Southwestern University

Stephen F. Englehart
California State Polytechnic University

Richard M. Golden
University of North Texas

Jonathon Grant
Florida State University

Tim Keirn
California State University, Long Beach

James Long
Colorado State University

Thomas C. Mackey
University of Louisville

Farid Mahdavi
San Diego State University

Pamela McVay
Ursuline College

James Overfield
University of Vermont

Melvin E. Page
East Tennessee State University

Phyllis E. Pobst
Arkansas State University

Dennis Reinhertz
University of Texas at Arlington

John A. Ricks
Middle Georgia College

Robert E. Rook
Fort Hays State University

David R. Smith
California State Polytechnic University, Pomona

Alice Spitzer
Washington State University

Tracy Steele
Sam Houston State University

Sara W. Tucker
Washburn University

Kenneth H. Williams
Alcorn State University

Richard S. Williams
Washington State University

Margaret A. Wingate
Broome Community College

PETER N. STEARNS

MICHAEL ADAS

STUART B. SCHWARTZ

MARC JASON GILBERT

Supplements

FOR QUALIFIED COLLEGE ADOPTERS

Companion Website (www.awl.com/stearns) Instructors can take advantage of the online course companion that supports this text. The instructor section of the website includes the instructor's manual, a list of instructor links, downloadable images from the text, and Syllabus Builder, our comprehensive course management system.

Instructor's Resource Manual by Norman Bennett of Boston University. The manual includes chapter summaries, discussion suggestions, critical thinking exercises, map exercises, primary source analysis suggestions, and term paper and essay topics. A special "Instructor's Tool Kit" by George Jewsbury of Oklahoma State University includes audiovisual suggestions.

Guide to Advanced Media and Internet Resources for World History, Second Edition, by Richard Rothaus of St. Cloud State University. This guide provides a comprehensive review of CD-ROM, software, and Internet resources for world civilization study, including a list of the primary resources, syllabi and articles, and discussion groups available online.

Discovering World History Through Maps and Views, Second Edition, by Gerald Danzer, University of Illinois, Chicago, winner of the AHA's James Harvey Robinson Award for his work in developing map transparencies. The second edition of this set of 100 four-color transparencies is updated to include the newest reference maps and the most useful source materials. These transparencies are bound with introductory materials in a three-ring binder with an introduction about teaching history, maps, and detailed commentary on each transparency. The collection includes source and reference maps, views and photos, urban plans, building diagrams, and works of art.

Test Bank by Elizabeth Williams of Oklahoma State University. A total of 2300 questions includes 50 multiple-choice questions and 5 essay questions per chapter. Each test is referenced by topic, type, and text page number.

TestGen Computerized Testing System. This easy-to-customize test generation software package presents a wealth of multiple-choice, true-false, short answer, and essay questions and allows users to add, delete, and print test items.

Map Transparencies to Accompany World Civilizations: The Global Experience, Third Edition. These text-specific transparencies are available to all adopters.

FOR THE STUDENT

Companion Website (www.awl.com/stearns) The online course companion provides a wealth of resources for students using *World Civilizations.* Students can access chapter summaries, practice test questions, a guide to doing research on the Internet, and over 400 annotated web links with critical thinking questions.

Student Study Guide in two volumes, prepared by Elizabeth Williams of Oklahoma State University. Each volume includes chapter outlines, timelines, map exercises, multiple-choice practice tests, and critical thinking and essay questions.

StudyWizard Computerized Tutorial. This interactive program, prepared by Elizabeth Williams of Oklahoma State University, features multiple-choice, true-false, and short answer questions. It also contains a glossary and gives users immediate test scores and answer explanations.

Longman World History Atlas. This four-color atlas contains 56 historical maps designed especially for world history courses. It is free when bundled with the text.

World History Map Workbook, Second Edition, in two volumes. Volume I (to 1600) prepared by Glee Wilson of Kent State University. Each volume includes more than 40 maps accompanied by more than 120 pages of exercises. Each volume is designed to teach the location of various countries and their relationship to one another. Also includes exercises that enhance students' critical thinking abilities.

Mapping World Civilizations: Student Activities, a free student workbook by Gerald Danzer, University of Illinois, Chicago. The workbook features map skill exercises written to enhance students' basic geographic literacy. The exercises provide ample opportunities for interpreting maps and analyzing cartographic materials as historical documents. The instructor is entitled to one free copy of *Mapping World Civilizations: Student Activities* for each copy of the text purchased from Longman.

Documents in World History in two volumes: Volume I, *The Great Tradition: From Ancient Times to 1500;* Volume II, *The Modern Centuries: From 1500 to the Present,* edited by Peter N. Stearns of Carnegie Melon University. This collection of primary source documents illustrates the human characteristics of key civilizations during major stages of world history.

Prologue

The study of history is the study of the past. Knowledge of the past gives us perspective on our societies today. It shows different ways in which people have identified problems and tried to resolve them, as well as important common impulses in the human experience. History can inform through its variety, remind us of some human constants, and provide a common vocabulary and examples that aid in mutual communication.

The study of history is also the study of change. Historians analyze major changes in the human experience over time and examine the ways in which those changes connect the past to the present. They try to distinguish between superficial and fundamental change, as well as between sudden and gradual change. They explain why change occurs and what impact it has. Finally, they pinpoint continuities from the past along with innovations. History, in other words, is a study of human society in motion.

World history is not simply a collection of the histories of various societies but a subject in its own right. World history is the study of historical events in a global context. It does not attempt to sum up everything that has happened in the past. It focuses on two principal subjects: the evolution of leading societies and the interaction among different peoples around the globe.

THE EMERGENCE OF WORLD HISTORY

Serious attempts to deal with world history are relatively recent. Many historians have attempted to locate the evolution of their own societies in the context of developments in a larger "known world:" Herodotus, though particularly interested in the origins of Greek culture, wrote also of developments around the Mediterranean; Ibn Khaldun wrote of what he knew about developments in Africa and Europe as well as in the Muslim world. But not until the 20th century, with an increase in international contacts and a vastly expanded knowledge of the historical patterns of major societies, did a full world history become possible. In the West, world history depended on a growing realization that the world could not be understood simply as a mirror reflecting the West's greater glory or as a stage for Western-dominated power politics. This hard-won realization continues to meet some resistance. Nevertheless, historians in several societies have attempted to develop an international approach to the subject that includes but goes beyond, merely establishing a context for the emergence of their own civilizations.

Understanding of world history has been increasingly shaped by two processes that define historical inquiry: debate and detective work. Historians are steadily uncovering new data not just about particular societies but about lesser-known contacts. Looking at a variety of records and artifacts, for example, they learn how an 8th century battle between Arab and Chinese forces in Central Asia brought Chinese prisoners who knew how to make paper to the Middle East, where their talents were quickly put to work. And they argue about world history frameworks: how central European actions should be in the world history of the past five hundred years, and whether a standard process of modernization is useful or distorting in measuring developments in modern Turkey or China. Through debate come advances in how world history is understood and conceptualized, just as the detective work advances the factual base.

WHAT CIVILIZATION MEANS

Most humans have always shown a tendency to operate in groups that provide a framework for economic activities, governance, and cultural forms-beliefs and artistic styles. These groups, or societies, may be quite small-hunting and gathering bands often numbering no more than 60 people. World history usually focuses on somewhat larger societies, with more extensive economic relationships (at least for trade) and cultures.

One vital kind of grouping is called civilization. The idea of civilization as a type of human society is central to most world history, though it also generates debate and though historians are now agreed that it is not the only kind of grouping that warrants attention. Civilizations, unlike some other societies, generate surpluses beyond basic survival needs. This in turn promotes a variety of specialized occupations and heightened social differentiation, as well as regional and long-distance trading networks. Surplus production also spurs the growth of cities and the development of formal states, with some bureaucracy, in contrast to more informal methods of governing. Most civilizations have also developed systems of writing.

Civilizations are not necessarily better than other kinds of societies. Nomadic groups have often demonstrated great creativity in technology and social relationships, as well as promoting global contacts more vigorously than settled civilizations sometimes did. And there is disagreement about exactly what defines a civilization—for example, what about cases like the Incas where there was not writing?

Used carefully, however, the idea of civilization as a form of human social organization, and an unusually extensive one, has merit. Along with agriculture (which developed earlier), civilizations have given human groups the capacity to fundamentally reshape their environments and to dominate most other living creatures. The history of civilizations embraces most of the people who have ever lived; their literature, formal scientific discoveries, art, music, architecture, and inventions; their most elaborate social, political, and economic systems; their brutality and destruction caused by conflicts; their exploitation of other species; and their degradation of the environment—a result of changes in technology and the organization of work.

To be truly global in scope, our inquiry into the history of civilizations must not be constricted by the narrow, Western-centric standards for determining what is civilized. Many "civilized" peoples have regarded outsiders with different physical features and cultures as uncouth "barbarians" or even subhumans. Even more recently, in awarding a society civilized status, most European and American writers have insisted that monumental buildings, cities, writing, and a high level of technology be present.

In fact, different civilizations have stressed different facets of human creativity. The Chinese have consistently built large and effective political systems. But Chinese thinkers have formulated only one major religion, Daoism, and it has had only a limited appeal within and beyond East Asia. By contrast, the peoples of India have produced some of humankind's most sophisticated and sublime religions, in Hinduism and Buddhism, but they have rarely known periods of political unity and strong government. The civilizations of the Maya made remarkable discoveries in astronomy and mathematics, but their technology remained roughly equivalent to that of Stone-Age peoples as late as the arrival of the Spaniards in the 16th century. These examples suggest that rather than stressing particular attainments such as the capacity to build pyramids or wheeled vehicles, a genuinely global definition of what it means to be civilized should focus on underlying patterns of social development that are common to complex societies throughout history. The attributes that determine whether a particular society is civilized or not should be freed from *ethnocentrism*—the tendency to judge other peoples' cultural forms solely on the basis of how much they resemble one's own.

THE COMPARATIVE APPROACH TO THE HISTORY OF CIVILIZATIONS

Much of world history can be organized through careful comparisons of the leading characteristics of the major civilizations, such as formal governments, family structures, and art. Remembering what civilizations have in common helps us to manage the complexity of world history and to highlight the key distinctions that also exist among major societies. Comparison gives us a means of connecting historical developments within different civilizations and allows us to identify key patterns that ought to be remembered and explained. It also helps capture the process of historical change. A situation new to one society can be compared with similar situations elsewhere. Many key changes, furthermore, developed independently within a civilization, and here analysis at the civilization level is inescapable.

INTERNATIONAL CONTACTS AND TIME PERIODS

World history is not, however, simply a progression of separate civilizations that can be compared in various ways. An understanding of the kinds of contacts different civilizations developed—and their responses to the forces that crossed their boundaries-is as important as the story of the great societies themselves. For example, when the rate of international trade picked up, it presented questions for each major society to answer: How would the society participate in the trading system? What domestic impact did international trade have? How did one society's reactions to the new levels of trade compare with those of other major societies?

Often, contacts were mediated by nomadic groups, whose freedom of movement and (sometimes) warlike qualities gave them special roles in moving between civilization boundaries. Explicit international relations ultimately developed among civilizations themselves. Early examples included emissaries that regularly attended on seats of power, like those from Japan, Korea, and Vietnam that visited the Chinese emperor by the 7th century, but also trade operations with organized outlets in farflung ports.

Changes in patterns of contact organize much of the chronology of world history. Historians treat time not in terms of one event after another but by defining *periods* in which basic patterns emerge. Some time periods see a particular trend toward the formation of empires; others involve the spread of major religions; others stress the impact of new technologies or production systems. Not all societies, in a given time period, neatly responded to the larger world forces-isolation from the wider world remained possible until just a few centuries ago—but enough did to enable us to define a coherent chronology for world history.

This book emphasizes six major time periods in world history. In the first, covered in Part I, civilization emerged. Early civilizations arose after people had formed a wide variety of local societies over most of the inhabitable globe. The early civilizations were regional, but they pulled local groups together into some shared institutions and beliefs, and some of them developed limited contacts with other civilizations.

The second period of world history saw the formation of much larger civilization units: the great classical societies of China, India, and the Mediterranean. This period emphasizes the integration of these larger civilization areas, and the level of contact among them.

The third, postclassical period in world history emerged as the classical civilizations declined. After about 500 C.E., civilization spread to new areas and new kinds of contact developed, involving the spread of novel religious systems, the increase of commercial exchange, and even the acceleration of international disease transmission.

In the fourth period of world history, beginning around 1450 C.E., the Americas and other previously isolated areas came into the international framework as trade and exchange reached another level of intensity.

The fifth period of world history, between 1750 and 1920, was shaped particularly by the advent of industrial society in western Europe. New rates of interaction and a new, and complex, balance of forces developed among the major civilization areas.

Finally, world history periodization took a sixth turn during the 20th century, again because of complicated changes in the nature of international contacts and the impact of those contacts on particular societies. The new global patterns of this century gain added meaning against the perspective of previous world trends.

The basic framework for managing and understanding world history resembles a weaving loom, in which two sets of threads interweave. One set consists of the major civilizations and key nomadic societies, identified through their principal characteristics and traced over time. The second set involves parallel processes and contacts that delineate the principal time periods of world history. The interaction between civilizations and international forces forms the warp and weave of world history, from civilization's origin to the present day.

MAJOR THEMES

To help organize the study of civilizations, including their comparison and the evolution of international contacts, this book stresses several major themes. These can be traced from one period to the next, as a means of charting change and continuity. Two themes involve the tension between established traditions and forces of change, as they affected key societies, and the tension between regional patterns and the contacts brought by developments such as trade and migration. Other themes involve technology and its environmental impact, and also social inequalities, between the two genders and among different social levels. The issue of human agency is crucial: what roles did individuals play in shaping historical forces, compared to other causes? Two final themes involve the interplay between civilizations and other types of societies, particularly nomadic groups that could spur both disruption and fruitful contact; and the development of more regular kinds of connections among societies, by organized trading groups, government representatives, missionaries and the like.

In sum: basic concerns about tradition/change and regionalism/contact are supplemented by the theme of technology and the environment. The second specific theme highlights changing patterns of inequality. A third features discussion of human agency as part of world-historical causation. Themes four and five deal with nomads and with the organization of international connections. The themes should be used as vehicles for comparison (how two civilizations managed inequality, for example) and as part of the assessment of the nature of periodization over time.

ANALYSIS IN WORLD HISTORY

World history involves comparison, assessment of global interaction, and consideration of more general formulas about how human societies operate. Through these issues, including consideration of the causes of significant change, the world's past can be used to help explain its present patterns. There are facts to be learned, but the greater analytical challenge is to use the facts to compare civilizations, to identify key periods of world history and the patterns of change from one period to the next, and to test general propositions about historical causation and development. With this approach world history becomes something to think about, not simply something to memorize and regurgitate. With this approach the task of learning world history gains focus and purpose.

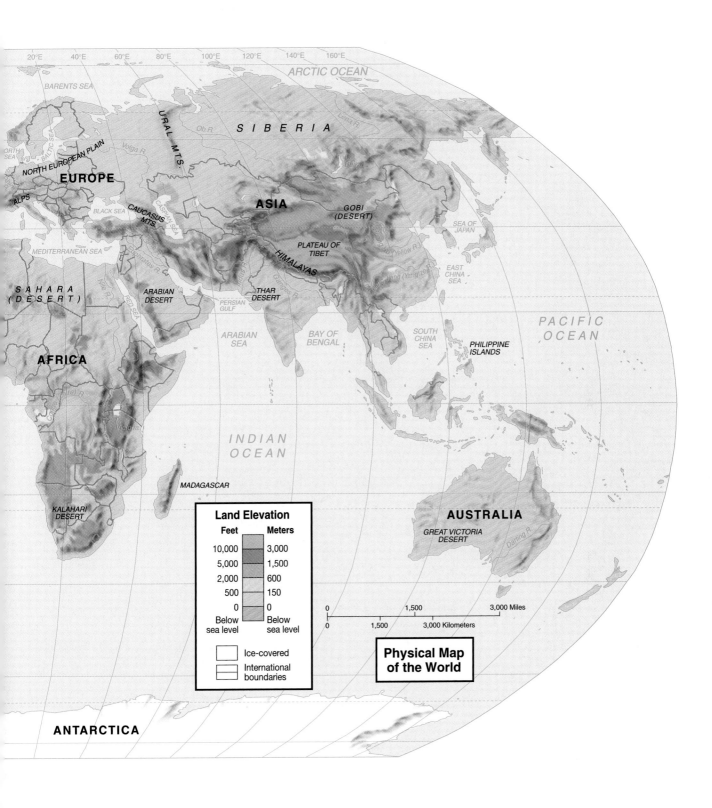

Physical Map
of the World

World Civilizations

PART 4
The World Shrinks, 1450–1750

INTRODUCTION

Many developments highlighted world history between 1450 and 1750, which marked a major new period—the early modern—in the global experience. As in most new world history periods, the balance of power among major civilizations shifted; western Europe became the most dynamic force worldwide. Contacts among many civilizations intensified. The world became smaller as international trade affected diverse societies and the speed and range of sailing ships increased. This growth of commerce affected western Europe and areas under its economic influence, such as Africa and the Americas, but commerce grew in China and Japan as well. Partly on the basis of innovations in weaponry, particularly gunpowder, new or revamped empires formed important regional political units in many parts of the world. These developments were especially significant in Asia. In addition to European colonial empires in various parts of the world, land-based empires formed in Russia, Persia, the Middle East and the Mediterranean, and India.

The early modern period was launched during the 15th century when European countries, headed by Portugal and Spain, began new explorations and soon new colonization efforts in Africa, Asia, and the Americas. It was launched also by the formation of the powerful Ottoman Empire in the Middle East, the Mughal and Ming empires in Asia, and the emergence of Russia from two centuries of Mongol control.

ON THE EVE OF THE EARLY MODERN PERIOD: THE WORLD AROUND 1450

A number of societies had expanded during the postclassical period. Russia was one, as a Russian monarchy formed. Western Europe failed to gain political unity, but slowly recovered from the 5th-century collapse of the Roman Empire. Western Europeans built important regional kingdoms while expanding the role of urban commerce and establishing an elaborate culture around Catholic Christianity. In sub-Saharan Africa, another set of regional kingdoms formed, although vital areas there were organized more loosely. African trade and artistic expression gained ground steadily. Finally, areas in contact with China built increasingly elaborate societies. Japan, like western Europe, emphasized a decentralized feudal system in politics. But it copied many aspects of Chinese culture and some social forms, including a more *patriarchal* approach to the status of women.

Other areas of the world featured civilizations or elaborate cultures developing in isolation from any global contacts. This was true of the expanding Polynesian zone in the Pacific Islands and of the populous civilizations of the Americas, focused in Mesoamerica, under the Aztecs, and in the Andes, which by the 15th century were under the vast Inca realm.

The structure of the postclassical world began to shift between the 13th and 15th centuries, setting the stage for a new period in world history. The great Aztec and Inca empires were showing signs of strain and overextension by the later 15th century. In Asia, Africa, and Europe, the key development was the decline of Arab political power and cultural dynamism. Islam continued to expand, but its political and commercial units fragmented. At the same time, there was a new round of invasions from central Asia, launched by the Mongols. In the 13th century, they attacked China, the Middle East, and eastern Europe, toppling established kingdoms and allowing new contacts between Asia and Europe.

By 1400 the Mongol surge was receding, though only slowly in Russia. A new empire emerged in China. The Arab caliphate had perished. But a new Islamic political force, under the Ottoman Turks, was taking shape. The Ottomans unified much of the Middle East and positioned themselves to destroy the venerable Byzantine Empire. Using their growing commercial vigor but also terrified by the emergence of a new Islamic power, western Europeans looked for ways to gain greater control over international trade. The Chinese briefly experimented with a series of mighty trading expeditions across the Indian Ocean. But a shift in emperors led to a retreat, with a decision to concentrate on traditions of internal political, cultural, and commercial development. As it turned out, this left the way open for the western European overseas expeditions. Western explorers and merchants benefited from technologies newly learned from China and the Islamic world, such as the compass and triangular sail, while adding important innovations such as guns and faster oceangoing ships.

1300 C.E.	1400 C.E.	1500 C.E.	1550 C.E.
1281 Founding of Ottoman dynasty	**1405–1433** Chinese expedition period	**1500–1600** Europe's commercial revolution	**1552** Russia begins expansion in central Asia and western Siberia
1350s Ottoman invasion of southeastern Europe	**1434–1498** Portuguese expeditions down West African coast	**1501–1510** Safavid conquest of Iran	**1570** Portuguese colony of Angola (Africa)
1368 Ming dynasty in China	**1441** Beginning of European slave trade in Africa	**1509** Spanish colonies on American mainland	**1571** Ottoman naval defeat at Lepanto
1390 Ming restrictions on overseas trade	**1453** Ottoman conquest of Constantinople	**1510–1511** Portugal conquers Goa (India), Malacca (Malaysia)	**1590** Hideyoshi unifies Japan
	1480 Moscow region free of Mongol control	**1517–1541** Protestant Reformation (Europe)	**1591** Fall of Songhay (Africa)
	1492 Columbus expeditions	**1519–1521** Magellan circumnavigates globe	
	1498–1499 Vasco da Gama expedition opens seas to Asia	**1519–1524** Cortes conquers Mexico	
		1520–1566 Suleiman the Magnificent (Ottoman)	
		1526 Babur conquest in northern India (Mughal)	
		1533 Pizarro wins Peru	
		1548 Portuguese government in Brazil	

THE RISE OF THE WEST

Between 1450 and 1750, western Europe, headed initially by Spain and Portugal and then by Holland, Britain, and France, gained control of the key international trade routes. It established colonies in the Americas and, on a much more limited basis, in Africa and parts of Asia.

At the same time, partly because of its new international position, the West itself changed rapidly, becoming an unusual kind of agricultural civilization. Commerce began to change the social structure and also affected basic attitudes toward family life and the natural environment. A host of new ideas, some of them springing from religious reformers, created a novel cultural climate in which scientific principles were increasingly valued. The scientific revolution gradually reshaped Western culture as a whole. More effective political structures emerged by the 17th century, as Western monarchs began to introduce bureaucratic principles similar to those pioneered long before in China.

A vital facet of the early modern period, then, was the West's expansion as an international force and its internal transformation. Like the previous global civilization, Arab Islam, the West developed a diverse and dynamic culture and society, which was both a result and a cause of its rising international prominence.

THE WORLD ECONOMY AND GLOBAL CONTACTS

Fed by new naval technologies, the world network intensified and took on new dimensions. The change involved more than the fact that the Europeans, not the Muslims, dominated international trade. It featured an expansion of the world network to global proportions, well beyond previous international linkages. The Americas were brought into contact with other cultures and included in global exchanges for the first time. At the end

1600 C.E.	1650 C.E.	1700 C.E.	1750 C.E.
1600 Dutch and British merchants begin activity in India	**1652** Dutch colony South Africa	**1713** New Bourbon dynasty, Spain	**1756–1763** Seven Years' War
1600–1690 Scientific revolution (Europe)	**1658–1707** Aurangzeb reign, beginning of Mughal decline	**1722** Fall of Safavid dynasty (Iran)	**1763** Britain acquires "New France"
1603 Tokugawa shogunate	**1682–1699** Turks driven from Hungary	**1759–1788** Reforms of Latin American colonial administration	**1764** British East India Company controls Bengal (India)
1607 First British colonies in North America	**1689–1725** Peter the Great (Russia)		**1770s** European—Bantu conflicts in southern Africa
1608 First French North American colonies			**1772–1795** Partition of Poland
1637 Russian pioneers to Pacific			**1775–1783** American Revolution
1640s Japan isolation			**1781** Indian revolts in New Grenada and Peru (Latin America)
1641 Dutch colonies in Indonesia			**1792** Slave uprising in Haiti
1642–1727 Isaac Newton			
1644 Qing dynasty, China			

of the period, in the 18th century, Polynesian and Australian societies began to undergo the same painful integrating experience.

By 1750 there were no fully isolated societies of any great size. The new globalism of human contacts had a host of consequences that ran through early modern centuries. The human disease pool became fully international for the first time, and peoples who had previously been isolated from the rest of the world suffered greatly from exposure to diseases for which they had developed no immunities. The global network also permitted a massive exchange of plants and animals. Cows and horses were introduced to the Americas, prompting significant changes in American Indian societies and economies. American food crops were spread around the world, bringing sweet potatoes, corn, and manioc to China, corn to Africa, and potatoes and tobacco to Europe. One result through most of the world, beginning in Asia as well as western Europe, was rapid population expansion.

As part of this new globalization, highly unequal relationships were established among many civilizations. During the postclassical millennium, 450–1450 C.E., a few areas contributed inexpensive raw materials (including labor power in the form of slaves) to more advanced societies, notably China and the Islamic world. These supply areas have included western Europe and parts of Africa and southeast Asia. Although economic relationships in these instances were unequal, they did not affect the societies that produced raw materials too severely because international trade was not sufficient to do so. After 1450 or 1500, as Western commerce expanded internationally, the West began to set up unequal relationships with a number of areas. Areas such as Latin America depended heavily on sales to export merchants, on imports of processed goods, and on Western ships and merchants to handle international trade. Dependence of this sort skewed labor relations by encouraging commercial exploitation of slaves and serfs. It is vital to stress that much of the world, particularly in the great Asian civilizations, remained outside this set of relationships. But the global network spread: Western overseas expansion began to engulf India and parts of Indonesia by the 18th century.

WORLD BOUNDARIES

The period of 1450–1750 saw an unusual number of boundary changes in world history. The spread of Western colonies was the most obvious development, but the establishment or extension of a number of large land-based empires was almost as significant.

Compare the two maps by tracing the areas of Western penetration. You will see the different forms this penetration took in different parts of the world. Note also what parts of the world offered particular opportunities for rivalries between the leading Western colonial powers and what parts were immune to Western expansion.

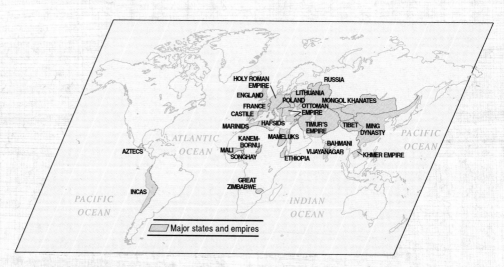

World Boundaries, c. 1453

World Boundaries, c. 1700. Compare with the 1453 map. What were the main changes? What areas were most stable? Why did Western colonies spread in some parts of the world and not in others?

THE GUNPOWDER EMPIRES

The rise of western Europe and its growing dominance of world trade was not the only major theme of early modern world history. The centuries after 1450 could also be called the age of the gunpowder empires. The development of cannons and muskets in the 15th and 16th centuries, through the combination of Western technology and previous Chinese invention, spurred the West's expansion. Ship-based artillery was fundamental to the West's mastery of international sea lanes and many ports and islands. But gunnery was picked up by other societies as well. The Ottoman Turks used huge cannons in their successful siege of Constantinople in 1453. The subsequent Ottoman Empire relied heavily on field guns to supplement trained cavalry. The rise of a new Russian Empire after 1480 was also built on the growing use of guns, and the Russian economy was later reshaped to ensure the manufacture of the new military hardware. Three other key empires—the Mughal in India, the Safavid in Persia, and the 17th-century Qing dynasty in China—relied on the new strength of land armies armed with guns. Guns also played a role in Japanese and African history during the period.

Guns supported the forging of new land empires throughout much of Asia and eastern Europe and, to some extent, in Africa. These developments were largely independent of Western influence, and they counterbalanced the growth of Western power. The rise of the

The power of gunpowder: The gun was introduced into Japan in 1542 through the Portuguese. By 1562, 10,000 Japanese soldiers carried muskets. The scenes depicted here are from a military manual written by one of the greatest generals of the period, Nobunaga.

Russian empire ran through the whole period, and though not as important as the expansion of the West, it was certainly a vital theme. The rise of the Ottomans, Safavids, and Mughals was a bit shorter-lived but echoed through the first two centuries of the period and, in the case of the Ottomans, created one of the most durable empires in world history.

THEMES

Many of the key themes of world history changed during the early modern centuries. Most strikingly, the impact of nomadic societies—once vital to world history dynamics—declined dramatically after the Mongol incursions. The new gunpowder empires, particularly Russia and China, conquered many of the old nomad strongholds. In many areas nomadic intermediaries were replaced by more direct relations among states or merchant groups. For example, European governments began regular diplomatic contacts, recognizing the importance of consistent interchange. China had received foreign representatives for centuries. In Europe, the practice started among Italian city-states in the Renaissance and then spread more widely. Representation to governments in Africa and Asia was a bit more haphazard, but formal emissaries were sent out to negotiate on trade and other matters.

Developments in the changing world economy had major effects on patterns of inequality. Gender relations did not change greatly in most areas, but labor systems were transformed throughout much of the world. The massive expansion of slavery and harsh serfdom in key parts of the world created new social hierarchies. The same developments also reduced human agency for millions of people who were captured or otherwise forced into slavery or serfdom. Growing wealth and new cultural currents, including the rise of science, created new opportunities for a small number of Europeans, and individual genius in art, trade, science, or military organization ultimately had global effects. Conquests created opportunities for human agency elsewhere as well, as with the imaginative leaders who first established the Mughal empire in India.

Finally, the early modern centuries saw drastic environmental change, though more because of the exchanges of foods, animals, and diseases with the Americas than because of new technology. Imported horses, sheep, and cattle, reproducing rapidly, had great effects on American grasslands and densely settled Indian farmlands. Imported diseases such as measles and smallpox had even more devastating results. Soil conditions were changed in some places by the introduction of new crops such as sugar, which often replaced native vegetation. From North America to China, settlers in search of land to farm began clearing temperate forests. And in a number of regions, the clearing of the world's great rainforests began.

CIVILIZATIONS AND LARGER TRENDS

As in earlier times, many developments during these early modern centuries occurred within individual civilizations, with little or no relationship to more general world trends. Only the Americas came close to being overwhelmed by outside influences. Nevertheless, the impact of the three international trends—Western expansion, intensification and globalization of the world commercial network, and the military and political results of gunpowder—affected patterns in the separate societies in many ways. Each civilization had to respond to these trends. Reactions were diverse, ranging from the eager embrace of new international currents to forced compliance or deliberate isolation.

International pressures increased with time. By 1700 western Europe's activities were looming larger, not just in key areas such as the Americas, the Asian island groups, and the coast of west Africa, but in mainland Asia and eastern Europe as well. A new Russian urge to selectively copy aspects of the West, and the establishment of growing British control in parts of India, were two facets of this shift. Even Japan, which initially responded to the new world economy by effective isolation, began to show a new but modest openness, exemplified by the end of a long-standing ban on translating Western books.

The first two chapters in this section focus on changes within the West and the emergence of Western colonies and Western-dominated world trade. Then, two chapters deal with two societies that had particular links with the West: Russia, whose expansion was an important theme in its own right, and a new kind of emerging civilization in Latin America. The last three chapters deal with major societies in Asia and Africa, where contacts with the West and the new world economy were significant, particularly as the early modern period wore on, but where separate patterns of activity remained vital.

Chapter 22

The Transformation of the West, 1450–1750

Anatomy as science and as art: The anatomical sketches and notes by Leonardo da Vinci demonstrate his study of the human form. In keeping with the scientific spirit of the age, artists of the late Renaissance sometimes turned to science in order to portray the human body as realistically as possible.

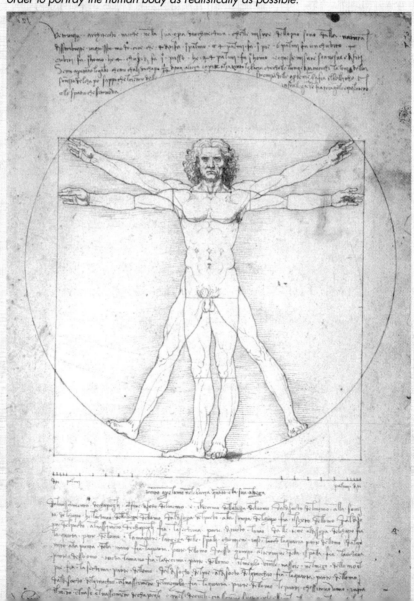

During the three centuries after 1450, Western civilization changed in dramatic ways. Still a largely agricultural society in 1750, the West had become unusually commercially active and had laid out a growing manufacturing sector. Government powers had expanded, and new political ideas complicated the picture. Beliefs had changed. Science came to form the center of Western intellectual life for the first time in the history of any society. Popular beliefs, including ideas about family and nature, also had shifted. In some respects, the West in this period was following a path that other civilizations had already laid out, such as increased bureaucratization in government. But in other areas, such as popular belief and family structure, the West was striking out in new directions.

Changes within western Europe resulted in part from overseas expansion and growing dominance in international trade. In turn, Europe's evolution furthered this international role.

Europe's internal changes unfolded amid much internal conflict. A host of terms, such as *Renaissance* and *Enlightenment*, describe key phases of change. Although there was no master plan, there were focal points: Europe's transformation centered on commerce, the state, and culture, with some support from technology. Between 1450 and 1650, a series of cultural shifts held center stage along with the rise in trade. Thereafter, the scientific revolution and the advent of new political forms introduced additional changes, which were amplified in the 18th-century Enlightenment.

THE FIRST BIG CHANGES: CULTURE AND COMMERCE

During the 15th century the Renaissance emphasized new styles and beliefs. This was followed by even more sweeping cultural and political change in the 16th century, with the Protestant Reformation and the Catholic response to it. A new commercial and social structure grew up as well, creating new opportunities and intense new grievances.

The Italian Renaissance

The move away from earlier patterns began with the Renaissance, which first developed in Italy during the 14th and 15th centuries. The significance of this rebirth should not be exaggerated; more fundamental changes came later and somewhat separately. But the Renaissance did challenge medieval intellectual values and styles. It suggested a certain amount of political innovation and built on a more commercialized economy. The Renaissance also sketched a new, brasher spirit that may have

523

1300 C.E.	1450 C.E.	1500 C.E.	1550 C.E.	1650 C.E.	1750 C.E.
1300–1450 Italian Renaissance	**1450–1519** Leonardo da Vinci **1450–1600** Northern Renaissance **1455** First European printing press in Mainz, Germany **1469–1527** Machiavelli **1475–1514** Michelangelo **1490s** France and Spain invade Italian city-states; beginning of Italian decline	**1500–1600** "Commercial revolution" **1515–1547** Francis I of France **1517** Luther's 95 theses; beginning of Protestant Reformation **1534** Beginning of Church of England **1541–1564** Calvin in Geneva **1543** "Copernican revolution"; Copernicus' work on astronomy	**1550–1649** Religious wars in France, Germany, and Britain **1555–1603** Elizabeth I, England **1564–1642** Galileo **1588** Defeat of Spanish Armada by English **17th century** Scientific Revolution **1609** Independence of Netherlands **1618–1648** Thirty Years' War **1642–1649** English civil wars **1642–1727** Newton **1643–1715** Louis XIV in France; absolute monarchy **1647–1648** Culmination of popular rebellion	**1670–1692** Decline of witchcraft trials **1682–1699** Hapsburgs drive Turks from Hungary **1688–1690** Glorious Revolution in Britain; parliamentary monarchy; some religious toleration; political writing of John Locke **18th century** Enlightenment **1712–1786** Frederick the Great of Prussia; enlightened despotism **1730–1850** European population boom **1733** James Kay invents flying shuttle loom **1736** Beginnings of Methodism	**1756–1763** Seven Years' War; France, Britain, Prussia, and Austria **1776** Adam Smith's *Wealth of Nations* **1780–1790** Joseph II, Austria and Hungary **1792** Mary Wollstonecraft's *Vindication of the Rights of Women*

encouraged a new Western interest in exploring strange waters or urging that old truths be reexamined.

Italy was already well launched in the development of Renaissance culture by the 15th century, based on its unusually extensive urban, commercial economy and its competitive city-state politics. Writers such as Petrarch and Boccaccio had promoted classical literary canons against medieval logic and theology, writing in Italian as well as the traditional Latin and emphasizing secular subjects such as love and pride. Painting turned to new realism and classical and human-centered themes. Religion declined as a central focus. The Italian Renaissance blossomed further in the 15th and early 16th centuries. This was a great age of Western art, as Leonardo da Vinci advanced the realistic portrayal of the human body and Michelangelo applied classical styles in painting and sculpture. In political theory, *Niccolo Machiavelli* emphasized realistic discussions of how to seize and maintain power. Like the artists, Machiavelli bolstered his realism with Greek and Roman examples. In history, scholars portrayed a past unencumbered by divine intervention and they established new critical standards that could be used to disprove traditional church claims.

Overall, Italian Renaissance culture stressed themes of *humanism:* a focus on humankind as the center of intellectual and artistic endeavor. Religion was not attacked, but its principles were no longer predominant. Historians have debated the reasons for this change. Italy's more urban, commercial environment was one factor, but so was the new imitation of classical Greek and Roman literature and art.

These Renaissance themes had some bearing on politics and commerce. Renaissance merchants improved their banking techniques and became more openly profit seeking than their medieval counterparts had been. City-state leaders experimented with new political forms and functions. They justified their rule not on the basis of heredity or divine guidance but more on the basis of what they could do to advance general well-being and their city's glory. Thus, they sponsored cultural activities and tried to improve the administration of the economy. They also developed more professional armies, for wars among the city-states were common, and gave new attention to military tactics and training. They also rethought the practice of diplomacy, introducing the regular exchange of ambassadors for the first time in the West. Clearly, the Renaissance encouraged innovation, although it also produced some dependence on classical models.

The Renaissance Moves Northward

Italy began to decline as a Renaissance center by about 1500. French and Spanish monarchs invaded the peninsula, reducing political independence. At the same time, new Atlantic trade routes reduced the importance of Mediterranean ports, a huge blow to the Italian economy.

As Renaissance creativity faded in its Italian birthplace, it passed northward. The *Northern Renaissance*—focused in France, the Low Countries, Germany, and England—began after 1450. Renaissance styles also affected Hungary and Poland in east central Europe. Classical styles in art and architecture became the rage. Knowledge of Greek and Latin literature gained ground, although many northern humanists wrote in their own languages (English, French, and so on). Northern humanists were more religious than their Italian counterparts, trying to blend secular interests with continued Christian devotion. Renaissance writers such as Shakespeare in England and Rabelais in France also mixed classical themes with an earthiness—a joy in bodily functions and human passions—that maintained elements of medieval popular culture. Renaissance literature established a new set of classics for literary traditions in the major Western languages: Shakespeare in England, Cervantes in Spain, and so on.

The Northern Renaissance produced some political change, providing another move toward greater state powers. As their revenues and operations expanded, Renaissance kings increased their pomp and ceremony. Kings such as *Francis I* in France became patrons of the arts, even importing Italian sculptors and architects to create their classical-style palaces. By the late 16th century, many monarchs were sponsoring trading companies and colonial enterprises. Interest in military conquest was greater than in the Middle Ages. Francis I was even willing to ally with the Ottoman sultan, the key Muslim leader. His goal was to distract his main enemy, the Habsburg ruler of Austria and Spain. In fact, it was an alliance in name only, but it illustrated how power politics was beginning to abandon the feudal or religious justifications that had previously clothed it in the West.

Yet the impact of the Renaissance should not be overstated, particularly outside Italy. Renaissance kings had new ceremonies, but they were still confined by the political powers of feudal landlords. A new political form had yet to emerge. Ordinary people were little touched by Renaissance values; the life of most peasants and artisans went on much as before. Economic life also changed little, particularly outside the Italian commercial centers. Rural people sometimes were pressed for new taxes to support cities and kings. Even in the upper classes, women sometimes encountered new limits as Renaissance leaders touted men's public bravado over women's domestic roles.

The Commercial Economy and a New Family Pattern

More fundamental changes were brewing in Western society by 1500, beneath the glittering surface of the Renaissance. Spurred by trading contacts with Asia, workers in the West improved the quality of pulleys and pumps in mines and learned how to forge stronger iron products. Printing was introduced in the 15th century when the German *Johannes Gutenberg* introduced movable type, building on Chinese printing technology. Soon books were distributed in greater quantities in the West, which helped expand the audience for Renaissance writers and disseminated religious ideas. Literacy began to gain ground and became a fertile source of new kinds of thinking. Technology clearly was poised to spur a variety of changes.

Family structure was also changing. A *European-style family* pattern came into being by the 15th century. This pattern involved a late marriage age and a primary emphasis on nuclear families of parents and children rather than the extended families characteristic of most agricultural civilizations. By the 16th century, ordinary people usually did not marry until their late 20s—a marked contrast to most agricultural societies. These changes emphasized the importance of husband–wife relations. They also closely linked the family to individual property holdings, for most people could not marry until they had access to property. Late marriage also provided a certain amount of birth control, which limited overcrowding even as economic activity began to speed up again in the West.

The Protestant and Catholic Reformations

In the 16th century, religious upheaval and a new commercial surge began to define the directions of change more fully.

In 1517, a German monk named *Martin Luther* nailed a document containing 95 *theses,* or propositions, to the door of the castle church in Wittenberg. He was protesting claims made by a papal representative in selling *indulgences,* or grants of salvation, for money, but in fact his protest went deeper. Luther's reading of the Bible convinced him that only faith could gain salvation. Church sacraments were not the path, for God could not be manipulated. Luther's protest, which was rebuffed by the papacy, soon led him to challenge many Catholic beliefs, including the authority of the pope himself. Luther would soon argue that monasticism was wrong, that priests should marry (as he did), and that the Bible should be translated from Latin so ordinary people could have direct access to its teachings. Luther did not want to break Christian unity, but the church he wanted should be on his terms (or, as he would have argued, the terms of the true faith).

Luther picked up wide support for his views during the mid-16th century and beyond. Many Germans, in a somewhat nationalist reaction, resented the authority and taxes of the Roman pope. German princes saw an opportunity to gain more power because their nominal leader, the holy Roman emperor, remained Catholic. Princes who turned Protestant could increase their independence and seize church lands. The Lutheran version of *Protestantism* (as the general wave of religious dissent was called) urged state control of the church as an alternative to papal authority, and this had obvious political appeal.

There were reasons for ordinary people to shift their allegiance as well. Some German peasants saw Luther's attack on authority as a sanction for their own social rebellion against landlords, although Luther specifically renounced this reading. Some townspeople were drawn to Luther's approval of work in the world; because faith alone gained salvation, Lutheranism could sanction money-making and other earthly pursuits more wholeheartedly than did traditional Catholicism. Unlike Catholicism, Lutherans did not see special vocations as particularly holy; monasteries were abolished, along with some of the Christian bias against money-making.

Once Christian unity was breached, other Protestant groups sprang forward. In England, Henry VIII began to set up an *Anglican church*, initially to challenge papal attempts to enforce his first marriage, which had failed to produce a male heir. (Henry ultimately had six wives in sequence, executing two of them, a particularly graphic example of the treatment of women in power politics.) Henry was also attracted to some of the new doctrines, and his most durable successor, his daughter Elizabeth I, was Protestant outright. Still more important were the churches inspired by *Jean Calvin*, a Frenchman who established his base in the Swiss city of Geneva. Calvinism insisted on God's *predestination*, or prior determination, of those who would be saved. Calvinist ministers became moral guardians and preachers of God's word. Calvinists sought the participation of all believers in local church administration, which promoted the idea of a wider access to government. They also promoted broader popular education so that more people could read the Bible. Calvinism was accepted not only in part of Switzerland but also in portions of Germany, in France (where it produced strong minority groups), in the Netherlands, in Hungary, and in England and Scotland. By the early 17th century, Puritan exiles brought it to North America.

The Catholic church did not sit still under Protestant attack. It did not restore religious unity, but it defended southern Europe, Austria, Poland, much of Hungary, and key parts of Germany for the Catholic faith. Under a *Catholic Reformation*, a major church council revived Catholic doctrine and refuted key Protestant tenets such as the idea that priests had no special sacramental power and could marry. They also attacked popular superstitions and remnants of magical belief, which meant that Catholics and Protestants alike were trying to find new ways to shape the outlook of ordinary folk. A new religious order, the *Jesuits,* became active in politics, education, and missionary work, regaining some parts of Europe for the church. Jesuit fervor also sponsored Catholic missionary activity in Asia and the Americas.

The End of Christian Unity in the West

The Protestant and Catholic Reformations had several results in Europe during the late 16th and early 17th centuries. Most obvious was an important series of religious wars. France was a scene of bitter battles between Calvinist and Catholic forces. These disputes ended only with the granting of tolerance to Protestants through *the edict of Nantes* in 1598, although in the next century French kings progressively cut back on Protestant rights. In Germany, the *Thirty Years' War* broke out in 1618, pitting German Protestants and allies such as Lutheran Sweden against the holy Roman emperor, backed by Spain. The war was so devastating that it reduced German power and prosperity for a full century, cutting population by as much as 60 percent in some regions. It was ended only by the 1648 *Treaty of Westphalia*, which agreed to the territorial tolerance concept: Some princely states and cities chose one religion, some another. This treaty also finally settled a rebel-

Figure 22.1. Hans Holbein's "The Dance of Death" illustrated encouraged by the continuing plague as well as religious conflict.

lion of the Protestant Netherlands against Spain, giving the former its full independence.

Religious fighting punctuated British history, first before the reign of Elizabeth in the 16th century, then in the *English Civil War* in the 1640s. Here too, religious issues combined with other problems, particularly in a battle between the claims of parliament to rights of control over royal actions and some rather tactless assertions of authority by a new line of English kings. The civil war ended in 1660 (well after King Charles I had been beheaded; Figure 22.2), but full resolution came only in 1688–1689, when limited religious toleration was granted to most Protestant (but not Catholic) faiths.

Religious issues thus dominated European politics for almost a century. The religious wars led to a grudging and limited acceptance of the idea of religious pluralism: Christian unity could not be restored, although in most individual countries (the Netherlands came closest to a full exception), any idea of full religious liberty was still in the future. The religious wars persuaded some people that religion itself

was suspect; if there was no dominant single truth, why all the cruelty and carnage? Finally, the wars affected the political balance of Europe, as Map 22.1 shows. After a period of weakness during its internal strife, France was on the upswing. The Netherlands and Britain were galvanized toward a growing international role. Spain, briefly ascendant, fell back. Internally, some kings and princes benefited from the decline of papal authority by taking a stronger role in religious affairs. This was true in many Catholic and Protestant domains. In some cases, however, Protestant dissent encouraged popular political movements and enhanced parliamentary power.

The impact of religious change went well beyond politics. Popular beliefs changed most in Protestant areas, but Catholic reform produced new impulses as well. Western people gradually became less likely to see an intimate connection between God and nature. Protestants resisted the idea of miracles or other interventions in nature's course. Religious change also promoted greater concentration on family life. Religious writers encouraged love between husband and wife. As one English Protestant put it, "When love is absent between husband and wife, it is like a bone out of joint: there is no ease, no order." This promotion of the family had ambiguous implications for women. Protestantism, abolishing religious convents, made marriage more necessary for women than before; there were fewer alternatives for women who could not marry. Fathers were also responsible for the religious training of the children. On the other hand, women's emotional role in the family improved with the new emphasis on affection.

Religious change accompanied and promoted growing literacy along with the spread of the printing press. In the town of Durham, England, around 1570, only 20 percent of all people were literate, but by 1630 the figure had climbed to 47 percent. Growing literacy opened people to additional new ideas and ways of thinking.

The Commercial Revolution

Along with religious upheaval during the 16th century, the economic structure of the West was fundamentally redefined. The level of European trade rose sharply, and many Europeans had new goods available to them. Involvement with markets and merchants increased.

A basic spur to greater commercialization was price inflation that occurred throughout western Europe

Figure 22.2. Civil war resulted in the execution of Charles I in London, England, in 1649.

during the 16th century. The massive import of gold and silver from Spain's new colonies in Latin America forced prices up. The availability of more money, based on silver supply, generated this price rise. New wealth heightened demand for products to sell, both in the colonies and in Europe, but Western production could not keep pace, hence the price inflation. Inflation encouraged merchants to take new risks, for borrowing was cheap when money was losing value. A sum borrowed one year would be worth less, in real terms, five years later, so it made sense to take loans for new investments.

Inflation and the new colonial opportunities led to the formation of great trading companies, often with government backing, in Spain, England, the Netherlands, and France. Governments granted regional monopolies to these giant concerns; thus, the Dutch East Indies Company long dominated trade with the islands of Indonesia. European merchants brought new profits back to Europe and developed new managerial skills and banking arrangements.

Colonial markets stimulated manufacturing. Most peasants continued to produce mainly for their own needs, but agricultural specialty areas developed in the production of wines, cheeses, wool, and the like. Some of these industries favored commercial farming and the use of paid laborers on the land. Shoemaking, pottery, metalworking, and other manufacturing specializations arose in both rural villages and the cities.

Technical improvements followed in many branches of manufacture, particularly in metals and mining.

Prosperity increased for many ordinary people as well as for the great merchants. One historian has estimated that by about 1600 the average Western peasant or artisan owned five times as many "things" as his or her counterpart in southeastern Europe. A 16th-century Englishman noted that whereas in the past a peasant and his family slept on the floor, having only a pan or two as kitchenware, by the final decades of the century a farmer might have "a fair garnish of pewter in his cupboard, three or four feather beds, so many coverlets and carpets of tapestry, a silver salt, a bowl for wine … and a dozen spoons." It was about this time that French peasants began to enjoy wine fairly regularly rather than simply at special occasions—the result of higher productivity and better trade and transport facilities.

There were victims of change as well, however. Growing commercialization created the beginnings of a new *proletariat* in the West—people without access to wealth-producing property. Population growth and rising food prices hit hard at the poor, and many people had to sell their small plots of land. Some proletarians became manufacturing workers, depending on orders from merchant capitalists to keep their tools busy in their cottages. Others became paid laborers on agricultural estates, where landlords were eager for a more manipulable work force to take

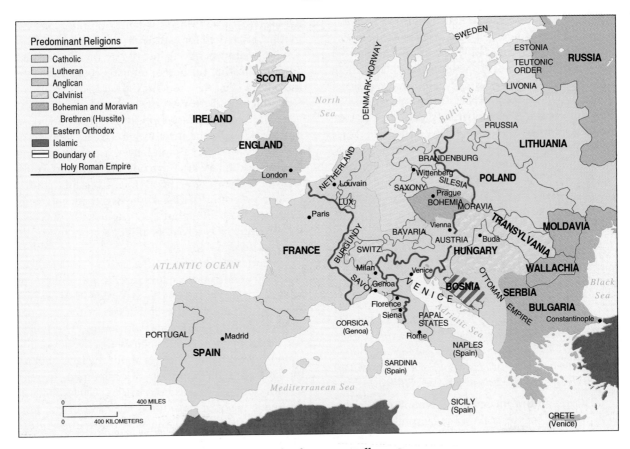

Map 22.1 *Western Europe During the Renaissance and Reformation. Different Protestant denominations made inroads in much of northwestern Europe with the Reformation, but Catholicism maintained its hold on significant portions of the continent.*

advantage of business opportunities in the cities. Others pressed into the cities, and a growing problem of beggars and wandering poor began to affect Western society. By blaming the poor for moral failings, a new, tough attitude toward poverty took shape that has lasted to some extent to the present day.

Not surprisingly, the shifts in popular economic and cultural traditions provoked important outcries. A huge wave of popular protest in western Europe developed at the end of the 16th century and extended until about 1650. Peasants and townspeople alike rose for greater protection from poverty and proletarianization. The uprisings did not deflect the basic currents of change, but they revealed the massive insecurity of many workers.

The popular rebellions of the 17th century revealed social tension and new ideas of equality. Peasant songs voiced such sentiments as this: "The whole country must be overturned, for we peasants are now to be the lords, it is we who will sit in the shade." Uprisings in 1648 produced demands for a popular political voice; an English group called the Levelers gained 100,000 signatures on a petition for political rights. Elsewhere, common people praised the kings while attacking their "bad advisors" and high taxes. One English agitator said that "we should cut off all the gentlemen's heads.... We shall have a merrier world shortly." In France, Protestant and Catholic peasants rose together against landlords and taxes: "They seek only the ruin of the poor people for our ruin is their wealth."

An unprecedented outburst against suspected witches arose in the same decades in various parts of western Europe and also in New England. Although attacks on witches had developed before, the new scale reflected intense social and cultural upheaval. Between 60,000 and 100,000 suspected witches were accused and killed. The *witchcraft persecution* reflected new resentments against the poor, who were often accused of witchcraft by communities unwilling to accept responsibility for their poverty. The hysteria also revealed new tensions about family life and the role of women, who were the most common targets of persecution. A few of the accused witches actually believed they had magical powers, but far more were accused by fearful or self-serving neighbors. The whole witchcraft experience revealed a society faced with forces of unusual complexity.

SCIENCE AND POLITICS: THE NEXT PHASE OF CHANGE

▓ *As the impact of the Reformation and commercialization continued, new scientific discoveries and political forms took shape from 1600 onward. These two forces shaped a new round of change that continued into the 18th century.*

The revolution in science, culminating in the 17th century, set the seal on the cultural reorientation of the West. Although the *scientific revolution* most obviously affected formal intellectual life, it also promoted changes in popular outlook.

At the same time, after the political upheavals of the Reformation, a more decisive set of new government forms arose in the West, centering on the emergence of the nation-state. The functions of the state expanded. The Western nation-state was not a single form, because key variants such as absolute monarchies and parliamentary regimes emerged, but there were some common patterns beneath the surface.

Science: The New Authority

During the 16th century, scientific research quietly built on the traditions of the later Middle Ages. A Polish clergyman, called *Copernicus* in the West, used astronomical observation and mathematical calculation to disprove the Hellenistic belief that the earth was the center of the universe. Rather, the earth moved around the sun. Johannes Kepler (1571–1630; Figure 22.3) was another important early figure in the study of planetary motion. Unusual for a major researcher, Kepler was from a poor fam-

ily; his father abandoned the family outright, and his mother, once tried for witchcraft, was unpleasant. But Kepler made his way to university on scholarship, aiming for the Lutheran ministry but drawn to astronomy and mathematics. Using the work of Copernicus and his own observations, he resolved basic issues of planetary motion. He also worked on optics and, with the mixed interests so common in real intellectual life, also practiced astrology, casting horoscopes for wealthy patrons. Also around 1600, anatomical work by the Belgian Vesalius gained greater precision. These key discoveries not only advanced knowledge but also implied a new power for scientific research in its ability to test and often overrule accepted ideas.

A series of empirical advances and wider theoretical generalizations extended the possibilities of science from the 1600s onward. New instruments such as the microscope and improved telescopes allowed gains in biology and astronomy. The Italian *Galileo* publicized Copernicus's discoveries while adding his own basic findings about the laws of gravity and planetary motion. Condemned by the Catholic church for his innovations, Galileo proved the inadequacy of traditional ideas about the universe. He also showed the new pride in scientific achievement, writing modestly how he, "by marvelous discoveries and clear demonstrations, had enlarged a thousand times" the knowledge produced by "the wise men of bygone ages." Chemical research advanced understanding of the behavior of gasses. English physician *John Harvey* demonstrated the circular movement of the blood in animals, with the heart as the "central pumping station."

These advances in knowledge were accompanied by important statements about science and its impact. Francis Bacon urged the value of careful empirical research and predicted that scientific knowledge could advance steadily, producing improvements in technology as well. *René Descartes* established the importance of a skeptical review of all received wisdom, arguing that human reason could develop laws that would explain the fundamental workings of nature.

The capstone to the 17th-century scientific revolution came in 1687, when *Isaac Newton* published his *Principia Mathematica*. This work drew the various astronomical and physical observations and wider theories together in a neat framework of natural laws. Newton set forth the basic principles of all motion

Figure 22.3. Johannes Kepler.

(for example, that a body in motion maintains uniform momentum unless affected by outside forces such as friction). Newton defined the forces of gravity in great mathematical detail and showed that the whole universe responded to these forces, which among other things explained the planetary orbits described by Kepler. Finally, Newton stated the basic scientific method in terms of a mixture of rational hypothesis and generalization and careful empirical observation and experiment. Here was a vision of a natural universe that could be captured in simple laws (although increasingly complex mathematics accompanied the findings). Here was a vision of a method of knowing that might do away with blind reliance on tradition or religious faith.

The scientific revolution was quickly popularized among educated Westerners, but not yet the wider populace. Here was a key step in the cultural transformation of western Europe in the early modern period. New scientific institutes were set up, often with government aid, to advance research and disseminate the findings. Lectures and easy-to-read manuals publicized the latest advances and communicated the excitement that researchers shared in almost all parts of Europe. Attacks on beliefs in

witchcraft became more common, and magistrates grew increasingly reluctant to entertain witchcraft accusations in court. Public hysteria began to die down after about 1670. There were growing signs of a new belief that people could control and calculate their environment. Insurance companies sprang up to help guard against risk. Doctors increased their attacks on popular healers, promoting a more scientific diagnosis of illness. Newsletters, an innovation by the late 17th century, began to advertise "lost and found" items, for there was no point leaving this kind of problem to customary magicians, called cunning men, who had poked around with presumably enchanted sticks.

By the 1680s writers affected by the new science, though not themselves scientists, began to attack traditional religious ideas such as miracles, for in the universe of the scientific revolution there was no room for disruption of nature's laws. Some intellectuals held out a new conception of God, called *Deism*, arguing that although there might be a divinity, its role was simply to set natural laws in motion. In England, *John Locke* argued that people could learn everything they needed to know through their senses and reason; faith was irrelevant. Christian beliefs in human sinfulness crumbled in the view of these intellectuals, for they saw human nature as basically good. Finally, scientific advances created wider assumptions about the possibility of human progress. If knowledge could advance through concerted human effort, why not progress in other domains? Even literary authorities joined this parade, and the idea that past styles set timeless standards of perfection came under growing criticism.

Science had never before been central to intellectual life. Science had played important roles in other civilizations, as in China, classical Greece, and Islam. Generally, however, wider religious or philosophical interests predominated. In China most notably, despite some real interest in generalizations about the physical universe derived from Daoism, science continued to be construed mainly in terms of practical, empirical advances. The Western passion for combining empiricism with more sweeping rational formulations—the idea of general laws of nature—clearly built on traditions that had come from Greek thought as mediated by Christian theology and Islamic philosophy during the postclassical period. In sum, the West was not alone in developing crucial scientific data, but it had become the most vibrant center for scientific advance, and its leading thinkers stood alone for some time in seeing science as the key to gaining and defining knowledge.

Absolute and Parliamentary Monarchies

The feudal monarchy—the balance between king and nobles—that had defined Western politics since the late postclassical period finally came undone in the 17th century. In most countries, after the passions of religious wars finally cooled, monarchs gained new powers, curtailing the tradition of noble pressure or revolt. At the same time, more ambitious military organization, in states that defined war as a central purpose, required more careful administration and improved tax collection.

The model for this new pattern was France, now the West's most important nation. French kings steadily built up their power in the 17th century. They stopped convening the medieval parliament and passed laws as they saw fit, although some provincial councils remained strong. They blew up the castles of dissident nobles, another sign that gunpowder was undercutting the military basis of feudalism. They appointed a growing bureaucracy drawn from the merchants and lawyers. They sent direct representatives to the outlying provinces. They professionalized the army, giving more formal training to officers, providing uniforms and support, and creating military hospitals and pensions.

So great was the power of the monarch, in fact, that the French system became known as *absolute monarchy*. Its most glorious royal proponent, King *Louis XIV*, summed up its principles succinctly: "I am the state." Louis became a major patron of the arts, giving government a cultural role beyond any previous levels in the West. His academies not only encouraged science but also worked to standardize the French language. A sumptuous palace at Versailles was used to keep nobles busy with social functions so that they could not interfere with affairs of state.

Using the new bureaucratic structure, Louis and his ministers developed additional functions for the state. They reduced internal tariffs, which acted as barriers to trade, and created new, state-run manufacturing. The reigning economic theory, *mercantilism*, held that governments should promote the internal economy to improve tax revenues and to limit imports from other nations, lest money be lost to enemy states. Therefore, absolute monarchs such as Louis XIV set tariffs on imported goods, tried to encourage their merchant fleets, and sought colonies to provide raw materials and a guaranteed market for manufactured goods produced at home.

The basic structure of absolute monarchy developed in other states besides France (see Map 22.2). Spain tried to imitate French principles in the 18th century, which resulted in efforts to tighten control over its Latin American colonies. However, the most important spread of absolute monarchy occurred in the central European states that were gaining in importance. A series of kings in Prussia, in eastern Germany, built a strong army and bureaucracy. They promoted economic activity and began to develop a state-sponsored school system. Habsburg kings in Austria–Hungary, though still officially rulers of the Holy Roman Empire, concentrated increasingly on developing a stronger monarchy in the lands under their direct control. The power of these Habsburg rulers increased after they pushed back the last Turkish invasion threat late in the 17th century and then added the kingdom of Hungary to their domains.

Most absolute monarchs saw a strong military as a key political goal, and many hoped for territorial expansion. Louis XIV used his strong state as the basis for a series of wars from the 1680s onward. The wars yielded some new territory for France but finally attracted an opposing alliance system that blocked further advance. Prussian kings, though long cautious in exposing their proud military to the risk of major war, turned in the 18th century to a series of conflicts that won new territory.

Britain and the Netherlands, both growing commercial and colonial powers, stood apart from the trend toward absolute monarchy in the 17th century. They emphasized the role of the central state, but they also built parliamentary regimes in which the kings shared power with representatives selected by the nobility and upper urban classes. The English civil wars produced a final political settlement in 1688 and 1689 (the so-called *Glorious Revolution*) in which parliament won basic sovereignty over the king. The English parliament no longer depended on the king to convene, for regular sessions were scheduled. Its rights to approve taxation allowed it to monitor or initiate most major policies.

Furthermore, a growing body of political theory arose in the 17th century that built on these parliamentary ideas. John Locke and others argued that power came from the people, not from a divine right to royal rule. Kings should therefore be restrained

Visualizing THE PAST

Versailles

This picture shows Louis XIV's grand 17th-century palace at Versailles. It displays the sheer opulence of this absolute monarchy, in what was Europe's richest and most populous and influential nation. It also shows the renewed hold of a classical style, seen to be most prestigious for public buildings. What else does it suggest?

Architecture is sometimes thought to be the most socially and historically revealing of all the arts because it depends most heavily on public support; it is harder for architects, particularly dealing with public buildings, to be as idiosyncratic as painters or poets may be.

Questions: What kinds of intentions on the part of Louis and his advisers does this building represent? How can Versailles be interpreted as a statement of absolute monarchy in addition to its obvious showiness? What are the relationships to nature and to spatial arrangement? What would the palace represent to an ordinary French person? To an aristocrat?

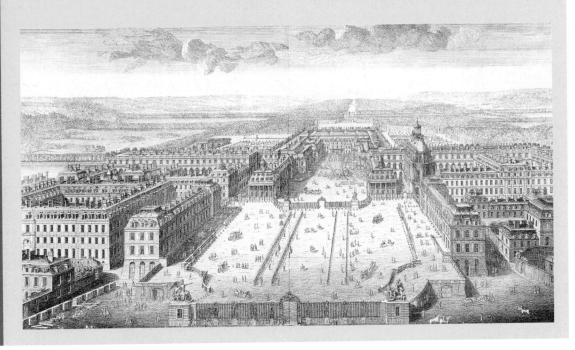

by institutions that protected the public interest, including certain general rights to freedom and property. A right of revolution could legitimately oppose unjust rule.

Overall, western Europe developed important diversity in political forms, between absolute monarchy and a new kind of *parliamentary monarchy*. It maintained a characteristic tension between government growth and the idea that there should be some limits to state authority. This tension was expressed in new forms, but it recalled some principles that had originated in the Middle Ages.

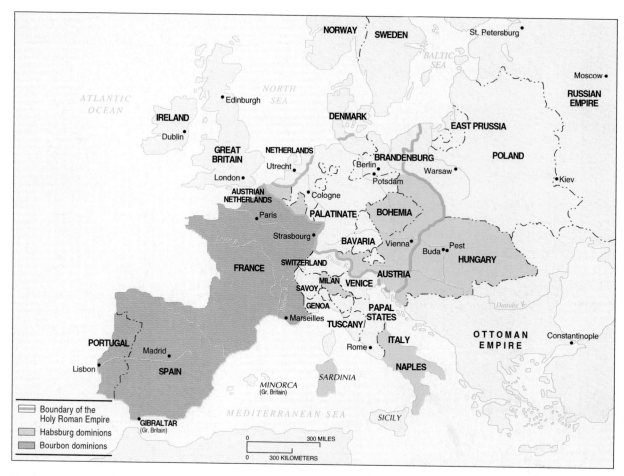

Map 22.2 *Europe Under Absolute Monarchy, 1715. The rise of absolute monarchies led to consolidation of national borders as states asserted full control of areas within their boundaries. For example, a recent study shows that villages that straddled the French–Spanish border were undifferentiated before 1600, but by 1700 they showed marked national differences because of different state policies and the greater impact of belonging to one state or another.*

The Nation-State

The absolute monarchies and the parliamentary monarchies shared important characteristics as nation-states. Unlike the great empires of many other civilizations, they ruled peoples who shared a common culture and language, some important minorities apart. They could appeal to a certain loyalty that linked cultural and political bonds. This was as true of England, where the idea of special rights of Englishmen helped feed the parliamentary movement, as it was of France. Not surprisingly, ordinary people in many nation-states, even though not directly represented in government, increasingly believed that government should act for their interests. Thus, Louis XIV faced recurrent popular riots based on the assumption that when bad harvests drove up food prices, the government was obligated to help people out.

In sum, nation-states developed a growing list of functions, particularly under the banner of mercantilism, whose principles were shared by monarchists and parliamentary leaders alike. They also promoted new political values and loyalties that were very different from the political traditions of other civilizations. They kept the West politically divided and often at war.

ⅰⅡ DEPⴕH

Elites and Masses

What caused the end of witchcraft hysteria in the West by the later 17th century? Did wise rulers calm a frenzied populace or did ordinary people themselves change their minds? One explanation focuses on new efforts by elites, such as local magistrates, to discipline mass impulses. Authorities stopped believing in demonic disruptions of natural processes, and so forced an end to persecutions. But many ordinary people were also thinking in new ways. Without converting fully to a scientific outlook, they became open to new ideas about how to handle health problems, reducing their belief in magical remedies; they needed witches less. Potential "witches" may have become more cautious. Older women, threatened by growing community suspicion, learned to maintain a lower profile and to emphasize benign, grandmotherly qualities rather than seeking a more independent role. Without question, there was a decline both in witchcraft beliefs, once a key element in the Western mentality, and in the hysteria specifically characteristic of the 16th and 17th centuries. This decline reflected new ways of thinking about strangeness and disruption. It involved complex interactions between various segments of Western society: magistrates and villagers, scientists and priests, husbands and widows.

The transformation of Western society after 1450 raises fascinating questions about the role of elites—particularly powerful groups and creative individuals—versus the ordinary people in causing change. The growing importance of social history has called attention to ordinary people, as we have seen, but it has not answered all the questions about their actual role. This role varies by place and time, of course. Some social historians tend to see ordinary people as victims of change, pushed around by the power groups. Others tend to stress the positive historical role of ordinary people in partly shaping the context of their own lives and affecting the larger course of history.

It is easy to read the early modern transformation of western Europe as an operation created by elites, with the masses as passively watching or futilely protesting. Not only the Renaissance and Reformation, but also the commercial revolution, took decisive action by key leadership groups. Leading merchants spurred economic change, and they ultimately began to farm out manufacturing jobs. The resultant rise of dependent wage labor, which tore a growing minority of western Europeans away from property and so from economic control of their lives, illustrates the power disparities in Western society. Ordinary people knuckled under or protested, but they were reacting, not initiating.

The rise of science rivets our attention on the activities of extraordinarily creative individuals, such as Newton, and elite institutions, such as the scientific academies. Some historians have suggested that the rise of science opened a new gap between the ways educated upper classes and masses thought.

Yet the ordinary people of western Europe were not passive, nor did they simply protest change in the name of tradition. Widespread shifts came from repeated decisions by peasants and artisans, not just from those at the top. The steady technological improvements in manufacturing thus flowed upward from practicing artisans, not downward from formal scientists. The European-style family that had taken shape by the 16th century was an innovation by ordinary people long ignored by the elite. It encouraged new parent–child relations and new tensions between young adults and the old that might spur other innovations, including a willingness to settle distant colonies in search of property. The fact that young people often had to wait to marry until their property-owning fathers died could induce many to seek new lands or new economic methods. In other words, ordinary people changed their habits too, and these changes had wide impact.

Questions: Did elites gain new power over the masses in early modern Western society? Are ordinary people more conservative by nature, more suspicious of change, than groups at the top? Can you describe at least two other historical cases in which it is important to determine whether change was imposed on ordinary people from above or whether ordinary people themselves produced important innovations?

THE WEST BY 1750

❖ *The three great currents of change—commercialization, cultural reorientation, and the rise of the nation-state—continued to operate in the West after 1700, along with the growing international influence of the West. Each current produced new changes that furthered the overall transformation of the West.*

Political Patterns

On the whole, during the mid-18th century political changes seemed least significant. During much of the century English politics settled into a bloated parliamentary routine in which key political groups competed for influence without major policy differences. Popular concern for greater representation surfaced in the 1760s, as a movement for wider voting rights surged briefly, but there was no consistent reform current. Absolute monarchy in France changed little institutionally, but it became less effective. It could not force changes in the tax structure that would give it more solid financial footing because aristocrats refused to surrender their traditional exemptions.

Political developments were far livelier in central Europe. In Prussia, *Frederick the Great,* building on the military and bureaucratic organization of his predecessors, introduced greater freedom of religion while expanding the economic functions of the state. His government actively encouraged better agricultural methods; for example, it promoted use of the American potato as a staple crop. It also enacted laws promoting greater commercial coordination and greater equity; harsh traditional punishments were cut back. Rulers of this sort claimed to be enlightened despots, wielding great authority but for the good of society at large.

Enlightened or not, the policies of the major Western nation-states produced recurrent warfare. France and Britain squared off in the 1740s and again in the *Seven Years' War* (1756–1763); their conflicts focused on battles for colonial empire. Austria and Prussia also fought, with Prussia gaining new land. Wars in the 18th century were carefully modulated, without devastating effects, but they demonstrated the continued linkage between statecraft and war that was characteristic of the West.

Enlightenment Thought and Popular Culture

In culture, the aftermath of the scientific revolution spilled over into a new movement known as the *Enlightenment,* centered particularly in France but with adherents throughout the Western world. Enlighten-ment thinkers continued to support scientific advance. Although there were no Newton-like breakthroughs, chemists gained new understanding of major elements, and biologists developed a vital new classification system for the natural species.

The Enlightenment also pioneered in applying scientific methods to the study of human society, sketching the modern social sciences. The basic idea was that rational laws could describe social as well as physical behavior and that knowledge could be used to improve policy. Thus, criminologists wrote that brutal punishments failed to deter crime, whereas a decent society would be able to rehabilitate criminals through education. Political theorists wrote about the importance of carefully planned constitutions and controls over privilege, although they disagreed about what political form was best. A new school of economists developed. In his classic book *Wealth of Nations,* Scottish philosopher *Adam Smith* set forth a number of principles of economic behavior. He argued that people act according to their self-interest but, through competition, promote general economic advance. Government should avoid regulation in favor of the operation of individual initiative and market forces. This was an important statement of economic policy and an illustration of the growing belief that general models of human behavior could be derived from rational thought.

Single individuals could sum up part of the Enlightenment's impressive range. Denis Diderot (1713–1784; Figure 22.4) was a multifaceted leader of the French Enlightenment, best known for his editorial work on the *Encyclopédie* that compiled scientific and social scientific knowledge. Trained initially by the Jesuits, Diderot also wrote widely on philosophy, mathematics, and the psychology of deaf–mutes and also tried his hand at literature. An active friend of other philosophers, Diderot also traveled to foreign courts as advisor and visiting intellectual. A visit to Catherine the Great of Russia in 1773–1774, to thank her for generous patronage, harmed his health, but he maintained his relationship with his mistress, Sophie Volland.

More generally still, the Enlightenment produced a set of basic principles about human affairs: Human beings are good, at least, improvable, and they can be educated to be better, reason is the key to truth, and religions that rely on blind faith or refuse to tolerate diversity are wrong. Enlightenment thinkers attacked the Catholic church with particular vigor. Progress was possible, even inevitable, if people could be set free. Society's goals should center on improving material and social life.

Figure 22.4. Denis Diderot.

discuss the latest reform ideas. Leading writers and compilations of scientific and philosophical findings, such as the *Encyclopaedia Britannica*, won a wide audience and, for a few people, a substantial fortune from the sale of books.

Other changes in popular outlook paralleled the new intellectual currents, although they had deeper sources than philosophy alone. Attitudes toward children began to shift in many social groups. Older methods of physical discipline were criticized in favor of more restrained behavior that would respect the goodness and innocence of children. Swaddling—wrapping infants in cloth so they could not move or harm themselves—began to decline as parents became interested in freer movement and greater interaction for young children. Among wealthy families, educational toys and books for children reflected the idea that childhood should be a stage for learning and growth.

Family life generally was changed by a growing sense that old hierarchies should be rethought and revised toward greater equality in the treatment of women and children in the home. Love between family members gained new respect, and an emotional bond in marriage became more widely sought. Parents grew more reluctant to force a match on a son or daughter if the emotional vibrations were not right. Here was a link not only with Enlightenment ideas of proper family relations but with the novels such as Richardson's *Pamela* that poured out a sentimental view of life.

Ongoing Change in Commerce and Manufacturing

Ongoing economic change paralleled changes in popular culture and intellectual life. Commerce continued to spread. Ordinary Westerners began to buy processed products, such as refined sugar and coffee or tea obtained from Indonesia and the West Indies, for daily use. This was a sign of the growing importance of Europe's new colonies for ordinary life and of the beginnings of mass consumerism in Western society. Another sign of change was the growing use of paid professional entertainment as part of popular leisure, even in rural festivals. Circuses, first introduced in France in the 1670s, began to redefine leisure to include spectatorship and a taste for the bizarre.

Agriculture began to change. Until the late 17th century, western Europe had continued to rely largely on the methods and techniques characteristic of the

Although it was not typical of the Enlightenment's main thrust, a few thinkers applied these general principles to other areas. A handful of *socialists* argued that economic equality and the abolition of private property must become important goals. A few feminist thinkers, such as *Mary Wollstonecraft* in England, argued—against the general male-centered views of most Enlightenment thinkers—that new political rights and freedoms should extend to women. Several journals written by women for women made their first appearance during this extraordinary cultural period. Madame de Beaumere took over the direction of the French *Journal des Dames* from a man, and in Germany, Marianne Ehrmann used her journal to suggest that men might be partly to blame for women's lowly position.

The popularization of new ideas encouraged further changes in the habits and beliefs of many ordinary people. Reading clubs and coffeehouses allowed many urban artisans and businessmen to

ᴅᴏᴄᴜᴍᴇɴᴛ

Controversies About Women

Changes in family structure and some shifts in the economic roles of women, as well as ambivalent Protestant ideas about women that emphasized the family context but urged affection and respect between wives and husbands, touched off new gender tensions in Western society by the 17th century. Some of these tensions showed in witchcraft trials, so disproportionately directed against women. Other tensions showed in open debate about women's relationships to men; women not content with a docile wifeliness vied with new claims of virtue and prowess by some women. Although the debate was centered in the upper class of Protestant nations such as England, it may have had wider ramifications. Some of these ramifications, though quieter during the 18th century, burst forth again in arguments about inequality and family confinement in the 19th century, when a more durable feminist movement took shape in the West. In the selections here, the antiwoman position is set forth in a 1615 pamphlet by Joseph Swetham; the favorable view implicitly urging new rights is in a 1640 pamphlet pseudonymously authored by "Mary Tattle-Well and Ioane Hit-Him-Home, spinsters."

Swetham's "Arraignment of Women"

Men, I say, may live without women, but women cannot live without men: for Venus, whose beauty was excellent fair, yet when she needed man's help, She took Vulcan, a clubfooted Smith....

For women have a thousand ways to entice thee and ten thousand ways to deceive thee and all such fools as are suitors unto them: some they keep in hand with promises, and some they feed with flattery, and some they delay with dalliances, and some they please with kisses. They lay out the folds of their hair to entangle men into their love; betwixt their breasts in the vale of destruction; and in their beds there is hell, sorrow and repentance. Eagles eat not men till they are dead, but women devour them alive....

It is said of men that they have that one fault, but of women it is said that they have two faults: that is to say, they can neither say well nor do well. There is a saying that goeth thus: that things far fetched and dear bought are of us most dearly beloved. The like may be said of women; although many of them are not far fetched, yet they are dear bought, yea and so dear that many a man curseth his hard pennyworths and bans his own heart. For the pleasure of the fairest woman in the world lasteth but a honeymoon; that is, while a man hath glutted his affections and reaped the first fruit, his pleasure being past, sorrow and repentance remaineth still with him.

Tattle-Well and Hit-Him-Home's "Women's Sharp Revenge"

But it hath been the policy of all parents, even from the beginning, to curb us of that benefit by striving to keep us under and to make us men's mere Vassals even unto all posterity. How else comes it to pass that when a Father hath a numerous issue of Sons and Daughters, the sons forsooth they must be first put to the Grammar school, and after perchance sent to the University, and trained up in the Liberal Arts and Sciences, and there (if they prove not Blockheads) they may in time be book-learned?...

When we, whom they style by the name of weaker Vessels, though of a more delicate, fine, soft, and more pliant flesh therefore of a temper most capable of the best Impression, have not that generous and liberal Education, lest we should be made able to vindicate our own injuries, we are set only to the Needle, to prick our fingers, or else to the Wheel to spin a fair thread for our own undoing, or perchance to some more dirty and debased drudgery. If we be taught to read, they then confine us within the compass of our Mother Tongue, and that limit we are not suffered to pass; or if (which sometimes happeneth) we be brought up to Music, to singing, and to dancing, it is not for any benefit that thereby we can engross unto ourselves, but for their own particular ends, the better to please and content their licentious appetites when we come to our maturity and ripeness. And thus if we be weak by Nature, they strive to make us more weak by our Nurture; and if in degree of place low, they strive by their policy to keep us more under.

Now to show we are no such despised matter as you would seem to make us, come to our first Creation, when man was made of the mere dust of the earth. The woman had her being from the best part of his body, the Rib next to his heart, which difference even in our complexions may be easily decided. Man is of a dull, earthy, and melancholy aspect, having shallows in his face and a very forest upon his Chin, when our soft and smooth Cheeks are a true representation of a delectable garden of intermixed Roses and Lilies.... Man might consider that women were not created to be their slaves or vassals; for as they had not their Original out of his head (thereby to command him), so it was not out of his foot to be trod upon, but in a medium out of his side to be his fellow feeler, his equal, and companion....

Thus have I truly and impartially proved that for Chastity, Charity, Constancy, Magnanimity, Valor, Wisdom, Piety, or any Grace or Virtue whatsoever, women have always been more than equal with men, and that for Luxury, Surquidant obscenity, profanity, Ebriety, Impiety, and all that may be called bad we do come far short of them.

Questions: What are the main disagreements in these 17th-century texts? What kind of approach was more novel, judging by the Western gender tradition to that point? What conditions prompted a more vigorous public debate about gender in the 17th century? How does it connect to religious, commercial, and political change? How does the favorable argument compare with more modern views about women? What kinds of change does it advocate? Did the new arguments about women's conditions suggest that these conditions were improving?

Middle Ages—a severe economic constraint in an agricultural society. The three-field system still meant that a full third of all farmland was left unplanted each year to restore fertility. First in the Netherlands and then elsewhere, new procedures for draining swamps added available land. Reformers touted nitrogen-fixing crops to reduce the need to leave land idle. Stockbreeding improved, and new techniques such as seed-drills and the use of scythes instead of sickles for harvesting increased productivity. Some changes spread particularly fast on large estates, but other changes affected ordinary peasants as well. Particularly vital in this category was the spread of the potato from the late 17th century onward.

A New World crop, the potato had long been shunned because it was not mentioned in the Bible and was held to be the cause of plagues. Enlightened government leaders, and the peasants' desire to win greater economic security and better nutrition, led to widespread use of this crop. In sum, the West improved its food supply and agricultural efficiency, leaving more labor available for other pursuits.

These changes, along with the steady growth of colonial trade and internal commerce, spurred increased manufacturing. Capitalism—the investment of funds in hopes of larger profits—also spread from big trading ventures to the production of goods. The 18th century witnessed a rapid spread of household production of textiles and metal products, mostly by rural workers who alternated manufacturing with some agriculture. Here was a key use of labor that was no longer needed for food. Hundreds of thousands of people were drawn into this domestic system, in which capitalist merchants distributed supplies and orders and workers ran the production process for pay (Figure 22.5). Although manufacturing tools were still

Figure 22.5. A family of woolmakers at home.

operated by hand, the spread of domestic manufacturing spurred important technical innovations designed to improve efficiency. In 1733, James Kay in England introduced the flying shuttle, which permitted automatic crossing of threads on looms; with this, an individual weaver could do the work of two. Improvements in spinning soon followed as the Western economy began to move toward a full-fledged Industrial Revolution (see Chapter 28).

Human changes accompanied and sometimes preceded technology. Around 1700, most manufacturers who made wool cloth in northern England were artisans, doing part of the work themselves. By 1720, a group of loom owners were becoming outright manufacturers with new ideas and behaviors. How were manufacturers different? They spent their time organizing production and sales rather than doing their own work. They moved work out of their homes. They stopped drinking beer with their workers. And they saw their workers as market commodities, to be treated as the conditions of trade demanded. In 1736, one such manufacturer coolly wrote that because of slumping sales, "I have turned off a great many of my makers, and keep turning more off weekly."

Finally, agricultural changes, commercialism, and manufacturing combined, particularly after about 1730, to produce a rapidly growing population in the West. With better food supplies, more people survived, particularly with the aid of the potato. Furthermore, new manufacturing jobs helped landless people support themselves, promoting in some cases earlier marriage and sexual relationships. Population growth, in turn, promoted further economic change, heightening competition and producing a more manipulable labor force. The West's great population revolution, which continued into the 19th century, both caused and reflected the civilization's dynamism, although it also produced great strain and confusion.

Conclusion

Innovation and Instability

By the 18th century, the various strands of change were increasingly intertwined in Western civilization. Stronger governments promoted agricultural improvements, which helped prod population growth. Changes in popular beliefs were fed by new economic structures; both encouraged a reevaluation of the family and the roles of children. New beliefs also raised new political challenges. Enlightenment

ideas about liberty and fundamental human equality could be directed against existing regimes. New family practices might have political implications as well. Children, raised with less adult restraint and encouraged to value their individual worth through parental love and careful education, might see traditional political limitations in new ways. There was no perfect fit, no inevitable match, in the three strands of change that had been transforming the West for two centuries or more: the commercial, the cultural, and the political. However, by 1750 all were in place. The combination had already produced an unusual version of an agricultural civilization, and it promised more upheaval in the future.

Further Readings

For an overview of developments in Western society during this period, with extensive bibliographies, see Sheldon Watts's *A Social History of Western Europe, 1450–1720* (1984), Michael Anderson's *Approaches to the West European Family* (1980), and Peter N. Stearns's *Life and Society in the West: The Modern Centuries* (1988). Charles Tilly's *Big Structures, Large Processes, Huge Comparisons* (1985) offers an analytical framework based on major change; see also Tilly's edited volume, *The Formation of National States in Western Europe* (1975).

On more specific developments and periods, J. H. Plumb's *The Italian Renaissance* (1986), F. H. New's *The Renaissance and Reformation: A Short History* (1977), O. Chadwick's *The Reformation* (1983), and Steven Ozment's *The Age of Reform, 1520–1550* (1980) are fine introductions to early changes. See also Hubert Jedin and John Dolan, eds., *Reformation and Counter Reformation* (1980). Later changes are sketched in Thomas Munck's *Seventeenth Century Europe: 1598–1700* (1990) and Jeremy Black's *Eighteenth Century Europe: 1700–1789* (1990). On England in the Civil War period, see Christopher Hill, *A Nation of Change and Novelty* (1990).

Key aspects of social change in this period can be approached through Peter Burke's *Popular Culture in Early Modern Europe* (1978), Robin Biggs's *Communities of Belief: Cultural and Social Tensions in Early Modern France* (1989), Keith Thomas's *Religion and the Decline of Magic* (1971), Lawrence Stone's *The Family, Sex and Marriage in England 1500–1800* (1977), and James Sharpe's *Instruments of Darkness: Witchcraft in Early Modern England* (1997). On popular protest, see Charles Tilly's *The Contentious French* (1986) and H.A.F. Kamen's *The Iron Century: Social Change in Europe 1550–1660* (1971).

On science, A. R. Hall's *From Galileo to Newton, 1630–1720* (1982) is a fine introduction. Relations between science and technology are covered in C. Cipolla's *Before the Industrial Revolution* (1976).

On the Web

Daily life in Renaissance Italy is examined at http://history.evansville.net/renaissa.html.

The lives and art of da Vinci (http://sunsite.unc.edu/cjackson/vinci), Michelangelo (http://www.michelangelo.com.br/) and Raphael (http://www.hipernet.ufsc.br.wm/paint/tl/it-ren) were closely intertwined with the city of Florence, whose history is addressed at http://www.mega.it.eng/egui/epo/secrepu.htm.

Martin Luther's life (http://www.luther.de/legenden.html and http://www.wittenberg.de/seiten/personen/luther.html) and the course of the Protestant Reformation/Catholic Counter-Reformation are discussed via text and documents http://www.fordham.edu/halsall/sbook1.htm#-Protestant, http://www.educ.msu.edu/homepages/http:/reformation/Counter/Counter/htm and http://angelfire.com/mi/spanogle/medieval.html.

Links to sites illuminating the art and literature of the Northern Renaissance can be found at http://pilot.msu.edu/~cloudsar/nrweb.html, while http://communication.ucsd.edu/bjones/laurance/luther.html illustrates the role of the printing press in the reformation.

The Web provides insight into the role of two of the leading absolute monarchs of Europe, Frederick the Great (http://members. tripod.com/~Nevermore/king7.html) and Louis XIV (http://www.geocities.com/Paris?Rue-1663/index.html and http://www.chateauversailles.fr/en/400.asp).

Isaac Newton's life and letters can be examined at http://www.cannylink.com/historyissacnewton.htm, while other leading figures of the scientific revolution can be explored at (http://www.fordham.edu/halsall/mod/hs1000.html#scirev).

The development of modern political and economic theory can be traced through the lives of Niccolo Machiavelli (http://sol.brunel.ac.uk/~jarvis/bola/ethics/mach.html), the Medici family (http://ES.RICE.EDU/es/HUMAN-SOC/galileo/People/medici.html), Adam Smith (http://www.ridgenet.net/~smitty/adam.html) and through the study of the Glorious Revolution of 1688 (http:// 129.109.57.188/louisvix.htm and http://www. lawsch.uga.edu/~glorious/index.html).

A rich web site, dealing with Renaissance women and their texts, can be found at http://www.stg.brown.edu.1081/dyna-web/rwo/rwo.

Chapter 23

The West and the World

In this 16th century Japanese painting, the artist depicted the Europeans and their African slaves as exotic and unfamiliar.

This chapter deals with the consequences of some key developments long celebrated in American school texts: the voyages of Columbus and the explorers and the empires built by European conquerors and missionaries. The result was a power shift in world affairs, but another set of crucial developments in world history also resulted: the redefinition of interchanges between world societies and civilizations.

Previous periods had seen important steps toward greater diffusion of goods and ideas. During the classical era, most attention was given to developing larger regional economies and cultural zones, such as the Chinese Middle Kingdom and the Mediterranean basin. Wider international contacts existed, but they were not of fundamental importance to the societies involved. The level and significance of contacts increased in the postclassical era. Missionary religions spilled across civilization boundaries, as with Buddhism in eastern and southeast Asia and above all with Islam. For the Middle East, parts of Africa and Europe, and much of India, international trade became an important feature of the basic economic structure, with some regions dominating trade in particular goods.

Despite these important precedents, the international relationships that developed after 1450, mainly but not exclusively sponsored by western Europe, spelled a new period in world history. New areas of the world were for the first time brought into the international complex, particularly the Americas. The rate of international trade also increased in some portions of the Old World, such as the islands of southeast Asia. Furthermore, international trade became so significant that it forged different relationships between key societies, based on the kind of goods and amount of control contributed to the surging world economy.

This chapter deals with several interrelated developments between about 1450 and 1750—the same centuries when western Europe was changing rapidly within its own borders. We start with a discussion of the West's acquisitions as it became the world's leading international trader and colonial power. Next we discuss the larger international economic system the West created, which turned out to have a life of its own. New exchanges of ideas, foods, and diseases followed from the emergence of this new system. Finally, we try to sort out the different kinds of responses the new economic framework generated, ranging from attempts at isolation to outright subjection.

1400 C.E.	1500 C.E.	1600 C.E.	1700 C.E.
1394–1460 Prince Henry the Navigator **1433** China ends great expeditions **1434** Portugal extends expeditions down West African coast **1488** Portuguese round Cape of Good Hope **1492** Columbus's first expedition **1497–1498** Vasco da Gama to India	**1509** First Spanish colonies on Latin American mainland **1514** Expedition to Indonesia **1519–1521** Magellan circumnavigates globe **1534** First French explorations in Canada **1542** Portuguese reach Japan **1562** Britain begins its slave trade **1571** Ottoman fleet defeated in Battle of Lepanto **1588** British defeat Spanish Armada **1597** Japan begins isolation policy	**1607** First British colony in Virginia **1608** First French colonies in Canada; first trading concession in India to England **1641** Dutch begin conquests on Java, in Indonesia **1652** Dutch launch colony in southern Africa	**1744** French–British wars in India **1756–1763** Seven Years' War, in Europe, India, and North America **1763** British acquire New France **1775–1783** American Revolution **1756** "Black hole" of Calcutta **1764** East India Company control of Bengal

THE WEST'S FIRST OUTREACH: MARITIME POWER

 Between 1450 and 1650, various western European nations gained unprecedented mastery of the world's oceans. Trading patterns and colonial expansion focused on Europe's maritime power. Pioneering efforts by Spain and Portugal were followed by the surge of Britain, Holland, and France.

Various European leaders, particularly merchants but also some princes and clergy, had become increasingly aware of the larger world around them since 1100. The Crusades brought knowledge of the Islamic world's superior economy and the goods that could be imported from Asia. The Mongol Empire, which sped up exchanges between the civilizations of Asia, also spurred European interest. The fall of the Khans in China disrupted this interchange, as China became once again a land of mystery to Europeans. Europe's upper classes had by this time become accustomed to imported products from southeast Asia and India, particularly spices. These goods were transported to the Middle East in Arab ships, then brought overland, where they were loaded again onto vessels (mainly from Genoa and Venice, in Italy) for the Mediterranean trade.

Europeans entered into this era of growing contacts with the wider world with several disadvantages. They remained ignorant of the wider world. Viking adventurers from Scandinavia had crossed the Atlantic in the 10th century, reaching Greenland and then North America, which they named Vinland. However, they quickly lost interest beyond establishing settlements on Greenland and Iceland, in part because they encountered Indian warriors whose weaponry was good enough to cause them serious problems. And many Europeans continued to believe that the earth was flat, although scientists elsewhere knew otherwise; this belief made them fearful of distant voyages lest they fall off the world's edge.

Europeans did launch a more consistent effort at expansion from 1291 onward, as discussed in Chapter 21. They were pressed by new problems: fear of the strength of the emerging Ottoman Empire and the lack of gold to pay for Asian imports. Initial settlements in island groups in the south Atlantic fed their hopes for further gains. However, the first expeditions were limited by the small, oar-propelled ships used in the Mediterranean trade, which could not travel far into the oceans.

New Technology: A Key to Power

During the 15th century, a series of technological improvements began to change the equation. Europeans developed deep-draft, round-hulled sailing ships for the Atlantic, capable of carrying heavy armaments. They also began to use the compass for navigation (an instrument they copied from the Arabs, who had learned it from the Chinese). Mapmaking and other navigational devices improved as well. Finally, European knowledge of explosives, another Chinese invention, was adapted into gunnery. European metalwork, steadily advancing in sophistication, allowed Western metalsmiths to devise the first guns and cannons. Though not very accurate, these weapons were awesome by the standards of the time (and terrifying to many Europeans, who had reason to fear the new destructive power of their own armies and navies). The West began to forge a military advantage over all other civilizations of the world, at first primarily on the seas—an advantage it would retain into the 20th century. With an unprecedented ability to kill and intimidate from a distance, western Europe was ready for its big push.

Portugal and Spain Lead the Pack

The specific initiative came from the small kingdom of Portugal, whose Atlantic location made it well-suited for new initiatives. Portugal's rulers were drawn by the excitement of discovery, the harm they might cause to the Muslim world, and a thirst for wealth—a potent mix. A Portuguese prince, *Henry the Navigator* (Figure 23.1), organized a series of expeditions along the African coast and also outward to islands such as the Azores. Beginning in 1434 the Portuguese began to press down the African coast, each expedition going a little farther than its predecessor. They brought back slaves, spices such as pepper, and many stories of gold hoards they had not yet been able to find.

Later in the 15th century, Portuguese sailors ventured around the *Cape of Good Hope* in an attempt to find India, where direct contact would give Europeans easier access to luxury cloths and spices. They rounded the cape in 1488, but weary sailors forced the expedition back before it could reach India. Then, after news of Columbus's discovery of America for Spain in 1492, Portugal redoubled its efforts, hoping to stave off the new Spanish competition. *Vasco da Gama's* fleet of four ships reached India in 1498, with the aid of a Hindu pilot picked up in east Africa. The Portuguese mistakenly believed that the Indians were Christians, for they thought the Hindu temples were churches. They faced the hostility of Muslim merchants, who had long dominated trade in this part of the world, and they brought only crude goods for sale, like iron pots. But fortunately they had a lot of gold as well. They managed to return with a small load of spices.

This success set in motion an annual series of Portuguese voyages to the Indian Ocean, outlined in Map 23.1. One expedition, blown off course, reached

Figure 23.1. *Prince Henry the Navigator, of Portugal, sent annual expeditions down the western coast of Africa. He was not a sailor, but his sponsorship was essential.*

Brazil, where it proclaimed Portuguese sovereignty (Figure 23.2). Portugal began to set up forts on the African coast and also in India—the forerunners of such Portuguese colonies as Mozambique, in east Africa, and Goa, in India. By 1514 the Portuguese had reached the islands of Indonesia, the center of spice production, and China. In 1542 one Portuguese expedition arrived in Japan, where a missionary effort was launched that met with some success for several decades.

Meanwhile, only a short time after the Portuguese quest began, the Spanish reached out with even greater force. Here also was a country only recently freed from Muslim rule, full of missionary zeal and a desire for riches. The Spanish had traveled into the Atlantic during the 14th century. Then in 1492, the same year that the final Muslim fortress was captured in Spain, the Italian navigator *Christopher Columbus*, operating in the name of the newly united Spanish monarchy, set sail for a westward route to India, convinced that the round earth would make his quest possible. As is well known, he failed, reaching the Americas instead and mistakenly naming their inhabitants Indians. Although Columbus believed to his death that he had sailed to India, later Spanish explorers realized that they had voyaged to a region where Europeans, Africans, and Asians had

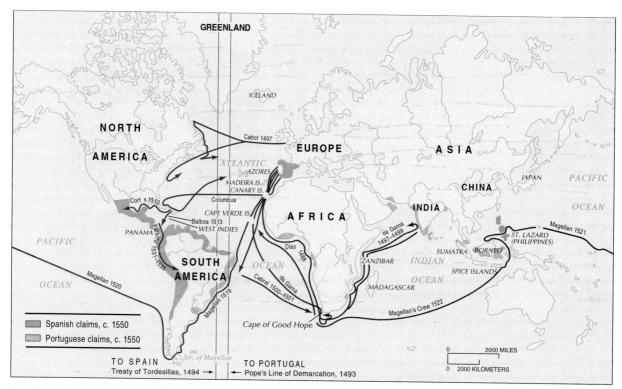

Map 23.1 *Spain and Portugal: Explorations and Colonies, c. 1600. In the early years of new exploration, Spanish and Portuguese voyages surveyed much of the coast of South America and some choice ports in Africa and Asia.*

not traveled previously. One expedition, headed by Amerigo Vespucci, gave the New World its name. Spain, eager to claim this new land, won papal approval for Spanish dominion over most of what is now Latin America, although a later treaty awarded Brazil to Portugal.

Finally, a Spanish expedition under *Ferdinand Magellan* set sail westward in 1519, passing the southern tip of South America and sailing across the Pacific, reaching the Indonesian islands in 1521 after incredible hardships. It was on the basis of this voyage, the first trip around the world, that Spain claimed the Philippines, which it held until 1898.

Portugal emerged from this first round of exploration with coastal holdings in parts of Africa and in the Indian port of Goa, a lease on the Chinese port of Macao, short-lived interests in trade with Japan, and, finally, the claim on Brazil. Spain asserted its hold on the Philippines, various Pacific islands, and the bulk of the Americas. During the

16th century, the Spanish backed up these claims by military expeditions to Mexico and South America. The Spanish also held Florida and sent expeditions northward from Mexico into California and other parts of what later became the southwestern United States.

Northern European Expeditions

Later in the 16th century, the lead in exploration passed to northern Europe, as newly strong monarchies, such as France and England, got into the act and zealous Protestants in Britain and Holland strove to rival Catholic gains (Map 23.2). In part this shift in dynamism occurred because Spain and Portugal were busy digesting the gains they had already made; in part it was because northern Europeans, particularly the Dutch and the British, improved the design of oceanic vessels, producing lighter, faster ships than those of their Catholic

Figure 23.2. This is the earliest European sketch of American Indians at the time of a Portuguese expedition to northern South America about 1500. "The people are thus naked, handsome, brown.... They also eat each other ... and hang the flesh of them in the smoke. They become a hundred and fifty years of age, and have no government."

adversaries. Britain won a historic sea battle with Spain in 1588, routing a massive Spanish Armada. From this point onward, the British, the Dutch, and to some extent the French vied for dominance on the seas, although in the Americas they aimed mainly northward because they could not challenge the Spanish and Portuguese colonies. Only in the sugar-rich West Indies did northern Europe seize islands initially claimed by Spain.

The new adventurers, like their Spanish and Portuguese predecessors, appreciated the economic potential of such voyages. Two 16th-century English explorers, trying to find an Arctic route to China, were told to keep an eye out for any native populations en route, for such people would provide a perfect market for warm English woolens. And if the territory was unpopulated, it might be put to use as a source of fish for Britain. A quest for profit had become a dominant policy motive.

French explorers crossed the Atlantic first in 1534, reaching Canada, which they claimed. In the 17th century, various expeditions pressed down from Canada into the Great Lakes region and the Mississippi valley.

The British also turned their attention to North America, starting with a brief expedition as early as 1497. The English hoped to discover a northwest passage to spice-rich India, but accomplished little beyond exploration of the Hudson Bay area of Canada during the 16th century. England's serious work began in the 17th century, with the colonization of the east coast of North America. Holland also had holdings in North America and, for a time, in Brazil.

The Dutch entered the picture after winning independence from Spain, and Holland quickly became a major competitor with Portugal in southeast Asia. The Dutch sent many sailors and ships to the region, ousting the Portuguese from the Indonesian islands by the early 17th century. Voyagers from the Netherlands explored the coast of Australia, though without much immediate result. Finally, toward the mid-17th century, Holland established a settlement on the southern tip of Africa, mainly to provide a relay station for its ships bound for the East Indies.

The Netherlands, Britain, and France all chartered great trading companies, such as the *Dutch East India Company* and the British firm of similar name. These companies were given government monopolies of trade in the regions designated, but they were not rigorously supervised by their own states. They had rights to raise armies and coin money on their own. Thus, semiprivate companies, amassing great commercial fortunes, long acted

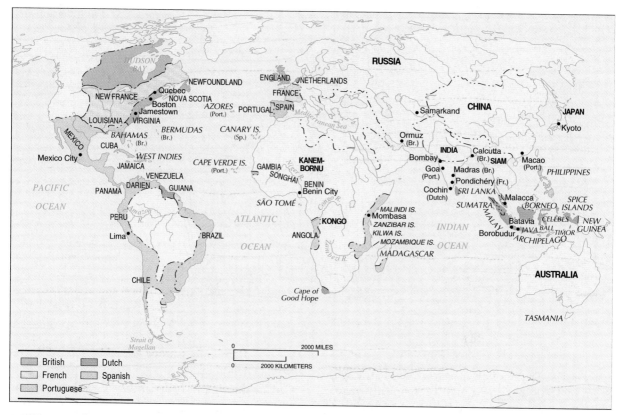

Map 23.2 *French, British, and Dutch Holdings, c. 1700. During the 17th century, northwestern Europe took the initiative in explorations, venturing into North America and seeking convenient trading stations elsewhere.*

almost like independent governments in the regions they claimed. For some time, a Dutch trading company effectively ruled the island of Taiwan off the coast of China; the *British East India Company* played a similar role in parts of India during much of the 18th century. The companies in North America traded actively in furs.

No matter where in Europe they came from, explorers and their crews faced many hardships at sea. The work was tiring and uncertain, with voyages lasting many months or years, and diseases such as scurvy were rampant. One expedition accepted only bachelors for its crew because married men would miss their families too much. A sailor on another trip complained that "he was tired of being always tired, that he would rather die once than many times, and that they might as well shut their eyes and let the ship go to the bottom."

IN DEPTH

Causation and the West's Expansion

Because of their interest in social change, historians inevitably deal with causation. What prompted the fall of Rome? Why did Islam spread so widely? What factors explain why most agricultural civilizations developed patriarchal family structures? Historical causation differs from the kinds of causation many scientists test. When experiments or observations can be repeated, scientists can gain a fairly precise understanding of the factors that produce a phenomenon: Remove an ingredient and the product changes. Historical causation is more complex. Major developments may resemble each other, but they never happen the same way twice. Definitive proof that factor X explains 40 percent of the spread of Buddhism in east Asia is impossible. This is why historians often disagree about causation. But if precision is impossible, high probability is not. We can get a fairly good sense of why things happen, and sloppy causation claims can be disproved. Furthermore, probing causation helps us explore the phenomenon itself. We know more about the nature of Western expansion in the 15th and 16th centuries if we discuss what caused it.

Some historians and other social scientists look to a single kind of cause as the explanation of a variety of circumstances. Some anthropologists are cultural determinists. They judge that a basic set of cultural factors, usually assumed to be very durable, causes the ongoing differences between societies: Chinese and Greeks, on average, respond differently to emotional stimuli because of their different cultural conditioning. More common is a technological or economic determinism. Some historians see technological change as setting other changes in motion. Others, including Marxists, argue that economic arrangements—how the economy is structured and what groups control it—produce at least the basic framework for innovations. At another pole, some historians used to claim "great men" as the prime movers in history. The causes of change thus became Chinggis Khan or Ashoka, with no need to look much farther.

Various approaches to causation have been applied to the West's explorations and colonial conquests in the early modern period. There is room for a "great man" analysis. Many descriptive accounts that dwell on explorers and conquerors (Vasco da Gama and Cortés, for example) and on leaders who sponsored them (such as Henry the Navigator) suggest that the key cause of the West's new role stemmed from the daring and vision of exceptional individuals.

Cultural causation can also be invoked. Somehow, Europe's expansion must relate to the wonders of innovation introduced by the Renaissance. The link with Christian culture is even easier to prove, for a missionary spirit quickly supplemented the efforts of early explorers, leading to more voyages and settlements in Asia and the Americas.

Political causation enters in, if not in causing the initial surge, at least in confirming it. Starting in the 16th century, rivalries between the nation-states motivated a continuing quest for new trade routes and colonies.

There is also room for a simpler, technologically determinist approach. In this view, Europe's gains came from a handful of new inventions. Benefiting from knowledge of advances in China and the Middle East, Europeans introduced naval cannons. Along with steady improvements in navigation and ship design, new techniques explain why Europe gained as it did. Except in the Americas, where they had larger technical and organizational advantages, Europeans advanced in areas they could reach by sea and dominate by ships' guns—port cities, islands, and trade routes—and not elsewhere. Put simply, Europe gained because of these few technical edges.

Like all determinisms, however, this technological approach raises as many questions as it answers. Why were Europeans so ready to adopt new inventions? (What caused the cause?) Why did other societies that were aware of Europe's innovations, such as China, deliberately scorn any adoption of Western naval techniques? Here a different culture determined a reaction different from that of the West. Technology and culture went hand in hand. Clearly, some combined causal framework is needed in this case.

We cannot expect uniform agreement on a precise ordering of causation. However, we can expect fruitful debate—the kind of debate that has already moved our understanding beyond surface causes, such as the powerful personalities of a few people, to a grasp of more underlying contexts.

Questions: If you had to choose a single determinism (cultural, technological, or economic) as basic to social change, which one would you pick? Why? In what ways might the professed motives of Western explorers and colonists have differed from their real motives? Would they necessarily have been aware of the discrepancy?

TOWARD A WORLD ECONOMY

❖ Europe's maritime dominance and the opening of the Atlantic and Pacific oceans had three major consequences in world history. They created a new international pool for basic exchanges of foods, diseases, and a few manufactured products. They created a new world economy, involving the first embrace of the Americas in international trade but setting a different framework even for Europe and Asia. And they created the conditions for direct Western penetration of some parts of the world through colony formation.

The "Colombian Exchange" of Disease and Food

The impact of wider exchange became visible quickly. The extension of international contacts spread disease. The victims were millions of native Americans who had not previously been exposed to Afro-Eurasian diseases such as smallpox and measles and who therefore had no natural immunities (Figure 23.3). During the 16th and 17th centuries, they died in huge numbers. Overall, in North and South America, more than half the native population would die; some estimates run as high as 80 percent. Whole island populations in the West Indies were wiped out. This was a major blow to earlier civilizations in the Americas as well as an opportunity for Europeans to forge a partially new population of their own citizens and slaves imported from Africa. The devastation occurred over a 150-year period, although in some areas it was more rapid. When Europeans made contact with Polynesians and Pacific Coast Indians in the 18th century, the same dreadful pattern played out, again devastating vibrant cultures.

Other exchanges were less dire. New World crops were spread rapidly via Western merchants. American corn and sweet potatoes were taken up widely in China (where merchants learned of them from Spaniards in the Philippines), the Mediterranean, and parts of Africa. In some cases these productive new crops, along with local agricultural improvements, triggered large population increases. For example, China began to experience long-term population pressure in the 17th century, and new crops played a key role. Ironically, Europe itself was slower to take advantage of them.

The use of tobacco, sugar, and coffee spread, but corn and particularly the potato were adopted only in the late 17th century, at which point they spurred major population upheaval in Europe as well.

Animal husbandry became more similar across the world as European and Asian animals, such as horses and cattle, were introduced to the New World. The spread of basic products and diseases formed an important backdrop to world history from the 16th century on, with varying effects on population structures in diverse regions.

The West's Commercial Outreach

Europeans did not displace all Asian shipping from the coastal waters of China and Japan, nor did they completely monopolize the Indian Ocean (see Chapter 28). Along the east African coast, while a few European bases were established, Muslim traders remained active, and commerce continued to move toward the

Figure 23.3. A 16th-century print of Aztec Indians suffering from smallpox during the Cortés invasion (1518–1519).

Middle East. Generally, however, western Europe dominated a great deal of oceanic shipping, even muscling in on trade between other societies, as between India and southeast Asia. This greatly increased Europe's overall profits, and disproportionate control by the great merchant companies increased the European ability to determine the framework for international trade. In the eastern Mediterranean, for example, a Spanish-directed fleet defeated the navy of the Ottoman Empire in the battle of *Lepanto* in 1571. With this setback, any hope of successful Muslim rivalry against European naval power ended. The Turks rebuilt their fleet and continued their activity in the eastern Mediterranean, but they could not challenge the Europeans on the larger international routes.

Although western Europe did not conquer much inland territory in Africa or Asia, it did seek a limited network of secure harbors. Led by Spain and Portugal, then followed by the various northern powers, European ports spread along the west coast of Africa, several parts of the Indian subcontinent, and the islands of southeast Asia by the 17th century. Even in China, where unusually strong governments limited the Europeans' ability to seize harbors outright, the Portuguese won effective control over the island port of Macao. European-controlled ports served as areas for contact with overland traders (usually local merchants) and provided access to inland goods not directly within the reach of the West.

Where direct control was not feasible, European influence led to the formation of special Western enclaves in existing cities, where Western traders won special legal rights. This was the pattern in the Ottoman Empire, where Western merchants set up colonies within Constantinople, and in Russia, where Western factors (shipping agents) set up first in Moscow and then in St. Petersburg. Elements of this system even emerged in Japan after a firm isolationist policy was launched about 1600, as Dutch traders had some special access to the port of Nagasaki. The point was obvious: International trade gained growing importance in supplementing regional economies. Because western Europe now ran this trade, it won special rights of access.

Imbalances in World Trade

The greatest competition in world trade emerged between European nations themselves. Spain briefly dominated, thanks to its imports of silver from the Americas. But it lacked a good banking system and could not support a full commercial surge. England, France, and Holland, where merchants had firmer status, soon pulled in the lion's share of profits from world trade.

Western Europe quickly expanded its manufacturing operations, so that it could export expensive finished goods, such as guns and cloth, in return for unprocessed goods, such as silver and sugar, traded by other societies. Here was another margin for profit.

The dominant *core nations* in the new world system supplemented their growing economic prowess by self-serving political policies. The doctrines of *mercantilism,* which urged that a nation-state not import goods from outside its own empire but sell exports as widely as possible in its own ships, both reflected and encouraged the new world system. Tariff policies discouraged manufacturing in colonial areas and stimulated home-based manufacturing.

Beyond western Europe lay areas that were increasingly enmeshed in the world economy but on a strictly dependent basis. These areas produced low-cost goods: precious metals and cash crops such as sugar, spice, tobacco, and later cotton. Human labor was a vital item of exchange. Parts of sub-Saharan Africa entered the new world economy mainly as suppliers of slaves. The earlier west African patterns of trade across the Sahara yielded to a dominant focus on the Atlantic and therefore to activities organized by Western shippers. In return for slaves and unprocessed goods, Europeans traded their manufactured items while profiting from their control of commercial and shipping services.

A System of International Inequality

The new world economic relationships proved highly durable. Most of the areas established as dependent by the 17th century still carry some special burdens in world trade today. The core–dependent system should not be exaggerated, in part because most of the world, including most of Asia and much of Africa, was not yet fully embraced by it. In dependent areas such as Latin America and the slave-supplying parts of Africa, not all people were mired in poverty. African slave traders and princes who taxed the trade might grow rich. In Latin America the silver mines and commercial estates required regional merchants and farmers to supply food. Furthermore, many peasants in Latin America and even more in Africa were not yet involved in a market economy at all—whether regional or international—but rather produced for local subsistence with traditional motives and methods. However, significant minorities were involved in production for the world market. Also, most African and Latin American merchants and landlords did not fully control their own terms of trade. They might prosper, but their wealth did not stimulate much local manufacturing or general economic advance. Rather, they tended to import European-made goods, including (in the case of American planters) art objects and luxury items.

Coercive labor systems spread. Because dependent economies relied on cheap production of unprocessed goods, there was a tendency to build a system of forced labor that would cost little even when the overall labor supply was precarious. In the Americas, given the population loss from disease, this led to the massive importation of African slaves. Also in the Americas, for many Indians and *mestizos* (people of mixed European and Indian blood), systems of estate management developed that demanded large amounts of labor. More limited examples of estate agriculture, in which peasants were forced into labor without the legal freedom to leave, arose for spice production in the Dutch East Indies and, by the 18th century, in British-dominated agricultural operations in India.

How Much World in the World Economy?

Huge areas of the world were not yet caught up in contact with the world economy. The societies that

Visualizing THE PAST

West Indian Slaveholding

The following table describes the rise of the plantation system, and attendant slaveholding, on the British West Indian island of Antigua, where sugar growing for export gained increasing hold.

Trends of the sort indicated in this table raise further analytical issues about cause and effect. What might have caused the main changes in Antigua's estate system? How might the changes have related to the larger framework of the world economy? What do the trends suggest about the European demand for sugar and about production methods used to meet this demand? What impact would the trends have had on slaves themselves? Laws in the British Caribbean soon began to enforce the estate system, exempting masters from murder charges when slaves died from beatings administered as punishment and fining groups such as the Quakers for daring to bring slaves to religious meetings. How do the statistical trends help explain the imposition of new laws of this sort?

Questions: What main trends in the social and economic structure of this part of Antigua during the 18th century do these figures suggest? What were the main changes in the relationship of slaveholding to property ownership? In the size of estates? In the comparative growth rates of owner and slave populations? Did the estate economy become more or less labor intensive, given the acreage involved? What do the trends suggest about the nature of the European-born or European-derived elite of Antigua?

	1688	1706	1767
Taxables	53	36	65
Slaveholders	16	30	65
Planters with 20 + slaves	6	16	46
Planters with 100 + slaves	0	4	22
Slaves	332	1,150	5,610
Acreage	5,811	5,660	12,350

remained outside the world system did not gain ground as rapidly as the core areas of Europe because they did not have the profit opportunities in international trade. Their technologies changed less rapidly. But until the 18th century, they did not face great international problems. East Asia remained most fully and consciously outside the burgeoning world economy. The Chinese government, having renounced large-scale international trade of its own early in the 15th century, deliberately avoided involvement with international trade on someone else's terms. It did copy some firearms manufacturing from the Europeans, but at a fairly low level. Beyond this it depended on extensive government regulation, backed up by a coastal navy, to keep European activities in check. Most of the limited trade that existed was channeled through Macao. European visitors wrote scornfully of China's disdain for military advances. A Jesuit wrote that "the military … is considered mean among them." The Chinese were also disparaged for adhering to tradition. One Western missionary in the 17th century described how, in his opinion, the Chinese could not be persuaded "to make use of new instruments and leave their old ones without an especial order from the Emperor to that effect. They are more fond of the most defective piece of antiquity than of the most perfect of the modern, differing much in that from us who are in love with nothing but what is new."

So China opted out, not keeping up with European developments but also not subservient to European merchants. The world economy played only a minor role in Chinese history through the 18th century. Chinese manufacturing gains led to a strong export position, and Europeans sent a great deal of American silver to China to pay for the goods they wanted. Indeed, more silver ended up in China than in any other country. But official isolation persisted. Indeed, at the end of the 18th century, a famous British mission, appealing to the government to open the country to greater trade, was rebuffed. The imperial court, after insisting on extreme deference from the British envoy, haughtily informed him that the Chinese had no need for outside goods. European eagerness for Chinese goods—attested to by the habit adopted in the 17th century of calling fine porcelain "china"—was simply not matched by Chinese enthusiasm, but a trickle of trade continued. Westerners compensated in part by developing their own porcelain industry by the 18th century, which contributed

to the early Industrial Revolution, particularly in Britain. Still, there were hopes for commercial entry to China that remained unfulfilled.

Japan, though initially attracted by Western expeditions in the 16th century, also quickly pulled back. The Japanese showed some openness to Christian missions, and they were fascinated by Western advances in gunnery and shipping. Artists captured the interest in exotic foreigners. Guns had particular relevance to Japan's ongoing feudal wars, for there was no disdain here for military life. Yet Japanese leaders soon worried about undue Western influence and the impact this could have on internal divisions among warring lords, as well as the threat guns posed to samurai military dominance. They encouraged a local gunmaking industry that matched existing European muskets and small cannon fairly readily, but having achieved this they cut off most contact with any world trade. Japanese were forbidden to travel or trade abroad, the small Christian minority was suppressed, and from the 17th until the 19th centuries Japan entered a period of almost complete isolation except for some Chinese contact and trading concessions to the small Dutch enclave near Nagasaki.

Several other societies remained largely untouched by new world trade, participating at levels too low to have significant impact. The rulers of India's new Mughal Empire in the 16th century were interested in Western traders and even encouraged the establishment of small port colonies, but most of their attention was riveted on internal development and land-based expansion and commerce; world trade was a sideline. The same held true for the Ottoman and Safavid empires in the Middle East through the 17th century, despite the presence of small European enclaves in key cities. Russia also lay outside the world economic orbit until the 18th century. A largely agricultural society, Russia conducted much of its trade with nomadic peoples in central Asia, which further insulated it from west European demands. Finally, much of Africa, outside the slave-trading orbit in western regions, was untouched by world trade patterns.

The Expansionist Trend

The world economy was not stationary; it tended to gain ground over time. South America, the West Indies, a part of North America, and some regions in west Africa were first staked out as dependencies beginning in the 16th century, and the list later expanded. Portions of southeast Asia that produced for world markets, under the dominance of the great Western trading companies, were brought into the orbit by the 17th century.

By the late 17th century, Western traders were advancing in India as the Mughal Empire began to fall apart. The British and French East India Companies staked out increasing roles in internal trade and administration. Early in the 18th century, Britain passed tariffs against the import of cotton cloth made in India as a means of protecting Britain's own cotton industry. The intent was to use India as a market for British-processed goods and a source of outright payments of gold, which the British were requiring by the late 18th century. Indian observers were aware of the shifting balance. An 18th century account noted,

> But such is the little regard which they [the British] show to the people of this kingdom, and such their apathy and indifference for their welfare, that the people under their dominion groan everywhere, and are reduced to poverty and distress.

India maintained a complex regional economy still, with much internal manufacturing and trade; it was not forced into such complete dependency as Latin America, for example. However, what had initially been a position outside the world economy was changing, to India's disadvantage.

Eastern Europe also was brought into a growing relationship with the world economy and the west European core. The growth of cities in the West created a growing market for imported grains by the 18th century. Much of this demand was met by east European growers, particularly in Prussia and Poland but also in Russia. Export grains, in turn, were produced mainly on large estates by serfs, who were subjected to prolonged periods of labor service. This relationship was similar to that which prevailed in Latin America, with one exception: Outside of Poland, east European governments were much stronger than their Latin American counterparts.

COLONIAL EXPANSION

🔢 *Along with the larger world economic system, a new wave of colonialism took shape after the early Spanish and Portuguese explorations.*

Key European nations developed direct overseas empires. Two sets of American colonies developed, one in Latin America and the Caribbean, one in parts of North America. The Americas hosted the largest colonies, but colonialism also spread to Africa and Asia.

The Americas: Loosely Controlled Colonies

Opportunities to establish colonies were particularly inviting in the Americas, where European guns, horses, and iron weapons offered special advantages and where political disarray and the population losses provided openings in many cases (see Chapter 25). Spain moved first. The Spanish colonized several West Indian islands soon after Columbus's first voyage, starting with Hispaniola and then moving into Cuba, Jamaica, and Puerto Rico. Only in 1509 did they begin settlement on the mainland, in search of gold; the first colony was established in what is now Panama, under an able but unscrupulous adventurer, *Vasco de Balboa*. Several expeditions fanned out in Central America, and then a separate expedition from Cuba launched the Spanish conquest of the Aztecs in Mexico. Another expedition headed toward the Inca realm in the Andes in 1531, where hard fighting was needed before ultimate victory. From this base several colonial expeditions spread to Colombia, other parts of the Andes, and portions of Argentina.

Expansion resulted from the efforts of a motley crew of adventurers, many of them violent and treacherous, like Francisco Pizarro (1478?–1541), admittedly one of the more successful examples (Figure 23.4). Pizarro first came to the Americas in 1502 and settled on the island of Hispaniola. Later, he joined Balboa's colony in Panama, where he received a cattle ranch. Learning of wealth in Peru, he joined with an illiterate soldier and a priest, mounting two expeditions that failed. In 1528 he returned to Spain to gain the king's support and also his agreement that he would be governor of the new province. With these pledges and a force of about 180 men, he attacked the divided Inca empire. Capturing Emperor Atahuallpa, he accepted a large ransom and then strangled him. Several revolts followed during Pizarro's rule from Lima, a coastal city he founded. But the Spanish king ennobled Pizarro for his success. At a dinner in 1541, Pizarro was assassinated by a group of Inca rebels.

Early colonies in the Americas typically were developed by small bands of gold-hungry Europeans, often loosely controlled by colonial administrations back home. Colonial rulers often established only loose controls over Indian populations at first, content to exact tribute without imposing detailed administration and sometimes leaving existing leaders in place. Gradually, more formal administration spread as agricultural settlements were established and official colonial systems took shape under control of bureaucrats sent from Spain and Portugal. Active missionary efforts, designed to Christianize the Indians, added another layer of detailed administration throughout the Spanish holdings in North and South America.

France, Britain, and Holland, though latecomers to the Americas, also staked out colonial settlements. French explorations along the St. Lawrence River in Canada led to small colonies around Quebec, from 1608 onward, and explorations in the Mississippi River basin. Dutch and English settlers moved into portions of the Atlantic coastal regions early in the 17th century. Also in the 17th century, all three countries seized and colonized several West Indian islands, which they soon involved in the growing slave trade.

British and French North America: Backwater Colonies

Colonies of European settlers developed in North America, where patterns differed in many respects from those in Latin America and the Caribbean. English colonies along the Atlantic received religious refugees, such as the Calvinists who fled religious tensions in Britain to settle in New England. Government grants of land to major proprietors such as William Penn led to explicit efforts to recruit settlers. New York began as a Dutch settlement but was taken over easily by an English expedition in 1664.

In Canada, the first substantial European settlements were launched by the French government under Louis XIV. The initial plan involved setting up manorial estates under great lords whose rights were carefully restricted by the state. French peasants were urged to emigrate, although it proved difficult to develop an adequate labor force. However, birth rates were high, and by 1755 *New France* had about 55,000 settlers in a peasant society that proved extremely durable as it fanned out around the fortress of Quebec. Strong organization by the Catholic church completed this partial replica of French

Figure 23.4. Francisco Pizarro.

provincial society. Britain attacked the French strongholds as part of a worldwide colonial struggle between the two powers, the Seven Years' War. France lost its colony under the terms of the *Treaty of Paris,* which in 1763 settled war. France eagerly regained its West Indian sugar islands, along with trading posts in Africa, and Britain took control of Canada and the Mississippi basin. Relations between British officials and the French Canadian community remained strained as British settlements developed in eastern Canada and in Ontario. The flight of many American loyalists after the 1776 revolution added to the English-speaking contingent in Canada.

Colonial holdings along the Atlantic and in Canada were generally of modest interest to Western

Ɖ O C U ϕ E N T

Western Conquerors: Tactics and Motives

In the first passage quoted here, Columbus writes to the Spanish monarchy on his way home from his 1492 expedition. In the second passage, the brother of Francisco Pizarro, the Spanish conqueror of Peru, describes in 1533 how the Inca ruler, Atahuallpa, was defeated.

Columbus's 1492 Expedition

Sir, believing that you will take pleasure in hearing of the great success which our Lord has granted me in my voyage, I write you this letter, whereby you will learn how in thirty-three days' time I reached the Indies with the fleet which the most illustrious King and Queen, our Sovereigns, gave to me, where I found very many islands thickly peopled, of all which I took possession without resistance for their Highnesses by proclamation made and with the royal standard unfurled. To the first island that I found I gave the name of *San Salvador*, in remembrance of His High Majesty, who hath marvelously brought all these things to pass; the Indians call it *Guanaham*....

Espanola is a wonder. Its mountains and plains, and meadows, and fields, are so beautiful and rich for planting and sowing, and rearing cattle of all kinds, and for building towns and villages. The harbours on the coast, and the number and size and wholesomeness of the rivers, most of them bearing gold, surpass anything that would be believed by one who had not seen them. There is a great difference between the trees, fruits, and plants of this island and those of *Juana*. In this island there are many spices and extensive mines of gold and other metals. The inhabitants of this and of all the other islands I have found or gained intelligence of, both men and women, go as naked as they were born, with the exception that some of the women cover one part only with a single leaf of grass or with a piece of cotton, made for that purpose. They have neither iron, nor steel, nor arms, nor are they competent to use them, not that they are not well-formed and of handsome stature, but because they are timid to a surprising degree....

Although I have taken possession of all these islands in the name of their Highnesses, and they are all more abundant in wealth than I am able to express ... yet there was one large town in *Espanola* of which especially I took possession, situated in a locality well adapted for the working of the gold mines, and for all kinds of commerce, either with the main land on this side, or with that beyond which is the land of the great Khan, with which there is great profit....

I have also established the greatest friendship with the king of that country, so much so that he took pride in calling me his brother, and treating me as such. Even should these people change their intentions towards us and become hostile, they do not know what arms are, but, as I have said, go naked, and are the most timid people in the world; so that the men I have left could, alone, destroy the whole country, and this island has no danger for them, if they only know how to conduct themselves.... Finally, and speaking only of what has taken place in this voyage, which has been so hasty, their Highnesses may see that I shall give them all the gold they require, if they will give me but a very little assistance; spices also, and cotton, as much as their Highnesses shall command to be shipped; and mastic, hitherto found only in Greece ... slaves, as many of these idolators as their Highnesses shall command to be shipped....

But our Redeemer hath granted this victory our illustrious King and Queen and their kingdoms, which have acquired great fame by an event of such high importance, in which all Christendom ought to rejoice, and which it ought to celebrate with great festivals and the offering of solemn thanks to the Holy Trinity with many solemn prayers, both for the great exaltation which may accrue to them in turning so many nations to our holy faith, and also for the temporal benefits which will bring great refreshment and gain, not only to Spain, but to all Christians.

Why and How Atahuallpa Was Defeated

The messengers came back to ask the Governor to send a Christian to Atahuallpa, that he intended to come at once, and that he would come unarmed. The Governor sent a Christian, and presently Atahuallpa moved, leaving the armed men behind him. He took with him about five or six thousand Indians without arms, except that under their shirts they had small darts and slings with stones.

He came in a litter, and before went three or four hundred Indians in liveries, cleaning straws from the road and singing. Then came Atahuallpa in the midst of his chiefs and principal men, the greatest among them being also borne on men's shoulders.... A Dominican Friar, who was with the Governor, came forward to tell him, on the part of the Governor, that he waited for him in his lodgings, and that he was sent to speak with him. The Friar then told Atahuallpa that he was a Priest, and that he was sent there to teach the things of the Faith, if they should desire to be Christians. He showed Atahuallpa a book ... and told him that book contained the things of God. Atahuallpa asked for the book, and threw it on the ground, saying: "I will not leave this place until you have restored all that you have taken in my land. I know well who you are, and what you have come for." ... The Friar went to the Governor and reported what was being done, and that no time was to be lost. The Governor sent to me; and I had arranged with the Captain of the artillery that, when a sign was given, he should discharge his pieces, and that, on hearing the reports, all the troops should come forth at once. This was done, and as the Indians were unarmed, they were defeated without danger to any Christian. Those who carried the litter, and the chiefs who surrounded Atahuallpa, were all killed, falling around him. The Governor came out and seized Atahuallpa, and in protecting him, he received a knife cut from a Christian in the hand. The troops continued the pursuit as far as the place where the armed Indians were stationed, who made no resistance whatever, because it was night. All were brought into town, where the Governor was quartered.

Next morning the Governor ordered us to go to the camp of Atahuallpa, where we found forty thousand pesos worth of gold and two or three pounds of silver.... The Governor said that he had not come to make war on the Indians, but that our Lord the Emperor, who was Lord of the whole world, had ordered him to come that he might see the land, and let Atahuallpa know the things of our Faith.... The Governor also told him that that land, and all other lands, belonged to the Emperor, and that he must acknowledge him as his Lord. He replied that he was content, and, observing that the Christians had collected some gold, Atahuallpa said to the Governor that they need not take such care of it, as if there was so little; for that he could give them ten thousand plates, and that he could fill the room in which

he was up to a white line, which was the height of a man and a half from the floor.

Questions What were the main bases for initial European judgments about the characteristics of American Indians? How might the Indians have judged the Europeans? What motives does Columbus appeal to in trying to interest Spanish rulers in the new land?

These documents raise obvious problems of interpretation. They interpret interactions with another, very foreign culture from the European standpoint only. They also attribute motives to the adventurers that may or may not have been predominant. Figuring out how to gain useful, valid information from documents of this sort, which are undeniably revealing of key passages in world history, is a major challenge. What parts of the accounts seem most reliable, and what criteria can be used to sort out degrees of accuracy?

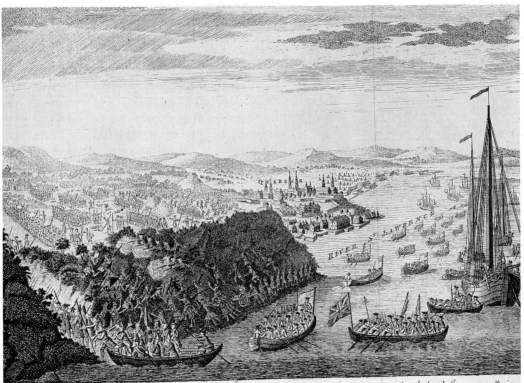

View of the Taking of QUEBECK *by the English Forces Commanded by Gen.ᶩ Wolfe Sep: 13 1759*

Figure 23.5. British naval power allowed the light infantry to scale the French fort from the St. Lawrence River and capture Quebec in 1759. The attack nullified the cannon in the French fort in what turned out to be a crucial event in Canada's history.

colonial powers in the 17th and even the 18th centuries. The Dutch were more attached to their Asian colonies. British and French leaders valued their West Indian holdings much more than their North American colonies. The value of North American products, such as timber and furs, was not nearly as great as profits from the Caribbean or Latin America, so much less attention was given to economic regulation. As a result, some merchant and manufacturing activities emerged among new Americans themselves.

North America remained unimportant in world history through the 18th century. The American colonies that would become the United States had a population of a mere 3 million, far smaller than the powerful colonies in Latin America. The value of imports and exports also remained insignificant. Southern colonies that produced tobacco and sugar, and then cotton, became important. Patterns there were similar to those of Latin America, with large estates based on imported slave labor, a wealthy planter class bent on importing luxury products from western Europe, and weak formal governments. Still, in world historical terms the Atlantic colonies in North America were a backwater amid the larger colonial holdings staked out in the early modern centuries.

Yet European settlers did arrive. Driven by religious dissent, ambition, and other motives, Europeans, many from the British Isles, colonized the Atlantic coastal region, where Indian populations were quickly reduced by disease and war. The society that developed in the British colonies was far closer to west European forms than was that of Latin America. The colonies operated their own assemblies, which provided the people with political experience. Calvinist and Quaker church assemblies gave governing power to groups of elders or wider congregations. Many colonists thus had reason to share with some west Europeans a sense of the importance of representative institutions and self-government.

Colonists were also avid consumers of political theories written in Europe, such as the parliamentary ideas of John Locke. There was also wide reading and discussion of Enlightenment materials, and institutions such as the 18th-century American Philosophical Society deliberately imitated European scientific institutes. Hundreds of North Americans contributed scientific findings to the British Royal Society. The colonies remained modest in certain cultural attainments. Art was rather primitive, although many stylistic cues came from Europe. There was no question that in formal culture, North American leaders saw themselves as part of a larger Western world.

By the late 18th century, some American merchants were trading with China, their ships picking up medicinal herbs along the Pacific coast and exchanging them for Chinese artifacts and tea. Great Britain tried to impose firmer limits on this modestly thriving local economy after the Seven Years' War. It hoped to win greater tax revenues and to guarantee markets for British goods and traders, but the effort came too late and helped encourage rebellion in key colonies. Unusual among the colonies, North America developed a merchant class and some stake in manufacturing in a pattern similar to that taking shape in western Europe itself.

The spread of Western values in the Atlantic colonies and in British and French settlements in Canada was facilitated by the modest impact of Native Americans in these settled areas. The Indian population of this part of North America had always been less dense than in Central America or the Andes region. Because few Indian groups in these regions practiced settled agriculture, instead combining hunting with slash-and-burn corn growing, European colonists found it easy to displace them from large stretches of territory. The ravages of European-imported disease reduced the Indian population greatly. Many forest peoples were pushed westward. Some abandoned agriculture, turning to a new horse-based hunting economy on the plains (the horse was brought to Mexico by the Spaniards). Many territorial wars further distracted the North American Indian groups. The net result of these factors was that although colonists interacted with Indians, learned from them, and feared and mistreated them, they did not combine with them to forge new cultural groups like those emerging in much of Latin America.

By 1700, the importation of African slaves proved to be a more important addition to the North American experience, particularly in the southern colonies. The practice of slaveholding and interactions with African culture distinguished North American life from its European counterpart. By the 18th century, 23 percent of the population of the English colonies was of African origin.

North America and Western Civilization

On balance, most white settlers intended to transplant key Western habits into their new setting. For

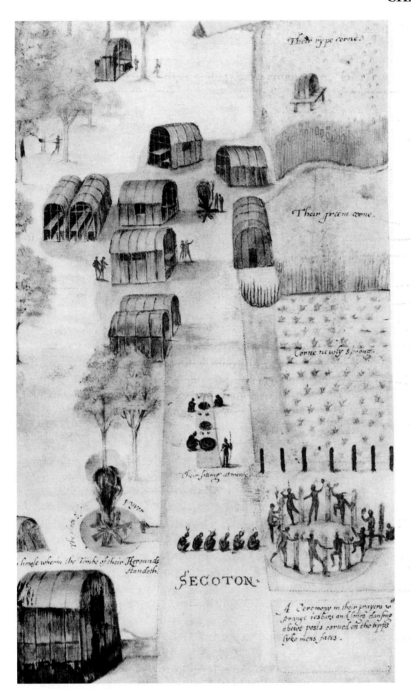

Figure 23.6. Watercolor by John White (c. 1590) of the Indian settlement of Secoton, Virginia. White was one of the pioneer settlers on Roanoke Island, North Carolina, and was also a pioneer of straightforward observation.

example, family patterns were similar. American colonists were able to marry slightly earlier than ordinary western Europeans because of the greater abundance of land, and they had larger families. Still, they reproduced most features of the European-style family, including the primary emphasis on the nuclear unit. The new Americans did have unusual concern for children, if only because they depended so heavily on their work in a labor-scarce environment. European visitors commented on the child-centeredness of American families and the freedom of children to speak up. These variations, though significant, played on trends also becoming visible in Europe, such as the new emphasis on family affection.

Even when key colonies rebelled against European control, as they did in 1776, they moved in the name of Western political ideas and economic goals against the dependency the British tried to impose. They established a government that responded to the new Western political theories, implementing some key ideas for the first time.

Africa and Asia: Coastal Trading Stations

Europeans for the most part contented themselves with small coastal fortresses in Africa, negotiating with African kings and merchants but not trying to claim large territories on their own. Generally, Europeans were deterred by climate, disease, and nonnavigable rivers from trying to reach into the interior. There were two important exceptions. From initial coastal settlements, Portugal sent expeditions into Angola in search of slaves. These expeditions had a more direct and more disruptive impact in this part of southwestern Africa than elsewhere along the Atlantic coast. More important still was the *Cape Colony* planted by the Dutch on the Cape of Good Hope in 1652. The intent was to form another coastal station to supply Dutch ships bound for Asia. But some Dutch farmers were sent, and these *Boers* (the Dutch word for farmers) began to fan out on large farms in a region still lightly populated by Africans. They clashed with local hunting groups, enslaving some of them. Only after 1770 did the expanding Boer settlements directly conflict with Bantu farmers, opening a long battle for control of southern Africa that raged until the late 20th century in the nation of South Africa.

European colonies in Asia were also exceptional. Spain set up an administration for the Philippines and sent active Catholic missionaries. The Dutch East India company administered portions of the main islands of present-day Indonesia and also (for a time) Taiwan, off the China coast.

Colonization in Asia entered a new phase as the British and French began to struggle for control of India, beginning in the late 17th century when the Mughal Empire weakened. Even before the Mughals faltered after the death in 1707 of their last great emperor, Aurangzeb, French and British forts dotted

the east and west coasts, along with Portuguese Goa. As Mughal inefficiency increased, with a resultant surge of regional states ruled by Indians, portions of the subcontinent became an arena for the growing international rivalry between Britain and France.

The British East India Company had two advantages in this competition. Through negotiation with local princes, it had gained a station at *Calcutta*, which gave it some access to the great wealth of the Ganges valley. Furthermore, the company had enormous influence over the British government and, through Britain's superior navy, excellent communication on the ocean routes. Its French rivals, in contrast, had less political clout at home, where the government often was distracted by European land wars. The French also were more interested in missionary work than the British, who like most Protestants became deeply committed to efforts at conversion in colonial territories only in the 19th century. Before then, the British were content to leave Hindu customs alone and devote themselves to commercial profits.

French–British rivalry raged bitterly through the mid-18th century. Both sides recruited Indian princes and troops as allies. Outright warfare erupted in 1744 and then again during the Seven Years' War. In 1756, an Indian ruler in Bengal attacked and captured the British base at Calcutta. In the aftermath of the battle, English prisoners were placed in their own jail, where humidity and overcrowding led to perhaps as many as 120 deaths before Indian officials became aware of their plight and released them. The English used this incident, which they dubbed the "black hole" of Calcutta, to rally their forces. The East India Company's army recaptured Calcutta and then seized additional Indian and French territory, aided by abundant bribes to many regional princes. French power in India was destroyed, and the East India Company took over administration of the Bengal region, which stretched inland from Calcutta. Soon after this, the British also gained the island of Ceylon (Sri Lanka) from the Dutch.

The full history of British India did not begin until late in the 18th century, when the British government took a more active hand in Indian administration, supplementing the unofficial government of the East India Company (Figure 23.7). Indeed, British control of the subcontinent was incomplete. The Mughal Empire remained, although it was increasingly weak and it controlled scant territory, as did other regional kingdoms, including the Sikh state. Britain gained some new territories by force but was also content to form alliances with local princes without disturbing their internal administration.

In most colonies, European administration long remained fairly loose. Few settlers arrived, except in South Africa and the Americas. Outside the Americas, cultural impositions were slight. Missionary activity won many converts in the Philippines but not elsewhere in Asia or in Africa at this point. The main impact of colonies supplemented the more general development of the world economy: Colonial administrations pressed for economic advantage for the home country by opening markets and prompting commercial production of cheap foods and raw materials. Here, of course, the consequences to colonial peoples were very real.

Impact on Western Europe

Conclusion to paper

Western Europe was affected by its own colonial success, not only economically but also diplomatically. Colonial rivalries and wars added to the existing hostilities between key nation-states. England and Holland early turned against Spanish success, with great effect. The Dutch and the English competed, engaging in many skirmishes in the 17th century. Then attention turned to the growing competition between the British and the French. This contest had extensive geographic scope: The Seven Years' War (1756–1763), fought in Europe, India, and North America, has been called the first world war.

There were also lesser effects on European society. For example, from the mid-17th century onward, the use of colonially produced sugar spread widely. Previously, sugar had been a costly, upper-class item. Now for the first time, except for salt, a basic product available to ordinary people was being traded over long distances. The spread of sugar had cultural as well as social and economic significance in giving ordinary Europeans the ability to obtain pleasurable sensations in quick doses—an interesting foreshadowing of later features of Western consumer behavior. It also promoted a growing role for dentists by the 18th century.

Conclusion

The Impact of a New World Order

The development of the world economy and European colonialism had immense impact. Western Europe was affected in many ways. In the world at large, economic pressures caused immense internal changes. The loss of mainly young people to the slave trade disrupted population patterns in many parts of Africa. By the 18th century, Indian manufacturing levels began to decline as a result of

Figure 23.7. This Indian portrait of two women in European dress illustrates the English influence in 18th-century India.

British pressure. In many areas, new labor systems spread in response to European markets. It remains important to see developments as part of an interaction, not simply European imposition. For example, missionary efforts did not always succeed. When they did, as in much of Latin America, they did not produce full replicas of European Christianity but combined with more traditional regional ideas, practices, and artistic representations. Diversity persisted, and different responses to colonialism and the world economy simply added a new element to this familiar world history framework.

The world economy brought some advantages, even aside from the obvious European gains and despite intense hardships such as the slave trade. Knowledge of new foodstuffs and increased trade helped many agricultural societies expand their populations and deal with some problems of scarcity.

Unquestionably, the creation of the world economic framework and the West's new military advantages presented key challenges to every civilization in the world. Even when the choice involved a conscious effort at isolation, some innovation was needed. However, even societies that sought stability above all found their environment shifting, so that they needed new policies simply to stand still.

Further Readings

Excellent discussions of Western exploration and expansion are Carlo Cipolla's *Guns, Sails and Empires: Technological Innovation and the Early Phases of European Expansion 1400–1700* (1997), J. H. Parry's *The Age of Reconnaissance* (1982), Richard S. Dunn's *Sugar & Slaves: The Rise of the Planter Class in the English West Indies, 1624–1713* (1972), and D. Boorstin's *The Discoverers* (1991 Recent works include Alan K. Smith's *Creating a World Economy: Merchant Capital, Colonialism and World Trade 1460–1825* (1991) and James Tracy, ed., *The Rise of Merchant Empires* (1986) and *The Political Economy of Merchant Empires* (1991). Somewhat more specific facets are treated in D. K. Fieldhouse's *The Colonial Empires* (1971), J. H. Parry's *The Discovery of South America* (1979), and S. Subrahmanyam's *The Portuguese Empire in Asia, 1500–1700* (1993). A vital treatment of the international results of new trading patterns of foods and disease is Alfred Crosby's *The Columbian Exchange: Biological and Cultural Consequences of 1492* (1972); see also Elinor G. Melville's *A Plague of Sheep: Environmental Consequences of the Conquest of Mexico* (1994). For a stimulating reemphasis on Asia Andre Geuder Frank's, *ReOrient: Global Economy in the Asian Age* (1998).On slavery and its trade, see Eric Williams's *Capitalism and Slavery* (1964), Orlando Patterson's *Slavery and Social Death: A Comparative Study* (1982), and D. B. Davis's *Slavery and Human*

Progress (1984); the last two are important comparative and analytical statements in a major field of recent historical study. See also Philip D. Curtin's *Atlantic Slave Trade* (1972) and his edited volume, *Africa Remembered: Narratives by West Africans from the Era of the Slave Trade* (1967). A good recent survey of developments in Africa and in the period is Paul Bohannan and Philip Curtin's *Africa and Africans* (3rd ed., 1988).

New world trading patterns are discussed in K.N.N. Shanduri's *Trade and Civilization in the Indian Ocean* (1985) and Philip Curtin's *Cross-Cultural Trade in World History* (1984). A controversial theoretical statement about new trade relationships and their impact on politics and social structure is Immanuel Wallerstein's *The Modern World System: Capitalist Agriculture and the Origins of the European World Economy in the Sixteenth Century* (1974) and *The Modern World System: Mercantilism and the Consolidation of the European World Economy 1600–1750* (1980); see also his *Politics of the World Economy: The States, the Movements and the Civilizations* (1984).

For discussions on where colonial North America fits in this period of world history, see Jack Greene and J. R. Pole, eds., *Colonial British America: Essays on the New History of the Early Modern Era* (1984); William J. Eccles, *France in America* (rev. ed., 1990); and Gary Nash, *Red, White and Black: The Peoples of Early America* (rev. ed., 1982).

On the Web

Biographies of leaders of the European age of discovery, from Henry the Navigator to Vasco De Gama, are offered at http://www.win.tue.nl/cs/fm/engels/discovery/index.html. This site also traces the lives of the world's great explorers of every region and era.

Information about contacts between conquistadors and Indians in North America can be found at http://www.FloridaHistory.com.

A virtual version of an exhibit mounted by the Library of Congress and other materials which look at the multicultural dimensions of the events of 1492, the life of Christopher Columbus and the Colombian Exchange his voyages initiated can be found at http://metalub.unc.edu/expo/1492.exhibit/Intro.html and http://www.colums.ohio-state.edu/English/people/odin.1/courses/571/columbex.htm.

Most discussions on the nature of that exchange rightly focus on the material outcomes of the Atlantic slave trade, such as the development of plantation economies and the exchange of crops, animals and diseases.

However, one site, http://daphne.palomar.edu/scrout/colexc.htm, also examines what it admits to be the controversial notion that the indigenous peoples of the Americas may have contributed toward the evolution of important modern ideas, including Western conceptions of liberty, ecology and even corporate structure. At the very least, such speculation reminds us that the relationship between the indigenous people of the Americas and their European conquerors was complex.

The relationship between conquistador Hernando Cortez and Donna Maria/La Malinche, his female Nahuatl-speaking translator, certainly was as complicated as Cortez's relations with his Aztec-hating Mesoamerica allies. Both relationships are discussed at http://thedagger.com/conquest.html.

Another site, http://www.fordham.edu/halsall/mod/aaztecsl.html, offers a text of the discussions between Cortez and Montezuma, which Malinche facilitated as a translator, that foreshadowed the end of the Aztec empire.

Francisco Pizarro's encounter with Inca leaders and the imposition of Spanish rule over their empire is presented at http://www.fll.vt.edu/culture-civ/spanish/texts/spainlatinamerica/pizarro.html and http://www.acs.u.calgary.ca/HIST/tutor/eurvoya/ inca.html.

The controversy over the demographic catastrophe that accompanied the conquest of Mexico is analyzed from the perspective of contemporary Spanish and Nahuatl records at http://www.hist.umn. edu/~rmccaa/vircatas/vir6.htm.

Dutch and British traders soon outstripped their Iberian competitors in the new global economy, a process described at http://www.fordham.edu/halsall/mod/modsbook/ 03.html.

This site contains the chief primary documentation for the early modern world system and includes a summary of Immanuel Wallerstein's World System Theory (http://www.fordham.edu/halsall/mod/wallerstein.html).

Accounts of the Dutch and British East India Companies can be found at http://hewwy-savenije.demon.nl/links6. htm and http://www.theeastindiacompany.com/history. html.

Chapter 24

The Rise of Russia

Peter I of Russia (1672–1725), commonly known as Peter the Great, is shown here in a herios pose. An autocrat who put down revolts against his rule with great cruelty, he was also a reformist who traveled widely in the West and took many steps toward westernizing Russia.

ussia's great land empire was formed between 1450 and 1750. Unlike Western colonial empires, Russia's expansion involved only limited commercial exchange. Nevertheless, it fundamentally altered power balances from Europe to Asia.

Russian leaders, casting off Tatar (Mongol) domination between 1450 and 1480, proceeded on a fairly steady course of expansion. Much of the new territory was Asian, but Russia also gained the leading role in eastern Europe by the 17th century. Regional kingdoms remained in eastern Europe, and many of them differed from Russia in important ways. Poland and Lithuania continued to rival Russia into the 17th century. But Russia was increasingly the focal point as it became a significant force in world history.

Russia was a minor actor on the world stage before the 15th century. Culture in Russia had developed in close connection with the Byzantine Empire, from roughly the 9th century onward. Russia had also converted to Orthodox Christianity, with its vibrant cultural traditions and rich art (see Chapter 15). Two centuries of Mongol rule had reduced Russia's cities and trade and lowered its cultural and educational levels.

Russia's evolution after 1450 draws our attention not just because of territorial expansion and growing importance but because of the fascinating changes the nation underwent as part of its surge onto the world scene. Building on a strong sense of separate identity, the Russians also entered into new contacts with Western society. Controversy over Western influence—whether to embrace it, select from it, or shun it—has continued in Russian culture to this day.

The period from 1450 to 1750, in sum, formed many of the characteristics of eastern Europe that have lasted into our own time: the dominance of Russia, the formation of a Eurasian Russian Empire, the capacity for change, and an ambivalence toward the West. Defining a Russian civilization, amid influences from several regions and the conscious if selective Westernization process, illustrates the difficulties in identifying modern civilization units.

1450 C.E.	1600 C.E.	1750 C.E.
1462 Much of Russia freed from Tartars by Ivan III (Ivan the Great) **1480** Moscow region free; Russian expansion presses south **1533–1584** Ivan IV (Ivan the Terrible), first to be called tsar, boyar power reduced **1552–1556** Russian expansion in central Asia, western Siberia	**1604–1613** Time of Troubles **1613–1917** Romanov dynasty **1637** Russian pioneers to pacific **1649** Law enacted making serfdom hereditary **1689–1725** Peter the Great **1700–1721** Wars with Sweden **1703** Founding of St. Petersburg	**1762–1796** Catherine the Great **1773–1775** Pugachev revolt **1772, 1793, 1795** Partition of Poland **1785** Law enacted tightening landlord power over serfs

RUSSIA'S EXPANSIONIST POLITICS UNDER THE TSARS

Between 1450 and 1650, Russia began its process of territorial expansion while working to strengthen the tsarist state in what proved to be the first phase of the empire's early modern development.

Russia's emergence as a new power in eastern Europe and central Asia initially depended on its gaining freedom from Mongol (Tatar) control. The Duchy of Moscow was the center for the liberation effort beginning in the 14th century. Local princes began to carve out greater autonomy, and the effectiveness of Mongol control began to diminish. Ironically, the Moscow princes initially gained political experience as tax collectors for the Mongols, but gradually they moved toward regional independence. Under *Ivan III*—Ivan the Great, who claimed succession from the Rurik dynasty and the old Kievan days—a large part of Russia was freed after 1462. Ivan organized a strong army, giving the new government a military emphasis it would long retain. He also used loyalties to the Orthodox Christian faith and to Russia—that is, to a blend of nationalism and religion—to win support for his campaigns. By 1480, Moscow had been freed from any payment to the Mongols and had gained a vast territory running from the borders of the Polish Lithuanian kingdom to the Ural mountains.

The Need for Revival

Mongol control never reshaped basic Russian values, for the rulers were interested in tribute, not full government. Many Russian landlords adopted Mongol styles of dress and social habits. However, most Russians remained Christians, and most local administrative issues remained in the hands of regional princes, landlords, or peasant villages. In these senses, Russia was set to resume many of its earlier patterns when full independence was achieved. On the other hand, the Mongol period reduced the vigor of Russian cultural life, lowering the levels of literacy among the priesthood, for example. Economic life deteriorated as well: With trade down and manufacturing limited, Russia had become a purely agricultural economy dependent on peasant labor. In these senses, independence brought a challenge for revival and reform.

Ivan the Great claimed an earlier tradition of centralized rule, which went back to the Rurik dynasty and Byzantine precedents, and added to it a new sense of imperial mission. He married the niece of the last Byzantine emperor, which gave him the chance to assert control over all Orthodox churches, whether in Russia or not.

Encouraged by his advisors, Ivan also insisted that Russia had succeeded Byzantium as a *third Rome*, with all that this implied in terms of grandeur and expansionist potential. Ivan accordingly called himself tsar, or Caesar, the "autocrat of all the Russians."

The next important tsar, *Ivan IV*, justly called Ivan the Terrible, continued the policy of Russian expansion. He also placed greater emphasis on controlling the tsarist autocracy, earning his nickname by killing many of the Russian nobles, or boyars, whom he suspected of conspiracy. Russian aristocrats lacked the tradition of political assertion of their counterparts in western Europe, and Ivan's policies of terror confirmed this fact.

Map 24.1 *Russian Expansion Under the Early Tsars, 1462–1598. From its base in the Moscow region, Russia expanded in three directions; the move into Siberia involved pioneering new settlements and political control.*

Patterns of Expansion

The territorial expansion policy focused particularly on central Asia. It was motivated by a desire to push the former Mongol overlords farther back. Russia was a country of vast plains, with few natural barriers to invasion. The early tsars turned this drawback to an advantage by pushing southward toward the Caspian Sea; they also moved east into the Ural mountains and beyond. Both Ivan III and Ivan IV recruited peasants to migrate to the newly seized lands, particularly in the south. These peasant–adventurers, or *cossacks,* were Russian pioneers, combining agriculture with daring military feats on horseback. The expansion territories long had a rough-and-ready frontier quality, only gradually settling down to more regular administration. The cossack spirit provided volunteers for further expansion, for many of the pioneers—like their American counterparts in the 19th century—chafed under detailed tsarist control and were eager to move on to new settlements. During the 16th century, the cossacks not only conquered the Caspian Sea area but also moved into western Siberia, across the Urals, beginning the gradual takeover and settlement of these vast plains, which previously had been sparsely inhabited by nomadic Asian peoples (see Map 24.1).

Expansion also offered tsars a way to reward loyal nobles and bureaucrats by giving them estates in new territories. This practice provided new agricultural areas and sources of labor; Russia used slaves for certain kinds of production work into the 18th century. Although Russia never became as dependent on expansion for social control and economic advance as the later Roman Empire or the Ottoman Empire had, it certainly had many reasons to continue the policy. Russia also created trading connections with its new Asian territories and their neighbors.

Russia's early expansion, along with that of the Ottoman Empire to the south, eliminated independent central Asia—that age-old source of nomadic cultures and periodic invasions in both the east and the west. The same expansion, though driven by the movement of Russian peasants and landlords to new areas, also added to Russia diverse new peoples, making this a multicultural empire, like that of the Mughals and Ottomans. Particularly important was the addition of a large Muslim minority, overseen by the tsarist government but not pressed to integrate with Russian culture.

Western Contact and Romanov Policy

Along with expansion and enforcement of tsarist primacy, the early tsars added one element to their overall approach: carefully managed contacts with western Europe. The tsars realized that Russia's cultural and economic subordination to the Mongols had put them at a commercial and cultural disadvantage. Ivan III was eager to launch diplomatic missions to the leading Western states. During the reign of Ivan IV, British merchants established trading contacts with Russia, selling manufactured products in exchange for furs and other raw materials. Soon, Western merchants established outposts in Moscow and other Russian centers. The tsars also imported Italian artists and architects to design church buildings and the magnificent royal palace in the Kremlin in Moscow. The foreign architects modified Renaissance styles to take Russian building traditions into account, producing the ornate, onion-shaped domes that became characteristic of Russian (and other east European) churches and creating a distinctive form of classicism. A tradition of looking to the West, particularly for emblems of upper-class art and status, was beginning to emerge by the 16th century, along with some reliance on Western commercial initiative (Figure 24.1).

Ivan IV died without an heir. This led to some new power claims by the boyars—*The Time of Troubles*—plus Swedish and Polish attacks on Russian territory. In 1613, however, an assembly of boyars chose a member of the Romanov family as tsar. This family, the *Romanov dynasty,* was to rule Russia until the great revolution of 1917. Although many individual Romanov rulers were weak, and tensions with the claims of nobles recurred, the Time of Troubles did not produce any lasting constraints on tsarist power.

The first Romanov, Michael, reestablished internal order without great difficulty. He also drove out the foreign invaders and resumed the expansionist policy of his predecessors. A successful war against Poland brought Russia part of the Ukraine, including Kiev; in the south, Russia's boundaries expanded to meet those of the Ottoman Empire. Expansion at this point was beginning to have new diplomatic implications as Russia encountered other established governments.

Alexis Romanov, Michael's successor, abolished the assemblies of nobles and gained new powers over the Russian church. He was eager to purge the

Figure 24.1. This icon, from the early 15th century, depicts Mary and the Christ Child. The Russian icon tradition used styles derived from Byzantine art that under Western influence became more naturalistic by the 17th century.

church of many superstitions and errors that, in his judgment, had crept in during Mongol times. His policies resumed the Orthodox tradition of state control over the church. Dissident religious conservatives, called *Old Believers,* were exiled to Siberia or to southern Russia, where they maintained their religion and extended Russia's colonizing activities.

RUSSIA'S FIRST WESTERNIZATION, 1690–1790

By the late 17th century, Russia was poised for dramatic, if selective, internal change. Peter the Great led the first Westernization effort in history, changing Russia permanently and providing a model for later Westernization attempts elsewhere. Peter and his successors used Westernization to bolster Russia's expansionist empire, without intending to become a truly Western society.

By the end of the 17th century Russia had become one of the great land empires, but it remained unusually agricultural by the standards of the West and the great Asian civilizations. The reign of *Peter I*, the son of Alexis and known with some justice as Peter the Great, built many new features into this framework between 1689 and 1725. In essence, Peter extended his predecessors' policies of building up tsarist control and expanding Russian territory (Map 24.2). He added a more definite interest in changing selected aspects of Russian economy and culture by imitating Western forms.

Peter the Great was a vigorous leader of exceptional intelligence and ruthless energy. A giant, standing 6 feet 8 inches, he was eager to move his country more fully into the Western diplomatic and cultural orbit without making it fully Western. He traveled widely in the West, incognito, seeking Western allies for a crusade against Turkish power in Europe—for which he found little enthusiasm. He also visited many Western manufacturing centers, even working as a ship's carpenter in Holland; through these activities he gained an interest in Western science and technology. He brought scores of Western artisans back with him to Russia.

Map 24.2 *Russia Under Peter the Great. From 1696 to 1725, Peter the Great allowed his country only one year of peace. For the rest of this time he radically changed the form of his government to pursue war. By the end, he had established his much-desired "Windows on the West" on the Baltic.*

Tsarist Autocracy of Peter the Great

In politics, Peter was clearly an autocrat. He put down revolts against his rule with great cruelty, in one case executing some of the ringleaders personally. He had no interest in the parliamentary features of Western centers such as Holland, seizing instead on the absolutist currents in the West at this time. Peter enhanced the power of the Russian state by using it as a reform force, trying to show that even aristocratic habits could be modified by state decree. Peter also extended an earlier policy of recruiting bureaucrats from outside aristocratic ranks and giving them noble titles to reward bureaucratic service. Here was a key means of freeing the state from exclusive dependence on aristocratic officials, who might maneuver from their separate power bases. Peter imitated Western military organization, creating a specially trained fighting force that put down local militias. Furthermore, Peter the Great set up a secret police to prevent dissent and to supervise the bureaucracy, paralleling an earlier Chinese innovation but going well beyond the bureaucratic control impulses of Western absolutists at that time. Peter's Chancery of Secret Police survived, under different names and with changing functions, to the 1990s; it was reinstituted after 1917 by a revolutionary regime that in other respects worked to undo key features of the tsarist system.

Peter's foreign policy maintained many well-established lines. He attacked the Ottoman Empire, but he won no great victories. He warred with Sweden, at the time one of the leading northern powers in Europe, and gained territory on the eastern coast of the Baltic Sea, thus reducing Sweden to second-rate military status. Russia now had a window on the sea, including a largely ice-free port. From this time onward, Russia became a major factor in European diplomatic and military alignments. The tsar commemorated Russia's shift of interests westward by moving his capital from Moscow to a new Baltic city that he named *St. Petersburg*.

What Westernization Meant

As a reformist, Peter concentrated on improvements in political organization, on selected economic development, and on cultural change. He tried to streamline Russia's small bureaucracy and alter military structure by using Western organizational principles. He created a more well-defined military hierarchy while developing functionally specialized bureaucratic departments. He also improved the army's weaponry and, with aid from Western advisors, created the first Russian navy. He completely eliminated the old noble councils, creating a set of advisors under his control. Provincial governors were appointed from St. Petersburg, and although town councils were elected, a tsar-appointed town magistrate served as final authority. Peter's ministers systematized law codes to extend through the whole empire and revised the tax system, with taxes on ordinary Russian peasants increasing steadily. New training institutes were established for aspiring bureaucrats and officers—one way to bring talented nonnobles into the system.

Peter's economic efforts focused on building up metallurgical and mining industries, using Russia's extensive iron holdings to feed state-run munitions and shipbuilding facilities. Without urbanizing extensively or developing a large commercial class, Peter's reforms changed the Russian economy. Landlords were rewarded for using serf labor to staff new manufacturing operations. This was a limited goal but a very important one, giving Russia the internal economic means to maintain a substantial military presence for almost two centuries.

Finally, Peter was eager to make Russia culturally respectable in Western eyes. Cultural change was not all superficial; it supplemented bureaucratic training and provided greater technical expertise. Peter was also eager to cut the Russian elite off from its traditions, to enhance state power, and to commit the elite to new identities. Thus, he required nobles to shave off their beards (Figure 24.2) and wear Western clothes; in symbolic ceremonies he cut off the long, Mongol-type sleeves and pigtails that were characteristic of the boyars. This was the first of many instances in which traditional appearance was forcibly altered as part of Western-oriented change, although in this case only the upper class was involved. Of greater substance were attempts to provide more education in mathematics and other technical subjects for the nobility. Peter and his successors founded scientific institutes and academies along Western lines, and serious discussion of the latest scientific and technical findings became common. At the elite level, Peter built Russia into a Western cultural zone, and Western fads and fashions extended easily into the glittering new capital city. Ballet, initially encouraged in the French royal court, was imported and became a Russian specialty. The use of Christmas trees came from Germany.

Figure 24.2. This contemporary Russian cartoon lampoons Peter the Great's order to his nobility to cut off their beards.

Peter also pressed for improvements in the condition of upper class women. They could now attend public events like their sisters in Western Europe. An old wedding tradition where a bride's father handed a whip to the groom as a symbol of power was abolished.

This Westernization effort had several features that can be compared with imitation processes in other societies later on. In the first place, the changes were selective. Peter did not try to touch the ordinary people of Russia or to involve them in the technological and intellectual aspects of Westernization. New manufacturing involved labor that was partially coerced, not the more independent (though not necessarily higher-paying) system of wage labor spreading in the West. There was no interest in building the kind of worldwide export economy characteristic of the West. Peter wanted economic development to support military strength rather than to achieve wider commercial goals. Finally, Westernization was meant to encourage the autocratic state, not to challenge it with some of the new political ideas circulating in the West. This was real change, but it did not fold Russia into Western civilization outright. Selectivity was crucial, and there was no interest in abandoning particularly Russian goals.

Furthermore, the Westernization that did occur brought hostile responses. Many peasants resented the Westernized airs and expenses of their landlords, some of whom no longer even knew Russian but spoke only French. Elements of the elite opposed Peter's thirst for change, arguing that Russian traditions were superior to those of the West. As one priest wrote to tsar Alexis, "You feed the foreigners too well, instead of bidding your folk to cling to the old customs." This tension continued in Russian history from this point forward, leading to important cycles of enthusiasm and revulsion toward Western values.

Consolidation Under Catherine the Great

The death of Peter the Great in 1724 was followed by several decades of weak rule, dominated in part by power plays among army officers who guided the selection of several ineffective emperors and empresses. The weakness of tsardom in these years encouraged new grumblings about undue Westernization and some new initiatives by church officials eager to gain more freedom of maneuver, but no major new policy directions were set. Russian territorial expansion continued, with several clashes with the Ottoman Empire and further exploration and settlement in Siberia. In 1761, Peter III, nephew of Peter the Great's youngest daughter, reached the throne. He was retarded, but his wife, a German-born princess who changed her name to Catherine—later *Catherine the Great*—soon took matters in hand and continued to rule as empress after Peter III's death (see Figure 24.3). Catherine resumed Peter the Great's interests in several respects. She defended the powers of the central monarch. She put down a vigorous peasant uprising, led by Emelian Pugachev, butchering Pugachev himself. She used the *Pugachev rebellion* as an excuse to extend the powers of the central government in regional affairs.

Catherine II (the Great) (1729–1796) is one of the fascinating women leaders of history. Born a Prussian princess, she converted to the Orthodox faith after her marriage to the heir to the Russian throne was arranged. Her married life was miserable, with frequent threats of divorce from her husband. She also disliked her son, the future tsar Paul I. Carefully cultivating the Russian court, Catherine benefited from a plot to dethrone her husband, Peter III, after an unpopular foreign policy move. Officers of the palace guard

DOCUMENT

The Nature of Westernization

Peter the Great and Catherine the Great were the two chief reformist rulers in Russia before 1800. In the first of the following edicts, Peter focuses on educational change; his approach reflected a real desire for innovation, Russia's autocratic tradition in government, and its hierarchical social structure. Catherine's "Instruction" borrowed heavily from Western philosophers and was hailed by one French intellectual as "the finest monument of the century." This document also showed distinctively Russian traditions and problems. However, the reforms in law and punishment were not put into practice, and the document itself was banned as subversive by Catherine's successor, as Russia's rulers began to fear the subversive qualities of Western influence after the French Revolution.

Decrees on Compulsory Education of the Russian Nobility, January 12 and February 28, 1714

Send to every *gubernia* [region] some persons from mathematical schools to teach the children of the nobility—except those of freeholders and government clerks—mathematics and geometry; as a penalty [for evasion] establish a rule that no one will be allowed to marry unless he learns these [subjects]. Inform all prelates to issue no marriage certificates to those who are ordered to go to schools....

The Great Sovereign has decreed: in all *gubernias* children between the ages of ten and fifteen of the nobility, of government clerks, and of lesser officials, except those of freeholders, must be taught mathematics and some geometry. Toward that end, students should be sent from mathematical schools [as teachers], several into each *gubernia,* to prelates and to renowned monasteries to establish schools. During their instruction these teachers should be given food and financial remuneration of three altyns and two dengas per day from *gubernia* revenues set aside for that purpose by personal orders of His Imperial Majesty. No fees should be collected from students. When they have mastered the material, they should then be given certificates written in their own handwriting. When the students are released they ought to pay one ruble each for their training.

Without these certificates they should not be allowed to marry or receive marriage certificates.

The "Instruction" of 1767

6. Russia is a European State.
7. This is clearly demonstrated by the following Observations: The Alterations which Peter the Great undertook in Russia succeeded with the greater Ease, because the Manners, which prevailed at that Time, and had been introduced amongst us by a Mixture of different Nations, and the Conquest of foreign Territories, were quite unsuitable to the Climate. Peter the First, by introducing the Manners and Customs of Europe among the European People in his Dominions, found at that Time such Means as even he himself was not sanguine enough to expect.
8. The Possessions of the Russian Empire extend upon the terrestrial Globe to 32 Degrees of Latitude, and to 165 of Longitude.
9. The Sovereign is absolute; for there is no other Authority but that which centers in his single Person, that can act with a Vigour proportionate to the Extent of such a vast Dominion.
10. The Extent of the Dominion requires an absolute Power to be vested in that Person who rules over it. It is expedient so to be, that the quick Dispatch of Affairs, sent from distant Parts, might make ample Amends for the delay occasioned by the great Distance of the Places.
11. Every other Form of Government whatsoever would not only have been prejudicial to Russia, but would even have proved its entire Ruin.
12. Another Reason is: That it is better to be subject to the Laws under one Master, than to be subservient to many.
13. What is the true End of Monarchy? Not to deprive People of their natural Liberty; but correct their Actions, in order to attain the supreme Good....
272. The more happily a People live under a government, the more easily the Number of the Inhabitants increases....
519. It is certain, that a *high* opinion of the *Glory* and *Power* of the Sovereign, would *increase* the *Strength* of his Administration; but a *good Opinion of his Love of Justice, will increase it at least as much.*
520. All this will never please those flatterers, who are daily instilling this pernicious Maxim into all the Sovereign on Earth, That their People are created for them only. But We think, and esteem it Our Glory to declare, "That We are created for Our People; and, of this Reason, We are obliged to Speak of Things just as they ought to be." For God forbid! That, after this Legislation is finished, any Nation on

Earth should be more just; and, consequently, should flourish, more than Russia; otherwise the Intention of Our Laws would be totally frustrated; an Unhappiness which I do not wish to survive.

Questions: In what sense did reformist measures strengthen Russian autocracy? Why might 18th-century Western thinkers admire reformist tsars? What relationships to the West did the reform measures suggest? What do the documents suggest about the motivations of leaders such as Peter and Catherine? Were they similar? Which Westernizer maintained a closer match between their claims and appearances and Russia's real conditions?

installed her as empress in 1762. The tsar was later murdered, possibly with Catherine's consent. Catherine's reign combined genuine Enlightenment interests with her need to consolidate power as a truly Russian ruler—a combination that explains the complexities of her policies. Like many male rulers, Catherine maintained an active personal life and had a succession of lovers, some of them politically influential.

Like Peter, Catherine was also a selective Westernizer, as her "instruction of 1767" (see the Document section) clearly demonstrated. She flirted with the ideas of the French Enlightenment, importing several French philosophers for visits and patronizing the arts and sciences. She summoned various reform commissions to discuss new law codes and other Western-style measures, including reduction of traditionally severe punishments.

Catherine's image was not always consistent with her policies, however. She was a centralizer and certainly an advocate of a strong tsarist hand. But Catherine also gave new powers to the nobility over their serfs, maintaining a trade-off that had been developing over the previous two centuries in Russia. In this trade-off, nobles served a strong central government and staffed it as bureaucrats and officers. They were in this sense a service aristocracy, not an independent force. They also accepted into their ranks newly ennobled officials chosen by the tsars. In return, however, most of the actual administration over local peasants, except for those on government-run estates, was wielded by the noble landlords. These landlords could requisition peasant labor, levy taxes in money and goods, and even impose punishments for crimes because landlord-dominated courts administered local justice. Catherine increased the harshness of punishments nobles could decree for their serfs.

Catherine patronized Western-style art and architecture, continuing to build St. Petersburg in the classical styles popular at the same time in the West and encouraging leading nobles to tour the West and even send their children to be educated there. But she also tried to avoid cultural influence from the West. When the great French Revolution broke out in 1789, Catherine was quick to close Russia's doors to the "seditious" writings of liberals and democrats. She also censored a small but emerging band of Russian intellectuals who urged reforms along Western lines. One of the first Western-inspired radicals, a noble named Radishev, who sought abolition of serfdom and more liberal political rule, was

Figure 24.3. Catherine the Great. Test your stereotypes: Does her appearance correspond to your expectations as you read about what Catherine did?

vigorously harassed by Catherine's police, and his writings were banned.

Catherine pursued the tradition of Russian expansion with energy and success. She resumed campaigns against the Ottoman Empire, winning new territories in central Asia, including the Crimea, bordering the Black Sea. The Russian–Ottoman contest became a central diplomatic issue for both powers, and Russia became increasingly ascendant. Catherine accelerated the colonization of Russia's holdings in Siberia and encouraged further exploration, claiming the territory of Alaska in Russia's name. Russian explorers also moved down the Pacific coast of North America into what is now northern California, and tens of thousands of pioneers spread over Siberia.

Finally, Catherine pressed Russia's interests in Europe, playing power politics with Prussia and Austria, though without risking major wars. She increased Russian interference in Polish affairs. The Polish government was extremely weak, almost paralyzed by a parliamentary system that let members of the nobility veto any significant measure, and this invited interest by more powerful neighbors. Russia was able to win agreements with Austria and Prussia for the *partition of Poland*. Three partitions, in 1772, 1793, and 1795, eliminated Poland as an independent state, and Russia held the lion's share of the spoils. The basis for further Russian involvement in European affairs had obviously been created, and this would show in Russia's ultimate role in putting down the French armies of Napoleon after 1812—the first time Russian troops moved into the heartland of western Europe.

By the time of Catherine's death in 1796, Russia had passed through three centuries of extraordinary development. It had won independence and constructed a strong central state, though one that had to maintain a balance with the local political and economic interests of a powerful nobility. It had brought new elements into Russia's culture and economy, in part by borrowing from the West. And it had extended its control over the largest land empire in the world (Map 24.3). In the east it bordered China, where an 18th-century Amur River agreement set new frontiers. A tradition of careful but successful military aggrandizement had been established, along with a real pioneering spirit of settlement. It is no wonder that not long after 1800, a perceptive French observer, Alexis de Tocqueville, likened the expanded and increasingly

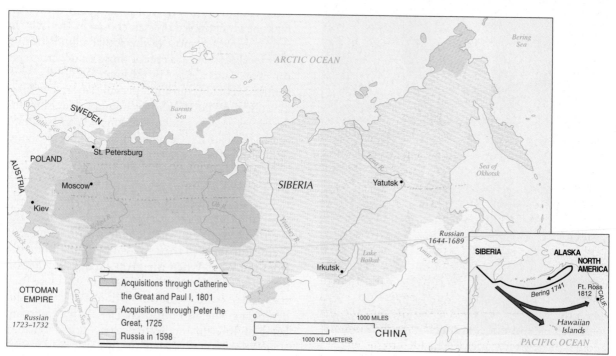

Map 24.3 *Russia's Holdings by 1800. Expansion fluctuated from one decade to the next but persisted, bringing Russia into encounters with three other civilization areas.*

important Russia to the new country emerging in the Western Hemisphere, the United States of America, as the two new giants of future world history.

THEMES IN EARLY MODERN RUSSIAN HISTORY

> *Russian society differed greatly from that of the West. It focused on serfdom and a deep-rooted peasant culture. The gap between Russia's traditional economic and social structure and its Westernization efforts at the top set up some durable tensions on the nation's history, visible even today. Although Russian serfdom was particularly severe, a similar social system developed in other east European areas.*

Because of its great estates, its local political power, and its service to the state, the Russian nobility maintained a vital position in Russian society. In Russia and in eastern Europe generally, landed nobles tended to be divided between a minority of great magnates, who lived in major cities and provided key cultural patronage, and smaller land owners, whose culture was less Westernized and whose lifestyle was much less opulent.

Serfdom: The Life of East Europe's Masses

During the 17th and 18th centuries, the power of the nobility over the serfs increased steadily. Before the Mongol conquest, Russian peasants had been largely free farmers with a legal position superior to that of their medieval Western counterparts. After the expulsion of the Tatars, however, increasing numbers of Russian peasants fell into debt and had to accept servile status to the noble land owners when they could not repay. They retained access to much of the land, but not primary ownership. The Russian government actively encouraged this process from the 16th century onward. Serfdom gave the government a way to satisfy the nobility and regulate peasants when the government itself lacked the bureaucratic means to extend direct controls over the common people. As new territories were added to the empire, the system of serfdom was extended accordingly, sometimes after a period of free farming.

By 1800, half of Russia's peasantry was enserfed to the landlords, and much of the other half owed comparable obligations to the state. Laws passed during the 17th and 18th centuries tied the serfs to the land and increased the legal rights of the landlords. An act in 1649 fixed the hereditary status of the serfs, so that people born to that station could not legally escape it.

Russia was setting up a system of serfdom very close to outright slavery in that serfs could be bought and sold, gambled away, and punished by their masters. The system was a very unusual case in which a people essentially enslaved many of its own members, in contrast to most slave systems, which focused on "outsiders."

Rural conditions in many other parts of eastern Europe were similar. Nobles maintained estate agriculture in Poland, Hungary, and elsewhere. They used the system to support their political control and distinctive lifestyle, as in Russia.

The intensification of estate agriculture and serf labor also reflected eastern Europe's growing economic subordination to the West; in this sense the systems should be compared with developments in Latin America, despite very different specific origins (see Chapter 25). Coerced labor was used to produce grain surpluses sold to Western merchants for the growing cities of western Europe. In return, Western merchants brought in manufactured goods, including the luxury furnishings and clothing essential to the aristocratic lifestyle.

Serfs on the estates of eastern Europe were taxed and policed by their landlords. In Russia, whole villages were sold as manufacturing labor—a process Peter the Great actively encouraged. Peasants were not literally slaves. They continued to use village governments to regulate many aspects of their lives, relying more heavily on community ties than their counterparts in the Western countryside. Yet most peasants were illiterate and quite poor. They paid high taxes or obligations in kind, and they owed extensive labor service to the landlords or the government—a source not only of agricultural production but also of mining and manufacturing. The labor obligation, or *obrok*, tended to increase steadily. Both the economic and the legal situation of the peasantry continued to deteriorate. Although Catherine the Great sponsored a few model villages to display her enlightenment to Western-minded friends, she turned the government of the serfs over to the landlords more completely than ever before. A law of

1785 allowed landlords to punish harshly any serfs convicted of major crimes or rebellion.

Trade and Economic Dependence

In between serfs and landlords, there were few layers of Russian society. Cities were small, and 95 percent of the population remained rural. (Most manufacturing took place in the countryside, so there was no well-defined artisan class.) Government growth encouraged some nonnoble bureaucrats and professionals. Small merchant groups existed as well, although most of Russia's European trade was handled by Westerners posted to the main Russian cities and relying on Western shipping. The nobility, concerned about this potential social competition, prevented the emergence of a substantial merchant class.

Russia's social and economic system worked well in many respects. It produced enough revenue to support an expanding state and empire. Russia was able to trade in furs and other commodities with areas in central Asia outside its boundaries, which meant that its export economy was not totally oriented toward the more dynamic West. It underwrote the aristocratic magnates and their glittering, Westernized culture. The system, along with Russia's expansion, yielded significant population growth: Russia's population doubled during the 18th century to 36 million. For an empire burdened by a harsh climate in most regions, this was no small achievement. Despite periodic famines and epidemics, there was no question that the overall economy had advanced.

Yet the system suffered from important limitations. Most agricultural methods were highly traditional, and there was little motivation among the peasantry for improvement because increased production usually was taken by the state or the landlord. Landlords themselves debated agricultural improvements in their academies, but when it came time to increase production they concentrated on squeezing the serfs. Manufacturing lagged behind Western standards, despite the important extension developed under Peter the Great.

Social Unrest

Russia's economic and social system led to protest. By the end of the 18th century, a small but growing number of Western-oriented aristocrats such as Radishev were criticizing the regime's backwardness, urging measures as far-reaching as the abolition of serfdom. Here were the seeds of a radical intelligentsia that, despite government repression, would grow with time. More significant still were the recurring peasant rebellions. Russian peasants for the most part were politically loyal to the tsar, but they harbored bitter resentments against their landlords, whom they accused of taking lands that were rightfully theirs. Periodic rebellions saw peasants destroy manorial records, seize land, and sometimes kill landlords and their officials. Peasant rebellions had occurred from the 17th century onward, but the Pugachev uprising of the 1770s was particularly strong. Pugachev (Figure 24.4), a cossack chieftain who claimed to be the legitimate tsar, promised an end to serfdom, taxation, and military conscription along with the abolition of the landed aristocracy. His forces roamed over southern Russia until they were finally defeated. Pugachev was brought to Moscow in a case and cut into quarters in a public square. The triumph of Catherine and the nobility highlighted the mutual dependence of government and the upper

Figure 24.4. After the great serf revolt, Pugachev was imprisoned and then executed.

Visualizing THE PAST

Oppressed Peasants

This painting is from the early 20th century (1907), when revolutionary currents were swirling in Russia and the status of the peasantry was widely discussed. This raises obvious issues of interpretation. The subject of the painting, tax collection and the poor material conditions of 17th-century peasants, is accurate.

Questions: Does this painting suggest early-20th-century rather than 17th-century sympathies in Russian culture? If so, in what ways? Does the painting include any glaring inaccuracies? Given the lack of popular art from the 17th century itself, except religious art, does the painting provide useful material for understanding peasant conditions? What elements were probably guesswork on the artist's part? What aspects of the tax collector's appearance suggest that the artist was striving for an accurate rendition of the ways officials looked *before* the reforms of Peter the Great?

class but did not end protest. Radishev, finding peasants barely able to work their own plots of land and sometimes tortured to work harder, thought he saw the handwriting on the wall: "Tremble, cruel hearted landlord! On the brow of each of your peasants I see your condemnation written."

IN DEPTH

Multinational Empires

Of all the new multinational empires created in the early modern period, Russia's was the most successful, lasting until 1991 and to an extent beyond. In contrast, India's Mughal Empire disappeared completely by the mid-19th century, and the Ottoman and Habsburg Empires flickered until after World War I. All the multinational empires were reasonably tolerant of internal diversity (like the Roman and Arab empires of the past, two other "multinational" entities). The Russian tsar, for example, called himself "Khan of the north" to impress central Asian people and took oaths of loyalty from this region on the Koran. However, Russia differed from Asian empires and the Hapsburgs in having a larger core of ethnic groups ready to fan out to the frontiers and establish pioneer settlements that sometimes developed into larger Russian enclaves. Russia also benefited from its willingness and ability to copy the West selectively, in contrast most obviously to the Ottoman Empire in the same period. This copying provided access to new military technologies and some new organizational forms.

Ironically, the same period that saw the creation of so many new empires also confirmed the importance of the culturally more cohesive nation-state, the dominant form in western Europe. England and France, prototypical nation-states, were not culturally homogeneous; they had important pockets of minorities who differed linguistically or religiously from the majority culture. But both maintained a clear basis for joining the political unit to the cultural one to foster loyalty. Efforts by the 17th-century French kings to purify and standardize the French language, or by English parliamentarians to claim empowerment from the "rights of freeborn Englishmen," were early signs that politics and national culture were coming together.

The clash between national loyalties and multinational empires did not become serious until the 19th century, and it has continued in the 20th. In the long run, most multinational states have not been able to sustain themselves in the face of increasing demands from individual national groups. The collapse of several multinational units in the 20th century—the Ottomans in the Middle East, the Hapsburgs in east central Europe, and recently the Russians themselves—created new diplomatic trouble spots quite obvious in the world today, for stable nation-states have had a hard time developing in these regions.

Questions: Why have nation-states been more successful, as political units, in modern world history than multinational empires have been? In what ways did the Russian empire develop some nation-state characteristics? What were its principal multinational features? Amid new needs for international economic coordination in the late 20th century, is it possible to build multinational organizations on some new basis?

Conclusion

Russia and Eastern Europe

Russian history did not include the whole of eastern Europe after the 15th century, although Russia's expansion, particularly its final acquisition of much of Poland, did merge much of the larger region into the Russian embrace. Regions west of Russia continued to form a fluctuating borderland between west European and east European influences. Even in the Balkans, under Ottoman control, growing trade with the West sparked some new cultural exchange by the 18th century, as Greek merchants, for example, picked up many Enlightenment ideas.

Areas such as present-day Poland or the Czech and Slovak regions operated more fully within the Western cultural orbit. The Polish scientist Copernicus was an early participant in fundamental discoveries in what became the scientific revolution. Western currents such as the Reformation also echoed in parts of east central Europe such as Hungary.

At the same time, many smaller east European nationalities lost political autonomy during the early modern era. Hungary, freed from the Turks, became part of the German-dominated Habsburg Empire. This empire also took over the Czech lands, then called Bohemia. Prussian territory pushed eastward into Polish areas.

The decline of Poland was particularly striking. In 1500, Poland, formed in 1386 by a union of the regional kingdoms of Poland and Lithuania, was the largest state in eastern Europe aside from Russia. Polish cultural life, linked with the West through shared Roman Catholicism, flourished in the 16th century. By 1600, however, economic and political setbacks mounted. Polish aristocrats, charged with electing the king, began deliberately choosing weak figures. The central government became powerless, and the aristocrats ran roughshod over poor peasants. As in Russia, urban centers, and thus a merchant class, were lacking. The aristocratic parliament vetoed any reform efforts until late in the 18th century, after Poland began to be partitioned by its more powerful neighbors. The eclipse of Poland highlighted Russian emergence in the European as well as the Eurasian stage.

Further Readings

For excellent survey coverage on this period, as well as additional bibliography, see Nicholas Riasanovsky's *History of Russia* (5th ed., 1992). Two excellent source collections for this vital period of Russian history are T. Riha, ed., *Readings in Russian Civilization. Vol. II, Imperial Russia 1700–1917* (1969) and Basil Dmytryshyn, *Imperial Russia: A Sourcebook 1700–1917* (1967).

On important regimes, see J.L.I. Fennell's *Ivan the Great of Moscow* (1961), R. Massie's *Peter the Great* (1981), and N. V. Riasanovsky's *The Image of Peter the Great in Russian History and Thought* (1985). This last book is a very interesting interpretive effort. On Catherine, see I. de Madariaga's *Russia in the Age of Catherine the Great* (1981).

Three good studies deal with cultural history: H. Rogger, *National Consciousness in Eighteenth Century Russia*

(1963), Marc Raeff, *Origins of the Russian Intelligentsia: The Eighteenth Century Nobility* (1966), and Marc Raeff, ed., *Russian Intellectual History* (1986).

For economic and social history, A. Kahan's *The Knout and the Plowshare: Economic History of Russia in the 18th Century* (1985) is an important treatment. For the vital peasant question, see Jerome Blum's *Lord and Peasant in Russia from the Ninth to the Nineteenth Century* (1961); see also Richard Hellie's *Slavery in Russia, 1450–1725* (1982). For an analytical overview, see Marc Raeff's *Understanding Imperial Russia: State and Society in the Old Regime* (1984). A very revealing comparison is Peter Kolchin, *Unfree Labor: American Slavery and Russian Serfdom* (1987). A fine recent survey on military and diplomatic strategy is William Fuller, *Strategy and Power in Russia, 1600–1914* (1992).

On the Web

A vivid introduction to Russian history is offered at http://www.bucknell.edu/departments/russian/index.html. Russia before the Romanovs is examined at http://garrard.russian.arizona.edu/atheneum/ivantheterrible.htm. Peter the Great's maritime interests are examined at http://www.nmm.ac.uk/education/fact_peter.html. His achievements as Czar are given careful treatment at http://garrard.russian.arizona.edu/atheneum/peterthegreat.htm. The lives of Peter the Great and Catherine the Great are seen against the backdrop of early modern Russia at http://www.english.upenn.edu/~jlynch/FrankDemo/People/russia.html and at http://www.english.upenn.edu/~jlynch/FrankDemo/Places/catherin.html

A virtual tour of their capital is available at http://www.cityvision2000.com/city_tour/index.htm. A colorful slice of Czarist life is revealed by a virtual exhibit on the snuffboxes of Catherine the Great at http://www.hermitage.ru/html_En/12/hm12_1_2.html. A rosy view of Cossack life is presented at http://www.max.K12.nd.us./cossack.html.

Catherine the Great's response to the rebellion led by a Don Cossack, Emelian Pugachev, and how it illuminated the differences in the political landscape of revolutionary France and absolutist Russia, is described at http://mars.acnet.wnec.edu/~grempel/courses/russia/lectures/16catherine.html.

Chapter 25

Early Latin America

The arrival of the Spaniards in Mexico brought Europeans into contact for the first time with the great civilizations of Mesoamerica. This depiction of the Spaniards by an Indian artist drawn after the conquest, demonstrates a fusion of European and indigenous forms of representation.

During the 15th and 16th centuries, Spain and Portugal created empires in the Americas. In contrast to Russia, which was also building an empire at this time, these were dependent empires, and both their economies and their cultural relationships to the West differed accordingly.

The new Latin American empires, like Russia by the 18th century, maintained special contacts with the West—and, as with Russia, this fact has continued to shape key characteristics to the present day. Whereas Russian leaders decided what aspects of the West to borrow, however, Western forms were simply imposed on many Latin American people. The new empires were examples also of the potency of gunpowder, which the conquerors used to establish their sway. Spanish and Portuguese conquerors had advantages besides gunpowder: metal equipment, horses, and the fearsome power of European diseases. This explains why the conquerors were able to force highly unequal relationships on the subject populations.

Latin America was immediately drawn into the New World economy, playing a central role in providing silver, new crops, and other goods. The new hierarchy of world economic relationships shaped conditions in this new civilization for several centuries.

The societies of Latin America also created important new political and cultural forms. The Spaniards and Portuguese, often called Iberians because they came from the Iberian peninsula in Europe, mixed with Native Americans and their earlier civilization forms and were influenced by imported African slaves. The formative period for Latin American civilization extended from initial contacts in the 1490s through the 18th century, when colonial structures began to decline. This span ran slightly longer than the early modern period in Europe; the early 1800s, rather than 1750, is the appropriate terminal point. This period spanned a number of stages, from raw conquest to growing economic and political complexity by the 18th century.

New societies, created by the intrusion of Spaniards and Portuguese and by the incorporation or destruction of Native American cultures, arose throughout the American continents. Both Europeans and Indians drew heavily on their previous experiences as they grappled with the problems created by their encounter with one other. Much of what the Iberians did in the Americas followed the patterns and examples of their European traditions. The Indians who survived, although they were battered and profoundly transformed, showed a vitality and resiliency that shaped later societies in many ways. What resulted drew on European and Indian precedents, but it was something new: the world's latest addition to the list of distinctive civilizations.

1450 C.E.	1500 C.E.	1600 C.E.	1750 C.E.
1493–1520 Exploration and settlement in the Caribbean	**1500** Cabral lands in Brazil	**1630–1654** Dutch capture northeastern Brazil	**1755–1776** Marquis of Pombal, Prime minister of Portugal
1494 Treaty of Tordesillar	**1519–1524** Cortés leads conquest of Mexico	**1654** English take Jamaica	**1759** Jesuits expelled from Brazil
1492 Fall of Granada, last Muslim kingdom in Spain; expulsion of the Jews; Columbus landfall in the Caribbean	**1533** Cuzco, Peru falls to Francisco Pizarro	**1695** Gold discovered in Brazil	**1756–1763** Seven Years' War
1493 Columbus's second expedition; beginnings of settlement in the Indies	**1541** Santiago, Chile founded	**1702–1713** War of the Spanish succession; Bourbon dynasty rules Spain	**1759–1788** Carlos III rules Spain; Bourbon reforms
	1540–1542 Coronado explores southwestern United States		**1763** Brazilian capital moved to Rio de Janeiro
	1549 Royal government established in Brazil		**1767** Jesuits expelled from Spanish America
	1580–1640 Spain and Portugal united under same rulers		**1781** Comunero revolt in New Granada; Tupac Amaru rebellion in Peru
			1788 Conspiracy for independence in Minas Gerais, Brazil

Various European peoples sought the same ends in the New World: economic gain and social mobility. The Portuguese, English, Spanish, and French all created large landed estates, or plantations, worked by coerced laborers—ultimately African slaves—wherever tropical conditions and European demand made such enterprises feasible. The Europeans exploited precious metals when they were discovered, and those who did not find the metals followed rumors of gold or emeralds.

SPANIARDS AND PORTUGUESE: FROM RECONQUEST TO CONQUEST

▓▓ *The Spaniards and Portuguese came from societies long in contact with peoples of other faiths and cultures in which warfare and conquest were well-established activities. In the Caribbean, these traditions were modified by American realities as people with the backing of the state moved to conquer the mainlands. By the 1570s, much of the Americas had been brought under Iberian control.*

The peoples who inhabited the Iberian peninsula had long lived at the frontier of Mediterranean Europe. The peninsula had known many inhabitants—Phoenicians, Carthaginians, Romans, and Goths—and during the Middle Ages had become a cultural frontier between Christianity and Islam. Conflict created a strong tradition of military conquest and rule over peoples of other beliefs and customs. Christian kingdoms had emerged, such as Portugal on the Atlantic coast, Aragon in eastern Spain, and in the center of the peninsula, Castile, the largest of all. By the mid-15th century, the religious and ethnic diversity in these kingdoms was being submerged by a process of political and religious unification under *Ferdinand of Aragon* and his wife, *Isabella of Castile*. With the fall in 1492 of Granada, the last Muslim kingdom, the cross had triumphed throughout the peninsula. Political savvy and religious fervor moved Isabella. Immediately upon the fall of Granada, Isabella ordered the Jews of her realm to convert or leave the country. As many as 200,000 may have left, severely disrupting some aspects of the Castilian economy. It was also in 1492, with the Granada War at an end and religious unification established, that Isabella and Ferdinand were willing to support the project of a Genoese mariner named Christopher Columbus, who hoped to reach the East Indies by sailing westward around the globe.

Iberian Society and Tradition

Like many Mediterranean people, the Spanish and Portuguese were heavily urban, with many peasants living in small towns and villages. The desire to live in an urban setting helped set up a pattern of Spanish cities amid a largely Indian countryside in many parts of the Americas.Many commoners who came to America as conquerors sought to recreate themselves as a new nobility, with Indians as their serfs. Patriarchal notions were heavily emphasized, although women had an active role in family life. The patriarchal family was readily adapted to Latin America, where large estates and grants of Indian laborers, or *encomiendas,* provided the framework for relations based on economic dominance. The Iberian peninsula maintained a tradition of holding slaves—part of its experience as an ethnic frontier—in contrast to most of medieval Europe, and African slaves had been imported from the trans-Sahara trade. The extension of slavery to America built on this tradition.

The political centralization of both Portugal and Castile depended on a professional bureaucracy, usually made up of men trained as lawyers and judges. This system is worthy of comparison with China and other great empires. Religion and the church served as the other pillar of Iberian politics; close links between church and state resulted from the reconquest of the peninsula from the Muslims, and these links, including royal nomination of church officials, were also extended to the New World.

Spanish and particularly Portuguese merchants also shaped traditions that became relevant in the American colonies. Portugal had been moving down the African coast since 1415, establishing trading posts rather than outright colonies. In the Atlantic islands, however, more extensive estates were established, leading to a slave trade with Africa and a highly commercial agricultural system based on sugar. Brazil would extend this pattern, starting out as a trade factory but then shifting, as in the Atlantic islands, to plantation agriculture.

The Chronology of Conquest

The Spanish and Portuguese conquest and colonization of the Americas falls roughly into three periods during the early modern centuries: first, an era of conquest from 1492 to about 1570, during which the main lines of administration and economy were set out; second, a phase of consolidation and maturity from 1570 to about 1700 in which the colonial institutions and societies took their definite form; and finally, during the 18th century, a period of reform and reorganization in both Spanish America and Portuguese Brazil that intensified the colonial relationship and planted the seeds of dissatisfaction and revolt (Map 25.1).

The period from 1492 to about 1570 or in some places 1600 witnessed a remarkable spurt of human destruction and creation. During roughly a century, vast areas of two continents and millions of people were brought under European control. The bases of an economic system that linked these areas to an emerging Atlantic economy were created, and a flow of immigration and commerce was set in motion. These processes were accompanied and made possible by the conquest and destruction of many Indian societies and the transformation of others, as well as by the introduction in some places of African slaves. Mexico and Peru, with their large sedentary populations and mineral resources, attracted the Spaniards and became, after the short initial Caribbean stage, the focus of immigration and institution building. Other conquests radiated outward from the Peruvian and Mexican centers.

The Caribbean Crucible

The *Caribbean* experience served Spain as a model for its actions elsewhere in the Americas. After Columbus's original voyage in 1492, a return expedition in the next year established a colony on the island of Santo Domingo (*Hispaniola;* Figure 25.1). From there and from Spain, expeditions carried out new explorations and conquests. Puerto Rico (1508) and Cuba (1511) fell under Spanish control, and by 1513 settlements existed in Panama and on the northern coast of South America.

In the Caribbean, the agricultural Taino Indians of the islands provided enough surplus labor to make their distribution to individual Spaniards feasible, and thus began what would become the *encomienda,* or grants of Indians to individual Spaniards in a kind of serfdom. Gold hunting, slaving, and European diseases rapidly depopulated the islands, and within two decades little was left there to hold Spanish attention. A few strongly fortified ports, such as Havana, San Juan, and Santo Domingo, guarded Spain's commercial lifeline, but on the whole the Caribbean became a colonial backwater for the next two centuries until sugar and slaves became the basis of its resurgence.

DOCUMENT

A Vision from the Vanquished

history usually is written by the victors, so it is rare to find a detailed statement from the vanquished. In the 17th century, Guaman Poma de Ayala, an acculturated Peruvian Indian who claimed to trace his lineage to the provincial nobility of Inca times, composed a memorial outlining the history of Peru under the Incas and reporting on the current conditions under Spanish rule. Guaman Poma was a Christian and a loyal subject. He hoped that his report would reach King Philip III of Spain, who might then order an end to the worst abuses, among which were the Spanish failure to recognize the rank and status of Indian nobles. His book was not published in his lifetime and was not recovered until the 20th century.

Guaman Poma was an educated, bilingual Indian who spoke Quechua as well as Spanish and who had a profound understanding of Andean culture. His book is remarkable for its revelations of Indian life, for its detailed criticism of the abuses suffered by the Indians, and especially because Guaman Poma illustrated his memorial with a series of drawings that give his words a visual effect. The illustrations also reveal the worldview of this interesting man. The drawings and text offer a critical inside view not of the laws, but of the workings of Spain's empire in America from an Indian point of view.

Miners

At the mercury mines of Huancavelica the Indian workers are punished and ill-treated to such an extent that they die like flies and our whole race is threatened with extermination. Even the chiefs are tortured by being suspended by their feet. Conditions in the silver-mines of Potosí and Chocllococha, or at the gold-mines of Carabaya are little better. The managers and supervisors, who are Spaniards or mestizos have virtually absolute power. There is no reason for them to fear justice, since they are never brought before the courts.

Beatings are incessant. The victims are mounted for this purpose on a llama's back, tied naked to a round pillar or put in stocks. Their hair is cut off and they are deprived of food and water during detention.

Any shortage in the labor gangs is made an excuse for punishing the chiefs as if they were common thieves or traitors instead of the nobility of the country. The work itself is so hard as to cause permanent injury to many of those who survive it. There is no remuneration for the journey to the mines and a day's labor is paid at the rate for half a day.

Proprietors

Your Majesty has granted large estates, including the right to employ Indian labor, to a number of individuals of whom some are good Christians and the remainder are very bad ones. These encomenderos, as they are termed, may boast about their high position, but in reality they are harmful both to the labor force and to the surviving Indian nobility. I therefore propose to set down the details of their life and conduct.

They exude an air of success as they go from their card games to their dinners in fine silk clothes. Their money is squandered on these luxuries, as well it may, since it costs them no work or sweat whatever. Although the Indians ultimately pay the bill, no concern is ever felt for them or even for Your Majesty or God himself.

Official posts like those of royal administrator and judge ought not to be given to big employers or mine-owners or to their obnoxious sons, because these peoples have enough to live on already. The appointments ought to go to Christian gentlemen of small means, who have

rendered some service to the Crown and are educated and humane, not just greedy.

Anybody with rights over Indian labor sees to it that his own household is well supplied with servant girls and indoor and outdoor staff. When collecting dues and taxes, it is usual to impose penalties and detain Indians against their will. There is no redress since, if any complaint is made, the law always favors the employer.

The collection of tribute is delegated to stewards, who make a practice of adding something in for themselves. They too consider themselves entitled to free service and obligatory presents, and they end up as bad as their masters. All of them, and their wives as well, regard themselves as entitled to eat at the Indians' expense.

The Indians are seldom paid the few reales a day which are owed to them, but they are hired out for the porterage of wine and making rope or clothing. Little rest is possible either by day or night and they are usually unable to sleep at home.

It is impossible for servant girls, or even married women, to remain chaste. They are bound to be corrupted and prostituted because employers do not feel any scruple about threatening them with flogging, execution, or burial alive if they refuse to satisfy their master's desires.

The Spanish grandees and their wives have borrowed from the Inca the custom of having themselves conveyed in litters like the images of saints in processions. These Spaniards are absolute lords without fear of either God or retribution. In their own eyes they are judges over our people, whom they can reserve for their personal service or their pleasure, to the detriment of the community.

Great positions are achieved by favour from above, by wealth or by having relations at Court in Castile. With some notable exceptions, the beneficiaries act without consideration for those under their control. The encomenderos call themselves conquerors, but their Conquest was achieved by uttering the words: Ama mancha noca Inca, or "Have no fear. I am Inca." This false pretense was the sum total of their performance.

Questions: What are the main abuses Guaman Poma complains about? What remedies does he recommend? What relationship do his views have to traditional Inca values? How might a white landlord or colonial official have answered his attacks?

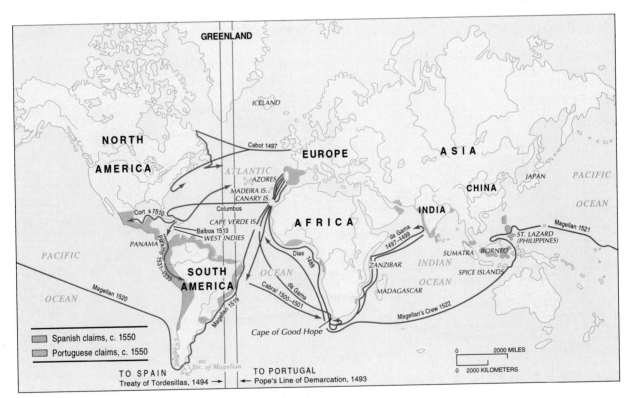

Map 25.1 *Spanish and Portuguese Explorations, 1400–1600*

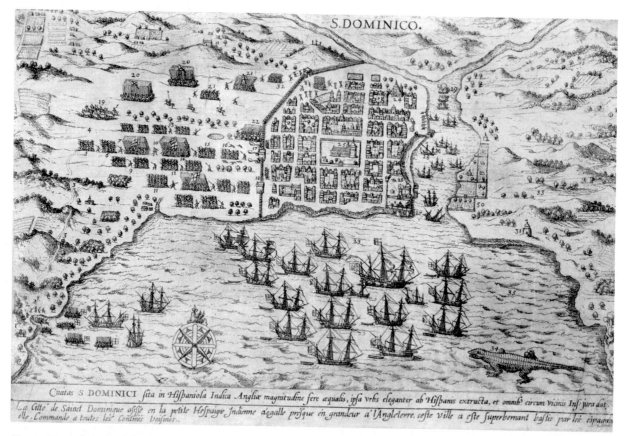

Figure 25.1. The city and port of Santo Domingo was the principal Spanish settlement in the Caribbean in the 16th century.

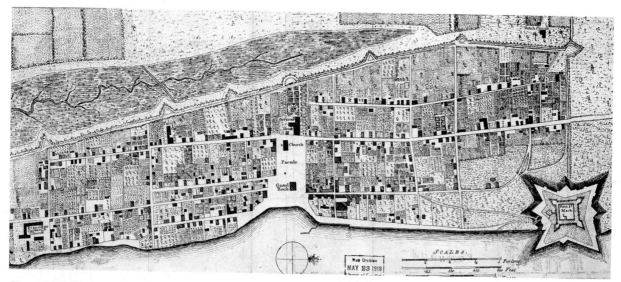

Figure 25.2. St. Augustine, Florida, the oldest city in the United States (founded in 1565), reflects its Spanish heritage in the central plaza and the checkerboard layout that can be seen in this 18th-century engraving.

In the 40 years between the first voyage of Columbus and the conquest of Mexico, the Caribbean served as a testing ground. The Spaniards established Iberian-style cities but had to adapt them to American realities. Hurricanes and Indians caused many towns to be moved or abandoned, but the New World also provided opportunities to implant new ideas and forms. Unlike cities in Europe, Spanish American cities usually were laid out according to a grid plan or checkerboard form with the town hall, major church, and governor's palace in the central plaza (Figure 25.2). Spaniards applied Roman models and rational town planning ideas to the new situation. Conquest came to imply settlement.

A move from private control by Columbus and his family to royal administration was marked by the creation of administrative institutions: the governorship, the treasury office, and the royal court of appeals staffed by professional magistrates. Spanish legalism was part of the institutional transfer. Notaries accompanied new expeditions, and a body of laws was developed based on those of Spain and augmented by American experience. The church, represented at first by individual priests and then by missionaries such as the Dominicans, participated in the enterprise. By 1530, a cathedral was being built on Hispaniola, and a university soon followed. The new area had to be provisioned and its commerce regularized. The Genoese participated in this process at first, but by the turn of the century, Spanish merchants were fully involved.

Rumors and hopes stimulated immigration from Spain, and by the 1510s the immigrants included larger numbers of Spanish women. Also, Spanish and Italian merchants began to import African slaves to work on the few sugar plantations that operated on the islands. The arrival of both Spanish women and African slaves represented a shift from an area of conquest to one of settlement. The gold-hunting phase had given out in the islands by the 1520s and was replaced by the establishment of ranches and sugar plantations. The adventurous, the disappointed, and the greedy repeated the pattern. Expeditions spun off in new directions, repeating the processes already set in motion but in each case drawing on the experience already gained.

Among these experiences was the virtual annihilation of the Indians of the Caribbean. Depopulation of the laboring population led to slaving on other islands, and in 30 years or so, most of the Indian population had died or been killed. The Indians of the lesser Antilles, or "Caribs," whom the Spanish accused of cannibalism and who were thus always subject to enslavement, held out longer because their islands were less attractive to European settlement. The pattern of European concentration on areas of denser Indian populations was already forming. The destruction of the Indians led to further expeditions toward the mainland; it also caused a transformation of the islands' economies toward activities such as sugar production, which called forth the African slave trade.

As early as 1510, the mistreatment and destruction of the Indians led to attempts by clerics and royal administrators to end the worst abuses. The activities of men such as Dominican friar *Bartolomé de Las Casas* (1484–1566; Figure 25.3), a conquistador turned priest, initiated the struggle for justice. Expeditions leaped from island to island. Where the

D. FR. BARTHOLOME DE LAS CASAS
Del Orden de Predicadores, Obispo de Chiapa
Varon apostolico, y el mas zeloso de la felicidad
de los Indios.
Nació en Sevilla el año de 1474, y murió en Madrid
el de 1566.

Figure 25.3. Father Bartolomé de Las Casas.

Indian peoples and cultures were more resilient, their impact on the societies that emerged was greater than in the Caribbean, but the process of contact was similar.

By the time of the conquest of Mexico in the 1520s and Peru in the 1530s, all the elements of the colonial system of Latin America were in place. Even in Brazil, which the Portuguese began to exploit after 1500, a period of bartering with the Indians was slowly replaced by increasing royal control and development of a sugar plantation economy. There, as in the Caribbean, Indian resistance and subsequent depopulation led to the importation of African laborers.

The Paths of Conquest

No other race can be found that can penetrate through such rugged lands, such dense forests, such great mountains and deserts and cross such broad rivers as the Spaniards have done … solely by the valor of their persons and the forcefulness of their breed.

These words, written by Pedro Cieza de Leon, one of the conquistadors of Peru, underlined the Spaniards' pride in their accomplishments. In less than a century, a large portion of two continents and islands in an inland sea, inhabited by millions of people, was brought under Spanish control. Spanish expeditions, usually comprising 50 to 500 men, provided the spearhead of conquest, and in their wake followed the women, missionaries, administrators, and artisans who began to form civil society.

The conquest was not a unified movement but rather a series of individual initiatives that usually operated with government approval. The conquest of the Americas was two-pronged: One prong was directed toward Mexico, and the other aimed at South America.

We can use the well-documented campaign in Mexico as an example of a conquest. In 1519, *Hernán Cortés,* an educated man with considerable ability as a leader, led an expedition of 600 men to the coast of Mexico. After hearing rumors of a great kingdom in the interior, he established a base at Veracruz on the coast and then began to strike inland. Pitched battles were fought with towns subject to the Aztec Empire, but after gaining these victories, Cortés was able to enlist the Indians' support against their overlords. With the help of the Indian allies, Cortés eventually reached the great Aztec island capital of Tenochtitlan.

By a combination of deception, boldness, ruthlessness, and luck, the Aztec emperor *Moctezuma II* was captured and killed. Cortés and his followers were forced to flee the Aztec capital and retreat toward the coast, but with the help of the Aztecs' traditional enemies, they cut off and besieged Tenochtitlan. Although the Aztec confederacy put up a stiff resistance, disease, starvation, and battle brought the city down in 1521. Tenochtitlan was replaced by *Mexico City.* The Aztec poets later remembered,

We are crushed to the ground,

we lie in ruins.

There is nothing but grief and suffering

in Mexico and Tlatelolco,

where once we saw beauty and valor.

By 1535, most of central Mexico, with its network of towns and its dense, agricultural populations, had been brought under Spanish control as the kingdom of *New Spain.* From there, the Spanish pushed their conquest southward into Guatemala and Honduras and northward into the area of the nomadic Indians of north central Mexico.

The second trajectory of conquests led from the Caribbean outposts to the coast of northern South America and Panama. From Panama, the Spaniards followed rumors of a rich kingdom to the south. In 1535, after a false start, *Francisco Pizarro* led his men to the conquest of the Inca Empire, which was already weakened by a long civil war. Once again, using guile and audacity, fewer than 200 Spaniards and their Indian allies brought a great Indian empire down. The Inca capital of Cuzco, high in the Andes, fell in 1533, but the Spanish decided to build their major city, Lima, closer to the coast. By 1540, most of Peru was under Spanish control, although an active resistance continued in remote areas for another 30 years.

From the conquests of densely populated areas, such as Mexico and Peru, where there were surpluses of food and potential laborers, Spanish expeditions spread out in search of further riches and strange peoples. Spanish expeditions penetrated the zones of semisedentary and nomadic peoples, who often offered stiff resistance. Expeditions from Mexico moved into the northern frontiers inhabited by nomadic hunters. From 1540 to 1542, in one of the most famous expeditions, *Francisco Vázquez de Coro-*

nado, searching for mythical cities of gold, penetrated what is now southwestern United States as far as Kansas. At the other end of the Americas, *Pedro de Valdivia* conquered the tenacious Araucanian Indians of central Chile and set up the city of Santiago in 1541, although the Araucanians continued to fight long after. Buenos Aires, in the southern part of the continent, founded by an expedition from Spain in 1536, was abandoned because of Indian resistance and was not refounded until 1580. Expeditions such as that led by Gonzalo Pizarro (1541–1542) penetrated the Amazon basin, and others explored the tropical forests of Central and South America during these years, but there was little there to attract permanent settlement. By 1570, there were 192 Spanish cities and towns throughout the Americas, one-third of which were in Mexico and Central America.

The Conquerors

We can make some general statements about the conquerors and the organization of conquest. The captains led by force of will and personal power. "God in the sky, the king in Spain, and me here" was the motto of one captain, and sometimes absolute power could lead to tyranny. Usually, an agreement was drawn up between the leader of the conquest and the representatives of the Spanish crown that granted authority in return for a promise to pay one-fifth of all treasure or other gains to the crown. Men signed up on a shares basis; those who brought horses or who had special skills might get double shares. Rewards were made according to the contract, and premiums were paid for special service and valor. There was a tendency for leaders to reward their friends, relatives, and men from their home province more liberally than others, so that after each conquest there was always a group of unhappy and dissatisfied conquerors ready to organize a new expedition. As one observer put it, "if each man was given the governorship, it would not be enough."

Few of the conquerors were professional soldiers; they represented all walks of Spanish life, including a scattering of gentlemen. Some of the later expeditions included a few Spanish women such as Ines Suárez, the heroine of the conquest of Chile, but such cases were rare. In general, the conquerors were men on the make, hoping to better themselves and serve God by converting the heathen at the same time. Always on the lookout for treasure, most con-

querors were satisfied by grants of Indians, who could be taxed or put to work. They took a distinct pride in the fact that they were not paid soldiers but rather volunteers who risked their lives for king and church. These adventurous men, many of humble origins, came to see themselves as a new nobility entitled to dominion over a new peasantry: the Indians.

The reasons for Spanish success were varied. Horses, firearms, and more generally steel weapons gave them a great advantage over the stone technology of the Indians. This technological edge, combined with effective and ruthless leadership, produced remarkable results. Europeans were also aided by the silent ally of epidemic disease, which sometimes even preceded a conquest and weakened the Indian resistance. Finally, internal divisions and rivalries within Indian empires, and their high levels of centralization, made the great civilizations particularly vulnerable. It is no accident that the Indian peoples who offered the stiffest and most continuous resistance were usually the mobile, tough nomadic tribes rather than the centralized states of sedentary peasants.

By about 1570, the age of the conquest was coming to a close. The generation of the conquerors was replaced by bureaucrats, merchants, and colonists as the institutions of colonial rule and the basis of the economy were regularized. The transition was not easy. In Peru a civil war erupted in the 1540s, and in Mexico there were grumblings from the old followers of Cortés. But the establishment of viceroys in the two main colonies and the creation of law courts in the main centers signaled that Spanish America had become a colony rather than a conquest.

Conquest and Morality

Conquest involved violence, domination, and theft. The Spanish conquest of the Americas created a series of important philosophical and moral questions for Europeans. Who were the Indians? Were they fully human? Was it proper to convert them to Christianity? Was the conquest of their lands justified? Driven by greed, many of the conquistadors argued that conquest was necessary to spread the gospel and that control of Indian labor was essential for Spain's rule. In 1548 Juan Gines de Sépulveda, a noted Spanish scholar, basing his arguments on Aristotle, published a book claiming that the conquest was fully justified. The Spaniards had come to free the Indians from their unjust lords and to bring the light of salvation. Most importantly, he argued, the Indians were not fully human, and that some peoples "were born to serve."

In 1550, the Spanish king suspended all further conquests and convoked a special commission in Valladolid to hear arguments for and against this position. Father Bartolomé de Las Casas—former conqueror and *encomendero*, Dominican priest, bishop of Chiapas, untiring defender of the Indians, and critic of Spanish brutality—presented the contrary opinion against Sépulveda. Las Casas had long experience in the Indies, and he believed that the inhabitants were rational people who, unlike the Muslims, had never done harm to Christians. Thus, the conquest of their lands was unjustified. The Indians had many admirable customs and accomplishments, he said. He argued that "the Indians are our brothers and Christ has given his life for them." Spanish rule in order to spread the Christian faith was justified, but conversion should take place only by peaceful means.

The results of the debate were mixed. The crown had reasons to back Las Casas against the dangerous ambitions of the Spanish conquerors. Sépulveda's book was censored, but the conquests nevertheless continued. Although some of the worst abuses were moderated, in reality the great period of conquest was all over by the 1570s. It was too little, too late. Still, the Spanish government's concern with the legality and morality of its actions and the willingness of Spaniards such as Las Casas to speak out against abuses are also part of the story.

THE DESTRUCTION AND TRANSFORMATION OF INDIAN SOCIETIES

To varying degrees, all the indigenous societies suffered the effects of the conquest. Demographic loss was extreme in many areas. The Spanish created institutions such as the encomienda to tax the native population or make them work. These policies disrupted indigenous societies.

The various Indian peoples responded in many different ways to the invasion of America and the transformation of their societies. All of them suffered a severe decline of population—a demographic catastrophe (Figure 25.4). On the main islands of the Caribbean, the Indian population had nearly disappeared by 1540 as the result of slaving, mistreat-

ment, and disease. In central Mexico, war, destruction, and above all disease brought the population from an estimated 25 million in 1519 to less than 2 million in 1580. In Peru, a similar process brought a loss from 10 million to 1.5 million between 1530 and 1590. Elsewhere in the Americas a similar but less well documented process took place. Smallpox, influenza, and measles wreaked havoc on the Indian population, which had developed no immunities against these diseases.

Although epidemic was the major cause of depopulation, the conquest and the weakening of indigenous societies contributed to the mortality and made the Indian populations more susceptible to disease. Population losses of this size disrupted Indian societies in many ways. For example, in central Mexico the contraction of the Indian population led the Spanish to concentrate the remaining population in fewer towns, and this led in turn to the seizure of former communal farming lands by Spanish landowners. Demographic collapse made maintaining traditional social and economic structures very difficult.

The case of Mexico is particularly stark. The tremendous decline of the Indian population was matched by the rapid increase in European livestock.

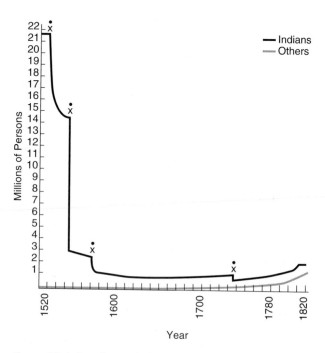

Figure 25.4. Population decline in New Spain.

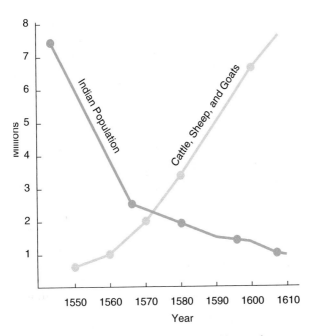

Figure 25.5. A comparison of human and livestock populations in central Mexico.

Cattle, sheep, and horses flourished on the newly created Spanish farms or on unclaimed lands. In a way, the Indian population of Mexico was replaced by European livestock (Figure 25.5).

Exploitation of the Indians

The desire to use Indians as laborers or to extract a tribute from them led the Spanish to maintain the aspects of Indian life that served colonial goals or at least did not openly conflict with Spanish authority or religion. Thus, in Mexico and Peru, while the old Indian religion and its priestly class were eliminated, the traditional Indian nobility remained in place, supported by Spanish authority, as middlemen between the tax and labor demands of the new rulers and the majority of the population.

The enslavement of Indians, except those taken in war, was prohibited by the mid-16th century in most of Spanish America. Instead, different forms of labor or taxation were imposed. At first, encomiendas were given to the individual conquerors of a region. The holders of these grants, or encomenderos, were able to use their Indians as workers and servants or to tax them. Whereas commoners had owed tribute or labor to the state in the Inca and Aztec empires, the new demands were arbitrary, often excessive, and usually without the recip-

rocal obligation and protection characteristic of the Indian societies. Encomiendas were introduced after the initial conquest from New Mexico in the north to Chile in the south. In general, the encomiendas were destructive to Indian societies, and as depopulation continued, the holders of the grants became dissatisfied. Finally, the Spanish crown, unwilling to see a new nobility arise in the New World among the conquerors with their grants of Indian serfs, moved to end the institution in the 1540s. The crown limited the inheritability of encomiendas and prohibited the right to demand certain kinds of labor from the Indians. Although encomiendas continued to exist in marginal regions at the fringes of the empire, they were all but gone by the 1620s in the central areas of Mexico and Peru. With the disappearance of the encomienda, the colonists and descendants of the conquerors increasingly sought grants of land rather than Indians as the basis of wealth.

Meanwhile, the colonial government increasingly extracted labor and taxes from native peoples. In many places, communities were required to send groups of laborers to work on state projects, such as church construction or road building, or in labor gangs for mining or agriculture. This forced labor, called the *mita* in Peru, mobilized thousands of Indians to work in the mines and on other projects. Although the Indians were paid a wage for this work, there were many abuses of the system by the local officials, and community labor requirements often were disruptive and destructive to Indian life. By the 17th century, many Indians left their villages to avoid the labor and tax obligations, preferring instead to work for Spanish land owners or to seek employment in the cities. This process eventually led to the growth of a wage labor system in which Indians, no longer resident in their villages, worked for wages on Spanish-owned mines and farms or in the cities.

In the wake of this disruption, Native American culture also demonstrated great resiliency in the face of Spanish institutions and forms, adapting and modifying them to indigenous ways. In New Spain, the Spanish municipal councils established in Indian towns were staffed by the indigenous elite. In Peru and Mexico, native peoples learned to use the legal system and the law courts so that litigation became a way of life. At the local level, many aspects of Indian life remained, and Indians proved to be selective in their adaptation of European foods, technology, and culture.

IN DEP†H

The Great Exchange

The arrival of the Spaniards and the Portuguese in the Americas began one of the most extensive and profound changes in the history of humankind. The New World, which had existed in isolation since the end of the last Ice Age, was now brought into continual contact with the Old World. The peoples and cultures of Europe and Africa came to the Americas through voluntary or forced immigration. Between 1500 and 1850, perhaps to 10 to 15 million Africans and 5 million Europeans crossed the Atlantic and settled in the Americas as part of the great migratory movement. Contact also initiated a broader biological and ecological exchange that changed the face of both the Old World and the New World—the way people lived, what they ate, and how they died—as the animals, plants, and diseases of the two hemispheres were transferred. Historian Alfred Crosby has called this process the *Columbian exchange*, and he has pointed out its profound effects as the first stage of the "ecological imperialism" that accompanied the expansion of the West. In this chapter we have discussed the devastating impact of Old World disease on Native American peoples. Long separated from the populations of the Old World and lacking immunities to diseases such as measles and smallpox, populations throughout the Americas suffered disastrous losses after initial contact. Not only among the dense populations in Peru and Mexico, but in the forests of Brazil and the woodlands of North America, contact with Europeans and Africans resulted in epidemics that devastated the indigenous populations. Only after many generations did immunities build up in the remaining populations that allowed them to withstand the diseases.

Disease may have also moved in the other direction. Some authorities believe that syphilis had an American origin and was brought to Europe only after 1492. In general, however, forms of life in the Old World—diseases, plants, and animals— were more complex than those in the Americas and thus displaced the New World varieties in open competition. The diseases of Eurasia and Africa had a greater impact on America than American diseases had on the Old World.

With animals also, the major exchange was from the Old World to the New World. From the beginning of contact, Europeans noted with curiosity the strange fauna of America, so different from that of Europe. The birds were a hit. Parrots were among the first creatures brought to Europe from America. Many early observers commented on the smaller size of the mammals in the New World and the absence of certain types, not realizing that mastodons, horses, camels, and other animals that had once roamed the Americas had long since disappeared. American Indians had domesticated dogs, guinea pigs, some fowl, and llamas, but in general domesticated animals were far less important in the Americas than in the Old World. Protein resources were thus also more restricted. The absence of cattle and horses had also left the peoples of the Americas without beasts of burden except for the llamas of the Andes.

In the first years of settlement in the Caribbean, the Spanish introduced horses, cattle, sheep, chickens, and domestic goats and pigs, all of which were considered essential for civilized life as the Iberians understood it. Some of these animals thrived in the New World. In the scrub brush and prairies of North America, in the tropical grasslands of Venezuela and on the South American pampas, vast herds of cattle began to roam freely. A hundred head of cattle abandoned by the Spanish in the Rio de la Plata area in 1587 had become 100,000 head 20 years later. Both for the consumption of meat, tallow, and hides in the Americas and eventually for the export of hides and meat to Europe and the rest of the world, the arrival of cattle in the Americas was a revolutionary occurrence. In Mexico, livestock and Spanish *haciendas* grew as rapidly as the Indian population declined and Indian communities contracted. The replacement of Indians by cattle became a metaphor of the conquest of Mexico.

The success of other European livestock was no less impressive. In the Andes and in Mexico, sheep thrived and supported an active textile industry, which eventually supplied most of the local needs. Horses were adopted quickly by the nomadic peoples of North and South America. This adaptation transformed their societies and gave them added mobility, allowing them to meet the Europeans on an almost equal basis. With horses, the Apaches of Arizona and the Indians of the Argentine pampas were able to hold off the Europeans for 300 years.

European livestock, even pigs and chickens, transformed indigenous life in America. Native Americans acquired some animals, such as oxen, slowly, but other animals, such as horses and sheep, had obvious benefits and were acquired more rapidly. The chieftain in Panama who answered that the greatest benefit Spain had brought to his people was the chicken egg may have disappointed his questioner, but his statement reflected a keen appreciation of the importance of the interchange. The newly introduced animals changed the ecological balance in the New World. Not only animals that were purposefully introduced, but species such as the sparrow and the brown rat, whose arrival was unplanned, changed the nature of life in the Americas.

The Europeans also brought their crops and their weeds. It was hard for Iberians to live without the Mediterranean necessities: wheat bread, olive oil, and wine. Columbus on his second voyage in 1499 introduced wheat, peas, melons, onions, grapes, and probably olives as well as sugar cane. Some crops, such as sugar cane, thrived and provided the basis for the rise of plantation economies; other crops such as wheat, olives, and grapes needed cooler or drier environments and had to wait until the Spanish reached the more temperate zones before they flourished. Later, Europeans introduced all of their own crops and even some crops such as bananas, coconut trees, coffee, and breadfruit that they had found in Africa, Asia, and the Pacific. They also inadvertently introduced other plants, such as tumbleweed, which spread quickly.

In the exchange of foods and stimulants, the contribution of America probably outweighed that of Europe, however. It is difficult today to imagine the diet of the Old World before the discovery of America. New World plants, such as tomatoes, squash, sweet potatoes, types of beans, and peppers, became essential foods in Europe. Tobacco and cacao, or chocolate, both American in origin, became widely distributed throughout the world.

Even more important were basic crops, such as the potato, maize, and manioc, all of which yielded more calories per acre than all the Old World grains except rice. The high yield of calories per acre of maize and potatoes had supported the high population densities of the American civilizations. After the Columbian voyages, these foods began to produce similar effects in the rest of the world. Manioc, or casava (we know it as tapioca), was a basic Indian food in the Caribbean and tropical South America. Particularly well suited to the tropics, manioc was never popular in Europe, but it spread widely in Asia and Africa, where it became a basic food by the 18th century. The potato, a staple of the Andean civilizations, was easy to grow and yielded large numbers of calories. By the 18th century it was well known from Ireland to Russia. Maize was a great success. It yielded as many calories per acre as rice, but it was easier to grow and could flourish in a wide variety of situations. By the 17th century it had spread to Spain and France, and by the 18th century it was found in Italy, Turkey, Greece, and Russia. The Europeans also introduced it to west Africa and China. Maize became a staple across the globe. At present, at least one-third of the crops raised to feed the world's population are of New World origin.

After 1750, the world population experienced a dramatic rise. The reasons for this expansion were many, but the contribution of the American foodstuffs with their high yields was a central one. Manioc, potatoes, sweet potatoes, and maize—to say nothing of peanuts, beans, and tomatoes—greatly expanded the food resources available throughout the world and continue to do so today. The balance sheet of the Columbian exchange was mixed, but the world was undeniably different after it began.

Questions: Why and in what ways was the Columbian exchange a particularly significant case of global contact? Was western Europe the chief beneficiary of the exchange? What balance was there between the economic dependency of the Americas and the ideas, technology, and goods they received from Europe?

COLONIAL ECONOMIES AND GOVERNMENTS

Agriculture and mining were the basis of the Spanish colonial economy. Eventually, Spanish farms and ranches competed with Indian villages, but they also depended on Indians as laborers. Over this economy Spain built a bureaucratic empire in which the church was an essential element and a major cultural factor.

Spanish America was an agrarian society in which perhaps 80 percent of the population lived and worked on the land. Yet in terms of America's importance to Spain, mining was the essential activity and the basis of Spain's rule in the Indies. Until the 18th century, the whole Spanish maritime commercial system was organized around the mining economy and the exchange of America's precious metals for manufactured goods from Europe. This exchange began to fit Latin America into the New World economy as a somewhat dependent area producing raw goods to trade with western Europe.

Although the booty of conquest provided some wealth, most of the precious metal sent across the Atlantic came from the postconquest mining industry. Gold was found in the Caribbean, Colombia, and Chile, but it was silver far more than gold that formed the basis of Spain's wealth in America.

The Silver Heart of Empire

The major silver discoveries were made in Mexico between 1545 and 1565 and in Peru at roughly the same time. Great silver mining towns developed. *Potosí* in Upper Peru (in what is now Bolivia) was the largest mine of all, producing about 80 percent of all the Peruvian silver. In the early 17th century, more than 160,000 people lived and worked in the town and its mine. Peru's Potosí and Mexico's Zacatecas became wealthy mining centers with opulent churches and a luxurious way of life for some, but as one viceroy of Peru commented, it was not silver that was sent to Spain "but the blood and sweat of Indians."

Mining labor was provided by a variety of workers. The early use of Indian slaves and encomienda workers in the 16th century gradually was replaced by a system of labor drafts. By 1572 the mining mita in Peru was providing about 13,000 workers a year to Potosí alone. Similar labor drafts were used in Mexico, but by the 17th century the mines in both places also had large numbers of wage workers willing to brave the dangers of mining in return for the good wages.

Although indigenous methods were used at first, most mining techniques were European in origin. After 1580, silver mining depended on a process of amalgamation with mercury to extract the silver from the ore-bearing rock. The Spanish discovery of a mountain of mercury at *Huancavelica* in Peru aided

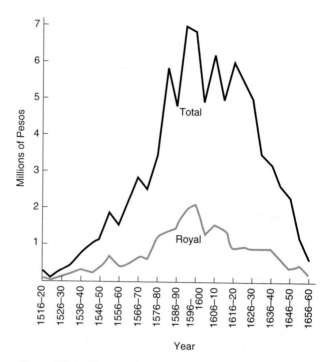

Figure 25.6. Silver production in Spanish America, 1516–1660.

American silver production. Potosí and Huancavelica became the "great marriage of Peru" and the basis of silver production in South America.

According to Spanish law, all subsoil rights belonged to the crown, but the mines and the processing plants were owned by individuals, who were permitted to extract the silver in return for paying one-fifth of production to the government, which also profited from its monopoly on the mercury needed to produce the silver (Figure 25.6).

Mining stimulated many other aspects of the economy, even in areas far removed from the mines. Workers had to be fed and the mines supplied. In Mexico, where most of the mines were located beyond the area of settled preconquest Indian population, large Spanish-style farms developed to raise cattle, sheep, and wheat. The Peruvian mines high in the Andes were supplied from distant regions with mercury, mules, food, clothing, and even coca leaves, used to deaden hunger and make the work at high altitudes less painful. From Spain's perspective, mining was the heart of the colonial economy.

Haciendas and Villages

Spanish America remained predominantly an agrarian economy. In highland Peru, Mexico, Guatemala, and New Granada, where large sedentary populations lived, Indian communal agriculture of traditional crops continued. As populations dwindled, Spanish ranches and farms began to emerge. The colonists, faced with declining Indian populations, also found land ownership more attractive. Family-owned rural estates, which produced grains, grapes, and livestock, developed throughout the central areas of Spanish America. Most of the labor force on these estates came from Indians who had left the communities and from people of mixed Indian and European heritage. These rural estates, or haciendas, producing primarily for consumers in America, became the basis of wealth and power for the local aristocracy in many regions. Although some plantation crops, such as sugar and later cacao, were exported to Europe from Spanish America, they made up only a small fraction of the value of the exports in comparison with silver. In some regions where Indian communities continued to hold traditional farming lands, an endemic competition between haciendas and village communities emerged.

Industry and Commerce

In areas such as Ecuador, New Spain, and Peru, sheep raising led to the development of small textile sweatshops, where common cloth was produced, usually by women. America became self-sufficient for its basic foods and material goods and looked to Europe only for luxury items not locally available.

Still, from Spain's perspective and that of the larger world economy taking shape in the early modern centuries, the American "kingdoms" had a silver heart, and the whole Spanish commercial system was organized around that fact. Spain allowed only Spaniards to trade with America and imposed tight restrictions. All American trade from Spain after the mid-16th century was funneled through the city of Seville and, later, the nearby port of Cádiz. The *Casa de Contratación*, or Board of Trade, in Seville registered ships and passengers, kept charts, collected duties, and in general controlled the Indies trade. It often worked in conjunction with a merchant guild, or *consulado*, in Seville that controlled goods shipped to America and handled much of the silver received

in return. Linked to branches in Mexico City and Lima, the consulados kept tight control over the trade and were able to keep prices high in the colonies.

Other Europeans looked on the Indies trade with envy. To discourage foreign rivals and pirates, the Spanish eventually worked out a convoy system in which two fleets sailed annually from Spain, traded their goods for precious metals, and then met at Havana, Cuba, before returning to Spain.

The fleet system was made possible by the large, heavily armed ships, called *galleons,* that were used to carry the silver belonging to the crown. Two great galleons a year also sailed from Manila in the Philippines to Mexico loaded with Chinese silks, porcelain, and lacquer. These goods were then shipped on the convoy to Spain along with the American silver. In the Caribbean, heavily fortified ports, such as Havana and Cartegena (Colombia), provided shelter for the treasure ships, while coast guard fleets cleared the waters of potential raiders. Although cumbersome, the convoys (which continued until the 1730s) were successful. Pirates and enemies sometimes captured individual ships, and some ships were lost to storms and other disasters, but only one fleet was lost—to the Dutch in 1627.

In general, the supply of American silver to Spain was continuous and made the colonies seem worth the effort, but the reality of American treasure was more complicated. Much of the wealth flowed out of Spain to pay for Spain's European wars, its long-term debts, and the purchase of manufactured goods to be sent back to the Indies. Probably less than half of the silver remained in Spain itself. The arrival of American treasure also contributed to a sharp rise in prices and a general inflation, first in Spain and then throughout western Europe during the 16th century. At no time did the American treasure make up more than one-fourth of Spain's state revenues, which is to say that the wealth of Spain depended more on the taxes levied on its own population than it did on the exploitation of its Native American subjects. However, the seemingly endless supply of silver did stimulated bankers to continue to lend money to Spain because the prospect of the great silver fleet was always enough to offset the falling credit of the Spanish rulers and the sometimes bankrupt government. As early as 1619, Sancho de Moncada wrote that "the poverty of Spain resulted from the discovery of the Indies," but there were few who could see the long-term costs of empire.

Ruling an Empire: State and Church

Spain controlled its American empire through a carefully regulated bureaucratic system. Sovereignty rested with the crown, based not on the right of conquest but on a papal grant that awarded the Indies to Castile in return for its services in bringing those lands and peoples into the Christian community. Some Native Americans found this a curious idea, and European theologians agreed, but Spain was careful to bolster its rule in other ways. The *Treaty of Tordesillas* (1494) between Castile and Portugal clarified the spheres of influence and right of possession of the two kingdoms by drawing a hypothetical north–south line around the globe and reserving to Portugal the newly discovered lands (and their route to India) to the east of the line and to Castile all lands to the west. Thus, Brazil fell within the Portuguese sphere. Other European nations later raised their own objections to the Spanish and Portuguese claims.

The Spanish Empire became a great bureaucratic system built on a juridical core and staffed to a large extent by *letrados,* university-trained lawyers from Spain. The modern division of powers was not clearly defined in the Spanish system, so that judicial officers also exercised legislative and administrative authority. Laws were many and contradictory at times, but the *Recopilación* (1681) codified the laws into the basis for government in the colonies.

The king ruled through the *Council of the Indies* in Spain, which issued the laws and advised him. Within the Indies, Spain created two *viceroyalties* in the 16th century, one based on Mexico City and the other on Lima. Viceroys, high-ranking nobles who were direct representatives of the king, wielded broad military, legislative, and, when they had legal training, judicial powers. The viceroyalties of New Spain and Peru were then subdivided into ten judicial divisions controlled by superior courts, or *audiencias,* staffed by professional royal magistrates who helped to make law as well as apply it. At the local level, royally appointed magistrates applied the laws, collected taxes, and assigned the work required of Indian communities. It is little wonder that they often were highly criticized for bending the law and taking advantage of the Indians under their control. Below them were myriad minor officials, customs and tax collectors, municipal officers, and inspectors, who made bureaucracy both a living and a way of life.

To some extent, the clergy formed another branch of the state apparatus, although it had other functions and goals as well. Catholic religious orders such as the Franciscans, Dominicans, and Jesuits carried out the widespread conversion of the Indians, establishing churches in the towns and villages of sedentary Indians and setting up missions in frontier areas where nomadic peoples were forced to settle.

Taking seriously the pope's admonition to Christianize the peoples of the new lands as the primary justification for Spain's rule, some of the early missionaries became ardent defenders of Indian rights and even admirers of aspects of Indian culture. For example, Franciscan priest Fray Bernardino de Sahagún (1499–1590) became an expert in the Nahuatl language and composed a bilingual encyclopedia of Aztec culture, which was based on methods very similar to those used by modern anthropologists. Other clerics wrote histories, grammars, and studies of Indian language and culture. Some were like Diego de Landa, Bishop of Yucatán (1547), who admired much about the culture of the Maya but who so detested their religion that he burned all their ancient books and tortured many Maya suspected of backsliding from Christianity. The recording and analysis of Indian cultures were designed primarily to provide tools for conversion.

In the core areas of Peru and New Spain, the missionary church eventually was replaced by an institutional structure of parishes and bishoprics. Archbishops sat in the major capitals, and a complicated church hierarchy developed. Because the holders of all such positions were nominated by the Spanish crown, the clergy tended to be major supporters of state policy as well as a primary influence on it.

The Catholic church profoundly influenced the cultural and intellectual life of the colonies in many ways. The construction of churches, especially the great baroque cathedrals of the capitals, stimulated the work of architects and artists, usually reflecting European models but sometimes taking up local themes and subjects. The printing presses, introduced to America in the early 16th century, always published a high percentage of religious books as well as works of history, poetry, philosophy, law, and language. Much intellectual life was organized around religion. Schools—such as those of Mexico City and Lima, founded in the 1550s—were run by the clergy, and universities were created to provide training primarily in law and theology, the foundations of state and society. Eventually, more than 70 universities flourished in Spanish

America. A stunning example of colonial intellectual life was the nun *Sor Juana Inés de la Cruz* (1651–1695; Figure 25.7), author, poet, musician, and social thinker. Sor Juana was welcomed at the court of the viceroy in Mexico City, where her beauty and intelligence were celebrated. She eventually gave up secular concerns and her library, at the urging of her superiors, to concentrate on purely spiritual matters. Even secular authors were heavily influenced by Catholicism. To control the morality and orthodoxy of the population, the tribunal of the Inquisition set up offices in the major capitals. Although Indians usually were exempt from its jurisdiction, Jews, Protestants, and other religious dissenters were not and were sometimes executed in an attempt to impose orthodoxy. Overall, church and state combined to create an ideological and political framework for the society and economy of Spanish America.

BRAZIL: THE FIRST PLANTATION COLONY

In Brazil, the Portuguese created the first great plantation colony of the Americas, growing sugar with the use of Indian and then African slaves. In the 18th century, the discovery of gold opened up the interior of Brazil to settlement and the expansion of slavery. Whereas Spanish America seemed to fulfill dreams of mineral wealth, Brazil—Portugal's American colony—became the first major plantation zone, organized to produce a tropical crop, sugar, in great demand and short supply in Europe.

The first official Portuguese landfall on the South American coast took place in 1500 when *Pedro Alvares Cabral,* leader of an expedition to India, stopped briefly on the tropical Brazilian shore. There was little at first to attract European interest except for the dyewood trees that grew in the forests, and thus the Portuguese crown paid little attention to Brazil for 30 years, preferring instead to grant licenses to merchants who agreed to exploit the dyewood in return for tax benefits and services. Pressure from French merchants also interested in dyewood finally moved the Portuguese crown to military action. The coast was cleared of the French, and a new system of settlement was established in 1532. Minor Portuguese nobles were given strips of land along the coast to colonize and develop. The nobles who held these *capitaincies* combined broad, seemingly feudal powers

Figure 25.7. Sor Juana Inés de la Cruz was the remarkable Mexican poet and writer whose talents won her recognition rarely given to women for intellectual achievements in colonial Latin America.

ers with a strong desire for commercial development. Most of them lacked the capital needed to carry out the colonization, and some had problems with the local Indian population. In a few places, towns were established, colonists were brought over, relations with the Indians were peaceful, and, most importantly, sugar plantations were established using first Indian, then African slaves.

In 1549, the Portuguese king sent a governor general and other officials to create a royal capital at Salvador. The first Jesuit missionaries also arrived. By 1600, Indian resistance had been broken in many places by military action, missionary activity, or epidemic disease. A string of settlements extended along the coast, centered on port cities such as Salvador and Rio de Janeiro. These served roughly 150 sugar plantations, a number that doubled by 1630. The plantations were increasingly worked by African slaves. By 1600, the Brazilian colony had about 100,000 inhabitants: 30,000 Europeans, 15,000 black slaves, and the rest Indians and people of mixed origin.

Sugar and Slavery

During most of the next century, Brazil held its position as the world's leading sugar producer. Sugar cane had to be processed in the field. It was cut and pressed in large mills, and the juice was then heated to crystallize into sugar. This combination of agriculture and industry in the field demanded large amounts of capital for machinery and large quantities of labor for the backbreaking work (Figure 25.8). Although there were always some free workers who had skilled occupations, slaves did most of the work. During the 17th century, about 7000 slaves a year were imported from Africa. By the end of the century, Brazil had about 150,000 slaves—about half its total population.

On the basis of a single crop produced by slave labor, Brazil became the first great plantation colony and a model that later was followed by other European nations in their own Caribbean colonies. Even after the Brazilian economy became more diverse, Brazil's social hierarchy still reflected its plantation and slave origins. The white planter families became an aristocracy linked by marriage to resident merchants and to the few Portuguese bureaucrats and officials, and they dominated local institutions. At the bottom of society were the slaves, distinguished by their color and their status as property. However, a growing segment of the population was composed of people of mixed origins, the result of *miscegenation* between whites, Indians, and Africans who—alongside poorer whites, freed blacks, and free Indians—served as artisans, small farmers, herders, and free laborers. In many ways, society as a whole reflected the hierarchy of the plantation.

Like Spain, Portugal created a bureaucratic structure that integrated this colony within an imperial system. A governor general ruled from Salvador, but the governors in each captaincy often acted independently and reported directly to the overseas council in Lisbon. The missionary orders were particularly important in Brazil, especially the Jesuits. Their extensive cattle ranches and sugar mills supported the construction of churches and schools as well as a network of missions with thousands of Indian residents.

As in Spanish America, royal officials trained in the law formed the core of the bureaucracy. Unlike the Spanish Empire, which except for the Philippines was almost exclusively American, the Portuguese Empire included colonies and outposts in Asia, Africa, and Brazil. Only gradually, in the 17th century, did Brazil become the predominant Portuguese colony. Even then, Brazil's ties to Portugal

Figure 25.8. Sugar was introduced to the Caribbean in 1493, and Brazil became the greatest producer by the next century. Sugar plantations using slave labor characterized Brazil and the Caribbean. This early European engraving is wrong in some details, but it does convey an image of the almost factorylike conditions in the sugar mills.

were in some ways stronger and more dependent than those between Spanish America and Spain. Unlike Spanish America, Brazil had neither universities nor printing presses. Thus, intellectual life was always an extension of Portugal, and Brazilians seeking higher education and government offices or hoping to publish their works always had to turn to the mother country. The general economic dependency of Latin America was matched by an intellectual subordination more intense in Brazil than in Spanish America.

Brazil's Age of Gold

As overseas extensions of Europe, the American colonies were particularly susceptible to changes in European politics. For 60 years (1580–1640), Spain and Portugal were ruled by the same monarchs, a situation that promoted their cooperation and gave the Habsburg kings of Spain and Portugal a worldwide empire. From 1630 to 1654, as part of a global struggle against Spain, the Dutch seized a portion of northeastern Brazil and controlled its sugar production. Although the Dutch were expelled from Brazil in 1654, by the 1680s the Dutch, English, and French had established their own plantation colonies in the Caribbean and were producing sugar, once again with slave laborers. This competition, which led to a rising price for slaves and a falling world price for sugar, undercut the Brazilian sugar industry, and the colony entered into hard times. Eventually, each European nation tried to establish an integrated set of colonies that included plantations (the Caribbean, Brazil), slaving ports (Africa), and food-producing areas (New England, southern Brazil).

Although Brazil's domination of the world sugar market was lost, throughout the 17th century *Paulistas,* hardy backwoodsmen from São Paulo (an area with few sugar plantations), had been exploring the interior, capturing Indians, and searching for precious metals. These expeditions not only established Portuguese claims to much of the interior of the continent but eventually were successful in their quest for wealth. In 1695, gold strikes were made in the mountainous interior in a region that came to be called *Minas Gerais* (General Mines), and the Brazilian colony experienced a new boom.

A great gold rush began. People deserted coastal towns and plantations to head for the gold washings, and they were soon joined by waves of about 5000 immigrants a year who came directly from Portugal. Labor in the mines, as in the plantations, was provided mostly by slaves. By 1720 there were more than 35,000 slaves in Minas Gerais, and by 1775 there were over 150,000 (out of a total population of 300,000 for the region). Wild mining camps and a wide-open society eventually coalesced into a network of towns such as the administrative center of Ouro Prêto, and the government, anxious to control the newfound wealth, imposed a heavy hand to collect taxes and rein in the unruly population. Gold production reached its height between 1735 and 1760 and averaged about 3 tons a year in that period, making Brazil the greatest source of gold in the Western world.

The discovery of gold was a mixed blessing in the long run. Further discovery of gold—and later of diamonds—opened the interior to settlement, once again with disastrous effects on the Indian population and with the expansion of slavery. The early disruption of coastal agriculture caused by the gold strikes was overcome by government control of the slave trade, and exports of sugar and tobacco continued to be important to the colony. Mining did stimulate the opening of new areas to ranching and farming, to supply the new markets in the mining zone. *Rio de Janeiro*, the port closest to the mines, grew in size and importance. It became capital of the colony in 1763. In Minas Gerais, a distinctive society developed in the mining towns: The local wealth was used to sponsor the building of churches, which in turn stimulated the work of artists, architects, and composers. Like the rest of Brazil, however, the hierarchy of color and the legal distinctions of slavery marked life in the mining zones, which were populated by large numbers of slaves and free persons of color.

Finally, gold allowed Portugal to continue economic policies that were detrimental in the long run. With access to gold, Portugal could buy the manufactured goods it needed for itself and its colonies, as few industries were developed in the mother country. With pressure from Portuguese wine producers, a treaty was signed with England in 1703 that guaranteed a trading arrangement with that country. As a result, much of the Brazilian gold flowed from Portugal to England to pay for manufactured goods and to compensate for a trade imbalance because the value of English manufactures was greater than that of Portuguese wine. After 1760, as the supply of gold began to dwindle, Portugal was again in a difficult position—in some ways an economic dependency of England.

Visualizing THE PAST

Race or Culture? A Changing Society

The process of marriage sexual contact between Spaniards, Indians, and Africans began to complicate the demographic and the social structures of the American colonies. The rise of a significant number of people of mixed origin could be noted in both Peru and Mexico. These graphs point out the differences in the two areas and may imply something about the situation of the indigenous communities as well as that of the castas. We should also remember that these categories were not necessarily biological and that Indians might be classified as castas if they spoke Spanish or wore Spanish-style clothes. What seems to be precise demographic measurement, may, in fact, be imprecise social definition.

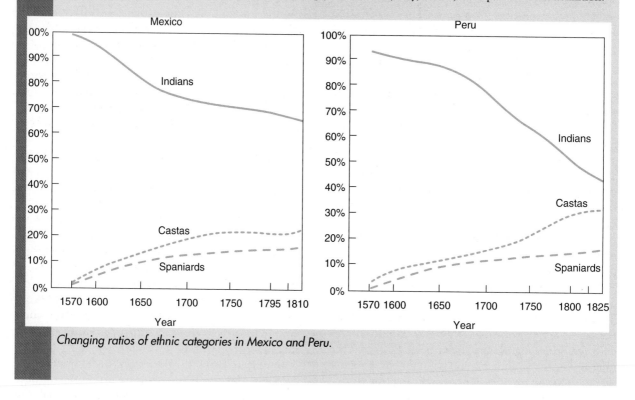

Changing ratios of ethnic categories in Mexico and Peru.

MULTIRACIAL SOCIETIES

■ *The mixture of whites, Africans, and Indians created the basis of multiracial societies in which hierarchies of color, status, and occupation all operated. By the 18th century, the castas, people of mixed origin, began to increase rapidly and had become a major segment of the population.*

The conquest and settlement of Latin America created the conditions for the formation of multiethnic societies on a large scale. The three major groups—

Indians, Europeans, and Africans—had been brought together under very different conditions: the Europeans as conquerors and voluntary immigrants, the Indians as conquered peoples, and the Africans as slaves. This situation created hierarchies of masters and servants, Christians and pagans, that reflected the relationships of power and the colonial condition. In such as central Mexico, where an Indian nobility had existed, aspects of preconquest social organization were maintained because they served the ends of Spanish government. In theory, there was a separation between the "republic of the Spaniards," which included all non-Indians, and the "republic of the Indians," which was supposed to have its own social rankings and its own rules and laws. This separation was never a reality, however, and the "republic of the Indians" always formed the base on which all society rested. Indians paid tribute, something not required of others in society.

The Society of Castas

Spaniards had an idea of society drawn from their own medieval experience, but American realities soon altered that concept. The key was miscegenation. The conquest had involved the sexual exploitation of Indian women and occasional alliances formed by the giving of concubines and female servants. Marriages with indigenous women, especially of the Indian nobility, were not unknown. As early as 1516, the Spanish crown tried to sponsor mixed marriages, although later it tried to limit the opportunities for mixed offspring. With few European women available, especially in frontier regions, mixed marriages and informal unions were common. The result was the growth of a large population of mixed background, the so-called mestizos. Although they were always suspected of illegitimacy, their status, especially in the early years, was higher than that of Indians. More acculturated than the Indians and able to operate in two worlds, mestizos became members of an intermediate category, not fully accepted as equals to Spaniards and yet expected to live according to the standards of Spanish society and often acting as auxiliaries to it. A similar process took place in areas such as Brazil and the Caribbean coasts, where large numbers of African slaves were imported. Slave owners exploited their female slaves or took slave women as mistresses, and then sometimes freed their mulatto children. The result was the growth of a large population of mixed background.

Throughout the Spanish Indies, European categories of noble, priest, and commoner continued, as did hierarchies based on wealth and occupation. But American realities created new distinctions in which race and place of birth also played a crucial role. This was the sociedad de castas, based on racial origins, in which Europeans or whites were at the top, black slaves or Indians were at the bottom, and the many kinds of mixes filled the intermediate categories. This accompanied the great cultural fusion in the formation of Latin America.

From the three original ethnic categories, many combinations and crosses were possible: mestizos, mulattoand so on. By the 18th century, this segment of the population had grown rapidly, and there was much confusion and local variation in terminology. A whole genre of painting developed simply to identify and classify the various combinations (Figure 25.7). Together, the people of mixed origins were called the castas, and they shopkeepers, and small farmers. In 1650, the castas made up perhaps 5 to 10 percent of the population of Spanish America, but by 1750, with made up 35 to 40 percent (see Visualizing the Past). In Brazil, still dominated by slavery, free people of color made up about 28 percent of the population—a proportion equal to that of whites. Together, however, free and slave blacks and mulattos made up two-thirds of the inhabitants of Brazil in the late 18th century.

As the mixed population grew in Spanish America, increasing restrictions were placed on them, but their social mobility could not be halted. their ethnic labels as their occupations, wealth, or marital status changed. A successful Indian might call himself a mestizo; a mestizo who married a Spanish woman might be called white. The ranks of the castas were also swelled by former slaves who had been given or had bought their freedom and by Indians who left their communities, spoke Spanish, and lived within the orbit of the Hispanic world. Thus, physical characteristics were only one criterion of rank and status, but color and ethnicity mattered, and they created a pseudoracial hierarchy. European or white status was a great social advantage. Not every person of European background was wealthy, but most of the wealthy merchants, land owners, bureaucrats, and miners were white. As one visitor wrote, "In America, every white is a gentleman."

Originally, all whites had shared the privileged status of Spaniards regardless of the continent of their birth, but over time distinctions developed between *peninsulares,* or those actually born in Spain, and *Creoles,* or those born in the New World.

Creoles thought of themselves as loyal American Spaniards, but with so many mestizos around, the shadow of a possible Indian ancestor and illegitimacy always made their status suspect as far as the Europeans were concerned. Still, Creoles dominated the local economies, held sway over large numbers of dependents at their haciendas and mines, and stood at the top of society, second only to the peninsulares. Increasingly, they developed a sense of identity and pride in their accomplishments, and they were sensitive to any suggestion of inferiority or to any discrimination because of their American birth. That growing sense of self-identity eventually contributed to the movements for independence in Latin America.

The hierarchy of race intersected with traditional Iberian distinctions based on gender, age, and class. The father of a family had legal authority over his children until they were 25. Women were in a subordinate position; they could not serve in government and were expected to assume the duties of motherhood and household (Figure 25.9). After marriage, women came under the authority of their husbands, but many a widow assumed the direction of her family's activities. Lower-class women often controlled small-scale commerce in towns and villages, worked in the fields, and labored at the looms of small factories. Marriages often were arranged and accompanied by the payment of a dowry, which remained the property of the woman throughout the marriage. Women also had full rights to inheritance. Upper-class women who did not marry at a young age were placed in convents to prevent contacts or marriages with partners of unsuitable backgrounds.

THE 18TH-CENTURY REFORMS

■■ *Increasing attacks on the Iberian empires by foreign rivals led to the Bourbon reforms in Spanish America and the reforms of Pombal in Brazil. These changes strengthened the two empires but also generated colonial unrest that eventually led to movements for independence.*

No less than in the rest of Europe, the 18th century was a period of intellectual ferment in Spain and Portugal as well as in their empires. In Spain and its colonies, small clubs and associations, calling themselves *amigos del país*, or friends of the country, met in many cities to discuss and plan all kinds of reforms.

Figure 25.9. Women in colonial Latin America engaged in agriculture and manufacturing, especially in textile workshops, but social ideology still reserved the household and the kitchen as the proper sphere for women, as seen in this scene of a kitchen in a large Mexican home.

Their programs were for material benefits and improvements, not political changes. In Portugal, foreign influences and ideas created a group of progressive thinkers and bureaucrats open to new ideas in economy, education, and philosophy. Much of the change that came in both empires resulted as much from the changing European economic and demographic realities as from new ideas. The expansion of population and economy in Europe, and the increased demands for American products, along with the long series of wars in the 18th century, gave the American colonies a new importance. Both the Spanish and Portuguese empires revived, but with some long-term results that eventually led to the fall of both.

The Shifting Balance of Politics and Trade

By the 18th century, it was clear that the Spanish colonial system had become outmoded and that Spain's exclusive hold on the Indies was no longer secure. To some extent the problem lay in Spain itself. The Spanish kings were weak by the late 17th century and did not provide adequate leadership. Beset by foreign wars, increasing debt, declining population, and internal revolts, a weakened Spain was threatened by a powerful France and by the rising mercantile strength of England and Holland, whose Protestantism also made them natural rivals of Catholic Spain. Since the 16th century, French, Dutch, and English ship captains had combined contraband trade with raiding in the Spanish Empire, and although Spain's European rivals could not seize Mexico or Peru, the sparsely populated islands and coasts of the Caribbean became likely targets. Buccaneers, owing allegiance to no nation, raided the Caribbean ports in the late 17th century. Meanwhile, the English took Jamaica in 1654, the French took control of western Hispaniola (Haiti) by 1697, and other islands fell to the English, French, and Dutch. Many of the islands turned to sugar production and the creation of slave and plantation colonies much like those in Brazil. These settlements were part of a general process of colonization, of which the English settlement of eastern North America and the French occupation of Canada and the Mississippi valley were also part.

Less apparent than the loss of territories, but equally important, was the failure of the Spanish mercantile and political system. The annual fleets became irregular. Silver payments from America declined, and most goods shipped to the Indies and even the ships that carried them were non-Spanish in origin. The colonies became increasingly self-sufficient in basic commodities, and as central government became weaker, local aristocrats in the colonies exercised increasing control over the economy and government of their regions, often at the expense of the Indian and the lower-class populations. Graft and corruption were rampant in many branches of government. The empire seemed to be crumbling. What is most impressive is that Spain was able to retain its American possessions for another century.

Even with Spain in decline, the Indies still seemed an attractive prize coveted by other powers, and the opportunity to gain them was not long in coming. A final crisis was set in motion in 1701 when the Spanish king, Charles II, died without an heir. Other European nations backed various claimants to the Spanish throne, hoping to win the prize of the Spanish monarchy and its American colonies. Philip of Anjou, a Bourbon and thus a relative of the king of France, was named successor to the Spanish throne. The *War of the Spanish Succession* (1702–1713) ensued, and the result at the Treaty of Utrecht (1713) was recognition of a branch of the Bourbon family as rulers of Spain; the price was some commercial concessions that allowed French merchants to operate in Seville and permitted England to trade slaves in Spanish America (and even to send one ship per year to trade for silver in the Americas). Spain's commercial monopoly was now being broken not just by contraband trade but by legal means as well.

The Bourbon Reforms

The new and vigorous Bourbon dynasty in Spain launched a series of reforms aimed at strengthening the state and its economy. In this age of "enlightened despotism," the Spanish Bourbon monarchs, especially *Charles III* (1759–1788), were moved by economic nationalism and a desire for strong centralized government to institute economic, administrative, and military reforms in Spain and its empire. The goal of these rulers and their progressive ministers was to revive Spain within the framework of its traditional society by applying the principles of rational and planned government. Thus, the aim was to make government more effective, more powerful, and better able to direct the economy. Certain groups or institutions that opposed these measures or stood in the way might be punished or suppressed. The Jesuit order, with its special allegiance to Rome, its rumored wealth, and its missions in the New World (which controlled almost 100,000 Indians in Paraguay alone), was a prime target. The Jesuits were expelled from Spain and its empire in 1767, as they had been from the Portuguese empire in 1759. In general, however, the entrenched interests of the church and the nobility were not frontally attacked as long as they did not conflict with the authority of the crown. The reforms were aimed at material improvements and a more powerful state, not social or political upheaval.French bureaucratic models were introduced. Ministers who took direct responsibility for policy were appointed. The system of taxation was tightened. The navy was reformed, and new ships were built. The convoy fleet system was abandoned, and new ports were opened in Spain and America for the Indies trade. In 1778, the policy of *commercio libre* opened trade to many ports in Spain and the Indies, although trade still was restricted to Spaniards or to ships sailing under Spanish license. Still, the more open policy undercut the monopoly of the consulados, and by stimulating trade, it made contraband less attractive.

In the Indies, the Bourbons initiated a broad program of reform. New viceroyalties were created in New Granada (1739) and the Rio de la Plata (1778) to provide better administration and defense to the growing populations of these regions. Royal investigators were sent to the Indies. The most important of them, *José de Gálvez,* spent six years in Mexico before returning to Spain to become Minister of the Indies and a chief architect of reform. His investigations, as well as reports by others, revealed the worst abuses of graft and corruption, which implicated the local magistrates and the Creole American land owners and aristocracy. Gálvez moved to eliminate the Creoles from the upper bureaucracy of the colonies. New offices were created. After 1780, the corregidores, or local magistrates, were removed from the Indian villages, and that office was replaced by a new system of intendants, or provincial governors, based on French models. This intendancy system was introduced throughout the Indies. Such measures did improve tax collection and made government more effective, but the reforms also disrupted the patterns of influence and power, especially among the Creole bureaucrats, miners, and land owners as their political power declined.

Many of the reforms in America were linked directly to defense and military matters. During the century, Spain often was allied with France, and the global struggle between England and France for

world hegemony made Spain's American possessions a logical target for English attack. During the Seven Years' War (1756–1763), the loss of Florida and the English seizure of Havana shocked Spain into action, particularly because when England held Havana in 1762, Cuban trade boomed. Regular Spanish troops were sent to New Spain, and militia units, led by local Creoles who were given military rank, were created throughout the empire. Frontiers were expanded, and previously unoccupied or loosely controlled regions, such as California, were settled by a combination of missions and small frontier outposts. In the Rio de la Plata, foreign competitors were resisted by military means. Spain sought every means to strengthen itself and its colonies.

During the Bourbon reforms, the government took an active role in the economy. State monopolies were established for items the government considered essential, such as tobacco and gunpowder. Whole new areas of Spanish America were opened to development. Monopoly companies were granted exclusive rights to develop certain colonial areas in return for developing the economies of those regions. The Caracas Company, formed in 1728, stimulated the development of cacao production in Venezuela and ensured an inexpensive supply of chocolate for Spain, but by eliminating contraband and controlling the price of imports, it also provoked complaints and even rebellion from the colonists.

The commerce of the Caribbean greatly expanded under the more liberal trading regulations. Cuba became another full-scale plantation and slave colony, exporting sugar, coffee, and tobacco and importing large numbers of Africans. Buenos Aires, on the Rio de la Plata, proved to be a great success story. Its population had grown rapidly in the 18th century, and by 1790 it had a booming economy based on ranching and the export of hides and salted beef. A newly prosperous merchant community in Buenos Aires dominated the region's trade.

The commercial changes were a double-edged sword. As Spanish and English goods became cheaper and more accessible, they undercut locally produced goods so that some regions that had specialized in producing cloth or other goods were unable to compete with the European imports. Links to international trade tightened as the diversity of Latin America's economy decreased. Later conflicts between those who favored free trade and those who wanted to limit imports and protect local industry often were as much about regional interests as about economic philosophy.

Finally, and most importantly, the major centers of the Spanish Empire also experienced rapid growth in the second half of the 18th century. Mining inspectors and experts had been sent to Peru and New Spain to suggest reforms and introduce new techniques. These improvements, as well as the discovery of new veins, allowed production to expand, especially in New Spain, where silver output reached new heights. In fact, silver production in Mexico far outstripped that of Peru, which itself saw increased production.

All in all, the Bourbon reforms must be seen from two vantage points: Spain and America. Undoubtedly, in the short run, the restructuring of government and economy revived the Spanish Empire. In the long run, the removal of Creoles from government, the creation of a militia with a Creole officer corps, the opening of commerce, and other such changes contributed to a growing sense of dissatisfaction among the elite, which only their relative well-being and the existing social tensions of the sociedad de castas kept in check.

Pombal and Brazil

The Bourbon reforms in Spain and Spanish America were paralleled in the Portuguese world during the administration of the *Marquis of Pombal* (1755–1776), Portugal's authoritarian prime minister. Pombal had lived as ambassador in England and had observed the benefits of mercantilism at firsthand. He hoped to use these same techniques, along with state intervention in the economy, to break England's hold on the Portuguese economy, especially on the flow of Brazilian gold from Portugal to England. This became crucial as the production of Brazilian gold began to decline after 1760. In another example of "enlightened despotism," Pombal brutally suppressed any group or institution that stood in the way of royal power and his programs. He developed a particular dislike for the Jesuits because of their allegiance to Rome and their semi-independent control of large areas in Brazil. Pombal expelled the Jesuits from the Portuguese Empire in 1759.Pombal made Brazil the centerpiece of his reforms. Vigorous administrators were sent to the colony to enforce the changes. Fiscal reforms were aimed at eliminating contraband, gold smuggling, and tax evasion. Monopoly companies were formed to stimulate agriculture in older plantation zones and were given the right to import large numbers of slaves.

New crops were introduced. Just as in Spanish America, new regions in Brazil began to flourish. Rio de Janeiro became the capital, and its hinterland was the scene of agricultural growth. The undeveloped Amazonian region, long dominated by Jesuit missionaries, received new attention. A monopoly company was created to develop the region's economy, and it stimulated the development of cotton plantations and the export of wild cacao from the Amazonian forests. These new exports joined the traditional sugar, tobacco, and hides as Brazil's main products.

Pombal was willing to do some social tinkering as part of his project of reform. He abolished slavery in Portugal to stop the import of slaves there and to ensure a steady supply to Brazil, the economic cornerstone of the empire. Because Brazil was vast and needed to be both occupied and defended, he removed Indians from missionary control in the Amazon and encouraged whites to marry them. Immigrant couples from Portugal and the Azores were sent to colonize the Amazon basin and the plains of southern Brazil, which began to produce large quantities of wheat and cattle. In 1778, a treaty between Spain and Portugal established the frontier between their American colonies. Like the Bourbons in Spain, Pombal hoped to revitalize the colonies as a way of strengthening the mother country. Although new policies were instituted, little changed within the society. Brazil was just as profoundly based on slavery in the late 18th century as it had ever been: The levels of slave imports reached 20,000 a year.

Even in the long run, Pombal's policies were not fully effective. Although he reduced Portugal's trade imbalance with England during this period, Brazilian trade suffered because the demand for its products on the world market remained low. This was a classic problem for the American colonies. Their economies were so tied to the sale of their products on the European market and so controlled by policies in the metropolis that the colonies' range of action was always limited. Although Pombal's policies were not immediately successful, they provided the structure for an economic boom in the last 20 years of the 18th century that set the stage for Brazilian independence.

Reforms, Reactions, and Revolts

By the mid-18th century, the American colonies of Spain and Portugal, like the rest of the world, were experiencing rapid growth in population and productive capacity. Scholars disagree on the roles of the

Bourbon and Pombaline reforms in this process, but the growth was undeniable. By the end of the century, Spanish America had a population of almost 13 million. Between 1740 and 1800, the population of Mexico, the most populous area, increased from 3.5 million to almost 6 million, about half of whom were Indians. In Brazil, the population reached about 2 million by the end of the century. This overall increase resulted from declining mortality rates, increasing fertility levels, increasing immigration from Europe, and the thriving slave trade. The opening of new areas to development and Europe's increasing demand for American products accompanied the population growth. The American colonies were experiencing a boom in the last years of the 18th century. Reformist policies, tighter tax collection, and the presence of a more activist government in both Spanish America and Brazil disrupted old patterns of power and influence, raised expectations, and sometimes provoked violent colonial reactions. Urban riots, tax revolts, and Indian uprisings were not unknown before 1700, but serious and more protracted rebellions broke out after that date. In New Granada (present-day Colombia), popular complaints against the government's control of tobacco and liquor consumption, and rising prices as well as new taxes, led to the widespread *Comunero Revolt* in 1781. A royal army was defeated, the viceroy fled from Bogota, and a rebel army almost took the capital. Only tensions between the various racial and social groups, and concessions by the government, brought an end to the rebellion.

At the same time, in Peru, an even more threatening revolt erupted. A great Indian uprising took place under the leadership of Jose Gabriel Condorcanqui, known as *Tupac Amaru*. A mestizo with a direct link to the family of the Incas, Tupac Amaru led a rebellion against "bad government." For almost three years the whole viceroyalty was thrown into turmoil while more than 70,000 Indians, mestizos, and even a few Creoles joined in rebellion against the worst abuses of the colonial regime. Tupac Amaru was captured and brutally executed, but the rebellion smoldered until 1783. It failed mostly because the Creoles, although they had their own grievances against the government, feared that a real social upheaval might take place if they upset the political balance.

This kind of social upheaval was not present in Brazil, where a government attempt to collect back taxes in the mining region led in 1788 to a plot against Portuguese control. A few bureaucrats, intellectuals, and miners planned an uprising for independence, but their conspiracy was discovered. The plotters were arrested, and one conspirator, a militia officer nicknamed Tiradentes, was hanged.

Despite their various social bases, these movements indicated that activism by governments increased dissatisfaction in the American colonies. The new prosperity of the late 18th century contributed to a sense of self-confidence and economic interest among certain colonial classes, which made them sensitive to restrictions and control by Spain and Portugal. Different groups had different complaints, but the sharp social and ethnic divisions within the colonies acted as a barrier to cooperation for common goals and tended to undercut revolutionary movements. Only when the Spanish political system was disrupted by a crisis of legitimacy at the beginning of the 19th century did real separation and independence from the mother countries become a possibility.

Conclusion

The Diverse Ingredients of Latin American Civilization

In three centuries, Spain and Portugal created large colonial empires in the Americas. These American colonies provided a basis of power to their Iberian mother countries and took a vital place in the expanding world economy as suppliers of precious minerals and certain crops to the growing economy of Europe. By the 18th century, the weakened positions of Spain and Portugal within Europe allowed England and France to benefit directly from the Iberian trade with American colonies. To their American colonies, the Iberian nations transferred and imposed their language, laws, forms of government, religion, and institutions. Large numbers of immigrants, first as conquerors and later as settlers, came to the colonies. Eventually, the whole spectrum of Iberian society was recreated in the New World as men and women came to seek a better life, bringing with them their customs, ideas, religion, laws, and ways of life. By government and individual action, a certain homogeneity was created, both in Spanish America and in Brazil. That seeming unity was most apparent among the Europeanized population.

Underlying the apparent continuity with Spain and Portugal and homogeneity among the various colonies were great variations. Latin America, with its distinct environments, its various economic possibilities, and its diverse Indian peoples, imposed new realities. In places such as Mexico and Peru, Indian cultures emerged from the shock of conquest, battered but still vibrant. Indian communities adapted to the new colonial situation. A distinctive multiethnic and multiracial society developed, drawing on Iberian precedents but also dependent on the Indian population and the proportion of various mixed racial categories. In areas where slavery predominated, African cultures also played a major role. Argentina with few Indians, Cuba with its slaves and plantations, and Mexico with its large rural Indian population all shared the same Hispanic traditions and laws, and all had a predominantly white elite, but their social and economic realities made them very different places. Latin America developed as a composite civilization—distinct from the West but related to it—combining European and Indian culture and society or creating the racial hierarchies of slave societies in places such as Brazil.

From the perspective of the world economy, despite the decline in production of precious metals, Latin American products remained in great demand in Europe's markets. As Latin Americans began to seek political independence in the early 19th century, they were confronted by this basic economic fact and by their continued dependence on trade with the developing world economy. Latin America's world economic position, with its labor force organization and outside commercial control, was yet another difference between this new civilization and that of Western Europe.

Further Readings

James Lockhart and Stuart B. Schwartz's *Early Latin America* (1982) provides an interpretation and overview. Lyle N. Macalister's *Spain and Portugal in the New World* (1984) is particularly good on the Iberian background and the formation of societies in Latin America. John H. Parry's *The Spanish Seaborne Empire* (1966) is well written and particularly good on commerce and government. On the conquest period there are excellent regional studies. Geographer Carl O. Sauer's *The Early Caribbean* (1966) describes the discovery, settlement, and conquest of that region, with much attention to Indian culture. James Lockhart's *Spanish Peru* (1968) is a model reconstruction of conquest society, and his *Men of Cajamarca* (1972) is an in-depth look at a group of conquistadors. The conquest of Mexico can be seen from two different angles in Bernal Díaz del Castillo's *The Discovery and Conquest of Mexico*, trans. A. P. Maudsley (1956), and in James Lockhart's edition of the Aztec testimony gathered after the conquest by Bernardino de Sahun, published as *We Peoples Here* (1962).

The transformation of Indian societies has been studied in books such as Steve J. Stern's *Peru's Indian Peoples* and *The Challenge of Spanish Conquest* (1982) on the early colonial era and William B. Taylor's *Drinking, Homicide, and Rebellion in Colonial Mexican Villages* (1979) on the 18th century. Another approach to the impact of conquest is presented in Noble David Cook's *Demographic Collapse: Indian Peru, 1520–1620* (1981), and Murdo MacLeod's *Spanish Central America* (1973) presents an integrated regional study of society and economy. Particularly sensitive to Indian views is Nancy Farriss's *Maya Society Under Colonial Rule* (1984).

Social and economic history have received considerable attention. The establishment of colonial economies has been studied in detail in books such as Eric Van Young's *Hacienda and Market in Eighteenth-Century Mexico* (1981), Stuart Schwartz's *Sugar Plantations and the Formation of Brazilian Society* (1985), and Peter J. Bakewell's *Silver Mining and Society in Colonial Mexico* (1971). Very good social history is now being written. For example, Susan Socolow's *Women in Colonial Latin America* (2000) examines the changing role of women. In Louisa Schell Hoberman and Susan Migden Socolow, eds., *Cities and Society in Colonial Latin America* (1986), urban social types are examined. A different kind of social history that examines popular thought can be seen in Jacques Lafaye's *Quetzalcoatl and Guadalupe* (1974).

The best starting place on the Bourbon reforms is David Brading's *Miners and Merchants in Bourbon Mexico* (1971), and John L. Phelan's study, *The Comunero Revolt, The People and the King* (1978), examines the Bourbon reforms' unintended effects. Dauril Alden's *Royal Government in Colonial Brazil* (1968) shows Pombal's effects on Brazil.

On the Web

The methods by which Europeans extracted wealth from Latin America by the manipulation of old or imposition of new patterns of mining, labor and land ownership (the mita and encomendero systems) and the impact these new patterns of economic life had on both the indigenous population and the imported African slave population is examined at http://www.emory.edu/COLLEGE/CULPEPER/BAKEWELL/index.html and http://www.hist.umw.edu/~rmccaa/colonial/potosi/outline.html. Both sites also illuminate the efforts of Portugal's Marquis of Pombal and the parallel policies of the Bourbon kings of Spain to gain control over the new economies of Latin America.

Indigenous resistance to Latin America's dependent economic position is given a human face through a discussion of the rebellions of Tupac Amaru and Juan Santos Atalhualpa at http://www.dickshovel.com/500.html. The composite nature of Latin American civilization is revealed in its celebration of the "Day of the Dead," (http://www.daphne.palomar.edu/muentos).

Chapter 26

The Muslim Empires

A portrait of a Safavid notable, probably Shah Suleyman I (1667–1693), by a Persian court artist. He is surrounded by courtiers, including a European visitor bearing presents for the Persian leader. From the time of Abbas, Europeans of different nationalities vied fiercely with each other for influence at the Safavid court.

The great nomadic invasions by the Mongols in the first half of the 13th century and by the armies of Timur in the last decades of the 14th century had made a shambles of much of the Muslim world. The pretense of Muslim unity, which had been preserved by the Seljuk Sultans' retention of the powerless caliphs after 1055, was shattered in 1258 by the conquest and sacking of the Abbasid capital and the extinction of the long-lived caliphate. Regional dynasties in areas as distant as Asia Minor and India were also crushed by nomadic armies, and many splendid Islamic cities were laid to waste. But in the wake of the most powerful incursions of the nomadic peoples of central Asia into the civilized heartlands of Eurasia, three new Muslim dynasties arose. These produced a new flowering of Islamic civilization. Competition between them also led to important political divisions and periodic military clashes within the Muslim world. The largest of the three empires, the *Ottoman,* stretched at its peak in the 17th century from North Africa to southern Russia, and from Hungary to the port of Aden on the southern end of the Red Sea (see Map 26.1). To the east in what is now Iran and Afghanistan, the *Safavid dynasty* arose to challenge the Ottomans for leadership of the Islamic world. Finally, yet another Muslim empire in India, centered like most of the earlier ones on the Delhi region of the Ganges plain, was built under the leadership of a succession of remarkable *Mughal* rulers.

The combination of these three empires—Ottoman, Safavid, and Mughal—produced the greatest political and military power the Islamic world had yet attained. The striking similarities between the three empires are the focus of this chapter. Each empire had its origins in the Turkic nomadic cultures of the central Asian steppe. Religious fervor and zeal for Islamic conversion were central to the rise of both the Ottoman and Safavid dynasties. The founders of the *Mughal Empire* were displaced princes in search of a new kingdom rather than religious zealots. But their successors often were preoccupied with questions of how far to push conversion efforts aimed at the Hindu majority of the peoples of South Asia. Each empire was based on military conquest, and, at least in its early stages, was oriented to the support of its armies and military classes. Both the early conquests and the continued strength of each of the dynasties depended on its effective use of firearms on the battlefield and in siege warfare.

Each of the Muslim empires was ruled by a succession of absolute monarchs whose imperial pretensions and courtly rituals were patterned after those of earlier Islamic dynasties. Support of the expanding bureaucracies

1250 C.E.	1400 C.E.	1500 C.E.	1525 C.E.	1550 C.E.	1650 C.E.	1700 C.E.
1243 Mongol invasion of Asia Minor	**1402** Timur's invasion; Ottoman setbacks under Bayazid	**1501–1510** Safavid conquest of Persia (present-day Iran)	**1526** Battle of Panipat; Babur's conquest of India	**1556** Mughal Empire reestablished in north India	**1657–1658** Great war of succession between sons of Shah Jahan	**1722** First Turkish-language printing press founded
1281 Founding of the Ottoman dynasty	**c. 1450s** Shi'ite influences enter Safavid teachings	**1507** Portuguese victory over Ottoman–Arab fleet at Diu in the Indian Ocean	**1529** First Ottoman siege of Vienna	**1556–1605** Reign of Akbar	**1658–1707** Reign of Aurangzeb	**1722** Fall of the Safavid dynasty
1334 Death of the first Safavid Sufi master at Ardabil	**c. 1450s** Beginning of large-scale recruitment of Janissary troops	**1514** Ottoman victory over Safavids at Chaldiran	**1540–1545** Mughal ruler Humayan in exile at Safavid court	**1571** Battle of Lepanto	**1683** Last Ottoman siege of Vienna	**1730** Ottoman armies are defeated by Persian forces under Nadir Khan (later Nadir Shah, emperor of Persia)
1350s Ottoman invasion of Europe; conquest of much of the Balkans and Hungary	**1453** Ottoman capture of Constantinople	**1517** Ottoman capture of Syria and Egypt	**1540** Babur's successor, Humayan, driven from India	**1582** Akbar's proclamation of his new religion	**1680s** Rajput and peasant revolts in North India	**1730s** First Western-modeled military schools established
		1520–1566 Rule of Suleyman the Magnificent; construction of Suleymaniye mosque in Constantinople	**1540–1545** Humayan in exile at the Safavid court	**1588–1629** Reign of Abbas I (the Great) in Persia	**1699** Treaty of Carlowitz; Ottomans cede territories in Europe	**1736–1747** Reign of Nadir Shah
						1739 Nadir Shah invades India from Persia, sacks the Mughal capital at Delhi

and military establishments of each empire was drawn primarily from taxes levied on the peoples of the ancient agrarian societies that each empire conquered and ruled. Under each dynasty, unique styles of artistic and literary expression developed. These drew both on earlier Islamic expression and on the skills and sensibilities of the conquered peoples, both Muslim and non-Muslim.

These similarities were counterbalanced by significant differences between the rival Muslim empires. Although each dynasty was Muslim, the Mughals ruled a predominantly non-Muslim population. Thus, the political tactics and social policies followed by the Mughal rulers in India differed from those of their Safavid rivals in Persia, whose subjects were for the most part Muslims. The Ottomans in this respect were midway between the Mughals and Safavids. For the first centuries of Ottoman rule, their subjects were largely Christian. Although extensive conversions to Islam from the 15th century onward resulted in a Muslim majority, throughout their reign the Ottoman sultans had to keep the interests of the empire's large Christian minority in mind. The empires were also divided by the Sunni–Shi'a split, which, as we have seen, emerged in the early decades of Islamic history and persisted through the centuries. Enmity was particularly intense between the Ottoman champions of Sunni Islam and the Shi'ite Safavids. These neighboring powers often warred over territory and persecuted the adherents of their rivals' brand of Islam. Sunni and Shi'a differences also led to varying religious practices, legal codes, and social organization in each Islamic empire.

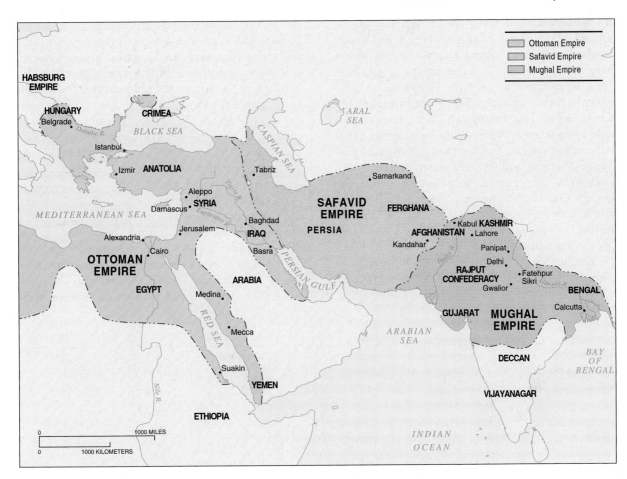

Map 26.1 *The Ottoman, Safavid, and Mughal Empires*

THE OTTOMANS: FROM FRONTIER WARRIORS TO EMPIRE BUILDERS

❖ *From the devastation that the Mongol invasions brought to much of the Islamic heartlands, a new power arose in the 13th and 14th centuries. Founded by yet another Turkic nomadic people migrating from the central Asian steppes, the Ottoman dynasty gradually built an empire in the eastern Mediterranean that rivaled the Abbasid imperium at its height. The Ottomans finally put an end to the long-besieged civilization of Byzantium and advanced deep into eastern and central Europe, where they came to rule large numbers of Christians. The Ottomans built much of their empire on the ideas and institutions of earlier Muslim civilizations. But in warfare, architecture, and engineering, they carried Islamic civilization in new directions. Internal weaknesses and the counteroffensives of their Muslim and European rivals had considerably reduced Ottoman power by the late 17th and early 18th centuries. Increasingly the dynasty was forced to attempt administrative and social reforms to cope with the challenges from the expansive Western powers.*

For centuries before the rise of the Ottoman dynasty, Turkic-speaking peoples from central Asia had played key roles in Islamic civilization as soldiers and administrators, often in the service of the Abbasid caliphs. But the collapse of the Seljuk Turkic kingdom of Rum in eastern Anatolia in Asia Minor (Map 26.2), after the invasion by the Mongols in 1243, opened the way for the Ottomans to seize power in their own right. The Mongols raided but did not directly rule Anatolia, which fell into a chaotic period of warfare between would-be successor states to the Seljuk sultans. Turkic peoples, both those fleeing the Mongols and those in search of easy booty, flooded into the region in the last decades of the 13th century. One of these peoples, called the Ottomans after an early leader named Osman, came to dominate the rest, and within decades they had begun to build a new empire based in Anatolia.

By the 1350s, the Ottomans had advanced from their strongholds in Asia Minor across the Bosporus straits into Europe. Thrace was quickly conquered,

and by the end of the century large portions of the Balkans had been added to their rapidly expanding territories (see Map 26.2). The Ottoman rise to power was severely but only temporarily set back in 1402 when the armies of Timur swept into Anatolia and defeated the Ottoman sultan Bayazid at Angora. For nearly a decade afterward, the region was torn by civil war between Bayazid's sons, each hoping to occupy his father's throne. The victory of Mehmed I led to the reunification of the empire and new conquests in Europe and Asia Minor.

In moving into Europe in the mid-14th century, the Ottomans had bypassed rather than conquered the great city of Constantinople, long the capital of the once powerful Byzantine Empire. By the mid-15th century, the Ottomans, who had earlier alternated between alliances and warfare with the Byzantines, were strong enough to undertake the

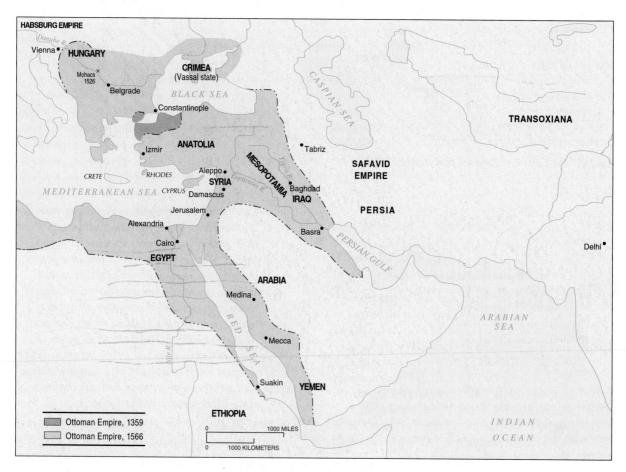

Map 26.2 *The expansion of the Ottoman Empire*

capture of the well-fortified city. For seven weeks in the spring of 1453, the army of *Mehmed II,* "The Conqueror," which numbered well over 100,000, assaulted the triple ring of land walls that had protected the city for centuries (Figure 26.1). The outnumbered forces of the defenders repulsed attack after attack until the sultan ordered his gunners to batter a portion of the walls with their massive siege cannon. Wave after wave of Ottoman troops struck at the gaps in the defenses that had been cut by the guns, quickly overwhelmed the defenders, and raced into the city to loot and pillage for the three days that Mehmed had promised as their reward for victory.

In the two centuries after the conquest of Constantinople, the armies of a succession of able Ottoman rulers extended the empire into Syria and Egypt and across North Africa, thus bringing under their rule the bulk of the Arab world (Map 26.2). The empire also spread through the Balkans into Hungary in Europe and around the Black and Red Seas. The Ottomans became a formidable naval power in the Mediterranean Sea. Powerful Ottoman galley fleets made possible the capture of major island bases on Rhodes, Crete, and Cyprus. The Ottoman armies also drove the Venetians and Genoese from much of the eastern Mediterranean and threatened southern Italy with invasion on several occasions. From their humble origins as frontier vassals, the Ottomans had risen to become the protectors of the Islamic heartlands and the scourge of Christian Europe. As late as 1683, Ottoman armies were able to lay siege to the capital of the Austrian Habsburg dynasty at Vienna. Even though the Ottoman Empire was in decline by this time, and the threat the assault

Figure 26.1 *An illuminated French manuscript from the 15th century shows the Ottoman siege of Constantinople in 1453. The Muslim capture of the great eastern bastion of Christian Europe aroused fears throughout the continent, resulting in demands for new crusades to recapture the city. The advance of the Ottomans in the east also provided impetus to the overseas expansion of nations such as Spain and Portugal on the western coasts of Europe. Both of these Catholic maritime powers saw their efforts to build overseas empires as part of a larger campaign to outflank the Muslim powers and bring areas that they controlled into the Christian camp.*

posed to Vienna was far less serious than a previous attack in the early 16th century, the Ottomans remained a major force in European politics until the late 19th century.

A State Geared to Warfare

Befitting an empire that had been founded and extended to spread Islam through the waging of the jihad, or holy war, military leaders played a dominant role in the Ottoman state, and the economy of the empire was geared to warfare and expansion. The Turkic cavalry, chiefly responsible for the Ottomans' early conquests from the 13th to the 16th centuries, gradually developed into a warrior aristocracy. They were granted control over land and peasant producers in annexed areas for the support of their households and military retainers. From the 15th century onward, members of the warrior class also vied with religious leaders and administrators drawn from other social groups for control of the expanding Ottoman bureaucracy. As the power of the warrior aristocracy shrank at the center, they built up regional and local bases of support. These inevitably competed with the sultans and the central bureaucracy for revenue and labor control. From the mid-15th century, the imperial armies were increasingly dominated by infantry divisions made up of troops called *Janissaries.* Most of the Janissaries had been forcibly conscripted as adolescent boys in conquered areas, such as the Balkans, where the majority of the population retained its Christian faith. Sometimes the boys' parents willingly turned their sons over to the Ottoman recruiters because of the opportunities for advancement that came with service to the Ottoman sultans. Though legally slaves, the youths were given fairly extensive schooling for the time and converted to Islam. Some of them went on to serve in the palace or bureaucracy, but most became Janissaries.

Because the Janissaries controlled the artillery and firearms that became increasingly vital to Ottoman success in warfare with Christian and Muslim adversaries, they rapidly became the most powerful component in the Ottoman military machine. Their growing importance was another factor contributing to the steady decline of the role of the aristocratic cavalry. Just like the mercenary forces that had earlier served the caliphs of Baghdad, the Janissaries eventually tried to translate military service into political influence. By the late 15th century they were deeply involved in court politics; by the mid-16th century they had the power to depose sultans and decide which one of a dying ruler's sons would mount the throne.

The Sultans and Their Court

Nominally, the Ottoman rulers were absolute monarchs. But even the most powerful sultan maintained his position by playing factions in the warrior elite off each other and pitting the warriors as a whole against the Janissaries and other groups. Chief among the latter were the Islamic religious scholars and legal experts, who retained many of the administrative functions they had held under the Arab caliphs of earlier centuries. In addition to Muslim traders, commerce within the empire was in the hands of Christian and Jewish trading groups, who as dhimmis, or "peoples of the Book," were under the protection of the Ottoman rulers. Although they have often been depicted in Western writings as brutal and corrupt despots, Ottoman sultans, especially in the early centuries of their sway, often were very capable rulers. Ottoman conquest often meant effective administration and tax relief for the peoples of areas annexed to the empire.

Like the Abbasid caliphs, the Ottoman sultans grew more and more distant from their subjects as their empire increased in size and wealth. In their splendid marble palaces and pleasure gardens, surrounded by large numbers of slaves and the many wives and concubines of their harems, Ottoman rulers followed elaborate court rituals based on those of earlier Byzantine, Persian, and Arab dynasties. Day-to-day administration was carried out by a large bureaucracy headed by a grand *vizier* (*wazir* in Arabic). The vizier was the overall head of the imperial administration, and he often held more real power than the sultan himself. Early sultans took an active role in political decisions and often personally led their armies into battle. Their sons usually were made provincial administrators or military commanders. This practice gave the potential successors to the ruler vital leadership training, and it does much to explain the high quality of many of the Ottoman monarchs until the late 16th century.

Like earlier Muslim dynasties, however, the Ottomans suffered greatly because they inherited Islamic principles of political succession that remained vague and contested. The existence of many talented and experienced claimants to the throne meant constant danger of civil strife. The death of a sultan could, and increasingly did, lead to protracted warfare among his sons. Defeated claimants sometimes fled to the domains of Christian or Muslim rulers hostile to the Ottomans, thereby becoming rallying points for military campaigns against the son who had gained the throne.

Constantinople Restored and the Flowering of Ottoman Culture

An empire that encompassed so many and such diverse cultures from Europe, Africa, and Asia naturally varied greatly from one province to the next in its social arrangements, artistic production, and physical appearance. But the Ottomans' ancient and cosmopolitan capital at Constantinople richly combined the disparate elements of their extensive territories. Like the Byzantine Empire as a whole, Constantinople had fallen on hard times in the centuries before the Ottoman conquest in 1453. Soon after Mehmed II's armies had captured and sacked the city, however, the Ottoman ruler set about restoring its ancient glory. He had the cathedral of Saint Sophia converted into one of the grandest mosques in the Islamic world, and new mosques and palaces were built throughout the city. This construction benefited greatly from architectural advances the Ottomans derived from the Byzantine heritage. Aqueducts were built from the surrounding hills to supply the grow-ing population with water, markets were reopened, and the city's defenses were repaired.

Each sultan who ruled in the centuries after Mehmed strove to be remembered for his efforts to beautify the capital. The most prominent additions were further mosques that represent some of the most sublime contributions of the Ottomans to Islamic and human civilization. The most spectacular of these was the Suleymaniye, pictured in Figure 26.2. As its name suggests, the mosque was built at the behest of the most successful of the sultans, Suleyman the Magnificent (1520–1566). Although it smacks of hometown pride, the following description by a 17th-century Ottoman chronicler of the reaction of some Christian visitors to the mosque conveys a sense of the awe that the structure still evokes:

> The humble writer of these lines once himself saw ten Frankish infidels skillful in geometry and architecture, who, when the door-keeper had changed their shoes for slippers, and had introduced them into the mosque for the purpose of showing it to them, laid their finger on their mouths, and each bit his finger from astonishment when they saw the minarets; but when they beheld the dome they tossed up their hats and cried Maria! Maria! and on observing the four arches which supported the dome … they could not find terms to express their admiration, and the ten … remained a full hour

Figure 26.2 *Built in the reign of Suleyman I in the 1550s and designed by the famous architect Sinan, the Suleymaniye mosque is among the largest domed structures in the world, and it is one of the great engineering achievements of Islamic civilization. The pencil-thin minarets flanking the great central dome are characteristic of Ottoman architecture, which was quite distinct from its Safavid and Mughal counterparts (shown in Figures 26.4 and 26.6).*

looking with astonishment on those arches. [One of them said] that nowhere was so much beauty, external and internal, to be found united, and that in the whole of Frangistan [Christian Europe] there was not a single edifice which could be compared to this.

In addition to the mosques, sultans and powerful administrators built mansions, rest houses, religious schools, and hospitals throughout the city. Both public and private gardens further beautified the capital, which Ottoman writers compared to paradise itself. The city and its suburbs stretched along both sides of the Bosporus, the narrow strait that separates Europe from Asia (see Map 26.2). Its harbors and the Golden Horn, a triangular bay that formed the northern boundary of the city, were crowded with merchant ships from ports throughout the Mediterranean and the Black Sea. Constantinople's great bazaars were filled with merchants and travelers from throughout the empire and places as distant as England and Malaya. They offered the seasoned shopper all manner of produce, from the spices of the East Indies and the ivory of Africa to slaves and forest products from Russia and fine carpets from Persia. Coffeehouses—places where men gathered to smoke tobacco (introduced from America in the 17th century by English merchants), gossip, do business, and play chess—were found in all sections of the city. They were pivotal to the social life of the capital. The coffeehouses also played a major role in the cultural life of Constantinople as places where poets and scholars could congregate, read their latest works aloud, and debate about politics and the merits of each other's ideas.

Beneath the ruling classes, a sizable portion of the population of Constantinople and other Ottoman cities belonged to the merchant and artisan classes. The Ottoman regime closely regulated commercial exchanges and handicraft production. Government inspectors were employed to ensure that standard weights and measures were used and to license the opening of new shops. They also regulated the entry of apprentice artisans into the trades and monitored the quality of the goods they produced. Like their counterparts in medieval European towns, the artisans were organized into guilds. Guild officers set craft standards, arbitrated disputes between their members, and provided financial assistance for needy members. They even arranged popular entertainments, often linked to religious festivals. The guilds

of Ottoman towns were much more closely supervised by government officials than was the case in Europe. In addition, a wider array of occupational groups—including entertainers, prostitutes, and even ordinary laborers—were organized into guilds than in the empires to the west.

The early Ottomans had written in Persian, and Arabic remained an important language for works on law and religion throughout the empire's history. But by the 17th century, the Turkish language of the Ottoman court had become the preferred mode of expression for poets and historians as well as the language of the Ottoman bureaucracy. In writing, as in the fine arts, the Ottomans' achievements have been somewhat overshadowed by those of their contemporary Persian and Indian rivals. Nonetheless, the authors, artists, and artisans of the Ottoman Empire have left a considerable legacy, particularly in poetry, ceramics, carpet manufacturing, and above all in architecture.

The Problem of Ottoman Decline

Much of the literature on the Ottoman Empire concentrates on its slow decline from the champion of the Muslim world and the great adversary of Christendom to the "sick man" of Europe in the 18th and 19th centuries. This approach provides a very skewed view of Ottoman history as a whole. Traced from its origins in the late 13th century, the Ottoman state is one of the great success stories in human political history. Vigorous and expansive until the late 17th century, the Ottomans were able to ward off the powerful enemies that surrounded their domains on all sides for nearly four centuries. The dynasty endured for more than 600 years, a feat matched by no other in all human history.

From one perspective, the long Ottoman decline, which officials and court historians actively discussed from the mid-17th century onward, reflects the great strength of the institutions on which the empire was built. Despite internal revolts and periodic conflicts with such powerful foreign rivals as the Russian, Austrian, Spanish, and Safavid empires, the Ottomans ruled into the 20th century. Yet the empire had reached the limits of its expansive power centuries earlier, and by the late 17th century the long retreat from Russia, Europe, and the Arab lands had begun. In a sense, some contraction was inevitable. Even when it was at the height of its power, the empire was too large to be maintained, given the resource base that the sultans had at their disposal and the primitive state of transport and communications in the preindustrial era.

The Ottoman state had been built on war and steady territorial expansion. As possibilities for new conquests ran out and lands began to be lost to the Ottomans' Christian and Muslim enemies, the means of maintaining the oversized bureaucracy and army shrank. The decline in the effectiveness of the administrative system that held the empire together was signaled by the rampant growth of corruption among Ottoman officials. The venality and incompetence of state bureaucrats prompted regional and local officials to retain more revenue for their own purposes. Poorly regulated by the central government, many local officials, who also controlled large landed estates, squeezed the peasants and the laborers who worked their lands for additional taxes and services. At times the oppressive demands of local officials and estate owners sparked rebellions. Peasant uprisings and flight resulted in the abandonment of cultivated lands and in social dislocations that further drained the resources of the empire.

From the 17th century onward, the forces that undermined the empire from below were compounded by growing problems at the center of imperial administration. The practice of assigning the royal princes administrative or military positions, to prepare them to rule, died out. Instead, possible successors to the throne were kept like hostages in special sections of the palace, where they remained until one of them ascended the throne. The other princes and potential rivals were also, in effect, imprisoned for life in the palace. Although it might have made the reigning sultan more secure, this solution to the problem of contested succession produced monarchs far less prepared to rule than those in the formative centuries of the dynasty. The great warrior–emperors of early Ottoman history gave way, with some important exceptions, to weak and indolent rulers, addicted to drink, drugs, and the pleasures of the harem. In many instances, the later sultans were little more than pawns in the power struggles of the viziers and other powerful officials with the leaders of the increasingly influential Janissary corps. Because the imperial apparatus had been geared to strong and absolute rulers, the decline in the caliber of Ottoman emperors had devastating effects on the empire as a whole. Civil strife increased, and the discipline and leadership of the armies on which the empire depended for survival deteriorated.

Military Reverses and the Ottoman Retreat

Debilitating changes within the empire were occurring at a time when challenges from without were growing rapidly. The Ottomans had made very effective use of artillery and firearms in building their empire. But their reliance on huge siege guns, and the Janissaries' determination to block all military changes that might jeopardize the power they had gained within the state, caused the Ottomans to fall further and further behind their European rivals in the critical art of waging war. With the widespread introduction of light field artillery into the armies of the European powers in the 17th century, Ottoman losses on the battlefield multiplied rapidly, and the threat they posed for the West began to recede.

On the sea, the Ottomans were eclipsed as early as the 16th century. The end of their dominance was presaged by their defeat by a combined Spanish and Venetian fleet at Lepanto in 1571. The great battle is depicted in the painting in Figure 26.3. Although the Ottomans had completely rebuilt their war fleet within a year after Lepanto and soon launched an assault on North Africa that preserved that area for Islam, their control of the eastern Mediterranean had been lost. Even more ominously, in the decades before Lepanto, the Ottomans and the Muslim world had been outflanked by the Portuguese seafarers who sailed down and around the coast of Africa. The failure in the early 1500s of the Ottomans and their Muslim allies in the Indian Ocean to drive the Portuguese from Asian waters proved far more harmful in the long run than Ottoman defeats in the Mediterranean.

Portuguese naval victories in the Indian Ocean revealed the decline of the Ottoman galley fleets and Mediterranean-style warships more generally. The trading goods, particularly spices, that the Portuguese carried around Africa and back to Europe enriched the Ottomans' Christian rivals. In addition, the fact that a large portion of the flow of these products was no longer transmitted to European ports through Muslim trading centers in the eastern Mediterranean meant that merchants and tax collectors in the Ottoman Empire lost critical revenues. As if this were not enough, from the late 16th century on, large amounts of silver flowed into the Ottomans' lands from mines worked by American Indian laborers in the Spanish empire in Peru and Mexico. This sudden influx of bullion into the rigid and slow-growing

Figure 26.3 *The clash of the galley fleets at Lepanto was one of the greatest sea battles in history. But despite devastating losses, the Ottomans managed to replace most of their fleet and go back on the offensive against their Christian adversaries within a year. Here the epic encounter is pictured in one of the many paintings devoted to it in the decades that followed. The tightly packed battle formations that both sides adopted show the importance of ramming rather than cannon fire in naval combat in the Mediterranean in this era. This pattern was reversed in the Atlantic and the other oceanic zones in which the Europeans had been expanding since the 14th century.*

economy of the Ottoman empire set off a long-term inflationary trend that further undermined the finances of the empire.

Several able sultans took measures to shore up the empire in the 17th century. The collapse of the Safavid dynasty in Persia and conflicts between the European powers at this time also gave the Ottomans hope that their earlier dominance might be restored. But their reprieve was temporary. With the scientific, technological, and commercial transformations occurring in Europe (discussed in Chapter 22), the Ottomans were falling behind their Christian rivals in most areas. But the growing gap was most critical in trade and warfare. The Ottomans inherited from their Arab, Persian, and Turkic predecessors the conviction that little of what happened in Europe was important. This belief, which is seen as a major cause of Ottoman decline by the traveler Aub Taleb quoted in the Document, prevented them from taking seriously the revolutionary changes that were transforming western Europe. The intense conservatism of powerful groups such as the Janissaries and, to a lesser extent, the reli-

gious scholars reinforced this fatal attitude. Through much of the 17th and 18th centuries, these groups blocked most of the Western-inspired innovations that reform-minded sultans and their advisors tried to introduce. As a result of these narrow and potentially dangerous attitudes, the isolated Ottoman imperial system proved incapable of checking the forces that were steadily destroying it.

THE SHI'ITE CHALLENGE OF THE SAFAVIDS

In the first years of the 16th century, after decades of warfare against established Muslim states, rival sects, and Christian communities in what is today southern Russia, the Safavids founded a dynasty and conquered the region that makes up the present-day nation of Iran (Map 26.3). From that point onward, Iran

ᴅᴏᴄᴜᴍᴇɴᴛ

An Islamic Traveler Laments the Muslims' Indifference to Europe

Although most of the travelers and explorers in this era were Europeans who went to Africa, Asia, and the Americas, a few people from these lands visited Europe. One of these, Abu Taleb, was a scholar of Turkish and Persian descent whose family had settled in India. At the end of the 18th century, Abu Taleb traveled in Europe for three years and later wrote an account in Persian of his experiences there. Although his was one of the few firsthand sources of information about Europe available to Muslim scholars and leaders, Abu Taleb was deeply disturbed by the lack of interest shown by other Muslims in his observations and discoveries. He wrote,

> When I reflect on the want of energy and the indolent dispositions of my countrymen, and the many erroneous customs which exist in all Mohammedan countries and among all ranks of Mussulmans, I am fearful that my exertions [in writing down his experiences in Europe] will be thrown away. The great and the rich intoxicated with pride and luxury, and puffed up with the vanity of their possessions, consider universal science as comprehended in the circle of their own scanty acquirements and limited knowledge; while the poor and common people, from the want of leisure, and overpowered by the difficulty of procuring a livelihood, have not time to attend to his personal concerns, much less to form desires for the acquirement of information of new discoveries and inventions, although such a person has been implanted by nature in

every human breast, as an honour and an ornament to the species. I therefore despair of their reaping any fruit from my labours, being convinced that they will consider this book of no greater value than the volumes of tales and romances which they peruse merely to pass away their time, or are attracted thereto by the easiness of the style. It may consequently be concluded, that as they will find no pleasure in reading a work which contains a number of foreign names, treats on uncommon subjects, and alludes to other matters which cannot be understood at first glance, but require a little time for consideration, they will, under pretense of zeal for their religion, entirely abstain and refrain from perusing it.

Questions: What reasons does Abu Taleb give for his fellow Muslims' indifference to his travel reports on Europe? What other factors can be added as a result of our study of long-standing Islamic attitudes toward Europe and conditions in the Ottoman Empire in this period? In what ways might the Muslims' neglect of events in Europe have hindered their efforts to cope with this expansive civilization in the centuries that followed?

Were there Western counterparts to Abu Taleb in these centuries, and how were their accounts of distant lands received in Europe?

---

has been one of the strongest and most enduring centers of Shi'ism within the Islamic world. Under the Safavid dynasty, which lasted until 1722, the Iranian region was also restored as a center of political power and cultural creativity at a level that it had rarely enjoyed since the collapse of the Sasanian Empire in the mid-7th century. With the Ottoman and Mughal empires that bordered it on the west and east, Safavid Iran was one of the three core regions of Islamic civilization in the gunpowder age.

Like the Ottomans, the Safavid dynasty arose from the struggles of rival Turkic nomadic groups in the wake of the Mongol and Timurid invasions of the 13th and 14th centuries. Also like the Ottomans, the Safavids rose to prominence as the frontier warrior

champions of a highly militant strain of Islam. But unlike the Ottomans, who became the champions of the Sunni majority of the Muslim faithful, the Safavids espoused the Shi'ite variant of Islam. As we saw in Chapter 12, in the early decades of Muslim expansion a split developed in the community of the faithful between the Sunnis, who recognized the legitimacy of the first three successors to Muhammad (Abu Bakr, Umar, and Uthman) and the Shi'ites, who believed that only the fourth successor (Ali, Muhammad's cousin and son-in-law) had the right to succeed the prophet. Over time, differences in doctrine, ritual, and law were added to the disagreements over succession that originally divided the Islamic community. Divisions have also arisen within both the Shi'ite and Sunni groupings, but bitter hostility and violent conflict most often have developed along Sunni–Shi'i lines. The long

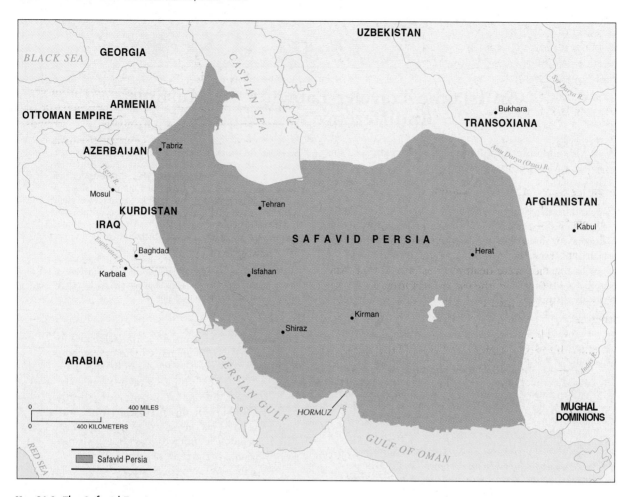

Map 26.3 *The Safavid Empire*

rivalry between the Sunni Ottomans and the Shi'ite Safavids proved to be one of the most pivotal episodes in the long history of these sectarian struggles.

The Safavid dynasty had its origins in a family of Sufi mystics and religious preachers, whose shrine center was at Ardabil near the Caspian Sea (Map 26.3). In the early 14th century, one of these Sufis, *Sail al-Din*, who gave the dynasty its name, began a militant campaign to purify and reform Islam and spread Muslim teachings among the Turkic tribes of the region. In the chaos that followed the collapse of Mongol authority in the mid-14th century, Sail al-Din and other Safavid Sufi leaders gained increasing support. But as the numbers of the *Red Heads* (as the Safavids' followers were called because of their distinctive headgear) grew, and as they began in the mid-15th century to preach Shi'ite doctrines, their enemies multiplied. After decades of fierce local struggles in which three successive Safavid leaders

perished, a surviving Sufi commander, *Ismâ'il,* led his Turkic followers to a string of victories on the battle-field. In 1501, Ismâ'il's armies took the city of Tabriz, where he was proclaimed *shah,* or emperor.

In the next decade, Ismâ'il's followers conquered most of Persia, drove the Safavid's ancient enemies, the Ozbegs—a neighboring nomadic people of Turkic stock—back into the central Asian steppes, and advanced into what is now Iraq. The Safavid successes and the support their followers received in the Ottoman borderlands from Turkic-speaking peoples brought them into conflict with Ottoman rulers. In August 1514, at *Chaldiran* in northwest Persia, the armies of the two empires met in one of the most fateful battles in Islamic history. Chaldiran was more than a battle between the two most powerful dynasties in the Islamic world at the time. It was a clash between the champions of the Shi'i and Sunni variants of Islam. The religious fervor with which both sides fought the battle was intensified by the long-standing Safavid persecutions of the Sunnis and the slaughter of Shi'is living in Ottoman territories by the forces of the Ottoman sultan, Selim.

The battle also demonstrated the importance of muskets and field cannon in the gunpowder age. Because his artillery was still engaged against enemies far to the east, Ismâ'il hoped to delay a decisive confrontation with the Ottoman forces under the Sultan Selim. When battle could not be avoided, Ismâ'il threw his cavalry against the cannon and massed muskets of the Ottoman forces. Despite desperate attempts to make up through clever maneuvers what he lacked in firepower, Ismâ'il's cavalry proved no match for the well-armed Ottomans.

The Safavids were dealt a devastating defeat. In the years that followed, the victorious Ottomans were able to concentrate their forces in campaigns to defeat other enemies in Egypt far to the west. Thus, their victory at Chaldiran buttressed the Ottomans' efforts to build the most powerful empire in the Islamic world. But the Ottomans could not follow up the battle with conquests that would have put an end to their Safavid rivals. The latter's capital at Tabriz was too far from Ottoman supply areas to be held through the approaching winter. The withdrawal of the Ottoman armies gave the Safavids the breathing space they needed to regroup their forces and reoccupy much of the territory they had originally conquered. Nonetheless, defeat at Chaldiran put an end to Ismâ'il's dreams of further westward expansion, and most critically it checked the rapid spread of conversions to Shi'i Islam in the western borderlands that had resulted from the Safavid's recent successes in battle. The outcome at Chaldiran determined that Shi'ism would be confined largely to Persia, or present-day Iran, and neighboring areas in what is today southern Iraq. Although the Ottoman and Safavid empires periodically waged wars over the next centuries, Chaldiran set limits to which either could expand and extend its variant of the Islamic faith.

IN DEPTH

The Gunpowder Empires and the Shifting Balance of Global Power

Like so many of their predecessors, each of the great Muslim dynasties of the premodern era came to power with the support of nomadic warrior peoples. Each based the military forces that won and sustained its empire on massed cavalry. But in each case, there was a significant divergence from past conditions. As the outcome of the critical battle of Chaldiran between the Ottomans and Safavids made clear, by the 16th century firearms had become a decisive element in armed conflict—the key to empire building. In military and political terms, global history had entered a new phase.

Although the Chinese had invented gunpowder and were the first to use it in war, the Mongols were the first to realize the awesome potential of the new type of weaponry based on explosive formulas. The Mongols continued to build their armies around swift cavalry and their skill as mounted archers. But siege cannons became critical to Mongol conquests once they ventured into the highly urbanized civilizations that bordered on their steppe homelands. Mongol successes against intricately walled and heavily fortified cities in China, Russia, and the Islamic heartlands impressed their sedentary and nomadic adversaries with the power of the new weaponry and contributed much to its spread throughout the Eurasian world in the late 13th and 14th centuries.

Innovation in the use of gunpowder spread quickly to many areas, especially Europe and the Muslim Middle East. By the late 15th century, muskets and field cannon, however heavy and clumsy the latter might be, were transforming warfare from Europe to China. In the Middle East, Janissary musketeers and heavy artillery became the driving force of Ottoman expansion. The Safavids' lack of artillery was critical to their defeat at Chaldiran. In Europe, armies were increasingly built around musket and artillery regiments. Rival states vied to attract gunsmiths who could provide them with the latest weaponry or, even better, invent guns that would give them decisive advantages over their rivals. In the Atlantic and the Mediterranean, handguns and cannon were introduced into sea warfare—an innovation that proved essential to the Europeans' ability to project their power overseas from the 16th century onward.

In many areas, the new military technology contributed to broader social and political changes. In Europe and somewhat later in Japan, for example, siege cannon reduced feudal castles to rubble. In so doing, they struck a mortal blow at the warrior aristocracies that had dominated these societies for centuries. But the success of the new weaponry forced a revolution in the design of fortifications and defense strategies. The defense systems that resulted, which were expensive and elaborate, spawned corps of professional officers and engineers, vast military supply industries, and urban centers enclosed by low-lying walls and star-shaped bastions. The cost of the field artillery, siege weapons, and new defense industries promoted state centralization, as the experience of the Muslim empires and the history of Europe and Japan in the gunpowder age demonstrate. Rulers with national or imperial ambitions had the firepower to level the fortresses of regional lords and thus more effectively control the populations and resources of their domains. Successful nation and empire builders came to control sufficient resources to build and maintain the very costly military machines essential for survival in the new era. Equally critically, they were able to deny the necessary resources to their rivals and vassals.

Although the new weaponry was vital to the rise and sustenance of nation-states and empires, some political systems were more compatible than others with efforts to exploit and improve on it. At one extreme, the Chinese scholar–gentry limited innovations in gunpowder weaponry and its use in warfare because they feared that these changes would lead to the dominance of the military in Ming and later Qing society. After the early 1600s, the shoguns, or military leaders, of neighboring Japan virtually banned the firearms that had done so much to bring them to power. In this case, a military caste feared that the spread of firearms to the general populace would destroy what was left of the feudal order they had built centuries earlier.

The obstacles faced by nomadic peoples such as the Mongols were very different. Their sparse populations and arid lands simply did not generate the resources or sustained invention that would allow them to keep up with their sedentary neighbors in the expensive arms races that the new technology spawned. As the advantages of sedentary societies grew more pronounced in the 17th and 18th centuries, nomadic peoples found not only that they could no longer raid or conquer the agrarian cores but also that sedentary adversaries could advance into and occupy their homelands on the steppe and desert fringes.

Nomadic dynasties, such as the Ottomans, Safavids, and Mughals, who had won their empires in the early stages of the gunpowder revolution, did control the agrarian bases and skilled artisans needed to supply their armies with muskets and siege cannons. But they were confronted by internal conflicts and, perhaps more critically in the long run, formidable external rivals. To begin with, their military technology was far in advance of the transport and communication systems of their far-flung empires. This fact, and their failure to build effective imperial bureaucracies, left them at the mercy of the warrior elites who brought them to power. In each of the three empires, the regional bases of the warrior classes became increasingly independent of the ruling dynasty. This meant that the rulers were denied revenue and other resources that were vital to maintaining competitive military establishments. Their fragile and overstretched administrative systems proved difficult to reform and more and more ineffective at administering the peasant populations in their charge. Internal revolts further sapped the resources of the hard-pressed Muslim dynasties.

In each Muslim empire, decline was hastened by the rise of European rivals, who proved more adept at taking advantage of the gunpowder revolution. The smaller but highly competitive nation-states of western Europe were better able to mobilize their smaller human and natural resources than their Muslim counterparts. Constant struggles for survival in the multistate European system also made the elites of Spain, England, and France more receptive to technological innovation, which became a central ingredient of political success in the gunpowder era. Emulating the more advanced states of western Europe, for example, Peter the Great forced social reforms and military innovations that transformed a weak and backward Russia into a powerful adversary of the Ottomans and the nomadic peoples of the steppes. Thus, although it began in China and was initially spread by the Mongol nomads, the gunpowder revolution eventually tipped the global balance of power in favor of the peoples of Christian Europe. This shift was an essential condition for Europe's rise to global power in the centuries that followed.

Questions: What advantages would gunpowder weaponry give to those who used it over those who did not in the early modern era? Were these advantages as decisive as they were later in the industrial age? Why would the use of muskets and early field cannons take a higher level of military organization and troop discipline and training than had been needed in earlier time periods? What made the new military technology so expensive? Why did the Europeans adopt it more readily than most other peoples, and why were they so intent on improving it?

Politics and War Under the Safavid Shahs

After his defeat at Chaldiran, Ismâ'il, once a courageous warrior and a popular leader, retreated to his palace and tried to escape his troubles through drink. His seclusion and struggles between the factions backing each of his sons for the right to succeed him left openings for subordinate Turkic chiefs to attempt to seize power. After years of turmoil, a new shah, Tahmasp I (1534–1576), won the throne and set about restoring the power of the dynasty. The Turkic chiefs were foiled in their bid for supreme power, and the Ozbegs were again and again driven from the Safavid domains. Under Shah Abbas I (1587–1629) the empire reached the height of its strength and prosperity, although the territories it controlled remained roughly equivalent to those ruled by Ismâil and Tahmasp I.

Under Tahmasp I and his successors, repeated efforts were made to bring the Turkic chiefs under control. They were gradually transformed into a warrior nobility comparable to that in the Ottoman domains. Like their Ottoman counterparts, the Safavid warrior nobles were assigned villages, whose peasants were required to supply them and their troops with food and labor. The most powerful of the warrior leaders occupied key posts in the imperial administration, and from the defeat at Chaldiran onward they posed a constant threat to the Safavid monarchs. To counterbalance this threat, Safavid rulers recruited Persians for positions at the court and in the rapidly expanding imperial bureaucracy. The struggle for power and influence between Turkic and Persian notables was further complicated by the practice, initiated by Ismâ'il's successor, Tahmasp I, of

recruiting into the bureaucracy and army slave boys who were captured in campaigns in southern Russia. Like the Janissaries in the Ottoman Empire, many of these slaves rose to positions of power. Also like the Janissaries, the slave regiments soon became a major force in Safavid political struggles.

Of all of the Safavid shahs, Abbas I, known also as *Abbas the Great,* made the greatest use of the youths who were captured in Russia and then educated and converted to Islam. They not only came to form the backbone of his military forces but were granted provincial governorships and high offices at court. Like the Janissaries, "slave" regiments, which were wholly dependent on Abbas's support, monopolized the firearms that had become increasingly prominent in Safavid armies. The Persians had artillery and handguns long before the arrival of the Portuguese by sea in the early 16th century. But Abbas and his successors showed little reluctance to call on the knowledgeable but infidel Europeans for assistance in their wars with the Ottomans. Abbas turned to European advisors, such as the one portrayed in the illustration at the beginning of this chapter. Of special importance were the Sherley brothers from England. They provided instruction in the casting of cannon and the training of Abbas's slave infantry and a special regiment of musketeers recruited from the Iranian peasantry. By the end of his reign, Abbas had built up a standing army of nearly 40,000 troops and an elite bodyguard. These measures to strengthen his armies and his victories on the battlefield appeared to promise security for the Safavid domains for decades to come—a promise that was not fulfilled.

State and Religion

The Safavid family was originally of Turkic stock, and early shahs such as Ismâ'il wrote in Turkish, unlike their Ottoman rivals, who preferred to write in Persian. After Chaldiran, however, Persian gradually supplanted Turkish as the language of the court and bureaucracy. Persian influences were also felt in the organization of court rituals and in the more and more exalted position of the Safavid shahs. Abandoning all pretense of the egalitarian camaraderie that had marked their earlier dealings with the warrior chiefs, the Safavids took grand titles, such as *padishah,* or king of kings, often derived from those used by the ancient Persian emperors. Like the Ottoman rulers, the Safavids presided from their high thrones over opulent palace complexes crowded with servants and courtiers. The pattern of palace life was set by elaborate court rituals and social interaction governed by a refined sense of etiquette and decorum. Although the later Safavid shahs played down claims to divinity that had been set forth under Ismâ'il and his predecessors, they continued to claim descent from one of the Shi'ite *imams,* or successors of Ali.

Changes in the status accorded to the Safavid rulers were paralleled by shifts in the religious impulses that had been so critical to their rise to power. The militant, expansive cast of Shi'ite ideology was modified as the faith became a major pillar of dynasty and empire. The early Safavids imported Arabic-speaking Shi'i religious experts. But later shahs came to rely on Persian religious scholars who entered into the service of the state and were paid by the government. *Mullahs,* who were both local mosque officials and prayer leaders, were also supervised by the state and given some support from it. All religious leaders were required to curse the first three caliphs and mention the Safavid ruler in the Friday sermon. Teaching in the mosque schools was also planned and directed by state religious officials.

Through these agents, the bulk of the Iranian population was converted to Shi'ism during the centuries of Safavid rule. Sunni Muslims, Christians, Jews, Zoroastrians, and the followers of Sufi preachers were pressured to convert to Shi'ism. Shi'i religious festivals, such as that commemorating the martyrdom of Husayn and involving public flagellation and passion plays, and pilgrimages to Shi'i shrines, such as that at Karbala in central Iraq, became the focal points of popular religion in Iran. Thus, Shi'ism not only provided ideological and institutional support for the Safavid dynasty but also came to be an integral part of Iranian identity, setting the people of the region off from most of their Arab and Turkic neighbors.

When the dynasty weakened, some of the religious experts and mullahs grew more independent. They found support in their local communities and voiced interpretations of the sacred texts that were based more on their own study than on the dictates of Safavid functionaries. Some religious scholars disputed the legitimacy of the dissolute shahs who occupied the throne in the latter stages of the dynasty. But it would be wrong to equate the power of these religious thinkers with that the *ayatollahs,* or highest religious authorities, have gained in present-day Iran. In Safavid times, no religious leader tried to seize power in his own right. Most continued to serve the dynasty or the rulers who succeeded the Safavids, or they withdrew from political affairs altogether.

Elite Affluence and Artistic Splendor

Although earlier rulers had built or restored mosques and religious schools and financed public works projects, Abbas I surpassed them all. After securing his political position with a string of military victories, Abbas I set about establishing his empire as a major center of international trade and Islamic culture. He had a network of roads and rest houses built, and he strove to make merchants and travelers safe within his domains. He set up workshops to manufacture the silk textiles and splendid Persian carpets that were in great demand. Abbas I encouraged Iranian merchants to trade not only with their Muslim neighbors and India and China to the east but also with the Portuguese—and later the Dutch and English—whose war and merchant ships were becoming a familiar sight in the Persian Gulf and Arabian Sea.

Although Abbas I undertook building projects throughout his empire, he devoted special attention to his capital at *Isfahan.* The splendid seat of Safavid power was laid out around a great square, shown in Figure 26.4, which was lined with two-story shops interspersed with great mosques, government offices, and soaring arches that opened onto formal gardens. Abbas I founded several colleges and oversaw the construction of numerous public baths and rest houses. He patronized workshops where intricately detailed and brilliantly colored miniatures were produced by master painters and their apprentices.

Above all, the great mosques that Abbas I had built at Isfahan were the glory of his reign. The vividly colored ceramic tiles, which Iranian builders had begun to use centuries earlier, turned the massive domes and graceful minarets of Safavid mosques and royal tombs into creations of stunning beauty. Geometric designs, floral patterns, and verses from the Quran written in stylized Arabic added movement and texture to the deep blue tiles that distinguished the monumental construction of the Safavid era. Gardens and reflecting pools were built near the mosques and rest houses. By combining graceful

Figure 26.4 *The great square of the Safavid capital at Isfahan was built by Abbas I to project the splendor and power of his empire. The buildings of the square made up one of the most splendid architectural complexes of the early modern era.*

arches, greenery, and colorful designs, Persian architects and artisans created lush, cool refuges (perhaps duplicating heaven itself, as it is described in the Quran) in a land that is dry, dusty, and gray-brown for much of the year.

Society and Gender Roles: Ottoman and Safavid Comparisons

Although the Ottomans and Safavids were bitter political rivals and religious adversaries, the social systems that developed under the two dynasties had much in common. Both were dominated, particularly in their earliest phases, by warrior aristocracies, which shared power with the absolutist monarchs of each empire and enjoyed prestige and luxury in the capital and on rural estates. In both cases, the warrior aristocrats gradually retreated to the estates, making life increasingly difficult for the peasants on whom they depended for the support of their grand households and many retainers. During the early phases of Safavid and Ottoman rule, the strength of the court and traditional peasant defenses such as the underreporting of crop yields and the threat of flight kept in check the demands of the warrior elite, now predominantly a rural land-owning class. But as the real power of the rulers of each empire diminished and as population increases reduced the uncultivated lands to which

peasants might flee, the demands of the landlord class grew harsher. Foreign invasions, civil strife, and the breakdown in vital services once provided by the state added to the growing misery of the peasantry. The resulting spread of banditry, peasant uprisings, and flight from the land further drained the resources of both empires and undermined their legitimacy.

The early rulers of both the Ottoman and the Safavid empires encouraged the growth of handicraft production and trade in their realms. Both dynasties established imperial workshops where products ranging from miniature paintings and rugs to weapons and metal utensils were manufactured. The rulers of each empire lavishly patronized public works projects that provided reasonably well-paid work for engineers, stonemasons, carpenters, and other sorts of artisans. Some of the more able emperors of these dynasties also pursued policies that they believed would increase both internal and international trade. In these endeavors, the Ottomans gained in the short run from the fact that large-scale traders in their empire often were from minority groups, such as Christians and Jews, who had extensive contacts with overseas traders that the bazaar merchants of the Safavid realm normally lacked. Although Safavid cooperation with Portuguese traders remedied this shortcoming to some extent, the Safavid economy remained much more constricted, less market oriented, and more technically backward than that of their Ottoman rivals.

Significantly, the Ottomans' advantages in trade and handicraft production were only relative; the European kingdoms to the west were superior in these areas. Whereas European techniques and technology were changing dramatically, even before 1750 and the beginnings of the Industrial Revolution, Ottoman manufacturing stagnated. In addition, its most dynamic trade sectors, still controlled by non-Muslim minorities, developed in increasing isolation from Ottoman society as a whole, often in defiance of imperial restrictions.

Women in Islamic societies under Ottoman or Safavid rule faced legal and social disadvantages comparable to those we have encountered in most civilized areas so far. Within the family, women were subordinated to their fathers and husbands. They seldom had political or religious power, and they had surprisingly meager outlets for artistic or scholarly expression. Even women of nomadic Turkic and Mongol backgrounds gradually lost their independence when they settled in the towns of conquered areas. There, the dictates of increasingly patriarchal codes and restrictive practices such as seclusion and veiling were imposed on women of all classes, but most strictly on those of the elite.

However, recent evidence suggests that many women in the Islamic heartlands in this era, perhaps clinging to the memory of the lives led by their nomadic predecessors, struggled against these restrictions. Travelers to Persia in the time of Abbas I remarked on the brightly colored robes worn by women in the capital and elsewhere, and noted that many women made no effort to cover their faces in public. At both the Ottoman and Safavid courts, the wives and concubines of the rulers and royal princes continued to exert influence behind the throne and remained deeply involved in palace conspiracies. More important for ordinary women in each of these societies was the fact that many were active in trade and some in moneylending. Court records also suggest that women often could invoke provisions in Islamic law that protected their rights to inheritance, decent treatment by their spouses, and even divorce in marital situations that had become intolerable.

How typical these instances of assertion and expression were is not clear. Although some women were a good deal better off than we had once thought, perhaps as well off as or even better off than their counterparts in China and India, most women probably lived unenviable lives. Limited largely to contacts with their own families and left with little more than household chores and domestic handicrafts such as embroidery to occupy their time, the overwhelming majority of women in effect disappeared from the history of two of the great centers of Islamic civilization.

The Rapid Demise of the Safavid Empire

Given the power and splendor the Safavid Empire had achieved by the end of the reign of Abbas I, its collapse was stunningly rapid. Abbas's fears of usurpation by one of his sons, which were fed by plots on the part of several of his closest advisors, had led during his reign to the death or blinding of all who could legitimately succeed him. A grandson, who was weak and thus thought by high state officials to be easily manipulated, was placed on the throne after Abbas's death. From this point, the dynasty's fortunes declined. As was true of the Ottomans, the practice of confining the princes to the atmosphere of luxury and intrigue that permeated the court led to a sharp fall in the quality of Safavid rulers. Able shahs, such as Abbas II (1642–1666), were too few to halt the decline of the imperial administration or to deal effectively with the many foreign threats to the empire. Factional disputes and rebellions shook the empire from within, and nomadic raiders and Ottoman and Mughal armies steadily reduced the territory the Safavids could tap for labor and revenue.

By March 1722, Isfahan was besieged by Afghani tribes. In October, after over 80,000 of the capital's inhabitants had died of starvation and disease, the city fell and Safavid power was ended. One of those who fought for the throne in the decade of war and destruction that followed claimed descent from the Safavid line. But a soldier–adventurer named *Nadir Khan Afshar* eventually emerged victorious from these bloody struggles. Although he began as a champion of Safavid restoration, Nadir Khan proclaimed himself shah in 1736. Despite the title, his dynasty and those that followed were short-lived. The area that had once made up the Safavid Empire was reduced for generations to a battleground for its powerful neighbors and a tempting target for nomadic raiders.

THE MUGHALS AND THE APEX OF MUSLIM CIVILIZATION IN INDIA

In the first decades of the 16th century, another wave of nomadic invaders established what was to become the most powerful of a succession of Muslim dynasties in South Asia. A warrior prince, Babur, and his remarkable descendants spread the power of the Mughal dynasty through much of the Indian subcontinent (Map 26.4). Under their rule, Islam peaked as a force in South Asian history, and a blend of Hindu–Islamic civilization produced architecture and art as splendid as that created in Persia under the Safavids. By the early 17th century, however, a familiar pattern of dynastic decline took hold. Wars of succession between claimants to the Mughal throne, nomadic incursions from Persia and Afghanistan, and internal revolts by the Mughals' non-Muslim subjects led to a recurrence of the political fragmentation and sectarian strife that had dominated so much of south Asia's long history.

Despite the fact that the founder of the Mughal dynasty, *Babur,* traced his descent on one side from the Mongol khans, the Mughal in the dynasty's name was not derived from the earlier nomadic conquerors. Babur was also descended from Turkic warriors, like Timur, and most of his followers were from Turkic or mixed nomadic origins. Unlike the Ottomans and Safavids, Babur's motives for conquest and empire building had little to do with religious fervor. He led his followers into India in 1526 because he had lost his original kingdom, centered on Farghana in central Asia, in the preceding decades.

After his father's death in 1498, Babur, then only a boy of 16, was thrown into a fierce struggle with the Ozbeg tribes for control of his ancestral realm. By 1504, Babur and his supporters had been driven back to Kabul in what is now Afghanistan. Originally, he directed raids into the fertile and heavily populated plains of India only to gain booty to support his campaigns to win back Farghana. Although India had much greater potential as a base on which to build an empire, Babur cared little for the green and well-watered subcontinent. Even after he later conquered

India, he continued to long for the arid steppe and blue-domed mosques of his central Asian birthplace. But after decades of wars that repeatedly ended in defeat, he was forced to give up his dream of reclaiming his homeland and to turn his full energies to the conquest of northern India.

In 1526, Babur—by then a seasoned military commander—entered India at the head of an experienced and well-organized army. At Panipat, north of Delhi, his army of 12,000 met the huge force of more than 100,000 sent to crush it by the last ruler of the Muslim Lodi dynasty, which then ruled much of northern India. Using gun carts, movable artillery, and cavalry tactics similar to those that had brought the Ottomans victory at Chaldiran, Babur routed the Lodi army. In addition to the superior firepower and mobility of his forces, their victory owed a great deal to the tactic of frightening the hundreds of war elephants that led the Lodi army into battle. The

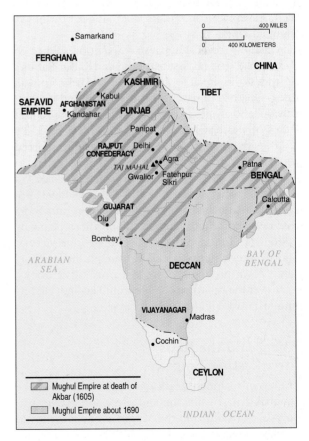

Map 26.4 *The Growth of the Mughal Empire, from Akbar to Aurangzeb*

elephants stampeded, trampling thousands of Lodi infantrymen or sending them into flight. A year later, Babur's forces, again vastly outnumbered, defeated a confederation of Hindu warrior–kings at Khanua, a small village near Agra. Within two years, he had conquered large portions of the Indus and Ganges plains and established a dynasty that would last more than 300 years.

The founder of the Mughal dynasty was a remarkable man. A fine military strategist and fierce fighter who went into battle alongside his troops, in the decades when he was continually fighting for his very life, Babur also cultivated a taste for the arts and music. He wrote one of the great histories of India, was a fine musician, and designed wonderful gardens for his new capital at Delhi. But he was a better conqueror than administrator. He did little to reform the very ineffective Lodi bureaucracy he had taken over—a project that would have solidified the Mughals' hold on the empire he had conquered. In 1530, at the age of 48, Babur suddenly fell ill and died, leaving his son, *Humayan,* to inherit the newly founded kingdom.

Like his father, Humayan was a good soldier; in fact, he had won his first battle at age 18. But Babur's death was the signal for his enemies to strike from all sides. One of Humayan's brothers disputed his succession, and armies from Afghanistan and the Rajput states of western India marched on his capital. By 1540, with his armies shattered, Humayan was forced to flee to Persia. There he remained in exile, an embarrassed guest at the Safavid court, for nearly a decade. Having gained a foothold at Kabul in 1545, Humayan launched a series of campaigns into India that restored Mughal rule to the northern plains by 1556. But Humayan did not live to savor his victory. Shortly after entering Delhi in triumph, he was hurrying down his library steps, his arms full of books, to answer the call to prayer. He stumbled and fell, hitting his head. He died within days.

Akbar and the Basis for a Lasting Empire

Humayan's sudden death once again imperiled the Mughal dynasty. His son and successor, *Akbar,* was only 13 years old, and the Mughals' enemies moved quickly to take advantage of what they saw as a very favorable turn of events. Their expectations were soon dashed because Akbar proved to be one of the greatest leaders of all history. Interestingly, Akbar's reign was contemporaneous with those of several other remarkable monarchs, including Elizabeth I of England, Philip of Spain, and the Muslim rulers Suleyman the Magnificent and Abbas I. Akbar was a match for any one of these very formidable rivals.

Like his father and grandfather, Akbar was a fine military commander with great personal courage. But unlike his predecessors, Akbar also had a vision of empire and sense of mission that hinged on uniting India under his rule. A workaholic who seldom slept more than three hours a night, Akbar personally oversaw the building of the military and administrative systems that would form the backbone of the Mughal Empire for centuries. He also patronized the arts and entered into complex religious and philosophical discussions with learned scholars from throughout the Muslim, Christian, and Hindu worlds. In addition, Akbar found time to carry out social reforms and invent his own universalistic religion. Though illiterate—there had been little time for book learning when his father fought for survival in the wilderness—Akbar had an insatiable curiosity and an incredible memory. By having others read aloud to him, he became educated in many fields.

At first with the help of senior advisors, but soon on his own, Akbar routed the enemies who had hoped to capitalize on the Mughals' misfortunes. In the decades after 1560, when he took charge of the government, Akbar's armies greatly extended the empire with conquests throughout north and central India. But it was Akbar's social policies and administrative genius that made it possible to establish the foundations of a lasting dominion in the subcontinent. He pursued a policy of reconciliation and cooperation with the Hindu princes and the Hindu majority of the population of his realm. He encouraged intermarriage between the Mughal aristocracy and the families of the Hindu Rajput rulers. Akbar also abolished the much-hated *jizya,* or head tax, that earlier Muslim rulers had levied on Hindu unbelievers. He promoted Hindus to the highest ranks in the government, ended a long-standing ban on the building of new Hindu temples, and ordered Muslims to respect cows, which the Hindu majority viewed as sacred.

Despite the success of these policies in reconciling the Hindu majority to Muslim rule, Akbar viewed tolerance as merely the first stage in a longer strategy to put an end to sectarian divisions in the subconti-

THE PAST

The Basis of Imperial Power in the Rival Muslim Empires

The tables below provide the vital statistics of each of the three great Muslim empires of the early modern era. Use these to determine the relative strengths and weaknesses of each of the empires. Also make use of the maps provided throughout this chapter to include geographical factors and incorporate points from the text with relevance to the questions posed below.

Questions: Which of the rival empires has the largest resource base? On the basis of your impressions from the text discussion, which is the most formidable in terms of artisan production and external trade? Which empire does geography favor the most in terms of defending itself and projecting its power? Which was the most secure/most threatened by a) rival powers? b) internal enemies? Which of these threats proved the most powerful and why? How would you rank the three empires in terms of overall military strength? What long-term problems can you identify regarding the survival of these imperial systems in the changing global system of the early modern era?

Vital Statistics of the Gunpowder Empires

	Land Area	Approximate Population	Religious Composition	Estimated Size of Military Forces	Source of Cannon/Firearms
Ottoman Empire c. 1566	c. 1,200,000 sq. mi.	30–35 million	Large majority Sunni Muslim; plus significant Jewish and Christian minorities	Largest army recorded— 200,000 cavalry, infantry, artillery; 90 warships+	Produced locally
Safavid Empire 1600	c. 750,000 sq. mi.	No reliable consensus; perhaps 10–15 million	Majority Sh'ia Muslim; small Sunni, Jewish and Christian minorities	40–50,000 cavalry, infantry, artillery; no navy	Imported cannon not widely used, except by European mercenaries
Mughal Empire c. 1600	c. 1,000,000 sq. mi.	105–110 million	10–15% Muslim (divided Sunni/Sh'ia); great majority Hindu and Sikh, Jewish, Christian minorities	Armies in hundreds of thousands reported; cavalry, infantry, artillery; no navy	Imported and produced locally

c. = approximations or rough estimates

nent. Blending elements of the many religions with which he was familiar, he invented a new faith, the *Din-i-Ilahi*, that he believed could be used to unite his Hindu and Muslim subjects. If the adherents of India's diverse religions could be convinced to embrace this common creed, Akbar reasoned, sectarian quarrels and even violent conflict could be brought to an end.

Like their counterparts in the Ottoman and Safavid empires, the Muslim and Hindu warrior aristocrats who formed the core of the supporters of the Mughal dynasty were granted peasant villages for their support. In turn, they were required to main-tain a specified number of cavalry and to be on call if the emperor needed their services. The court and the central bureaucracy were supported by revenues drawn from the tribute paid by the military retainers and from taxes on lands set aside for the support of the imperial household. Because of a shortage of administrators, in most areas local notables, many of whom were Hindu, were left in place as long as they swore allegiance to the Mughal rulers and paid their taxes on time. These arrangements left the control and welfare of the village population largely in the hands of the military retainers of the dynasty and local power brokers.

Social Reform and Social Change

In addition to his administrative reforms, Akbar pushed for social changes that he believed would greatly benefit his subjects. Beyond the public works typically favored by able Muslim rulers, Akbar sought to improve the calendar, to establish living quarters for the large population of beggars and vagabonds in the large cities, and to regulate the consumption of alcohol. Whatever success the latter campaign may have had in Indian society as a whole, it apparently failed in Akbar's own house-hold, for one of his sons was reputed to drink 20 cups of double-distilled wine per day.

More than any of Akbar's many reform efforts, those involving the position of women demon-strated how far the Mughal ruler was in advance of his time. He encouraged widow remarriage, at that point taboo for both Hindus and Muslims, and dis-couraged child marriages. The latter were so wide-spread among the upper classes that he did not try to outlaw them, and it is doubtful that his disap-proval did much to curb the practice. Akbar did legally prohibit sati, or the burning of high-caste Hindu women on their husbands' funeral pyres (Figure 26.5). Because this custom was deeply entrenched among the Rajput princes and warrior classes that were some of his most faithful allies, this was a risky move on Akbar's part. But he was so determined to eradicate sati, particularly in cases where the widow was pressured to agree to be burned alive, that he once personally rescued a young girl despite the protestations of her angry relatives. He also tried to provide relief for women trapped in purdah, or seclusion in their homes, by encouraging the merchants of Delhi and other cities to set aside special market days for women only.

Figure 26.5 *This engraving from a late 16th-century German traveler's account of India shows a European artist's impression of an Indian widow committing sati. Not surprisingly, this practice of burning high-caste widows on their deceased husbands' funeral pyres often was described at great length by European visitors in this era. There was some disagreement in their accounts as to whether the women went willingly into the fire, as some early authors claimed. Later inquiries in the British period revealed that some of the widows had been drugged and others tied to the funeral pyre itself. It is likely that most simply caved in to the relentless pressure applied by their dead spouse's relatives and their own children.*

Mughal Splendor and Early European Contacts

Despite his many successes and the civil peace and prosperity his reign brought to much of northern India, Akbar died a lonely and discouraged man. By 1605, he had outlived most of his friends and faced revolts by sons eager to claim his throne. Above all, he died knowing that Din-i-Ilahi, the religion he had created to reconcile his Hindu and Muslim subjects, had been rejected by both.

Although neither of his successors, Jahangir (1605–1627) or Shah Jahan (1627–1658), added much territory to the empire Akbar had left them, in their reigns Mughal India reached the peak of its splendor. European visitors marveled at the size and opulence of the chief Mughal cities: Delhi, Agra, and Lahore. The huge Mughal armies, replete with elephant and artillery corps, dwarfed those of even the most powerful European rulers at the time. Some of the more perceptive European observers, such as Francois Bernier, also noted the poverty in which the lower classes in both town and country-side lived and the lack of discipline and training of most of the soldiers in the Mughal armies. Perhaps most ominously, Bernier added that in invention and the sciences, India had fallen far behind western Europe in most areas.

Nonetheless, by the late 17th century, Mughal India had become one of the major overseas destinations for European traders. They brought products from throughout Asia, though little from Europe itself, to exchange for a variety of Indian manufactures, particularly the subcontinent's famed cotton textiles. The trade gap that the demand for Indian cotton cloth and clothing had created in the West in Roman times persisted millennia later. The 17th- and 18th-century rage for Indian textile products is reflected in the following ditty from *Prince Butler's Tales*, written in England in 1696:

> Our ladyes all were sent a gadding
>
> After these toys they ran a madding
>
> And nothing then would please their fancies
>
> Nor dolls, nor joans [cotton caps]
>
> Nor wanton nancies.
>
> Unless it be of Indian making.

The importance of the Indian textile trade is also indicated by the names we still use for different kinds of cotton cloth, from calico (after the Indian port city of Calicut) to chintz and muslin, as well as by our names for cotton clothes such as pajamas.

Because they were easily washed and inexpensive, Indian textiles first won a large market among the working and middle classes in Britain and elsewhere in Europe. In the reigns of Queen Mary and Queen Anne, fine Indian cloth came into fashion at the court as well. An incident from the reign of the Mughal emperor *Aurangzeb*, who succeeded Shah Jahan, suggests just how fine the cloth in question was. Aurangzeb, a religious zealot, scolded his favorite daughter for appearing in his presence in garments that revealed so much of her body. The daughter protested that she had on three layers of fine cotton clothing. It is thus no wonder that even after industrialization had revolutionized cotton textile manufacture in England, European visitors to India continued to observe and write in great detail about the techniques Indian artisans used to weave and dye cotton cloth. The popularity of Madras cloth today demonstrates that this interest has not died out.

Artistic Achievement in the Mughal Era

Both Jahangir and Shah Jahan continued Akbar's policy of tolerance toward the Hindu majority and retained most of the alliances he had forged with Hindu princes and local leaders. They made little attempt to change the administrative apparatus they had inherited from Akbar, and they fought their wars in much the same way as the founders of the dynasty had. Both mounted campaigns to crush potential enemies and in some cases to enlarge the empire. But neither was as interested in conquest and politics as in enjoying the good life. Both were fond of drink, female dancers, and the pleasure gardens they had laid out from Kashmir to Allahabad. Both were delighted by polo matches (a game invented by the princes of India), ox and tiger or elephant fights, and games of pachisi, which they played on life-sized boards with palace dancers as chips. Both took great pleasure in the elaborate court ceremonies that blended Indian and Persian precedents, lavish state processions, their palaces and jewel-studded wardrobes, and the scented and sweetened ices that were rushed from the cool mountains in the north to their capitals on the sweltering plains.

Jahangir and Shah Jahan are best remembered as two of the greatest patrons of the fine arts in human history. They expanded the painting workshops that had been started by the early Mughals so that thousands of exquisite miniatures could be produced during their reigns. Some of these paintings show the influence of European painting: at times superficial, as in the addition of halos and cherubs to portraits of Jahangir; at times more fundamental, as when Indian artists tried to introduce true perspective or Christian religious themes into their work. However, most of the miniatures are devoted to more traditional Islamic subjects, such as battles, scenes of life at court, and wonderfully detailed paintings of animals and plants.

Both Jahangir and Shah Jahan also devoted a good deal of money and effort to building some of the most stunning architectural works of all time. The best known of these is the *Taj Mahal* (Figure 26.6), which has become a symbol for India itself. But structures such as the audience hall in the Red Fort at Delhi, Akbar's tomb at Sikandra, and the tomb of Itimad al-Dowleh at Agra rival the Taj Mahal in design and perhaps surpass it in the beauty of their detail and decoration.

At its best, Mughal architecture blends what is finest in the Persian and Hindu traditions. It fuses the Islamic genius for domes, arches, and minarets and the balance between them with the Hindu love of ornament. In place of the ceramic tiles the Persians used to finish their mosques and tombs, Indian artisans substituted gleaming white marble, inset with semiprecious stones arranged in floral and geometric patterns. Extensive use was also made of marble reflecting pools, the most famous of which mirrors the beauty of the Taj Mahal. When these pools were inlaid with floral patterns and provided with fountains, the rippling water appeared to give life to the stone plant forms. Like the architects and artisans of the Ottoman Empire and Safavid Persia, those who served the Mughal rulers strove to create paradise on earth, an aspiration that was carved in marble on the audience hall of the Red Fort at Delhi. Around the ceiling of the great hall, it is written "If there is paradise on earth—It is here … it is here."

Court Politics and the Position of Elite and Ordinary Women

Not surprisingly, two rulers who were so absorbed in the arts and the pursuit of pleasure left most of the

Figure 26.6 *Perhaps no single building has come to symbolize Indian civilization more than the Taj Mahal. The grace and elegance of the tomb that Shah Jahan built in his wife's honor provide an enduring source of aesthetic delight. The white marble of the tomb is inlaid with flowers and geometric designs cut from semiprecious stones. The windows of the central chamber, which houses the tombs of Shah Jahan and Mumtaz Mahal, are decorated with carved marble screens, which add a sense of lightness and delicacy to the structure.*

mundane tasks of day-to-day administration largely in the hands of subordinates. In both cases, strong-willed wives took advantage of their husbands' neglect of politics to win positions of power and influence at the Mughal court. Jahangir's wife, *Nur Jahan,* continually amassed power as he became more and more addicted to wine and opium. She packed the court with able male relatives, and her faction dominated the empire for most of the later years of Jahangir's reign. Nur Jahan was a big spender, but not only on pomp and luxury. She became a major patron of much-needed charities in the major cities. Despite her success at pursuits that were normally reserved for males, she was defeated in the end by the roles of wife and mother to which many felt she should confine herself. She died giving birth to her 19th child.

Shah Jahan's consort, *Mumtaz Mahal,* also became actively involved in court politics. But Shah Jahan was a much more engaged and able ruler than Jahangir, and thus her opportunities to amass power behind the throne were more limited. She is remembered not for her political acumen but for the love and devotion Shah Jahan bestowed upon her, a love literally enshrined in the Taj Mahal, the tomb where she is buried. Shah Jahan's plans to build a companion tomb for himself in black marble across the Jumna River were foiled by the revolt of his sons and by his imprisonment. He was buried next to his wife in the Taj Mahal, but her tomb is central and far larger than that of her husband.

Although the position of women at the Mughal court improved in the middle years of the dynasty's power, that of women in the rest of Indian society declined. Child marriage grew more popular, and the age limit was lowered. It was not unheard of for girls to be married at age nine. Widow remarriage among Hindus nearly died out. Seclusion was more and more strictly enforced for upper-caste women, both Hindu and Muslim. Muslim women rarely ventured forth from their homes unveiled, and those who did risked verbal and even physical abuse. The governor of one of the provinces of the Mughal Empire divorced his wife because she was seen scrambling for her life, unveiled, from a runaway elephant. Among upper-caste Hindus, the practice of sati spread despite Shah Jahan's renewed efforts to outlaw it. The dwindling scope of productive roles left to women, combined with the burden of the dowry that had to be paid to marry them off, meant that the birth of a girl was increasingly seen as an inauspicious event. At court as well as in the homes of ordinary villagers, only the birth of a son was greeted with feasting and celebrations.

The Beginnings of Imperial Decline

Aurangzeb, Shah Jahan's son and successor, seized control of an empire that was threatened by internal decay and growing dangers from external enemies. For decades, the need for essential administrative, military, and social reforms had been ignored. The Mughal bureaucracy had grown bloated and corrupt. The army was equally bloated and backward in weaponry and tactics. Peasants and urban workers had seen their productivity and living standards fall steadily. The Taj Mahal and other wonders of the Mughal artistic imagination had been paid for by the mass of the people at a very high price.

Though not the cruel bigot he is often portrayed as, Aurangzeb was not the man to restore the dynasty's declining fortunes. Courageous, honest, intelligent, and hard-working, he seemed an ideal successor to two rulers who had so badly neglected the affairs of state. But Aurangzeb was driven by two ambitions that proved disastrous to his schemes to strengthen the empire. He was determined to extend Mughal control over the whole of the Indian subcontinent, and he believed that it was his duty to purify Indian Islam and rid it of the Hindu influences he was convinced were steadily corrupting it.

The first ambition increased the number of the empire's adversaries, strained the allegiance of its vassals and allies, and greatly overextended its huge but obsolete military forces. By the time of his death in 1707, after a reign of nearly 50 years, Aurangzeb had conquered most of the subcontinent and extended Mughal control as far north as Kabul in what is now Afghanistan. But the almost endless warfare of his years in power drained the treasury and further enlarged an inefficient bureaucracy and army without gaining corresponding increases in revenues to support them.

Equally critically, the long wars occupied much of Aurangzeb's time and energies, diverting him from the administrative tasks and reforms essential to the dynasty's continued strength. While he was leading his massive armies in the south, there were peasant uprisings and revolts by Muslim and Hindu princes in the north. Perhaps even more harmful to the imperial system was the growing autonomy of local leaders, who diverted more and more revenue from the central administration into their own coffers. On the northern borders, incursions by Persian and Afghan warrior bands were increasing.

While Aurangzeb's military campaigns strained the resources of the empire, his religious policies gravely weakened the internal alliances and disrupted the social peace Akbar had so skillfully established. Aurangzeb continued to employ Hindus in the imperial service; in fact, he did not have the Muslim replacements to do without them. But non-Muslims were given far fewer posts at the upper levels of the bureaucracy, and their personal contact with the emperor was severely restricted. Aurangzeb also took measures that he and his religious advisors felt would help rid their Muslim faith and culture of the Hindu influences that had permeated it over the centuries. He forbade the building of new temples and put an end to Hindu religious festivals at court. Aurangzeb also reinstated the hated head tax on unbelievers—a measure he hoped might prod them to convert to Islam. The tax fell heavily on the Hindu poor and in some cases drove them to support sectarian movements that rose up to resist Aurangzeb.

By the end of Aurangzeb's reign, the Mughal Empire was far larger than it had been under any of the earlier emperors, but it was also more unstable. Internal rebellions, particularly those mounted by the *Marattas* in western India, put an end to effective Mughal control over large areas. The rise of new sects, such as the *Sikhs* in the northwest, further strained the declining resources of an imperial system that was clearly overextended. The early leaders of the Sikhs originally tried to bridge the differences between Hindu and Muslim. But Mughal persecution of the new sect, which was seen as religiously heretical and a political threat to the dynasty, eventually transformed Sikhism into a staunchly anti-Muslim force within the subcontinent. In addition, Muslim kingdoms in central and east India continued to resist Mughal hegemony, and Islamic invaders waited at the poorly guarded passes through the Himalayas to strike and plunder once it was clear that the Mughals could no longer fend them off.

As centralized political control broke down and warfare increased throughout much of the subcontinent, regional lords became the keys to social cohesion and cultural creativity. In a sense, this shift from fairly centralized to regional political control marked a return to a pattern that had long been predominant in south Asian civilization. However, the fragmentation of political power in the early 18th century left tempting openings in many parts of India for foreign intervention and the economic exploitation of Indian artisans and peasants by local lords and foreign and local merchants. None would take fuller advantage of these opportunities than the English, who began the century as just one of many Asian and European contenders for the fallen crown of the Mughal

emperors. (On England's expansion in India, see Chapters 23 and 30.)

Conclusion

The Rise of Europe and the Eclipse of Islamic Civilization as the Pivot of the World Order

The internal causes of decline discussed in this chapter for the early modern Muslim empires probably were sufficient to destroy the great gunpowder empires of Islam. But each was also undermined by further weaknesses that had profound significance for Islamic civilization as a whole. Captivated by their rivalries with each other and the problems of holding together their empires, none of the dynasties took the rising threat from Europe seriously. They called on Western travelers and missionaries for advice in casting cannon or military tactics. But none of these Islamic peoples systematically monitored technological advances in Europe.

This failure to take strong measures to meet the challenges that European overseas expansion was creating for Islamic civilization was also responsible for the weakening of the economic basis of each of the empires. Key tax revenues and merchant profits were drained off by the rise of European trading empires in Asia (see Chapters 23 and 28). The Europeans' gains in ways to generate wealth and economic growth meant increasing losses for Muslim societies and political systems. These setbacks eventually proved critical to the failure of Muslim efforts to compete politically and militarily with their Christian rivals.

Despite these trends, Muslim rulers and scholars continued to take little interest in European learning. Thus, they were largely oblivious to the scientific ideas that were transforming the European worldview and steadily enhancing the Westerners' ability to tap new sources of power for production, communications, and war. The Muslims' contempt for Europeans and their culture was centuries old, but by the 16th century it was also a dangerous anachronism. In the 18th and 19th centuries, Muslim peoples and cultures paid a high price for this arrogance and their leaders' failure to recognize and match the intellectual and material accomplishments of the West.

Further Readings

The Lapidus survey suggested in the earlier chapters on Islam provides a fine introduction to the empires that are the focus of this chapter. The best detailed studies of the

Ottoman Empire can be found in the works of Halil Inalcik, especially his chapters in *The Cambridge History of Islam.* For a different perspective on the Ottomans, see Stanford Shaw's *History of the Ottoman Empire and Modern Turkey, vol. I (1780–1808)* (1976). Bernard Lewis's *Istanbul and the Civilization of the Ottoman Empire* (1963) provides internal perspectives of life at the center of the Ottoman Empire. Peter F. Sugar's *Southeastern Europe Under Ottoman Rule, 1354–1804* (1977) is a fine account of life in the Christian portions of the empire. R. M. Savory's writings, including his chapters in *The Cambridge History,* are the most reliable of a very limited literature in English on the Safavid period. Though quite specialized, Michel Mazzaoui's *The Origins of the Safavids* (1972) provides the fullest account of the beginnings and rise of the Safavid dynasty. The contributions to the volume that Savory edited on *Islamic Civilization* (1976) include good discussions of the arts and society in the Turkic and Persian sectors of the Islamic heartland. The introductory sections of Nikki Keddi's *Roots of Revolution* (1981) provide a good discussion of the relationship between religion and the state in the Safavid period.

The Ikram and Ahmad books cited in Chapter 13 on expansion of Islam in India are also good on the Mughals. Though specialized, the works of Muhammad Habib and Athar Alli on the Mughal Empire are also critical. Of the many works on Mughal art and architecture, Gavin Hambly's *Mughal Cities* (1968) has some of the best color plates and an intelligent commentary.

On the Web

Virtual visits to the palaces of the Mughals (http://rubens.anu.edu.au/student.projects/tajmahal/mughal.html), the Ottomans (http://www.ee.bilkent.edu.tr/~history/topkapi.html and http://interactive.m2.org/) and the Safavids (http://bridge.anglia.ac.uk/~trochford/Khakopol.html) provide clear evidence of the splendor of their empires.

A simulated interview with the Mughal Emperor Akbar (http://itihaas.com/medieval/akbar2.html) lends insight into his early struggles with his tutors, his skill as an empire-builder and the wisdom of his policy of religious toleration as embodied in his Din-i-Illahi.

The brilliant art and literary record left by some Mughal and Ottoman emperors provides glimpses into the working of their regimes as is revealed by the *Akbarnama* (http://www.bampfa.berkley.edu/exhibits/indian/u0300.htm and http://faculty-wed.at.nwu.edu/art-history/fraser/b40/ mughal_India.html).

Further insight into the everyday politics of gunpowder empires can be obtained through a reading of the memoirs of a Serb janissary, Konstantin Mihailovic, excerpts from which are offered at http://www.humanities.ccny.ccny.edu/History/reader/jan.htm.

Chapter 27

Africa and the Africans in the Age of the Atlantic Slave Trade

West African slave market.

While the new empires dominated the core areas of the Muslim world during the early modern centuries, sub-Saharan Africa, previously linked to the Muslim world in many ways, moved into a different orbit. Islam remained important, and in eastern Africa so did trade with western Asia, but the rise of the West and of the Western-dominated world economy proved to be a powerful force in recasting the framework of African history. The strength of earlier African cultural and political traditions persisted in many places, but the impact of the West was the newest influence in Africa and in some respects an immensely powerful one. African history had its own pace and rhythm, and this chapter therefore exceeds the chronological boundaries of the early modern period. The influences of Islam and the West initiated or intensified processes of religious conversion, political reorganization, and social change that persisted in some cases to the 19th century. The distinctive nature and chronology of African history should not blind us to its role in world history.

During the age of European maritime and commercial expansion, large areas of Africa were brought into the orbit of the expanding world economy and were influenced by the transformation taking place. Not all parts of Africa were influenced in the same way or at the same time. After 1450, the growing and often bitter contacts between Europeans and Africans, primarily through the slave trade, linked the destiny of Africa to broader external trends and resulted in a diaspora of millions of Africans to the Middle East, Europe, and especially the Americas. Not all European contact with Africa was centered on the slave trade, nor was the desire for slaves the only impulse behind European explorations, but the slave trade after 1600 overshadowed other activities until the mid-19th century.

This process had a direct impact on certain areas of Africa, and it also made Africans an important element in the changing balance of world civilizations. The forced movement of Africans as captive laborers and the creation of slave-based societies in the Americas were major aspects of the formation of the modern world and the growth of the economies of western Europe. This forced migration was part of the international exchange of foods, diseases, animals, and ideas that marked the era and had a profound influence on the indigenous peoples in various regions, as we saw in the case of the Americas. Moreover, in large areas of the Americas colonized by Europeans, where slavery came to be the predominant form of labor, African culture was transferred, contributing to the creation of new cultural forms. In this chapter we examine the history of parts of Africa in the age of the slave trade and the creation of slave societies in the Atlantic world as part of the general process of European expansion and the creation of a world economy.

1400 c.e.	1500 c.e.	1600 c.e.	1700 c.e.	1800 c.e.
1415 Portuguese capture Ceuta (Morocco); beginning of European expansion **1441** First shipment of African slaves brought directly from Africa to Portugal **1481** Portuguese fort established at El Mina	**1562** Beginnings of English slave trade **1570** Portuguese establish colony in Angola **1591** Fall of Songhay Empire	**1652** Dutch establish colony at Cape of Good Hope	**1700–1717** Osei Tutu unifies the Asante kingdom **1713** English get right to import slaves to Spanish Empire **1720s** Rise of the kingdom of Dahomey **1790s** Abolitionist movement gains strength in England **1792** Slave uprising in Haiti	**1804** Usuman Dan Fodio leads Hausa expansion **1815** Cape colony comes under formal British control **1818–1828** Shaka forges Zulu power and expansion; *Mfecane* under way **1833** Great Britain abolishes slavery in the West Indies **1834** Boers make "great trek" into Natal

Although much of the analysis in this chapter emphasizes the increasing linkage between Africa and the wider world, it should be made clear at the outset that many fundamental processes of African development, as discussed in Chapters 10 and 14, continued throughout this period. Almost all of Africa remained independent of outside political control, and most cultural development was autonomous as well. Africa differed profoundly from Latin America in these respects during the early modern centuries.

A variety of trends affected various parts of the sub-Saharan region. Islam consolidated its position in east Africa and the Sudan. In Ethiopia, the Christian kingdom of the highlands continued to hold off its Muslim rivals. In many places in Africa, as in Europe, independent states continued to form and expand, perhaps as a result of a population expansion that followed the spread of iron tools and improved agriculture. Kingdoms spread to new areas. Scholars disagree on the extent to which these long-term developments were affected by Europeans and the rise of the Atlantic slave trade. Some argue that the enlarged political scale—the growth of large kingdoms through much of the subcontinent—was the dominant theme of the period and that slavery was one of its byproducts. Others see European demand as a major impulse in political expansion. In this chapter we emphasize the impact of slavery and the slave trade because our focus is not simply the geographic region of Africa but the African peoples who were swept into the expanding international economy.

THE ATLANTIC SLAVE TRADE

⚫⚫ *Early Portuguese contacts set the patterns for contact with the African coast. The slave trade expanded to meet the demand for labor in the new American colonies, and millions were exported in an organized commerce that involved Europeans and Africans.*

Portuguese ships pushed down the west African coast and finally reached the Cape of Good Hope in 1487 (Map 27.1). Along the coast, the Portuguese established *factories:* forts and trading posts with resident merchants. The most important of these was *El Mina* (1482) in the heart of the gold-producing region of the forest zone. These forts allowed the Portuguese to exercise some control with few personnel. Although the early voyagers carried out some raids, once out of range of their cannons, the Portuguese simply were not powerful enough to enforce their will on the larger west African states. Therefore, most forts were established with the consent of local rulers, who benefited from access to European commodities and sometimes from the military support the Portuguese provided in local wars.

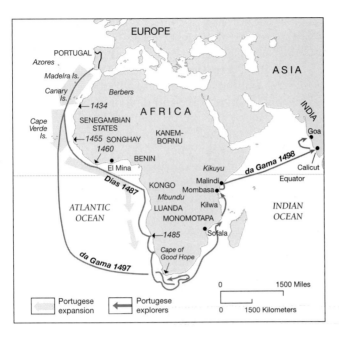

Map 27.1 *Portuguese Expansion and Major African Kingdoms*

Africans acquired goods from the Portuguese, who sometimes provided African rulers with slaves brought from other stretches of the coast. In return, the Portuguese received ivory, pepper, animal skins, and gold. From El Mina, Accra, and other trade forts, routes led directly into the gold-producing regions of the interior, so that the Portuguese eventually traded with Mande and Soninke merchants from Mali and Songhay. Much of the Portuguese success resulted from their ability to penetrate the existing African trade routes, to which they could also add specialized items. Portuguese and African–Portuguese mulatto traders struck out into the interior to establish trade contacts and collection points. These isolated *lança-dos* provided essential links between the economies of the African interior and the nodules of European mercantilism on the coast.

Trade was the basis of Portuguese relations with Africans, but in the wake of commerce came political, religious, and social relations. The small states of the Senegambian coast did not impress the Portuguese, and they were particularly suspicious of Muslims, their traditional enemies. When they reached the Gold Coast (modern Ghana) and found the kingdom of Benin, they were impressed both by the power of the ruler and by the magnificence of his court. Other large African states also provoked similar responses.

Missionary efforts were made to convert the rulers of Benin, Kongo, and other African kingdoms. The Portuguese contacted the Kongo kingdom south

of the Zaire River about 1484. The missionaries achieved a major success in Kongo, where members of the royal family were converted. The ruler, *Nzinga Mvemba* (1507–1543), with the help of Portuguese advisors and missionaries, brought the whole kingdom to Christianity. Attempts were made to "Europeanize" the kingdom. Portugal and Kongo exchanged ambassadors and dealt with each other with a certain equality in this early period, but eventually enslavement of his subjects led Nzinga Mvemba to try to end the slave trade and limit Portuguese activities. He was only partially successful because of Portugal's control of Kongo's ability to communicate with the outside world and its dominance over Kongo's trade.

These first contacts were marked by cultural preconceptions as well as by appreciation and curiosity. Africans found the newcomers strange and at first tried to fit them into their existing concepts of the spiritual and natural world. Images of Portuguese soldiers and traders began to appear in the bronzes of Benin and the carved ivory sculptures of other African peoples (see Figure 27.1). The Portuguese tended to look on Africans as savages and pagans who were also capable of civilized behavior and conversion.

Portuguese exploration continued southward toward the Cape of Good Hope and beyond in the 16th century. Early contacts were made with the Mbundu peoples south of Kongo in the 1520s, and

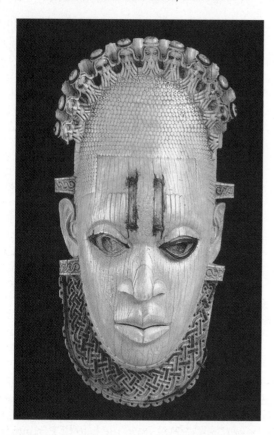

Figure 27.1. *African artists were impressed by Europeans and sometimes incorporated them in their own work, as can be seen in the headpiece of this beautifully carved ivory head of a Benin monarch. Europeans in turn employed African artisans to produce decorative luxury goods.*

a more permanent Portuguese settlement was established there in the 1570s with the foundation of *Luanda* on the coast. This became the basis for the Portuguese colony of Angola. As we have already seen, the Portuguese tried to dominate the existing trading system of the African ports in the Indian Ocean and Red Sea. They established a base on Mozambique Island and then secured bases at Kilwa, Mombasa, Sofala, and other ports that gave them access to the gold trade from Monomotapa (Mwenemutapa) in the interior. In east Africa, as on the west African coast, the number of permanent Portuguese settlers was minimal. The Portuguese effort was primarily commercial and military, although it was always accompanied by a strong missionary effort.

The patterns of contact established by the Portuguese were followed by others. In the 17th century, the Dutch, English, French, and others competed with the Portuguese and displaced them to some extent, but the system of fortified trading stations, the combination of force and diplomacy, alliances with local rulers, and the predominance of commercial relations continued as the principal pattern of European contact with Africa.

Although for a long time Portugal's major interest was in gold, pepper, and other products, a central element in this pattern was the slave trade. Slavery as an institution had been extensive in the Roman Empire but had died out in most of Europe during the Middle Ages, when it was replaced by serfdom. In the Mediterranean and in Iberia, however, where there was an active military frontier between Christians and Muslims, it had remained important. Moreover, the trans-Saharan slave trade had brought small numbers of black Africans into the Mediterranean throughout the period. The Portuguese voyages now opened a direct channel to sub-Saharan Africa. The first slaves brought directly to Portugal from Africa arrived in 1441, and after that date slaves became a common trade item. The Portuguese and later other Europeans raided for slaves along the coast, but the numbers acquired in this way were small. After initial raids, Europeans found that trade was a much more secure and profitable way to get these human cargoes. For example, the Portuguese sent about 50 slaves per year to Portugal before 1450, when raiding was prevalent, but by 1460 some 500 slaves per year arrived in Portugal as a trade with African rulers developed. Whether the victims were acquired by raiding or by trade, the effects on them were similar. An eyewitness to the unloading of slaves in Portugal in 1444 wrote,

> But what heart could be so hard as not to be pierced with piteous feelings to see that company? For some kept their heads low and their faces bathed in tears, looking one upon another; others stood groaning very dolorously, looking up to the height of heaven, fixing their eyes upon it, crying out loudly, as if asking help of the Father of Nature.

The slave trade was given added impetus when the Portuguese and the Spanish began to develop sugar plantations on the Atlantic islands of Madeira (Portugal) and the Canaries (Spain) and off the

African coast on Portuguese São Tomé. Sugar production demanded many workers and constant labor under difficult conditions, usually in a tropical or subtropical environment. The plantation system of organization associated with sugar, in which managers were able to direct and control laborers over long periods with little restraint, was later extended to America and then to other crops. Although the system did not depend only on Africans, they became the primary plantation laborers in the Atlantic world. The slave trade grew significantly in volume and complexity after 1550 as the American plantation colonies, especially Brazil, began to develop. By 1600, the slave trade predominated over all other kinds of commerce on the African coast.

Trend Toward Expansion

Although debate and controversy surround many aspects of the history of slavery, it is perhaps best to start with the numbers. Estimates of the volume of the trade vary widely, and scholars still debate the figures and their implications, but the range of calculations has been narrowed by recent research. Between 1450 and 1850, it is estimated that about 12 million Africans were shipped across the Atlantic, and with a mortality rate of 10 to 20 percent on the ships, about 10 or 11 million Africans actually arrived in the Americas. How many people died in Africa as a result of the slaving wars or in the forced marches to the coast is unknown, but estimates have been as high as one-third of the total captured. The volume changed over time. In the 16th century, the numbers were small, but they increased to perhaps 16,000 per year in the 17th century. The 18th century was the great age of the Atlantic slave trade; probably more than 7 million slaves, or more than 80 percent of all those embarked, were exported between 1700 and 1800. By the latter date, about 3 million slaves lived in the Americas. Even in the 19th century, when slavery was under attack, the trade to some places continued. Cuba received some 700,000 slaves, and Brazil took more than 1 million in that century alone.

The high volume of the slave trade was necessary to the slave owners because in most of the slave regimes in the Caribbean and Latin America slave mortality was high and fertility was low (partly because more men than women were imported). Thus, over time there was usually a loss of population. The only way to maintain or expand the number of slaves was by importing more from Africa. The one exception to this pattern was the southern United States, where the slave population grew, perhaps because of the temperate climate and the fact that few worked in the most dangerous and unhealthy occupations, such as sugar growing and mining. By 1860, almost 6 million slaves worked in the Americas, about 4 million of them in the southern United States, an area that depended more on natural population growth than on the Atlantic slave trade. In terms of total population, however, slaves in British North America were never more than one-fourth of the whole population, whereas in the British and French Caribbean they made up 80 to 90 percent of the population.

The dimensions of the trade varied over time, reflecting the economic and political situation in the Americas. From 1530 to 1650, Spanish America and Brazil received the majority of African slaves, but after the English and French began to grow sugar in the

---

TABLE 27-1
Slave Exports from Africa, 1500–1900 (thousands)

	1500–1600 (%)	1600–1700 (%)	1700–1800 (%)	1800–1900 (%)	Total
Red Sea	200 (17)	200 (7)	200 (3)	450 (8)	1050 (6)
Trans-Sahara	550 (47)	700 (24)	700 (9)	1200 (22)	3150 (19)
East Africa and Indian Ocean	100 (9)	100 (4)	400 (5)	442 (8)	1042 (6)
Trans-Atlantic	325 (28)	1868 (65)	6133 (83)	3330 (61)	11,656 (69)
					16,898

Source: Adapted from Paul Lovejoy, *Transformations in Slavery: A History of Slavery in Africa* (1983).

Caribbean, the islands of Jamaica, Barbados, and St. Domingue (Haiti) became important terminals for the slavers. By the 18th century, Virginia and the Carolinas in North America had also become major destinations, although they never rivaled the Caribbean or Brazil.

Between 1550 and 1850, Brazil alone received 3.5 to 5 million Africans, or about 42 percent of all those who reached the New World. The Caribbean islands, dedicated to sugar production, were the other major destination of Africans. The island colonies of St. Domingue and Jamaica each received more than 1 million slaves in the 18th century alone.

It should be emphasized that these figures represent only the volume in the Atlantic slave trade. The older trans-Sahara, Red Sea, and east African slave trades in the hands of Muslim traders continued throughout the period and added another 3 million people to the total of Africans exported as slaves in this period.

The Atlantic slave trade drew slaves from across the continent, and its concentration shifted over time. In the 16th century, the majority of slaves were exported from the Senegambia region, but by the 17th century, west central Africa (modern Zaire and Angola) was the major supplier. That area was joined by the areas of the Gold Coast and the Slave Coast—Dahomey and Benin—at the end of the century, when Benin alone was exporting more than 10,000 slaves per year. In the century that followed, wars for control of the interior created the large states of *Asante* among the Akan peoples of the Gold Coast and *Dahomey* among the Fon peoples. These wars were both the cause and the result of increasing slave exports from these regions.

TABLE 27-2
Destinations of African Slaves in the Atlantic Slave Trade

	Thousands	Percent
British North America	523	5
Spanish America	1687	15
British Caribbean	2443	21
French Caribbean	1655	15
Dutch Caribbean	500	4
Danish Caribbean	50	0.4
Brazil	4190	37
Old World	297	2.6
	11,345	

Source: James Rawley, *The Transatlantic Slave Trade* (1981), 428.

Demographic Patterns

The majority of the trans-Saharan slave trade consisted of women to be used as concubines and domestic servants in north Africa and the Middle East, but the Atlantic slave trade concentrated on men. To some extent this was because planters and mine owners in the Americas were seeking workers for heavy labor and were not eager to risk buying children because of the high levels of mortality. Also, African societies that sold captives into slavery often preferred to sell the men and keep the women and children as domestic slaves or to extend existing kin groups.

The Atlantic trade seems to have had a demographic impact on at least certain parts of west and central Africa. One estimate is that the population of about 25 million in 1850 in those regions was about one-half what it would have been had there been no slave trade. It is true that the trans-Atlantic trade carried more men than women and more women than children, but captive women and children who remained in Africa swelled the numbers of enslaved people and skewed the proportion of women to men in the African enslaving societies. Finally, as the Atlantic trade developed, new crops, such as maize and manioc, were introduced to Africa that provided new food resources for the population and helped it recover from the losses to the slave trade.

Organization of the Trade

The patterns of contact and trade established by the Portuguese at first were followed by rival Europeans on the African coast. Control of the slave trade or a portion of it generally reflected the political situation in Europe. For one and a half centuries, until about 1630, the Portuguese controlled most of the coastal trade and were the major suppliers of their own colony of Brazil and the Spanish settlements in America. The growth of slave-based plantation colonies in the Caribbean and elsewhere led other Europeans to compete with the Portuguese. The Dutch became major competitors when they seized El Mina in 1637 and temporarily took Angola (1641–1648) to supply their conquests in northeastern Brazil. By the 1660s, the English were eager to have their own source of slaves for their growing colonies in Barbados, Jamaica, and Virginia. The *Royal African Company* was chartered for that purpose. The French made similar arrangements in the 1660s, but not until the 18th century did France become a major carrier. Like other small European

Figure 27.2. *The annual yam harvest festival was an occasion when the power and authority of the Asante ruler could be displayed. The English observers who painted this scene were impressed by the might of this West African kingdom.*

nations, even Denmark had its agents and forts on the African coast. Each nation established merchant towns or trade forts at places such as Axim, Nembe, Bonny, Whydah, and Luanda from which a steady source of captives could be obtained. For the Europeans stationed on the coast, Africa was also a graveyard because of the tropical diseases they encountered. Fewer than 10 percent of the employees of the Royal Africa Company who went to Africa ever returned to England, and the majority died in the first year out. European mortality among the crews of slave ships was also very high because of tropical diseases such as malaria. The slave trade proved deadly to all involved, but at least some of the Europeans had a choice, whereas for the enslaved Africans there was none.

European agents for the companies often had to deal directly with local rulers, paying a tax or offering gifts. Various forms of currency were used, such as iron bars, brass rings, and cowrie shells. The Spanish developed a complicated system in which a healthy man was called an *Indies piece*, and children and women were priced at fractions of that value. Slaves were brought to the coast by a variety of means. Sometimes, as in Angola, European military campaigns produced captives for slaves, or African and mulatto agents purchased captives at interior trade centers. In Dahomey, a royal monopoly was established to control the flow of slaves. Some groups used their position to tax or control the movement of slaves from the interior to the coast. Although African and European states tried to establish monopolies over the trade, private merchants often circumvented restrictions.

Clearly, both Europeans and Africans were actively involved in the slave trade. It was not always clear which side was in control. One group of English merchants on the Gold Coast complained of African insolence in 1784 because in negotiations the Africans had emphasized that "the country belongs to them." In any case, the result of this collaboration was to send millions of Africans into bondage in foreign lands.

Historians have long debated the profitability of the slave trade. Some argue that the profits were so great and constant that they were a major element in the rise of commercial capitalism and, later, the origins of the Industrial Revolution. Undoubtedly, many people profited from the trade in African slaves. A single slaving voyage might make a profit of as much as 300 percent, and merchants in the ports that specialized in fitting out ships for the slave trade, such as Liverpool, England, or Nantes, France—as well as African suppliers—derived a profit from the slave trade. But the slave trade also involved risks and costs, so that in the long run, profitability levels did not remain so high. In the late 18th century, profitability in the English slave trade probably ran from 5 to 10 percent on average, and in the French and Dutch trades it was slightly lower. The slave trade was little more profitable in the long run than most business activities of the age, and by itself was not a major source of the capital needed in the Industrial Revolution.

However, it is difficult to calculate the full economic importance of slavery to the economies of Europe because it was so directly linked to the plantation and mining economies of the Americas. During some periods, a *triangular trade* existed in which slaves were carried to the Americas; sugar, tobacco, and other goods were then carried to Europe; and European products were sent to the coast of Africa to begin the triangle again. Were profits from the slave trade accumulated in Liverpool invested in the textile industry of England? And if so, how important were these investments for the growth of that industry? We would need to calculate the value of goods produced in Europe for exchange in the slave trade as well as the profits derived from the colonies to measure the importance of slavery to the growth of the European economies. Still, the very persistence of the slave trade indicates its viability. The slave trade surely contributed to the formation of emerging capitalism in the Atlantic world. In Africa itself, the slave trade often drew economies into dependence on trade with Europeans and suppressed the growth of other economic activities.

It is clear that by the late 18th century, the slave trade and slavery were essential aspects of the economy of the Atlantic basin, and their importance was increasing. More than 40 percent of all the slaves that crossed the Atlantic embarked during the century after 1760, and the plantation economies of Brazil, the Caribbean, and the southern United States were booming in the early 19th century. The slave trade was profitable enough to keep merchants in it, and it contributed in some way to the expanding economy of western Europe. It was also the major way in which Africa was linked to the increasingly integrated economy of the world.

AFRICAN SOCIETIES, SLAVERY, AND THE SLAVE TRADE

The slave trade influenced African forms of servitude and the social and political development of African states. Newly powerful states such as Asante and Dahomey emerged in west Africa, and in the Sudan and east Africa, slavery also produced long-term effects.

Europeans in the age of the slave trade sometimes justified the enslavement of Africans by pointing out that slavery already existed on that continent. However, although forms of bondage were ancient in Africa, and the Muslim trans-Sahara and Red Sea trades already were established, the Atlantic trade interacted with and transformed these earlier aspects of slavery.

African societies had developed many forms of servitude, which varied from a peasant status to something much more like chattel slavery, in which people were considered things: "property with a soul," as Aristotle put it. African states usually were nonegalitarian, and because in many African societies all land was owned by the state or the ruler, the control of slaves was one of the few ways, if not the only way, in which individuals or lineages could increase their wealth and status. Slaves were used as servants, concubines, soldiers, administrators, and field workers. In some cases, as in the ancient empire of Ghana and in Kongo, there were whole villages of enslaved dependents who were required to pay tribute to the ruler. The Muslim traders of west Africa who linked the forest region to the savanna had slave porters as well as villages of slaves to supply their caravans. In many situations, these forms of servitude were fairly benign and were an extension of lineage and kinship systems. In others, however, they were exploitative economic and social relations that reinforced the hierarchies of various African societies and allowed the nobles, senior lineages, and rulers to exercise their power. Among the forest states of west Africa, such as Benin, and in the Kongo kingdom in central Africa, slavery was already an important institution before the European arrival, but the Atlantic trade opened up new opportunities for expansion and intensification of slavery in those societies.

Despite great variation in African societies and the fact that slaves sometimes attained positions of command and trust, in most cases slaves were denied choice about their lives and actions. They were placed in dependent or inferior positions, and they were often considered aliens. It is important to remember that the enslavement of women was a central feature of African slavery. Although slaves were used in many ways in African societies, domestic slavery and the extension of lineages through the addition of female members remained a central feature in many places. Some historians believe that the excess of women led to polygyny (having more than one wife at a time) and the creation of large harems by rulers and merchants, whose power was increased by this process, and the position of women was lowered in some societies.

In the Sudanic states of the savanna, Islamic concepts of slavery had been introduced. Slavery was viewed as a legitimate fate for nonbelievers but was illegal for Muslims. Despite the complaints of legal scholars such as Ahmad Baba of Timbuktu (1556–1627) against the enslavement of Muslims, many of the Sudanic states enslaved their captives, both pagan and Muslim. In the Niger Valley, slave communities produced agricultural surpluses for the rulers and nobles of Songhay, Gao, and other states. Slaves were used for gold mining and salt production and as caravan workers in the Sahara. Slavery was a widely diffused form of labor control and wealth in Africa.

The existence of slavery in Africa and the preexisting trade in people allowed Europeans to mobilize the commerce in slaves quickly by tapping existing routes and supplies. In this venture they were aided by the rulers of certain African states, who were anxious to acquire more slaves for themselves and to supply slaves to the Europeans in exchange for aid and commodities. In the 16th-century Kongo kingdom, the ruler had an army of 20,000 slaves as part of his household, and this gave him greater power than any Kongo ruler had ever held. In general, African rulers did not enslave their own people, except for crimes or in other unusual circumstances; rather, they enslaved their neighbors. Thus, expanding, centralizing states often were the major suppliers of slaves to the Europeans as well as to societies in which slavery was an important institution.

Slaving and African Politics

As one French agent put it, "The trade in slaves is the business of kings, rich men, and prime merchants." European merchants and royal officials were able to tap existing routes, markets, and institutions, but the new and constant demand also intensified enslavement in Africa and perhaps changed the nature of slavery itself in some African societies.

In the period between 1500 and 1750, as the gunpowder empires and expanding international commerce of Europe penetrated sub-Saharan Africa, existing states and societies often were transformed. As we saw in Chapter 14, the empire of Songhay controlled a vast region of the western savanna until its defeat by a Moroccan invasion in 1591, but for the most part the many states of central and western Africa were small and fragmented. This led to a situation of instability caused by competition and warfare as states tried to expand at the expense of their neighbors or to consolidate power by incorporating subject provinces. The warrior or soldier emerged in this situation as an important social type in states such as the Kongo kingdom and Dahomey as well as along the Zambezi River. The endless wars promoted the importance of the military and made the sale of captives into the slave trade an extension of the politics of regions of Africa. Sometimes, as among the Muslim states of the savanna or the Lake Chad region, wars took on a religious overtone of believers against nonbelievers, but in much of west and central Africa that was not the case. Some authors see this situation as a feature of African politics; others feel it was the result of European demand for new slaves. In either case, the result was the capture and sale of millions of human beings. Although increasing centralization and hierarchy could be seen in the enslaving African societies, a contrary trend of self-sufficiency and antiauthoritarian ideas developed among the peoples who bore the brunt of the slaving attacks.

One result of the presence of Europeans on the coast was a shift in the locus of power within Africa. Just as states such as Ghana and Songhay in the savanna took advantage of their position as intermediaries between the gold of the west African forests

Figure 27.3 *The size of African cities and the power of African rulers often impressed European observers. Here the city of Loango, capital of a kingdom on the Congo coast, is depicted as a bustling urban center. At this time it was a major port in the slave trade.*

and the trans-Saharan trade routes, the states closer to the coast or in contact with the Europeans could play a similar role. Those right on the coast tried to monopolize the trade with Europeans, but European meddling in their internal affairs and European fears of any coastal power that became too strong blocked the creation of centralized states under the shadow of European forts. Just beyond the coast it was different. With access to European goods, especially firearms, iron, horses, cloth, tobacco, and other goods, western and central African kingdoms began to redirect trade toward the coast and to expand their influence. Some historians have written of a gun and slave cycle in which increased firepower allowed these states to expand over their neighbors, producing more slaves, which they traded for more guns. The result was unending warfare and the disruption of societies as the search for slaves pushed ever farther into the interior.

Asante and Dahomey

Perhaps the effects of the slave trade on African societies are best seen in some specific cases. Several large states developed in west Africa during the slave trade era. Each represented a response to the realities of the European presence and the process of state formation long under way in Africa. Rulers in these states grew in power and often surrounded themselves with ritual authority and a luxurious court life as a way of reinforcing the position that their armies had won.

In the area called the Gold Coast by the Europeans, the empire of Asante (Ashanti) rose to prominence in the period of the slave trade. The Asante were members of the Akan people (the major group of modern Ghana) who had settled in and around Kumasi, a region of gold and kola nut production that lay between the coast and the Hausa and

Mande trading centers to the north. There were at least 20 small states, based on the matrilineal clans that were common to all the Akan peoples, but those of the Oyoko clan predominated. Their cooperation and their access to firearms after 1650 initiated a period of centralization and expansion. Under the vigorous *Osei Tutu* (d. 1717), the title *asantehene* was created to designate the supreme civil and religious leader. His golden stool became the symbol of an Asante union that was created by linking the many Akan clans under the authority of the asantehene but recognizing the autonomy of subordinate areas. An all-Asante council advised the ruler, and an ideology of unity was used to overcome the traditional clan divisions. With this new structure and a series of military reforms, conquest of the area began. By 1700, the Dutch on the coast realized that a new power had emerged, and they began to deal directly with it.

With control of the gold-producing zones and a constant supply of prisoners to be sold as slaves for more firearms, Asante maintained its power until the 1820s as the dominant state of the Gold Coast. Although gold continued to be a major item of export, by the end of the 17th century, slaves made up almost two-thirds of Asante's trade.

Farther to the east, in the area of the Bight of Benin (between the Volta and Benin rivers on what the Europeans called the Slave Coast), several large states developed. The kingdom of *Benin* was at the height of its power when the Europeans arrived. It traced its origins to the city of Ife and to the Yoruba peoples that were its neighbors, but it had become a separate and independent kingdom with its own well-developed political and artistic traditions, especially in the casting of bronze. As early as 1516, the ruler, or oba, limited the slave trade from Benin, and for a long time most trade with Europeans was controlled

Visualizing THE PAST

Symbols of African Kinship

*I*n many African societies, the symbols of authority and kingship had a ritual power. African kings were sacred or sacredness resided in the symbols of their authority. Art and design, by creating impressive ritual and civil objects, were often used to emphasize the power and prestige of the ruler and the links between the community and the king. In Dahomey, for example, royal treasures were paraded by the people as a way of creating a sense of pride and of awe among the viewers. Among the Fante people, young males of the chief's family carry staffs and decorative swords, each of which carries a message or symbolic meaning. Such ceremonies solidify the image of the king and link the generations. Arts can serve kingship and rulers by mobilizing artists, and by defining the images and messages to be conveyed, help to create culture. This was a technique of rule in no way limited to Africa.

Fante boys in Ghana holding symbolic swords.

directly by the king and was in pepper, textiles, and ivory rather than slaves. Eventually, European pressure and the goals of the Benin nobility combined to generate a significant slave trade in the 18th century, but Benin never made the slave trade its primary source of revenue or state policy.

The kingdom of Dahomey, which developed among the Fon (or Aja) peoples, had a different response to the European presence. It began to emerge as a power in the 17th century from its center at Abomey, about 70 miles from the coast. Its kings ruled with the advice of powerful councils, but by the 1720s access to firearms allowed the rulers to create an autocratic and sometimes brutal political regime based on the slave trade. In the 1720s, under King Agaja (1708–1740), the kingdom of Dahomey moved toward the coast, seizing in 1727 the port town of Whydah, which had attracted many European traders. Although Dahomey became to some extent a subject of the powerful neighboring Yoruba state of Oyo, whose cavalry and archers made it strong, Dahomey maintained its autonomy and turned increasingly to the cycle of firearms and slaves. The trade was controlled by the royal court, whose armies (including a regiment of women) were used to raid for more captives. As Dahomey expanded it eliminated the royal families and customs of the areas it conquered and imposed its own traditions. This resulted in the formation of a unified state, which lasted longer than some of its neighbors. Well into the 19th century, Dahomey was a slaving state, and dependence on the trade in human beings had negative effects on the society as a whole. More than 1.8 million slaves were exported from the Bight of Benin between 1640 and 1890.

This emphasis on the slave trade should not obscure the creative process within many of the African states. The growing divine authority of the rulers paralleled the rise of absolutism in Europe. It led to the development of new political forms, some of which had the power to limit the role of the king. In the Yoruba state of Oyo, for example, a governing council shared power with the ruler. In some states, a balance of offices kept central power in check. In Asante, the traditional village chiefs and officials whose authority was based on their lineage were increasingly challenged by new officials appointed by the asantehene as a state bureaucracy began to form.

The creativity of these societies was also seen in traditional arts. In many places, crafts such as bronze casting, woodcarving, and weaving flourished. Guilds of artisans developed in many societies, and their specialization produced crafts executed with great skill. In Benin and the Yoruba states, for example, remarkable and lifelike sculptures in wood and ivory continued to be produced. Often, however, the best artisans labored for the royal court, producing objects designed to honor the ruling family and reinforce the civil and religious authority of the king. This was true in architecture, weaving, and the decorative arts as well. Much of this artistic production also had a religious function or contained religious symbolism; African artists made the spiritual world visually apparent.

Europeans came to appreciate African arts and skills. In the 16th century the Portuguese began to employ African artists from Benin, Sierra Leone, and Kongo to work local ivory into ladles, saltcellars (containers), and other decorative objects that combined African and European motifs in beautifully carved designs. Although commissioned by Europeans and sometimes including European religious and political symbols, African artists found ways to incorporate traditional symbols and themes from motherhood to royal power. Many of these objects ended up in the collections of nobles and kings throughout Renaissance Europe. They demonstrated the growing contact between Africa and the wider world.

East Africa and the Sudan

West Africa obviously was the region most directly influenced by the trans-Atlantic slave trade, but there and elsewhere in Africa, long-term patterns of society and economy continued and intersected with the new external influences.

On the east coast of Africa, the Swahili trading cities continued their commerce in the Indian Ocean, adjusting to the military presence of the Portuguese and the Ottoman Turks. Trade to the interior continued to bring ivory, gold, and a steady supply of slaves. Many of these slaves were destined for the harems and households of Arabia and the Middle East, but a small number were carried away by the Europeans for their plantation colonies. The Portuguese and Indo-Portuguese settlers along the Zambezi River in Mozambique used slave soldiers to increase their territories, and certain groups in interior east Africa specialized in supplying ivory and slaves to the east African coast.

Figure 27.4 *Ivory hunting horn.*

Europeans did establish some plantation-style colonies on islands such as Mauritius in the Indian Ocean, and these depended on the east African slave trade.

On Zanzibar and other offshore islands, and later on the coast itself, Swahili, Indian, and Arabian merchants followed the European model and set up clove-producing plantations using African slave laborers. Some of the plantations were large, and by the 1860s Zanzibar had a slave population of about 100,000. The sultan of Zanzibar alone owned more than 4000 slaves in 1870. Slavery became a prominent feature of the east African coast, and the slave trade from the interior to these plantations and to the traditional slave markets of the Red Sea continued until the end of the 19th century.

Much less is known about the interior of eastern Africa. The well-watered and heavily populated region of the great lakes of the interior supported large and small kingdoms. Bantu speakers predominated, but many peoples inhabited the region. Linguistic and archeological evidence suggests that pastoralist peoples from the Upper Nile Valley with a distinctive late Iron Age technology moved southward into what is today western Kenya and Uganda, where they came into contact with Bantu speakers and with the farmers and herders who spoke another group of languages called Cushitic. The Bantu states absorbed the immigrants, even when the newcomers established ruling dynasties. Later Nilotic migrations, of people who spoke languages of the Nilotic group, especially of the *Luo* peoples, resulted in the construction of related dynasties among the states in the area of the large lakes of east central Africa. At Bunyoro, the Luo eventually established a ruling dynasty among the existing Bantu population. This kingdom exercised considerable power in the 16th and 17th centuries. Other related states formed in the region. In Buganda, near Lake Victoria, a strong monarchy ruled a heterogeneous population and dominated the region in the 16th century. These developments in the interior, as important as they were for the history of the region, were less influenced by the growing contact with the outside world than were other regions of Africa.

Across the continent in the northern savanna at the end of the 18th century, the process of Islamization, which had been important in the days of the Mali and Songhay empires, entered a new and violent stage that not only linked Islamization to the external slave trade and the growth of slavery in Africa but also produced other long-term effects in the region. After the breakup of Songhay in the 16th century, several successor states had developed. Some, such as the Bambara kingdom of Segu, were pagan. Others, such as the Hausa kingdoms in northern Nigeria, were ruled by Muslim royal families and urban aristocracies but continued to contain large numbers of animist subjects, most of whom were rural peasants. In these states the degree of Islamization was slight, and an accommodation between Muslims and animists was achieved. Beginning in the 1770s, Muslim reform movements began to sweep the western Sudan. Religious brotherhoods advocating a purifying Sufi variant of Islam extended their influence throughout the Muslim trade networks in the Senegambia region and the western Sudan. This movement had an intense impact on the *Fulani* (Fulbe), a pastoral people who were spread across a broad area of the western Sudan.

In 1804, Usuman Dan Fodio, a studious and charismatic Muslim Fulani scholar, began to preach the reformist ideology in the Hausa kingdoms. His movement became a revolution when in 1804, seeing himself as God's instrument, he preached a jihad against the Hausa kings, who, he felt, were not following the teachings of Muhammad. A great upheaval followed in which the Fulani took control of most of the Hausa states of northern Nigeria in the western Sudan. A new kingdom, based on the city of Sokoto, developed under Dan Fodio's son and brother. The Fulani expansion was driven not only by religious zeal but by political ambitions, as the attack on the well-established Muslim kingdom of Bornu demonstrated. The result of this upheaval was the creation of a powerful Sokoto state under a caliph, whose authority was established over cities such as Kano and Zaria and whose rulers became emirs of provinces within the Sokoto caliphate.

By the 1840s, the effects of Islamization and the Fulani expansion were felt across much of the interior of west Africa. New political units were created, a reformist Islam that tried to eliminate pagan practices spread, and social and cultural changes took place in the wake of these changes. Literacy became more widely dispersed, and new centers of trade, such as Kano, emerged in this period. Later jihads established other new states along similar lines. All of these changes had long-term effects on the region of the western Sudan.

These upheavals, moved by religious, political, and economic motives, were affected by the external pressures on Africa. They fed into the ongoing processes of the external slave trade and the development of slavery within African societies. Large numbers of captives resulting from the wars were exported down to the coast for sale to the Europeans, while another stream of slaves crossed the Sahara to north Africa. In the western and central Sudan, the level of slave labor rose, especially in the larger towns and along the trade routes. Slave villages, supplying royal courts and merchant activities as well as a plantation system, developed to produce peanuts and other crops. Slave women spun cotton and wove cloth for sale, slave artisans worked in the towns, and slaves served the caravan traders, but most slaves did agricultural labor. By the late 19th century, regions of the savanna contained large slave populations—in some places as much as 30 to 50 percent of the whole population. From the Senegambia region of Futa Jallon, across the Niger and Senegal basins, and to the east of Lake Chad, slavery became a central feature of the Sudanic states and remained so through the 19th century.

WHITE SETTLERS AND AFRICANS IN SOUTHERN AFRICA

In southern Africa, a Dutch colony eventually brought Europeans into conflict with Africans, especially the southern Bantu-speaking peoples. One of these groups, the Zulu, created under Shaka a powerful chiefdom during the early 19th century in a process of expansion that affected the whole region.

One area of Africa little affected by the slave trade in the early modern period was the southern end of the continent. As we saw in Chapter 14, this region was still occupied by non-Bantu hunting peoples, the San (Bushmen); by the Khoikhoi (Hottentots), who lived by hunting and sheep herding; and, after contact with the Bantu, by cattle-herding peoples. Peoples practicing farming and using iron tools were living south of the Limpopo River by the 3rd century C.E. Probably Bantu speakers, they spread southward and established their villages and cattle herds in the fertile lands along the eastern coast, where rainfall was favorable to their agricultural and pastoral way of life. The drier western regions toward the Kalahari Desert were left to the Khoikhoi and San. Mixed farming and pastoralism spread throughout the region in a complex process that involved migration, peaceful contacts, and warfare.

By the 16th century, Bantu-speaking peoples occupied much of the eastern regions of southern Africa. They practiced agriculture and herding;

worked iron and copper into tools, weapons, and adornments; and traded with their neighbors. They spoke related languages such as Tswana and Sotho as well as the Nguni languages such as Zulu and Xhosa. Among the Sotho, villages might have contained as many as 200 people; the Nguni lived in hamlets made up of a few extended families. Men worked as artisans and herders; women did the farming and housework, and sometimes organized their labor communally. Politically, chiefdoms of various sizes—many of them small, but a few with as many as 50,000 inhabitants—characterized the southern Bantu peoples. Chiefs held power with the support of relatives and with the acceptance of the people, but there was great variation in chiefly authority. The Bantu-speaking peoples' pattern of political organization and the splitting off of junior lineages to form new villages created a process of expansion that led to competition for land and the absorption of newly conquered groups. This situation became intense at the end of the 18th century, either because of the pressures and competition for foreign trade through the Portuguese outposts on the east African coast or because of the growth of population among the southern Bantu. In any case, the result was farther expansion southward into the path of another people who had arrived in southern Africa.

In 1652, the Dutch East India Company established a colony at the Cape of Good Hope to serve as a provisioning post for ships sailing to Asia. Large farms developed on the fertile lands around this colony. The Cape Colony depended on slave labor brought from Indonesia and Asia for a while, but it soon enslaved local Africans as well. Expansion of the colony and its labor needs led to a series of wars with the San and Khoikhoi populations, who were pushed farther to the north and west. By the 1760s, the Dutch, or Boer, farmers had crossed the Orange River in search of new lands. They saw the fertile plains and hills as theirs, and they saw the Africans as intruders and a possible source of labor. Competition and warfare resulted. By about 1800 the Cape Colony had about 17,000 settlers (or Afrikaners, as they came to be called), 26,000 slaves, and 14,000 Khoikhoi.

As the Boers were pushing northward, the southern Bantu were extending their movement to the south. Matters were also complicated by European events when Great Britain seized the Cape Colony in 1795 and then took it under formal British control in 1815. While the British government helped the settlers to clear out Africans from potential farming lands, government attempts to limit the Boer settlements and their use of African labor were unsuccessful. Meanwhile, competition for farming and grazing land led to a series of wars between the settlers and the Bantu during the early 19th century.

Various government measures, the accelerating arrival of English-speaking immigrants, and the lure of better lands caused groups of Boers to move to the north. These *voortrekkers* moved into lands occupied by the southern Nguni, eventually creating a number of autonomous Boer states. After 1834, when Britain abolished slavery and imposed restrictions on landholding, groups of Boers staged a *great trek* far to the north to be free of government interference. This movement eventually brought them across the Orange River and into Natal on the more fertile east coast, which the Boers believed to be only sparsely inhabited by Africans. They did not realize or care that the lack of population resulted from a great military upheaval taking place among the Bantu peoples of the region.

The Mfecane and the Zulu Rise to Power

Among the Nguni peoples, major changes had taken place. A unification process had begun in some of the northern chiefdoms, and a new military organization had emerged. In 1818, leadership fell to Shaka, a brilliant military tactician, who reformed the loose forces into regiments organized by lineage and age. Iron discipline and new tactics were introduced, including the use of a short stabbing spear to be used at close range. The army was made a permanent institution, and the regiments were housed together in separate villages. The fighting men were allowed to marry only after they had completed their service. Shaka's own Zulu chiefdom became the center of this new military and political organization, which began to absorb or destroy its neighbors. Shaka demonstrated talent as a politician, destroying the ruling families of the groups he incorporated into the growing Zulu state. He ruled with an iron hand, destroying his enemies, acquiring their cattle, and crushing any opposition. His policies brought power to the Zulu, but his erratic and cruel behavior also earned him enemies among his own people. Although he was assassinated in 1828, Shaka's reforms remained in place, and his

Figure 27.5. This Zulu royal kraal, drawn in the 1830s, gives some idea of the power of the Zulu at the time that Shaka was forging Zulu dominance during the mfecane.

successors built on the structure he had created. Zulu power was still growing in the 1840s, and the Zulu remained the most impressive military force in black Africa until the end of the century.

The rise of the Zulu and other Nguni chiefdoms was the beginning of the *mfecane,* or wars of crushing and wandering. As Zulu control expanded, a series of campaigns and forced migrations led to constant fighting as other peoples sought to survive by fleeing, emulating, or joining the Zulu. Groups spun off to the north and south, raiding the Portuguese on the coast, clashing with the Europeans to the south, and fighting with neighboring chiefdoms. New African states, such as the *Swazi,* that adapted aspects of the Zulu model emerged among the survivors. One state, *Lesotho,* successfully resisted the Zulu example. It combined Sotho and Nguni speakers and defended itself against Nguni armies. It eventually developed as a kingdom far less committed to military organization, one in which the people had a strong influence on their leaders.

The whole of the southern continent, from the Cape Colony to Lake Malawi, had been thrown into turmoil by raiding parties, remnants, and refugees. Superior firepower allowed the Boers to continue to hold their lands, but it was not until the Zulu Wars of the 1870s that Zulu power was crushed by Great Britain, and even then only at great cost. During that process, the basic patterns of conflict between Africans and Europeans in the largest settler colony on the continent were created. These patterns included competition between settlers and Africans for land, the expanding influence of European government control, and the desire of Europeans to use Africans as laborers.

IN DEPTH

Slavery and Human Society

Slavery is a very old and widespread institution. It has been found at different times all over the globe, among simple societies and in the great centers of civilization. In some of these societies, it has been a marginal or secondary form of labor, whereas in others it became the predominant labor form or "mode of production" (in the jargon of Marxist analysis). The need for labor beyond the capacity of the individual or the family unit is very old, and as soon as authority, law, or custom could be established to set the conditions for coercion, the tribe, the state, the priests, or some other group or institution extracted labor by force. Coerced labor could take different forms. There are important distinctions between indentured servants, convict laborers, debt-peons, and chattel slaves.

Although most societies placed some limits on the slaveholder's authority or power, the denial of the slave's control over his or her own labor and life choices was characteristic of this form of coercion throughout history. In most societies that had a form of chattel slavery, the slave was denied a sense of belonging in the society—the idea of kinship. The honor associated with family or lineage was the antithesis of slavery. Joseph in Egypt, and the viziers of the sultans of Turkey, might rise to high positions, but the fact that they were slaves meant that they were instruments of their masters' will. In fact, because they were slaves and thus unconstrained by kinship or other ties and obligations, they could be trusted in positions of command.

Because slaves became nonpersons—or, as one modern author has put it, because they suffered a "social death"—it was always easier to enslave "others" or "outsiders": those who were different in some way. Hebrews enslaved Canaanites, Greeks enslaved "barbarians," and Muslims made slaves of nonbelievers. If the difference between slave and master was readily seen, it made enforcement of slave status that much easier. Racism as such did not cause modern slavery, but differences in culture, language, color, and other physical characteristics always facilitated enslavement. The familiarity of Europeans and Muslims with black Africans in an enslaved status contributed to the development of modern racism. To paraphrase English historian Charles Boxer, no people can enslave another for 400 years without developing an attitude of superiority.

Slavery was not only a general phenomenon that existed in many societies. Rarely questioned on any grounds, it was seen as a necessary and natural phenomenon. Slavery is accepted in the texts of ancient India, the Old Testament, and the writings of 5th-century Greece. Aristotle specifically argued that some people were born to rule and others to serve. In Christian theology, although all people might be free in spirit in the kingdom of God, servitude was a necessary reality in the real world. Voices might be raised arguing for fair treat-

ment or against the enslavement of a particular group, but the condition of servitude itself usually was taken as part of the natural order of the world.

In this context, the attack on slavery in Western culture that grew from the Enlightenment and the social and economic changes in western Europe and its Atlantic colonies at the end of the 18th century was a remarkable turning point in world history. Whether one believes that slavery was an outdated labor form that was incompatible with industrial capitalism and was therefore abolished or that it was destroyed because its immorality became all too obvious, its demise was quick. In about a century and a half, the moral and religious underpinning of chattel slavery was cut away and its economic justifications were questioned seriously. Although slavery lingered in at least a few places well into the 20th century, few people were willing to defend the institution publicly.

Although slavery historically existed in many places, it has become intimately associated with Africa because of the scope of the Atlantic slave trade and the importance of slavery in forming the modern world system. There was nothing inevitable about Africa's becoming the primary source of slaves in the modern world. Europeans did use American Indians and European indentured workers when they could, but historical precedents, maritime technology, and availability combined to make Africa the source of labor for the expanding plantation colonies of Europe.

African slavery obviously played an important role in shaping the modern world. The African slave trade was one of the first truly international trades, and it created an easy access to labor that enabled Europeans to exploit the Americas. Some have argued that it was an important, even a necessary feature in the rise of capitalism and the international division of labor. Others disagree. In this question, as in nearly every other question about modern slavery, controversies still abound.

In the context of African history, the interpretation of slavery is still changing rapidly. A recent and careful estimate of the volume involved in the Atlantic trade (10–12 million) has been questioned seriously, especially by African scholars, who see this new figure as an attempt to downplay the exploitation of Africa. Another debate centers on the impact of the trade on the population and societies within Africa. The slave trade was important to the economy of the Atlantic, but how important was this external trade in Africa itself? Early researchers, reacting to the preabolitionist European self-justifications that the slave trade was no great crime because Africans had long become familiar with slavery and were selling already enslaved people, argued that African "slavery" often was an extension of kinship or other forms of dependency and was quite unlike the chattel slavery of western Europe. But further research has demonstrated that in many African societies, slavery was an integral part of the economy and that although specific conditions sometimes differed greatly from those in the Americas, the servile condition in Africa had much in common with chattel slavery. For example, the Sokoto caliphate in the 19th century had a proportion of slaves similar to that in Brazil and the southern United States. Slave societies did exist in Africa.

Now, controversy rages over the extent to which the development of African slavery resulted from the long-term impact of the slave trade and the European demand for captive labor. African societies did not live in isolation from the pressures and examples of the wider world economy into which they were drawn. The extent to which that contact transformed slavery in Africa is now in question. These controversies among historians reflect current concerns and a realization that the present social and political situation in Africa and in many places in the Americas continues to bear the burden of a historical past in which slavery played an essential role. In evaluating slavery, as in all other historical questions, what we think about the present shapes our inquiry and our interpretation of the past.

Questions: Why did Africa become the leading source of slaves in the early modern world economy? What are some of the leading issues in interpreting African slavery? What were the roles of Africans and Europeans in the early modern slave trade?

THE AFRICAN DIASPORA

The slave trade and the horrifying Middle Passage carried millions of Africans from their original homelands. In the Americas, especially in plantation colonies, they became a large segment of the population, and African cultures were adapted to new environments and conditions. Africans also resisted enslavement.

The slave trade was the means by which the history of the Americas and Africa became linked and a principal way in which African societies were drawn into the world economy. The import into Africa of European firearms, Indian textiles, Indonesian cowrie shells, and American tobacco in return for African ivory, gold, and especially slaves demonstrated Africa's integration into the mercantile structure of the world. Africans involved in the trade learned to deal effectively with this situation. Prices of slaves rose steadily in the 18th century, and the terms of trade increasingly favored the African dealers. In many African ports, such as Whydah, Porto Novo, and Luanda, African or Afro-European communities developed that specialized in the slave trade and used this position to advantage.

Slave Lives

For the slaves themselves, slavery meant the destruction of their villages or their capture in war, separation from friends and family, and then the forced march to an interior trading town or to the slave pens at the coast. Conditions were deadly; perhaps as many as one-third of the captives died along the way or in the slave pens. Eventually the slaves were loaded onto the ships. Cargo sizes varied and could go as high as 700 slaves crowded into the dank, unsanitary conditions of the slave ships, but most cargoes were smaller. Overcrowding was less of a factor in mortality than the length of the voyage or the point of origin in Africa; the Bights of Benin and Biafra were particularly dangerous. The average mortality rate for slaves varied over time, but it ran at about 18 percent or so until the 18th century, when it declined somewhat. Still, losses could be catastrophic on individual ships, as on a Dutch ship in 1737, where 700 of the 716 slaves died on the voyage. The Middle Passage, or slave voyage to the Americas, was traumatic. Taken from their homes, branded, confined, and shackled, they faced not only the dangers of poor hygiene, dysentery, disease, and bad treatment but also the fear of being eaten or worse by the Europeans. Their situation sometimes led to suicide or resistance and mutiny on the ships. However traumatic, the Middle Passage certainly did not strip Africans of their culture, and they arrived in the Americas retaining their languages, beliefs, artistic traditions, and memories of their past.

Africans in America

The slaves carried across the Atlantic were brought mainly to the plantations and mines of America. Landed estates using large amounts of labor, often coerced, became characteristic of American agriculture, at first in sugar production and later for rice, cotton, and tobacco. The plantation system already used for producing sugar on the Atlantic islands of Spain and Portugal was transferred to the New World. After attempts to use Indian laborers in places such as Brazil and Hispaniola, Africans were brought in. West Africans, coming from societies in which herding, metallurgy, and intensive agriculture were widely practiced, were sought by Europeans for the specialized tasks of making sugar. In the English colonies of Barbados and Virginia, indentured servants from England eventually were replaced by enslaved Africans when new crops, such as sugar, were introduced or when indentured servants became less available. In any case, the plantation system of farming with a dependent or enslaved work force characterized the production of many tropical and semitropical crops in demand in Europe, and thus the plantation became the locus of African and American life.

Slaves did many other things as well. As we saw in Chapter 25, gold mining in Brazil made extensive use of black slaves, and the Spanish used slaves in the silver mines of Mexico. Urban slavery was characteristic of Latin American cities, where slaves were often artisans, street vendors, and household servants. In early 17th-century Lima, Peru, the capital of Spain's colony in South America, blacks outnumbered Europeans. Later cities such as Charleston and New Orleans also developed a large slave and free African

population. In short, there was almost no occupation that slaves did not perform, although most were agricultural laborers.

American Slave Societies

Each American slave-based society reflected the variations of its European origin and its component African cultures, but there were certain similarities and common features. Each recognized distinctions between African-born *salt water slaves,* who were almost invariably black (by European standards) and their American-born descendants, the *Creole slaves,* some of whom were mulattos as a result of the sexual exploitation of slave women or other forms of miscegenation. In all the American slave societies, a hierarchy of status evolved in which free whites were at the top, slaves were at the bottom, and free people of color had an intermediate position. In this sense, color and "race" played a role in American slavery it had not played in Africa. Among the slaves, slaveholders also created a hierarchy based on origin and color. Creole and especially mulatto slaves were given more opportunities to acquire skilled jobs or to work as house servants rather than in the fields or mines. They were also more likely to win their freedom by manumission, the voluntary freeing of slaves.

This hierarchy was a creation of the slaveholders and did not necessarily reflect perceptions among the slaves. There is evidence that important African nobles or religious leaders, who for one reason or another were sold into slavery, continued to exercise authority within the slave community. Still, the distinctions between Creole and African slaves tended to divide that community, as did the distinctions between different African groups whose members maintained their ties and affiliations in America. Many of the slave rebellions in the Caribbean and Brazil were organized along African ethnic and political lines. In Jamaica, there were several Akan-led rebellions in the 18th century, and the largest escaped slave community in 17th century Brazil apparently was organized and led by Angolans.

Although economic factors imposed similarities, the slave-based societies also varied in their composition. In the 18th century, for example, on the Caribbean islands where the Indian population had died out or had been exterminated and where few Europeans settled, Africans and their descendants

DOCUMENT

An African's Description of the Middle Passage

During the era of the slave trade, enslaved Africans by one means or another succeeded in telling their stories. These accounts, with their specific details of the injustice and inhumanities of slavery, became particularly useful in the abolitionist crusade. The biography of Frederick Douglass is perhaps the most famous of these accounts.

The biography of Olaudah Equiano, an Ibo from what is today eastern Nigeria on the Niger River, presents a personal description of enslavement in Africa and the terrors of the Middle Passage. Equiano and his sister were kidnapped in 1756 by African slave hunters and sold to British slave traders. Separated from his sister, Equiano was carried to the West Indies and later to Virginia, where he became servant to a naval officer. He traveled widely on his master's military campaigns and was later sold to a Philadelphia Quaker merchant, who eventually allowed him to buy his freedom. Later, he moved to England and became an active member in the movement to end slavery and the slave trade. His biography was published in 1789. The political uses of this kind of biography and Equiano's association with the abolitionists should caution us against accepting the account at face value, but it does convey the personal shock and anguish of those caught in the slave trade.

The first object which saluted my eyes when I arrived on the coast was the sea, and a slaveship, which was riding at anchor, and waiting for its cargo. These filled me with astonishment, which was soon converted into terror, which I am yet at a loss to describe, nor the then feelings of my mind. When I was carried on board I was immediately handled, and tossed up, to see if I were sound, by some of the crew; and I was now persuaded that I had got into a world of bad spirits, and that they were going to kill me. Their complexions too differing so much from ours, their long hair, and the language they spoke, which was very different from any I had ever heard, united to confirm me in this belief. Indeed, such were the horrors of my views and fears at that moment, that if ten thousand worlds had been my own, I would have freely parted with them all to have exchanged my condition with that of the meanest slave in my own country. When I looked round the ship too, and saw a large furnace or copper boiler, and a multitude of black people of every description chained together, every one of their countenances expressing dejection and sorrow, quite overpowered with horror and anguish, I fell motionless on the deck and fainted. When I recovered a little, I found some black people about me, who I believed were some of those who brought me on board, and had been receiving their pay; they talked to me in order to cheer me, but all in vain. I asked them if we were not to be eaten by those white men with horrible looks, red faces, and long hair. They told me I was not.... I now saw myself deprived of all chance of returning to my native country, or even the least glimpse of hope of gaining the shore, which I now considered as friendly; and I even wished for my former slavery, in preference to my present situation, which was filled with horrors of every kind, still heightened by my ignorance of what I was to undergo. I was not long suffered to indulge my grief; I was soon put down under decks, and there I received such a salutation in my nostrils as I had never experienced in my life; so that with the loathsomeness of the stench, and the crying together, I became so sick and low that I was not able to eat, nor had I the least desire to taste anything. I now wished for the last friend, death, to relieve me; but soon, to my grief two white men offered me eatables; and on my refusing to eat, one of them held me fast by the hands, and laid me across, I think, the windlass, and tied my feet while the other flogged me severely. I had never experienced anything of this kind before; and, although not being used to the water, I naturally feared that element the first time I saw it; yet, nevertheless, could I have got over the nettings, I would have jumped over the side; but I could not; and, besides the crew used to watch us very closely who were not chained down to the decks, lest we should leap into the water; and I have seen some of these poor African prisoners most severely cut for attempting to do so, and hourly whipped for not eating. This, indeed was often the case with myself. In a little time after amongst the poor chained men, I found some of my own nation, which in a small degree gave ease to my mind. I inquired of them what was to be done with us? They gave me to understand we were to be carried to these white people's country to work for them. I then was a little revived, and thought, if it were no worse than working, my situation was not so desperate; but still I feared I should be put to death, the white people looked and acted, as I thought, in so savage a manner; for I had never seen among any people such instances of brutal cruelty; and this was not only shown to us blacks, but also to some of the whites themselves....

At last when the ship we were in had got in all her cargo, they made ready with many fearful noises, and we were all put under deck, so that we could not see how they managed the vessel. But this disappointment was the least of my sorrow. The stench of the hold while we were on the coast was so intolerably loathsome, that it was dangerous to remain there for any time, and some of us had been permitted to stay on deck for the fresh air; but now the whole ship's cargo was confined together, it became absolutely pestilential. The closeness of the place, and the heat of the climate, added to the number in the ship, which was so crowded that each had scarcely room to turn himself, almost suffocated us. This produced copious perspirations, so that the air soon became unfit for respiration, from a variety of loathsome smells, and brought on a sickness amongst the slaves, of which many died, thus falling victims to the improvident avarice, as I may call it, of their purchasers. This wretched situation was again aggravated by the galling of the chains, now become insupportable; and the filth of the necessary tubs, into which the children fell, and were almost suffocated. The shrieks of the women, and the groans of the dying, rendered the whole a scene of horror almost inconceivable.

Questions: In what ways does Equiano's description contradict a previous understanding of the slave trade? What opportunities existed for the captives to resist? What effect might the experience of Africans on the slave ships have had on their perceptions of each other and of the Europeans?

formed the vast majority. In Jamaica and St. Domingue, slaves made up more than 80 percent of the population, and because mortality levels were so high, a large proportion were African-born. Brazil also had large numbers of imported Africans, but its more diverse population and economy, as well as a tradition of manumitting slaves and high levels of miscegenation, meant that slaves made up only about 35 percent of the population. However, free people of color, the descendants of former slaves, made up about another one-third, so that together slaves and free colored people made up two-thirds of the total population.

The Caribbean and Brazil differed significantly from the southern colonies of British North America, which depended less on imported Africans

1. Moulin. 2. Fourneaux. 3. Formes. 4. Vinaigrerie. 5. Cannes   SVCRERIE.   6. Gros 7. Latanir. 8. Pajomirioba 9. Choux 10. Cafes   11. Figuir.

Figure 27.6..Africans performed all kinds of labor in the Americas, from domestic service to mining and shipbuilding. Most worked on plantations like this sugar mill in the Caribbean.

because of natural population growth among the slaves. There, Creoles predominated, but manumission was less common, and free people of color made up less than 10 percent of the total Afro-American population. The result was that slavery in North America was less influenced by Africa. By the mid-18th century, the slave population in most places in North America was reproducing itself. By 1850, fewer than 1 percent of the slaves there were African-born. The combination of natural growth and the small direct trade from Africa reduced the degree of African cultural reinforcement.

The People and Gods in Exile

Africans brought as slaves to America faced a peculiar series of problems. Working conditions were exhausting, and life for most slaves often was difficult and short. Family formation was made difficult because of the general shortage of female slaves; the ratio of men to women was as much as three to one in some places. To this was added the insecurity of slave status: Family members might be separated by sale or by a master's whim. Still, most slaves lived in family units, even though their marriages were not always sanctioned by the religion of their masters. Throughout the Americas, wherever Africans were brought, aspects of their language, religion, artistic sensibilities, and other cultural elements survived. To some extent, the amount of continuity depended on the intensity and volume of the slave trade from a particular area. For example, Yoruba culture was particularly strong in northeastern Brazil because the trade between it and the Bight of Benin was heavy and continuous in the early 19th century. During certain periods, Akan peoples predominated in Jamaica, and Ewe or Dahomeans predominated in Haiti. Some slaveholders tried to mix up the slaves on their plantations so that strong African identities would be lost, but colonial dependence on slavers who consistently dealt with the same region tended to undercut such policies. In the Americas, African slaves had to adapt and to incorporate other African peoples' ideas and customs into their own lives. Moreover, the ways and customs of the masters were also imposed. Thus, what emerged as Afro-American culture reflected specific African roots adapted to a new reality. Afro-American culture was dynamic and creative in this sense.

Figure 27.7 *African, American, or both? In Suriname, descendants of escaped slaves maintain many aspects of African culture but have adapted, modified, and transformed them in many ways. This wooden door shows the imaginative skills of African-American carvers.*

Religion was an obvious example of continuity and adaptation. Slaves were converted to Catholicism by the Spaniards and the Portuguese, and they showed fervent devotion as members of Black Catholic brotherhoods, some of which were organized by African origins. Still, African religious ideas and practices did not die out, and many African slaves were accused of witchcraft by the Inquisition in those colonies. In the English islands, *obeah* was the name given to the African religious practices, and the men and women knowledgeable in them were held in high regard within the community. In Brazilian *candomble* (Yoruba) and Haitian *Vodun* (Aja), fully developed versions of African religion flourished and continue today, despite attempts to suppress them.

The reality of the Middle Passage meant that religious ideas were easier to transfer than the institutional aspects of religion. Without religious specialists or a priestly class, aspects of African religions were changed by contact with other African peoples as well as with colonial society. In many cases, slaves held their new faith in Christianity and their African beliefs at the same time, and tried to fuse the two. For Muslim Africans this was more difficult. In 1835 in Bahia, the largest slave rebellion in Brazil was organized by Muslim Yoruba and Hausa slaves and directed against the whites and against nonbelievers.

Resistance and rebellion were other aspects of African-American history. Recalcitrance, running away, and direct confrontation were present wherever slaves were held. As early as 1508, African runaways disrupted communications on Hispaniola, and in 1527, a plot to rebel was uncovered in Mexico City. Throughout the Americas, communities of runaway slaves formed. In Jamaica, Colombia, Venezuela, Haiti, and Brazil, runaway communities were persistent. In Brazil, during the 17th century, *Palmares,* an enormous runaway slave kingdom with many villages and a population of perhaps 8000 to 10,000 people, resisted Portuguese and Dutch attempts to destroy it for a century. Although its inhabitants were both Creoles and Africans of various backgrounds, its origins, organization, and leadership were Angolan. In Jamaica, the runaway Maroons were able to gain some independence and a recognition of their freedom. So-called ethnic slave rebellions organized by a particular African group were common in the Caribbean and Brazil in the 18th century. In North America, where reinforcement from the slave trade was less important, resistance was also important, but it was based less on African origins or ethnicities.

Perhaps the most remarkable story of African-American resistance is found in the forests of *Suriname,* a former Dutch plantation colony. There, large numbers of slaves ran off in the 18th century and mounted an almost perpetual war in the rainforest against the various expeditions sent to hunt them down. Those captured were brutally executed, but eventually a truce developed. Today about 50,000 Maroon descendants still live in Suriname and French Guiana. The Suriname Maroons maintained many aspects of their west African background in terms of language, kinship relations, and religious beliefs, but these were fused with new forms drawn from European and American Indian contacts resulting from their New World experience. From this fusion based on their own creativity, a truly Afro-American culture was created.

Africa and the End of the Slave Trade

The end of the Atlantic slave trade and the abolition of slavery in the Atlantic world resulted from economic, political, and religious changes in Europe and in its overseas American colonies and former colonies. These changes, which were manifestations of the Enlightenment, the Age of Revolution, Christian revivalism, and perhaps the Industrial Revolution, were external to Africa, but once again they determined the pace and nature of change within Africa.

Like much else about the history of slavery, there is disagreement about the end of the slave trade. It is true that some African societies began to export other commodities, such as peanuts, cotton, and palm oil, which made their dependence on the slave trade less important, but the supply of slaves to European merchants was not greatly affected by this development. In general, the British plantation economies were booming in the period from 1790 to 1830, and plantations in Cuba, Brazil, and the southern United States flourished in the decades that followed. Thus, it is difficult to find a direct and simple link between economic self-interest and the movement to suppress the slave trade.

Opponents of slavery and the brutality of the trade had appeared in the mid-18th century, in relation to new intellectual movements in the West. Philosopher Jean-Jacques Rousseau in France and political economist Adam Smith in England both wrote against it. Whereas in ancient Rome during the spread of Christianity and Islam, and in 16th-century Europe, the enslavement of "barbarians" or nonbelievers was seen as positive—a way to civilize others—slavery during the European Enlightenment and bourgeois revolution came to be seen as backward and immoral. The slave trade was particularly criticized. It was the symbol of slavery's inhumanity and cruelty.

England, as the major maritime power of the period, was the key to the end of the slave trade. Under the leadership of religious humanitarians, such as John Wesley and *William Wilberforce,* an abolitionist movement gained strength against the merchants and the West Indies interests. After much parliamentary debate, the British slave trade was abolished in 1807. Having set out on this course, Britain tried to impose abolition of the slave trade on other countries throughout the Atlantic. Spain and Portugal were pressured to gradually suppress the trade and the British navy was used to enforce these agreements by capturing illegal slave ships. The full end of slavery in the Americas did not occur until 1888, when it was abolished in Brazil.

Conclusion

The Impact of Slavery on Africa

Africa was drawn into the world economy in the era of the slave trade, at first slowly, but with increasing intensity after 1750. Its incorporation produced differing effects on African societies, reinforcing authority in some places, creating new states in others, and sometimes provoking social, religious, and political reactions. Although many aspects of African life followed traditional patterns, contact with the world economy forced many African societies to adjust in ways that often placed them at a disadvantage and facilitated Europe's colonization of Africa in the 19th century. Well into the 20th century, as forced labor continued in Africa under European direction, the legacy of the slave trade era proved slow to die.

Further Readings

Aside from the general books on Africa already mentioned in the Further Readings for previous chapters, some specific readings are particularly useful. Martin Hall's *The Changing Past: Farmers, Kings, and Traders in Southern Africa* (1987)

discusses the use of archeological evidence in African history. D. Birmingham and Phyllis Martin, eds., *History of Central Africa,* 2 vols. (1983) presents extended essays on a number of regions. On west Africa in the age of the slave trade, a good introduction is J.F.A. Ajayi and Michael Crowder, eds., *History of West Africa,* 2 vols. (1975), especially volume 2. On southern Africa, Leonard Thompson's *A History of South Africa* (1990) presents a broad survey, and J. D. Omer-Cooper's *The Zulu Aftermath* (1969) is a classic account.

There are many histories of the slave trade, but Herbert S. Klein's *The Atlantic Slave Trade* (1999) provides an up-to-date and intelligent overview. On the quantitative aspects of the slave trade, Philip Curtin's *The Atlantic Slave Trade: A Census* (1969) is the proper starting point, while David Ettis' *The Rise of African Slavery in the Americas* (2000) is an important new study. All new quantitative studies will depend on the CD-ROM *The Atlantic Slave Trade* (1998), edited by David Eltis et al. Roger Anstey's *The Atlantic Slave Trade and British Abolition* (1975) deals with the economic and religious aspects of the end of the slave trade.

On Africa, Paul Lovejoy's *Transformations in Slavery: A History of Slavery in Africa* (1983) and Patrick Manning's *Slavery and African Life* (1990) provide comprehensive overviews, and J. E. Inikori's *Forced Migration: The Impact of the Export Slave Trade on African Societies* (1982) brings together essays by leading scholars. Joseph Miller's *Way of Death* (1989) is a detailed study of the effects of the slave trade on Angola and a fine example of an in-depth study of one region.

John K. Thornton, *Africa and Africans in the Making of the Atlantic World* (1994) is an excellent argument for the centrality of slavery in Africa, and Walter Rodney's essay "Africa in Europe and the Americas," *Cambridge History of Africa,* vol. 4, 578–622, is a succinct overview of the African diaspora. Herbert Klein's *African Slavery in Latin America and the Caribbean* (1987) is an up-to-date survey. Excellent overviews based on the best secondary literature are Robin Blackburn's *The Making of New World Slavery* (1997), and his *The Overthrow of Colonial Slavery* (1988).

On the general theoretical issues of slavery, Orlando Patterson's *Slavery and Social Death* (1982) is a broad comparative sociological study. David B. Davis's *Slavery and Human Progress* (1984) takes a historical approach to many of the same questions and then places the abolitionist movement in context.

On the Web

The African slave trade as described by the slaves themselves can be found at http://www.fordham.edu/halsall/africa/africasbook.html (scroll down to "Enslaved People") and http://vi.uh.edu/pages/mintz/primary.html.

Narratives of slaves who lived in the American South can be encountered at http://metalab.unc.edu/docsouth/narratives.html.

The role of the Royal African Company in the trade is des-cribed at http://www.pbs.org/wgbh/aia/part1/1p269.html.

The career of the *Amistad*, a slave schooner which became the subject of a major film, is closely analyzed at http://www.law.umkc.edu/faculty/projects/ftrials/amistad/AMI_ACT.HTM.

The Asante of what is now the nation of Ghana(http://www.ashanti.com.au/ and http://www.uiowa.edu/~africart/toc/people/Asante.html) built an empire out of the slave trade, while the people of Benin, less dependent upon it, were still able to maintain their rich artistic heritage and religious traditions (http://www.skidmore.edu/academics/laronson/ AH_207/BeninArt/BeninArt.html).

At the same time, the Swahili (http://www.uiowa.edu/~africart/toc/people/ Swahili.html) joined with Arabs and Indians in establishing spice plantations in Zanzibar and Shaka Zulu built an empire in the southern regions of the continent.

Biographies of Shaka can be found at http://campus.northpark.edu/history/WebChron/ Africa/ShakaZulu.htm and http://www.shaka.iafrica.com/history.html.

Chapter 28

Asian Transitions in an Age of Global Change

A number of the major forms of interaction between expansive European peoples and those of Asia are vividly illustrated in this panoramic Japanese silk screen painting from the early 1600s. The strong impression made by the size and power of the Portuguese ship that has just arrived in harbor is evident in the artist's exaggeration of the height of its fore and aft castles. The trade goods being unloaded, mainly Chinese silks, which are also being sold in the market place to the left of the painting, but also exotic products such as peacocks and tiger skills, demonstrate the ways in which the Portuguese had become carriers between different areas in Asia, including Japan. The cluster of black-robed missionaries waiting to greet the arriving Portuguese sea captain (under the umbrella in the center) suggest that efforts to convert the Japanese to Christianity were in full swing, at least in this area of the kingdom.

When Vasco da Gama's ships returned to Lisbon in 1499, it was clear that tiny Portugal rather than mighty Spain had won the race to the fabled Indies. Columbus's voyages to the Americas, with the support of the Spanish rulers, opened up new worlds to the civilizations of Europe, Asia, and Africa. But Da Gama's 1498 expedition accomplished the task that had been the ultimate aim of all the explorations launched by the Europeans as early as the 14th century. He and his sailors had found a sea link between an expansive and insecure Europe and the powerful and wealthy civilizations of Asia.

Although da Gama's voyage marked a major turning point for much of western Europe, its impact on most of Asia was much less decisive, at least in the 16th and 17th centuries. The Portuguese, and the Dutch, French, and English who followed them into Asia, soon found that they had little to offer the Indians, southeast Asians, or Chinese in exchange for the silks and spices they risked their lives to carry back to Europe. They were disappointed to find that few Asian peoples were interested in converting to Christianity. They also quickly realized that however feisty and well-armed they might be, they were far too few in numbers to make much headway

1350 C.E.	1500 C.E.	1550 C.E.	1600 C.E.	1650 C.E.	1700 C.E.
1368 Ming dynasty comes to power in China **1368–1398** Reign of the Hongwu emperor **1390** Ming restrictions on overseas commerce **1403–1424** Reign of the Yunglo emperor in China **1405–1423** Zhenghe expeditions from China to Southeast Asia, India, and East Africa **1498–1499** Vasco da Gama opens the sea route around Africa to Asia	**1507** Portuguese defeat a combined Muslim war fleet at Diu off the coast of western India **1510** Portuguese conquest of Goa in western India **1511** Portuguese conquer Malacca on the tip of Malayan peninsula **1540s** Francis Xavier makes mass converts in India	**1573** End of the Ashikaga Shogunate **1573–1620** Reign of the Wanli emperor **1580s** Jesuits arrive in China **1590** Hideyoshi unifies Japan **1592** First Japanese invasion of Korea **1597** Second Japanese invasion of Korea	**1600s** Dutch and British assault on Portuguese Empire in Asia; decline of Portuguese power **1603** Tokugawa Shogunate established **1614** Christianity banned in Japan **1619–1620** Dutch East India Company established at Batavia on Java **1640s** Japan moves into self-imposed isolation **1641** Dutch capture Malacca from the Portuguese; Dutch confined to Deshima Island off Nagasaki	**1644** Nomadic Manchus put an end to the Ming dynasty; Manchu Qing dynasty rules China **1654–1722** Reign of the Kangxi emperor in China	**1755–1757** Dutch become the paramount power on Java; Qing conquest of Mongolia

against even the smaller kingdoms of Asia, such as Siam or Vietnam, much less against mighty empires such as those ruled by the Chinese or the Mughals.

The Europeans used their sea power to control the export of specific products, especially spices such as pepper, cinnamon, and nutmeg. They also sought to regulate the seaborne commerce in some sections of the vast Asian trading network that stretched from the ports of the Red Sea to south China. But efforts at trade control proved expensive and were difficult to sustain in the face of widespread Asian resistance. The Portuguese—and after them the Dutch and the English—found that it was better to fit into the Asian system rather than to attempt to capture it. They neither controlled the commerce of the Indian Ocean network nor significantly changed the course of social, economic, or political development in most Asian societies.

As was the case with the Mughal and Safavid empires (see Chapter 26), the central themes in the history of Asian civilizations in the 16th and 17th centuries often had little or nothing to do with European expansion. They emerged from long-term processes rooted in the inner workings of these ancient civilizations and their interaction with neighboring states and nomadic peoples. For example, the Europeans had nothing to do with the impressive expeditions by which the Chinese tried in the early 14th century to begin their own global expansion. A century later, threats from elsewhere in Asia, not Europe, convinced the rulers of China to attempt to cut their kingdom off from the world. European missionaries and firearms played important roles in the civil wars that raged in Japan in the 16th century. But these struggles were part of a pattern of feudal fragmentation and a quest for political unity that had long preceded the coming of the Europeans.

Thus, although the European presence was felt in each of the areas considered in this chapter, the impact of Europe's global expansion was of secondary importance except in island southeast Asia, which is the focus of the first section. The sections on China and Japan that follow emphasize the longer-term unfolding of civilization in each of these areas and the effects of their interaction on each other. The continuing importance of nomadic challenges to Chinese civilization is also stressed. Though fascinating in their own right, European responses to China and Japan, and their activities there, are worked into these larger patterns because this perspective more accurately conveys the reality of this era. European seafarers may have sailed across much of the globe. But European peoples had not yet gained the military strength and economic power to dominate the civilizations of Asia or change the course of their development.

THE ASIAN TRADING WORLD AND THE COMING OF THE EUROPEANS

Several European seafaring nations were actively involved in south and southeast Asia in the centuries after Vasco da Gama rounded the Cape of Good Hope in 1498. Most European enterprise in the region was centered on trade, as all the European powers struggled to find the most profitable ways to obtain the many products they wanted from Asia. Some Europeans went to Asia in search of Christian converts rather than personal gain. Small numbers of Europeans also settled in coastal enclaves in both India and the Indonesian archipelago. But trade and commercial profits motivated most Europeans who explored, fought wars, and struggled to survive in Asia during the first centuries of European overseas expansion.

Vasco da Gama and his Portuguese crew received a rather rude shock soon after arriving in India in 1498. Still congratulating themselves on having found a sea route around Africa, which Portuguese explorers had been seeking for generations, they successfully made their way across the Arabian Sea to India. At Calicut, a prosperous commercial center on the southwest coast (see Map 28.1), they went ashore to trade for the spices, fine textiles, and other Asian products that were among the main objectives of the voyages of exploration. Reveling in the fine quality and abundance of the products from all over Asia that were available in the town's great marketplace, the Portuguese were startled to learn that the local merchants were not interested in the products they had brought to trade for Asian goods. In fact, their cast-iron pots, coarse cloth, and coral beads elicited little more than sneers from the merchants they approached. Suddenly da Gama and his crews faced the humbling prospect of returning home with little proof that they had reached Asia and begun to tap its fabled wealth. Reluctantly, they concluded that they had little choice but to use the small supply of silver bullion they had brought along for emergencies. They found that the Asian merchants were willing to take their precious metal. But they also discovered that their meager provision did not go very far toward filling the holds of their ships with Asian treasures.

Much of what the Europeans did in Asia in the 16th and 17th centuries was devoted to working out the implications of that first encounter in Calicut. The very fact of Da Gama's arrival demonstrated both the needs and curiosity that had driven the Europeans halfway around the world as well as the seaworthiness of their *caravel* ships. Their stops at Calicut and ports on the eastern coast of Africa also made the Portuguese acutely aware of the fact that their old rivals, the Muslims, had arrived in east Africa and south and southeast Asia well ahead of them. This unpleasant discovery promised resistance to Portuguese trading and empire building in Asia. It also meant major obstacles to their plans for converting the peoples of the area to Roman Catholicism. But the Portuguese observed that the Muslims and Asian peoples were deeply divided and that they rarely understood the potential threat posed by what was, after all, a handful of strangers from across the world.

Bonds of Commerce: The Asian Sea Trading Network, c. 1500

As later voyages by Portuguese fleets revealed, Calicut and the ports of east Africa, which Da Gama had found on the initial foray into Asia, made up only a small segment of a larger network of commercial exchange and cultural interaction. This trading system stretched thousands of miles from the Middle East and Africa along all the coasts of the giant Asian continent. Both the products exchanged in this network and the main routes followed by those who sailed it had been established for centuries—in many cases, millennia.

In general, the *Asian sea trading network* can be broken down into three main zones, each of which was focused on major centers of handicraft manufacture (Map 28.1). In the west was an Arab zone anchored on the glass-, carpet-, and tapestry-making Islamic heartlands at the head of the Red Sea and the Persian Gulf. India, with its superb cotton textiles, dominated the central portions of the system, and China, which excelled in producing paper, porcelain, and silk textiles,

formed the eastern pole. In between or on the fringes of the three great manufacturing centers were areas such as Japan, the mainland kingdoms and island states of southeast Asia, and the port cities of east Africa that fed mainly raw materials—precious metals, foods, and forest products—into the trading network.

Of the raw materials circulating in the system, the broadest demand and highest prices were paid for spices, which came mainly from Ceylon and the islands at the eastern end of what is today the Indonesian archipelago. Long-distance trade was largely in high-priced commodities such as spices, ivory from Africa, and precious stones. But silk and cotton textiles also were traded over long distances. Bulk items, such as rice, livestock, and timber, normally were exchanged between the ports within each of the main trading zones. Though less profitable than luxury commodities, bulk staples made up a large portion of the volume of goods traded in some segments of the system.

Since ancient times, monsoon winds and the nature of the ships and navigational instruments avail-

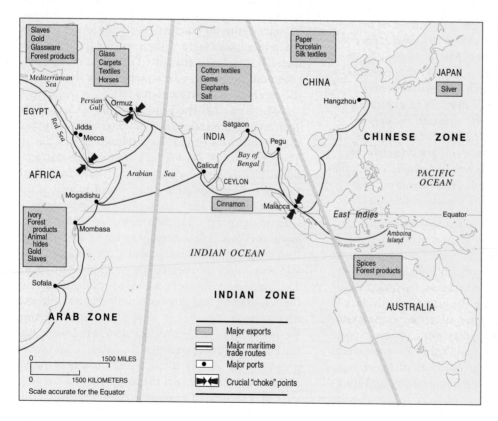

Map 28.1 *Routes and Major Products Exchanged in the Asian Trading Network, c. 1500*

able to sailors had dictated the main trade routes in the Asian network. Much navigation was of the coasting variety, that is, sailing along the shoreline and charting distances and location with reference to towns and natural landmarks. The Arabs and Chinese, who had compasses and large, well-built ships, could cross large expanses of open water such as the Arabian and South China seas. But even they preferred established coastal routes rather than the largely uncharted and less predictable open seas. As the Portuguese quickly learned, there were several crucial points where segments of the trade converged or where geography funneled it into narrow areas. The mouths of the Red Sea and Persian Gulf were two of these points, as were the Straits of Malacca, which separated mainland from island southeast Asia (see Map 28.1).

Two general characteristics of the trading system at the time of the Portuguese arrival were critical to European attempts to regulate and dominate it. First, there was no central control. Second, military force was usually absent from commercial exchanges within it. Although Arab sailors and merchants were found in ports throughout much of the network, they had no sense of common cause. They sailed and traded to provide for their own livelihood and to make profits for the princes or merchants who financed their expeditions. The same was true for the Chinese, southeast Asian, and Indian merchants and sailors who were concentrated in particular segments of the trading complex. Because all the peoples participating in the network had something to trade for the products they wanted from others, exchanges within the system were largely peaceful. Trading vessels were lightly armed for protection against attack by pirates.

Trading Empire: The Portuguese Response to the Encounter at Calicut

The Portuguese were not prepared to abide by the informal rules that had evolved over the centuries for commercial and cultural exchanges in the great Asian trading complex. It was apparent after the trip to the market in Calicut that the Portuguese had little, other than gold and silver, to exchange with Asian peoples. In an age in which prominent economic theorists, called *mercantilists,* taught that a state's power depended heavily on the amount of precious metals a monarch had in his coffers, a steady flow of bullion to Asia was unthinkable. It was particularly objec-

tionable because it would enrich and thus strengthen merchants and rulers from rival kingdoms and religions, particularly the Muslims, whose position the Portuguese had set out to undermine through their overseas enterprises. Unwilling to forgo the possibilities for profit that a sea route to Asia presented, the Portuguese resolved to take by force what they could not get through fair trade.

The decision by the Portuguese to use force to extract spices and other goods from Asia resulted largely from their realization that they could offset their lack of numbers and trading goods with their superior ships and weaponry (see Figure 28.1). Except for the huge war fleets of Chinese junks, no Asian people could muster fleets able to withstand the firepower and maneuverability of the Portuguese squadrons. Their sudden appearance in Asian waters and their interjection of sea warfare into a peaceful trading system gained the European intruders an element of surprise that kept their adversaries off balance in the critical early years of empire building. The Portuguese forces were small in numbers but united in their drive for wealth and religious converts. This allowed them to take advantage of the deep divisions that separated their Asian competitors and the Asians' inability to combine their forces effectively in battle. Thus, when Da Gama returned for a second expedition to Asian waters in 1502, he was able to force ports on both the African and Indian coasts to submit to a Portuguese tribute regime. He also assaulted towns that refused to cooperate. When a combined Egyptian–Indian fleet was finally sent in reprisal in 1509, it was defeated off Diu on the western Indian coast. The Portuguese would not have to face so formidable an alliance of Asian sea powers again.

The Portuguese soon found that sea patrols and raids on coastal towns were not sufficient to control the trade in the items they wanted, especially spices. Thus, from 1507 onward they strove to capture towns and build fortresses at a number of strategic points on the Asian trading network (Map on p.671). In that year they took *Ormuz* at the southern end of the Persian Gulf; in 1510 they captured *Goa* on the western Indian coast; and, most critical of all, in the next year they successfully stormed *Malacca* on the tip of the Malayan peninsula. These ports served both as naval bases for Portuguese fleets patrolling Asian waters and as *factories,* or points where spices and other products could be stored until they were shipped to Europe. Ships and naval stations became the key components

Figure 28.1. *In the 15th and 16th centuries, the port of Lisbon in tiny Portugal was one of the great centers of international commerce and European overseas exploration. Although aspects of the early, streamlined caravel design can be detected in the ships pictured here, additional square sails, higher fore and aft castles, and numerous cannons projecting from holes cut in the ships' sides exemplify a later stage of naval development.*

of a Portuguese trading empire that was financed and directed by the kings of Portugal.

The aim of the empire was to establish Portuguese monopoly control over key Asian products, particularly spices, such as the cinnamon being processed in Figure 28.2. Ideally, all the spices produced were to be shipped in Portuguese galleons to Asian or European markets. There they would be sold at high prices, which the Portuguese could dictate because they controlled the supply of these goods. The Portuguese also sought, with little success, to impose a licensing system on all merchant ships that traded in the Indian Ocean from Ormuz to Malacca. The combination of monopoly and the licensing system, backed by force, was intended to give the Portuguese control of a sizeable portion of the Asian trading network.

Portuguese Vulnerability and the Rise of the Dutch and English Trading Empires

The plans for empire that the Portuguese drew up on paper never became reality. They managed for some decades to control much of the flow of spices, such as nutmeg and mace, which were grown in very limited areas. But control of the market in key condiments, such as pepper and cinnamon, eluded them. At times the Portuguese resorted to severe punishments such as cutting off the hands of the rival traders and ships' crews caught transporting spices in defiance of their monopoly. But they simply did not have the soldiers or the ships to sustain their monopolies, much less the licensing system. With just over a million people in all of Portugal and never more than 15,000 Portuguese in Asia at one time, the trading empire was stretched thin. Even this small community soon became deeply divided. Many of the Portuguese who went out to serve the empire became independent traders in defiance of the crown monopoly. The resistance of Asian rivals, poor military discipline, rampant corruption among crown officials, and heavy Portuguese shipping losses caused by overloading and poor design had taken a heavy toll on the empire by the end of the 16th century.

The overextended and declining Portuguese trading empire proved no match for the Dutch and English rivals, whose war fleets challenged it in the early 17th century. The Portuguese had grown so weak that they were unable to exploit the deep hos-

Figure 28.2. *Sinhalese workers peeling the bark from the branches of cinnamon trees are depicted in this photo taken in the era of British rule on Ceylon. Similar techniques were used by cinnamon peelers in the pre-European, the Portuguese, and the Dutch periods to extract the cinnamon sticks and powder that were in great demand in Europe. Like the other spices European traders carried home from Asia, cinnamon had many uses that would seem strange to us today. It was mixed into medicines and used as an effective mouthwash and, of course, a popular ingredient in pastries and other sweets.*

tility and frequent clashes between their northern European rivals. Of the two, the Dutch emerged, at least in the short term, as the victors. They captured the critical Portuguese port and fortress at Malacca and built a new port of their own in 1620 at *Batavia* on the island of Java (see Map on p.671). The latter location, which was much closer to the island sources of key spices, reflected the improved European knowledge of Asian geography. It also reflected the Dutch decision to concentrate on the monopoly control of certain spices rather than on Asian trade more generally. The English, who fought hard but lost the struggle for control of the spice islands, were forced to fall back to India. At the time this appeared to be a disheartening reversal. In the 18th century, however, when the demand for Indian textiles soared and India emerged as the keystone of Britain's global empire, it came to be seen as an incredible stroke of good fortune.

The *Dutch trading empire* (see Map on p.671) was made up of the same basic components as the Portuguese: fortified towns and factories, warships on patrol, and monopoly control of a limited number of products. But the Dutch had more numerous and better armed ships and went about the business of monopoly control in a much more systematic fash-

ion. To regulate the supply of cloves, nutmeg, and mace, for example, they uprooted the plants that produced these spices on islands they did not control. They also forcibly removed or wiped out island peoples who cultivated these spices without Dutch supervision and dared to sell them to their trading rivals.

Although the profits from the sale of these spices in Europe in the mid-17th century helped sustain Holland's golden age, the Dutch found that the greatest profits in the long run could be gained from peacefully working themselves into the long-established Asian trading system. The demand for spices declined and their futile efforts to gain control over crops such as pepper that were grown in many places became more and more expensive. In response, the Dutch came to rely mainly (as they had long done in Europe) on the fees they charged for transporting products from one area in Asia to another. They also depended on profits gained from buying Asian products, such as cloth, in one area and trading them in other areas for goods that could be sold in Europe at inflated prices. The English also adopted these trading patterns, although their enterprises were concentrated along the coasts of India and on the cloth trade rather than on the spices of southeast Asia. For both the Dutch and the English, peaceful commerce was

Visualizing THE PAST

Intruders: The Pattern of Early European Expansion into Asia

Compare the map shown here with Map 28.1. Note the new routes, major port centers, and fortified factory centers added by the different European powers as they moved into Asia. Compare these with the traditional regions of spice growing, textile manufacture, and other industries.

Also note the areas where the different European powers began to establish substantial territorial empires and the dates when these areas were brought under Western control. Compare the routes favored by the Portuguese, Dutch, English, French, and Spanish, and the areas where their fortified outposts and territorial conquests are centered.

Questions: What do the shifting areas where European routes and fortified trading centers are located tell us about the main goals and relative power of each of the European countries? What advantages did those who entered later in the process have in this regard? On the basis of the discussion in Chapters 22 and 23, which of these states would you argue had the strongest power base in Europe itself? Why was the Spanish pattern of expansion so radically different from those of the other powers? What do the areas conrtolled by different European powers tell us about the objectives of establishing colonial empires, as opposed to the trading empires favored in the early decades of European expansion into the region? Which areas of Asia were the most impervious to European expansionism in this period, and why?

more profitable than forcible control, and monopolistic measures were increasingly aimed at European rather than Asian rivals.

Going Ashore: European Tribute Systems in Asia

Their ships and guns allowed the Europeans to force their way into the Asian trading network in the 16th and 17th centuries. But as they moved inland and away from the sea, their military advantages and their ability to dominate the Asian peoples rapidly disappeared. Because the vastly superior numbers of Asian armies offset the Europeans' advantage in weapons and organization for waging war on land, even small kingdoms such as those on Java and in mainland southeast Asia were able to resist European inroads into their domains. In the larger empires such as those in China, India, and Persia—and when confronted by martial cultures such as Japan's—the

Europeans quickly learned their place. That they were often reduced to kowtowing or humbling themselves before the thrones of Asian potentates is demonstrated by the instructions given by a Dutch envoy about the proper behavior for a visit to the Japanese court:

> Our ministers have no other instruction to take there except to look to the wishes of that brave, superb, precise nation in order to please it in everything, and by no means to think on anything which might cause greater antipathy to us.... That consequently the Company's ministers frequenting the scrupulous state each year must above all go armed in modesty, humility, courtesy, and amity, always being the lesser.

In certain situations, however, the Europeans were drawn inland away from their forts, factories, and war fleets in the early centuries of their expansion into Asia (see Map on p.671). The Portuguese, and

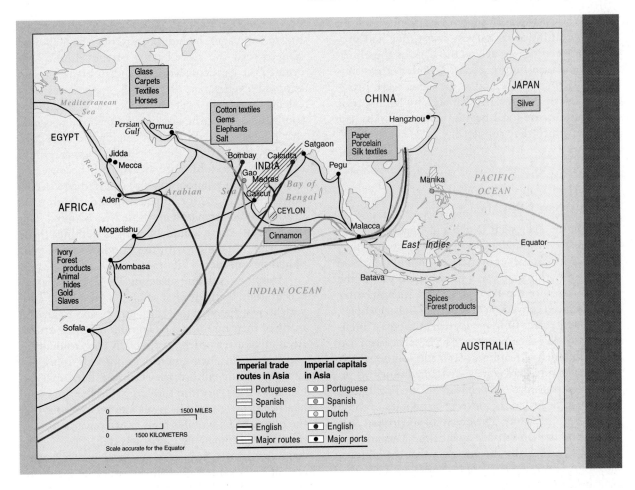

Imperial trade routes in Asia
- Portuguese
- Spanish
- Dutch
- English
- Major routes

Imperial capitals in Asia
- Portuguese
- Spanish
- Dutch
- English
- Major ports

0 — 1500 MILES
0 — 1500 KILOMETERS
Scale accurate for the Equator

the Dutch after them, felt compelled to conquer the coastal areas of Ceylon to control the production and sale of cinnamon, which grew in the forests of the southern portions of that island. The Dutch moved slowly inland from their base at Batavia into the highlands of western Java. They discovered that this area was ideal for growing coffee, which was in great demand in Europe by the 17th century. By the mid-18th century, the Dutch not only controlled the coffee-growing areas but were the paramount power on Java. The *Treaty of Gijanti* in 1757 reduced the remaining Javanese princes to vassals of the Dutch East India Company.

The Spanish, taking advantage of the fact that the Philippine Islands lay in the half of the world the pope had given them to explore and settle in 1493, invaded the islands in the 1560s. The conquest of *Luzon* and the northern islands was facilitated by the fact that their animistic inhabitants lived in small states the Spanish could subjugate one by one. The

repeated failure of Spanish expeditions to conquer the southern island of *Mindanao,* which was ruled by a single kingdom whose Muslim rulers were determined to resist Christian dominance, dramatically underscores the limits of the Europeans' ability to project their power on land in this era.

In each area where the Europeans went ashore in the early centuries of expansion, they set up tribute regimes that closely resembled those the Spanish imposed on the American Indian peoples of the New World (see Chapter 25). The European overlords were content to let the indigenous peoples live in their traditional settlements, controlled largely by hereditary leaders drawn from their own communities. In most areas, little attempt was made to interfere in the daily lives of the conquered peoples as long as their leaders met the tribute quotas set by the European conquerors. The tribute was paid in the form of agricultural products grown by the peasantry under forced labor systems supervised by the peasants' own elites. In some cases, the indigenous peoples continued to harvest crops they had produced for centuries, such as the bark of the cinnamon plant (see Figure 28.2). In other areas new crops, such as coffee and sugar cane, were introduced. But in all cases, the demands for tribute took into account the local peasants' need to raise the crops on which they subsisted.

Spreading the Faith: The Missionary Enterprise in South and Southeast Asia

Although the Protestant Dutch and English were little interested in winning converts to Christianity during the early centuries of overseas expansion, the spread of Roman Catholicism was a fundamental part of the global mission of the Portuguese and Spanish. After the widespread conversion of American Indian peoples, the meager returns from the Iberian missionary offensive in Asia were disappointing. The fact that Islam had arrived in much of maritime south and southeast Asia centuries before Da Gama's arrival had much to do with the indifference or open hostility the Portuguese met when they tried to convert the peoples of these regions to Christianity. The dream of a Christian Asia joining the Iberian crusade against the Muslims was also dealt a setback by the discovery that the Hindus, whom Da Gama and some of his entourage had originally believed to be Christians, had a sophisticated and deeply entrenched set of religious ideas and rituals. As a result, widespread conversion in south Asia was limited to outcaste groups in coastal areas.

Despite these setbacks, of all the Asian areas where European enclaves were established in the early centuries of expansion, India appeared to be one of the most promising fields for religious conversion. From the 1540s onward, Franciscan and Dominican missionaries, as well as the Jesuit *Francis Xavier,* who were willing to minister to the poor, low-caste fisherfolk and untouchables along the southwest coast, converted tens of thousands. But these missionary orders soon found that they were making little headway among high-caste groups. In fact, taboos against contact with untouchables and other low-caste groups made it nearly impossible for the missionaries to approach prospective upper-caste converts.

To overcome these obstacles, an Italian Jesuit named *Robert Di Nobili* devised a different conversion strategy in the early 1600s. He learned several Indian languages, including Sanskrit, which allowed him to read the sacred texts of the Hindus. He donned the garments worn by Indian brahmans and adopted a vegetarian diet. All these measures were calculated to win over the upper-caste Hindus in south India, where he was based. Di Nobili reasoned that if he succeeded in Christianizing the high-caste Hindus, they would then bring the lower Hindu castes into the fold. But, he argued, because the ancient Hindu religion was sophisticated and deeply entrenched, Indian brahmans and other high-caste groups would listen only to those who adopted their ways. Meat eaters would be seen as defiling; those who were unfamiliar with the Hindus' sacred texts would be considered ignorant.

Despite some early successes, Di Nobili's strategy was undone by the refusal of high-caste Hindu converts to worship with low-caste groups and to give up many of their traditional beliefs and religious rituals. Rival missionary orders, particularly the Dominicans and Franciscans, denounced his approach. In assimilating to Hindu culture, they claimed, Di Nobili and his co-workers, not the Indians, were the ones who had been converted. His rivals also pointed out that the refusal of Di Nobili's high-caste converts to worship with untouchable Christians defied one of the central tenets of Christianity: the equality of all believers before God. His rivals finally won the ear of the pope, and Di Nobili was recalled to Rome. Deprived of his energy and knowledge of Indian ways, his mission in south India quickly collapsed.

Beyond socially stigmatized groups such as the untouchables, the conversion of the general populace in Asia occurred only in isolated areas. Perhaps the greatest successes of the Christian missions occurred in the northern islands of the Philippines, which had not previously been exposed to a world religion such as Islam or Buddhism. Because the Spanish had conquered the island of Luzon and the smaller islands to the south, and then governed them as part of their vast intercontinental empire, they were able launch a major missionary effort. Once areas had been "pacified" by Spanish conquistadors, the administration of the Filipinos, or at least of those who lived outside the capital at Manila, was turned over to the missionary orders. The *friars,* as the priests and brothers who went out to convert and govern the rural populace were called, became the main channel for transmitting European influences. The friars first converted local Filipino leaders. These leaders then directed their followers to build new settlements that were centered, like those in Iberia and the New World, on town squares where the local church, the residences of the missionary fathers, and government offices were located. Beyond tending to the spiritual needs of the villagers in their congregation, the friars served as government officials. They dispensed justice, oversaw the collection of the tribute payments and public works projects, and were responsible for what little education rural Filipinos received. Very often, the friars were the only Europeans most Filipinos saw for years or even decades.

Like the American Indian peoples of Spain's New World empire, most Filipinos were formally converted to Catholicism. But also like the American Indians, the Filipinos' brand of Christianity represented a creative blend of their traditional beliefs and customs and the religion preached by the friars. Because key tenets of the Christian faith were taught in Spanish for fear that they would be corrupted if put in the local languages, it is doubtful that most of the converts had a very good grasp of Christian beliefs. Many converted because Spanish dominance and their own leaders' conversion gave them little choice. Others adopted the new faith because they believed that the Christian God could protect them from illness or because they were taken with the notion that they would be equal to their Spanish overlords in heaven.

Almost all Filipinos clung to their traditional ways and in the process seriously compromised Christian beliefs and practices. Most attended confession, for example, at best once a year to be absolved of all the "heathenish" sins the missionaries accused them of committing. The veneration of Catholic saints easily fused with preconquest idolatry, and Christian miracles were easily assimilated into indigenous magical practices. The Filipinos continued public bathing, which the missionaries condemned as immodest, and refused to give up ritual drinking. They also continued to commune with deceased members of their families, often in sessions that were disguised as public recitations of the rosary. Thus, even in the Asian area where European control was the strongest and pressures for acculturation to European ways the greatest, much of the preconquest way of life and approach to the world was maintained.

Modest Returns: The Early Impact of Europeans in Maritime Asia

In 1700, after two centuries of European involvement in south and southeast Asia, most of the peoples of the area had been little affected by efforts to build trading empires and win Christian converts. European sailors had added several new routes to the Asian trading network. The most important of these were the link around the Cape of Good Hope between Europe and the Indian Ocean and the connection between the Philippine Islands and Mexico in the Americas. The Europeans' need for safe harbors and storage areas led to the establishment and rapid growth of trading centers such as Goa, Calcutta, and Batavia. It also resulted in the gradual decline of existing indigenous commercial centers, especially the Muslim cities on the east coast of Africa and somewhat later the fortress town of Malacca. The Europeans introduced the principle of sea warfare into what had been a peaceful commercial world. But the Asian trading system as a whole survived the initial shock of this innovation, and the Europeans eventually concluded that they were better off adapting to the existing commercial arrangements rather than dismantling them.

Because exchanges had been taking place between Europe and Asia for millennia, few new inventions or diseases were spread in the early centuries of expansion. This low level of major exchanges was particularly striking compared with the catastrophic interaction between Europe and the Americas. But, as in Africa, European discoveries in the long-isolated Western Hemisphere did result in the introduction of important new food plants into India, China, and other areas from the 1600s onward. Otherwise, Europeans died mainly of diseases that they contracted in Asia, such as new strains of malaria and dysentery. They spread diseases only to the more isolated parts of Asia, such as the Philippines, where the coming of the Spanish was accompanied by a devastating smallpox epidemic. The impact of European ideas, inventions, and modes of social organization was also very limited during the first centuries of expansion. Key European devices, such as clocks, were seen as toys by Asian rulers to whom they were given as presents. Christianity aroused more hostility than interest from the adherents of the ancient faiths of Asia and the more recent converts to Islam.

MING CHINA: A GLOBAL MISSION REFUSED

■■ *With the restoration of ethnic Chinese rule and the reunification of the country under the Ming dynasty (1368–1644), Chinese civilization enjoyed a new age of splendor. Renewed agrarian and commercial growth supported a population that was the largest of any center of civilization at the time, probably exceeding that of all western Europe combined. The Ming empire's resources were vast, and it had some of the world's most advanced technology as well as large numbers of skilled engineers and artisans to put its rich soils and mineral wealth to productive use. China's centralized bureaucracy remained the best organized and most efficient in the world. Although the firearms of its armies began to fall somewhat behind those of the West, China still had a formidable military establishment in numbers, organization, and leadership. A return to the examination system under the Ming rulers also ensured that the Chinese elite was one of the largest and best educated of any major civilization. In its early decades, the Ming dynasty also pursued a policy of overseas expansion that had no precedent in Chinese history. When China again turned inward in the last centuries of the dynasty, a potentially formidable obstacle to the rise of European dominance in Asia was removed.*

Zhu Yuanzhang, a military commander of peasant origins who founded the Ming dynasty, had suffered a great deal under the Mongol yoke. Both his parents and two of his brothers had died in a plague in 1344, and he and a remaining brother were reduced to begging for the land in which to bury the rest of their family. Threatened with the prospect of starvation in one of the many famines that ravaged the countryside in the later, corruption-riddled reigns of the Mongols, Zhu alternated between begging and living in a Buddhist monastery to survive. When the neighboring countryside rose in rebellion in the late 1340s, Zhu left the monastery to join a rebel band. His courage in combat and his natural capacity as a leader had soon made him one of the more promi-

nent of several rebel warlords attempting to overthrow the Yuan dynasty. After protracted military struggles against rival rebel claimants to the throne and the Mongol rulers themselves, Zhu's armies conquered most of China. Zhu declared himself the *Hongwu* emperor in 1368. He reigned for 30 years.

Immediately after he seized the throne, Zhu launched an effort to rid China of all traces of the "barbarian" Mongols. Mongol dress was discarded, Mongol names were dropped by those who had adopted them and were removed from buildings and court records, and Mongol palaces and administrative buildings in some areas were raided and sacked. The nomads themselves fled or were driven beyond the Great Wall, where Ming military expeditions pursued them on several occasions.

Another Scholar–Gentry Revival

Because the Hongwu emperor, like the founder of the earlier Han dynasty, was from a peasant family and thus poorly educated, he viewed the scholar–gentry with some suspicion. But he also realized that their cooperation was essential to the full revival of Chinese civilization. Scholars well versed in the Confucian classics were again appointed to the very highest positions in the imperial government. The generous state subsidies that had supported the imperial academies in the capital and the regional colleges were fully restored. Most critically, the civil service examination system, which the Mongols had discontinued, was reinstated and greatly expanded. In the Ming era and the Qing that followed, the examinations played a greater role in determining entry into the Chinese bureaucracy than had been the case under any earlier dynasty. At times, as many as half of all government officials had earned their positions through success in the exam competitions. This left many positions to be won by virtue of being born male in the right family or of giving timely gifts to high officials. But the exams ensured that there was a high level of education and talent for Ming administrators as a whole.

In the Ming era, the examination system was routinized and made more complex than before. Prefectural, or county, exams were held in two out of three years. The exams were given in large compounds, like the one depicted in Figure 28.3, surrounded by walls and watchtowers from which the examiners could keep an eye on the thousands of candidates. Each can-

ᴅᴏᴄᴜᴍᴇɴᴛ

Exam Questions as a Mirror of Chinese Values

The subjects and specific learning tested on the Chinese civil service exams give us insight into the behavior and attitudes expected of the literate, ruling classes of what was perhaps the best-educated preindustrial civilization. Sample questions from these exams can tell us a good deal about what sorts of knowledge were considered important and what kinds of skills were necessary for those who aspired to successful careers in the most prestigious and potentially the most lucrative field open to Chinese youths: administrative service in the imperial bureaucracy. The very fact that such a tiny portion of the Chinese male population could take the exams and an even smaller number could successfully pass them says a lot about gender roles and elitism in Chinese society. In addition, the often decisive role of a student's calligraphy—the skill with which he was able to brush the Chinese characters—reflects the emphasis the Chinese elite placed on a refined sense of aesthetics.

> Question 1: Provide the missing phrases and elaborate on the meaning of the following:
>
> The Duke of She observed to Confucius: "Among us there was an upright man called Kung who was so upright that when his father appropriated a sheep, he bore witness against him." Confucius said …
>
> [The missing phrases are, "The upright men among us are not like that. A father will screen his son and a son his father—yet uprightness is to be found in that."]

> Question 2: Write an eight-legged essay [one consisting of eight sections] on the following:
>
> Scrupulous in his own conduct and lenient only in his dealings with the people.

> Question 3: First unscramble the following characters and then comment on the significance of this quotation from one of the classic texts:
>
> Beginning, good, mutually, nature, basically, practice, far, near, men's
>
> (The correct answer is, "Men's beginning nature is basically good. Nature mutually near. Practice mutually far.")

Questions: Looking at the content of these questions, what can we learn about Chinese society and attitudes? For example, where do the Chinese look for models to orient their social behavior? What kinds of knowledge are important to the Chinese? Do they stress specialist skills or the sort of learning that we associate with a broad liberal arts education? If we take SAT exams as equivalent gauges of our social values, how would you compare Ming China and modern America? What are the advantages and drawbacks of each system?

didate was assigned a small cubicle where he struggled to answer the questions, slept, and ate over the several days that it took to complete the arduous exam. Those who passed and received the lowest degree were eligible to take the next level of exams, which were given in the provincial capitals every three years. Only the most gifted and ambitious went on because the process was fiercely competitive—in some years as many as 4000 candidates competed for 150 degrees. Success at the provincial level brought a rise in status and opened the way for appointments to positions in the middle levels of the imperial bureaucracy. It also permitted particularly talented scholars to take the imperial examinations, which were given in the capital every three years. Those who passed the imperial exams were eligible for the highest posts in the realm and were the most revered of all Chinese, except members of the royal family.

Reform: Hongwu's Efforts to Root Out Abuses in Court Politics

Hongwu was mindful of his dependence on a well-educated and loyal scholar–gentry for the day-to-day administration of the empire. But he sought to put clear limits on their influence and to institute reforms that would check the abuses of other factions at court. Early in his reign, Hongwu abolished the position of chief minister, which had formerly been the key link between the many ministries of the central government. The powers that had been amassed by those who occupied this office were transferred to the emperor himself. Hongwu also tried to impress all officials with the honesty, loyalty, and discipline he expected from them by introducing the practice of public beatings for bureaucrats found guilty of corruption or incompetence. Officials charged with mis-

Figure 28.3. *A 19th-century engraving shows the cubicles in which Chinese students and bureaucrats took the imperial civil service examinations in the capital at Beijing. Candidates were confined to the cubicles for days and completed their exams under the constant surveillance of official proctors. They brought their own food, slept in the cubicles, and were disqualified if they were found talking to others taking the exams or going outside the compound where the exams were being given.*

deeds were paraded before the assembled courtiers and beaten a specified number of times on their bare buttocks. Many died of the wounds they received in the ordeal. Those who survived never recovered from the humiliation, which was to a certain extent shared by all the scholar–gentry by virtue of the very fact that such degrading punishments could be meted out to any of them.

Hongwu also introduced measures to cut down on the court factionalism and never-ending conspiracies that had eroded the power of earlier dynasties. He decreed that the emperor's wives should come only from humble family origins. This was intended to put an end to the power plays of the consorts from high-ranking families, who built palace cliques that

were centered on their influential aristocratic relatives. He warned against allowing eunuchs to occupy positions of independent power and sought to limit their numbers within the Forbidden City. To prevent plots against the ruler and fights over succession, Hongwu established the practice of exiling all potential rivals to the throne to estates in the provinces, and he forbade them to become involved in political affairs. On the darker side, Hongwu condoned thought control, as when he had some sections from Mencius's writings that displeased him deleted forever from the writings included on the imperial exams. Although many of these measures went far to keep peace at court under Hongwu and his strong successor, the Yunglo emperor (1403–1424), they were allowed to lapse under later, less capable, rulers, with devastating consequences for the Ming Empire.

A Return to Scholar–Gentry Social Dominance

Perhaps because his lowly origins and personal suffering made him sensitive to the plight of the peasantry, Hongwu introduced measures that would improve the lot of the common people. Like most strong emperors, he promoted public works projects, including dike building and the extension of irrigation systems aimed at improving the farmers' yields. To bring new lands under cultivation and encourage the growth of a peasant class that owned the lands it toiled so hard to bring into production, Hongwu decreed that unoccupied lands would become the tax-exempt property of those who cleared and cultivated them. He lowered forced labor demands on the peasantry by both the government and members of the gentry class. Hongwu also promoted silk and cotton cloth production and other handicrafts that provided supplemental income for peasant households.

Although these measures led to some short-term improvement in the peasants' condition, they were all but offset by the growing power of rural landlord families, buttressed by alliances with relatives in the imperial bureaucracy. Gentry households with members in government service were exempted from land taxes and enjoyed special privileges, such as permission to be carried about in sedan chairs and to use fans and umbrellas. Many gentry families engaged in moneylending on the side; some even ran lucrative gambling dens. Almost all added to their estates either by buying up lands held by peasant landholders or by foreclosing on loans made to farmers in times of need in exchange for mortgages on their family plots. Peasants displaced in these ways had little choice but to become tenants of large landowners or landless laborers moving about in search of employment.

More land meant ever larger and more comfortable households for the gentry class. They justified the growing gap between their wealth and the poverty of the peasantry by contrasting their foresight and industry with the lazy and wasteful ways of the ordinary farmers. The virtues of the gentry class were celebrated in stories and popular illustrations. The latter showed members of gentry households hard at work weaving and storing grain to see them through the cold weather, while commoners, who neglected these tasks, wandered during the winter, cold and hungry, past the walled compounds and closed gates of gentry households.

At most levels of Chinese society, the Ming period continued the subordination of youths to elders and women to men that had been steadily intensifying in earlier periods. If anything, neo-Confucian thinking was even more influential than under the late Song and Yuan dynasties. Some of its advocates proposed draconian measures to suppress challenges to the increasingly rigid social roles. For example, students were expected to venerate and follow the instructions of their teachers, no matter how muddle-headed or tipsy the latter might be. A terrifying lesson in proper decorum was drawn from an incident in which a student at the imperial academy dared to dispute the findings of one of his instructors. The student was beheaded, and his severed head was hung on a pole at the entrance to the academy. Not surprisingly, this rather unsubtle solution to the problem of keeping order in the classroom merely drove student protest underground. Anonymous letters critical of poorly prepared teachers continued to circulate among the student body.

Women were also driven to underground activities to ameliorate their subordination and, if they dared, expand their career opportunities. At the court, they continued, despite Hongwu's measures, to play strong roles behind the scenes. Even able rulers such as Hongwu were swayed by the advice of favorite wives or dowager mothers and aunts. On one occasion, Hongwu chided the empress Ma for daring to inquire into the condition of the common people. She replied that because he was the father of the people, she was the mother, and thus it was quite proper for her to be concerned for the welfare of her children. Weak emperors such as *Wanli* (1573–1620) could become so embroiled in disputes arising from rivalry between their wives and concubines and their allies at court that the rulers' ability to govern was seriously impaired.

Even within the palace, the plight of most women was grim. Hundreds, sometimes thousands of attractive young women were brought to the court in the hope that they would catch the emperor's fancy and become one of his concubines or perhaps even be elevated to the status of wife. Because few actually succeeded, many spent their lives in loneli-

ness and inactivity, just waiting for the emperor to glance their way.

In society at large, women had to settle for whatever status and respect they could win within the family. As before, their success in this regard hinged largely on bearing male children and, when they were married, moving from the status of daughter-in-law to mother-in-law. The daughters of upper-class families were often taught to read and write by their parents or brothers, and many composed poetry, painted, and played musical instruments (Figure 28.4). But as in earlier centuries, even well-read women were barred from taking the civil service exams and obtaining positions in the bureaucracy.

Although women from the nonelite classes still worked the fields and in some areas sold goods in the local market, the main avenues for some degree of independence and self-expression remained becoming courtesans or entertainers. The former should be clearly distinguished from prostitutes in that they served a very different clientele and were literate and often accomplished in painting, music, and poetry. Even the most successful courtesans made their living by gratifying the needs of upper-class men for uninhibited sex and companionship. But they often enjoyed lives of luxury and much greater personal freedom than even women from scholar–gentry households.

An Age of Growth: Agriculture, Population, Commerce, and the Arts

The first decades of the Ming period were an age of buoyant economic growth in China that both was fed by and resulted in unprecedented contacts with other civilizations overseas. The territories controlled by the Ming emperors were never as extensive as those ruled by the Tang dynasty. But in the Ming era, the great commercial boom and population increase that had begun in the late Song were renewed and accelerated. The peopling of the Yangtze region and the areas to the south was given a great boost by the importation, through Spanish and Portuguese merchant intermediaries, of new food crops from the Americas, particularly root crops from the Andes highlands. Three plants—maize (or corn), sweet potatoes, and peanuts—were especially important. Because these crops could be grown on inferior soils without irrigation, their cultivation spread quickly through the hilly and marginal areas that bordered on the irrigated rice lands of southern China. They became vital supplements to the staple rice or millet diet of the Chinese people, particularly those of the rapidly growing southern regions.

Because these plants were less susceptible to drought, they also became an important hedge

Figure 28.4. *The varied diversions of the wives and concubines of Ming emperors are depicted in this scene of court life. In addition to court intrigues and maneuvers to win the emperor's favor, women of the imperial household occupied themselves with dance, music, games, and polite conversation. With eunuchs, officials, and palace guards watching them closely, the women of the palace and imperial city spent most of their lives in confined yet well appointed spaces.*

against famine. The introduction of these new crops was an important factor behind the great surge in population growth that was under way by the end of the Ming era. By 1600, the population of China had risen to about 120 million from 80 to 90 million in the 14th century. Two centuries later, in 1800, it had more than doubled and surpassed 300 million.

Agrarian expansion and population increase were paralleled in early Ming times by a renewal of commercial growth. The market sector of the domestic economy became ever more pervasive, and overseas trading links multiplied. Because China's advanced handicraft industries produced a wide variety of goods, from silk textiles and tea to fine ceramics and lacquerware, that were in high demand throughout Asia and in Europe, the terms of trade ran very much in China's favor. In addition to the Arab and Asian traders, Europeans arrived in increasing numbers at the only two places—*Macao* and, somewhat later and more sporadically, *Canton*—where they were officially allowed to do business in Ming China.

Not surprisingly, the merchant classes, particularly those engaged in long-distance trade, reaped the biggest profits from the economic boom. But a good portion of their gains was transferred to the state in the form of taxes and to the scholar–gentry in the form of bribes for official favors. Much of the merchants' wealth was invested in land rather than being plowed back into trade or manufacturing, because land owning, not commerce, remained the surest route to social status in China.

Ming prosperity was reflected in the fine arts, which found generous patrons both at court and among the scholar–gentry class more generally. Although the monochromatic simplicity of the work of earlier dynasties was sustained by the ink brush paintings of artists such as Xuwei, much of the Ming output was busier and more colorful. Portraits and scenes of court, city, or country life were more prominent. Nonetheless, the Chinese continued to delight in depicting individual scholars or travelers contemplating the beauty of mountains, lakes, and marshes, which dwarf the human observers.

Whereas the painters of the Ming era concentrated mainly on developing established techniques and genres, major innovation was occurring in literature. Most notable in this regard was the full development of the Chinese novel, which had had its beginnings in the writings of the Yuan era. The novel form was given great impetus by the spread of literacy among the upper classes in the Ming era. This was facilitated by the growing availability of books that had resulted from the spread of woodblock printing from the 10th century onward. Ming novels, such as *The Water Margin, Monkey,* and *The Golden Lotus,* were recognized as classics in their own time and continue to set the standard for Chinese prose literature today. Thus, although Chinese technical inventiveness slowed at a critical time, given the great advances in science and technology in contemporary Europe, Ming achievements in the fine arts were impressive, even in comparison with those of the glorious Tang and Song eras.

An Age of Expansion: The Zhenghe Expeditions

The seemingly boundless energy of the Chinese in early decades of Ming rule drove them far beyond the traditional areas of expansion in central Asia and the regions south of the Yangtze. In the reign of the third Ming emperor, Yunglo, they launched a series of expeditions that had no precedent in Chinese history. Between 1405 and 1423, a court eunuch named *Zhenghe,* one of Yunglo's most trusted subordinates, led seven major expeditions overseas (Map 28.2). A mix of motives, including a desire to explore other lands and proclaim the glory of the Ming empire to the wider world, prompted the voyages. The early expeditions were confined largely to southeast Asian seas and kingdoms. The last three expeditions reached as far as Persia, southern Arabia, and the east coast of Africa—distances comparable to those covered by the Portuguese in their early voyages around Africa.

The ships and fleets involved in each of the overseas missions were truly impressive. The initial fleet contained 62 ships (compared with 3 for Columbus in 1492 and 4 for Da Gama 6 years later) that carried nearly 28,000 sailors, merchants, and soldiers (compared with 150 for Da Gama's first voyage around Africa). Some of the larger ships in Zhenghe's fleet were more than 400 feet long and displaced up to 1500 tons of water; the largest of Da Gama's caravels could not have been much more than 60 feet long and displaced about 300 tons of water. Taken together, the expeditions led by Zhenghe leave little doubt that the Chinese had the capacity to expand on a global scale at least a century before the Europeans rounded the Cape of Good Hope and entered Asian waters.

Although they had ample means, the Chinese were ambivalent about the worth of the voyages. It was gratifying to have "barbarian" peoples from the southern seas do homage to the emissaries of the Ming ruler. In addition, the giraffes and other curious animals that were carried home made interesting additions to the imperial zoo. But there were few tangible returns from these expensive undertakings. The scholar–gentry rivals of Zhenghe and other court eunuchs could convincingly argue that the voyages were a luxury that the empire simply could not afford. When they noted that the Mongols were once again restless beyond the defenses of the Great Wall (for which repair and reinforcements were needed), it was hard to refute their insistence that the defense of the empire must come before seemingly frivolous overseas exploration. There was one more voyage after Yunglo's death in 1424, but his successors shared little of his enthusiasm for the voyages, so they were abandoned in the early 1430s. China's spectacular entry onto the world stage proved a short run indeed.

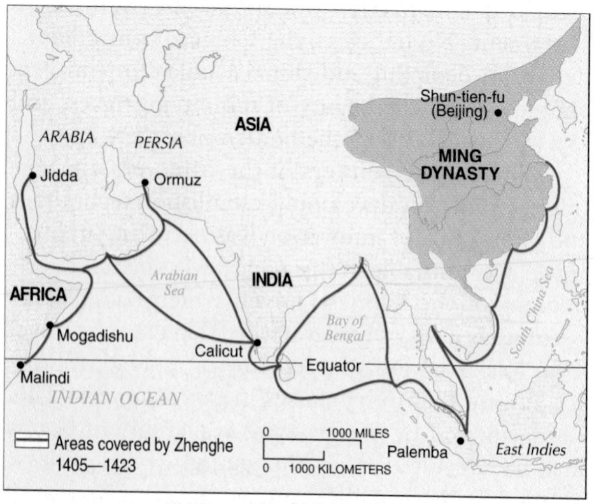

Map 28.2 *Ming China and the Zhenghe Expeditions, 1405–1423*

IN DEPTH

Means and Motives for Overseas Expansion: Europe and China Compared

Given China's capacity for overseas expansion and the fateful consequences for global history that resulted from the fact that Europe, not China, eventually took the lead, the reasons for the Chinese failure to follow up on their early voyages of exploration merit serious examination. The explanations for the Chinese refusal to commit to overseas expansion can be best understood if they are contrasted with the forces that drove the Europeans with increasing determination into the outside world. In broad terms, such a comparison underscores the fact that although both the Europeans and the Chinese had the means to expand on a global scale, only the Europeans had strong motives for doing so.

The social and economic transformations that occurred in European civilization during the late Middle Ages and the early Renaissance had brought it to a level of development that compared favorably with China in many areas (see Chapters 21, 22, and 23). Although the Chinese empire was far larger and more populous than tiny nation-states such as Portugal, Spain, and Holland, the European kingdoms had grown more efficient at mobilizing their more limited resources. Rivalries between the states of a fragmented Europe had also fostered a greater aggressiveness and sense of competition on the part of the Europeans than the Chinese rulers could even imagine. China's armies were far larger than those of any of the European kingdoms, but European soldiers were on the whole better led, armed, and disciplined. Chinese wet rice agriculture was more productive than European farming, and the Chinese rulers had a far larger population to cultivate their fields, build their dikes and bridges, work their mines, and make tools, clothing, and weapons. But on the whole, the technological innovations of the medieval period had given the Europeans an advantage over the Chinese in the animal and machine power they could generate—a capacity that did much to make up for their deficiencies in human power.

Despite their differences, both civilizations had the means for sustained exploration and expansion overseas, although the Chinese were ready to undertake such enterprises a few centuries earlier than the Europeans. As the voyages of Da Gama, Columbus, and Zhenghe demonstrated, both civilizations had the shipbuilding and navigational skills and technology needed to tackle such ambitious undertakings. Why, then, were the impressive Zhenghe expeditions a dead end, whereas the more modest probes of Columbus and Da Gama were the beginning of half a millennium of European overseas expansion and global dominance?

The full answer to this question is as complex as the societies it asks us to compare. But we can learn a good deal by looking at the groups pushing for expansion within each civilization and the needs that drove them into the outside world. There was widespread support for exploration and overseas expansion in seafaring European nations such as Portugal, Spain, Holland, and England. European rulers financed expeditions they hoped would bring home precious metals and trade goods that could be sold at great profits. Both treasure and profits could be translated into warships and armies that would strengthen these rulers in their incessant wars with European rivals and, in the case of the Iberian kingdoms, with their Muslim adversaries.

European traders looked for much the same benefits from overseas expansion. Rulers and merchants also hoped that explorers would find new lands whose climates and soils were suitable for growing crops such as sugar that were in high demand and thus would bring big profits. Leaders of rival branches of the Christian faith believed that overseas expansion would give their missionaries access to unlimited numbers of heathens to be converted or would put them in touch with the legendary lost king, Prester John, who would ally with them in their struggle with the infidel Muslims.

By contrast, the Chinese Zhenghe expeditions were very much the project of a single emperor and a favored eunuch, whose Muslim family origins may go a long way toward accounting for his wanderlust. Yunglo appears to have been driven by little more than curiosity and the vain desire to impress his greatness and that of his empire on peoples whom he considered inferior. Although some Chinese merchants went along for the ride, most felt little need for the voyages. They already traded on favorable terms for all the products Asia, and in some cases Europe and Africa, could offer. The merchants had the option of waiting for other peoples to come to them, or, if they were a bit more ambitious, of going out in their own ships to southeast Asia.

The scholar–gentry were actively hostile to the Zhenghe expeditions. The voyages strengthened the position of the much-hated eunuchs, who vied with the scholar–gentry for the emperor's favor and the high posts that went with it. In addition, the scholar–gentry saw the voyages as a foolish waste of resources that the empire could not afford. They believed it would be better to direct the wealth and talents of the empire to building armies and fortifications to keep out the hated Mongols and other nomads. After all, the memory of foreign rule was quite fresh.

As this discussion makes clear, the elites of western European nations had very good reasons for pushing voyages of exploration and projects of overseas expansion. The rulers and bureaucrats of China, on the other hand, had no reasons that were very convincing. In fact, there were very persuasive reasons, rooted in centuries of struggle against the nomads, for diverting resources that might have gone into overseas expeditions into projects on the home front. As had happened so often before in their history, the Chinese were drawn inward, fixated on internal struggles and the continuing threat from central Asia. As the Chinese retreated, the Europeans surged outward. It is difficult to exaggerate the magnitude of the consequences for both civilizations and all humankind.

Questions: How might history have been changed if the Chinese had mounted a serious and sustained effort to project their power overseas in the decades before Da Gama rounded the Cape of Good Hope? Why did the Chinese fail to foresee the threat that European expansion would pose for the rest of Asia and finally for China itself? Did other civilizations have the capacity for global expansion in this era? What prevented them from launching expeditions similar to those of the Chinese and Europeans? In terms of motivation for overseas expansion, were peoples such as the Muslims, Indians, and American Indians more like the Europeans or the Chinese?

Chinese Retreat and the Arrival of the Europeans

Just over a half century after the last of the Zhenghe expeditions, China had purposely moved from the position of a great power reaching out overseas to an increasingly isolated empire. In 1390, the first imperial edict aimed at limiting Chinese overseas commerce was issued. In the centuries that followed, the Ming war fleet declined dramatically in the number and quality of its ships, and strict limits were placed on the size and number of masts with which a seagoing ship might be fitted. As the Chinese shut themselves in, the Europeans probed ever farther across the globe and were irresistibly drawn to the most legendary of all overseas civilizations, the Middle Kingdom of China. In addition to the trading contacts noted earlier, Christian missionaries infiltrated Chinese coastal areas and tried to gain access to the court, where they hoped to curry favor with the Ming emperors. While religious orders such as the Franciscans and Dominicans toiled to win converts among the common people and made modest progress that could be counted in the tens of thousands, the Jesuits adopted the top-down strategy that Di Nobili had pursued in India (Figure 28.5). In China, however, a single person, the Ming emperor, instead of a whole

Figure 28.5. *Jesuits in Chinese dress at the emperor's court. The Jesuits believed that the best way to convert a great civilization such as China was to adopt the dress, customs, language, and manners of its elite. They reasoned that once the scholar–gentry elite had been converted, they would bring the rest of China's vast population into the Christian fold.*

caste, sat at the top of the social hierarchy, and for that reason the rulers and their chief advisors became the prime targets of the Jesuit mission.

Some Chinese scholars showed interest in Christian teachings and Western thinking more generally. But the Jesuit missionaries who made their way to Beijing clearly recognized that their scientific knowledge and technical skills were the keys to maintaining a presence at the Ming court and eventually interesting the Chinese elite in Christianity. Beginning in the 1580s, a succession of brilliant Jesuit scholars, such as *Matteo Ricci* and *Adam Schall*, spent most of their time in the imperial city correcting faulty calendars, forging cannon, fixing clocks imported from Europe, and astounding the Chinese scholar–gentry with the accuracy of their instruments and their ability to predict eclipses. They won a few converts among the elite. However, most court officials were suspicious of these strange-looking "barbarians" with large noses and hairy faces, and they tried to limit their contacts with the imperial family. Some at the court, especially the scholar–officials who were humiliated by the foreigners' corrections to their calendars, were openly hostile to the Jesuits. Despite serious harassment, however, the later Ming emperors remained sufficiently fascinated by these very learned and able visitors that they allowed a handful to remain. When the Ming were overthrown by the *Manchu* nomads from the north, the Jesuits were able to hold and even strengthen their position at court.

Ming Decline and the Chinese Predicament

By the late 1500s, the Ming retreat from overseas involvement had become just one facet of a familiar pattern of dynastic decline. The highly centralized, absolutist political structure, which had been established by Hongwu and had been run well by able successors such as Yunglo, became a major liability under the mediocre or incompetent men who occupied the throne through much of the last two centuries of Ming rule. Decades of rampant official corruption, exacerbated by the growing isolation of weak rulers by the thousands of eunuchs who gradually came to dominate life within the Forbidden City, eventually eroded the foundations on which the empire was built.

Public works projects, including the critical dike works on the Yellow River, fell into disrepair, and

floods, drought, and famine soon ravaged the land. Peasants in afflicted districts were reduced to eating the bark from trees or the excrement of wild geese. Some peasants sold their children into slavery to keep them from starving, and peasants in some areas resorted to cannibalism. Rapacious local landlords built huge estates by taking advantage of the increasingly desperate peasant population. As in earlier phases of dynastic decline, farmers who had been turned off their land and tortured for taxes, or had lost most of the crop they had grown, turned to flight, banditry, and finally open rebellion to confiscate food and avenge their exploitation by greedy landlords and corrupt officials.

True to the pattern of dynastic rise and fall, internal disorder resulted in and was intensified by foreign threats and renewed assaults by nomadic peoples from beyond the Great Wall. One of the early signs of the seriousness of imperial deterioration was the inability of Chinese bureaucrats and military forces to put an end to the epidemic of Japanese (and ethnic Chinese) pirate attacks that ravaged the southern coast in the mid-16th century. Despite an official preoccupation with the Mongols early in the Ming era and with the Jurchens or Manchus to the northeast of the Great Wall in later times, the dynasty was finally toppled in 1644, not by the Mongols in the west but by rebels from within. By that time, the administrative apparatus had become so feeble that the last Ming emperor, *Chongzhen*, did not realize how serious the rebel advance was until enemy soldiers were scaling the walls of the Forbidden City. After watching his wife withdraw to her chambers to commit suicide, and after bungling an attempt to kill his young daughter, the ill-fated Chongzhen retreated to the imperial gardens and hanged himself rather than face capture.

Although they managed to topple the dynasty, none of the divided rebel forces that challenged the Ming in the 1640s proved a viable replacement. A political vacuum within China once again opened the way for invasions and conquest by a nomadic people from beyond the Great Wall. This time, the Jurchens or Manchus, not the Mongols, seized power after a series of military victories and the capture of the imperial capital. The Manchu leader, Nurhaci, established a new dynasty, the Qing, which would rule China for nearly three and a half centuries and prove to be the last of a succession of imperial houses that extended back more than two millennia.

FENDING OFF THE WEST: JAPAN'S REUNIFICATION AND THE FIRST CHALLENGE

■■ *Fortunately for the Japanese, their ability to defend their island home was not tested in the early centuries of expansion. In the decades just after the Europeans began to arrive in the islands in the 1540s, the Japanese found leaders who had the military and diplomatic skills and ruthlessness needed to restore the shogunate. To do so it was necessary to force the daimyo, or most powerful warlords, to acknowledge a supreme commander, if not a true sovereign. By the early 1600s, with the potential threat from the Europeans looming ever larger in the Japanese imagination, the new Tokugawa shoguns had gained sufficient control to let them gradually shut down contacts with outsiders (Map 28.3). They succeeded in enveloping the islands in a state of isolation that lasted nearly two and a half centuries. One of the main casualties of this move into isolation was the Christian missionary effort, which in the 1580s seemed on the verge of converting the shogun and the majority of his subjects.*

By the 16th century, the daimyo stalemate and the pattern of recurring civil war were so entrenched in Japanese society that a succession of three remarkable military leaders was needed to restore unity and internal peace. *Nobunaga*, the first of these leaders, was from a minor warrior household. But his skills as a military leader soon vaulted him into prominence in the ongoing struggles for power among the daimyo lords. As a leader Nobunaga combined daring, a willingness to innovate, and ruthless determination—some would say cruelty. He was not afraid to launch a surprise attack against an enemy that outnumbered him ten to one, and he was one of the first of the daimyos to make extensive use of the firearms that the Japanese had begun to acquire from the Portuguese in the 1540s. The measures Nobunaga took against those who resisted him, such as the slaughter of thousands of monks and villagers attached to the Buddhist monastery at Mount Hiei near Kyoto, may have cowed some of the weaker daimyos into submission.

In 1573, Nobunaga deposed the last of the Ashikaga shoguns, who had long ruled in name only.

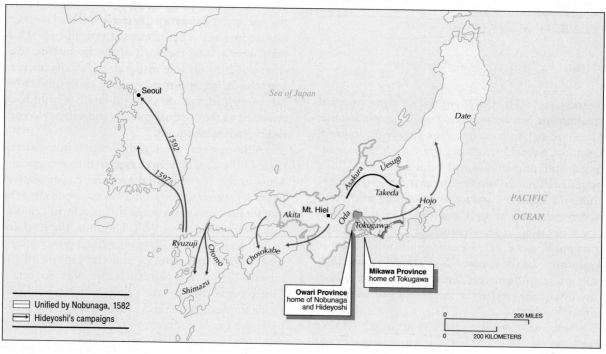

Map 28.3 *Japan During the Rise of the Tokugawa Shogunate*

By 1580, he had unified much of central Honshu under his command. As his armies drove against the powerful western daimyo in 1582, Nobunaga was caught off guard by one of his vassal generals and was killed when the Kyoto temple where he had taken refuge was burned to the ground.

At first it appeared that Nobunaga's campaigns to restore central authority to the islands might be undone. But his ablest general, *Toyotomi Hideyoshi* (Figure 28.6), moved quickly to punish those who had betrayed Nobunaga and to renew the drive to break the power of the daimyos who had not yet submitted to him. Though the son of a peasant, Hideyoshi matched his master in military prowess but was far more skillful at diplomacy. A system of alliances and a string of victories over the last of the resisting daimyos made Hideyoshi the military master of Japan by 1590.

Figure 28.6. *In this late 16th-century portrait, Hideyoshi (1536–1598) grasps the sword that catapulted him to power and exudes the discipline and self-confidence that impelled his campaigns to unify Japan. Although warrior skills were vital in his rise to power, he and other members of the samurai class were expected to be literate, well-mannered by the conventions of the day, and attuned to the refined aesthetics of rock gardens and tea ceremonies.*

The ambitious overlord had much more grandiose schemes of conquest in mind. He dreamed of ruling China and even India, although he knew little about either place. Hideyoshi also threatened, among others, the Spanish in the Philippines. Apparently as the first step toward fulfilling this vision of empire building on a grand scale, Hideyoshi launched two attacks on Korea in 1592 and 1597, each of which involved nearly 150,000 soldiers. After initial successes, both campaigns stalled. The first ended in defeat; the second was still in progress when Hideyoshi died in 1598.

Although Hideyoshi had tried to ensure that he would be succeeded by his son, the vassals he had appointed to carry out his wishes tried to seize power for themselves after his death. One of these vassals, *Tokugawa Ieyasu*, had originally come from a minor daimyo house. But as an ally of Hideyoshi, he had been able to build up a powerful domain on the heavily populated Kanto plain. Ieyasu soon emerged triumphant from the renewed warfare that resulted from Hideyoshi's death. Rather than continue Hideyoshi's campaigns of overseas expansion, Ieyasu concentrated on consolidating power at home. In 1603, he was granted the title of shogun by the emperor, an act that formally inaugurated centuries of rule by the Tokugawa family.

Under Ieyasu's direction, the remaining daimyos were reorganized. Most of the lands in central Honshu either were controlled directly by the Tokugawa family, who now ruled the land from the city of *Edo* (later Tokyo), or were held by daimyos who were closely allied with the shoguns. Although many of the outlying or vassal daimyos retained their domains, they were carefully controlled and were required to pledge their personal allegiance to the shogun. Over time, the estates of numerous vassal daimyos were reduced in size or broken up and absorbed by the Tokugawa family or its close allies. It was soon clear that the Tokugawas' victory had put an end to the civil wars and brought a semblance of political unity to the islands.

Dealing with the European Challenge

All through the decades when the three unifiers were struggling to bring the feisty daimyos under control, they also had to contend with a new force in Japanese history: the Europeans. From the time in 1543 when shipwrecked Portuguese sailors were washed up on the shore of Kyushu island, European traders and missionaries had been visiting the islands in increasing numbers. The traders brought the Japanese goods that were produced mainly in India, China, and southeast Asia and exchanged them for silver, copper, pottery, and lacquerware. Perhaps more important, European traders and the missionaries who followed them to the islands brought firearms, printing presses, and other Western devices such as clocks. The firearms, which the Japanese could themselves manufacture within years and were improving in design within a generation, revolutionized Japanese warfare and contributed much to the victories of the unifiers. Commercial contacts with the Europeans also encouraged the Japanese to venture overseas to trade in nearby Formosa and Korea and in places as distant as the Philippines and Siam.

Soon after the merchants, Christian missionaries, including Francis Xavier (Figure 28.7), arrived in the islands and set to work converting the Japanese to Roman Catholicism. Beginning in the outlying daimyos' domains, the missionaries worked their way toward the political center that was beginning to coalesce around Nobunaga and his followers by the 1570s. Seeing Christianity as a counterforce to the mil-

itant Buddhist orders that were resisting his rise to power, Nobunaga took the missionaries under his protection and encouraged them to preach their faith to his people. The Jesuits, adopting the same top-down strategy of conversion that they had followed in India and China, converted many of the daimyos and their samurai retainers. Some of the Jesuits were also convinced that they were on the verge of winning over Nobunaga, who delighted in wearing Western clothes, encouraged his artists to copy Western paintings of the Virgin Mary and scenes from the life of Christ, and permitted the missionaries to build churches in towns throughout the islands. The missionaries were persuaded that Nobunaga's conversion would bring the whole of the Japanese people into the Christian fold. Even without it, they reported converts in the hundreds of thousands by the early 1580s.

In the late 1580s, quite suddenly, the missionaries saw their carefully mounted conversion campaign collapse. Nobunaga was murdered, and his successor, Hideyoshi, though not yet openly hostile, was lukewarm toward the missionary enterprise. In part, the missionaries' fall from favor resulted from the fact that

Figure 28.7. *The arrival of Francis Xavier and his entourage in Japan is depicted in this 16th-century screen painting. The painting wonderfully conveys Japanese perceptions of these strangers from distant lands as exotic, awkward, and curiously dressed. Other than differences in skin color, to which the Japanese were highly sensitive, all have rather similar facial features, perhaps because the Japanese thought that all the Westerners looked alike.*

the resistance of the Buddhist sects had been crushed. More critically, Hideyoshi and his followers were alarmed by reports of converts refusing to obey their overlords' commands when they believed them to be in conflict with their newly adopted Christian beliefs. Thus, the threat that the new religion posed for the established social order was growing more apparent. That threat was compounded by signs that the Europeans might follow up their commercial and missionary overtures with military expeditions aimed at conquering the islands. The Japanese had been strongly impressed with the firearms and pugnacity of the Europeans, and they did not take threats of invasion lightly.

Japan's Self-Imposed Isolation

Growing doubts about European intentions, and fears that both merchants and missionaries might subvert the existing social order, led to official measures to restrict foreign activities in Japan, beginning in the late 1580s. First, Hideyoshi ordered the Christian missionaries to leave the islands—an order that was not rigorously enforced, at least at the outset. By the mid-1590s, Hideyoshi was actively persecuting both Christian missionaries and converts. His successor, Ieyasu, continued this persecution and then officially banned the faith in 1614. European missionaries were driven out of the islands; those who remained underground were hunted down and killed or expelled. Japanese converts were compelled to renounce their faith; those who refused were imprisoned, tortured, and executed. By the 1630s, the persecutions, even against Christians who tried to practice their faith in secret, had become so intense that thousands of converts in the western regions joined in hard-fought but hopeless rebellions against the local daimyos and the forces of the shogun. With the suppression of these uprisings, Christianity in Japan was reduced to an underground faith of isolated communities. As in India and China, a promising start toward conversion had died out.

Under Ieyasu and his successors, the persecution of the Christians grew into a broader campaign to isolate Japan from outside influences. In 1616, foreign traders were confined to a handful of cities; in the 1630s, all Japanese ships were forbidden to trade or even sail overseas. One after another, different European nations were either officially excluded from Japan (the Spanish) or decided that trading there was no longer worth the risk (the English). By the 1640s, only a limited number of Dutch and Chinese ships were allowed to carry on commerce on the small island of *Deshima* in Nagasaki Bay. The export of silver and copper was greatly restricted, and Western books were banned to prevent Christian ideas from reentering the country. Foreigners were permitted to live and travel only in very limited areas.

By the mid-17th century, Japan's retreat into almost total isolation was complete. Much of the next century was spent in consolidating the internal control of the Tokugawa Shogunate by extending bureaucratic administration into the vassal daimyo domains throughout the islands. In the 18th century, a revival of neo-Confucian philosophy, which had marked the period of the Tokugawa's rise to power, increasingly gave way to the influence of thinkers who championed the *school of National Learning*. As its name implies, the new ideology laid great emphasis on Japan's unique historical experience and the revival of indigenous culture at the expense of Chinese imports such as Confucianism. In the centuries that followed, through contacts with the small Dutch community at Deshima, members of the Japanese elite also followed developments in the West. Their avid interest in European achievements contrasted sharply with the indifference of the Chinese scholar–gentry in this period to the doings of the "hairy barbarians" from Europe.

The openings the Japanese left to the outside world meant that when the second push by the Western powers for entry into Japan came, beginning in the 1850s, the Japanese knew much more clearly than the Chinese what they were up against. The indifference of the Chinese left them blind to the intentions and power of their European adversaries and thus unable to deal effectively with European demands and ultimately military incursions in the mid-19th century. After much debate within the daimyo elite, the Japanese first followed a policy of concession and evasion in the face of the Western challenge. They then concentrated on building up their strength by adopting European innovations that they had monitored over the centuries through contacts with the Dutch at Deshima.

Conclusion

Asia and the First Phase of Europe's Global Expansion

During the early modern period in global history, the West's surge in exploration and commercial expansion touched most of Asia only peripherally. This was particularly true of east Asia, where the political cohesion and military strength of the vast Chinese empire and the Japanese warrior-dominated states blocked all hope of European advance. Promising missionary inroads in the 16th century were stifled by hostile Tokugawa shoguns in the early 17th century. They were also carefully contained by the Ming emperors and the nomadic Qing dynasty in the mid-1600s. Strong Chinese and Japanese rulers limited trading contacts with the aggressive Europeans and confined European merchants to a few ports—Macao and Canton in China, Deshima in Japan—that were remote from their respective capitals. Change in China, Japan, Korea, and central Asia arose mainly from internal factors. Continuity was ensured by the persistence of centuries-old cultural and social patterns and techniques of handling alien intruders such as the European seafarers.

Even in most of south and southeast Asia, where the European impact in the early centuries of Western overseas expansion was much more pronounced, most Asians remained in charge of their own destinies. European control was limited to the coastal periphery of great empires, such as that built by the Mughals in India, and the kingdoms of mainland and island southeast Asia. Sea power allowed the Portuguese, and after them the Spanish, Dutch, and English, to control trading outposts in ports such as Goa, Malacca, Batavia, and Bombay. In some instances they were even able to conquer parts of island kingdoms, such as the southwest corner of Ceylon or the northwest end of Java. Christian missionaries won few converts except in areas such as the northern Philippines where none of the major Asian religions had previously spread. Even in commerce and seafaring, endeavors in which the influence of the West in Asia was the greatest, the Europeans found that it was better to blend into existing networks and to cooperate with local rulers and merchants than to build expensive and vulnerable trading empires.

found in the works of J. C. van Leur, M.A.P. Meilink-Roelofsz, K. N. Chaudhuri, Ashin Das Gupta, Sanjay Subrahmanyam, and Michael Pearson. C. R. Boxer's *The Portuguese Seaborne Empire* (1969) and *The Dutch Seaborne Empire* (1965) are still essential reading, although the latter has little on the Europeans in Asia. Boxer's *Race Relations in the Portuguese Colonial Empire, 1415–1852* (1963) provides a stimulating, if contentious, introduction to the history of European social interaction with overseas peoples in the early centuries of expansion. Important correctives to Boxer's work can be found in the more recent contributions of George Winius. G. B. Sansom's *The Western World and Japan* (1968) includes a wealth of information on the interaction between Europeans and, despite its title, peoples throughout Asia, and it has good sections on the missionary initiatives in both China and Japan.

The period of the Ming dynasty has been the focus of broader and more detailed studies than the dynasties that preceded it. An important early work is Charles O. Hucker's *The Censorial System of Ming China* (1966). Two essential recent works are Albert Chan's *The Glory and Fall of the Ming Dynasty* (1982) and Edward Dreyer's more traditional political history, *Early Ming China, 1355–1435* (1982). There are also wonderful insights into daily life at various levels of Chinese society in Roy Huang's very readable *1587: A Year of No Significance; The Ming Dynasty in Decline* (1981) and into the interaction between the Chinese and the Jesuits in Jonathan Spence's *The Memory Palace of Matteo Ricci* (1984). Frederic Wakeman Jr.'s *The Great Enterprise*, 2 vols. (1985), is essential to an understanding of the transition from Ming to Manchu rule. The early chapters of Spence's *The Search for Modern China* (1990) also provide an illuminating overview of that process.

Perhaps the best introductions to the situation in Japan in the early phase of European expansion are provided by G. B. Sansom's survey, *A History of Japan, 1615–1867* (1963), and Conrad Totman's *Politics in the Tokugawa Bakufu, 1600–1843* (1967). Numerous studies on the Europeans in Japan include those by Donald Keene, Grant Goodman, Noel Perrin, and C. R. Boxer. Intellectual trends in Japan in this era are most fully treated in H. D. Harootunian's *Toward Restoration: The Growth of Political Consciousness in Tokugawa Japan* (1970).

Further Readings

C.G.F. Simkins's *The Traditional Trade of Asia* (1968) provides an overview of the Asian trading network from ancient times until about the 18th century. Much more detailed accounts of specific segments of the system, as well as the impact of the Dutch and Portuguese on it, can be

On the Web

The achievement of the Ming and later Qing Dynasties are on view at virtual tours of their versions of the Great Wall and Forbidden City offered at http://www.chinavista.com/travel/greatwall/greatwall.html and http://www.chinavista.com/beijing/gugong/!start.html.

Perhaps the finest of all virtual tour sites on the Web is that which provides a glimpse into the rich cultural life of the Tokugawa capital of Edo at http://www.us-japan.org/edomatsu/Start/frame.html. This shogunate was established after a civil war that followed the reigns of Nobunaga Oda (http://www.ox.compsoc.net/~gemini/simons/historyweb/oda–nobunaga.html) and Toyotomi Hideyoshi, developer of the grand Osaka Castle (http://www.tourism.city.osaka. jp/en/castle/mainmenu.htm). It marked the ascension of Tokugawa Ieyasu who is the subject of a web page (http://www.namos.co.jp/aichi-hatsu/english/ittop.htm) that offers insight into his military and economic strategies as well as some panoramic views of places that figured in his rise to power.

The period that saw the rise and development of the Tokugawa witnessed much exchange between Asians and Christian missionaries elsewhere in Asia. An exceptional on-line study of these exchanges and the lives of Mateo Ricci, Adam Schall and Robert Di Nobili can be found at http://acc6.its.brooklyn.cuny.edu/~phalsall/texts/ric-jour.html and http://metalab.unc.edu/expo/vatican.exhibit/exhibit/i-rome_to_china/Rome_to_china.html. These exchanges were made possible by earlier developments in sea-going transportation, trade and exploration, such as the travels of Zhenghe or Chengho (http://chinapage.com/chengho.html), the development of the caravel (http://www.mariner.org/age/portuguese.html and http://www.pfri.hr/pov/pov07.html) and the development of Portuguese and Dutch trading empires (http://www.geocities.com/Athens/Styx/6497/).

The homepage of the Dutch East Indian Company (http://allserv.rug.ac.be/~sdconinc/VOC/welcome.htm) provides luminous virtual tours of both Batavia and Deshima that demonstrate the still peripheral role of Europeans in Asia at this time.

PART 5

Industrialization and Western Global Hegemony, 1750–1914

Test #2 material starts

INTRODUCTION

Between 1750 and 1918, world history was dominated by growing European imperialism. These were the decades in which Western civilization (embracing much of North America as well as western Europe) experienced the Industrial Revolution, which transformed the bases of production through new technology and new sources of power. European dominance in the world economy became almost overwhelming.

In contrast to the early modern period, when Western power on land was limited, no area could escape the possibility of extensive European or United States penetration. Africa, previously able to resist Western power while strengthening internal political units, was carved up into a patchwork of colonies. The West's new hegemony was also expressed through growing commercial penetration of areas such as China and the Ottoman Empire that were not held as colonies. Finally, Western hegemony was expressed by the need for leaders in every civilization to decide what Western institutions and values to imitate and how.

International commercial contacts increased steadily. They were enhanced by major technological innovations, notably the steamship, railroad, and telegraph. Cultural contacts reflected Western power as well. Just as Christianity and commercial penetration went hand in hand in Latin America during the early modern period, by the end of the 19th century religious conversion began to accompany imperialist entry into Africa's heartlands, and Western science and new ideas such as nationalism spread even more widely.

By the 1850s, the leading issues in all civilizations began to revolve around what to do about the West's new power: how and whether to resist, and what could or should be imitated. Common responses included growing interest in establishing new kinds of schools and, in many cases, even parliaments and constitutions.

CHRONOLOGY: FROM INDUSTRIAL REVOLUTION TO THE BEGINNINGS OF A WESTERN BREAKDOWN

The beginning this new period, 1750, focuses on no particular event. The war that opened in that decade, which produced battles in Europe, North America, and India as well as on the seas, has some claim to being history's first global conflict. More important is the fact that during the 1750s, the forces that produced Europe's Industrial Revolution began to take shape: rapid population growth, expansion of manufacturing, and a surge of new inventions. The real Industrial Revolution is properly dated a few decades later, but the second half of the 18th century included its formative stages.

With Western industrialization under way, signs of its impact on the wider world followed quickly. In 1798, a modest French expeditionary force seized Egypt from its Muslim rulers—a clear sign of a new power balance in the eastern Mediterranean. In the 1820s, Britain's hold over India began to intensify. In the 1830s, the West forced open China's markets, using insistence on the right to sell opium in China as its entering wedge. In the 1850s, Britain and France defeated Russia in a war in its own Crimean backyard, while the United States and Britain pried open Japanese markets under threat of naval bombardment. The American Civil War (1861–1865) saw the industrial North prevail over the slaveholding South. Also in the 1860s, the scramble for new African colonies began. In the 1870s, a new level of commercial penetration started to transform the Latin Ameri-

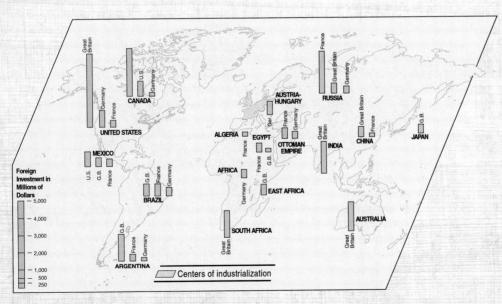

Industrial Development in Key Regional Centers, c. 1900

1700 C.E.	1800 C.E.	1825 C.E.
1730–1850 Population boom in western Europe	**1805–1849** Muhammad Ali rules Egypt	**1825–1855** Repression in Russia
1770 James Watt's steam engine; beginning of Industrial Revolution	**1808–1825** Latin-American wars of independence	**1826** New Zealand colonization begins
1776–1783 American Revolution	**1815** Vienna settlement	**1830, 1848** Revolutions in Europe
1786–1790 First British reforms in India	**1815** British annexation of Cape Town and region of southern Africa	**1835** English education in India
1788 Australian colonization begins	**1822** Brazil declares independence	**1838** Ottoman trade treaty with Britain
1789–1815 French Revolution and Napoleon	**1823** Monroe Doctrine	**1839–1841** Opium War between England and China
1798 Napoleon's invasion of Egypt		**1839–1876** Reforms in Ottoman Empire
		1840 Semiautonomous government in Canada
		1846–1848 Mexican-American War
		1848 ff. Beginnings of Marxism

can economy and social relationships. Between the 1850s and 1900, the islands of Polynesia were brought under Western control as colonies, and the Maoris of New Zealand were subjected to a government of European settlers.

The industrial–imperialist period drew to a close with the outbreak of World War I in 1914 simply because, in the wake of this massive conflict, the West's world hold began to recede. Revolutions in Russia, Japanese expansion, and the beginnings of colonial revolt signaled the end of the undisputed dominance of the industrial West.

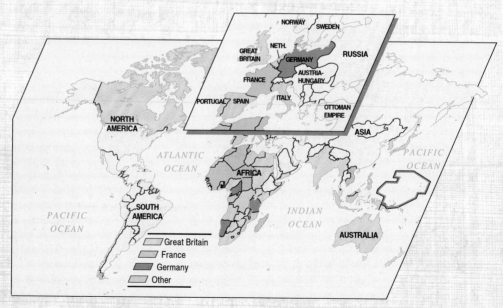

Main Colonial Holdings, c. 1914

1850 C.E.	1875 C.E.	1900 C.E.
1850–1864 Taiping rebellion in China	**1877–1878** Ottomans out of most of Balkans; Treaty of San Stefano	**1901** Commonwealth of Australia
1853 Perry expedition to Edo Bay in Japan	**1879–1890s** Partition of West Africa	**1903** Construction of Panama Canal begins
1854–1856 Crimean War	**1882** British takeover of Egypt	**1904–1905** Russo-Japanese War
1867 Union of central and eastern Canada	**1884–1914** Russian industrialization	**1905–1906** Revolution in Russia; limited reforms
1858 British Parliament assumes control over India	**1885** Formation of National Congress Party in India	**1908** Young Turk rising
1860–1868 Civil strife in Japan	**1886–1888** Slavery abolished in Cuba and Brazil	**1910** Japan annexes Korea
1861 Emancipation of serfs in Russia; reform era begin	**1890** Japanese constitution	**1911–1912** Revolution in China; of empire
1861–1865 American Civil War	**1890s** Partition of East Africa	**1914–1918** World War I
1863 Emancipation of slaves in U.S.	**1890s** European leases in China	
1864–1871 German unification	**1894–1895** Sino-Japanese War	
1868–1912 Meiji (reform) era in Japan	**1895** Cuban revolt against Spain	
1870 Establishment of Japanese Ministry of Industry	**1898** Formation of Marxist Social Democratic Party in Russia	
1870–1910 Acceleration of "demographic transition" in western Europe and the United States	**1898** Spanish-American War; U.S. acquires the Philippines, Puerto Rico, and Hawaii; U.S. intervenes in Cuba	
1870–1910 Expansion of commercial export economy in Latin America	**1898–1901** Boxer Rebellion in China	
1871–1912 High point of European imperialism		

POPULATION MOVEMENTS

Western industrialization and imperialism led to huge shifts in the population structures of various parts of the world. Both basic dynamics and migration patterns were involved. In the West, including the United States, the birth rate began to decline to historically low levels. This *demographic transition* to low birth rates reflected the fact that child labor was being displaced by machines; children were far less useful than they had been in agricultural societies. But high birth rates continued elsewhere in the world, and new public health measures began to reduce the death rates. The West's percentage of total world population began to slip by 1900 even as the West's world power reached its brief peak.

Industrialization drew workers from populous agricultural regions to the new factory centers. European areas that were slow to industrialize, especially in southern and eastern Europe, sent hundreds of thousands of immigrants to centers in Germany and France and especially to the United States, Australia, and Canada. Italian, Portuguese, and Spanish immigrants also flooded to the more prosperous Latin American nations in the late 19th century. The slave trade from Africa was ended under British leadership early in the 19th century; only a trickle continued, mainly to the Middle East. Humanitarian considerations, as well as the new ability of industrial factories to organize free workers more effectively for production, fed this development.

Various immigration patterns arose to replace the slave trade. Asian and European immigrants were recruited. New Asian minorities became important factors in various parts of the world, beginning a pattern that continued in the 20th century. Though not slaves, most immigrants were poorly paid and often were restricted by harsh contracts and forced to pay inflated prices at company-owned stores. Many Asian immigrants, replacing former slave labor, were signed to restrictive indentures. Others served as shopkeepers and other commercial agents in their new societies.

DIVERSITY IN THE AGE OF WESTERN DOMINANCE

Western industrialization and imperialist expansion were not the only major developments in the world between 1750 and 1914. A major surge of popular conversion to Islam began in sub-Saharan Africa at the end of the 18th century, marking an important shift in the continent's religious map. Latin American nations, for the most part winning freedom from Spain and Portugal by the 1820s after a series of wars for independence, launched an important process of new nation building. Significant developments elsewhere echoed more traditional themes. Thus, in China, major social unrest in the mid-19th century recalled earlier periods of dynastic decline in which rural elements rose against population pressure and unchecked control by landlords.

The principal complexity in describing the period from 1750 to 1914 lies in detailing the diverse reactions to the growth of Western military and industrial might.

One reaction was incorporation into an expanded Western civilization. The West enlarged during the 19th century through the emergence of strong immigrant societies in the United States, Canada, Australia, and New Zealand, each with its own important modifications of basic Western patterns.

Two societies, Russia and Japan, underwent dramatic internal change, imitating key Western gains without becoming entirely Western.

China and the Ottoman Empire both lost territories to Western imperialism but preserved a degree of independence amid growing weakness, outside interference, and agonizing indecision about the most effective way to counter the challenge from the West. Latin American nations that were newly independent also grappled with reform currents, but under intense economic constraints. Most of the rest of the world, including north Africa, was colonized outright. Colonial rule was not a constant, having somewhat different effects in India, for example, than in Africa, where imperialism was a later arrival and where a harsher racism characterized Western policy.

The different reactions to the industrial, imperialist West affected traditional civilization alignments. The growing gap between Japan and China is a case in point. New economic inequalities arose in different areas of the world; industrial societies gained new levels of wealth and some raw material producers declined, beset by population pressure and falling export prices.

What was Western civilization by this point? Was it Christianity or one of the newer political worldviews such as nationalism or socialism? Was the Western political message liberal, or did it consist of tighter bureaucratic organization and more effective military force, both definite aspects of the West's 19th-century experience? Different Western faces obviously affected the responses by other societies.

MAJOR THEMES TRANSFORMED

One indication of the global power of industrialization was the recasting of some crucial human themes in world history. New machines and higher population densities intensified human ability to change the environment, often for the worse. In the industrializing areas, chemical and smoke pollution was exacerbated by higher levels of sewage disposal; waterways suffered particularly. Food needs prompted farmers and estate owners elsewhere to cut down forests and to plant crops not compatible with local soil conditions. Rubber trees, spread widely in Brazil from their native home in southeast Asia, caused massive erosion; so did the spread of palm plantations (used for vegetable oil) in Africa. New transportation and worldwide trade and military pressures made isolation more difficult for any civilization (although renewed efforts surfaced after 1918). With contacts and growing Western dominance also came new forms of international relations. Independent nations began to exchange diplomatic representatives worldwide. Furthermore, from the 1860s onward, international agencies arose for the first time, setting rules for such matters as postal exchange and commercial licensing across national boundaries. These agencies, soon joined by other groups such as the Red Cross and a new Olympic committee, were long dominated by the West, but they created unprecedented conduits for relationships between states.

Industrialization had complex effects on social and economic inequality. Inequality between regions increased: Mexicans, whose standard of living was about two-thirds as high as that of U.S. Americans in 1800, had dropped to one-third by 1900. Inequality within many societies also increased with the spread of wage labor. On the other hand, the most blatant forced labor systems, including slavery, were abolished in this period. Legal equality increased, but other, more complex forms of inequality persisted. Gender relations took on new dimensions, and they continued to vary between societies. Machines and male labor replaced or devalued women's work in many settings; one clear indicator was the worldwide rise of female domestic servants. Yet new Western beliefs began to idealize women in other respects, giving them unprecedented credit for beauty and moral purity.

The sweeping forces of industrialization and imperialism reduced human agency in some respects. Many people had to do work or accept rulers they neither liked nor chose. Even peasants were subjected to new taxes and pressure to change the ways they produced food. In some cases, technology gained supremacy over human agency. A French factory owner every week put a garland of flowers on the machine that had been most productive, offering the workers nothing at all. Yet human agency was not entirely crushed. Most groups of workers, immigrants, or colonial laborers managed to preserve or invent some rituals and values that gave them a certain identity. Nevertheless, the question of human agency for all but the very rich and powerful became more complex in the 19th century.

Chapter 29

The Industrialization of the West, 1760–1914

Romantic painters delighted in evocative scenes and a mysterious Gothic presence, as depicted by John Constable in The Cornfields.

Three themes dominate the complex history of Western society between 1750 and 1914. First was industrialization as an economic and social transformation. Next was political upheaval, highlighted by the age of revolution, 1789–1848. Third was the importation of western European institutions and values to settler societies such as the United States and Australia, which expanded Western civilization's geographic range. Change is measured by befores and afters. In 1760, western Europe consisted almost entirely of monarchies. By 1914 many monarchies had been overthrown, and everywhere powerful parliaments, based on extensive voting systems, defined much of the political apparatus. In 1760, western Europe was largely agricultural, albeit highly commercial; by 1914 it was industrialized, with urban populations beginning to surpass rural populations in size.

In the century and a half after 1760, Western society went through a dizzying series of disruptions. Dramatic new cultural styles developed, some challenging 18th-century Enlightenment thought and some building on it through scientific research or political theory. A host of diplomatic upheavals accompanied internal change. New states rose to power—Germany and the United States were particularly noteworthy—and at the end of the period, a new alliance system brought the West to a catastrophic war.

The greatest change of all involved the West's industrialization. The Industrial Revolution featured the creation of radical new technological and economic structures, transforming agricultural society much as the Neolithic revolution had once transformed hunting-and-gathering cultures. The force of the industrial upheaval spilled over into all facets of Western life, changing intimate popular habits such as sexuality and family life and basic social processes such as the making of war.

European values and institutions were exported. Important extensions of Western civilization arose not only in the United States but also in Canada, Australia, and New Zealand. In Europe, industrialization and the principles of the French Revolution touched the whole world.

The best way to untangle the complexity of the Western transformation is to proceed historically—that is, to identify key subperiods within the longer span. These subperiods involve a growing crisis, late in the 18th century, that helped create changes in a variety of areas from sex to machinery; then a phase of experimentation, from roughly 1789 to 1850, in which political revolution vied for attention with industrialization; and finally, from 1850 to 1914, a more mature stage in which the implications of industrial society were more fully worked out.

1700 C.E.	1820 C.E.	1840 C.E.	1860 C.E.
1730 ff. Massive population rise	**1820** Revolutions in Greece and Spain; rise of liberalism and nationalism	**1840** Union act reorganizes Canada, provides elected legislature	**1860–1870** Second Maori War
c. 1770 James Watt's steam engine; beginning of Industrial Revolution	**1820s ff.** Industrialization in U.S.	**1843–1848** First Maori War in New Zealand	**1861–1865** American Civil War
1788 First convict settlement in Australia	**1823** First legislative council in Australia	**1846–1848** Mexican-American War	**1863** Emancipation of slaves
1789 Washington, first president of the U.S.	**1826-1837** Active European colonization begins in New Zealand	**1848 ff.** Writings of Karl Marx; rise of socialism	**1864–1871** German unification
1789–1799 French Revolution	**1829** Jackson, seventh president of United States	**1848–1849** European Revolutions	**1867** British North America Act, unites eastern and central Canada
1790 ff. Beginning of per capita birthrate decline (U.S.)	**1830, 1848** Revolutions in several European countries	**1850** Australia's Colonies Government Act allows legislature and more autonomy	**1870–1879** Institution of French Third Republic
1793 First free European settlers in Australia	**1832** Reform Bill of 1832 (England)	**1852** New constitution in New Zealand; elected councils	**1870s ff.** Rapid birthrate decline
1793–1794 Radical phase	**1837** Rebellion in Canada	**1859** Darwin's *Origin of Species*	**1870s ff.** Spread of compulsory education laws
1799–1815 Reign of Napoleon	**1837–1842** U.S.–Canada border clashes	**1859–1870** Unification of Italy	**1871–1914** High point of European imperialism
1800–1850 Romanticism in literature and art	**1839** New British colonial policy allows legislature and more autonomy		**1879–1907** Alliance system: Germany-Austria (1879); Germany-Austria-Russia (1881); Germany-Italy-Austria (1882); France-Russia (1891); Britain-France (1904); Britain-Russia (1907)
1803 Louisiana Purchase (U.S.)			
1810–1826 Rise of democratic suffrage in U.S.			
1815 Congress of Vienna; more conservative period			

FORCES OF CHANGE

▓▓ *Even before industrialization, new ideas and social pressures caused a series of political revolutions, beginning with the American Revolution in 1775. The French Revolution of 1789 had an impact throughout Europe and beyond and encouraged new movements of liberalism and nationalism. Lesser revolutions followed in 1820 and 1830.*

Intellectual Challenge and Population Pressure

Three forces were working to shatter Europe's calm by the mid-18th century. In combination, they help explain both industrialization and the surge of political revolts. The first of the forces was cultural, for intellectual ferment was running high. Enlightenment thinkers challenged regimes that did not grant full religious freedom or that insisted on aristocratic privilege, and a few called for widespread popular voice in government. Jean-Jacques Rousseau argued for government based on a general will, and this could be interpreted as a plea for democratic voting. A gap had opened between leading intellectuals and established institutions, and this played a role in the revolutions that lay ahead. Enlightenment thinkers also encouraged economic and technical change and policies that would promote industry; manufacturers

and political reformers alike could take inspiration from these ideas.

Along with cultural change, ongoing commercialization continued to stir the economy. Business-people, gaining new wealth, might well challenge the idea that aristocrats alone should hold the highest political offices. They certainly were growing interested in new techniques that might spur production. Commercial practices might also draw attack, from artisans or peasant villagers who preferred older economic values. This could feed revolution as well.

A final source of disruption was occurring more quietly at all social levels. Western Europe experienced a huge population jump after about 1730. Within half a century, the population of France rose by 50 percent; that of Britain and Prussia rose 100 percent. This *population revolution* was caused by better border policing by the efficient nation-state governments, which reduced the movement of disease-bearing animals. More important was improved nutrition resulting from the growing use of the potato. These factors reduced the death rate, particularly for children; instead of more than 40 percent of all children dying by age 2, the figure by the 1780s was closer to 33 percent. More children surviving also meant more people living to have children of their own, so the birth rate increased as well.

Population pressure at this level always has dramatic impact. Upper-class families, faced with more surviving children, tried to tighten their grip on exist-

1880 C.E.	1900 C.E.
1880s ff. High point of impressionism in art	**1901** Commonwealth of Australia, creates national federation
1881–1914 Canadian Pacific Railway	**1907** New Zealand dominion status in British Empire
1881–1889 German social insurance laws enacted	**1912–1913** Balkan Wars
1882 U.S. excludes Chinese immigrants	**1914** Beginning of World War I
1891–1898 Australia and New Zealand restrict Asian immigration	**1917** U.S. enters World War I
1893 U.S. annexes Hawaii	
1893 Women's suffrage in New Zealand	
1898 Spanish-American War; U.S. acquires Puerto Rico, Guam, Philippines	
1899 U.S. acquires part of Samoa	

began to change their dress to more urban styles; this suggests an early form of new consumer interest. Premarital sex increased, and out-of-wedlock births rose to 10 percent of all births. Among groups with little or no property, parental authority began to decline because the traditional threat of denying inheritance had no meaning. Youthful independence became more marked, and although this was particularly evident in economic behavior as many young people looked for jobs on their own, the new defiance of authority might have had political implications as well.

The Tide of Revolution, 1789–1830

Against the backdrop of intellectual challenge, commercial growth, and population pressure, the placid politics of the 18th century were shattered by the series of revolutions that took shape in the 1770s and 1780s. The wave of revolutions caught up many social groups with diverse motives, some eager to use revolution to promote further change and some hoping to turn back the clock and recover older values.

The American Revolution

The first concrete development occurred when Britain's Atlantic colonies rebelled in 1775 in what was primarily a war for independence rather than a full-fledged revolution. A large minority of American colonists resisted Britain's attempt to impose new taxes and trade controls on the colonies after 1763. Many settlers also resented restrictions on movement into the frontier areas. The colonists also invoked British political theory to argue that they should not be taxed without representation. The Stamp Act of 1765, imposing tax on documents and pamphlets, particularly roused protest against British tyranny. Other grievances were involved. Crowding along the eastern seaboard led some younger men to seek new opportunities, including political office, that turned them against the older colonial leadership. Growing commerce antagonized some farmers and artisans, who looked for ways to defend the older values of greater social equality and community spirit.

Colonial rebels set up a new government, which issued the Declaration of Independence in 1776 and authorized a formal army to pursue its war. The persistence of the revolutionaries combined with British military blunders and significant aid from the French

ing offices. In the late 18th century, it became harder for anyone who was not an aristocrat to gain a high post in the church or state. This reaction helped feed demands for change by other groups. Business families faced with more children often decided to expand their operations, sometimes adopting new equipment. This change led to a new willingness to take risks. Above all, population pressure drove many people into the working class as they lost any real chance of inheriting property. These people were eager to take advantage of new labor opportunities simply to survive. They thus formed the nucleus of a new working class in agriculture and, above all, in manufacturing.

The population growth of the 18th century prompted a rapid expansion of domestic manufacturing in western Europe and, by 1800, in the United States. Hundreds of thousands of people became full- or part-time producers of textile and metal products, working at home but in a capitalist system in which materials, work orders, and sales depended on urban merchants. This development has been called *proto-industrialization*, and it ultimately encouraged new technologies to expand production further because of the importance of new market relationships and manufacturing volume.

Population upheaval and the spread of a propertyless class that worked for money wages had a sweeping impact on a variety of behaviors in Western society, including North America. Many villagers government, designed to embarrass its key enemy. After several years of fighting, the United States won its freedom and, in 1789, set up a new constitutional structure based on Enlightenment principles, with checks and balances between the legislature and the executive branches of government, and formal guarantees of individual liberties. Voting rights, though limited, were widespread, and the new regime was for a time the most advanced in the world. Socially, the revolution accomplished less; slavery was untouched.

Crisis in France in 1789

The next step in the revolutionary spiral occurred in France. It was the *French Revolution* that most clearly set in motion the political restructuring of western Europe. Several factors combined in the 1780s in what became a classic pattern of revolutionary causation. Ideological insistence on change won increasing attention from the mid-18th century onward, as Enlightenment thinkers urged the need to limit the powers of the Catholic church, the aristocracy, and the monarchy. Social changes reinforced the ideological challenge. Some middle-class people, proud of their business or professional success, wanted a greater political role. Many peasants, pressed by population growth, wanted fuller freedom from landlords' demands.

The French government and upper classes proved incapable of reform. Aristocrats tightened their grip in response to their own population pressure, and the government proved increasingly ineffective—a key ingredient in any successful revolution. Finally, a sharp economic slump in 1787 and 1788, triggered by bad harvests, set the seal on revolution.

The French king, *Louis XVI*, called a meeting of the traditional parliament to consider tax reform for his financially pinched regime. But middle-class representatives, inspired by Enlightenment ideals, insisted on turning this assembly (which had not met for a century and a half) into a modern parliament, with voting by head and with majority representation for nonnoble property owners. The fearful king caved in after some street riots in Paris in the summer of 1789, and the revolution was under way.

Events that summer were crucial. The new assembly, with its middle-class majority, quickly turned to devising a new political regime. A stirring *Declaration of the Rights of Man and the Citizen* proclaimed freedom of thought. Like the American Declaration of Independence, this law enacted natural rights to "liberty, property, security, and resistance to oppression" and specifically guaranteed free expression of ideas. A popular riot stormed a political prison, the Bastille, on July 14, in what became the revolution's symbol; ironically, almost no prisoners were there. Soon after this, peasants seized manorial records and many landed estates. This triggered a general proclamation abolishing manorialism, giving peasants clear title to much land and establishing equality under the law. Although aristocrats survived for some time, the principles of aristocratic rule were undercut. The privileges of the church were also attacked, and church property was seized. A new constitution proclaimed individual rights, including freedom of religion, press, and property. A strong parliament was set up to limit the king, and about one-half the adult male population—those with property—were eligible to vote.

The French Revolution: Radical and Authoritarian Phases

By 1792, the initial push for reform began to turn more radical. Early reforms provoked massive opposition in the name of church and aristocracy, and civil war broke out in several parts of France. Monarchs in Britain, Prussia, and Austria trumpeted their opposition to the revolution, and France soon moved toward European war as well. These pressures led to a takeover by radical leaders, who wanted to press the revolution forward and to set up firmer authority in the revolution's defense. The radicals abolished the monarchy. The king was decapitated on the *guillotine,* a new device introduced, Enlightenment-fashion, to provide more humane executions that instead became a symbol of revolutionary bloodthirst. The radicals also executed several thousand opponents in what was named the Reign of Terror, even though by later standards it was mild.

The leader of the radical phase was Maximilien Robespierre (1758–1794), a classic example of a revolutionary ideologue. Born into a family of lawyers, he gained his law degree in 1781 and soon was publishing Enlightenment-style political tracts. The new philosophies inspired passion in Robespierre, particularly the democratic ideas of Rousseau. Elected to all the initial revolutionary assemblies, Robespierre headed the prosecution of the king in 1792 and then took over the leadership of government. He put down many factions, sponsored the Terror, and worked to centralize the government. In 1794, he set

Visualizing THE PAST

The French Revolution in Cartoon

This cartoon, titled *The Former Great Dinner of the Modern Gargantua with His Family*, appeared in 1791 or 1792, as the revolution was becoming more radical. It pictures the king and his wife as latter-day Gargantuas, referring to a French literary figure who was a notoriously great eater.

Questions: How does the cartoon characterize the relationship between French society and economy and the monarchy? What social struc-

ture is implied? What conclusions might readers of the cartoon draw about what should happen to the monarchy?

With improvements in printing and literacy, cartoons were becoming more available, and they have continued to be important into the present day. Why were they effective as a means of communicating ideas? Did they spur people to action, or might they deflect action by provoking a good laugh?

up a civic religion, the "cult of the Supreme Being," to replace Catholicism. Personally incorruptible, Robespierre came to symbolize the single-minded revolutionary, although he shied away from significant social reforms that might have drawn urban support. He was convinced that he knew the people's will, but opposition mounted, and when he called for yet another purge of moderate leaders he was arrested

and guillotined on the same day, abandoned by the popular factions that had once spurred him on.

Robespierre and his colleagues pushed the revolution further. A new constitution, never fully put into practice, proclaimed universal adult male suffrage. The radicals introduced a metric system of weights and measures, the product of the rationalizing genius of the Enlightenment. They also proclaimed universal military conscription, claiming that men who were free citizens owed loyalty and service to the government. And revolutionary armies began to win major success. Not only were France's enemies driven out, but the regime began to acquire new territory in the Low Countries, Italy, and Germany, spreading revolutionary gains farther in western Europe.

A new spirit of popular *nationalism* surfaced during the revolution's radical phase. Many French people felt an active loyalty to the new regime—to a state they believed they had helped create. A new symbol was a revolutionary national anthem, with its rousing first lines, "Come, children of the nation, the day of glory has arrived." Nationalism could replace older loyalties to church or locality.

The fall of the radicals led to four years of moderate policies. Then in 1799 the final phase of the revolution was ushered in with the victory of Napoleon Bonaparte, a leading general who soon converted the revolutionary republic to an authoritarian empire. Napoleon reduced the parliament to a rubber stamp, and a powerful police system limited freedom of expression. However, Napoleon confirmed other liberal gains, including religious freedom, while enacting substantial equality—though for men, not women—in a series of new law codes. To train bureaucrats, Napoleon developed a centralized system of secondary schools and universities.

Driven by insatiable ambition, Napoleon devoted most of his attention to expansion abroad (Map 29.1). A series of wars brought France against all of Europe's major powers, including Russia. At its height, about 1812, the French empire directly held or controlled as satellite kingdoms most of western Europe, and its success spurred some reform measures even in Prussia and Russia. The French Empire crumbled after this point. An attempt to invade Russia in 1812 failed miserably. French armies perished in the cold Russian winter even as they pushed deep into the empire. An alliance system organized by Britain crushed the emperor definitively in 1814 and 1815. Yet Napoleon's campaigns had done more than dominate European diplomacy for one and a half decades. They had also spread key revolutionary legislation—the idea of equality under the law and the attack on privileged institutions such as aristocracy, church, and craft guilds—throughout much of western Europe.

The revolution and Napoleon encouraged popular nationalism outside of France as well as within.

French military success continued to draw great excitement at home. Elsewhere, French armies tore down local governments, as in Italy and Germany, which whetted appetites there for greater national unity. And the sheer fact of French invasion made many people more conscious of loyalty to their own nations; popular resistance to Napoleon, in parts of Spain and Germany, played a role in the final French defeat.

A Conservative Settlement and the Revolutionary Legacy

The allies who had brought the proud emperor down met at Vienna in 1815 to reach a peace settlement that would make further revolution impossible. Diplomats at the *Congress of Vienna* did not try to punish France too sternly, on the grounds that the European balance of power should be restored. Still, a series of stronger powers was established around France, which meant gains for Prussia within Germany and for the hitherto obscure nation of Piedmont in northern Italy. The old map was not restored, and the realignments ultimately facilitated national unifications. Britain gained new colonial territories, confirming its lead in the scramble for empire in the wider world. Russia, newly important in European affairs, maintained its hold over most of Poland.

These territorial adjustments kept Europe fairly stable for almost half a century—a major achievement, given the crisscrossed rivalries that had long characterized Western society. But the Vienna negotiators were much less successful in promoting internal peace. The idea was to restore monarchy in France and to link conservative powers in defense of churches and kings.

But political movements arose to challenge conservatism. They involved concrete political agitation, but also an explosion of ideals. Many of the ideals would resonate in many parts of the world during the 19th and 20th centuries. *Liberals* focused primarily on issues of political structure. They looked for ways to limit state interference in individual life and urged representation of propertied people in government. Liberals touted the importance of constitutional rule and protection for freedoms of religion, press, and assembly. Largely representing the growing middle class, many liberals also sought economic reforms, including better education, which would promote industrial growth.

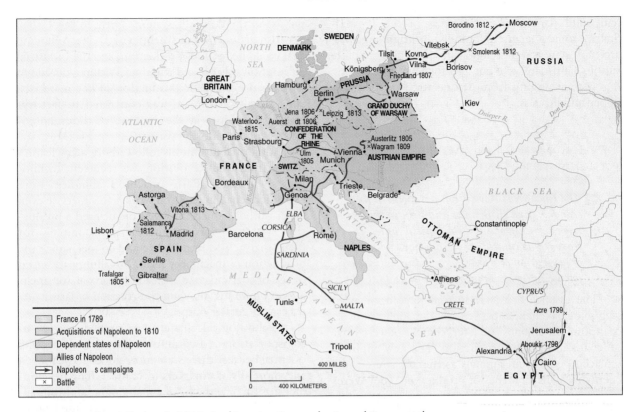

Map 29.1 *Napoleon's Empire in 1812. By this point, France dominated Europe to the borders of Russia, whose cold winters would weaken Napoleon's army. Napoleon's redrawing of satellite states stoked nationalist fervor, particularly in Italy and Germany.*

Radicals accepted the importance of most liberal demands, but they also wanted wider voting rights. Some advocated outright democracy. They also urged some social reforms in the interest of the lower classes. A smaller current of socialism urged an attack on private property in the name of equality and an end to capitalist exploitation of workers.

Nationalists, often allied with liberalism or radicalism, urged the importance of national unity and glory.

Political protest found support among students and among urban artisans, concerned about economic changes that might displace craft skills. Revolutions broke out in several places in 1820 and again in 1830. The 1820 revolts involved a nationalist *Greek Revolution* against Ottoman rule—a key step in gradually dismantling the Ottoman Empire in the Balkans—and a rebellion in Spain. Another French Revolution of 1830 installed a different king and a somewhat more liberal monarchy. Uprisings also

occurred in key states in Italy and Germany, though without durable result; the Belgian Revolution of 1830 produced a liberal regime and a newly independent nation.

Britain and the United States also participated in the process of political change, though without revolution. Key states in the United States granted universal adult male suffrage (except for slaves) and other political changes in the 1820s, leading to the election of a popular president, Andrew Jackson, in 1828. In Britain, *the Reform Bill of 1832,* a response to popular agitation, gave the parliamentary vote to most middle-class men. This change ushered in a period during which urban governments gained new powers as they came under control of business leaders, and the aristocrats who still controlled the national ministries began to adopt measures that increasingly favored commercial development.

By the 1830s, regimes in France, Britain, Belgium, the United States, and several other countries had solid parliaments (Congress in the United States), some guarantees for individual rights against arbitrary state action, religious freedom not only for various Christian sects but also for Jews, and a voting system ranging from democratic (for men) to upper middle class.

THE INDUSTRIAL REVOLUTION

■■ *The Industrial Revolution restructured the economy, first in Britain and then in the rest of western Europe and the United States. It featured dramatic new technology and a new organization of work. Early industrialization fed a final wave of revolutions in 1848.*

The essence of the Industrial Revolution was technological change, particularly the application of coal-powered engines (or, later, engines powered by other fossil fuels) to production. The new engines replaced people and animals as the key sources of energy in many branches of production. They were joined by new production equipment that could apply power to manufacturing through more automatic processes. Thus, spindles were invented that wrapped fiber automatically into thread, and looms mixed threads automatically without direct human intervention. Engines were also used in sugar refining, printing, and other processes.

The British Industrial Revolution resulted from a host of factors, including favorable natural resources. Industrialization was fed also by the late 18th-century crisis. Population pressure forced innovations at all social levels. The Industrial Revolution also built on previous trends in Western society, including the growth of the large manufacturing sector and the huge advantages in world trade. Prior development in science set a basis on which creative artisans could widen their efforts at technical innovation. Governments already committed to policies of economic growth also supported industrialization by instituting laws encouraging new inventions and new trading and banking systems.

Origins of Industrialization, 1770–1840

The key inventions of early industrialization developed in Britain during the 18th century. Automatic machinery in textiles initially was intended for man-

ual use in the domestic system. Then, in the 1770s, Scottish artisan James Watt devised a steam engine that could be used for production, and the Industrial Revolution was off and running. Within a decade in Britain, the domestic production of key materials, such as cotton thread, was converted to factory-housed machines at the expense of thousands of home workers, mostly women.

Additional inventions followed, for a key feature of the Industrial Revolution was recurrent technological change. Early machine spindles were expanded, enabling a given worker to supervise even faster output. American inventors devised a production system of interchangeable parts, initially for rifles, that helped standardize and so mechanize the production of machinery itself. Metallurgy advanced by use of coal and coke, instead of charcoal, for smelting and refining, allowing the creation of larger furnaces and greater output.

Technological change was applied quickly to transportation and communication, which became essential because there were more goods to be moved and more distant markets to contact. The development of the telegraph, steam shipping, and the railway, all early in the 19th century, provided faster movement of information and goods.

The Industrial Revolution depended on improvements in agriculture. Industrialization concentrated increasing amounts of manufacturing in cities, where power sources could be brought together with labor. City growth was dizzying during the first decades of industrialization. Sleepy villages such as Manchester, England, grew to cities of several hundred thousand people. This kind of growth depended on better agricultural production, accomplished through improved equipment and seeds and the growing use of fertilizers.

Industrialization also meant a *factory system*. Steam engines had to be concentrated because their power could not be widely diffused until the later application of electricity. Factory labor separated work from the home—one of the basic human changes inherent in the Industrial Revolution. It also allowed manufacturers to introduce greater specialization of labor and more explicit rules and discipline, which along with the noisy machines permanently changed the nature of human labor.

Industrialization had profound and complex environmental impact. Use of coal and iron reduced pressure on Europe's remaining forests. But smoke pollution in factory areas was an early issue, and both factory wastes and growing cities quickly affected water quality. Industrial demands for raw materials created desolate slagheaps around mines, both in Europe and in areas where raw materials were produced. The Industrial Revolution, and particularly its new uses of energy, transformed human use of nature, with an accelerating impact that stretched through the 20th century.

The Spread of Industry

Once Britain launched industrialization, other Western nations quickly saw the need to imitate (Map 29.2). Britain's industrial power helped the nation hold out against Napoleon and led to huge profits for successful businesses by the early 19th century. Hence, both governments and individual entrepreneurs in places such as Belgium, Germany, and New England soon rushed to copy. On the European continent, French revolutionary laws helped unleash industrialization by destroying local restrictions on trade, protecting private property, and abolishing artisan guilds that had often tried to defend older production techniques. With guilds and manors destroyed, propertyless workers were commodities to be used and paid as the market required.

Belgium and France began to industrialize in the 1820s, and the United States and Germany followed soon thereafter. Industrialization did not immediately sweep all before it, even in Britain; artisan production actually expanded for a time as cities grew, and rural labor remained vital. But the forms of the Industrial Revolution gained ground steadily once they were implanted in the West, and factory workers and their managers multiplied rapidly.

The Disruptions of Industrial Life

The Industrial Revolution was not just a technological change; indeed, the changing role of technology and work organizations reshaped human life. The process involved huge movements of people from countryside to city. Families were disrupted, as young adults proved to be the prime migrants. Cities themselves, poorly equipped to begin with and crowded beyond all precedent, became hellholes for many new residents (see Figure 29.1). Health conditions worsened in poor districts because of packed housing and inadequate sanitation. Crime increased for a time. New social divisions opened up as middle-class families moved away from the city, beginning a pattern of suburbanization that continued

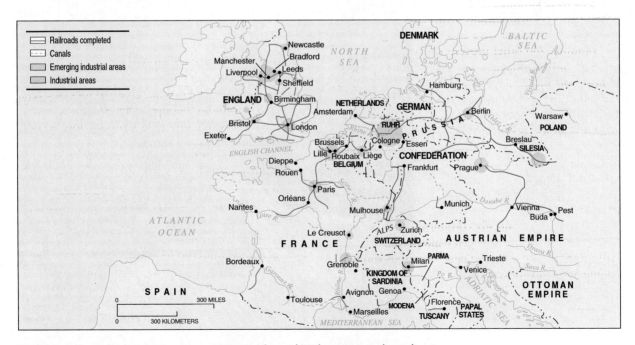

Map 29.2 *Industrialization in Europe, c. 1850. By the mid-19th century, industrialization had spread across Europe, aided by the development of railroad links that brought resources to the new factories and transported their finished goods to world markets.*

into the late 20th century. Work became more unpleasant for many people. Not only was it largely separated from family, but the new machines and factory rules compelled a rapid pace and coordination that pulverized traditional values of leisurely, high-quality production. First in Britain, and then elsewhere, groups of workers responded to the new machines by outright attack; *Luddite* protests, named after a mythical British machine-breaker called Ned Ludd, failed to stop industrialization, but they showed the stress involved.

The early Industrial Revolution also forced new constraints on traditions of popular leisure. Factory owners, bent on getting as much work as possible from their labor force to help pay for expensive machines, tried to ban singing, napping, drinking, and other customary frivolities on the job. Punctuality and efficiency were cast as virtues, and anything that took time away from work was considered almost sinful. A typical tract, called "The Duty and Advantage of Early Rising," issued in 1786, warned workers that "by *soaking* ... so long between warm sheets, the flesh is as it were parboiled, and becomes soft and flabby. The nerves, in the meantime, are quite unstrung."

Family life changed. Middle-class people quickly enhanced the redefinition of the family already begun in the early modern centuries. The family for them served as an image of affection and purity. Children and women were to be sheltered from the storms of the new work world. Women, traditionally active partners to merchants, now withdrew from formal jobs. They gained new roles in caring for children and the home, and their moral status in many ways improved, but their sphere was more separate from that of men than had been true before. As the Document suggests, magazines began to lavish new praise on women's family virtue. Children also were rede-

Figure 29.1. *Population growth, factory-promoted unemployment, and the growing potency of industrially produced alcoholic drinks helped create a slum life in English cities in the 18th and early 19th centuries. Pictures of this sort roused indignation and hostility in the middle classes.*

Ꭰ O C U Ꮇ E N T

Women in the Industrial Revolution

The West's Industrial Revolution changed the situation of women in many ways. Some of the changes have recurred more recently in other civilizations, and others were particularly characteristic of the 19th-century West. Industrialization cut into women's traditional work and protest roles (for example, in spearheading bread riots as attention shifted to work-based strikes), but it tended to expand the educational opportunities for women. Some new work roles and protest outlets, including feminism, developed by 1914. Important changes occurred in the home as well. New ideas and standards elevated women's position and set up more demanding tasks. Relationships between women were also affected by the growing use of domestic servants (the most common urban job for working-class women) and new attitudes of middle- and lower-class women. The first document that follows sketches the idealization of middle-class women; it comes from an American moral tract of 1837, written anonymously, probably by a man. The second document, written by a woman in an English women's magazine, shows new household standards of another sort, with a critical tone also common in middle-class literature. Finally, a British housewife discusses her servant problems, reflecting yet another facet of women's lives. How could women decide what their domestic roles were and whether they brought satisfaction?

Women as Civilizers (1837)

As a sister, she soothes the troubled heart, chastens and tempers the wild daring of the hurt mind restless with disappointed pride or fired with ambition. As a mistress, she inspires the nobler sentiment of purer love, and the sober purpose of conquering himself for virtue's sake. As a wife, she consoles him in grief, animates him with hope in despair, restrains him in prosperity, cheers him in poverty and trouble, swells the pulsations of his throbbing breast that beats for honorable distinction, and rewards his toils with the undivided homage of a grateful heart. In the important and endearing character of mother, she watches and directs the various impulses of unfledged genius, instills into the tender and susceptible mind the quickening seeds of virtue, fits us to brave dangers in time of peril, and consecrates to truth and virtue the best affections of our nature.

Motherhood as Power and Burden (1877)

Every woman who has charge of a household should have a practical knowledge of nursing, simple doctoring and physicianing. The professional doctor must be called in for real illness. But the Home Doctor may do so much to render professional visits very few and far between. And her knowledge will be of infinite value when it is necessary to carry out the doctor's orders....

The Mother Builder

It is a curious fact that architects who design and builders who carry out their plans must have training for this work. But the Mother Builder is supposed to have to know by instinct how to put in each tiny brick which builds up the "human." The result of leaving it to "instinct" is that the child starts out with bad foundations and a jerry-built constitution....

When one considers that one child in every three born dies before the age of five years, it is evident how wide-spread must be the ignorance as to the feeding and care of these little ones. It is a matter of surprise to those who understand the constitution and needs of infants that, considering the conditions under which the large number of them are reared, the mortality is not greater....

The Risks Babies Run

To begin with, the popular superstition that a young baby must be "hungry" because it lives on milk, and is on this plea the recipient of scraps and bits of vegetables, potato and gravy, crusts, and other heterogeneous articles of diet, has much to answer for. Then, the artistic sense of the mother which leads her to display mottled necks, dimpled arms, and chubby legs, instead of warmly covering these charming portions of baby's anatomy, goes hugely to swell the death-rate. Mistakes in feeding and covering have much to answer for in the high mortality of infants.

The Servant "Problem" (1860)

So we lost Mary, and Peggy reigned in her stead for some six weeks....

But Peggy differed greatly from her predecessor Mary. She was not clean in her person, and my mother declared that her presence was not desirable within a few feet. Moreover she had no notion of putting things in their places, but always left all her working materials in the apartment where they were last used. It was not therefore pleasant, when one wanted a sweeping brush, to have to sit down and think which room Peggy had swept the last, and so on with all the paraphernalia for dusting and scrubbing. But this was not the worst. My mother, accustomed to receive almost reverential respect from her old servants could not endure poor Peggy's familiar ways....

Now, though I am quite willing to acknowledge the mutual obligation which exists between the employer and employed, I do not agree with my charwoman that she is the only person who ought to be considered as conferring a favor. I desire to treat her with all kindness, showing every possible regard to her comfort, and I expect from her no more work than I would cheerfully and easily perform in the same time. But when I scrupulously perform my part of the bargain, both as regards food and wages, not to mention much thought and care in order to make things easy for her and which were not in the agreement at all, I think she ought not only to keep faith with me if possible, but to abstain from hinting at the obligation she confers in coming.

It is not pleasant, as my mother says, to beg and pray for the help for which we also pay liberally. But it is worse for my kitchen helper to be continually reminding me that she need not go out unless she likes, and that it was only to oblige me she ever came at all. I do not relish this utter ignoring of her wages, etc., or her being quite deaf because I choose to offer a suggestion as to the propriety of dusting out the corners, or when I mildly hint that I should prefer her doing something in my way....

But if I were to detail all my experiences, I should never have done. I have had many good and willing workers; but few on whose punctuality and regularity I could rely.

Questions: In what ways did industrialization increase differences between women and men in the 19th-century West? What were the main changes in women's roles and ideals? How did middle-class and working-class women differ? These magazine articles were prescriptive, suggesting what women should be like. Middle-class audiences consumed vast amounts of this kind of prescriptive literature from the 19th century onward, as sources of both praise and constructive criticism. Did the women's images projected in these materials bolster or undermine women's position? Would they generate contentment or dissatisfaction among their readers? Finally, do they reflect real life or merely idealized standards (for wives, mothers, and servants)? What are the problems in using prescriptive materials to describe 19th-century women's history?

fined. The middle class came to see education, not work and apprenticeship, as the logical role for children to prepare them for a complex future.

The changes in family roles and values show how deeply the Industrial Revolution could reach into personal life. The confusion of change worried many people, even businesspeople actively building the new industrial world. As a leading French industrialist noted, "Progress is not necessarily progressive. If it were not inevitable, it might be better to stop it."

The Revolutions of 1848

By the 1840s, the impacts of political revolution and industrial transformation were beginning to coalesce. Western history was being shaped by reactions to these two forces in combination.

Government functions shifted. For example, all Western governments encouraged railway development; Prussia built many lines directly, and the United States government gave large land grants to promote a national rail system. All governments began to organize technical fairs and to promote engineering and science education. Most governments took an interest in education more generally, on the grounds that a more literate work force would be more productive. Thus, France began to encourage (though not yet require) primary schools

throughout the nation after the revolution of 1830. Another area that cried out for government attention involved urban conditions. Again by the 1830s, governments began to build new sewer systems, to promote some housing regulation, and in general to launch the process of making the new cities more habitable. They also developed formal urban police forces, another vital extension of government power.

Key lower-class groups turned to political protest as a means of compensating for industrial change. Artisans and workers in Britain generated a new movement to gain the vote in the 1830s and 1840s; this *Chartist movement* hoped that a democratic government would regulate new technologies and promote popular education.

A final, extraordinary wave of *revolutions in 1848 and 1849* brought protest to a head. Paris was again the center. In the popular uprising that began in February 1848, the French monarchy was once again expelled, this time for good, and a democratic republic was established briefly. Urban artisans pressed for serious social reform—perhaps some version of socialism, and certainly government-supported jobs for the unemployed. Groups of women schoolteachers, though fewer in number, agitated for the vote and other rights for women. The social demands were far wider than those of a great uprising of 1789.

Figure 29.2. *In 1848, crowds—mainly urban artisans—stormed the military arsenal in Berlin during the last great revolution in the industrial West.*

Revolution quickly spread to other centers. Major revolts occurred in Germany (Figure 29.2), Austria, and Hungary. Revolutionaries in these areas devised liberal constitutions to modify conservative monarchies, artisans pressed for social reforms that would restrain industrialization, and peasants sought a complete end to manorialism. Revolts in central Europe also pressed for nationalist demands: German nationalists worked for the unity of their country, and various nationalities in Austria–Hungary, including Slavic groups, sought greater autonomy. A similar liberal nationalist revolt occurred in various parts of Italy.

The revolutionary fires burned only briefly. The social demands of artisans and some factory workers were put down quickly; not only conservatives but middle-class liberals opposed these efforts. Nationalist agitation also failed for the moment, as the armies of Austria–Hungary and Prussia restored the status quo to central Europe and Italy. Democracy persisted in France, but a nephew of the great Napoleon soon replaced the liberal republic with an authoritarian empire that lasted until 1870. Peasant demands were met, and serfdom was fully abolished throughout western Europe. Many peasants, uninterested in other gains, supported conservative forces.

The substantial failure of the revolutions of 1848 drew the revolutionary era in western Europe to a close. Failure taught many liberals and working-class leaders that revolution was too risky; more gradual methods should be used instead. Improved transportation reduced the chance of food crises, the traditional trigger for revolution in Western history. Bad harvests in 1846 and 1847 had driven up food prices and helped promote insurgency in the cities, but famines of this sort did not recur in the West. Many governments also installed better riot control police.

By 1850, an industrial class structure had come to predominate. Earlier revolutionary gains had reduced the aristocrats' legal privileges, and the rise of business had eroded their economic dominance. With industrialization, social structure came to rest less on privilege and birth and more on money. Key divisions by 1850 pitted middle-class property owners against workers of various sorts. The old alliances that had produced the revolutions were now dissolved.

THE CONSOLIDATION OF THE INDUSTRIAL ORDER, 1850–1914

❖❖ *Industrial society developed more fully after 1850 and contained new family and leisure patterns. Political consolidation brought national unifications in Italy and Germany and new constitutions. Governments developed new functions, and the rise of socialism changed the political spectrum.*

In most respects, the 65 years after 1850 seemed calmer than the frenzied period of political upheaval and initial industrialization. City growth continued in the West; indeed, several countries, starting with Britain, passed the 50-percent mark in urbanization—the first time in human history that more than a minority of a population had lived in cities. But city governments began to gain ground on the pressing problems growth had created. Sanitation improved, and death rates fell below birth rates for the first time in urban history. Parks, museums, effective regulation of food and housing facilities, and more efficient police forces all added to the safety and the physical and cultural amenities of urban life. Revealingly, crime rates began to stabilize or even drop in several industrial areas, a sign of more effective social control but also of a more disciplined population.

Adjustments to Industrial Life

Family life adjusted to industrialization. Birth rates began to drop as Western society began a *demographic transition* to a new system that promoted fairly stable population levels through a new combination of low birth rates and low death rates. Children were now seen as a source of emotional satisfaction and parental responsibility, not as workers contributing to a family economy.

Material conditions generally improved after 1850. By 1900, probably two-thirds of the Western population enjoyed conditions above the subsistence level. People could afford a few amenities such as newspapers and family outings, their diet and housing improved, and their health got better. The decades from 1880 to 1920 saw a real revolution in children's health, thanks in part to better hygiene during childbirth and better parental care. Infancy and death separated for the first time in human history: Instead of one-third or more of all children

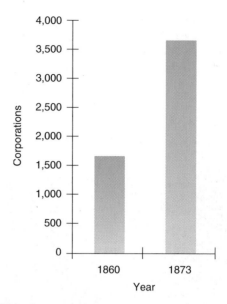

Figure 29.3. *Corporations in Western Europe, 1860–1873: The expansion in numbers.*

dying by age 10, child death rates fell to less than 10 percent and continued to plummet. The discovery of germs by *Louis Pasteur* led by the 1880s to more conscientious sanitary regulations and procedures by doctors and other health care specialists; this reduced the deaths of women in childbirth. Women began to outlive men by a noticeable margin, but men's health also improved.

Important labor movements took shape among industrial workers by the 1890s, with massive strike movements by miners, metalworkers, and others from the United States to Germany. The new trade union movement stressed the massed power of workers. Hosts of labor leaders sprang up amid detested work conditions and political repression. For example, Jean Dumay was born in a metallurgical center in France in 1841. His radical ideas shocked his stepfather, who believed rich people were necessary sources of jobs, and he was banned from the factory as an "unruly worker hothead" and later exiled from France for eight years for agitation. He later returned and became an elected urban official as protest began to turn into new political power. Many workers learned to bargain for better pay and shorter hours.

In the countryside, peasant protests declined. Many European peasants gained a new ability to use market conditions to their own benefit. Some, as in Holland and Denmark, developed cooperatives to market goods and purchase supplies efficiently. Many peasants specialized in new cash crops, such as dairy products. Still more widely, peasants began to send their children to school to pick up new knowledge that would improve farming operations. The traditional isolation of rural areas began to decline.

Political Trends and the Rise of New Nations

Western politics consolidated after the failed revolutions of 1848. Quite simply, issues that had dominated the Western political agenda for many decades were largely resolved within a generation. The great debates about fundamental constitutions and government structure, which had emerged in the 17th century with the rise of absolutism and new political theory and then raged during the decades of revolution, at last grew quiet.

Many Western leaders worked to reduce the need for political revolution after 1850. Liberals decided that revolution was too risky and became more willing to compromise. Key conservatives strove to develop reforms that would save elements of the old regime, including power for the landed aristocracy and the monarchy. A British conservative leader, *Benjamin Disraeli*, took the initiative of granting the vote to working-class men in 1867. *Count Camillo di Cavour*, in the Italian state of Piedmont, began even earlier to support industrial development and extend the powers of the parliament to please liberal forces. In Prussia, a new prime minister, *Otto von Bismarck*, similarly began to work with a parliament and to extend the vote to all men (though grouping them in wealth categories that blocked complete democracy). Other Prussian reforms granted freedom to Jews, extended (without guaranteeing) rights to the press, and promoted mass education. The gap between liberal and conservative regimes narrowed in the West, although it remained significant.

The new conservatives also began to use the force of nationalism to win support for the existing social order. Previously, nationalism had been a radical force, challenging established arrangements in the name of new loyalties. Many liberals continued to defend nationalist causes. However, conservative politicians learned how to wrap themselves in the flag, often promoting an active foreign policy in the interest of promoting domestic calm. Thus, British conservatives became champions of expanding the empire, while in the United States, by the 1890s, the

Republican party became increasingly identified with imperialist causes.

The most important new uses of nationalism in the West occurred in Italy and Germany. After wooing liberal support, Cavour formed an alliance with France that enabled him to attack Austrian control of northern Italian provinces in 1858. The war set in motion a nationalist rebellion in other parts of the peninsula that allowed Cavour to unite most of Italy under the Piedmontese king (Map 29.3). This led to a reduction of the political power of the Catholic pope, already an opponent of liberal and nationalist ideas—an important part of the general reduction of church power in Western politics.

Following Cavour's example, Bismarck in Prussia staged a series of wars in the 1860s that expanded Prussian power in Germany. He was a classic diplomatic military strategist, a key example of an individual agent seizing on larger trends such as nationalism to produce results that were far from inevitable. For example, in 1863 Bismarck used the occasion of Danish incorporation of two heavily German

Map 29.3 *The Unification of Italy. The mid-19th century saw both Italy and Germany fused into single nations, as strong leaders brought together numerous small regional states.*

Legend:
- Kingdom of Sardinia to 1859
- To Sardinia, 1860
- Annexed to Sardinia, 1861; establishes kingdom of Italy
- To Italy, 1866
- To Italy, 1870

provinces, Schleswig and Holstein, to justify the Prussian and Austrian defeat of Denmark. Then he maneuvered a pretext for Prussian declaration of war against Austria. In 1866, Prussia emerged as the supreme German power. A final war, against France, led to outright German unity in 1871 (Map 29.4). The new German Empire boasted a national parliament with a lower house based on universal male suffrage and an upper house that favored conservative state governments. This kind of compromise, combined with the dizzying joy of nationalist success, won support for the new regime from most liberals and many conservatives.

Other key political issues were resolved at about the same time. The bloody *American Civil War*— the first war based extensively on industrial weaponry and transport systems, carefully watched by European military observers—was fought between 1861 and 1865. The war resolved by force the simmering dispute over sectional rights between the North and South in the new nation and also brought an end to slavery. France, after its defeat by Germany in 1870, overthrew its short-lived echo of the Napoleonic Empire and established a conservative republic with votes for all men, a reduction of church power, and expansion of education, but no major social reform. Just as conservative Bismarck could be selectively radical, France proved that liberals could be very cautious.

Almost all Western nations now had parliamentary systems, usually democracies of some sort, in which religious and other freedoms were widely protected. In this system, liberal and conservative ministries could alternate without major changes of internal policy. Indeed, Italy developed a process called *trasformismo,* or transformism, in which parliamentary deputies, no matter what platforms they professed, were transformed once in Rome to a single-minded pursuit of political office and support of the status quo.

The Social Questions and New Government Functions

The decline of basic constitutional disputes by the 1870s promoted the fuller development of an industrial-style state. A new set of political movements emerged.

Government functions and personnel expanded rapidly throughout the Western world after 1870. All Western governments introduced civil service examinations to test applicants on the basis of talent rather than on connections or birth alone, thus unwittingly imitating Chinese innovations more than a thousand years before. With a growing bureaucracy and improved recruitment, governments began to extend their regulatory apparatus, inspecting factory safety, the health of prostitutes, hospital conditions, and even (through the introduction of passports and border controls) personal travel.

Schooling expanded, becoming generally compulsory up to age 12. Governments believed that education provided essential work skills and the basis for new levels of political loyalty. Many American states by 1900 began also to require high school education, and most Western nations expanded their public secondary school systems. Here was a huge addition to the ways in which governments and individuals interacted. The new school systems promoted literacy; by 1900, 90 to 95 percent of all adults in western Europe and the United States could read. Schools also encouraged certain social agendas. Girls were carefully taught about the

Prussia, 1815—1866
Annexed by Prussia, 1866
Joined Prussia in forming the North German Confederation, 1867
German Confederation, 1815—1866
Joined with Prussia to form the German Empire, 1871
Alsace-Lorraine ceded to German Empire by France, 1871

Map 29.4 *The Unification of Germany, 1815–1871.*

importance of home and women's moral mission in domestic science programs. Schools also carefully propounded nationalism, teaching the superiority of the nation's language and history as well as attacking minority or immigrant cultures.

Governments also began to introduce wider welfare measures, replacing or supplementing traditional groups such as churches and families. Bismarck was a pioneer in this area in the 1880s as he tried to wean German workers from their attraction to socialism. His tactic failed, as socialism steadily advanced, but his measures had lasting importance. German social insurance began to provide assistance in cases of accident, illness, and old age. Some measures to aid the unemployed were soon added, initially in Britain. These early welfare programs were small and their utility limited, but were sketched a major extension of government power.

Accompanying the quiet revolution in government functions was a realignment of the political spectrum in the Western world during the late 19th century. Constitutional issues were replaced by social issues—what people of the time called the *social question*—as the key criteria for political partisanship. Socialist and feminist movements surged to the political fore, placing liberals and conservatives in a new defensive posture.

The rise of *socialism* depended above all on the power of grievance of the working class, with allies from other groups. It also reflected *Karl Marx's* redefinition of political theory. Early socialist doctrine, from the Enlightenment through 1848, had focused on human perfectibility: Set up a few exemplary communities, where work and rewards would be shared, and the evils of capitalism would end. Marx's socialism, worked out between 1848 and 1860, was toughminded, and he blasted earlier theorists as giddy utopians. Marx saw socialism as the final phase of an inexorable march of history, which could be studied dispassionately and scientifically. History for Marx was shaped by the available means of production and who controlled those means, an obvious reflection of the looming role of technology in the industrial world forming at that time. According to Marx, class struggle always pitted a group out of power with the group controlling the means of production; hence, in the era just passed, the middle class had battled the feudal aristocracy and its hold on the land. Now the middle class had won; it dominated production and, through this, the state and the culture as well. But it had created a new class enemy, the propertyless pro-

letariat, that would grow until revolution became inevitable. Then, after a transitional period in which proletarian dictatorship would clean up the remnants of the bourgeois social order, full freedom would be achieved. People would benefit justly and equally from their work, and the state would wither away; the historic class struggle would at last end because classes would be eliminated.

Marx's vision was a powerful one. It clearly identified capitalist evil. It told workers that their low wages were exploitive and unjust. It urged the need for violent action but also ensured that revolution was part of the inexorable tides of history. The result would be heaven on earth—ultimately, an Enlightenment-like vision of progress.

By the 1860s, when working-class activity began to revive, Marxist doctrine provided encouragement and structure. Marx himself continued to concentrate on ideological development and purity, but leaders in many countries translated his doctrine into practical political parties.

Germany led the way. As Bismarck extended the vote, socialist leaders in the 1860s and 1870s were the first to understand the implications of mass electioneering. Socialist movements provided fiery speakers who courted popular votes. By the 1880s, socialists in Germany were cutting into liberal support, and by 1900, the party was the largest single political force in the nation. Socialist parties in Austria, France, and elsewhere followed a roughly similar course, everywhere emerging as a strong minority force.

The rise of socialism terrified many people in Western society, who took the revolutionary message literally. In combination with major industrial strikes and unionization, it was possible to see social issues portending outright social war. But socialism itself was not unchanging. As socialist parties gained strength they often allied with other groups to achieve more moderate reforms. A movement called *revisionism* arose, which argued that Marx's revolutionary vision was wrong and that success could be achieved by peaceful democratic means. Many socialist leaders denounced revisionism but put their energies into building electoral victories rather than plotting violent revolution.

Socialism was not the only challenge to the existing order. By 1900, powerful *feminist movements* had arisen. These movements sought various legal and economic gains for women, such as equal access to professions and higher education as well as the right to vote. Feminism won support particularly from middle-class women, who argued that the very moral superiority granted to women in the home should be translated into political voice. Many middle-class women also chafed against the confines of their domestic roles, particularly as family size declined. In several countries, feminism combined with socialism, but in Britain, the United States, Australia, and Scandinavia, a separate feminist current arose that petitioned widely and even conducted acts of violence in order to win the vote. Several American states and Scandinavian countries extended the vote to women by 1914, in a pattern that would spread to Britain, Germany, and the whole United States after 1918.

The new feminism, like the labor movement, was no mere abstraction but the fruit of active, impassioned leadership, in this case, largely from the middle classes. Emmeline Pankhurst (1858–1928; Figure 29.4) was typical of the more radical feminist leadership both in background and tactics. Born to a reform-minded English middle-class family, she was active in women's rights issues, as was her husband. She collaborated with Richard Pankhurst, whom she

had married in 1879, to work for improvements in women's property rights, and she participated in the Socialist Fabian Society. But then she turned more radical. She formed a suffrage organization in 1903 to seek the vote for women, and with her daughter Christabel sponsored attention-getting public disturbances, including planting a bomb in St. Paul's Cathedral. Window-smashing, arson, and hunger strikes rounded out her spectacular tactical arsenal. Often arrested, she engaged in a huge strike in 1912. The suffragists supported the war effort, which gained public sympathy, in 1914. Pankhurst moved to Canada for a time, leaving the English movement to her daughter, but returned as a respected figure to run for Parliament after women had gained the vote in 1928.

CULTURAL TRANSFORMATIONS

❖ *Western culture changed dramatically during the 19th century. Growing emphasis on consumers introduced new values and leisure forms. Science*

Figure 29.4. *Emmeline Goulden Pankhurst.*

increased its hold but generated a new, complex view of nature, and new artistic movements demonstrated innovation and spontaneity.

Emphasis on Consumption and Leisure

Key developments in popular culture differentiated Western society after 1850 from the decades of initial industrialization. Better wages and the reduction of work hours gave ordinary people new opportunities (Figure 29.5). Alongside the working class grew a large white-collar labor force of secretaries, clerks, and salespeople, who served the growing bureaucracies of big business and the state. These workers, some of them women, adopted many middle-class values, but they also insisted on interesting consumption and leisure outlets. The middle class itself became more open to the idea that pleasure could be legitimate.

Furthermore, the economy demanded change. Factories could now spew out goods in such quantity that popular consumption had to be encouraged simply to keep pace with production. Widespread advertising developed to promote a sense of need where none had existed before. Product crazes emerged. The bicycle fad of the 1880s, in which middle-class families flocked to purchase the new machine, was the first of many consumer fads in modern Western history. People just had to have them. Bicycles also changed previous social habits, as women needed less cumbersome garments and young couples could out-pedal chaperones during courtship.

Mass leisure culture began to emerge. Popular newspapers, with bold headlines and compelling human interest stories, won millions of subscribers in the industrial West. They featured shock and entertainment more than appeals to reason or political principle. Crime, imperialist exploits, sports, and even comics became the items of the day. Popular theater soared. Comedy routines and musical revues drew thousands of patrons to music halls; after 1900, some of these entertainment themes dominated the new

Figure 29.5. *Middle-class and working-class families made trips to the seaside popular before appropriate clothing had been designed, as can be seen in this scene from Yarmouth, England.*

medium of motion pictures. Vacation trips became increasingly common, and seaside resorts grew to the level of big business.

The rise of team sports readily expressed the complexities of the late 19th-century leisure revolution. Here was another Western development, which soon had international impact. Soccer, American football, and baseball surged into new prominence at both amateur and professional levels. These new sports reflected industrial life. Though based on traditional games, they were organized by means of rules and umpires. They taught the virtues of coordination and discipline and could be seen as useful preparation for work or military life. They were suitably commercial: Sports equipment, based on the ability to mass-produce rubber balls, and professional teams and stadiums quickly became major businesses. But sports also expressed impulse and violence. They expressed irrational community loyalties and even, as the Olympic Games were reintroduced in 1896, nationalist passions.

Overall, new leisure interests suggested a complex set of attitudes on the part of ordinary people in Western society. They demonstrated growing secularism. Religion still counted among some groups, but religious practice had declined as people increasingly looked for worldly entertainments. Many people would have agreed that progress was possible on this earth through rational planning and individual self-control. Yet mass leisure also suggested a more impulsive side to popular outlook, one bent on the display of passion or at least vicarious participation by spectators in emotional release.

Advances in Scientific Knowledge

Science and the arts took separate paths, with influential developments in each area. The size of the intellectual and artistic community in the West expanded steadily with rising prosperity and advancing educational levels. A growing audience existed for various intellectual and artistic products. The bulk of the new activity was resolutely secular. Although new churches were built as cities grew, and missionary activity reached new heights outside the Western world, the churches no longer served as centers for the most creative intellectual life. Continuing advances in science kept alive the rationalist tradition. Universities and other research establishments increasingly applied science to practical affairs, linking science and technology in the popular mind under a general aura of

progress. Improvements in medical pathology and the germ theory combined science and medicine, although no breakthrough therapies resulted yet. Science was applied to agriculture through studies of seed yields and chemical fertilizers, with Germany and then the United States in the lead.

The great advance in theoretical science came in biology with the evolutionary theory of *Charles Darwin*, whose major work was published in 1859. Darwin argued that all living species had evolved into their present form through the ability to adapt in a struggle for survival. Biological development could be scientifically understood as a process taking place over time, with some animal and plant species disappearing and others—the fittest in the survival struggle—evolving from earlier forms. Darwin's ideas clashed with traditional Christian beliefs that God had fashioned humankind as part of initial creation, and the resultant debate further weakened the hold of religion. Darwin also created a more complex picture of nature than Newton's simple physical laws had suggested. In this view, nature worked through random struggle, and people were seen as animals with large brains, not as supremely rational.

Developments in physics continued as well, with work on electromagnetic behavior and then, about 1900, increasing knowledge of the behavior of the atom and its major components. New theories arose, based on complex mathematics, to explain the behavior of planetary motion and the movement of electrical particles, where Newtonian laws seemed too simple. After 1900, *Albert Einstein's* theory of relativity formalized this new work by adding time as a factor in physical measurement. Again, science seemed to be steadily advancing in its grasp of the physical universe, although it is also important to note that its complexity surpassed the understanding even of educated laypeople.

The social sciences also continued to use observation, experiment, and rationalist theorizing. Great efforts went into compiling statistical data about populations, economic patterns, and health conditions. Sheer empirical knowledge about human affairs had never been more extensive. At the level of theory, leading economists tried to explain business cycles and the causes of poverty, and social psychologists studied the behavior of crowds. Toward the end of the 19th century, Viennese physician *Sigmund Freud* began to develop his theories of the workings of the human subconscience. He argued that much behavior is determined by impulses but that emotional problems can be relieved if they are brought into the light of rational discussion.

New Directions in Artistic Expression

A second approach in the Western culture developed in the 19th century. This approach emphasized artistic values and often glorified the irrational. To be sure, many novelists, such as Charles Dickens in England, bent their efforts toward realistic portrayals of human problems, trying to convey information that would inspire reform. Many painters built on the discoveries of science, using knowledge of optics and color. For example, French painter Georges Seurat was inspired by findings about how the eye processes color, applying tiny dots of paint to his canvasses so that they would blend into a coherent whole in a style aptly called pointillism.

Nevertheless, the central artistic vision, beginning with *romanticism* in the first half of the century, held that emotion and impression, not reason and generalization, were the keys to the mysteries of human experience and nature. Artists portrayed intense passions, even madness, not calm reflection. Romantic novelists wanted to move readers to tears, not philosophical debate; painters sought empathy with the beauties of nature (as in Constable's painting in the opening of this chapter) or the storm-tossed tragedy of shipwreck. Romantics and their successors after 1850 also deliberately tried to violate traditional Western artistic standards. Poetry did not have to rhyme; drama did not necessarily need plot; painting could be evocative, not literal (Figure 29.6). (For literal portrayals, painters could now argue, use a camera.) Each generation of artists proved more defiant than the last. By 1900, painters and sculptors were becoming increasingly abstract, and musical composers worked with atonal scales that defied long-established conventions. Some artists talked of art for art's sake, arguing essentially that art had its own purposes unrelated to the larger society around it.

Figure 29.6. *Cézanne's The Large Bathers (1898–1905). This painting illustrates the artist's abandonment of literal pictorial realism to concentrate on what he considered fundamental. His use of nudity further alienated the "respectable" public.*

At neither the formal nor the popular levels, then, did Western culture produce a clear synthesis in the 19th century. New scientific discipline and rationalism warred with impulse—even with evocations of violence. The earlier certainties of Christianity and even the Enlightenment gave way to greater debate. Some observers worried that this debate also expressed tensions between different facets of the same modern mind and that these tensions could become dangerous. Perhaps the Western world was not put together quite as neatly as the adjustments and consolidations after 1850 might suggest.

WESTERN SETTLER SOCIETIES

■■ *Western industrial growth and nationalist rivalry brought an explosion of imperialist expansion in the late 19th century. Along with this expansion, several societies, including the growing United States, extended many Western values and institutions to new areas. This expansion of the West to a number of vast settler societies was one of the crucial developments of the 19th century.*

The Industrial Revolution prompted a major expansion of the West's power in the world. Western nations could pour out far more processed goods than before, which meant that they needed new markets. They also needed new raw materials and agricultural products, which spurred the development of more commercial agriculture in places such as Africa and Latin America. The vast ships and communication networks created by industrial technology spurred the intensification of the Western-led world economy.

Industrialization also extended the West's military advantage in the wider world. Steamships could navigate previously impassable river systems, bringing Western guns inland as never before. The invention of the repeating rifle and machine gun gave small Western forces superiority over masses of local troops. These new means combined with new motives: European nations competed for new colonies as part of their nationalistic rivalry, businesspeople sought new chances for profit, and missionaries sought opportunities for conversion. Haltingly before 1860, then rapidly, Europe's empires spread through Africa, southeast Asia, and parts of China and the Middle East.

Many of the same forces, and also massive European emigration, created Western settler societies overseas in areas where indigenous populations were decimated by disease. The most important "overseas Western" nation, and the only one to become a major world force before 1914, was the United States.

Emerging Power of the United States

The country that was to become the United States did not play a substantial role in world history in its colonial period. Its export products were far less significant than those of Latin America and the Caribbean. The American Revolution caused a stir in Europe, but the new nation emphasized internal development through the early 19th century. The Monroe Doctrine (1823) warned against European meddling in the Americas, but it was British policy and naval power that kept the hemisphere free from new colonialism. American energies were poured into elaboration of the new political system, internal commercial growth and early industrialization, and westward expansion. The Louisiana purchase, the acquisition of Texas, and the rush to California rapidly extended the United States beyond the Mississippi. The nation stood as a symbol of freedom to many Europeans, and it was often invoked in the revolutions of 1848, as in the earlier Latin American wars for independence. It began to receive a new stream of immigrants, particularly from Ireland and Germany, during the 1840s. Its industrialists also borrowed heavily from European investors to fund national expansion.

The crucial event for the United States in the 19th century was the Civil War, fought between 1861 and 1865. Profound differences separated the increasingly industrial North, with its growing farms, from the slaveholding South, with its export-oriented plantation economy and distinctive value system. Disputes over slaveholding led the Southern states to try secession; the North opposed these actions in the interests of preserving national unity and, somewhat hesitantly, ending the slavery system. The Civil War produced an anguishing level of casualties and maimings. The North's victory brought important gains for the freed slave minority, although by the late 1870s, white politicians in the South had begun to severely constrain the political and economic rights of African Americans.

The Civil War also accelerated American industrialization. Heavy industry boomed in a push to produce for the war effort. The completion of a rail link to the Pacific opened the west to further settlement, leading to the last bitter round of wars with Native Americans. Economic expansion brought the United States into the industrial big leagues, its growth rivaling that of Germany. After the Civil War, American armaments manufacturers began to seek export markets. Other industrial producers soon followed as the United States became a major competitor worldwide. American firms, such as the Singer sewing machine company, set up branches in other countries. American agriculture, increasingly mechanized, began to pour out exports of grain and meats (the latter thanks to the development of refrigerated shipping), particularly to European markets where peasant producers could not fully compete.

American diplomacy was not particularly influential outside the Western Hemisphere, although a wave of imperialist expansion from the late 1890s onward brought American interests to the Pacific and Asia. American culture was also seen as largely parochial. Despite increasingly varied art and literature, American work had little impact abroad. Many artists and writers, such as Henry James and James McNeill

Whistler, sought inspiration in European centers, sometimes becoming expatriates. Even in technology, American borrowing from Europe remained extensive, and American scientific work gained ground only in the late 19th century, partly through the imitation of German-style research universities. These developments confirmed the role of the new giant in extending many larger Western patterns.

European Settlements in Canada, Australia, and New Zealand

During the 19th century, Canada, Australia, and New Zealand filled with immigrants from Europe and established parliamentary legislatures and vigorous commercial economies that aligned them with the dynamics of Western civilization (Map 29.5). Sparse and disorganized hunting-and-gathering populations (particularly in Canada and Australia) offered little resistance. Like the United States, these new nations looked primarily to Europe for cultural styles and intellectual leadership. They also followed common Western patterns in such areas as family life, the status of women, and the extension of mass education and culture. Unlike the United States, however, these

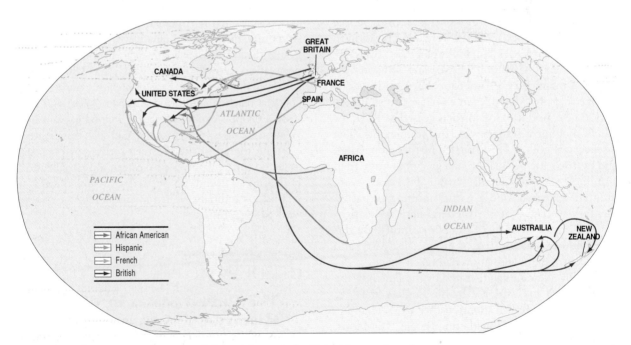

Map 29.5 *19th-Century Settlement and Consolidation in the United States, Canada, Australia, and New Zealand. Immigration led European settlers (and, in North America, enslaved Africans) to key areas previously populated by peoples vulnerable to imported diseases.*

nations remained part of the British Empire, though with growing autonomy.

Canada, won by Britain in wars with France in the 18th century, had remained apart from the American Revolution. Religious differences between French Catholic settlers and British rulers and settlers troubled the area recurrently, and several uprisings occurred early in the 19th century. Determined not to lose this colony as it had lost the United States, the British began in 1839 to grant increasing self-rule. Canada set up its own parliament and laws but remained attached to the larger empire. Initially, this system applied primarily to the province of Ontario, but other provinces were included, creating a federal system that describes Canada to this day. French hostilities were eased somewhat by the creation of a separate province, Quebec, where the majority of French speakers were located. Massive railroad building, beginning in the 1850s, brought settlement to the western territories and a great expansion of mining and commercial agriculture in the vast plains. As in the United States, new immigrants from southern and particularly eastern Europe poured in during the last decades of the century, attracted by Canada's growing commercial development.

Britain's Australian colonies originated in 1788, when a ship deposited convicts to establish a penal settlement at Sydney. Australia's only previous inhabitants had been a hunting-and-gathering people called the aborigines, and they were in no position to resist European settlement and exploration. By 1840, Australia had 140,000 European inhabitants, engaged mainly in a prosperous sheep-raising agriculture that provided needed wool for British industries. The exportation of convicts ceased in 1853, by which time most settlers were free immigrants. The discovery of gold in 1851 spurred further pioneering, and by 1861 the population had grown to more than a million. As in Canada, major provinces were granted self-government with a multiparty parliamentary system. A unified federal nation was proclaimed on the first day of the 20th century. By this time, industrialization, a growing socialist party, and significant welfare legislation had taken shape.

Finally, New Zealand, visited by the Dutch in the 17th century and explored by the English in 1770, began to receive British attention after 1814. Here the Polynesian hunting-and-gathering people, the Maoris, were well organized politically. Missionary efforts converted many of them to Christianity between 1814 and the 1840s. The British government, fearful of French interest in the area, moved to take official control in 1840, and European immigration followed. New Zealand settlers relied heavily on agriculture (including sheep raising), selling initially to Australia's booming gold-rush population and then to Britain. Wars with the Maoris plagued the settlers during the 1860s, but after the Maori defeat, generally good relations were established, and the Maoris won some representation in Parliament. As in Canada and Australia, a parliamentary system was created that allowed the new nation to rule itself as a dominion of the British Empire without interference from the mother country.

Canada, New Zealand, and Australia each had distinct national flavors and national issues. These new countries were far more dependent on the European, particularly the British, economy than was the United States. Industrialization did not overshadow commercial agriculture and mining, even in Australia, so that exchanges with Europe remained important. Nevertheless, despite their distinctive features, these countries followed the basic patterns of Western civilization, from political forms to key leisure activities. The currents of liberalism, socialism, modern art, and scientific education that described Western civilization to 1900 and beyond largely characterized these important new extensions.

It was these areas, along with the United States and part of Latin America, particularly Brazil and Argentina, that received new waves of European emigrants during the 19th century. Although Europe's population growth rate slowed after 1800, it still advanced rapidly on the basis of previous gains as more children reached adulthood and had children of their own. Europe's export of people helped explain how Western societies could take shape in such distant areas.

The spread of the Western settler societies also reflected the new power of Western industrialization. Huge areas could be settled quickly, thanks to steamships and rails, while remaining in close contact with western Europe.

iN DEP†H

The United States in World History

Placing United States history in world history raises some important issues. Should the United

States be treated as a separate civilization (perhaps along with Canada and other places that mixed dominant Western settlement with frontier conditions)? Latin America, because of its ongoing position in the world economy and its blending of European, Indian, and African influences, usually is not treated as part of Western civilization. Does the same hold true for the United States?

Because the United States is so often treated separately in history courses, there is a ready assumption of American uniqueness. The United States had purer diplomatic motives than did western Europe—look at the idealism of Woodrow Wilson. It had its own cultural movements, such as the religious "great awakening" of the 18th century and transcendentalism in the 19th. The United States had the unique experience of wave after wave of immigrants reaching its shores, contributing great cultural diversity but also promoting cultural and social integration under the banners of Americanization. Many thoughtful historians argue for American exceptionalism—that is, the United States as its own civilization, not as part of larger Western patterns. *American exceptionalists* do not contend that the United States was immune from contact with western Europe, which would be ridiculous, but they argue that this contact was incidental to the larger development of the United States on its own terms.

American exceptionalists can point to several factors that caused the development of a separate United States civilization. Although colonial immigrants often intended to duplicate European styles of life, the vastness and wealth of the new land quickly forced changes. As a result, American families gave greater voice to women and children, and abundant land created a class of independent farmers rather than a traditional peasantry with tight-knit villages. The successful revolution continued to shape a political life different from that of western Europe. The frontier, which lasted until the 1890s and had cultural impact even beyond that date, would continue to make Americans unusually mobile and restless while draining off some of the social grievances that arose in western Europe.

Distinctive causes produced distinctive results. There is no question that the United States, into the 20th century, had a different agricultural setup from that of western Europe. American politics,

with the exception of the Civil War, emphasized small disagreements between two major political parties; third-party movements typically were pulled into the mainstream rather quickly. There was less political fragmentation and extremism than in western Europe and more stability (some would say boredom). No strong socialist movement took shape. Religion was more important in American than in European life by the late 19th century. Religion served immigrants as a badge of identity and helped all Americans, building a new society, retain some sense of their moorings. The absence of established churches in the United States kept religion out of politics, in contrast to Europe, where churches got caught up in more general attacks on the political establishment.

The American exceptionalist argument often appeals particularly to things Americans like to believe about themselves—more religious than people in other societies, less socialistic, full of the competence that came from taming a frontier—but it must embrace some less savory distinctiveness as well. The existence of slavery, and then the racist attitudes and institutions that arose after its abolition, created ongoing issues in American life that had no direct counterpart in western Europe. Correspondingly, Europe had less direct contact with African culture; jazz was one of the key products of this aspect of American life.

Yet from a world history standpoint, the United States must be seen also, and perhaps primarily, as an offshoot of Western civilization. The colonial experience and the revolution showed the powerful impact of Western political ideas, culture, and even family styles. American history in the 19th century followed patterns common in western Europe. The development of parliamentary life and the spread of democracy, though occurring unusually early in the United States, fit a larger Western pattern. American industrialization was a direct offshoot of that in Europe and followed a common dynamic. Labor strikes and trade unionism spread in similar ways in western Europe and the United States in the late 19th century. American intellectuals kept in close contact with European developments, and there were few purely American styles. Conditions for women and wider patterns of family life, in areas such as birth control and disciplining children, were similar on both sides of the North Atlantic, which shows that the United States not only imitated western Europe but paralleled it.

In some important cases, because the United States was freer from peasant and aristocratic traditions, it pioneered developments that surfaced later in western Europe. This was true in the development of mass consumer culture and mass media (such as the popular press and popular films).

American exceptions remain, such as the Civil War, racial issues, and the absence of serious socialism. American distinctiveness remains in another respect: The United States was rising to world power just as key European nations, notably Britain, began to decline. The trajectory of American history is somewhat different from that of western Europe, and the 20th century revealed a growing American ability to play power politics in western Europe itself. Just as American exceptionalists must admit crucial western European influences, those who see the United States as part of the West must factor in special features and dynamics.

The main point is to analyze American history in careful comparative terms, removing the nation's history from the isolation in which it is so often taught and viewed.

Questions: Which argument has the greater strength in describing 19th-century history: the United States as a separate civilization or the United States as part of the West? Have the United States and western Europe become more or less similar in the 20th century? Why?

DIPLOMATIC TENSIONS AND WORLD WAR I

■■ *Diplomatic and military tensions within Europe began to increase, particularly from the 1890s onward. Rival alliance systems built up their military arsenals. A series of crises, particularly in the Balkans, accelerated the tension.*

The unification of Germany and its rapid industrial growth profoundly altered the power balance within Europe. Bismarck was very conscious of this, and during the 1870s and 1880s, still a skilled manipulator, he built a complex alliance system designed to

protect Germany and divert European attention elsewhere. France, Germany's deepest enemy, was largely isolated. But even the French concentrated on imperialist expansion in Africa and Asia.

By 1900, however, few parts of the world were available for Western seizure. Latin America was independent but under extensive United States influence, so that a new intrusion of colonialism was impossible. Africa was almost entirely carved up. The few final colonies taken after 1900—Morocco by France and Tripoli (Libya) by Italy—caused great diplomatic furor on the part of other colonial powers worried about the balance of forces. China and the Middle East were technically independent, but were in fact crisscrossed by rivalries between the Western powers and Russia (and in China's case, Japan). No agreement was possible on further takeovers.

Yet imperialist expansion had fed the sense of rivalry between key nation-states. Britain, in particular, grew worried about Germany's overseas drive and its construction of a large navy. Economic competition between a surging Germany and a lagging Britain added fuel to the fire. France, eager to escape the Bismarck-engineered isolation, was willing to play down its traditional rivalries with Britain. The French also took the opportunity to ally with Russia, when after 1890 Germany dropped this particular alliance because of Russian–Austrian enmity.

The New Alliance System

By 1907, most major European nations were paired off in two alliance systems: Germany, Austria–Hungary, and Italy formed the *Triple Alliance,* and Britain, Russia, and France formed the newer *Triple Entente.* Three against three seemed fair, but Germany grew increasingly concerned about facing potential enemies to the east (Russia) and west (France). These powers steadily built up their military arsenals in what turned out to be the first of several arms races in the 20th century. All powers save Britain had instituted peacetime military conscription to provide large armies and even larger trained reserves. Artillery levels and naval forces grew steadily—the addition of a new kind of battleship, the Dreadnought, was a key escalation—and discussions about reducing armament levels went nowhere. Each alliance system depended on an unstable partner. Russia suffered a revolution in 1905, and its allies worried that any further diplomatic setbacks might paralyze the eastern giant. Austria–Hungary was plagued by nationality disputes, particularly by minority Slavic groups; German leaders fretted that a diplomatic setback might bring chaos. Both Austria and Russia were heavily involved in maneuverings in the Balkans, the final piece in what became a nightmare puzzle.

Small Balkan nations had won independence from the Ottoman Empire during the 19th century; as Turkish power declined, local nationalism rose, and Russian support for its Slavic neighbors paid off. But the nations were intensely hostile to one another. Furthermore, *Balkan nationalism* threatened Austria, which had a large southern Slav population. Russia and Austria nearly came to blows on several occasions over Balkan issues. Then, in 1912 and 1913, the Balkan nations engaged in two internal wars, which led to territorial gains for several states but satisfied no one (Map 29.6). Serbia, which bordered Austria to the south, had hoped for greater stakes. At the same time, Austria grew nervous over the gains Serbia had achieved. In 1914, a Serbian nationalist assassinated an Austrian archduke on behalf of Serbian claims. Austria vowed to punish Serbia. Russia rushed to the defense of Serbia and mobilized its troops against Austria. Germany, worried about Austria and also eager to be able to strike against France before Russia's cumbersome mobilization was complete, called up its reserves and then declared war on August 1. Britain hesitated briefly, then joined its allies. World War I had begun, and with it came a host of new problems for Western society.

Conclusion

Diplomacy and Society

The tensions that spiraled into major war are not easy to explain. Diplomatic maneuverings can seem quite remote from the central concerns of most people, if only because key decisions—for example, with whom to ally—are made by a specialist elite. Even as the West became more democratic, few ordinary people placed foreign affairs high on their election agendas.

The West had long been characterized by political divisions and rivalries. In comparison with some other civilizations, this was an inherent weakness of the Western political system. In a sense, what happened by the late 19th century was that the nation-state system got out of hand, encouraged by the absence of serious challenge from any other civilizations. The rise of Germany and new tensions in the Balkans simply complicated the growing nationalist competition.

This diplomatic escalation also had some links to the strains of Western society under the impact of industrialization. Established leaders in the West continued to worry about social protest. They tended to seek diplomatic successes to distract the people. This procedure worked nicely for a few decades when imperialist gains came easily. But then it backfired: Around 1914 German officials, fearful of the power of the socialists, wondered

Map 29.6 *The Balkan Wars, 1912–1913: Before and after the two wars.*

whether war would aid national unity, and British leaders, beset by feminist dissent and labor unrest, failed to think through their own diplomatic options. Leaders also depended on military buildups for economic purposes. Modern industry, pressed to sell the soaring output of its factories, found naval purchases and army equipment a vital supplement.

The masses themselves had some role to play. Although some groups, particularly socialists, were hostile to the alliance system and to imperialism, many workers and clerks found the diplomatic successes of their nations exciting. In an increasingly disciplined and organized society, with work routine if not downright boring, the idea of violence and energy—even of war—could be appealing. Mass newspapers, which fanned nationalist pride with stories of conquest and tales of the evils of rival nations, helped shape this belligerent popular culture.

In other words, the consolidation of industrial society in the West continued to generate strain at various levels. Consolidation meant more powerful armies and governments and a more potent industrial machine. It also meant continued social friction and an ongoing tug of war between rational restraint and a desire to break out.

Thus, just a few years after celebrating a century of material progress and peace, ordinary Europeans went to war almost gaily in 1914. Troops departed for the front convinced that war would be exciting, with quick victories. Their departure was hailed by enthusiastic civilians, who draped their trains with flowers. Four years later, almost everyone would have agreed that war had been unmitigated hell. However, the complexities of industrial society were such that war's advent seemed almost a welcome breath of the unexpected, a chance to get away from the disciplined stability of everyday life.

Further Readings

Two excellent studies survey Europe's Industrial Revolution: Sidney Pollard's *Peaceful Conquest: The Industrialization of Europe* (1981) and David Landes's *The Unbound Prometheus: Technological Change and Industrial Development in Western Europe from 1700 to the Present* (1969). See also Phyllis Deane's *The First Industrial Revolution* (1980) on Britain. For a more general survey, see Peter N. Stearns's *The Industrial Revolution in World History* (1993). On the demographic experience, see Thomas McKeown's *The Modern Rise of Population* (1977).

For the French Revolution and political upheaval, Isser Woloch's *The New Regime: Transformations of the French Civic Order, 1789–1829* (1994) is a useful introduction. Lynn Hunt's *Politics, Culture and Class in the French Rev-*

olution (1984) is an important recent study. Other revolutionary currents are treated in *The Crowd in History: Popular Disturbances in France and England* (1981) by George Rudé and *1848: The Revolutionary Tide in Europe* (1974) by Peter Stearns.

Major developments concerning women and the family are covered in Louise Tilly and Joan Scott's *Women, Work and Family* (1978) and Steven Mintz and Susan Kellogg's *Domestic Revolutions: A Social History of American Family Life* (1989). See also R. Evans's *The Feminists: Women's Emancipation in Europe, America and Australia* (1979). An important age group is treated in John Gillis's *Youth and History* (1981).

For an overview of social change, see Peter Stearns and Herrick Chapman's *European Society in Upheaval* (1991). On labor history, see Michael Hanagan's *The Logic of Solidarity* (1981) and Albert Lindemann's *History of European Socialism* (1983). Eugen Weber's *Peasants into Frenchmen: The Modernization of Rural France* (1976) and Harvey Graff, ed., *Literacy and Social Development in the West* (1982) deal with important special topics.

On political and cultural history, see Gordon Wright's *France in Modern Times* (1981), Gordon Craig's *Germany, 1866–1945* (1978), and Louis Snyder's *Roots of German Nationalism* (1978). J. H. Randall's *The Making of the Modern Mind* (1976) is a useful survey; see also O. Chadwick's *The Secularization of the European Mind in the Nineteenth Century* (1976). On major diplomatic developments, see D. K. Fieldhouse's *Economics and Empire, 1830–1914* (1970) and David Kaiser's *Politics and War: European Conflict from Philip II to Hitler* (1990).

For working-class materials from 1830s Britain, see the Web site http://www.history.rochester.edu/pennymag.

On the Web

The sights and sounds of the French Revolution of 1789 are offered at http://otal.umd.edu/~fraistat/romrev/frbib.html, http://history.hanover.edu/modern/frenchrv.htm, http://www.hs.port.ac.uk/Users/david.andress/frlinks.htm,http://marseillaise.org/English, http://fmc.utm.edu/~geverett/marseil.htm and http://www.admi.net/marseillaise.html.

The American Revolution and the Revolutionary War is explored at http://www.cfcsc.dnd.ca/links/milhist/usrev.html, http://users.southeast.net/~dixe/amrev/index.htm and at http://www.revwar.com/.

A bibliography of the women of the American Revolution is provided at http://wwwcarleton.ca/~pking/arbib/

z.htm. Many web pages offer insight into the personalities of the age of revolution, such as Marie Antoinette (http://www2.lucidcafe.com/lucidcafe/library/ 95 nov/antoinette.html), Napoleon (http://napoleonic-literature.simplenet.com/Book15/ V1C1.htm) and Thomas Paine (http://odur.let.rug.nl/~usa/B/ tpaine/paine.htm). Also readily available are web resources addressing the lives of key figures in the Industrial Revolution, such as James Watt (whose reconception of the steam engine can be found at http://www.geocities.com/Athens/Acropolis/6914/ watte.htm, http://www.spartacus.schoolnet.co.uk/ SCwatt.htm and http://homepages.westminster. org.uk/hooke/issue10/watt.htm), Eli Whitney (http://www.eliwhitney.org/ew.htm) and Ned Ludd (http://www.fastlink.com.au/subscrib/hit/smash. htm), whose name became synonymous with resistance to technological change.

The life of industrial workers in 19th century England is examined at http://applebutter.freeservers.com/worker/ index.html and http://www.history.rochester.edu/ pennymag.

Other Web sites explore the world of working women (http://home.earthlink.net/~womenwhist/lesson7.html) and working children (http://www.spartacus.schoolnet. co.uk/IRchild.main.htm).

The impact of industrialization gave thrust to the writings of Karl Marx and others whose critiques and assessments of the future of capitalism were to usher in a new revolutionary period in human history. A brief essay at http://landow.stg.brown.edu/victorian/religion/phil2.html manages to illuminate key forms of Marxian analysis, including the role of ideology in human society. Two of the best sites for accessing and comparing the ideas of Marxist writers are http://csf.colorado.edu/mirrors /marxists.org/ admin/intro/index.htm and http://www.anu.edu.au/polsci/marx/marx.html (which includes a very clear RealAudio file of the "Internationale" sung by an Irish folksinger accompanied on the guitar).

Chapter 30

Industrialization and Imperialism: The Making of the European Global Order

A romantic depiction of the 1879 battle of Isandhlwana in the Natal province of Southern Africa. The battle demonstrated that despite their superior firepower, the Europeans could be defeated by well-organized and determined African or Asian resistance forces.

The process of industrialization that began to transform western European societies in the last half of the 18th century fundamentally changed the nature and impact of European overseas expansion. In the centuries of expansion before the industrial era, Europeans went overseas because they sought material things they could not produce themselves and because they felt threatened by powerful external enemies. They initially sought precious metals, for which they traded in Africa and waged wars of conquest in the Americas. In the Americas, they also seized land on which they could grow high-priced commercial crops such as sugar and coffee. In Asia, European traders and adventurers sought either manufactured goods, such as cotton and silk textiles (produced mainly in India, China, and the Middle East), or luxury items, such as spices, that would improve the living standards of the aristocracy and rising middle classes.

In the Americas, Africa, and Asia, missionaries from Roman Catholic areas such as Spain and Portugal sought to convert what they saw as "heathen" peoples to Christianity. Both the wealth gained from products brought home from overseas and the souls won for Christ were seen as ways of strengthening Christian Europe in its long struggle with the Muslim empires that threatened Europe from the south and east.

In the industrial era, from roughly 1800 onward, the things that Europeans sought in the outside world as well as the source of the insecurities that drove them there changed dramatically. Raw materials—metals, vegetable oils, dyes, cotton, and hemp—needed to feed the machines of Europe, not spices or manufactured goods, were the main products the Europeans sought overseas. Industrialization began to transform Europe into the manufacturing center of the world for the first time. As a result, overseas markets for machine-made European products became a key concern of those who pushed for colonial expansion.

Christian missionaries, by then as likely to be Protestant as Roman Catholic, still tried to win converts overseas. But unlike the rulers of Portugal and Spain in the early centuries of expansion, European leaders in the industrial age rarely took initiatives overseas to promote Christianity. In part, this reflected the fact that western Europe itself was no longer seriously threatened by the Muslims or any other non-European people. The fears that fueled European imperialist expansion in the industrial age arose from internal rivalries between the European powers themselves. Overseas peoples might resist the European advance, but different European national groups feared each other far more than even the largest non-European empires.

1600 C.E.	1700 C.E.	1750 C.E.	1800 C.E.
1619 Dutch established trading post at Batavia in Java	**1707** Death of Mughal emperor, Aurangzeb; beginning of imperial breakdown	**1750s** Civil war and division of Mataram; Dutch become the paramount power on Java	**1815** British annex Cape Town and surrounding area
1620s Sultan of Mataram's attacks on Batavia fail	**1739** Nadir Shah's invasion of India from Persia	**1756–1763** Seven Years' War, British–French global warfare	**1830** Start of the Boers' Great Trek in South Africa
1652 First Dutch settlement in South Africa at Cape Town	**1740–1748** War of Austrian Succession; global British–French struggle for colonial dominance	**1757** Battle of Plassey; British dominant power in Bengal	**1835** Decision to give support for English education in India; English adopted as the language of Indian law courts
1661 British port-trading center founded at Bombay		**1769–1770** Great Famine in Bengal	
1690 Calcutta established at center of British activities in Bengal		**1775–1782** War for independence by American colonists; another British–French struggle for global preeminence	
		1786–1790 Cornwallis's political reforms in India	
		1790–1815 Wars of the Revolution and Napoleonic era	
		1798 Napoleon's invasion of Egypt	

The contrast between European expansion in the preindustrial era and in the age of industrialization was also reflected in the extent to which the Europeans were able to build true empires overseas. In the early centuries of overseas expansion, European conquests were concentrated in the Americas, where long isolation had left the indigenous peoples particularly vulnerable to the technology and diseases of the expansive Europeans (see Chapter 25). In much of the rest of the world (see Chapters 23, 26, and 28), European traders and conquistadors were confined largely to the sea-lanes, islands, and coastal enclaves. Now, industrial technology and the techniques of organization and discipline associated with the increasing mechanization of the West gave the Europeans the ability to reach and infiltrate any foreign land. From the populous, highly centralized, and technologically sophisticated Chinese Empire to small bands of hunters and gatherers struggling to survive in the harsh environment of Tierra del Fuego on the southern coast of South America, few peoples were remote enough to be out of reach of the steamships and railways that carried the Europeans to and across all continents of the globe. No culture was strong enough to remain untouched by the European drive for global dominance in this era. None could long resist the profound changes unleashed by European conquest and colonization.

The shift from the preindustrial to the industrial phase of European overseas expansion was gradual and cumulative, extending roughly from 1750 to 1850. By the mid-19th century, few who were attuned to international events could doubt that a turning point had been reached. The first section of this chapter explores the initial stages of this transformation. It traces the advance of the Dutch inland on Java and the rise in India of what can be seen as the first empire of the industrial era. The middle sections of the chapter are devoted to the forces in Europe and the outside world that led to the great burst of

1850 C.E.	1900 C.E.
1850s Boer republics established in the Orange Free State and Transvaal	**1914** Outbreak of World War I
1853 First railway line constructed in India	
1857 Calcutta, Madras, and Bombay universities founded	
1857–1858 "Mutiny" or Great Rebellion in north India	
1858 British parliament assumes control over India from the East India Company	
1867 Diamonds discovered in Orange Free State	
1869 Opening of the Suez Canal	
c. 1879–1890s Partition of West Africa	
1879 Zulu victory over British at Isandhlwana; defeat at Rourke's Drift	
1882 British invasion of Egypt	
1885 Indian National Congress Party founded in India; gold discovered in the Transvaal	
1890s Partition of East Africa	
1898 British–French crisis over Fashoda in the Sudan	
1899–1902 Angolo-Boer War in South Africa	

imperialist expansion, which was a dominant feature of global history in the last decades of the 19th century. The final sections explore the patterns of European conquest and rule that persisted from earlier colonization efforts and the innovations that were dictated by the ambitions and aspirations of late 19th-century advocates of the new imperialism.

THE SHIFT TO LAND EMPIRES IN ASIA

✖ *From the mid-18th century onward, the European powers began to build true empires in Asia similar to those they had established in the Americas beginning in the 16th century. Using divide-and-conquer tactics, first the Dutch on Java and then the British in India began the process of carving up Asia, Africa, and Oceania into colonial possessions (see Map 30.1). In this first phase of the colonization process, Europeans overseas were willing to adapt their lifestyles to the climates and cultures of the peoples they had gone out to rule.*

The Dutch were hesitant to promote major changes in Javanese society. But the British in India pushed for social reforms, Western education, and other transformations that would become quite familiar in the age of "high" imperialism in the late 19th century.

Although we usually use the term *partition* to refer to the European division of Africa at the end of the 19th century, the Western powers had actually been carving up the globe into colonial enclaves for centuries. At first, this process was haphazard and often was quite contrary to the interests and designs of those in charge of European enterprises overseas. For example, the directors who ran the Dutch and English East India Companies (which were granted monopolies of the trade between their respective countries and the East in the 17th and 18th centuries) had little interest in territorial acquisitions. In fact, they were actively opposed to involvement in the political rivalries of the Asian princes. Wars were expensive, and direct administration of African or Asian possessions was even more so. Both cut deeply into the profits gained through participation in the Asian trading system, and profits—not empires—were the chief concern of the Dutch and English directors.

Whatever policies company directors may have instructed their agents in Africa and Asia to follow, these men were often drawn into local power struggles. After all, they had to defend their forts, warehouses, and occasionally their ships from the attacks of local lords who resented their competition or laid claim to the land that the Europeans occupied. The company directors had to learn to write off these political entanglements as part of the overhead of their trading empires. But they continued to resist initiatives by their overseas agents that would involve them in governing large numbers of Asians or Africans. But before the Industrial Revolution produced the telegraph and other methods of rapid communication, company directors and European prime ministers had very little control over those who actually ran their trading empires. In the 18th century, a letter took months to reach Calcutta from London; the reply took many months more. Commanders in the field, or *men-on-the-spot* as they are often called in historical accounts, thus had a great deal of leeway. They could conquer whole provinces or kingdoms before home officials even learned that their armies were on the move. Thus, the land empires the European powers began to build before the Industrial

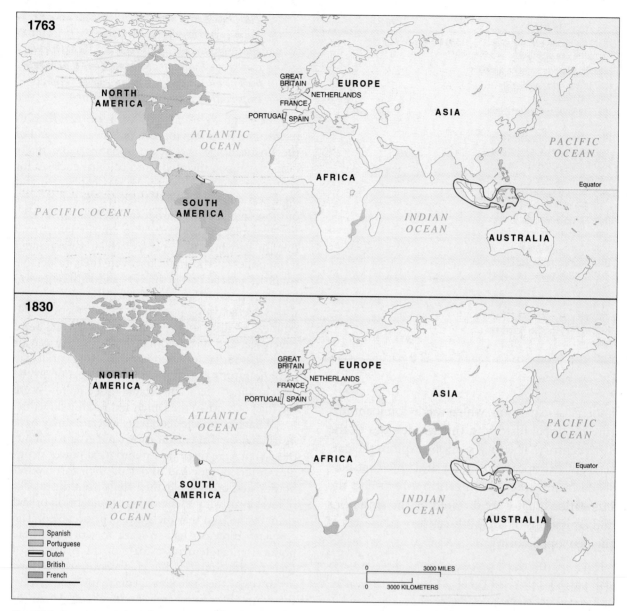

Map 30.1 *European Colonial Territories, Before and After 1800*

Revolution were very much the product of initiatives by local commanders, often acting against the wishes and belated orders of their superiors in Europe.

Prototype: The Dutch Advance on Java

One of the earliest empires to be built in this fashion was that pieced together in the late 17th and 18th centuries by the Dutch in Java (see Map 30.2). Java was then and is now the most populous of the chain of hundreds of islands that today makes up the country of Indonesia. In the early years after the Dutch established their Asian headquarters at Batavia on the northwest coast of the island in 1619, it was a struggle just to survive. After beating back major attacks against Batavia launched in the late 1620s by *Sultan Agung*—the ruler of the kingdom of *Mataram*, which controlled most of the Javanese interior—the Dutch were content to become his vassals and pay an annual tribute. In the decades that followed, the Dutch concentrated on gaining monopoly control over the spices produced on the smaller islands of the Indonesian archipelago to the east. But in the 1670s, the Dutch repeatedly intervened in the wars between rival claimants to the throne of Mataram. The Dutch backed the side that eventually won. As the price for their assistance, they demanded that the territories around Batavia be turned over to them to administer.

This episode was the first of a long series of Dutch interventions in the wars of succession between the princes of Mataram. Dutch armies were made up mainly of troops recruited from the island peoples of the eastern archipelago, led by Dutch commanders. Their superior organization and discipline, even more than their firearms, made the Dutch a potent ally of whichever prince won them to his side. But the price the Javanese rulers paid was very high. Each succession dispute and Dutch intervention led to more and more land being ceded to the increasingly land-hungry Europeans. By the mid-18th century, the sultans of Mataram controlled only the south central portions of Java. A failed attempt by Sultan Mangkubumi to restore Mataram's control over the Dutch in the 1750s ended with a Dutch-dictated division of the kingdom that signified Dutch control of the entire island. Java had been transformed into the core of an Asian empire that would last for 200 years.

Pivot of World Empire: The Rise of the British Rule in India

In many ways, the rise of the British as a land power in India resembled the Dutch capture of Java. The directors of the English East India Company were as hostile as the Dutch financiers to territorial expansion. But British agents of the company in India repeatedly meddled in disputes and conflicts between local princes. In these interventions, the British, adopting a practice pioneered by the French, relied heavily on Indian troops, called *sepoys* (some of whom are pictured in Figure 30.1) recruited from peoples throughout the subcontinent. As had been the case in Java, Indian princes regarded the British as allies, whom they could use and control to crush Indian rivals or put down usurpers who tried to seize their thrones. As had happened in Java, the European pawns gradually emerged as serious rivals to the established Indian rulers and eventually dominated the region.

Partly because the struggle for India came later, there were also important differences between the patterns of colonial conquest in India and Java as well as between the global repercussions of each. In contrast to the Dutch march inland, which resulted largely from responses to local threats and opportunities, the rise of the *British Raj* (the Sanskrit-derived name for the British political establishment in India) owed much to the fierce global rivalry between the British and the French. In the 18th century, the two powers found themselves on opposite sides in five major wars. These struggles were global in a very real sense. On land and sea, the two old adversaries not only fought in Europe but also squared off in the Caribbean, where each had valuable plantation colonies; in North America; and on the coasts and bays of the Indian Ocean (Map 30.1). With the exception of the American War of Independence (1775–1782), these struggles ended in British victories. The British loss of the American colonies was more than offset by earlier victories in the Caribbean and especially in India. These triumphs gradually gave the British control of the entire south Asian subcontinent.

Although the first victories of the British over the French and the Indian princes came in the south in the late 1740s, their rise as a major land power in Asia hinged on victories won in Bengal to the northeast (see Map 30.3). The key battle at *Plassey* in 1757, in which fewer than 3000 British troops and Indian

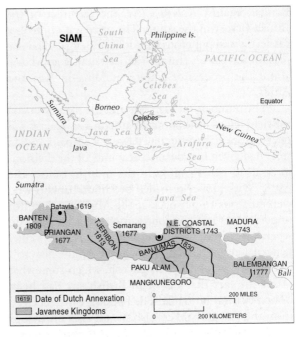

Map 30.2 *The Stages of Dutch Expansion in Java*

Figure 30.1. *Indian soldiers, or sepoys, made up a large portion of the rank-and-file troops in the armies of British India. Commanded by European officers and armed, uniformed, and drilled according to European standards, troops such as those pictured here were recruited from the colonized peoples and became one of the mainstays of all European colonial regimes. The European colonizers preferred to recruit these soldiers from subject peoples whom they saw as particularly martial. In India, these included the Sikhs (pictured here) and Marattas, as well as Gurkhas recruited from neighboring but independent Nepal.*

sepoys defeated an Indian army of nearly 50,000, is traditionally pictured as the heroic triumph of a handful of brave and disciplined Europeans over a horde of ill-trained and poorly led Asians. The battle pitted the *Nawab Sirāj-ud-daula,* who was then the ruler of Bengal, against *Robert Clive,* the architect of the British victory in the south. The prize was control of the fertile and populous kingdom of Bengal. The real reasons for Clive's famous victory tell us a good deal about the process of empire building in Asia and Africa.

The numbers on each side and the maneuvers on the field tell us little about a battle that in a sense was over before it had begun. Clive's well-paid Indian spies had given him detailed accounts of the divisions in Sirāj-ud-daula's ranks in the months before the battle. With money provided by Hindu bankers who were anxious to get back at the Muslim prince for unpaid debts and for confiscating their treasure on several occasions, Clive bought off the Nawab's chief general and several of his key allies. Even the Nawab's leading spy was on Clive's payroll, which somewhat offset the fact that the main British spy had been bribed by Sirāj-ud-daula. The backing Clive received from the Indian bankers also meant that his troops were well paid, whereas those of the Nawab were not.

Thus, when the understandably nervous ruler of Bengal rode into battle on June 23, 1757, his fate had already been sealed. At the time, the Nawab was still a teenager, who acted against the British out of justifiable suspicions that they meant to take over his kingdom as they had those in south India. The Nawab's troops under French officers and one of his Indian commanders fought well. But his major Indian allies defected to the British or remained stationary on his flanks when the two sides were locked in combat. These defections wiped out the Nawab's numerical advantage, and Clive's skillful leadership and the superiority of his artillery did the rest. The British victors had once again foiled their French rivals. As the Nawab had anticipated, they soon took over the direct administration of the sizable Bengal–Bihar region. The foundations of Britain's Indian and global empire had been laid.

The Consolidation of British Rule

In the decades after Plassey, the British officials of the East India Company repeatedly went to war with Indian princes whose kingdoms bordered on the company's growing possessions (Map 30.3). Like the Dutch on Java, the British often became

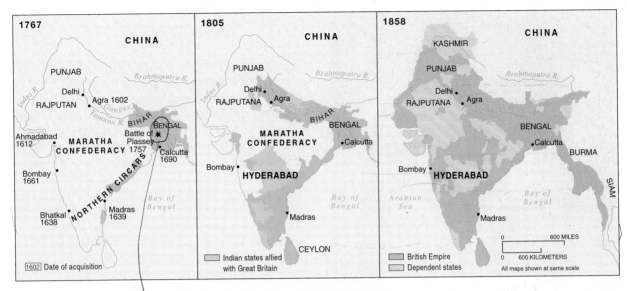

Map 30.3 *The Growth of the British Empire in India, from the 1750s to 1858*

involved in succession disputes and ended up controlling the kingdoms being contested. All of these pulls grew stronger and stronger as the Mughal Empire broke down in the last decades of the century. In its ruins, regional Indian princes fought to defend or expand their territories at the expense of their neighbors. Interventions in these conflicts or assaults on war-weakened Indian kingdoms allowed the British to advance steadily inland from their three trading towns on the Indian coast: Madras, Bombay, and Calcutta. These cities became the administrative centers of the three *Presidencies* that eventually made up the bulk of the territory the British ruled directly in India. In many areas, the British were content to leave defeated or allied Indian princes on the thrones of their *Princely States* and to control their kingdoms through agents stationed at the rulers' courts (for a Dutch–Javanese example of this pattern, see Figure 30.2).

In attempting to prevent the conquest of their kingdoms by the British, the princes of India, like those before them in Java, were handicapped in a number of critical ways. Because there was no sense of Indian national identity, it was impossible to appeal to the defense of the homeland or the need for unity to drive out the foreigners. Indian princes continued to fear and fight with each other despite the ever-growing power of the British Raj. Old grudges and

hatreds ran deeper than the new threat of the British, and there was a sense that the British would someday just go away. Many ordinary Indians were eager to serve in the British regiments, which had better weapons, brighter uniforms, and higher and more regular pay than all but a handful of the armies of the Indian rulers. The British were equally eager to recruit these volunteers, especially those drawn from Indian peoples whom the British deemed especially warlike, such as the Gurkhas of Nepal and the Sikhs of the Punjab. By the mid-19th century, Indian soldiers in the pay of the British outnumbered British officers and enlisted men in India by almost five to one (Figure 30.1).

From the first decades of the 19th century, India was clearly the pivot of the great empire being built by Britain on a global scale. Older colonies with large numbers of white settlers, such as Canada and Australia, contributed more space to the total square miles of empire the British were so fond of calculating. But India had by far the greater share of colonized peoples. Britain's largest and most powerful land forces were the armies recruited from the Indian peoples, and these were rapidly becoming the policemen of the entire British Indian Empire. In the mid-19th century, Indian soldiers were sent to punish the Chinese and Afghans, conquer Burma and Malaya, and begin the conquest of south and

Figure 30.2. *The close alliances that the European colonizers often struck with the "native" princes of conquered areas are graphically illustrated by this photo of the Susuhunan of Surakarta, a kingdom in central Java, standing arm-in-arm with a high Dutch official. At the upper levels of the administration, Dutch leaders were paired with Javanese rulers and aristocrats. The Dutch official always had the last say in joint decisions. But because he was closely linked to subordinate administrators, his Javanese "partner" often had a good deal more to say about how effectively the decision was carried out.*

east Africa. Indian ports were essential to British sea power east of the Cape of Good Hope. As the century progressed, India became the major outlet for British overseas investments and manufactured goods as well as a major source of key raw materials.

Early Colonial Society in India and Java

Although they slowly emerged as the political masters of Java and India, the Dutch and the British were at first content to leave the social systems of the peoples they ruled pretty much as they had found them. The small numbers of European traders and company officials who lived in the colonies for any length of time simply formed a new class atop the social hierarchies that already existed in Java and different parts of India. Beneath them, the aristocratic classes and often the old ruling families were preserved. They were left in charge of the day-to-day administration at all but the very highest levels (Figure 30.2). Although Dutch monopolies and attacks by the sultans of Mataram on the northern coastal towns decimated the Javanese trading classes, Chinese and Chinese–Javanese mestizo (mixed-race) merchants soon emerged to take their place and increasingly allied themselves with the Dutch overlords.

To survive in the hot tropical environments of south and southeast Asia, the Dutch and English were forced to adapt to the ancient and sophisticated host cultures of their Asian colonies. After establishing themselves at Batavia, for example, the Dutch initially tried to create a little Holland in Java. They built high, close-packed houses overlooking canals, just like those they had left behind in Amsterdam and Rotterdam. But they soon discovered that the canals were splendid breeding grounds for insects and microbes that (though the Europeans did not make the connection until somewhat later) carried debilitating or lethal diseases such as malaria, dysentery, and typhoid. By the late 17th century, the prosperous merchants and officials of Batavia had begun to move away from the unhealthy center of the city to villas in the suburbs. Their large dwellings were set in gardens and separated by rice paddies and palm groves. The tall houses of the inner city gave way in the countryside to low, sprawling dwellings with many open spaces to catch the tropical breezes. Each was ringed with long porches with overhanging roofs to block the heat and glare of the sun. Similar dwellings, from which we get our term *bungalow*, came into fashion in India in the 18th century.

Europeans living in the tropical colonies also adopted, to varying degrees, the dress, the eating and work habits, and even the political symbols and styles of the Asian peoples they ruled. Some Englishmen refused to give up their tight-fitting woolen clothing, at least in public. But many (one suspects most of those who survived) took to wearing looser-fitting cotton clothing. Dutch gentlemen even donned the long skirt-like sarongs of the Javanese aristocrats (Figure 30.2). British and Dutch officials learned to appreciate the splendid cuisines of India and Java—a taste that the Dutch would never lose and the British would revive at home in the postindependence era. Englishmen smoked Indian *hookahs*, or water pipes, and delighted in performances of Indian dancing "girls." Adjusting to the heat of the colonies, both the Dutch and the English worked hard in the cool of the morning, took a long lunch break (often with a siesta), and then returned to the office for the late afternoon and early evening. Large clusters of subordinates followed Dutch colonial officials as they paraded about under umbrellas, which like those of the Javanese nobility were colored and decorated in accordance with their rank. British governors rode about on lavishly attired elephants and received visitors in settings that would have done justice to the throne rooms of the more ostentatious Asian princes.

Because the Europeans who went to Asia until the mid-19th century were overwhelmingly male, Dutch and British traders and soldiers commonly had liaisons with Asian women. In some cases these involved little more than visits to the local brothel, but very often European men lived with Asian women, and sometimes they married them. Before the end of the 18th century, mixed marriages on the part of prominent traders or officers were widely accepted, particularly in Java. Thus, examples of racial discrimination against the subject peoples on the basis of their physical appearance can certainly be found during the early decades of European overseas empire. But the frequency of liaisons that cut across racial boundaries suggests a social fluidity and a degree of interracial interaction that would be unthinkable by the last half of the 19th century, when the social distance between colonizers and colonized was consciously marked in a variety of ways.

Social Reform in the Colonies

Until the early 19th century, neither the Dutch nor the British had much desire to push for changes in the social or cultural life of their Asian subjects. The British enforced the rigid divisions of the Hindu caste system, and both the British and the Dutch made it clear that they had little interest in spreading Christianity among the Indians or the Javanese. In fact, for fear of offending Hindu and Muslim religious sentiments, the British refused to allow Christian missionaries to preach in their territories until the second decade of the 19th century.

Beginning in the 1770s, however, rampant corruption on the part of company officials forced the British Parliament to enact significant reforms in the administration of the East India Company and its colonies. By that time most of those who served in India saw their brief tenure as a chance to strike it rich quickly. They made great fortunes by cheating the company and exploiting the Indian peasants and artisans. The bad manners and conspicuous consumption of these upstarts, whom their contemporaries scornfully called *nabobs*, were satirized by leading novelists of the age, such as William Thackeray.

When the misconduct of the nabobs resulted in the catastrophic Bengal famine of 1770, in which as much as one-third of the population of that once prosperous province died, their abuses could no longer be ignored. Parliament passed several acts that restructured the company hierarchy and made it much more accountable to the British government. A succession of political reforms culminated in sweeping measures taken in the 1790s by the same *Lord Charles Cornwallis* whose surrender at Yorktown had sealed Britain's loss of the American colonies. By cleaning up the courts and reducing the power of local British administrators, Cornwallis did much to check widespread corruption. Because of his mistrust of Indians, his measures also severely limited their participation in governing the empire.

In this same period, forces were building, in both India and England, that caused a major shift in British policy toward social reform among the subject peoples. The Evangelical religious revival, which had seen the spread of Methodism among the English working classes, soon spilled over into Britain's colonial domains. Evangelicals were in the vanguard of the struggle to put an end to the slave trade, and by the early 19th century they also added the eradication of Indian social abuses to their campaigns for human improvement. Their calls for reforms were warmly supported by Utilitarian philosophers such as Jeremy Bentham and James Mill. These prominent British thinkers believed that there were common principles by which human societies ought to be run if decent living conditions were to be attained by people at all class levels. Mill and other Utilitarians were convinced that British society, though flawed, was far more advanced than Indian society. Thus, they pushed for the introduction of British institutions and ways of thinking in India as well as the eradication of what they considered Indian superstitions and social abuses.

The Utilitarians had little use for the spread of Christianity that the Evangelicals saw as the ultimate solution to India's ills. But both agreed that Western education was the key to revitalizing an ancient but decadent Indian civilization. Both factions were contemptuous of Indian learning. Influential British historian Thomas Babington Macaulay put it most bluntly when he declared in the 1830s that one shelf of an English gentleman's library was worth all the writings of Asia. Consequently, the Evangelicals and the Utilitarians pushed for the introduction of English-language education for the children of the Indian elite. But their determination to change Indian society went far beyond introducing Western learning. Such officials pushed for major reforms in Indian society and advocated a large-scale infusion of Western technology.

At the center of the reformers' campaign was the effort to put an end to sati, the ritual burning of Hindu widows on the funeral pyres of their deceased husbands. This practice, which was clearly a corruption of Hindu religious beliefs, had spread fairly widely among upper-caste Hindu groups by the era of the Muslim invasions in the 11th and 12th centuries. In fact, the wives of proud warrior peoples, such as the Rajputs, had been encouraged to commit mass suicide rather than risk dishonoring their husbands by being captured and molested by Muslim invaders. By the early 19th century, some Brahman castes and even lower-caste groups in limited areas had adopted the practice of sati.

In the 1830s, bolstered by the strong support and active cooperation of Western-educated Indian leaders, such as *Ram Mohun Roy,* the British outlawed sati. A confrontation between the British and those affected by their efforts to prevent widow burnings illustrates the confidence of the reformers in the righteousness of their cause and the sense of moral and social superiority over the Indians that the British felt in this era. A group of Brahmans complained to a British official, Charles Napier, that his refusal to allow them to burn the widow of a prominent leader of their community was a violation of their social customs. Napier replied,

> The burning of widows is your custom. Prepare the funeral pyre. But my nation also has a custom. When men burn women alive, we hang them and confiscate all their property. My carpenters shall therefore erect gibbets on which to hang all concerned when the widow is consumed. Let us all act according to our national customs.

The range and magnitude of the reforms the British enacted in India in the early 19th century marked a watershed in global history. During these years, the alien British, who had become the rulers of one of humankind's oldest centers of civilization, consciously began to transmit the ideas, inventions, modes of organization, and technology associated with western Europe's scientific and industrial revolutions to the peoples of the non-Western world. English education, social reforms, railways, and telegraph lines were only part of a larger project by which the British tried to remake Indian society along Western lines. India's croplands were measured and registered, its forests were set aside for scientific management, and its people were drawn more and more into the European-dominated global market economy. British officials promoted policies that they believed would teach the Indian peasantry the merits of thrift and hard work. British educators lectured the children of India's rising middle classes on the importance of emulating their European masters in matters as diverse as being punctual, exercising their bodies, and mastering the literature and scientific learning of the West. Ironically, the very values and ideals that the British preached so earnestly to the Indians would soon be turned against colonizers by those leading India's struggle for independence from Western political domination.

IN DEPTH

Western Education and the Rise of an African and Asian Middle Class

To varying degrees and for many of the same reasons as the British in India, all European colonizers educated the children of African and Asian elite groups in Western-language schools. The early 19th-century debate over education in India was paralleled by an equally hard-fought controversy among French officials and missionaries regarding the proper schooling for the peoples of Senegal in west Africa. The Dutch did not develop European-language schools for the sons of the Javanese elite until the mid-19th century, and many young Javanese men continued to be educated in the homes of the Dutch living in the colonies until the end of the century. Whatever their particular views on education, all colonial policymakers realized that they needed administrative assistants and postal clerks and that they could not begin to recruit enough Europeans to fill these posts. Therefore, all agreed that Western education for some segments of the colonized population was essential for the maintenance of colonial order.

One of the chief advantages of having Western-educated African and Asian subordinates—for they were always below European officials or traders—was that their salaries were much lower than what Europeans would have been paid for doing the same work. The Europeans had no trouble rationalizing this inequity. Africans and Asians served in their own lands and thus were accustomed to life in the hot, humid, insect- and disease-ridden tropics. For the Europeans who worked in the colonies, life in these environments was deemed difficult, even dangerous. Higher pay was thought to compensate them for the sacrifices involved in colonial service. The Europeans also had a higher standard of living than Africans or Asians, and colonial officials assumed that European employees would be more hard-working and efficient.

Beyond the need for government functionaries and business assistants, each European colonizer stressed different objectives in designing Western-language schools for the children of upper-class families. The transmission of Western scientific learning and production techniques was a high priority for the British in India. The goal of educational policymakers, such as Macaulay, was to teach the Indians Western literature and manners and to instill in them a Western sense of morality. As Macaulay put it, they hoped that English-language schools would turn out brown English gentlemen,

who would in turn teach their countrymen the ways of the West.

The French, at least until the end of the 19th century, went even further. Because they conceived of French nationalism as a matter of culture rather than birth, it was of prime importance that Africans and other colonial students master the French language and the subtleties of French cuisine, dress, and etiquette. The French also saw the process of turning colonial subjects into black, brown, and yellow French citizens as a way to increase their stagnant population to keep up with rival nations, especially Germany and Great Britain. Both of these rivals and the United States had much higher birth rates in this period.

When the lessons had been fully absorbed and the students fully assimilated to French culture, they could become full citizens of France, no matter what their family origins or skin color. Only a tiny minority of the population of any French colony had the opportunity for the sort of schooling that would qualify them for French citizenship. But by the early 20th century, there were thousands of Senegalese and hundreds of Vietnamese and Tunisians who could carry French passports, vote in French elections, and even run for seats in the French Parliament. Other European colonial powers adopted either the British or the French approach to education and its aims. The Dutch and the Germans followed the British pattern, whereas the Portuguese pushed assimilation for even smaller numbers of the elite classes among the peoples they colonized.

Western education in the colonies succeeded in producing clerks and railway conductors, brown Indian gentlemen and black French citizens. It also had effects that those who shaped colonial educational policy did not intend, effects that within a generation or two would produce major challenges to European colonial dominance.

The population of most colonized areas was divided into many different ethnic, religious, and language groups with separate histories and identities. Western-language schools gave the sons (and, in limited instances, the daughters) of the leading families a common language in which to communicate. The schools also spread common attitudes and ideas and gave the members of diverse groups a common body of knowledge. In all European colonial societies, Western education led to similar occupational opportunities: in government service, with Western business firms, or as professionals (e.g., lawyers, doctors, journalists). Thus, within a generation after their introduction, Western-language schools had created a new middle class in the colonies that had no counterpart in precolonial African or Asian societies.

Occupying social strata and economic niches in the middle range between the European colonizers and the old aristocracy on one hand and the peasantry and urban laborers on the other, Western-educated Africans and Asians became increasingly aware of the interests and grievances they had in common. They often found themselves at odds with the traditional rulers or the landed gentry, who, ironically, were often their fathers or grandfathers. Members of the new middle class also felt alienated from the peasantry, whose beliefs and way of life were so different from those they had learned in Western-language schools.

For more than a generation they clung to their European tutors and employers. Eventually, however, they grew increasingly resentful of their lower salaries and of European competition for scarce jobs. They were also angered by their social segregation from the Europeans, which intensified in the heightened racist atmosphere of the late 19th century). European officials and business managers often made little effort to disguise their contempt for even the most accomplished Western-educated Africans and Asians. Thus, members of the new middle class in the colonies were caught between two worlds: the traditional ways and teachings of their fathers and the modern world of their European masters. Finding that they would be fully admitted to neither world, they rejected the first and set about supplanting the Europeans and building their own versions of the second, or modern, world.

Questions: Why did the Europeans continue to provide Western-language education for Africans and Asians once it was clear they were creating a class that might challenge their position of dominance? Why were challenges from this new class much more effective than resistance on the part of the peasantry or movements led by the traditional religious and political elites? What factors prevented the Europeans from doing a better job to satisfy the demands of the new middle classes? Would they have been satisfied in the long run by concessions by the Europeans in salaries, more jobs, and less racial discrimination? Do you think the European colonial order would have lasted longer if Western-language education had been denied to colonized peoples?

INDUSTRIAL RIVALRIES AND THE PARTITION OF THE WORLD, 1870–1914

The spread of the Industrial Revolution from the British Isles to continental Europe and North America greatly increased the advantages the Western powers already enjoyed in manufacturing capacity and the ability to wage war, relative to all other peoples and civilizations. These advantages resulted in ever higher levels of European and American involvement in the outside world and culminated in the domination of the globe by Western powers by the late 19th century. Beginning in the 1870s, the Europeans indulged in an orgy of overseas conquests that reduced most of Africa, Asia, and the Pacific Ocean region to colonial possessions by the time of the outbreak of World War I in 1914 (see Maps 30.4 and 30.5). In these empires, there were major shifts in the social interaction between Europeans and colonized peoples, in the means by which Europeans extracted wealth from their overseas possessions, and in the Europeans' attitudes toward the spread of what they saw as their superior ideas and institutions.

Although science and industry gave the Europeans power over the rest of the world, they also heightened economic competition and political rivalries between the European powers. In the first half of the 19th century, industrial Britain, with its seemingly insurmountable naval superiority, was left alone to dominate overseas trade and empire building. By the

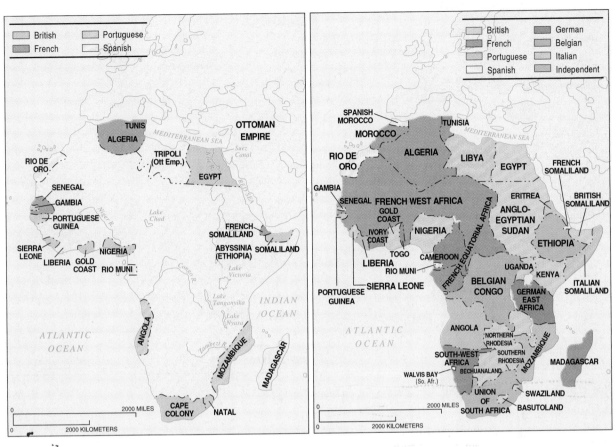

Map 30.4 *The Partition of Africa between c.1870 and 1914*

last decades of the century, Belgium, France, and especially Germany and the United States were challenging Britain's industrial supremacy and actively building (or in the case of France, adding to) colonial empires of their own. Many of the political leaders of these expansive nations saw colonies as essential to states that aspired to status as great powers. Colonies were also seen as insurance against raw material shortages and the loss of overseas market outlets to European or North American rivals.

Thus, the concerns of Europe's political leaders were both political and economic. The late 19th century was a period of recurring economic depressions in Europe and the United States. The leaders of the newly industrialized nations had little experience in handling the overproduction and unemployment that came with each of these economic crises. They were deeply concerned about the social unrest and, in some cases, what appeared to be stirrings of revolu-

tion that each phase of depression created. Some political theorists argued that as destinations to which unemployed workers might migrate and as potential markets for surplus goods, colonies could serve as safety valves to release the pressure built up in times of industrial slumps.

In the era of the scramble for colonial possessions, political leaders in Europe played a much more prominent role in decisions to annex overseas territories than they had earlier, even in the first half of the 19th century. In part, this was because of improved communications. Telegraphs and railways not only made it possible to transmit orders much more rapidly from the capitals of Europe to their representatives in the tropics but also allowed ministers in Europe to play a much more active role in the ongoing governance of the colonies. But more than politicians were involved in late 19th-century decisions to add to the colonial empires. The popular

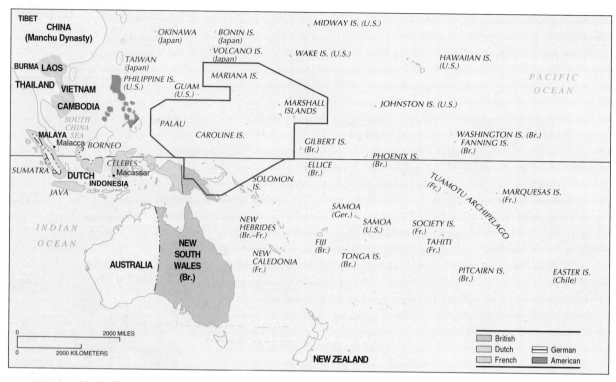

Map 30.5 *The Partition of Southeast Asia and the Pacific Islands to 1914*

press and the extension of the vote to the lower middle and working classes in industrial Europe and the United States made public opinion a major factor in foreign policy. Although stalwart explorers might on their own initiative make treaties with local African or Asian potentates who assigned their lands to France or Germany, these annexations had to be ratified by the home government. In most cases, ratification meant fierce parliamentary debates, which often spilled over into press wars and popular demonstrations. Empires were now only rarely the personal projects of private trading concerns and ambitious individuals; they had become the property and pride of the nations of Europe and North America.

Quarrels over the division of the colonial spoils were cited by those who sought to justify the arms buildup and general militarism of the age. Colonial rivalries greatly intensified the growing tension that dominated the interaction of Western powers in the decades before World War I. As Europe divided into armed camps, successive crises over control of the Sudan, Morocco, and the Balkans (which the great powers treated very much like colonies) had much to

do with the alliances that formed and the crisis mentality that contributed so much to the outbreak of war in August 1914.

Unequal Combat: Colonial Wars and the Apex of European Imperialism

Industrial change not only justified the Europeans' grab for colonial possessions but made them much easier to acquire. By the late 19th century, scientific discoveries and technological innovations had catapulted the Europeans far ahead of all other peoples in the capacity to wage war. The Europeans could tap mineral resources that most peoples did not even know existed, and European chemists mixed ever more deadly explosives. Advances in metallurgy made possible the mass production of light, mobile artillery pieces that rendered suicidal the massed cavalry or infantry charges that were the mainstay of Asian and African armies. Advances in artillery were matched by great improvements in hand arms. Much more accurate and faster firing, breech-loading rifles replaced the clumsy muzzle-loading muskets of the first phase of empire building. By the 1880s, after decades of experimentation, the machine gun had become an effective battlefield weapon. Railroads gave the Europeans the mobility of the swiftest African or Asian cavalry and the ability to supply large armies in the field for extended periods of time. On the sea, Europe's already formidable advantages (amply illustrated in Figure 30.3) were increased by industrial transformations. After the opening of the Suez canal in 1869, steam power supplanted the sail, iron hulls replaced wood, and massive guns, capable of hitting enemy vessels miles away, were introduced into the fleets of the great powers.

The dazzling array of new weaponry with which the Europeans set out on their expeditions to the Indian frontiers or the African bush made the wars of colonial conquest very lopsided. This was particularly true when the Europeans encountered resistance from peoples such as those in the interior of Africa or the Pacific islands (see Maps 30.4 and 30.5). These areas had been cut off from most preindustrial advances in technology, and thus their peoples were forced to fight European machine guns with spears, arrows, and leather shields. One African leader, whose followers struggled with little hope to halt the German advance into east Africa, resorted to natural imagery to account for the power of the invaders' weapons:

> On Monday we heard a shuddering like Leviathan, the voice of many cannon; we heard the roar like waves of the rocks and rumble like thunder in the rains. We heard a crashing like elephants or monsters and our hearts melted at the number of shells. We knew that we were hearing the battle of Pangani; the guns were like a hurricane in our ears.

Not even peoples with advanced preindustrial technology and sophisticated military organization, such as the Chinese and the Vietnamese, could stand against, or really comprehend, the fearful killing devices of the Europeans. In advising the Vietnamese emperor to give in to European demands, one of his officials, who had led the fight against the French invaders, warned,

> Nobody can resist them. They go where they choose.... Under heaven, everything is feasible to them, save only the matter of life and death.

Figure 30.3. *An engraving from the popular* Illustrated London News *shows British warships and gunboats bombarding the east African port of Mombasa in 1874. As in the early centuries of European expansion, sea power remained a critical way for the British and other colonizers to project their power throughout the 19th century. Raids, such as the one shown in the illustration, were so heavily relied upon to control local rulers that the term* gunboat diplomacy *became a staple of international parlance in the mid-19th century.*

Despite the odds against them, African and Asian peoples often fiercely resisted the imposition of colonial rule. West African leaders, such as Samory and Ahmadou Sekou, held back the European advance for decades. When rulers such as the Vietnamese emperors refused to fight, local officials organized guerrilla resistance in defense of the indigenous regime. Martial peoples such as the Zulus in South Africa had the courage and discipline to face and defeat sizable British forces in or conventional battles such as that at Isandhlwana in 1879 (depicted in the illustration that opens this chapter). But conventional resistance eventually ended in defeat. The guerrilla bands in Vietnam were eventually run to the ground. Even at *Isandhlwana*, 3000 Zulus lost their lives in the massacre of 800 British and 500 African troops. In addition, within days of the Zulu victory, a tiny force of 120 British troops at a nearby outpost held off an army of thousands of Zulus. Given European advantages in conventional battles, guerrilla resistance, sabotage, and in some cases banditry proved the most effective means of fighting the Europeans' attempts to assert political control. Religious leaders were often in the forefront of these struggles, which occurred across the globe from the Ghost Dance religion in the late 19th-century American West to the Maji Maji uprisings in German East Africa in 1907 and the Boxer rebellion in China in 1898. The magic potions and divine assistance they offered to protect their followers seemed to be the only way to offset the demoralizing killing power of the Europeans' weapons.

However admirable the courage of those who resisted the European advance, and despite temporary setbacks, by the eve of World War I in 1914 very little of the earth was left for the Europeans to conquer. Except Ethiopia, all of Africa had been divided between the European powers (see Map 30.4). Maps of the continent became a patchwork of colors, each designating one of the European powers. In southeast Asia (see Map 30.5), only Siam remained independent, in part because Britain and France could not decide which of them should have it. The Americans had replaced the Spanish as the colonial overlords of the Philippines, and the Dutch were completing the conquest of the outer islands of the Indonesian archipelago. Even the island clusters of the Pacific had been divided between the hungry industrial powers. China, Persia, and the Middle East had not yet been occupied, but many believed that the informal political and economic influences the European powers exerted in these areas were the prelude to formal annexation.

PATTERNS OF DOMINANCE: CONTINUITY AND CHANGE

Widespread conquests were only the most dramatic manifestation of the great disparity in power that industrialization had created between the Europeans (including the North Americans) and all other peoples of the globe. The Europeans' sense of their own uniqueness and superiority, heightened by their unparalleled scientific and technological achievements, also led to major changes in their economic, social, and cultural relations with the colonized. Europeans living in the colonies increasingly distanced themselves from the peoples they ruled. Europe and North America became even more dominant in the world market system, with much of the rest of the globe supplying them with low-priced raw materials in return for the more highly priced, mass-produced consumer goods of the West. The demand for Western learning on the part of the elite and middle classes of colonized peoples in Africa and Asia rose sharply.

By the end of the 19th century, the European colonial order was made up of two different kinds of colonies. The greater portion of the European empires consisted of the so-called *tropical dependencies* in Africa, Asia, and the South Pacific. In these colonies, small numbers of Europeans ruled large populations of non-Western peoples. The tropical dependencies were a vast extension of the pattern of dominance the British, Dutch, and French had worked out earlier in India, Java, and African enclaves such as Senegal. Most of these colonies had been brought, often quite suddenly, under European rule in the late 19th and early 20th century.

Settlement colonies were the second major type of European overseas possession, but within this type there were two different patterns of European occupation and indigenous response. The first pattern was exhibited by colonies such as Canada and Australia, which the British labeled the *White Dominions*. The White Dominions accounted for a good portion of the land area but only a tiny minority of the population of Britain's global empire. The descendants of European settlers made up most of the population in these colonies, in which small numbers of native inhabitants had been decimated by diseases and wars of conquest. These patterns of European settlement and the sharp decline of the indigenous population were also found in the portions of North America that came to form the United States. Although colonies such as Canada and Australia remained within the British Empire, each moved steadily toward self-government and parliamentary rule in the late 19th century.

In some of the areas where large numbers of Europeans had migrated, a second major variation on the settlement colony developed. Both in regions that had been colonized as early as North America, such as South Africa, and in those the Europeans and Americans had begun to occupy only in the mid- or late 19th century, such as Algeria, Kenya, New Zealand, and Hawaii, the key demographic characteristics of the settler colonies and tropical dependencies were combined. Temperate climates and mild disease environments in these areas made it possible for tens or hundreds of thousands of Europeans to settle permanently. Despite the Europeans' arrival, large indigenous populations survived and then began to increase rapidly. As a result, in these areas for which the label *contested settler colonies* seems most apt, Europeans and indigenous peoples increasingly clashed over land rights, resource control, social status, and cultural differences.

From the 19th century onward, the history of contested settler societies has been dominated by the interaction between European settlers and indigenous peoples. The last sections of this chapter are devoted to case studies of three of the most important and representative examples of the contested settler colony variation on the settlement colony pattern: south Africa, New Zealand, and Hawaii. Because the pattern of colonization involved in the White Dominions is considered in some depth in Chapter 23, developments in Canada and Australia are covered largely through comparisons to patterns in South Africa and other contested settlement areas.

Colonial Regimes and African and Asian Peoples

As the Europeans imposed their rule over tens of millions of additional Africans and Asians in the late 19th century, they drew heavily on precedents set in older colonies, particularly India, in establishing administrative, legal, and educational systems. As in India (or in Java and Senegal), the Europeans exploited long-standing ethnic and cultural divisions between the peoples of their new African or Asian colonies to put down resistance and maintain control. In west and east Africa in particular, they used the peoples who followed *animistic religions* (those that focused on the proposition of nature or ancestral spirits) or those who had converted to Christianity against the Muslim communities that existed in most colonies. In official reports and censuses, colonial administrators strengthened existing ethnic differences by dividing the peoples in each colony into "tribes." The label itself, with its connotations of primitiveness and backwardness, says a great deal about general European attitudes toward the peoples of sub-Saharan Africa. In southeast Asia, the colonizers attempted to use hill-dwelling "tribal" minorities against the majority populations that lived in the lowlands. In each colonial area, favored minorities, often Christians, were recruited into the civil service and police. Their collaboration not only resulted in a sense of loyalty to the colonizers but antagonized less favored ethnic and religious groups, thus bolstering the divide-and-rule strategy of the Europeans.

As had been the case in India, Java, and Senegal, small numbers of Europeans lived mainly in the capital city and major provincial towns. From these urban centers they oversaw the administration of the African and Asian colonies, which was actually carried out at the local level mainly by hundreds or thousands of African and Asian subordinates. Some of these subordinates, normally those in positions of the greatest authority, were Western educated. But the majority were recruited from indigenous elite groups, including village leaders, local notables, and regional lords (Figure 30.4). In Burma, Malaya, and east Africa, numerous Indian administrators and soldiers helped the British to rule new additions to their empire. The Europeans also recruited promising young men in the newly colonized areas for Western schooling that would make them fit for jobs as government clerks or railway mechanics.

THE PAST

Capitalism and Colonialism

In the century since the European powers divided up much of Africa, Asia, and the Pacific into their colonial fiefdoms, historians have often debated how much this process had to do with capitalism. They have also debated, perhaps even more intensely, over how much economic benefit the European colonial powers and the United States were able garner from their colonies. The tables shown here pair Great Britain, the premier industrialized colonial power, with Germany, Europe, the United States, and key areas of the British empire. For each Western society and colonized area, various indices of the amount or intensity of economic interaction are indicated. A careful examination of each set of statistics and a comparison among them should enable you to answer the questions that follow on the connections between capitalism and colonialism.

Questions: To which areas did the bulk of British foreign investment flow? Which areas invested most

British Investment Abroad on the Eve of the First World War (1913)

Circa (1913)	% of Total British Investment	% of Total British Imports	Main Products Exported to GB	% of Total British Exports	Main Products Imported fr. GB
Germany	%0.17	%8.98	Manufactures	%9.82	Manufactures Foods
Rest of Europe	%5.64	%27	Foodstufs Manufactures	%30	Textiles, Machinery, Manufactures
"White" Dominions (ANZAC)	%24.75	%10.93	Wool, Foodstuffs Ores, Textiles	%12.28	Machinery, Textiles, Foods
United States of America	%20.05	%16.95	Manufactures Foodstuffs	%9.37	Manufactures
India (may inlcude Ceylon)	%10.07	%6.30	Cotton, Jute Narcotics, Tea, Other Comestibles	%11.29	Machinery, Coal, Comestibles
Egypt	%1.29	%0.74	Cotton	%1.25	Manufactures Textiles, Coal
West Africa	%0.99		Foodstuffs, Plant Oils, Ores, Timber		Manufactures, Textiles, Machinery
South Africa	%9.84	%1.60	Diamonds, Gold, Wool Other Ores	%3.79	

heavily in Great Britain? With which areas did the British have the highest volume of trade? On which was it the most dependent for outlets for its manufactured goods? On which was it the most dependent for raw materials? On which for raw materials that had strategic importance? Do these patterns suggest that colonized areas were more or less important than independent nations; great power rivals, such as Germany and the United States; or settler colonies, such as Canada and Australia? On the basis of this information, would you say that Britain's "true" colonies (e.g., India, Malaya, sub-Saharan Africa) were vital to its economic well-being and defense? If so, which were the most important?

In contrast to Java and India, where schools were heavily state supported, Western-language education in Africa was left largely to Protestant and Catholic missionaries. As a result of deep-seated racial prejudices held by nearly all the colonizers, higher education was not promoted in Africa. As a result, college graduates were few in Africa compared with India, the Dutch East Indies, or even smaller Asian colonies such as Burma and Vietnam. This policy stunted the growth of a middle class in black Africa, a consequence that European colonial officials increasingly intended. As nationalist agitation spread among the Western-educated classes in India and other Asian colonies, colonial policymakers warned against the dangers posed by college graduates. According to this argument, those with advanced educations among the colonized aspired to jobs that were beyond their capacity and were disgruntled when they could not find employment.

Changing Social Relations Between Colonizer and Colonized

In both long-held and newly acquired colonies, the growing tensions between the colonizers and the rising African and Asian middle classes reflected a larger shift in European social interaction with the colonized peoples. This shift had actually begun long before the scramble for colonies in the late 19th century. Its causes are complex, but the grow-

Figure 30.4. A dramatized engraving of the submission in 1896 of King Prempeh of the powerful Asante kingdom in present-day Ghana. The picture underscores the importance the European colonizers placed on alliances with or the forced submission of indigenous African rulers and local leaders. It also shows a rare case of the public humiliation of indigenous leaders, who in this case had recently conspired to drive the British out by force. Normally, indigenous elites who cooperated with the colonizers were included in pageants celebrating the colonizers' power and were treated with respect, lest their hold over the mass of the colonized peoples be undermined.

ing size and changing makeup of European communities in the colonies were critical factors. As more and more Europeans went to the colonies, they tended to keep to themselves on social occasions rather than mixing with the "natives." New medicines and increasingly segregated living quarters made it possible to bring to the colonies the wives and families of government officials and European military officers (but not of the rank and file until well into the 20th century). Wives and families further closed the social circle of the colonized, and European women looked disapprovingly on liaisons between European men and Asian or African women. Brothels were off limits for upper-class officials and officers, and mixed marriages or living arrangements met with more and more vocal disapproval within the constricted world of the colonial communities and back home in Europe. The growing numbers of missionaries and pastors for European congregations in the colonies obviously strengthened these taboos.

Historians of colonialism once put much of the blame on European women for the growing social gap between colonizer and colonized. But recent research has shown that male officials bore much of the responsibility. They established laws restricting or prohibiting miscegenation and other sorts of interracial liaisons. They also pushed for housing arrangements and police practices designed specifically to keep social contacts between European women and the colonized at a minimum. These measures locked European women in the colonies into an almost exclusively European world. They had many "native" servants and "native" nannies for their children. But they rarely came into contact with men or women of their own social standing from the colonized peoples. When they did, the occasions were highly public and strictly formal.

The trend toward social exclusivism on the part of Europeans in the colonies and their open disdain for the culture of colonized peoples were reinforced by notions of *white racial supremacy*, which peaked in acceptance in the decades before World War I. It was widely believed that the mental and moral superiority of whites over the rest of humankind, usually divided into racial types according to the crude criterion of skin color, had been demonstrated by what were then believed to be scientific experiments. Because the inferior intelligence and weak sense of morality of non-Europeans were seen as inherent and

permanent, there seemed to be little motivation for Europeans to socialize with the colonized. There were also good reasons to fight the earlier tendency to adopt elements of the culture and lifestyle of subject peoples. As photos from the late 19th century reveal, stiff collars and ties for men and corsets and long skirts for women became obligatory for respectable colonial functionaries and their wives. The colonizers' houses were filled with the overstuffed furniture and bric-a-brac that the late Victorians loved so dearly. European social life in the colonies revolved around the infamous clubs, where the only "natives" allowed were the servants. In the heat of the summer, most of the administrators and nearly all of the colonizers' families retreated to hill stations, where the cool air and quaint architecture made it seem almost as if they were home again, or at least in a Swiss mountain resort.

Shifts in Methods of Economic Extraction

The relationship between the colonizers and the mass of the colonized remained much as it had been before. District officers, with the help of many "native" subordinates, continued to do their paternal duty to settle disputes between peasant villagers, punish criminals, and collect taxes. European planters and merchants still relied on African or Asian overseers and brokers to manage laborers and purchase crops and handicraft manufactures. But late 19th-century colonial bureaucrats and managers tried to instruct African and Asian peasants in scientific farming techniques and to compel the colonized peoples more generally to work harder and more efficiently. These efforts involved an important extension of dependent status in the Western-dominated world economy. Pressure for new work habits supported the drive for cheap raw materials to export, and drew in a growing segment of the colonial labor force.

A wide range of incentives were devised to expand export production. Some of them benefited the colonized peoples, such as cheap consumer goods that could be purchased with cash earned by producing marketable crops or working on European plantations. In many instances, however, colonized peoples were simply forced to produce, for little or no pay, the crops or raw materials that the Europeans wanted. Head and hut taxes were imposed that could be paid only in ivory, palm nuts, or wages earned working on European estates. Under the worst of these forced-labor schemes, such as those inflicted on the peoples of the Belgian Congo in the late 19th century, villagers were flogged and killed if they failed to meet production quotas, and women and children were held hostage to ensure that the men would deliver the products demanded on time. Whether appealing to the colonized peoples' self-interest or using terror tactics, the colonial overlords were determined to draw their subjects into fuller participation in the European-dominated global market economy.

As increasing numbers of the colonized peoples were involved in the production of crops or minerals intended for export, the economies of most of Africa, India, and southeast Asia were reorganized to serve the needs of the industrializing European economies. Roads and railways were built primarily to move farm produce and raw materials from the interior of colonized areas to port centers from which they could be shipped to Europe. Benefiting from Europe's technological advances, mining sectors grew dramatically in most of the colonies. Vast areas that had previously been uncultivated or (more commonly) had been planted in food crops were converted to the production of commodities—such as cocoa, palm oil, rubber, and hemp—in great demand in the markets of Europe and, increasingly, the United States.

The profits from the precious metals and minerals extracted from Africa's mines or the rubber grown in Malaya went mainly to European merchants and industrialists. The raw materials themselves were shipped to Europe to be processed and sold or used to make industrial products. The finished products were intended mainly for European consumers. The African and Asian laborers who produced these products were generally poorly paid—if they were paid at all. The laborers and colonial economies as a whole were steadily reduced to dependence on the European-dominated global market. Thus, economic dependence complemented the political subjugation and social subordination of colonized African and Asian peoples in a world order loaded in favor of the expansionist nations of western Europe. It is little wonder then that, as the contrasting quotes in the Document section reveal, that African and Asian assessments of the impact of colonial rule differed sharply from those of the European overlords.

Settler Colonies and White Dominions: South Africa

The contested settler colonies that developed in Africa and the Pacific in the 19th century were similar to the White Dominions in important ways. In fact, the early history of South Africa, one of the largest contested settler colonies, had interesting parallels with those of Canada and Australia, the largest of the White Dominions. European settlers began to move into the southwest corner of south Africa and eastern Canada in the mid-17th century, long before the settlement of Australia began in the 1840s. The initial Dutch colony at Cape Town was established to provide a way station where Dutch merchant ships could take on water and fresh food in the middle of their long journey from Europe to the East Indies. In contrast to Canada, where French fur trappers and missionaries quickly moved into the interior, the small community of Dutch settlers stayed near the coast for decades after their arrival. But like the settlers in Australia, the Boers (or farmers), as the Dutch in South Africa came to be called, eventually began to move into the vast interior regions of the continent.

Although the settlers in each of the three areas were confronted by wild, uncharted, and in some ways inhospitable frontier regions, they also found a temperate climate in which they could grow the crops and raise the livestock they were accustomed to in Europe. Equally important, they encountered a disease environment they could withstand. The Boers and Australians found the areas into which they moved sparsely populated. In this respect their experience was somewhat different from that of the settlers in Canada, where the American Indian population, though far from dense, was organized into powerful tribal confederations. The Boers and Australians faced much less resistance as they took possession of the lands once occupied by hunting-and-gathering peoples.

The Boer farmers and cattle ranchers enslaved these peoples, the *Khoikhoi*, while integrating them into their large frontier homesteads. Extensive miscegenation between the Boers and Khoikhoi in these early centuries of European colonization produced the sizeable "colored" population that exists in South Africa today. The coloreds are seen as distinct from the black African majority. The Australian and Canadian settlers drove the aborigines they encountered into the interior, eventually leaving many of those who survived their invasions the uneasy occupants of remote tracts

ᴅᴏᴄᴜᴍᴇɴᴛ

Contrary Images: The Colonizer Versus the Colonized on the "Civilizing Mission"

Each of the following passages from novels written in the colonial era expresses a different view of the reasons behind European colonization in Africa and Asia and its consequences. The first is taken from an adventure story written by John Buchan titled *Prester John,* a favorite in the pre–World War I decades among English schoolboys, many of whom would go out as young men to be administrators in the colonies. Davie, the protagonist in the story, is a "tall, square-set lad.... renowned [for his] prowess at Rugby football." In the novel, Davie summarizes key elements of the "civilizing mission" credo by which so many European thinkers and political leaders tried to justify their colonization of most of the rest of the world.

> I knew then [after his struggle to thwart a "native" uprising in South Africa] the meaning of the white man's duty. He has to take all the risks, reck[on]ing nothing of his life or his fortunes and well content to find his reward in the fulfillment of his task. That is the difference between white and black, the gift of responsibility, the power of being in a little way a king; and so long as we know this and practise it, we will rule not in Africa alone but wherever there are dark men who live only for the day and their own bellies. Moreover the work made me pitiful and kindly. I learned much of the untold grievances of the natives and saw something of their strange, twisted reasoning.

The second passage is taken from René Maran's *Batouala,* which was first published in 1921 just after World War I. Though a French colonial official in west Africa, like Edward Blyden, Maran was an African-American, born in Martinique, who was highly sensitive to the plight of the colonized in Africa. Here his protagonist, a local African leader named Batouala, complains of the burdens rather than the benefits of colonial rule and mocks the self-important European agents of the vaunted civilizing mission.

> But what good does it do to talk about it? It's nothing new to us that men of white skin are more delicate than men of black skin. One example of a thousand possible. Everyone knows that the whites, saying that they are "collecting taxes," force all blacks of a marriageable age to carry voluminous packages from when the sun rises to when it sets.
>
> These trips last two, three, five days. Little matter to them the weight of these packages which are called "sandoukous." They don't sink under the burden. Rain, sun, cold? They don't suffer. So they pay no attention. And long live the worst weather, provided the whites are sheltered.
>
> Whites fret about mosquito bites.... They fear mason bees. They are also afraid of the "prankongo," the

Figure 30.4. *Edward Blyden was a model product of European–in this case British–efforts to produce a Westernized middle class through education. Born in St. Thomas in the Caribbean, Blyden was the son of slaves, who excelled in the missionary schools on the island. He later became the editor of Liberia's most prominent newspaper, and the author of numerous books and articles. In his published work and in a lively correspondence with leading British and American politicians, he became one of Africa's most outspoken defenders and a much-quoted opponent of racism.*

> scorpion who lives, black and venomous, among decaying roofs, under rubble, or in the midst of debris.
>
> In a word, everything worries them. As if a man worthy of the name would worry about everything which lives, crawls, or moves around him.

Questions: What sorts of roles does Davie assume that the Europeans must play in the colonies? What benefits accrue to colonized peoples from their rule? What impression does he convey of the thinking and behavior of the colonized peoples? In what ways do Batouala's views of the Europeans conflict with Davie's assumptions about himself and other colonizers? Does Batouala agree with Davie's conviction that colonial rule is beneficial for the Africans? What sorts of burdens does Batouala believe it imposes? According to Batouala, what advantages do Africans have over Europeans?

of waste that were not worth settling. In both cases, the indigenous population was also decimated by many of the same diseases that had turned contacts with the Europeans into a demographic disaster for the rest of the Americas in the early centuries of expansion.

Thus, until the early 19th century, the process of colonization in South Africa paralleled that in Canada and Australia quite closely. Small numbers of Europeans had migrated into lands that they considered empty or undeveloped. After driving away or subjugating the indigenous peoples, the Europeans farmed, mined, and grazed their herds on these lands (see Figure 30.5), which they claimed as their own. Whereas the settler societies in Canada and Australia went on to develop, rather peacefully, into loyal and largely self-governing dominions of the British empire, the arrival of the same British overlords in South Africa in the early 19th century sent the Boers reeling onto a very different historical course. The British captured Cape Town during the wars precipitated by the French Revolution in the 1790s, when Holland was overrun by France, thus making its colonies subject to British attack. The British held the colony during the Napoleonic conflicts that followed, and they annexed it permanently in 1815 as a vital link on the route to India.

Made up mainly of people of Dutch and French Protestant descent, the Boer community differed from the British newcomers in almost every way pos-

sible. The Boers spoke a different language, and they lived mostly in isolated rural homesteads that had missed the scientific, industrial, and urban revolutions that had transformed British society and attitudes. Most critically, the evangelical missionaries who entered South Africa under the protection of the new British overlords were deeply committed to eradicating slavery. They made no exception for the domestic pattern of enslavement that had developed in Boer homesteads and communities. By the 1830s, missionary pressure and increasing British interference in their lives drove a handful of Boers to open but futile rebellion, and many of the remaining Boers fled the Cape Colony.

In the decades of the *Great Trek* that followed, tens of thousands of Boers migrated in covered wagons pulled by oxen, first east across the Great Fish River and then over the mountains into the veld, or rolling grassy plains that make up much of the South African interior (see Map 30.4). In these areas, the Boers collided head-on with populous, militarily powerful, and well-organized African states built by Bantu peoples such as the Zulus and the Xhosa. Throughout the mid-19th century, the migrating Boers clashed again and again with Bantu peoples, who were determined to resist the seizure of the lands where they pastured their great herds of cattle and grew subsistence foods. The British followed the

Figure 30.5. *In both New Zealand and Australia, sheepherding was a major impetus for the spread of European settlement into interior areas. In Australia, the sparse indigenous population and vast land area meant that there was ample room for the large herds that became a dominant feature of the landscape. On the smaller islands of New Zealand, the advance of the sheepherding frontier was often at the expense of the more populous Maori peoples and the cause of tension, even open conflict.*

Boer pioneers along the southern and eastern coast, eventually establishing a second major outpost at Durban in *Natal*. Tensions between the Boers and Britain remained high, but the British often were drawn into the frontier wars against the Bantu peoples, even though they were not always formally allied to the Boers.

In the early 1850s, the hard-liners among the Boers established two *Boer Republics* in the interior, named the Orange Free State and the Transvaal, which they tried to keep free of British influence. For more than a decade, the Boers managed to keep the British out of their affairs. But when diamonds were discovered in the Orange Free State in 1867, British entrepreneurs, such as *Cecil Rhodes,* and prospectors began to move in, and tensions between the Boers and the British began to build anew. In 1880–1881, these tensions led to a brief war in which the Boers were victorious. However, the tide of British immigration into the republics rose even higher after gold was discovered in the Transvaal in 1885.

Although the British had pretty much left the Boers to deal with the African peoples who lived in the republics as they pleased, British migrants and financiers grew more and more resentful of Boer efforts to limit their numbers and curb their civil rights. British efforts to protect the settlers and bring the feisty and independent Boers into line led to the republics' declaration of war against the British in late 1899 and to Boer attacks on British bases in Natal, the Cape Colony, and elsewhere. The *Boer War* (1899–1902) that followed began the process of decolonization for the European settlers of South Africa. At the same time, it opened the way for the dominance of the Boer minority over the African majority that would become the central problem in South African history for most of the 20th century.

Pacific Tragedies

The territories the Europeans, Americans, and Japanese claimed throughout the South Pacific in the 19th century were in some cases outposts of true empire and in others contested settler colonies. In both situations, however, the coming of colonial rule resulted in demographic disasters and social disruptions of a magnitude that had not been seen since the first century of European expansion into the Americas. Like the American Indian peoples of the New World, the peoples of the South Pacific had long lived in isola-tion. This meant that, like the American Indians, they had no immunities to many of the diseases European explorers and later merchants, missionaries, and settlers carried to their island homes from the 1760s onward. In addition, their cultures were extremely vulnerable to the corrosive effects of outside influences, such as new religions, different sexual mores, more lethal weapons, and sudden influxes of cheap consumer goods. Thus, whatever the intentions of the incoming Europeans and Americans—and they were by no means always benevolent—their contacts with the peoples of the Pacific islands almost invariably ushered in periods of social disintegration and widespread human suffering.

Of the many cases of contact between the expansive peoples of the West and the long-isolated island cultures of the South Pacific, the confrontations in New Zealand and Hawaii are among the most informative. As we saw in Chapters 10 and 21, sophisticated cultures and fairly complex societies had developed in each of these areas. In addition, at the time of the European explorers' arrivals the two island groups contained some of the largest population concentrations in the whole Pacific region. Both areas were subjected to European influences carried by a variety of agents, from whalers and merchants to missionaries and colonial administrators. After the first decades of contact, the peoples of New Zealand and Hawaii experienced a period of crisis so severe that their continued survival was in doubt. In both cases, however, the threatened peoples and cultures rebounded and found enduring solutions to the challenges from overseas. Their solutions combined accommodation to outside influences with revivals of traditional beliefs and practices.

New Zealand The Maoris of New Zealand actually went through two periods of profound disruption and danger. The first began in the 1790s, when timber merchants and whalers established small settlements on the New Zealand coast. Maoris living near these settlements were afflicted with alcoholism and the spread of prostitution. In addition, they traded wood and food for European firearms, which soon revolutionized Maori warfare—in part by rendering it much more deadly—and upset the existing balance between different tribal groups. Even more devastating was the impact of diseases, such as smallpox, tuberculosis, and even the common cold, that ravaged Maori communities throughout the north island. By the 1840s, only 80,000 to 90,000 Maoris remained of a population that had been as high as 130,000 less than a century earlier. But the Maoris survived these calamities and began to adjust to the imports of the foreigners. They took up farming with European implements, and they grazed cattle purchased from European traders. They cut timber, built windmills, and traded extensively with the merchants who visited their shores. Many were even converted to Christianity by the missionaries, who established their first station in 1814.

The arrival of British farmers and herders in search of land in the early 1850s, and the British decision to claim the islands as part of their global empire, again plunged the Maoris into misery and despair. Backed by the military clout of the colonial government, the settlers occupied some of the most fertile areas of the north island. The warlike Maori fought back, sometimes with temporary successes, but they were steadily driven back into the interior of the island. In desperation, in the 1860s and 1870s they flocked to religious prophets who promised them magical charms and supernatural assistance in their efforts to drive out the invaders. When the prophets also failed them, the Maoris seemed for a time to face extinction. In fact, some British writers predicted that within generations the Maoris, like the Arawaks and Tasmanians before them, would die out.

The Maoris displayed surprising resilience. As they built up immunities to new diseases, they also learned to use European laws and political institutions to defend themselves and preserve what was left of their ancestral lands. Because the British had in effect turned the internal administration of the islands over to the settlers' representatives, the Maoris' main struggle was with the invaders who had come to stay. Western schooling and a growing ability to win British colonial officials over to their point of view eventually enabled the Maoris to hold their own in their ongoing legal contests and daily exchanges with the settlers. A multiracial society has evolved that reflects a reasonable level of European and Maori accommodation and interaction, and the Maori have preserved much of value in their traditional culture.

Hawaii The conversion of Hawaii to settler colony status followed familiar basic imperialist patterns but with specific twists. Hawaii did not become a colony until the United States proclaimed annexation in 1898, although an overzealous British official had briefly claimed the islands for his nation in 1843.

Hawaii came under increasing Western influence from the late 18th century onward—politically at the hands of the British, and culturally and economically from the United States, whose westward surge quickly spilled into the Pacific Ocean.

Although very occasional contact with Spanish ships during the 16th and 17th centuries probably occurred, Hawaii was effectively opened to the West through the voyages of *Captain James Cook* from 1777 to 1779. Cook was first welcomed as a god, partly because he had the good luck to land during a sacred period when war was forbidden. A later and less well-timed visit brought Cook's death as Hawaiian warriors tried to take over his ship for its metal nails. These humble objects were much prized by a people whose elaborate culture rested on a Neolithic technology and thus was without iron or steel. The Cook expedition and later British visits convinced a young Hawaiian prince, *Kamehameha,* that some imitation of Western ways could produce a unified kingdom under his leadership, replacing the small and warring regional units that had previously prevailed. A series of vigorous wars, backed by British weapons and advisors, won Kamehameha his kingdom between 1794 and 1810. The new king and his successors promoted economic change, encouraging Western merchants to establish export trade in Hawaiian goods in return for increasing revenues to the royal treasury.

Hawaiian royalty began to imitate Western habits, in some cases traveling to Britain and often building Western-style palaces. Two powerful queens advanced the process of change by insisting that traditional taboos subordinating women be abandoned. In this context, vigorous missionary efforts from Protestant New England, beginning in 1819, brought extensive conversions to Christianity. As with other conversion processes, religious change had wide implications. Missionaries railed against traditional Hawaiian costumes, insisting that women cover their breasts, and a new garment, the muumuu, was made from homespun American nightgowns with the sleeves cut off. Backed by the Hawaiian monarchy, missionaries quickly established an extensive school system, which by 1831 served 50,000 students from a culture that had not previously developed writing.

The combination of Hawaiian interest and Western intrusion produced creative political and cultural changes, though at the expense of previous values. Demographic and economic trends had more insidious effects. Western-imported diseases, particularly sexually transmitted diseases and tuberculosis, had the usual tragic consequences for a previously isolated people: By 1850 only about 80,000 Hawaiians remained of a prior population of about half a million. Westerners more consciously exploited the Hawaiian economy. Whalers helped create raucous seaport towns. Western settlers from various countries (called haoles by the Hawaiians) experimented with potential commercial crops, soon concentrating on sugar. Many missionary families, impatient with the subsistence habits of Hawaiian commoners, turned to leasing land or buying it outright. Most settlers did not entirely forget their religious motives for migrating to the islands, but many families who came to Hawaii to do good ended by doing well.

Western businesses usually were encouraged by the Hawaiian monarchy, eager for revenues and impressed by the West's military power. In 1848, an edict called the *Great Mahele* imposed Western concepts of property on Hawaiian land, which had previously been shared by commoners and aristocrats. Most of the newly defined private property went to the king and the nobles, who gradually sold most of it to investors from the West. As sugar estates spread, increasing numbers of Americans moved in to take up other commercial and professional positions. Hence, an increasingly "settler" pattern developed in a technically independent state. Because of the Hawaiian population decline, it was also necessary to import Asian workers to staff the estates. The first Chinese contract workers had been brought in before 1800, and after 1868, a larger current of Japanese arrived.

Literal imperialism came as an anticlimax. The abilities of Hawaiian kings declined after 1872, in one case because of disease and alcoholism. Under a weakened state, powerful planter interests pressed for special treaties with the United States that would promote their sugar exports, and the American government claimed naval rights at the Pearl Harbor Base by 1887. As the last Hawaiian monarchs turned increasingly to promoting culture, writing a number of lasting Hawaiian songs but also spending money on luxurious living, American planters concluded that their economic interests required outright United States control. An annexation committee persuaded American naval officers to "protect American lives and property" by posting troops around Honolulu in 1893. The Hawaiian ruler was deposed, and an imperialist-minded United States Congress formally took over the islands in 1898.

As in New Zealand, Western control was combined with respect for Polynesian culture. Because Hawaiians were not enslaved and soon ceased to threaten those present, Americans in Hawaii did not apply the same degree of racism found in earlier relations with African slaves or North American Indians. Hawaii's status as a settler colony was further complicated by the arrival of many Asian immigrants. Nevertheless, Western cultural and particularly economic influence extended steadily, and the ultimate political seizure merely ratified the colonization of the islands.

Conclusion

The Pattern of the Age of Imperialism

Although the basic patterns of domination in European colonial empires remained similar to those worked out in Java and India in the early industrial period, the style of colonial rule and patterns of social interaction between colonizer and colonized changed drastically in the late 19th century. Racism and social snobbery became pervasive in contacts between the colonizers and their African and Asian subordinates. The Europeans consciously renounced the ways of dressing, eating habits, and pastimes that had earlier been borrowed from or shared with the peoples of the colonies. The colonizers no longer saw themselves simply as the most successful competitors in a many-sided struggle for political power. They were convinced that they were inherently superior beings—citizens of the most powerful, civilized, and advanced societies on earth. Colonial officials in the age of "high imperialism" were much more eager than earlier administrators to pull Asian and African peasants into the market economy and to teach them the value of hard work and discipline. Colonial educators were determined to impress upon the children of the colonized elite classes the superiority of Western learning and of everything Western, from political organization to clothing styles.

The European colonizers assumed that it was their God-given destiny to remake the world in the image of industrial Europe. But in pushing for change within colonized societies that had ancient, deeply rooted cultures and patterns of civilized life, the Europeans often aroused resistance to specific policies and to colonial rule more generally. The colonizers were able to put down protest movements led by displaced princes and religious prophets. But much more enduring and successful challenges to their rule came, ironically, from the very leaders their social reforms and Western-language schools had done so much to nurture. These *nationalists* reworked European ideas and resurrected those of their own cultures. They borrowed European organizational techniques and used the communication systems and common language the Europeans had introduced into the colonies to mobilize the resistance to colonial domination that became one of the dominant themes of global history in the 20th century.

Further Readings

The literature on various aspects of European imperialism is vast. Useful general histories on the different empires include Bernard Porter's *The Lion's Share: A Short History of British Imperialism 1850–1970* (1975), Raymond Betts's *Tricouleur* (1978), James J. Cooke's *The New French Imperialism, 1880–1910* (1973), and Woodruff D. Smith's *The German Colonial Empire* (1978). For the spread of Dutch power in Java and the "outer islands," see Merle Ricklets, *A History of Modern Indonesia* (1981). There is no satisfactory general history of the growth of British Empire in India, but Edward Thompson and G. T. Garratt provide a lively chronology in the *Rise and Fulfillment of British Rule in India* (1962), which can be supplemented by the essays in R. C. Majumdar, ed., *British Paramountcy and Indian Renaissance, Part I* (1963). More recent accounts of specific aspects of the rise of British power in India are available in C. A. Bayley's *Indian Society and the Making of the British Empire* (1988) and P. J. Marshall's *Bengal: The British Beachhead, 1740–1828* (1987), both part of *The New Cambridge History of India.*

Of the many contributions to the debate over late 19th-century imperialism, some of the most essential are those by D.C.M. Platt, Hans-Ulrich Wehler, William Appleman Williams, Jean Stengers, D. K. Fieldhouse, and Henri Brunschwig, as well as the earlier works by Lenin and J. A. Hobson. Winfried Baumgart's *Imperialism* (1982) provides a good overview of the literature and conflicting arguments. Very different perspectives on the partition of Africa can be found in Jean Suret-Canale's *French Colonialism in Tropical Africa, 1900–1945* (1971) and Ronald Robinson and John Gallagher's *Africa and the Victorians* (1961).

Most of the better studies on the impact of imperialism and social life in the colonies are specialized monographs, but Percival Spear's *The Nabobs* (1963) is a superb place to start on the latter from the European viewpoint, and the works of Frantz Fanon, Albert Memmi, and O. Mannoni provide many insights into the plight of the colonized. The impact of industrialization and other changes in Europe on European attitudes toward the colonized are treated in several works, including Philip Curtin's *The Image of Africa* (1964), William B. Cohen's *The French Encounter with Africans* (1980), and Michael Adas's *Machines as the Measure of Men* (1989). Ester Boserup's *Women's Role in Economic Development* (1970) provides a good overview of the impact of colonization on African and Asian women and families, but it should be supplemented by more recent monographs on the position of women in colonial settings. One of the best of these is Jean Taylor's *The Social World of Batavia* (1983).

On the Web

The causes of imperialism in the nineteenth century are explored at http://www.fordham.edu/halsall/mod/modsbook34.html. The nature and scope of British imperialism is examined at http://www.wrl.utexas.edu/~scoggins/316british/ twentieth/eco.htm.

The Web offers the means to closely examine the trends, events and personalities involved in the age of imperialism in Africa (http://pw2.netcom.com/~giardina/colony.html), German imperialism in China (http://www2.h-net.msu.edu/~germany/gtext/Kaiserreich/china.htm) and Africa (http://www.fordham.edu/halsall/africasbook.html), American imperialism in the Philippines and the rest of Asia (http://smplanet.com/imperialism/toc.html), and Japanese imperialism in Korea (http://socrates.berkeley.edu/~korea/colony.html), which included the use of chôngsindae ("Comfort Women").

The onset of British imperialism in India, including studies of key personalities such as Robert Clive and key events such as the Battle of Plassey, receives careful treatment at http://www.sscnet.ucla.edu/southasia/History/British/EAco.html.

The British debacle at Isandhlwana and the Zulu wars are given fulsome treatment from a leading British historian at http://www.kwazulu.co.uk/.

An African nationalist perspective of these anti-colonial struggle is offered at http://www.anc.org.za/ancdocs/history/misc/ isandhlwana.html.

The "white man's burden" carried by Rudyard Kipling's prose and poetry is examined at http://wwwhost.cc.utexas.edu/ftp/pub/das/.html/south.asia/sagar/spring.1994.issue/nandi.bhatia.art.html. The American anti-imperialist attack on Kipling's famous poem on race and empire is presented at http://www.boondocksnet.com/kipling/.

Chapter 31
The Consolidation of Latin America, 1830–1920

Benito Juárez, an Indian from southern Mexico, rose to the presidency and began a series of sweeping reforms. His uncompromising resistance to foreign intervention and monarchy made him a symbol of Mexican sovereignty and independence. That symbolism as a nationalist and a man of law is portrayed in a mural by Mexican artist Diego Rivera.

The spread of Western imperialism, along with its consolidation in prior holdings such as Indonesia, carved up much of the world during the 19th century. Africa, both north and south of the Sahara, was almost entirely swallowed up. Australia, New Zealand, and all the clusters of smaller Pacific islands, including Polynesia, were seized. Southeast Asia was taken, and in combination with earlier acquisitions, this meant a solid colonial swath from India in the west to the Philippines in the east.

Four major parts of the world were not caught up in the full imperialist scramble. Russia, most of the Middle East, and much of east Asia were exempt, although imperialist rivalries cut into the latter two civilizations to some extent. Inherited political strength or new initiatives prevented Western control. The fourth exception, Latin America, was the most surprising of all, for in a century of imperialism this society cast off previous colonial controls. The force of the industrial West was deeply felt; like other non-Western and noncolonial areas, Latin America was reshaped by the dominant international forces of the day. New and independent political and cultural initiatives also formed a major part of this civilization's 19th-century experience.

Most Latin American nations gained their political independence early in the 19th century. These former American colonies of Spain and Portugal were swept by the same winds of change that transformed Europe's society and economy and led to the separation of England's North American colonies. Although at present Latin America is sometimes considered part of the Third World along with many Asian and African nations, in reality its political culture was formed in the 18th century by the ideas of the Western Enlightenment. Thus, Latin American leaders in the 19th century, despite their many differences, often shared with Western political figures a firm belief in the virtues of progress, reform, representational and constitutional government, and private property rights. At the same time, Latin American leaders often faced insurmountable problems different from those of Europe and the United States. The colonial heritage had left little tradition of participatory government among the majority of the Latin American population. A highly centralized colonial state had intervened in many aspects of life and had created both dependence on central authority and resentment of it. Class and regional interests deeply divided the new nations, and wealth was very unequally distributed. Finally, the rise of European industrial capitalism created an economic situation that often placed the new nations in a weak or dependent position. These problems and tensions are the focus of our examination of Latin America in the 19th century.

1800 C.E.	1820 C.E.	1840 C.E.	1860 C.E.	1880 C.E.	1900 C.E.
1792 Slave rebellion in St. Domingue (Haiti)	**1821** Mexico declares independence; empire under Iturbide lasts to 1823	**1846–1848** Mexican–American War	**1862–1867** French intervention in Mexico	**1886–1888** Cuba and Brazil finally abolish slavery	**1903** Panamanian independence; beginning of Panama Canal (opens in 1914)
1804 Haiti declares independence	**1822** Brazil declares independence; empire established under Dom Pedro I	**1847–1855** Caste War in Yucatan	**1865–1870** War of the Triple Alliance (Argentina, Brazil, and Uruguay against Paraguay)	**1889** Fall of Brazilian Empire; republic established	
1808–1825 Spanish–American wars of independence	**1823** Monroe Doctrine indicates U.S. opposition to European ambitions in the Americas	**1850s** Beginnings of railroad construction in Cuba, Chile, and Brazil	**1868–1878** Ten-year war against Spain in Cuba	**1895–1898** Cuban Spanish–American War; U.S. acquires Puerto Rico and Philippines	
1808 Portuguese court flees Napoleon, arrives in Brazil; French armies invade Spain	**1829–1852** Juan Manuel de Roses rules Rio de la Plata	**1854** Benito Juárez leads reform in Mexico	**1869** First school for girls in Mexico		
1810 In Mexico, Father Hidalgo initiates rebellion against Spain	**1830** Bolívar dies; Gran Colombia dissolves into separate countries of Venezuela, Columbia, and Ecuador		**1876–1911** Porfirio Díaz rules Mexico		

FROM COLONIES TO NATIONS

■■ *Internal developments and the international situation of the Napoleonic wars set the independence movements in motion. Hidalgo in Mexico, Bolívar in northern South America, and San Martín in the Rio de la Plata led the successful revolutions. In Brazil, an independent monarchy was created.*

By the late 18th century, the elites of American-born whites or Creoles (*criollos*) expressed a growing self-consciousness as they began to question the policies of Spain and Portugal and the need to remain in a colonial relationship. At the same time, these elites were joined by the majority of the population in resenting the increasingly heavy hand of government, as demonstrated by the new taxes and administrative reforms of the 18th century. But the shared resentment was not enough to overcome class conflicts and divisions. Early movements for independence usually failed because of the reluctance of the colonial upper classes to enlist the support of the Indian, mestizo, and mulatto masses, who might later prove too difficult to control. The actual movements were set in motion only when events in Europe precipitated actions in America.

Causes of Political Change

Latin American political independence was achieved as part of the general Atlantic revolution of the late 18th and early 19th centuries, and Latin American leaders were moved by the same ideas as those seeking political change elsewhere in the Atlantic world. Four external events had a particularly strong impact on political thought in Latin America. The American Revolution, from 1776 to 1783, provided a model of how colonies could break with the mother country. The French Revolution of 1789 provoked great interest in Latin America, and its slogan, "liberty, equality, and fraternity," appealed to some sectors of the population. As that revolution became increasingly radical it was rejected by the Creole elites, who could not support regicide, rejection of the church's authority, and the social leveling implied by the Declaration of the Rights of Man.

The third external event was partially an extension of the French Revolution but had its own dynamic. Torn by internal political conflict during the turmoil in France, the whites and free people of color in St. Domingue, France's great sugar colony in the Caribbean, became divided. The slaves seized the moment in 1791 to stage a great general rebellion. Under able leadership by *Toussaint L'Overture* and other blacks, various attempts to subdue the island were defeated, and in 1804 the independent republic of Haiti was proclaimed. For Latin American elites, Haiti was an example to be avoided. The specter of general social upheaval and of slaves becoming their own masters so frightened them that they became even more unwilling to risk political change. It was not accidental that neighboring Cuba and Puerto Rico, whose elites had plantations and slaves and were acutely aware of events in Haiti, were among the last of Spain's colonies to gain independence. For slaves and free people of color throughout the Americas, however, Haiti became a symbol of freedom and hope.

What eventually precipitated the movements for independence in Latin America was the confused Iberian political situation caused by the French Revolution and its aftermath. France invaded Portugal and Spain, and a general insurrection erupted in 1808 and was followed by a long guerrilla war. During the fighting, a central committee, or junta central, ruled in the Spanish king's name in opposition to Napoleon's brother, whom Napoleon appointed king.

Who was the legitimate ruler? By 1810, the confusion in Spain had provoked a crisis in the colonies. In places such as Caracas, Bogotá, and Mexico, local elites, pretending to be loyal to the deposed king Ferdinand, set up juntas to rule in his name, but they ruled on their own behalf. The *mask of Ferdinand* fooled few people, and soon the more conservative elements of the population—royal officials and those still loyal to Spain—opposed the movements for autonomy and independence. A crisis of legitimacy reverberated throughout the American colonies.

Spanish American Independence Struggles

The independence movements divided into three major theaters of operation. In Mexico, a conspiracy among leading Creoles moved one of the plotters, the priest *Father Miguel de Hidalgo,* to call for help from the Indians and mestizos of his region in 1810. He won a number of early victories but eventually lost the support of the Creoles, who feared social rebellion more than they desired independence. Hidalgo was captured and executed, but the insurgency smoldered in various parts of the country. Eventually, after 1820 when events in Spain weakened the king and the central government, conservative Creoles in Mexico were willing to move toward independence by uniting with the remnants of the insurgent forces. *Augustín de Iturbide,* a Creole officer at the head of an army that had been sent to eliminate the insurgents, drew up an agreement with them instead, and the combined forces of independence occupied Mexico City in September 1821. Soon thereafter, with the support of the army, Iturbide was proclaimed emperor of Mexico.

This was a conservative solution. The new nation of Mexico was born as a monarchy, and little recognition was given to the social aspirations and programs of Hidalgo and his movement. Central America was briefly attached to the Mexican Empire, which collapsed in 1824. Mexico became a republic, and the Central American states, after attempting union until 1838, split apart into independent nations.

In South America and the Caribbean, the chronology of independence was a mirror image of the conquest of the 16th century. Formerly secondary areas such as Argentina and Venezuela, slowest to be settled in the 16th century, were among the first to opt for independence and the best able to achieve it, and the old colonial center in Peru was among the last to break with Spain. The Caribbean islands of Cuba and Puerto Rico—among the first of Spain's American possessions—fearful of slave rebellion and occupied by large Spanish garrisons, remained loyal until the end of the 19th century.

In northern South America, a movement for independence centered in Caracas had begun in 1810. After early reverses, *Simon Bolívar,* a wealthy Creole officer, emerged as the leader of the revolt against Spain (see Figure 31.1). With considerable military skill and a passion for independence, he eventually mobilized support, and between 1817 and 1822 he won a series of victories in Venezuela, Colombia, and Ecuador. Until 1830, these countries were united into a new nation called *Gran Colombia.* Political differences and regional interests led to the breakup of Gran Colombia. Bolívar became disillusioned and fearful of anarchy. "America is ungovernable," he said, and "those who have served the revolution have plowed the sea." To his credit, however, Bolívar rejected all attempts to crown him as king, and he remained until his death in 1830 firmly committed to the cause of independence and republican government.

Meanwhile, in southern South America, another movement had coalesced under *José de San Martín* in the Rio de la Plata. Buenos Aires had become a booming commercial center in the late 18th century, and its residents, called *porteños,* particularly resented Spanish trade restrictions. Pushing for freedom of trade, they opted for autonomy in 1810 but tried to keep the outlying areas, such as Paraguay, under their control. The myth of autonomy rather than independence was preserved for a while. By 1816, however, the independence of the United Provinces of the Rio de la Plata had been proclaimed, although the provinces were far from united. Upper Peru (Bolivia) remained under Spanish control, Paraguay declared independence

Figure 31.1 *Simon Bolívar led the struggle for political independence in northern South America. Son of a wealthy Creole family, he became an ardent proponent of independence and a firm believer in the republican form of government.*

in 1813, and the Banda Oriental (Uruguay) resisted the central authority of Buenos Aires.

In Buenos Aires, San Martín had emerged as a military commander willing to speak and act for independence. From Argentina his armies crossed the Andes to Chile to help the revolutionary forces in that colony. After winning victories there, the patriot forces looked northward. Peru, the seat of the old viceroyalty, remained under Spanish rule. Its upper class was deeply conservative and not attracted to the movements for independence. San Martín's forces entered Peru, and Creole adherence was slowly won. With victories such as the battle of Ayacucho in 1824, royalist forces were defeated. By 1825, all of Spanish South America had gained its political independence. Despite various plans to create some form of monarchy in many of the new states, all of them emerged as independent republics with representative governments. The nations of Spanish America were born of the Enlightenment and the ideas of 19th-century liberalism. The wars of independence became the foundational moments of their heroic birth.

Brazilian Independence

Although the movement for independence in Brazil was roughly contemporaneous with those in Spanish America, and many of the causes were similar, independence there was achieved by a very differ-

ent process. By the end of the 18th century, Brazil had grown in population and economic importance. The growth of European demand for colonial products, such as sugar, cotton, and cacao, contributed to that growth and to the increase in slave imports to the colony. Although Brazilian planters, merchants, and miners sometimes longed for more open trade and fewer taxes, they feared that any upsetting of the political system might lead to a social revolution or, even worse, a Haitian-style general slave uprising. Thus, incipient movements for independence in Minas Gerais in 1788 and Bahia in 1798 were unsuccessful. As one official said, "Men established in goods and property were unwilling to risk political change."

The Napoleonic invasions provoked a different outcome in Portugal than in Spain. When in 1807 French troops invaded Portugal, the whole Portuguese royal family and court fled the country and, under the protection of British ships, sailed to Brazil. A new court was established at Rio de Janeiro, which then became the capital of the Portuguese Empire. Brazil was raised to equal status with Portugal, and all the functions of royal government were set up in the colony. As a partial concession to England and to colonial interests, the ports of Brazil were opened to world commerce, thus satisfying one of the main desires of the Brazilian elites. Unlike Spanish America, where the Napoleonic invasions provoked a crisis of authority and led Spanish Americans to consider ruling in their own name, in Brazil the transfer of the court brought royal government closer and reinforced the colonial relationship.

Until 1820, the Portuguese king, *Dom João VI*, lived in Brazil and ruled his empire from there. Rio de Janeiro was transformed into a capital city with a public library, botanical gardens, and other improvements. Printing presses began to operate in the colony for the first time, schools were created, and commerce, especially with England, boomed in the newly opened ports. The arrival of many Portuguese bureaucrats and nobles with the court created jealousy and resentment, however. Still, during this period Brazil was transformed into the seat of empire, a fact not lost on its most prominent citizens.

Matters changed drastically in 1820 when, after the defeat of Napoleon in Europe and a liberal revolution in Portugal, the king was recalled and a parliament convoked. João VI, realizing that his return was inevitable, left his young son Pedro as regent, warning him that if independence had to come, he should lead the movement. Although Brazilians were allowed representation at the Portuguese parliament, it became clear that Brazil's new status was doomed and that it would be recolonized. After demands that the prince regent also return to Europe, Pedro refused, and in September 1822 he declared Brazilian independence. He became *Dom Pedro I*, constitutional emperor of Brazil. Fighting against Portuguese troops lasted a year, but Brazil avoided the long wars of Spanish America. Brazil's independence did not upset the existing social organization based on slavery, nor did it radically change the political structure. With the brief exception of Mexico, all of the former Spanish American colonies became republics, but Brazil became a monarchy under a member of the Portuguese ruling house.

NEW NATIONS CONFRONT OLD AND NEW PROBLEMS

The new nations confronted difficult problems: social inequalities, political representation, the role of the church, and regionalism. These problems led to political fragmentation. Personalist leaders, representing various interests and their own ambitions, rose to prominence.

By 1830, the former Spanish and Portuguese colonies had become independent nations. The roughly 20 million inhabitants of these nations looked hopefully to the future. Many of the leaders of independence had shared ideals: representative government, careers open to talent, freedom of commerce and trade, the right to private property, and a belief in the individual as the basis of society. There was a general belief that the new nations should be sovereign and independent states, large enough to be economically viable and integrated by a common set of laws.

On the issue of freedom of religion and the position of the church, however, there was less agreement. Roman Catholicism had been the state religion and the only one allowed by the Spanish crown. While most leaders attempted to maintain Catholicism as the official religion of the new states, some tried to end the exclusion of other faiths. The defense of the church became a rallying cry for the conservative forces.

The ideals of the early leaders of independence often were egalitarian. Bolívar had received aid from Haiti and had promised in return to abolish slavery in the areas he liberated. By 1854, slavery had been abolished everywhere except Spain's remaining colonies, Cuba and Puerto Rico, as well as in Brazil; all were places where the economy was profoundly based on it. Early promises to end Indian tribute and taxes on people of mixed origin came much slower because the new nations still needed the revenue such policies produced. Egalitarian sentiments often were tempered by fears that the mass of the population was unprepared for self-rule and democracy. Early constitutions attempted to balance order and popular representation by imposing property or literacy restrictions on voters. Invariably, voting rights were reserved for men. Women were still disenfranchised and usually were not allowed to hold public office. The Creole elite's lack of trust of the popular classes was based on the fact that in many places the masses had not demonstrated a clear preference for the new regimes and had sometimes fought in royalist armies mobilized by traditional loyalties and regional interests. Although some mestizos had risen to leadership roles in the wars of independence, the old color distinctions did not disappear easily. In Mexico, Guatemala, and the Andean nations, the large Indian population remained mostly outside of national political life. The mass of the Latin American population—Indians and people of mixed origins—waited to see what was to come, and they were suspicious of the new political elite, who were often drawn from

export raw materials + consume

the old colonial aristocracy but were also joined by a new commercial and urban bourgeoisie.

Political Fragmentation

The new nations can be grouped into regional blocks. Some of the early leaders for independence had dreamed of creating a unified nation in some form, but regional rivalries, economic competition, and political divisions soon made that hope impossible. Mexico emerged as a short-lived monarchy until a republic was proclaimed in 1823, but its government remained unstable until the 1860s because of military coups, financial failures, foreign intervention, and political turmoil. Central America broke away from the Mexican monarchy and formed a union, but regional antagonisms and resentment of Guatemala, the largest nation in the region, eventually led to dissolution of the union in 1838. Spain's Caribbean colonies, Cuba and Puerto Rico, suppressed early movements for independence and remained outwardly loyal. The Dominican Republic was occupied by its neighbor Haiti, and after resisting its neighbor as well as France and Spain, it finally gained independence in 1844. The Dominican example and the fear of a Haitian-style slave revolt tended to keep the Creole leaders of Cuba and Puerto Rico quiet.

In South America, the old colonial viceroyalty of New Granada became the basis for Gran Colombia, the large new state created by Bolívar that included modern Ecuador, Colombia, Panama, and Venezuela. The union, made possible to some extent by Bolívar's personal reputation and leadership, disintegrated as his own standing declined, and it ended in 1830, the year of his death. In the south, the viceroyalty of the Rio de la Plata served as the basis for a state that the peoples of Argentina hoped to lead. Other parts of the region resisted. Paraguay declared and maintained its autonomy under *Dr. José Rodríguez de Francia,* who ruled his isolated and landlocked country as a dictator until 1840. Modern Uruguay was formed by a revolution for independence against the dominant power of its large neighbors, Argentina and Brazil. It became an independent buffer between those two nations in 1828. The Andean nations of Peru and Bolivia, with their large Indian populations and conservative colonial aristocracies, flirted with union from 1829 to 1839 under the mestizo general *Andrés Santa Cruz,* but once again regional rivalries and the fears of their neighbors undermined the effort. Finally, Chile, somewhat isolated and blessed by the opening of trade in the Pacific, followed its own political course in a fairly stable fashion.

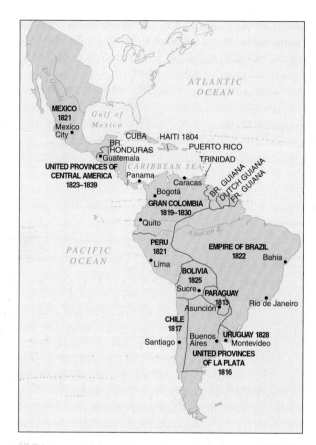

Map 31.1 *Independent States of Latin America*

Most attempts at consolidation and union failed. Enormous geographic barriers and great distances separated nations and even regions within nations. Roads were poor and transportation rudimentary. Geography, regional interests, and political divisions were too strong to overcome. The mass of the population remained outside the political process. The problems of national integration were daunting. What is striking is not that Spanish America became 18 separate nations but that it did not separate into even more.

Caudillos, Politics, and the Church

The problems confronting the new nations were many. More than a decade of warfare in places such as Venezuela, Colombia, and Mexico had disrupted the economies and devastated wide areas. The mobilization of large armies whose loyalty to regional commanders was often based on their personal qualities, rather than their rank or politics, led to the rise of *caudillos,* independent leaders who dominated local areas by force and sometimes seized the national government itself. In times of intense division between civilian politicians, a powerful regional army commander became the arbiter of power, and thus the army sometimes made and unmade governments. Keeping the army in the barracks became a preoccupation of governments, and the amount of money spent on the military far exceeded the needs. The military had become important in the 18th century as Spain tried to shore up the defense of its empire, but it became a preserver of order.

Military commanders and regional or national caudillos usually were interested in power for their own sake, but they could represent or mobilize different groups in society. Many often defended the interests of regional elites, usually land owners, but others were populists who mobilized and claimed to speak for Indians, peasants, and the poor and sometimes received their unquestioning support. A few, such as the conservative Rafael Carrera, who ruled Guatemala from 1839 to 1865, sincerely took the interest of the Indian majority to heart, but other personalist leaders disregarded the normal workings of an open political system and the rule of law.

Other common issues confronted many of the new nations. Most political leaders were agreed on the republic as the basic form of government, but could not agree on what kind of republic. A struggle often developed between *centralists,* who wanted to create strong, centralized national governments with broad powers, and *federalists,* who wanted tax and commercial policies to be set by regional governments. Other tensions developed between liberals and conservatives. Liberals stressed the rights of the individual and attacked the corporate (membership in a group or organization) structure of colonial society. They dreamed of a secular society and looked to the United States and France as models. Often they wanted a decentralized, or federalist, form of government. Conservatives usually believed in a strong centralized state, and they often wanted to maintain aspects of colonial society. They believed that a structure in which corporate groups (such as the Indians), artisan guilds, or institutions (such as the church) provided the most equitable basis of social action should be recognized in law. To the conservatives, society was not based on open competition and individualism but was organic: Each group was linked to the other like parts of a body whose health depended on the proper functioning of each part. Not all conservatives resisted change, and some—such as Mexican intellectual and politi-

cian Lucas Alamán—were among the most enlightened leaders in terms of economic and commercial reforms, but as a group the conservatives were skeptical of secularism and individualism and strove to keep the Catholic Iberian heritage alive.

The role of the church became a crucial issue in politics. It divided proclerical conservatives from the more secular liberals. In Mexico, for example, the church had played a major role in education, the economy, and politics. Few questioned its dogma, but liberals tried to limit its role in civil life. The church fought back with the aid of its proclerical supporters and with the power of the papacy, which until the 1840s refused to fill vacant positions in the hierarchy or to cooperate with the new governments.

Political parties, often calling themselves Liberal or Conservative, sprang up throughout Latin America. They struggled for power and tried to impose their vision of the future on society. However, their leaders usually were drawn from the same social class of land owners and urban bourgeoisie, with little to differentiate them except their position in the church or on the question of federalism versus centralization. The general population might be mobilized by the force and personality of a particular leader such as *Juan Manuel de Rosas* in Argentina or *Antonio López de Santa Anna* in Mexico, but political ideology rarely was an issue for most of the population.

The result was political turmoil and insecurity in much of Latin America in the first 50 years after independence. Presidents came and went quickly. Written constitutions, which both liberals and conservatives thought were a positive thing, were often short-lived and were overturned with a change in government because the margin for interpretation of the constitution was slight. Great efforts were made to make constitutions precise, specific, and definitive, but this resulted in an attempt to change them each time there was a change in government. Some nations avoided the worst aspects of instability. After enacting a constitution in 1833 that gave the president broad powers, Chile established a functioning political system that allowed compromise. Brazil, with its monarchical rule, despite a period of turmoil from 1832 to 1850, was able to maintain a political system of compromise, although it was dominated by the Conservatives, who were favored by the emperor. Its 1824 constitution remained in force until 1889.

It is fair to say that in much of Latin America the basic questions of government and society

DOCUMENT

Confronting the Hispanic Heritage: From Independence to Consolidation

Simon Bolívar (1783–1830), "The Liberator," was a man of determination and perception. His campaigns for independence were defeated on several occasions, yet he did not despair. In 1815, while in exile on the island of Jamaica, he penned a letter to a newspaper that gave his evaluation of Latin America's situation and his vision for the future for its various parts. He advocated a republican form of government and rejected monarchy, but he warned against federalism and against popular democracies that might lead to dictatorships: "As long as our countrymen do not acquire the abilities and political virtues that distinguish our brothers to the north, wholly popular systems, far from working to our advantage, will, I greatly fear, bring about our downfall." Spain had left America unprepared, and in this letter Bolívar summarized many of the complaints of Latin Americans against Spanish rule and underlined the difficulty of the tasks of liberation—political, social, and economic. The famous "Letter of Jamaica" is one of the most candid writings by a leader of Latin American independence. The following excerpts suggest its tone and content.

"Bolívar's Jamaica Letter" (1815)

We are young people. We inhabit a world apart, separated by broad seas. We are young in the ways of almost all the arts and sciences, although, in a certain manner, we are old in the ways of civilized society. I look upon the present state of America as similar to that of Rome after its fall. Each part of Rome adopted a political system conforming to its interest and situation or was led by the individual ambitions of certain chiefs, dynasties, or associations. But this important difference exists: those dispersed parts later reestablished their ancient nations, subject to the changes imposed by circumstances or extent. But we scarcely retain a vestige of what once was; we are, moreover, neither Indian nor European, but a species midway between the legitimate proprietors of this country and the Spanish usurpers. In short, although Americans by birth we derive our rights from Europe, and we have to assert these rights against the rights of the natives, and at the same time we must defend ourselves against the invaders. This places us in a most extraordinary and involved situation....

The role of the inhabitants of the American hemisphere has for centuries been purely passive. Politically they were nonexistent. We are still in a position lower than slavery, and therefore it is more difficult for us to rise to the enjoyment of freedom.... States are slaves because of

either the nature or the misuse of their constitutions; a people is therefore enslaved when the government, by its nature or its vices infringes on and usurps the rights of the citizen or subject. Applying these principles, we find that America was denied not only its freedom but even an active and effective tyranny....

We have been harassed by a conduct which has not only deprived us of our rights but has kept us in a sort of permanent infancy with regard to public affairs. If we could have at least managed our domestic affairs and our internal administration, we could have acquainted ourselves with the processes and mechanics of public affairs. We should also have enjoyed a personal consideration, thereby commanding a certain unconscious respect from the people, which is so necessary to preserve amidst revolutions. That is why I say we have even been deprived of an active tyranny, since we have not been permitted to exercise its functions.

Americans today, and perhaps to a greater extent than ever before, who live within the Spanish system occupy a position in society no better than that of serfs destined to labor, or at best they have no more status than that of mere consumers. Yet even this status is surrounded with galling restrictions, such as being forbidden to grow European crops, or to store products which are royal monopolies, or to establish factories of a type the Peninsula (Spain) itself does not possess. To this add the privileges, even in articles of prime necessity, and the barriers between the American provinces, designed to prevent all exchange of trade, traffic, and understanding. In short, do you wish to know what our future held?—simply the cultivation of the fields of indigo, grain, coffee, sugar cane, cacao, and cotton; cattle raising on the broad plains, hunting wild game in the jungles; digging in the earth to mine its gold—but even these limitations could never satisfy the greed of Spain. So negative was our existence that I can find nothing comparable in any other civilized society....

By mid-century, Latin American political leaders were advocating "progress" and attempting to bring Latin America closer to the norms of life set by Europe. For liberals such as Argentine soldier, statesman, and author *Domingo F. Sarmiento* (1811–1888), his nation's task was to overcome the "barbarism" of rural life and implant the "civilization" of the Europeanized cities. Sarmiento saw in the bands of mounted rural workers, or *gauchos,* and their caudillo leaders an anachronistic way of life that held the nation back. His comparison of the gauchos to the Berbers of north Africa demonstrates the ancient hostility of "civilized" urban-dwellers to the nomadic way of life. In a way, Sarmiento saw the dictatorship of Juan Manuel de Rosas as a result of the persistence of the gauchos and the manipulation of the lower classes—a sort of living example of what Bolívar had warned against. The following excerpt from Sarmiento's classic *Life in the Argentine Republic in the Days of the Tyrants or Civilization and Barbarism* (1868) demonstrates his admiration for European culture, including that of Spain, and his desire to model his nation on it. That such a program might involve economic and cultural dependency did not concern Sarmiento and others like him.

The Search for Progress

Before 1810 two distinct, rival, and incompatible forms of society, two differing kinds of civilization existed in the Argentine Republic: one being Spanish, European, and cultivated, the other barbarous, American, and almost wholly of native growth. The revolution which occurred in the cities acted only as the cause, the impulse, which set these two distinct forms of national existence face to face, and gave occasion for a contest between them, to be ended, after lasting many years, by the absorption of one into the other.

I have pointed out the normal form of association, or want of association, of the country people, a form worse a thousand times, than that of a nomad tribe. I have described the artificial associations formed in idleness, and the sources of fame among the gauchos—bravery, daring, violence and opposition to regular law, to the civil law, that is, of the city. These phenomena of social organization existed in 1810, and still exist, modified in many points, slowly changing in others, and yet untouched in several more. These foci about which were gathered the brave, ignorant, free, and unemployed peasantry, were found by thousands through the country. The revolution of 1810 carried everywhere commotion and the sound of arms. Public life, previously wanting in this Arabo-Roman society, made its appearance in all the taverns, and the revolutionary movement finally brought about provincial, warlike associations, called montoneras [mounted gaucho guerrilla bands] legitimate offspring of the tavern and the field, hostile to the city and to the army of revolutionary patriots. As events succeed each other, we shall see the provincial montoneras headed by their chiefs; the final triumph, in Facundo Quiroga [a caudillo leader], of the country over the cities throughout the land; and by their subjugation in spirit, government, and civilization, the final formation of the central consolidated despotic government of the landed proprietor, Don Juan Manuel de Rosas, who applied the knife of the gaucho to the culture of Buenos Aires, and destroyed the work of centuries—of civilization, law, and liberty....

They [revolutions for independence] were the same throughout America, and sprang from the same source, namely, the progress of European ideas. South America pursued that course because all other nations were pursuing it. Books, events, and the impulses given by these, induced South America to take part in the movement imparted to France by North American demands for liberty, and to Spain by her own and French writers. But what my object requires me to notice is that the revolution—except in its external symbolic independence of the king—was interesting and intelligible only to the Argentine cities, but foreign and unmeaning to the rural districts. Books, ideas, municipal spirit, courts, laws, statues, education, all points of contact and union existing between us and the people of Europe, were to be found in the cities, where there was a basis of organization, incomplete and comparatively evil, perhaps, for the very reason it was incomplete, and had not attained the elevation which it felt itself capable of reaching, but it entered into the revolution with enthusiasm. Outside the cities, the revolution was a problematical affair, and [in] so far [as] shaking off the king's authority was shaking off judicial authority, it was acceptable. The pastoral districts could only regard the question from this point of view. Liberty, responsibility of power, and all the questions which the revolution was to solve, were foreign to their mode of life and to their needs. But they derived this advantage from the revolution, that it tended to confer an object and an occupation upon the excess of vital force, the presence of which among them has been pointed out, and was to add a broader base of union than that to which throughout the country districts the men daily resorted.

The Argentine Revolutionary War was twofold: first, a civilized warfare of the cities against Spain; second, a war against the cities on the part of the country chieftains with the view of shaking off all political subjugation and satisfying their hatred of civilization. The cities overcame the Spaniards, and were in their turn overcome by the country districts. This is the explanation of the Argentine Revolution, the first shot of which fired in 1810, and the last is still to be heard.

Questions: To what extent did the leaders of independence see their problems as a result of their Hispanic heritage? What would have been the reaction of the mass of the population to Sarmiento's idea of progress? Were the leaders naive about Latin America's possibilities for political democracy?

remained unresolved after independence. Some observers attributed these problems to personalism, a lack of civic responsibility, and other defects in the "Latin" character. Nevertheless, the parallel experience of later emerging nations in the 20th century suggests that these problems were typical of former colonial dependencies searching for order and economic security in a world in which their options were constrained by their own potential and by external conditions.

LATIN AMERICAN ECONOMIES AND WORLD MARKETS, 1820–1870

▓▓ *In the mid-19th century, Latin American economies stagnated in the aftermath of the wars of independence. Dependence on exports created neocolonial ties. Toward mid-century, a new prosperity began as some nations found new markets for their exports. The revenues thus earned allowed liberal governments to advocate a variety of social and political changes. The examples of Mexico, Argentina, and Brazil illustrate the general pattern from political instability or economic stagnation to the emergence of stable liberal regimes by the end of the century.*

The former colonies of Spain and Portugal now entered the world of diplomatic relations and international commerce. The new nations sought diplomatic recognition and security. In the 1820s, while Europe was undergoing the post-Napoleonic conservative reaction and monarchies were being restored, various plans to help Spain recolonize Latin America were put forward. Great Britain generally opposed those ideas, and because Great Britain was the dominant power at sea, its recognition of Latin American sovereignty was crucial. Moreover, the newly independent United States also felt an affinity and sympathy for the new nations to the south. The *Monroe Doctrine* of 1823 stated clearly that any attempt by a European power to colonize in the Americas would be considered an unfriendly act by the United States. The United States at the time probably could have done little to prevent such actions, but Britain could, and its support of Latin American independence provided needed protection.

There was a price for this support. During the turmoil of the 1820s, British foreign minister Lord Canning had once said, "Spanish America is free and if we do not mismanage our affairs sadly, she is English." He was referring to the broad economic and commercial advantages that the new nations offered. British commerce had penetrated the area in the 18th century, when various concessions for trade had been won from the Spanish government, and Britain had profited from illegal trade as well. Now it could afford to offer its diplomatic recognition in exchange for the freedom to trade with the new nations. Although little capital had been invested directly in Latin America before 1850, Latin American governments now turned to foreign governments and banks for loans. Meanwhile, Britain became a major consumer of Latin American products. In return Britain sold about 5 million pounds worth of manufactured goods to the new nations each year, about half of which went to Brazil, where British merchants were especially strong. Although some historians argue that this was a small portion of Britain's overseas trade, it was crucial for Latin America. In some ways, Britain replaced Spain as a dominant economic force over the area in a sort of neocolonial commercial system. Although other nations, notably France and the United States, also traded with Latin America, Britain remained predominant before 1860.

Open ports and the influx of foreign goods, often of better quality and cheaper than local products, benefited the port cities that controlled customhouses and the large land owners whose hides, sugar, and other products were exported. But these policies tended to damage local industries or regions that had specialized in producing for internal markets. Little capital was available for investment in local industries, and often the governments controlled by liberal free-traders or conservative land owners would not or could not impose tariffs on imports needed to protect or stimulate local industry. Latin America became increasingly dependent on foreign markets and foreign imports and thereby reinforced the old colonial economic heritage in which land was the basis of wealth and prestige.

Mid-Century Stagnation

From about 1820 to 1850, the economy of Latin America was stagnant. Its mining sector was slow to recover after the wars of independence, its transportation network and port facilities were still underdeveloped, and it lacked capital for investment or found that so much capital was tied up in land that it was unavailable for investment in industry. Only Cuba, with its booming sugar economy, expanded, but Cuba was still a colony of Spain. After 1850, however, this situation began to change as the expansion of the European economy created new demands for Latin American products. Coffee in Brazil, hides and beef in Argentina, and minerals and grains in Chile provided the basis of growth and allowed some Latin American governments to address social issues.

For example, Peru exploited enormous *guano* (bird droppings) deposits on islands off its coast. Between 1850 and 1880, exports of this fertilizer earned Peru more than 10 million pounds, and this income allowed the government to end Indian tribute and to abolish slavery by compensating the owners. Latin American cities began to grow and provide good internal markets, and the introduction of steamships and railroads began to overcome the old problems of transportation. By the 1840s, steamship lines improved communication within countries and opened up new possibilities for international commerce, and by the 1860s, railroads like the one in Figure 31.2 were being built, usually to link export-producing regions to the ports. Landed wealth and exports continued to characterize the economies of the region, as they had in the colonial era. As the levels of exports and the governments' dependence on them increased, Latin America's vulnerability to the vagaries of the world economy increased as well.

Without detailing all the complex changes within the Latin American nations during the 19th century, we can discern a few general patterns. After the turmoil of independence, liberal reformers tried to institute a series of programs in the 1820s and 1830s intended to break the patterns of the colonial heritage and to follow the main social and economic trends of western Europe. These ideas often were imposed on societies and economies unprepared for drastic change, especially because the strength of opposing institutions, such as the church and the army, remained intact. By the 1840s, conservatives had returned to power in many places to slow or stop the reform measures. Some of them tried to speak for the lower classes or the Indians, who wanted to see the paternal aspects of the old colonial state reimposed to protect them from the reforms of the liberals. In some ways, an alliance between the land owners and the peasantry emerged in opposition to the changes suggested by the middle-class, urban modernizers.

Economic Resurgence and Liberal Politics

By the last quarter of the century, as the world economy entered a phase of rapid expansion, there was a

Figure 31.2 *The drive for progress made Latin American nations anxious to accept foreign investment. Railroads were important for economic growth in that they often linked key exports to the ports and were designed principally to serve the needs of foreign capital. However, railroad workers often proved to be the most radical segment of the Latin American work force.*

shift in attitude and possibilities in Latin America. Liberals returned to power in many places in Latin America and initiated a series of changes that began to transform their nations. The ideological basis of the new liberal surge was also changing. Based on the ideas of *positivism* of the French philosopher *Auguste Comte,* who stressed observation and a scientific approach to the problems of society, Latin American politicians and intellectuals found a guiding set of principles and a justification of their quest for political stability and economic growth.

This shift was caused in large part by the general economic expansion of the second industrial revolution and the age of imperialism. The application of science to industry created new demands for Latin American products, such as copper and rubber, to accompany the increasing demand for its consumer products such as wheat, sugar, and coffee. The population of Latin America doubled to more than 43 million inhabitants in the 60 years between 1820 and 1880. After 1850, economies grew rapidly; the timing varied greatly, but the expansion of exports in places such as Colombia, Argentina, and Brazil stimulated prosperity for some and a general belief in the advantages of the liberal programs. The desire to participate in the capitalist expansion of the Western economy dominated the thinking of Latin American leaders. Foreign entrepreneurs and bankers joined hands with philosophical liberals, land owners, and urban merchants in Latin America to back the liberal programs, which now became possible because of the increased revenues generated by exports.

The leaders of the post-1860 governments were a new generation of politicians who had matured during the chaotic years of postindependence politics. Their inspiration came from England, France, and the United States. They were firm believers in progress, education, and free competition within a secular society, but they were sometimes distrustful of the mass of their own people, who seemed to represent an ancient "barbarism" in contrast to the "civilization" of progress. That distrust and their sometimes insensitive application of foreign models to a very different reality in their own countries—what one Brazilian author has called "ideas out of place"—prevented many from achieving the progress they so ardently desired.

Economic growth and progress were costly. Responding to international demand, land owners increased their holdings, often aided by the governments they controlled or influenced. Peasant lands were expropriated in Chile, Peru, and Bolivia; small farmers were displaced in Brazil and Costa Rica; and church lands were seized in Mexico. Labor was needed. Immigrants from Europe flooded into Argentina and Brazil, and in other countries new forms of tenancy, peonage, and disguised servitude developed.

Mexico: Instability and Foreign Intervention

After the short monarchical experiment, a Mexican republic was established. Its constitution of 1824, based on the examples of France, the United States, and Spain, was a federalist document that guaranteed basic civil rights. Nevertheless, this constitution did not address the nation's continuing social problems and needs: the maldistribution of land, the status of the Indians, the problems of education, and the situation of vast numbers of poor people among the approximately 7 million people in Mexico, the most populous of the new nations. Politics soon became a complicated struggle between the conservative centralists and the liberal federalists and was made even more complicated by jockeying for advantage by commercial agents of Great Britain and the United States. For a short period from 1832 to 1835, the liberals, led by Valentín Gómez Farias, were in control and tried to institute a series of sweeping social and economic reforms, but their attack on the church led to violent reaction and the assumption of power by General Antonio López de Santa Anna.

The mercurial Santa Anna remained until his death the maker of Mexican politics. He was a typical caudillo, a personalist, autocratic leader. But Mexico's instability resulted not only from his personality. Santa Anna was merely the symptom of deeper problems.

Mexico's instability and financial difficulties made it a target for foreign intervention. A Spanish invasion was repulsed in 1829, and a French expedition landed to collect unpaid debts in 1838. More seriously, Texas, the vast area of Mexico's northern frontier, was increasingly occupied by Anglo-American settlers, who brought their language, customs, and religion despite restrictions on the latter. Although the Texans at first sought more autonomy as federalists within the Mexican nation, as had been done in Yucatan and other Mexican provinces, ethnic and religious differences as well as Santa Anna's attempts to suppress the Texans in 1836 led to widespread fighting and the declaration of Texan independence. Santa

Anna, captured for a while by the Texans, returned to dominate Mexican politics, but the question of Texas festered and became acute when in 1845 the United States, with its eye on California and moved by *manifest destiny*—a belief that it was destined to rule the continent from coast to coast—voted to annex Texas.

The result was war. A border dispute and the breakdown of negotiations over California led to hostilities in 1846. Santa Anna, who had been in exile, returned to lead the Mexican forces, but United States armies seized California, penetrated northern Mexico, and eventually occupied the Mexican capital. Mexico was forced to sign the disadvantageous *Treaty of Guadalupe-Hidalgo* (1848), in which the United States acquired about one-half of Mexico's national territory but less than 5 percent of its population. The *Mexican–American War* and the treaty left a bitter legacy of distrust of the northern neighbor, not only in Mexico but throughout the region. For Mexico there was also a serious loss of economic potential, but the heroic battle against the better-equipped Americans produced a sense of nationalism and a desire to confront the nation's serious internal problems, which also bore some responsibility for the war and the defeat.

Politics could not return to the prewar situation. Santa Anna did return to office for a while, more mercurial and despotic than ever, but now he was opposed by a new generation of liberals: intellectuals, lawyers, and some rural leaders, many of them from middle-class backgrounds, some of them mestizos and even a few Indians. Perhaps the most prominent of them was *Benito Juárez* (1806–1872), a humble Indian who had received a legal education and had eventually become the governor of his state. He shared the liberal vision of a secular society based on the rule of law in which the old privileges of the church and the army would be eliminated as a way of promoting economic change and growth. The liberal revolt, called *La Reforma*, began in 1854 and triumphed within a year. In a series of laws integrated into a new constitution in 1857, the liberals set the basis for their vision of society. Military and clerical privileges were curtailed, and church property was placed on sale. Indian communal lands also were restricted, and the government forced the sale of these lands to individuals—to Indians, it was hoped. The goal of these programs was to create a nation of small independent farmers. However, the lands often were bought up by speculators or already wealthy hacendados (land owners), and the result was that the peasants and Indians lost what land they had. By 1910,

about half of Mexico's rural population was landless. Good intentions had brought disastrous results.

The liberal program produced the expected conservative reaction. The church threatened to excommunicate those who upheld the new constitution. Civil war erupted, and in reaction, Juárez, now president, pushed forward even more radical measures. Losing ground in the war, the conservatives turned to Europe and convinced Napoleon III of France to intervene. Attracted by possible economic advantage, dreams of empire, and a desire to please Catholics in France, Napoleon III justified French intervention by claims of a shared "Latin" culture (this was the origin of the term *Latin America*). Under cover of a joint expedition, French forces landed in 1862 and soon took the capital. At the urging of the French, *Maximilian von Habsburg*, an Austrian archduke, was convinced to take the throne of Mexico. Well-intentioned but ineffective, Emperor Maximilian tried to get the support of Juárez and the liberals and even kept many of the laws of the Reforma in place, to the dismay of his conservative supporters. But Juárez absolutely rejected the idea of a foreign prince ruling Mexico. French bayonets and the United States' preoccupation with its own Civil War allowed Emperor Maximilian and his Empress Carlota to rule. When French troops were withdrawn, the regime crumbled. Maximilian and his loyal generals were captured and executed in 1867. His death shocked Europeans. The famous painter Eduard Manet commemorated the event (see Figure 31.3). Juárez' message to Europe was "hands off Mexico."

Juárez returned to office, but his administration was increasingly autocratic—a reality that he felt was unavoidable after so long a period of instability. By his death in 1872, the force of his personality, his concern for the poor, and his nationalist position against foreign intervention had identified liberalism with nationalism in Mexico and made Juárez a symbol of the nation. By 1880, Mexico was poised on the edge of a period of strong central government and relative political stability, which under the virtual dictator *Porfirio Díaz* led to rapid economic growth, penetration of the economy by foreign capital, the expansion of the large landed estates, political repression, and a revolution.

Argentina: The Port and the Nation

Whereas Mexico and its silver had been the core of Spain's empire in America, the rolling plains, or pam-

Figure 31.3 *Emperor Maximilian was finally captured after his attempt, with French help, to reestablish a monarchy in Mexico. Well-meaning, he eventually lost the support of the conservatives. Juárez refused to spare his life, as a warning to other ambitious nations that Mexico would remain independent.*

pas, of the Rio de la Plata in southern South America had been a colonial backwater until the 18th century, when direct trade had begun to stimulate its economy. The Rio de la Plata was dominated by the port of Buenos Aires and its merchants, but the other areas of the region had their own interests and resented the power and growth of the port city and its surrounding countryside. The United Provinces of the Rio de la Plata, which declared their independence in 1816, soon split apart, and local caudillos, able to call on the support of gauchos, dominated each region. In Buenos Aires, the liberals gained control in the 1820s, and instituted a series of broad reforms in education, finance, agriculture, and immigration. These included a program of public land sales, which stimulated the growth of cattle ranches and the power of the rancher class.

In many ways the secular and progressive program of the Argentine liberals paralleled the program of Gómez Farías in Mexico and produced a similar negative reaction from conservatives and the church, especially when church lands were confiscated and freedom of religion was legislated. But the liberals' main sin was centralism, a desire to create a strong national government. Centralists (called Unitarians in the Argentine context) provoked the reaction of the federalists, who by 1831 had taken power under Juan Manuel de Rosas, who commanded the loyalty of the gaucho employees of the ranchers.

Under Rosas, the federalist program of a weak central government and local autonomy was instituted, but Rosas's federalism favored the ranchers of the Buenos Aires province and the merchants of the great port. He campaigned against the Indians to the south to open new lands to the cattle ranchers. Exports of hides and salted meat increased, but the revenues collected at the port were not shared with the other provinces. Although popular with the gauchos and the urban poor and remembered today as a nationalist who resisted British and French economic pressure, Rosas proved to be a despotic leader, crushing his opponents and forcing people to display his slogan "Death to the savage, filthy Unitarians." His brand of populist, authoritarian, personalist politics drove liberal opponents into exile, where they plotted his overthrow. Meanwhile, his policies continued to favor the ranching and meat-exporting interests of Buenos Aires. Eventually, the liberal exiles joined forces with the caudillos who, while federalists, resented Rosas's brand of federalism that had so favored the Buenos Aires province. In 1852, this coalition defeated Rosas and drove him from power.

There followed a confused decade of rival governments because the questions of federalism and the role of Buenos Aires within the nation remained unresolved. A new constitution was issued in 1853 under the influence of Juan Bautista Alberdi, an able and progressive journalist who was also a strong believer in the need to encourage immigration. This constitution incorporated the programs of the federalists but guaranteed national unity through the power of the presidency over the provincial governors. By 1862, after considerable fighting, a compromise was worked out and the new, unified nation, now called the *Argentine Republic,* entered into a period of prosperity and growth under a series of liberal presidents whose programs paralleled the Reforma in Mexico. The age of the liberals was now in full swing.

Between 1862 and 1890, able and intelligent presidents, such as Bartolomé Mitre (1821–1876) and Domingo F. Sarmiento (1811–1888), initiated a wide series of political reforms and economic measures designed to bring progress to Argentina. Sarmiento was an archetype of the liberal reformers of the mid-century. A great admirer of England and the United States, a firm believer in the value of education, and an ardent supporter of progress, Sarmiento had been a constant opponent of Rosas and had been driven into exile. During that time, he wrote *Facundo,* a critique of the caudillo politics of the region, in which the "barbarism" of the gauchos and their leaders was contrasted to the "civilization" of the liberal reformers. (See the Document in this chapter.)

Now in power, Sarmiento and the other liberal leaders were able to put their programs into practice. They were aided by several factors. Political stability made investment more attractive to foreign banks and merchants. The expansion of the Argentine economy, especially exports of beef, hides, and wool, created the basis for prosperity. Foreign trade in 1890 was five times as great as it had been in 1860. The population tripled to more than 3 million as the agricultural expansion, high wages, and opportunities for mobility attracted large numbers of European immigrants. Buenos Aires became a great, sprawling metropolis (Figure 31.4). With increased revenues, the government could initiate reforms in education, transportation, and other areas, often turning to foreign models and foreign investors. There was also an increased feeling of national unity. A long and bloody war waged by Argentina, Brazil, and Uruguay against their neighbor Paraguay from 1865 to 1870 created a sense of unity and national pride.

That sense was also heightened by the final defeat of the Indians south of Buenos Aires by 1880 as more land was opened to ranching and agriculture. At about the same time as in the United States, the railroad, the telegraph, and the repeating rifle brought an end to the Indians' resistance and opened their lands to settlement. The Indians, who were pushed far to the south, and the gauchos, whose way of life was displaced by the tide of immigrants, received little sympathy from the liberal government. By 1890, Argentina seemed to represent the achievement of a liberal program for Latin America.

The Brazilian Empire

It was sometimes said that despite its monarchical form, Brazil was the only functioning republic in South America in the 19th century. At first glance it seemed that Brazil avoided much of the political instability and turmoil found elsewhere in the continent and that through the mediation of the emperor a political compromise was worked out. However, problems and patterns similar to those in Spanish America lay beneath that facade. The transition to nationhood was smooth, and thus the basic foundations of Brazilian society—slavery, large landholdings, and an export economy—remained securely in place, reinforced by a new Brazilian nobility created for the new empire.

Brazilian independence had been declared in 1822, and by 1824 a liberal constitution had been

Figure 31.4 *The tremendous boom in the Argentine economy was reflected in the growth of Buenos Aires, the so-called Paris of the Americas, as a cosmopolitan urban center.*

issued by Dom Pedro I, the young Brazilian monarch, although not without resistance from those who wanted a republic or at least a very weak constitutional monarch. But Dom Pedro I was an autocrat. In 1831, he was forced to abdicate in favor of his young son, Pedro (later to become Dom Pedro II), but the boy was too young to rule, and a series of regents directed the country in his name. What followed was an experiment in republican government, although the facade of monarchy was maintained.

The next decade was as tumultuous as any in Spanish America. The conflict between liberalism and conservatism was complicated by the existence of monarchist and antimonarchist factions in Brazil. The centralism of the government in Rio de Janeiro was opposed by the provinces, and a series of regional revolts erupted, some of which took on aspects of social wars as people of all classes were mobilized in the fighting. The army suppressed these movements. By 1840, however, the politicians were willing to see the young Dom Pedro II begin to rule in his own name.

Meanwhile, Brazil had been undergoing an economic transformation brought about by a new export crop: coffee. Coffee provided a new basis for agricultural expansion in southern Brazil. In the provinces of Rio de Janeiro and then São Paulo, coffee estates, or *fazendas,* began to spread toward the interior as new lands were opened. By 1840, coffee made up more than 40 percent of Brazil's exports, and by 1880, that figure reached 60 percent.

Along with the expansion of coffee growing came an intensification of slavery, Brazil's primary form of labor. For a variety of humanitarian and economic reasons, Great Britain pressured Brazil to end the slave trade from Africa during the 19th century, but the slave trade continued on an enormous scale up to 1850. More than 1.4 million Africans were imported to Brazil in the last 50 years of the trade, and even after the trans-Atlantic slave trade ended, slavery continued. At mid-century, about one-fourth of Brazil's population were still enslaved. Although some reformers were in favor of ending slavery, a real abolitionist movement did not develop in Brazil until after 1870. Brazil did not finally abolish slavery until 1888.

As in the rest of Latin America, the years after 1850 saw considerable growth and prosperity in Brazil. Dom Pedro II proved to be an enlightened man of middle-class habits who was anxious to reign over a tranquil and progressive nation, even if that tranquility was based on slave labor. The trappings of a monarchy, a court, and noble titles kept the elite attached to the regime. Meanwhile, railroads, steamships, and the telegraph began to change communication and transportation. Foreign companies invested in these projects as well as in banking and other activities. In growing cities such as Rio de Janeiro and São Paulo, merchants, lawyers, a middle class, and an urban working class began to exert pressure on the government. Less wedded to landholding and slavery, these new groups were a catalyst for change, even though the right to vote was still very limited. Moreover, the nature of the labor force was changing.

After 1850, a tide of immigrants, mostly from Italy and Portugal, began to reach Brazil's shores, increasingly attracted by government immigration schemes. Between 1850 and 1875, more than 300,000 immigrants arrived in Brazil; more than two-thirds of them went to work in the coffee trees of southern Brazil. Their presence lessened the dependence on slavery, and by 1870 the abolitionist movement was gaining strength. A series of laws freeing children and the aged, the sympathy of Dom Pedro II himself, the agitation by abolitionists (both black and white), and the efforts of the slaves (who began to resist and run away in large numbers) brought in 1888 an end to slavery in Brazil, the last nation in the Western Hemisphere to abolish it.

Support for the monarchy began to wither. The long war of the Triple Alliance against Paraguay (1865–1870) had become unpopular, and the military began to take an active role in politics. Squabbles with the church undercut support from the clergy. The planters now turned increasingly to immigrants for their laborers, and some began to modernize their operations. The ideas of positivism, a modernizing philosophy that attempted to bring about material progress by applying scientific principles to government and society, attracted many intellectuals and key members of the army. Politically, a Republican party formed in 1871 began to gather support in urban areas from a wide spectrum of the population. The Brazilian monarchy, long a defender of the planter class and its interests, could not survive the abolition of slavery. In 1889, a nearly bloodless military coup deposed the emperor and established a republic under military men strongly influenced by positivist intellectuals and Republican politicians.

But such "progress" came at certain costs in many nations in Latin America. In the harsh backlands of northeastern Brazil, for example, the change to a republic, economic hardship, and the secularization of society provoked peasant unrest. Antonio Conselheiro, a religious mystic, began to gather followers in the 1890s, especially among the dispossessed peasantry. Eventually, their community, Canudos, contained thousands. The government feared these "fanatics" and sent four military expeditions against Canudos, Conselheiro's "New Jerusalem." The fighting was bloody, and casualties were in the thousands. Conselheiro and his followers put up a determined guerilla defense of their town and their view of the world. The tragedy of Canudos' destruction moved journalist Euclides da Cunha to write *Rebellion in the Backlands (Os sertões,* 1902), an account of the events. Like Sarmiento, he saw them as a struggle between civilization and barbarism. However, da Cunha maintained great sympathy for the followers of Antonio Conselheiro (Figure 31.5), and he argued that civilization could not be spread in the flash of a cannon. The book has become a classic of Latin American literature, but the problems of national integration and the disruption of traditional values in the wake of modernization and change remained unresolved.

SOCIETIES IN SEARCH OF THEMSELVES

There was a tension in cultural life between European influences and the desire to express an American reality, or between elite and folk culture. Social change came very slowly for Indians, blacks, and women, but by the end of the century the desire for progress and economic resurgence was beginning to have social effects.

As colonial subjects of Spain and Portugal, the elites of Latin America had shared the culture and values of Europe. Recognition of that shared experience continued among the upper classes, who still looked to Europe for their inspiration, but political independence also provoked feelings of Americanism and at least a partial separation from, and rejection of, the old forms. Many times, however, this was simply a denial of the Hispanic traditions associated with the old colonial status and an acceptance of English and French models that seemed to represent the new age.

Cultural Expression After Independence

The end of colonial rule opened up Latin America to direct influences from the rest of Europe. Scientific observers, travelers, and the just plain curious—often

Figure 31.5 *Refugees of Canudos.*

accompanied by artists—came to see and record, and while doing so introduced new ideas and fashions. Artistic and cultural missions sometimes were brought directly from Europe by Latin American governments.

The tastes and fashions of Europe were adopted by the elite in the new nations. The battles and triumphs of independence were celebrated in paintings, hymns, odes, and theatrical pieces in the neoclassical style in an attempt to use Greece and Rome as a model for the present. Latin Americans followed the lead of Europe, especially France. The same neoclassical tradition also was apparent in the architecture of the early 19th century.

In the 1830s, the generation that came of age after independence turned to romanticism and found the basis of a new nationality in historical images, the Indian, and local customs. This generation often had a romantic view of liberty. They emphasized the exotic as well as the distinctive aspects of American society. In Brazil, for example, poet António Gonçalves Dias (1823–1864) used the Indian as a symbol of Brazil and America. In Cuba, novels sympathetic to slaves began to appear by mid-century. In Argentina, writers celebrated the pampas and its open spaces. Sarmiento's critical account of the caudillos in

Facundo described in depth the life of the gauchos, but it was José Hernández who in 1872 wrote *Martín Fierro,* a romantic epic poem about the end of the way of the gaucho. Historical themes and the writing of history itself became a political act because studying the past became a way of organizing the present. Many of Latin America's leading politicians were also excellent historians: Mitre in Argentina, Alamán in Mexico, and a remarkable group of liberal Chilean historians deeply influenced by positivism.

By the 1870s, a new realism emerged in the arts and literature that was more in line with the scientific approach of positivism and the modernization of the new nations. As the economies of Latin America surged forward, novelists appeared who were unafraid to deal with human frailties such as corruption, prejudice, and greed. Chilean Alberto Blest Gana and Brazilian mulatto J. Machado de Assis (1839–1908; Figure 31.6) wrote critically about the social mores of their countries during this era.

Throughout the century, the culture of the mass of the population had been little affected by the trends and tastes of the elite. Popular arts, folk music, and dance flourished in traditional settings, demonstrating a vitality and adaptability to new situations that was often lacking in the more imitative fine arts. Sometimes authors in the romantic tradition or poets such as Hernández turned to traditional themes for their subject and inspiration, and in that way they brought these traditions to the greater attention of their class and the world. For the most part, however, popular artistic expressions were not appreciated or valued by the traditional elites, the modernizing urban bourgeoisie, or the new immigrants.

Old Patterns of Gender, Class, and Race

Although significant political changes make it appealing to deal with the 19th century as an era of great change and transformation in Latin America, it is necessary to recognize the persistence of old patterns and sometimes their reinforcement. Changes took place, to be sure, but their effects were not felt equally by all classes or groups in society, nor were all groups attracted by the promises of the new political regimes and their views of progress.

For example, women gained little ground during most of the century. They had participated actively in the independence movements. Some had taken up arms or aided the insurgent forces, and some—such as

Figure 31.6 *Machado de Assis (1839–1908) was a gifted African–Brazilian author of humble origins whose psychological short stories and novels won him acclaim as Brazil's greatest novelist of the 19th century.*

Colombian Policarpa (La Pola) Salvatierra, whose final words were "Do not forget my example"—had paid for their activities on the gallows. After independence, there was almost no change in the predominant attitudes toward women's proper role. Expected to be wives and mothers, women could not vote, hold public office, become lawyers, or in some places testify in a court of law. Although there were a few exceptions, unmarried women younger than 25 remained under the power and authority of their fathers. Once married, they could not work, enter into contracts, or control their own estates without permission of their husbands. As in the colonial era, marriage, politics, and the creation of kinship links were essential elements in elite control of land and political power, and thus women remained a crucial resource in family strategies.

Lower-class women had more economic freedom—often controlling local marketing—and also more personal freedom than elite women under the constraints of powerful families. In legal terms, however, their situation was no better—and in material terms, much worse—than that of their elite sisters. Still, by the 1870s women were an important part of the work force.

The one area in which the situation of women began to change significantly was public education. There had already been a movement in this direction in the colonial era. At first, the idea behind education for girls and women was that because women were responsible for educating their children, they should be educated so that the proper values could be passed to the next generation. By 1842, Mexico City required girls and boys aged 7 to 15 to attend school, and in 1869 the first girls' school was created in Mexico. Liberals in Mexico wanted secular public education to prepare women for an enlightened role within the home, and similar sentiments were expressed by liberal regimes elsewhere. Public schools appeared throughout Latin America, although their impact was limited. For example, Brazil had a population of 10 million in 1873, but only about 1 million men and half that number of women were literate.

The rise of secular public education created new opportunities for women. The demand for teachers at the primary level created the need for schools in which to train teachers. Because most teachers were women, these teacher training schools gave women access to advanced education. Although the curriculum often emphasized traditional female roles, an increasing number of educated women began to emerge who were dissatisfied with the legal and social constraints on their lives. By the end of the 19th century, these women were becoming increasingly active in advocating women's rights and other political issues.

In most cases, the new nations legally ended the old society of castes in which legal status and definition depended on color and ethnicity, but in reality much of that system continued. The stigma of skin color and former slave status created barriers to advancement. Indians in Mexico, Bolivia, and Peru often continued to labor under poor conditions and to suffer the effects of government failures. There was conflict. In Yucatan, a great rebellion broke out, pitting the Maya against the central government and the whites, in 1839 and again in 1847. It smoldered for 10 years. Despite the intentions of governments, Indians resisted changes imposed from outside their communities and were willing to defend their traditional ways. The word *Indian* was still an insult in most places in Latin America. For some mestizos and others of mixed origin, the century presented opportunities for advancement in the army, professions, and commerce, but these cases were exceptions.

In many places, expansion of the export economy perpetuated old patterns. Liberalism itself changed during the century, and once its program of secularization, rationalism, and property rights were made law, it became more restrictive. Positivists of the end of the century still hoped for economic growth, but some were willing to gain it at the expense of individual freedoms. The positivists generally were convinced of the benefits of international trade for Latin America, and large landholdings increased in many areas at the expense of small farms and Indian communal lands as a result. A small, white Creole, landed upper class controlled the economies and politics in most places, and they were sometimes joined in the political and economic functions by a stratum of urban middle-class merchants, bureaucrats, and other bourgeois types. The landed and mercantile elite tended to merge over time to create one group that, in most places, controlled the government. Meanwhile, new social forces were at work. The flood of immigration, beginning in earnest in the 1870s, to Argentina, Brazil, and a few other nations began to change the social composition of those places. Increasingly, rapid urbanization also changed these societies. Still, Latin America, though politically independent, began the 1880s as a group of predominantly agrarian nations with rigid social structures and a continuing dependency on the world market.

---

in DEP†H

Explaining Underdevelopment

Whether we use the word *underdeveloped,* the more benign *developing,* or the old-fashioned *backward,* it is usually clear that the term describes a large number of nations in the world with a series of economic and social problems. Because Latin America was the first part of what we now call the Third World to establish its independence and begin to compete in the world economy, it had to confront the reasons for its relative position and problems early and without many models to follow. The Document section of this chapter offers two visions of Latin America's early problems that are similar because both emphasize the Hispanic cultural heritage, as well as its supposed deficiencies or strengths, as a key explanation for the region's history. Such cultural explanations were popular among 19th-century intellectuals and political leaders, and they continue today, although other general theories based on economics and politics have become more popular.

At the time of Latin American independence, the adoption of European models of economy, government, and law seemed to offer great hope. But as "progress," republican forms of government, free trade, and liberalism failed to bring about general prosperity and social harmony, Latin Americans and others began to search for alternative explanations of their continuing problems as a first step in solving them. Some critics condemned the Hispanic cultural legacy; others saw the materialism of the modern world as the major problem and called for a return to religion and idealism. By the 20th century, Marxism provided a powerful analysis of Latin America's history and present reality, although Marxists themselves could not decide whether Latin American societies were essentially feudal and needed first to become capitalist or whether they were already capitalist and were ready for socialist revolution.

Throughout these debates, Latin Americans often implicitly compared their situation with that of the United States and tried to explain the different economic positions of the two regions. At the beginning of the 19th century, both regions were still primarily agricultural, and although a few places in North America were starting small industries, the mining sector in Latin America was far stronger than that of its northern neighbor. In 1850, Latin America had a population of 33 million, compared with 23 million in the United States, and the per capita income in both regions was roughly equal. By 1940, however, Latin America's population was much larger and its economic situation was far worse than in the United States. Observers were preoccupied by why and how this disparity arose. Was there some flaw in the Latin American character, or were the explanations to be found in the economic and political differences between the two areas, and how could these differences be explained? The answers to these questions were not easy to obtain, but increasingly they were sought not in the history of individual countries but in analyses of a world economic and political system.

There had long been a Marxist critique of colonialism and imperialism, but the modern Latin American analysis of underdevelopment grew from different origins. During the 1950s, a number of European and North American scholars developed the concept of "modernization," or "Westernization." Basing their ideas on the historical experience of western Europe, they believed that development was a matter of increasing per capita production in any society, and that as development took place various kinds of social changes would follow. The more industrialized, urban, and modern a society became, the more social change and improvement were possible as traditional patterns and attitudes were abandoned or transformed. Technology, communication, and the distribution of material goods were the means by which the transformation would take place. Some scholars also believed that as this process occurred there would be a natural movement toward more democratic forms of government and popular participation.

Modernization theory held out the promise that any society could move toward a brighter future by following the path taken earlier by western Europe. Its message was one of improvement through gradual rather than radical or revolutionary change, and thus it tended to be politically conservative. It also tended to disregard cultural differences, internal class conflicts, and struggles for power within nations. Moreover, sometimes it was adopted by military regimes that believed that imposing order was the best way to promote the economic changes necessary for modernization.

The proponents of modernization theory had a difficult time convincing many people in the "underdeveloped" world, where the historical experience had been very different from that of western Europe. In 19th-century Latin America, for example, early attempts to develop industry were faced with competition from the cheaper and better products of already industrialized nations such as England and France, so a similar path to development was impossible. Critics argued that each nation did not operate individually but was part of a world system that kept some areas "developed" at the expense of others.

These ideas were first and most cogently expressed in Latin America. After World War II, the United Nations established an Economic Commission for Latin America (ECLA). Under the leadership of Argentine economist Raul Prebisch, the ECLA began to analyze the Latin American economies. Prebisch argued that "unequal exchange" between the developed nations at the center of the world economy and those like Latin America created structural blocks to economic growth. The ECLA suggested various policies to overcome the problems, especially the development of industries that would overcome the region's dependence on foreign imports.

From the structural analysis of the ECLA and from more traditional Marxist critiques, a new kind of explanation, usually called *dependency theory,* began to emerge in the 1960s. Rather than seeing underdevelopment or the lack of economic growth as the result of failed modernization, some scholars in Latin America began to argue that development and underdevelopment were not stages but part of the same process. They believed that the development and growth of some areas, such as western Europe and the United States, were achieved at the expense of, or because of, the underdevelopment of dependent regions such as Latin America. Agricultural economies at the periphery of the world economic system always were at a disadvantage in dealing with the industrial nations of the center, and thus they would become poorer as the industrial nations got richer. The industrial nations would continually draw products, profits, and cheap labor from the periphery. This basic economic relationship of dependency meant that production, capital accumulation, and class relations in a dependent country were determined by external forces. Some theorists went further and argued that Latin America and other nations of the Third World were culturally dependent in their consumption of ideas and concepts. Both modernization theory and Mickey Mouse were seen as the agents of a cultural domination that was simply an extension of economic reality. These theorists usually argued that socialism offered the only hope for breaking out of the dependency relationship.

These ideas, which dominated Latin American intellectual life, were appealing to other areas of Asia and Africa that had recently emerged from colonial control. Forms of dependency analysis became popular in many areas of the world in the 1960s and 1970s. By the 1980s, however, dependency theory was losing its appeal. As an explanation of what had happened historically in Latin America, it was useful, but as a theory that could predict what might happen elsewhere, it provided little help. Marxists argued that it overemphasized the circulation of goods (trade) rather than how things were produced and that it ignored the class conflicts they believed were the driving force of history. Moreover, with the rise of multinational corporations, the nature of capitalism itself was changing, and thus an analysis based on trade relationships between countries became somewhat outdated.

Whether development can be widespread, as modernization theory argued, or whether the underdevelopment of some countries is inherent in the capitalist world economy, as the dependency theorists believe, is still a matter of dispute, but recent events in eastern Europe have thrown the socialist alternative into question as well. The search for new explanations and new solutions to the problems of development will continue as peoples throughout the world work to improve their lives.

Questions: In what sense was 19th-century Latin America a dependent economy? Which explanation or prediction about dependency best fits world economic trends today?

THE GREAT BOOM, 1880–1920

■■ *Between 1880 and 1920, Latin America, like certain areas of Asia and Africa, experienced a tremendous spurt of economic growth, stimulated by the increasing demand in industrializing Europe and the United States for raw materials, foodstuffs, and specialized tropical crops. Mexico and Argentina are two excellent examples of the effects of these changes. By the end of the 19th century, the United States was beginning to intervene directly in Latin American affairs.*

Latin America was well prepared for export-led economic expansion. The liberal ideology of individual freedoms, an open market, and limited government intervention in the operation of the economy had triumphed in many places. Whereas this ideology had been the expression of the middle class in Europe, in Latin America it was adopted not only by the small urban middle class but also by the large land owners, miners, and export merchants linked to the rural economy and the traditional patterns of wealth and land owning. In a number of countries, a political alliance was forged between the traditional aristocracy of wealth and the new urban elements. Together they controlled the presidential offices and the congresses and imposed a business-as-usual approach to government at the expense of peasants and a newly emerging working class.

The expansion of Latin American economies was led by exports. Each nation had a specialty: bananas and coffee from Central America; tobacco and sugar from Cuba; rubber and coffee from Brazil; hennequen (a fiber for making rope), copper, and silver from Mexico; wool, wheat, and beef from Argentina; and copper from Chile. In this era of strong demand and good prices, these nations made high profits. This allowed them to import large quantities of foreign goods, and it provided funds for the beautification of cities and other government projects. But export-led expansion was always risky because the world market prices of Latin American commodities ultimately were determined by conditions outside the region. In that sense, these economies were particularly vulnerable and in some ways dependent.

Also, export-led expansion could result in rivalry, hostility, and even war between neighboring countries. Control of the nitrates that lay in areas between Chile, Peru, and Bolivia generated a dispute that led to the War of the Pacific (1879–1883), pitting Chile against Bolivia and Peru. Although all were unprepared for a modern war at first, eventually thousands of troops were mobilized. The Chileans occupied Lima in 1881 and then imposed a treaty on Peru. Bolivia lost Antofagasta and its access to the Pacific Ocean and became a landlocked nation. Chile increased its size by a third and benefited from an economic boom during and after the war. In Peru and Bolivia, governments fell, and a sense of national crisis set in after the defeat in the "fertilizer war."

The expansion of Latin American trade was remarkable. It increased by about 50 percent between 1870 and 1890. Argentina's trade was increasing at about 5 percent a year during this period—one of the highest rates of growth ever recorded for a national economy. "As wealthy as an Argentine" became an expression in Paris, reflecting the fortunes that wool, beef, and grain were earning for some in Argentina. In Mexico, an oligarchic dictatorship, which maintained all the outward attributes of democracy but imposed

"law and order" under the dictator Porfirio Díaz, created the conditions for unrestrained profits. Mexican exports doubled between 1877 and 1900. Similar figures could be cited for Chile, Costa Rica, and Bolivia.

This rapidly expanding commerce attracted the interest of foreign investors eager for high returns on their capital. British, French, German, and North American businesses and entrepreneurs invested in mining, railroads, public utilities, and banking. More than half the foreign investments in Latin America were British, which alone were 10 times more in 1913 than they had been in 1870. But British leadership was no longer uncontested; Germany and, increasingly, the United States provided competition. The United States was particularly active in the Caribbean region and Mexico, but not until after World War I did United States capital predominate in the region.

Foreign investments provided Latin America with needed capital and services but tended to place key industries, transportation facilities, and services in foreign hands. Foreign investments also constrained Latin American governments in their social, commercial, and diplomatic policies.

Mexico and Argentina: Examples of Economic Transformation

We can use these two large Latin American nations as examples of different responses within the same general pattern. In Mexico, the Liberal triumph of Juárez had set the stage for economic growth and constitutional government. In 1876, Porfirio Díaz, one of Juárez's generals, was elected president, and for the next 35 years he dominated politics. Díaz suppressed regional rebellions and imposed a strong centralized government. Financed by foreign capital, the railroad system grew rapidly, providing a new way to integrate Mexican regional economies, move goods to the ports for export, and allow the movement of government troops to keep order. Industrialization began to take place. Foreign investment was encouraged in mining, transportation, and other sectors of the economy, and financial policies were changed to promote investments. For example, United States investments expanded from about 30 million pesos in 1883 to more than 1 billion by 1911.

The forms of liberal democracy were maintained but were subverted to keep Díaz in power and to give his development plans an open track. Behind these policies were a number of advisors who were strongly influenced by positivist ideas and who wanted to impose a scientific approach on the national economy. These *cientificos* set the tone for Mexico while the government suppressed any political opposition to these policies. Díaz's Mexico projected an image of modernization led by a Europeanized elite who greatly profited from the economic growth and the imposition of order under Don Porfirio.

Growth often was bought at the expense of Mexico's large rural peasantry and its growing urban and working classes. This population was essentially native, because unlike Argentina and Brazil, Mexico had received few immigrants. They participated very little in the prosperity of export-led growth. Economic expansion at the expense of peasants and Indian communal lands created a volatile situation.

Strikes and labor unrest increased, particularly among railroad workers, miners, and textile workers. In the countryside, a national police force, the Rurales, maintained order, and the army was mobilized when needed. At the regional level, political bosses linked to the Díaz regime in Mexico City delivered the votes in rigged elections.

For 35 years, Díaz reigned supreme and oversaw the transformation of the Mexican economy. His opponents were arrested or driven into exile, and the small middle class, the land owners, miners, and foreign investors celebrated the progress of Mexico. In 1910, however, a middle-class movement with limited political goals seeking electoral reform began to mushroom into a more general uprising in which the frustrations of the poor, the workers, the peasants, and nationalist intellectuals of various political persuasions erupted in a bloody 10-year civil war, the Mexican Revolution.

At the other end of the hemisphere, Argentina followed an alternative path of economic expansion. By 1880, the Indians on the southern pampa had been conquered, and vast new tracts of land were opened to ranching. The strange relationship between Buenos Aires and the rest of the nation was resolved when Buenos Aires was made a federal district. With a rapidly expanding economy, it became "the Paris of South America," an expression that reflected the drive by wealthy Argentines to establish themselves as a modern nation. By 1914, Buenos Aires had more than 2 million inhabitants, or about one-fourth of the national population. Its political leaders, the "Generation of 1880," inherited the liberal program of Sarmiento and Mitre, and they were able to enact their programs because of the high levels of income the expanding economy generated.

Technological changes contributed to Argentine prosperity. Refrigerated ships allowed fresh beef to be sent directly to Europe, and this along with wool and wheat provided the basis of expansion. Labor was provided by a flood of immigrants. Some were golondrinas (literally, "swallows"), who were able to work one harvest in Italy and then a second in Argentina because of the differences in seasons in the two hemispheres, but many immigrants elected to stay. Almost 3.5 million immigrants stayed in Argentina between 1857 and 1930, and unlike the Mexican population, by 1914 about one-third of the Argentine population was foreign born. Italians, Germans, Russians, and Jews came to "hacer America"—that is, "to make America"—and remained. In a way, they really did Europeanize Argentina, as did not happen in Mexico, introducing the folkways and ideologies of the European rural and working classes. The result was a fusion of cultures that produced not only a radical workers' movement but also the distinctive music of the tango, which combined Spanish, African, and other musical elements in the cafe and red-light districts of Buenos Aires. The tango became the music of the Argentine urban working class.

As the immigrant flood increased, workers began to seek political expression. A Socialist party was formed in the 1890s and tried to elect representatives to office. Anarchists hoped to smash the political system and called for strikes and walkouts. Inspired to some extent by European ideological battles, the struggle spilled into the streets. Violent strikes and government repression characterized the decade after 1910, culminating in a series of strikes in 1918 that led to extreme repression. Development had its social costs.

The Argentine oligarchy was capable of some internal reform, however. A new party representing the emerging middle class began to organize. It was aided by an electoral law in 1912 that called for secret ballots, universal male suffrage, and compulsory voting. With this change, the Radical party, promising political reform and more liberal policies for workers, came to power in 1916, but faced with labor unrest it acted as repressively as its predecessors. The oligarchy made room for middle-class politicians and interests, but the problems of Argentina's expanding labor force remained unresolved, and Argentina's economy remained closely tied to the international market for its exports.

With many variations, similar patterns of economic growth, political domination by oligarchies formed by traditional aristocracies and "progressive" middle classes, and a rising tide of labor unrest or rural rebellion can be noted elsewhere in Latin America. Modernization was not welcomed by all sectors of society. Messianic religious movements in Brazil, Indian resistance to the loss of lands in Colombia, and banditry in Mexico were all to some extent reactions to the changes being forced on the societies by national governments tied to the ideology of progress and often insensitive to its effects.

Uncle Sam Goes South

After its Civil War, the United States began to take a more direct and active interest in the politics and economies of Latin America. Commerce and investments began to expand rapidly in this period, especially in Mexico and Central America. American industry was seeking new markets and raw materials, while the growing population of the United States created a demand for Latin American products. Attempts were made to create inter-American cooperation. A major turning point came in 1898 with the outbreak of war between Spain and the United States, which began to join the nations of western Europe in the age of imperialism.

The war centered on Cuba and Puerto Rico, Spain's last colonies in the Americas. The Cuban economy had boomed in the 19th century on the basis of its exports of sugar and tobacco grown with slave labor. A 10-year civil war for independence, beginning in 1868, had failed in its main objective but had won the island some autonomy. A number of ardent Cuban nationalists, including journalist and poet José Martí, had gone into exile to continue the struggle. Fighting erupted again in 1895, and the United States joined in 1898, declaring war on Spain and occupying Cuba, Puerto Rico, and the Philippines.

In fact, U.S. investments in Cuba had been increasing rapidly before the war, and the United States had become a major market for Cuban sugar. The Cuban *Spanish American War* opened the door to direct U.S. involvement in the Caribbean. The Cuban army was treated poorly by its American allies, and a U.S. government of occupation was imposed on Cuba and Puerto Rico, which had witnessed its own stirrings for independence in the 19th century. When the occupation of Cuba ended in 1902, a series of onerous conditions was imposed on independent Cuba that made it almost an American dependency— a status that was legally imposed in Puerto Rico.

For strategic, commercial, and economic reasons, Latin America, particularly the Caribbean and Mexico, began to attract American interest at the turn of the century. These considerations lay behind the drive to build a canal across Central America that would shorten the route between the Atlantic and Pacific. When Colombia proved reluctant to meet American proposals, the United States backed a Panamanian movement for independence and then signed a treaty with its representative that granted the United States extensive rights over the *Panama Canal*. President Theodore Roosevelt was a major force behind the canal, which was opened to traffic in 1908.

The Panama Canal was a remarkable engineering feat and a fitting symbol of the technological and industrial strength of the United States. North Americans were proud of these achievements and hoped to demonstrate the superiority of the "American way"— a feeling fed to some extent by racist ideas and a sense of cultural superiority. Latin Americans were wary of American power and intentions in the area. Many intellectuals cautioned against the expansionist designs of the United States and against what they saw as the materialism of American culture. Uruguayan José Enrique Rodó, in his essay *Ariel* (1900), contrasted the spirituality of Hispanic culture with the materialism of the United States. Elsewhere in Latin America, others offered similar critiques.

Latin American criticism had a variety of origins: nationalism, a Catholic defense of traditional values, and some socialist attacks on expansive capitalism. In a way, Latin America, which had achieved its political independence in the 19th century and had been part of European developments, was able to articulate the fears and the reactions of the areas that had become the colonies and semicolonies of western Europe and the United States in the age of empire.

Conclusion

New Nations, Old Problems

During the 19th century, the nations of Latin America moved from the status of colonies to that of independent nation-states. The process was sometimes exhilarating and often painful, but during the course of the century, these nations were able to create governments and to begin to address many social and economic problems. These problems were inherited from the colonial era and were intensified by internal political and ideological conflicts and foreign intervention. Moreover, the Latin American nations had to revive their economies after their struggles for independence and to confront their position within the world economic system as suppliers of agricultural products and consumers of manufactured goods.

The heritage of the past weighed heavily on Latin America. Political and social changes were many, and pressures for these changes came from a variety of sources, such as progressive politicians, modernizing military men, a growing urban population, dissatisfied workers, and disadvantaged peasants. Still, in many ways Latin America remained remarkably unchanged. Revolts were frequent, but revolutions that changed the structure of society or the distribution of land and wealth were few, and the reforms intended to make such changes usually were unsuccessful. The elite controlled most of the economic resources, a growing but still small urban sector had emerged politically but either remained weak or had to accommodate the elite, and most of the population continued to labor on the land with little hope of improvement. Latin America had a distinctive civilization, culturally and politically sharing much of the Western tradition yet economically functioning more like areas of Asia and Africa. Latin America was the first non-Western area to face the problems of decolonization, and many aspects of its history that seemed so distinctive in the 19th century proved to be previews of what would follow: decolonization and nation-building elsewhere in the world in the 20th century.

Further Readings

Stanley J. and Barbara Stein's *The Colonial Heritage of Latin America* (1970) is a hard-hitting interpretation of colonial and 19th-century Latin America that emphasizes its continued dependency and its neocolonial status after independence. David Bushnell and Neil Macauley's *The Emergence of Latin America in the Nineteenth Century* (1988) provides an excellent overview that is critical of the dependency thesis. The classic study from the dependency perspective is Fernando Henrique Cardoso and Enzo Faletto's *Dependency and Development in Latin America* (1979). Roberto Cortés Conde's *The First Stages of Modernization in Spanish America* (1974) provides a good economic analysis, as does S. Haber, *Why Latin America Fell Behind* (1997). The movements for independence are described in John Lynch's *The Spanish American Revolutions* (1973). Tulio Halperin Donghi's *The Aftermath of Revolution in Latin America* (1973) analyzes the first half of the 19th century. Claudio Veliz's *The Centralist Tradition in Latin America* (1980) tries to explain the divergent development of Latin America and western Europe, and E. Bradford Burns's *Poverty or Progress: Latin America in the Nineteenth Century* (1973) provides a challenging attack on the liberal programs and a defense of a folk political tradition. Jean Franco's *The Modern Culture of Latin America: Society and the Artist* (1967) is a lively discussion of literature and the arts. Volumes 3 to 5 of *The Cambridge History of Latin America* (1985–1986) contain up-to-date essays on major themes and individual countries. A good essay from the collection is Robert Freeman Smith's "Latin America, the United States, and the European Powers, 1830–1930," vol. 4, 83–120.

There are many single-volume country histories and monographs on particular topics. David Rock's *Argentina* (1985), E. B. Burns's *A History of Brazil* (1980), Michael Meyer and William Sherman's *The Course of Mexican History* (1979), and Herbert Klein's *Bolivia* (1982) are good examples of national histories. There are excellent rural histories,

such as Stanley Stein's *Vassouras: A Brazilian Coffee County* (2nd ed., 1989), Charles Berquist's *Coffee and Conflict in Colombia, 1886–1910* (1978), and Arnold Bauer's *Chilean Rural Society* (1975). Silvia Arrom's *The Women of Mexico City* (1985) is a fine example of the growing literature in women's history, some of which is also seen in June Nash and Helen Safa, eds., *Sex and Class in Latin America* (1980). Hobart Spalding Jr.'s *Organized Labor in Latin America* (1977) surveys urban labor, and Charles Berquist's *Labor in Latin America* (1986) is a comparative interpretative essay.

On the Web

Simon Bolivar's views on state formation and his ambivalent attitude toward the United States are examined at http://victorian.fortunecity.com/dadd/453, http://www.emory.edu/COLLEGE/CULPEPER/BAKEWELL/texts/jamaica-letter.html and http://www.airpower.maxwell.af.mil/airchronicles/ aureview/1986/jul-aug/bushnell.html.

The life and career of his co-revolutionist in the South, Jose San Martin, is beautifully illustrated at http://www.pachami.com/English/ressanmE.htm and described at http://geocities.com/TimesSquare/1848/martin.html.

Bolivar and San Martin lived to see their visions compromised or betrayed, but they avoided the tragic fate of the hero of the Mexican war for independence, Father Miguel de Hidalgo, described at http://www.mexconnect.com/mex_/history/stuck/jthidalgo.htm. Hidalgo's home village of Dolores can be visited at http://mexconnect.com/mex_/travel/ganderson/gadeloresh.html.

James Monroe's message to Congress in 1823, establishing what came to be known as the Monroe Doctrine, is analyzed at http://hkuhist2.hku.hk/firstyear/Roberts/robertse04.htm.

Thomas Jefferson's own analysis of Monroe's address available at http://www.mtholyoke.edu/acad/intre/thomas.htm, illuminates the process by which America evolved from a revolutionary upstart to a world power. Jefferson himself rejects a seizure of Cuba on moral grounds, but notes its value as a possible addition to his country. Later, other American leaders with fewer scruples would seize land from their neighbor to the South, a topic addressed at http://sunsite.dcaa.unam.mx/revistas/1847/ and http://www.grossmont.k12.ca.us/Mtmiguel/Library/MexicanWar.html.

The concept of Manifest Destiny as it relates to world history beyond the U.S.-Mexican conflict is discussed at http://odur.let.rug.nl/~usa/E/manifest/manifxx.htm.

For U.S. and Latin American relations generally, see http://darkwing.uoregon.edu/^caguirre/uslatam.html.

Chapter 32

Civilizations in Crisis: The Ottoman Empire, the Islamic Heartlands, and Qing China

In the late nineteenth century, the Chinese were forced to concede port and warehouse areas, such as the one in this painting, to rival imperialist powers. These areas were, in effect, colonial enclaves. They were guarded by foreign troops, flew foreign flags, and were run by Western or Japanese merchant councils.

By the early 18th century, it appeared that two of the civilizations—Middle Eastern Islamic and Chinese—still capable of contesting the European drive for global dominance were headed in very different directions. Under the Manchu rulers, whose seizure of the Chinese throne in the mid-17th century was noted in Chapter 28, China was enjoying yet another early dynastic period of growth and prosperity. The territory controlled by the Manchus was greater than that claimed by any Chinese dynasty since the Tang in the 7th century. China's population was growing steadily, and its trade and agricultural production were keeping pace. Like other "barbarian" peoples, the Europeans were closely controlled by the functionaries of the ruling Qing dynasty. European traders were confined to the ports of Macao and Canton on China's south coast. In the early 18th century, the Qing emperor had severely curtailed missionary activities in China without fear of foreign reprisals. Thus, despite signs of growing poverty and social unrest in some districts, the Manchus appeared to have restored good government and the well-being of the general populace of China.

At the other end of Asia, the fate of the Ottomans appeared to be exactly the reverse. After centuries of able rule and expansion at the expense of their Christian and Muslim neighbors (see Chapter 26), the Ottomans were in full retreat by the early 18th century. The Austrian Habsburgs chipped away at the Ottomans' European possessions from the west while a revived Russia closed in from the north. Muslim kingdoms in north Africa broke away from the empire, and imperial governors and local notables throughout the Arab portions of the Middle East grew more and more independent of the ruling Sultan in Istanbul (formerly Constantinople). Political decline was accompanied by rising economic and social disruption. Inflation was rampant throughout much of the empire, and European imports were rapidly destroying what was left of the already battered Ottoman handicraft industries. The empire was racked by social tensions, crime, and rebellion in some areas. The divided Ottoman elite could not agree on a strategy for reinvigorating state and society. Nor could they find a way to halt the advance of the Christian infidels, whose military victories and economic inroads were undoing centuries of hard-won conquests. With the ranks of its Ottoman defenders reduced, the very heartlands of the Islamic world were increasingly at risk.

In a little more than a century, the very different paths these two civilizations appeared to be following suddenly converged, and then the Ottomans gained strength as China fell apart. A combination of internal weaknesses and growing pressure from the industrializing European powers threw China into a prolonged crisis in the early 19th century. If anything,

1650 C.E.	1800 C.E.	1850 C.E.	1875 C.E.	1900 C.E.
1644 Manchu nomads conquer China; Qing dynasty rules	**1805–1849** Reign of Muhammad Ali in Egypt	**1850–1864** Taiping rebellion in China	**1876** Constitution promulgated for Ottoman Empire	**1905** Fatherland Party established in Egypt
1664–1722 Reign of the Kangxi emperor in China	**1807–1839** Reign of Ottoman Sultan Mahmud II	**1854–1856** Crimean War	**1876–1908** Reign of Ottoman Sultan Abdul Hamid	**1908** Young Turks seize power in Istanbul
1727 First printing press set up in the Ottoman Empire	**1826** Ottoman Janissary corps destroyed	**1856–1860** Anglo–French war against China	**1877** Treaty of San Stefano; Ottomans driven from most of the Balkans	
1736–1799 Reign of the Qianlong emperor in China	**1834** Postal system established in Ottoman Empire	**1866** First railway begun in Ottoman Empire	**1882** British invasion and occupation of Egypt; failed revolt led by Orabi in Egypt	
1768–1774 Disastrous Ottoman war with Russia	**1838** Ottoman treaty with British removing trade restrictions in the empire	**1869** Opening of the Suez Canal	**1883** Mahdist victory over British-led Egyptian expeditionary force at Shakyan	
1772 Safavid dynasty falls in Persia	**1839–1841** Opium War in China	**1870** Ottoman legal code reformed	**1889** Young Turks established in Paris	
1789–1807 Reign of Ottoman Sultan Selim III	**1839–1876** *Tanzimat reforms in the Ottoman Empire*		**1898** British–Egyptian army defeats the Mahdist army at Omdurman	
1798 British embassy to Qianlong emperor in China; French invasion of Egypt; Napoleon defeats Egypt's Mameluk rulers	**1839–1897** Life of Islamic thinker Al-Afghani		**1898–1901** Boxer Rebellion in China; 100 Days of Reform in China	
	1849–1905 Life of Muhammad Abduh			

Chinese civilization was revealed as even more vulnerable than the Islamic world, which the Ottomans sought to defend. The Ottomans began to find new sources of leadership and to introduce reforms on the basis of Western precedents. In sharp contrast, the Manchus were paralyzed by the shock of devastating defeats at the hands of the European "barbarians." Overpopulation, administrative paralysis, and massive rebellions sapped China's strength from within, while European gunboats and armies broke down its outer defenses. By the end of the 19th century, internal disruptions and external pressures had demolished the foundations of Chinese civilization—a civilization whose development we have traced over nearly four millennia.

As old China died, its leaders struggled to find a new and viable system to put in its place. That struggle was carried on throughout a half century (roughly from 1898 to 1949) of foreign invasion, revolution, and social and economic breakdown that produced suffering on a scale unmatched in all human history. In sharp contrast, by the end of the 19th century, new lead-

ers had emerged in the Ottoman Empire who were able to overthrow the sultanate with little bloodshed and to begin the process of nation-making in the Turkish portions of the empire. Unfortunately, Ottoman weaknesses in earlier decades left the rest of the Middle East exposed to European inroads, and a larger Islamic crisis proved impervious to Turkish solutions.

The first sections of this chapter focus on attempts to revive the declining Ottoman Empire. In dealing with these patterns, we also look at developments in the central Islamic lands. Here the focus is the great changes set in motion by Napoleon's invasion of Egypt in 1798 and the differing responses of Islamic thinkers and political leaders to the growing threat of industrial Europe. The second half of the chapter concentrates on the forces that led to the collapse of Chinese civilization in the last half of the 19th century. We also look at some of the early Chinese responses to the profound crisis engendered by this collapse and examine the legacy of the fall of the Qing, China's last imperial dynasty, in the early 20th century.

IN DEPTH

Western Dominance and the Decline of Civilizations

With Europe's emergence as the dominant global power from the 18th century onward, the patterns of the rise and fall of civilizations established in the classical age changed fundamentally. As we have seen in our examination of the forces that led to the breakup of the great civilizations in human history, each civilization has a unique history. But some general patterns have been associated with the decline of civilizations. Internal weaknesses and external pressures have acted over time to erode the institutions and break down the defenses of even the largest and most sophisticated civilizations. In the preindustrial era, slow and vulnerable communication systems were a major barrier to the long-term cohesion of the political systems that held civilizations together. Ethnic, religious, and regional differences, which were overridden by the confidence and energy of the founders of civilizations, reemerged. Self-serving corruption and the pursuit of pleasure gradually eroded the sense of purpose of the elite groups that had played a pivotal role in civilized development. The resulting deterioration in governance and military strength increased social tensions and undermined fragile preindustrial economies.

Growing social unrest from within was paralleled by increasing threats from without. A major factor in the fall of nearly every great civilization, from those of the Indus valley and Mesopotamia to Rome and the civilizations of Mesoamerica, was an influx of nomadic peoples, whom sedentary peoples almost invariably saw as barbarians. Nomadic assaults revealed the weaknesses of the ruling elites and destroyed their military base. Their raids also disrupted the agricultural routines and smashed the public works on which all civilizations rested. Normally, the nomadic invaders stayed to rule the sedentary peoples they had conquered, as has happened repeatedly in China, Mesoamerica, and the Islamic world. Elsewhere, as occurred after the disappearance of the Indus valley civilization in India and after the fall of Rome, the vanquished civilization was largely forgotten or lay dormant for centuries. But over time, the invading peoples living in its ruins managed to restore patterns of civilized life that were quite different from, though sometimes influenced by, the civilization their incursions had helped to destroy centuries earlier.

Neighboring civilizations sometimes clashed in wars on their frontiers, but it was rare for one civilization to play a major part in the demise of another. In areas such as Mesopotamia, where civilizations were crowded together in space and time in the latter millennia B.C.E., older, long-dominant civilizations were overthrown and absorbed by upstart rivals. In most cases, however, and often in Mesopotamia, external threats to civilizations came from nomadic peoples. This was true even of Islamic civilization, which proved the most expansive before the emergence of Europe and whose rise and spread brought about the collapse of several long-established civilized centers. The initial Arab explosion from Arabia that felled Sasanian Persia and captured Egypt was nomadic. But the incursions of the Arab bedouins differed from earlier and later nomadic assaults on neighboring civilizations. The Arab armies carried a new religion with them from Arabia that provided the basis for a new civilization, which incorporated the older ones they conquered. Thus, like other nomadic conquerors, they borrowed heavily from the civilizations they overran.

The emergence of western Europe as an expansive global force radically changed long-standing patterns of interaction between civilizations as well as between civilizations and nomadic peoples. From the first years of overseas exploration, the aggressive Europeans proved a threat to other civilizations. Within decades of Columbus's arrival in 1492, European military assaults had destroyed two of the great centers of high civilization in the Americas: the Aztec and Inca empires. The previous isolation of the American Indian societies and their consequent susceptibility to European diseases, weapons, plants, and livestock made them more vulnerable than most of the peoples the Europeans encountered overseas. Therefore, in the first centuries of Western expansion, most of the existing civilizations in Africa and Asia proved capable of standing up to the Europeans, except on the sea. With the scientific discoveries and especially the technological innovations that transformed Europe in the 17th and 18th centuries, all of this gradually changed. The unparalleled extent of the western Europeans' mastery of the natural world gave them new sources of power for resource extraction, manufacture, and war. By the end of the 18th century, this power was being translated into the economic, military, and increasingly the political domination of other civilizations.

A century later, the Europeans had either conquered most of these civilizations or reduced them to spheres they controlled indirectly and threatened to annex. The adverse effects of economic influences from the West, and Western political domination, proved highly damaging to civilizations as diverse as those of west Africa, the Islamic heartlands, and China. For several decades before World War I, it appeared that the materially advanced and expansive West would level all other civilized centers. In that era, most leading European, and some African and Asian, thinkers and political leaders believed that the rest of humankind had no alternative (except perhaps a reversion to savagery or barbarism) other than to follow the path of development pioneered by the West.

As we shall see in this chapter and those that follow, the challenges European global domination posed for other civilizations provoked a wide variety of responses. They ranged from retreat into an idealized past free of European influences to extensive transformation along European lines. The leaders and thinkers of all non-Western peoples debated how extensively their societies must adopt Western ways to survive the onslaught of the European imperialist powers, and whether it would be possible to confine Western influences to certain spheres. They also struggled to come up with ways of mobilizing popular support for movements aimed at resisting the advance of the European powers and driving them from areas in Africa and Asia where they were already in control. As we shall see in the sections that follow, some of these modes of resistance were more successful than others. Some civilizations managed to adapt and survive, and others collapsed entirely. But all non-Western peoples became preoccupied with coping with the powerful challenges posed by the industrial West to the survival of their civilized past and the course of their future development.

Questions: Can you think of instances in which one preindustrial civilization was a major factor in the collapse of another? Why do you think such an occurrence was so rare? Discuss the advantages that the American Indians' isolation from civilizations in Europe, Africa, and Asia gave the European intruders in the 16th century. What kinds of advantages did the scientific and industrial revolutions give the Europeans over all other civilized peoples from the 18th century onward? Can you think of specific historical, cross-civilization confrontations in which one or more of those advantages was apparent in determining the outcome? Is the West losing these advantages today? If so, what do you think the consequences will be? If not, how is the West managing to keep the upper hand in relation to non-Western civilizations?

FROM EMPIRE TO NATION: OTTOMAN RETREAT AND THE BIRTH OF TURKEY

◼ *By the early 18th century, the days of the Ottoman Empire appeared numbered. Weakened by internal strife, the Ottomans were unable to prevent their European rivals from whittling away territories on all sides. But beginning in the late 18th century, able Ottoman rulers and committed reformers devised strategies and initiated changes that slowed the decline of the empire and the advance of the European powers. Rather than crash and disappear like so many empires before it, the Ottoman regime was captured from within by leaders committed to remaking it in the image of Western nations.*

In part, the Ottoman crisis was brought on by a succession of weak rulers within a political and social order that was centered on the sultan at the top. Inactive or inept sultans opened the way for power struggles between rival ministers, religious experts, and the commanders of the Janissary corps. Competition between elite factions further eroded effective leadership within the empire, weakening its control over the population and resources it claimed to rule. Provincial officials colluded with the local land-owning classes, the ayan, to cheat the sultan of a good portion of the taxes due him, and they skimmed all the revenue they could from the already impoverished peasantry in the countryside.

At the same time, the position of the artisan workers in the towns deteriorated because of competition from imported manufactures from Europe. Particularly in the 18th and early 19th centuries, this led to urban riots in which members of artisan guilds and young men's associations often took a leading role. Merchants within the empire, especially those who belonged to minority religious communities such as the Jews and Christians, grew more and more dependent on commercial dealings with their European counterparts. This pattern accelerated the influx

of Western manufactured goods that was steadily undermining handicraft industries within the empire. In this way Ottoman economic dependence on some of its most threatening European political rivals increased alarmingly.

With the Ottoman leaders embroiled in internal squabbles and their armies deprived of the resources needed to match the great advances in weaponry and training made by European rivals, the far-flung Ottoman possessions proved an irresistible temptation for their neighbors (Map 32.1). In the early 18th century, the Austrian Habsburg dynasty was the main beneficiary of Ottoman decadence. The long-standing threat to Vienna was forever vanquished, and the Ottomans were pushed out of Hungary and the northern Balkans.

In the late 1700s, the Russian Empire, strengthened by Peter the Great's forced Westernization (see Chapter 24), became the main threat to the Ottomans' survival. As military setbacks mounted and the Russians advanced across the steppes toward warm water ports in the Black Sea, the Ottomans' weakness was

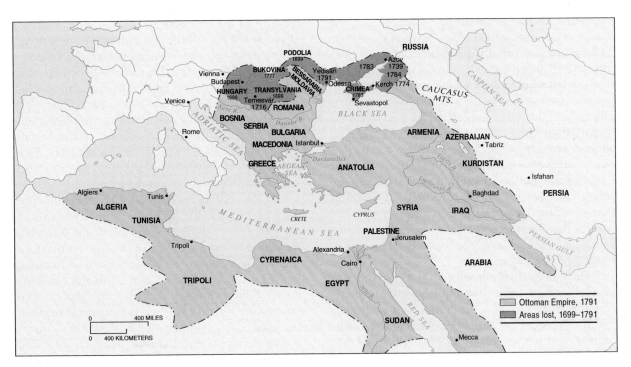

Map 32.1 *The Ottoman Empire in the Late 18th Century*

underscored by their attempts to forge alliances with other Christian powers. As the Russians gobbled up poorly defended Ottoman lands in the Caucasus and Crimea, the subject Christian peoples of the Balkans grew more and more restive under Ottoman rule. In 1804, a major uprising broke out in Serbia that was repressed only after years of difficult and costly military campaigns. But military force could not quell the Greek revolt that broke out in the early 1820s, and by 1830 the Greeks had regained their independence after centuries of Ottoman rule. In 1867, Serbia also gained its freedom, and by the late 1870s the Ottomans had been driven from nearly the whole of the Balkans and thus most of the European provinces of their empire. In the decades that followed, Istanbul itself was repeatedly threatened by Russian armies or those of the newly independent Balkan states.

Reform and Survival

Despite almost two centuries of unrelieved defeats on the battlefield and steady losses of territory, the Ottoman Empire somehow managed to survive into the 20th century. Its survival resulted in part from divisions between the European powers, each of which feared that the others would gain more from the total dismemberment of the empire. In fact, the British concern to prevent the Russians from controlling Istanbul—thus gaining direct access to and threatening British naval dominance in the Mediterranean—led them to prop up the tottering Ottoman regime repeatedly in the last half of the 19th century. Ultimately, the Ottomans' survival depended on reforms from within, initiated by the sultans and their advisors at the top of the imperial system and carried out in stages over most of the 19th century. At each stage, reform initiatives increased tensions within the ruling elite. Some factions advocated far-reaching change along European lines, others argued for reforms based on precedents from the early Ottoman period, and other elite groups had a vested interest in blocking change of any sort.

These deep divisions within the Ottoman elite made reform a dangerous enterprise. Although modest innovations, including the introduction of the first printing press in 1727, had been enacted in the 18th century, Sultan *Selim III* (1789–1807) believed that bolder initiatives were needed if the dynasty and empire were to survive. But his reform efforts, aimed at improving administrative efficiency and building a new army and navy, angered powerful factions within the bureaucracy. They were also seen by the Janissary corps, which had long been the dominant force in the Ottoman military (see Chapter 26), as a direct threat. Selim's modest initiatives cost him his throne—he was toppled by a Janissary revolt in 1807—and his life.

Two decades later, a more skillful sultan, *Mahmud II,* succeeded where Selim III had failed. After secretly building a small professional army with the help of European advisors, in 1826 Mahmud II ordered his agents to incite a mutiny of the Janissaries. This began when the angry Janissaries overturned the huge soup kettles in their mess area. With little thought given to planning their next move, the Janissaries poured into the streets of Istanbul, more a mob than a military force. Once on the streets, they were shocked to be confronted by the sultan's well-trained new army. The confrontation ended in the slaughter of the Janissaries, their families, and the Janissaries' religious allies.

After cowing the ayan, or provincial notables, into at least formal submission to the throne, Mahmud II launched a program of much more far-reaching reforms than Selim III had attempted. Although the ulama, or religious experts, and some of Mahmud's advisors argued for self-strengthening through a return to the Ottoman and Islamic past, Mahmud II patterned his reform program on Western precedents. After all, the Western powers had made a shambles of his empire. He established a diplomatic corps on Western lines and exchanged ambassadors with the European powers (Figure 32.1). The Westernization of the army was expanded from Mahmud's secret force to the whole military establishment. European military advisors, both army and navy, were imported to supervise the overhaul of Ottoman training, armament, and officers' education.

In the decades that followed, Western influences were pervasive at the upper levels of Ottoman society, particularly during the period of the *Tanzimat reforms* between 1839 and 1876. University education was reorganized on Western lines, and training in the European sciences and mathematics was introduced. State-run postal and telegraph systems were introduced in the 1830s, and railways were begun in the 1860s. Newspapers were established in the major towns of the empire. Extensive legal reforms were enacted, and in 1876 a constitution, based heavily on European prototypes, was promulgated. These legal reforms greatly improved the position of minority

Figure 32.1 *The European view of the Ottoman Empire as an exotic and bizarrely antique land is captured in this late 18th-century engraving of the Ottoman sultan entertaining the French ambassador and his entourage. Even though the sultans' power was greatly diminished, European diplomats continued to observe long-standing protocols in their visits to the Sublime Porte, where the Ottoman foreign ministry was located. In the 19th century, as a succession of sultans sought to Westernize the empire, foreign relations, including a regular exchange of resident ambassadors with each of the European powers, were increasingly brought in line with those of the Ottomans' European rivals.*

religious groups, whose role in the Ottoman economy increased steadily.

Some groups were adversely affected by these changes, which opened the empire more and more to Western influences. This was especially true of the artisans, whose position was gravely weakened by an 1838 treaty with the British that removed import taxes and other barriers to foreign trade that had protected indigenous producers from competition from the West. Other social groups gained little from the Tanzimat reforms. This was particularly true of

women. Proposals for women's education and an end to seclusion, polygamy, and veiling were debated in Ottoman intellectual circles from the 1860s onward. But few improvements in the position of women, even among the elite classes, were won until after the last Ottoman sultan was driven from power in 1908.

Repression and Revolt

The reforms initiated by the sultans and their advisors did improve the Ottomans' ability to fend off, or at least deflect, the assaults of foreign aggressors. But they increasingly threatened the dynasty responsible for them. Western-educated bureaucrats, military officers, and professionals came increasingly to view the sultanate as a major barrier to even more radical reforms and the full transformation of society. The new elites also clashed with conservative but powerful groups, such as the ulama and the ayan, who had a vested interest in preserving as much as possible of the old order.

The Ottoman Sultan *Abdul Hamid* responded to the growing threat from Westernized officers and civilians by attempting a return to despotic absolutism during his long reign from 1878 to 1908. He nullified the constitution and restricted civil liberties, particularly the freedom of the press. These measures deprived Westernized elite groups of the power they had gained in forming imperial policies. Dissidents or even suspected troublemakers were imprisoned and sometimes tortured and killed. But the deep impact of decades of reform was demonstrated by the fact that even Abdul Hamid continued to push for Westernization in certain areas. The military continued to adopt European arms and techniques, increasingly under the instruction of German advisors. In addition, railways, including the famous line that linked Berlin to Baghdad, and telegraph lines were built between the main population centers. Western-style educational institutions grew, and judicial reforms continued.

The despotism of Abdul Hamid came to an abrupt end in the nearly bloodless coup of 1908. Resistance to his authoritarian rule had led exiled Turkish intellectuals and political agitators to found the *Ottoman Society for Union and Progress* in Paris in 1889. Professing their loyalty to the Ottoman regime, the Young Turks (Figure 32.2), as members of the society came to be known, were determined to restore the 1876 constitution and resume far-reaching reforms within the empire. Clandestine printing presses operated by the Young Turks turned out tracts denouncing the regime and outlining further steps to be taken to modernize and thus save the empire. Assassinations were attempted and coups plotted, but until 1908 all were undone by a combination of divisions within the ranks of the Westernized dissidents and police countermeasures.

Sympathy within the military for the 1908 coup had much to do with its success. Perhaps even more important was the fact that only a handful of the sultan's supporters were willing to die defending the regime. Although a group of officers came to power, they restored the constitution and press freedoms and promised reforms in education, administration, and even the status of women. The sultan was retained as a political figurehead and the highest religious authority in Islam.

Unfortunately, the officers soon became embroiled in factional fights that took up much of the limited time remaining before the outbreak of World War I. In addition, their hold on power was shaken when they lost a new round of wars in the Balkans and a conflict against Italy over Libya, the Ottomans' last remaining possession in north Africa. Just as the sultans had before them, however, the Young Turk officers managed to stave off the collapse of the empire by achieving last-gasp military victories and by playing the hostile European powers against each other.

Although it is difficult to know how the Young Turks would have fared if it had not been for the outbreak of World War I, their failure to resolve several critical issues did not bode well for the future. They overthrew the sultan, but they could not bring themselves to give up the empire ruled by Turks for over 600 years. The peoples most affected by their decision to salvage what was left of the empire were the Arabs of the Fertile Crescent and coastal Arabia, who still remained under Ottoman control. Arab leaders in Beirut and Damascus had initially favored the 1908 coup because they believed it would bring about the end of their long domination by the Turks. To their dismay, the Arabs discovered that the Young Turks not only meant to continue their subjugation but were determined to enforce state control to a degree unthinkable to the later Ottoman sultans. The quarrels between the leaders of the Young Turk coalition and the growing resistance in the Arab portions of what was left of the Ottoman Empire were suddenly cut short in August 1914.

Figure 32.2 *Taken after Turkey's defeat in World War I and the successful struggles of the Turks to prevent the partition of their heartlands in Asia Minor by the victorious Greeks, this photo features a group of young Turks who have survived these challenges and grown a good deal older. The man in the business suit in the center is Mustafa Kemal, or Ataturk, who emerged as a masterful military commander during and after the war, and went on to become the founder of the modern nation of Turkey.*

The Young Turks' ineptitude was again demonstrated as they allowed the empire to become embroiled in the global conflict brought on by the outbreak of general war in Europe. Turkish entry into World War I on the side of the Germans in October, 1914, and its defeat several years later, brought about the end of the Ottoman Empire. These reversals also gave rise to a leader, *Mustafa Kemal*, or *Ataturk*, who was able to galvanize his people for the formidable tasks involved in building the modern nation of Turkey from the ruins of defeat.

WESTERN INTRUSIONS AND THE CRISIS IN THE ARAB ISLAMIC HEARTLANDS

▓▓ *The profound crisis of confidence brought on by successive reverses and the ever-increasing strength of the Muslims' old European rivals elicited a wide variety of responses in the Islamic world. Islamic thinkers debated the best way to reverse the decline and drive back the Europeans. Some argued for a return to the Islamic past, others favored a large-scale adoption of Western ways, and others tried to find ways to combine the two approaches. Reformist leaders, such as Muhammad Ali in Egypt, tried to graft on elements of Western culture while preserving the old state and society pretty much intact. Religious leaders, most spectacularly the Mahdi of the Sudan, who was regarded by his followers as a divinely appointed prophet, rose up to lead jihads, or holy wars, against the advancing Europeans.*

By the early 1800s, the Arab peoples of the Fertile Crescent, Egypt, coastal Arabia, and north Africa had lived for centuries under Ottoman–Turkish rule. Although most Arabs resented Turkish domination, they could identify with the Ottomans as fellow Muslims, who were both ardent defenders of the faith and patrons of Islamic culture. Still, the steadily diminishing capacity of the Ottomans to defend the Arab Islamic heartlands left them at risk of conquest by the aggressive European powers. The European capture of outlying but highly developed Islamic states, from those in the Indonesian archipelago and India to Algeria in north Africa, engendered a sense of crisis among the Islamic faithful in the Middle Eastern heartlands. From the most powerful adversaries of Christendom, the Muslims had become the besieged. The Islamic world had been displaced by the West as the leading civilization in a wide range of endeavors, from scientific inquiry to monumental architecture. Much of the Muslim community was forced to live under infidel European overlords; what remained was threatened by European conquest.

Muhammad Ali and the Failure of Westernization in Egypt

Although it did not establish a permanent European presence in the Islamic heartlands, Napoleon's invasion of Egypt in 1798 sent shock waves across what remained of the independent Muslim world (Figure 32.3). Significantly, Napoleon's motives for launching the expedition had little to do with designs for empire in the Middle East itself. Rather, he saw the Egyptian campaign as the prelude to destroying British power in India, where the French had come out on the short end of earlier wars for empire. Whatever his calculations, Napoleon managed to slip his fleet past the British blockade in the Mediterranean and put ashore his armies in July 1798 (see Map 32.1). There followed one of the most lopsided military clashes in modern history. As they advanced inland, Napoleon's forces were met by tens of thousands of cavalry bent on defending the Mamluk regime that then ruled Egypt as a vassal of the Ottoman sultans. The term *Mamluk* literally meant slave, and it suggested the Turkic origins of the regime in Egypt. Beginning as slaves who served Muslim overlords, the Mamluks had centuries earlier risen in the ranks as military commanders and seized power in their own name. *Murad*, the head of the coalition of Mamluk households that shared power in Egypt at the time of Napoleon's arrival, dismissed the invader as a donkey boy whom he would soon drive from his lands.

Murad's contempt for the talented young French commander was symptomatic of the profound ignorance of events in Europe that was typical of the Islamic world at the time. This ignorance led to a series of crushing defeats, the most famous of which came in a battle fought beneath the pyramids of the ancient Egyptian pharaohs. In that brief but bloody battle, the disciplined firepower of the French legions devastated the ranks of Mamluk cavalry, who were clad in medieval armor and wielded spears against the artillery Napoleon used with such devastating effect.

Figure 32.3 *This highly romanticized lithograph from the early-nineteenth century celebrates the stunning victory of the young Napoleon Bonaparte at the Battle of the Pyramids in 1798. Frenchmen of the time were thrilled by Napoleon's one-sided triumphs beneath the ancient Egyptian tombs that loom in the background. Ironically, the rubble in the foreground provides a more apt commentary on the outcome of the French invasion that was brought to an abrupt end by the British destruction of the French supply ships.*

Because the Mamluks had long been seen as fighters of great prowess in the Islamic world, their rout was traumatic. It revealed just how vulnerable even the Muslim core areas were to European aggression and how far the Muslims had fallen behind the Europeans in the capacity to wage war. Ironically, the successful invasion of Egypt brought little advantage to Napoleon or the French. The British caught up with the French fleet and sank most of it at the Battle of Aboukir in August 1798. With his supply line cut off, Napoleon was forced to abandon his army and sneak back to Paris, where his enemies were trying to use his reverses in Egypt to put an end to his rise to power.

Thus, Egypt was spared European conquest for a time. But the reprieve brought little consolation to thoughtful Muslims because the British, not Egypt's Muslim defenders, had been responsible for the French retreat.

In the chaos that followed the French invasion and eventual withdrawal in 1801, a young officer of Albanian origins named *Muhammad Ali* emerged as the effective ruler of Egypt. Deeply impressed by the weapons and discipline of the French armies, the Albanian upstart devoted his energies and the resources of the land that he had brought under his rule to building an up-to-date European-style military force. He introduced Western-style conscription among the Egyptian peasantry, hired French officers to train his troops, imported Western arms, and adopted Western tactics and modes of organization and supply. Within years he had put together the most effective fighting force in the Middle East. With it, he flaunted the authority of his nominal overlord, the Ottoman sultan, by successfully invading Syria and building a modern war fleet that threatened Istanbul on a number of occasions.

Although Muhammad Ali's efforts to introduce reforms patterned after Western precedents were not confined to the military, they fell far short of a fundamental transformation of Egyptian society. To shore up his economic base, he ordered the Egyptian peasantry to increase their production of cotton, hemp, indigo, and other crops that were in growing demand in industrial Europe. Efforts to improve Egyptian harbors and extend irrigation works met with some success and led to modest increases in the revenues that could be devoted to the continuing modernization of the military. Attempts to reform education were ambitious, but little was actually achieved. Numerous schemes to build up an Egyptian industrial sector were frustrated by the opposition of the European powers and the intense competition from imported, Western-manufactured goods.

To secure his home base, Muhammad Ali also found that he had little choice but to ally with the powerful rural landlords, the ayan, to control the peasantry. He sought to eliminate nonofficial intermediaries who collected taxes from the peasants, and he claimed all land as state property. But despite these measures, a hereditary landlord class was still firmly entrenched in the rural areas decades later. His forcible confiscation of the peasants' produce to pay for the rising costs of the military establishment and for his foreign entanglements further impoverished an already hard-pressed rural population.

The limited scope of Muhammad Ali's reforms ultimately checked his plans for territorial expansion and left Egypt open to inroads by the European powers. He died in 1848, embittered by the European opposition that had prevented him from mastering the Ottoman sultans and well aware that his empire beyond Egypt was crumbling. Lacking Muhammad Ali's ambition and ability, his successors were content to confine their claims to Egypt and the Sudanic lands that stretched from the banks of the Upper Nile to the south (see Map 32.1). Intermarrying with Turkish families that had originally come to Egypt to govern in the name of the Ottoman sultans, Muhammad Ali's descendants provided a succession of rulers who were known as *khedives* after 1867. The khedives were the formal rulers of Egypt until they were overthrown by the military coup that brought Nasser to power in 1952.

Bankruptcy, European Intervention, and Strategies of Resistance

Muhammad Ali's successors made a muddle of his efforts to reform and revitalize Egyptian society. While cotton production increased and the landlord class grew fat, the great majority of the peasants went hungry. The long-term consequences of these developments were equally troubling. The great expansion of cotton production at the expense of food grains and other crops rendered Egypt dependent on a single export. This meant that it was vulnerable to sharp fluctuations in demand (and thus price) on the European markets to which most of it was exported. Some further educational advances were made. But these were mainly at elite schools where French was the language of instruction. Therefore, the advances were too limited to benefit the broader populace by making government more efficient or stimulating public works projects and improved health care.

Much of the revenue the khedives managed to collect, despite the resistance of the ayan, was wasted on the extravagant pastimes of the mostly idle elite connected to the palace. Most of what was left was squandered on fruitless military campaigns to assert Egyptian authority over the Sudanic peoples along the upper Nile. The increasing inability of the khedives to balance their books led in the mid-19th century to their growing indebtedness to European financiers. The latter lent money to the khedives and members of the Turkish elite because the financiers wanted continued access to Egypt's cheap cotton. By the 1850s, they had a second motive: a share in the potentially lucrative schemes to build a canal across the Isthmus of Suez that would connect the Mediterranean and Red Seas. The completion of the *Suez Canal* in 1869, depicted while still under construction in Figure 32.4, transformed Egypt into one of the most strategic places on earth. The canal soon became a vital commercial and military link between the European powers and their colonial empires in Asia and east Africa. Controlling it became one of the key objectives of their peaceful rivalries and wartime operations through the first half of the 20th century.

The ineptitude of the khedival regime and the Ottoman sultans, who were their nominal overlords, prompted discussion among Muslim intellectuals and political activists as to how to ward off the growing European menace. In the mid-19th century, Egypt, and particularly Cairo's ancient Muslim University of al-Azhar, became key meeting places of these thinkers from throughout the Islamic world. Some prominent Islamic scholars called for a jihad to drive the infidels from Muslim lands. They also argued that the Muslim world could be saved only by a return to the patterns of religious observance and social interaction that they believed had existed in the golden age of Muhammad.

Other thinkers, such as *al-Afghani* (1839–1897) and his disciple *Muhammad Abduh* (1849–1905), stressed the need for Muslims to borrow scientific learning and technology from the West and to revive their earlier capacity to innovate. They argued that Islamic civilization had once taught the Europeans much in the sciences and mathematics, including such critical concepts as the Indian numerals. Thus, it was fitting that Muslims learn from the advances the Europeans had made with the help of Islamic borrowings. Those who advocated this approach also stressed the importance of the tradition of rational inquiry in Islamic history. They strongly disputed the views of religious scholars who contended that the Quran was the source of all truth and should be interpreted literally.

Although both religious revivalists and those who stressed the need for imports from the West agreed on the need for Muslim unity in the face of the growing European threat, they could not reconcile their very different approaches to Islamic renewal. Their differences, and the uncertainties they have injected into Islamic efforts to cope with the challenges of the West, remain central problems in the Muslim world today.

Figure 32.4. Building a canal across the desert Isthmus of Suez was a remarkable engineering feat. As this contemporary photo illustrates, a massive investment in up-to-date technology was needed. By creating a water route between the Mediterranean and Red seas, the canal greatly shortened the travel time between Europe and maritime Asia as well as the east coast of Africa. Combined with the growing predominance of steamships, it helped to expand global commerce as well as tourism, which became a major middle-class activity in the late 19th century.

The mounting debts of the khedival regime and the strategic importance of the canal gave the European powers, particularly Britain and France, a growing stake in the stability and accessibility of Egypt. French and British bankers, who had bought up a good portion of the khedives' shares in the canal, urged their governments to intervene militarily when the khedives proved unable to meet their loan payments. At the same time, French and British diplomats quarreled over how much influence each of their nations should exercise within Egypt.

In the early 1880s, a major challenge to the influence of foreign interests was mounted by the supporters of a charismatic young Egyptian officer named *Ahmad Orabi.* The son of a small farmer in lower Egypt, Orabi had attended Quranic school and studied under the reform-minded Muhammad Abduh at al-Azhar. Though a native Egyptian, Orabi had risen in the ranks of the khedival army and had become increasingly critical of the fact that the officer corps was dominated by Turks with strong ties to the khedival regime. An attempt by the khedive to save money by disbanding Egyptian regiments and dismissing Egyptian officers sparked a revolt led by Orabi in the summer of 1882. Riots in the city of Alexandria, associated with mutinies in the Egyptian armies, drove the frightened khedive to seek British assistance. After bombarding the coastal batteries set up by Orabi's troops, the British sent ashore an expeditionary force that crushed Orabi's rebellion and secured the position of the khedive.

Although Egypt was not formally colonized, the British intervention began decades of dominance by both British consuls, who ruled through the puppet khedives, and British advisors to all high-ranking Egyptian administrators. British officials controlled Egypt's finances and foreign affairs; British troops ensured that their directives were heeded by Egyptian administrators. Direct European control over the Islamic heartlands had begun.

Jihad: The Mahdist Revolt in the Sudan

As Egypt fell under British control, the invaders were drawn into the turmoil and conflict that gripped the Sudanic region to the south. Egyptian efforts to conquer and rule the Sudan, beginning in the 1820s, were resisted fiercely. The opposition forces were led by the camel- and cattle-herding nomads who occupied the vast, arid plains that stretched west and east from the Upper Nile (see Map 32.1). The sedentary peoples who worked the narrow strip of fertile land along the river were more easily dominated. Thus, Egyptian authority, insofar as it existed at all, was concentrated in these areas and in river towns such as *Khartoum*, which was the center of Egyptian administration.

Even in the riverine areas, Egyptian rule was greatly resented. The Egyptian regime was notoriously corrupt, and its taxes placed a heavy burden on the peasants compelled to pay them. The Egyptians were clearly outsiders, and the favoritism they showed some of the Sudanic tribes alienated the others. In addition, nearly all groups in the Muslim areas in the north Sudan were angered by Egyptian attempts in the 1870s to eradicate the slave trade. The trade had long been a great source of profit for both the merchants of the Nile towns and the nomads, who attacked non-Muslim peoples, such as the Dinka in the south, to capture slaves.

By the late 1870s, Egyptian oppression and British intervention had aroused deep resentment and hostility. But a leader was needed to unite the diverse and often divided peoples of the region and to provide an ideology that would give focus and meaning to rebellion. *Muhammad Achmad* proved to be that leader. He was the son of a boat builder, and he had been educated by the head of a local Sufi brotherhood. The fact that his family claimed descent from Muhammad and that he had the physical signs—a cleft between his teeth and a mole on his right cheek—that the local people associated with the promised deliverer, or *Mahdi*, advanced his reputation. The visions he began to experience, after he had broken with his Sufi master and established his own sectarian following, also suggested that a remarkable future was in store. What was seen to be a miraculous escape from a bungled Egyptian effort to capture and imprison Muhammad Achmad soon led to his widespread acceptance as a divinely appointed leader of revolt against the foreign intruders.

The jihad that Muhammad Achmad, who came to be known to his followers as the Mahdi, proclaimed against both the Egyptian heretics and British infidels was one of a number of such movements that had swept through sub-Saharan Africa since the 18th century. It represented the most extreme and violent Islamic response to what was perceived as the dilution of Islam in the African environment and the growing threat of Europe. Muhammad Achmad promised to purge Islam of what he saw as superstitious beliefs and degrading practices that had built up over the centuries, thus returning the faith to what he claimed was its original purity. He led his followers in a violent assault on the Egyptians, whom he believed professed a corrupt version of Islam, and on the European infidels. At one point, his successors dreamed of toppling the Ottoman sultans and invading Europe itself.

The Mahdi's skillful use of guerrilla tactics and the confidence his followers placed in his blessings and magical charms earned his forces several stunning victories over the Egyptians. Within a few years the Mahdist forces were in control of an area corresponding roughly to the present-day nation of Sudan (see Map 40.1). At the peak of his power, the Mahdi fell ill with typhus and died. In contrast to many movements of this type, which collapsed rapidly after the death of their prophetic leaders, the Mahdists found a capable successor for Muhammad Achmad. The *Khalifa Abdallahi* had been one of the Mahdi's most skillful military commanders. Under Abdallahi, the Mahdists built a strong, expansive state. They also sought to build a closely controlled society in which smoking, dancing, and alcoholic drink were forbidden, and theft, prostitution, and adultery were severely punished. Islamic religious and ritual practices were enforced rigorously. In addition, most foreigners were imprisoned or expelled, and the ban on slavery was lifted.

For nearly a decade, Mahdist armies attacked or threatened neighboring states on all sides, including the Egyptians to the north. But in the fall of 1896, the famous British General Kitchener was sent with an expeditionary force to put an end to one of the most serious threats to European domination in Africa. The spears and magical garments of the Mahdist forces proved no match for the machine guns and artillery of Kitchener's columns. At the battle of Omdurman in 1898, thousands of the Mahdist cavalry were slaughtered. Within a year the Mahdist state collapsed, and British power advanced yet again into the interior of Africa.

Retreat and Anxiety: Islam Imperiled

The 19th century was a time of severe reverses for the peoples of the Islamic world. Outflanked and outfought by their old European rivals, Islamic leaders became puppets of European overlords or their lands passed under the rule of colonial rulers. Diverse forms of resistance, from the reformist path taken by the Ottoman sultans to the prophetic rebellions of leaders such as Muhammad Achmad, slowed but could not halt the European advance. European products and demands steadily eroded the economic fabric and heightened social tensions in Islamic lands. The stunning military and economic successes of the Christian Europeans cast doubts on Muslim claims that theirs was the one true faith. By the century's end, it was clear that neither the religious revivalists, who called for a return to a purified Islam free of Western influences, nor the reformers, who argued that some borrowing from the West was essential for survival, had come up with a successful formula for dealing with the powerful challenges posed by the industrial West. Failing to find adequate responses and deeply divided, the Islamic community grew increasingly anxious over the dangers that lay ahead. Islamic civilization was by no means defeated. But its continued viability clearly was threatened by its powerful neighbor, which had become master of the world.

THE LAST DYNASTY: THE RISE AND FALL OF THE QING EMPIRE IN CHINA

Although China had been strong enough to get away with its policies of isolation and attitudes of disdain in the early centuries of Euro-

pean expansion, by the late 18th century these policies were outmoded and dangerous. Not only had the Europeans grown much stronger than they had been in the early centuries of expansion, but Chinese society was crumbling from within. More than a century of strong rule by the Manchus and a high degree of social stability, if not prosperity, for the Chinese people gave way to rampant official corruption, severe economic dislocations, and social unrest by the end of the 18th century. With the British in the lead, over the course of the 19th century, the Western powers took advantage of these weaknesses to force open China's markets, humiliate its military defenders, and reduce its Qing rulers to little more than puppets. By century's end, Chinese intellectuals were locked in heated debates over how to check the power of the advancing "barbarians" from the West and restore China's collapsing political and social order.

Although the Manchu nomads had been building an expansive state of their own north of the Great Wall for decades, their conquest of China was both unexpected and sudden. A local leader named *Nurhaci* (1559–1626) was the architect of unity among the quarrelsome Manchu tribes. He combined the cavalry of each tribe into extremely cohesive fighting units within eight *banner armies,* named after the flags that identified each. In the first decades of the 17th century, Nurhaci brought much of Manchuria, including a number of non-Manchu peoples, under his rule (Map 32.2). Although he remained the nominal vassal of the Chinese Ming emperor, Nurhaci's forces continually harassed the Chinese who lived north of the Great Wall, steadily driving them southward or in some cases incorporating them into his growing state.

During this period, the Manchu elite's adoption of Chinese ways, which had begun much earlier, was greatly accelerated. The Manchu bureaucracy was organized along Chinese lines, Chinese court ceremonies were adopted, and Chinese scholar–officials found lucrative employment in the growing barbarian state north of the Great Wall. Though less affected by Chinese influences, Manchu commoners had some exposure to Chinese ways. Most remained nomadic herders, but a fair percentage had become sedentary farmers by the time of the conquest of China proper.

The weakness of the declining Ming regime, rather than the Manchus' own strength, gave the

Map 32.2 *China During the Qing Era*

their Ming predecessors. They added to the court calendar whatever Confucian rituals they did not already observe. They made it clear that they wanted the scholar–officials who had served the Ming to continue in office. The Manchus even pardoned many who had been instrumental in prolonging resistance to their conquest. But at the same time, the new rulers assumed a much more direct role in appointing local officials than had the Ming. They also reduced the tax exemptions and privileges of these functionaries. For much of the first century of the dynasty, Chinese and Manchu officials were paired in appointments to most of the highest posts of the imperial bureaucracy, and Chinese officials predominated at the regional and local levels. Manchus, who made up less than 2 percent of the population of the Qing Empire, occupied a disproportionate number of the highest political positions. But there were few limits as to how high talented ethnic Chinese could rise in the imperial bureaucracy.

Unlike the Mongol conquerors who had abolished it, the Manchus retained the examination system and had their own sons educated in the Chinese classics. The Manchu emperors styled themselves the Sons of Heaven and rooted their claims to be the legitimate rulers of China in their practice of the traditional Confucian virtues. The early Manchu rulers were generous patrons of the Chinese arts, and at least one, *Kangxi* (1661–1722; Figure 32.5), was a significant Confucian scholar in his own right. Kangxi and other Manchu rulers employed thousands of scholars to compile great encyclopedias of Chinese learning.

Economy and Society in the Early Centuries of Qing Rule

The Manchu determination to preserve much of the Chinese political system was paralleled by an equally conservative approach to Chinese society as a whole. In the early centuries of their reign, the writings of Zhu Xi, which had been so influential in the preceding dynastic eras, continued to dominate official thinking. Thus, long-nurtured values such as respect for rank and acceptance of hierarchy—that is, old over young, male over female, scholar–bureaucrat over commoner—were emphasized in education and imperial edicts. Among the elite classes, the extended family remained the core unit of the social order, and the state grew increasingly suspicious of any forms of social organization, such as guilds and especially secret societies, that rivaled it.

Manchus an opportunity to seize control in China. Their entry into China resulted from a bit of luck. In 1644, an official of the Ming government in charge of the northern defenses called in the Manchus to help him put down a widespread rebellion in the region near the Great Wall. Having allowed the Manchus to pass beyond the wall, the official found that they were an even greater threat than the rebels. Exploiting the political divisions and social unrest that were destroying what was left of Ming authority, the Manchus boldly advanced on the Ming capital at Beijing, which they captured within the year. It took nearly two decades before centers of Ming and rebel resistance in the south and west were destroyed by the banner armies, but the Manchus soon found themselves the masters of China.

They quickly proved that they were up to the challenge of ruling the largest empire in the world. Their armies forced submission by nomadic peoples far to the west and compelled tribute from kingdoms such as Vietnam and Burma to the south. Within decades, the Manchu regime, which had taken the dynastic name *Qing* before its conquest of China, ruled an area larger than any previous Chinese dynasty with the exception of the Tang.

To reconcile the ethnic Chinese who made up the vast majority of their subjects, the Manchu rulers shrewdly retained much of the political system of

Figure 32.5 *The first Manchu emperor, Kangxi, whose long reign (1654–1722) brought such power and prosperity to China that a number of prominent European writers compared him to the philosopher–kings who were the ideal for the classical Greek philosopher Plato. Kangxi had many of the virtues of the accomplished Chinese gentleman. He was an able ruler, a talented writer, and a patron of literature and painting.*

The lives of women at all social levels remained centered on or wholly confined to the household. There the dominance of elder men was upheld by familial pressures and the state. Male control was enhanced by the practice of choosing brides from families slightly lower in social status than those of the grooms. Because they were a loss to their parents'

household at marriage and usually needed a sizable dowry, daughters continued to be much less desirable than sons. Despite the poor quality of the statistics relating to the practice, there are indications that the incidence of female infanticide rose in this period. In the population as a whole, males considerably outnumbered females, the reverse of the balance between the two in contemporary industrial societies.

Beyond the family compound, the world pretty much belonged to men, although women from lower-class families continued to work in the fields and sell produce in the local markets. The best a married woman could hope for was strong backing from her father and brother after she had gone to her husband's home, as well as the good luck in the first place to be chosen as the wife rather than as a second or third partner in the form of a concubine. If they bore sons and lived long enough, wives took charge of running the household. In elite families they exercised control over other women and even younger men. In contrast to India, where widow remarriage was all but prohibited, especially among the higher castes, in China it was permitted because widows were seen as a burden on family resources.

Some of the strongest measures the Manchus took after conquering China were aimed at alleviating the rural distress and unrest that had become so pronounced in the last years of Ming rule. Taxes and state labor demands were lowered. Incentives such as tax-free tenure were offered to those willing to resettle lands that had been abandoned in the turmoil of the preceding decades. A sizable chunk of the imperial budget (up to 10 percent in the early years of the dynasty) was devoted to repairing existing dikes, canals, and roadways and extending irrigation works. Peasants were encouraged to plant new crops, including those for which there was market demand, and to grow two or even three crops per year on their holdings. Like some of the earlier dynasties, the Qing tried to check the accumulation of great estates by rural landlords and to strengthen the bargaining position of the tenant classes.

Given the growing population pressure on the cultivable acreage and the near disappearance in most areas of open lands that could be settled, the regime had very little success in these efforts. After several decades of holding steady, the landed classes found that they could add to their estates by calling in loans to peasants or simply by buying them out. With a surplus of workers, tenants had less and less bargaining power in their dealings with landlords. If they objected to the share of the crop the landlords offered, they were turned off the land and replaced by those willing to accept even less. As a result, the gap between the rural gentry and ordinary peasants and laborers increased. One could not miss the old and new rich in the rural areas, as they rode or were carried in sedan chairs, decked out in silks and furs, to make social calls on their peers. To further display their superior social standing, many men of the gentry class let their nails grow long to demonstrate that they did not have to engage in physical labor.

The sector of Chinese society over which the Qing exercised the least control was also the most dynamic. The commercial and urban expansion that had begun in the Song era gained new strength in the long peace China enjoyed during the first century and a half of Manchu rule. Regional diversification in crops such as tea was matched by the development of new ways to finance agricultural and artisan production. Until the end of the 18th century, both the state and the mercantile classes profited enormously from the great influx of silver that poured into China in payment for its exports of tea, porcelain, and silk textiles. European and other foreign traders flocked to Canton, and Chinese merchants, freed from the restrictions against overseas travel of the late Ming, found lucrative market outlets overseas. Profits from overseas trade gave rise to a wealthy new group of merchants, the *compradors,* who specialized in the import–export trade on China's south coast. In the 19th century, these merchants proved to be one of the major links between China and the outside world.

Rot from Within: Bureaucratic Breakdown and Social Disintegration

By the late 18th century, it was clear that like so many Chinese dynasties of the past, the Qing was in decline. The signs of decline were pervasive and familiar. The bureaucratic foundations of the Chinese Empire were rotting from within. The exam system, which had done well in selecting able and honest bureaucrats in the early decades of the dynasty, had become riddled with cheating and favoritism. Despite formal restrictions, sons of high officials often were ensured a place in the ever-growing bureaucracy. Even more disturbing was the fact that nearly anyone with enough money could buy a post for sons or brothers. Poor scholars could be paid to take the exams for poorly educated or not-so-bright relatives. Examiners could be bribed to approve weak credentials or look the other way when candidates consulted cheat sheets while taking their exams. In one of the most notorious cases of cheating, a merchant's son won high honors despite the fact that he had spent the days of testing in a brothel hundreds of miles from the examination site.

Cheating had become so blatant by the early 18th century that in 1711 students who had failed the exams at Yangzhou held a public demonstration to protest bribes given to the exam officials by wealthy salt merchants. The growing influx of merchant and poorly educated landlords' sons into the bureaucracy was particularly troubling because few of them had received the classical Confucian education that stressed the responsibilities of the educated ruling classes and their obligation to serve the people. Increasingly, the wealthy saw positions in the bureaucracy as a means of influencing local officials and judges and enhancing family fortunes. Less and less concern was expressed for the effects of bureaucratic decisions on the peasantry and urban laborers.

Over several decades, the diversion of revenue from state projects to enrich individual families devastated Chinese society. For example, funds needed to maintain the armies and fleets that defended the huge empire fell off sharply. Not surprisingly, this resulted in a noticeable drop in the training and armament of the military. Even more critical for the masses were reductions in spending on public works projects. Of these, the most vital were the great dikes that confined the Yellow River in northern China. Over the millennia, because of the silting of the river bottom and the constant repair of and additions to the dikes, the river and dikes were raised high above the densely populated farmlands through which they passed. Thus, when these great public works were neglected for lack of funds and proper official supervision of repairs, leaking dikes and the rampaging waters of the great river meant catastrophe for much of northeastern China.

Nowhere was this disaster more apparent than in the region of the Shandong peninsula (see Map 32.2). Before the mid-19th century, the Yellow River emptied into the sea south of the peninsula. By the 1850s, however, the neglected dikes had broken down over much of the area, and the river had flooded hundreds of square miles of heavily cultivated farmland. By the 1860s, the main channel of the river flowed north of the peninsula. The lands in between had been flooded and the farms wiped out. Millions of peasants were left without livestock or land to cultivate. Tens—perhaps hundreds—of thousands of peasants died of famine and disease.

As the condition of the peasantry deteriorated in many parts of the empire, further signs of dynastic decline appeared. Food shortages and landlord demands prompted mass migrations. Vagabond bands clogged the roads, and beggars crowded the city streets. Banditry, long seen by the Chinese as one of the surest signs of dynastic decline, became a major problem in many districts. As the following verse from a popular ditty of the 1860s illustrates, the government's inability to deal with the bandits was seen as a further sign of Qing weakness:

When the bandits arrive, where are the troops?

When the troops come, the bandits have vanished.

Alas, when will the bandits and troops meet?

The assumption then widely held by Chinese thinkers—that the dynastic cycle would again run its course and the Manchus would be replaced by a new and vigorous dynasty—was belied by the magnitude of the problems confronting the leaders of China. The belief that China's future could be predicted from the patterns of its past ignored the fact that there were no precedents for the critical changes that had occurred in China under Manchu rule. Some of these changes had their roots in the preceding Ming era (see Chapter 28), in which, for example, food crops from the Americas, such as corn and potatoes, had set in motion a population explosion. An already large population had nearly doubled to reach a total of more than 200 million in the first century (c. 1650–1750) of Manchu rule; in the next century, it doubled again to reach 410 to 415 million. As successful as they had been in the past, Chinese social and economic systems could not carry such a large population. China desperately

needed innovations in technology and organization that would increase its productivity to support its exploding population at a reasonable level. The corrupt and highly conservative late Manchu regime was increasingly an obstacle to, rather than a source of, these desperately needed changes.

Barbarians at the Southern Gates: The Opium War and After

A second major difference between the forces sapping the strength of the Manchus and those that had brought down earlier dynasties was the nature of the "barbarians" who threatened the empire from outside. Out of ignorance, the Manchu rulers and their Chinese administrators treated the Europeans much like the nomads and other peoples whom they saw as barbarians. But the Europeans presented a very different sort of challenge. They came from a civilization that was China's equal in sophistication and complexity. In fact, although European nation-states such as Great Britain were much smaller in population (in the early 19th century, England had 7 million people to China's 400 million), the scientific and industrial revolutions allowed them to compensate for their smaller numbers with better organization and superior technology. These advantages proved critical in the wars between China and Britain and the other European powers that broke out in the mid-19th century.

The issue that was responsible for the initial hostilities between China and the British did little credit to the latter. For centuries, British merchants had eagerly exported silks, fine porcelains, tea, and other products from the Chinese Empire. Finding that they had little in the way of manufactured goods or raw materials that the Chinese were willing to take in exchange for these products, the British were forced to trade growing amounts of silver bullion. Unhappy about the unfavorable terms of trade in China, British merchants hit on a possible solution in the form of opium, which was grown in the hills of eastern India. Although opium was also grown in China, the Indian variety was far more potent and was soon in great demand in the Middle Kingdom. By the early 19th century an annual average of 4500 chests of opium, each weighing 133 pounds, were sold, either legally or illegally, to merchants on the south China coast (Figure 32.6). By 1839, on the

Figure 32.6 *An early 19th-century engraving of a British opium factory gives some sense of the massive scale of the opium trade with China. The opium paste was worked into balls, which were dried on racks like those shown in the illustration. The balls were then packed in chests for shipping to China and other overseas destinations. Although the British forbade the sale of opium in their Indian empire, they went to war with China in 1839–1841 because the Qing rulers tried to put an end to the import of a product that was contributing to the disintegration of Chinese civilization.*

eve of the *Opium War*, nearly 40,000 chests were imported by the Chinese.

Although the British had found a way to reverse the trade balance in their favor, the Chinese soon realized that the opium traffic was a major threat to their economy and social order. Within years, China's favorable trade balance with the outside world was reversed, and silver began to flow in large quantities out of the country. As sources of capital for public works and trade expansion decreased, agricultural productivity stagnated or declined, and unemployment spread, especially in the hinterlands of the coastal trading areas. Wealthy Chinese, who could best afford it, squandered increasing amounts of China's wealth to support their opium habits. Opium dens spread in the towns and villages of the empire at an alarming rate.

It has been estimated that by 1838, 1 percent of China's more than 400 million people were addicted to the drug. Strung-out officials neglected their administrative responsibilities, the sons of prominent scholar–gentry families lost their ambition, and even laborers and peasants abandoned their work for the debilitating pleasures of the opium dens.

From the early 18th century, Qing emperors had issued edicts forbidding the opium traffic, but little had been done to enforce them. By the beginning of the 19th century, it was clear to the court and high officials that the opium trade had to be stopped. When serious efforts were finally undertaken in the early 1820s, they only drove the opium dealers from Canton to nearby islands and other hidden locations on the coast. Finally, in the late 1830s, the emperor sent one of the most distinguished officials in the empire, *Lin Zexu,* with orders to use every means available to stamp out the trade. Lin, who was famous for his incorruptibility, took his charge seriously. After being rebuffed in his attempts to win the cooperation of European merchants and naval officers in putting an end to the trade, Lin ordered the European trading areas in Canton blockaded, their warehouses searched, and all the opium confiscated destroyed.

Not surprisingly, these actions enraged the European merchants, and they demanded military action to avenge their losses. Arguing that Lin's measures violated both the property rights of the merchants and principles of free trade, the British ordered the Chinese to stop their antiopium campaign or risk military intervention. When Lin persisted, war broke out in late 1839. In the conflict that followed, the Chinese were routed first on the sea, where their antiquated war junks were no match for British gunboats. Then they were soundly defeated in their attempts to repel an expeditionary force the British sent ashore. With British warships and armies threatening the cities of the Yangtze River region, the Qing emperor was forced to sue for peace and send Lin into exile in a remote province of the empire.

Their victories in the Opium War and a second conflict, which erupted in the late 1850s, allowed the European powers to force China to open trade and diplomatic exchanges. After the first war, Hong Kong was established as an additional center of British commerce. European trade was also permitted at five other ports, where the Europeans were given land to build more warehouses and living quarters (see the painting that opens the chapter). By the 1890s, 90 ports of call were available to more than 300,000 European and American traders, missionaries, and diplomats. Britain, France, Germany, and Russia had won long-term leases of several ports and the surrounding territory (see Map 32.2).

Although the treaty of 1842 made no reference to the opium trade, after China's defeat the drug poured unchecked into China. By the mid-19th century, China's foreign trade and customs were overseen by British officials. They were careful to ensure that European nationals had favored access to China's markets and that no protective tariffs, such as those the Americans were using at the time to protect their young industries, were established by the Chinese. Most humiliating of all for the Chinese was the fact that they

were forced to accept European ambassadors at the Qing court. Not only were ambassadors traditionally (and usually quite rightly) seen as spies, but the exchange of diplomatic missions was a concession that European nations were equal in stature to China. Given the deeply entrenched Chinese conviction that their Middle Kingdom was the civilized center of the earth and that all other peoples were barbarians, this was a very difficult concession to make. European battleships and firepower gave them little choice.

A Civilization at Risk: Rebellion and Failed Reforms

Although it was not immediately apparent, China's defeat in the Opium War greatly contributed to a building crisis that threatened not just the Qing dynasty but Chinese civilization as a whole. Defeat and the dislocations in south China brought on by the growing commercial encroachments of the West spawned a massive rebellion that swept through much of south China in the 1850s and early 1860s and at one point threatened to overthrow the Qing dynasty. Led by a mentally unstable, semi-Christianized prophet named *Hong Xiuquan,* the *Taiping rebellion* increased the already considerable stresses in Chinese society and further drained the diminishing resources of the ruling dynasty. Widespread peasant uprisings, incited by members of secret societies such as the White Lotus, had erupted as early as the 1770s. But the Taiping movement was the first to pose a serious alternative not only to the Qing dynasty but to Confucian civilization as a whole. The Taipings offered sweeping programs for social reform, land redistribution, and the liberation of women. They also attacked the traditional Confucian elite and the learning on which its claims to authority rested. Taiping rebels smashed ancestral tablets and shrines, and they proposed a simplified script and mass literacy that would have undermined one of the scholar–gentry's chief sources of power.

Their attack on the scholar–gentry was one of the main causes of the Taipings' ultimate defeat. Left no option but to rally to the Manchu regime, the provincial gentry became the focus of resistance to the Taipings. Honest and able Qing officials, such as Zeng Guofan, raised effective, provincially based military forces just in time to fend off the Taiping assault on northern China. Zeng and his allies in the government also carried out much-needed reforms to root out corruption in the bureaucracy and revive the stagnating Chinese economy.

In the late 19th century, these dynamic provincial leaders were the most responsible for China's *self-strengthening* movement, which was aimed at countering the challenge from the West. They encouraged Western investment in railways and even factories in the areas they governed, and they modernized their armies. Combined with the breakdown of Taiping leadership and the declining appeal of a movement that could not deliver on its promises, the gentry's efforts brought about the very bloody suppression of the Taiping rebellion. Other movements were also crushed, and banditry was brought under control for a time. But like the Ottoman sultans and their advisors, the Chinese gentry introduced changes that they saw as limited. They wanted to preserve the existing order, not fundamentally transform it. They continued to profess loyalty to the gravely weakened Manchu regime because they saw it as a defender of the traditional order. At the same time, their own power grew to such a point that the Manchus could control them only with great difficulty. Resources were drained from the court center to the provincial governors, whose growing military and political power posed a threat to the Qing court. The basis of China's political fragmentation was building behind the crumbling facade of Manchu rule.

Despite their clearly desperate situation by the late 19th century, including a shocking loss in a war with Japan in 1894 and 1895, the Manchu rulers stubbornly resisted the far-reaching reforms that were the only hope of saving the regime and, as it turned out, Chinese civilization. Manchu rulers occasionally supported officials who pushed for extensive political and social reforms, some of which were inspired by the example of the West. But their efforts were repeatedly frustrated by the backlash of members of the imperial household and their allies among the scholar–gentry, who were determined to preserve the old order with only minor changes and to make no concessions to the West.

The last decades of the dynasty were dominated by the ultraconservative dowager empress *Cixi*, who became the power behind the throne. In 1898, she and her faction crushed the most serious move toward reform. Her nephew, the emperor, was imprisoned in the Forbidden City, and leading advocates for reform were executed or driven from China.

On one occasion, Cixi defied the Westernizers by rechanneling funds that had been raised to build modern warships into the building of a huge marble boat in one of the lakes in the imperial gardens. With genuine reform blocked by Cixi and her faction, the Manchus relied on divisions between the provincial officials and between the European powers to maintain their position. Members of the Qing household also secretly backed popular outbursts aimed at expelling the foreigners from China, such as the *Boxer Rebellion* (Figure 32.7). The Boxer uprising broke

Figure 32.7 *During the Boxer uprisings from 1898 to 1901, allied armies—European, American, and Japanese—entered the Chinese capital at Beijing, where the foreign legations endured nearly 2 months of siege and assaults by Chinese resistance forces. Once the Boxers had been defeated, the allies imposed large fines on the Chinese, thus forcing them to pay for what was in effect a failed rebellion against the steady takeover of the empire by foreign economic and political interests. For the next half century, China was a major arena for conflict between the great powers, including the United States and Japan.*

out in 1898 and was put down only through the intervention of the imperialist powers in 1901. Its failure led to even greater control over China's internal affairs by the Europeans and a further devolution of power to provincial officials.

The Fall of the Qing

By the beginning of the 20th century, the days of the Manchus were numbered. With the defeat of the Taipings, resistance to the Qing came to be centered in rival secret societies such as the Triads and the Society of Elders and Brothers. These underground organizations inspired numerous local uprisings against the dynasty in the late 19th century. All of these efforts failed because of lack of coordination and sufficient resources. But some of the secret society cells became a valuable training ground that prepared the way for a new sort of resistance to the Manchus.

By the end of the 19th century, the sons of some of the scholar–gentry and especially of the merchants in the port cities were becoming more and more involved in secret society operations and other activities aimed at overthrowing the regime. Because many of these young men had received European-style educations, their resistance was aimed at more than just getting rid of the Manchus. They envisioned power passing to Western-educated, reformist leaders who would build a new, strong nation-state in China patterned after those of the West rather than simply establishing yet another imperial dynasty. For aspiring revolutionaries such as *Sun Yat-sen*, who emerged as one of their most articulate advocates, seizing power was also seen as a way to enact desperately needed social programs to relieve the misery of the peasants and urban workers.

Although they drew heavily on the West for ideas and organizational models, the revolutionaries from the rising middle classes were deeply hostile to the involvement of the imperialist powers in Chinese affairs. They also condemned the Manchus for failing control the foreigners. The young rebels cut off their *queues* (braided ponytails) in defiance of the Manchu order that all ethnic Chinese wear their hair in this fashion. They joined in uprisings fomented by the secret societies or plotted assassinations and acts of sabotage on their own. Attempts to coordinate an all-China rising failed on several occasions because of personal animosities or incompetence. But in late

1911, opposition to the government's reliance on the Western powers for railway loans led to secret society uprisings, student demonstrations, and mutinies on the part of imperial troops. When key provincial officials refused to put down the spreading rebellion, the Manchus had no choice but to abdicate. In February 1912, the last emperor of China, a small boy named *Puyi*, was deposed, and one of the more powerful provincial lords was asked to establish a republican government in China.

The End of a Civilization?

The revolution of 1911 toppled the Qing dynasty, but in many ways a more important turning point for Chinese civilization was reached in 1905. In that year, the civil service exams were given for the last time. Reluctantly, even the ultraconservative advisors of the empress Cixi had concluded that solutions to China's predicament could no longer be found in the Confucian learning the exams tested. In fact, the abandonment of the exams signaled the end of a pattern of civilized life the Chinese had nurtured for nearly 2500 years. The mix of philosophies and values that had come to be known as the Confucian system, the massive civil bureaucracy, rule by an educated and cultivated scholar–gentry elite, and even the artistic accomplishments of the old order came under increasing criticism in the early 20th century. Many of these hallmarks of the most enduring civilization that has ever existed were violently destroyed.

As we shall see in Chapter 41, however, even though Confucian civilization passed into history like so many before it, many of its ideas, attitudes, and ways of approaching the world survived. Some of them played critical roles in the violent and painful struggle of the Chinese people to build a new civilization to replace the one that had fallen. The challenge of blending and balancing the two remains to the present day.

Conclusion

Islamic and Chinese Responses to the Challenge of the West Compared

Both Chinese and Islamic civilizations were severely weakened by internal disruptions in the 18th and 19th centuries,

DOCUMENT

Building a New China

Faced with mounting intrusions by the Western powers into China, which the Manchu dynasty appeared powerless to resist, Chinese political leaders and intellectuals debated the ways by which China could renew itself and thus survive the challenges posed by industrialized West. As the following passages from his journal *A People Made New* (published from 1902 to 1905) illustrate, Liang Qichao, one of the main advocates of major reforms in Chinese society, recognized the need for significant borrowing from Europe and the United States. At the same time, late 19th- and early 20th-century champions of renewal such as Liang wanted to preserve the basic features of Chinese society as they had developed over two millennia of history.

> If we wish to make our nation strong, we must investigate extensively the methods followed by other nations in becoming independent. We should select their superior points and appropriate them to make up our own shortcomings. Now with regard to politics, academic learning, and techniques, our critics know how to take the superior points of others to make up for our own weakness; but they do not know that the people's virtue, the people's wisdom, and the people's vitality are the great basis of politics, academic learning, and techniques.

> [Those who are for "renovation"] are worried about the situation and try hard to develop the nation and to promote well-being. But when asked about their methods, they would begin with diplomacy, training of troops, purchase of arms and manufacture of instruments; then they would proceed to commerce, mining, and railways; and finally they would come, as they did recently, to officers' training, police, and education. Are these not the most important and necessary things for modern civilized nations? Yes. But can we attain the level of modern civilization and place our nation in an invincible position by adopting a little of this and that, or taking a small step now and then? I know we cannot.

> Let me illustrate this by commerce. Economic competition is one of the big problems of the world today. It is the method whereby the powers attempt to conquer us. It is also the method whereby we should fight for our existence. The importance of improving our foreign trade has been recognized by all. But in order to promote foreign trade, it is necessary to protect the rights of our domestic trade and industry; and in order to protect these rights, it is necessary to issue a set of commercial laws. Commercial laws, however, cannot stand by themselves, and so it is necessary to complement them with other laws. A law which is not carried out is tantamount to no law; it is therefore necessary to define the powers of the judiciary. Bad legislation is worse than no legislation, and so it is necessary to decide where the legislative power should belong. If those who violate the law are not punished, laws will become void as soon as they are proclaimed; therefore, the duties of the judiciary must be defined. When all these are carried to the logical conclusion, it will be seen that foreign trade cannot be promoted without a constitution, a parliament, and a responsible government.

> … What, then, is the way to effect our salvation and to achieve progress? The answer is that we must shatter at a blow the despotic and confused governmental system of some thousands of years; we must sweep away the corrupt and sycophantic learning of these thousands of years.

Questions: What does Liang see as the key sources of Western strength? What does he believe China needs most to borrow from Europe and the United States? Do his recommendations strike you as specific enough to rescue China from its many predicaments? If you were the emperor's advisor, what sorts of changes would you recommend, perhaps copying the approaches tried by the leaders of other civilizations in this era?

and each was thrown into prolonged crisis by the growing challenges posed by the West. Several key differences in the interaction between each civilization and the West do much to explain why Islam, though badly shaken, survived, whereas Chinese civilization collapsed under the burden of domestic upheavals and foreign aggression. For the Muslims, who had been warring and trading with Christian Europe since the Middle Ages, the Western threat had long existed. What was new was the much greater strength of the Europeans in the ongoing contest, which resulted from their global expansion and their scientific and industrial revolutions. For China, the challenges from the West came suddenly and brutally. Within decades, the Chinese had to revise their image of their empire as the center of the world and the source of civilization itself to take into account severe defeats at the hands of peoples they once dismissed as barbarians.

The Muslims could also take comfort from the fact that in the Judeo-Christian and Greek traditions they shared much with the ascendant Europeans. As a result, elements of their own civilization had played critical roles in the rise of the West. This made it easier to justify Muslim borrowing from the West, which in any case could be set in a long tradition of exchanges with other civilizations. Although some Chinese technology had passed to the West, Chinese and Western leaders were largely unaware of early exchanges and deeply impressed by the profound differences between their societies. For the Chinese, borrowing from the barbarians required a painful reassessment of their place in the world—a reassessment many were unwilling to make.

In countering the thrusts from the West, the Muslims gained from the fact that they had many centers to defend; the fall of a single dynasty or regime did not mean the end of Islamic independence. The Muslims also gained from the more gradual nature of the Western advance. They had time to learn from earlier mistakes and try out different responses to the Western challenges. For the Chinese, the defense of their civilization came to be equated with the survival of the Qing dynasty, a line of thinking that the Manchus did all they could to promote. When the dynasty collapsed in the early 20th century, the Chinese lost faith in the formula for civilization they had successfully followed for more than two millennia. Again, timing was critical. The crisis in China seemed to come without warning. Within decades, the Qing went from being the arrogant controller of the barbarians to being a defeated and humbled pawn of the European powers.

When the dynasty failed and it became clear that the "barbarians" had outdone the Chinese in so many fields of civilized endeavor, the Chinese had little to fall back on. Like the Europeans, they had excelled in social and political organization and in mastery of the material world. Unlike the Hindus or the Muslims, they had no great religious tradition with which to counter the European conceit that worldly dominance could be equated with inherent superiority. In the depths of their crisis, Muslim peoples clung to the conviction that theirs was the true faith, the last and fullest of God's revelations to humankind. That faith became the basis of their resistance and their strategies for renewal, the key to the survival of Islamic civilization and its continuing efforts to meet the challenges of the West in the 20th century.

Further Readings

The best general introductions to the Ottoman decline and the origins of Turkey are Bernard Lewis's *The Emergence of Modern Turkey* (1961) and the chapter "The Later Ottoman Empire" by Halil Inalcik in *The Cambridge History of Islam,* vol. 1 (1973). Other recent studies on specific aspects of this process include C. V. Findley's studies of Ottoman bureaucratic reform and the development of a modern civil service in what is today Turkey, Ernest Ramsaur's *The Young Turks* (1957), Stanford Shaw's *Between Old and New* (1971), and David Kusher's essay, *The Rise of Turkish Nationalism* (1977). On Egypt and the Islamic heartlands in this period, see P. M. Holt's *Egypt and the Fertile Crescent, 1516–1922* (1965) or P. J. Vatikiotis's *The History of Egypt* (1985). On the Mahdist movement in the Sudan, see P. M. Holt's *The Mahdist State in the Sudan* (1958) or the fine summary by L. Carl Brown in Robert Rotberg and Ali Mazrui, eds., *Protest and Power in Black Africa* (1970). The latter also includes many informative articles on African resistance to European conquest and rule. On women and changes in the family in the Ottoman realm, see Nermin Abadan-Unat's *Women in Turkish Society* (1981), and in the Arab world, see Nawal el Saadawi's *The Hidden Face of Eve* (1980).

On the Manchu takeover in China, see Frederic Wakeman Jr.'s *The Great Enterprise* (1985) and Jonathan Spence and John E. Willis, eds., *Ming to Ch'ing* (1979). On Qing rule, among the most readable and useful works are Spence's *Emperor of China: Portrait of K'ang-hsi* (1974) and the relevant sections in his recent study, *The Search for Modern China* (1990); Susan Naquin and Evelyn Rawski's *Chinese Society in the 18th Century* (1987); and the essays in John Fairbank, ed., *The Cambridge History of China: Late Ch'ing 1800–1911* (1978). A good survey of the causes and course of the Opium War is provided in Hsin-pao Chang's *Commissioner Lin and the Opium War* (1964). The Taiping rebellion is covered in Jen Yu-wen's *The Taiping Revolutionary Movement* (1973), and the first stages of the Chinese nationalist movement are examined in the essays in Mary Wright, ed., *China in Revolution: The First Phase* (1968). The early sections of Elisabeth Croll's *Feminism and Socialism in China* (1980) provide an excellent overview of the status and condition of women in the Qing era.

Web Sites:

The transitions from the Mongol to Ming to Qing dynasties are reviewed at http://www.bergen.org/AAST/ Projects/ChinaHistory/MING.HTM.The art of the Qing Empire is on view at http://www.op.net/~uarts/ lin/we_c6.html.The decline of the Qing (http://library. thinkquest.org/26469/history/1900.html) was accelerated by the failure of a reform effort which climaxed in the 103 days from June 11 to September 21, 1898 (http://www-chaos.umd.edu/history/modern3. html).This failure came on top of the Opium War (http://kizuna.ins.cwru.edu/asia110/projects/projects/ Tang3/tang3.html) which an astute observer notes has undercurrents that were not confined to China (http://mir.drugtext.org/druglibrary/schaffer/history/om/om/15htm).

A site at http://www.humanities.ccny.cuny.edu/history/reader/ opium.htm encourages discussion of Chinese Opium Commissioner Lin Zexu's letter to Queen Victoria.

The Taiping Rebellion (http://www-chaos.umd.edu/history/modern2.html) gravely weakened 2,000 years of traditional Chinese government. The Boxer Rebellion (http://www.geocities.com/CollegePark/Pool/6208/title_page.htm) provided the coup de grace.

Major General Charles "Chinese" Gordon (http://www.cis.upenn.edu/~homeier/interests/heros/gordon4.html), who took part in the suppression of the anti-foreign, anti-Qing Taiping Rebellion, also found himself addressing another indigenous revolt in Egypt led by Muhammad Ahmad ibn as Sayyid abd Allah, known as al- Madhi (http://webcrawler.com/education/art_and_humanities/

history/africa/empires_and _kingdoms/sahara_desert/?search=al%2DMahdi and http://lcweb2.loc.gov/cgi-bin/query/r?Find/ cstudy@Feild[DOCID+sdo 24]).

Unlike al-Mahdi, who sought the path of militant revivalism, Mohammad Abduh and Jamal al-din Afghani (http://www.afghan-web.com/history/afghani.html) sought Western-style modernization within the context of Islam.

Earlier, Mohammad Ali, ruler of Egypt, had sought the same goal through economic transformation, but even the efforts of his successors to build the Suez Canal backfired due to European control over capital flow which ultimately led to increased European control over Egypt. (http://www.emayzine.com/lectures/egypt1798-1924.html).

Much the same fate befell the Tanzimat (http://landow.stg.brown.edu/victorian/history/dora/dora9.html), the Ottoman effort that paralleled the Qing reformist experiment.

Chapter 33

Russia and Japan: Industrialization Outside the West

This silk factory, based on imported technology and designed mainly for the burgeoning export trade to the West, is representative of early Japanese industrialization.

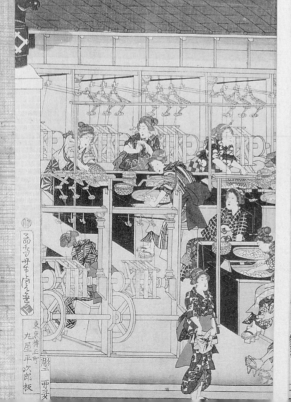

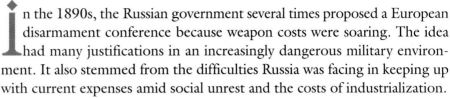

In the 1890s, the Russian government several times proposed a European disarmament conference because weapon costs were soaring. The idea had many justifications in an increasingly dangerous military environment. It also stemmed from the difficulties Russia was facing in keeping up with current expenses amid social unrest and the costs of industrialization.

On a more frivolous front, in 1896 a team of Japanese students defeated a group of American sailors in a baseball game, to their great delight. Growing foreign presence and an effort to imitate aspects of Western education had introduced new pastimes to Japan, including baseball, and within two decades the Japanese were prepared to beat Westerners at their own game.

This chapter deals with two important nations that defied the common pattern of growing Western domination during the 19th century: Russia and Japan. Both did so only after a heightened threat of Western interference, and both had to accept Western advisors and other intrusions. By 1914, however, Russia and Japan had managed to launch significant industrialization and to make other changes designed to strengthen their political and social systems. Neither Russia nor Japan rivaled the industrial might of the West at this point; both were trying to catch up after a late start. Their achievement was economic autonomy—not a share in the West's core position—which enabled both nations to gain sufficient power to participate in the imperialist scramble of the late 19th century.

Russia and Japan differed from the pattern of halting reforms characteristic of China and the Middle East in the 19th century. Theirs were the only societies outside the West to begin a wholesale process of industrialization before the 1960s.

The case of Japan was particularly striking. Japanese industrialization and related reforms seemed less expected in light of previous patterns than did Russia's, where an interest in selective borrowing from the West had developed by 1700. Japan pulled away from the rest of east Asia, at least for a time, whereas Russia continued a pattern of expanding influence in eastern Europe and central Asia.

Russia and Japan did have some common characteristics, which help explain why both could maintain economic and political independence during the West's century of power. They both had prior experience of imitation: Japan from China, Russia from Byzantium and then the West. They knew that learning from outsiders could be profitable and need not destroy their native cultures. They both had improved their political effectiveness

1700 c.e.	**1800 c.e.**	**1825 c.e.**	**1850 c.e.**
1720 End ban on Western books	**1800–1850** Growth of "Dutch school"	**1825** Decembrist Revolt	**1853** Perry expedition to Edo Bay
	1812 Failure of Napoleon's invasion	**1825–1855** Heightening of repression by Tsar Nicholas I	**1854** Follow-up American and British fleet visit
	1815 Russia reacquires Poland through the Treaty of Vienna; Alexander I and the Holy Alliance	**1829–1878** Serbia gains increasing autonomy in Ottoman Empire, then independence	**1854–1856** Crimean War
		1830–1831 Polish nationalist revolt repressed	**1856** Romania gains virtual independence
		1831 Greece wins independence after revolt against Ottomans	**1860–1868** Civil strife
		1833, 1853 Russian–Ottoman wars	**1860s–1870s** Alexander II reforms
		1841–1843 Brief shogun reform effort	**1861** Russian emancipation of serfs
			1865–1879 Russian conquests on central Asia
			1867 Mutsuhito, emperor of Japan
			1867 Russia sells Alaska to U.S.
			1868–1912 Meiji period
			1870 Ministry of Industry established
			1870–1940 Population growth
			1872 Universal military service established

during the 17th and 18th centuries, through the Tokugawa shogunate and the tsarist empire, respectively. Both nations could use the state to sponsor changes that in the West had rested in part with private businesses.

Ironically, soon after the reform period began in both countries, Russia and Japan met in new ways, as their expansionist interests brought a clash over influence in Korea. The resultant *Russo-Japanese War* symbolized the growing importance of both societies in world affairs. The war promoted further change, convincing Japanese leaders that they were on the right course while weakening the Russian establishment.

Reforms in both Russia and Japan raised new questions about civilization identity as change cut into distinctive traditions. Individual agents played a great role in initiating and directing the reform process in each country. Of course, rapid technological shifts figured directly in the policies Russia and Japan now sponsored because catching up with Western military and production technology was a key goal.

RUSSIA'S REFORMS AND INDUSTRIAL ADVANCE

▓▓ *After half a century of conservatism, Russia moved into an active reform period in 1861. Social and political changes set the basis for initial industrialization by the 1890s. But social strain persisted as Russian leaders tried to defend the tsarist autocracy.*

Russia Before Reform

Russian rulers, beginning with Catherine the Great in her later years, sought means to protect the country from the contagion of the French Revolution. The sense that Western policies might serve as models for Russia faded dramatically. Napoleon's 1812 invasion of Russia also led to a new concern with defense. Conservative intellectuals supported the move toward renewed isolation. In the eyes of these aristocratic writers, Russia knew the true meaning of community and stability. The system of serfdom provided ignorant peasants with the guidance and protection of paternalistic masters—an inaccurate social analysis but a comforting one. To resist Napoleon's pressure early in the 19th century, the government

1875 C.E.	*1900* C.E.
1875–1877 Russian Ottoman war; Russia wins new territory	**1902** Loose alliance with Britain
1877 Final samurai rising	**1904–1905** Russo–Japanese War
1878 Bulgaria gains independence	**1904–1905** Loss in Russo–Japanese War
1881 Anarchist assassination of Alexander II	**1905–1906** Revolution results in peasant reforms and duma
1881–1905 Growing repression, attacks on minorities	**1910** Annexation of Korea
1884–1887 New gains in central Asia	**1912** Growing party strife in Parliament
1884–1914 Beginnings of Russian industrialization; near-completion of trans-Siberian railway (full linkage 1916)	**1912–1918** Balkin Wars
1890 New constitution and legal code	**1914–1918** Entry to World War I
1892–1903 Sergey Witte, minister of finance	**1914** World War I
1894–1895 Sino–Japanese war	**1916–1918** Seizure of former German holdings in Pacific and China
1898 Formation of Marxist Social Democratic Party	**1917** Revolution and Bolshevik victory

introduced some improvements in bureaucratic training. A new tsar, Alexander I, flirted with liberal rhetoric, but at the Congress of Vienna he sponsored the *Holy Alliance* idea. In this Alliance, the conservative monarchies of Russia, Prussia, and Austria would combine in defense of religion and the established order. The idea of Russia as a bastion of sanity in a Europe gone mad was appealing, although in fact the Alliance itself accomplished little.

Defending the status quo produced some important new tensions, however. Many intellectuals remained fascinated with Western progress. Some praised political freedom and educational and scientific advance while deploring the West's neglect of social issues amid the squalor of early industrialization. Others focused more purely on Western cultural styles. Early in the 19th century, Russia began to contribute creatively to Europe's cultural output. The poet Pushkin, for example, descended from an African slave, used romantic styles to celebrate the beauties of the Russian soul and the tragic dignity of the common people. Because of its compatibility with the use of folklore and a sense of nationalism, the romantic style took deep root in eastern Europe. Russian musical composers would soon make their contributions, again using folk themes and sonorous sentimentality within a Western stylistic context.

While Russia's ruling elite continued to welcome Western artistic styles and took great pride in Russia's growing cultural respectability, they increasingly censored intellectuals who tried to incorporate liberal or radical political values. A revolt of Western-oriented army officers in 1825—the *Decembrist uprising* (see Figure 33.1)—inspired the new tsar, Nicholas I, to still more adamant conservatism. Repression of political opponents stiffened, and the secret police expanded. Newspapers and schools, already confined to a small minority, were tightly supervised. What political criticism there was flourished mainly in exile in places such as Paris and London; it had little impact on Russia.

Partly because of political repression, Russia avoided the wave of revolutions that spread through Europe in 1830 and 1848. Russia seemed to be operating in a different political orbit from that of the West, to the great delight of most Russian officials. In its role as Europe's conservative anchor, Russia even intervened in 1849 to help Austria put down the nationalist revolution in Hungary—a blow in favor of monarchy but also a reminder of Russia's eagerness to flex its muscles in wider European affairs.

While turning more conservative than it had been in the 18th century, Russia maintained its tradition of territorial expansion. Russia had confirmed its hold over most of Poland at the Congress of Vienna in 1815 after Napoleon briefly sponsored a separate Polish duchy. Nationalist sentiment, inspired by the growth of romantic nationalism in Poland and backed by many Polish land owners with ties to western Europe, roused recurrent Polish opposition to Russian rule. An uprising occurred in 1830 and 1831, triggered by news of the revolutions in the West and led by liberal aristocrats and loyal Catholics who chafed under the rule of an Orthodox power. Tsar Nicholas I put down this revolt with great brutality, driving many leaders into exile.

At the same time, Russia continued its pressure on the Ottoman Empire, whose weakness attracted their eager attention. A war in the 1830s led to some territorial gains. France and Britain repeatedly tried to prop up Ottoman authority in the interest of countering Russian aggression. Russia also supported many nationalist movements in the Balkans, including the Greek independence war in the 1820s; here, a desire to cut back the Turks outweighed Russia's commitment to conservatism. Overall, although no

Figure 33.1 *In the military Decembrist revolt in St. Petersburg, Loyalist troops put down the insurgent regiments in 1825.*

massive acquisitions marked the early 19th century, Russia continued to be a dynamic diplomatic and military force (Map 33.1).

Economic and Social Problems: The Peasant Question

Russia's economic position did not keep pace with its diplomatic aspirations. As the West industrialized and central European powers such as Prussia and Austria introduced at least the beginnings of industrialization, including some rail lines, Russia largely stood pat. This meant that it began to fall increasingly behind the West in technology and trade. Russian landlords eagerly took advantage of Western markets for grain, but they increased their exports not by improving their techniques but by tightening the labor obligations on their serfs. This was a common pattern in much of eastern Europe in the early 19th century, as Polish and Hungarian nobles also increased labor service to gain ground in the export market. In return for low-cost grain exports, Russia and other east European areas imported some Western machinery and other costly equipment as well as luxury goods for the great aristocrats to display as badges of cultured respectability. A few isolated factories that used foreign equipment were opened up in imitation of west European industrialization, but there was no significant change in overall manufacturing or transportation mechanisms. Russia remained a profoundly agricultural society based mainly on serf labor, but it was now a visibly stagnant society as well.

The widening gap between Russia and the West was driven home dramatically by a minor war in the Crimea between 1854 and 1856. Nicholas I provoked conflict with the Ottoman Empire in 1853, arguing among other things that Russia was responsible for protecting Christian interests in the Holy Land. This time, however, France and Britain were not content with diplomatic maneuverings to limit Russian gains but came directly to the sultan's aid. Britain was increasingly worried about any great power advance in the region that might threaten its hold on India, whereas France sought diplomatic glory and also represented itself as the Western champion of Christian rights. The resultant *Crimean War* was fought directly in Russia's back yard on the Black Sea, yet the Western forces won, driving the Russian armies from their entrenched positions. The loss was profoundly disturbing to Russian leadership, for the Western powers won this little war not because of great tactics or inspired principles but because of their industrial advantage. They had the ships to send masses of military supplies long distances, and their artillery and other weapons were vastly superior to Russia's home-produced models. This severe blow to a regime that prided itself on military vigor was a frightening portent for the future.

The Crimean War helped convince Russian leaders, including the new tsar, Alexander II, that it was time for a change. Reform was essential, not to copy the West but to allow sufficient economic adjustments for Russia to keep pace in the military arena. First and foremost, reform meant some resolution of Russia's leading social issue, the issue that most dis-

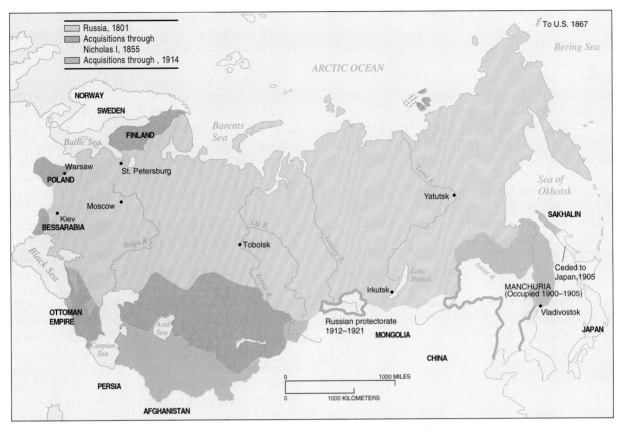

Map 33.1 *Russian Expansion, 1815–1914. Russia continued to push to the west, south, and east.*

tinguished Russian society from that of the West: serfdom. Only if the status of serfs changed could Russia develop a more vigorous and mobile labor force and so be able to industrialize. Russian concern about this issue paralleled the attacks on slavery in the Americas in the same period, reflecting a desire to meet Western humanitarian standards and a need for cheap, flexible labor.

So for two decades Russia returned to a policy of reform, based on Western standards and examples; serfdom had been abolished in western Europe after 1789 and in east central regions such as Prussia and Hungary in the aftermath of the revolutions of 1848. As before, however, the intention was not to duplicate Western measures fully but to protect distinctive Russian institutions, including the landed aristocracy and tightly knit peasant communities. The result was an important series of changes that, with tragic irony, created more grievances than they resolved while opening the way to further economic change.

The Reform Era and Early Industrialization

The final decision to emancipate the serfs in 1861 came at roughly the same time that the United States and Brazil decided to free slaves. Neither slavery nor rigorous serfdom suited the economic needs of a society seeking an independent position in Western-dominated world trade.

In some ways, the *emancipation of the serfs* was more generous than the liberation of slaves in the Americas. Although aristocrats retained part of the land, including the most fertile holdings, the serfs got most of it, in contrast to slaves, who received their freedom but nothing else. However, Russian emancipation was careful to preserve essential aristocratic power; the tsar was not interested in destroying the nobility, who remained his most reliable political ally and the source of most bureaucrats. Even more, emancipation was designed to retain the tight grip of the tsarist state. The serfs obtained no new political rights at a national level. They were still tied to their villages until they could pay for the land they were given. The redemption money went to the aristocrats to help preserve this class. Redemption payments added greatly to peasants' material hardship (Figure 33.2), and peasants thought that the land belonged to them with no need to pay for its return.

Emancipation did bring change; it helped create a larger urban labor force. But it did not spur a revolution in agricultural productivity because most peasants continued to use traditional methods on their small plots. And it did not bring contentment. Indeed, peasant uprisings became more common as hopes for a brighter future seemed dashed by the limits of change. Explosive rural unrest in Russia was furthered by substantial population growth as some of the factors that had earlier swelled the West's population now spread to Russia, including increased use of the potato.

In sum, after 1861 Russia was a classic case of a society in the midst of rapid change where reform did not go far enough to satisfy key protest groups. Peasants used their village structures, so often praised by

Figure 33.2 *This roadside scene in the late 19th century depicts the poverty of a Russian peasant village. What forces produced such poor conditions, even after serfdom had been abolished?*

Russian conservatives, to provide organization and goals for recurrent attacks on landlords and state tax officials, usually while professing loyalty to the tsar.

To be sure, the reform movement did not end with emancipation. Alexander II introduced a host of further measures in the 1860s and early 1870s. New law codes cut back the traditional punishments now that serfs were legally free in the eyes of the law (though subject to important transitional restrictions). The tsar created local political councils, the *zemstvoes,* which had a voice in regulating roads, schools, and other regional policies. Some form of local government was essential now that the nobles no longer directly ruled the peasantry. The zemstvoes gave some Russians, particularly middle-class people such as doctors and lawyers, new political experience, and they undertook important inquiries into local problems. However, the councils had no influence on national policy; the tsar resolutely maintained his own authority and that of his extensive bureaucracy. Another important area of change was the army; the Crimean War had shown the need for reform. The officer corps was improved through promotion by merit and a new organization of essential services. Recruitment was extended, and many peasants learned new skills through their military service. Some strides also were made in providing state-sponsored basic education, although schools spread unevenly.

From the reform era onward, literacy increased rapidly in Russian society. A new market developed for popular reading matter that had some similarities to the mass reading culture developing in the West. Interestingly, Russian potboiler novels, displaying a pronounced taste for excitement and exotic adventure, also attested to distinctive values. For example, Russian "bad guys" never were glorified in the end but always were either returned to social loyalty or condemned—a clear sign of the limits to individualism. Women gained new positions in this climate of change. Some won access to higher education, and, as in the West, a minority of women mainly from the upper classes began to penetrate professions such as medicine. Even sexual habits began to change, as had occurred in the West a century earlier. Fathers' control over their children's behavior loosened a bit, particularly where nonagricultural jobs were available, and sexual activity before marriage increased.

The move toward industrialization was part of the wider process of change. State support was an industrial effort, for Russia lacked a preexisting middle class and capital. State enterprises had to make up part of the gap, in the tradition of economic activity that went back to Peter the Great.

Russia began to create an extensive railroad network in the 1870s. The establishment of the *trans-Siberian railroad*, which connected European Russia with the Pacific, was the crowning achievement of this drive when it was nearly completed by the end of the 1880s. The railroad boom directly stimulated expansion of Russia's iron and coal sectors. Railroad development also stimulated the export of grain to the West, which now became essential to earn foreign currency needed in payment for advanced Western machinery. The railroads also opened Siberia up to new development, which in turn brought Russia into a more active and contested Asian role.

By the 1880s, when Russia's railroad network had almost quintupled since 1860, modern factories were beginning to spring up in Moscow, St. Petersburg, and several Polish cities, and an urban working class was growing rapidly (Figure 33.3). Printing factories and metalworking shops expanded the skilled artisanry in the cities, and metallurgy and textile plants recruited a still newer semiskilled industrial labor force from the troubled countryside.

Figure 33.3 *Early Russian industrialization is depicted in this 1888 photo of the commercial department of the Abrikosova and Son factory.*

Under *Count Witte,* minister of finance from 1892 to 1903 and an ardent economic modernizer, the government enacted high tariffs to protect new Russian industry, improved its banking system, and encouraged Western investors to build great factories with advanced technology. As Witte put it, "The inflow of foreign capital is … the only way by which our industry will be able to supply our country quickly with abundant and cheap products." By 1900, approximately half of Russian industry was foreign owned and much of it was foreign operated, with British, German, and French industrialists taking the lead. Russia became a debtor nation as huge industrial development loans piled up. By 1900, Russia had surged to fourth rank in the world in steel production and was second to the United States in the newer area of petroleum production and refining. Russian textile output was also impressive. Long-standing Russian economic lags were beginning to yield.

This industrial revolution was still in its early stages. Russia's world rank was a function more of its great size and population, along with its rich natural resources, than of thorough mechanization. Many Russian factories were vast—on average, the largest in the world—but they usually were not up to Western technical standards, nor was the labor force highly trained. Agriculture also remained backward, as peasants, often illiterate, had neither capital nor motives to change their ways.

Other reforms also produced ambiguous results. Russia remained a traditional peasant society in many ways. Beneath the official military reorganization, many peasant–soldiers continued to see their officers as landlord–patrons. Discipline and military efficiency were lax. It was not clear that the Russian masses had experienced the kinds of attitudinal changes that had occurred in the West at the time of initial industrialization or even before. Even more obvious was the absence of a large, self-confident middle class of the sort that had arisen earlier in the West. Businesspeople and professionals grew in numbers, but often they were dependent on state initiatives, such as zemstvo employment for doctors and economic guidance for businesspeople. They also lacked the numbers and tradition to become as assertive as their Western counterparts had been (for example, in challenging aristocratic power and values).

ᴅ ᴏ ᴄ ᴜ ᴍ ᴇ ɴ ᴛ

Conditions for Factory Workers in Russia's Industrialization

Russia passed several laws protecting workers, but enforcement was minimal. The Ministry of Finance established a factory inspectorate in the 1880s, which dutifully reported on conditions; these reports usually were ignored. The following passages deal with a number of Moscow factories in the 1880s.

In the majority of factories there are no special quarters for the workers. This applies to workers in paper, wool, and silk finishing. Skilled hand craftsmen like brocade weavers can earn good wages, and yet most of them sleep on or under their looms, for lack of anything else. Only in a few weaving factories are there special sleeping quarters, and these are provided not for the weavers, but for other workers—the winders and dyers, etc. Likewise, the velveteen cutters almost always sleep on the tables where they work. This habit is particularly unhealthy, since the work areas are always musty and the air is saturated with dye fumes—sometimes poisonous ones. Carpenters also generally sleep on their workbenches. In bastmatting factories, workers of both sexes and all ages sleep together on pieces and mats of bast which are often damp. Only the sick workers in these bast factories are allowed to sleep on the single stove.... Work at the mill never stops, day or night. There are two twelve-hour shifts a day, which begin at 6:00 A.M. and 6:00 P.M. The men have a half-hour for breakfast (8:30–9:00) and one hour for dinner (1:00–2:00).

The worst violations of hygienic regulations were those I saw in most of the flax-spinning mills where linen is produced.... Although in western Europe all the dust-producing carding and combing machines have long been covered and well ventilated, I saw only one Russian linen mill where such a machine was securely covered. Elsewhere, the spools of these machines were completely open to the air, and the scutching apparatus is inadequately ventilated....

In many industrial establishments the grounds for fines and the sizes of fines are not fixed in advance. The factory rules may contain only one phrase like the following: "Those found violating company rules will be fined *at the discretion of the manager.*"

The degree of arbitrariness in the determination of fines, and thus also in the determination of the worker's wages, was unbelievably extreme in some factories. In Podolsk, for instance, in factories No. 131 and No. 135, there is a ten-ruble forfeit for leaving the factory before the expiration of one's contract. But as applied, this covers much more than voluntary breach of contract on the worker's part. This fine is exacted from every worker who for any reason has to leave the factory. Cases are known of persons who have had to pay this fine three times. Moreover, fines are levied for so many causes that falling under a severe fine is a constant possibility for each worker. For instance, workers who for any reason came into the office in a group, instead of singly, would be fined one ruble. After a second offense, the transgressors would be dismissed—leaving behind, of course, the ten-ruble fine for breach of contract.

In factory No. 135 the workers are still treated as serfs. Wages are paid out only twice a year, even then not in full but only enough to pay the workers' taxes (other necessities are supplied by the factory store). Furthermore this money is not given to the workers directly, but is sent by mail to their village elders and village clerks. Thus the workers are without money the year around. Besides they are also paying severe fines to the factory, and these sums will be subtracted from their wages at the final year-end accounting.

Extreme regulations and regimentation are very common in our factories—regulations entangle the workers at every step and burden them with more or less severe fines which are subtracted from their often already inadequate wages. Some factory administrators have become real virtuosos at thinking up new grounds for fines. A brief description of a few of the fines in factory No. 172 is an excellent example of this variety: on October 24, 1877, an announcement was posted of new fines to be set at the discretion of the office for fourteen different cases of failure to maintain silence and cleanliness. There were also dozens of minor fines prescribed for certain individual offenses: for example, on August 4, 1883, a huge fine of five rubles was set for singing in the factory courtyard after 9:30, or at any time in any unauthorized place. On June 3, 1881, a fine was to be levied from workers who took tea and sugar, bread, or any kind of foodstuffs into the weaving building, "in order to avoid breeding any insects or vermin." On May 14, 1880, a fine was set for anyone who wrote with pencil, chalk, or anything else on the walls in the dyeing or weaving buildings.

Questions: What were the worst features of Russian factories? Were conditions worse than in western Europe during early industrialization, and if so in what ways and why? (Relatedly, what conditions probably were common in the first stages of factory industry everywhere?) How did working conditions and management attitudes help create a revolutionary mood among Russian workers? Think also about the nature of this source. Why would a conservative government sponsor such a critical report? What does the report suggest about tensions at the top of Russian society, between government and business? Would a conservative government be more likely to undertake this kind of inquiry than the more reform-minded regime that had existed a decade earlier? What do you think the results of such a report would be, in the Russian context, or indeed in any early industrial context?

PROTEST AND REVOLUTION IN RUSSIA

⬛ *A rising tide of unrest accompanied Russia's period of transformation by the 1880s, from nationalist agitation to outright revolution. Russia became a profoundly unstable society.*

The Road to Revolution

Alexander II's reforms, as well as economic change and the greater population mobility it involved, encouraged minority nationalities to make demands of the great empire. Intellectuals explored the cultural traditions of Ukrainians and other groups. Nationalist beliefs initially were imported from western Europe, but here and elsewhere in eastern Europe, they encouraged divisive minority agitation that multinational states, such as Russia and Austria–Hungary, found very hard to handle. Nationalist pressures were not the main problem in Russia, but given Russia's mainstream nationalist insistence on the distinctive superiorities of a Russian tradition, they did cause concern.

Social protest was more vigorous still, and it was heightened not only by the limitations of reform but by industrialization itself. Recurrent famines provoked peasant uprisings. Peasants deeply resented redemption payments and taxes and often seized and burned the records that indicated what they owed.

Many educated Russians, including some aristocrats, also clamored for revolutionary change. Two strands developed. Many business and professional people, though not very aggressive, began to seek a fuller political voice and new rights such as greater freedom in the schools and press; they argued for liberal reforms. At the same time, a group of radical *intelligentsia*—a Russian term for articulate intellectuals as a class—became increasingly active. As Russian universities expanded, student groups grew as well, and many were impatient with Russia's slow development and with the visible restrictions on political activity.

Some intellectuals later toned down their goals as they entered the bureaucracy or business life. But many remained inspired by radical doctrines, and more than a few devoted their lives to a revolutionary cause. This kind of intellectual alienation rested on some of the principles that had roused intellectuals in the West, but it went deeper in Russia. It was the first example of a kind of intellectual radicalism, capable of motivating terrorism, that would characterize other societies caught in tense transitions during the 20th century. The Russian intelligentsia wanted political freedom and deep social reform while maintaining a Russian culture different from that of the West, which they saw as hopelessly materialistic. Their radicalism may have stemmed from the demanding task they set themselves: attacking key Russian institutions while building a new society that would not reproduce the injustices and crippling limitations of the Western world.

Many Russian radicals were *anarchists*, who sought to abolish all formal government. Although anarchism was not unknown in the West, it took on particular force in Russia in opposition to tsarist autocracy. Many early anarchists in the 1860s hoped that they could triumph by winning peasant support, and a host of upper-class radicals fanned out to teach the peasantry the beauties of political activism. Failure here led many anarchists to violent methods and thus to the formation of the first large terrorist movement in the modern world. Given the lack of popular support and other political outlets, assassinations and bombings seemed the only way to attack the existing order. As anarchist leader Bakunin put it,

> We have only one plan—general destruction. We want a national revolution of the peasants. We refuse to take any part in the working out of schemes to better the conditions of life; we regard as fruitless solely theoretical work. We consider destruction to be such an enormous and difficult task that we must devote all our powers to it, and we do not wish to deceive ourselves with the dream that we will have enough strength and knowledge for creation.

Not surprisingly, the recurrent waves of terrorism merely strengthened the tsarist regime's resolve to avoid further political change in what became a vicious circle in 19th-century Russian politics.

By the late 1870s, Alexander II was pulling back from his reform interest, fearing that change was getting out of hand. Censorship of newspapers and political meetings tightened; many dissidents were arrested and sent to Siberia. Alexander II was assassinated by a terrorist bomb in 1881 after a series of botched attempts. His successors, while increasing the effort to industrialize, continued to oppose further political reform. New measures of repression also were directed against minority nationalities, partly to dampen their unrest and partly to gain the support of upper-class conservatives. The Poles and other groups were supervised carefully. Russian language instruction was forced on peoples such as Ukrainians. Persecution of the large Jewish minority was stepped up, resulting in many mass executions—called pogroms—and seizures of property. As a consequence, many Russian Jews emigrated.

By the 1890s, the currents of protest gained new force. Marxist doctrines spread from the Western socialist movement to a segment of the Russian intelligentsia, who became committed to a tightly organized proletarian revolution. One of the most active Marxist leaders was *Vladimir Ilyich Ulyanov,* known as Lenin. Lenin, a man from a bureaucratic family whose brother had been killed by the political police, introduced important innovations in Marxist theory to make it more appropriate for Russia. He argued that because of the spread of international capitalism, a proletariat was developing worldwide in advance of industrialization. Therefore, Russia could have a proletarian revolution without going through a distinct middle-class phase. Lenin also insisted on the importance of disciplined revolutionary cells that could maintain doctrinal purity and effective action even under severe police repression. Lenin's approach animated the group of Russian Marxists known as *Bolsheviks,* or majority party (though, ironically, they were actually a minority in the Russian Marxist movement as a whole). The approach proved ideal for Russian conditions.

Working-class unrest in the cities grew with the new currents among the intelligentsia. Russian workers became far more radical than their Western counterparts. They formed unions and conducted strikes—all illegal—but many of them also had firm political goals in mind. Their radicalism stemmed partly from the absence of legal political outlets. It arose also from rural unrest—for these new workers pulled in peasant grievances against the existing order—and from the severe conditions of early industrialization, with its large factories and frequent foreign ownership. Although many workers were not linked to any particular doctrine, some became interested in Bolshevism, and they were urged on by passionate organizers.

By 1900, the contradictory currents in Russian society may have made revolution inevitable. The forces demanding change were not united, but the importance of mass protest in both countryside and city, as well as the radical intelligentsia, made it difficult to find a compromise. Furthermore, the regime remained resolutely opposed to compromise. Conservative ministers urged a vigorous policy of resistance and repression.

The Revolution of 1905

Military defeat in 1904 and 1905 finally lit this tinderbox. Russia had maintained its expansionist foreign policy through the late 19th century, in part because of tradition and in part because diplomatic success might draw the venom from internal unrest. It also wanted to match the imperialist strides of the Western great powers. A war with the Ottoman Empire in the 1870s brought substantial gains, which were then pushed back at the insistence of France and Britain. Russia also successfully aided the creation in the Balkans of new Slavic nations, such as Serbia and Bulgaria, the "little Slavic brothers" that filled nationalist hearts with pride. Some conservative writers even talked in terms of a pan-Slavic movement that would unite the Slavic people—under Russian leadership, of course. Russia participated vigorously in other Middle Eastern and central Asian areas. Russia and Britain both increased their influence in Persia and Afghanistan, reaching some uneasy truces that divided spheres of activity early in the 20th century. Russia was also active in China. The development of the trans-Siberian railroad encouraged Russia to incorporate some northern portions of Manchuria, violating the 18th-century Amur River agreement. Russia also joined Western powers in obtaining long-term leases to Chinese territory during the 1890s.

These were important gains, but they did not satisfy growing Russian ambitions, and they also brought trouble. Russia risked an overextension because its diplomatic aspirations were not backed by real increases in military power. The problem first came to a head in 1904. Increasingly powerful Japan became worried about further Russian expansion in northern China and efforts to extend influence into Korea. War broke out in 1904. Against all expectations save Japan's, the Japanese won. Russia could not move its fleet quickly to the Pacific, and its military organization proved too cumbersome to oppose the more effective Japanese maneuvers. Japan gained the opportunity to move into Korea as the balance of power in the Far East began to shift.

Unexpected defeat in war unleashed massive protests on the home front in the Russian Revolution of 1905. Urban workers mounted well-organized general strikes that were designed above all for political gains. Peasants led a series of insurrections, and liberal groups also agitated. After trying brutal police repression, which only infuriated the urban crowds, the tsarist regime had to change course. It wooed liberals by creating a national parliament, the *duma*. The minister *Stolypin* introduced an important series of reforms for the peasantry. Peasants gained greater freedom from redemption payments and village controls. They could buy and sell land more freely. The goal was to create a stratified, market-oriented peasantry in which successful farmers would move away from the peasant masses, becoming rural capitalists. Indeed, peasant unrest did die down, and a minority of aggressive entrepreneurs, called *kulaks*, began to increase agricultural production and buy additional land. Yet the reform package quickly came unglued. Not only were a few new workers' rights withdrawn, triggering a new series of strikes and underground activities, but the duma was progressively stripped of power. Nicholas II, a weak man who was badly advised, could not surrender the tradition of autocratic rule, and the duma became a hollow institution, satisfying no one. Police repression also resumed, creating new opponents to the regime.

Pressed in the diplomatic arena by the Japanese advance yet eager to counter internal pressures with some foreign policy success, the Russian government turned once again to the Ottoman Empire and the Balkans. Various strategies to acquire new rights of access to the Mediterranean and to back Slavic allies in the Balkans yielded no concrete results, but they did stir the pot in this vulnerable area and helped lead to World War I. And this war, in which Russia participated to maintain its diplomatic standing and live up to the billing of Slavic protector, led to one of the great revolutions of modern times.

Russia and Eastern Europe

A number of Russian patterns were paralleled in smaller east European states such as Hungary (joined to Austria but autonomous after 1866), Romania, Serbia, Bulgaria, and Greece. These were new nations—unlike Russia—and emerging after long Ottoman dominance, they had no access to the diplomatic influence of their giant neighbor. Most of the new nations established parliaments, in imitation of Western forms, but carefully restricted voting rights and parliamentary powers. Kings—some of them new, as the Balkan nations had set up monarchies after gaining independence from the Ottoman Empire—ruled without many limits on their power. Most east European nations abolished serfdom either in 1848 or soon after Russia's move, but landlord power remained more extensive than in Russia, and peasant unrest followed. Most of the smaller east European nations industrialized much less extensively than Russia, and as agricultural exporters they remained far more dependent on Western markets.

Amid all the problems, eastern Europe enjoyed a period of glittering cultural productivity in the late 19th century, with Russia in the lead. Development of the romantic tradition and other Western styles continued. National dictionaries and histories, along with the collection of folk tales and music, helped the smaller Slavic nations gain a sense of their heritage. The Russian novel enjoyed a period of unprecedented brilliance. Westernizers such as Turgenev wrote realistic novels that promoted what they saw as modern values, whereas writers such as Tolstoy and Dostoevsky tried to portray a special Russian spirit. Russian music moved from the romanticism of Tchaikovsky to more innovative, atonal styles of the early 20th century. Polish and Hungarian composers such as Chopin and Liszt also made an important mark. Russian painters began participating in modern art currents, producing important abstract work. Finally, scientific research advanced at levels of fundamental importance. A Czech scientist, Gregor Mendel, furthered the understanding of genetics, and a Russian physiologist, Ivan Pavlov, experimenting on conditioned reflexes, explained unconscious responses in human beings. Eastern Europe thus participated more fully than ever before in a cultural world it shared with the West.

JAPAN: TRANSFORMATION WITHOUT REVOLUTION

Like Russia, Japan faced new pressure from the West during the 1850s, although this pressure took the form of a demand for more open trade rather than outright military conflict. Japan's response was more direct than Russia's and more immediately successful. Despite Japan's long history of isolation, its society was better adapted than Russia's to the challenge of industrial change. Market forms were more extensive, reaching into peasant agriculture, and literacy levels were higher. Nevertheless, Japan had to rework many of its institutions during the final decades of the 19th century, and the process produced significant strain.

The Final Decades of the Shogunate

On the surface, Japan experienced little change during the first half of the 19th century, and certainly this was a quiet time compared with the earlier establishment of the Tokugawa shogunate (see Chapter 28) or the transformation introduced after the 1850s.

During the first half of the 19th century, the shogunate continued to combine a central bureaucracy with semifeudal alliances between the regional daimyos and the samurai. The government repeatedly ran into financial problems. Its taxes were based on agriculture, despite the growing commercialization of the Japanese economy; this was a severe constraint. At the same time, maintaining the feudal shell was costly. The government paid stipends to the samurai in return for their loyalty. A long budget reform spurt late in the 18th century built a successful momentum for a time, but a shorter effort between 1841 and 1843 was notably unsuccessful. This weakened the shogunate by the 1850s and hampered its response to the crisis induced by Western pressure.

Japanese intellectual life and culture also developed under the Tokugawa regime. Neo-Confucianism continued to gain among the ruling elite at the expense of Buddhism. Japan gradually became more secular, particularly among the upper classes. This was an important precondition for the nation's response to the Western challenge in that it precluded a strong religious-based resistance to change. Various Confucian schools actively debated into the mid-19th century, keeping Japanese intellectual life fairly creative. Schools and academies expanded, reaching well below the upper class through commoner schools, or *terakoya,* which taught reading, writing, and the rudiments of Confucianism to ordinary people. By 1859, more than 40 percent of all men and over 15 percent of all women were literate—a far higher percentage than anywhere else in the world outside the West, including Russia, and on a par with some of the fringe areas of the West (including the American South).

Although Confucianism remained the dominant ideology, there were important rivals. Tensions between traditionalists and reformist intellectuals were emerging, as in Russia in the same decades. A national studies group praised Japanese traditions, including the office of emperor and the Shinto religion. One national studies writer expressed a typical sentiment late in the 18th century: "The 'special dispensation of our Imperial Land' means that ours is the native land of the Heaven-Shining Goddess who casts her light over all countries in the four seas. Thus our country is the source and fountainhead of all other countries, and in all matters it excels all the others." The influence of the national studies school grew somewhat in the early 19th century, and it would help inspire ultranationalist sentiment at the end of the century and beyond.

A second minority group consisted of what the Japanese called *Dutch Studies.* Although major Western works had been banned when the policy of isolation was adopted, a group of Japanese translators kept alive the knowledge of Dutch to deal with the traders at Nagasaki. The ban on Western books was ended in 1720, and thereafter a group of Japanese scholars interested in "Dutch medicine" created a new interest in Western scientific advance, based on the realization that Western anatomy texts were superior to those of the Chinese. In 1850, there were schools of Dutch studies in all major cities, and their students urged freer exchange with the West and a rejection of Chinese medicine and culture. "Our general opinion was that we should rid our country of the influences of the Chinese altogether. Whenever we met a young student of Chinese literature, we simply felt sorry for him."

Just as Japanese culture showed an important capacity for lively debate and fruitful internal tension, so the Japanese economy continued to develop into the 19th century. Commerce expanded as big merchant companies established monopoly privileges in many centers. Manufacturing gained ground in the countryside in such consumer goods industries as soy sauce and silks, and much of this was organized by city merchants. Some of these developments were comparable to slightly earlier changes in the West and have given rise to arguments that economically Japan had a running start on industrialization once the Western challenge revealed the necessity of further economic change.

By the 1850s, however, economic growth had slowed—a situation that has prompted some scholars to stress Japan's backwardness compared with the West. Technological limitations constrained agricultural expansion and population increase. At the same time, rural riots increased in many regions from the late 18th century onward. They were not overtly political but rather, like many rural protests, aimed at wealthy peasants, merchants, and landlord controls. Although the authorities put down this unrest with little difficulty, the protests contributed to a willingness to consider change when they were joined by challenge from the outside.

The Challenge to Isolation

Some Japanese had become increasingly worried about potential outside threats. In 1791, a book was issued advocating a strong navy. Fears about the West's growing power and particularly Russia's Asian expansion fed these concerns in later decades.

Fear became reality in 1853 when American commodore *Matthew Perry* arrived with a squadron in Edo Bay near Tokyo and used threats of bombardment to insist that Americans be allowed to trade. The United States, increasingly an active part of the West's core economy, thus launched for Japan the same kind of pressure the Opium War had created for China: pressure from the heightened military superiority of the West and its insistence on opening markets for its burgeoning economy. In 1854, Perry returned and won the right to station an American consul in Japan; in 1856, through a formal treaty, two ports were opened to commerce. Britain, Russia, and Holland quickly won similar rights. As in China, this meant that Westerners living in Japan would be governed by their own representatives, not by Japanese law.

The bureaucrats of the shogunate saw no alternative but to open up Japan, given the superiority of Western navies. And of course, there were Japanese who had grown impatient with strict isolation; their numbers swelled as the Dutch schools began to expand. On the other hand, the daimyos, intensely conservative, were opposed to the new concessions, and their opposition forced the shogun to appeal to the emperor for support. Soon, samurai opponents of the bureaucracy were also appealing to the emperor, who began to emerge from his centuries-long confinement as a largely religious and ceremonial figure. Whereas most daimyos defended the status quo, the samurai were more divided. Some saw opportunity in change, including the possibility of unseating the shogunate. The fact was that the complex shogunate system had depended on the isolation policy; it could not survive the stresses of foreign influence and inter-

nal reactions. The result was not immediate collapse; indeed, into the late 1850s, Japanese life seemed to go on much as before.

In the 1860s, political crisis came into the open. The crisis was spiced by samurai attacks on foreigners, including one murder of a British official, matched by Western naval bombardments of feudal forts. Civil war broke out in 1866 as the samurai eagerly armed themselves with American Civil War surplus weapons, causing Japan's aristocracy to come to terms with the advantages of Western armaments. When the samurai defeated a shogunate force, many Japanese were finally shocked out of their traditional reliance on their own superiority. One author argued that the nation, compared with the West with its technology, science, and humane laws, was only half civilized.

This multifaceted crisis came to an end in 1868 when the victorious reform group proclaimed a new emperor named Mutsuhito but commonly called "Meiji," or "Enlightened One." In his name, key samurai leaders managed to put down the troops of the shogunate. The crisis period had been shocking enough to allow further changes in Japan's basic political structure—changes that went much deeper at the political level than those introduced by Russia from 1861 onward.

iπ DEP†H
The Separate Paths of Japan and China

Japan's ability to change in response to new Western pressure contrasted strikingly with the sluggishness of Chinese reactions into the 20th century. The contrast draws particular attention because China and Japan had been part of the same civilization orbit for so long, which means that some of the assets Japan possessed in dealing with change were present in China as well. Indeed, Japan turned out to benefit, by the mid-19th century, from having become more like China in key respects during the Tokugawa period. The link between Chinese and Japanese traditions should not be exaggerated, of course, and earlier differences help explain the divergence that opened so clearly in the late 19th century. The east Asian world now split apart, with Japan seizing eagerly on Chinese weakness to mount a series of attacks from the 1890s to 1945, which only made China's troubles worse.

Japan and China had both chosen isolation from larger world currents from about 1600 until the West forced new openings between 1830 and 1860. Japan's isolation was the more complete. Both countries lagged behind the West because of their self-containment, which was why Western industrialization caught them unprepared. China's power and wealth roused Western greed and interference first, which gave Japan some leeway.

However, China surpassed Japan in some areas that should have aided it in reacting to the Western challenge. Its leadership, devoted to Confucianism, was more thoroughly secular and bureaucratic in outlook. There was no need to brush aside otherworldly commitments or feudal distractions to deal with the West's material and organizational power. Government centralization, still an issue in Japan, had a long history in China. With a rich tradition of technological innovation and scientific discovery in its past as well, China might have appeared to be a natural to lead the Asian world in responding to the West.

However, that role fell to Japan. Several aspects of Japanese tradition gave it a flexibility that China lacked. It already knew the benefits of imitation, which China, save for its period of attraction to Buddhism, had never acknowledged. Japan's slower government growth had allowed a stronger, more autonomous merchant tradition even as both societies became more commercial in the 17th and early 18th centuries. Feudal traditions, though declining under the Tokugawa shogunate, also limited the heavy hand of government controls while stimulating some sense of competitiveness, as in the West. In contrast, China's government probably tried to control too much by the 18th century and quashed initiative in the process.

China was also hampered by rapid population growth from the 17th century onward. This population pressure consumed great energy, leaving scant capital for other economic initiatives. Japan's population stability into the 19th century pressed resources less severely. Japan's island status made the nation more sensitive to Western naval pressures.

Finally, China and Japan were on somewhat different paths when the Western challenge intruded in the mid-19th century. China was suffering one of its recurrent dynastic declines. Government became less efficient, intellectual life stagnated, and popular unrest surged. A cycle of renewal might have followed, with a new dynasty seizing more vigorous reins. But Western interference disrupted this process, complicating reform and creating various new discontents that ultimately overturned the imperial office.

In contrast, Japan maintained political and economic vigor into the 19th century. Whereas by the late 19th century China needed Western guidance simply to handle such bureaucratic affairs as tariff collection and repression of peasant rebellion, Japan suffered no such breakdown of authority, using foreign advisors far more selectively.

Once a different pattern of response was established, every decade increased the gap. Western exploitation of Chinese assets and dilution of government power made conditions more chaotic, while Japanese strength grew steadily after a very brief period of uncertainty. By the 20th century, the two nations were enemies—with Japan, for the first time, the stronger—and seemed to be in different orbits. Japan enjoyed increasing industrial success and had a conservative state that would yield after World War II to a more fully parliamentary form. China, after decades of revolution, finally won its 20th-century political solution; communism.

Yet today, at the onset of the 21st century, it is unclear whether east Asia was split as permanently as 19th- and early 20th-century developments had suggested. Japan's industrial lead remains, but China's economy is stirring. Common cultural habits of group cooperation and decision making remind us that beneath different political systems, a fruitful shared heritage continues to operate. The heritage is quite different from that of the West but fully adaptable to the demands of economic change. And so Westerners begin to wonder whether a Pacific century is about to dawn.

Questions: What civilization features had Japan and China shared before the 19th century? In what ways were Japanese political institutions more adaptable than Chinese institutions? Why was Russia also able to change earlier and more fundamentally than 19th-century China?

Industrial and Political Change in the Meiji State

The new Meiji government promptly set about abolishing feudalism, replacing the daimyos in 1871 with a system of nationally appointed prefects (district administrators carefully chosen from different regions; the perfect system was copied from French practice). Political power was effectively centralized, and from this base the Meiji rulers—the emperor and his close advisors, drawn from loyal segments of the aristocracy—began to expand the power of the state to effect economic and social change.

Quickly, the Japanese government sent samurai officials abroad, to western Europe and the United States, to study economic and political institutions and technology. These samurai, deeply impressed by what they saw, pulled back from their earlier antiforeign position and gained increasing voice over other officials in the government. Their basic goal was Japan's domestic development, accompanied by a careful diplomatic policy that would avoid antagonizing the West.

Fundamental improvements in government finance soon followed. Between 1873 and 1876, the Meiji ministers introduced a real social revolution. They abolished the samurai class and the stipends this group had received. The tax on agriculture was converted to a wider tax, payable in money. The samurai were compensated by government-backed bonds, but these decreased in value, and most samurai became poor. This development sparked renewed conflict, and a final samurai uprising occurred in 1877. However, the government had introduced an army based on national conscription, and by 1878 the nation was militarily secure. Individual samurai found new opportunities in political and business areas as they adapted to change. One former samurai, Iwasoki Yataro (1834–1885; Figure 33.4), who started his career buying weapons for a feudal lord, set up the Mitsubishi company after 1868, winning government contracts for railroad and steamship lines designed to compete with British companies in the region. Despite his overbearing personality, Iwasaki built a loyal management group, including other former samurai, and by his death had a stake in shipbuilding, mining, and banking as well as transportation. The continued existence of the samurai, reflecting Japan's lack of outright revolution, would yield diverse results in later Japanese history.

Figure 33.4 *Iwasaki Yataro.*

The process of political reconstruction crested in the 1880s. Many former samurai organized political parties. Meiji leaders traveled abroad to discover modern political forms. In 1884 they created a new conservative nobility, stocked by former nobles and Meiji leaders, that would operate a British-style House of Peers. Next, the bureaucracy was reorganized, insulated from political pressures, and opened to talent on the basis of civil service examinations. The bureaucracy began to expand rapidly; it grew from 29,000 officials in 1890 to 72,000 in 1908. Finally, the constitution, issued in 1889, ensured major prerogatives for the emperor along with limited powers for the lower house of the *Diet,* as the new parliament was called. Here, Germany provided the model, for the emperor commanded the military directly (served by a German-style general staff) and also directly named his ministers. Both the institution and its members' clothing were Western, as the Visualizing the Past segment shows. The Diet could pass laws, upon agreement of both houses, and could approve budgets, but failure to pass a budget would simply reinstate the budget of the previous year. Parliament could thus advise government, but it could not control it. Finally, the conservative tone of this parliamentary experiment was confirmed by high property qualifications set for voting rights. Only about 5 percent of Japanese men had enough wealth to be allowed to vote for representatives to the lower house.

Visualizing THE PAST

Two Faces of Western Influence

These pictures show an 1850s cartoon portraying American Commodore Matthew Perry as a greedy warlord and the first meeting of the Japanese Parliament in 1890.

Questions: What was the cartoon meant to convey? What kinds of attitudes toward the West does it represent? What does the picture of parliament convey about attitudes toward the West? What was the model for the design of the meeting room? What do the two pictures suggest about uses of costume in a time of rapid change?

Japan's political structure thus came to involve centralized imperial rule, wielded by a handful of Meiji advisors, combined with limited representative institutions copied from the West. This combination gave great power to a group of wealthy businesspeople and former nobles who influenced the emperor and also pulled strings within the parliament. Political parties arose, but a coherent system overrode their divisions into the 20th century. Japan thus followed its new policy of imitating the West, but it retained its own identity. The Japanese political solution compared interestingly to Russian institutions after Alexander II's reforms: Both states were centralized and authoritarian, but Japan had incorporated business leaders into its governing structure, whereas Russia defended a more traditional social elite.

Japan's Industrial Revolution

Political decisions were essential after the crisis of the 1860s, but they were soon matched by other initiatives. The new army, based on the universal conscription of young men, was further improved by formal officer training and by upgrading armaments according to Western standards. With the aid of Western advisors, a modern navy was established.

Attention also focused on creating the conditions necessary for industrialization. New government banks funded growing trade and provided capital for industry. State-built railroads spread across the country, and the islands were connected by rapid steamers. New methods raised agricultural output to feed the people of the growing cities.

The new economic structure depended on the destruction of many older restrictions. Guilds and internal road tariffs were abolished to create a national market. Land reform created clear individual ownership for many farmers, which helped motivate expansion of production and the introduction of new fertilizers and equipment.

Government initiative dominated manufacturing not only in the creation of transportation networks but also in state operation of mines, shipyards, and metallurgical plants. Scarce capital and the unfamiliarity of new technology seemed to compel state direction, as occurred in Russia at the same time. Government control also helped check the many foreign advisors needed by early Japanese industry; here, Japan maintained closer supervision than its Russian neighbor. Japan established the Ministry of Industry in 1870, and it quickly became one of the key government agencies, setting overall economic policy as well as operating specific sectors. By the 1880s, model shipyards, arsenals, and factories provided experience in new technology and disciplined work systems for many Japanese. Finally, by expanding technical training and education, setting up banks and post offices, and regularizing commercial laws, the government provided a structure within which Japan could develop on many fronts. Measures in this area largely copied established practices in the West, but with adapta-tion suitable for Japanese conditions; thus, well before any European university, Tokyo Imperial University had a faculty of agriculture.

Private enterprise quickly played a role in Japan's growing economy, particularly in the vital textile sector. Some businesspeople came from older merchant families, although some of the great houses had been ruined with the financial destruction of the samurai class. There were also newcomers, some rising from peasant ranks. Shuibuzawa Eiichi, for example, born a peasant, became a merchant and then an official of the Finance Ministry. He turned to banking in 1873, using other people's money to set up cotton-spinning mills and other textile operations. By the 1890s huge new industrial combines, later known as *zaibatsu,* were being formed as a result of accumulations of capital and far-flung merchant and industrial operations.

By 1900, the Japanese economy was fully launched in an industrial revolution. It rested on a political and social structure different from that of Russia—one that had in most respects changed more profoundly. Japan's success in organizing industrialization, including its careful management of foreign advice and models, proved to be one of the great developments of later 19th-century history.

It is important to keep these early phases of Japanese industrialization in perspective. Pre-World War I Japan was far from the West's equal. It depended on imports of Western equipment and raw materials such as coal; for industrial purposes, Japan was a resource-poor nation. Although economic growth and careful government policy allowed Japan to avoid Western domination, Japan was newly dependent on world economic conditions and was often at a disadvantage. It needed exports to pay for machine and resource imports, and these in turn took hordes of low-paid workers. Silk production grew rapidly, the bulk of it destined for Western markets. Much of this production was based on the labor of poorly paid women who worked at home or in sweatshops, not in mechanized factories. Some of these women were sold into service by farm families. Efforts at labor organization or other means of protest were met by vigorous repression.

Social and Cultural Effects of Industrialization

The Industrial Revolution and the wider extensions of manufacturing and commercial agriculture, along with political change, had significant ramifications within Japanese culture and society. Japanese society was disrupted by massive population growth. Better nutrition and new medical provisions reduced death rates, and the upheaval of the rural masses cut into traditional restraints on births. The result was steady population growth that strained Japanese resources and stability, although it also ensured a constant supply of low-cost labor. This was one of the causes of Japan's class tensions.

The Japanese government introduced a universal education system, providing primary schools for all. This education stressed science and the importance of technical subjects along with political loyalty to the nation and emperor. Elite students at the university level also took courses that emphasized science, and many Japanese students went abroad to study technical subjects in other countries.

Education also revealed Japanese insistence on distinctive values. After a heady reform period in the 1870s, when hundreds of Western teachers were imported and a Rutgers University professor brought in for high-level advice about the whole system, the emperor and conservative advisors stepped back after 1879. Innovation and individualism had gone too far: A traditional moral education was essential, along with new skills, that would stress "loyalty to the Imperial House, love of country, filial piety toward parents, respect for superiors, faith in friends, charity toward inferiors and respect for oneself." The use of foreign books on morality was prohibited, and intense government inspection of textbooks was intended to promote social order.

Many Japanese copied Western fashions as part of the effort to become modern. Western-style haircuts replaced the samurai shaved head with a top-knot—another example of the Westernization of hair in world history. Western standards of hygiene spread, and the Japanese became enthusiastic toothbrushers and consumers of patent medicines. Japan also adopted the Western calendar and the metric system. Few Japanese converted to Christianity, however, and despite Western popular cultural fads, the Japanese managed to preserve an emphasis on their own values. What the Japanese wanted and got from the West involved practical techniques; they planned to infuse them with a distinctively Japanese spirit. As an early Japanese visitor to the American White House wrote in a self-satisfied poem that captured the national mood,

We suffered the barbarians to look upon

The glory of our Eastern Empire of Japan.

Western-oriented enthusiasms were not meant to destroy a distinctive Japanese spirit.

Japanese family life retained many traditional emphases. The birth rate dropped as rapid population growth forced increasing numbers of people off the land. Meanwhile, the rise of factory industry, separating work from home, made children's labor less useful. This trend, developed earlier in the West, seems inseparable from successful industrialization. There were new signs of family instability as well; the divorce rate exploded until legal changes made procedures more difficult. On the more traditional side, the Japanese were eager to maintain the inferiority of women in the home. The position of Western women offended them. Japanese government visitors to the United States were appalled by what they saw as the bossy ways of women: "The way women are treated here is like the way parents are respected in our country." Standards of Japanese courtesy also contrasted with the more open and boisterous behavior of Westerners, particularly Americans. "Obscenity is inherent in the customs of this country," noted another samurai visitor to the United States. Certain Japanese religious values were also preserved. Buddhism lost some ground, although it remained important, but Shintoism, which appealed to the new nationalist concern with Japan's distinctive mission and the religious functions of the emperor, won new interest.

Economic change, and the tensions as well as the power it generated, also produced a shift in Japanese foreign policy. With only one previous exception, the abortive late 16th-century invasion of Korea, the Japanese had never before been interested in territorial expansion, but by the 1890s they joined the ranks of imperialist powers. This shift was partly an imitation of Western models. Imperialism also relieved some strains within Japanese society, giving displaced samurai the chance to exercise their military talents elsewhere. Even more than Western countries, which used similar arguments for imperialism, the Japanese economy also needed access to markets and raw materials. Because Japan was poor in many basic materials, including coal and oil for energy, the pressure for expansion was particularly great.

Japan's quick victory over China in the *Sino-Japanese War* for influence in Korea (1894–1895) was a first step toward expansion (Map 33.2). Japan convincingly demonstrated its new superiority over all other Asian powers. Humiliated by Western insistence that it abandon the Liaotung peninsula it had just taken from China, the Japanese planned a war with Russia as a means of striking out against the nearest European state. A 1902 alliance with Britain was an important sign of Japan's arrival as an equal nation in the Western-dominated world diplomatic system. The Japanese were also eager to dent Russia's growing strength in east Asia after the development of the trans-Siberian railroad. Disputes over Russian influence in Manchuria and Japanese influence in Korea led to the Russo-Japanese War in 1904, which Japan won handily because of its superior navy. Japan annexed Korea in 1910, entering the ranks of imperialist powers.

The Strain of Modernization

Japanese achievement had its costs, including poor living standards in the crowded cities. Many Japanese conservatives resented the passion other Japanese displayed for Western fashions. Disputes between generations, with the old clinging to traditional standards and the young more interested in Western styles, were very troubling in a society that stressed the importance of parental authority.

Some tension entered political life. Political parties in Japan's parliament clashed with the emperor's ministers over rights to determine policy. The government often had to dissolve the Diet and call for new elections, seeking a more workable parliamentary majority. Political assassinations and attempted assassinations reflected grievances, including direct action impulses in the samurai tradition.

Another kind of friction emerged in intellectual life. Many Japanese scholars copied Western philosophies and literary styles, and there was enough adaptation to prevent the emergence of a full Russian-style intelligentsia. Other intellectuals expressed a deep pessimism about the loss of identity in a changing world. The underlying theme was confusion about a Japan that was no longer traditional, but not Western either. What *was* it? Thus, some writers spoke of Japan's heading for a "nervous collapse from which we will not be able to recover." Others dealt with more personal conflicts such as those in the following poem:

> Do not be loved by others; do not accept their charity, do not promise anything…. Always wear a mask. Always be ready for a fight—be able to hit the next man on the head at any time. Don't forget that when you make friends with someone you are sooner or later certain to break with him.

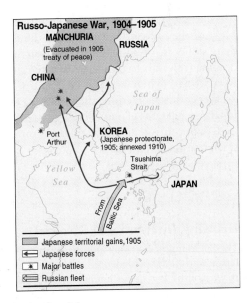

Map 33.2 *Japanese Colonial Expansion to 1914. What were the principal gains? Why did Japan feel frustrated by the ultimate results of its victories?*

As an antidote to social and cultural insecurity, Japanese leaders urged national loyalty and devotion to the emperor, and with some success. The official message promoted Japanese virtues of obedience and harmony that the West lacked. School texts thus stressed,

> Our country takes as its base the family system: the nation is but a single family, the imperial family is our main house. We the people worship the unbroken imperial line with the same feeling of respect and love that a child feels toward his parents…. The union of loyalty and filial piety is truly the special character of our national polity.

Japanese nationalism built on traditions of superiority, cohesion, and deference to rulers, as well as on the new tensions generated by rapid change. It became a deep force, probably in Japan more than elsewhere, that played a unique role in justifying sacrifice and struggle in a national mission to preserve independence and dignity in a hostile world. Nationalism, along with firm police repression of dissent and the sweeping changes of the early Meiji years, certainly helps explain why Japan avoided the revolutionary pressure that hit Russia, China, and other countries after 1900.

Yet Japan's very success reminds us of how unusual it was. No other society outside the Western world was yet able to match its achievements. Russia, responding to Western example in its own way, continued its growth as a world power, but amid such social disarray that further upheaval was inevitable. Most of the rest of the world faced the more immediate concern of adjusting to or resisting Western dominance; industrialization was a remote prospect. Even today, when many societies are striving for greater industrialization, the ability to emulate the Japanese pattern of rapid change seems very limited—concentrated, interestingly enough, in other small east Asian nations.

Conclusion

Growing International Rivalries

The beginnings of serious industrialization in Russia and Japan, and the unprecedented entry of Japan into world affairs, contributed important new ingredients to the world diplomatic picture by the early 20th century. These developments, along with the rise of the United States, added

to the growing sense of competition between the established Western powers. Japan's surge promoted a fear in the West of a new *yellow peril* that should be opposed through greater imperialist efforts. Outright colonial acquisitions by the new powers added directly to the competitive atmosphere, particularly in the Far East. Japan was not yet a major world player, but it was beginning to make its muscle felt.

Further Readings

A. Gerschenkron, *Economic Backwardness in Historical Perspective: A Book of Essays* (1962) helps define the conditions of latecomer industrialization. On Russia, see Geoffrey Hosking, *Russia: People and Empire, 1532–1917* (1997). Russian reforms and economic change are discussed in W. Blackwell, *The Industrialization of Russia*, 2nd ed. (1982), and Jerome Blum, *Lord and Peasant in Russia from the Ninth to the Nineteenth Century* (1961). On social and cultural developments, see Victoria Bonnell, ed., *The Russian Worker: Life and Labor Under the Tsarist Regime* (1983); Barbara Engel, *Mothers and Daughters: Women of the Intelligentsia in Nineteenth Century Russia* (1983); and Jeffrey Brooks, *When Russia Learned to Read: Literacy and Popular Culture* (1987). On another vital area of eastern Europe, see A. Stavrianos, *The Balkans, 1815–1914* (1963). Japan in the 19th century is viewed from a modernization perspective in R. Dore, ed., *Aspects of Social Change in Modern Japan* (1967). See also W. W. Lockwood, *The Economic Development of Japan: Growth and Structural Change 1868–1938* (1954); J. C. Abegglen, *The Japanese Factory: Aspects of Its Social Organization*, rev. ed. (1985); Hugh Patrick, ed., *Japanese Industrialization and Its Social Consequences* (1973); Andrew Gordon, *The Evolution of Labor Relations in Japan* (1985); R. H. Myers and M. R. Beattie, eds., *The Japanese Colonial Empire 1895–1945* (1984); E. O. Reischauer, *Japan, the Story of a Nation* (1981); and Peter N. Stearns, *Schools and Students in Industrial Society: Japan and the West* (1997).

On the Web

The glories of Czarist Russia are revealed by a virtual tour of the Alexander Palace at http://www.alexanderplace.org/palace. However, the riches of the Czars could not conceal the dismal world of the Russian peasantry whose lot was little improved by Russian economic modernization.

This world and how it was illuminated by the works of the Russian writer Nikolai Gogal is addressed at http://

russianculture.miningco.com/culture/russianculture/library/weekly/aa081098.htm.

Russian liberalism reached its high-water mark in the abolition of serfdom, an institution whose rise and demise is described at http://www.yale.edu/lawweb/avalon/econ/koval6.htm.

But reaction soon set in. A copy of the Emancipation Manifesto ending serfdom, an essay on post-emancipation village life, and exhibits on the training of Russian aristocrats and the Russian imperial style can be found at http://russianculture.about.com/culture/russianculture/msub23.htm.

The failure of the Revolution of 1905 (http://web.mit.edu/napoli/www/guided.html) to achieve any significant degree of political and social reform paved the way for those favoring more radical change, such as the Bolsheviks, led by Vladimir Ilyich Ulanov, whose life is examined at http://www.soften.ktu.lt/~kaleck/Lenin/.

The Meiji Restoration's industrial policy, including its first industrial fair and Japan's wars with China and Russia is discussed at http://www.Meiji.com/index.html.

A key to understanding the process of modernization in Japan is the Constitution of the Empire of Japan (1889) which is reproduced at http://history.hanover.edu/texts/1889con.html. For further insight into this process, this document can be compared with the Constitution of Japan (1947) at http://history.hanover.edu/texts/1947con/html.

Life in Meji Japan can be glimpsed through an exhibition of contemporary woodblock art at http://www.students.haverford.edu/east/meiji/exhibithome.html.

PART 6
The 20th Century in World History

Exam #3 = Final Exam material. Start here →

Chapters

INTRODUCTION

Describing the 20th century is one of the most challenging tasks facing a historian. We are so close to the patterns involved that objectivity is difficult. Previous periods, although they generate continued debate, at least constitute stories whose endings are known. We can easily see that the Industrial Revolution ushered in profound changes for the West and some other parts of the world by 1900. We can even more easily see that during the 19th century, Western nations gained unprecedented power in the world. In other words, it is not difficult to define the 19th century in terms of its contrasts with the early modern period, to see what its new ingredients were and how many of them turned out.

We are still engaged in the 20th century and its immediate aftermath, which makes judgment far more tentative. This is not a new problem. In the 19th century, for example, many people were not aware of the Industrial Revolution, even when they were involved in it. They were much more likely to point to some recent political event or cultural current in defining their era. It is hard to get perspective on one's own time. How significant in world history was the surge of Nazism during the 1930s? Here was a fearsome new political movement that at the time seemed to signify permanent changes in political trends and the whole character of European society. Almost any historian writing in the 1950s, at least in the West, would have seen the rise of Nazism as a major turning point. Yet from the vantage point of the 1990s Nazism seems one of many developments that mark a key subperiod rather than a fundamental feature of the whole century. Many Americans in the 1990s would rate the rise of Japan to the status of industrial superpower far more important in creating a novel international context for our century than Nazism was. Nazism's decisive focus has diluted with the passage of time. Even the cold war now seems more an episode than a decisive stage in world history.

Given the problems of perspective, two contradictory impulses can affect historians' efforts to place their century as part of a larger scheme of periodization. One impulse is to emphasize the continuities, lest we be misled into exaggerating the novelty of our time and downplay the importance of the past. From the end of the 1980s well into the 1990s, nationalist sentiment revived in the Balkans and several other ethnic regions. Bulgaria tried to eliminate a Turkish minority by expelling them or making them adopt Bulgarian names; Christians fought with Muslims in the former Yugoslavia. Despite more than 50 years of war, revolution, and profound political change in this region, passions dating from before the 19th century remained lively. Which is more important: all these new developments or the fact that in the minds of many, basic loyalties had changed so little?

At the other extreme, many other observers reflect a modern culture that emphasizes rapid and fundamental change. They write of the 20th century as a third revolution, comparable only to the Neolithic and Industrial Revolutions of the past in setting up basic new conditions for human existence. Or they talk of unprecedented environmental change that is about to do us in.

The middle path may prove the most valid, urging a balance between continuity and change in judging our own age.

The key question is whether the 20th century opened up a new basic period in world history or whether it simply modified the fundamental patterns of the 19th century. The answer seems clear: The 20th century has provided a rare break in world history, comparable in scope to the 15th century or the 5th century. The contemporary period in world history was just taking shape even at the end of the 1990s, so it is harder to define than earlier watersheds. We cannot be sure of some ultimate directions.

Previous periods in world history have met three criteria: They involved basic geographic rebalancing among major civilization areas, they measurably increased the intensity and extent of contact among civilizations, and partly as a result of new contacts, they demonstrated some new and roughly parallel patterns among many of the major civilizations. The 20th century meets these criteria.

THE REPOSITIONING OF THE WEST

The decline of the West is a key feature of the new balance between civilizations in the 20th century. This resulted in part from the two highly destructive wars fought between 1914 and 1945. Both wars were global in causes, conduct, and results, but bitter European rivalries played a key role, and the weakening of western Europe's world position was a key consequence.

The West's global position changed in several respects. Western population (including that of the United States) decreased rapidly as a percentage of the world total. Western birth control practices and rapid population growth rates elsewhere combined to produce this result. The West's population stagnation opened Europe and the United States to rapid immigration from other societies.

1910–1920 Mexican Revolution

1912 African National Congress party formed in South Africa

1912 Fall of Qing dynasty in CHina; beginning of Chinese revolution

1914–1918 World War I

1916 Arab revolts against Ottomans

1917 United States' entry to World War I

1917 Russian Revolution

1917 Balfour Declaration promises Jews a homeland in Palestine

1919 Versailles peace settlement; League of Nations

1919 Revolt in Egypt; first Pan-African Nationalist Congress

1920 Treaty of Sèvres reorganizes Middle East

1921 Foundation of Chinese Communist party

1927–1928 Stalin heads Soviet Union; five-year plans and collectivization

1929–1933 Height of Great Depression

1930–1945 Vargas regime in Brazil

1931 Japan invades Manchuria

1931–1947 Gandhi-led resistance in India

1933 Nazis rise to power in Germany

1933–1939 New Deal in United States

1934–1940 Cárdenas reform period in Mexico

1935 German rearmament; Italy conquers Ethiopia

1937 Army officers in power in Japan; invasion of China

1939–1945 World War II

1939 Nazi–Soviet Pact

1941 United States enters war

1942–1945 Holocaust

1945 Formation of United Nations

1945 Atomic bomb

1945 Communists proclaim Vietnam independence

1945–1948 Soviet takeover of Eastern Europe

1946 Philippines proclaim independence

1946–1947 Decolonization in Asia, Africa, and Oceania

1947 Peronism in Argentina

1947 India and Pakistan gain independence

1947–1975 Cold war; Marshall Plan

1948 Division of Korea

1948 Israel–Palestine partition; first Arab–Israeli war

1949 Formation of NATO

1949 Communist victory in China

1950–1953 Korean War

1951 End U.S. occupation in China

1955 Warsaw Pact

1955 Bandung conference; nonaligned movement

1956 Partial end of Stalinism

1957 European Economic Community (Common Market)

1957 Ghana becomes first independent African Nation

1959 Cuban Revolution

More decisive was the decline and then the virtual end of the great Western empires, a process clearly under way by the 1920s and then culminating after 1945. The West, which dominated most of the world directly or indirectly by 1920, ruled little beyond its own borders by 1980. Monopoly over the most advanced weapon systems, a key Western advantage since the 16th century, also ended, although many Western nations, led after 1945 by the United States, retained a major share in leadership. Japan and then the Soviet Union joined the West as world military giants, while other societies, though not quite as advanced, gained ground. Furthermore, alternative forms of warfare, particularly the guerrilla tactics used in colonial struggles, allowed many regions to counter Western military supremacy. From a Western standpoint, the world became more complicated after centuries of steadily advancing edge in military power.

In 1991, the United States and various allies decisively defeated Iraq in the Persian Gulf War, using a variety of high-technology weapons. Western-dominated military advantages meant that only a few hundred allied soldiers died in combat, compared with perhaps 100,000 Iraqis. But even this war showed how the 20th century had become more complex than the easy days of Western imperialism. It took months of military buildup, a force of more than half a million men and women, and expenditures of more than $50 billion to defeat a medium-sized Arab state.

The West also lost its unchallenged preeminence as a world trader and manufacturer. Of course, much of the world economic system established in the 16th century persisted. Impor-

1960 C.E.	1970 C.E.	1980 C.E.	1990 C.E.
1960s Civil rights movement in U.S.; revival of feminism	**1972, 1979** Oil crises; height of OPEC power	**1980–1988** Iran–Iraq War	**1990** Reunification of Germany
1962 Algeria declares independence	**1975–1898** Democratic regimes spread in Latin America	**1985 ff.** Gorbachev heads Soviet Union; reforms and unrest through Eastern Europe	**1990–1991** Iraq invades Kuwait; Persian Gulf crisis; U.S.–Allied defeat of Iraq
1965–1973 U.S. military intervention in Vietnam	**1976** Death of Mao; new reform pattern in China	**1989** Reform movement in South Africa	**1991** Collapse of the Soviet Union
1965–1968 Cultural revolution in China	**1979** Iranian Revolution; spread of Islamic fundamentalism	**1989** New regimes throughout Eastern Europe	**1992** Full economic integration of Common Market
1968–1973 Student protests in West	**1975** Communist victory in Vietnam		**1994** Palestinian autonomy in Israel; Full democracy in South Africa, Nelson Mandela President

tant regions still sent cheap raw materials, supplied by low-paid labor, into international trade. Only a few societies made the bulk of the profits from international trade because they ran the shipping and banking facilities and produced the most expensive processed products. In this basic sense, there was strong continuity from earlier periods in world history. But the actors changed, which is where the West's decline showed up. Although the West continued to be among the dominant economic agents, by the 1960s it was joined by Japan and an increasing number of other east Asian centers. Still others societies, such as Brazil and China, gained new ability to compete with the West in selected industrial areas.

On many fronts, the rise of the West, one of the leading processes in world history since the 15th century, leveled off, with the 1920s and 1930s forming a key turning point. No single civilization emerged by the end of the 20th century to claim the kind of growing world leadership the West had long produced. In part, this was because the West itself still remained strong.

Nevertheless, the West's decline opened opportunities for other regional centers. The proliferation of new nations around the world after 1945 brought new opportunities for independence. Successful liberation movements created new opportunities for human agency outside the West. Individual leaders such as Gandhi in India, Mao Zedong in China, and Lenin in Russia put a personal stamp on developments outside the West. The 20th century added to the forces of conformity and mass organization, but there were opportunities for individual initiative in shaping cultural and political change.

INTERNATIONAL CONTACTS

The intensification of international contacts was a basic feature of the 20th century. Technology was critical: Innovations included faster communication via wireless radio and, later, satellite and computer; faster transport, using the airplane; and larger capacity for communication and the movement of goods. Levels of world trade steadily increased, and more and more corporations (particularly from the West and Japan) operated internationally.

World wars and peacetime alliances demonstrated the new levels of international contact on other fronts. Diplomatic contacts were internationalized as never before. International cultural influences also increased in tandem with improved communication and the efforts of multinational corporations. Films, scientific research, and artistic styles all spread widely at both popular and elite levels. By the 1990s, children in nearly every society could identify Mickey Mouse. The result was no single world culture, for regional reactions and the extent of penetration varied widely. But most cultures had to come to some terms with the impact of Hollywood movies, Parisian art, and British–American popular music. International interest in sports was another unprecedented development across civilization lines. Soccer won mass enthusiasm almost everywhere; the Olympic Games, which were reestablished in 1896, shifted from initial dominance by the West to genuine global participation.

The growth of international contacts also created unprecedented complexity in international relations. Under the League of Nations and then, after World War II, the United Nations and the World Bank, international agencies proliferated. Government embassies

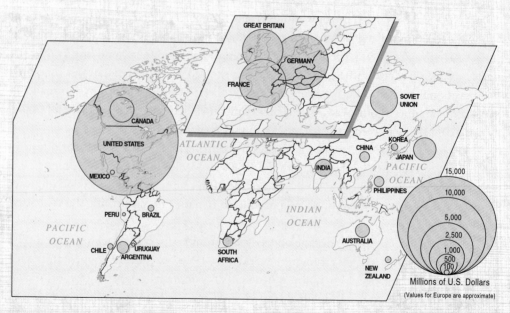

World Distribution of Manufacturing, 1930

spread to and from the new nations; never had so many foreign service professionals flourished. More and more businesses divided production and sales facilities between many countries in what came to be called multinational corporations. New streams of immigrants from Africa, Asia, and the Caribbean headed toward the leading industrial centers from the 1920s onward. Some observers wondered whether the balance was shifting away from regional identities toward global homogenization.

INTERNATIONAL CHALLENGES IN POLITICS AND CULTURE

Change undermined long-standing traditions in politics, social structures, and culture. Very few societies had the same form of government by 2000 that they had in 1900. Monarchies crumbled and were replaced by democracies, totalitarian governments, or authoritarian regimes. Politically, major civilizations tried to come to terms with Western examples while developing governments vigorous enough to gain or maintain independence. Along with new political forms came new functions. Governments generally took on new roles in trying to further economic growth. They also accepted new responsibilities in areas such as education and health care, and their contact with masses of citizens increased greatly as a result.

Changes in previous belief systems formed another current that swept over most national and civilization boundaries. Most of the world's people in 1850 adhered to one of the great religions or philosophical systems created during the classical or postclassical eras, such as Confucianism, Christianity, and Islam. These systems were still lively in 1950, and some were even winning new converts. In most parts of the world, however, they had been modified or challenged by new systems of belief that were more secular in orientation, such as liberalism, nationalism, or communism. They were also challenged by growing interest in science, a staple of the burgeoning mass education systems.

Changes in ideas and politics related to a third general international current: the displacement of long-standing beliefs in rigid social inequalities. All the great agricultural civilizations had developed highly structured systems of inequality. Western ideas, expressed in great movements such as the French Revolution of 1789, had attacked assumptions of structured inequality and legal privilege. Also, the abolition of slavery through most of the world in the 19th century signaled the end of another traditional institution of inequality. The further spread of Western ideas, as well as new movements such as Russian and Chinese communism and the nationalisms of Asia and Africa, brought a more widespread attack on rigid inequalities in the 20th century. Caste systems and aristocracies officially crumbled, with rare exceptions. Societies turned to new efforts at equality or at least equality of opportunity, including widespread voting rights, although countercurrents such as racist beliefs or gender inequalities complicated the picture. Inequality did not end, but older ideas yielded to new beliefs.

Innovation did not mean uniformity. Major civilizations developed different political, cultural, and social responses to change. It was the need to innovate that had global force.

THE 20TH CENTURY AS A NEW PERIOD IN WORLD HISTORY

The 20th century as a new period in world history unfolded in three phases. Between 1914 and 1945, the world was shaken by a series of catastrophic events—two world wars and an international depression—that led to the new international order, reflecting the West's decline and facilitating the emergence of new centers of activity. Several political upheavals accompanied the West's crises, ushering in new regimes in Russia, Mexico, China, and Turkey.

After 1945, decolonization entered high gear, creating a host of novel governments. New social mobility, changes in gender relations, and redefinitions of government functions moved to center stage. The decades after World War II were also defined by a tense struggle between most communist societies, headed by the Soviet Union, and the United States and its allies. This cold war ushered in unprecedented military buildups and daunting new weaponry, though no catastrophic "hot" wars broke out.

The late 20th century saw the end of the cold war after the collapse of the Soviet Union. The result was a more uncertain, if in some ways less menacing, international diplomatic and military framework. Regional conflicts took on new importance. At the same time, the continued advance of societies such as China, the impact of worldwide manufacturing growth, and the results of proliferating information technology added to the pressures for change.

The chapters that follow deal with the 20th century by discussing a combination of major themes and particular societies. First, key global patterns are outlined, particularly in the period of the world wars but also later cold war and post–cold war stages. Then two

The World in 1995

chapters deal with major changes in the West itself and with the revolutionary era and its aftermath in Russia and eastern Europe. The rise of the Pacific Rim organizes the next chapter around the theme of rapid industrialization. Chapter 38 deals with Latin America, another scene of significant revolution amid larger efforts at political, economic, and social change. Two chapters then focus on the decolonization movement and its aftermath in the formation of new states; these chapters highlight developments in south and southeast Asia, the Middle East, and sub-Saharan Africa. Then revolution and its aftermath again take center stage, with discussion of China and Vietnam. A final chapter returns to overall patterns and questions for the future.

Chapter 34

International Contacts and Conflicts, 1914–1999

With the German invasion into France in 1914, northern France was pockmarked with trenches from which little advance was possible. The Western Front, as it was known, pitted attacking German troops against French and British defenders. Trench warfare, depicted in the painting here, employed the awesome technology of modern war.

This chapter deals with the international framework of 20th-century world history. It stresses World War I and later dislocation as a launching pad for 20th-century change. It also studies World War II, the cold war, and the end of the cold war as later stages of change. Through each phase, the intensification of international military, diplomatic, and economic contacts underlies specific events. Each major phase also defined a new balance between the world's major societies.

War, depression, and cold war set the context for world history. Every society was deeply affected as global relationships gained greater influence than ever before.

A series of international arrangements and organizations formed. These activities, in influencing world affairs, offered an alternative path to the recurrent global crises.

International economic and diplomatic events were not the whole story. Several trends cut a somewhat different chronological path. Massive global population growth began in the 1890s and accelerated in mid-century, slowing only at the century's end; the 20th century more than tripled global numbers. New global migration streams resulted. Western, particularly American, popular culture began to gain international attention soon after 1900; in the century's second decade, Hollywood film companies began to set up distribution branches in Australia, Latin America, and Asia. Forces of this sort must be considered with the more spectacular conflicts highlighted in this chapter.

Confidence and Internationalism on the Eve of World War I

Widespread Western optimism before 1914 had an international dimension. Imperialists believed that Western leadership was bringing new enlightenment to the inferior peoples of the rest of the world. Beyond outright imperialism, during the later 19th century there had been some interesting first steps at international organization, which might foreshadow a more peacefully functioning world.

In 1851, for example, an International Statistical Congress began meeting to standardize the practices of statistical services of the European governments. A more informal committee met in 1863 to prepare policies on the rights of neutral parties to aid the wounded during wars. An official diplomatic conference redrafted these policies in 1864 as the Geneva Convention, establishing the Red Cross, an international agency for humanitarian service in wartime. The Telegraphic Union of 1865 blazed a new trail,

1910 C.E.	1920 C.E.	1930 C.E.	1940 C.E.
1914–1918 World War I	**1920** Treaty of Sèvres dissolves Ottoman Empire; French and British mandates set up in Middle East	**1931** Japan invades Manchuria	**1940** Axis agreement (Germany, Italy, Japan)
1915 Italy enters war		**1933** Nazis rise to power in Germany	**1940** Fall of France
1916 Beginning of Arab revolt against Ottoman Empire	**1923** Treaty of Lausanne recognizes independence of Turkey	**1935** Germany rearms; Italy invades Ethiopia	**1941** Japanese attack Pearl Harbor, United States enters war
1917 Russian Revolution	**1929–1939** Great Depression	**1936–1939** Spanish Civil War	**1941** German invasion of Soviet Union
1917 British Balfour Declaration promises Jews a homeland in Palestine		**1937** New Japanese attack on China; beginning of war in Asia	**1942** Tide begins to turn in both war theaters; Soviet Union repulses attack on Stalingrad; Allies invade North Africa
1917 United States enters war		**1938** Germany's union (Anschluss) with Austria; Germany invades Czechoslovakia; Munich conference	**1942–1945** Allied conferences in Teheran, Yalta, Potsdam
1918 German emperor abdicates		**1939** World War II begins; Germany and Soviet Union invade Poland	**1944** Invasion of France by Allies
1918 Treaty of Brest–Litovsk; Russia withdraws from war		**1939** Nazi–Soviet Pact	**1945** U.S. drops atomic bomb on Japan
1919 Versailles conference and treaty; League of Nations established			**1945** End of World War II
1919 Treaty of St. Germain recognizes Czechoslovakia, Yugoslavia, Poland, and Hungary			**1945** United Nations established
1919–1939 Period of United States isolation			**1946** United States grants Philippines independence
			1947 Cold war begins between United States and Soviet Union
			1947 Wider decolonization begins with independence of India and Pakistan
			1949 Formation of NATO

followed 10 years later by the Postal Union. Both unions set international procedures for regular exchanges of letters and messages. Some of these steps were serious modifications of the idea that an individual national government could do as it pleased. If nothing else, the practical agreements facilitated the development of international business arrangements. The habit of thinking internationally seemed to spread. Scientists met often in international conferences. Industrialists showed their wares at international fairs and exhibitions, starting with London's great Crystal Palace display in 1851 and extending through regular world's fairs in various parts of Europe and the United States. Western socialists formed an international movement, based on the idea that working peoples should unite across national boundaries. Athletes gained a new forum for international competition with the establishment of the modern Olympic games in 1896.

These various moves toward *internationalization* were an important development in world history, both recognizing and furthering the intensification of the world network. Many of the international systems and habits established during the late 19th century still facilitate world exchanges today. Some, like easy international mailing, are so routine that they barely merit thought.

Despite its significance, however, the international movement had two related weaknesses. First, it was based heavily on Western dominance and control of empires. A few other governments from North America, Latin America, and Asia fit in, but most of the initial arrangements were made by Europeans and for Europeans. The process of weaning internationalism from Western control would be a long and painful one and would take place particularly after 1945. Furthermore, internationalization gained ground at the same time that nationalism was rising in Europe and elsewhere. Here was another limit on internationalist thinking, quickly visible in areas such as the Olympic games, which turned into an international forum for fierce athletic competition between rival nations.

1950 C.E.	1960 C.E.	1970 C.E.	1980 C.E.
1950–1953 Korean War	**1960 ff.** Diminution of cold war **1962** Cuban Missile Crisis **1963** Nuclear Test Ban Treaty **1964–1973** U.S. and Vietnam War	**1972 and 1974** Strategic Arms Limitation Treaties, U.S. and Soviet Union	**1989** End of cold war

The limits of internationalism showed clearly when the movement turned away from economic and goodwill areas to more directly political matters. In 1898, the Russian tsar called for a peace conference designed to seek agreement on reducing armament levels among the world's great powers. The discussions, held in The Hague in 1899, amplified international agreements on the treatment of war prisoners, temporarily prohibited weapons thrown from balloons, and banned gas warfare and some other new technologies. (The latter measures were ignored in the great world war that broke out 15 years later.) A permanent court of arbitration was established that nations could use to settle disputes. This court, now called the *World Court*, still sits in The Hague and has ruled on conflicts in such areas as economic rights and boundary questions. Disarmament and the idea of compulsory arbitration of international disputes were rejected. Obviously, the promising move toward more genuine international discussion of the issues that might cause war was not possible, given the intense national rivalries.

WORLD WAR I

World War I launched many trends of the 20th century. Bitter nationalist warfare weakened western Europe while nationalism and revolution stirred elsewhere. An inadequate peace settlement after Germany's defeat guaranteed further tensions in Europe, east Asia, and the Middle East.

The Onset of World War I

World War I gave birth to the 20th century. It was a messy beginning, setting a host of new forces in motion, including complex new international relationships. By 1918, a new world balance was beginning to emerge.

Diplomatic tensions had escalated steadily between the major European powers—Britain, France, Russia, Germany, and Austria–Hungary—from the 1890s onward (see Chapter 29). Two rival alliances had formed, theoretically pitting the first three nations against Germany, Austria–Hungary, and Italy. Rapid imperialist gains in Africa and Asia had accustomed the European nations to territorial expansion and easy diplomatic prestige, yet by 1900 most of the world's available territory had already

Visualizing THE PAST

Trench Warfare

This World War I photograph highlights soldiers in the trenches during one of the many lulls in battle.

Questions: What can be read from the picture? Photographs are an important visual experience in modern history; how can they be interpreted? What were the trenches like? Can the expressions and poses of the soldiers be read to suggest what war meant to them? How did it compare with their previous lives in industrial society and with expectations in an age that had vaunted manliness and nationalism? Does the picture raise issues of bias or staging on the part of the photographer, or is it a neutral piece of evidence? Finally, can one move from this picture of war to some speculations about what peacetime life would be like for the veterans who returned?

been carved up. Tensions within Europe became prominent once again. Many nations tended to use military growth, such as the battleship-building rivalry that seized Britain and Germany, as a means of distracting people from difficult social tensions at home. This was particularly tempting in central and eastern Europe. Austria–Hungary was beset by bitter national struggles between several Slavic groups against the control of German and Hungarian leadership. Russia faced a revolutionary mood in its workers and peasants. The two alliance systems focused increasingly on the leading European trouble spot, the Balkans, where bitterly competitive small nations fought two wars in 1912 and 1913. Russia was interested in these struggles because of its vaunted kinship with other Slavic peoples; Austria–Hungary was interested because it feared south Slavic nationalism.

In July 1914, a Serbian nationalist shot the Austrian Archduke Ferdinand, the emperor's nephew, hoping to strike a blow for Serbian acquisition of Slavic territories controlled by Austria. After years of tension, this was the last straw for Austria–Hungary: Serbia had to be attacked. Germany supported Austria, partly out of loyalty to a weak ally and partly because some leaders believed that world war was inevitable and sooner was better than later because both France and Russia were in early stages of military reforms that would strengthen them in the long run. Russia refused to let Austria bully Serbia, lest it lose all Balkan influence. France vowed to support Russia. When Austria declared war on Serbia on July 28, Russia launched a general mobilization in the belief that it had to prepare right away because its procedures were slow. This mobilization frightened Germany, whose strategy called for it to defeat France quickly before turning to Russia, so Germany declared war on both allies on August 1. Britain entered the fray on August 4. After a century of peace in Europe, the nation-states once again launched a general war. But this one, fed by the new powers of the state, new nationalist passions, and the devastating armaments produced by industrialization, would have far more awesome and global consequences than any previous struggle.

Patterns of War in Europe

Quickly, two major fronts were established as hostilities opened (see Map 34.1). One, mainly in France,

pitted attacking German troops against French and British defenders. The second developed in eastern Europe, particularly in Russian Poland, where German armies battled Russian forces while trying to support the weaker Austrian–Hungarian army to the south. After 1915, when Italy entered the war on the side of France and Britain, wooed by promises of territory to be seized from Austria and the Middle East, a third *Italian front* developed between the Italians and the Austrians. There was also an important contest for the seas. The large German surface fleet was bottled up by the British for most of the war, but German submarines played havoc with Atlantic sea lanes, particularly through 1916. German *submarine warfare*, featuring attacks on U.S. ships bringing people and supplies to Britain, was the most important single cause of America's entry into the war in 1917.

On the *western front*, northern France was soon pockmarked with trenches, from which little advance was possible. The awesome technology of modern war was revealed in all its power as devastating artillery, machine guns, barbed-wire fences, and the use of poison gas added to the horrors of the stalemate. By 1916 stagnation on the western front had turned into a nightmare as the Germans lost 850,000 men, the French 700,000, and the British 410,000, without any appreciable change in the lines of battle. A German novelist later described life in the rat-infested trenches:

> The front is a cage in which we must await fearfully whatever may happen. We lie under the network of arching shells and live in a suspense of uncertainty. Over us Chance hovers.

Most of the fighting on the *eastern front* took place in the western portions of Russia, with some momentous battles. Fighting also spread to the Balkans, where Austria crushed Serbia, and the other small states aligned in the hope of gaining local advantage.

The war led to unprecedented growth of government. Whole industrial sectors, such as railroads in the United States, were administered outright by the state. Within government, the executive branch increasingly took over from parliament, particularly in Germany, where by 1917 a top general ran the country. Governments also leaned heavily on public opinion. Dissent was censored, and dissenters were arrested. Newspapers and other media were

Map 34.1 *World War I Fronts in Europe and the Middle East. The central powers initially pushed out to the east, west, and south, but the expected major advances did not materialize.*

manipulated to create the most favorable public opinion possible. Thus the British (and through them, the Americans) were sold exaggerated stories of German violence, whereas Germans were so carefully shielded from military setbacks after 1917 that many did not know they were losing until the end came.

Even spying took on new dimensions, if only because popular nationalism was so inflamed. Mata Hari (Margarette MacLeod, née Zelle, 1876–1917;

Figure 34.1) was accused of spying and was executed by the French in World War I. A Dutch dancer, she married, then separated from her husband and began a dancing career in Paris. She changed her name to focus attention on her East Indian dances. Dancing with few clothes, she gained a series of lovers, including many army officers. The French accused her of passing military information to a German diplomat in neutral Holland. Mata Hari claimed she was spying for the French in German-occupied Belgium. Amid a welter of accusations, Mata Hari was shot by a firing squad. Her name survives to characterize the modern image of a seductive female spy.

The War Outside Europe

World War I was originally a European conflict, a particularly cruel result of the political divisions and rivalries that had long marked the Western experience, now exacerbated by nationalism. Nevertheless, given the West's world dominance, it was inevitable that the war would spill over into other areas and that some of its most important effects were felt outside Europe.

British dominions, notably Canada, Australia, and New Zealand, were drawn into the war early on as loyal members of the British Empire. Forces from these countries fought bravely on several fronts and in the process brought their new nations into greater world involvements.

World War I also brought the United States into world power politics as a major player, culminating a development that had been brewing for some time. Distant from the battlefields, Americans initially dis-

agreed over which side, if either, was in the right. American businesspeople, in the meantime, profited greatly from the war by selling goods to the various combatants and taking advantage of Europeans' distraction to gain new ground in other world markets. Rapidly rising exports, combined with loans to European governments that needed credit to buy war materials and food, converted the United States from an international debtor to a creditor nation for the first time in the nation's history. Despite all the gains resulting from noninvolvement, American leadership was on balance pro-British. Clumsy German attempts to influence American opinion and the submarine warfare that affected American ships, including passenger vessels, moved the country toward a more interventionist mood. In 1917, the United States entered the war, soon sending fresh troops and needed supplies to the western front and helping to turn the tide against the Germans. The United States also brought into the war a new current of idealism, choosing to see its unaccustomed role as fighting for international justice and democracy; this input played an important role in the war's results.

Combatants in Africa, Asia, and the Middle East

The involvement of the United States and the British Commonwealth was only part of the war's international story. Minor skirmishes of the war were fought around the German colonies in Africa, involving Africans as colonial troops, and France used many Africans in its armies on the European front. Experience in fighting in a European war could be important for the Africans involved, increasing their awareness of European standards and the contradiction between fierce nationalist pride in Europe and the subjection of their own peoples. It was no accident that the first Pan-African Nationalist Congress occurred in 1919. There, emerging African leaders pursued nationalist goals similar to those they had seen in Europe, though without the internal divisiveness.

The war also spread to east Asia, where it fit into a new pattern of conflict. Japan entered the war on the side of Britain and France, honoring its previous alliance with Britain. Australia and New Zealand took over German Samoa to forestall a Japanese advance to the south. China declared war on Germany in 1917, hoping not to be ignored by the European

Figure 34.1 *Mata Hari.*

powers. But Japan was the big gainer in the region, moving into German holdings in China's Shantung province and presenting additional demands for Chinese concessions. World War I in the Far East advanced an already aggressive Japanese policy, setting the stage for further conflict.

Large numbers of troops from India fought for the British in Europe. Many Indian nationalists backed the war effort, hoping that a British victory would promote India's freedom. Allied wartime declarations about national liberation, though aimed mainly at minority groups in enemy countries such as the Habsburg Monarchy, inspired hope in India, as in Africa and elsewhere, again promoting new issues for the future. India was promised limited self-government after the war.

World War I had still wider ramifications in the Middle East. The Ottoman Empire, long attached to German military advisors, joined Germany in the war effort. The Germans even hoped that the Turks could sponsor a Muslim uprising against British and French holdings in north Africa, but this did not happen. Rather, the war weakened the already feeble Ottoman state. The British sponsored a rebellion by Arab nationalists against their Ottoman overlords, winning important allies along the eastern Mediterranean. They also promised support to Jewish settlers in Israel, in the *Balfour Declaration* of 1917. Allied actions set in motion various forces among people who were hostile to Ottoman rule and eager for some kind of independence, although they also encouraged contradictory goals in the Middle East itself. With Germany defeated, the Ottoman Empire split apart.

Overall, the war's international result was a substantial decrease in Europe's world power. Two new players, the United States and Japan, won new prestige or new territory and gained ground. Europe's need for colonial support and its devotion to belligerent nationalism gave many leaders in India, Africa, and the Middle East a higher level of awareness of their own national rights and merits.

The War's End

In March 1917 the pressures of war, added to the earlier strains in Russian society, caused a major revolution that toppled the tsarist government (see Chapter 36). Soon a new revolt, in October 1917, brought Lenin and the communists to power. This

leadership, bent on restructuring Russian society and wanting to escape the pressures of war, signed the *Brest–Litovsk Treaty* with the Germans in March 1918, giving the Germans substantial territories in western Russia in return for peace.

This proved to be the peak of German success, however, and the treaty was a partial mistake. The Germans had to commit more troops to occupying its new territory than was sensible, reducing the abilities of a thoroughly war-torn nation to push new energy into the crucial western front. Heavy fighting there during 1917 caused massive losses on both sides before the arrival of fresh American troops. A series of last-ditch German offensives in 1918 failed, leaving the nation with no reserves. Then a French–British–American counteroffensive pressed forward, aided by the collapse of Habsburg forces in Italy and the Balkans. The German military generals, by now running the country, installed a new civilian government so that blame for defeat would not fall directly on their forces. This government, led ultimately by socialists when the German emperor abdicated, had no choice but to sue for peace in November 1918.

TABLE 34-1
World War I Losses

The number of known dead was placed at about 10 million men and the wounded at about 20 million, distributed among chief combatants as follows (round numbers):

	Dead	Wounded	Prisoner
Great Britain	947,000	2,122,000	192,000
France	1,385,000	3,044,000	446,000
Russia	1,700,000	4,950,000	500,000
Italy	460,000	947,000	530,000
United States	115,000	206,000	4,500
Germany	1,808,000	4,247,000	618,000
Austria–Hungary	1,200,000	3,620,000	200,000
Turkey	325,000	400,000	

The total direct cost of the war was figured at $180 billion and the indirect cost at $151.612 billion.

The Peace and the Aftermath

Settlement of the war was difficult, even with the military apparatus of Germany temporarily dismantled or underground. Diplomats of the victorious nations convened at Versailles, near Paris, where they debated the fate of much of the world (Figure 34.2). Russia, Germany, and indeed most of the world were unrepresented. France was bent on revenge against Germany. It got back the provinces of Alsace and Lorraine surrendered after its 1871 war loss but not the security it yearned for. Italy wanted new territory; it received less than it wanted and emerged unsatisfied as well. Japan hoped for a great power role but was largely ignored, which heightened Japanese discontent despite concrete war gains. The United States, led by president Woodrow Wilson, espoused great ideals and hoped for just settlement of all nationalist issues—particularly in eastern Europe, where many nationalities struggled for recognition—and a new *League of Nations* to deal with future disputes and to make war unnecessary. But ideals were

hard to put into practice amid conflicting interests, and domestic public opinion prevented the United States from taking a consistently active role. The United States did not even join the League of Nations its president had conceived. American political *isolationism* contributed to French and British fears for the future.

China suffered greatly because of its losses to a surging Japan and the internal unrest that followed the war. China refused to sign away the Shantung province to Japan but was powerless to resist. The Austro-Hungarian Empire collapsed entirely as nationalist uprisings carved out the new nations of Czechoslovakia and Hungary, and Yugoslavia emerged as an enlarged south Slavic state. This left a somewhat fragile Germanic Austria cut off from its traditional markets, one of many small countries in a weakened region of Europe. Germany lost territory

Figure 34.2 *At the Paris Peace Conference of 1919, the Arabs sought a new voice. The Arab representatives included Prince Feisal of Jordan and an Iraqi general. A British delegation member, T. E. Lawrence, was a long-time friend of the Arabs. The Arabs did not win full national self-determination for their homelands.*

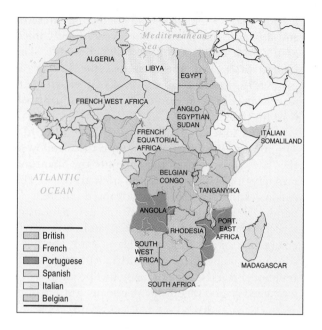

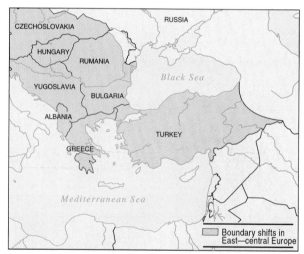

Map 34.2 *The Postwar World in 1920. New colonial holdings in Africa and Asia and the collapse of two multinational empires.*

to France as well as to a revived Polish state in the east. Germany's global empire was also taken away and it was branded unfit for colonial rule. It was also blamed for causing the war and faced large reparation payments to the Allies, particularly France and Belgium. These impositions created huge discontent in Germany, and many leaders vowed revenge on France as the leader of the punitive peacemakers.

Russia, ignored as a communist pariah after its revolution in 1917, was also reduced by the creation of additional small states in eastern Europe, including Poland and several Baltic republics. Here was potential for future trouble. The Versailles peace settlement set up important preconditions for future strife in Europe, the Middle East, and east Asia by creating discontented great powers, insecure or disappointed victors, and a new series of small states that might tempt future expansionists (Map 34.2).

The War's Devastations and Dislocations

The legacy of World War I weakened Europe internally and reduced its strength in the world at large. More than 10 million people had died, meaning that almost every European family had a death to mourn. Never before had a war approached this level of devastation. Countries such as France and Serbia, partic-

ularly hard hit, lost more than one-tenth of their total populations. Truly, this war was "the blood-red dawn of the 20th century." Loss of men also decreased the European birth rate, for families that might have formed could not. Massive destruction of industrial property and agricultural land temporarily dislocated many economies, leading to a period of postwar instability, which ended only in 1923. More serious than these largely repairable setbacks was an imbalance produced by the methods of financing the war. Most combatant regimes had borrowed heavily, unwilling to raise taxes too much lest civilian morale be destroyed. Even during the last years of war, despite government restrictions, prices began to rise because of the inflationary impact of increased government spending. And after the war, inflation soared in many countries. Many people with fixed savings were nearly wiped out.

Outside Europe, colonialism was only mildly changed on the surface. There was little outright loss of colonies; indeed, the 1920s were (on paper) the peak of Western imperialism. Germany's African colonies were taken over by Britain and France. The new colonies were held as mandates of the League of Nations, not as outright possessions. The implication was that although colonial administrations might be established, they were only temporarily responsible, with an obligation to prepare these areas for independence. In many parts of the world, nationalist leaders, including Gandhi and Ho Chi Minh, seized on Wilsonian principles of self-determination, asking why they were applied only within Europe and not to the wider world. Here was a vital pressure for heightened agitation against imperialist rule.

A crucial area of change involved the Middle East. The Ottoman Empire collapsed. Italy and Greece led an initial attempt to carve up even the areas around Constantinople and Asia Minor where Turks were in the majority. But by 1923 a vigorous new Turkish republic led by Mustafa Kemal, or Ataturk, repulsed those efforts through war and negotiation. The rest of the Ottoman holdings were divided up as mandates of the League of Nations, with Britain taking Palestine and Iraq and France gaining Syria and Lebanon. A few new or renewed monarchies, such as Iran and the kingdom of Saudi Arabia, sprang up in the Persian Gulf region. The Middle East was politically fragmented, a legacy that proved disruptive in world affairs later in the 20th century. Here, as in central Europe, the postwar settlement simply asked for further trouble.

Beyond the peace settlement itself, the international economic results of the war continued to reverberate. American and Japanese businesspeople had captured many European export markets, which complicated Europe's immediate postwar recovery. Even when European states had regained greater health, they forced unprecedented international competition. Britain, in particular, never recovered the export position on which its global domination had so long depended. European debts to impatient U.S. creditors further complicated the international economy.

The war also gave birth to a new international organization. Here, trends before the war resumed, but the results were feeble. The League of Nations established several subsidiary organizations that gathered information and focused on international social concerns. However, the league itself proved to be little more than a discussion group, as real diplomacy continued on a nation-to-nation basis. Several disarmament conferences held in the 1920s, intended particularly to reduce naval competition, were ineffective as well. The international idea advanced but it lacked muscle.

THE GREAT DEPRESSION

The economic depression that dominated the 1930s was international in scope. Economic shocks were particularly severe in western Europe and the United States. Latin America, Africa, and Japan, as world exporters, were also heavily involved. The depression triggered important new government policies but also furthered extremist political forces in many countries. The Great Depression resulted from new problems in the industrial economy of Europe and the United States, combined with the long-term weakness in other parts of the world. The result was a worldwide collapse that spared only a few economies and brought political and economic pressures on virtually every society. International economic dislocation followed international dislocation in war.

Causes of Economic Instability

The impact of World War I on the European economy led to several rocky years into the early 1920s. War-induced inflation was a particular problem in Germany, where prices soared daily and ordinary purchases took huge quantities of currency. Forceful government action finally resolved this crisis in 1923, but only by a massive devaluation of the mark, its monetary unit, which did nothing to restore lost savings. Great Britain, an industrial pioneer and already the victim of a loss of dynamism before the war, recovered more slowly, in part because of its unusually great dependence on an export market that was now open to wider competition.

Structural problems affected other areas of Europe besides Britain and lasted well beyond the predictable readjustments to peacetime. Farmers throughout the Western world, including the United

States, faced almost chronic overproduction of food and resulting low prices. Food production had soared in response to wartime needs; then, during postwar inflation many farmers in western Europe and North America borrowed heavily to buy new equipment, overconfident that their good markets would be sustained. But rising European production combined with large imports from the Americas sent prices down, which made debts harder to repay. One response was continued flight from the countryside. The remaining farmers were hard pressed, unable to sustain high demand for manufactured goods.

Furthermore, most of the dependent areas in the world economy, colonies and noncolonies alike, were suffering badly. Pronounced tendencies toward overproduction developed in the smaller nations of eastern Europe, which sent agricultural goods to western Europe, as well as among tropical producers in Africa and Latin America. Here, continued efforts to earn export revenue drove local estate owners to expand output in such goods as coffee, sugar, and rubber. As European governments and businesspeople organized their African colonies for more profitable exploitation, they set up large estates devoted to goods of this type. Production often exceeded demand, which drove prices and earnings down not only in Africa but also in Latin America. This meant that many colonies and dependent economies were unable to buy many industrial exports, which weakened the demand for Western products precisely when output tended to rise amid growing United States and Japanese competition.

The governments of the leading industrial nations provided scant leadership during the emerging crisis of the 1920s. Nationalistic selfishness predominated. Western nations were more concerned about insisting on repayment of debts owed to them or enacting tariff barriers to protect their own industries than about balancing world economic growth. Protectionism, as practiced even by traditionally free-trade Great Britain and by the many new nations in eastern Europe, simply reduced market opportunities and made a bad situation worse. Italy turned to a new kind of government under fascism (see Chapter 35).

Collapse and Crisis

The formal advent of depression occurred in October 1929, when the New York stock market crashed.

Stock values tumbled as investors quickly lost confidence in issues that had been pushed ridiculously high. United States banks, which had depended heavily on their stock investments, rapidly echoed the financial crisis, and many institutions failed, dragging their depositors along with them. Even before this collapse, Americans had begun to call back earlier loans to Europe. When one piece of the speculative spiral was withdrawn, the whole edifice quickly collapsed. Key bank failures in Austria and Germany followed the American crisis. Throughout most of the industrial West, investment funds dried up as creditors went bankrupt or tried to call in their loans.

With investment receding, industrial production quickly began to fall, beginning in the industries that produced capital goods and extending quickly to consumer products. Falling production (levels dropped by as much as one-third by 1932) meant falling employment and lower wages, which in turn withdrew more demand from the economy and led to further hardship. New problems developed among workers, now out of jobs or suffering from reduced hours and reduced pay, as well as the middle classes. The statistics were grim: Up to one-third of all blue-collar workers in the West lost their jobs for prolonged periods (Figure 34.3). White-collar unemployment, though not quite as severe, was also unparalleled. In Germany 600,000 of 4 million white-collar workers had lost their jobs by 1931. The depression fed on itself, growing steadily worse from 1929 to 1933.

Worldwide Impact

A few economies were buffered from the depression. The Soviet Union, busy building an industrial society under communist control, had cut off all but the most insignificant economic ties with other nations to promote *socialism in one country*. The result placed great hardships on many Russian people, who were called to sustain rapid industrial development without outside capital, but it did prevent a depression from happening during the 1930s. As the Document section suggests, Soviet leaders pointed with pride to the lack of serious unemployment and steadily rising production rates, in contrast with the miseries of Western capitalism at the time.

For most of the rest of the world, however, the depression worsened an already bleak economic picture. Western markets could absorb fewer commod-

Figure 34.3 *This photo of a United States woman exemplifies unemployment and poverty during the Great Depression.*

ity imports as production fell and incomes dwindled. Hence, the nations that produced foods and raw materials saw their prices and earnings drop even more than before. Unemployment rose rapidly in the export sectors of the Latin American economy, creating a major political challenge not unlike that faced by the Western leaders.

Japan, as a new industrial country still heavily dependent on export earnings for financing its imports of essential fuel and raw materials, was hit hard too. Luxury purchases of silk exports collapsed, leading to severe unemployment and, again, a crucial political crisis. Japanese farmers were reduced to eating the bark from trees.

Between 1929 and 1931, the value of Japanese exports plummeted by 50 percent. Workers' real income dropped by almost one-third, and more than 3 million were unemployed. The depression was compounded by bad harvests in several regions, leading to rural begging and near-starvation, although the Japanese economy rebounded strongly after the initial shock.

For Latin America, the depression stimulated new kinds of effective political action, particularly greater state involvement in planning and direction. New government vigor did not cure the economic effects of the depression, which escaped the control of most individual states, but it did begin an important new phase in the civilization's political evolution. For Japan, the depression increased suspicion of the West and helped promote new expansionism, designed to win more assured markets in Asia. In the West, the depression led to new welfare programs that stimulated demand and helped restore confidence, but it also led to radical social and political experiments such as German Nazism (see Chapter 35). What was common in these reactions was the global quality of the depression, which made it impossible for any purely national policy to restore full prosperity. Even Nazi Germany, which boasted of regaining full employment, continued to suffer from low wages and other dislocations, aside from its increasing dependence on military production.

Finally, the reactions to the depression, including a sense of weakness and confusion in many quarters inside and outside policy circles, contributed to the last great crisis of the first half of the 20th century: a second, more fully international world war. Again, international contacts and rebalancing took a violent turn.

WORLD WAR II

■■ *World War II involved major battles in Asia, Europe, and the Mediterranean as offensive moves by Germany, Japan, and Italy gradually gave way to defeat. The war furthered the exhaustion of Europe as a colonial power and propelled the United States and the Soviet Union to new world status.*

The war broke out formally in 1939 but actually was prepared by a series of clashes through the 1930s. The causes of the war were global, spanning from Europe to east Asia. Deliberate strides toward military expansion by new regimes in Japan and Germany brought the clouds of war to Asia and the Pacific as well as to Europe and the Mediterranean. Feeble

ᴆocuᴍeɴᴛ

The Leader of the Soviet Union Evaluates the Depression

In March 1939, Joseph Stalin, the uncontested leader of the Soviet state, spoke to the 18th Communist Party Congress on the state of the world and the implications for the Soviet Union. His evaluation of the nature of the depression and its implications were central to his overall policy statement.

New Economic Crisis in the Capitalist Countries. Intensification of the Struggle for Markets and Sources of Raw Material, and for a New Redivision of the World

The economic crisis which broke out in the capitalist countries in the latter half of 1929 lasted until the end of 1933. After that the crisis passed into a depression, and was then followed by a certain revival, a certain upward trend of industry. But this upward trend of industry did not develop into a boom, as is usually the case in a period of revival. On the contrary, in the latter half of 1937 a new economic crisis began which seized the United States first of all and then England, France and a number of other countries.

The capitalist countries thus found themselves faced with a new economic crisis before they had even recovered from the ravages of the recent one.

This circumstance naturally led to an increase of unemployment. The number of unemployed in capitalist countries, which had fallen from 30,000,000 in 1933 to 14,000,000 in 1937, has now again risen to 18,000,000 as a result of the new crisis.... The present crisis will be more severe and more difficult to cope with than the previous crisis.

Further, the present crisis has broken out not in time of peace, but at a time when a second imperialist war has already begun; when Japan, already in the second year of her war with China, is disorganizing the immense Chinese market and rendering it almost inaccessible to the goods of other countries; when Italy and Germany have already placed their national economies on a war footing, squandering their reserves of raw material and foreign currency for this purpose; and when all the other big capitalist powers are beginning to reorganize themselves on a war footing. This means that capitalism will have far less resources at its disposal for a normal way out of the present crisis than during the preceding crisis.

Lastly, as distinct from the preceding crisis, the present crisis is not universal, but as yet involves chiefly the economically powerful countries which have not yet placed themselves on a war economy basis. As regards the aggressive countries, such as Japan, Germany and Italy, who have already reorganized their economies on a war footing, they, because of the intense development of their war industry, are not yet experiencing a crisis of overproduction, although they are approaching it. This means that by the time the economically powerful, nonaggressive countries begin to emerge from the phase of crisis the aggressive countries, having exhausted their reserves of gold and raw material in the course of the war fever, are bound to enter a phase of very severe crisis....

The Soviet Union is the only country in the world where crises are unknown and where industry is continuously on the upgrade. Naturally, such an unfavorable turn of economic affairs could not but aggravate relations among the powers. The preceding crisis had already mixed the cards and sharpened the struggle for markets and sources of raw materials. The seizure of Manchuria and north China by Japan, the seizure of Abyssinia by Italy—all this reflected the acuteness of the struggle among the powers. The new economic crisis was bound to lead, and is actually leading, to a further sharpening of the imperialist struggle. It is no longer a question of competition in the markets, of a commercial war, of dumping. These methods of struggle have long been recognized as inadequate. It is now a question of a new redivision of the world, of spheres of influence and colonies, by military action. It is a distinguishing feature of the new imperialist war that it has not yet become universal, a world war. The war is being waged by aggressor states, who in every way infringe upon the interests of the nonaggressive states, primarily Britain, France and the U.S.A., while the latter draw back and retreat, making concession after concession to the aggressors.

Thus we are witnessing an open redivision of the world and spheres of influence at the expense of the nonaggressive states, without the least attempt at resistance, and even with a certain connivance, on their part.

Incredible, but true.

To what are we to attribute this one-sided and strange character of the new imperialist war?

How is it that the nonaggressive countries, which possess such vast opportunities, have so easily and without resistance abandoned their positions and their obligations to please the aggressors?

Is it to be attributed to the weakness of the nonaggressive states? Of course not! Combined, the nonaggressive, democratic states are unquestionably stronger than the fascist states, both economically and militarily.

To what then are we to attribute the systematic concessions made by these states to the aggressors?

It might be attributed, for example, to the fear that a revolution might break out if the nonaggressive states were to go to war and the war were to assume world-wide proportions. The bourgeois politicians know, of course, that the first imperialist world war led to the victory of the revolution in one of the largest countries. They are afraid that the second imperialist world war may also lead to the victory of the revolution in one or several countries.

Questions: How did Stalin compare his nation's economy with that of the capitalist leaders? How did he relate the depression to the diplomatic crisis? Was his judgment accurate, or was it unduly biased by communist theory? What were the implications of this kind of analysis for Soviet foreign policy by 1939?

Reading this document is complicated by two factors. In the first place, Soviet (Russian) economic claims may sound quaint at the outset of the 21st century, given the problems of the Russian economy. As with many sources, interpreting Stalin's remarks takes an effort of historical empathy, putting oneself back into the context of the Great Depression. Second, Stalin's remarks attack the motivations of Western countries, both "aggressive" and "nonaggressive"; it is demanding to evaluate a document that blasts a capitalist system that most Americans esteem. What are the best ways around these difficulties, to understand what Stalin meant and what the significance of his remarks were in the context of the 1930s and of Soviet ideology? What are the most telling points he makes? Which are the flimsiest, and why? What were the motives behind his remarks?

responses from the other powerful states in Europe and North America resulted in nationalistic and ideological divisions, including widespread Western suspicion of the communist regime in the Soviet Union.

New Authoritarian Regimes

The beginnings of this tragedy involved the advent of militaristic governments as key national forces. The early phases of the depression triggered growing political fragmentation in Japan, particularly through the rise of various ultranationalist groups. Some of these groups opposed Western values in the name of Shintoism and Confucianism, while others urged a Nazi-style authoritarian government free from parliamentary restraint and undue tradition. A military group, backed by many younger officers, advocated a "defense state" under their control. This group attacked key government and business offices and killed the prime minister in 1932. The result, satisfactory to no major group, was four years of moderate military rule under an older admiral, followed in 1936 and 1937 by a tougher military regime after another officers' rebellion failed. Japanese voters continued to prefer more moderate parties, but leadership fell increasingly into militaristic hands.

The advent of military rule developed in a context of regional diplomatic crisis. During the late 1920s, Chinese nationalist forces seemed to be gaining ground in their effort to unify their chaotic nation after the 1911 revolution. Their success worried Japan's army leaders, who wanted to be able to influence the Manchurian province of China as a buffer between their new colony of Korea and the Soviet Union. In fact, Japan had dominated the Manchurian warlord since its victory over Russia in 1905. Fearful of losing ground and unimpeded by the weak civilian government in Tokyo, the Japanese army marched into Manchuria in 1931, proclaiming it an independent state. Japan's action was condemned by the League of Nations. But the action was ineffective, as Japan simply withdrew from the league. This advance set the scene for the next round of crisis, the outbreak of World War II in the Far East, in 1937.

In the meantime, a more decisive change of regime had occurred in Germany, where the depression triggered political chaos. The *National Socialist* (Nazi) *party*, led by *Adolf Hitler*, began to pick up strength after nearly fading from existence during the mid-1920s. Nazis advocated many things, but among their leading goals was an aggressive foreign policy that would reverse the humiliation of the Versailles treaty and gain for Germany military glory and new territory for expansion. Sponsored by conservatives who erroneously thought they could control him, Hitler took power legally in 1933. He soon abolished the parliamentary regime and built a totalitarian state with himself at the helm.

The Nazi state was a radically new kind of regime involving the deliberate construction of a war machine. Hitler expanded armament production, creating new jobs, and also built up the army and separate Nazi military forces. In Hitler's view, the essence of the state was authority, and the function of the state was war.

Hitler's advent galvanized the authoritarian regime of Italy. Here, a fascist state had been formed in the 1920s, led by *Benito Mussolini*. Like Hitler,

Mussolini had promised an aggressive foreign policy and new nationalist glories, but his first decade had been rather moderate diplomatically. With Hitler in power, however, Mussolini began to experiment more boldly, if only to avoid being overshadowed. This was another destabilizing element in world politics.

The Steps Toward War

Hitler moved first. He suspended German reparation payments, thus renouncing this part of the Versailles settlement; he walked out of a disarmament conference and withdrew from the League of Nations. He announced German rearmament in 1935 and brought military forces into the Rhineland in 1936. Both moves were in further violation of Versailles. When these challenges were greeted by loud protests from France and Britain, but nothing more serious, Hitler was poised for the further buildup of German strength and new diplomatic adventures that would ultimately lead to World War II.

In 1935, Mussolini attacked Ethiopia, planning to avenge Italy's failure to conquer this ancient land during the imperialist surge of the 1890s. Again the League of Nations condemned the action, but again neither it nor the democratic powers in Europe and North America took action. Consequently, after some hard fighting, the Italians won their new colony.

In 1936, a civil war engulfed Spain, pitting authoritarian and military leaders against republicans and leftists. Germany and Italy quickly moved to support the Spanish right, sending in supplies and troops and gaining not only new glory but also precious military training in such specialties as bombing civilian targets. France, Britain, and the United States, though vaguely supporting the Spanish republic, could agree on no concrete action. Only the Soviet Union sent effective support for the government, and by 1939 the republican forces in the Spanish Civil War had been defeated.

In 1938, Hitler proclaimed a long-sought union, or *Anschluss*, with Austria as a fellow German nation. Western powers complained and denounced but did nothing. In the same year Hitler marched into a German-speaking part of Czechoslovakia. War threatened, but a *Munich conference* convinced French and British leaders that Hitler might be satisfied with acquiescence. Czechoslovakia was dismembered and its western (Sudeten) region was turned over to Ger-

many as the British prime minister, Neville Chamberlain, duped by Hitler's apparent eagerness to compromise, proclaimed that his *appeasement* had won "peace in our time." ("Our time" turned out to be slightly over a year.) Emboldened by Western weakness, Hitler took over all of Czechoslovakia in March 1939 and began to press Poland for territorial concessions. He also concluded an agreement with the Soviet Union, which was not ready for war with Germany and had despaired of Western resolve. The Soviets also coveted parts of Poland, the Baltic states, and Finland for their own, and when Hitler invaded Poland, Russia launched its own war to undo the Versailles settlement. Hitler attacked Poland on September 1, 1939, not necessarily expecting general war but clearly prepared to risk it; Britain and France, now convinced that nothing short of war would stop the Nazis, made their own declaration in response.

War had already broken out in China. Japan, continuing to press the ruling Chinese government lest it gain sufficient strength to threaten Japanese gains, became involved in a skirmish with Chinese forces in the Beijing area in 1937. Fighting spread, initially unplanned. Most Japanese military leaders opposed more general war, arguing that the nation's only interest was to defend Manchuria and Korea. However, influential figures on the General Staff held that China's armies should be defeated decisively to prevent future trouble. This view prevailed, and Japanese forces quickly occupied the cities and railroads of eastern China. The Chinese army refused to give in, and a stalemate resulted that lasted until 1945; neither side was capable of major new advance (Figure 34.4).

In 1940, the two main areas of conflict, Europe and the Pacific, drew together when Germany and Italy (already uneasy allies) signed an agreement with Japan. Japanese leaders had long admired Germany and welcomed Hitler's hostility to the Soviet Union and communism. Early German successes in the European war, and the realization by the Japanese that expansion in the Pacific would pit them against the United States, combined to argue for a more formal alliance. A *Tripartite Pact* was signed by Germany, Japan, and Italy in September 1940. In fact, Japan and Germany never collaborated closely. Japan refused to participate in Germany's ultimate war with the Soviet Union despite long-standing opposition to Russian strength. Nevertheless, the union of the aggressor states, however hollow in practice, seemed to align the powers of the world between those on the attack and those on the defense, a symbolism particularly influential for the United States.

As war broke out from 1937 to 1939, the powers most interested in preserving the status quo remained unprepared, hopeful that war could be averted by talk and concessions. France and Britain continued to feel the debilitating effects of World War I and were not eager for another conflict. Depression-induced tensions made it difficult for these governments to agree on any active policy, and political leftists and conservatives even disagreed over which was the greater enemy: Germany or the Soviet Union. The United States was less polarized but was eager to maintain its policy of isolationism in order not to complicate the delicate process of building a new set of government programs to fight the depression. Only by late 1938 did Western leaders begin to admit that war was likely and to launch some measures of military preparedness, including army expansion and aircraft production. Britain took the lead here, and its efforts proved vital in allowing successful defense of the nation in the first stages of the war with Germany. But the Western effort was too little and too late to prevent war itself.

The Course of the War: Japan's Advance and Retreat

The background to World War II made it obvious that war would be fought in two major centers: the Pacific and the European regions, the latter spilling over into north Africa and the Middle East (see Map 34.3). The background also made it inevitable that the first years of the war would feature almost unremitting German and Japanese success against ill-prepared opponents. Only in 1942 and 1943 did the tide begin to change because the powers that had been drawn into war were more powerful, economically and in population size, than their ambitious taunters.

The bitter war in Asia, pitting Japan against China and the United States with Britain in an important supporting role, followed a fairly simple course of thrust and counterthrust. Stalemated in China, Japan used the outbreak of war in Europe as an occasion to turn its attention to other parts of Asia. It seized Indochina from France's troops. Later, as the Japanese attacked Malaya and Burma, their desire for an Asian empire put them on a collision course with the United States, which as a Pacific power was unwilling to allow Japan to become a predominant

Figure 34.4 *These Japanese soldiers were captured by Chinese forces in the interior of China after a bitter battle in 1942.*

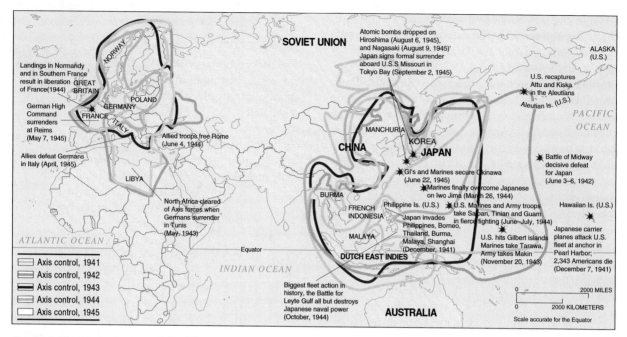

Map 34.3 *The Main Theaters of World War II. Gains by the Axis powers to 1942 were reversed steadily by Allied military action.*

force in the Far East. The United States' holdings in Hawaii and the Philippines, along with American attempts to withhold materials necessary to Japan's war economy, convinced Japanese leaders that a clash was inevitable. Negotiations with the United States broke down with the American insistence that Japan renounce all gains acquired since 1930. It was in this setting that the Japanese attacked *Pearl Harbor* on December 7, 1941, and then seized American possessions in the eastern Pacific, including the Philippine Islands. It also attacked Malaysia and Burma. Only toward the middle of 1942 did the United States begin to gain ground, using its greater numbers and superior level of industrialization. Scattered islands were reconquered in 1943, and the Philippines were regained in 1944, while massive air raids began an onslaught on Japan itself. Meanwhile, American, British, and Chinese forces continued to tie down a large Japanese army on the Asian mainland.

Germany Overreaches

In Europe, Germany initially seemed unstoppable, and the Western democracies suffered accordingly.

German strategy focused on the *Blitzkrieg*, or "lightning war," involving rapid movement of troops, tanks, and mechanized carriers. With this strategy the Germans crushed Poland and, after a brief lull, pushed early in 1940 into Denmark and Norway. The next targets were Holland, Belgium, and France, where invasion was prepared for by massive bombardments of civilian targets. Rotterdam, for example, was flattened at the cost of 40,000 lives.

German dynamism was matched, as in the 1930s, by Allied weakness. France fell surprisingly quickly, partly because the French were unprepared for war and reliant on an outdated defensive strategy and partly because French troops were quickly demoralized because of the deep tensions within their own society. By the summer of 1940, most of France lay in German hands, and a semifascist collaborative regime, based in the city of Vichy, ruled the remainder. Only Britain stood apart, able to withstand Hitler's air offensive and win the contest for its skies known as the Battle of Britain. Imaginative air force tactics combined with solid new leadership under a coalition government headed by *Winston Churchill*, as well as iron resolve on the part of British citizens

Figure 34.5 *Erwin Rommel and German forces in north Africa.*

to resist the devastating air raids. Hitler's hopes for a British collapse were dashed.

In 1940, Germany controlled the bulk of the European continent. It aided its ally, Italy, in a conquest of Yugoslavia and Greece. It moved into north Africa to press British and French holdings (Figure 34.5). Conquered territories were forced to supply materials, troops, and slave labor to the German war machine.

The balance in the war began to shift in 1941. Blocked from invading Britain, Hitler turned toward the tempting target of Russia. The goal was to provide space for German colonization in this vast agricultural area. Germany's attack began in June, all pretense of alliance abandoned, and the Germans easily penetrated into central Russia. Yet the Soviet forces, while losing ground amid massive loss of life, did not collapse. They moved back, relocating Soviet industry eastward. As with Napoleon's invasion attempt over a century before, weather also came to the Russians' aid. The Germans, counting on another quick victory, were caught off guard by a harsh winter. As in Britain, civilian morale in Russia greatly aided the war effort, and although German forces continued to advance through 1942, the ability to deliver a knockout blow eluded them.

Late 1941 also brought the United States' entry into the war, spurred initially by the Japanese attack on Pearl Harbor. The U.S. leaders had already supported Britain with loans and supplies, and they now eagerly used the bombing of Pearl Harbor to enter the war in Europe and Asia against what seemed a clear threat to Western democracy, perhaps to Western civilization itself. American involvement, delayed because of a lack of preparation, began to make itself felt in 1942 when American and British forces challenged the Germans in north Africa. In the same year, the Soviet Union pushed back an intensive German *siege of Stalingrad,* which if successful might have opened the way to the Ural Mountains and Russia's new industrial heartland. A large portion of the German force on the Russian front surrendered, and the Red armies began a gradual push westward that would take them past their own borders, through eastern Europe, and by 1945 deep into Germany itself.

In the meantime, British and American forces moved into the Italian peninsula from north Africa, ousting Mussolini while bombing German industrial and civilian targets. Then, in 1944, the Allies invaded France, again pushing the Germans back with the aid of French forces hostile to fascism. Amid bitter fighting—Hitler decided to resist as fiercely as possible, goaded in part by Allied insistence that Germany surrender without conditions—the Anglo-American forces gradually surged into western Germany. Massive bombing preceded the Allied invasion. In late April 1945, Russian and American troops met on the Elbe River. On April 30, Hitler committed suicide in his Berlin bunker, and in the next month German military commanders surrendered their country to the victorious invaders.

The war in the Pacific also ended a few months later. This conflict had become primarily a duel between Japan and the United States, but British and Chinese forces were also engaged. After the European theater of operations closed, the Soviet Union turned its attention eastward as well. Japan's collapse was precipitated by American use of atomic bombs on two cities, *Hiroshima* and *Nagasaki,* which helped secure the second unconditional surrender of an Axis power and a period of American occupation. This birth of atomic warfare opened a new period in the world's military history, even as the world war drew to a close.

Human Costs

World War II had been a huge killer, with wanton cruelty adding to the effect of weapons of unprecedented power. Japanese troops in China had killed hosts of civilians, often after torturing them, when they captured cities that had tried to hold out. In Nanking, for example, as many as 300,000 were killed after the city had fallen. Hitler's decision to eliminate Jews throughout Europe resulted in 6 million deaths in the gas chambers of the *Holocaust,* an unprecedented modern effort at genocide (see Chapter 35). Other groups, including gypsies and various political dissidents, were also brutalized. Hitler's forces also deliberately attacked civilian centers through bombing raids, in the usually mistaken belief that such destruction would destroy morale. Allied forces, as they became more powerful, paid back in kind. The British air force firebombed the German city of Dresden in retaliation for earlier German raids. Firebombing of Japanese cities led to as many as 80,000 deaths in a single raid. The American decision to drop its newly developed atomic bomb on Japan was made in this environment. American officials wanted to force Japan to surrender without costly invasion, and they also hurried to prevent Soviet advance in Asia. The bombing of Hiroshima killed more than 78,000 civilians, and the raid on Nagasaki two days later also killed tens of thousands. Radiation fallout ultimately killed thousands more. The new American president, *Harry Truman,* called the bombing "the greatest thing in history." Overall, at least 35 million people were killed in the war, 20 million in the Soviet Union alone.

IN DEPTH

Total War

War had changed long before the 20th century. With civilization, war lost its ritual characteristics. It became more commonly an all-out battle, using any tactics and weapons that would aid in victory. In other words, war became less restrained than it had been among more "primitive" peoples, who often used bluff and scare more than all-out violence.

The 20th century most clearly saw the introduction of a fundamentally new kind of war: *total war,* in which vast resources and emotional commitments of the belligerent nations were marshaled to support military effort. The two world wars were thus novel not only in their geographic sweep but in their mobilization of the major combatants. The features of total war also colored other forms of struggle, helping to explain brutal guerrilla and terrorist acts by groups not powerful enough to mount total wars but nonetheless affected by their methods and passions.

Total war resulted from the impact of industrialization on military effort, reflecting both the technological innovation and the organizational capacity that accompanied the industrial economy. Key steps in the development of total war thus emerged in the West from the end of the 18th century. The French Revolution, building new power for the state in contact with ordinary citizens, introduced mass conscription of men, forming larger armies than had ever before been possible. New citizen involvement was reflected in incitements to nationalism and stirring military songs, including aggressive national anthems—a new idea in itself. Industrial technology was first applied to war on a large scale in the American Civil War. Railroads allowed wider movement of mass armies, and mass-produced guns and artillery made a mockery of earlier cavalry charges and redefined the kind of personal bravery needed to fight in war.

However, it was World War I that fully revealed the nature of total war. Steadily more destructive technology included battleships, submarines, tanks, airplanes, poison gas (which had been banned by international agreement before the war), machine guns, and long-range artillery.

Organization for war included not only massive, compulsory recruitment—the draft—but also government control of economic activity via obligatory planning and rationing. It included unprecedented control of media, not only through effective censorship and the jailing of dissidents but through powerful propaganda designed to incite passionate, all-out commitment to the national cause and deep, unreasoned hatred of the enemy. Vivid posters, flaming speeches, and outright falsehood were combined in the emotional mobilization effort. All of these features returned with a vengeance in World War II, from the new technology of bombing, rocketry, and ultimately the atomic bomb to the enhanced economic mobilization organized by government planners.

The people most affected by the character of total war were the troops themselves, who directly endured—bled from and died from—the new technology. But one measure of total war was a blurring of the distinction between military and civilians, a distinction that had often limited war's impact earlier in world history. Whole civilian populations, not just those unfortunate enough to be near the front lines, were forced into certain types of work and urged to certain types of beliefs. The bombing raids, including the German rockets directed against British cities late in World War II, subjected civilians to some of the most lethal weapons available, as many belligerents deliberately focused their attacks on densely populated cities. Correspondingly, psychological suffering, though less common among civilians than among front-line soldiers, could spread throughout the populations involved in war.

Total war, like any major historical development, had mixed results. Greater government economic direction often included new measures to protect workers and give them a voice on management boards. Mobilization of the labor force often produced at least temporary breakthroughs for women. And intense efforts to organize technological research often produced side effects of more general economic benefit, such as the invention of synthetic rubber and other new materials.

Still, total war was notable especially for its devastation. The idea of throwing all possible resources into a military effort made war more economically disruptive than had been the case before. The possibilities unleashed in total war produced embittered veterans who might vent their anger by attacking established political values. It certainly made postwar diplomacy more difficult. One result of total war was a tendency for the victor to be inflexible in negotiations at war's end: People who fought so hard found it difficult to treat enemies generously. The results of a quest for vengeance often produced new tensions that led directly, and quickly, to further conflict. War-induced passions and disruptions could also spark new violence at home, as crime rates often soared not only right after the war ended (a traditional result) but more durably. Children's toys started to reflect the most modern weaponry. How much of the nature of 20th-century life has been determined by the consequences of total war?

Questions: How did the experience of total war affect social and political patterns after the war's end? Why do many historians believe that total war made rational peacetime settlements more difficult than did earlier types of warfare?

The Settlement of World War II

World War II did not produce the sweeping peace settlement, untidy as it was, that had officially ended World War I. The major Allies opposed to Germany and Japan met on several occasions, earnestly trying to build a peace that would avoid the mistakes of Versailles. A key result of Allied discussions was agreement on the *United Nations*. This new international organization from the outset featured better representation than did the League of Nations. The United States pledged to join, and it ultimately housed the United Nations headquarters in New York. The Soviet Union was included, and China (represented by the Nationalist government) attained great status for the first time in modern history. Britain and France rounded out the key group of great powers that would have a permanent seat on the Security Council, the steering committee for the new organization. Internationalism now moved beyond the conventional Western orbit, although the Western leaders sought to retain dominance. Like the

League, the United Nations had as its primary mission providing a forum for negotiating disputes, but it also took over the apparatus of more specialized international agencies that addressed world problems in agriculture, labor, and the like. Although U.N. efforts to preserve peace encountered many difficulties, the organization played a vital role in various international police and relief operations. It also sponsored conferences that exercised strong influences over issues such as child labor, women's conditions, and environmental protection. Its role accelerated as the cold war ended in the 1980s.

The wartime Allies found it increasingly difficult to reach accord on more specific aspects of the postwar world. Some leaders wanted to destroy Germany's industrial structure, to prevent any recurrence of threat from this quarter, but others held out for milder measures. All agreed that Hitler's regime must go and that Germany must surrender unconditionally. The key problem that emerged involved a growing tension between the Soviet Union and the United States, along with British representatives who feared Soviet ambitions.

Initial discussions between the U.S., British, and Soviet governments began in 1942, focusing at first on purely military issues. The heads of the three states met in 1943 in Teheran, Iran, where the Soviet government pressed the Western powers to open a new front in France, which was done with the invasion of Normandy in 1944. The decision at this *Teheran Conference* to focus on France rather than moving up from the Mediterranean gave the Soviet forces a free hand to move through the smaller nations of eastern Europe as they pushed the Nazi armies back. Britain negotiated separately with the Soviets to ensure Western dominance in postwar Greece as well as equality in Hungary and Yugoslavia, in exchange for Soviet control of Romania and Bulgaria, but the United States resisted this kind of scorn for the rights of small nations.

With the war nearly over, the next settlement meeting was the *Yalta Conference* in the Soviet Crimea, early in 1945. Franklin Roosevelt of the United States was eager to press the Soviet Union for assistance against Japan, and to this end the Soviets were promised important territorial gains in Manchuria and the northern Japanese islands. About Europe, however, agreement was more difficult. The three powers easily arranged to divide Germany into four occupation zones (with liberated France getting a chunk), which would be disarmed and purged of Nazi influence. However, Britain resisted Soviet zeal to eliminate German industrial power, seeing a viable Germany as a potential ally in a subsequent Western–Soviet contest. Bitter disagreement also raged over the smaller nations of eastern Europe. That they should be friendly to their Soviet neighbor was undisputed, but the Western leaders also wanted them to be free and democratic. Stalin, the Soviet leader, had to make some concessions by including noncommunist leaders in what was already a Soviet-controlled government in liberated Poland—concessions that he soon violated.

The final postwar conference occurred in Potsdam, a Berlin suburb, in July 1945. Russian forces occupied not only most of eastern Europe but eastern Germany as well (Map 34.4). This situation prompted the agreement that the Soviet Union could take over much of what had been eastern Poland, with the Poles gaining part of eastern Germany in compensation. The *Potsdam Conference* divided Germany pending a final peace treaty (which was not to come for over 40 years). Austria was also divided and occupied, gaining unity and independence only in 1956 on condition of neutrality between the United States and the Soviet Union. Amid great difficulty, treaties were worked out for Germany's other allies, including Italy, but the United States and, later, the Soviet Union signed separate treaties with Japan.

All these maneuvers had several results. Japan was occupied by the United States. Its wartime gains were stripped away, and even Korea, taken earlier, was freed but divided between United States and Soviet zones of occupation (the basis for the north–south Korean division still in effect today). Former Asian colonies were returned to their old "masters," though often briefly as new independence movements quickly challenged the control of the weakened imperialist powers. China regained most of its former territory; here, too, stability was quickly challenged by renewed fighting between Communist and Nationalist parties within the nation, aided by the Soviet Union and the United States, respectively.

The effort to confirm old colonial regimes applied also to the Middle East, India, and Africa. Indian and African troops had fought for Britain during the war,

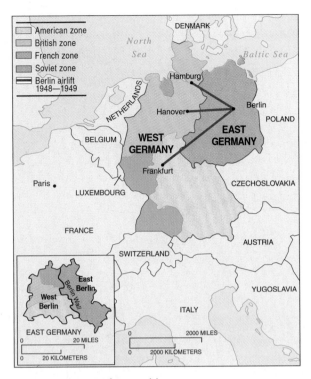

Map 34.4 *Europe After World War II*

Europe were free to set up or confirm democratic regimes. But most of them lived under the shadow of growing U.S. influence, as manifested in continued occupation by American troops, economic aid and coordination, and outright policy manipulation.

The stage was set for two great movements that would shape international contacts in the next decades. The first was the challenges by subject peoples to the remaining control by the great European empires—the movement known as decolonization. This profound upheaval created scores of new nations in Asia, Africa, and the West Indies from 1946 to the 1970s. The second was the confrontation between the two great powers that emerged from the war, the United States and the Soviet Union, each with new international influence and new military might. This confrontation was called the *cold war,* and many believed it would soon become a war in a more literal and devastating sense.

THE COLD WAR AND DECOLONIZATION, 1945–1989

> *Like the world wars before them, cold war rivalries began in Europe. The Soviet Union, its troops occupying most east European countries, staunchly defended the communist regimes it sponsored between 1945 and 1948. An eastern bloc shaped up that included Poland, Czechoslovakia, Bulgaria, Romania, and Hungary. Soviet occupation of the eastern zone of Germany gave Russia a base closer to the heart of Europe than the tsars had ever dreamed possible (see Map 34.5).*

Offended by Russia's heavy-handed manipulation of eastern Europe, United States and British policymakers tried to counter. The new American president, Harry Truman, was less eager for smooth relations with the Soviets than Franklin Roosevelt had been; he was emboldened by the U.S. development of the atomic bomb in 1945. Britain's wartime leader, Winston Churchill, had long feared communist aggression; it was he in 1946 who coined the phrase *iron curtain* to describe the division between free and repressed societies that he saw taking shape in Europe. But Britain lacked the power to resist Soviet

although Britain had imprisoned key nationalist leaders and put independence plans on hold. African leaders had participated actively in the French resistance to its authoritarian wartime government. The Middle East and north Africa had been shaken by German invasions and Allied counterattacks. With Europe's imperial powers further weakened by their war effort, adjustments seemed inevitable, as in the parts of Asia invaded by the Japanese.

In Europe, the Soviet Union pushed its boundaries westward, erasing nearly all the losses after World War I. Independent nations created in 1918 were for the most part restored (although the former Baltic states of Latvia, Lithuania, and Estonia became Soviet provinces because they had been Russian provinces before World War I). Except for Greece and Yugoslavia, the nations in this region quickly fell under Soviet domination, with communist governments forced on them, and Soviet troops occupied them. This included Hungary, Czechoslovakia, Romania, and Bulgaria. The nations of western

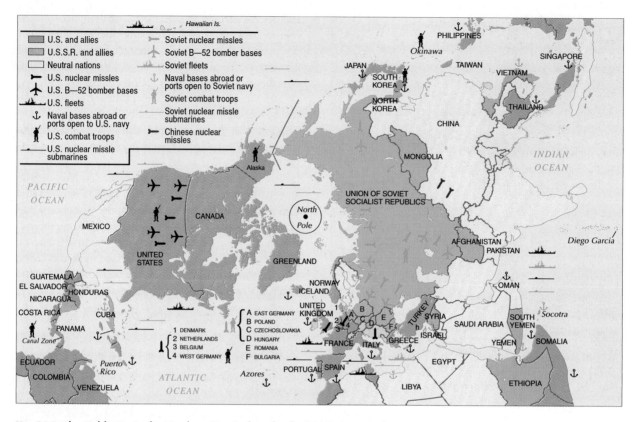

Map 34.5 *The Cold War in the Northern Hemisphere by the 1980s (as seen from space over the North Pole). Two rival alliance systems and leading noninvolved states.*

pressure, and under the Labour party government it explicitly left the initiative to the United States.

The United States responded to Russia's power plays with vigor. It criticized Russian policies and denied Russian applications for reconstruction loans. It bolstered regimes in Iran, Turkey, and Greece that were under Soviet pressure. In Greece, particularly, Americans took over British resistance to a powerful communist guerrilla campaign. Then, in 1947, the United States proclaimed its Marshall Plan, a program of substantial loans that was designed to aid Western nations in rebuilding from the war's devastation. In Soviet eyes, the Marshall Plan was a vehicle for American economic dominance, and there is little question that in addition to humanitarian motives the United States intended to beat back domestic communist movements in countries such as France and Italy by promoting economic growth.

Germany was the focal point of the cold war in these early years. Soviet policy in Germany initially concentrated on seizing goods and factories as reparation. The Western Allies soon prevented Russian intervention in their own zones and turned to some rebuilding efforts in the interests of playing a modest "German card" against growing Soviet strength in the east. Allied collaboration started building a unified West Germany in 1946, and local political structures, followed by more national political structures, were established through elections. When in 1947 the West moved to promote German economic recovery by creating a stable currency, the Soviet Union responded by blockading the city of Berlin, the divided former capital that sat in the midst of the Russian zone. The United States responded with a massive airlift to keep the city supplied, and the crisis finally ended in 1948, with two separate Germanies—

East and West—beginning to take clear shape along a tense, heavily fortified frontier.

Cold war divisions spread from Germany to Europe more generally with the formation of two rival military alliances. *The North Atlantic Treaty Organization (NATO)* was formed in 1949, under U.S. leadership, to group most of the western European powers and Canada in a defensive alliance against possible Soviet aggression. The NATO pact soon authorized some rearmament of West Germany in the context of resistance to communism. In response, the Soviet Union organized the Warsaw Pact among its eastern European satellites. When the Soviets developed their own nuclear capacity, the world—particularly, the European world—was starkly divided between two rival camps, each dominated by one of the two superpowers. Numerous American and Soviet military units were stationed in Europe on either side of the iron curtain.

In 1949, the Soviet Union developed its own atomic bomb. From this point into the 1980s, the Soviet Union and the United States built ever more fearsome nuclear arsenals, with more sophisticated weapons and various kinds of missile systems to deliver them. Conventional forces, including those from NATO and Warsaw Pact allies, also were large and well equipped.

With Europe uneasily stabilized between the two power blocs, cold war tensions in the 1950s turned to the global arena. North Korea's invasion of South Korea in 1949 ultimately was backed by Soviet and Chinese aid (although North Koreans initially acted on their own), and U.S. opposition, partially successful, was billed as a battle against international communism. During the 1950s, the United States busily formed alliances with Australia and New Zealand, several noncommunist countries in southeast Asia, and several Middle Eastern countries, all in the name of resisting communist advance. Soviet and American propagandists competed in every part of the world. Economic aid and military assistance were used to cultivate governments in Africa and Asia. Tensions between the two superpowers seemed to threaten nuclear confrontation at several points, particularly when the Soviets began to install missiles on the soil of their new Western Hemispheric ally, Cuba (Figure 34.7). However, actual war broke out only once more, in a regional theater. American fears of possible communist advance in South Vietnam, after

the French withdrew from their former colony in the 1950s, brought on a United States military response based on the assumption that communist advance must be opposed anywhere. In this case, after a costly and demoralizing engagement, the United States was forced to retreat, but the immediate consequences did not spill beyond Indochina.

The Cold War was more than a power struggle between two international camps. It was also a battle of ideas. Communism put forth a vision of greater justice, independence from Western control, and industrialization free from both capitalism and Western dominance. The United States saw itself as defender of a free world that highlighted democracy, relatively free markets under capitalism, and personal liberties. The battle of ideas affected the societies involved, with bitter suspicion of the opposing values it also raged around the world, as many leaders were pressed to choose one or the other visions for the future.

Overall, the peak intensity of the cold war passed after the 1950s. New Soviet leaders began to

Figure 34.6 *May Day celebration in Red Square, Moscow.*

Figure 34.7 *Site of Cuban missile base in San Cristobal in October 1962. Discovery of Soviet installations threatened war, but Soviet prime minister Khruschev removed the missiles under pressure from the United States.*

negotiate with the United States; these discussions reduced tension and in the 1970s led to several important arms limitation agreements. Individual countries—Egypt was an example for a time—played off the two superpower rivals, gaining economic assistance from both. Rivalries between China and the Soviet Union, from the late 1950s onward, also softened cold war hostilities. In sum, the cold war affected but did not determine major world developments after 1960.

Even before this, the cold war had intertwined with the other major post–World War II international development, the process of decolonization and the rise of new states in Asia and Africa. From 1946 into the 1970s, first in Asia, then in Africa and other areas, almost all former Western colonies won independence. China and Vietnam also experienced sweeping revolutions. The process of decolonization, whether accompanied by revolution or not, was at least as important as the cold war. It led to the cre-

ation of a host of new or revived nations, many of which quickly developed strong governments and regional military arsenals of their own. Some of these new states moved quickly into one of the alliance systems. For example, Vietnam maintained close ties with the Soviet Union, whereas Thailand and Malaysia favored the United States. But many new nations, headed by giants such as India, proclaimed *nonalignment* in the cold war, seeking and often gaining workable diplomatic relations with both the United States and the Soviet Union. In the long run, the results of decolonization proved more durable in world history than the cold war.

Additional international connections developed during the cold war. Among most nations (the communist bloc stayed somewhat isolated until the 1970s and 1980s), economic interactions increased. There were no global depressions of the magnitude of the 1930s, but economic problems in one area often affected others. Oil shortages in 1973 and 1979, caused by supply manipulation by the oil-producing countries, had international impact. On another front, many multinational companies, based in North America, western Europe, or Japan, began production operations in various parts of the world, often influencing individual governments in unprecedented ways. Exploitation of cheap labor was one of the goals of the multinationals, which brought new industries but also often new hardships to many parts of the world. International pollution problems were a final fruit of the increasingly global character of the world economy.

TABLE 34-2
U.S. Defense Spending in the Cold War (exclusive of veterans' and interest payments)

	National Defense (in billions of 1987 dollars)	% of Gross Domestic Product	% of Federal Budget
1940	18.1	1.7	17.5
1950	94.6	5.2	32.2
1960	217.9	9.5	52.2
1970	264.4	8.3	41.8
1980	187.1	5.1	22.7
1985	261.2	6.4	26.7
1990	272.3	5.5	23.9
1993 (estimated)	239.5	4.7	19.6

Source: U.S. Office of Management and Budget, *Budget of the United States Government*, annual.

The cold war finally wound down in the 1980s. A nationalistic new American president, Ronald Reagan, increased military spending. The Soviet Union, already in economic difficulty, was hard pressed to respond. The Soviet economic crisis was openly acknowledged in 1985 by its new leader, Mikhail Gorbachev. Gorbachev encouraged several significant arms reduction agreements with the United States and in 1989 was obliged to recognize the full independence of satellite states of eastern Europe. With the collapse of the communist system in Europe (including the end of the Soviet Union itself in 1991), the cold war had ended.

Period III: The 1990s and Beyond

The end of the cold war, coming also after the near completion of the decolonization process, set up yet another 20th-century period in world history, one that may extend well into the 21st century. In terms

of international military and economic relations, several features seem to predominate, at least initially.

First, the United States had no full rival as a military superpower. For the moment at least, the alliance systems that had marked Western and world history for more than a century began to close down. The United States preserved elements of its anti-communist alliance, particularly NATO, and extended it into some of the newly independent nations of eastern Europe such as Poland.

Second, regional conflicts demanded new attention in the aftermath of changes in eastern Europe and the lack of a clear international framework. Tensions involving Iraq, the conflict between India and Pakistan, fighting in the former Yugoslavia, and massive killings in central Africa commanded the headlines. The United States and, often, the United Nations played roles in forming alliances that tried to reduce hostilities, but with varying success. In key cases, such as India and Pakistan, concerns about the spread of nuclear weapons added to the regional emphasis.

Third, heightening a trend visible since the 1970s, reassertions of regional identities also accompanied the end of the cold war. Various east Asian leaders commented on weaknesses in Western values, including excessive individualism. The revival of Islam continued to generate tensions within the Middle East, affecting even well-established secular states such as Turkey. Hindu nationalism surged in India.

Fourth, new emphasis was placed on regional but supranational trade blocs, designed to support economic growth by generating wider markets and labor supplies. The European Union expanded its membership and proposed further growth. A North American free trade agreement joined the United States, Mexico, and Canada, with possibilities of extension to Latin America. Looser groupings occurred between states of the former Soviet Union, between Latin American nations headed by Brazil, and in the Pacific region.

Fifth, spurred by the economic success of the United States and western Europe, most major societies in all regions moved toward more common commercial policies. Countries from Mexico to India to China reduced state-run enterprises in favor of greater competition and freer market forces, believing the reforms would promote economic growth. China, ending revolutionary experiments, made an early commitment to the new policies in 1978. Economic structures still varied, but there were fewer policy disparities than at any previous point in the 20th century. Less widely, an interest in democratic political processes spread to many different societies, continuing another trend that had begun in the late 1970s.

Developments of this sort reflected the steady growth in the importance of international economic contacts in the post–cold war context. What they added up to was not entirely clear, although some observers talked of a new framework of rivalry (economic and cultural, if not military) among zones of Western cultural heritage, zones of Confucian heritage, and zones of Islamic heritage. However, no single framework had emerged in the international arena, with superpower rivalry a thing of the past.

Conclusion

A Legacy of Uncertainty

World war and cold war brought new destruction and new levels of fear to many parts of the world. Both kinds of war weakened western Europe in the world by sapping its strength and then replacing its leadership with that of the new superpowers. The rise of the United States was particularly strong in the global economy, military intervention, and the cold war arms race. American cultural influence ranged from Hollywood to Christian missionaries. But the decline of Europe's world role also opened new opportunities for leaders in Asia and Africa, who were able to seize on Europe's weakness and in many cases fruitfully play off suitors from the United States and the Soviet Union. The rebalancing of world power, along with the steady increase in the importance of the global economy, were the main results of the first two diplomatic eras of the 20th century. This rebalancing continued to develop during the century's final decade.

Further Readings

Several important books have dealt with the origins of World War I. L. Lafore's *The Long Fuse* (1965) is a very readable introduction; see also James Joll's *Origins of World War I* (1984), which is slightly more up to date. A controversial interpretation is F. Fischer's *Germany's Aims in the First World War* (1967); see also P. Kennedy's *The Rise of the Anglo-German Antagonism 1860–1914* (1980). I. Geiss's *July 1914* (1967) is a collection of documents on the subject.

For a wider perspective, G. Barraclough's *An Introduction to Contemporary History* (1968) is extremely interesting. On the war's cultural impact, P. Fussell's *The Great War and Modern Memory* (1975) is a brilliant treatment. See also R. J. Sontag's *A Broken World, 1919–1939* (1971) for a survey of the period, dealing mainly with Europe. On the war itself, see K. Robbins's *The First World War* (1984); see also J. Williams's *The Other Battleground: The Home Fronts, Britain, France, and Germany, 1911–1918* (1972) and R. Wohl's *The Generation of 1914* (1979). On the peace settlement, see A. J. Mayer's *The Politics and Diplomacy of Peacemaking* (1968).

On the Great Depression, C. Kindleberger's *The World in Depression, 1929–1939* (1973) is a solid introduction. See also J. Galbraith's *The Great Crash of 1929* (1980) and, for a useful collection of articles, W. Laqueur and G. L. Mosse, eds., *The Great Depression* (1970). Japan's experience is covered in I. Morris, ed., *Japan, 1931–1945: Militarism, Fascism, Japanism?* (1963).

A good introduction to World War II is Gordon Wright's *The Ordeal of Total War, 1939–1945* (1968); see also W. Murray's *The Change in the European Balance of Power* (1984). On the war itself, see B. H. Liddell Hart's *History of the Second World War*, vol. 2 (1971). The U.S. role is the subject of R. A. Divine's *The Reluctant Belligerent: American Entry into World War II* (1979). On the Asian front, see J. H. Boyle's *China and Japan at War, 1937–1945* (1972) and R. Butow's *Japan's Decision to Surrender* (1954). See also S. Ienaga's *The Pacific War* (1978) and Chi Hsi-sheng's *Nationalist China at War* (1982).

On the war's immediate aftermath, see H. Feis's *From Trust to Terror: The Onset of the Cold War, 1945–1950* (1970) and Martin Sherwin's *A World Destroyed: The Atomic Bomb and the Grand Alliance* (1975). For a more general assessment of war's role in the 20th century, see Raymond Aron's *Century of Total War* (1985).

On the cold war, see Walter Lafeber, *America, Russia and the Cold War, 1949–1980* (1980), and Thomas Patterson, *On Every Frontier, the Making of the Cold War* (1979).

Recent work includes R. Douglas's *The World War, 1939–1945: The Cartoonist's Version* (1991); R. Hilberg's *Perpetrators, Victims, Bystanders: The Jewish Catastrophe 1933–1945* (1992); H. James and M. Stone, eds. *When the Wall Came Down: Reactions to German Unification* (1992); and T. Rosenberg's *The Haunted Land: Facing Europe's Ghosts After Communism* (1995).

On the Web

The Great War is examined at http://www.pitt.edu/~pngachec/greatwar/ww1.html and http://www.worldwar1.com/index.html.

The battle of the Somme is illuminated at http://www.stemnetnf.ca/beaumont/somme.htm and http://www.spartacus.schoolnet.co.uk/FWWsomme.htm.

The Battle of Verdun is revisited at http://dut:ta.a0.twi.tudelf.nl/nsens/bunnik.verdun.html.

The concept of blitzkrieg is explained at http:www.achtungpanzer.com/blitz.htm.

The artistic representation of the effects of the techniques of modern warfare is examined at http://www.emory.edu/PHILOSOPHY/ART/guernica.html.

The role of the American homefront and American women in World War II is explored through photographs and interviews at http://pomperaug.com/socstud/stumuseum/ web/ARHome.htm.

World War II as seen through Russian eyes is studied at http://wwiithroughrussianeyes.com.

Dramatic recreations or virtual visits to key sites of that conflict abound on the Web. These sites include D-Day (http://www.nando.net/sproject/dday/dday.html), Hiroshima (http://titan.iwu.edu/~rwilson/hiroshima/, http://www.he.net/~donglong/index.html and http://www.lclark.edu/~history/Hiroshima/), the 1941- 44 siege of Leningrad (http://www.cityvision2000.com/history/900days.htm), and Pearl Harbor (http://brilliacomp.ust.edu/~mportil/assign.html and http://www.execpc.com/~dschaaf/mainmenu.html). Many Japanese interment camps in America now have a dedicated web site, such as that at http://www.library.arizona.edu/wracamps/. One site, however, http:www.oz.net/~cyu/Internment/main.html, has links to many of these sites and also to documents relating to the interment program.

The Holocaust receives effective treatment at the National Holocaust Museum (http://www.remember.org) and at the Simon Wiesenthal Center (http://www.wiesenthal.com/).

It is possible to make an online tour and view special exhibits of The Museum of Tolerance, a division of the Simon Wiesenthal Center that focuses on the dynamics of racism and prejudice in America as well as Holocaust history. Of particular interest is the manner in which its interactive and interview-driven "The Making of a Skinhead" program bears comparison to the content of sites devoted to the Hitler Youth movement (http://www.historyplace.com/worldwar2/hitleryouth/index.html) and the Italian fascist youth movement (http://www.library.wisc.edu/libraries/dpf/Facism/Youth/html).

A virtual visit to the Anne Frank homepage (http://www.annefrank.nl/) lends a human face to both fascist oppression and the quest for a world without hatred.

Chapter 35

The West in the 20th Century

Campus unrest was a Western-wide phenomenon in the 1960s. Student uprisings in France in 1968 created a near revolution. Here, students and workers demonstrate in Paris.

This chapter deals with developments in western Europe and the extensions of Western society in North America, Australia, and New Zealand between 1914 and the present. Western history was profoundly marked by the framework of global events discussed in Chapter 34, dividing into two strongly contrasting periods.

World War I and its economic, cultural, and demographic devastation led to three decades that were among the most troubled in Western history. Several major societies cast off democratic political forms and mainstream cultural values in favor of radical new experiments, and others stopped functioning effectively. After 1945, however, despite the cold war and the pressure of decolonization, western Europe and the United States alike found new sources of dynamism. The West was hardly problem free in the decades after World War II partly because adjustments to its new world position raised new uncertainties. But the level of conflict and confusion declined as new structures began to take hold in the 1950s and 1960s. Many Europeans argued that they were building a new kind of society.

The United States along with Canada, Australia, New Zealand, and the leading nations of western Europe was very flexible in dealing with major political and economic issues. The West also continued to provide leadership in scientific research and popular consumer culture. In these areas Western patterns continued to have influence well beyond the borders of the civilization itself. Developments since 1945 drove home the point that although its world power declined, Western society retained great vitality.

1915 C.E.	1935 C.E.	1955 C.E.	1975 C.E.	1985 C.E.
1918–1923 Postwar adjustments; new republic in Germany, economic recession and recovery; emergence of communist movement	**1935** Nuremberg laws deprive German Jews of citizenship	**1957** Establishment of European Economic Community (Common Market)	**1979** Thatcher and new conservatism in Britain	**1992** End of economic restrictions within Common Market
1922 Mussolini takes power in Italy	**1936** Popular Front government in France	**1958** De Gaulle's Fifth Republic in France	**1979** Significant recession	
1925 Locarno agreements regularize Germany's diplomatic relations	**1938** Attacks on German Jews increase	**1960s** Civil rights movement in U.S.	**1981** Reagan president in U.S.	
1928 Kellogg–Briand Pact	**1942** Hitler decides on extermination of European Jews	**1960s** Emergence of new feminist movement		
1930 Rapid rise of Nazi party	**1945** End of World War II	**1968–1973** Massive student protests		
1933 Hitler becomes chancellor of Germany	**1945–1948** New constitutions in Italy, Germany, and France; Labour party victory in Britain; basic measures of welfare states	**1970s** Democratic regimes in Spain, Portugal, and Greece		
1933–1937 New Deal in United States	**1947** Marshall Plan	**1973, 1979** Oil crises		
	1947–1974 Decolonization			
	1947–1960s Emergence and most intense phase of cold war			
	1948 East and West German regimes established			
	1948 Publication of *The Second Sex*			
	1949 North Atlantic Treaty Organization established			

THE DISARRAY IN THE WEST, 1914–1945

World War I was a traumatic experience for western Europe. Despite important innovation, particularly in the 1920s, the West could not resolve the key postwar problems in politics and economics until after another world war.

World War I quickly shattered the confidence many Europeans felt at the turn of the century. It also damaged the European economy, diplomatic relations between Western states, and political systems in many countries. The key battlegrounds for four bloody years had been in Europe. The sheer rate of death and maiming, as well as the frustration of nearly four years of stalemate, had a devastating material and psychological impact on the European combatants. More than 10 million Europeans died. In key countries such as Britain, France, and Germany, the percentage killed had a serious demographic impact, reducing the number of young men available for work and family life. Vast amounts of property had been destroyed. Key prewar regimes were toppled when the German emperor abdicated and the Habsburg Empire collapsed.

The Roaring '20s

Despite all the disruptions, a brief period of stability, even optimism, emerged in the mid-1920s. Diplomatic tensions eased somewhat within Europe as Germany made some moves to adapt to its weakened position in return for partial relief from the reparation payments. Although Germany refused to accept its new eastern boundaries, it did promise friendship all around. Hopes that the Versailles settlement could be permanent ran so high that an American and a French leader coauthored a treaty outlawing war forever (the *Kellogg–Briand Pact* of 1928, which a number of nations dutifully ratified), a sign of the naive hopes of the decade.

Internal politics harbored new but potentially manageable tensions. The war's end and immediate economic dislocations, as well as the impact of the Russian Revolution, had inspired a new political polarization in many countries. Many veterans, embittered by the war experience, joined groups on the far right that wanted an authoritarian government and recovery of national honor. The labor movement on the left split, and a minority wing became communist, taking cues from the revolutionary regime in the Soviet Union. Germany produced an admirable constitution for its new democratic republic, but many groups did not accept it and there were understandable fears for its survival. Even Britain, long known for its political stability, saw a major shift as the Labour party replaced the Liberals as the second major political force. Generally, the liberal middle sector of European politics was weakened. Nevertheless, the mid-1920s brought a brief respite as the extremist groups declined in force. Few leaders of great stature emerged. Even in the United States, a series of colorless presidents captured the political timidity of the decade.

Economic prosperity buoyed hopes in the middle of the decade. Industrial production boomed, though more markedly in the United States than in western Europe. Mass consumption standards rose for several years. Radios became widespread, and new products were developed, such as the artificial fiber rayon. Particularly in the United States, the automobile became a mass consumption item, and its effects ranged from reducing rural isolation to changing teenage dating habits. Household appliances proliferated, and technology's impact on daily life reached a new level. Advertising became more pervasive and visually alluring, as Figure 35.1 suggests.

Finally, the 1920s saw a burst of cultural creativity and social change in many parts of the West. Filmmakers experimented with this genre for artistic expression and mass entertainment. Modern artists such as Picasso developed geometric cubist styles and other innovations. Writers and playwrights such as Luigi Pirandello and James Joyce pioneered new forms, reducing plot lines and, in the case of drama, often seeking audience involvement.

Women, particularly in the middle class, made important changes. Women's involvement in the labor force during the war was short-lived, as men pushed them out at war's end. However, postwar legislation granted suffrage to women in Britain, Germany, and the United States. Furthermore, prosperity and the falling birth rate gave many women the chance to develop new leisure habits and less restrictive fashions. Young women in the United States began to date more freely as a preliminary to courtship. Wives in Britain wrote of new interests in sexual pleasure while maintaining their commitment to marriage. A new generation of advice writers, such as Marie Stopes in England, talked about bodily pleasures as "mystical, alluring, enchanting in their promise." These developments, like the more general rise of consumerism, gained further momentum later.

Figure 35.1 *Consumer society, 1920s style: cars, cosmetics, a "new woman," and more open pleasure seeking.*

The Impact of the Depression

All the hopeful signs seemed to vanish with the onset of depression in 1929, and the Great Depression revealed that the economic and political achievements of the mid-1920s had not been as solidly based as people had hoped. Political consequences were inevitable, with so many people out of work or threatened with unemployment. The weak Western governments responded to the onset of the catastrophe counterproductively. They raised national tariffs to keep out the goods of other countries, but this merely worsened the international economy and weakened sales for everyone. The depression heightened political polarization. People sought solutions from radical parties or movements, both on the left and on the right. Support for communist parties went up in many countries, and in important cases an authoritarian movement on the radical right gained increased attention. Even in stable nations, such as Britain, battles between conservative and labor movements made decisive policy difficult.

There were a few cases of constructive political response. Scandinavian states, directed by moderate socialist movements, increased government spending, providing new levels of social insurance against illness and unemployment and foreshadowing the modern *welfare state*. In the United States, Franklin Roosevelt's *New Deal*, from 1933 onward, enacted several social insurance measures and used government spending to stimulate the economy. The New Deal did not cure the American depression, but it alleviated the worst effects. The New Deal also brought the United States more in line with the government traditions of other Western nations by increasing the power of the state in what had been, by European standards, a rather loosely governed society. Under Roosevelt, the government became much more active, regulating banks and other economic activities and sponsoring huge public works. A new social security system provided assistance to the unemployed and retirees; correspondingly, older people began to expect less economic support from their families and more from the state.

In key cases, however, the Great Depression led to either of two effects: a parliamentary system that became increasingly incapacitated, too divided to take vigorous action even in foreign policy, or the outright overturning of the parliamentary system itself.

France was a prime example of the first pattern. The French government responded sluggishly to the depression. Voters reacted by moving toward political extremes. Socialist and then communist parties expanded. Rightist movements calling for a strong leader and fervent nationalism grew, often disrupting political meetings to discredit the parliamentary system. In response, liberal, socialist, and communist parties allied in a *Popular Front* in 1936, winning the election. However, the Popular Front government was unable to take strong social reform measures because of the ongoing strength of conservative republicans and the authoritarian right. The same paralysis crept into foreign policy in response to the growing militarism of Nazi Germany. The Popular Front fell in 1938, but even before this France was close to a standstill.

The Challenge of Fascism

In Germany, the impact of the depression led directly to the new fascist regime. The shock of loss in World War I was exacerbated by treaty arrangements that cast blame for the war on the German nation. Modern parliamentary traditions were new and shaky in any event. Many factors combined to make Germany a breeding ground for *fascism,* although it took the depression to bring this current to the fore.

Fascism was a product of the war. The movement's advocates, many of them former veterans, attacked the weakness of parliamentary democracy and the corruption and class conflict of Western capitalism. They proposed a strong state ruled by a powerful leader who would revive the nation's forces through vigorous foreign and military policy. Fascists vaguely promised social reforms to alleviate class antagonisms, and their attacks on trade unions as well as socialist and communist parties pleased landlords and business groups. A first fascist regime took power in Italy in 1922 as Mussolini marched to power. The word *fascism* came from the Italian movement's Roman symbol, a bundle of sticks (*fasci*). It was the advent of the National Socialist, or Nazi, regime in Germany under Adolf Hitler that made this new political movement a major force in world history.

In his vote-gathering campaigns, Hitler repeated standard fascist arguments about the need for unity and the hopeless weakness of parliamentary politics. The state should provide guidance, for it was greater than the sum of individual interests, and the leader should guide the state. Middle-class elements, including big business leaders, were attracted to Hitler's firm stance against socialism and communism. Hitler also focused grievances against various currents in modern life, from big department stores to feminism, by attacking Jewish influences in Germany. And he promised a glorious foreign policy to undo the wrongs of the Versailles treaty. Finally, Hitler represented a hope for effective action against the depression. Although the Nazi party never won a majority vote in a free election, it did win the largest single slice in 1932, and this enabled Hitler to make arrangements with other political leaders for his rise to power legally in 1933.

Once in power, Hitler quickly set about constructing a *totalitarian state,* a new kind of government that would exercise direct control over nearly all the activities of its subjects. Hitler eliminated all opposition parties; he purged the bureaucracy and military, installing loyal Nazis in many posts. His secret police, the *Gestapo*, arrested hundreds of thousands of political opponents. Trade unions were replaced by government-sponsored bodies that tried to appease low-paid workers by offering full employment and various welfare benefits. Government economic planning helped restore production levels, with particular emphasis on armament construction. The Nazi regime also disputed dominant Western cultural trends. It attacked modern art, urging more realistic, heroic styles, often in the classical mode, and even challenged scientific education, with praise for sports and physical training over intellectual life. Hitler cemented his regime with constant, well-staged propaganda bombardments, strident nationalism, and an incessant attack on Germany's large Jewish minority.

Hitler's hatred of Jews ran deep. He blamed them for various personal misfortunes and for movements such as socialism and excessive capitalism that in his view had weakened the German spirit. Obviously, anti-Semitism served as a catch-all for a host of diverse dissatisfactions and therefore appealed to many Germans. Anti-Semitism also provided a scapegoat that could rouse national passions and distract the population from other problems. Measures against Jews became more and more severe: They were forced to wear special emblems, their property was attacked and seized, and increasing numbers were sent to concentration camps. After 1940, Hitler's policy turned to eliminating the European Jewish population, and the Holocaust raged in the concentration camps of Germany and its conquered territories. Other groups were also fiercely attacked, including gypsies and gays.

Hitler's foreign and military policies were based on preparation for war. He wanted not only to recoup Germany's World War I losses but to create a land empire that would extend across much of Europe, particularly toward the east against what he saw as the inferior Slavic peoples. When war finally broke out in 1939, Hitler's forces pressed forward for three years before his opponents were able to regroup.

World history from one war through the next read like a tragic drama in Western history. One dire event led to the next, with none of the major participants able to stop them. Historians have debated whether better leadership in the West could have stemmed the tide or whether human agency was powerless in light of the crisis forces.

AFTER WORLD WAR II: INTERNATIONAL SETTING FOR THE WEST

▓ *Western Europe seemed at an all-time low in 1945, as wartime damage combined with pressures against colonialism and the rise of two superpowers. The new cold war seemed to dwarf European concerns. But western Europe bounced back, with U.S. collaboration, in what was one of the most innovative periods in Europe's history. New economic vitality combined with a resurgence of democracy designed to right the wrongs of Europe's recent past.*

World War II left western Europe in shambles. The sheer physical destruction, caused particularly by bombing raids, disrupted housing and transportation. Downed bridges and rail lines complicated food shipments, leaving many people ill-fed and unable to work at full efficiency. German use of forced foreign labor and the many boundary changes generated hundreds of thousands of refugees trying to return home or find a new home. For at least two years after 1945, it was unclear whether recovery would be possible. Sheer survival proved difficult enough.

Europe and Its Colonies

Decolonization added to Europe's postwar problems. European nations tried to restore colonial administrations worldwide, but they faced growing resistance. It was soon clear that many colonies could be maintained only at great cost, and the European nations decided that the colonies were not worth the expense.

A few colonial clashes proved divisive. France tried to defend its holdings in Vietnam against nationalist guerrillas, yielding only in 1954 after some major defeats. The French clung even more fiercely to Algeria, its oldest African colony and one with a large European minority. The French military joined Algerian settlers in insisting on a war to the death against nationalist forces, and bitter fighting went on for years. Tension even threatened civil war in France until a new president, Charles de Gaulle, realized the hopelessness of the struggle and negotiated Algeria's independence in 1962.

Overall, decolonization proceeded more smoothly, without prolonged fighting that might have drained the Western nations themselves. Many west European governments maintained close relations with former colonies.

The impact of decolonization on the West should not be minimized. Important minorities of former settlers and officials came home embittered. Europe's overt power in the world was reduced dramatically. Efforts by Britain and France to attack independent Egypt in 1956, to protest Egypt's nationalization of the Suez Canal, symbolized the new state of affairs. The United States and the Soviet Union forced a quick end to hostilities, and what was once a colonial lifeline came into non-Western hands.

The Cold War

The cold war, the second postwar international trend, had many implications for western Europe. It brought new pressures from the United States on internal and foreign policy. Through the 1950s and beyond, the United States pressed for acceptance of German rearmament and for acceptance of American forces and weapons systems. The United States' wishes were not always met, but the Americans had vital negotiating leverage in the economic aid they offered, the troops they stationed in Europe, and the nuclear "umbrella" they developed. The nuclear weapons seemed to offer the only realistic protection against a direct Soviet attack. For their part, the Soviet Union influenced western Europe not only through its perceived aggressive intent but also by funding and supporting communist movements in France and Italy.

Although tensions receded after the high point of the late 1940s, western Europe could no longer plan to defend itself against its major external enemy. Although Great Britain and, after 1958, France developed small nuclear capabilities, they simply could not afford the massive stockpiles and rockets of the two superpowers. To some extent, western Europeans grew comfortable in their reliance on U.S. protection. Not only during the lean postwar years but even after prosperity returned, European nations kept their military budgets modest, in comparison with the United States and the Soviet Union. The perceived Soviet threat and the decline of Great Britain also pressed Canada, Australia, and New Zealand into increasing diplomatic and economic ties with the United States.

As western Europe abandoned its military preeminence, the United States, never before a major peacetime military power, devoted growing resources to its military capacity and gave a growing voice to its mili-

tary leaders. Regardless of the political party in power, the percentage of the U.S. government budget going to the military remained stable from the 1950s to the 1980s, when it went up. In contrast, some European leaders boasted that their societies had made a transition toward preeminence of civilian values and goals. Although American and European values and institutions became more similar in key respects after World War II, the difference in military roles signaled ongoing distinctions within Western society.

New Directions in the West

Although decolonization and the cold war left their mark, western Europe demonstrated surprising resiliency. A new set of leaders emerged in many countries, some from wartime resistance movements eager to avoid the mistakes that had led to depression and war. Resistance thinking, suggested in the Document section, sought dramatic new solutions for previous problems. Although this vision was not always realized, western Europe moved forward from 1945 onward on three important fronts: the extension of democratic political systems, a modification of nation-state rivalries within Europe, and a commitment to rapid economic growth that reduced social and gender tensions.

The Spread of Liberal Democracy

In politics, defeat in war greatly discredited fascism and other rightist movements that had opposed parliamentary democracy. Vestiges of these movements continued, periodically surfacing in countries such as France and Italy, but rarely with much muscle. At the same time, key leftist groups, including the strong communist movements that emerged from the war in France and Italy, were committed to democratic politics. While social protest continued, outright revolutionary sentiment declined. Finally, several new political movements surfaced, notably the important *Christian Democratic movement,* which was wedded to democratic institutions and moderate social reform. Despite national variations, western Europe experienced a shift in the political spectrum toward fuller support for democratic constitutions and greater agreement on the need for government planning and welfare activities.

New regimes had to be established in Germany and Italy after the defeat of fascist and Nazi leadership, whereas France established a new republic once occupation ended. France, Britain, and the United States progressively merged their occupation zones in

ᴅᴏᴄᴜᴍᴇɴᴛ

The Resistance Spirit

In most countries occupied by Nazi Germany, resistance movements sprang up during the war to contest the short-lived empire. Resistance fighters in Holland, France, and elsewhere also formulated plans for a new Europe after the war that would redress the social and diplomatic tensions that had bedeviled the West for decades. The battles against the Nazis, but also their ideas, lead one historian to label the Resistance the wildest period of revolt in Europe since 1848. This resistance spirit was far from fully realized as Europe rebuilt after 1945, but it helps explain some of the West's new directions and unexpected comeback. The first of the following selections comes from a document adopted by the French National Resistance Council in 1944, representing various movements. The second selection contains excerpts from underground newspapers in the previous year.

The Resistance Council Pledged to Remain United After the War

In order to assure: the establishment of the broadest possible democracy by allowing the people to voice their desires through the reestablishment of universal suffrage; full liberty of thought, conscience and expression; freedom of the press—an honest press, independent of the State, powerful economic interests and foreign influences; freedom of association, freedom to meet and demonstrate; the inviolability of the home and of private correspondence; respect for the individual; absolute equality of all citizens before the law.

In order to effect the necessary reforms:

1. Economic: the establishment of a true economic and social democracy, with the requisite eviction of the great economic and financial feudatories from the direction of the economy; rational organization of the economy, assuring the subordination of special interests to the general interest, and freed from the professional dictatorship installed in the image of the fascist states; the development of national production following a state plan, established after consultation with the representatives of all interested groups; the return to the nation of the great monopolies, fruits of the labor of all, of energy resources, of the underground riches of the country, of the insurance companies and the major banks; the development and support of producers', buyers', and sellers' cooperatives in both agriculture and manufacturing; the right of qualified workers to rise to administrative and management positions in business, and workers' participation in the running of the economy.

2. Social: the right to work and the right to leisure, in particular by the reestablishment and the improvement of labor contracts; a major readjustment of wages and the guarantee of a level of wages and working conditions which will assure every worker and his family security, dignity, and the chance of a decent life; a complete social security system, providing all citizens with the means of existence when they are unable to secure it themselves—a system whose management is shared by those concerned and by the State; a meaningful opportunity for all French children to have the benefits of education and access to the best of French culture, whatever their family's financial status, so that the highest positions in society are truly open to all those with the capacity to fill them, thus bringing into being a real elite, of merit rather than of birth, constantly renewed from the people.

From La Revue Libre and L'ecole D'Uriage, 1943

The visible causes of the war are not the main causes: racist imperialism, megalomania of the totalitarian leaders, etc. All these factors stem from an essential main cause, to wit the need for people to adapt their social and economic organization to the progress of science and technology....

Like it or not, this war is revolutionary, in several senses. First, it destroys the last vestiges of the decaying capitalist order.... Under the Nazi oppression the masses in Europe, long so apathetic, are gradually regaining the taste for liberty. To use their energies we must give this war a goal, which can rouse their enthusiasm, to win their agreement to the construction of a world where they are no longer pariahs, but with the completion of democracy, truly sovereign....

As to France, we think that some kind of Western grouping effected with us, mainly on an economic basis and as extensive as possible, can offer great advantages. Such a grouping, extended in Africa, in close relations with the Orient and notably the Arab states which legitimately seek to unite their interests, and for which the English Channel, the Rhine, the Mediterranean will be like arteries, can constitute a chief center in the worldwide organization of production, exchange and security.

Questions: What did resistance leaders identify as Europe's big problems? What economic and social changes were sought? What was the resistance approach to nationalism? Sources of this sort invite analysis in terms of cause and effect. How might resistance thinking help explain European recovery after 1945? What components of resistance thinking did not come to pass? By examining the main resistance ideas in terms of what happened to western Europe earlier in the 20th century, the causes of these same ideas can be suggested. What other causes might have come into play? What kinds of people (age, social class, gender, cultural and political affiliation) were most likely to generate resistance ideas in France?

Germany into what became the *Federal Republic of Germany* (West Germany), encouraging a new constitution that would avoid the mistakes of Germany's earlier Weimar Republic by outlawing extremist political movements. The new constitutions set up after 1945 in many European countries, although they varied in particulars, uniformly established effective parliaments with universal suffrage. And the regimes endured. Only France, pressed by the Algerian War, changed its constitution in 1958, forming a Fifth Republic, still democratic but with stronger presidential authority.

Western Europe's movement toward more consistent democracy was extended in the 1970s when Spain and Portugal shifted from their authoritarian, semifascist constitutions to democratic, parliamentary systems. Greece, increasingly linked to the West, followed the same pattern. By the 1980s, western Europe had become more politically uniform than ever before. Party dominance shifted, with conservatives, including Christian Democrats, alternating with socialist coalitions, but all major actors agreed on the constitutional system itself.

The Welfare State

The consolidation of democracy also entailed a general movement toward a welfare state. Resistance ideas and the shift leftward of the political spectrum helped explain the new activism of the state in economic policy and welfare issues. Wartime planning in the British government had pointed to the need for new programs to reduce the impact of economic inequality and to reward the lower classes for their loyalty. Not surprisingly, the governments that emerged at the war's end—Britain's Labour party and communist–socialist–Christian Democrat coalitions in France and Italy—quickly moved to set up a new government apparatus that would play a vigorous role in economic planning and develop new social activities as well. By 1948 the basic nature of the modern welfare state had been established throughout western Europe. The United States, though somewhat more tentative in welfare measures, added to its New Deal legislation in the 1960s, under president Lyndon Johnson's *Great Society* programs, creating medical assistance packages for the poor and the elderly. Canada enacted a still more comprehensive medical insurance plan.

The European welfare state elaborated a host of social insurance measures. Unemployment insurance

was improved. Medical care was supported by state-funded insurance or, as in Britain where it became a centerpiece of the new Labour program, the basic health care system was nationalized. State-run medical facilities provided free care to the bulk of the British population from 1947 onward, although some small fees were introduced later. All western European governments provided family assistance payments to families with several children, the amount increasing with family size. Governments also became more active in the housing field—a necessity given wartime destruction and postwar population growth. Britain embarked on an ambitious program of *council housing*, providing many single-family units that deliberately mixed working-class and middle-class families in new neighborhoods. By the 1950s more than one-fourth of the British population was housed in structures built and run by the government.

The welfare state that emerged in the postwar years was a compromise product. It recognized a large private sector and tried to limit and cushion individual initiative rather than replace it with state action alone, as in the communist system. It provided aid for citizens at many income levels. Middle-class people used state medical insurance and disproportionately benefited from expanded educational systems and university scholarships. In other words, although the welfare state focused particularly on problems of workers and the poor, it won support from other groups by dealing with some of their special needs as well. An important new definition of government functions, the welfare state increased contacts between government and citizens and produced a host of new regulations that framed European life.

An increased government role in economic policy paralleled the welfare state. Most postwar governments nationalized some industry sectors outright. Most European countries also set up new planning offices, responsible for developing multiyear economic projections and for setting goals and the means to meet them. By coordinating tax concessions and directing the flow of capital from state banks, government planners had genuine power to influence economic activity. Planning extended to agriculture as well. Officials regulated crop sizes and encouraged consolidation of land for greater efficiency, and they could require farmers to participate in cooperatives that would improve marketing and purchasing procedures.

Of the Western nations, only the United States shunned an economic planning office, although it maintained government regulation of the financial system. American government growth consisted more of expanding military activities and piecemeal welfare measures.

Despite important variations, the role of the state loomed large throughout the West from the 1940s onward. A new breed of bureaucrat, often called a *technocrat* because of intense training in engineering or economics and because of a devotion to the power of national planning, came to the fore in government offices.

Political Stability and the Question Marks

Welfare states and economic planning reduced political protest during most of the post-World War II decades. For better or worse, Europeans seemed to accept the state's new social and economic role as well as its constitutional structure. Political debates often were fierce and partisan loyalties intense, but few sweeping issues were raised. Political power oscillated between moderate conservative and reformist socialist parties.

The new Western patterns of political compromise were jolted severely by a series of student protests that developed in the late 1960s. Even before this, in the United States a vigorous civil rights movement had developed to protest unequal treatment of African Americans (Figure 35.2). Massive demonstrations, particularly in southern cities, attacked segregation and limitations on African-American voting rights.

Campus unrest was a Western-wide phenomenon in the 1960s. At major American universities, student protest focused on the nation's involvement in the war in Vietnam. Young people in Europe and the United States also targeted the materialism of their societies, seeking more idealistic goals and greater justice. Student uprisings in France in 1968 created a near revolution. By the early 1970s, new rights for students as well as other reforms, combined with police repression, ended the most intense student protests, and the passage of civil rights legislation in the United States reduced urban rioting and demonstrations. The flexibility of postwar Western democracy seemed triumphant. Some additional political concerns, including a new wave of feminism and environmentalist movements, entered the arena

Figure 35.2 *The great civil rights rally in Washington, D.C., August 1963.*

during the 1970s, partly as an aftermath of the student explosion. The rise of the Green movement in several countries in the 1970s signaled a new political tone, hostile to uncontrolled economic growth. Green parliamentary deputies in Germany refused even to wear coats and ties in their efforts to defy established political habits.

As economic growth slowed in the 1970s and the Western world faced its greatest economic recession since the immediate postwar years, other signs of political change emerged. New leadership sprang up within the British Conservative party and the United States Republican party. In 1979, British Conservative leader *Margaret Thatcher* began the longest-running prime ministership in history, working to cut welfare and housing expenses and to promote free enterprise. Neither she nor her American counterpart, Ronald Reagan, fully dismantled the welfare state, but they did reduce its impact. Another attack on the welfare state emerged with the triumph of a Republican congressional majority in the United States in November 1994. In response, leaders such as Bill Clinton in the United States and the British Labor Party's Tony Blair rode to power in the 1990s with more pragmatic versions of the welfare state that focused more on economic growth than social protections.

Despite all the portents of change, however, the main lines of postwar government persisted into the 1990s. Democratic institutions often failed to command great excitement as voting levels went down throughout the West (particularly in the United States), but they roused no widespread, coherent resistance either. The Western world remained freer from major political upheavals than most other civilizations in the postwar decades, and freer than Western society itself had been during the 1920s and 1930s. The main question was, how long would harmony last?

The Diplomatic Context

Western Europe addressed some traditional diplomatic problems, notably recurrent nationalistic rivalry, as part of its postwar political renewal. United States guidance combined with innovative thinking in the new European governments to produce a dramatic new diplomatic framework in Europe itself.

Many wartime resistance leaders combined their hatred of Nazism with a plea for a reconstruction of the European spirit. The Christian Democratic movement in particular produced important new advocates of harmony among European nations.

Furthermore, by 1947, American leaders grew eager to spur western Europe's economic recovery, and they judged that coordination across national boundaries was an essential precondition. Thus the American *Marshall Plan* required discussion of tariffs and other development issues between recipient nations. With simultaneous American insistence on the partial rearmament of Germany and German participation in NATO, the framework for diplomatic reform was complete.

Faced with these pressures and aware of the failure of nationalistic policies between the wars, several French leaders proposed coordination between France and Germany as a means of setting up a new Europe. The nations of the Low Countries and Italy soon were linked in these activities. The idea was to tie German economic expansion to an international framework so that the nation's growing strength would not again threaten European peace. A measure to establish a united European military force proved too ambitious and collapsed under nationalist objections. But in 1958, the six west European nations (West Germany, France, Italy, Belgium, Luxembourg, and the Netherlands) set up the *European Economic Community,* or Common Market, to begin to create a single economic entity across national political boundaries. Tariffs were reduced between the member nations, and a common tariff policy was set for the outside world. Free movement of labor and investment was encouraged. A Common Market bureaucracy was established, ultimately in Brussels, to oversee these operations. The Common Market set up a court system to adjudicate disputes and prevent violations of coordination rules; it also administered a development fund to spur economic growth in laggard regions such as southern Italy or western France.

The Common Market did not move quickly toward a single government. Important national disputes limited the organization's further growth. For example, France and Germany routinely quarreled over agricultural policy, with France seeking more payments to farmers. But the Common Market managed to establish an advisory international parliament, ultimately elected by direct vote. Then, in the 1980s, arrangements were made to dismantle all trade and currency exchange barriers between member states in 1992, creating economic unity. And the Common Market's success expanded its hold within western Europe. After long hesitation, Britain, despite its tradition of proud island independence, decided to join, as did Ireland, Denmark, and later Greece, Spain, and

Map 35.1 *NATO Boundaries and Neutral Nations. Plans for a wider European Union; the Common Market and its growth.*

Portugal. In the mid-1990s, Finland, Sweden, and Austria joined, and the community (now called the European Union) planned further coordination measures, including a single currency. Nationalist tensions within western Europe receded to a lower point than ever before in modern history.

Economic Expansion

Accompanying political and diplomatic change was striking economic growth after a short, agonizing time of postwar rebuilding. The welfare state and the Common Market may have encouraged this growth by improving purchasing power for the masses and facilitating market expansion across national boundaries; economic growth encouraged the success of new political and diplomatic systems in turn.

There was no question that by the mid-1950s, western Europe had entered a new economic phase. Agricultural production and productivity increased rapidly as peasant farmers, backed by the technocrats, adopted new equipment and seeds. Retooled industries poured out textiles and metallurgical products. Expensive consumer products such as automobiles and appliances supported rapidly growing factories.

Overall growth in gross national product surpassed the rates of any extended period since the beginning of the Industrial Revolution; it also surpassed the growth rates of the U.S. economy during the 1950s and 1960s. Once some basic reconstruction and currency stabilization had occurred by 1948, the German economy took off at a 6 percent annual expansion during the 1950s; with few modest setbacks, this pace continued into the early 1970s. France attained an 8 percent growth rate by the late 1950s, maintained almost this level during the 1960s, and returned to rates of more than 7 percent annually by the early 1970s. By 1959 the Italian economy, a newcomer to the industrial big leagues, was expanding at an 11 percent annual rate. Admittedly, these were the clearest success stories. Scandinavian growth was more modest, and Britain, also expanding but falling rapidly in rank among the European national economies, managed at best a 4 percent increase annually. However, even this contrasted sharply with the stagnation of the 1920s and early 1930s.

These growth rates depended on rapid technological change. Europe's rising food production was achieved with a steadily shrinking agricultural labor force. France's peasant population—16 percent of the labor force in the early 1950s—fell to 10 percent two decades later, but overall output was much higher than before. During the 1950s the industrial work force grew as part of factory expansion, but by the 1960s, despite rising production, the proportion of factory workers also began to drop. Workers in the service sector, filling functions as teachers, clerks, medical personnel, insurance and bank workers, and performers and other leisure industry personnel, rose rapidly in contrast. Europe, like the United States, began to convert technological advance into the provision of larger bureaucracies and service operations without jeopardizing the expanding output of goods. In France, half of all paid workers were in the service sector by 1968, and the proportion rose steadily thereafter.

The high rates of economic growth also ensured low unemployment after the immediate postwar dislocations passed. Even Britain, with lagging development, averaged no more than 4 percent unemployment per year during the 1950s and 1960s, and countries such as France and Germany had rates of 2 to 3 percent a year. Indeed, many parts of the continent were short of labor and had to seek hundreds of thousands of workers from other areas—first from southern Europe, then, as that region industrialized, from Africa, the Middle East, and parts of Asia. The rise of immigrant minorities was a vital development in western Europe and the United States, where the influx of Asian and Latin-American immigrants increased markedly.

Economic growth and low unemployment meant large increases in incomes, even with the taxation necessary to sustain welfare programs. Per capita disposable income rose 117 percent in the United States between 1960 and 1973 and soared 258 percent in France, 312 percent in Germany, and 323 percent in Denmark. Scandinavia, Switzerland, and the Federal Republic of Germany surpassed the United States in standard of living by the 1980s, and France, long an apparent laggard in modern economic development, pulled even. New spending money rapidly translated into huge increases in the purchase of durable consumer goods, as Western civilization became more affluent. Shopping malls and supermarkets, the agents of affluence and extensive but efficient shopping that had first developed in the United States, spread widely at the expense of more traditional, specialist small shops. With the consumer society, promptings to buy, to smell good, to look right, and to express one's personality in the latest car style quickly began to describe European as well as American life (Figure 35.3). The frenzy to find good vacation spots was intense. Millions of Germans poured annually into Italy and Spain, seeking the sun. Britons thronged to Spanish beaches. Europeans were bent on combining efficient work with indulgent leisure.

The West's economic advance was not without some dark spots. Many immigrant workers from Turkey, north Africa, Pakistan, and the West Indies suffered very low wages and unstable employment. These immigrants, euphemistically called "guest workers," often were residentially segregated and were the victims of discrimination by employers and police. Racism continued to be an important factor in Western society.

More troubling still was the slowing of economic growth after 1970. In 1973, the oil-producing states of the Middle East cut their production and raised prices, initially in response to a Middle Eastern war with Israel. A second orchestrated oil crisis in 1979 led to a severe recession throughout Western society, with unusually high rates of unemployment. Growing competition from east Asia and other areas cut into traditional staples such as steel and automobile production, making it difficult to recover the dynamism of the two postwar decades.

Then in the 1990s, renewed recession hit first the United States, then western Europe, where unemployment rates surged past 10 percent. Governments everywhere cut back welfare benefits, although in most of western Europe a high-wage economy persisted for those employed. Postwar prosperity continued to fuel life in the West, but there were serious questions about the future.

Chevy puts the purr in performance!

Figure 35.3 *In the United States, as well as in Japan and western Europe, advertisements increasingly evoked a good life to be achieved by buying the right goods. The newest car was associated with a prosperous home, a loving family, and even happy pets.*

SOCIETY AND CULTURE IN THE WEST

◼ *Political and economic changes in Western society changed the contours of earlier industrial development. They also reduced many earlier differences within Western society, particularly between the United States and western Europe, as the two key Western spaces converged in many respects. The West became the first example of an advanced industrial society, especially from the 1950s onward, and both the United States and western Europe played key roles in this change.*

Postindustrial Social Structure

Economic growth eased some earlier social conflicts throughout the West. Workers were still propertyless as producers, but they owned many consumer goods, such as appliances and vehicles. Social lines were blurred by rapid social mobility as educational opportunities opened further and the size of the white-collar sector expanded. Much unskilled labor was left to immigrants. Economic and political change also changed conditions for west Europe's peasantry. Peasants became commercial agents, eager to improve their standards of living, and, through car trips and television, participants in consumer culture.

Social distinctions remained, to be sure. Middle-class people had more abundant leisure opportunities and a more optimistic outlook than did most workers. Signs of tension continued. Crime rates went up throughout Western society after the 1920s, and the levels were particularly high in the United States. Race riots punctuated American life in the 1950s and 1960s and exploded in immigrant sections of British cities in the 1980s.

The Women's Revolution

A key facet of postwar change involved women and the family; again, both western Europe and the United States participated in this upheaval. Although family ideals persisted in contradictory ways, with workers urging that "a loving family is the finest thing, something to work for, to look to and to look after," the realities of family life changed in contradictory ways. Family leisure activities expanded. Extended family contacts were facilitated by telephones and automobiles. More years of schooling increased the importance of peer groups for children, and the authority of parents declined.

The clearest innovation in family life came through the new working patterns of women. World War II brought more factory and clerical jobs for women, as World War I had done. After a few years of downward adjustment, the trends continued. From the early 1950s onward, the number of working women, particularly married women, rose steadily in western Europe, the United States, and Canada. Women's earlier educational gains had improved their work qualifications; the growing number of service jobs created a need for additional workers. Many women also sought entry into the labor force as a means of adding to personal or family income, affording some of the con-

sumer items now becoming feasible but not yet easy to buy or fulfilling themselves personally in a society that associated worth with work and earnings.

The growing employment of women brought the female segment of the labor force up to 44 percent of the total in most Western countries by the 1970s. To be sure, full job equality was not achieved. Most women were concentrated in clerical jobs rather than spread through the occupational spectrum, despite a growing minority of middle-class women who were entering professional and management ranks. Clearly, however, the trends of the 19th-century Industrial Revolution, which had kept women and family separate from work outside the home, had yielded to a dramatic new pattern.

THE PAST

Women at Work: The Female Labor Force in France and the United States

A statistical table of this sort is essentially descriptive. What patterns are described here? Is there a major change, and how can it be defined? What are the main differences between these two nations? Were they converging, becoming more similar, in 1962? In 1982? Do they end up in a similar situation with regard to women's work roles, or are they more different in 1982 than they were in 1946?

From description, questions of causation arise; statistical patterns provide a precise framework for a challenging analysis. Why were the United States and France so different in 1946? What might have caused the changes in patterns (for example, in the United States during the 1950s)? What was the role of new feminist demands in 1963? What might have caused the differences in the timing of trends in France and the United States?

Women at Work: The Female Labor Force in France and the United States

	France		United States	
	Women Workers (thousands)	Percentage of Total Force	Women Workers (thousands)	Percentage of Total Force
1946	7,880	37.903	16,840	27.83
1954	6,536	33.93	19,718	29.43
1962	6,478	33.23	24,047	32.74
1968	6,924	34.62	29,242	35.54
1975	7,675	36.48	37,553	39.34
1982	8,473	39.46	47,894	42.81

Sources: B. R. Mitchell, *International Historical Statistics: Europe, 1750–1988;* U.S. Bureau of the Census, *Historical Statistics of the United States, Colonial Times to 1970, Bicentennial Edition, Part 1;* U.S. Bureau of the Census, *Statistical Abstract of the United States: 1984.*

Other new rights for women accompanied this shift. Where women had lacked the vote before, as in France, they now got it. Women made gains in higher education, although again full equality remained elusive. Family rights improved, at least in the judgment of most women's advocates. Access to divorce increased, which many observers viewed as particularly important to women. Abortion law eased, though more slowly in countries of Catholic background than in Britain or Scandinavia; it became increasingly easy for women to regulate their reproduction. The development of new birth control methods, such as the contraceptive pill, introduced in 1960, and growing knowledge and acceptability of birth control, decreased unwanted pregnancies. Sex and procreation became increasingly separate considerations. Although women continued to differ from men in sexual outlook and behavior—for example, more than twice as many French women as men hoped to link sex, marriage, and romantic love, according to 1960s polls—more women than before tended to define sex in terms of pleasure.

Predictably, changes in the family, including the roles of women, raised new issues and redefined ideals of companionship. The first issue involved children. A brief increase in the Western birth rate ended in the early 1960s, and a rapid decline ensued. By the 1990s, countries such as Italy and Greece were no longer maintaining population levels except by immigration. The greater number of employed women and the desire to use income for high consumer standards worked against having children, or very many children, particularly in the middle class. Increasingly, children were sent, often at an early age, to day care centers, one of the amenities provided by the European welfare state. At the same time, however, some observers worried that Western society was becoming indifferent to children in an eagerness for adult work and consumer achievements. For example, between the 1950s and 1980s American adults shifted their assessment of family satisfaction away from parenthood by concentrating on shared enjoyments between husbands and wives.

Family stability also showed new cracks. Pressures to readjust family roles, women working outside the family context, and growing legal freedom for women caused men and women alike to turn more readily to divorce. In 1961, 9 percent of all British marriages ended in divorce; by 1965, the figure was 16 percent and rising. By the late 1970s, one-third of all British marriages ended in divorce, and the U.S. rate was even higher.

A new surge of feminist protest showed the strains caused by women's new activities amid continued limitations. The growing divorce rate produced an increase of female poverty. New work roles revealed the persistent earnings gap between men and women.

A *new feminism* began to take shape with the publication in 1949 of *The Second Sex* by French intellectual Simone de Beauvoir. Betty Friedan (Figure 35.4) popularized and Americanized this thinking with her 1963 book *The Feminine Mystique*. Friedan, a college graduate who had worked in psychology before marrying, had moved to the suburbs and raised three children in the 1950s. Her role left her deeply dissatisfied, and she urged women's work and equality, writing for women's magazines and interviewing many women equally frustrated with the suburban dream. Divorced in 1969, Friedan helped found the National Organization for Women (NOW) in 1966. Efforts of this sort, throughout the West, launched a new wave of women's rights agitation after three decades of calm. Compared to earlier efforts, the new feminism tended to emphasize a more literal equality that would play down special domestic roles and qualities (Figure 35.5).

Figure 35.4 *Betty Friedan.*

Figure 35.5 *The feminist movement focused particularly on economic gains for women and a rejection of purely domestic roles. The movement first gained momentum in the United States in the late 1960s, in the wake of civil rights agitation, but soon spread to western Europe.*

Thus, even as social class tensions declined in the West, compared with the century of industrialization, new divisions became important. Gender conflict was an obvious new issue, but so was the gap between racial minorities, new or old, and established white populations.

iñ DEP†H
The Decline of the West?

At various points in the 20th century, various kinds of Westerners have worried about the decline of Western society. Sometimes their concern focuses on the undeniable *relative* decline of the West in the world, which sets the 20th century off from the periods in world history between 1450 and 1920. In the 1980s, for example, various U.S. news magazines began to trumpet the idea of an emerging "Pacific century," dominated by east

Asian powers, that would replace the period of Western (and recently, American) preponderance.

The idea of *absolute* decline has had its proponents as well. The West's relative loss of power over the past 60 years might well suggest absolute decline. Some societies—such as the Roman Empire and the Ottoman Empire—depended on continued expansion to provide labor or booty for the upper class and then began to lose their vitality when further growth became impossible. The West no longer needs colonies to provide slaves, but it may have become so dependent on its ability to dominate other economies that relative decline will spell the beginning of a new period of internal woes.

Furthermore, many other factors suggest decline. Early in the 20th century, pondering the growing pleasure seeking of Western culture and its internal divisions, a German philosopher named

Oswald Spengler wrote a book called *The Decline of the West* in which he predicted that Western civilization was going the way of Rome—doomed to fall before the onslaught of such vigorous but less civilized peoples as the Russians or the Americans. His book was hugely popular after World War I, when it looked as if Western nations had indeed inflicted grievous injury on their own society. Other historians, though somewhat less pessimistic than Spengler, have picked up the theme of what they see as an inevitable decline of societies after periods of vigor. The theme seemed to fit western Europe again immediately after World War II, when both victors and vanquished were suffering through the immense problems of reconstruction. It was revived again in the late 1980s, when the world dominance of the United States seemed in retreat.

Other observers, though less systematic, saw internal decay. Some focused on cultural trends, bemoaning the lack of standards in art—the tendency to play with novel styles, however frivolous, simply to win attention. Or they criticized popular culture for what they claimed was a shallow materialism and vulgar sexuality; some critics saw analogies between Western commercialism and the Roman "bread and circuses" approach to the urban masses that had weakened the empire's moral fiber and reduced its capacity for work and military valor. However, analogies are inexact, and the role of moral decline in causing Rome's downfall is debatable. One of the problems in comparing current Western trends with past cases of decline is that modern conditions as shaped by industrialization may weaken the applicability of past standards.

Western demography is a case in point. There is no question that the demographic vitality of the West weakened in the late 19th and 20th centuries; the baby boom era, from 1943 to 1963, is a brief but interesting exception. Birth rates have gone down fairly steadily, in the 1930s and again by the 1980s, reaching a rate close to the replacement level. Moreover, slow or zero population growth has been accompanied by increased aging, the result of increasing life expectancy combined with a smaller number of children being born. In most historical situations, slowing population growth has signaled a general decrease in vitality, causing further decline as competition and the opportunity provided by population increase waned. Unquestionably, the West's demographic trends have reduced its percentage of world population, opening it to new immigration from various parts of the world. But the total package is hard to measure, for in the context of an industrial society, which provides a variety of technical aids to human labor and is a heavy consumer of resources, stable populations might be a source of strength, not weakness, whereas rapid population increase might be a burden that limits development.

Finally, judgments about decline are complicated by the cycles of Western history during the 20th century and the nature of modern Western expectations. Periods of great disarray, such as the 1930s, have not led thus far to long-term chaos, as Western nations have seemed able to bounce back. Other decades roused anxiety mainly because of the heavy Western commitment to steady progress. Thus, during the 1970s, when economic growth slowed, many polls showed that Americans had stopped believing that their society would advance in the future (although they still believed that their own lives would get better). Yet the 1970s brought no huge crisis, simply a slowing in the pace of improvement. The Western habit of expecting steady economic advance could easily lead to temporary exaggerations of what 1970s Americans called malaise.

Clearly, to paraphrase Mark Twain, reports of the death of the West seemed premature. Yet past examples from world history suggest one other caution: Social decline, if it does set in, typically takes a long time to work through. Rome declined for three centuries before it fell; the Ottoman Empire began to turn downward two centuries before it became known as weak. The first century of decline may be hard to perceive, yet it is important to monitor.

Questions: Has the West shown signs of cultural decline in the 20th century? What is the best case for arguing that 20th-century Western history does not suggest cultural decline? If the West is in decline, what can be done about it? Does world history suggest that decline is reversible?

Western Culture: Creativity and Uncertainty

Western culture in the 20th century displayed important creativity and change but also signs of tension. Artists and composers stressed stylistic innovation. Scientific work flourished, as the West remained the center of most fundamental inquiry in the theoretical sciences. But complex discoveries, such as the principle of relativity in physics, qualified older ideas that nature can be captured in a few sweeping scientific laws. And the sheer specialization of scientific research removed much of it from ready public understanding. Disciplines that once provided an intellectual overview, such as philosophy, declined in the 20th century or were transformed into specialized research fields; for example, many philosophers turned to the scientific study of language, and sweeping political theory virtually disappeared.

The dynamism of scientific research continued to form the clearest central thread in Western culture after 1920. Growing science faculties commanded the greatest prestige in the expanding universities. Individual scientists made striking discoveries, and an army of researchers cranked out more specific findings than scientists had ever before produced. In addition, the wider public continued to maintain a faith that science held the keys to understanding nature and society and to improving technology and human life. Finally, while scientific findings varied widely, belief in a central scientific method persisted: Form a rational hypothesis, test that hypothesis through experiment or observation, and emerge with a generalization that will show regularities in physical behaviors.

By the 1930s, physicists began to experiment with bombarding basic matter with neutrons, or particles that carry no electric charge; this work culminated during World War II in the development of the atomic bomb. Research in physics continued after World War II with a combination of increasingly sophisticated means of observation that were made possible by improved telescopes, atom smashers, and then lasers and space satellites, and the complex mathematical theories facilitated by the theory of relativity. Astronomers made progress in identifying additional galaxies and other phenomena in space. The debate about the nature of matter also continued.

Breakthroughs in biology involved primarily genetics. Earlier identification of the principles of inheritance received wide attention only after 1900. By the 1920s, researchers who used the increasingly familiar fruit fly had established exact rules for genetic transmission. Discovery in the 1950s by British and American scientists of the structure of the basic genetic unit, the famous double-helix pattern of deoxyribonucleic acid (DNA), advanced the understanding of how genetic information is transmitted and how it can be altered.

Biologists produced major improvements in health care. New drugs, beginning with penicillin in 1928, revolutionized the treatment of common diseases, and immunization virtually eliminated scourges such as diphtheria. By the 1970s, genetics gave rise to a host of industries that used scientific principles to produce new medicines, seeds, and pesticides. At the same time, use of genetics to clone complex animals—the first sheep was cloned in Scotland in 1997—raised new ethical issues about human capacity to reshape natural processes.

The rational method, broadly conceived, also advanced in the social sciences from 1920 onward. In economics, while sweeping theories were downplayed, quantitative models of economic cycles or business behavior increasingly gained ground. Work by British economist *John Keynes,* which emphasized the importance of government spending to compensate for loss of purchasing power during a depression, played a great role in the policies of the American New Deal and in efforts by European planners to control the economic cycles after World War II.

Like the sciences, the social sciences became increasingly diverse and specialized. Many social scientists sought practical applications for their work. Psychologists became involved not only in dealing with mental illness but in trying to promote greater work efficiency. The rise of anthropology in the 1920s, and the development of social history as a branch of inquiry into human behavior, swam against the social scientific current by pointing to the importance of diversity and chronology in understanding human life. However, most leading social scientists continued to emphasize the quest for consistency in human and social behavior. After World War II, the increasing use of mathematical models and laboratory experiments in the social sciences enhanced this emphasis.

Most 20th-century artists, concerned with capturing the world through impressions, worked against the grain of science and social science. Painting became increasingly nonrepresentational. *The cubist movement,* headed by Pablo Picasso, rendered familiar objects as geometric shapes; after cubism, modern art moved even further from normal perception, stressing purely geometrical design or wild swirls of color. The focus was on mood—the individual reaction of viewers to the individual reality of the artist (Figure 35.6). Musical composition involved the use of dissonance and experimentation with new scales; after World War II, a growing interest in electronic instrumentation added to this diversity. In poetry, the spread of unfamiliar forms, ungrammatical constructions, and sweeping imagery continued the movement of the late 19th century. In literature, the novel remained dominant, but it turned toward exploring moods and personalities.

The modern artistic vision was not simply a preoccupation of artists. Designs and sculptures based on abstract art began to grace public places from the 1920s onward; furnishings and films also reflected the modernist themes. Most revealing of the cross-currents between art, modern technology, and public taste was the development of a characteristic 20th-century architectural style, the modern or international style. The use of new materials, such as reinforced concrete and massive sheets of glass, allowed architects to abandon much that was traditional. The need for new kinds of buildings, particularly for office use, and the growing cost of urban space also encouraged the introduction of new forms such as the skyscraper (Figure 35.7), pioneered in the United States. Soaring structures, free-floating columns, and new combinations of angles and curves characterized leading Western buildings in the 20th century. After World War II, when reconstruction in Europe and the expansion of new regional centers in the southwestern United States provided new opportunities for building, the face of urban space in Western society was transformed.

The 20th-century cultural themes in the West were largely secular. Protestant and Catholic theologians ventured major statements, but they no longer commanded center stage. In western Europe, despite an important reform movement in the Catholic church that simplified the traditional ceremonies in favor of more direct contact between priests and worshipers, religion played a minor role in both formal and popular culture. Regular church attendance fell, attracting only 5 percent of the British population by the 1970s. The increasing use of cremation rather than burial showed a radical change in the traditional Christian approaches to death. In the United States, religion maintained a greater hold, and both church attendance and popular belief remained at higher levels than elsewhere in Western society. Both in the

Figure 35.6 *Marcel Duchamp, using a modified cubist style, achieved a dramatic visual effect in an approach characteristic of Western art from the 1920s onward.*

1920s and again after World War II, the United States also saw a greater variety of popular revival movements and attempts to use religion to maintain or restore traditional values.

Western culture was not a monopoly of European civilization in the 20th century. Western art forms, particularly in architecture, spread widely because of their practicality and their currency in what remained a highly influential society. The achievements of Western science, particularly those related to technology and medicine, won wide attention. By the same token, Western art and science were greatly enriched by many practitioners from other cultures: Japanese artists, for example, or Indian medical researchers and computer scientists. Feminism was also echoed elsewhere in the world. Elements of Western culture thus have now become international, and we must trace their interweaving into other civilizations. Yet no other culture created quite the same balance between an overwhelming interest in science and a frenzied concern for stylistic innovation and individual expression in the arts.

TABLE 35-1
Two Measures of Rising Consumer Prosperity in Europe, 1957 and 1965

Automobiles	1957	1965
France	3,476,000	7,842,000
Germany (Federal Republic)	2,456,288	8,103,600
Italy	1,051,004	(1956) 5,469,981
The Netherlands	375,676	1,272,890
Sweden	796,000	1,793,000

Televisions	1957	1965
France	683,000	6,489,000
Germany	789,586	11,379,000
Italy	367,000	6,044,542
The Netherlands	239,000	2,113,000
Sweden	75,817	2,110,584

(*Source:* Adapted from *The Europa Year Book 1959* (London: Europa Publications, 1959) and *The Europa Year Book 1967*, vol. 1 (London: Europa Publications, 1967).)

Figure 35.7 *The skyscraper, developed first in the United States, became a major expression of artistic innovation and dramatic new structural materials, including novel uses of glass. This Chicago tower was designed by European master Ludwig Mies van der Rohe.*

Conclusion

Will the Real West Please Stand Up?

Twentieth-century Western society reflected increasing tensions between industrial values and Western traditions. Western intellectuals thus insisted on the primacy of rational inquiry while relying on artistic forms that seemed bent on portraying a world gone mad. Ordinary Europeans and Americans accepted a disciplined work environment that stressed control over emotion while reveling in scenes of violence and sexual ecstasy in their leisure hours, sometimes embellished by the use of drugs.

Leisure interests appealed to individual pleasure seeking, including an interest in sexuality profoundly shocking to many other cultures. But most jobs involved routine activities that were controlled by an elaborate supervisory apparatus. Leisure, appealing to individual self-expression in one sense, generally meant mass, commercially manipulated outlets for all but a handful of venturesome souls. By the 1950s, television watching had become the leading recreational interest of Western peoples, and most television fare was deliberately standardized. Ironically, individualism and its outlets in consumer behavior often made collective protest against bureaucratization and routine extremely difficult. One of the reasons for the decline of organized labor throughout the West was workers' growing need to spend time earning money for their new cars or using the new cars they had.

To critics within Western society and without, Western society at times seemed badly confused. Poverty and job boredom coexisted with affluence and continued appeals to the essential value of work. Youth protest—including defiant costumes and pulsating rock music—family instability, and growing crime might be signs of a fatally flawed society. Rising rates of suicide and increasing incidence of mental illness were other troubling symptoms. At the least, Western society continued to display the strains of change.

Further Readings

For an excellent general survey, see Robert Paxton's *Europe in the 20th Century* (1985). See also Morris Janowitz's *The Last Half Century: Social Change and Politics in America* (1978). A good factual compendium is Tony Howarth's *Twentieth-Century History: The World Since 1900* (1979).

Some excellent national interpretations enhance the general coverage. See A. F. Havighurst's *Twentieth-Century Britain* (1982) and John Ardagh's highly readable *The New French Revolution: A Social and Economic Survey of France* (1968) and *France in the 1980s* (1982). Volker Berghahn's *Modern Germany: Society, Economy and Politics in the 20th Century* (1983) is also useful.

On Europe between the wars, Charles Maier's *Recasting Bourgeois Europe* (1975) is a penetrating comparative approach. On fascism and Nazism, see F. Carsten's *The Rise of Fascism* (1980) and S. Payne's *Fascism: Comparison and Definition* (1984). David Schoenbaum's *Hitler's Social Revolution* (1980) is an excellent study of how Nazism worked in practice. See also Gerald Fleming's *Hitler and the Final Solution* (1984) on the holocaust. R. Stromberg's *Intellectual History of Modern Europe* (1966) and K. D. Bracher's *Age of Ideologies: A History of Political Thought in the Twentieth Century* (1989) provide a factual framework in a complex area. See also H. S. Hughes's *Consciousness and Society* (1976).

On post-World War II social and economic trends, see C. Kindleberger, *Europe's Postwar Growth* (1967); V. Bogdanor and R. Skidelsky, eds., *The Age of Affluence* (1970); and R. Dahrendorf, ed., *Europe's Economy in Crisis* (1982). On the welfare state, see Stephen Cohen's *Modern Capitalist Planning: The French Model* (1977) and E. S. Einhorn and J. Logue's *Welfare States in Hard Times* (1982)

Important overviews of recent European history are Walter Laqueur's *Europe Since Hitler* (1982), R. von Albertini's *Decolonization* (1982), Miles Kahler's *Decolonization in Britain and France: The Domestic Consequences of International Relations* (1984), Helen Wallace et al.'s *Policy-Making in the European Community* (1983), and Alfred Grosser's *The Western Alliance* (1982). On the United States, see David Oshinsky's *A Conspiracy So Immense: The World of Joe McCarthy* (1983), Richard Polenberg's *One Nation Divisible: Class, Race and Ethnicity in the United States Since 1938* (1980), Harvard Sitkoff's *The Struggle for Black Equality, 1954–1980* (1981), William Chafe's *The American Woman: Her Changing Social, Economic and Political Roles* (1972),

and Haynes Johnson's *Sleepwalking Through History: America in the Reagan Years* (1991).

On the relevant Commonwealth nations, see Charles Doran's *Forgotten Partnership: U.S.–Canada Relations Today* (1983), Edward McWhinney's *Canada and the Constitution, 1979–1982* (1982), and Stephen Graubard, ed., *Australia: Terra Incognita?* (1985).

On the Web

Life in the United States in the 1920s is illuminated at http://www.louisville.edu/~kpraybol/1920s. The causes of the Great Depression are examined at http://www.escape.com/~paulg53/politics/ great_depression.shtml. Personal remembrances of the Great Depression are recorded at http://www.sos.state.mi.us/history/ museum/techstuf/depressn/teacup.html. One of the finest web sites running is that focussed on the New Deal at http://newdeal.feri.org/.

The nature of the totalitarian state and the relationship between politics and art is addressed through close analysis of individual Nazi and Soviet artists and their work at http://www.primenet.com/~byoder/artofnz.htm. An excellent overview of the Cold War is available at http://history.acusd.edu/gen/20th/coldwarO.html and http://cwihp.si.edu/default.htm. The European quest for union is explored at http://www.eurunion.org. Analyses of recent events and significant speeches in Europe, as well as analyses of NATO actions, can be found at http://www.nato.int/.

The place of Simone de Beauvior (http:// members.aol.com/CazadoraKE/private/Philo/Beau/ USimone.html) and Betty Friedan (http://www.lycos.com/wguide/tools/pgview.html?wwbestof=Y&wwtitle=Betty%20Friedan&wwdoc=http%3a%2f%2fwww.feminist.com%2fbeyond.htm&wwmid=99447&wwdocid=1052400&wwprate=0.79&wwdoctype=2) in the "new feminist movement" leaves little doubt that this revolutionary effort ultimately sought the liberation of both men and women. Sites devoted to the women's liberation movement include http://scriptorium.lib.duke.edu/ wlm and http://lists.village.virginia.edu/sixties/1960s.

A militant view of the alleged ills of the affluent society and the growing dominance of multinational and non-state organizations in the post-modern era is presented at http://www.socialconscience.com/. A less radical view that nonetheless suggests that the twin pillars of Western Civilization (the market economy and democracy) are more likely to undermine than support each other can be found at http://www.mtholyoke.edu/acad/intrel/ attali.html.

Chapter 36

Russia and
Eastern Europe

Breaching the Berlin Wall in 1989: West and East Germany meet.

East European history in the 20th century has been dominated by Russia's 1917 revolution, one of the great upheavals of modern times. Into the 1990s, contemporary Russian history was shaped by the revolution's impact and the attempt to build a society on new communist principles. Russia's struggles merged with those of the rest of eastern Europe after 1945, as Soviet-dominated regimes emerged throughout the region.

Russian history also had an unprecedented importance in wider world history during the 20th century. China and Cuba used Russian models and added their own twists; revolutionaries elsewhere in Latin America and Asia, and also in Africa and the West, drew inspiration from the Soviet system. Spurred by the revolution and ongoing industrialization, the new Soviet Union emerged after 1945 as one of the two great world powers. For several decades after 1945, as Western colonial controls receded, Soviet ideological influence seemed to rival the West's cultural outreach.

Russian history in the 20th century divides into four subperiods: the revolution and immediate aftermath, 1917–1928; Stalinism, isolation, and the new Soviet Empire, 1928–1953; consolidation and superpower status, 1953–1985; and dissolution of the communist system from 1985 onward.

Through all four periods, older Russian themes, such as state power, expansionism, and ambivalence about the West, blended with revolutionary innovations.

1920 C.E.	1940 C.E.	1960 C.E.	1980 C.E.
1917 Russian Revolution; Bolshevik takeover (October)	**1941** German invasion of Soviet Union	**1961** Berlin Wall erected	**1985** Gorbachev to power
1918–1919 Independent smaller nations in Eastern Europe	**1943** Soviet army pushes west	**1962** Cuban missile crisis	**1988–1989** Liberalization movements throughout Eastern Europe; new constitutions, economic reforms; agitation by nationalities in Soviet Union
1921 Lenin's New Economic Policy	**1945–1948** Soviet takeover of Eastern Europe	**1968** Revolt in Czechoslovakia and its repression; Soviet policy (Brezhnev doctrine) proclaims right to intervene in any Socialist country	**1988** New Soviet constitution; establishment of the Congress of People's Deputies
1923 New constitution in Russia	**1949** Soviet Union develops atomic bomb	**1979** Uprisings in Poland and their suppression	**1990** Gorbachev selected as president; new elections throughout much of Eastern Europe; economic unification in Germany
1927 Stalin in full power	**1953** Stalin's death	**1979** Soviet invasion of Afghanistan	**1991** End of Soviet Union, collapse of Communist party in Russia; Yeltsin chief leader
1928 Beginning of collectivization of agriculture and five-year plans	**1955** Formation of Warsaw Pact		**1991–1994** Collapse of Yugoslavia; civil war in Bosnia
1936–1938 Stalin's great purges	**1956** Stalinism attacked by Khrushchev		**1993–2000** Yeltsin clashes with parliament, new constitution
1939 Signing of Russo–German pact; Soviet invasion of eastern Poland and Finland	**1956** Hungarian revolt and its suppression		**1995** Russian army attempts to suppress independence of Chechnya, a Muslim region
			2000 Election of Putin as President

THE RUSSIAN REVOLUTION

▓▓ *The active period of the Russian revolution lasted from 1917 to the mid-1920s. Internal and foreign opposition complicated the revolutionary process, as in France in 1789, but key patterns of the new regime were set in less than a decade.*

In March 1917, strikes and food riots broke out in Russia's capital, St. Petersburg (later named Leningrad and renamed St. Petersburg in 1991). Spurred by wartime misery, the outbursts protested the conditions of early industrialization set against incomplete rural reform and an unresponsive political system. They quickly assumed revolutionary proportions. The rioters called not just for more food and work but for a new political regime. A council of workers, called a *soviet*, took over the city government and arrested the tsar's ministers. Unable to rely on his own soldiers, the tsar abdicated, thus ending the long period of imperial rule.

Liberalism to Communism

For eight months, a liberal provisional government struggled to rule the country. Like Western liberals, revolutionary leaders such as *Alexander Kerensky* were eager to see genuine parliamentary rule, religious and other freedoms, and a host of political and legal changes. But liberalism was not deeply rooted in Russia, if only because of the small middle class. The liberal leaders tried to maintain their war effort, which increased economic misery and popular discontent. Liberal leaders also held back from the massive land reforms expected by the peasantry. Serious popular unrest continued, and in November (October, by the Russian calendar) a second revolution took place that expelled liberal leadership and soon brought the Bolshevik leader, Lenin, to power (Figure 36.1).

Lenin and the Bolsheviks—soon renamed the *Russian Communist Party*—faced several immediate problems. They handled the war by signing a humiliating peace treaty with Germany that gave up huge sections of western Russia in return for an end to hostilities. This treaty was soon nullified by Germany's defeat at the hands of the Western allies, but Russia was ignored at the Versailles peace conference, treated as a pariah by the fearful Western powers. A revived Poland built heavily on land Russia had controlled for more than a century, and new, small Baltic states cut into even earlier acquisitions. Still, although Russia harbored deep grievances against the Versailles treaty, the early end to the war was vital to Lenin's consolidation of power.

A second problem involved internal political rivals. The communists created the *Council of People's*

Commissars, headed by Lenin and drawn from soviets across the nation, to govern the state. But a parliamentary election produced a clear majority for the *Social Revolutionary party,* which emphasized peasant support and rural reform. Lenin shut down the Parliament, replacing it with a Bolshevik-dominated *Congress of Soviets.* He pressed the Social Revolutionaries to disband, arguing that "the people voted for a party which no longer existed." Russia was to have not a Western-style multiparty system but rather a communist monopoly in the name of the true people's will. Indeed, communist control of the government apparatus persisted from this point to 1989 thanks to a combination of effective party leadership and police repression.

However, Russia's revolution did produce a familiar backlash that revolutionaries in other eras would have recognized quite easily: foreign hostility and, even more important, domestic resistance. Britain, France, the United States, and Japan all sent troops against the communist threat, although they pulled back quickly.

The internal civil war was a more serious matter as it raged from 1918 to 1921. Tsarist generals, religiously faithful peasants, and many minority nationalities made a common cause against the communist regime. Their efforts were aided by continuing economic distress. Lenin quickly decreed a redistribution of land to the peasantry and also launched a *nationalization,* or state takeover, of basic industry. The measures roused widespread opposition, particularly among landed peasants, and agriculture and manufacturing declined (see Figure 36.2).

Stabilization of the New Regime

Communist leadership restored order on several key foundations. First, a powerful new army was raised under the inspiration of Leon Trotsky, who recruited able generals and masses of loyal conscripts. This *Red Army* was an early beneficiary of two ongoing sources of strength for communist Russia: a willingness to use people of humble background but great ability and an ability to inspire mass loyalty in the name of a

Figure 36.1 *Moscow workers guard the Bolshevik headquarters during the Russian Revolution of 1917.*

Figure 36.2 *Civil war and peasant resistance to collectivization dramatically reduced food supplies, forcing a temporary change in government policy. Children were the victims of the famine of 1922.*

brighter communist future. Economic disarray was reduced in 1921 when Lenin issued his *New Economic Policy* (NEP). The NEP promised freedom of action for small businesspeople and peasant land owners. The state continued to set basic economic policies, but its efforts were combined with individual initiative. Under this temporary policy, food production began to recover, and the regime gained time to prepare the more durable structures of the communist system. Lenin stressed the importance of sheer economic growth, arguing that "electrification plus Soviet power equals communism."

By 1923, the *Bolshevik Revolution* was an accomplished fact. A new constitution set up a federal system of socialist republics. This system recognized the multinational character of the nation, known now not as Russia but the *Union of Soviet Socialist Republics.* The dominance of ethnic Russians was preserved in the central state apparatus, however, and certain groups, notably Jews, were given no distinct representation. With the separate republics firmly controlled by the national Communist party, and with

basic decisions centralized, the impact of the new nationalities policy was somewhat mixed. It was also true that direct protest from the nationalities declined notably from the 1920s until the late 1980s.

The apparatus of the central state was another mixture of appearance and reality. *A Supreme Soviet* had many of the trappings of a parliament and was elected by universal suffrage. But competition in elections normally was prohibited, which meant that the Communist party easily controlled this body—which, in any event, served mainly to ratify decisions made by the party's central executive. The Soviet political system was elaborated over time. A new constitution in the 1930s spoke glowingly of human rights. In fact, to consolidate their power the communists quickly reestablished an authoritarian system, under central party bureaucracy, complete with updated versions of the political police to ensure loyalty.

Rivalries between leaders at the top also had to be sorted out. Lenin sickened and then died in 1924, creating an unexpected leadership gap. Key lieutenants jostled for power, including the Red Army's flamboyant Trotsky and a Communist party member of worker origins who had taken the name *Stalin,* meaning "steel." After a few years of jockeying, *Joseph Stalin* emerged as undisputed leader of the Soviet state, his victory a triumph for party control over all branches of government. Stalin represented a strongly nationalist version of communism in contrast to the more ideological and international visions of many rivals. Lenin set up the *Comintern,* or Communist International office, to guide international revolutionary activity. But revolution did not spill over, despite a few brief uprisings in places such as Hungary and Germany right after World War I. Under Stalin, the revolutionary leadership, while still committed in theory to an international movement, pulled back to concentrate on Russian developments pure and simple—building "socialism in one country," as Stalin put it. Stalin in many ways represented the anti-Western strain in Russian tradition, though in new guise. Rival leaders were killed or expelled, and competing visions of the revolution were downplayed.

The communists had managed to create a new political, economic, and cultural structure without serious internal challenge between the initial, chaotic years and the late 1980s. However, revolutions do not end quickly. Although the formal revolutionary period spanned only a few vivid years, the actual force

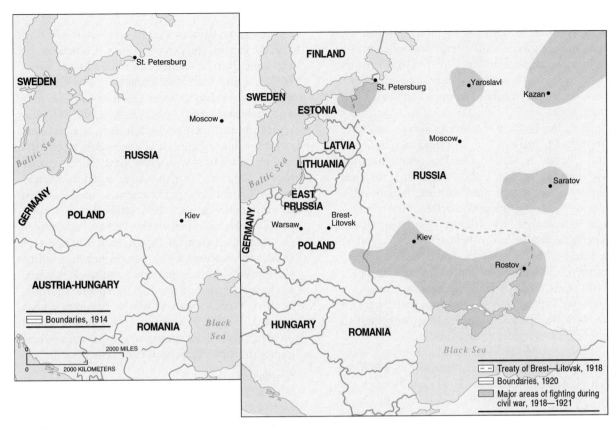

Map 36.1 *Eastern Europe and the Soviet Union, 1919–1939. The Soviet Union regained some territory ceded to Germany in the 1918 Treaty, but it lost ground to a number of east European States.*

of the revolution continued until the mid-1930s—that is, through a period of fascinating experimentation during the 1920s and into the establishment of a full Stalinist regime from 1928 onward.

IN DEP†H
20th-Century Revolutions

Never in world history have there been as many revolutions, in not one but a host of different civilizations, as in the 20th century. These include a minor and a major revolution in Russia; one or perhaps two major revolutions in China (the whole span from 1911 to 1949 can be seen as either a single revolutionary process or a sequence

of two outbreaks); a major upheaval in Mexico; then, much later, significant revolutions in Cuba, Bolivia, and Nicaragua; and more recently a revolution in Iran. A number of smaller revolutions add to the number.

What are the patterns of 20th-century revolution? Revolutions occurred in societies in which significant changes were under way—such as the earliest phases of industrialization in Russia, the economic development undertaken by the prerevolutionary regime in Iran, and the initial political and educational changes in China—but had not yet had a chance to coalesce. In other words, the revolutionary moment sees some groups antagonized by the shifts that have occurred and other groups eager for still more rapid change. Like earlier revolts, 20th-century revolutions involved several different groups with diverse demands and revolutionary attributes. Most of the 20th-century revolutions had a strong peasant component and took place where landlord controls had helped spur rural grievances.

The 20th-century revolutions always involved a prior intellectual buildup. Doctrines of democracy and liberalism, nationalism, or some form of socialism (most often Marxism) provided the most common ideological spurs, but the Iranian revolution—one of the most distinctive in the group—was dominated by Islamic fundamentalism. Revolutions also fed on an absence of effective political outlets for key groups as well as a weakening of the established state. Most revolutionary cases involved a government structure strong in principle but with weak new leaders (the tsarist case, for example) or the aging of an authoritarian figure (as in Mexico, Cuba, and Iran).

Some historians have tried to develop a standard revolutionary dynamic, based on earlier Western models more than on 20th-century cases. In this model, revolutions begin with initially liberal impulses, seeking greater freedom and control from below. Then as economic problems continue, often along with civil strife and foreign intervention, the liberal phase gives way to greater authority, even outright dictatorship. Elements of this pattern are visible in several 20th-century cases (such as China, Russia to some extent, Mexico, and Iran briefly), but the authoritarian strand in most instances emerges very quickly.

An important common ingredient of 20th-century revolutions was the need to come to terms with Western influence and often to reassert greater national autonomy. Mexico, Russia, and China all grappled with growing Western economic control and cultural influence in the early 20th century, and all tried to come up with alternative development models. Many revolutions thus heightened anti-Western sentiment, at least for a time, and all tried to reduce Western power to interfere with internal affairs. Thus, the Russian revolution reduced foreign business involvement, and Stalinism went on the attack against "decadent" Western cultural influence.

No model for 20th-century revolutions should ignore two basic points. First, each revolution,

including the Russian, had its own flavor—its own specific causes, its own outcomes. Individual flavor came from distinctive cultural traditions, social balances, and individual leadership. For example, not every revolution had a Lenin who could unify and galvanize the whole experience. Second, although 20th-century revolutions shared some common ingredients, it is impossible to predict where revolution will strike next. Right before World War I, an Austrian banker urged investment in the Russian Empire because it seemed so much more durable than the harassed regimes of western Europe; right before the Iranian Revolution, the American Central Intelligence Agency sent back rosy reports of the government's solidity. Revolutions do have patterns, and these patterns suggest a great deal about the dynamic of 20th-century world history where revolution has loomed so large. Revolutions must also be evaluated through their spontaneous qualities—their ability to make predictions look ridiculous.

Questions: How did 20th-century revolutions compare with liberal Western revolutions from 1789 to 1848? Why did Marxism prove to be such an important revolutionary ideology in the 20th-century context? Will revolutions affect other societies in the 21st century? Are there reasons to believe that the causes of the 20th-century revolutionary movement are exhausted?

BUILDING SOVIET SOCIETY

After a lively experimental phase in the 1920s, Stalinism dominated the Soviet system for nearly two decades. Stalin's system involved increased police repression, rapid industrialization, agricultural collectivization, and ultimately the Soviet Union's successful defense against German attack in World War II.

The mid-1920s were a surprisingly open-ended period in Soviet history, partly because those at the top of the power pyramid were jockeying for power. A host of new groups found a voice. The Communist party, though not eager to recruit too many members lest it lose its tight organization and elite status, encouraged all sorts of subsidiary organizations.

Youth movements, women's groups, and particularly organizations of workers all actively debated policies. Workers were able to influence management practices, and women's groups helped carve out legal equality and new educational and work opportunities for their members.

The atmosphere of excited debate spilled over into such areas as family policy. At various points, Soviet policy seemed to downplay the importance of family in favor of individual rights, thus making it easy to obtain divorces and abortions. Ultimately, by the 1930s the pendulum swung back toward greater conservatism, featuring protection of the family unit and an effort to encourage the birth rate, but only after some fascinating fluctuations. One key to the creative mood of these years was the rapid spread of education, along with the educational and propaganda activities sponsored by various adult groups. Literacy gained ground quickly. The new educational system was also bent on reshaping popular culture away from older peasant traditions, especially religion, and toward beliefs in communist political analysis and science. Access to new information, new modes of inquiry, and new values promoted controversy.

Stalinism

The experimental mood began to fade after 1927, when Joseph Stalin acquired full power over potential rivals. Stalin, eager for authoritarian control, was also eager to renew the momentum toward socialism that had been deflected by the New Economic Policy. By this time, the bulk of the land lay in the hands of a minority of wealthy, commercially oriented peasants, the *kulaks,* who were particularly attuned to a profit-based market agriculture. Stalin devoted himself to a double task: making the Soviet Union a fully industrial society and doing so under full control of the state rather than through private initiative and individual ownership of producing property. In essence, Stalin wanted modernization but with a revolutionary, noncapitalist twist. And although he was willing to borrow Western techniques and advice—importing a few foreign engineers, for example—he insisted on Russian control and largely Russian endeavor.

Centralized Economic Policies

A massive program to collectivize agriculture began in 1928. *Collectivization* meant creating large, state-run farms rather than individual holdings as in the West. Communist party agitators pressed peasants to join in collectives. Collectivization promised to facilitate the mechanization of agriculture by sharing scarce machines while increasing Communist party control over peasants.

Although some rural laborers welcomed collectivization, most kulaks refused to cooperate, often destroying livestock and other property rather than submitting to collectivization. Devastating famine resulted from Stalin's insistence on pressing forward. In addition, millions of kulaks were killed or deported to Siberia during the early 1930s in one of the most brutal oppressions of what turned out to be a brutal century in world history. Gradually, rural resistance collapsed and production began to increase once again. But collectivization was never a smashing success, for even the peasants who participated often seemed unmotivated. Agricultural production remained a major weakness in the Soviet economy, demanding a higher percentage of the labor force than was common under industrialization.

If Stalin's approach to agriculture had serious flaws, his handling of industry was in most ways a stunning success. A system of *five-year plans* under the state planning commission began to set clear priorities for industrial development, including expected output levels and new facilities. The government built massive factories for metallurgy, mining, and electric power to make Russia an industrial country independent of Western-dominated world banking and trading patterns. There was more than a hint of Peter the Great's policies here, updating the economy without really Westernizing it. But industrialization was a greater departure from previous conditions than anything Peter had contemplated. As before, the focus was on heavy industry, which built on Russia's great natural resources and also prepared for possible war with Hitler's anticommunist Germany. Stalin relied not on price competition but on formal, centralized resource allocation to distribute equipment and supplies. This led to bottlenecks and waste because quotas for individual factories were set in Moscow, but there was no question that rapid industrial growth occurred. During the first two five-year plans, to 1937—that is, during the same period the West was mired in the depression—Soviet output of machinery and metal products grew 14-fold. The Soviet Union had become the world's third industrial power, behind Germany and the United States. A long history of backwardness seemed to have ended.

Toward an Industrial Society

For all its distinctive features, Soviet industrialization produced many results similar to those in the West. Increasing numbers of people were crowded into cities, often cramped in inadequate housing, for Soviet planners, like earlier Western capitalists, were reluctant to put too many resources into mass housing. Factory discipline was strict as communist managers tried to instill new habits into former peasants. Incentive procedures were introduced to motivate higher production. At the same time, communist policy quickly built up a network of welfare services, surpassing the West in this area and reversing decades of tsarist neglect. Workers had meeting houses and recreational programs, as well as protection in cases of illness and old age. Soviet industrial society provided only modest standards of living at this point, but a host of collective activities compensated to some degree.

Totalitarian Rule

Stalin combined his industrialization program with a new intensification of government police procedures. He used the party and state apparatus to monopolize power even more thoroughly than Hitler's state attempted. Opponents and imagined opponents of his version of communism were executed. During the great purge of party leaders that culminated in 1937 and 1938, hundreds of people were intimidated into confessing imaginary crimes against the state, and most of them were put to death. Many thousands more were sent to Siberian labor camps. Any possibility of vigorous internal initiative was crushed, as both the state and the Communist party were bent under Stalin's suspicious will. News outlets were monopolized by the state and the party, and informal meetings also risked a visit from the secret police, renamed the Ministry of Internal Affairs (MID) in 1934. Party congresses and meetings of the executive committee, or *Politburo*, became mere rubber stamps. An atmosphere of terror spread in Soviet society.

Stalin also had to pay attention to foreign policy. Nazi Germany threatened the Soviet Union from the west, and Hitler was vocal about his scorn for Slavic peoples and communism and about his desire to create "living room" for Germany to the east.

Stalin initially hoped that he could cooperate with the Western democracies in blocking the German threat. The Soviet Union thus tried to partici-

pate in a common response to German and Italian intervention during the Spanish Civil War in 1936 and 1937. But France and Britain were incapable of forceful action and were almost as suspicious of the Soviets as of the Nazis. So the Soviet Union, unready for war and greatly disappointed in the West, signed the historic agreement with Hitler in 1939. The Ribbentrop–Molotov pact bought some time for greater war preparation and also enabled Soviet troops to attack eastern Poland and Finland in an effort to regain territories lost in World War I. Here was the first sign of a Soviet revival of Russia's long interest in conquest, which would be intensified by the experience of World War II.

The awkward honeymoon with Hitler did not last. The Nazis, having completed their sweep of France but blocked from invading Britain, quickly regained their eastern appetites, sharpened by concern about the Soviet Union's territorial gains. The

Map 36.2 *Soviet and East European Boundaries by 1948. The new communist empire was joined in the Warsaw Pact, formed to respond to the West's North Atlantic Treaty Organization (itself formed in response to a perceived communist threat).*

invasion of the Soviet Union was launched in 1941 and soon brought a new Soviet alliance with the Western powers, including, by the end of the year, the United States.

The war was devastating but also exhilarating for the Soviet Union. The country's new industrial base, hastily relocated in the Ural Mountains and beyond, proved vital in providing the material needed for war, but the effort was extremely costly. Great cities such as Leningrad and Stalingrad were besieged by the Germans for months, with huge loss of life. The war heightened the age-old Russian fear of invasion and foreign interference, already enhanced by World War I and Western intervention during the revolution. But as the Red Army pressed westward after 1943, finally penetrating to the Elbe River in Germany, there was new opportunity for aggrandizement. Russia was able to regain its former western boundaries at the expense of nations such as Poland; some small states set up by the Treaty of Versailles were swallowed entirely. Larger east European states were allowed to remain intact, but their regimes were quickly brought under the control of communist parties backed by the Soviet occupation forces.

THE SOVIET UNION AS A SUPERPOWER

■■ *Despite the massive dislocations caused by World War II, the initial postwar decades saw the high-water mark of the Soviet system. In weaponry and space exploration, the Soviet Union competed with the United States as a superpower. The Soviet empire spread to embrace the smaller nations of eastern Europe, now under communist control. Soviet culture blossomed, combining distinctive communist themes with a new expressiveness by certain intellectuals.*

As a result of Soviet industrialization and its World War II push westward, the Soviet Union emerged as a world power. Continued concentration on heavy industry and weapon development, plus strategic alliances and links to communist movements in various parts of the world, helped maintain this status.

Soviet participation in the late phases of the war against Japan brought an opportunity to seize some islands in the northern Pacific. The Soviet Union established a protectorate over the communist regime of North Korea to match the American protectorate in South Korea. Soviet aid to the victorious Communist party in China brought new influence in that country for a time. In the 1970s the Soviet Union gained a new ally in communist Vietnam, which among other things provided naval bases for the Russian fleet. Growing military and economic strength gave the postwar Soviet Union new leverage in the Middle East, Africa, and even parts of Latin America; the alliance with a newly communist Cuba was a key step during the 1960s. The Soviet Union's superpower status was confirmed by its development of the atomic and then hydrogen bombs from 1949 onward and by its deployment of missiles and naval forces to match the rapid expansion of U.S. arsenals.

The New Soviet Empire in Eastern Europe

The clearest extension of the Soviet sphere developed right after World War II in eastern Europe. Here the Soviets made it clear that they intended to stay, pushing their sphere of influence farther to the west than ever before in history. Soviet insistence on this empire helped launch the cold war, as the Soviet Union demonstrated its willingness to confront the West rather than relax its grip.

The small nations of eastern Europe, mostly new or revived after World War I, had gone through a troubled period between the world wars, and this helped make them vulnerable to Nazi and then Soviet advances. Most were consumed by nationalist excitement at independence by 1918 as well as by intense grievances about territories not acquired. Bitter rivalries among the east European states weakened them diplomatically and economically. Most of the new nations began the interwar period with some form of parliamentary democracy but soon converted to authoritarian rule, either through a dictator (as in Poland) or by a monarch's seizure of new power (as in Yugoslavia, the new nation expanded from Serbia). This political pattern resulted from more underlying social tensions. Most east European countries remained primarily agricultural and heavily dependent on sales to western Europe. They were hard hit by the collapse of agricultural prices in the 1920s, and then they were further damaged by the depression. Furthermore, most countries refused to undertake serious land reform. Aristocratic estate owners tried desperately to repress peasant movements, which brought them to the support of authoritarian regimes, often complete with vaguely fascist trappings.

Only Czechoslovakia stood as an exception, where an unusually advanced industrialization process and an extensive urban culture, combined with land reform, produced the basis for an effective parliamentary democratic regime. Most of the rest of eastern Europe remained caught between Western patterns that seemed impossible or irrelevant and a revolutionary Soviet Union now feared for its communism as well as its Russian strength. The situation was predictably unstable. Although the interwar experience enhanced nationalist loyalties, it did not create a viable economic or diplomatic system for the region.

Then came the Nazi attack and ineffective Western response. Czechoslovakia, Poland, and Yugoslavia were seized by German or Italian forces. Several other east European authoritarians allied themselves directly with Hitler because of shared ideological leanings and a fear of the Soviet Union. Eastern Europe fell under Nazi control for four years, compelled to provide troops and labor and subject to Hitler's Holocaust attack on the Jews.

The Red Armies came next, directly liberating all of eastern Europe and the eastern part of Germany to the Elbe River, except for Greece and Yugoslavia. Soviet military might and collaboration with local communist movements crushed opposition parties and forced out noncommunist regimes by 1948. Only three east European nations stood out from the common pattern: Greece, which moved toward the Western camp; Albania, which formed a rigid Stalinist regime; and Yugoslavia, where a communist regime formed under the resistance leader Tito quickly proclaimed its neutrality in the cold war and tried to form a more open-ended, responsive version of the communist economic and social system.

Through most of eastern Europe, a standard dynamic emerged by the early 1950s. The new Soviet-sponsored regimes attacked possible rivals for power, including the Roman Catholic church. Mass education and propaganda outlets spread quickly. Collectivization of agriculture ended the large estate system without creating a property-owning peasantry. Industrialization was pushed through successive five-year plans, though with some limitations because of Soviet insistence on easy access to key natural resources. After the formation of NATO in western Europe, most east European nations were enfolded in a common defense alliance, the Warsaw Pact, and a common economic planning organization. Soviet troops continued to be stationed in most countries both to confront the Western alliance and to monitor the new regimes and their loyalty to the common cause.

The imposition of the Soviet system created obvious tensions. Dissatisfaction with particularly tight controls in East Germany brought a workers' uprising in 1953, which was vigorously repressed by Soviet troops, and widespread exodus to West Germany until the *Berlin Wall* was built in 1961 to contain the flow. All along the new borders of eastern Europe, barbed wire fences and armed patrols kept the people in. The relaxation of Stalinism within the Soviet Union in 1956 created new hopes that controls might be loosened. More liberal communist leaders arose in Hungary and Poland, with massive popular backing, seeking to create greater freedom within communism. In Poland, the Soviets accepted a new leader more popular with the Polish people; Poland was allowed to halt agricultural collectivization, establishing widespread peasant ownership in its place, and the Catholic church, now the symbol of Polish independence, gained greater tolerance. However, a new regime in Hungary was cruelly crushed by the Soviet army (Figure 36.3) and replaced by hard-line Stalinist leadership.

A few modest deviations were allowed. For example, Hungary developed new intellectual vigor and experimented with slightly less centralized economic planning.

But the limits of experimentation in eastern Europe were brought home again in 1968, when a more liberal regime came to power in Czechoslovakia. Again the Soviet army responded, expelling the reformers and setting up a particularly rigid leader in their stead. Striving and repression had very human faces. The leader of the Czech uprising, Alexander Dubcek, was a fervent communist whose father had been educated in the Soviet Union. Dubcek fought against the Nazis in the illegal communist resistance movement in World War II and then, with communism in power, moved up quickly in the ranks. But when the reform movement crested in 1968, he stood firm against Soviet interference in the name of a democratic communism, advocating freedoms of the press and speech. But Soviet military pressure forced him to Moscow, where he made huge concessions to the Soviets, appealing for Czech cooperation in an emotional speech on his return. He was steadily demoted after the reform movement ended, finally ending in a remote forestry position. But he did live to see the end of the communist regime in 1989 and was hailed as a hero by joyous demonstrators.

Poland was the center of the challenge to the Soviet system in the late 1970s as widespread Catholic unrest combined with an independent labor movement, *Solidarity,* all against the backdrop of a stagnant economy and low morale. The Polish army took over the state, under careful Soviet supervision.

With all the discontents, change occurred. Communist-imposed social policies brought real social upheaval by abolishing the once-dominant aristocracy and remaking the peasant masses through collectivization and industrial urban growth. Earlier cultural ties with the West persisted, but now Russian, not French or English, was the first foreign language learned.

East European allies aided Soviet ventures in other parts of the world, providing supplies and advisors for activities in Africa, Latin America, and elsewhere. But the recurrent unrest in eastern Europe acted as a check on Soviet policy; the need for a con-tinued military presence limited Soviet adventurism in other parts of the world.

Evolution of Domestic Policies

Stalinist policies continued within the Soviet Union after World War II. They combined strict Communist party and police controls with popular support. During the cold war, after 1947, news media blasted America as an evil power and a corrupt society. Many people in the Soviet Union, fearful of a new war that American aggressiveness seemed to threaten, agreed that strong government authority remained necessary. Strict limits on travel, outside media, and uncensored glimpses of the outside world kept the Soviet Union unusually isolated in the mid-20th century; its culture, like its economy, was largely removed from world currents.

Stalin's political structure continued to emphasize central controls and the ever-present party bureaucracy, strengthened by loyalty to Stalin himself. Party membership was the ticket to bureaucratic promotion, and the party deliberately kept its mem-

Figure 36.3 *As Soviet troops moved into Hungary to crush the revolt of 1956, freedom fighters in Budapest headed for the front with whatever weapons they could find. This truckload of supporters is being urged on by the crowd.*

ᴅ ᴏ ᴄ ᴜ ᴍ ᴇ ɴ ᴛ

Socialist Realism

One of the most fascinating features of the Soviet system was the attempt to create a distinctive art, different from Western cultures (seen as decadent) and appropriate to the communist mission. This effort involved censorship and forced orthodoxy, but it also was an attempt to resolve earlier Russian problems of relating formal culture to the masses and trying to preserve a national distinctiveness amid the seductions of Western influence. The following effort to define Soviet artistic policy was written by Andrey Zhdanov in 1934, the year Stalin made him the party's spokesperson at the Congress of Soviet Writers.

There is not and never has been a literature making its basic subject-matter the life of the working class and the peasantry and their struggle for socialism. There does not exist in any country in the world a literature to defend and protect the equality of rights of the working people of all nations and the equality of rights of women. There is not, nor can there be in any bourgeois country, a literature to wage consistent war on all obscurantism, mysticism, hierarchic religious attitudes and threats of hell-fire, as our literature does.

Only Soviet literature could become and has in fact become such an advanced, thought-imbued literature. It is one flesh and blood with our socialist construction....

What can the bourgeois writer write or think of, where can he find passion, if the worker in the capitalist countries is not sure of his tomorrow, does not know whether he will have work, if the peasant does not know whether he will be working on his bit of land or thrown on the scrap heap by a capitalist crisis, if the working intellectual is out of work today and does not know whether he will have work tomorrow?

What can the bourgeois author write about, what source of inspiration can there be for him, when the world, from one day to the next, may be plunged once more into the abyss of a new imperialist war?

The present position of bourgeois literature is such that it is already incapable of producing great works. *The decline and decay of bourgeois literature derive from the decline and decay of the capitalist system and are a feature and aspect characteristic of the present condition of bourgeois culture and literature.* The days when bourgeois literature, reflecting the victories of the bourgeois system over feudalism, was in the heyday of capitalism capable of creating great works, have gone, never to return. Today a degeneration in subject matter, in talents, in authors and in heroes, is in progress....

A riot of mysticism, religious mania and pornography is characteristic of the decline and decay of bourgeois culture. The "celebrities" of that bourgeois literature which has sold its pen to capital are today thieves, detectives, prostitutes, pimps and gangsters....

The proletariat of the capitalist countries is already forging its army of writers and artists—revolutionary writers, the representatives of whom we are glad to be able to welcome here today at the first Soviet Writers' Congress. The number of revolutionary writers in the capitalist countries is still small but it is growing and will grow with every day's sharpening of the class struggle, with the growing strength of the world proletarian revolution.

We are firmly convinced that the few dozen foreign comrades we have welcomed here constitute the kernel, the embryo, of a mighty army of proletarian writers to be created by the world proletarian revolution in foreign countries....

Comrade Stalin has called our writers "engineers of the human soul." What does this mean? What obligations does such an appellation put upon you?

It means, in the first place, that you must know life to be able to depict it truthfully in artistic creations, to depict it neither "scholastically" nor lifelessly, nor simply as "objective reality," but rather as reality in its revolutionary development. The truthfulness and historical exactitude of the artistic image must be linked with the task of ideological transformation, of the education of the working people in the spirit of socialism. This method in fiction and literary criticism is what we call the method of socialist realism.

Our Soviet literature is not afraid of being called tendentious, for in the epoch of class struggle there is not and cannot be "apolitical" literature.

And it seems to me that any and every Soviet writer may say to any dull-witted bourgeois, to any philistine or to any bourgeois writers who speak of the tendentiousness of our literature: "Yes, our Soviet literature is tendentious and we are proud of it, for our tendentiousness is to free the working people—and the whole of mankind—from the yoke of capitalist slavery."

To be an engineer of the human soul is to stand four-square on real life. And this in turn means a break with old-style romanticism, with the romanticism which depicted a nonexistent life and nonexistent heroes, drawing the reader away from the contradictions and shackles of life into an unrealizable and utopian world. Romanticism is not alien to our literature, a literature standing firmly on a materialistic basis, but ours is a romanticism of a new type, revolutionary romanticism. We say that socialist realism is the fundamental method of Soviet fiction and literary criticism, and this implies that revolutionary romanticism will appear as an integral part of any literary creation, since the whole life of our Party, of the working class and its struggle, is a fusion of the hardest, most matter-of-fact practical work, with the greatest heroism and the vastest perspectives. The strength of our Party has always lain in the fact that it has united and unites efficiency and practicality with broad vision, with an incessant forward striving and the struggle to build a communist society.

Soviet literature must be able to portray our heroes and to see our tomorrow. This will not be utopian since our tomorrow is being prepared by planned and conscious work today....

Questions: What were the reasons for culture according to Stalinist intellectuals? How did Soviet cultural leaders analyze Western intellectual life? What were the proper tasks of an artist in Soviet society? How were these tasks expressed in socialist realism? What would the Soviet response be to a Western intellectual claiming objectivity for his work?

bership low—at about 6 percent of the population—to ensure selection of the most dedicated elements. New candidates for the party vowed unswerving loyalty and group consciousness. A 1939 party charter stated the essential qualities:

> The Party is a united militant organization bound together by a conscious discipline which is equally binding on all its members. The Party is strong because of its solidarity, unity of will, and unity of action, which are incompatible with any deviation from its program and rules, with any violation of Party discipline, with factional groupings, or with double-dealing. The Party purges its ranks of persons who violate its program, rules, or discipline.

Under Stalinism, bureaucratic caution increased. Top officials who kept their posts tended to be colorless figures, competent but above all extremely loyal both to official ideology and to Stalin as leader. For example, one durable foreign minister, Molotov, was described by Stalin as having a "mind like a file clerk."

Soviet Culture: Promoting New Beliefs

The government and party also maintained a vigorous cultural agenda. Although this had been foreshadowed by the church–state links of tsarist days, it had no full precedent. The regime quickly declared war on the Orthodox church and other religions, attempting to shape a secular population that would maintain a Marxist, scientific orthodoxy. Artistic and literary styles, as well as purely political writings, were monitored carefully to ensure that they reflected the party line. The educational system was used to train and recruit technicians and bureaucrats and to create a loyal, right-thinking citizenry. New mass ceremonies, such as May Day parades, stimulated devotion to the Soviet Union and to communism.

Although the new regime did not try to abolish the Orthodox church outright, it greatly limited the church's outreach. Thus, the church was barred from giving religious instruction to anyone under age 18, and state schools vigorously preached that religion was mere superstition. Although loyalties to the church persisted, they seemed concentrated in a largely elderly minority. The Soviet regime also limited freedom of religion for the Jewish minority, often holding up Jews as enemies of the state in a manipulation of traditional Russian anti-Semitism. The larger Muslim minority was given greater latitude on condition of loyalty to the regime.

The Soviet state also opposed the strong Western cultural orientation of the 19th-century tsarist elite, which had never widely touched the masses in any event. Modern Western styles of art and literature were attacked as decadent. Earlier styles, appropriated as Russian, were maintained. Thus, Russian orchestras performed a wide variety of classical music, and the Russian ballet, though rigid and conservative by 20th-century Western standards, commanded wide attention and enforced rigorous standards of excellence. Soviet culture emphasized a new style of *socialist realism* in the arts (Figure 36.4), a style bent on glorifying heroic workers, soldiers, and peasants. As the Document section shows, socialist realism was seen as a vital educational tool and an antidote to Western cultural decadence. A vigorous strand of modern art in prerevolutionary and 1920s Russia yielded under Stalin to grandiose, neoclassical paintings and sculpture. Although care was taken to preserve older buildings, Soviet architecture emphasized functional, classical lines and a pronounced taste for the monumental. The principles of socialist realism spread to eastern Europe after World War II, particularly in public displays and monuments. After 1960, however, Soviet and east European artists began to

Visualizing THE PAST

Socialist Realism

How does the picture illustrate the purposes of this style? How does it compare to the stated purposes of socialist realism in the Document section? Why would it be seen as an inspiration to the Soviet people? How did its themes fit the larger Stalinist system? Was the picture realistic by Western standards? How would official artists defend it against charges of inaccuracy? How did the style and themes compare with the modern, abstract art gaining ground in the West at this point (see Chapter 35)? How did it compare with the popular art shown in commercials for products in the United States and western Europe? Is the picture a good summary of Soviet culture?

In this example of Socialist realism, heroic women workers labor at a bustling, productive factory.

interact somewhat more with Western styles. At the popular level, jazz and rock music bands began to emerge by the 1980s, though official suspicion of Western culture persisted.

Soviet literature remained diverse and creative, despite official controls sponsored by the communist-dominated Writers' Union. Leading authors wrote movingly of the travails of the civil war and World War II, maintaining the earlier tradition of sympathy with the Russian people, great patriotism, and a concern for the Russian soul.

The most creative Soviet artists, and particularly the writers, often skirted a fine line between conveying some of the sufferings of the Russian people in the 20th century and courting official disapproval. Their freedom also varied, depending on the mood of the leadership. Thus, censorship eased after Stalin and then tightened somewhat, though not to previous levels. Yet even authors critical of aspects of the

Soviet regime maintained distinctive Russian values. *Aleksandr Solzhenitsyn,* who was exiled to the West because of the publication of his trilogy about the Siberian prison camps, *The Gulag Archipelago,* found the West too materialistic and individualistic for his taste. Barred from his homeland for many years, he continued to seek some alternative both to communist policy and to Westernization and retained a continuing belief in the solidarity and faith of the Russian national soul.

Soviet culture placed strong emphasis on science and social science. Scientists enjoyed great prestige and power. Social scientific work, heavily colored by Marxist theory, nonetheless produced important analyses of current trends and history. Scientific research was even more heavily funded, and Soviet scientists made several fundamental discoveries in physics, chemistry, and mathematics. Like their counterparts in the West, they also contributed to technology and weaponry. Scientists felt the heavy hand of official disapproval at times. Biologists and psychiatrists in particular were urged to reject Western theories that called human rationality and social progress into question. Thus Freudianism was banned, and biologists who overemphasized the uncontrollability of genetic evolution were jailed under Stalin. After the heyday of Stalinism, scientists gained greater freedom from ideological dictates, and exchanges with Western researchers became more common in what was, at base, a common scientific culture.

For many intellectuals, cultural expression became a risk and a personal survival tool. Nadezhda Mandelstam (1899–1980; her first name means "hope"), born to a family of Jewish origin but converted to Christianity, saw her poet husband arrested in 1938 and never saw him again. She devoted her literary life to his memory while staying out of police purview by teaching English in obscure teachers' training institutes. Two volumes (*Hope Against Hope* and *Hope Abandoned*), essentially autobiography, told her story and that of her husband. They were published first in the West but then circulated secretly in Russia, winning her a large following. She entertained a wide circle, harassed by communist officials who denied her all postal service and even, at her death, tried to prevent her Christian burial (ultimately returning her body to her friends, however). As communism collapsed, nearly everything she wrote was printed in Russia.

Figure 36.4 *In his 1949 painting* Creative Fellowship, *Shcherbakov shows the cooperation of scientists and workers in an idealized factory setting. The painting exemplifies the theories and purposes of Socialist realism.*

Economy and Society

The Soviet Union became a fully industrial society between the 1920s and the 1950s. Manufacturing grew rapidly, and city populations rose to more than 50 percent of the total. Most of the rest of eastern Europe was also fully industrialized by the 1950s. However, Soviet and east European modernization had some distinctive features. State control of nearly all economic sectors was one key element. The Soviet Union also lagged in the priorities it placed on consumer goods—not only Western staples such as automobiles, but also housing construction and simple items such as bathtub plugs. Thus, despite an occasional desire to beat the West at its own game, eastern Europe and the Soviet Union did not develop the kind of consumer society that came to characterize the West. Living standards improved, and extensive welfare services provided security for some groups that was lacking in the West, but complaints about poor consumer products and long lines to obtain desired goods remained a feature of Soviet and eastern European life.

Eastern European society also echoed many themes of contemporary Western social history simply because of the shared fact of industrial life. For example, work rhythms became roughly similar. Industrialization in Russia brought massive efforts to speed the pace of work and introduce regularized supervision. The incentive systems designed to encourage able workers resembled those used in Western factories. Similar leisure activities developed as well. Sports provided excitement for the peoples of eastern Europe, as did mass media such as films and television. Family vacations to the beaches of the Black Sea became cherished respites.

East European social structure also grew closer to that of the West, despite the continued importance of the rural population and despite the impact of Marxist theory. Particularly interesting was a tendency for urban society to divide along class lines between workers and a better-educated, managerial middle class. Perks for managers and professional people, particularly Communist party members, set them off from the masses.

Finally, the Soviet family reacted to some of the same pressures of industrialization the Western family experienced. Massive movement to the cities and crowded housing focused on the nuclear family unit as ties to a wider network of relatives loosened. The birth rate dropped. The official Soviet policy on birth rates varied for a time, but the basic trends became similar to those in the West. Declining infant death rates caused by improved diets and medical care, along with growing periods of schooling and some increase in consumer expectations, made large families less desirable than before. By the 1970s, the Soviet growth rate was about the same as that of the West. As in the West, some minority groups, particularly Muslims in the southern Soviet republics, maintained higher birth rates than the majority ethnic group (in this case, ethnic Russians), which caused some concern about maintaining Russian cultural dominance.

Patterns of child-rearing showed some similarities to those in the West. Parents, especially in the managerial middle class, devoted great attention to promoting their children's education. At the same time, children were more strictly disciplined than in the West, both at home and in school. Russian families could never afford the domestic idealization of women that had prevailed in the West during industrialization. Most married women worked, an essential feature of an economy struggling to industrialize and offering low wages to individual workers. Women performed many heavy physical tasks. They also dominated some professions, such as medicine. Russian propagandists took pride in the constructive role of women and their official equality, but there were signs that many women suffered burdens from demanding jobs with little help from their husbands at home.

Despite state repression, popular culture was expressive. Concerns about acquisition, romance, and school success had a very Western, or more properly a modern industrial, ring. Thus, 1970s graffiti on a church wall in Leningrad—a traditional site of wish lists since the last tsarist days—expressed familiar personal aspirations:

> "Lord, grant me luck, and help me to be accepted into the Art Academy in four years." "Happiness and health to me and Volodya." "Lord strangle Tarisyn." "Lord, help me get rid of Valery." "Lord, help me in love." "Lord make Charlotte fall in love with me." "Lord, I'm hungry." "Lord, help me pass the exam in political economics." "Lord, help me pass the exam in: (1) electrical technology; (2) electrical vacuum instruments; (3) Marxism–Leninism." "Help me pass my driver's license test, Lord." "Lord, take the arrogance out of my wife." "Lord, help me win a transistor radio, model AP–2–14, in the lottery." Added on by another person: "All we have is P–20–1. Archangel Gabriel."

De-Stalinization

The rigid government apparatus, created by Stalin and sustained after World War II by frequent arrests and exiles to forced labor camps, was put to a major test after Stalin's death in 1953. The results gradually loosened, without totally reversing, Stalinist cultural isolation.

The focus on one-man rule might have created immense succession problems; indeed, jockeying for power often developed among aspiring candidates. Yet the system held together. Years of bureaucratic experience gave most Soviet leaders a taste for coordination and compromise. Stalin's death was answered by a ruling committee that balanced interest groups, notably the army, the police, and the party apparatus. This mechanism encouraged conservatism, as each bureaucratic sector defended its existing prerogatives, but it also ensured fundamental stability.

In 1956, however, a new Soviet leader, *Nikita Khrushchev,* emerged from the committee pack to gain primary power. In a stirring speech delivered to the party congress, Khrushchev attacked Stalinism for its concentration of power and arbitrary dictatorship. He condemned Stalin for his treatment of political opponents, his narrow interpretations of Marxist doctrine, and even his failure to prepare adequately for World War II. The implications of this startling blast changed the Soviet political climate and led to some decentralization of decision making. Political trials became less common, and the most overt police repression eased. A few intellectuals were allowed to raise new issues, dealing with the purges and other Stalinist excesses. Outright critics of the regime were less likely to be executed and more likely to be sent to psychiatric institutions or, in the case of internationally visible figures such as a handful of novelists, exiled to the West or confined to house arrest. But party control and centralized economic planning remained intact.

After the de-Stalinization furor and Khrushchev's fall from power, patterns in the Soviet Union remained stable into the 1980s, at times stagnant. Economic growth continued but with no dramatic breakthroughs. Recurrent worries over sluggish productivity, especially during inadequate harvests, compelled expensive grain deals with Western nations, including the United States. Several changes of leadership occurred as party chieftains aged and died, but the transitions were handled smoothly.

Cold war policies eased somewhat upon Stalin's death. Khrushchev vaunted the Soviet ability to outdo the West at its own industrial game, bragging on a visit to the United States, "We will bury you." The Khrushchev regime produced one of the most intense moments of the cold war with the United States as it probed for vulnerabilities. The Soviet government installed missiles in Cuba, yielding only to firm American response in 1962. Khrushchev had no desire for war, and both before and after the Cuban missile crisis, he promoted a new policy of peaceful coexistence. He hoped to beat the West economically, and he actively expanded the Soviet space program. *Sputnik,* the first satellite, was sent into space in 1957, and Yuri Gagarin went up in the first manned flight in 1961, both before the U.S. equivalents. Khrushchev maintained a competitive tone, but he shifted away from the exclusively military emphasis. Lowered cold war tensions with the West permitted a small influx of Western tourists by the 1960s as well as greater access to the Western media and a variety of cultural exchanges that gave some Soviet citizens a renewed sense of contact with a wider world.

At the same time, the Soviet leadership continued a steady military buildup, adding increasingly sophisticated rocketry. The Soviets maintained a lead in manned space flights into the late 1980s. Both in space and in the arms race, the Soviet Union demonstrated great technical ability combined with a willingness to settle for somewhat simpler systems than those the United States attempted. An active sports program, resulting in a growing array of victories in the Olympic games, also showed the Soviet Union's new ability to compete on an international scale and its growing pride in international achievements.

The nation faced several new foreign policy problems while maintaining superpower status. The rift with China grew from the mid-1950s onward, and the two great communist nations shared a massive border. The rise of Muslim awareness in the 1970s was deeply troubling to the Soviet Union, with its own large Muslim minority; this prompted an invasion of Afghanistan to promote a friendly puppet regime, which bogged down amid guerrilla warfare in the late 1980s. On balance, the Soviet Union played a cautious diplomatic game, almost never engaging directly in warfare but maintaining a high level of preparedness.

Problems of work motivation and discipline loomed larger in Russia than in the West by the 1980s, after the heroic period of building an industrial society under Stalinist exhortation and threat. With highly bureaucratized and centralized work

Figure 36.5 *Young capitalist selling Pepsi on a Moscow street, 1993.*

plans, as well as a lack of consumer goods, many workers found little reason for great diligence. High rates of alcoholism, so severe as to cause an increase in death rates, also burdened work performance. More familiar were problems of youth agitation. Although Soviet statistics tended to conceal crime problems, it was clear that many Soviet youths became impatient with the disciplined life and were eager to have greater access to Western culture, including rock music and blue jeans.

THE EXPLOSION OF THE 1980S AND 1990S

> ■ *Beginning in the mid-1980s, a growing economic crisis forced political change. Piecemeal experiments within the Soviet Union led to an explosion by 1989, when the independent nations renounced communism and the Russian empire itself split apart. Instability persisted into the late 1990s as the region found it difficult to define a new political and economic order.*

From 1985 onward, the Soviet Union entered a period of intensive reform. This was matched by a host of new political movements in eastern Europe that dismantled the Soviet empire. The initial cause of this extraordinary upheaval lay in the deteriorating Soviet economic performance, intensified by the costs of military rivalry with the United States.

Economic Stagnation

Despite satisfaction with the Soviet Union's world prestige, the economy was grinding to a standstill by the 1980s. Forced industrialization had produced extensive environmental damage throughout eastern Europe. According to Soviet estimates, half of all rivers were severely polluted, and more than 40 percent of all agricultural land was endangered by the late 1980s; more than 20 percent of Soviet citizens lived in regions of ecological disaster. The rates and severity of respiratory and other diseases rose, impairing both morale and economic performance. Infant mortality rates also rose in several regions, sometimes matching the highest levels anywhere in the world.

Industrial production began to stagnate and even drop as a result of rigid central planning, health problems, and poor worker morale. As economic growth stopped, the percentage of resources allocated to military production approached one-third of all national income as Soviet–American rivalry became steadily more costly. This reduced funds available for other investments and for consumer needs. Younger leaders began to recognize, at first privately, that the system was near collapse.

Reform and Agitation

In 1985, after a succession of leaders whose age or health precluded major initiatives, the Soviet Union brought a new, younger official to the fore. *Mikhail Gorbachev* quickly renewed some of the earlier attacks on Stalinist rigidity and replaced some of the old-line party bureaucrats. He conveyed a new and more Western style, dressing in fashionable clothes (and accompanied by his wife, who did the same), holding open press conferences, and even allowing Soviet media to engage in active debate and to report on problems as well as successes.

Gorbachev also changed the Soviet Union's cold war stance. He urged a reduction in nuclear armaments, and in 1987 he negotiated a new agreement with the United States that limited medium-range missiles in Europe. He ended the war in Afghanistan, bringing Soviet troops home. Internally, Gorbachev proclaimed a policy of *glasnost,* or openness, which implied new freedom to comment and criticize. He pressed particularly for a reduction in bureaucratic decision making and for the use of market incentives to stimulate greater output. The sweep of Gorbachev's reforms, accompanied by a new tone in Soviet public relations, remained difficult to assess. Strong limits on political freedom persisted, and it was unclear whether Gorbachev could cut through the centralized planning apparatus that controlled the main lines of the Soviet economy.

In many ways, Gorbachev's policies restored a characteristic ambivalence about the West as he reduced Soviet isolation while continuing to criticize aspects of Western political and social structure. Gorbachev clearly hoped to use some Western management techniques and cultural styles without intending to abandon the basic controls of the communist state. Western analysts wondered whether the Soviet economy could improve worker motivations without embracing a Western-style consumerism or whether computers could be introduced more widely without admitting wider freedom to the exchange of information.

Gorbachev also tried to open the Soviet Union to fuller participation in the world economy, recognizing that isolation in a separate empire had limited access to new technology and motivation to change. Although the new leadership did not rush to make foreign trade or investment too easy because suspicion persisted, the economic initiatives brought symbolic changes, such as the opening of a McDonald's restaurant in Moscow, and a whole array of new contacts with foreigners for various Soviet citizens.

The keynote of the reform program was *perestroika*, or economic restructuring, which Gorbachev translated into more leeway for private ownership and decentralized control in industry and agriculture. For example, farmers won the chance to lease land for 50 years with rights of inheritance, and industrial concerns were authorized to buy from either private or state operations. Foreign investment was newly encouraged. Gorbachev pressed for reductions in Soviet military commitments, particularly through agreements with the United States on troop reductions and limitations on nuclear weaponry, to free resources for consumer goods industries. He urged more self-help by the general population, arguing that he wanted to "rid public opinion of . . . faith in a 'good Tsar,' the all powerful center, the notion that someone can bring about order and organize perestroika from on high." Politically, he encouraged a new constitution in 1988, giving power to a new parliament, the Congress of People's Deputies, and abol-

ishing the communist monopoly on elections. Important opposition groups developed both inside and outside the party, pressing Gorbachev between conservative hard-liners and radicals wanting faster reforms. Gorbachev was elected to a new, powerful presidency of the Soviet Union in 1990.

Reform, amid continued economic stagnation, provoked agitation among minority nationalities in the Soviet Union from 1988 onward. Muslims and Armenian Christians rioted in the south, both against each other and against the central state. Baltic nationalists and other European minorities also stirred, some insisting on independence (notably in Lithuania) and some pressing for greater autonomy. In early 1991 several regions, including Lithuania as well as Georgia in the south, voted for independence, although their efforts were thwarted temporarily by the central state.

Dismantling the Soviet Empire

Gorbachev's new approach prompted more definitive results outside the Soviet Union than within, as the smaller states of eastern Europe uniformly moved for greater independence and internal reforms. Bulgaria opted for economic liberalization in 1987 but was held back by the Soviets; pressure resumed in 1989 as the Bulgarian party leader was ousted and free elections were arranged. Hungary changed leadership in 1988 and installed a noncommunist president. A new constitution and free elections were planned in Hungary, where the Communist party renamed itself Socialist. Hungary also reviewed its great 1956 uprising, formally declaring it "a popular uprising . . . against an oligarchic system . . . which had humiliated the nation." The nation moved rapidly toward a free market economy.

Poland installed a noncommunist government in 1988 and worked quickly to dismantle the state-run economy; prices rose rapidly as government subsidies were withdrawn. The Solidarity movement, combining noncommunist labor leaders and Catholic intellectuals, became the dominant political force. East Germany displaced its communist government in 1989, expelling key leaders and moving rapidly toward unification with West Germany. The Berlin Wall was dismantled, and in 1990 noncommunists won a free election. Full German unification occurred toward the end of 1990. Czechoslovakia installed a new government in 1989, headed by playwright Vaclav Havel, and again worked to introduce free elections and a more market-driven economy.

Map 36.3 *Post–Soviet Union Russia, Eastern Europe, and Central Asia. The boundaries of east central Europe and central Asia were redrawn.*

Although mass demonstrations played a key role in several of these political upheavals, only in Romania was there outright violence, as an exceptionally authoritarian communist leader was swept out by force. As in Bulgaria, the Communist party retained power, though under new leadership, and reforms moved less rapidly there than in places such as Hungary and Czechoslovakia.

Reform in eastern Europe, as in the Soviet Union itself, was complicated by clashes between nationalities. Change and uncertainty brought older attachments and antagonisms to the fore. Romanians and ethnic Hungarians fought, and Bulgarians attacked a Turkish minority left over from the Ottoman period. Yugoslavia witnessed bitter clashes between rival Slavic groups. The Yugoslav federation fell apart as south Slavic groups such as the Croats claimed their own country. Bitter fighting broke out in Bosnia, a region divided between nationalities, with Serbs,

Croats, and Muslims all clamoring for territory. Later, in 1998–1999, bloody clashes between Serbs and Albanians in the province of Kosovo prompted heavy-handed outside interventions.

Amid this rapid and unexpected change, the prospects for the future were wide open. Few of the new governments fully defined their constitutional structures. Amid innovation, the range of new political parties almost compelled later consolidations. Like the Soviet Union itself, all the east European states suffered from sluggish production. In 1993–1994, economic grievances propelled former Communist parties to election majorities in both Poland and Hungary, although there was no attempt to restore a full communist system. Environmental problems also played a role. Diplomatic linkages between small states, a critical problem area between the two world wars, also had not been resolved. What remained clear was the dramatic change in Russian policy. Gorbachev reversed postwar imperialism completely, stating that "any nation has the right to decide its fate by itself," and his successor, *Boris Yeltsin,* confirmed this stance. Soviet troops were withdrawn rapidly from the former empire, and it seemed unlikely that a change of heart toward a repressive attempt to reestablish empire would be possible.

Shocks in 1991: The End of the Soviet Union

The uncertainties of the situation within the Soviet Union were confirmed in the summer of 1991, when an attempted coup was mounted by military and police elements. Gorbachev's presidency and democratic decentralization were threatened. However, popular demonstrations asserted the strong democratic current that had developed in Russia since 1986. The contrast with earlier Soviet history and with the suppression of democracy in China two years before was striking.

The failed coup led to new attacks on the Communist party and to new independence movements by minority nationalities. The Baltic republics declared independence again, this time with wide international recognition. Independence movements spread to

other parts of the Soviet Union, notably its European borders (Belarus, Ukraine, Moldova) and the Muslim areas of central Asia, where several new republics surfaced. By December 1991, the Soviet Union was dismantled, replaced by a loose union of the successor republics, the Commonwealth of Independent States. Gorbachev, unwilling to accept this final indignity and increasingly on the margins of power in Russia itself, resigned. The elected president of the Russian Republic, Boris Yeltsin, became the leading political figure. The Communist party was dissolved.

Internal struggles between ethnic groups convulsed several of the new republics. Large Russian minorities and the continued presence of Russian troops were additional factors in a very volatile diplomatic situation. Most of the republics, which had been tied into the larger Soviet economy, faced serious economic problems.

In the new Russian Federation itself, recurrent crisis prevailed as well. Despite considerable personal popularity, Yeltsin struggled to gain a political base. He was pitted against the parliament, composed mainly of former communists, and an armed clash occurred in 1993 from which Yeltsin and the army emerged victorious (Figure 36). The ensuing elections produced yet

Figure 36.5 *Using the army to attack the parliament building, Boris Yeltsin consolidated his position against dissident delegates, many of them former communists, but he lost ensuing parliamentary elections.*

another constitution, designed to stabilize democracy, but a divided parliament (Figure 36.7). Ardent nationalists, urging a restoration of Russian greatness, formed the largest group; Yeltsin's supporters, loosely organized, and a bloc of former communists divided most of the remainder. In this muddy situation, Yeltsin slowed economic reforms, generating a set of policies that combined some drive toward private enterprise with protection for state-run operations. On the diplomatic front, Yeltsin continued collaboration with the West in such trouble spots as the Balkans, although he faced pressures to take a more independent Russian line. Cultural creativity remained high, with greater freedom to publish, although funding problems paralyzed scientific research.

The economy remained very weak in the late 1990s. Production levels were down. Some successful new enterprises had emerged. But supplies to consumers were uncertain, and unemployment was a growing problem. In 1998, the economy came near collapse as the value of the ruble plummeted. This jeopardized market reforms and political stability alike as former communists urged new government controls. At the same time, there were signs of a larger breakdown of values and discipline. Organized crime gained ground. Rampant profiteering created a much-resented wealthy class, complete with fancy cars and new nightclubs. Many Russians, convinced that communism had failed but unclear what the alternatives were, simply struggled to define their own beliefs. There was no clear precedent for this sort of crisis in world history, short of defeat in war, and predictions for the future were uncertain at best. Election of a new President in 2000, Vladimir Putin, did not initially clarify Russia's political or economic directions.

Conclusion

What Next?

Current Soviet and east European history is dominated by the surprising events of the past decade. Recent events have made clear that much less changed in this region during the 20th century than had been believed, even by Soviet citizens themselves. Soviet law had long trumpeted women's equality, and Soviet women played vital roles in the labor force, but inequality in household chores continued. Soviet constitutions had featured a system of federated republics, but central government control and Russian ethnic dominance spurred minority nationalism, and divisive nationalist hostilities burned brightly. Religion also remained a vital force despite decades of secularization.

Revolution and a totalitarian state had also made less of a dent in traditional attraction to Western standards than might have been imagined. Indeed, several east European states rushed to proclaim a Western-style devotion to individual liberty as well as a market economy.

Continuities from the communist period persist as well. Many Russian leaders resent this loss of superpower status. The use of the Russian army to put down rebellious delegates to the parliament in 1993 increased the conservative strain in the new Russian regime, as did the 1995 attack on a rebellious Muslim region, Chechnya. The prospects for democratic leadership were by no means secure.

Many east Europeans continue to value the welfare protections of communist society and the limitations on social inequality. Many hope to combine elements of collective protection with more capitalism. Many Russians oppose blatant individual profiteering, maintaining earlier communal traditions that predated communism; for some, equality in poverty seems preferable to individual self-seeking. Many continue to attack aspects of Western individualism that seem unattractive, such as high crime rates and youth unrest, even as these trends gain ground in their own region. And many citizens appreciate the ear-

Figure 36.7 *Russian elections, 1993.*

lier achievements of the Soviet system—in destroying the landlord class, for example—and in revolutionizing access to education. Tensions in relationship to Western values, an old theme redefined under communism, persist as well.

Eastern Europe had been a dynamic factor in world history for centuries, which means that the questions about its future, unanswerable at the end of the 20th century, affect far more than the region itself. Throughout the turmoil of 20th-century war and revolution, Russia retained a pivotal position in European and Asian power balances, and ultimately in world affairs more widely. Is this role to be redefined, or will it gradually recede, and with what consequences?

Further Readings

On the Russian Revolution, Sheila Fitzpatrick's *The Russian Revolution, 1917–1932* (1982) is a recent overview with a rich bibliography. See also A. Rabinowitch's *The Bolsheviks Come to Power* (1976), Robert Tucker's *Stalin as Revolutionary* (1972), and R. Conquest's *The Great Terror* (1968). Edmund Wilson's *To the Finland Station* (1972) offers a dramatic account of the revolution's early phase. On nationality issues, see R. Pipes's *The Formation of the Soviet Union* (1964).

More recent Soviet history is treated in Richard Barnet's *The Giants: Russia and America* (1977), A. Rubinstein's *Soviet Foreign Policy Since World War II* (1981), Alec Nove's *The Soviet Economic System* (1980), Stephen Cohen et al., eds., *The Soviet Union Since Stalin*, and Ben Eklof's *Gorbachev and the Reform Period* (1988).

Other parts of eastern Europe are treated in H. Setson Watson's *Eastern Europe Between the Wars* (1962), F. Fetjo's *History of the People's Democracies: Eastern Europe Since Stalin* (1971), J. Tampke's *The People's Republics of Eastern Europe* (1983), Timothy Ash's *The Polish Revolution: Solidarity* (1984), H. G. Skilling's *Czechoslovakia: Interrupted Revolution* (1976) (on the 1968 uprising), and B. Kovrig's *Communism in Hungary from Kun to Kadar* (1979).

A major interpretation of the communist experience is T. Skocpol's *States and Social Revolutions* (1979). On the early signs of explosion in eastern Europe, see K. Dawisha's *Eastern Europe, Gorbachev and Reform: The Great Challenge* (1988). Bohdan Nahaylo and Victor Swoboda's *Soviet Disunion: A History of the Nationalities Problem in the USSR* (1990) provides important background. See also Rose Brady's *Kapitalizm: Russia's Struggle to Free Its Economy* (1999). On women's experiences, see Barbara Engel and Christine Worobec, eds., *Russia's Women: Accommodation, Resistance, Transformation* (1990).

On the Web

A relevant Web site on Soviet constitutions and other early Soviet documents and pictures is http://www.hutman.com/~nusides/Soviet.

For a brief look at Lenin, the father of the Russian Revolution, go to http://www.soften.ktu.lt/~kaleck/lenin/ and http://history.hanover.edu/modern/lenin.htm. For a critical view of Lenin set against more recent events in that country, go to http://flag.blackened.net/revolt/ws91/lenin31.html. These men and ideas responsible for the Soviet Union's rise to power and its demise, from Stalin to Boris Yeltsin and from the New Economic Policy to perestroika are examined at http://home.mira.net/~andy/bs/index.htm.

Leon Trotsky's role as an exiled critic of that regime (http:www.anu.edu.au/polsci/marx/contemp/pamsetc/socfrombel/sfb_7.htm) can be enlivened by a virtual visit to the house in Mexico where he was assassinated by a Stalinist agent (http://old.myhouse.com/pub/bigjohn/STORY12.html). This fate was narrowly avoided by others who sought a different socialist path in close proximity to the Soviet state such as Alexander Dubcek (http://rferl.org/nca/special/invasion1968), Vaclav Havel (http://www.hrad.cz/president/Havel/cvp_uk.html) and his Velvet Revolution http://www.radio.cz/history/history15.html) and Lech Walesa (http://www.nobel.se/laureates/peace-1983-1-bio.html).

The rise and demise of the Berlin Wall is traced in text, video and photographs at http://207.25.71.25/resources/video.almanac/1989/index3.html, http://userpage.chemie.fu_berlin.ed/B|W/wall.html, http://members.aol.com/johball/berlinw2.htm and http://www.novaonline.nv.cc.va.us/eli/evans/his135/MODULES/events/Berlinwall.htm.

Changes in the former Soviet Union since 1991, including the attempted breakaway of Chechnya from the Russian Federation, are explored at http://www.learner.org/exhibits/russia.

The history of Lenin's mausoleum in text and photographs can be found at http://www.aha.ru/~mausoleu/m-hist_e.htm.

Chapter 37

Japan and the Pacific Rim

Tokyo at night at the beginning of the 21st century epitomizes the resurgence of Asian economies following World War II.

The rebalancing of major societies in the 20th century showed in the rise of east Asia's coastal areas. This chapter covers several political units in eastern Asia—Japan, Korea, Taiwan, and the city-states of Singapore and Hong Kong—that underwent unusual economic growth during the second half of the 20th century.

The *Pacific Rim states* joined the West as the center of the world's greatest industrial strength. The Pacific Rim states also shared a fascinating effort to blend successful industrial forms with a distinctive cultural and political tradition They provided the clearest alternative to the West of what a vigorous modern society might look like.

The key actor was Japan. Japan's rise to new eminence was launched in the 19th century with the reforms of the Meiji era. During the 1930s, the Japanese military surge continued with the attacks on China and large stretches of southeast Asia and the Pacific. After defeat in World War II and a new series of internal reforms, Japan concentrated on dynamic economic growth. This small, resource-poor island nation reached toward control of almost one-fifth of total world trade. Japanese competition challenged the United States and western Europe, and its demand for raw materials figured prominently in Canada, Australia, Latin America, and the Middle East as well as Asia.

After World War II, Japan's success was mirrored by the rapid rise of other centers in eastern Asia. South Korea, Taiwan, and the city-states of Hong Kong and Singapore, though not yet attaining Japanese levels of prosperity and influence, gained ground rapidly.

1920 C.E.	1930 C.E.	1940 C.E.	1950 C.E.	1980 C.E.
1920 Advance of heavy industry **1923** Tokyo earthquake **1923** Defeat of Japanese bill for universal suffrage	**1931** Rebellion in Korea; Japanese repression **1931** Rise of nationalism; new hostility to West **1931** Height of depression, impact on Japan; bad harvests **1936** Assassination of several Japanese political leaders; young army officer rebellion **1938** Japan's war budget; state control of economic life **1937** Increasingly open role by military officers; arrest of opposition politicians	**1945** Japan defeated; American occupation **1946–1948** Kuomintang (Nationalist) regime consolidates in Taiwan **1948** Korea divided	**1950–1953** Korean War after invasion by North Korea **1951** American occupation ends in Japan **1954** U.S.–Taiwan defense treaty **1955** Merger forms Liberal Democratic party in Japan **1955** Japanese production reaches prewar levels **1959** Singapore declares independence **1961** Military regime in South Korea **1965** Growing Hong Kong autonomy	**1980** End U.S.–Taiwan treaty alliance **1984** British–Chinese agreement to return Hong Kong to China in 1997 **1988–1989** Growing student agitation for liberal political reform in South Korea; elected civilian government installed **1993–1994** Liberal Democrats ousted from power in Japan; corruption scandals and coalition governments amid economic recession

DECADES OF TURMOIL: THE WORLD WARS AND THEIR CONSEQUENCES

■■ *The first decades of the 20th century brought important changes to east Asia as China was consumed with internal problems and Japan surged ahead economically and militarily. Japan's economic strength showed in its quick rebound from the depression, but after some experiments with fuller democracy, its political system moved toward growing militarism.*

During the initial decades of the 20th century, Japan concentrated heavily on diplomatic and military gains as well as the difficult process of adjusting to the parliamentary, constitutional government established during the Meiji period. After 1900, the government party struggled to maintain a working political majority against various opposition factions. By this time Japan was an expansionist power; it formally annexed Korea in 1910. Japan ruled its new Asian colonies firmly, exacting taxes and raw materials while securing markets for its growing industrial output.

Japan's Ongoing Development

Along with international gains came continued industrial advance. Japanese industry continued to lag behind Western levels, relying heavily on low-wage labor and the export of a small number of items such as silk cloth. Silk production, at 16 million pounds in 1890, soared to 93 million pounds in 1929. Agricultural productivity improved steadily, led by progressive landlords who introduced fertilizers and new equipment. Rice production more than doubled between the 1880s and the 1930s. Modern industry advanced as Japan entered a second industrial phase in the 1920s. Great industrial combines—the *zaibatsu*—sponsored rapid expansion in fields such as shipbuilding and metallurgy, usually relying heavily on tight links with the government bureaucracy. The use of electric power grew faster in Japan than anywhere else in the world in the 1920s. A popular consumer culture developed, at least in the cities, as workers began to attend movies and read newspapers. Education advanced rapidly, with primary school attendance universal by 1925. Enrollments in secondary schools and technical colleges swelled, improving the capacity to assimilate the newer Western technologies.

The limits on Japanese economic advance included vulnerability to economic conditions abroad. Even before the depression, competition from artificial fibers such as rayon, produced by Western chemical companies, weakened silk exports. Population growth was another burden, or at least a mixed blessing. Japan's population soared from 30 million in 1868, to 45 million in 1900, and then to 73 million by 1940. Growth at this rate limited improvements in living standards and created social dislocation in the crowded, migrant-filled cities. Periodic protests through strikes, demonstrations, and some socialist agitation were met with vigorous police response. Conditions worsened (see Chapter 34) in the first phase of the Great Depression of the 1930s. The economy recovered quickly, however, under the twin stimuli of a new export boom and government-organized military procurement as Japan began to build up its war machine. Under the 1930s minister of finance, *Korekiyo Takahashi,* the government increased its spending to provide jobs, which in turn generated new demands for food and manufactured items.

By 1937, Japan boasted the third largest merchant marine in the world. The nation became self-sufficient in machine tools and scientific equipment, the fruit of the growth in technical training. The quality of Japanese industrial goods rose, producing the first Western outcry against Japanese exports, even though in 1936 the Japanese controlled only 3.6 percent of world trade.

Political Crisis and Growing Militarism

While the economy gained, political crisis seized center stage, leading to a new and risky round of military and diplomatic experiments that culminated in World War II. Social tensions played a role in this transition as Japan moved further from its basic tradition of noninvolvement in elaborate foreign ventures. Military leaders began to take a growing role in setting general diplomatic policy from the mid-1920s onward, at the expense of the civilian parties and politicians. The military leaders were trained in separate schools and saw themselves as the true guardians of the modern Japanese state as well as of older traditions. They reported not to civilian authority but directly to the emperor. A reduction of military budgets during the 1920s hit military leaders hard, and the army's prestige declined to such a point that officers wore civilian clothing when off base. Naval officers were appalled at decisions accepted from a great power Naval Conference in 1930 that limited fleet levels. In essence, Japan experimented during the 1920s with a liberal political pattern, which seemed to give primacy to party maneuverings and electoral appeals but also antagonized the military and other conservative elite groups.

This was the context in which military officials began to make separate decisions about Manchuria, leading to the 1931 seizure of this key Chinese region, while the civilian government tried to equiv-

ocate. Then, as political divisions increased in response to the initial impact of the depression, a variety of nationalist groups emerged, some advocating a return to Shinto or Confucian principles against the more Western values of urban Japan. As in Germany, various groups used the depression for a more sweeping protest against parliamentary forms.

In May 1932, a group of younger army officers attacked key government and banking officers and murdered the prime minister. They did not take over the state directly, but for the next four years moderate military leaders headed the executive branch, frustrating both the military firebrands and the political parties. Another attempted military coup in 1936 was put down by forces controlled by the established admirals and generals, but this group, including the vigorous General *Tojo Hideki,* increasingly interfered with civilian cabinets. The result, after 1936, was a series of increasingly militaristic prime ministers. By the end of 1938, Japan controlled a regional empire, including Manchuria, Korea, and Taiwan, within which the nation sold half its exports and from which it bought more than 40 percent of all imports, particularly food and raw materials. Both the military leadership and economic leaders, interested in such Asian resources as the rubber of British Malaya and the oil of the Dutch East Indies, soon pressed for wider conquests as Japan surged into World War II.

Change in Other Pacific Rim Areas

During the interwar decades, the experiences of other parts of eastern Asia were diverse. Japan's firm control over Korea created important resentments, and Japanese economic policies did little to stimulate major new developments in the Korean economy. The period of Japanese rule did disrupt Korean traditions, including the tendency to look toward Chinese superiority. The Japanese had replaced the Korean king with his feeble-minded son in 1908, and then, when a Korean patriot assassinated the resident general in 1909, they abolished the monarchy altogether. Korea's elaborate court aristocracy was undermined in this process. Colonial status, which lasted until Japan's World War II defeat in 1945, prevented the generation of new institutions, but there was new potential for innovation after the long centuries of Yi dynasty rule.

Almost from the outset, the Japanese launched an effort to suppress Korean culture and promote the adoption of Japanese ways. Korean-language newspapers were banned, Korean teachers were required to wear Japanese uniforms and carry swords, and Japanese money, weights and measures, and language instruction were introduced throughout the country. Korean resources were put at the disposal of Japanese industrialists, many of whom invested in factories in the new colony. The Korean peasantry was compelled to concentrate on rice production for export to Japan and other foreign markets. During World War II, the Japanese military police forcibly conscripted increasing numbers of Korean youths for labor gangs and troops to support their expanding war effort, and the population was exhorted to join the Japanese people in "training to endure hardship."

As in other colonial areas such as India, economic exploitation may have had some promising side effects, without being any less exploitive. Historians have recently found some keys to Korea's later economic success in industrial opportunities developed under the Japanese. Korea's large Christian minority also consolidated under the Japanese as the religion became less a missionary import, more a basis for some independent identity amid occupation.

Singapore, a city with a largely Chinese population held as part of Britain's colony of Malaya, underwent important development during the late 1930s when the British tried to build it into an invulnerable naval base. Singapore served as a growing international seaport linked by road and rail to the rubber- and tin-producing areas of Malaya, although its people remained separate in identity from the Muslim Malays themselves. It suffered greatly during the Japanese World War II occupation, emerging with widespread unemployment and poverty.

World War II increased pressures for change throughout the Pacific Rim. The Japanese temporarily dislodged Western colonial rule in places such as Malaya, causing great hostility but spurring interest in independence from the West.

Figure 37.1 *During the early stages of World War II in Asia, the Japanese bombed Shanghai, China, in 1937.*

Figure 37.2 *In March 1919, the Korean people declared their independence and rose in revolt against Japanese imperialism. Japanese police executed many Koreans during the movement.*

EAST ASIA IN THE POSTWAR SETTLEMENTS

▓ *Adjustments at the end of World War II defined the Pacific Rim into the 1950s, as a zone of reasonably stable noncommunist states developed. Linked to the West, these states maintained a neo-Confucian emphasis on the importance of conservative politics and a strong state.*

The victors in World War II had some reasonably clear ideas about how east Asia was to be restructured. Korea was divided between a Russian zone of occupation in the north and an American zone in the south. *Taiwan* was restored to China, which in principle was ruled by a Kuomintang government headed by Chiang Kai-shek. The United States regained the Philippines and pledged to grant independence quickly, retaining some key military bases. European powers restored controls over their holdings in Vietnam, Malaya, and Indonesia. Japan was occupied by American forces bent on introducing major changes that would prevent a recurrence of military aggression.

New Divisions and the End of Empires

Not surprisingly, the Pacific regions of Asia did not quickly settle into agreed-upon patterns. A decade after the war's end, not only the Philippines but also Indonesia and Malaya were independent, as part of the postwar tide of decolonization. Taiwan was still ruled by Chiang Kai-shek, but the Chinese mainland was in the hands of a new and powerful communist regime. Chiang's nationalist regime claimed a mission to recover China, but in fact Taiwan was a separate republic. Korea remained divided but had undergone a brutal north–south conflict in which only U.S. intervention preserved South Korea's independence. Japan was one of the few Pacific regions where matters had proceeded somewhat according to plan, as the nation began to recover while accepting a very different political structure.

Japanese Recovery

Japan in 1945 was in shambles. Its cities were burned, its factories destroyed or idle, its people impoverished and shocked by the fact of surrender and the trauma of bombing, including the atomic devastation of Hiroshima and Nagasaki. However, like the industrial nations of the West, Japan was capable of reestablishing a vigorous economy with surprising speed. And its occupation by U.S. forces, eager to reform Japan but also eager to avoid punitive measures, provided an opportunity for a new period of selective Westernization.

The American occupation government, headed by *General Douglas MacArthur*, worked quickly to tear down Japan's wartime political structure. (Occupation

ᴆ ᴏ ᴄ ᴜ ᴍ ᴇ ɴ ᴛ

Japan and the Loss in World War II

Japan's defeat brought moral and material confusion. The government was so uncertain of the intentions of the victorious Americans that it evacuated its female employees to the countryside. The following excerpt from the 1945 diary of Yoshizawa Hisako (who became a writer on home economics) reveals more popular attitudes and the mixed ingredients that composed them. The passage also suggests how the American occupation force tried to present itself and the reception it received.

August 15. As I listened to the Emperor's voice announcing the surrender, every word acquired a special meaning and His Majesty's voice penetrated my mind. Tears streamed down my cheeks. I kept on telling myself that we must not fight ourselves and work hard for our common good. Yes, I pledged myself, I must work [for Japan's recovery].

The city was quiet.

I could not detect any special expression in people's faces. Were they too tired? However, somehow they seemed brighter, and I could catch an expression showing a sign of relief. It could have been a reflection of my own feelings. But I knew I could trust what I saw....

The voluntary fighting unit was disbanded, and I was no longer a member of that unit. Each of us burned the insignia and other identifications.

I cannot foresee what kind of difficulty will befall me, but all I know is that I must learn to survive relying on my health and my will to live.

August 16. People do not wear expressions any different from other days. However, in place of a "good morning" or "good afternoon," people are now greeting each other with the phrase "What will become of us?"

During the morning, the city was still placed under air-raid alert.

My company announced that until everything becomes clearer, no female employees were to come to work, and urged all of us to go to the countryside, adding that we should leave forwarding addresses. This measure was taken to conform to the step already taken by governmental bureaus. Are they thinking that the occupation army will do something to us girls? There are so many important questions we have to cope with, I cannot understand why governmental officials are so worried about these matters.

We did not have enough power and lost the war.

The Army continued to appeal to the people to resist the enemy to the end. This poses a lot of problems. People can show their true colors better when they are defeated than when they win. I just hope we, as a nation, can show our better side now.

Just because we have been defeated, I do not wish to see us destroying our national characteristics when we are dealing with foreign countries.

August 17. It was rumored that a number of lower echelon military officers were unhappy with the peace, and were making some secret moves. There were other rumors, and with the quiet evacuation of women and children from the cities, our fear seemed to have intensified. After all we have never experienced a defeat before. Our fear may simply be the manifestation of fear of the unknown.

Our airplanes dropped propaganda leaflets.

One of the leaflets was posted at the Kanda Station which said: "Both the Army and Navy are alive and well. We expect the nation to follow our lead." The leaflet was signed. I could understand how those military men felt. However, we already have the imperial rescript to surrender. If we are going to rebuild, we must open a new path. It is much easier to die than to live. In the long history of our nation, this defeat may become one of those insignificant happenings. However, the rebuilding after the defeat is likely to be treated as a far more important chapter in our history.

We did our best and lost, so there is nothing we have to say in our own defense. Only those people who did not do their best may now be feeling guilty, though.

Mr. C. said that everything he saw in the city was so repugnant that he wanted to retreat to the countryside. I was amazed by the narrowness of his thought process. I could say that he had a pure sense of devotion to the country, but that was only his own way of thinking. Beautiful perhaps, but it lacked firm foundation. I wish men like him would learn to broaden their perspectives.

August 18. Rationed bread distribution in the morning. I went to the distribution center with Mrs. A.

August 21. We heard that the allied advance units will be airlifted and arrive in Japan on the 26th. And the following day, their fleet will also anchor in our harbors. The American Army will be airlifted and land in Atsugi airport.

According to someone who accompanied the Japanese delegation which went to accept surrender conditions, the Americans behaved like gentlemen. They explained to the Americans that certain conditions were unworkable in light of the present situation in Japan. The Americans immediately agreed to alter those conditions. They listened very carefully to what the Japanese delegation had to say.

An American paper, according to someone, reported that meeting as follows: "We cooked thick beefsteak expecting seven or eight Japanese would appear. But seventeen of them came, so we had to kill a turkey to prepare for them. We treated them well before they returned." ... When I hear things like this, I immediately feel how exaggerated and inefficient our ways of doing things are. They say that Americans will tackle one item after another at a conference table, and do not waste even 30 seconds....

In contrast, Japanese administration is conducted by many chairs and seals. For example when an auxiliary unit is asked to undertake a task for a governmental bureau, before anything can be done, twenty, or thirty seals of approval must be secured. So there is no concept of not wasting time. Even in war, they are too accustomed to doing things the way they have been doing, and their many seals and chairs are nothing but a manifestation of their refusal to take individual responsibilities.

The fact of a defeat is a very serious matter and it is not easy to accept. However, it can bring some positive effects, if it can inculcate in our minds all the shortcomings we have had. I hope this will come true some day, and toward that end we must all endeavor. Even if we have to suffer hunger and other tribulations we must strive toward a positive goal.

Questions: How did Japanese attitudes in defeat help prepare Japan for postwar redevelopment? Did defeat produce new divisions in attitudes among the Japanese? What other kinds of reactions might have been expected? How would you explain the rather calm and constructive outlook the passage suggests? Would American reactions to a Japanese victory have been similar?

lasted until 1952, a year after Japan signed a peace treaty with most of its wartime opponents.) The military forces were disbanded, the police decentralized, many officials removed, and political prisoners released. For the long run, American authorities pressed for a democratization of Japanese society by giving women the vote, encouraging labor unions, and abolishing Shintoism as a state religion. Several economic reforms were also introduced, breaking up landed estates for the benefit of small farmers—who quickly became politically conservative—and dissolving the holdings of the zaibatsu combines, a measure that had little lasting effect as Japanese big business regrouped quickly.

A new constitution tried to cut through older limitations by making the parliament the supreme government body. Several civil liberties were guaranteed, along with gender equality in marriage and collective bargaining rights. Military forces with "war potential" were abolished forever, making Japan a unique major nation in its limited military strength. The emperor became merely a symbolic figurehead, without political power and with no claims to Shinto divinity. Even as Japan accepted many political and legal concepts, it inserted its own values into the new constitution. Thus, a 1963 law called for special social obligations to the elderly, in obvious contrast to Western

Figure 37.3 *The United States advanced on Japan with the invasion and capture of Okinawa in March 1945.*

approaches: "The elders shall be loved and respected as those who have for many years contributed toward the development of society, and a wholesome and peaceful life shall be guaranteed to them."

These new constitutional measures were embraced by the Japanese people, many of whom became avid opponents of any hint of military revival. Military power and responsibility in the region were retained by the United States, which long after the occupation period kept important bases in Japan. Many of the political features of the new constitution worked smoothly—in large part because the Japanese had experienced parliamentary and political party activity for extended periods in previous decades. Two moderate parties merged in 1955 into the new *Liberal Democratic party,* which monopolized Japan's government into the 1990s.

Japan became a genuine multiparty democracy but with unusual emphasis on one-party control in the interests of order and elite control. It granted women the vote, but women's conditions differed markedly from men's. In education, American occupation forces insisted on reducing the nationalism in textbooks and opening secondary schools to more social groups. These changes merged with existing Japanese enthusiasm for education, heightening the emphasis on school success. Japan developed one of the most meritocratic systems in the world, with students advanced to university training on the basis of rigorous examinations. But once the occupation ended, the government reasserted some traditional components in this education package, including careful controls over textbooks. In 1966, for example, the Ministry of Education attacked "egotistic" attitudes in Japan, which were producing "a feeling of spiritual hollowness and unrest." Schools in this situation should generate ethical discipline and group consciousness, touching base with more customary goals while preparing students for their role in Japan's expanding economy. As one conservative put it in the 1980s, "You have to teach tradition [to the children] whether they like it or not."

Korea: Intervention and War

Korea's postwar adjustment period was far more troubled than Japan's. The leaders of the great Allied powers during World War II had agreed in principle that Korea should be restored as an independent state. But the United States' eagerness to obtain Soviet help against Japan resulted in Soviet occupation of the northern part of the peninsula. As the cold war intensified, American and Soviet authorities could not agree on unification of the zones, and in 1948 the United States sponsored a *Republic of Korea* in the south, matched by a Soviet-dominated *People's Democratic Republic of Korea* in the north. North Korea's regime drew on an earlier Korean Communist party founded in exile in the 1900s. North Korea quickly became a communist state with a Stalinist-type emphasis on the power of the leader, Kim Il-Sung, until his death in 1994. The South Korean regime, bolstered by an ongoing American military presence, was headed by nationalist Syngman Rhee. Rhee's South Korea developed parliamentary institutions in form but maintained a strongly authoritarian tone.

In June 1950, North Korean forces attacked South Korea, hoping to impose unification on their own terms. The United States reacted quickly (after some confusing signals about whether South Korea was inside the U.S. "defense perimeter"). President Truman insisted on drawing another line against communist aggression, and he orchestrated United Nations sponsorship of a largely American "police action" in support of South Korean troops. In the ensuing *Korean War,* under General MacArthur's leadership, Allied forces pushed North Korea back, driving on toward the Chinese border; this action roused concern on the part of China's communist regime, which sent "volunteers" to force American troops back toward the south. The front stabilized in 1952 near the original north–south border. The stalemate dragged on until 1953, when a new American administration was able to agree to an armistice.

Korea then continued its dual pattern of development. North Korea produced an unusually isolated version of one-man rule as Kim concentrated his powers over the only legal political party, the military, and the government. Even Soviet liberalization in the late 1980s brought little change. South Korea and the United States concluded a mutual defense treaty in 1954; American troop levels were reduced, but the South Korean army gained more sophisticated military equipment and the United States poured economic aid into the country, initially to prevent starvation in a war-ravaged land. The political tenor of South Korea continued to be authoritarian. In 1961, army officers took over effective rule of the country, although sometimes a civilian government served as a front.

Figure 37.4 *This tank unit of the North Korean People's Army assembled in September 1950. Military buildup was part of the preparation for invading South Korea.*

However, economic change began to gain ground in South Korea, ushering in a new phase of activity and international impact. Tensions between the two Koreas continued to run high, with many border clashes and sabotage, but outright warfare was avoided.

Emerging Stability in Taiwan, Hong Kong, and Singapore

Postwar adjustments in Taiwan involved yet another set of issues. As the communist revolutionary armies gained the upper hand in mainland China, between 1946 and 1948 the Kuomintang (Nationalist) regime prepared to fall back on its newly reacquired island, which the communists could not threaten because they had no navy. The result was imposition over the Taiwanese majority of a new leadership plus a massive military force drawn from the mainland.

The authoritarian political patterns the nationalists had developed in China, centered on Chiang Kai-shek's personal control of the government, were amplified by the need to keep disaffected Taiwanese in check. Hostility with the communist regime across the Taiwan Strait ran high. In 1955 and 1958, the communists bombarded two small islands controlled by the nationalists, Quemoy and Matsu, and wider conflict threatened as the United States backed up its ally. Tensions were defused when communist China agreed to fire on the islands only on alternate days, while United States ships supplied them on the off-days, thus salvaging national honor. Finally, the United States induced Chiang to renounce any intentions of attacking the mainland, and conflict eased into mutual bombardments of propaganda leaflets. During this period, as in South Korea, the United States gave economic aid to Taiwan, ending assistance only in the 1960s when growing prosperity seemed assured.

Two other participants in the economic advances of the Pacific Rim were distinguished by special ties to Britain. *Hong Kong* remained a British colony after World War II; only in the 1980s was an agreement reached between Britain and China for its 1997 return to the Chinese fold. Hong Kong gained increasing autonomy from direct British rule. Its Chinese population swelled at various points after 1946 as a result of flights from communist rule.

Singapore retained a large British naval base until 1971, when Britain abandoned all pretense of power in east Asia. Singapore gained independence as a vigorous free port in 1959.

Overall, by the end of the 1950s a certain stability had emerged in the political situation of many smaller east Asian nations. From the 1960s onward these same areas, combining Western contacts with important traditions of group loyalty, moved from impressive economic recovery to new international influence on the basis of manufacturing and trade.

JAPAN, INCORPORATED

◼◼ *The keynotes of Japanese history from the 1950s onward were a fierce concentration on economic growth and distinctive political and cultural forms as the nation proved that industrial success did not depend on a strict Western pattern.*

The Distinctive Political and Cultural Style

The chief emphasis of Japanese politics lay in conservative stability. The Liberal Democratic party held the reins of government from 1955 onward.

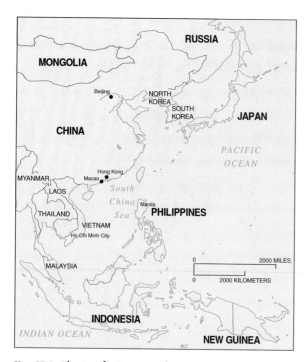

Map 37.1 *The Pacific Rim Area by 1960. Geographic locations and political systems created new contacts and alignments.*

This meant that Japan, uniquely among the democratic nations of the postwar world, had no experience with shifts in party administration until 1993. Changes in leadership, which at times were frequent, were handled through negotiations among the Liberal Democratic elite, not directly as a result of shifts in voter preference.

Clearly, this system revived many of the oligarchic features of Meiji Japan and the Japan of the 1920s. During the prosperous 1970s and 1980s, economic progress and the Liberal Democrats' willingness to consult opposition leaders about major legislation reinforced Japan's effective political unity. Only at the end of the 1980s, when several Liberal Democratic leaders were branded by corruption of various sorts, were new potential questions raised.

Japan's distinctive political atmosphere showed clearly in strong cooperation with business. The state set production and investment goals while actively lending public resources to encourage investment and limit imports. The government–business coordination to promote economic growth and export expansion prompted the half-admiring, half-derisory Western label "Japan, Incorporated."

The government actively campaigned to promote birth control and abortion, and population growth slowed. This was another product of the strong national tradition of state-sponsored discipline.

As in politics and education, Japanese culture preserved important traditional elements, which provided aesthetic and spiritual satisfactions amid rapid economic change. Customary styles in poetry, painting, tea ceremonies, and flower arrangements continued. Each New Year's Day, for example, the emperor presided at a poetry contest, and masters of traditional arts were honored by being designated as Living National Treasures. Kabuki and No theater also flourished. Japanese films and novels often recalled the country's earlier history. Japanese painters and architects participated actively in the "international style" pioneered in the West, but they often infused it with earlier Japanese motifs such as stylized nature painting. City orchestras played the works of Western composers and native compositions that incorporated passages played on the Japanese flute and zither. At the same time, aside from interior decoration and film, Japanese contributions to world culture were negligible; this was not where national creativity showed an international face.

Cultural combinations were not always smooth. Both before and after World War II, key intellectuals

Figure 37.5 *Traditional settings are found in modern Japan. The yomei-mon gateway, at the mausoleum of Ieyasu in Nikko, is a traditional place for contemplation.*

used art and literature to protest change, not merely to blend Western and traditional styles. The flamboyant postwar writer Hiraoka Kimitoke (pen name Yukio Mishima, 1925–1970) was a case in point. His novels and dramas began to appear in 1949, dealing with controversial themes such as homosexuality while also updating versions of the No plays. A passionate nationalist, he was too sickly for military service in World War II but then built up his body. At first he enjoyed many Western contacts and interests, but he came to hate Western ways. In 1968 he formed a private army centered on restoring Japanese ideals. After finishing a final major novel, Mishima performed his own ritual suicide in 1970. He wrote to an American friend shortly before his death, "I came to wish to sacrifice myself for this old beautiful tradition of Japan, which is disappearing very quickly day by day."

The Economic Surge

Particularly after the mid-1950s, rapid economic growth made Japan's clearest mark internationally and commanded the most intense energies at home. By 1983, the total national product was equal to the combined totals of China, both Koreas, Taiwan, India, Pakistan, Australia, and Brazil. Per capita income, though still slightly behind that of the leading Western nations such as West Germany, had passed that of many countries, including Britain. Annual economic growth reached at least 10 percent regularly from the mid-1950s onward, surpassing the regular levels of every other nation during the 1960s and 1970s as Japan became one of the top two or three economic powers in the world. Leading Japanese corporations, such as the great automobile manufacturers and electronic equipment producers, became known not simply for the volume of their international exports but for the high quality of their goods.

A host of factors fed this astounding economic performance. Active government encouragement was a major ingredient. Educational expansion played a major role as Japan began to turn out far more engineers than did more populous competitors such as the United States. Foreign policy also played a role. Japan was able to devote almost its whole capital to investment in productive technology, for its military expenses were negligible given its reliance on United States protection.

Japan's distinctive labor policies functioned well. Workers were organized mainly in company

Figure 37.6 *Hiraoka Kimitoke.*

unions that were careful not to impair their companies' productivity. Leading corporations solidified this cooperation, which spurred zealous work from most employees. Social activities, including group exercise sessions before the start of the working day, promoted and expressed group loyalty, and managers took active interest in suggestions by employees. The Japanese system also ensured lifetime employment to an important part of the labor force, a policy aided by economic growth, low average unemployment rates, and an early retirement age. This network of policies and attitudes made Japanese labor seem both less class-conscious and less individualistic than labor forces in the advanced industrial nations of the West; it reflected older traditions of group solidarity in Japan, going back to feudal patterns.

Japanese management displayed a distinctive spirit, again as a result of adapting older traditions of leadership. There was more group consciousness, including a willingness to abide by collective decisions and less concern for quick personal profits than was characteristic of the West, particularly the United States. Few corporate bureaucrats changed firms, which meant that their efforts were concentrated on their company's success. Leisure life remained meager by Western standards, and many Japanese were reluctant to take regular vacations.

Japan's distinctiveness extended to family life, despite some features similar to the West's industrial experience. Japanese women, though increasingly well educated and experiencing an important decline in birth rates, did not follow Western patterns precisely. A feminist movement was confined to a small number of intellectuals. Within the family, women shared fewer leisure activities with their husbands, concentrating more heavily on domestic duties and intensive child-rearing than was true in the West by the 1970s. In child-rearing, conformity to group standards was emphasized far more than in the West or in communist China. A comparative study of nursery schools showed that Japanese teachers were bent on effacing their own authority in the interests of developing strong bonds between the children. Shame was directed toward nonconformist behaviors, a disciplinary approach the West had largely abandoned in the early 19th century. Japanese television game shows, superficially copied from those of the West, imposed elaborate, dishonoring punishment on losing contestants.

The nation had few lawyers, for it was assumed that people could make and abide by firm arrangements through mutual agreement. Psychiatrists reported far fewer problems of loneliness and individual alienation than in the West. Conversely, situations that promoted competition between individuals, such as university entrance tests, produced far higher stress levels than did analogous Western experiences. The Japanese had particular ways to relieve tension as well. Bouts of heavy drinking were more readily tolerated than in the West, seen as a time when normal codes of conduct could be suspended under the helpful eyes of friends. Businessmen and some politicians had recourse to traditional geisha houses for female-supplied cosseting, a normal and publicly accepted activity.

Japanese popular culture was not static, both because of ongoing attraction to Western standards and because of rapid urbanization and economic growth. The U.S. presence after World War II brought a growing fascination with baseball, and professional teams flourished. Japanese athletes began also to excel in such sports as tennis and golf. In the mid-1980s, the government, appalled to discover that a majority of Japanese children did not use chopsticks but preferred knives and forks in order to eat more rapidly, invested money to promote chopsticks training in the schools. This was a minor development, but it indicates the ongoing tension between change, with its Western connotations, and a commitment to Japanese identity. The veneration of old age was challenged by some youthful assertiveness and by the sheer cost of supporting the rapidly growing percentage of older people, for Japan relied heavily on family support for elders.

Other issues were associated with change. By the 1960s, pollution became a serious problem as cities and industry expanded rapidly; traffic police, for example, sometimes wore protective masks to protect their lungs. The government (eager to preempt a potential opposition issue) paid increasing attention to environmental issues after 1970.

The 1990s brought some new questions to Japan. Mired in political corruption, the Liberal Democrats were replaced by shaky coalition governments. A severe economic recession caused widespread unemployment. Even as Japanese methods were being touted in the West as a basis for economic and social revitalization, some of the critical patterns of postwar development were at least temporarily disrupted.

Figure 37.7 *Crowding and commerce in contemporary Japan are depicted in this photo of the lively Shinjuku district of Tokyo at night. Japanese cities mix dense populations with other familiar features of commercial urban centers.*

THE PACIFIC RIM: NEW JAPANS?

Economic and to some extent political developments in several other middle-sized nations and city-states on Asia's Pacific coast mirrored important elements of Japan's 20th-century history, though at a slightly later date. Political authoritarianism was characteristic, though usually with periodic bows to parliamentary forms and with recurrent protests from dissidents who wanted greater freedom. Government functions extended to careful economic planning and rapid expansion of the educational system, which emphasized technical training. Group loyalties promoted diligent labor and a willingness to work hard for low wages. Economic growth burgeoned, although new clouds appeared on the horizon at the end of the 1990s.

The Korean Miracle

South Korea was the most obvious example of the spread of new economic dynamism to other parts of the Pacific Rim. The Korean government rested normally in the hands of a political strongman, usually from army ranks. Syngman Rhee was forced out of office by student demonstrations in 1960; a year later, a military general, Chung-hee, seized power. He retained his authority until his assassination in 1979 by his director of intelligence. Then another general seized power. Intense student protest, backed by wider popular support, pressed the military from power at the end of the 1980s, but a conservative politician won the ensuing general election, and it was not clear how much the political situation had changed. Opposition activity was possible in South Korea, though usually heavily circumscribed, and many leaders were jailed. There was some freedom of the press except for publications from communist countries.

As in postwar Japan, the South Korean government from the mid-1950s onward placed its primary emphasis on economic growth, which in this case started from a much lower base after the Korean War and previous Japanese exploitation. Huge industrial firms were created by a combination of government aid and active entrepreneurship. By the 1970s, when growth rates in Korea began to match those of Japan, Korea was competing successfully in the area of cheap consumer goods, as well as in steel and automobiles, in a variety of international markets. In steel, Korea's surge—based on the most up-to-date technology, a skilled engineering sector, and low wages—pushed past Japan's. The same held true in textiles, where Korean growth (along with that of Taiwan) erased almost one-third of the jobs held in the industry in Japan.

Huge industrial groups such as Daewoo and *Hyundai* resembled the great Japanese holding companies before and after World War II and wielded great political influence. For example, Hyundai was the creation of entrepreneur Chung Ju Yung, a modern folk hero who walked 150 miles to Seoul, South Korea's capital, from his native village to take his first job as a day laborer at age 16. By the 1980s, when Chung was in his sixties, his firm had 135,000 employees and 42 overseas offices throughout the world. Hyundai virtually governed Korea's southeastern coast. It built ships, including petroleum supertankers; it built thousands of housing units sold to low-paid workers at below-market rates; it built schools, a technical college, and an arena for the practice of the traditional Korean martial art Tae Kwon Do. With their lives carefully provided for, Hyundai workers responded in kind, putting in six-day weeks with three vacation days per year and participating in almost worshipful ceremonies when a fleet of cars was shipped abroad or a new tanker launched.

South Korea's rapid entry into the ranks of newly industrialized countries produced a host of more general changes. The population soared: By the 1980s more than 40 million people lived in a nation about the size of the state of Indiana, producing the highest population density on earth: about 1000 people per square mile. This was one reason why, even amid growing prosperity, many Koreans emigrated. The government gradually began to encourage couples to limit their birth rates. Seoul expanded to embrace 9 million people; it developed intense air pollution and a hothouse atmosphere of deals and business maneuvers. Per capita income increased despite the population increase, rising almost 10 times from the early 1950s to the early 1980s but to a level still only one-ninth of that of Japan. Huge fortunes coexisted with widespread poverty in this setting, although the poor were better off than those of less developed nations.

Advances in Taiwan and the City-States

The Republic of China, as the government of Taiwan came to call itself, experienced a high rate of economic development. Productivity in both agriculture and industry increased rapidly, the former spurred by land reform that benefited small commercial farmers. The government concentrated increasingly on economic gains as its involvement in plans for military action against the mainland communist regime declined. As in Japan and Korea, formal economic planning reached high levels, though allowing latitude for private business. Money was poured into education, and literacy rates and levels of technical training rose rapidly. The result was important cultural and economic change for the Taiwanese people. Traditional medical practices and ritualistic popular religion remained lively but were expanded to allow simultaneous use of modern, Western-derived medicine and some of the urban entertainment forms popular elsewhere.

The assimilation of rapid change gave the Taiwanese government great stability despite a host of new concerns. The U.S. recognition of the People's Republic of China brought with it a steadily decreasing official commitment to Taiwan. In 1978, the United States severed diplomatic ties with the Taiwanese regime, although unofficial contacts—through the American Institute in Taiwan and the Coordination Council for North American Affairs, established by the republic in Washington—remained strong. The Taiwanese also built important regional contacts with other governments in eastern and southeastern Asia that facilitated trade. For example, Japan served as the nation's most important single trading partner, purchasing foodstuffs, manufactured textiles, chemicals, and other industrial goods.

Taiwan also developed some informal links with the communist regime in Beijing, although the latter continued to claim the island as part of its territory. The republic survived the death of Chiang Kai-shek and the accession of his son, *Chiang Ching-kuo,* in 1978. The young Chiang emphasized personal authority less than his father had, and he reduced somewhat the gap between mainland-born military personnel and native Taiwanese in government ranks. However, a strong authoritarian strain continued, and political diversity was not encouraged.

Conditions in the city-state of Singapore, though less tied to great power politics, resembled those in Taiwan in many ways. The prime minister, *Lee Kuan Yew,* took office in 1959, when the area first gained independence, and held power for the next three decades. The government established tight controls over its citizens, going beyond anything attempted elsewhere in the Pacific Rim. Sexual behavior and potential economic corruption, as well as more standard aspects of municipal regulation and economic planning, were scrutinized carefully. The government proclaimed the necessity of unusual discipline and

THE PAST

Pacific Rim Growth

How can these figures be used to illustrate the industrial emergence of the Pacific Rim? Which countries most clearly have been undergoing an industrial revolution since the 1960s, and how can this be measured? How do the key Pacific Rim areas compare in growth to the neighboring "little tigers," Indonesia, Malaysia and Thailand? Do the two tables suggest that China should be counted part of the Pacific Rim? What are some of the problems in making the judgment? Do the Philippines constitute another "little tiger?" Finally, how do Japanese patterns compare with the newer areas of the Pacific Rim, and how can this relationship be explained?

Note: Growth at 2.3 percent per year doubles the category in 30 years. 7 percent per year doubles in 10 years.

Indices of Growth and Change in the Pacific Rim
Gross National Product (GNP) 1965–1996 Per Capita GNP
East and Southeast Asia, annual growth rates (%)

	1965	1996
China	8.5	6.7
Hong Kong	7.5	5.6
Indonesia	6.7	4.6
Japan	4.5	3.6
Korea (South Korea only)	8.9	7.3
Malaysia	6.8	4.1
Philippines	3.5	.9
Singapore	8.3	6.3
Thailand	7.3	5.0

for comparison

	1965	1996
All preeisiting industrial countries	3.0	2.2
United States	2.4	1.4
India	4.5	2.3

social and economic data

	% Labor force in agriculture		% population urban	
China	78	72	17	31
Indonesia	66	55	41	82
Japan	20	7	71	78
Korea (South)	49	18	41	82
Malaysia	54	27	34	54
Thailand	80	64	13	20

Adapted from World Bank, World Development Indicators (Washington, D.C., 1998) restraint because such a large population crowded into a limited space. One result was unusually low reported crime rates, and another was the near impossibility of serious political protest. The dominant People's Action party suppressed opposition movements. The authoritarian political style was rendered somewhat more palatable by extraordinarily successful economic development, based on a combination of government controls and initiatives and free enterprise. Already the world's fourth largest port, Singapore saw manufacturing and banking surpass shipping as sources of revenue. Electronics, textiles, and oil refining joined shipbuilding as major sectors. By the 1980s Singapore's population enjoyed the second highest per capita income in Asia. Educational levels and health conditions improved accordingly.

Finally, Hong Kong retained its status as a major world port and branched out as a center of international banking, serving as a bridge between the communist regime in China and the wider world. Export production combined high-speed technology with low wages and long hours for the labor force, yielding highly competitive results. Textiles and clothing formed 39 percent of total exports by the 1980s, but other sectors, including heavy industry, developed impressively as well. As in other Pacific Rim nations, a prosperous middle class emerged, with links to many other parts of the world, Western and Asian alike. In 1997, after careful negotiation with the British, Hong Kong was returned to China. The communist government promised to respect the territory's free market economic system and maintain democratic political rights, although the changeover raised questions for the future.

Common Themes and New Problems

The Pacific Rim states had more in common than their rapid growth rates and expanding exports. They all stressed group loyalties against excessive individualism or protest and in support of hard work. Confucian morality often was used, implicitly or explicitly, as part of this effort. The Pacific Rim states also shared reliance on government planning and direction amid limitations on dissent and instability. Of course, they benefited greatly from the expansion of the Japanese market for factory goods, such as textiles, as well as raw materials.

The dynamism of the Pacific Rim spilled over to neighboring parts of southeast Asia by the 1980s. "Little tigers" such as Indonesia, Malaysia, and Thailand began to experience rapid economic growth, along with the pollution problems that accompanied new manufacturing and larger cities.

However, the final years of the 20th century revealed unexpected weaknesses in this dynamic region. Growth faltered, unemployment rose, and currencies from South Korea to Indonesia took a drastic hit. Many Western observers argued that this crisis could be resolved only by reducing the links between governments and major firms and introducing more free-market competition. In essence, they contended that only a Western industrial model could be successful, and agencies such as the World Bank tried to insist on reforms in this direction as a condition for economic assistance. In the meantime, political pressures increased amid economic distress, and in 1998 the long-time authoritarian ruler of Indonesia was overturned in favor of pledges for future democracy. By 1999, however, economic growth rates in the region began to pick up. It was not clear that basic patterns had to be rethought.

IN DEPTH

The Pacific Rim as a U.S. Policy Issue

Whenever power balances change between nations or larger civilizations, a host of policy issues arises for all parties involved. The rise of the Pacific Rim economies posed some important questions for the West, particularly for the United States because of its military role in the Pacific as well as its world economic position. The United States had actively promoted economic growth in Japan, Korea, and Taiwan as part of its desire to discourage the spread of communism. Although American aid was not solely responsible for Pacific Rim advance, and although it tapered off by the 1960s, the United States took some satisfaction in demonstrating the vitality of noncommunist economies. The United States also was not eager to relinquish its military superiority in the region, which gave it a stake in Asian opinion.

Yet the threats posed by growing Pacific Rim economic competition were real and growing. Japan seemed to wield a permanent balance-of-payments superiority; its exports to the United States regularly exceeded imports by the 1970s and 1980s, which contributed greatly to the United

States' unfavorable overall trade balance. Japanese investment in American companies and real estate increased the United States' growing indebtedness to foreign nations. The symbolic problems were real as well. Japanese observers pointed out with some justice that Americans seemed more worried about Japanese investments than about larger British holdings in the United States, an imbalance that smacked of racism. Certainly, Americans found it harder to accept Asian competition than they did European, if only because it was less familiar. Japanese ability to gain near monopolies in key industries such as electronic recording systems and the growing Korean challenge in steel and automobiles meant or seemed to mean loss of jobs and perhaps a threat of more fundamental economic decline in years to come.

In the 1980s, several observers urged American imitation of the bases of Pacific Rim success: The United States should open more partnerships between government and private industry and do more economic planning, it should teach managers to commit themselves to group harmony rather than individual profit seeking, and it should build a new concord between management and labor, based on greater job security and cooperative social programs. Some firms in the United States did introduce certain Japanese management methods, including more consultation with workers, with some success.

Other observers, also concerned about long-term erosion of American power on the Pacific Rim, urged a more antagonistic stance. A few wanted the United States to pull out of costly Japanese and Korean bases so that the Pacific Rim would be forced to shoulder more of its own defense costs. Others wanted to impose tariffs on Asian goods, at least until the Pacific Rim nations made it easier for American firms to compete in Asian markets. Aggrieved American workers sometimes smashed imported cars and threatened Asian immigrants, although many American consumers continued to prefer Pacific Rim products. The options were complex, and no clear change in American policy emerged.

Pacific Rim nations also faced choices about their orientation toward the West, particularly the United States. Questions that arose earlier about what Western patterns to copy and what to avoid continued to be important, as the Japanese concern about forks and chopsticks suggests. Added were issues about how to express pride and confidence in modern achievements against what were seen as Western tendencies to belittle and patron-

Figure 37.8 *Hyundai loading dock for export to the United States.*

ize. In 1988, the summer Olympic games were held in South Korea, a sign of Korea's international advance and a source of great national pride. During the games, Korean nationalism flared against the U.S. athletes and television commentators, based on their real or imagined tendencies to seek out faults in Korean society. South Korea, like Japan, continued to rely on Western markets and U.S. military assistance, but there was a clear desire to put the relationship on a more fully equal footing. This desire reflected widespread public opinion, and it could have policy implications.

The Pacific Rim crisis in 1998 raised a new set of questions. American leaders urged assistance to beleaguered economies such as those of South Korea and Indonesia, but they also, with some self-satisfaction, tried to insist on introducing a more Western-style market economy. Asian leaders recognized the need for some change, but they did not welcome advice that seemed to ignore successful components from the past and threatened some of the privileges of established political and business elites.

Questions: How great were the challenges posed by the Pacific Rim to the U.S. world position and well-being? What are the most likely changes in American–Pacific Rim relations over the next two decades?

Conclusion

The Pacific Rim as Exception or Model

The rise of the Pacific Rim nations was based on a combination of several factors. First, the nations shared in aspects of the Confucian cultural and political heritage, mediated, as in Japan, by many adaptations and additions. Second, the Pacific Rim nations shared some special contacts with the West through unusually intense interaction with the British or through postwar dealings with the United States. Finally, the principal Pacific Rim centers, including Japan, were rocked by 20th-century events, which forced rethinking and innovation.

Pacific Rim success raised obvious questions about China and Vietnam, where different issues had dominated much of the 20th century. As China and then Vietnam experimented with new economic forms in the late 1970s and early 1980s and experienced rapid industrial growth, many observers wondered whether these Asian mainstays,

or at least their coastal cities, would soon join in the Pacific Rim ascendancy.

The rise of the Pacific Rim has been an unusual development in world history, quite apart from its contrast with the region's isolation in earlier eras. Its basis rests on economics rather than military power or a missionary culture. As a vital new world history development, the position of the Pacific Rim continues to raise questions about the area's ultimate international role, with some pundits predicting an "east Asian century" in the near future, replacing the long period of Western dominance.

Further Readings

The best account of contemporary Japanese society and politics is E. O. Reischauer's *The Japanese* (1988). For a recent history, see M. Howe's *Modern Japan: A Historical Survey* (1986). On the economy, consult H. Patrick and H. Rosovsky's *Asia's New Giant: How the Japanese Economy Works* (1976), E. F. Vogel's *Japan as Number One: Lessons for America* (1979), and K. Ohkawa and H. Rosovsky's *Japanese Economic Growth: Trend Acceleration in the Twentieth Century* (1973).

Several novels and literary collections are accessible and useful. J. Tanizaki's *The Makioka Sisters* (1957) deals with a merchant family in the 1930s; see also H. Hibbett, ed., *Contemporary Japanese Literature: An Anthology of Fiction, Film and Other Writing Since 1945* (1977), and John and Asako McKinstry, eds., *Jinsei Annai, "Life's Guide": Glimpses of Japan Through a Popular Advice Column* (1991). An important study of change, focusing on postwar rural society, is G. Bernstein's *Haruko's World: A Japanese Farm Woman and Her Community* (1983). Another complex 20th-century topic is assessed in R. Storry's *The Double Patriots: A Story of Japanese Nationalism* (1973).

On the Pacific Rim concept and its implications for the world economy, see David Aikman, *Pacific Rim: Area of Change, Area of Opportunity* (1986); Philip West et al., eds., *Pacific Rim and the Western World: Strategic, Economic and Cultural Perspectives* (1987); Stephen Haggard and Chung-in Moon, *Pacific Dynamics: The International Politics of Industrial Change* (1988); Ronald A. Morse et al., *Pacific Basin: Concept and Challenge* (1986); and Staffan B. Linder, *Pacific Century: Economic and Political Consequences of Asian-Pacific Dynamism* (1986).

Excellent introductions to recent Korean history are Bruce Cumings's *Korea's Place in the Sun: A Modern History* (1997), Robert E. Bedeski's *The Transformation of South Korea: Reform and Reconstitution Under Roh Tae Woo, 1987–1992* (1994), and David Rees's *A Short History of Modern Korea* (1988). Various special topics are addressed in Marshall R. Pihl, ed., *Listening to Korea* (1973). See also David Steinberg's *The Republic of Korea:*

Economic Transformation and Social Change (1989), Paul Kuznets's *Economic Growth and Structure in the Republic of Korea* (1977), and Dennis McNamara's *The Colonial Origins of Korean Enterprise 1910–1945* (1990).

For a fascinating exploration of cultural change and continuity in Taiwan around issues in health and medicine, see Arthur Kleinman's *Patients and Healers in the Context of Culture* (1979). On Singapore, Janet W. Salaff's *State and Family in Singapore* (1988) is an excellent study; see also R. N. Kearney, ed., *Politics and Modernization in South and Southeast Asia* (1975). See also Robert E. Bedeski's *The Transformation of South Korea: Reform and Reconstitution in the Sixth Republic Under Roh Tae Woo, 1987–1992* (1994).

On the Web

The career arc of leading personalities in the rise of modern Korea, such as Syngman Rhee and Kim Il-Song (http://socrates.berkeley.edu/korea/jhmenul.html), and much of the history of post-war Japan was shaped by the Korean War (http://socrates.berkeley.edu/~korea/koreanwar.html).

The life of General Douglas MacArthur and the art and society of the occupation or "Confusion" era in Japan is discussed at http://educate.si.edu/spotlight/korean.html. Japan's difficulty in accepting responsibility fo its wartime atrocities, particularly the abuse of Korean women by Japanese occupation troops, is discussed at http://witness.peacemaker.or.kr/symereport.htm.

Korekiyo Takahashi's role in the building of the modern Japanese economy and his conflict with the war party led by Tojo Hideki is examined at http://www.historynet.com/worlwarII/articles/11963-text.htm. The place of Takahashi's policies in today's Japan is examined at http://www.atimes.com/Japan-econ/AB12Dh01.html.

The rapid post-war industrialization of East Asia owed much to Japan's participation in the post-war revolution in technology (http://www.iss.u-tokyo.ac.jp/Newsletter/SSJ1/gluck.html).

In East Asia, that revolution was facilitated by very close cooperation between business and government (http://www.ccnet.com/~suntzu.75/japaninc.htm, http://www.kimsoft.com/1997/sk-econ.htm and http://cweb2.loc.gov/cgi-bin/query/D?cstudy:3:./temp/~frd_db3s::) which recently has been criticized even in Japan, where politicians were caught with trunks full of cash provided by leading Japanese companies. This pattern was followed by the eastern Pacific Rim's economic tigers as part of an authoritarian development strategy most clearly expressed by Singapore's leader, Lee Kuan Yew (http://landow.stg.brown.edu/post/singapore/government/leekuanyew/leekuanyewov.html), who has made comparisons between himself and Machiavelli (http://www.gn.apc.org/sfd/Link%pages/Link%20Folders/Hunan%20Rights/fear.html).

A recent economic recession in the region (http://www.rice.edu/rtv/speeches/19981023lee.html) has forced some to question whether the East Asian model of economic growth is worthy of emulation elsewhere. The difficulty in constructing historical paradigms even for post-war EastAsia is explored at http://www.iss.utokyo.ac.jp/Newsletter/SSJ1/gluck.html.

Chapter 38

Latin America: Revolution and Reaction in the 20th Century

The construction of a strong nation built on socialist principles was the message conveyed in public murals after the Mexican Revolution like this one by David Siqueros.

The focus of the previous three chapters—the West, eastern Europe, and the Pacific Rim—involved societies with very different 20th-century institutions and experiences but with one common bond: the experience of industrialization or its growth. The chapters that follow deal with societies grouped in what is sometimes called the *Third World,* in contrast to the capitalist industrial nations of the First World and the communist industrial nations of the Second World. Third World societies displayed great diversity, depending on their political traditions—the presence or absence of revolutionary experience, for example—and on cultural emphasis. However, they all faced issues of economic development and the inequality of relating to economically more powerful societies as part of their 20th-century history.

Latin America fit the Third World definition closely, despite great regional variety, but it also showed how loose this definition was. During the 20th century, Latin America continued to take an intermediate position between the nations of the North Atlantic and the developing countries of Asia and Africa. Although Latin America shared many problems with these other areas of the Third World, its earlier political independence and its often more Western social and political structures placed it in a distinct category. During the century, the Latin American elites led their nations into closer ties with the growing international capitalist economy, admittedly over increasing objections from critics within their nations. Investments and initiative often came from Europe and the United States, and Latin American economies continued to concentrate on exports. As a result, Latin America became increasingly vulnerable to changes in the world financial system.

For many Latin Americans, this dependency on the markets, the financial situation, and the economic decisions made outside the region was also reflected in a political and even cultural dependency in which foreign influence and foreign models shaped all aspects of national life.

Throughout the century, Latin Americans grappled with the problem of finding a basis for social justice, cultural autonomy, and economic security by adopting ideologies from abroad or by developing a specifically Latin American approach to the problem. Thus, in Latin America the struggle for decolonization has been primarily one of economic disengagement and a search for political and cultural forms appropriate to Latin American realities rather than a process of political separation and independence, as in Asia and Africa.

New groups began to appear on the political stage. Although Latin America continued its 19th-century emphasis on agrarian and mineral production, an industrial sector also grew in some places, and as this movement gathered strength, workers' organizations began to emerge as a political force. Industrialization was accompanied by immigration to some countries

1910 C.E.	1920 C.E.	1930 C.E.	1940 C.E.	1960 C.E.	1980 C.E.
1910–1920 Mexican Revolution	**1920–1940** Mexican muralist movement active	**1930** Revolution in Brazil brings Getúlio Vargas to power	**1942** Brazil joins the Allies; sends troops to Europe	**1961** U.S.–backed invasion of Cuba is defeated	**1982** Argentina and Great Britain clash over the Falkland Islands (Malvinas Islas)
1910 Madero's revolt	**1929** Women get the right to vote in Ecuador	**1930** Military takes control of the Argentine government	**1944–1954** Arevalo and Arbenz reforms in Guatemala	**1964** Military coup topples Brazilian government	**1983** U.S. invades Grenada
1911 Zapata promises land reform		**1932** Women win voting rights in Cuba and Brazil	**1947** Juan Péron elected president of Argentina	**1970–1973** Salvador Allende, Socialist government in Chile; overthrown and assassinated by the military in 1973	**1989** Sandinistas lose election in Nicaragua
1914 Panama Canal opens		**1933** Death of August César Sandino, leader of Nicaraguan resistance to U.S. occupation	**1952–1964** Bolivian Revolution	**1979** Sandinista Revolution takes control in Nicaragua	**1989** U.S. invades Panama, deposes General Noriega
1917 Mexican Constitution includes revolutionary changes		**1934–1940** President Cárdenas enacts many of the reforms promised by the Mexican Revolution	**1954** Arbenz overthrown with help from U.S.		
		1938 Mexico nationalizes its petroleum resources	**1959** Castro leads revolution in Cuba		

and urban growth in many places. A growing urban middle class linked to commerce, industry, and the expanding state bureaucracies also began to play a role in the political process.

With variation from country to country, overall the economy and the political process were subject to a series of broad shifts. There was a pattern to these shifts, with economic expansion (accompanied by conservative regimes that, although sometimes willing to make gradual reforms, hoped to maintain a political status quo) alternating with periods of economic crisis during which various attempts were made to provide social justice or to break with old social and political patterns. Thus, the political pendulum swung broadly across the region and often affected several countries at roughly the same time, indicating the relationship between international trends and the internal events in these nations.

Latin Americans have long debated the nature of their societies and the need for change. Although much of the rhetoric of Latin America has stressed radical reform and revolutionary change in the 20th century, the region has remained remarkably unchanged as the old institutions and political and economic patterns have adapted to new situations and provided a sometimes disheartening continuity. Revolutionaries have not been lacking, but the task of defeating

the existing political and social order and creating a new one on which the majority of the population will agree is difficult, especially when this must be done within an international as well as a national context. Thus, the few revolutionary political changes that have had long-term effects stand in contrast to the general trends of the region's political history. At the same time, however, significant changes in education, social services, the position of women, and the role of industry have taken place over the course of the century and have begun to transform many areas of Latin American life.

THE MEXICAN REVOLUTION AND THE GREAT WAR

■■ *The Mexican Revolution (1910–1920) was a violent reaction to authoritarian modernization. It produced a new sense of nationalism, reforms (especially in the 1930s), and an institutionalized party that took over the presidency and remained in power in the mid-1990s.*

Two cataclysmic events launched Latin America into the 20th century and set in motion trends that would determine much of the region's subsequent history. The first of these events was the 10-year civil war and political upheaval of the *Mexican Revolution*, caused primarily by internal forces. Eventually, the

Mexican Revolution was also influenced by another major event: the outbreak of World War I. Although most Latin American nations avoided direct participation in the Great War, as World War I was called at the time, the disruption of traditional markets for Latin American exports and the elimination of European sources of goods caused a realignment of the economies of several nations in the region. They were forced to rely on themselves. A spurt of manufacturing continued the process begun after 1870, and some small steps were taken to overcome the traditional dependence on outside supply. Finally, at the end of World War I, the United States emerged as the dominant foreign power in the region, replacing Great Britain in both economic and political terms. That position created a reality that Latin Americans could not ignore and that greatly influenced the economic and political options in the region.

Mexico's Upheaval

The regime of Porfirio Díaz had been in power since 1876 and seemed unshakable. During the Díaz dictatorship, tremendous economic changes had been made, and foreign concessions in mining, railroads, and other sectors of the economy had created a sense of prosperity among the Mexican elite. However, this progress had been bought at considerable expense. Foreigners controlled large sectors of the economy. The hacienda system of extensive landholdings by a small elite dominated certain regions of the country. The political system was corrupt, and any complaint was stifled. The government took repressive measures against workers, peasants, and Indians who opposed the loss of their lands or the unbearable working conditions. Political opponents often were imprisoned or forced into exile. In short, Díaz ruled with an iron fist through an effective political machine.

By 1910, however, Díaz was 80 years old and seemed willing to allow some political opposition. *Francisco Madero,* a wealthy son of an elite family, proposed to run against Díaz. Madero believed that some moderate democratic political reforms would relieve social tensions and allow the government to continue its economic development with a minimum of popular unrest. This was more than Díaz could stand. Madero was arrested, a rigged election put Díaz back in power, and things returned to normal. When Madero was released from prison, he called for a revolt.

A general rebellion developed. In the north, small farmers, railroaders, and cowboys coalesced under the colorful former bandit and able commander *Pancho Villa.* In the southern province of Morelos, an area of old conflicts between Indian communities and large sugar estates, a peasant-based guerrilla movement began under *Emiliano Zapata,* whose goal of land reform was expressed in his motto "Tierra y Libertad" ("Land and Liberty"). Díaz was driven from power by this coalition of forces, but it soon became apparent that Madero's moderate programs would not resolve Mexico's continuing social problems. Zapata rose in revolt, demanding a sweeping land reform, and Madero steadily lost control of his subordinates. In 1913, with at least the tacit agreement of the American ambassador in Mexico, who wanted to forestall revolutionary changes, a military coup removed Madero from government and he was then assassinated.

General Victoriano Huerta sought to impose a Díaz-type dictatorship supported by the large land owners, the army, and the foreign companies, but the tide of revolution could not be stopped so easily. Villa and Zapata rose again against the government and were joined by other middle-class political opponents of Huerta's illegal rule. By 1914, Huerta was forced from power, but the victorious leaders now began to fight over the nature of the new regime and the mantle of leadership. An extended period of warfare followed, and the tides of battle shifted constantly. The railroad lines built under Díaz now moved large numbers of troops, including *soldaderas* (Figure 38.1), women who sometimes shouldered arms. Matters were also complicated by U.S. intervention, aimed at bringing "order" to the border regions, and by diplomatic maneuverings after the outbreak of World War I in Europe. Villa and Zapata remained in control in their home territories, but they could not wrest the government from the control of the more moderate political leaders in Mexico City. *Alvaro Obregón,* an able general who had learned the new tactics of machine guns and trenches from the war raging in Europe and had beaten Villa's cavalry in a series of bloody battles in 1915, emerged as leader of the government.

The Mexican Revolution was roughly contemporaneous with revolutions in other agrarian societies that had also just undergone a period of rapid and disruptive modernization. The Boxer Rebellion in China (1899–1901) and the toppling of the emperor in 1911, the 1905 revolution in Russia, and a revolution in Iran in the same year underlined the rapid changes in these societies, all of which had received large foreign investments from either the United States or western Europe. In each of these countries,

Figure 38.1. *The Mexican Revolution mobilized large segments of the population, both men and women. The Villista forces shown here included soldaderas among the railroad workers, peasants, cowboys, and townsfolk who took up arms in northern Mexico.*

governments had tried to establish strong centralized control and had sought rapid modernization, but in doing so they had made their nations increasingly dependent on foreign investments and consequently on world financial markets. Thus, the world banking crisis of 1907 and 1908 cut Mexico and these other countries off from their needed sources of capital and created severe strains on their governments. This kind of dependency, and the fact that in Mexico more than 20 percent of the nation's territory was owned directly by citizens or companies from the United States, fed a growing nationalism that spread through many sectors of society. That nationalist sentiment played a role in each of these revolutions.

By 1920 the civil war had ended and Mexico began to consolidate the changes that had taken place in the previous confused and bloody decade. Obregón was elected president in that year. He was followed by a series of presidents from the new "revolutionary elite" who tried to consolidate the regime. There was much to be done. The revolution had devastated the country: 1.5 million people had died, major industries were destroyed, and ranching and farming were disrupted. But there was great hope because the revolution also promised (although it did not always deliver) real changes.

What were some of these changes? A new *Mexican Constitution of 1917* promised land reform, limited the foreign ownership of key resources, guaranteed the rights of workers, placed restrictions on clerical education and church ownership of property, and promised educational reforms. The workers who had been mobilized were organized in a national confederation and were given representation in the government. The promised land reforms were slow in coming, but under *President Lázaro Cárdenas* (1934–1940), more than 40 million acres were distributed, most of it in the form of ejidos, or communal holdings. The government launched an extensive program of primary and especially rural education.

Culture and Politics in Postrevolutionary Mexico

Nationalism and indigenism, or the concern for the Indians and their contribution to Mexican culture, lay beneath many reforms. Having failed to integrate the Indians into national life for a century, Mexico now attempted to *"Indianize"* the nation through secular schools that emphasized nationalism and a vision of the Mexican past that glorified the Indian heritage and denounced Western capitalism. Artists such as *Diego Rivera* and *José Clemente Orozco* recaptured that past and outlined a social program for the future in stunning murals on public buildings such as those in Figure 38.2, designed to inform, convince, and entertain at the same time. The Mexican muralist movement had a wide impact on artists throughout Latin America—even though, as Orozco himself stated, it sometimes created simple solutions and strange utopias by mixing a romantic image of the Indian past with Christian symbols and communist ideology. Novelists such as Mariano Azuela found in the revolution itself a focus for the examination of Mexican reality. Popular culture celebrated the heroes and events of the revolution in scores of ballads (*corridos*) that were sung to celebrate and inform.

> Gabino Barrera
> rose in the mountains
> his cause was noble,
> protect the poor and give them the land.
> Remember the night he was murdered
> three leagues from Tlapehuala;
> 22 shots rang out
> leaving him time for nothing.

Figure 38.2. *Diego Rivera's mural of modern Mexico in the Nacional Palace (1929–1935) illustrates the struggle of classes and ideologies and mixes Marxist symbols with a critique of capitalism.*

Gabino Barrera and his loyal steed

fell in the hail of rounds,

the face of this man of the Revolution

finally rested, his lips pressed to the ground.

In literature, music, and the arts, the revolution and its themes provided a stimulus to a tremendous burst of creativity.

The gains of the revolution were not made without opposition. Although the revolution preceded the Russian Revolution of 1917 and had no single ideological model, many of the ideas of Marxian socialism were held by leading Mexican intellectuals and a few politicians. The secularization of society and especially education met strong opposition from the church and the clergy, especially in states where socialist rhetoric and anticlericalism were extreme. In the 1920s, a conservative peasant movement backed by the church erupted in central Mexico. These *Cristeros,* backed by conservative politicians, fought to stop the slide toward secularization. The fighting lasted for years until a compromise was reached.

The United States intervened diplomatically and militarily during the revolution, motivated by a desire for "order," fear of German influence on the new government, and economic interests. An incident provoked a short-lived U.S. seizure of Veracruz in 1914, and when Pancho Villa's forces had raided across the border, the United States sent an expeditionary force into Mexico to catch him. The mission failed. For the most part, however, the war in Europe dominated American foreign policy efforts until 1918. The United States was suspicious of the new government, and a serious conflict arose when American-owned oil companies ran into problems with workers. When President Cárdenas expropriated the companies in 1934, the companies called for U.S. intervention or pressure. An agreement was worked out, however, and Mexico nationalized its petroleum industry in a state-run monopoly. This nationalization of natural resources was considered a declaration of economic independence. It symbolized the nationalistic basis of many of the revolution's goals.

As in any revolution, the question of continuity arose when the fighting ended. The revolutionary leadership hoped to institutionalize the new regime by creating a one-party system. This organization, called the *Party of the Institutionalized Revolution (PRI),* developed slowly during the 1920s and 1930s into a dominant force in Mexican politics. It incorporated labor, peasant, military, and middle-class sectors and proved flexible enough to incorporate new interest groups as they developed. Although Mexico became a multiparty democracy in theory, in reality the PRI controlled politics and, by accommodation and sometimes repression, maintained its hold on national political life. Some presidents governed much as the strongmen in the 19th century had done, but the party structure and the need to incorporate various interests within the government coalition limited the worst aspects of caudillo, or personalist, rule. The presidents were strong, but the policy of limiting the presidency to one six-year term ensured some change in leadership. The question of whether a revolution could be institutionalized remained in debate.

By the 1990s, many Mexicans believed that little remained of the principles of the revolutionaries of 1910. The PRI government hoped that expanding the economy through such arrangements as the *North American Free Trade Agreement (NAFTA)* would offer new hope to the nation. By 1997, it was still not clear what effect the agreement would have on Mexico, and it had generated considerable opposition among U.S. labor groups, who feared job losses because of the lower wages of Mexican workers. Charges of corruption reached to the highest levels of the Mexican government, but the PRI continued to hold power despite serious challenges from both the right and the left.

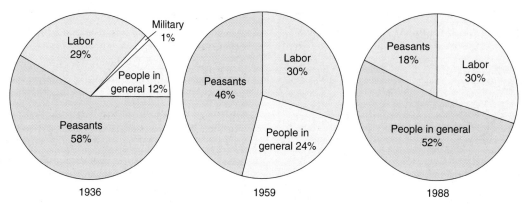

Figure 38.3 *Participation in the PRI: These graphs reflect party membership by sectors. Note that the population shifted away from rural areas and that labor remained fairly steady.*

Perhaps the most serious challenge to the status quo was the outbreak in January 1994 of an armed guerilla movement in the heavily Indian southern state of Chiapas where young rebels sought to improve conditions. Calling themselves Zapatistas in honor of Emiliano Zapata, the peasant leader in the Mexican Revolution of 1910, some 2000 poorly armed, masked men and women (Figure 38.4) attacked and captured four towns at exactly the moment when the Mexican government was negotiating the North American Free Trade Agreement. Although the government claimed that many of the rebels were foreigners or leftist revolutionaries from Guatemala, their demands for work, land, housing, food, health care, and education were widely supported by the long-neglected indigenous population of Chiapas. The Mexican government moved to suppress the rebels but also entered into negotiations, agreeing to many demands in an attempt to prevent the movement from growing as the country prepared for a presidential election. Discussions with the rebels were disrupted when the government candidate was assassinated, and for the first time since the 1920s, it seemed that the PRI candidate might not win.

The development and trade policies of the Mexican government in the 1990s had resulted in a growing economy and higher per capita income, but great disparities remained between rich and poor, especially Mexico's Indians. By choosing Zapata as a symbol of their movement, the Zapatistas tried to show that the basic problems of a fair society remained unsolved, that the revolution was incomplete, and that armed struggle could be successful, but they were willing to wait and see what the democratic process would produce.

Figure 38.4. *Zapatistas mobilized in Chiapas, one of Mexico's poorest states, and have been able to resist government suppression.*

ECONOMIC CHANGE AND NEW POLITICAL ACTORS

During and after World War I, Latin American economies expanded and the population continued to increase, especially in the cities. The growth of middle-class and working-class populations challenged traditional oligarchies and resulted in new political parties, often populist and nationalist. These new parties and the traditional elites both attacked liberalism and laissez-faire capitalism, which were clearly in crisis by the time of the world economic crash in 1929.

The Mexican Revolution had a limited immediate impact beyond the borders of Mexico, but the outbreak of World War I affected most of Latin America directly. The economic boom of the late 19th century had continued into the early 20th century. Each nation had its specialized crop or set of exports: coffee from Colombia, Brazil, and Costa Rica; minerals from Bolivia, Chile, and Peru; bananas from Ecuador and Central America; and sugar from Cuba. As long as European demand remained high, groups in control of these exports profited greatly.

World War I had some immediate effects on the Latin American economies. Cut off from supplies of traditional imports, these countries experienced a spurt of industrial growth in what economists call *import substitution industrialization.* Latin Americans had to produce for themselves some of what they had formerly imported. Most of this involved light industry such as textiles. Latin America continued to suffer from a lack of capital, limited markets (because so many people had so little to spend), and low technological levels. Still, changes took place. Moreover, during the war European demand for some products increased. World War I had stimulated the economy, but it was a false start. After the war, a general inflation meant that the real wages of the working classes declined and their worsening condition contributed to increasing political unrest.

That unrest also resulted from population growth, which was rapid in some countries. Immigrants continued to pour into Argentina, Brazil, and some of the other countries with a temperate climate, swelling the ranks of the rural and urban working classes. Cities grew in size and importance. Some, such as Lima, Montevideo, Quito, and Mexico City, so dominated the economic and political resources of their countries that growth outside the capital was difficult. By 1920, for example, 20 percent of Argentina's total population lived in Buenos Aires, and 14 percent of the population of Chile and Cuba lived in their respective capitals, Santiago and Havana. Rapid urban growth created a series of social problems that reflected the transformation of Latin America from agrarian to industrializing societies.

Labor and the Middle Class

The rising importance of urban labor, such as the workers we see in Figure 38.5, and the growth of an urban middle class led to changes in the political structure of some Latin American nations. The traditional land-owning oligarchy in countries such as Argentina, Chile, and Brazil began to open up the political system to meet the desire of the growing middle class to share political power. In Argentina, for example, a new electoral law in 1912 resulted in the 1916 triumph of the middle-class–based Radical party. After some preliminary attempts to forge an alliance with workers, however, that strategy was abandoned in favor of closer ties with the traditional elites. In Brazil, after the establishment of a republic in 1889, a series of conservative presidents from the Republican party in the wealthiest and most powerful states held control of the government. This alliance of traditional landed interests and urban middle classes maintained political stability and a business-as-usual approach to government, but it began to encounter a series of opponents during the 1920s. Reformist military officers, disaffected state politicians, social bandits, and millenarian peasant movements seeking a return to a golden age all acted in different ways against the political system and the system of export–import capitalism that seemed to produce increasing inequality while it produced great wealth. Similar criticisms were voiced throughout Latin America.

As in western Europe, in Latin America the growing industrial and urban labor forces began to exert some influence on politics during the first decades of the century. Not surprisingly, many workers were engaged in export production or in related transportation activities. Immigrants from Spain, Italy, and elsewhere in Europe sometimes came with well-developed political goals and ideologies. These ideologies ranged from *anarchism,* which aimed to smash the state entirely by using the general strike to gain power, to *syndicalism,* which aimed to use the organization of labor to achieve that goal. Railroad, dock, and mining workers often were among the most radical and the first to organize; usually they were met with force. Hundreds of miners in Iquique, Chile, striking against awful conditions in 1907, were shot down by government forces. Between 1914 and 1930, a series of general strikes and labor unrest swept through much of Latin America. Sometimes, as in Argentina in 1919 during the *Tragic Week,* the government reaction to "revolutionary workers," many of whom were foreign born, led to brutal repression under the guise of nationalism.

A growing sense of class conflict developed in Latin America as in western Europe during this period. Some gains were made, however, as it became increasingly clear that governments now had to con-

Figure 38.5. The growing labor force that resulted from Latin American industrialization began to change the nature of urban life and politics around the time of World War I. Here, women in Orizaba, Mexico, are making sacks for coffee.

sider organized labor as a force to be confronted or accommodated. It should be emphasized that most workers in Latin America, unlike those in western Europe, were still agrarian and for the most part were not organized. Thus, the history of the labor movement tells only a small part of the story.

Ideology and Social Reform

In the 1920s and 1930s, the failures of liberalism were becoming increasingly apparent. A middle class had emerged and had begun to enter politics, but unlike its western European counterpart, it gained power only in conjunction with the traditional oligarchy or the military. In Latin America, the ideology of liberalism discussed in Chapter 31 was not an expression of the strength of this class but rather a series of ideas not particularly suited to the realities of Latin America, where large segments of the popula-

tion were landless, uneducated, and destitute. Increasing industrialization did not dissolve the old class boundaries, nor did public education and other classic liberal programs produce as much social mobility as had been expected.

Disillusioned by liberalism and World War I, artists and intellectuals who had looked to Europe for inspiration turned to Latin America's own populations and history for values and solutions to Latin American problems. Increasingly, during the 1920s, intellectuals complained that Latin America was on a race to nowhere. In literature and the arts, the ideas of rationality, progress, and order associated with liberalism and the outward appearances of democracy were under attack.

Ideas of reform and social change were in the air. University students in Cordoba, Argentina, began a reform of their university system that gave the university more autonomy and students more power within it. This movement soon spread to other countries. Movements for social reform gathered strength in Brazil, Chile, and Uruguay. Many of those who criticized the failure of the liberal regimes claimed that Latin America should seek its own solutions rather than import ideas from Europe. There were other responses as well. Socialist and Communist parties were formed or grew in strength in several Latin American nations in this period, especially after the Russian Revolution of 1917. The strength of these parties of the left originated in local conditions but sometimes was aided by the international Communist movement. Although criticism of existing governments and of liberalism as a political and economic philosophy came from these left-leaning parties, it also came from traditional elements in society such as the Roman Catholic church, which disliked the secularization represented by a capitalist society.

Populist Politics: The Case of Peru

We can use Peru as an example of this ferment. That Andean nation, with its predominantly Indian population, followed the general trend of export-oriented development based on nitrates and a few agricultural products. The foreign capital invested there controlled many crucial transportation facilities and vital industries. The elites profited from economic expansion, but a war with Chile (the War of the Pacific, 1879–1883) led to the loss of territory and nitrate resources. Many peasants were landless, and government corruption was rampant. By the 1920s, critics had emerged. José Carlos Mariateguí (1895–1930), a young essayist, wrote nationalistic analyses of Peru's ills from a socialist perspective that glorified the Indian past and denounced political and economic conditions in Peru. His *Seven Essays of Peruvian Reality* (1928) became a classic of social criticism.

Another young Peruvian, *Victor Raul Haya de la Torre* (1895–1979) created a new party, the American Popular Revolutionary Alliance (APRA), in 1924. This party, drawing on the models of the Mexican Revolution, socialism, and nationalism as well as on some aspects of Mussolini's fascism, aimed at being an international party throughout the hemisphere. However, its greatest success was in Peru itself, where by the 1930s its members had made an impact on politics. Anti-imperialist, nationalistic, and in favor of nationalizing lands and basic industries, APRA's program won wide support. Haya de la Torre depended on his own personal charisma and on middle-class and proletarian support for the success of APRA. This was a mix of personal qualities and programs that could be seen in a number of Latin American regimes in the period. Electoral battles and political strife between right and left in the 1930s kept APRA from power. Although opposed by the military and other sectors of society, Apristas remained a force in Peruvian politics and finally gained the presidency in 1985 with the victory of Alan García, but the origins of the movement were tied to the political disillusionment of the period between the wars.

APRA represented the new populist political parties in Latin America that began to mobilize mass support among workers, small farmers, and urban sectors under the direction of personalist leaders. Populism usually was nationalist and seemingly anti-establishment. It gained broad support from urban masses and rural peasants, but it was often led by politicians from the military or the elites, who channeled this support into policies that did not challenge the government structure. With an emphasis on personal charisma, direct appeals to the masses, and the political mobilization of people previously excluded from politics, populist leaders, such as *Juan Perón* in Argentina, became powerful forces in the region.

The Great Crash and Latin American Responses

The economic dependency of Latin America and the internal weaknesses of the liberal regimes were made clear by the great world financial crisis of 1929. After the crash, the foreign investments so essential to the continued growth of the Latin American economies

ceased, and purchases of the region's products declined. Unemployment and economic dislocation were general. The liberal political and economic programs that had brought the changes of the late 19th and early 20th centuries were now bankrupt. Within three years, there were violent military coups in 12 countries as new alternatives to the deepening crisis of the area were sought. Among these alternatives were various adaptations of socialism or *corporatism*, a political ideology that emphasized the organic nature of society and made the state a mediator, adjusting the interests of different social groups. This philosophy often appealed to conservative groups and to the military because it stressed cooperation and the avoidance of class conflict and because it placed the state at the center of power. Moreover, the fact that corporatism was adopted by Catholic European regimes, such as Italy, Spain, and Portugal, contributed to its popularity in Latin America. Aspects of Italian and later German fascism also appealed to conservatives in Latin America. During the 1930s, fascist groups formed, complete with their own militant rhetoric and uniforms, and sometimes gained political power in Brazil, Mexico, and Chile.

Unrestrained capitalism had created deep social divisions. By the 1930s, many Western societies, including Latin America, began to moderate the principles and policies of unbridled laissez-faire capitalism by trying to bring about some kind of social reform to provide a broader basis for governments. The New Deal in the United States and the corporatist governments of Italy and Spain were responses to the failures and problems of capitalism. Latin America also participated in this trend.

PROMISES OF SOCIAL REFORM

■■ *The regimes of the 1930s enacted broad reforms and mobilized the mass of the population in politics as never before in the region. Cárdenas in Mexico, Vargas in Brazil, and Perón in Argentina drew ideas from socialist and fascist models and instituted broad reforms.*

New regimes, as well as a new concern with social problems, characterized much of Latin America in the 1930s. We have already mentioned the reforming administration of President Cárdenas (1934–1940) in Mexico, when land reform and many of the social aspects of the revolution were initiated on a large scale. Cárdenas distributed more than 40 million acres of land and created communal farms and a credit system to support them. He expropriated foreign oil companies that refused to obey Mexican law and created a state oil monopoly. He expanded rural education programs. These measures made him broadly popular in Mexico and seemed to give the promise of the revolution substance.

Cárdenas in Mexico was perhaps the most successful example of the new political tide that could be seen elsewhere in Latin America. In Cuba, for example, the leaders of a nationalist revolution in 1933 aimed at social reform and breaking the grip of the United States took power, and although their rule soon was taken over by moderate elements, important changes and reforms did take place. To some extent, such new departures underlined both the growing force of nationalism and the desire to integrate new forces into the political process. Nowhere was this more apparent than in the populist regimes of Brazil and Argentina.

The Vargas Regime in Brazil

In Brazil, a contested political election in 1929, in which the state elites could not agree on the next president, resulted in a short civil war and the emergence of *Getúlio Vargas* (1872–1954) as the new president. The Brazilian economy, based on coffee exports, had collapsed in the 1929 crash. Vargas had promised liberal reforms and elimination of the worst abuses of the old system. Once in power, he launched a new kind of centralized political program, imposing federal administrators over the state governments. He held off attempted coups by the communists in 1935 and by the green-shirted fascist "integralists" in 1937. With the support of the military, Vargas imposed a new constitution in 1937 that established the Estado Novo (New State), based on ideas from Mussolini's Italy. It imposed an authoritarian regime within the context of nationalism and economic reforms, limiting immigration and eliminating parties and groups that resisted national integration or opposed the government.

For a while, Vargas played off Germany and the Western powers in the hope of securing armaments and favorable trade arrangements. Despite Vargas's authoritarian sympathies, he eventually joined the Allies, supplied bases to the United States, and even sent troops to fight against the Axis powers in Italy. In return, Brazil obtained arms, financial support for industrial development, and trade advantages. Meanwhile, Vargas ran a corporatist government, allowing some room for labor negotiations under strict government supervision. Little open opposition to the government was allowed. The state organized many other aspects of the economy. Opposition to Vargas and his repressive policies was building in Brazil by 1945, but by then he was turning increasingly to the left, seeking support from organized labor and coming to terms with the Communist party leaders whom he had imprisoned.

In 1945, Vargas was deposed by a military coup, but he did not disappear from Brazilian political life. After an interim of five years, Vargas returned to the presidency, this time on a program of nationalism and with support from the left and from a new Workers' party. Under his supporter, João Goulart, the party mobilized the urban labor force. Limitations were put on foreign profit-making in Brazil. As in Mexico and Argentina, a state monopoly of petroleum was established. Vargas's nationalist and populist stance had a broad appeal, but his policies often were more conservative than his statements. Under criticism from both the right and the left, Vargas committed suicide in 1954. His suicide note emphasized his populist ties and blamed his death on Brazil's enemies:

> Once more the forces and interests which work against the people have organized themselves again and emerge against me.... I was a slave to the people, and today I am freeing myself for eternal life. But this people whose slave I was will no longer be slave to anyone. My sacrifice will remain forever in their souls and my blood will be the price of their ransom.

Much of Brazilian history since Vargas has been a struggle over his mantle of leadership. In death, Vargas became a martyr and a nationalist hero, even to the groups he had repressed and imprisoned in the 1930s.

Argentina: Populism, Perón, and the Military

Argentina was something of an anomaly. There, the middle-class Radical party, which had held power during the 1920s, fell when the economy collapsed in 1929. A military coup backed by a strange coalition of nationalists, fascists, and socialists seized power, hoping to return Argentina to the golden days of the great export boom of the 1890s. The coup failed. Argentina became more dependent as foreign investments increased and markets for Argentine products declined. However, industry was growing, and with it grew the numbers and strength of industrial workers, many of whom had migrated from the countryside. By the 1940s, the workers were organized in two major labor federations. Conservative governments backed by the traditional military held power through the 1930s, but in 1943 a military group once again took control of the government.

The new military rulers were nationalists who wanted to industrialize and modernize Argentina and make it the dominant power of South America. Some were admirers of the fascist powers and their programs. Although many of them were distrustful of the workers, the man who became the dominant political force in Argentina recognized the need to create a broader basis of support for the government. Colonel Juan D. Perón (1895–1974; Figure 38.6) emerged as a power in the government. Using his position in the Ministry of Labor, he appealed to workers, raising their salaries, improving their benefits, and generally supporting their demands. Attempts to displace him failed, and he increasingly gained popular support, aided by his wife, *Eva Duarte,* known as Evita. She became a public spokesperson for Perón among the lower classes. During World War II, Perón's admiration for the Axis powers was well known. In 1946, Perón successfully manipulated an attempt by the United States to discredit him, because of his pro-fascist sympathies, into nationalist support for his presidential campaign.

Perón forged an alliance between the workers, the industrialists, and the military. Like Vargas, he learned the effectiveness of the radio, the press, and public speeches in mobilizing public support. He depended on his personal charisma and on repression of opponents to maintain his rule. The Peronist program was couched in nationalistic terms. The government nationalized the foreign-owned railroads and telephone companies as well as the petroleum resources. The foreign debt was paid off, and for a while the Argentine economy boomed in the immediate postwar years. But by 1949, there were economic problems again. Meanwhile, Perón ruled by a combination of inducements and repression, while his wife, Evita, became a symbol to the descamisados, or the poor and downtrodden, who saw in Peronism a glimmer of hope. Her death in 1952 at age 33 caused national mourning.

Perón's regime was a populist government with a broader base than had ever been attempted in Argentina. Nevertheless, holding the interests of the various components of the coalition together became increasingly difficult as the economy worsened. A democratic opposition developed and complained of Perón's control of the press and his violation of civil liberties. Industrialists disliked the strength of labor organizations. The military worried that Perón would

arm the workers, and they feared Perón would begin to cut back on the military's gains. The Peronist party became more radical and began a campaign against the Catholic church. In 1955, anti-Perón military officers drove him into exile.

Argentina spent the next 20 years in the shadow of Perón. The Peronist party was banned, and a succession of military-supported civilian governments tried to resolve the nation's economic problems and its continuing political instability. But Peronism could survive even without Perón, and the mass of urban workers and the strongly Peronist unions continued to agitate for his programs, especially as austerity measures began to affect the living conditions of the working class. Perón and his new wife, Isabel, returned to Argentina in 1973, and they won the presidential election in that year, she as vice president. When Perón died the next

Figure 38.6. *The populist politics of Juan Perón and his wife, Evita, brought new forces, especially urban workers, into Argentine politics. Their personal charisma attracted support from groups formerly excluded from politics but eventually led to opposition from the Argentine military and Perón's overthrow in 1955.*

year, however, it was clear that Argentina's problems could not be solved by the old formulas. Argentina slid once more into military dictatorship.

RADICAL OPTIONS IN THE 1950S

■■ *Frustration with the failures of social, political, and economic reforms led to radical solutions that were often influenced by socialist ideas. In Bolivia, Guatemala, and Cuba, revolutionaries tried to change the nature of government and society, but such changes also had to accommodate the reality of the cold war and the interests of the United States.*

The Argentine and Brazilian changes begun by Perón and Vargas were symptomatic of the continuing problems of Latin America, but their personalistic authoritarian solutions were only one possible response. By the 1940s, pressure for change had built up through much of Latin America. Across the political spectrum there was a desire to improve the social and economic conditions throughout the region and a general agreement that development and economic strength were the keys to a better future. How to achieve those goals remained in question, however. In Mexico, one-party rule continued, and the "revolution" became increasingly conservative and interested in economic growth rather than social justice. In a few countries, such as Venezuela and Costa Rica, reform-minded democratic parties were able to win elections in an open political system. In other places, such a solution was less likely or less attractive to those who wanted reform. Unlike the Mexican revolutionaries of 1910–1920, those seeking change in the post–World War II period could turn to the well-developed political philosophy of Marxian socialism as a guide. However, such models were fraught with dangers because of the context of the cold war and the ideological struggle between western Europe and the Soviet bloc.

Throughout Latin America, the failures of political democratization, economic development, and social reforms led to consideration of radical and revolutionary solutions to national problems. In some cases, the revolutions at first were successful but ultimately were unable to sustain the changes. In predominantly Indian Bolivia, where as late as 1950 90 percent of the land was owned by 6 percent of the population, a revolution erupted in 1952 in which miners, peasants, and urban middle-class groups participated. Although mines were nationalized and some land redistributed, fear of moving too far to the left brought the army back into power in 1964, and subsequent governments remained more interested in order than in reform.

Guatemala: Reform and United States Intervention

The first place where more radical solutions were tried was Guatemala. This predominantly Indian nation had some of the worst of the region's problems. Its population was mostly illiterate and suffered poor health conditions and high mortality rates. Land and wealth were distributed very unequally, and the whole economy depended on the highly volatile prices for its main exports of coffee and bananas. In 1944, a coalition of middle-class and labor elected a reformer, *Juan José Arevalo,* as president. Under a new constitution, he began a series of programs within the context of "spiritual socialism" that included land reform and an improvement in the rights and conditions of rural and industrial workers. An income tax, the first in the nation's history, was projected and educational reforms were planned. These programs and Arevalo's sponsorship of an intense nationalism brought the Arevalo government into direct conflict with foreign interests operating in Guatemala, especially the *United Fruit Company,* the largest and most important foreign concern there. That company had operated in Guatemala from the turn of the century and had acquired extensive properties. It also controlled transportation and shipping facilities. Its workers often were better paid than the average, and their health and other benefits were more extensive, but because it was a foreign company with such a powerful role in Guatemala, United Fruit was the target of nationalistic anger.

In 1951, after a free election, the presidency passed to Colonel Jacobo Arbenz, whose nationalist program was more radical and whose public statements against foreign economic interests and the landholding oligarchy were more extreme than under Arevalo. Arbenz announced several programs to improve or nationalize the transportation network, the hydroelectric system, and other areas of the economy. A move to expropriate unused lands on large estates in 1953 provoked opposition from the landed oligarchy and from United Fruit, which eventually was threatened with the loss of almost half a million acres of reserve land. The U.S. government, fearing "communist" penetration of the

Arbenz government and under considerable pressure from the United Fruit Company, denounced the changes and began to impose economic and diplomatic restrictions on Guatemala. At the same time, the level of nationalist rhetoric intensified, and the government increasingly received the support of the political left in Latin America and in the socialist bloc.

In 1954, with the help of the U.S. Central Intelligence Agency, a dissident military force was organized and invaded Guatemala. The Arbenz government fell, and the pro-American regime that replaced it turned back the land reform and negotiated a settlement favorable to United Fruit. The reform experiment was thus brought to a halt. By the standards of the 1960s and later, the programs of Arevalo and Arbenz seem rather mild, although Arbenz's statements and his acceptance of arms from eastern Europe undoubtedly contributed to U.S. intervention. The reforms promised by the U.S.-supported governments were minimal. Guatemala continued to have a low standard of living, especially for its Indian population. The series of military governments after the coup failed to address the nation's social and economic problems. That failure led to continual violence and political instability. A coalition of coffee planters, foreign companies, and the military controlled political life. A guerrilla movement grew and provoked brutal military repression, which fell particularly hard on the rural Indian population. Guatemala's attempt at radical change, an attempt that began with an eye toward improving the conditions of the people, failed because of external intervention. The failure was a warning that change would not come without internal and foreign opposition.

The Cuban Revolution: Socialism in the Caribbean

The differences between Cuba and Guatemala underline the diversity of Latin America and the dangers of partial revolutions. The island nation had a population of about 6 million, most of whom were the descendants of Spaniards and the African slaves who had been imported to produce the sugar, tobacco, and hides that were the colony's mainstays. Cuba had a large middle class, and its literacy and health care levels were better than in most of the rest of the region. Rural areas lagged behind in these matters, however, and there the working and living conditions were poor, especially for the workers on the large sugar estates. Always in the shadow of the United States, Cuban politics and economy were rarely free of American interests. By the 1950s, about three-fourths of what Cuba imported came from the United States. American investments in the island were heavy during the 1940s and 1950s. Although the island experienced periods of prosperity, fluctuations in the world market for Cuba's main product, sugar, revealed the tenuous basis of the economy. Moreover, the disparity between the countryside and the growing middle class in Havana underlined the nation's continuing problems.

From 1934 to 1944, Cuba had been ruled by *Fulgencio Batista,* a strong-willed, authoritarian reformer who had risen from the lower ranks of the army. Among his reforms were a democratic constitution of 1940 that promised major changes, nationalization of natural resources, full employment, and land reform. However, Batista's programs of reform were marred by corruption, and when in 1952 he returned to the presidency, there was little left of the reformer but a great deal of the dictator. Opposition developed in various sectors of the society. Among the regime's opponents was *Fidel Castro,* a young lawyer experienced in leftist university politics and an ardent critic of the Batista government and the ills of Cuban society. On July 26, 1953, Castro and a few followers launched an unsuccessful attack on some military barracks. Captured, Castro faced a trial, an occasion he used to expound his revolutionary ideals, aimed mostly at a return to democracy, social justice, and the establishment of a less dependent economy.

Released from prison, Castro fled to exile in Mexico where, with the aid of *Ernesto "Che" Guevara,* a militant Argentine revolutionary, he gathered a small military force. They landed in Cuba in 1956 and slowly began to gather strength in the mountains. By 1958, the "26th of July Movement" had found support from students, some labor organizations, and rural workers and was able to conduct operations against Batista's army. The bearded rebels, or barbudos, won a series of victories. The dictator, under siege and isolated by the United States (which because of his excesses refused to support him any longer), was driven from power, and the rebels took Havana amid wild scenes of joy and relief (Figure 38.7).

What happened next is highly debatable, and Castro himself has offered alternative interpretations at different times. Whether Castro was already a Marxist–Leninist and had always intended to introduce a socialist regime (as he now claims) or whether the development of this program was the result of a series of pragmatic decisions is in question. Rather than simply returning to the constitution of 1940 and enacting moderate reforms, Castro launched a program of sweeping change. Foreign properties were expropriated, farms were collectivized, and a centralized socialist economy was put in place. Most of these changes were accompanied by a nationalist and anti-imperialist foreign policy. Relations with the United States were broken off in 1961, and Cuba increasingly depended on the financial support and arms of the Soviet Union to maintain its revolution. With that support in place, Castro was able to survive the increasingly hostile reaction of the United States. That reaction included a disastrous U.S.–sponsored invasion by Cuban exiles in 1961 and an embargo on trade with Cuba. Dependence on the Soviet Union led to a crisis in 1961, when Soviet nuclear missiles, perhaps placed in Cuba in case of another U.S. invasion, were discovered and a confrontation between the superpowers ensued. Despite these problems, to a large extent the Cuban Revolution survived because the politics of the cold war provided Cuba with a protector and a benefactor.

The results of the revolution have been mixed. The social programs were extensive. Education, health, and housing have improved greatly and rank Cuba among the world's leaders—quite unlike most other nations of the region. This is especially true in the long-neglected rural areas. A wide variety of social and educational programs have mobilized all sectors of the population. The achievements have been accompanied by severe restrictions of basic freedoms.

Attempts to diversify and strengthen the economy have been less successful. An effort to industrialize in the 1960s failed, and Cuba turned again to its ability to produce sugar. The world's falling sugar and rising petroleum prices led to disaster. Only by subsidizing Cuban sugar and supplying petroleum below the world price could the Soviet Union maintain the Cuban economy. Since the breakup of the Soviet Union in the 1990s, the Cuban situation has deteriorated; along with China, the island has become one of the last socialist bastions.

Despite these problems, the Cuban Revolution offered an example that has proved attractive to those seeking to transform Latin American societies. Early direct attempts to spread the model of the Cuban Revolution, such as Che Guevara's guerrilla operation in Bolivia, where he lost his life in 1967, were failures, but the Cuban model and the island's ability to resist the pressure of a hostile United States has proved attractive to other nations in the Caribbean and Central Amer-

Figure 38.7. *Fidel Castro and his guerrilla army brought down the Batista government in January 1959, to the wild acclaim of many Cubans. Castro initiated sweeping reforms in Cuba that eventually led to the creation of a socialist regime and the hostility of the United States.*

ica, such as Grenada and Nicaragua, that have also exercised the revolutionary option. U.S. reaction to such movements has been containment or intervention.

THE SEARCH FOR REFORM AND THE MILITARY OPTION

Programs based in Catholic, Marxist, and capitalist doctrines continued to seek solutions to Latin America's problems. Military governments in the 1960s and 1970s based on nationalism and advocating economic development created new "bureaucratic authoritarian" regimes, which for a while served the cold war interests of the United States. By the 1980s a new wave of democratic regimes was emerging.

The revolutionary attempts of the 1950s, the durability of the Cuban Revolution, and the general appeal of Marxist doctrines in the Third World underlined Latin America's tendency to undertake revolutionary change that left its economic and social structures unchanged. How could the traditional patterns of inequality and international dependency be overcome? What was the best path to the future?

For some, the answer was political stability, imposed if necessary, to promote capitalist economic growth. The one-party system of Mexico demonstrated its capacity for repression when student dissidents were brutally killed during disturbances in 1968. Mexico enjoyed some prosperity from its petroleum resources in the 1970s, but poor financial planning, corruption, and foreign debt again caused problems by the 1980s, and the PRI seemed to be losing its ability to maintain control of Mexican politics.

For others, the church, long a power in Latin America, provided a guide. Christian Democratic parties formed in Chile and Venezuela in the 1950s, hoping to bring reforms through popularly based mass parties that would preempt the radical left. The church often was divided politically, but the clergy took an increasingly engaged position and argued for social justice and human rights, often in support of government opponents. A few, such as Father Camilo Torres in Colombia, actually joined armed revolutionary groups in the 1960s.

More common was the emergence within the church hierarchy of an increased concern for social justice. By the 1970s, a *liberation theology* combined Catholic theology and socialist principles in an effort to improve conditions for the poor. When criticized for promoting communism in his native Brazil, Dom Helder da Camara, archbishop of Pernambuco, remarked, "The trouble with Brazil is not an excess of communist doctrine but a lack of Christian justice." The position of the church in Latin American societies was changing, but there was no single program for this new stance or even agreement among the clergy about its validity. Still, this activist position provoked attacks against clergy such as the courageous Archbishop Oscar Romero of El Salvador, who was assassinated in 1980. The church also played an important role in the fall of the Paraguayan dictatorship in 1988.

Out of the Barracks: Soldiers Take Power

The success of the Cuban Revolution also impressed and worried those who feared revolutionary change within a Communist political system. The military forces in Latin America had been involved in politics since the days of the caudillos in the 19th century, and in several nations military interventions had been common. As the Latin American military became more pro-

fessionalized, however, a new philosophy underlay the military's involvement in politics. The soldiers began to see themselves as above the selfish interests of political parties and as the true representatives of the nation. With technical training and organizational skills, military officers by the 1920s and 1930s believed that they were best equipped to solve their nations' problems, even if that meant sacrificing the democratic process and imposing martial law.

In the 1960s, the Latin American military establishments, made nervous by the Cuban success and the swing to leftist or populist regimes, began to intervene directly in the political process, not simply to clean out a disliked president or party, as they had done in the past, but to take over government itself. In 1964, the Brazilian military (with the support of the United States and Brazilian the middle class) overthrew the elected president after he threatened to make sweeping social reforms. In Argentina, growing polarization between the Peronists and the middle class led to a military intervention in 1966. In Chile, the socialist government of president *Salvador Allende* was overthrown in 1973 by the Chilean military, which until then had remained for the most part out of politics. Allende had nationalized industries and banks and had sponsored peasant and worker expropriations of lands and factories. His government was caught in an increasing polarization between groups trying to halt these changes and those pushing for faster and more radical reforms. By 1973, the economy was in serious difficulty, undermined by resistance in Chile and by U.S. policies designed to isolate the country. Allende was killed during the military coup against him, and throughout Latin America there were demonstrations against the military and U.S. involvement. But Chile was not alone. Similar coups took place in Uruguay in 1973 and in Peru in 1968.

The soldiers in power imposed a new type of bureaucratic authoritarian regime. Their governments were supposed to stand above the competing demands of various sectors and establish economic stability. Now, as arbiters of politics, the soldiers would place the national interest above selfish interests by imposing dictatorships. Government was essentially a presidency, controlled by the military, in which policies were formulated and applied by a bureaucracy organized like a military chain of command. Political repression and torture were used to silence critics, and stringent measures were imposed to control inflation and strengthen the economies. Laws limited political freedoms, and repression often was brutal and illegal.

Visualizing THE PAST

Murals and Posters: Art and Revolution

*P*ublic art for political purposes has been used since ancient Egypt, but with the development of lithography (a color printing process), the poster emerged as a major form of communication. First developed in the late 19th century as a cheap form of advertising using image and text to sell soap, wine, or chocolate or to advertise dance halls and theaters, by the 1880s posters were adapted to political purposes, and in World War I all the major combatants used them. But those opposed to governments could also use posters to convey a revolutionary message to a broad public. In Latin America, as we have seen, the Mexican Revolution made use of public art in great murals, but these were often expensive and took a long time to complete. Both the Cuban revolution of the 1960s and the Nicaraguan Revolution of the 1980s turned to the poster as a way to convey its policies and goals to a broad public.

Questions: What are the advantages of the poster over the mural and vice versa? Is poster art really art? Why are images of the past often the subjects of revolutionary art? To whom is political art usually directed?

In Argentina, violent opposition to military rule led to a counteroffensive and a "dirty war" in which thousands of people "disappeared," kidnapped and tortured or killed by government security forces.

Government economic policies fell heaviest on the working class. The goal of the military in Brazil and Argentina was development. To some extent, in Brazil at least, economic improvements were achieved, although income distribution became even more unequal than it had been. Inflation was reduced, industrialization increased, and gains were made in literacy and health, but basic structural problems such as land ownership and social conditions for the poorest people remained unchanged.

There were variations within these military regimes. All were nationalistic. The Peruvian military tried to create a popular base for its programs and to mobilize support among the peasantry. It had a real social program, including extensive land reform, and was not simply a surrogate for the conservatives in Peruvian society. In Chile and Uruguay, the military was fiercely anticommunist. In Argentina, nationalism and a desire to gain popular support in the face of a worsening economy led to a confrontation with Great Britain over the Falkland Islands (Islas Malvinas), which both nations claimed. A short war in 1982 resulted in an Argentine defeat and a loss of the military's credibility that contributed to its loss of authority.

The New Democratic Trend

In Argentina and elsewhere in South America, by the mid-1980s the military had begun to return government to civilian politicians. Continuing economic problems and the pressures of containing opponents wore heavily on the military leaders, who began to realize that their solutions were no more destined to success than those of civilian governments. Moreover, the populist parties, such as the Peronists and Apristas, seemed less of a threat, and the fear of Cuban-style communism had diminished. Also, the end of the cold war meant that the United States was less interested in sponsoring regimes that, though "safe," were also repressive. In Argentina, elections were held in 1983. Brazil began to restore democratic government after 1985 and in 1989 chose its first popularly elected president since the military takeover. The South American military bureaucrats and modernizers were returning to their barracks.

The process of redemocratization was not easy, nor was it universal. In Peru, Sendero Luminoso (Shining Path), a long-sustained leftist guerrilla movement, controlled areas of the countryside and tried to disrupt national elections in 1990. In Central America, the military cast a long shadow over the government in El Salvador. After the elections of 1990, which removed the *Sandinista party* from control in Nicaragua, an uneasy truce continued between them and the centralist government of Violeta Chamorro, the newly elected president. By the late 1990s civilian government had returned to Guatemala as the country struggled to overcome the history of repression and rebellion and the animosities they had created. In 1999, a furor resulted when it was discovered that the "eyewitness" account of the military repression in that country, written by Rigoberta Menchu, an Indian who had won the Nobel Peace Prize, was not entirely accurate, although her defenders claimed it was still essentially true. The United States demonstrated its continuing power in the region in its invasion of Panama and the arrest of its strongman leader, Manuel Noriega.

Latin American governments in the last decades of the century faced tremendous problems. Large foreign loans taken in the 1970s for the purpose of development, sometimes for unnecessary projects, had created a tremendous level of debt that threatened the economic stability of countries such as Brazil, Peru, and Mexico. High rates of inflation provoked social instability as real wages fell. Pressure from the international banking community to curb inflation by cutting government spending and reducing wages often ignored the social and political consequences of such actions. An international commerce in drugs, which produced tremendous profits, stimulated criminal activity and created powerful international cartels that could even threaten national sovereignty, as they did in Colombia. In countries as diverse as Cuba, Panama, and Bolivia, the narcotics trade penetrated the highest government circles.

But despite the problems, the 1990s seemed to demonstrate that the democratic trends were well established. In Venezuela and Brazil, corruption in government led to the fall of presidents. In late 2000, Mexico prepared for an election that might introduce a true multiparty system, and in Brazil a leftist working-class presidential candidate, Lula (Luiz Inacio Lula da Silva), was the leading candidate as Brazilians went to the polls, although he lost to a moderate but honest reformer. More radical options were still possible. In Colombia an insurgency continued to threaten the nation's stability, and in other countries the military was sometimes troublesome, but a commitment to a more open political system in most of the region seemed firm.

DOCUMENT

The People Speak

Scholarly analysis of general trends often cannot convey the way in which historical events and patterns affect the lives of people or the fact that history is made up of the collective experience of individuals. It is often very difficult to know about the lives of common people in the past or to learn about their perceptions of their lives. In recent years in Latin America, however, a growing literature of autobiographies, interpreted autobiographies (in which another writer puts the story down and edits it), and collections of interviews have provided a vision of the lives of common people. These statements, like any historical document, must be used carefully because their authors or editors sometimes have political purposes, because they reflect individual opinions, or because the events they report may be atypical. Nevertheless, these personal statements do put flesh and blood on the bones of history and provide an important perspective from those whose voice in history often is lost.

A Bolivian Woman Describes Her Life

Domitilia Barrios de Chungara was a miner's wife who became politically active in the mine workers' political movement. Her presence at the United Nations–sponsored International Woman's Year Tribunal in 1975 moved a Brazilian journalist to organize her statements into a book about her life. This excerpt provides a picture of her everyday struggle for life.

> My day begins at four in the morning, especially when my compañero is on the first shift. I prepare his breakfast. Then I have to prepare salteñas [small meat pastries] because I make about one hundred salteñas every day and I sell them on the street. I do this in order to make up for what my husband's wage doesn't cover in terms of our necessities. The night before, we prepare the dough and at four in the morning I make the salteñas while I feed the kids. The kids help me.
>
> Then the ones that go to school in the morning have to get ready, while I wash the clothes left soaking over night.
>
> At eight I go out to sell. The kids that go to school in the afternoon help me. We have to go to the company store and bring home the staples. And in the store there are immensely long lines and you have to wait there until eleven in order to stock up. You have to line up for meat, for vegetables, for oil. So it's just one line after another. Since everything is in a different place, that's how it has to be.
>
> From what we earn between my husband and me, we can eat and dress. Food is very expensive: 28 pesos for a kilo of meat, 4 pesos for carrots, 6 pesos for onions....

Considering that my compañero earns 28 pesos a day, that's hardly enough is it?

> We don't ever buy ready made clothes. We buy wool and knit. At the beginning of each year, I also spend about 2,000 pesos on cloth and a pair of shoes for each of us. And the company discounts some of that each month from my husband's wage. On the pay slips that's referred to as the "bundle." And what happens is that before we finish paying the "bundle" our shoes are worn out. That's how it is.
>
> Well, from eight to eleven in the morning I sell the salteñas. I do the shopping in the grocery store, and I also work at the Housewives Committee talking with the sisters who go there for advice.
>
> At noon, lunch has to be ready because the rest of the kids have to go to school.
>
> In the afternoon I have to wash clothes. There are no laundries. We use troughs and have to get the water from a pump.
>
> I've got to correct the kids' homework and prepare everything I'll need to make the next day's salteñas.

From Peasant to Revolutionary

Rigoberta Menchú, a Quiché Indian from the Guatemalan highlands, came from a peasant family that had been drawn into politics during the repression of Indian communities and human rights in the 1970s. In these excerpts, she reveals her disillusionment with the government and her realization of the ethnic division between Indians and ladinos, or mestizos, that complicates political action in Guatemala.

> The CUC [Peasant Union] started growing; it spread like wildfire among the peasants in Guatemala. We began to understand that the root of all our problems was exploitation. That there were rich and poor and that the rich exploited the poor—our sweat, our labor. That's how the rich got richer and richer. The fact that we were always waiting in offices, always bowing to the authorities was part of the discrimination that we Indians suffered.
>
> The situation got worse when the murderous generals came to power although I did not actually know who was the president at the time. I began to know them from 1974 when General Kjell Langerud came to power. He came to our region and said: 9We're going to solve the land problem. The land belongs to you. You cultivate the land and I will share it out among you.9 We trusted him. I was at the meeting when [he] spoke. And what did he give us? My father tortured and imprisoned.
>
> Later I had the opportunity of meeting other Indians. Achi Indians, the group that lives closest to us. And I got to know some Mam Indians too. They all told me: 9The rich are bad. But not all ladinos are bad.9 And I started wondering: Could it be that not all ladinos are Achi Indians, the group that lives closest to us? And I know some Mam Indians too. They all told me: "The rich are bad?..."

There were poor ladinos as well as rich ladinos, and they were exploited as well. That's when I began recognizing exploitation. I kept on going to the finca [large farm] but now I really wanted to find out, to prove if that was true and learn the details. There were poor ladinos on the finca. They worked the same, and their children's bellies were swollen like my little brother's.... I was just beginning to speak a little Spanish in those days and I began to talk to them. I said to one poor ladino: "You are a poor ladino, aren't you?" And he nearly hit me. He said: "What do you know about it, Indian!" I wondered: "Why is that when I say poor ladinos are like us, I'm spurned?" I didn't know then that the same system which tries to isolate us Indians also puts barriers between Indians and ladinos.... Soon afterwards, I was with the nuns and we went to a village in Uspantán where mostly ladinos live. The nun asked a little boy if they were poor and he said: "Yes, we're poor but we're not Indians." That stayed with me. The nun didn't notice, she went on talking. She was foreign, she wasn't Guatemalan. She asked someone else the same question and he said: "Yes, we're poor but we're not Indians." It was very painful for me to accept that an Indian was inferior to a ladino. I kept on worrying about it. It's a big barrier they've sown between us, between Indian and ladino. I didn't understand it.

Questions: What was distinctive about lower-class life and outlook in late 20th-century Latin America? How had lower-class life changed since the 19th century?

The United States and Latin America: Continuing Presence

As a backdrop to the political and economic story we have traced thus far stands the continuing presence of the United States. After World War I, the United States emerged as the predominant power in the hemisphere, a position it had already begun to assume at the end of the 19th century with the Cuban–Spanish–American War and the building of the Panama Canal. European nations were displaced as the leading investors in Latin America by the United States. In South America, private investments by American companies and entrepreneurs, as well as loans from the American government, were the chief means of U.S. influence. U.S. investments rose to more than $5 billion by 1929, or more than one-third of all U.S. investments abroad.

Cuba and Puerto Rico experienced direct United States involvement and almost a protectorate status. But in the Caribbean and Central America, the face of U.S. power, economic interest, and disregard for the sovereignty of weaker neighbors was most apparent. Military interventions to protect U.S.–owned properties and investments became so common that there were more than 30 before 1933. Haiti, Nicaragua, the Dominican Republic, Mexico, and Cuba all experienced direct interventions by U.S. troops. Central America was a peculiar case because the level of private investments by U.S. companies such as United Fruit was very high and the economies of these countries were so closely tied to the United States. Those who resisted the U.S. presence were treated as bandits by expeditionary forces. In Nicaragua, *Augusto Sandino* led a resistance movement against occupying troops until his assassination by the U.S.–trained Nicaraguan National Guard in 1934. His struggle against U.S. intervention made him a hero and the figurehead of the Sandinista party, which carried out a socialist revolution in Nicaragua in the 1980s.

The grounds for these interventions were economic, political, strategic, and ideological. The direct interventions usually were followed by the creation or support of conservative governments, often dictatorships that would be friendly to the United States. These became *Banana Republics,* a reference not only to their dependence on the export of tropical products but also to their often subservient and corrupt governments.

Foreign interventions contributed to a growing nationalist reaction. Central America with its continuing political problems became a symbol of Latin America's weakness in the face of foreign influence and interference, especially by the United States. The Nobel Prize–winning Chilean communist poet Pablo Neruda, in his poem "The United Fruit Co." (1950), spoke of the dictators of Central America as 9circus flies, wise flies, learned in tyranny9 who buzzed over the graves of the people. He wrote the following eight lines with passion:

> When the trumpet sounded, all was prepared in the land,
>
> and Jehovah divided the world between Coca Cola Inc.,
>
> Anaconda, Ford Motors, and other companies:
>
> United Fruit Co. reserved for itself the juiciest part,
>
> the central coast of my land,
>
> the sweet waist of America
>
> and baptized again its lands
>
> as Banana Republics.

The actions of the United States changed after 1933. In that year, president Franklin Delano Roosevelt introduced the *Good Neighbor Policy,* which promised to deal more fairly with Latin America and to stop direct interventions. After World War II, however, the U.S. preoccupation with containment of the Soviet Union and communism as an ideology led to new strategies in Latin America. They included participation in regional organizations, the support of governments that at least expressed democratic or anticommunist principles, the covert undermining of governments considered unfriendly to U.S. interests, and, when necessary, direct intervention. Underlying much of this policy was also a firm belief that economic development would eliminate the conditions that contributed to radical political solutions. Thus, U.S. programs such as the *Alliance for Progress,* begun in 1961, aimed to develop the region as an alternative to those solutions. The alliance had limited success despite good intentions and more than $10 billion in aid. Because of its record, Latin Americans and North Americans both began to question the assumption that development was basically a problem of capital and resources and that appropriate

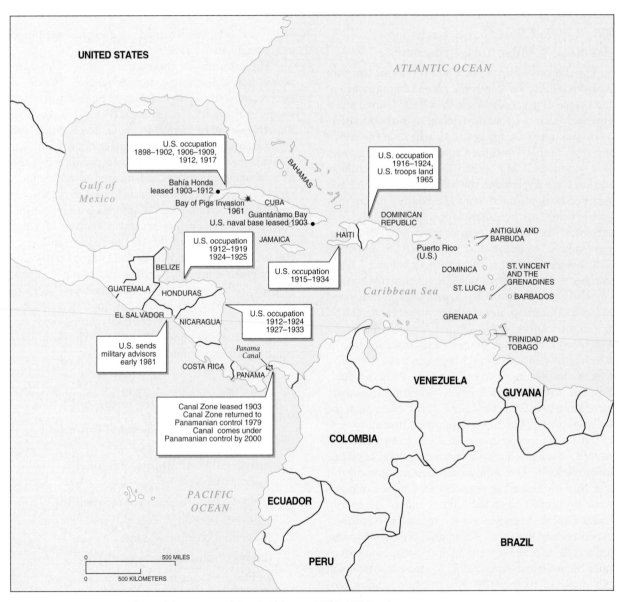

Map 38.1 *Intervention in Central America and the Caribbean, 1898–1981*

strategies would lead to social and economic improvement, which in turn would forestall revolution.

During the 1970s and 1980s, U.S. policy often was pragmatic, accepting Latin America as it was, which meant dealing on friendly terms with the military dictatorships. President Jimmy Carter (1976–1980) made a new initiative to deal with Latin America and to influence governments there to observe civil liberties. Most significantly, a treaty was signed with Panama that ceded to that nation eventual control of the Panama Canal.

Increasing violence in Central America in the 1980s and the more conservative presidencies of Ronald Reagan and George Bush led the United States back to policies based on strategic, economic, and defense considerations in which direct intervention or support of counterrevolutionary forces played a part. Thus, in 1989 and 1990, the United States toppled a government in Panama that was authoritarian, defied U.S. policies, and controlled drug smuggling, replacing it with a cooperative regime backed by American troops.

IN DEPTH

Human Rights in the 20th Century

In Latin America, the question of *human rights* became a burning issue in the 1960s and continued thereafter. The use of torture by repressive governments, the mobilization of death squads and other vigilante groups with government acquiescence, and the use of terrorism against political opponents by the state and by groups opposed to the state became all too common in the region. Latin America's record on the violation of human rights was no worse than that of some other areas of the world. However, the demonstrations by the Argentine "Mothers of the Plaza del Mayo" to focus attention on their disappeared children; the publication of prison memoirs recounting human rights violations in Brazil, Cuba, and Argentina; and films dramatizing events such as the assassination of Archbishop Oscar Romero in El Salvador have all focused attention on the problem in Latin America. Moreover, because Latin America shares in the cultural heritage of Western societies, it is difficult to make an argument that human rights

there have a different meaning or importance than in Europe or North America.

The concept of human rights—that is, certain universal rights enjoyed by all people because they are justified by a moral standard that stands above the laws of any individual nation—may go back to ancient Greece. The concept of natural law and the protection of religious or ethnic minorities also moved nations in the 19th century toward a defense of human rights. To some extent, the international movement to abolish the slave trade was an early human rights movement. In modern times, however, the concept of human rights has been strongly attached to the foundation of the United Nations. In 1948, that body, with the experience of World War II in mind, issued a Universal Declaration of Human Rights and created a commission to oversee the human rights situation. The Universal Declaration, which guaranteed basic liberties and freedoms regardless of color, sex, or religion, proclaimed that it should be the "common standard for all peoples and nations." However, one critic has stated that of the 160 nations in the United Nations, only about 30 have a consistently good record on human rights.

A major problem for the international community has been enforcing the Universal Declaration. The United Nations commission did not have any specific powers of enforcement, and much debate has taken place on the power of the United Nations to intervene in the internal affairs of any nation. More recently, various regional organizations have tried to establish the norms that should govern human rights and to create institutions to enforce these norms.

One specialist has claimed that "human rights is the world's first universal ideology." The defense of human rights seems to be a cause that most people and governments can accept without hesitation, but the question is complex. Although the rights to life, liberty, security, and freedom from torture or degrading punishment are generally accepted in principle by all nations, other rights remain open to question. What is a right, and to what extent are definitions of rights determined by culture?

The question of universality versus relativism emerged quickly in the debate over human rights. What seemed to be obvious human rights in Western societies were less obvious in other parts of the world, where other priorities were held. For example, laws prohibiting child labor were enforced by most Western societies, but throughout the world perhaps 150 million children worked, often in unhealthy and exploitive conditions. They worked because of economic necessity in many cases, but in some societies such labor was considered moral and proper. Such cultural differences have led to a position of relativism, which recognizes that there are profound cultural variations in what is considered moral and just. Critics of the original Universal Declaration contend that its advocacy of the right to own property and the right to vote imposed Western political and economic values as universals. Cultural relativism had the advantage of recognizing the variety of cultures and standards in the world, but it has also been used as a shield to deflect criticism and to excuse the continued violation of human rights.

The definition of human rights is also political. The West emphasizes the civil and political rights of the individual. The socialist nations place social and economic justice above individual rights, although by the 1990s movements in eastern Europe and China indicated that there was pressure to modify this approach. In the Third World, an argument for peoples' rights has emerged in which the "right to development," which calls for a major structural redistribution of the world's resources and economic opportunities, is a central concept (Figure 38.8). As Leopold Senghor of Senegal put it, "Human rights begin with breakfast"; or as a report on Ghana stated, "'One man, one vote' is meaningless unless accompanied by the principle of 'one man, one bread.'" Whereas the right to development is seen as a human right in the Third World, it is viewed as a political and economic demand in wealthier nations of the West.

Another dimension of human rights is the extent to which it influences national foreign policies. Governments may make statements pledging respect for human rights in their foreign policies, but considerations of national defense, sovereignty, or other goals often move human rights concerns into a secondary position. Disputes over the role of human rights in foreign policy sometimes are posed as a conflict between "moralistic utopians" who see the world as it should be and "pragmatists" who see the world as it is. Neither approach necessarily denies the importance of human rights, but there are differences in priority and strategy. Pragmatists might argue that it is better to maintain relations with a nation violating human rights in order to be able to exercise some influence over it in the future, or that other policy considerations must be weighed along with those of human rights in establishing foreign policy. Moralists would prefer to bring pressure by isolating and condemning a nation that violates international standards.

These different approaches have been reflected in the U.S. policy shifts toward Latin America. In the 1950s, human rights considerations were secondary to opposing the spread of communism in the hemisphere, and the United States was willing to support governments that violated human rights as long as they were anticommunist allies. During the 1960s, this policy continued, but increasing and systematic abuses by military regimes in Brazil, Uruguay, Chile, Nicaragua, and elsewhere in Latin America began to elicit some changes. In 1977, President Carter initiated a new policy in which human rights considerations would be given high priority in U.S. foreign policy. The U.S. refusal to support or aid governments that violated human rights contributed to the weakening of some regimes and stimulated resistance to human rights violations in Latin America, but by the 1980s a more pragmatic approach had returned to U.S. policy. Criticism of human rights violations sometimes was made selectively, and abuses in "friendly" governments were dismissed. The extent to which human rights concerns must be balanced against issues such as security, the maintenance of peace, and nonintervention continues to preoccupy policymakers.

Attention to human rights will continue to play an important role in international affairs. Problems of definition still remain, and there is no universal agreement on the exact nature of human rights. Controversy on the weight of political and civil rights and social, cultural, and economic rights continues to divide richer and poorer nations. Still, the United Nations Declaration of Human Rights, to which 160 nations are signatories, provides a basic guide and an outline for the future.

Questions: Why might various regimes oppose human rights, and on what basis? Is the human rights movement a Western replacement for imperialism as a way to exert international political influence? Have international human rights movements produced political change?

Figure 38.8. *The right to a secure life became the goal of many political movements. Here, in a church-sponsored demonstration in São Paulo, Brazil, women and men seek "Land and Peace for All Peoples."*

SOCIETIES IN SEARCH OF CHANGE

❖ *Social relations changed slowly in Latin America. Inequalities based on ethnicity continued in some places. Women had entered the labor force in large numbers but began to gain the vote only after 1929. However, their status was in many ways closer to that of women in western Europe than to those of Asia or Africa. Population growth, urbanization, and the migration of workers continued to challenge the region as both politicians and artists tried to identify and confront persistent problems.*

Despite the structural, political, and international conditions that have frustrated Latin American attempts at profound reform, there have been great changes during the 20th century. Problems of ethnicity, gender, and class continue to influence many of these societies. The movement of populations and their settlement has also been a major feature of the

century. These aspects of social life are just two of the continuing historical processes of Latin America.

Social and gender relations have changed during the century. We have already seen how countries such as Mexico, Peru, and Bolivia sought to enfranchise their Indian populations during this century in different ways and with differing degrees of success. National ideologies and actual practice often are not the same, and discrimination on the basis of ethnicity continues in many places. To be called Indian is still an insult in many places in Latin America. Although ethnic and cultural mixture characterizes many Latin American populations and makes Indian and African elements important features of national identity, relations with Indian populations often continue to be marked by exploitation and discrimination in nations as diverse as Brazil, Nicaragua, and Guatemala.

Slow Change in Women's Roles

The role of women has changed slowly. After World War I, women in Latin America continued to live under inequalities in the workplace and in politics. Women were denied the right to vote anywhere in Latin America until Ecuador enfranchised women in 1929 and Brazil and Cuba did the same in 1932. Throughout most of the region, those examples were not followed until the 1940s and 1950s. In some nations, the traditional associations of women with religion and the Catholic church in Hispanic life made reformers and revolutionaries fear that women would become a conservative force in national politics. This attitude, combined with traditional male attitudes that women should be concerned only with home and family, led to a continued exclusion of women from political life. In response, women formed various associations and clubs and began to push for the vote and other issues of interest to them.

Feminist organizations, suffrage movements, and international pressures eventually combined to bring about change. In Argentina, 15 bills for female suffrage were introduced in the senate before the vote was won in 1945. Sometimes the victory was a matter of political expediency for those in power: In the Dominican Republic and some other countries, the enfranchisement of women was a strategy used by conservative groups to add more conservative voters to the electorate in an effort to hold off political change. In Argentina, recently enfranchised women became a major pillar of the Peronist regime, although that regime suppressed female political opponents such as Victoria Ocampo, editor of the important literary magazine *Sur*.

Women eventually discovered that the ability to vote did not in itself guarantee political rights or the ability to have their specific issues heard. After achieving the vote, women tended to join the national political parties, where traditional prejudices against women in public life limited their ability to influence political programs. In Argentina, Brazil, Colombia, and Chile, for example, the integration of women into national political programs has been slow, and women have not participated in proportion to their numbers. In a few cases, however, such as in the election of Perón in Argentina in 1946 and Eduardo Frei in Chile in 1964, or in the popular opposition to Salvador Allende in 1973, women played a crucial role.

Some of the earliest examples of mobilization of women and their integration into the national labor force of various Latin American nations came in the period just before World War I and continued thereafter. The classic roles of women as homemakers, mothers, and agricultural workers were expanded as women entered the industrial labor force in growing numbers. By 1911 in Argentina, for example, women made up almost 80 percent of the textile and clothing industry's workers. But women found that their salaries often were below those of comparable male workers and that their jobs, regardless of the skill levels demanded, were considered unskilled and thus less well paid. Under these conditions, women, like other workers, joined the anarchist, socialist, and other labor unions and organizations.

Labor organizations are only a small part of the story of women in the labor force. In countries such as Peru, Bolivia, and Ecuador, women working in the markets control much small-scale commerce and have become increasingly active politically. In the growing service sectors, women have also become an important part of the labor force. Shifts in attitudes about women's roles have come more slowly than political and economic changes. Even in revolutionary Cuba, where a Law of the Family guaranteed equal rights and responsibilities within the home, enforcement has been difficult.

By the mid-1990s, the position of women in Latin America was closer to that in western Europe and North America than to the other areas of the world. Women made up 9 percent of the legislators in Latin America, a percentage higher than in any other region of the world. They also held 9 percent of the cabinet posts, standing second only to North America's 12 percent. In terms of demographic patterns, health, education, and place in the work force, the comparative position of women reinforced Latin America's intermediate position between the developed nations and the Third World.

The Movement of People

In 1950, the populations of North America (United States and Canada) and Latin America were both about 165 million, but by 1985 Latin America's population had grown to more than 400 million, compared with 265 million for North America. Declining mortality and continuing high fertility were responsible for this situation.

At the beginning of the 20th century, the major trend of population movement was immigration to Latin America, but the region has long experienced internal migration and the movement of people within the hemisphere. By the 1980s, this movement had reached significant levels, fed by the flow of workers seeking jobs, the demands of capital for cheap labor, and the flight of political refugees seeking basic freedoms. In the 1920s, Mexican workers crossed the border to the United States in large numbers at the same time Guatemalans were crossing the border to Mexico to work on coffee estates. During World War II, government programs to supply laborers were set up between the United States and Mexico, but these were always accompanied by extralegal migration, which fluctuated with the economy. Conditions for migrant laborers often were deplorable, although the extension of social welfare to them in the 1960s began to address some of the problems. By the 1970s, more than 750,000 illegal Mexican migrants a year were crossing the border—some more than once—as the United States continued to attract migrants.

This internationalization of the labor market was comparable in many ways with the movement of workers from poorer countries such as Turkey, Morocco, Portugal, and Spain to the stronger economies of West Germany and France. In Latin America it also reflected the fact that industrialization in the 20th century depended on highly mechanized industry that did not create enough new jobs to meet the needs of the growing population. Much of the migration has been to the United States, but there has also been movement across Latin American frontiers: Haitians migrate to work in the Dominican Republic, and Colombians illegally migrate to Venezuela. By the 1970s, about 5 million people per year were migrating in Latin America and the Caribbean.

Politics has also been a major impulse for migration. Haitians fleeing political repression and abysmal conditions have risked great dangers in small open boats to reach the United States. One of the great political migrations of the century has been caused by the Cuban Revolution. Beginning in 1959, when the Cuban middle class fled socialism, and continuing into the 1980s with the flight of Cuban workers, almost 1 million Cubans left the island. The revolutionary upheaval in Nicaragua and political violence in Central America have contributed to the flight of refugees. Often, it is difficult to separate political and economic factors in the movement of people from their homelands.

International migration is only part of the story. During the 20th century, there has been a marked movement in Latin America from rural to urban areas. Whereas in the 19th century, Latin America was an agrarian region, by the 1980s about one-half of the population lived in cities of more than 20,000, and more than 25 of these cities had populations of more than 1 million. Some of these cities had reached enormous size. In 1988 Mexico City had more than 16 million inhabitants, São Paulo had 10 million, and Buenos Aires had 8 million. Latin America was by far the most urbanized area of the developing world and only slightly less urbanized than western Europe.

The problem is not simply size but rate of growth. The urban populations have grown at a rate about three times that of the population as a whole, which itself has grown rapidly. Urban economies have not been able to create enough jobs for the rapidly increasing population. Often recent migrants lived in marginal neighborhoods or in shantytowns, which have become characteristic of the rapidly growing cities of Latin America. These favelas, to use the Brazilian term, have created awful living conditions, but over time some have become poorer neighborhoods within the cities, and community cooperation and action within them have secured basic urban services.

In socialist Cuba, a concerted effort to deemphasize Havana and other large cities and reverse the rural–urban migration pattern was made, but in most of the region, urbanization has continued as growing populations seek better opportunities. In part, this movement is explained by a general population growth rate of more than 2.5 percent per year since the 1960s.

Although Latin American urbanization has increased rapidly since 1940, the percentage of its people living in cities is still less than in western Europe but more than in Asia and Africa. Unlike the 19th-century European experience, the lack of employment in Latin American cities has kept rural migrants from becoming part of a laboring class with a strong identification with fellow workers. Those who do succeed in securing industrial jobs often join paternalistic labor organizations that are linked to the government. Thus, there is a separation between the chronically underemployed urban lower class and the industrial labor force. Whereas industrialization and urbanization promoted a strong class solidarity in 19th-century Europe, which led to the gains of organized labor, in contemporary Latin America nationalist and populist politics have weakened the ability of the working class to operate effectively in politics.

Cultural Reflections of Despair and Hope

Latin America remains an amalgamation of cultures and peoples trying to adjust to changing world realities. Protestant denominations have made some inroads, but the vast majority of Latin Americans are still Catholic. Hispanic traditions of family, gender relations, business, and social interaction influence everyday life and help to determine responses to the modern world.

Latin American popular culture remains vibrant. It draws on African and Indian traditional crafts, images, and techniques but arranges them in new ways. Also part of popular culture are various forms of Latin American music. The Argentine tango of the turn of the century began in the music halls of lower-class working districts of Buenos Aires and became an international craze. The African-influenced Brazilian samba and the Caribbean salsa have spread widely, a Latin American contribution to world civilization.

The struggle for social justice, economic security, and political formulas in keeping with the cultural and social realities of their nations has provided a dynamic tension that has produced tremendous artistic achievements. Latin American poets and novelists have gained worldwide recognition. We have already noted the artistic accomplishments of the Mexican Revolution. In 1922, Brazilian artists, composers, and authors staged a Modern Art Week in São Paulo, which emphasized a search for a national artistic expression that reflected Brazilian realities.

That theme also preoccupied authors elsewhere in Latin America. The social criticism of the 1930s produced powerful realist novels, which revealed the exploitation of the poor, the peasantry, and the Indians. Whether in the heights of the Andes or in the dark streets of the growing urban slums, the plight of the common folk provided a generation of authors with themes worthy of their effort. Social and political criticism has remained a central feature of Latin American literature and art and has played an important role in the development of newer art forms such as film.

The inability to bring about social justice or to influence politics has also sometimes led Latin American artists and intellectuals to follow other paths. In the 1960s a wave of literature took place in which novels that mixed the political, the historical, the erotic, and the fantastic were produced by a generation of authors who found the reality of Latin America too absurd to be described by the traditional forms or logic. Writers such as the Argentine Jorge Luis Borges (1899–1980) and the Colombian Gabriel García Marquez (b. 1928) won acclaim throughout the world. García Marquez's *One Hundred Years of Solitude* (1967) used the history of a family in a mythical town called Macondo as an allegory of Latin America and traced the evils that befell the family and the community as they moved from naive isolation to a maturity that included oppression, exploitation, war, revolution, and natural disaster but never subdued the spirit of its people. In that way, his book outlined the trajectory of Latin America in the 20th century.

Conclusion

Struggling Toward the Future

In the 1990s, Latin America continued to search for economic growth, social justice, and political stability. No easy solutions were available. In many ways, Latin American societies remained "unrevolutionary," unable to bring about needed changes because of deeply entrenched class interests, international conditions, or power politics. However, the struggle for change had produced some important results. The Mexican and Cuban revolutions brought profound changes in those countries and had a broad impact on the rest of the hemisphere, either as models to copy or as dangers to be avoided. Other nations, such as Bolivia, Peru, and Nicaragua, attempted their own versions of radical change with greater or lesser success. New forms of politics, sometimes populist and sometimes militarist, were tried. New political and social ideas, such as those of liberation theology, grew out of the struggle to find a just and effective formula for change. Latin American authors and artists served as a conscience for their societies and received worldwide recognition for their depiction of the sometimes bizarre reality they observed. Although tremendous problems continued to face the region, Latin America remained the most advanced part of the developing world.

Further Readings

A considerable literature in many disciplines deals with Latin America as a whole, and there are many country-specific studies. Two good introductory texts, both of which present variations of the "dependency" interpretation, are E. Bradford Burns's *Latin America: A Concise Interpretative History* (4th ed., 1986) and Thomas E. Skidmore and Peter H. Smith's *Modern Latin America* (1989). An excellent overview of Latin American literature and art is provided in Jean Franco's *The Modern Culture of Latin America* (2nd ed., 1970). Aspects of population history are discussed in Nicholas Sánchez-Albornoz's *The Population of Latin America* (1970) and Magnus Morner's *Adventurers and Proletarians: The Story of Migrants in Latin America* (1985). The role of women is presented briefly in June Hahner's *Women in Latin American History* (1976). A great deal on Latin American politics and social conditions can be gathered from the Internet. From a well-researched critical stance, see the North American Congress on Latin America (NACLA) reports (www.nacla.org).

The economic history of Latin America is summarized in the classic by Brazilian economist Celso Furtado, *Economic Development of Latin America* (2nd ed., 1976) and in John Sheahan's *Patterns of Development in Latin America* (1987). Two excellent studies of labor that have different emphases are Hobart Spalding Jr.'s *Organized Labor in Latin America* (1977) and Charles Berquist's *Labor in Latin America* (1986). An overview is provided by Richard Salvucci, ed. in *Latin America and the World Economy* (1996).

There are many good studies of Latin American politics, but Guillermo O'Donnell's *Modernization and Bureaucratic Authoritarianism* (1973) has influenced much recent scholarship. The role of the United States is discussed in Abraham Lowenthal's *Partners in Conflict: The United States and Latin America* (1987). Lester D. Langley's *The United States and the Caribbean in the Twentieth Century* (4th ed., 1989) gives a clear account of the recent history in that region, and Walter La Feber's *Inevitable Revolutions* (1984) is a critical assessment of U.S. policy in Central America. Lars Schoultz's *Human Rights and United States Policy Toward Latin America* (1981) details the influence of human rights on foreign policy.

A few good monographs on important topics represent the high level of scholarship on Latin America. Alan Knight's *The Mexican Revolution*, 2 vols. (1986) and John M. Hart's *Revolutionary Mexico* (1987) provide excellent analyses of that event. Freidrich Katz' *The Life and Times of Pancho Villa* (1998) is an outstanding biography. Florencia Mallon's *The Defense of Community in Peru's Central Highlands* (1983) looks at national change from a

TABLE 38-1
Population of Capital Cities as a Percentage of Total Population in Ten Latin American Nations

Nation	Capital	1880	1905	1930	1960	1983
Brazil	Rio de Janeiro	3	4	4	7	4*
Mexico	Mexico City	3	3	5	15	20
Argentina	Buenos Aires	12	20	20	32	34
Columbia	Bogotá	1	2	2	8	11
Peru	Lima	3	3	5	19	27
Chile	Santiago	6	10	13	22	37
Uruguay	Montevideo	12	30	28	31	40
Venezuela	Caracas	3	4	7	20	18
Cuba	Havana	13	15	15	18	20
Panama	Panama City	7	14	16	25	20

*No longer the capital city.

Source: From J. P. Cole, *Latin America: An Economic and Social Geography* (1965), 417.

community perspective. Robert Potash's *The Army and Politics in Argentina 1945–1962* (1980) is one of the best in-depth studies of a Latin American military establishment, and Richard Gott's *Guerilla Movements in Latin America* (1972) presents analysis and documents on the movements seeking revolutionary change. On the cultural aspects of the US influence on Latin America there is Gilbert Joseph, et. al. Eds., *Close Encounters Empire* (1998).

On the Web

The revolutions in Chile (http://www.neravt.com/left/allende.htm), Cuba (http://www.msstate.edu/Archives/History/text/ wolfe.html), Guatemala (www.gettysburg.edu/~mbecker/las273/guatemala/guatemala.html) and Mexico (http://ac.acusd.edu/History/projects/border/ page01.html) inspired both joy and deadly reaction.

The leaders of these movements, such as Jacobo Arbenz of Guatemala (http://www.multimedia.calpoly.edu/libarts/1call/Arbenz~1.htm), Cuba's Castro (http://cnn.com/resources/newsmakers/world/ namerica/castro.html) and Mexico's Emilio Zapata (http://www.

indians.org/welker/zapata.htm), often seem larger than life; none more so than Che Guevara (http://www.pbs.org/newshour/forum/november97/che.html), whose global reach can be gauged by a German exhibition of political posters devoted to his career at http://www.sul.stanford.edu/depts/hasrg/german/exhibit/GDRposters/che.html.

The hopes of many Latin Americans for a more egalitarian society were celebrated in the works of artists such as Diego Rivera (http://www.arts~history.mx/museomural.html and http://www.diegorivera.com/index.htm) and Jose Orozco (http://www.wfu.edu/academic-departments/History/Fyprojects/Kmason/Orozo.htm). These hopes were ultimately broken on the anvil of the Cold War (http://www.sfu.edu/~hsa/ex-post-facto/guat.html) and (http://turnerlearning.com/cnn/coldwar/backyard/byrd_ttl.html). They now largely rest with those who see the free market as the solution to poverty and inequality. There are doubts, however, that the free market is the panacea for the region's longstanding economic and social ills (http://owl.temple.edu/economics/econ52/news_clips/ ForeignTrade/1_1_99NAFTA), a doubt that is particularly strong among the Mayan farmers of Chiapas (http://www.igc.org/igc/pn/hg/chis.html.).

Chapter 39

Decolonization and the Decline of the European World Order

As this photograph of British forces near the walls of Jerusalem in 1929 suggests, both the British and French increased their empires in the 20th century by moving into areas like the Middle East that had not yet been colonized. But the sorry mess that colonial administrators made of annexed areas only served to underscore the bankrupcy of the European colonial order and hasten its demise.

All the great civilizations of Asia and Africa were shaken to their foundations by Europe's rise to global power in the 18th and 19th centuries. European political, economic, and later cultural dominance forced the thinkers and leaders of ancient centers of civilized development—from China and the Islamic heartlands to south Asia and Sudanic Africa (see Chapters 29, 30, and 32)—to reappraise their own beliefs, institutions, and traditions. However reluctantly, many of these thinkers and politicians came to see that if their civilizations were to be revitalized and freed from European domination, hard decisions had to be made. They had to determine which elements in their own cultures could be preserved and which must be rejected. They also had to decide how much to borrow from the Europeans and what aspects of Western culture could be refused.

Most accounts of African and Asian solutions to these questions stress ideas (such as nationalism and Marxism) and modes of political organization (such as political parties and boycotts) that the colonized peoples borrowed from the Europeans. But the African and Asian responses that eventually forced the Europeans to relinquish their colonial empires were also deeply rooted in their own religions, their long-standing patterns of political mobilization, and other facets of their ancient traditions of civilization. Striking a workable balance between the need to reinvigorate these distinctive civilized traditions and to borrow from the West has proved to be one of the central challenges for 20th-century African and Asian leaders.

In the late 19th century, when the global domination of the European powers peaked, forces were already beginning to build that would eventually lead to the loss of their colonial empires and greatly diminish their role in world affairs. Some of these forces came from within the colonies as a sense of community and common cause began to build among the Western-educated, middle-class groups that emerged in colonized areas of Asia and Africa (see Chapter 30). The political organizations established by these groups, and their efforts to arouse mass nationalist sentiment, increasingly challenged the right of the Europeans to subjugate foreign lands and peoples.

Although violence was sometimes used, particularly in colonial societies with large numbers of European settlers, African and Asian nationalists relied mainly on peaceful mass demonstrations, economic boycotts, and constitutional maneuvers in their struggles for independence. In these protracted contests, leaders such as Mohandas Gandhi and Kwame Nkrumah deftly turned the Europeans' own principles and values, especially those stressing human dignity and civil rights, against the colonial overlords. At the same time, they used indigenous religious beliefs and traditional symbols of legitimacy to rally

1880 c.e.	1890 c.e.	1900 c.e.	1910 c.e.	1920 c.e.	1930 c.e.
1876 Madras famine in India **1882** Orabi revolt in Egypt; British occupation of Egypt **1885** Founding of the Indian Congress party	**1890s** First Egyptian political parties formed **1897** World Zionist Organization founded; West African Aborigines Rights Protection Society founded	**1904–1905** Japanese victory over Russia; British partition of the province of Bengal in India **1906** Dinshawai incident in Egypt; Muslim League founded in India **1909** Morley–Minto political reforms in India	**1913** Rabindranath Tagore wins the Nobel Prize for literature **1914–1918** World War I; main theaters of war in European colonies; Mesopotamia, Arabia and Palestine, and Africa **1915–1916** McMahon-Hussein correspondence **1917** Balfour Declaration **1919** Revolt in Egypt, women a major force in demonstrations; Montagu–Chelmsford reforms in India; Rowlatt Act in India first all-India civil disobedience movement	**1920s** Pan–African Congresses in Paris; beginnings of the négritude movement **1921** René Maran wins the French Prix Goncourt for *Batouala* **1922** British granted the League of Nations mandate for Palestine; first stage in Egyptian independence **1927** Simon Commission in India	**1930s** Great Depression **1931** Gandhi-led Salt March revives Indian Nationalist movement; strikes and rebellion in Sierra Leone **1935** Government of India Act **1936–1939** Arab risings in Palestine

mass support to their cause. The fact that European colonial regimes had been built in collaboration with indigenous elite groups—including princes, landlords, and the new middle classes—and depended for their survival on these groups, as well as on soldiers and police recruited from the colonized peoples, rendered them particularly vulnerable to growing challenges from within.

In addition to internal forces that eroded the European colonial order, growing conflicts between the Western powers dealt heavy blows to the imperial edifice. The rivalries between the great powers that helped cause the late 19th-century scramble for colonies also contributed to the outbreak of the series of global conflicts that set the framework for 20th-century global history. Thus, World War I cast doubt on the Europeans' claims that by virtue of their racial superiority they were the fittest of all peoples to rule the globe.

The social and economic disruptions caused by the war in key colonies such as Egypt, India, and the Ivory Coast made it possible for nationalist agitators to build a mass base for their anti-colonial movements. The Great Depression of the 1930s, which hit most of the colonies very hard, gave further strength to the nationalist cause. Despite the ultimate victory of the old colonial powers over Nazi Germany and Japan, World War II dealt a series of crushing blows to the European colonial order. Within decades of the end of that conflict, most of Africa and Asia had been liberated from European rule.

This chapter explores several phases of the decolonization process, beginning with the first stirrings of nationalism in India and Egypt in the late 19th century. The sections that follow examine the interplay between international events, such as those associated with the two world wars and the Great Depression, and conditions and movements in the colonies. Because it is impossible to relate the history of the independence struggles in each of the colonies, key movements, such as those in India, Egypt, and British and French West Africa, are considered in some depth. These specific movements are then related to broader patterns in African and Asian decolonization or, in the case of South Africa, the winning of independence for a small minority of the colonial population.

1940 c.e.	1950 c.e.	1960 c.e.
1941–1945 World War II; main theatres of war in European colonies; North Africa, Southeast Asia, and Pacific Islands **1941** Fall of Singapore to the Japanese **1942** Cripps Mission to India; Quit India movement **1947** India and Pakistan gain independence **1948** Israel–Palestine partition, first Arab–Israeli war; beginning of apartheid legislation in South Africa	**1957** Ghana established as first independent African nation **1958** Afrikaner Nationalist party declares independence of South Africa	**1960** Congo granted independence from Belgian rule **1962** Algeria wins independence

PROTOTYPES FOR THE INDEPENDENCE STRUGGLES: THE FIRST PHASE OF DECOLONIZATION IN INDIA AND EGYPT

■■ *Because India and much of southeast Asia had been colonized long before Africa, movements for independence arose in Asian colonies somewhat earlier than in their African counterparts. By the end of the 19th century, the Western-educated minority of the colonized in India and the Philippines had been organized politically for decades. Their counterparts in Burma and the Netherlands Indies were also beginning to form associations to give voice to their political concerns. Because of India's size and the pivotal role it played in the British Empire (by far the largest of the European imperialist empires), the Indian nationalist movement pioneered patterns of nationalist challenge and European retreat that were followed in many other colonies. Although it had been under British control for only a matter of decades,*

Egypt also proved an influential center of nationalist organization and resistance in the pre–World War I era.

Local conditions elsewhere in Asia and in Africa led to important variations on the sequence of decolonization worked out in India and Egypt. But key themes—such as the lead taken by Western-educated elites, the importance of charismatic leaders in the spread of the anticolonial struggle to the peasant and urban masses, and a reliance on nonviolent forms of protest—were repeated again and again in other colonial settings.

India: The Makings of the Nationalist Challenge to the British Raj

The *Indian National Congress party* led the Indians to independence and has governed through most of the postcolonial era. It grew out of regional associations of Western-educated Indians that were originally more like study clubs than political organizations. These associations were centered in the cities of Bombay, Poona, Calcutta, and Madras (see Map 39.1). The Congress party that Indian leaders formed in 1885 had the blessing of a number of high-ranking British officials. These officials saw it as a forum through which educated Indians could make their opinions known to the government, thereby heading off potential discontent and political protest.

For most of its first decades, the Congress party, some of whose members are shown in Figure 39.1, served these purposes quite well. The organization had no mass base and very few ongoing staff members or full-time politicians who could sustain lobbying efforts on issues raised at its annual meetings. Some members of the Congress party voiced concern about the growing poverty of the Indian masses and the drain of wealth from the subcontinent to Great Britain. But the Congress party's debates and petitions to the government were dominated by elite-centric issues, such as removing barriers to Indian employment in the colonial bureaucracy and increasing Indian representation in all-Indian and local legislative bodies. Most of the members of the early Congress party were firmly loyal to the British rulers and confident that once their grievances were made known to the government, they would be remedied.

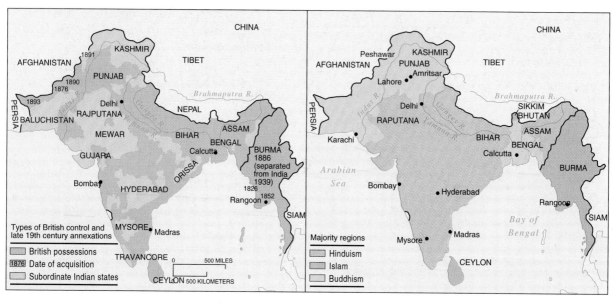

Map 39.1 *British India in the Nationalist Era*

However, many Western-educated Indians were increasingly troubled by growing British racism. They were convinced that this had much to do with their poor salaries and limited opportunities for advancement in the colonial administration. In their annual meetings, members of the Congress, who were now able to converse and write in a common English language, discovered that no matter where they came from in India, they were treated in a similar fashion. The Indians' shared grievances, their similar educational and class backgrounds, and their growing contacts through the Congress party gave rise to a sense of common Indian identity that had never before existed in a south Asian environment that was more diverse linguistically, religiously, and ethnically than Europe.

Social Foundations of a Mass Movement

By the end of the 19th century, the Western-educated elites had also begun to grope for causes that would draw a larger segment of the Indian population into their growing nationalist community. More than a century of British rule had generated in many areas of India the social and economic disruptions and the sort of discontent that produced recruits for nationalist campaigns. Indian businesspeople, many of

whom would become major financial backers of the Congress party, were angered by the favoritism the British rulers showed to British investors in establishing trade policies in India. Indian political leaders increasingly stressed these inequities and the more general loss to the Indian people resulting from what they called the drain of Indian resources under colonial rule. Although the British rebuttal was that a price had to be paid for the peace and good government that had come with colonial rule, nationalist thinkers pointed out that the cost was too high.

A large portion of the Indian government budget went to cover the expenses of the huge army that mainly fought wars elsewhere in the British Empire. The Indian people also paid for the generous salaries and pensions of British administrators, who occupied positions that the Indians themselves were qualified to assume. Whenever possible, as in the purchase of railway equipment or steel for public works projects, the government bought goods manufactured in Great Britain. This practice buttressed a British economy that was fast losing ground to the United States and Germany. It also maintained the classic colonial relationship between a manufacturing European colonizer and its raw-material–producing overseas dependencies.

In the villages of India, the shortcomings of British rule were equally apparent by the late 19th cen-

Figure 39.1 *As this photograph of some of the leaders of the "Non-Cooperative" Congress party illustrates, by the early 1920s even moderate Indian nationalist leaders were moving away from loyalty to the British and extensive Anglicization. In the decades that followed, the mix of Western coats and ties and Indian headgear and dhotis increasingly gave way to apparel that was entirely Indian, even among highly Anglicized nationalist families such as the Nehrus.*

tury. The needs of the British home economy often dictated policies that pushed the Indian peasantry toward producing cash crops such as cotton, jute, and indigo. The decline in food production that resulted played a major role in the regional famines that struck repeatedly in the pre–World War I era. Radical Indian nationalists often charged that the British were indifferent to food shortages and disease outbreaks, and that they did far too little to alleviate the suffering that resulted. In many areas, landlessness and chronic poverty, already a problem before British rule was established, increased. In most places, British measures to control indebtedness and protect small landholders and tenants were too little and came too late.

The Rise of Militant Nationalism

Some of the issues Indian nationalist leaders stressed in their early attempts to build a mass base had great appeal for devout Hindus. This was particularly true of campaigns to protect cows, which have long had a special status for the Hindu population of south Asia. But these religiously oriented causes often alienated the adherents of other faiths, especially the Muslims (Map 39.1). Not only did Muslims eat beef, but they made up nearly one-fourth of the population of the Indian Empire. Some leaders, such as *B. G. Tilak*, were little concerned by this split. They believed that because Hindus made up the overwhelming majority of the Indian population, nationalism should be built on appeals to Hindu religiosity. Tilak worked to promote the restoration and revival of what he believed to be the ancient traditions of Hinduism. On this basis, he opposed women's education and the raising of the very low marriage age for women. Tilak also turned festivals for Hindu gods into occasions for mass political demonstrations. He broke with more moderate leaders of the

Congress party by demanding the boycott of British-manufactured goods. Tilak also sought to persuade his fellow Indians to refuse to serve in the colonial administration and military. Tilak demanded full independence, with no deals or delays, and threatened violent rebellion if the British failed to comply.

Tilak's oratorical skills and religious appeal made him the first Indian nationalist leader with a genuine mass following. Nonetheless, his popularity was confined mainly to his home base in Bombay and in nearby areas in western India. At the same time, his promotion of a very reactionary sort of Hinduism offended and frightened moderate and progressive Hindus, the Muslims, and followers of other religions, such as the Sikhs. When evidence was found connecting Tilak's writings to underground organizations that advocated violent revolt, the British, who had grown increasingly uneasy about his radical demands and mass appeal, arrested and imprisoned him. Six years of exile for Tilak in Burma set back the mass movement he had begun to build among the Hindu population.

The other major threat to the British in India before World War I also came from Hindu communalists who advocated the violent overthrow of the colonial regime. But unlike Tilak and his followers, those who joined the terrorist movement favored clandestine operations over mass demonstrations. Although terrorists were active in several parts of India by the 1890s, those in Bengal built perhaps the most extensive underground network. Considerable numbers of young Bengalis, impatient with the gradualist approach advocated by moderates in the Congress party, were attracted to underground secret societies. These were led by quasireligious, guru-style leaders who exhorted them to build up their physiques with Western-style calisthenics and learn how to use firearms and make bombs. British officials and government buildings were the major targets of terrorist assassination plots and sabotage. But on occasion the young revolutionaries also struck at European civilians and collaborators among the Indian population. But the terrorists' small numbers and limited support from the colonized populace as a whole rendered them highly vulnerable to British repressive measures. The substantial resources the British devoted to crushing these violent threats to their rule had checked the terrorist threat by the outbreak of World War I.

Tilak's removal and the repression campaigns against the terrorists strengthened the hand of the more moderate politicians of the Congress party in the years before the war. Western-educated Indian lawyers came to be the dominant force in nationalist politics, and—as the careers of Gandhi, Jinnah, and Nehru demonstrate—they would provide many of the movement's key leaders throughout the struggle for independence. The approach of those who advocated a peaceful, constitutionalist route to decolonization was given added appeal by timely political concessions on the part of the British. The *Morley–Minto reforms* of 1909 provided educated Indians with greater opportunities to vote for and serve on local and all-India legislative councils.

Egypt and the Rise of Nationalism in the Middle East

Egypt is the one country in the Afro-Asian world in which the emergence of nationalism preceded European conquest and domination (Map 39.2). The uprisings touched off by the mutiny of Ahmad Orabi and other Egyptian officers (see Chapter 32), which led to the British occupation in 1882, were aimed at liberating the Egyptian people from their alien Turkish overlords as well as the meddling Europeans. British occupation meant double colonization for the Egyptian people by the Turkish khedives (who were left in power) and their British advisors.

In the decades after the British conquest, government policy was dominated by the strong-willed and imperious *Lord Cromer*. As High Commissioner of Egypt, he pushed for much-needed economic reforms that reduced but could not eliminate the debts of the puppet khedival regime. Cromer also oversaw sweeping reforms in the bureaucracy and the construction of irrigation systems and other public works projects. But the prosperity the British congratulated themselves for having brought to Egypt by the first decade of the 20th century was enjoyed largely by tiny middle and elite classes, often at the expense of the mass of the population. The leading beneficiaries included foreign merchants, the Turco-Egyptian political elite, a small Egyptian bourgeoisie in Cairo and other towns in the Nile delta, and the ayan, or the great landlords in the rural areas.

The latter were clearly among the biggest gainers. The British had been forced to rely heavily on local, estate-owning notables in extending their control into the rural areas. As a result, the ayan,

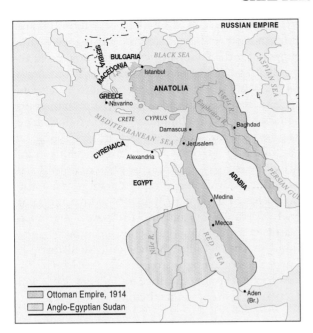

Map 39.2 *The Middle East, 1914–1922*

business and professional families that made up much of this new middle class. Even nationalist leaders who came from rural ayan families built their following among the urban middle classes. In contrast to India, where lawyers predominated in the nationalist leadership, in Egypt, journalists (some educated in France) led the way.

In the 1890s and early 1900s, newspapers in Arabic (and to a lesser extent French and English) vied to expose the mistakes of the British and the corruption of the khedival regime. Egyptian writers also attacked the British for their racist arrogance and their monopolization of well-paying positions in the Egyptian bureaucracy. Like their Indian counterparts, Egyptian critics argued that these could just as well have been filled by university-educated Egyptians. In the 1890s, the first nationalist party was formed. But again in contrast to India, where the Congress party dominated the nationalist movement from the outset, a variety of rival parties proliferated in Egypt. There were three main alternatives by 1907. But none could be said to speak for the great majority of the Egyptians, who were illiterate, poorly paid, and largely ignored urban laborers and rural farmers.

In the years before the outbreak of World War I in 1914, heavy-handed British repression was necessary on several occasions to put down student riots or retaliate for assassination attempts against high British and Turco-Egyptian officials. Despite the failure of the nationalist parties to unite or build a mass base in the decades before the war, the extent of the hostility felt by the Egyptian masses was demonstrated by the *Dinshawai incident* in 1906. This confrontation between the British and their Egyptian subjects exemplified the racial arrogance of most of the European colonizers. Although the incident at Dinshawai was seemingly a small clash resulting in limited numbers of fatalities, the excessive British response to it did much to undermine whatever support remained for their continued presence in Egypt.

Most Egyptian villages raised large numbers of pigeons, which were an important supplement to the meager peasant diet. Over the years, some of the British had turned the hunting of the pigeons of selected villages into a holiday pastime. A party of British officers on leave were hunting the pigeons of the village of Dinshawai in the Nile delta

not the impoverished mass of rural cultivators and laborers, received most of the benefits of the new irrigation works, the railways, and the increasing orientation of Egyptian agriculture to producing raw cotton for the export market. Unfettered by legal restrictions, the ayan amassed ever larger estates by turning small land owners into landless tenants and laborers. As their wealth grew, the contrast between the landlords' estate houses and the thatch and mud-walled villages of the great mass of the peasantry became more and more pronounced. Bored by life in the provinces, the landed classes spent most of their time in the fashionable districts of Cairo or in resort towns such as Alexandria. Their estates were run by hired managers, who were little more than rent collectors as far as the peasants were concerned.

With the khedival regime and the great landlords closely allied to the British overlords, resistance to the occupation was left mainly to the middle class. Since the mid-19th century, this new and small social class had been growing in numbers and influence, mainly in the towns in the Nile delta. With the memory of Orabi's revolt in 1882 still fresh, the cause of Egyptian independence was taken up mainly by the sons of the *effendi*, the prosperous when they accidentally shot the wife of the prayer leader of the local mosque. The angry villagers mobbed the greatly outnumbered shooting party, which in panic fired on the villagers. Both the villagers and the British soldiers suffered casualties in the clashes that followed. In reprisal for the death of one of the officers, the British hanged four of the villagers. Although the actual hanging was not photographed, the building of the scaffolding was captured in the photo in Figure 39.2. The British also ordered that other villagers connected to the incident be publicly flogged or sentenced to varying terms of hard labor.

The harsh British reprisals aroused a storm of protest in the Egyptian press and among the nationalist parties. Some Egyptian leaders later recalled that the incident convinced them that cooperation with the British was unacceptable and fixed their resolve

to agitate for an end to Egypt's occupation. Popular protests in several areas, and the emergence of ayan support for the nationalist cause, also suggested the possibility of building a mass base for anti-British agitation. More than anything else, the incident at Dinshawai had galvanized support for nationalist agitation across the communal and social boundaries that had so long divided the peoples of Egypt.

By 1913, the British had been sufficiently intimidated by the rising tide of Egyptian nationalism to grant a constitution and representation in a parliament elected indirectly by men of wealth and influence. World War I and the British declaration of martial law put a temporary end to nationalist agitation. But, as in India, the war unleashed forces in Egypt that could not be stopped and that would soon lead to the revival of the drive for independence with even greater strength than before.

Figure 39.2 *This photograph, probably taken without the knowledge of the British authorities, shows the construction of the gallows that were used to hang the four peasants who were executed in reprisal for the attacks on British soldiers at Dinshawai in 1906. The conical tower in the distance behind the scaffold was the roost for the pigeons that were the intended targets of the ill-fated hunting party. The Dinshawai incident exemplified the colonizers' tendency to overreact to any sign of overt resistance on the part of the colonized. Their frequent resort to execution and other violent reprisals in these situations was clearly linked to an undercurrent of paranoia that many commentators observed in the tiny communities of European officials, merchants, and planters who lived among large numbers of Africans or Asians.*

WORLD WAR I AND THE POSTWAR CRISIS OF THE EUROPEAN EMPIRES

The nationalist struggle against European colonial domination was given a great boost by the long, devastating war between the European great powers that broke out in 1914. Although the European colonizers had often quarreled over colonial possessions in the late 19th century, during the war they actually fought each other in the colonies for the first time. Major theaters of conflict developed during the war in west and east Africa and especially in the Middle East. British naval supremacy denied the Germans access to their colonies in Africa and the Pacific. With the blockade on their side, the British, French, and Belgians were able to draw heavily on their colonies for soldiers, laborers, and raw materials.

African and Asian soldiers in the hundreds of thousands served both on the Western Front and in the far-flung theaters of war from Egypt, Palestine, and Mesopotamia to east Africa. The French recruited tens of thousands of African and Asian laborers to replace workers in French industrial centers who had been conscripted into the armies fighting on the Western Front. The colonies also supplied food for the home populations of the Entente allies, as well as vital raw materials such as oil, jute, and cotton. Contrary to long-standing colonial policy, the British even encouraged expansion of industrial production in India to supplement the output of their overextended home factories. Thus, the war years contributed to the development in India of the largest industrial sector in the colonized world.

World War I showed the subjugated peoples of Africa and Asia the spectacle of the self-styled civilizers of humankind sending millions of young men to be slaughtered in the trench stalemate on the Western Front. For the first time, African and Asian soldiers were ordered by their European officers to kill other Europeans. In the process, the vulnerability of the seemingly invincible Europeans and the deep divisions between them were revealed. During the war years, European troops in the colonies were withdrawn to meet the need for soldiers on the many war fronts. The garrisons that remained were dangerously understaffed. The need to recall administrative personnel from both British and French colonies meant that colonial officials were compelled to fill their vacated posts with African and Asian administrators, many of whom enjoyed real responsibility for the first time.

To maintain the loyalty of their traditional allies among the colonized and to win the support of the Western-educated elites or new allies such as the Arabs, the British and French made many promises about the postwar settlement. Because these concessions often compromised their prewar dominance or their plans for further colonial expansion, the leaders of the victorious Allies repeatedly reneged on them after the war. The betrayal of these pledges contributed to postwar agitation against the continuation and spread of European colonial domination.

India: Gandhi and the Nationalist Struggle

In the months after the outbreak of the war, the British could take great comfort from the way in which the peoples of the empire rallied to their defense. Though already well on the way to independence, their subjects in the White Dominions—Canada, Australia, and New Zealand—lost no time in declaring war on the Central Powers and raising armies. Dominion troops served with distinction in both the Middle Eastern and European theaters of war. But botched campaigns such as at Gallipoli and the costly offensives on the Somme severely strained relations between the British high command and the colonials. Of the many colonies among the tropical dependencies, none played as critical a role in the British war effort as India. The Indian princes offered war loans, Indian soldiers bore the brunt of the war effort in east Africa and the Middle East, and nationalist leaders, including Gandhi and Tilak, toured India selling British war bonds. But as the war dragged on and Indians died on the battlefields or went hungry at home to sustain a conflict that had little to do with them, signs of unrest spread throughout the subcontinent.

Wartime inflation adversely affected nearly all segments of the Indian population. Indian peasants were angered at the ceilings set on the price of their market produce, despite rising costs. They were often

DOCUMENT

Lessons for the Colonized from the Slaughter in the Trenches

The prolonged and senseless slaughter of the youth of Europe in the trench stalemate on the Western Front did much to erode the image of Europeans as superior, rational, and more civilized beings that they had worked hard to propagate among the colonized peoples in the decades before the Great War. The futility of the seemingly endless slaughter cast doubts on the Europeans' fitness to rule themselves, much less the rest of the world. The destructive uses to which their science and technology were put brought into question the Europeans' long-standing claims that these material advancements demonstrated their intellectual and organizational superiority over all other peoples. The following quotations, taken from the writings of some of the leading thinkers and political leaders of the colonized peoples of Africa and Asia, reflect their disillusionment with the West as a result of the war and the continuing turmoil in Europe in the postwar era.

Rabindranath Tagore, Bengali poet, playwright, and novelist, who was one of the earliest non-European recipients of the Nobel Prize for literature, wrote the following:

> Has not this truth already come home to you now when this cruel war has driven its claws into the vitals of Europe? When her hoard of wealth is bursting into smoke and her humanity is shattered on her battlefields? You ask in amazement what she has done to deserve this? The answer is, that the West has been systematically petrifying her moral nature in order to lay a solid foundation for her gigantic abstractions of efficiency. She has been all along starving the life of the personal man into that of the professional.

Mohandas Gandhi, who emerged in the years after the war as India's leading nationalist figure warned his countrymen:

> India's destiny lies not along the bloody way of the West, but along the bloodless way of peace that comes from a simple and godly life. India is in danger of losing her soul.... She must not, therefore, lazily and helplessly say, "I cannot escape the onrush from the West." She must be strong enough to resist it for her own sake and that of the world. I make bold to say that the Europeans themselves will have to remodel their outlooks if they are not to perish under the weight of the comforts to which they are becoming slaves.

Léopold Sédar Senghor, Senegalese poet and political leader, who is widely regarded as one of the finest 20th-century writers in the French language, wrote in his poem "Snow Upon Paris,"

> Lord, the snow of your Peace is your
> proposal to a divided world to a divided
> Europe
> To Spain torn apart....
> And I forget
> White hands that fired the shots which
> brought the empires crumbling
> Hands that flogged the slaves, that flogged
> You [Jesus Christ]
> Chalk-white hands that buffeted You,
> powdered painted hands that buffeted me
> Confident hands that delivered me to
> solitude to hatred
> White hands that felled the forest of palm
> trees once commanding Africa, in the heart
> of Africa.

Aimé Cesaire, West Indian poet and founder of the négritude (assertion of black culture) movement in the late 1920s, wrote in "Return to My Native Land,"

> Heia [Praise] for those who have never
> invented anything
> those who never explored anything
> those who never tamed anything
> those who give themselves up to the
> essence of all things
> ignorant of surfaces but struck by the
> movement of all things

Questions: On the basis of this sample, what aspects of the West's claims to superiority were called into question by the suicidal conflict of the leading powers within European civilization? What aspects of their own civilizations do these writers champion as alternatives to the ways of the West? Are these writers in danger of stereotyping both the West and their own civilizations?

upset by their inability to sell what they had produced because of shipping shortages linked to the war. Indian laborers saw their already meager wages drop steadily in the face of rising prices. At the same time, their bosses grew rich from profits earned in war production. Many localities suffered from famines, worsened by wartime transport shortages that impeded relief efforts.

After the end of the war in 1918, moderate Indian politicians were frustrated by the British refusal to honor wartime promises. British leaders had promised the Indians that if they continued to support the war effort, India would move steadily to self-government within the empire once the conflict was over. Indian hopes for the fulfillment of these promises were raised by the *Montagu–Chelmsford reforms* of 1919. These measures increased the powers of Indian legislators at the all-India level and placed much of the provincial administration of India under their control. But the concessions granted in the reforms were offset by the passage later in the same year of the *Rowlatt Act*, which placed severe restrictions on key Indian civil rights such as the freedom of the press. These conditions fueled local protest during and immediately after the war. At the same time, a new leader, Mohandas Gandhi, emerged who soon forged this localized protest into a sustained all-India campaign against the policies of the colonial overlords.

Gandhi's remarkable appeal to both the masses and the Western-educated nationalist politicians resulted from a combination of factors. Perhaps the most important was the strategy for protest that he had worked out a decade earlier as the leader of a successful movement of resistance to the restrictive laws imposed on the Indian migrant community in South Africa. Gandhi's stress on nonviolent but aggressive protest tactics endeared him both to the moderates and to more radical elements within the nationalist movement. His advocacy of peaceful boycotts, strikes, noncooperation, and mass demonstrations—which he labeled collectively *satyagraha,* or truth force—proved an effective way to weaken British control while limiting opportunities for violent reprisals that would allow the British to make full use of their superior military strength.

It is difficult to separate Gandhi's approach to mass protest from Gandhi as a person and thinker. Though physically unimposing, he had an inner con-

fidence and sense of moral purpose that sustained his followers and wore down his adversaries. He combined the career of a Western-educated lawyer with the attributes of a traditional Hindu ascetic and guru. The former had exposed him to the world beyond India and gave him an understanding of the strengths and weaknesses of the British colonizers. These qualities and his soon legendary skill in negotiating with the British made it possible for Gandhi to build up a strong following among middle-class, Western-educated Indians, who had long been the dominant force behind the nationalist cause. But the success of Gandhi's protest tactics also hinged on the involvement of ever-increasing numbers of the Indian people in anticolonial resistance. The image of a traditional mystic and guru that Gandhi projected was critical in gaining mass support from peasants and laborers alike. Many of these "ordinary" Indians would walk for miles when Gandhi was on tour. Many did so to honor a saint rather than listen to a political speech. Gandhi's widespread popular appeal, in turn, gave him even greater influence among

Figure 39.3 As this photo of Mahatma Gandhi beside his spinning wheel suggests, he played many roles in the Indian nationalist struggle. The wheel evokes India's traditional status as a textile center and the economic boycotts of British machine-made cloth that were central to Gandhi's civil disobedience campaigns. Gandhi's meditative position projects the image of a religious guru that appealed to large segments of the Indian populace. The simplicity of his surroundings evokes the asceticism and detachment from the material world that had long been revered in Indian culture.

nationalist politicians. The latter were very aware of the leverage his mass following gave to them in their ongoing contests with the British overlords.

The Rise of Communalism and the Beginnings of Political Fragmentation

Gandhi's mystical ascetic side hampered his efforts to reach out to all Indians. Despite his constant stress on religious tolerance and communal harmony, some Muslim leaders mistrusted this Hindu guru and the Congress party politicians ho organized his civil disobedience campaigns. Even though Muslims had been and continued to be prominent leaders in the Congress party, a number of leaders of the Islamic community warned that the party was dominated by Hindus, who had taken much greater advantage of opportunities for higher education and political advancement. To better support their demands for separate electorates and legislative seats, several mostly well-educated and well-to-do Muslims founded a rival party, the *Muslim League,* in 1906. Although the League represented only a small percentage of even the Muslim minority until the 1940s, its presence signified a potentially dangerous potential division within the Indian national movement.

The League's stubbornness was matched on the Hindu side by a number of extremist, communalist parties that were vehemently opposed to Gandhi's call for tolerance and Hindu power sharing with minority religious groups. All the charisma and wisdom Gandhi could muster were not sufficient to bring these fringe groups into the Congress party's mainstream. Leaders of the Muslim League would destroy his vision of a united India; a Hindu extremist eventually took his life.

The success of Gandhian satyagraha tactics in local protest movements paved the way for his sudden emergence as the central figure in the all-Indian nationalist struggle. The India-wide campaign to repeal the Rowlatt Act demonstrated both the strengths and the weaknesses of Gandhi's approach. Congress party organizers rallied mass support for boycotts, noncooperation, and civil disobedience throughout the subcontinent. In fact, the response was so widespread and rapid that it stunned the British and put them on the defensive. But a lack of time and sufficient numbers of trained followers to instruct protesters in the discipline of nonviolent resistance led to

violent reprisals for police repression. Convinced that satyagraha could not be truly carried out under these conditions, Gandhi called off the anti-Rowlatt campaign. His decision delighted the British, who were fearful that it was about to succeed. But it angered many other nationalist politicians, including Jawaharlal Nehru, who like Gandhi was then emerging as one of the foremost leaders of the anticolonial struggle. Gandhi's withdrawal allowed the British to round up and imprison much of the nationalist leadership, including Nehru and Gandhi himself.

Although it was nearly a decade before Gandhi and the Congress party could launch a campaign on a scale comparable to the postwar satyagraha, British relief at the successful repression of dissent was short-lived. Throughout the 1920s, urban lawyers and peasant associations used Gandhian tactics to protest colonial policies and local abuses by both British and Indian officials. By the early 1930s, British insensitivity and the mounting effects of the global Great Depression paved the way for a revival of the civil disobedience campaign on an all-India basis. Growing dissent prompted the British to set up the *Simon Commission* in 1927 to consider future government responses to nationalist demands. Made up entirely of British officials and politicians and focused on tactics of repression, the commission simply aroused greater unrest. For a brief period, hostility to it unified nationalist politicians on both the left and the right and those representing Hindus, Muslims, and Sikhs. The depression created new openings for the revival of the mass struggle for decolonization. In the early 1930s, a sharp fall in the price of agricultural products hit nearly all segments of the rural population, which made up more than 80 percent of the Indian total.

Astutely gauging the mood of the Indian masses, Gandhi launched another round of all-India civil disobedience campaigns with the dramatic Salt March and satyagraha in early 1931. The British alternated between mass jailings, forcible repression, and round-table negotiations with nationalist leaders, especially Gandhi, in the next half decade. They ended by making major concessions to nationalist demands. These were embodied in the *Government of India Act of 1935.* Though retaining control of the central administration, the British agreed to turn the provincial governments over to Indian leaders, who would be chosen by a greatly expanded electorate. The nationalists' assumption of office in 1937 ended the already diminished civil disobedience agitation. This ushered in a period of British–nationalist accommodation that lasted until another global war shook the foundations of the European colonial order.

The Middle East: Betrayal and the Growth of Arab Nationalism

After World War I, resistance to European colonial domination, which had been confined largely to Egypt in the prewar years, spread to much of the rest of the Middle East. With Turkish rule in the area ended by defeat in the war, Arab nationalists in Beirut, Damascus, and Baghdad turned to face the new threat presented by the victorious Entente powers, France and Britain. Betraying promises to preserve Arab independence that the British had made in 1915 and early 1916, French and British forces occupied much of the Middle East in the years after the war. *Hussein, the Sherif of Mecca*, had used these promises to convince the Arabs to rise in support of Britain's war against the Turks, despite the fact that the latter were fellow Muslims. Consequently, the Allies' postwar violation of these pledges humiliated and angered Arabs throughout the Middle East. The occupying European powers faced stiff resistance from the Arabs in each of the *mandates* they carved out in Syria, Iraq, and Lebanon under the auspices of the League of Nations. The Arabs' sense of humiliation and anger was intensified by the disposition of Palestine, where British occupation was coupled with promises of a Jewish homeland (See Map 39.3).

The fact that the British had appeared to promise Palestine, for which they received a League of Nations mandate in 1922, to both the Jewish Zionists and the Arabs during the war greatly complicated an already confused situation. Despite repeated assurances to the Hussein and other Arab leaders that they would be left in control of their own lands after the war, *Lord Balfour*, the British foreign secretary, promised Zionist leaders in 1917 that his government would promote the establishment of a Jewish homeland in Palestine after the war. This pledge fed existing *Zionist* aspirations for the Hebrew people to return to their ancient Middle Eastern lands of origin, which had been nurtured by the Jews of the diaspora for millennia. In the decades before World War I, these dreams led to the formation of a number of organizations. Some of them were dedicated to promoting Jewish emigration to

Palestine; others were committed to establishing a Jewish state there.

These early moves were made in direct response to the persecution of the Jews of eastern Europe in the last decades of the 19th century. Particularly vicious *pogroms*, or violent assaults on the Jewish communities of Russia and Romania in the 1860s and 1870s, convinced Jewish intellectuals such as *Leon Pinsker* that assimilation of the Jews into, or even acceptance by, Christian European nations was impossible. Pinsker and other thinkers called for a return to the Holy Land. Like-minded people founded Zionist organizations, such as the Society for the Colonization of Israel, to promote Jewish migration to Palestine in the late 19th century. Until World War I, the numbers of Jews returning to Palestine were small—in the tens of thousands—although Zionist communities were established on lands purchased in the area.

Until the late 1890s, the Zionist effort was generally opposed by Jews in Germany, France, and other parts of western Europe who enjoyed citizenship and extensive civil rights. In addition, many in these communities had grown prosperous and powerful in their adopted lands. But a major defection to the Zionists occurred in 1894. *Theodor Herzl*, an established Austrian journalist, was stunned by French mobs shouting "death to the Jews" as they

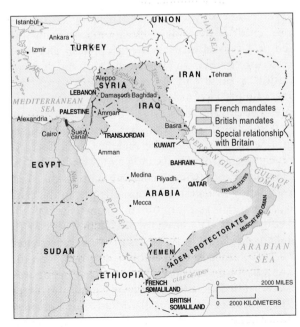

Map 39.3 *The Middle East in the Aftermath of World War I*

taunted an army officer named *Alfred Dreyfus*. Dreyfus was a French Jew who had been falsely accused of passing military secrets to the Germans. His subsequent mistreatment, including exile to the penal colony on Devil's Island, became the flashpoint for years of bitter debate between the left and right in France. Soon after this incident in 1897, Herzl and other prominent western European Jews joined with Jewish leaders from eastern Europe to form the *World Zionist Organization*. As Herzl made clear in his writings, the central aim of this increasingly well-funded organization was to promote Jewish migration to and settlement in Palestine until a Zionist state could be established in the area. Herzl's nationalist ambitions, as well as his indifference to the Arabs already living in the area, were captured in the often-quoted view of one of his close associates that Palestine was "a land without people for a people [the Jews] without a land."

Lord Balfour's promises to the Zionists and the British takeover of Palestine struck the Arabs as a double betrayal of wartime assurances that Arab support for the Entente powers against the Turks would guarantee them independence after the war. This sense of betrayal was a critical source of the growing hostility the Arabs felt toward Jewish emigration to Palestine and their purchase of land in the area. Rising Arab opposition convinced many British officials, especially those who administered Palestine, to severely curtail the open-ended pledges that had been made to the Zionists during the war. This shift led to Zionist mistrust of British policies and open resistance to them. It also fed the Zionists' determination to build up their own defenses against the increasingly violent Arab resistance to the Jewish presence in Palestine.

But British attempts to limit Jewish emigration and settlement were not matched by efforts to encourage, through education and consultation, the emergence of strong leadership among the Arab population of Palestine. Consequently, in the critical struggles and diplomatic maneuvers of the 1930s and 1940s, the Arabs of Palestine were rarely able to speak for themselves. They were represented by Arab leaders from neighboring lands, who did not always understand Palestinian needs and desires. These non-Palestinian spokespersons also often acted more in the interests of Syrian or Lebanese Arabs than those of the Christian and Muslim Arab communities in Palestine.

Revolt in Egypt, 1919

Because Egypt was already occupied by the British when the war broke out, and it had been formally declared a protectorate in 1914, it was not included in the promises made by the British to the Sherif Hussein. As a result, the anticolonial struggle in Egypt was rooted in earlier agitation and the heavy toll the war had taken on the Egyptian people, particularly the peasantry. During the war, the defense of the Suez Canal was one of the top priorities for the British. To guard against possible Muslim uprisings in response to Turkish calls for a holy war, martial law was declared soon after hostilities began. Throughout the war, large contingents of Entente and empire forces were garrisoned in Egypt. They drained the increasingly scarce food supplies of the area. Forced labor and confiscations by the military of the precious draft animals of the peasantry also led to widespread discontent. As the war dragged on, this unrest was further inflamed by spiraling inflation as well as food shortages and even starvation in some areas.

By the end of the war, Egypt was ripe for revolt. Mass discontent strengthened the resolve of the educated nationalist elite to demand a hearing at Versailles, where the victorious Allies were struggling to reach a postwar settlement. When a delegation (*wafd* in Arabic) of Egyptian leaders was denied permission to travel to France to make the case for Egyptian self-determination, most Egyptian leaders resigned from the government and called for mass demonstrations. What followed shocked British officials. Student-led riots touched off outright insurrection over much of Egypt. At one point, Cairo was cut off from the outside world, and much of the countryside was hostile territory for the occupying power. Although the British army was able to restore control, at the cost of scores of deaths, it was clear that some hearing had to be given to Egyptian demands. The emergence of the newly formed *Wafd party* under its hard-driving leader, *Sa'd Zaghlul*, provided the nationalists with both a focus for unified action and a mass base that far excelled any they had attracted before the war.

When a special British commission of inquiry into the causes of the upheaval in Egypt met with widespread civil disobedience and continuing violent opposition, it recommended that the British begin negotiations for an eventual withdrawal from Egypt.

Years of bargaining followed, which led to a highly qualified independence for the Egyptians. British withdrawal occurred in stages, beginning in 1922 and culminating in the British withdrawal to the Suez Canal zone in 1936. Although they pulled out of Egypt proper, the khedival regime was preserved and the British reserved the right to reoccupy Egypt should it be threatened by a foreign aggressor.

Although they had won a significant degree of political independence, the Egyptian leaders of the Wafd party, as well as its rivals in the Liberal Constitutionalist and Union parties, did little to relieve the increasing misery of the Egyptian people. Most Egyptian politicians regarded the winning of office as an opportunity to increase their own and their families' fortunes. Many politicians, both those from ayan households and those from the professional and merchant classes, used their influence and growing wealth to amass huge estates, which were worked by landless tenants and laborers. Locked in personal and interparty quarrels as well as the ongoing contest with the khedival regime for control of the government, few political leaders had the time or inclination to push for the land reforms and public works projects that the peasantry so desperately needed.

The social bankruptcy of the 40 years of nationalist political dominance that preceded the military coup and social revolution led by Gamal Abdul Nasser in 1952 is suggested by some revealing statistics compiled by the United Nations in the early 1950s. By that time, nearly 70 percent of Egypt's cultivable land was owned by 6 percent of the population. Some 12,000 families alone controlled 37 percent of the farmland. As for the mass of the people, 98 percent of the peasants were illiterate, malnutrition was chronic among both urban and rural populations, and an estimated 95 percent of rural Egyptians suffered from eye diseases. Such was the legacy of the very unrevolutionary process of decolonization in Egypt.

The Beginnings of the Liberation Struggle in Africa

Most of Africa had come under European colonial rule only in the decades before World War I. Nonetheless, precolonial missionary efforts had produced small groups of Western-educated Africans in parts of west and south-central Africa by the end of the 19th century. Like their counterparts in India, most Western-educated Africans were loyal to their British and French overlords during World War I. With the backing of both Western-educated Africans and the traditional rulers, the British and especially the French were able to draw on their African possessions for labor and raw materials throughout the war. But this reliance took its toll on their colonial domination in the long run. In addition to local rebellions in response to the forcible recruitment of African soldiers and laborers, the war effort seriously disrupted newly colonized African societies. African merchants and farmers suffered from shipping shortages and the sudden decline in demand for crops such as cocoa. African villagers were not happy to go hungry so that their crops could feed the armies of the Allies. As Lord Lugard, an influential colonial administrator, pointed out, the desperate plight of the British and French also forced them to teach tens of thousands of Africans

> how to kill white men, around whom [they had] been taught to weave a web of sanctity of life. [They] also know how to handle bombs and Lewis guns and Maxims—and [they have] seen the white men budge when [they have] stood fast. Altogether [they have] acquired much knowledge that might be put to uncomfortable use someday.

The fact that the Europeans kept few of the promises of better jobs and public honors, which they had made during the war to induce young Africans to enlist in the armed forces or serve as colonial administrations, contributed to the unrest of the postwar years. This was particularly true of the French colonies, where opportunities for political organization, much less protest, were limited before, during, and after the war. Major strikes and riots broke out in the interwar period. In the British colonies, where there was more tolerance for political organization, there were also strikes and a number of rebellions. Throughout colonized Africa, protest intensified in the 1930s in response to the economic slump brought on by the Great Depression.

Although Western-educated politicians did not link up with urban workers or peasants in most African colonies until the 1940s, disenchanted members of the emerging African elite began to organize in the 1920s and 1930s. In the early stages of this process, charismatic African-American political figures such as *Marcus Garvey* and *W.E.B. Du Bois* had a major impact on emerging African nationalist leaders. In the 1920s, attempts were made to arouse all-Africa loyalties and build *pan-African* organizations. The fact that the leadership of these organizations was mainly African-American and West Indian, and that delegates from colonized areas in Africa itself faced very different challenges under different colonial overlords, had much to do with the fact that pan-Africanism proved unworkable. But its well-attended conferences, especially the early ones in Paris, did much to arouse anticolonial sentiments among Western-educated Africans.

By the mid-1920s, nationalists from French and British colonies were going separate ways. Because of restrictions in the colonies and because small but well-educated groups of Africans were represented in the French Parliament, French-speaking west Africans concentrated their organizational and ideological efforts in Paris in this period. The *négritude* literary movement nurtured by these exiles did much to combat the racial stereotyping that had so long held the Africans in psychological bondage to the Europeans. Writers such as *L. S. Senghor, Léon Damas,* and the West Indian *Aimé Césaire* celebrated the beauty of black skin and the African physique. They argued that in the precolonial era African peo-

ples had built societies where women were freer, old people were better cared for, and attitudes toward sex were far healthier than they had ever been in the so-called civilized West.

Except in settler colonies, such as Kenya and Rhodesia, Western-educated Africans in British territories were given greater opportunities to build political associations within Africa itself. In the early stages of this process, African leaders sought to nurture organizations that linked the emerging nationalists of different British colonies, such as the National Congress of British West Africa. By the late 1920s, these pan-colony associations gave way to political groupings concerned primarily with issues within individual colonies such as Sierra Leone, the Gold Coast, or Nigeria. After the British granted some representation in colonial advisory councils to Western-educated Africans in this period, emphasis on colony-specific political mobilization became even more pronounced.

Although most of these early political organizations were too loosely structured to be considered true political parties, there was a growing recognition by some leaders of the need to build a mass base. In the 1930s, a new generation of leaders made much more vigorous attacks on British policies. Through their newspapers and political associations, they also reached out to ordinary African villagers and the young, who had hitherto played little role in nationalist agitation. Their efforts to win a mass following would come to full fruition only after European divisions plunged humanity into a second global war.

Figure 39.4 *In the post–World War I era, African and African-American intellectuals such as Léopold Sédar Senghor (pictured here), W.E.B. Du Bois, and Aimé Césaire explored in their writings the ravages wrought by centuries of suffering inflicted on the people of Africa by the slave trade and the forced diaspora that resulted. These intellectuals worked to affirm the genius of African culture and African patterns of social interaction.*

İN DEPȚH

Women in Asian and African Nationalist Movements

One important but often neglected dimension of the liberation struggles that Asian and African peoples waged against their colonial overlords was the emergence of educated, articulate, and politically active women in most colonial societies. The educational opportunities provided by the European colonizers often played as vital a role as they had in the formation of male leadership in nationalist movements. Missionary girls' schools were confined in the early stages of European involvement in Africa and

Asia to the daughters of low-class or marginal social groups. But by the end of the 19th century they had become respectable for women from the growing Westernized business and professional classes. In fact, in many cases some degree of Western education was essential if Westernized men were to find wives with whom they could share their career concerns and intellectual pursuits.

The seemingly insurmountable barriers that separated Westernized Asian and African men from their traditional—and thus usually without formal education—wives became a stock theme in the novels and short stories of the early nationalist era. This concern was perhaps best exemplified by the works of Rabindranath Tagore. The problem was felt so acutely by the first generation of Indian nationalist leaders that many took up the task of teaching their wives English and Western philosophy and literature at home. Thus, for many upper-class Asian and African women, colonization proved a liberating force. This trend was often offset by the male-centric nature of colonial education and the domestic focus of the curriculum in women's schools.

Although women played little role in the early, elitist stages of Asian and African nationalist movements, they often became more and more prominent as the early study clubs and political associations reached out to build a mass base. In India, women who had been exposed to Western education and European ways, such as Tagore's famous heroine in the novel *The Home and the World,* came out of seclusion and took up supporting roles, although they were still usually behind the scenes. Gandhi's campaign to supplant imported, machine-made British cloth with homespun Indian cloth, for example, owed much of its success to female spinners and weavers. As nationalist leaders moved their anticolonial campaigns into the streets, women became involved in mass demonstrations. Throughout the 1920s and 1930s, Indian women braved the *lathi,* or billy club, assaults of the Indian police; suffered the indignities of imprisonment; and launched their own newspapers and lecture campaigns to mobilize female support for the nationalist struggle.

In Egypt, the British made special note of the powerful effect that the participation of both veiled women and more Westernized upper-class women had on mass demonstrations in 1919 and the early 1920s. These outpourings of popular support did much to give credibility to the Wafd's demands for British withdrawal. In both India and Egypt, female nationalists addressed special appeals to British and American suffragists to support their struggles for political and social liberation. In India in particular, their causes were advanced by feminists such as the English champion of Hinduism, Annie Besant, who became a major figure in the nationalist movement both before and after World War I.

When African nationalism became popularly supported after World War II, women, particularly the outspoken and fearless market women in west Africa, emerged as a major political force. In settler colonies such as Algeria and Kenya, where violent revolt proved necessary to bring down deeply entrenched colonial regimes, women took on the dangerous tasks of messengers, bomb carriers, and guerrilla fighters. As Frantz Fanon argued decades ago, and as was later beautifully dramatized in the film *The Battle of Algiers,* this transformation was particularly painful for women who had been in seclusion right up to the time of the revolutionary upsurge. The cutting of their hair, as well as the wearing of lipstick and Western clothes, often alienated them from their own fathers and brothers, who equated such practices with prostitution.

In many cases, women's participation in struggles for the political liberation of their people was paralleled by campaigns for female rights in societies dominated by men. Upper-class Egyptian women founded newspapers and educational associations that pushed for a higher marriage age, educational opportunities for women, and an end to seclusion and veiling. Indian women took up many of these causes and also developed programs to improve hygiene and employment opportunities for lower-caste women. These early efforts, as well as the prominent place of women in nationalist struggles, had much to do with the granting of basic civil rights to women. These included suffrage and legal equality that were key features of the constitutions of many newly independent Asian and African nations. The majority of women in the new states of Africa and Asia have yet to enjoy most of these rights. Yet their inclusion in constitutions and postindependence laws provides crucial backing for the struggles for women's liberation in the nations of the postcolonial world.

Questions: Why might missionary education for women in the colonies have stressed domestic skills? In what ways do you think measures to modernize colonial societies were oriented to men? Can you think of women who have been or are major political figures in contemporary Africa and Asia? Why have there not been more? What sorts of traditional constraints hamper the efforts of women to achieve economic and social equality and major political roles in newly independent nations?

ANOTHER GLOBAL WAR AND THE COLLAPSE OF THE EUROPEAN WORLD ORDER

▦ *The effects of a second global conflict, brought on by the expansionist ambitions of Hitler's Germany and imperial Japan, proved fatal to the already weakened European colonial empires. The sobering casualties of yet another war between the industrialized powers sapped the will of the Western colonizers to engage in further conflicts that would clearly be needed to crush resurgent nationalist movements throughout Africa and Asia. From India and Pakistan to west Africa, independence was won in most of the nonsettler colonies with surprisingly little bloodshed and remarkable speed. But in areas such as Algeria, Kenya, and South Africa, where large European settler communities tried to block nationalist agitation, liberation struggles were usually violent and costly and at times far from complete.*

The Nazi rout of the French and the stunningly rapid Japanese capture of the French, Dutch, British, and U.S. colonies in southeast Asia put an end to whatever illusions the colonized peoples of Africa and Asia had about the strength of their colonial overlords. Because the Japanese were non-Europeans, their early victories over the Europeans and Americans played a

particularly critical role in destroying the myth of the white man's invincibility. The fall of the "impregnable" fortress at Singapore on the southern tip of Malaya, and the U.S. setbacks at Pearl Harbor and in the Philippines proved to be blows from which the colonizers never quite recovered, even though they went on to defeat the Japanese. The sight of tens of thousands of British, Dutch, and American troops, struggling under the supervision of the victorious Japanese to survive the death marches to prison camps in their former colonies, left an indelible impression on the Asian villagers who saw them pass by. The harsh regimes and heavy demands the Japanese conquerors imposed on the peoples of southeast Asia during the war further strengthened their determination to fight for self-rule and to look to their own defenses after the conflict was over.

The devastation of World War II, a total war fought in the cities and countryside over much of Europe, drained the resources of the European powers. It also sapped the will of the European people to hold increasingly resistant African and Asian peoples in bondage. The war also greatly increased the power and influence of the two giants on the European periphery: the United States and the Soviet Union. In Africa and the Middle East, as well as in the Pacific, the United States approached the war as a campaign of liberation. American propagandists made no secret of Franklin Roosevelt's hostility to colonialism in their efforts to win Asian and African support for the Allied war effort. In fact, American intentions in this regard were enshrined in the *Atlantic Charter* of 1941. This pact sealed an alliance between the United States and Great Britain that the latter desperately needed to survive in its war with Nazi Germany. In it Roosevelt persuaded a reluctant Churchill to include a clause that recognized the "right of all people to choose the form of government under which they live." The Soviets were equally vocal in their condemnation of colonialism and were even more forthcoming with material support for nationalist campaigns after the war. In the cold war world of the superpowers that emerged after 1945, there was little room for the domination that western Europe had once exercised over much of the globe.

The Winning of Independence in South and Southeast Asia

The outbreak of World War II soon put an end to the accommodation between the Indian National Congress and the British in the late 1930s. Congress leaders offered to support the Allies' war effort if the British would give them a significant share of power at the all-India level and commit themselves to Indian independence once the conflict was over. These conditions were rejected both by the viceroy in India and at home by Winston Churchill, who headed the coalition government that led Britain through the war. However, Labour members of the coalition government indicated that they were willing to negotiate India's independence. As tensions built between nationalist agitators and the British rulers, *Sir Stafford Cripps* was sent to India in early 1942 to see whether a deal could be struck with the Indian leaders. Indian divisions and British resistance led to the collapse of Cripps's initiative and the renewal of mass civil disobedience campaigns under the guise of the *Quit India* movement, which began in the summer of 1942.

The British responded with repression and mass arrests, and for much of the remainder of the war, Gandhi, Nehru, and other major Congress politicians were imprisoned. Of the Indian nationalist parties, only the Communists—who were committed to the anti-Fascist alliance—and, more ominously, the Muslim League rallied to the British cause. The League, now led by a former Congress party politician, the dour and uncompromising *Muhammad Ali Jinnah*, won favor from the British for its wartime support. As their demands for a separate Muslim state in the subcontinent hardened, the links between the British and Jinnah and other League leaders became a key factor in the struggle for decolonization in south Asia.

World War II brought disruptions to India similar to those caused by the earlier global conflict. Inflation stirred up urban unrest, and a widespread famine in 1943 and 1944, brought on in part by wartime transport shortages, engendered much bitterness in rural India. Winston Churchill's defeat in the first postwar British election in 1945 brought a Labour government to power that was ready to deal with India's nationalist leaders. The decolonization process between 1945 and 1947 focused on what sort of state or states would be carved out of the subcontinent after the British withdrawal. Jinnah and the League had begun to build a mass following among the Muslims. To rally support they played on widespread anxieties among the Muslim minority that a single Indian nation would be dominated by the Hindu majority and that the Muslims would become the targets of increasing discrimination. It was therefore essential, they insisted, that a separate Muslim state called Pakistan be created from the areas in northwest and east India where Muslims were the most numerous.

As communal rioting spread throughout India, the British and key Congress party politicians reluctantly concluded that a bloodbath could be averted only by *partition*, or the creation of two nations in the subcontinent: one secular, one Muslim. Thus, in the summer of 1947, the British handed power over to the leaders of the majority Congress party, who headed the new nation of India, and to Jinnah, who became the first president of Pakistan (see Map 40.2). In part because of the haste with which the British withdrew their forces from the deeply divided subcontinent, a bloodbath occurred anyway. Vicious Hindu–Muslim and Muslim–Sikh communal rioting, in which neither women nor children were spared, took the lives of hundreds of thousands in the searing summer heat across the plains of northwest India. Whole villages were destroyed; trains pulled into railway stations that were packed with corpses hacked to death by armed bands of rival religious adherents. These atrocities fed a huge exchange of refugee populations between Hindu–Sikh and Muslim areas that may have totaled 10 million people. This tragic displacement of populations that was and remains the largest in human history. Those who fled were so terrified that they were willing to give up their land, their villages, and most of their worldly possessions. The losses of partition were compounded by the fact that there was soon no longer a Gandhi to preach tolerance and communal coexistence. On January 30, 1948, he was shot by a Hindu fanatic while on his way to one of his regular prayer meetings.

In granting independence to India, the British in effect removed the keystone from the arch of an empire that spanned three continents. Burma (known today as Myanmar) and Ceylon (now Sri Lanka) won their independence peacefully in the years that followed. India's independence and Gandhi's civil disobedience campaigns, which had done so much to win a mass following for the nationalist cause, also inspired successful struggles for independence in Ghana, Nigeria, and other African colonies in the 1950s and 1960s.

The retreat of the most powerful of the imperial powers could not help but contribute to the weakening of lesser empires such as those of the Dutch, the French, and the Americans. In fact, the transfer of power from U.S. officials to moderate, middle-class Filipino politicians was well under way before World War II broke out. The loyalty to the Americans that most Filipinos displayed during the war, as well as the stubborn guerrilla resistance they put up against the Japanese occupation, helped bring about the rapid granting of independence to the Philippines once the war was ended.

The Dutch and French were less willing to follow the British example and relinquish their colonial possessions in the postwar era. From 1945 to 1949, the Dutch fought a losing war to destroy the nation of Indonesia, which nationalists in the Netherlands Indies had established when the Japanese hold over the islands broke down in mid-1945. The French struggle to retain Indochina is discussed in Chapter 41, which focuses on the successful communist revolutions in east Asia in the postwar period. No sooner had the European colonizers suffered these losses than they were forced to deal with new threats to the last bastions of the imperial order in Africa.

The Liberation of Nonsettler Africa

World War II was even more disruptive to the colonial order imposed on Africa than World War I. Forced labor and confiscations of crops and minerals returned, and inflation and controlled markets again reduced African earnings. African recruits in the hundreds of thousands were drawn once more into the conflict and had even greater opportunities to use the latest European weapons to destroy Europeans. African soldiers had witnessed British and French defeats in the Middle East and southeast Asia, and they fought bravely only to experience renewed racial discrimination once they returned home. Many were soon staunch supporters of postwar nationalist campaigns in the African colonies of the British and French. The swift and humiliating rout of the French and Belgians by Nazi armies in the spring of 1940 shattered whatever was left of the colonizers' reputation for military prowess. It also led to a bitter and, in the circumstances, embarrassing struggle between the forces of the puppet Vichy regime and those of de Gaulle's Free French, who continued fighting the Nazis mainly in France's north and west African colonies.

The wartime needs of both the British and the Free French led to major departures from long-standing colonial policies that had limited industrial development throughout Africa. Factories to process urgently needed vegetable oils, foods, and minerals were established in western and south central Africa. These in turn contributed to a growing migration on the part of African peasants to the towns and a sharp spurt in African urban growth.

The inability of many of those who moved to the towns to find employment made for a reservoir of disgruntled, idle workers that was skillfully tapped by nationalist politicians in the postwar decades.

There were two main paths to decolonization in nonsettler Africa in the postwar era. The first was pioneered by *Kwame Nkrumah* and his followers in the British Gold Coast colony, which, as the nation of Ghana, became the first independent black African state in 1957. Nkrumah epitomized the more radical sort of African leader that emerged throughout Africa after the war. Educated in African missionary schools and the United States, he had established wide contacts with nationalist leaders in both British and French west Africa and civil rights leaders in America before his return to the Gold Coast in the late 1940s. He returned to a land in ferment. The restrictions of government-controlled marketing boards and their favoritism for British merchants had led to widespread but nonviolent protest in the coastal cities. But after the police fired on a peaceful demonstration of ex-soldiers in 1948, rioting broke out in many towns.

Although both urban workers and cash crop farmers had supported the unrest, Western-educated African leaders were slow to organize these dissident groups into a sustained mass movement. Their reluctance arose in part from their fear of losing major political concessions, such as seats on colonial legislative councils, that the British had just made. Rejecting the caution urged by more established political leaders, Nkrumah resigned his position as chair of the dominant political party in the Gold Coast and established his own Convention Peoples Party (CPP). Even before the formal break, he signaled the arrival of a new style of politics by organizing mass rallies, boycotts, and strikes.

In the mid-1950s, Nkrumah's mass following, and his growing stature as a leader who would not be deterred by imprisonment or British threats, won repeated concessions from the British. Educated Africans were given more and more representation in legislative bodies, and gradually they took over administration of the colony. The British recognition of Nkrumah as the prime minister of an independent Ghana in 1957 simply concluded a transfer of power from the European colonizers to the Western-educated African elite that had been under way for nearly a decade.

The peaceful transfer of power to African nationalists led to the independence of the British nonsettler colonies in black Africa by the mid-1960s.

Figure 39.5 *Scenes such as the one in this photo were played out tens of times in the decades after World War II. British Home Secretary R. A. Butler is greeted by Kwame Nkrumah, whom Butler will soon swear in as the leader of the first independent nation, Ghana, to be carved out of Britain's African colonies.*

Independence in the comparable areas of the French and Belgian empires in Africa came in a somewhat different way. Hard pressed by costly military struggles to hold on to their colonies in Indochina and Algeria, the French took a much more conciliatory line in dealing with the many peoples they ruled in west Africa. Ongoing negotiations with such highly Westernized leaders as Senegal's Senghor and the Ivory Coast's Felix Houphouât-Boigny led to reforms and political concessions. The slow French retreat ensured that moderate African leaders, who were eager to retain French economic and cultural ties, would dominate the nationalist movements and the postindependence period in French west Africa. Between 1956 and 1960, the French colonies moved by stages toward nationhood, a process that sped up after de Gaulle's return to power in 1958. By 1960, all of France's west African colonies were free.

In the same year, the Belgians completed a much hastier retreat from their huge colonial possession in the Congo. There was little in the way of an organized nationalist movement to pressure them into concessions. In fact, by design there were scarcely any well-educated Congolese to lead resistance to Belgian rule. At independence in 1960, there were only 16 African college graduates in a Congolese population that exceeded 13 million. Although the Portuguese still clung to their impoverished and scattered colo-

nial territories, by the mid-1960s the European colonial era had come to an end in all but the settler societies of Africa.

Repression and Guerrilla War: The Struggle for the Settler Colonies

The pattern of peaceful withdrawal by stages that characterized decolonization in most of Asia and Africa proved unworkable in most of the settler colonies. These included areas such as Algeria, Kenya, and Southern Rhodesia, where substantial numbers of Europeans had gone to settle permanently in the 19th and early 20th centuries. South Africa, which had begun to be settled by Europeans centuries earlier, provided few openings for nationalist agitation except that mounted by the politically and economically dominant colonists of European descent. In each case, the presence of European settler communities, varying in size from over a million in South Africa and Algeria to tens of thousands in Kenya and Southern Rhodesia, blocked both the rise of indigenous nationalist movements and concessions on the part of the colonial overlords.

Because the settlers regarded the colonies to which they had emigrated as their permanent homes, they fought all attempts to turn political control over to the African majority or even to grant them civil

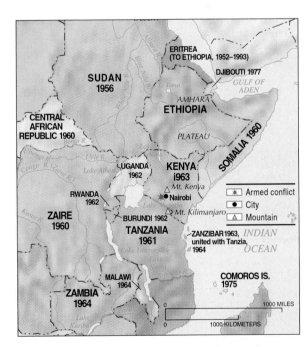

Map 39.4 *Kenya: The Struggle for Independence in the 1950s*

Visualizing
THE PAST

Nationalist Leaders:
Different Styles, Different Images

Throughout Africa and Asia, struggles for decolonization and national independence often led to the emergence of leaders with exceptional mass appeal and political skills. But the personal qualities, visions of the future, and leadership styles that made for widespread loyalty to these individuals varied widely depending on the cultures and social settings from which they emerged as well as the nature of the political contests that led to the colonizers' retreat and the establishment of new nations. The following are photos of four of the most charismatic and effective leaders of indepen-

dence movements in Africa and Asia. Study these photos and the background information on each of these individuals that is provided in earlier sections of this chapter and the relevant section of Chapter 40, and answer the questions about leadership styles and images that follow.

Questions: What do the dress and poses of each of these leaders tell us about the images they projected? Why did the style and approach each adopted win widespread popular support in each of the very different societies in which they emerged as pivotal leaders in the struggles for independence? How well do you think that each of their approaches to leadership served them in dealings with the European colonizers and contests with the rival leaders and political parties they faced in each of the societies in which they arose? What did charisma mean in each of these settings?

Gamal Abdul Nasser, Egypt

Kwame Nkrumah, Ghana

Mahatma Gandhi, India

Léopold Sédar Senghor, Senegal

rights. They also doggedly refused all reforms by colonial administrators that required them to give up any of the lands they had occupied, often at the expense of indigenous African peoples. Unable to make headway through nonviolent protest tactics, which were forbidden, or negotiations with British or French officials, who were fearful of angering the highly vocal settler minority, many African leaders turned to violent, revolutionary struggles to win their peoples' independence.

The first of these erupted in Kenya in the early 1950s (Map 39.3). Impatient with the failure of the nonviolent approach adopted by *Jomo Kenyatta* and the leading nationalist party, the Kenya African Union (KAU), an underground organization, coalesced around a group of more radical leaders. After forming the *Land Freedom Army* in the early 1950s, the radicals mounted a campaign of terror and guerrilla warfare against the British, the settlers, and Africans who were considered collaborators. At the height of the struggle in 1954, some 200,000 rebels were in action in the capital at Nairobi and in the forest reserves of the central Kenyan highlands. The British responded with an all-out military effort to crush the

guerrilla movement, which was dismissed as an explosion of African savagery and labeled by the colonizers, not the rebels, the Mau Mau. At the settlers' insistence, the British imprisoned Kenyatta and the KAU organizers, thus eliminating the nonviolent alternative to the guerrillas.

The rebel movement was defeated militarily by 1956, at the cost of thousands of lives. But the British were now in a mood to negotiate with the nationalists, despite strong objections from the European settlers. Kenyatta was released from prison, and he emerged as the spokesperson for the Africans of Kenya. By 1963, a multiracial Kenya had won its independence. Under what was in effect Kenyatta's one-party rule, it remained until the mid-1980s one of the most stable and more prosperous of the new African states.

The struggle of the Arab and Berber peoples of Algeria (see Map 39.4) for independence was longer and even more vicious than that in Kenya. For decades Algeria had been regarded by the French as an integral part of France, a department just like Provence or Brittany. The presence of more than a million European settlers in the colony only strengthened the resolve of French politicians to retain it at all costs. But in the decade after World War II, sporadic rioting grew into sustained guerrilla resistance. By the mid-1950s, the *National Liberation Front (FLN)* had mobilized large segments of the Arab and Berber population of the colony in a full-scale revolt against French rule and settler, or *colon*, dominance. High-ranking French army officers came to see the defeat of this movement as a way to restore a reputation that had been badly tarnished by recent defeats in Vietnam (see Chapter 41). As in Kenya, the rebels were defeated in the field. But they gradually negotiated the independence of Algeria after Charles de Gaulle came to power in 1958. The French people had wearied of the seemingly endless

war, and de Gaulle became convinced that he could not restore France to great power status as long as its resources continued to be drained by the Algerian conflict.

In contrast to Kenya, the Algerian struggle was prolonged and brutalized by a violent settler backlash. Led after 1960 by the *Secret Army Organization (OAS)*, it was directed against the Arabs and Berbers as well as French people who favored independence for the colony. With strong support from elements in the French military, earlier resistance by the settlers had toppled the government in Paris in 1958, thereby putting an end to the Fourth Republic. In the early 1960s, the OAS came close to assassinating de Gaulle

Figure 39.6 *Algerians celebrate in Oran as French barricades are torn down by members of the local Arab militia and Arab civilians just after independence is announced in July, 1962. The barricades were erected throughout the colony to deny access to areas where Europeans were resident to the Arabs and Berbers, who made up the overwhelming majority of the population. Although cities such as Oran and Algiers had long been segregated into "native" and European quarters, the protracted and bloody war for independence fought by the Arab and Berber peoples had resulted in full-scale occupation by the French army and the physical separation of settler and Arab–Berber areas.*

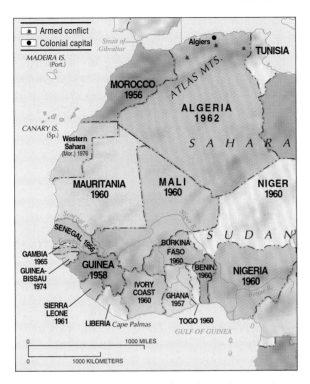

Map 39.5 *Algeria: The Struggle for Independence in the 1960s*

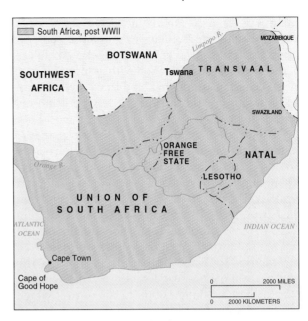

Map 39.6 *The Union of South Africa*

and overthrowing the Fifth Republic, which his accession to power had brought into existence. In the end, however, the Algerians won their independence in 1962. After the bitter civil war, the multiracial accommodation worked out in Kenya appeared out of the question as far as the settlers of Algeria were concerned. More than 900,000 left the new nation within months after its birth. In addition, tens of thousands of *harkis,* or Arabs and Berbers who had sided with the French in the long war for independence, fled to France. They and later migrants formed the core of the substantial "Algerian" population now resident in France.

The Persistence of White Supremacy in South Africa

In southern Africa, violent revolutions also put an end to white settler dominance in the Portuguese colonies of Angola and Mozambique in 1975 and in

Southern Rhodesia (now Zimbabwe) by 1980. Only in South Africa (Map 39.6) did the white minority manage to maintain its position of supremacy. Its ability to do so rested on several factors that distinguished it from other settler societies. To begin with, the white population of South Africa, roughly equally divided between the Dutch-descended Afrikaners and the more recently arrived English speakers, was a good deal larger than that of any of the other settler societies. Although they were only a small minority in a country of 23 million black Africans and 3.5 million East Indians and coloreds (mulattos, in American parlance), by the mid-1980s, South Africa's settler-descended population had reached 4.5 million.

Unlike the settlers in Kenya and Algeria, who had the option of retreating to Europe as full citizens of France or Great Britain, the Afrikaners in particular had no European homeland to fall back on. They had lived in South Africa as long as other Europeans had in North America, and they considered themselves quite distinct from the Dutch. Over the centuries, the Afrikaners had also built up what was for them a persuasive ideology of white racist supremacy. Though crude by European or American standards, Afrikaner racism was far more explicit and elaborate than that developed by the settlers of any other colony. Afrikaner ideology was grounded in selected biblical quotations and the celebration of their historic struggle to "tame a beautiful but hard land" in the face of opposition from both the African "savages" and the British "imperialists."

Ironically, their defeat by the British in the Anglo-Boer War from 1899 to 1902 (see Chapter 30) also contributed to the ability of the white settler minority to maintain its place of dominance in South Africa. A sense of guilt arising especially from their treatment of Boer women and children during the war; tens of thousands of whom died of disease in what the British called *concentration camps*—led the victors to make major concessions to the Afrikaners in the postwar decades. The most important of these was internal political control, which included turning over the fate of the black African majority to the openly racist Afrikaners. Not surprisingly, the continued subjugation of the black Africans became a central aim of the Afrikaner political organizations that emerged in the 1930s and 1940s, culminating in the *Afrikaner National Party*. From 1948, when it emerged as the majority party in the all-white South African legislature, the National party devoted itself to winning complete independence from Britain (which came without violence in 1961), and to establishing lasting white domination over the political, social, and economic life of the new nation.

A rigid system of racial segregation (which is discussed more fully in Chapter 40), called *apartheid* by the Afrikaners, was established after 1948 through the passage of thousands of laws. Among other things, this legislation reserved the best jobs for whites and carefully defined the sorts of contacts permissible between different racial groups. The vote and political representation were denied to the black Africans, and ultimately to the coloreds and Indians. It was illegal for members of any of these groups to hold mass meetings or to organize political parties or labor unions. These restrictions, combined with very limited opportunities for higher education for black Africans, hampered the growth of black African political parties and their efforts to mobilize popular support for the struggle for decolonization. The Afrikaners' establishment of a vigilant and brutal police state to uphold apartheid and their opportunistic cultivation of divisions between the diverse peoples in the black African population also contributed to their ability to preserve a bastion of white supremacy in an otherwise liberated continent.

Conflicting Nationalisms: Arabs, Israelis, and the Palestinian Question

Although nearly all Arab peoples who were not yet free by the end of World War II were liberated by the early 1960s, the fate of Palestine continued to present special problems. Hitler's campaign of genocide against the European Jews had provided powerful support for the Zionists' insistence that the Jews must have their own homeland, which more and more was conceived in terms of a modern national state. The brutal persecution of the Jews also won international sympathy for the Zionist cause. This resulted in part from the fact that the leaders of many nations, including the United States and Great Britain, were reluctant to admit Jews fleeing the Nazi terror into their own countries. As the Nazis stepped up their race war against the Jews, the tide of Jewish immigration to Palestine rose sharply. But growing Arab resistance to Jewish settlement and land purchases in Palestine, often expressed in communal rioting and violent assaults on Zionist communities, led to increasing British restrictions on the entry of Jews into the colony. A major Muslim revolt swept Palestine between 1936 and 1939. The British managed to put down this uprising but only with great difficulty. It decimated the leadership of the Palestinian Arab community and further strengthened the British resolve to stem the flow of Jewish immigrants to Palestine. Government measures to keep out Jewish refugees from Nazi oppression led in turn to violent Zionist resistance to the British presence in Palestine. The Zionist assault was spearheaded by a regular Zionist military force, the *Haganah*, and several underground terrorist organizations.

By the end of World War II, the major parties claiming Palestine were locked in a deadly stale-

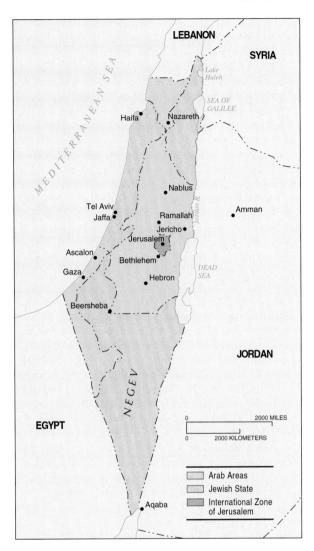

Map 39.7 *The Partition of Palestine After World War II*

commission of inquiry supplied a possible solution: partition. After World War II, the newly created United Nations provided an international body that could give a semblance of legality to the proceedings. In 1948, with sympathy for the Jews running high because of the postwar revelations of the horrors of Hitler's "Final Solution," the member states of the United Nations, with the United States and the Soviet Union in rare agreement, approved the partition of Palestine into Arab and Jewish countries (Map 39.7).

The Arab states that bordered the newly created nation of Israel had vehemently opposed the United Nations' action. Soon the two sides were engaged in all out warfare. Though heavily outnumbered, the Zionists proved to be better armed and much better prepared to defend themselves than almost anyone expected. Not only did they hold onto the tiny patchwork state they had been given by the United Nations, but they expanded it at the Arabs' expense. The brief but bloody war that ensued created hundreds of thousands of Palestinian Arab refugees. It also sealed the persisting hostility between Arabs and Israelis that has been the all-consuming issue in the region and a major international problem throughout the postindependence era. In Palestine, conflicting strains of nationalism collided. As a result, the legacy of colonialism proved even more of a liability to social and economic development than in much of the rest of newly independent Africa and Asia.

Conclusion

The Limits of Decolonization

Given the fragile foundations on which it rested, the rapid demise of the European colonial order is not surprising. The winning of political freedom in Asia and Africa also represented less of a break with the colonial past than the appearance of many new nations on the map of the world might lead one to assume. The decidedly nonrevolutionary, elite-to-elite transfer of power that was central to liberation in most colonies, even those where there were violent guerrilla movements, limited the extent of the social and economic transformation that occurred. The

mate. The Zionists were determined to carve out a Jewish state in the region. The Palestinian Arabs and their allies in neighboring Arab lands were equally determined to transform Palestine into a multireligious nation in which the position of the Arab majority would be ensured. Having badly bungled their responsibilities and under attack from both sides, the British wanted more than anything else to scuttle and run. The 1937 report of a British

Western-educated African and Asian classes moved into the offices and took the jobs—and often the former homes—of the European colonizers. But social gains for the rest of the population in most new nations were minimal or nonexistent. In Kenya, Algeria, and Zimbabwe (formerly Southern Rhodesia), abandoned European lands were distributed to Arab and African peasants and laborers. But in most former colonies, especially in Asia, the big landholders that remained were indigenous, and they have held their land tenaciously. Educational reforms were carried out to include more sciences in school curricula and the history of Asia or Africa rather than Europe. But Western cultural influences have remained strong in almost all of the former colonies. Indians and many west Africans with higher educations continue to communicate in English. Some of the most prominent of the leaders of former French colonies continue to pride themselves on their impeccable French, decorate their presidential palaces with French antiques, and keep closely in touch with trends in French intellectual circles.

The liberation of the colonies also did little to disrupt Western dominance of the terms of international trade or the global economic order more generally. In fact, in the negotiations that led to decolonization, Asian and African leaders often explicitly promised to protect the interests of Western merchants and businesspeople in the postindependence era. As we shall see in Chapter 40, these and other limits that sustained Western influence and often dominance, even after freedom was won, greatly reduced the options open to nationalist leaders struggling to build viable and prosperous nations. Although new forces have also played important roles, the postindependence history of colonized peoples cannot be understood without a consideration of the lingering effects of the colonial interlude in their history.

Further Readings

A thoughtful overview of decolonization in the British empire as a whole can be found in the works of John Darwin. The best introduction to the massive literature that has developed on the Indian nationalist movement, as well as a good general historical chronology of the struggle for independence, can be found in Sumit Sarkar's *Modern India 1885–1947* (1983). Mohandas Gandhi's autobiographical *The Story of My Experiments with Truth* (1927) remains an invaluable account of perhaps the most famous Africa or Asian nationalist leader. Louis Fischer's biography, *Gandhi* (1950), still yields valuable insights into the personality of one of the great nationalist leaders and the workings of nationalist politics. Judith Brown's studies of Gandhi as a political leader, including *Gandhi's Rise to Power* (1972), and her recent biography of his life and career provide an approach more in tune with current

research. The poems and novels of Tagore yield wonderful insights into the social and cultural life of India through much of this era.

P. J. Vatikiotis's *The History of Egypt* (especially the 1985 edition) has excellent sections on the nationalist era in that country. Interesting, but often less reliable, is Jacque Berque's *Colonialism and Nationalism in Egypt* (1972). Leila Ahmed's *Women and Gender in Islam* (1992) has excellent chapters on the role of women at various stages of the nationalist struggle and in the postindependence era. George Antonius's *The Arab Awakening* (1946) is essential reading on the history of the Palestine question. It can be balanced by Aaron Cohen's *The Arabs and Israel* (1970) and David Hirst's *The Gun and the Olive Branch* (1984). The period of the partition and the first Arab–Israeli conflict have been the subject of much revisionist scholarship in recent years. Some of the best of this is included in important books by Benny Morris, Walid Khalidi, Ilan Pappé, and Tom Segev.

The early stages of the nationalist struggle in west Africa are covered by Michael Crowder's *West Africa Under Colonial Rule* (1982), and the final drives for decolonization are surveyed in Ali A. Mazrui and Michael Tidy's *Nationalism and New States in Africa* (1984), J. D. Hargreaves's *Decolonization in Africa* (1988), and W. R. Louis and P. Gifford, eds., *Decolonization in Africa* (1984). On specific movements, see Alastair Horne's *A Savage War of Peace* (1977) on Algeria, C. Rosberg and J. Nottingham's *The Myth of "Mau Mau"* (1966) on Kenya, and the writings of Terrence Ranger on Rhodesia. Of the many works on South Africa, the general histories of S. Throup, B. Bunting, T. D. Moodie, and Leonard Thompson provide a good introduction to the rise of Afrikaner power.

On the Web

An overview of the process of decolonization with links to such sources as the works of Chinua Achebe, can be found at http://cedar.evansville.edu/~wc203/web/imperial.htm.

The African National Congress Party homepage at http://www.anc.org.za/ not only provides current information about the party, but also materials on the freedom struggle in South Africa, such as the life histories, speeches and writings of African National Congress freedom fighters and presidents, including Nelson Mandela. Apartheid in South Africa is discussed at http://www-cs-students.stanford.edu/~cale/cs201/apartheid.hist.html.

Colonial and post-colonial discourse that embraces issues such as negritude is the subject of analysis at http://www.stg.brown.edu/projects/hypertext/landow/post/poldiscourse/negritute.html. A survey of the struggle in the Middle East against colonialism is offered at http://www. fordham.edu/haalsall/Islam/islambook.html#Islamic nationalism.

The Palestinian National Charter is reproduced at http: //www.yale.edu/lawweb/avalaon/plocov.htm.

Insight into the casual brutality of imperialism can be obtained from an illustrated Egyptian account of the Dihshawai incident in Egypt at http://touregypt.net /denshwaymuseum.htm. The socio-economic context of this incident and its effects are examined at http:// lcweb2.loc.gov/cgi-bin/query/D?cstdy:1/ temp/ ~frd_7fru.

The Web offers sites that examine leading nationalists and nationalist movements. Thesse include Theodore Herzl and his leadership of the Zionist movement, (http:// www.israelemb.org/zioism/index.html),

Jomo Kenyatta and his role in the Land Freedom Army and Mau Mau movements (http://www.kenyaweb.com /history/ch10/index.html and http://www.kenyaweb. com/history/ch12/index.html), and Bal Gangadhar

Tilak and his place in the Indian freedom movement (http://www.indiasurvey.com/biodata/balgangadharti-lak.htm).

Of the many Web sites devoted to Mohandas Karamchand Gandhi, one of the best (http:// dwardmac.pitzer.edu/anarchist_archives/bright/ gandhi/Gandhi.html) also examines those who have succeeded him as champions of Satyagraha. Another site (http://www.historychannel.com/speeches/index.html) provides a short film covering a speech Gandhi made while on a visit to London.

Insight into Jawaharlal Nehru's mindset, a quick-time movie of his release from a British jail during the last years of colonialism and links to his writings and other materials can be found at http://www.india-info.com /arts_humani_history/ nehru_jawaharlal_1889_1964 _htm.

A sympathetic review of the life of Mohammad Ali Jinnah is provided at http://www.rediff.com/news/1998/sep /10jinnah.htm, while a short movie made of him delivering one of his key speeches is available at http://www. harappa.com/jinnahmov.html.

Chapter 40

Africa and Asia in the Era of Independence

Women played a vital role in the mass demonstrations that toppled the shah of Iran and brought Ayatollah Khomeini to power. In many ways women's support for political movements in the post-colonial period was a continuation of their active participation in earlier struggles against European colonial domination. But increasingly in the post-colonial era, women have organized not only to promote political change, but to force social and economic reforms that will improve the quality of their own lives.

In Gillo Pontecorvo's moving film on the struggle for independence in Algeria, *The Battle of Algiers,* one member of the high command of the National Liberation Front (FLN) reflects on the nature of the revolutionary struggle in a conversation with a young guerrilla fighter, the protagonist of the film. When the young man expresses his anxieties about the outcome of the general strike taking place in the city of Algiers, the thoughtful leader of the FLN seeks to put the immediate crisis in a larger perspective. Revolutions, he observes, are difficult to get going and even harder to sustain. But the real tests, he says, will come when the revolutionary struggle has been successfully concluded. Once independence has been won, the leaders of the liberation struggle must assume power and face the greatest challenges of all: building viable nations and prosperous societies for peoples disoriented and deprived by decades or in many cases centuries of colonial rule.

These reflections on the process of decolonization anticipated the actual experience of the peoples in the new nations carved out of the ruins of the European colonial empires. Once the European colonizers had withdrawn and the initial euphoria of freedom had begun to wear off, Western-educated nationalist leaders were forced to confront the realities of the fragile state structures and underdeveloped economies they had inherited. With the common European enemy gone, the deep divisions between the different ethnic and religious groups that had been thrown together in the postcolonial states became more and more apparent and disruptive. These related challenges, which were faced by all of the newly independent peoples of Africa and Asia, are explored in the opening sections of this chapter.

The leaders of the new nations found their efforts to spur economic growth limited by concessions made to the departing colonizers and by the nature of the international economy, which heavily favored industrialized nations. They saw their ambitious schemes to improve living standards among formerly colonized peoples frustrated by a shortage of expertise and resources and by population growth rates that quickly ate up whatever advances could be made. Population increase and efforts to spur economic development have also often had highly detrimental effects on the already ravaged environments of the newly independent nations. Loggers and land-hungry farmers have cut and burned vast swaths of the rainforests throughout much of Africa and Asia. Unable to afford the expensive antipollution devices that have reduced environmental degradation in wealthier industrialized countries, many developing nations have experienced an alarming fouling of their air, water, and soil in the decades since independence.

1920 B.C.E.	1940 B.C.E.	1950 B.C.E.	1960 C.E.	1970 C.E.	1980 C.E.
1912 African National Congress party formed	**1947** India and Pakistan achieve independence	**1951** India's first five-year plan for economic development launched	**1960** Sharpeville shootings in South Africa	**1970s** Peak period for the OPEC cartel	**1980–1988** Iran–Iraq War
1928 Founding of the Muslim Brotherhood in Egypt	**1948** First Arab–Israeli War; Afrikaner Nationalist party to power in South Africa; beginning of apartheid legislation	**1952** Farouk and khedival regime overthrown in Egypt; Nasser and Free Officers to power	**1966** Nkrumah overthrown by military coup in Ghana	**1971** Bangladesh revolt against West Pakistan; Indo-Pakistani War	**1989** De Klerk charts a path of peaceful reform in South Africa
1930s Free Officers movement develops in Egypt	**1949** Hassan al-Banna assassinated in Egypt	**1955** Bandung Conference; beginning of non-aligned movement	**1966–1970** Biafran secessionist war in Nigeria	**1972** Bangladesh becomes an independent nation	**1990** Nelson Mandela released from prison; Iraqi invasion of Kuwait
		1956 Abortive British-French-Israeli intervention in Suez	**1967** Six-Day War between Israel and the Arabs	**1973** Third Arab-Israeli War	**1991** Gulf War
		1958 South Africa completely independent of Great Britain		**1979** Shah of Iran overthrown; Khomaini-led Islamic republic declared	**1994** First democratic elections in South Africa

Increasing poverty, official corruption, and a growing concern for the breakdown of traditional culture and social values produced widespread social unrest. Dissent and civil disturbances called into question the leadership abilities of the nationalist politicians who had won independence but floundered as heads of new nations. Challenges to the existing order came both from communist and socialist parties on the left of the political spectrum and religious revivalist movements, whose positions were often a complex blend of radicalism and conservatism. Dissident socialist movements have frequently clashed with religious revivalists over a wide range of issues, from the place of religion in the newly independent nations to the proper roles and rights of women.

To remain in power and to ensure that they would be able to realize their visions of economic and social development in the postcolonial era, Western-educated nationalist leaders adopted various strategies to beat back these threats. As we shall see in the later sections of this chapter, these strategies met with widely varying degrees of success. The price for failure was often a fall from power and at times the execution of former nationalist heroes. In many instances, their places were taken by military commanders, who assumed dictatorial powers, forcibly silenced dissent, and suppressed interethnic and religious rivalries. In a few cases, the champions of religious revival and resistance to Western influences, most notably those in Iran, swept moderate reformers and dictators from power.

THE CHALLENGES OF INDEPENDENCE

In the early decades of independence, the very existence of the nation-states that were carved out of the Western colonial empires was often challenged by the internal rivalries, and in some cases civil wars, between different social and ethnic groups. Economic growth was hampered by unprecedented rates of population increase, the structure of the international market, and the underdeveloped state of most colonial economies at the time of independence. Some social groups benefited more than others from the opportunities created by independence, and women continued to find themselves disadvantaged in nearly all areas of their lives.

The nationalist movements that won independence for most of the peoples of Africa and Asia usually involved some degree of mass mobilization.

Peasants and working-class townspeople, who hitherto had little voice in politics beyond their village boundaries or local labor associations, were drawn into political contests that toppled empires and established new nations. To win the support of these groups, nationalist leaders promised them jobs, civil rights, and equality once independence was won. The leaders of many nationalist movements nurtured visions of postindependence utopias in the minds of their followers. They were told that once the Europeans, who monopolized the best jobs, were driven away and their exploitive hold on the economies of colonized peoples was brought to an end, there would be enough to give everyone a good life.

Unfortunately, postindependence realities in almost all new African and Asian nations made it impossible for nationalist leaders to fulfill the expectations they had aroused among their followers and, in varying degrees, among the colonized populace at large. Even with the Europeans gone and the terms of economic exchange with more developed countries somewhat improved, there was simply not enough to go around. Thus, the socialist-inspired ideologies that nationalist leaders had often embraced and promoted were misleading. The problem was not just that goods and services were unequally distributed, leaving some people rich and the great majority poor. The problem was that there were not enough resources to take care of everybody, even if it was possible to distribute them equitably.

When utopia failed to materialize, personal rivalries and long-standing divisions between different classes and ethnic groups, which had been muted by the common struggle against the alien colonizers, resurfaced or intensified. In almost all the new states, these rivalries and differences became dominant features of political life. They produced political instability and often threatened the viability of the nations themselves. They consumed resources that might have been devoted to economic development. They also blocked—in the name of the defense of subnational interests—measures designed to build more viable and prosperous states. Absorbed by the task of just holding their new nations together, African and Asian politicians neglected problems—such as soaring population increases, uncontrolled urban growth, rural landlessness, and environmental deterioration—that soon loomed just as large a threat as political instability to their young nations.

IN DEPTH

Artificial Nations and the Rising Tide of Communal Strife

Again and again in the postcolonial era, the new states of Africa and Asia have been torn by internal strife. Often much of what we in the industrialized West know of these areas is connected to the breakdown of their political systems and the human suffering that has resulted. In just the last few years, for example, international news reports have featured descriptions of famines generated by civil wars in Somalia, the Sudan, and Mozambique; by harrowing images of refugees fleeing for their lives from Rwanda, Angola, and Cambodia; by religious riots in India; and mass slaughter in Timor. Western observers are often tempted to take this instability and suffering as proof that African and Asian peoples are unfit to rule themselves, that they are incapable of building viable political systems. Some commentators have even begun to ask whether many of these areas were better off under colonial rule and to call for more active intervention by Japan and the West.

Although these responses are understandable given the crisis-focused coverage of African and Asian affairs by international news agencies, they fail to take into account the daunting obstacles that have confronted nation-builders in these areas. They ignore the important ways in which Western colonialism contributed to the internal divisions and political weaknesses of newly independent states. They also overlook the deep, often highly disruptive social divisions within Western societies (the long history of racial conflict in the United States, for example, or the vicious civil war in the former European nation of Yugoslavia). Clearly, a longer-term comparative perspective is needed if we are to understand the persistent difficulties that African and Asian peoples have had building viable nations and functioning pluralistic societies.

Any analysis of the recurring political crises of Africa and Asia should begin with the realization that nearly all the nations that emerged from decolonization were artifical creations. The way the European empires had been built and their boundaries demarcated ensured that this would be the case. European generals conquered and European explorers staked out claims to territories in ways that rarely, if ever, took into account the interests or history of the peoples who occupied these lands. As Lord Salisbury, one of the most prominent late 19th-century champions of imperialist expansion, confessed in the 1890s, the conquerors knew next to nothing about the lands they divided up around the green-felt tables at conferences in Berlin, Paris, and other European capitals:

> We have been engaged in drawing lines upon maps where no white man's foot ever trod; we have been giving away mountains and rivers and lakes to each other [Europeans] only hindered by the small impediment that we never knew exactly where the mountains and rivers and lakes were.

If they could not locate the mountains and rivers, European diplomats could hardly have been expected to know much about the peoples who lived on or along them. As a consequence, the division of Africa and Asia was arbitrary (see, for example, Map 40.1). Colonial boundaries cut peoples apart: the Shans of southeast Asia, the Kurds of the Middle East, the Somalis of the horn of east Africa. They also tossed together tens, sometimes hundreds, of very different and often hostile ethnic or religious groups. The roads and railways built by the colonizers, the marketing systems they established, and the educational policies they pursued all hardened the unnatural boundaries and divisions established in the late 19th century. It was these artificial units, these motley combinations of peoples that defied the logic of history and cultural affinity, that African and Asian nationalist leaders had to try to meld into nations after World War II.

The point is not that there was perfect harmony or unity among the peoples of Asia and Africa before the coming of colonial rule. As we have seen, there was a great diversity of ethnicity, languages, and religions among the peoples who built civilizations in these areas in the precolonial era. Intense competition, communal conflict, and countless wars occurred between different ethnic and religious groups. European colonization worsened these divisions while suppressing violent confrontations between different communities. In fact, European colonial regimes were built and maintained by divide-and-rule tactics. Very often the colonizers

selectively recruited minority ethnic or religious groups into their armies, bureaucracies, and police forces. For example, the Tutsi minority in strife-torn Rwanda and Burundi was much favored by first the Belgians and later the French. The Europeans admired the taller, fine-featured Tutsis. Their admiration was enhanced by the fact that Tutsi kingdoms had dominated the Hutu majority before the colonizers arrived. In the colonial period, the Tutsis had greater access to missionary education, military training, and government positions than the Hutu majority. These advantages gained a disproportionate share of political power and social standing for the Tutsis after independence. But they also made them the obvious target for persecution by disgruntled Hutus. Rivalry and violent conflict between the two groups has often made a shambles of nation-building initiatives in Rwanda and Burundi over the past several decades and reached catastrophic levels in the mid-1990s. It has continued to simmer in the years since, at times spilling over into political struggles in neighboring states such as Congo.

The inequities of the colonial order were compounded by the increasingly frequent use of divide-and-rule policies by European officials in the last years of their rule. In addition, the colonizers' desire to scuttle and run from their colonial responsibilities when it was clear that the days of colonial rule were numbered opened the way for the ethnic and religious strife. Communal violence in turn prompted the exodus of refugees that accompanied the winning of independence in many colonies, most notably in south Asia, Nigeria, the Belgian Congo, and Palestine. The Western-educated leaders who came to power in these and other newly independent states soon realized that only a small portion of the population was committed to an overarching nationalist identity. Even among the Westernized elite classes, which had led the decolonization struggle, national loyalties were often shallow and overridden by older, subnational ethnic and religious identities. As a result, many of the new nations of Africa and southeast Asia have been threatened by secessionist movements.

The most spectacular collapse of a new state came in Pakistan, the unwieldy patchwork of a nation the British threw together at the last minute in 1947 to satisfy Jinnah's demands for majority rule in Muslim areas of the Indian sub-

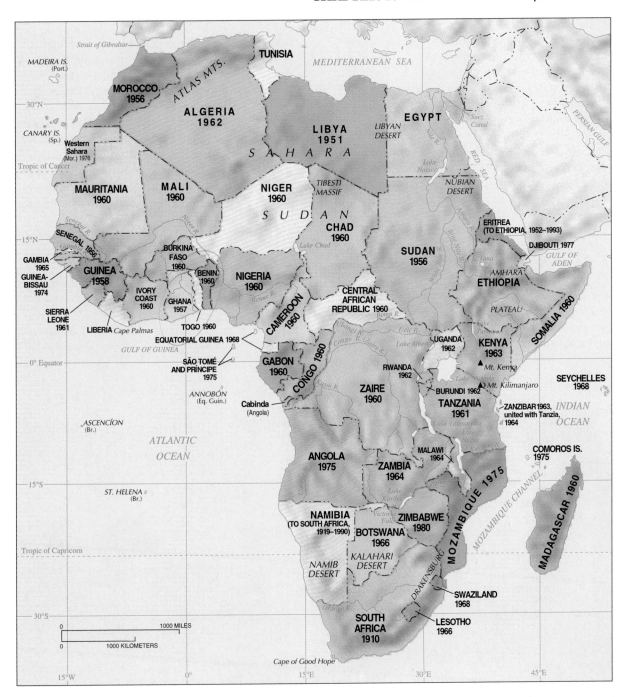

Map 40.1 *The Colonial Division of Africa and the Emergence of New Nations*

continent (Map 40.2). A glance at the map reveals the vulnerability of Pakistan, split into two parts: West and East Pakistan, separated by more than 1000 miles of hostile Indian territory. East and West Pakistan also differed greatly in their natural environments (Figure 40.1) and in the ethnic makeup of their peoples and the languages they used. They even differed in their approaches to the Islamic faith that had justified including them in the same country in the first place.

Fragile national ties were eroded rapidly by the East Pakistanis' perception that they had been in effect recolonized by West Pakistan. West Pakistanis held highly disproportionate shares of government jobs and military positions, and West Pakistan received the lion's share of state revenues despite the fact that the East generated most of Pakistan's foreign earnings. By the early 1970s, East and West Pakistan were locked in a bloody civil war, which ended with the creation of the nation of *Bangladesh* from East Pakistan in 1972.

India, which relished the chance to contribute to the breakup of Pakistan, has itself been repeatedly threatened by civil strife between different linguistic, religious, and ethnic groups. In the early 1980s, Sikh guerrillas carried on a violent campaign for separation in the north, and the Indian government was forced to intervene militarily in the vio-

lent struggle between different ethnic and religious groups in Sri Lanka (Ceylon), its neighbor to the south. In 1997, an avowedly Hindu communalist party came to power in New Delhi, in defiance of the staunch adherence to the principle of a secular state, by leading Indian nationalists figures in the colonial era and all of the earlier postindependence governments. The victory of the *Bharatya Janata party (BJP)* has intensified the anxieties of the large Muslim minority and other non-Hindu religious groups about the possibility of discrimination and even open persecution.

In Africa, where there was even less of a common historical and cultural basis on which to build nationalism than in south or southeast Asia, separatist movements have been a prominent feature of the political life of new states. Secessionist movements have raged from Morocco in the northwest to Ethiopia in the east and Angola in the south (see Map 40.1). Civil wars, such as the

Figure 40.1 *Like many of the nations of east and west Africa, one of the earliest states to be carved out of the former colonies, Pakistan, contained extreme contrasts of lush tropical and arid semidesert environments. The cultures of East and West Pakistan were equally diverse, a diversity that had much to do with the violent secession of what became the nation of Bangladesh in 1971. From the Sudan to Nigeria, similar differences have threatened the viability of the new nations of Africa.*

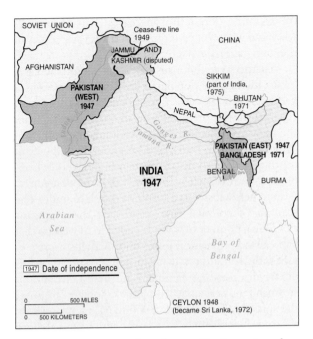

Map 40.2 *The Partition of South Asia: The Formation of India, Pakistan, Bangladesh, and Sri Lanka*

struggle of the non-Muslim peoples of the southern Sudan against the Muslim rulers from the northern parts of that country, have also abounded. Thus far, none of the secessionist movements have succeeded, although that of the Ibo peoples of eastern Nigeria, who proclaimed an independent state of *Biafra* in 1967, led to three years of bloody warfare in Africa's most populous nation (Figure 40.2).

Although Asian and African leaders have been acutely aware of the injustices and persecutions of minority groups that often precipitated these conflicts, none have seriously suggested changing the unnatural boundaries established in the colonial era. In fact, these divisions have become inviolable. African national leaders fear that a successful secession movement in a neighboring country might encourage dissident minorities in their own nation.

In all cases, the artificial nature of the new nations of Africa and Asia has proved costly. In addition to internal divisions, boundary disputes between newly independent nations have often led to border clashes and open warfare. India and Pak-

istan have fought three such wars since 1947. Iraq's *Saddam Hussein* justified his 1990 annexation of Kuwait with the argument that the tiny but oil-rich Arab "sheikhdom" was an artificial creation of the British colonizers, who had carved Kuwait out of land that historically had been part of Iraq.

Democracy has often been one of the main victims of the tensions between rival ethnic groups within African and Asian nations and threats from neighbors without. Politicians in nearly all the new states have been quick to play on communal fears as well as on ethnic and religious loyalties to win votes. As a result, freely elected legislatures have often been dominated by parties representing these special interests. Suspicions that those in power were favoring their own or allied groups has led to endless bickering and stalemates in national legislatures, which have become tempting targets for coup attempts by military strongmen. One of the more predictable reasons these usurpers have given for dictatorial rule has been the need to contain the communal tensions aroused by democratic election campaigns.

The threats from rival ethnic and religious groups felt by those in power have also contributed to exorbitant military spending by Asian and African leaders—spending that their societies can rarely afford. In countries where civil wars have actually occurred, such as Ethiopia, Mozambique, and Angola, economic development has ground to a standstill. At the same time, military clashes have resulted in widespread death, destruction, epidemic disease, and famines that have persisted in some areas for decades. These conflicts have often resisted international peacekeeping efforts, and the misery and despair they have inflicted on the peoples caught up in them often have overwhelmed even the best organized international relief agencies.

Questions: How might colonial policies have been changed to reduce the tensions between different ethnic and religious communities? Why were these measures not taken? What can be done now to alleviate these divisions? Should the United Nations or industrialized nations such as the United States or Japan intervene directly to contain communal clashes or civil wars in Africa and Asia? What is to be done with the rapidly growing refugee populations created by these conflicts?

Figure 40.2 *Since independence, famine has stalked much of the formerly colonized world, particularly in sub-Saharan Africa. Often, as in the case of these young refugees from the Nigerian civil war photographed in the late 1960s, starvation has been caused by human conflicts rather than natural disasters.*

The Population Bomb

The nationalist leaders who led the colonized peoples of Africa and Asia to independence had firmly committed themselves to promoting rapid economic development once colonial restraints were removed. In keeping with their Western-educated backgrounds, most of these leaders saw their nations following the path of industrialization that had brought national prosperity and international power to much of western Europe and the United States. This course of development was also fostered by representatives of the Soviet bloc, who had emphasized heavy industry in their state-directed drives to modernize their economies and societies. Of the many barriers to the rapid economic breakthroughs postcolonial leaders hoped for, the most formidable and persistent were the spiraling population increases that often overwhelmed whatever economic advances the peoples of the new nations managed to make.

Factors making for sustained population increases in already densely populated areas of Asia and Africa had begun to take effect even before the era of high colonialism (Figure 40.3). Food crops, mostly from the New World, contributed to dramatic population growth in China, India, and Java as early as the 17th century. They also helped sustain high levels of population in areas such as the Niger delta in west Africa, despite heavy losses as a result of the slave trade. The coming of colonial rule reinforced these upward trends in a number of ways. It ended local warfare that had caused population losses and, perhaps more significantly, had indirectly promoted the spread of epidemic diseases and famine. The new railroad and steamship links established by the colonizers to foster the spread of the market economy also cut down on the regional famines that had been a major check against sustained population increase since ancient times. Large amounts of food could be shipped from areas where harvests were good to those where drought or floods threatened the local inhabitants with starvation.

With war and famine—two of the main barriers to population increase—much reduced, growth began to speed up. This was particularly true in areas such as India and Java that had been under European control for decades. Death rates declined, but birth rates remained much the same, leading to increasingly larger net increases. Improved hygiene and medical treatment played little part in this rise until the early 20th century. From that time, efforts to eradicate tropical diseases, as well as global scourges such as smallpox, and to improve sewage systems and purify drinking water have led to further population increases.

Nearly all leaders of the emerging nations headed societies in which population was increasing at unprecedented levels. This increase continued in the early years of independence. In much of Asia, it has begun to level off in recent decades. But in most of Africa, population growth continues at very high rates. In some cases, most notably south Asia, moderate growth rates have produced huge total populations because they were adding to an already large base. As a result, in the 1970s population experts predicted that at the then-current rates, south Asia's population of more than 600 million would more than double by the year 2000. With more than 1 bil-

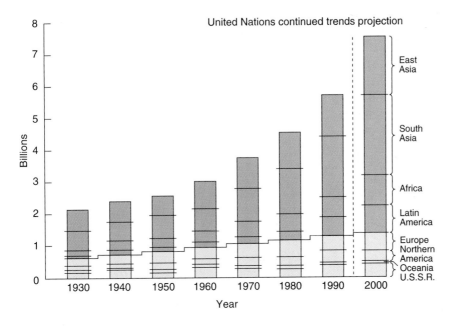

Figure 40.3 *This graph shows the growth of the world population by major global geographic areas between 1930 and the year 2000. It illustrates the near stabilization of the upswing in populations of the West and the states of the former Soviet Union that began with industrialization in the 18th century. It charts the explosion that occurred in recent decades in the areas of the globe that were colonized, both formally and informally, by the industrial powers in the 19th and early 20th centuries. These increases surpass those of any other epoch in human history.*

lion people in India alone at present, the prophecy has more than been fulfilled.

In Africa, by contrast, which began with low population levels, relative to its large land area, very high birth rates and diminished mortality rates have resulted in very steep population increases in recent decades. Some population experts predict that if present growth rates continue, by the mid-21st century Nigeria will have a population equal to that of present-day China. In view of the AIDS epidemic that has spread through much of central and eastern Africa in the 1980s and 1990s, some of the estimates for population increases in Africa as a whole may have to be revised downward. But recent measures of African productivity and per capita incomes suggest that even more moderate increases in population may be difficult to support at reasonable living standards. This prospect is underscored by estimates that the 400 million peoples of Africa are supported by a continental economy with a productive capacity equal to just 6 percent of that of the United States, or roughly equal to that of the state of Illinois.

On the face of it, the conquest of war, disease, and famine was one of the great achievements of European colonial regimes. It was certainly an accomplishment that colonial officials never tired of citing in defense of continued European dominance. But the European policy of limiting industrialization in their colonial dependencies meant that one of the key

ways by which Europe had met its own population boom in the 19th and early 20th centuries was not available to the new nations of Asia and Africa. They lacked the factories to employ the exploding population that moved to the cities from the rural areas, as well as the technology to produce the necessities of life for more and more people. Unlike the Europeans and the Americans, the emerging nations found it difficult to draw food and mineral resources from the rest of the world to feed this growing population. In fact, these were the very things the colonized peoples had been set up to sell to the industrialized nations. Even in countries such as India, where impressive advances in industrialization were made in the postcolonial era, gains in productivity were swallowed up rapidly by the population explosion.

In most African and Asian countries, there has been resistance to birth control efforts aimed at controlling population growth. Some of this resistance is linked to deeply entrenched social patterns and religious beliefs. In many of these societies, procreation is seen as a sign of male virility. In addition, the capacity to bear children, preferably male children, continues to be critical to the social standing of women. In some cases, resistance to birth control is linked to specific cultural norms. For example, Hindus believe that a deceased man's soul cannot begin the cycle of rebirth until his eldest son has performed special ceremonies over his funeral pyre. This belief increases the already great pressure on Indian women to have children, and it encourages families to have several sons to ensure that at least one survives the father.

In Africa, children are seen as indispensable additions to the *lineage:* the extended network of relatives (and deceased ancestors) that, much more than the nuclear family, makes up the core social group over much of the subcontinent. As in India, sons are essential for continuing the patrilineal family line and performing burial and ancestral rites. The key roles played by women in agricultural production and marketing make girls highly valued in African societies. This is not true in many Asian societies, where high dowries and occupational restrictions limit their contribution to family welfare.

Before the 20th century, the high rates of stillbirths and infant mortality meant that mothers could expect to lose many of the children they conceived. Ten or 12 deaths of 15 or 16 children conceived was not unheard of. Beyond the obvious psychological scars left by these high death rates, they also fostered the conviction that it was necessary to have many children to ensure that some would outlive the parents. In societies where welfare systems and old-age pensions were meager or unknown, surviving children took on special urgency because they were the only ones who would care for their parents once they could no longer work for themselves. The persistence of these attitudes in recent decades, when medical advances have greatly reduced infant mortality, has been a major factor contributing to soaring population growth.

In the early decades after independence, many African and Asian leaders were deeply opposed to state measures to promote family planning and birth control. Some saw these as Western attempts to meddle in their internal affairs; others proudly declared that the socialist societies they were building would be able to take care of the additional population. As it has become increasingly clear that excessive population increase makes significant economic advances impossible, many of these leaders have begun to reassess their attitudes toward birth control. A particular cause for alarm is the fact that in many developing countries a high percentage of the population is under age 15 (as high as 40 percent in some areas) and thus dependent on others for support. But even for those who now want to promote family planning, the obstacles are staggering. In addition to the cultural and social factors just discussed, African and

Asian leaders often find they lack sufficient resources and the educated personnel needed to make these programs effective. High rates of illiteracy, particularly among women, must be overcome, but education is expensive. Perhaps no form of financial and technical assistance from the industrialized to the developing world will be as critical in the coming decades as that devoted to family planning.

Parasitic Cities and Endangered Ecosystems

As population increase in the rural areas of emerging nations outstripped the land and employment opportunities available to the peasantry, mass migrations to urban areas ensued. The massive movement of population from overcrowded villages to the cities was one of the most dramatic developments in the postcolonial history of most African and Asian countries. Ambitious youths and the rural poor crowded into port centers and capital cities in search of jobs and a chance to find the "good life" that the big hotels and restaurants and the neon lights of the city center appeared to offer to all comers. But because most African and Asian cities lacked the rapidly expanding industrial sectors that had made possible the absorption of a similar migrant influx earlier in the West, they were often dead ends for migrants from the rural areas. There were few jobs, and heavy competition for them ensured that wages would remain low for most workers. The growing numbers of underemployed or unemployed migrants turned to street vending, scavenging, huckstering, begging, or petty crime to survive.

In the independence era, the urban poor have become a volatile factor in the political struggles of the elite. They have formed the crowds willing for a price to cheer on one contender or jeer down another, and ready to riot and loot in times of government crisis. In deeply divided societies, the poor, working-class, or idle youths of the urban areas have often formed the shock troops in communal clashes between rival ethnic and religious groups. Fear of outbursts by urban "mobs" has also forced Asian and African regimes to spend scarce resources to subsidize and thus keep low the price of staple foods, such as bread, kerosene, and other necessities.

The sudden population influx from the rural areas to cities without sufficient jobs or the infrastructure to support them has greatly skewed urban growth in the emerging nations. Within decades, Asian cities have become some of the largest in the world, and African urban areas have sprawled far beyond their modest limits in colonial times. As Figure 40.4 dramatically illustrates, the wealth of the upper- and middle-class areas, dominated by glitzy hotels and high-rises, contrasts disturbingly with the poverty of the vast slums that stretch in all directions from the city centers. Little or no planning was possible for the slum quarters that expanded as squatters erected makeshift shelters wherever open land or derelict buildings could be found. Originally, most of the slum areas lacked electricity, running water, or even the most basic sewage facilities. As shanties were gradually converted into ramshackle dwellings, many governments scrapped plans to level slum settlements and instead tried to provide them with electrical and sanitary systems. As an increasing number of development specialists have reluctantly concluded, slums often provide the only housing urban dwellers are likely to find for some time to come.

These conditions have burdened most African and Asian societies with parasitic rather than productive cities. This means that they are heavily dependent for survival on food and resources drawn from their own countryside or from abroad. In contrast to the cities of western Europe and North America, even during the decades of rapid urban expansion in the 19th century, few African or Asian cities have had the manufacturing base needed to generate growth in their surrounding regions or the nation as a whole. They take from the already impoverished countryside, but they are able to give little in return. Urban dependence on the countryside further stretches the already overextended resources of the rural areas.

Rural overpopulation in the decades after independence has led to soil depletion in many areas that have been worked for centuries or millennia. It has also resulted in an alarming rate of deforestation throughout Africa and Asia. Peasant villagers cut trees for fuel or clear land for farming and livestock grazing. Deforestation and overgrazing not only pose major threats to wild animal life but also upset the balance in fragile tropical ecosystems, producing further soil depletion and erosion and encouraging desertification. This environmental degradation is intensified by industrial pollution from both the developed countries and the emerging nations themselves. Although the industrial sectors in the latter are

Figure 40.4 *In the urban areas of undeveloped nations, the contrast between the wealth of the few and the poverty of the majority is revealed by the juxtaposition of the high-rise apartments of the affluent middle classes and the shantytowns of the urban poor. The city centers of Africa and Asia are much like those of the industrial West or Japan. But the cities as a whole in the emerging nations often are more like collections of large villages than integrated urban units. Many of these villages are vast shantytowns with varying levels of basic services such as running water, sewer systems, and transportation networks to the city center.*

small, pollution tends to be proportionally greater than in the developed world because African and Asian nations rarely can afford the antipollution technology introduced over the last few decades in western Europe, Japan, and North America.

Women's Subordination and the Nature of Feminist Struggles in the Postcolonial Era

The example of both the Western democracies and the communist republics of eastern Europe, where women had won the right to vote in the early and mid-20th century, encouraged the founders of the emerging nations to write female suffrage into their constitutions. The very active part women played in many nationalist struggles was perhaps even more critical to their earning the right to vote and run for political office. Women's activism also produced some semblance of equality in legal rights, education, and occupational opportunities under the laws of many new nations.

However, the equality that was proclaimed on paper often bore little resemblance to the actual rights that most African and Asian women could exercise. It also had little bearing on the conditions under which they lived their daily lives. Despite the media attention given to women such as *Indira Gandhi, Corazon Aquino,* and *Benazir Bhutto,* who have emerged in the decades since independence as national leaders, political life in most African and Asian countries continues to be dominated by men. The overwhelming majority of elected officials and government administrators, particularly at the upper levels of state bureaucracies, are men. Because they usually are less well educated than their husbands, women in societies where genuine elections are held often do not exercise their right to vote, or they simply vote for the party and candidates favored by their spouses.

Even the rise to power of individual women such as Indira Gandhi, who proved to be one of the most resolute and powerful of all Third World leaders, is deceptive. In every case, female heads of state in the Third World entered politics and initially won political support because they were connected to powerful men. Indira Gandhi was the daughter of *Jawaharlal Nehru,* India's first prime minister; Corazon Aquino's husband was the martyred leader of the Filipino opposition to Ferdinand Marcos; and Benazir Bhutto's father was a domineering Pakistani prime minister who had been toppled by a military coup and was executed in the late 1970s. Lacking these sorts of connections, most African and Asian women have been at best relegated to peripheral political positions and at worst are allowed no participation in the political process.

The limited gains made by African or Asian women in the political sphere are paralleled by the second-class position to which most are consigned in many societies. In some respects, their handicaps are comparable to those that constrict women in the industrialized democracies and communist nations. But the obstacles to female self-fulfillment, and in many cases mere survival, in emerging nations are usually much more blatant and fundamental than the restrictions women have to contend with in developed societies. To begin with, early marriage ages for women and large families are still the norm in most African or Asian societies. This means that women spend their youthful and middle-age years having children. There is little time to think of higher education or a career.

Because of the low level of sanitation in many African and Asian societies and the scarcity of food in many, all but elite and upper middle-class women experience chronic anxiety about such basic issues as adequate nutrition for their children and their susceptibility to disease. The persistence of male-centric customs directly affects the health and life expectancy of women themselves. For example, the Indian tradition that dictates that women first serve their husbands and sons and then eat what is left has obvious disadvantages. The quantity and nutritional content of the leftovers is likely to be lower than of the original meals, and in tropical environments flies and other disease-bearing insects are more likely to have fouled the food.

The demographic consequences of these social patterns can be dramatic. In the 1970s, for example, it was estimated that as much as 20 percent of the female population of India was malnourished and that another 30 percent had a diet that was well below acceptable United Nations levels. In sharp contrast to the industrial societies of Japan, the United States, and Europe, where women outnumber (because on the average they outlive) men, in India there are only 930 females for every 1000 males.

Although the highly secular property and divorce laws many new states passed after independence have given women much greater legal protection, many of these measures are ignored in practice. Very often, African and Asian women have neither the education nor the resources to exercise their legal rights. The spread of *religious revivalism* in many cases has further eroded these rights, even though advocates of a return to tradition often argue that practices such as veiling and stoning for women (but not men) caught in adultery actually enhance their dignity and status. Most Asian and African women continue to be dominated by male family members, are much more limited than men in their career opportunities, and are likely to be less well fed, educated, and healthy than men at comparable social levels.

Neocolonialism, Cold War Rivalries, and Stunted Development

The schemes of nationalist leaders aimed at building an industrial base that would support the rapidly increasing populations of their new nations soon yielded to the economic realities of the postcolonial world. Not only did most of the nations that emerged from colonialism have little in the way of an industrial base, but their means of obtaining one were meager. To buy the machines and hire or train the technical experts that were essential to get industrialization going, African and Asian countries needed to earn capital they could invest for these ends. Some funds could be accumulated by saving a portion of the state revenues collected from the peasantry. In most cases, however, there was little left once the bureaucrats had been paid, essential public works and education had been funded, and other state expenses had been met. Thus, most emerging nations have relied on the sale of cash crops and minerals to earn the money they need to finance industrialization. As their leaders soon discovered, the structure of the world market worked against them.

The pattern of exchange promoted in the colonial era left most newly independent countries dependent on the export production of two or three food crops or industrial raw materials. The former included cocoa, palm oil, coffee, jute, and hemp. Key among the latter were minerals, such as copper, bauxite, and oil, for which there was a high demand in the industrialized economies of Europe, North America, and increasingly Japan. Since World War II, the prices of these exports—which economists call *primary products*—have not only fluctuated widely but have declined steadily when compared to the prices of most of the manufactured goods emerging nations usually buy from the industrialized world. Price fluctuations have created nightmares for planners in Africa and Asia. Revenue estimates from the sale of coffee or copper in years when the price is high are used to plan government projects for building roads, factories, and dams. Market slumps can wipe out these critical funds, thereby retarding economic growth, and throw African or Asian countries deeply into debt. These setbacks are doubly frustrating because to get industrialization going, developing countries are often forced to export precious and finite mineral resources that they will need if they succeed in industrializing.

The leaders and planners of African and Asian countries have had little success in improving the terms under which they participate in the global market economy. Even the gains made by the oil cartel in the early 1970s proved to be confined to a few nations and to be temporary. They were soon offset to a large degree by divisions between the oil-producing states. More recently, they have been further reduced by high global production, which has driven down the price per barrel. These obstacles, which go a long way to explain Iraq's invasion of Kuwait in 1990, have made it difficult to maintain the production quotas that were essential to the great rise in the price of oil in the mid-1970s.

African and Asian leaders have been quick to blame the legacy of colonialism and what they have called the *neocolonial* structure of the global economy for the limited returns yielded thus far by their development schemes. Although there is much truth to these accusations, they do not tell the whole story. These leaders themselves must also share the responsibility for the slow pace of economic growth in much of the developing world. The members of the educated classes that came to dominate the political and business life of newly independent nations often used their positions to enrich themselves and their relatives at the expense of their societies as a whole. Corruption has been notoriously widespread in most of the new nations. Government controls on the import of goods, such as automobiles, television sets, and stereos, which are luxury items beyond the reach of most of the people, have often been lax. As a result, tax revenues and export earnings that could have fueled development have often gone to provide the good life for small minorities within emerging nations. The inability or refusal of many African and Asian regimes to carry out key social reforms, such as land redistribution, which would spread the limited resources available more equitably over the population, has contributed vitally to the persistence of these patterns.

Badly strapped for investment funds and essential technology, African and Asian nations have often turned to international organizations, such as the World Bank and the International Monetary Fund, or to rival industrial nations for assistance. Although resources for development have been gained in this way, the price for international assistance has often been high. Both the United States and the Soviet Union, as well as their allies, have demanded major concessions in return for their aid. These have ranged from commitments to buy the products of, and favor

DOCUMENT

Cultural Creativity in the Emerging Nations: Some Literary Samples

Despite, or perhaps because of, political instability and chronic economic difficulties, postcolonial African and Asian societies have generated a high level of artistic creativity over the past four or five decades. Nowhere has this creativity been more prominent and brilliant than in literary works, for which African and Asian writers have earned Nobel prizes and won a wide readership far beyond their own nations. The selections that follow are only a small sample of the vast and varied works of these talented writers, from poetry and drama to novels and short stories.

Much of the literature of Asian and African writers focuses on the predicament of the Western-educated elites who dominate the new nations that emerged from the European colonial empires. In the following stanza from the poem "I Run Around with Them," Indonesian poet Chairil Anwar reflects on the lack of purpose and malaise he believed to be widespread among the children of these elite groups.

> I run around with them, what else can I
> do, now—
> Changing my face at the edge of the street,
> I use their eyes
> And tag along to visit the fun house:
> These are the facts as I know them
> (A new American flic at the Capitol,
> The new songs they dance to).
> We go home: there's nothing doing
> Though this kind of Death is our neighbor,
> our friend, now.
> Hanging around at the corner, we wait for
> the city bus
> That glows night to day like a gold tooth;
> Lame, deformed, negative, we
> Lean our bony asses against lamp poles
> And jaw away the years.

In the next quotation from the novel *No Longer at Ease,* widely read Nigerian author Chinua Achebe identifies another dilemma: the pull between Western culture and the ancient civilization of one's own land.

Nothing gave him greater pleasure than to find another Ibo-speaking student in a London bus. But when he had to speak in English with a Nigerian student from another tribe he lowered his voice. It was humiliating to have to speak to one's countryman in a foreign language, especially in the presence of the proud owners of that language. They would naturally assume that one had no language of one's own. He wished they were here today to see. Let them come to Umuofia [the protagonist's home village] now and listen to the talk of men who made a great art of conversation. Let them come and see men and women and children who knew how to live, whose joy of life had not yet been killed by those who claimed to teach other nations how to live.

Like many of the more famous African and Asian novelists, V. S. Naipaul is an expatriate, born in the Caribbean and now living in rural England. In his moving and controversial account of his return to his Indian ancestral home, titled *An Area of Darkness,* Naipaul confronts the problem of massive poverty and the responses of foreigners and the Indian elite to it.

To see [India's] poverty is to make an observation of no value; a thousand newcomers to the country before you have seen and said as you. And not only newcomers. Our own sons and daughters, when they return from Europe and America, have spoken in your very words. Do not think that your anger and contempt are marks of your sensitivity. You might have seen more: the smiles on the faces of the begging children, that domestic group among the pavement sleepers waking in the cool Bombay morning, father, mother and baby in a trinity of love, so self-contained that they are as private as if walls had separated them from you; it is your gaze that violates them, your sense of outrage that outrages them…. It is your surprise, your anger that denies [them] humanity.

Questions: Can you think of parallels in U.S. history or contemporary society to the situations and responses conveyed in these passages from recent African and Asian writings? Do they suggest that it is possible to communicate even intimate feelings across cultures, or do you find them alien, different? What other issues would you expect African and Asian artists to deal with in their work?

investors from, the lending countries to entering into alliances and permitting military bases on the territory of the client state. Loans from international lending agencies almost invariably have been granted only after the needy nation agreed to *conditionalities*. These are regulations that determine how the money is to be invested and repaid, and they usually involve promises to make major changes in the economy of the borrowing nation.

In recent years, these promises have often included a commitment to remove or reduce state subsidies on food and other essential consumer items. State subsidies were designed to keep prices for staple goods at a level that the urban and rural poor—the great majority of the people in almost all emerging nations—could afford. When carried out, subsidy reductions often have led to widespread social unrest, riots, and the collapse or near collapse of postcolonial regimes. These violent outbursts are dramatic reminders of just how precarious social stability is in much of the developing world and of how limited and perilous are the solutions devised thus far for the problems confronting the new nations that won their independence from the European colonial empires.

PATHS TO ECONOMIC GROWTH AND SOCIAL JUSTICE

■■ *However much the leaders of the new nations of Africa and Asia might have blamed their societies' woes on the recently departed colonizers, they soon felt the need to deliver on the promises of social reform and economic well-being that had done so much to rally support to the nationalist cause. Different leaders adopted different approaches, and some tried one strategy after another. Although it is obviously impossible to deal with all of these efforts at nation-building and economic development in depth, the basic elements of several distinctive strategies are considered in this chapter. The discussion of each strategy focuses on a single, prominent case example.*

Depending on their own skills, their advisors and lieutenants, and the res... their disposal, African and Asian leaders have tack... the daunting task of development with varying degrees of success. Ways have been found to raise the living standards of a significant percentage of the population of some of the emerging nations. But these strategies have rarely benefited the majority. Solutions to specific problems have often given rise to new dilemmas. For example, the *Green Revolution* in agriculture that many development experts credit with averting global famine in the last three decades has rendered staple crops over much of the developing world more dependent on irrigation and oil-based fertilizers and more vulnerable to plant diseases. Strategies aimed at a genuine redistribution of wealth that will benefit all levels of society have suffered from bureaucratic paralysis, planning errors, and insufficient resources.

It may be too early to judge the outcomes of many development schemes. But so far, none has proved to be the path to the social justice and general economic development that nationalist leaders saw as the ultimate outcome of struggles for decolonization. Although some countries have done much better than others, successful overall strategies to deal with the challenges facing the nations of Africa and Asia have yet to be devised.

Charismatic Populists and One-Party Rule

One of the least successful responses on the part of African or Asian leaders who found their dreams for national renewal frustrated has been a retreat into authoritarian rule. This approach has often been disguised by calculated, charismatic appeals for support from the disenfranchised masses. Perhaps the career of Kwame Nkrumah, the leader of Ghana's independence movement, illustrates this pattern best (Map 40.3). There is little question that Nkrumah was genuinely committed to social reform and economic uplift for the Ghanaian people during the years of his rise to become the first prime minister of Ghana in 1957. After assuming power, he moved vigorously to initiate programs that would translate his high aspirations for his people into reality. But his ambitious schemes for everything

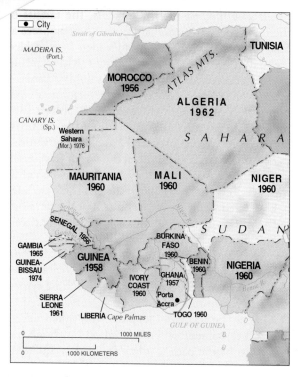

Map 40.3 *Ghana in the 1960s Under Kwame Nkrumah*

from universal education to industrial development soon ran into trouble.

Rival political parties, some representing regional interests and ethnic groups long hostile to Nkrumah, repeatedly challenged his initiatives and tried to block the efforts to carry out his plans. His leftist leanings won support from the Soviet bloc but frightened away Western investors, who had a good deal more capital to plow into Ghana's economy. They also led to growing hostility on the part of the United States, Great Britain, and other influential noncommunist countries. Most devastatingly, soon after independence, the price of cocoa—by far Ghana's largest export crop—began to fall sharply. Tens of thousands of Ghanaian cocoa farmers were hard hit and the resources for Nkrumah's development plans suddenly dried up.

Nkrumah's response to these growing problems was increasingly dictatorial. He refused to give up or cut back on his development plans. As a result, most failed miserably because of the lack of key supplies and official mismanagement. In the early 1960s, he forcibly crushed all political opposition by banning rival parties and jailing other political leaders. He

assumed dictatorial powers and ruled through functionaries in his own Convention People's Party.

Nkrumah also sought to hold on to the loyalty of the masses and mobilize their energies by highly staged "events" and the manipulation of largely invented symbols and traditions that were said to be derived from Ghana's past. Thus, he tried to justify his policies and leadership style with references to a uniquely African brand of socialism and the need to revive African traditions and African civilization. Even before independence, he had taken to wearing the traditional garb of the Ghanaian elite. The very name *Ghana*, which Nkrumah himself proposed for the new nation that emerged from the former Gold Coast colony, had been taken from an ancient African kingdom. The original Ghanaian kingdom actually was centered much farther to the north and had little to do with the peoples of the Gold Coast.

Nkrumah went about the country giving fiery speeches, dedicating monuments to the "revolution," which often consisted of giant statues of himself (Figure 40.5). He also assumed a prominent role in the nonaligned movement that was then sweeping the newly independent nations. As the French journalist Jean Lacouture reported in the mid-1960s, Nkrumah's posturing had become a substitute for his failed development schemes. His followers' adulation knew no bounds. Members of his captive parliament compared him to Confucius, Muhammad, Shakespeare, and Napoleon and predicted that his birthplace would serve as a "Mecca" for all of Africa's leaders. But his suppression of all opposition and his growing ties to the Communist party, coupled with the rapid deterioration of the Ghanaian economy, increased the ranks of his enemies, who waited for a chance to strike. That chance came early in 1966, when Nkrumah went off on one of his many trips, this time a peace mission to Vietnam. In his absence, he was deposed by a military coup. Nkrumah died in exile in 1972, and Ghana moved in a very different direction under its new military rulers.

Military Responses: Dictatorships and Revolutions

Nkrumah was just one of many civilian leaders in the postcolonial world who have been victims of military coups. In fact, it is far more difficult to find African and Asian (or, as we have seen in Chapter 38, Latin American) countries that have remained under civilian

Figure 40.5 *Many monumental statues of Kwame Nkrumah such as this one rose in the towns and villages of Ghana as he tried to cover the failure of his socialist-inspired development programs with dictatorial rule and self-glorification. Although Nkrumah's efforts to cover his regime's failures through self-glorifying displays and pageantry were extreme, they were not unique. The many photos of the "great leader" of the moment that one finds in many developing nations are a variation on Nkrumah's tactics. And these state campaigns to glorify the dictatorial figures are reminiscent of those mounted by the leaders of the communist revolutions in Russia, China, and Cuba.*

regimes since independence than those that have experienced military takeovers of varying durations. India, the Ivory Coast, Kenya, Zambia, and Zimbabwe are some of the more notable of the former; much of south and southeast Asia and the rest of Africa have been or are now governed by military regimes. Given the difficulties that leaders such as Nkrumah faced after

independence and the advantages the military have in crisis situations, the proliferation of coups in the emerging nations is not surprising.

The armed forces in African and Asian countries have at times been divided by the religious and ethnic rivalries that have been so disruptive in new nations. But the regimentation and emphasis on discipline and in-group solidarity in military training often render soldiers more resistant than other social groups to these forces. In conditions of political breakdown and social conflict, the military possesses the monopoly—or near monopoly—of force that is often essential for restoring order. Their occupational conditioning makes soldiers not only more ready than civilian leaders to use the force at their disposal but less concerned with its destructive consequences. Military personnel also tend to have some degree of technical training, which was usually lacking in the humanities-oriented education of civilian nationalist leaders. Because most military leaders have been staunchly anticommunist, they have often attracted covert technical and financial assistance from Western governments.

Once in control, military leaders have banned civilian political parties and imposed military regimes of varying degrees of repression and authoritarian control. Yet the ends to which these regimes have put their dictatorial powers have differed greatly. At their worst, military regimes—such as those in Uganda (especially under Idi Amin), Burma (now Myanmar), and Zaire—have quashed civil liberties while making little attempt to reduce social inequities or improve living standards. These regimes have existed mainly to enrich the military leaders and their allies. Military governments of this sort have been notorious for official corruption and for imprisoning, torturing, or eliminating political dissidents. Understandably uneasy about being overthrown, these regimes have diverted a high proportion of their nations' meager resources, which might have gone for economic development, into expenditures on expensive military hardware. Neither the Western democracies nor the countries of the Soviet bloc have hesitated to supply arms to these military despots. Military leaders of this type have also been ready to use quarrels and sometimes military conflicts with neighboring regimes to divert attention from the failure of their domestic policies.

In a few cases, military leaders have been radical in their approaches to economic and social reform. Perhaps none was more so than *Gamal Abdul Nasser*

(Figure 40.6), who took power in Egypt after a military coup in 1952. As we have seen in Chapter 39, the Egyptians won their independence in the mid-1930s except for the lingering British presence in the Suez Canal zone (Map 40.4). But self-centered civilian politicians and the corrupt khedival regime had done little to improve the standard of living of the mass of the Egyptian people. As conditions worsened and Egypt's governing parties did little but rake in wealth for their elitist memberships, revolutionary forces emerged in Egyptian society.

The radical movement that succeeded in gaining power, the *Free Officers movement*, evolved from a secret organization established in the Egyptian army in the 1930s. Founded by idealistic young officers of Egyptian rather than Turco-Egyptian descent, the secret Revolutionary Command Council studied conditions in the country and prepared to seize power in the name of a genuine revolution. For many decades, it was loosely allied to the *Muslim Brotherhood*, another revolutionary alternative to the khedival regime.

The brotherhood was founded by Hasan al-Banna (see Figure 40.7) in 1928. Al-Banna was a schoolteacher who had studied in his youth with the famous Muslim reformer Muhammad Abduh. While at Al-Azhar University in Cairo in the years after World War I, al-Banna had combined a deep interest in scientific subjects with active involvement in student demonstrations in support of Wafd demands for Egyptian independence. In this period, like many other Egyptian students, al-Banna developed contempt for the wealthy minority of Egyptians and Europeans who flourished in the midst of the appalling poverty of most of his people.

To remedy these injustices and rid Egypt of its foreign oppressors, al-Banna founded the Muslim Brotherhood in 1928. Although members of the organization were committed to a revivalist approach to Islam, the brotherhood's main focus, particularly in the early years, was on a program of social uplift and sweeping reforms. The organization became involved in a wide range of activities, from promoting trade unions and building medical clinics to educating women and pushing for land reform. By the late 1930s, the brotherhood's social service had become highly politicized. Al-Banna's followers fomented strikes and urban riots and established militant youth organizations and paramilitary assassination squads. Despite the murder of al-Banna by the Khedive Farouk's assassins in 1949, the members of the brotherhood continued to expand its influence in the early 1950s among both middle-class youths and the impoverished masses.

After Egypt's humiliating defeats in the first Arab–Israeli War of 1948 and in a clash with the British over the latter's continuing occupation of the

Figure 40.6 *After the Free Officers' seizure of power in the 1952 coup, a young general named Nasser emerged as the most charismatic and able of a number of rivals for power. For nearly two decades Nasser dominated Egyptian politics and was a major force in Middle Eastern history.*

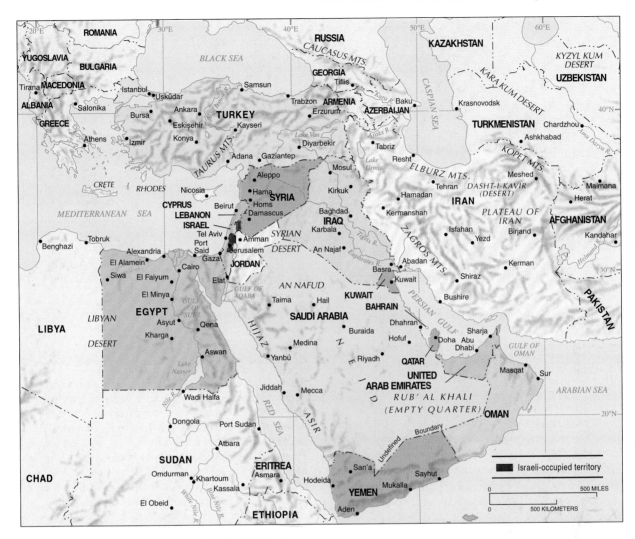

Map 40.4 *The Middle East in the Cold War Era*

Suez Canal zone in 1952, mass anger with a discredited khedival and parliamentary regime gave the officers their chance. In July 1952, an almost bloodless military coup toppled the corrupt khedive Farouk from his jewel-encrusted throne (Figure 40.8).

The revolution had begun. The monarchy was ended, and with the installation of Nasser and the Free Officers, Egyptians ruled themselves for the first time since the 6th century B.C.E. By 1954, all political parties had been disbanded, including the Muslim Brotherhood, which had clashed with its former allies in the military and had been suppressed after an attempt on Nasser's life. Nasser was only one of several officers at the head of the Free Officers move-

ment, and by no means was he initially the most charismatic. But after months of internal power struggles in the officer corps, he emerged as the head of a military government that was deeply committed to revolution.

Nasser and his fellow officers used the dictatorial powers they had won in the coup to force through programs that they believed would uplift the long-oppressed Egyptian masses. They were convinced that only the state had the power to carry out essential social and economic reforms, and thus they began to intervene in all aspects of Egyptian life. Land reform measures were enacted: Limits were placed on how much land an individual could own, and excess

Figure 40.7 *Hasan al-Banna, founder of the Muslim Brotherhood.*

Figure 40.8 *The growing Egyptian resistance to the British occupation of the Suez Canal zone was expressed in this effigy of a British soldier that was strung up on a Cairo street corner in January 1952. The Arabic banner that accompanies the mock hanging reminds Egyptians of the Dinshawai incident, discussed in Chapter 39, and the need to sustain resistance to British domination. Within months of this protest, mass demonstrations and a military coup freed the Egyptian people from both the British occupation and the repressive khedival regime.*

lands were seized and redistributed to landless peasants. State-financed education through the college level was made available to Egyptians. The government became Egypt's main employer; by 1980, more than 30 percent of Egypt's work force was on the state payroll. State subsidies were used to lower the price of basic food staples, such as wheat and cooking oil. State-controlled development schemes were introduced that emphasized industrial growth, modeled after the Five-Year Plans of the Soviet Union.

To establish Egypt's economic independence, stiff restrictions were placed on foreign investment. In some cases foreign properties were seized and redistributed to Egyptian investors. Nasser also embarked on an interventionist foreign policy that stressed the struggle to destroy the newly established Israeli state, forge Arab unity, and foment socialist revolutions in neighboring lands. His greatest foreign policy coup came in 1956, when he rallied international opinion to finally oust the British and their French allies from the Suez Canal zone. Despite the setbacks suffered by Egyptian military forces, Nasser made good use of the rare combined backing of the United States and the Soviet Union to achieve his aims in the crisis.

However well intentioned, many of Nasser's initiatives misfired. Land reform efforts were frustrated by bureaucratic corruption and the clever strategies devised by the landlord class to hold on to their estates. State development schemes often lacked proper funding and failed because of mismanagement and miscalculations. Even the Aswan Dam project, which was the cornerstone of Nasser's development drive, was a fiasco. Egypt's continuing population boom quickly canceled out the additional cultivable lands the dam produced. The dam's interference with the flow of the Nile resulted in increasing numbers of parasites that cause blindness. It also led to a decline in the fertility of farmlands in the lower Nile delta, which were deprived of the rich silt that normally was washed down by the river. Foreign investment funds from the West, which Egypt desperately needed, soon dried up. Aid from the much poorer Soviet bloc could not begin to match what was lost, and much of this assistance was military. In the absence of sufficient foreign investment and with Egypt's uncontrolled population rising at an alarming rate, the state simply could not afford all the ambitious schemes to which Nasser and the revolutionary officers had committed it. The gap between aspirations and means was increased in the later years of Nasser's reign (in the 1960s) by the heavy costs of his mostly failed foreign adventures, including the disastrous Six-Day War with Israel in 1967.

Although he had to move slowly at first, Nasser's successor, *Anwar Sadat,* had little choice but to dismantle the massive state apparatus that had been created. He favored private rather than state initiatives. During Sadat's tenure in office the middle class, which had been greatly restricted by Nasser, emerged again as a powerful force. After fighting the Israelis to a stalemate in 1973, Sadat also moved to end the costly confrontation with Israel as well as Egypt's support for revolutionary movements in the Arab world. He expelled the Russians and opened Egypt to aid and investment from the United States and western Europe.

Sadat's shift in direction has been continued by his successor, *Hosni Mubarak.* But neither the attempt at genuine revolution led by Nasser nor the move to capitalism and more pro-West positions under his successors has done much to check Egypt's alarming population increases and the corruption of its bloated bureaucracy. Neither path to development has had much effect on the glaring gap between the living conditions of Egypt's rich minority and its impoverished masses. No better gauge of the discontent that is bred by these inequities can be found than the proliferation of Muslim fundamentalist movements. One of these succeeded in assassinating Sadat; others have sustained terrorist campaigns aimed at overthrowing the Mubarak regime.

The Indian Alternative: Development for Some of the People

Although the approach to nation-building and economic development followed by the leaders of independent India has shared the Nasserite emphasis on socialism and state intervention, India's experience has differed from Egypt's in several significant ways. To begin with, the Indians have managed to preserve civilian rule throughout the nearly five decades since they won their independence from Great Britain. In fact, in India the military has consistently defended secular democracy against religious extremism and other would-be authoritarian trends. In addition, although India, like Egypt, has been saddled with a crushing burden of overpopulation, it came to independence with a larger industrial and scientific sector, a better communication system and bureaucratic grid, and a larger and more skilled middle class in proportion to its total population than any other African or Asian country.

During the first decades of its freedom, India had the good fortune to be governed by leaders such as Jawaharlal Nehru and his allies in the Congress party who were deeply committed to social reform and economic development as well as the preservation of civil rights and democracy. India's success at the latter has been remarkable. Despite continuous threats of secession by religious and linguistic minorities, as well as poverty, unemployment, and recurring natural disasters, India remains the world's largest functioning democracy. Except for brief periods of rule by coalitions of opposition parties, the Congress party has ruled at the center for most of the independence era. But opposition parties have controlled many state and local governments, and they remain vocal and active in the national parliament. Civil liberties, exemplified by a very outspoken press and free elections, have been upheld to an extent that sets India off from much of the rest of the emerging nations. Their staying power was perhaps most emphatically demonstrated by the heavy political price that Nehru's daughter and more dictatorially prone successor, Indira Gandhi, paid for trying to curtail press and political freedoms in the mid-1970s. That attempt led to one of the rare election defeats the Congress party has suffered until well into the 1990s.

Nehru's approach to government and development also differed from Nasser's in his more moderate mix of state and private initiatives. Nehru and his successors pushed state intervention in some sectors but also encouraged foreign investment from countries in both of the rival blocs in the cold war. As a consequence, India has been able to build on its initial advantages in industrial infrastructure and its skilled managerial and labor endowment. Its significant capitalist sector has encouraged ambitious farmers, such as those in the Punjab in the northwest, to invest heavily in the improved seed strains, fertilizers, and irrigation that are at the heart of the Green Revolution. Industrial and agrarian growth has generated the revenue for the Indian government to promote literacy and village development schemes, as well as family planning, village electrification, and other improvement projects in recent decades.

Despite its successes, India has suffered from the same gap between needs and resources that all developing nations have had to face. Whatever the government's intentions—and India has been hit by corruption and self-serving politicians like most nations—there have simply not been the resources to raise the living standards of even a majority of its huge population. The middle class has grown, perhaps as rapidly as that of any postcolonial nation. Its presence is striking in the affluent neighborhoods of cities such as Bombay and Delhi and is proclaimed by the Indian film industry, the world's largest, and in many sitcoms and dramas about the lives of Indian-style yuppies. But as many as 50 percent of India's people have gained little from the development plans and economic growth that have occurred since independence.

In part, this is because population growth has offset economic gains. But social reform has been slow in most areas, both rural and urban. Groups such as the wealthy landlords, who supported the nationalist drive for independence, have continued to dominate the great mass of tenants and landless laborers, just as they did in the precolonial and colonial eras. Some development measures, most notably those associated with the Green Revolution, have greatly favored cultivators with the resources to invest in new seeds and fertilizer. They have increased the gap between rich and poor people over much of rural India. India's literacy rate remains well below that of China (the only rival with which it can be compared usefully, given the size of each and the magnitude of the problems they face), and a far larger proportion of India's population remains malnourished. Thus, the poor have paid and will continue to pay the price for Indian gradualism. Consequently, those favoring more revolutionary solutions to India's social inequities and mass poverty have plenty of ammunition with which to attack the ruling parties.

Iran: Religious Revivalism and the Rejection of the West

No path of development adopted by a postcolonial society has provided more fundamental challenges to the existing world order than revolutionary Iran under the direction of *Ayatollah Khomeini*. In many respects, the Khomeini revolution of 1979 was a throwback to the religious fervor of such anticolonial resistance movements as that led by the Mahdi of the Sudan in the 1880s. Core motivations for the followers of both movements were provided by the emphasis on religious purification and the rejoining of religion and politics, which leaders such as the Mahdi and Khomeini have seen as central to the Islamic tradition. The call for a return to the kind of society believed to have existed in the past "golden age" of the prophet Muhammad was central to the policies pursued by both the Mahdist and Iranian regimes once they had gained power. Both movements were aimed at toppling Western-backed governments: the Mahdists' the Anglo-Egyptian presence in the Sudan, Khomeini's the autocratic Iranian shah and the Pahlavi dynasty.

Although they came from the Sunni and Shi'ite religious traditions, respectively, both the Mahdi and Khomeini claimed to be divinely inspired deliverers. Each promised to rescue the Islamic faithful from imperialist Westerners and from corrupt and heretical leaders within the Muslim world. Both leaders promised their followers magical protection and instant paradise should they fall while waging the holy war against the heretics and infidels. Each leader sought to build a lasting state and social order on the basis of what were believed to be Islamic precedents. Thus, each revivalist movement aimed at defending and restoring what its leaders believed to be the true beliefs, traditions, and institutions of Islamic civilization. The leaders of both movements sought to spread their revolutions to surrounding areas, both Muslim and infidel, and each believed he was setting in motion forces that would eventually sweep the entire globe.

Though proclaimed as an alternative path for development that could be followed by the rest of the emerging nations, Khomeini's revolution owed its initial success in seizing power to a combination of circumstances that was unique to Iran. Like China, Iran had not been formally colonized by the European powers but rather had been reduced to a sphere of informal influence, divided between Great Britain and Russia. As a result, neither the bureaucratic nor the communication infrastructures that accompanied colonial takeovers were highly developed there. Nor did a substantial Western-educated middle class emerge. Thus, the impetus for "modernization" came suddenly and was imposed from above by the Pahlavi shahs. The initiatives taken by the second shah in particular, which were supported by Iran's considerable oil wealth, wrenched Iran out of the isolation and backwardness in which most of the nation lived until the mid-20th century. The shah tried to impose economic development and social change by government directives. Although advances occurred, the regime managed to alienate the great mass of the Iranian people in the process.

The shah's dictatorial and repressive regime deeply offended the emerging middle classes, whom he considered his strongest potential supporters. His flaunting of Islamic conventions and his neglect of Islamic worship and religious institutions enraged the *ayatollahs,* or religious experts. They also alienated the *mullahs,* or local prayer leaders and mosque attendants, who guided the religious and personal lives of the great majority of the Iranian population. The favoritism the shahs showed foreign investors and a handful of big Iranian entrepreneurs with personal connections to highly placed officials angered the smaller bazaar merchants, who had long maintained close links with the mullahs and other religious leaders. The shah's half-hearted land reform schemes alienated the land-owning classes without doing much to improve the condition of the rural poor. Even the urban workers, who benefited most from the boom in construction and light industrialization the shah's development efforts had stimulated, were dissatisfied. In the years before the 1979 revolution, a fall in oil prices had resulted in an economic slump and widespread unemployment in urban areas such as the capital, Tehran.

Although he had treated his officers well, the shah had badly neglected the military rank-and-file, especially in the army. So when the crisis came in 1978, the shah found that few soldiers were prepared to defend his regime. His armies refused to fire on the growing crowds that demonstrated for his removal and the return of Khomeini, then in exile in Paris. Dying of cancer and disheartened by what he saw as betrayal by his people and by allies such as the United States, the shah fled without much of a fight. Khomeini's revolution triumphed over a regime that looked powerful but proved to be exceptionally vulnerable.

After coming to power, Khomeini, defying the predictions of most Western "experts" on Iranian affairs, followed through on his promises of radical change. Constitutional and leftist parties allied to the revolutionary movement were brutally repressed. Moderate leaders were replaced quickly by radical religious figures who were eager to obey Khomeini's every command. The "satanic" influences of the United States and western Europe were purged; at the same time, Iran also distanced itself from the atheistic communist world. Secular influences in law and government were supplanted by strict Islamic

legal codes, which included such punishments as the amputation of limbs for theft and stoning for women caught in adultery. Veiling became obligatory for all women (see chapter opener), and the career prospects for women of the educated middle classes, who had been among the most favored by the shah's reforms, suddenly were limited drastically.

Khomeini's planners also drew up grand schemes for land reform, religious education, and economic development that accorded with the dictates of Islam. Most of these measures came to little because soon after the revolution, Saddam Hussein, the military leader of neighboring Iraq, sought to take advantage of the turmoil in Iran by annexing its western, oil-rich provinces. The *First Gulf War* that resulted swallowed up Iranian energies and resources for almost the entire decade after Khomeini came to power. Although the struggle clearly was initially the fault of the invading Iraqis, it became a highly personal vendetta for Khomeini, who was determined to destroy Saddam Hussein and punish the Iraqis. His refusal to negotiate peace caused heavy losses and untold suffering to the Iranian people. This suffering continued long after it was clear that the Iranians' aging military equipment and handful of allies were no match for Hussein's more advanced military hardware and an Iraqi war machine bankrolled by its oil-rich Arab neighbors, who were fearful that Khomeini's revolution might spread to their own countries.

As the support of the Western powers, including the United States (despite protestations of neutrality), for the Iraqis increased, the position of the isolated Iranians became increasingly intolerable. Hundreds of thousands of poorly armed and half-trained Iranian conscripts, including tens of thousands of untrained and nearly weaponless boys, died before Khomeini finally agreed to a humiliating armistice in 1988. Peace found revolutionary Iran in shambles. Few of its development initiatives had been pursued, and shortages in food, fuel, and the other necessities of life were widespread.

Iran's decade-long absorption in the war and its continuing isolation makes it impossible to assess the potential of the religious revivalist, anti-Western option for other postcolonial nations. What had seemed at first to be a viable path to independent development for African and Asian peoples had become mired in brutal internal repression and misguided and failed development schemes.

Visualizing THE PAST

Globalization and Post-Colonial Societies

Although many of the areas colonized by the industrialized nations of the West had participated in long-distance trade from early times, colonial rule greatly intensified their integration into the capitalist-dominated world system. Colonization also brought more remote areas that had been only marginally affected by cross-cultural trade into the world system for the first time. As we have seen in Chapters 30 and 39, new market linkages not only affected the elites and trading classes of African and Asian societies, they increasingly involved the peasants, who made up the great majority of the population of colonial societies, as well as smaller numbers of workers in the towns and cities.

In the post-colonial era, this process of global market integration has accelerated steadily. One key feature of advancing globalization has been the specialized production of mineral and agricultural exports for foreign consumption. Another has been the growing proportion of uprooted farmers and urban laborers in post-colonial societes employed in factories manufacturing clothing, household furnishings, audio-visual equipment and other consumer goods for sale overseas, particularly in wealthy societies such as those in North America, western Europe and Japan. These shifts have greatly increased trading links and economic independence between post-colonial societies and those that had formerly colonized them.

Questions: The pervasiveness of these connections in the daily lives of peoples around the globe can be readily seen in the shoes, clothing and watches worn by the teacher and students in your class, and by the equipment and furnishings of your classrooms. Poll the class to determine where these items and other school supplies were produced. Discuss household and other personal items which were likely to have been manufactured, or at least assembled, in similar locales. Then consider the conditions under which the laborers who made these products were likely to have worked, and the international corporations which oversee and market these products. Who benefits the most from the profits made in the international marketing of such goods? How does the fact they are imported in massive quantities affect the wages and working conditions of American factory laborers? What measures can be taken to improve the situation of both workers overseas and those in the United States, or are the interests of the two irreconcilable?

South Africa: The Apartheid State and Its Demise

South Africa was by no means the only area still under some form of colonial dominance decades after India gained its independence in 1947. Portugal, the oldest and long considered the weakest of the European colonizers, held onto Angola, Mozambique, and its other African possessions until the mid-1970s. Until 1980, Zimbabwe (formerly Southern Rhodesia) was run by white settlers, who had unilaterally declared their independence from Great Britain. Southwest Africa became fully free of South African control only in 1989, and some of the smaller islands in the West Indies and the Pacific remain under European or American rule to the present day.

By the 1970s, however, South Africa was by far the largest, most populous, richest, and most strategic area where most of the population had yet to be liberated from colonial domination. Since the 1940s, the white settlers, particularly the Dutch-descended Afrikaners, had solidified their internal control of the country under the leadership of the Nationalist party. In stages and through a series of elections in which the blacks, who made up the majority of South Africans, were not allowed to vote, the Nationalists won complete independence from Great Britain in 1960. From 1948, when the Nationalist party first came to power, the Afrikaners moved to institution-alize white supremacy and white minority rule by passing thousands of laws that, taken together, made up the system of *apartheid* that dominated all aspects of South African life until the 1990s.

Apartheid was designed not only to ensure a monopoly of political power and economic domi-nance for the white minority, both British- and Dutch-descended, but also to impose a system of extreme segregation on all races of South Africa in all aspects of their lives. Separate and patently unequal facilities were established for different racial groups for recreation, education, housing, work, and medical care. Dating and sexual intercourse across racial lines were strictly prohibited, skilled and high-paying jobs were reserved for white workers, and nonwhites were required to carry passes that listed the parts of South Africa where they were allowed to work and live. If caught by the police without their passes or in areas where they were not permitted to travel, nonwhite South Africans were routinely given stiff jail sentences.

Spatial separation was also organized on a grander scale by the creation of numerous *homelands* within South Africa, each designated for the main ethnolin-guistic or "tribal" groups within the black African population. Though touted by the Afrikaners as the ultimate solution to the racial "problem," the home-lands scheme would have left the black African major-ity with a small portion of some of the poorest land in South Africa. Because the homelands were overpopu-lated and poverty-stricken, the white minority was guaranteed a ready supply of cheap black labor to work in their factories and mines and on their farms. Denied citizenship in South Africa proper, these labor-ers would have been forced eventually to return to the homelands, where they had left their wives and chil-dren while emigrating in search of work.

To maintain the blatantly racist and inequitable system of apartheid, the white minority had to build a police state and expend a large portion of the fed-eral budget on a sophisticated and well-trained mili-tary establishment. Because of the land's great mineral wealth, the Afrikaner nationalists were able to find the resources to fund their garrison state for decades. Until the late 1980s, the government prohibited all forms of black protest and brutally repressed even nonviolent resistance. Black organizations such as the *African National Congress* were declared illegal, and African leaders such as *Walter Sisulu* and *Nelson Man-dela* were shipped off to maximum-security prisons. Other leaders, such as *Steve Biko*, one of the young

organizers of the Black Consciousness movement, was murdered while in police custody.

Through spies and police informers, the regime tried to capitalize on personal and ethnic divisions within the black majority community. Favoritism was shown to some leaders and groups to keep them from uniting with others in all-out opposition to apartheid. With all avenues of constitutional negoti-ation and peaceful protest closed, many advocates of black majority rule in a multiracial society turned to guerrilla resistance from the 1960s onward. The South African government responded in the 1980s by declaring a state of emergency, which simply intensified the restrictions already in place in the gar-rison state. The government repeatedly justified its repression by labeling virtually all black protest as communist-inspired and playing on the racial fears of the white minority.

Through most of the 1970s and early 1980s, it appeared that the hardening hostility between the unyielding white minority and the frustrated black majority was building to a very violent upheaval. But from the late 1980s, countervailing forces were tak-ing hold in South African society. An international boycott greatly weakened the South African economy. In addition, the South African army's costly and futile involvement in wars in neighboring Namibia and Angola seemed to presage never-ending struggles against black liberation movements within the coun-try. Led by the courageous *F. W. De Klerk,* moderate Afrikaner leaders pushed for reforms that began to dis-mantle the system of apartheid. The release of key black political prisoners, such as the dramatic freeing of Nelson Mandela in 1990, signaled that at long last the leaders of the white majority were ready to nego-tiate the future of South African politics and society. Permission for peaceful mass demonstrations and ulti-mately the enfranchisement of all adult South Africans for the 1994 elections provided a way out of the dead end in which the nation was trapped under apartheid.

The well-run and remarkably participatory 1994 elections brought to power the African National Con-gress party, led by Nelson Mandela. He has proved to be one of the most skillful and respected political lead-ers on the world scene as well as a moderating force in the potentially volatile South African arena. The peaceful surrender of power by F. W. De Klerk's los-ing party, which was supported by most of the white minority, suggested that a pluralist democracy might well succeed in South Africa. But major obstacles remain. Bitter interethnic rivalries within the black

Figure 40.8 *This photograph of a long lines of newly enfranchised citizens waiting to vote in the 1995 election in South Africa provides a striking contrast with the decreasing participation in elections in the United States and other older democracies in the West. For the first time, the Bantu-speaking peoples, coloreds and Indians, who made up the vast majority of South Africa's population, were allowed to vote in free elections. Their determination to exercise their hard-won right to vote was demonstrated by the peoples' willingness to wait, often in stifling heat, for many hours in the long lines that stretched from polling stations throughout the country.*

majority community, which periodically flared into bloody battles between Zulus and Xhosas in 1990s, have yet to be fully resolved. Hard-line white supremacist organizations among the Afrikaners continue to defy the new regime. And the tasks of reforming the institutions and redistributing the wealth of South Africa in ways that will make for a just and equitable social order are formidable. Well into the 21st century, South Africa is likely to remain one of the most interesting and promising social experiments of an age in which communalism and ethnic hostility threatened to engulf much of the globe.

Conclusion

The Postcolonial Experience in Historical Perspective

Although the years of independence for the nations that have emerged from the colonial empires have been filled with political and economic crises and social turmoil, it is important to put the recent history of Africa and Asia in a larger perspective. Most of the new nations that emerged from colonialism have been in existence for only a few decades. They came to independence with severe handicaps, many of which were a direct legacy of their colonial experiences. It is also important to remember that developed countries, such as the United States, took decades and numerous boundary disputes and outright wars to reach their current size and structure. Nearly a century after the original 13 colonies broke from Great Britain and formed the United States, a civil war, the most costly war in the nation's history, was needed to preserve the union. If one takes into account the artificial nature of the emerging nations, most have held together rather well.

What is true in politics is true of all other aspects of the postcolonial experience of the African and Asian peoples. With much lower populations and far fewer industrial competitors, as well as the capacity to draw on the resources of much of the rest of the world, European and North American nations had to struggle to industrialize and thereby achieve a reasonable standard of living for most of their people. Even with these advantages, the human cost in terms of horrific working conditions and urban squalor was enormous, and we are still paying the high ecological price. African and Asian countries (and, as we saw in Chapter 33, this includes Japan) have had few or none of the West's advantages. They have begun the "great ascent" to development burdened by excessive and rapidly increasing populations that overwhelm the limited resources that developing nations often must export to earn the capital to buy food and machines. The emerging nations struggle to establish a place in the world market system that is structured in favor of the established industrial powers.

Despite the cultural dominance of the West, which was one of the great legacies or burdens of the colonial era, Asian and African thinkers and artists have achieved a great deal. If much of this achievement has depended on Western models, one should not be surprised, given the educational backgrounds and personal experiences of the first generations of African and Asian leaders. The challenge for the coming generations will be to find genuinely African and Asian solutions to the problems that have stunted political and economic development in the postcolonial nations. The solutions arrived at are likely to vary a great deal, given the diversity of the nations and societies involved. They are also likely to be forged from a combination of Western influences and the ancient and distinguished traditions of civilized life that have been nurtured by African and Asian peoples for millennia.

Further Readings

Much of the literature on political and economic development in the emerging nations is focused on individual countries, and it is more helpful to know several cases in some depth than to try to master them all. Robert Heilbroner's writings, starting with his *The Great Ascent* (1961), still provide the most sensible introduction to challenges to the new states in the early decades of independence. Peter Worsley's *The Third World* (1964) provides a provocative, if somewhat disjointed, supplement to Heilbroner's many works. Though focused mainly on south and southeast Asia, Gunnar Myrdal's *Asian Drama*, 3 vols. (1968) is the best exploration in a single cultural area of the complexities of the challenges to development. A good overview of the history of postindependence south Asia can be found in W. N. Brown's *The United States and India, Pakistan, and Bangladesh* (1984 ed.), despite its misleadingly Western-centric title. Perhaps the best account of Indian politics is contained in Paul Brass's *The Politics of Independence* (1990) in the *New Cambridge History of India* series. On development policy in India, see Francine R. Frankel's *India's Political Economy, 1947–1977* (1978). Ali Mazrui and Michael Tidy's *Nationalism and New States in Africa* (1984) provides a good survey of developments throughout Africa. Also useful are S. A. Akintoye's *Emergent African States* (1976) and H. Bretton's *Power and Politics in Africa* (1973). For the Middle East, John Waterbury's *The Egypt of Nasser and Sadat* (1983) provides a detailed account of the politics of development, and Peter Mansfield's *The Arabs* (1978) supplies a decent (if dated) overview.

On military coups, see Ruth First's *The Barrel of a Gun* (1971) and S. Decalo's *Coups and Army Rule in Africa* (1976). Shaul Bakash's *The Reign of the Ayatollahs* (1984) is perhaps the most insightful of several books that have appeared on Iran since the revolution. Brian Bunting's *The Rise of the South African Reich* (1964) traces the rise of the apartheid regime in great (and polemic) detail, and Gail Gerhart's *Black Power in South Africa* (1978) is one of the better studies devoted to efforts to tear apartheid down. Among the many fine African and Asian authors whose works are available in English, some of the best include (for Africa) Chinua Achebe, Wole Soyinka, and Ousmene Sembene; (for India) A. R. Narayan and V. S. Naipaul; (for Egypt) Nawal el Saadawi and Naguib Mahfouz; and (for Indonesia) Mochtar Lubis and P. A. Toer. For white perspectives on the South African situation, the fictional works of Nadine Gordimer and J. M. Coetzee are superb.

On the Web

Jawaharlal Nehru's views on Marxism, capitalism and non-alignment are presented at http://www.fordham. edu/halsall/mod/1941/nehru.html. A useful review of India's first fifty years of independence may be found at http://www.itihaas.com/independent/contrib7.html.

Kwame N'Krumah's classic indictment of neo-colonialism can be found at http://miavx1.acs.muohio.edu/~hstcwis /zinsser/ neoclasm.html, while a classically neo-conservative view condemning neo-colonialism, but not modernization, is offered at http://www.afbis.com/analysis /neo-colonialism.html.

Gamal Abdul Nasser's Cold War era experiments with Arab socialism as the best means of negotiating modernization are discussed at http://www.arab.net/egypt /history/et_nasser.html.

The debate over the role of religion as a solution to the moral malaise as well as the disparity of wealth that has come to characterize the post-modern era is illuminated by the works of Hasan al-Banna of the Muslim Brotherhood (http://www.prelude.co.uk/mb/banna/message.htm), by the life of Iran's Ayatollah Komaini (http://users. detanet.com/~cybrgbl/burning/ ayatollah-khomeini .html) and by the platform of India's Bharatiya Janata Party (http://www.bjp.com).

Chapter 41

War and Revolution in China and Vietnam

Mao Zezong as the friend and father of the people is the theme emphasized in this colorful poster from the Maoist era. Soldiers, peasants, women, children and peoples from many regions of China are pictured here rallying to Mao's vision of a strong, just and prosperous China.

延 安 新 春

In many respects, the recent histories of China and the peoples of Japan, Korea, and Vietnam, whose cultures were so profoundly affected by Chinese civilization, have been fundamentally different from that of much of the rest of Asia and Africa. Particularly in the past century, the experience of the Japanese has diverged the most from those of other African and Asian peoples (see Chapters 33 and 37). The ethnically homogenous, politically unified, and militarily adept Japanese not only were able to beat off Western imperialist advances against their island home but they have been one of the few non-Western peoples to achieve a high level of industrialization. Within decades of the forced "opening" of Japan by the United States in the 1850s, Japan also became the only African or Asian nation to join the ranks of the great powers. In imitation of its Western rivals, it embarked on its own campaign of imperialist expansion overseas. Although Korea was colonized early in the 20th century by its powerful Japanese neighbor, in the decades since World War II it has emerged as one of the new industrial centers on the Pacific Rim (see Chapter 37).

In contrast to industrialized Japan and to Korea in the past three decades or so, with their high standards of living and global economic power, the recent histories of China and Vietnam have had a good deal in common with the rest of the emerging nations. Both China and Vietnam suffered heavily from the assaults and exploitive terms of exchange imposed by imperialist powers, both Western and Japanese. Each has had to contend with underdevelopment, overpopulation, poverty, and environmental degradation. But unlike most of the rest of the formerly colonized peoples, the Chinese and the Vietnamese have had to deal with these awesome challenges in the midst of the collapse of the patterns of civilized life each had followed for thousands of years.

As disruptive imperialist conquest and its effects were in the rest of the African and Asian worlds, most colonized peoples managed to preserve much of their precolonial cultures and modes of social organization. The defense and revival of traditional customs, religious beliefs, and social arrangements played a key role in their struggles for decolonization. This was not the case in China and Vietnam, where a combination of external aggression and internal upheavals discredited and destroyed the Confucian system that had long been synonymous with civilized life.

With their traditional order in shambles, the peoples of China and Vietnam had no choice but to embark on full-scale revolutions that would clear away the rubble of the failed Confucian system. They needed to remove the obstacles posed by imperialist dominance and build new, viable states and

1750 C.E.	1910 C.E.	1925 C.E.	1940 C.E.	1955 C.E.	1970 C.E.
1770s Tayson rebellion in Vietnam	**1911** Revolution in China	**1925** VNQDD founded in Vietnam; first Communist organization established in Vietnam	**1942** Japanese occupation of French Indochina	**mid-1950s** Buildup of U.S. advisors in South Vietnam	**1975** Communist victory in Vietnam; collapse of the Republic of South Vietnam
1802 Establishment of the Nguyen dynasty; Vietnam unified	**1912** Fall of the Qing dynasty in China	**1927** Nationalists capture Shanghai; purge of Communists and workers	**1945** Ho Chi Minh proclaims the Republic of Vietnam	**1957** "Let a Thousand Flowers Bloom" campaign in China	**1976** Death of Zhou Enlai and Mao Zedong; purge of the Gang of Four
1858–1862 Beginning of the French conquest of Vietnam	**1919** May Fourth Movement begins; founding of Guomindang or Nationalist party	**1929** Failed VNQDD-inspired uprising	**1949** Victory of the Communists in China; People's Republic of China established	**1958–1960** "Great Leap Forward" in China	
1883 French conquest of Vietnam is completed	**1921** Communist party of China founded	**1930** Failed Communist uprising in Vietnam	**1950–1951** Purge of the landlord class in China	**1963** Beginning of state family planning in China	
		1931 Japanese invasion of Manchuria	**1950–1953** Korean War	**1965–1968** Era of the Cultural Revolution in China	
		1937 Japanese invasion of China proper	**1953** Beginning of China's first five-year plan	**1965–1973** Direct U.S. military intervention in Vietnam	
			1954 French defeated at Dien Bien Phu; Geneva accords, French withdrawal from Vietnam; beginning of the Sino–Soviet split	**1968** Tet offensive in Vietnam	

societies. In contrast to much of the rest of the colonized world, the countries of China and Vietnam derived few benefits from European domination, either informal or formal. Imperialist pressures eroded and smashed their political institutions rather than building up a bureaucratic grid and imparting political ideologies that could form the basis for nation-building. Both already had the strong sense of identity, common language, and a unifying polity that were among the major legacies of colonialism in other areas.

The distinctive forces that led to revolutionary upheavals in China and Vietnam are examined in this chapter. Special attention is given to why revolutionary rather than gradualist, reformist alternatives emerged victorious in each case. We also consider some of the major effects of the revolutionary solutions adopted on social organization, family and gender relationships, and cultural forms in each of these societies. In addition, we look at the development strategies envisioned or enacted in each of these societies and the often devastating environmental effects of some of these policies. In studying China, which has had a great impact on other emerging nations, we also explore in some depth the history of the period after the revolutionaries took

power. Perhaps more than any other part of the modern world, China and Vietnam provide us with the opportunity to study why civilizations break down and how new civilizations are fashioned from the ruins of the old.

THE STRUGGLE FOR CHINA

The abdication of Puyi, the Manchu boy–emperor in 1912, marked the end of a century-long losing struggle on the part of the Qing dynasty to protect Chinese civilization from foreign invaders and revolutionary threats from within, such as the massive Taiping movement (see Chapter 32). The fall of the Qing opened the way for an extended struggle over which leader or movement would be able to capture the mandate to rule the ancient society that for millennia had ordered the lives of one-fourth of humankind. The loose alliance of students, middle-class politicians, secret societies, and regional military commanders that overthrew the Manchus quickly splintered into several hostile contenders for the right to rule China. Both internal factors and foreign influences paved the way for the ultimate victory of the Chinese Communist party under Mao Zedong.

After the fall of the Qing dynasty, the best-positioned of the contenders for power were regionally based military commanders or warlords, who dominated Chinese politics for the next three decades. Many of the warlords combined in cliques or alliances, both to protect their own territories and to crush neighbors and annex their lands. The most powerful of these cliques, centered in north China (Map 41.1), was headed by the unscrupulous *Yuan Shikai*, who hoped to seize the vacated Manchu throne and found a new dynasty. By virtue of their wealth, the merchants and bankers of coastal cities such as Shanghai and Canton made up a second power center in post-Manchu China. Their involvement in politics resulted from their willingness to bankroll both favored warlords and Western-educated, middle-class politicians such as *Sun Yat-sen*.

Sometimes supportive of the urban civilian politicians and sometimes wary of them, university students and their teachers, as well as independent intellectuals, were another factor in the complex post-Qing political equation. Although the intellectuals and students played critical roles in shaping new ideologies to rebuild Chinese civilization, they were almost defenseless in a situation in which force was essential to those who hoped to exert political influ-

ence. Deeply divided but very strong in some regions, the secret societies were another contender for power. Like many in the military, they envisioned the restoration of monarchical rule but under a Chinese, not a foreign, dynasty. The situation was further complicated by the continuing intervention of the Western powers eager to profit from China's divisions and weakness. However, their inroads were increasingly overshadowed by those of the newest imperialist power, Japan. From the mid-1890s, when the Japanese had humiliated their much larger neighbor by easily defeating it in war, until 1945, when Japan's surrender ended World War II, the Japanese were a major factor in the long and bloody contest for control of China.

The May Fourth Movement and the Rise of the Marxist Alternative

Sun Yat-sen headed the Revolutionary Alliance, a loose coalition of anti-Qing political groups that had spearheaded the 1911 revolt. After the Qing were toppled, Sun claimed that he and the parties of the alliance were the rightful claimants to the mandate to

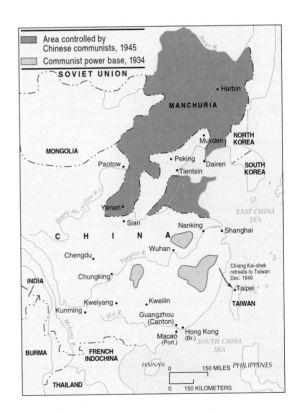

Map 41.1 *China in the Era of Revolution and Civil War*

rule China. But he could do little to assert civilian control in the face of warlord opposition. The Revolutionary Alliance had little power and almost no popular support outside the urban trading centers of the coastal areas in central and south China. Even in these areas, they were at the mercy of the local warlords. The alliance formally elected Sun president at the end of 1911, set up a parliament modeled after those in Europe, and chose cabinets with great fanfare. But their decisions had little effect on warlord-dominated China.

Sun Yat-sen conceded this reality when he resigned the acting presidency in favor of the northern warlord Yuan Shikai in 1912. As the most powerful of the northern clique of generals, Yuan appeared to have the best chance to unify China under a single government. He at first feigned sympathy for the democratic aims of the alliance leaders but soon revealed his true intentions. He took foreign loans to build up his military forces and buy out most of the bureaucrats in the capital at Beijing. When Sun and other leaders of the Revolutionary Alliance called for a second revolution to oust Yuan in the years after 1912, he made full use of his military power and more underhanded methods, such as assassinations, to put down their opposition. By 1915, it appeared that Yuan was well on his way to realizing his ambition of becoming China's next emperor. However, his schemes were foiled by the continuing rivalry of other warlords, republican nationalists such as Sun, and the growing influence of Japan in China. The latter increased dramatically as a result of World War I.

As England's ally according to terms of a 1902 treaty, Japan immediately entered the war on the side of the Entente (or Western allied) powers. Moving much too quickly for the comfort of the British and the other Western powers, the Japanese seized German-held islands in the Pacific and occupied the Germans' concessionary areas in China. With all the great powers except the United States embroiled in war, the Japanese sought to establish a hold on their giant neighbor. In early 1915, they presented Yuan's government with Twenty-One Demands, which, if accepted, would have reduced China to the status of a dependent protectorate. Although Sun and the Revolutionary Alliance lost much support by refusing to repudiate the Japanese demands, Yuan was no more decisive. He neither accepted nor rejected the demands but concentrated his energies on an effort to build popular enthusiasm for his accession to the throne. Disgusted by Yuan's weakness and ambition,

one of his warlord rivals plotted his overthrow. Hostility to the Japanese won Yuan's rival widespread support, and in 1916 Yuan was forced to resign the presidency. His fall was the signal for a free-for-all power struggle between the remaining warlords for control of China.

As one of the victorious allies, Japan managed to solidify its hold on northern China by winning control of the former German concessions in the peace negotiations at Versailles in 1919. But the Chinese had also allied themselves to the Entente powers during the war. Enraged by what they saw as a betrayal by the Entente powers, students and nationalist politicians organized mass demonstrations in many Chinese cities on May 4, 1919. One of largest of these is shown in the photograph in Figure 41.1. The demonstrations began a prolonged period of protest against Japanese inroads. This protest soon expanded from marches and petitions to strikes and mass boycotts of Japanese goods.

The fourth of May, the day when the resistance began, gave its name to a movement in which intellectuals and students played a leading role. Initially at least, the *May Fourth movement* was aimed at transforming China into a liberal democracy. Its program was spelled out in many speeches, pamphlets, novels, and newspaper articles. Confucianism was ridiculed and rejected in favor of a wholehearted acceptance of all that the Western democracies had to offer. Noted Western thinkers such as Bertrand Russell and John Dewey toured China, extolling the merits of science, industrial technology, and democratic government and basking in the cheers of enthusiastic Chinese audiences. Chinese thinkers called for the liberation of women, the simplification of the Chinese script to promote mass literacy, and the promotion of Western-style individualism.

Many of these themes are captured in the literature of the period. In the novel *Family* by Ba Jin, for example, a young man boldly tells his older brother that he will not accept the marriage partner the family has arranged for him. He sees his refusal as part of a more general revolt of the youth of China against the ancient Confucian social code.

> Big Brother, I'm doing what no one in our family has ever dared do before—I'm running out on an arranged marriage. No one cares about my fate, so I've decided to walk my own road alone. I'm determined to struggle against the old forces to the end. Unless you cancel the match, I'll never come back. I'll die first.

Figure 41.1 *Spearheaded by students and intellectuals in China's urban areas, the May Fourth demonstrations in 1919 proclaimed the end of nearly 2000 years of Confucian dominance in China and the opening of the country to ideologies from the West, both democratic and Marxist.*

As enthusiastic as the urban youth of China were, it was soon clear that mere emulation of the liberal democracies of the West could not solve China's problems. Civil liberties and democratic elections were meaningless in a China that was ruled by warlords. Gradualist solutions were folly in a nation where tens of millions of peasants were malnourished or dying of starvation. Even if fair elections could be held and a Western-style parliament installed as an effective ruling body, China's crisis had become so severe that there was little time for legislators to debate. The ministers of an elected government with little military clout would not have been able to implement well-meaning programs for land redistribution and subsidies for the poor in the face of entrenched regional opposition from the landlords and the military. It soon became clear to many Chinese intellectuals and students, as well as to some of the nationalist politicians, that more radical solutions were needed. In the 1920s, this conviction gave rise to the communist left within the Chinese nationalist movement.

The example of the Russian Revolution, rather than careful reading of the writings of Karl Marx and Friedrich Engels, made a number of Chinese thinkers aware of possible Marxist solutions to China's ills. The Bolshevik victory and the programs launched to rebuild Russia prompted Chinese intellectuals to give serious attention to the works of Marx and other socialist thinkers and the potential they offered for reviving China. But careful study of the writings of Marx, Engels, Lenin, and Trotsky in the wake of the Russian Revolution also impressed a number of Chinese intellectuals with the need for major changes in Marxist ideology if it was going to be of any relevance to China or other peasant societies. After all, Marx had foreseen socialist revolutions occurring in the more advanced industrial societies with well-developed working classes and a strong proletarian consciousness. He had thought that there would be little chance for revolution in Russia. In China, with its overwhelmingly rural, peasant population (and Marx saw the peasantry as a reactionary or, at best, a conservative, petty bourgeois social element), the prospects for revolution looked even more dismal.

The most influential of the thinkers who called for a reworking of Marxist ideology to fit China's situation was *Li Dazhao* (Figure 41.2). Li was from peasant origins, but he had excelled in school and eventually become a college teacher. He headed the Marxist study circle that developed after the May 1919 upheavals at the University of Beijing. His interpretation of Marxist philosophy placed heavy emphasis on its ability to promote renewal and harness the energy and vitality of a nation's youth. In contrast to Lenin, Li saw the peasants, rather than the urban workers, as the vanguard of revolutionary change. He justified this shift from the orthodox Marxist emphasis on the working classes, which made up only a tiny fraction of China's population at the time, by characterizing the whole of Chinese society as proletarian. All of China, he argued, had been exploited by the bourgeois, industrialized West. Thus, the oppressed Chinese as a whole needed to unite and rise up against their exploiters.

Li's version of Marxism, with changes that made it suitable for China, had great appeal for the students, including the young Mao Zedong, who joined

Figure 41.2 *Li Dazhao has proved to be one of the most influential thinkers of modern China. Following the lead of like-minded, revisionist Marxist theorists, Mao and other revolutionary leaders in the postcolonial world have relied mainly on the impoverished peasantry to bring them to power and to push through their programs for social transformation.*

Li's study circle. They too were angered by what they saw as China's betrayal by the imperialist powers. They shared Li's hostility (very much a throwback to the attitudes of the Confucian era) to merchants and commerce, which appeared to dominate the West. They longed for a return to a political system, like the Confucian, in which those who governed were deeply committed to social reform and social welfare. They also believed in an authoritarian state, which they felt ought to intervene constructively in all aspects of the people's lives.

The Marxist study club societies soon spawned a number of more broadly based, politically activist organizations. The Marxists' capture of prominent periodicals, such as the *New Youth* magazine, did much to spread the ideas of Marx and Lenin among the politically active youth of China's coastal cities. With support from Sun Yat-sen, Marxist intellectuals established the *Socialist Youth Corps* in 1920, which was dedicated to recruiting the urban working classes to the revolutionary movement. Students such as Mao returned to their provincial bases to win supporters for the leftist cause and to foment resistance to the oppressive rule of the local warlords.

In the summer of 1921, in an attempt to unify the growing Marxist wing of the nationalist struggle, a handful of leaders from different parts of China met in secret in the city of Shanghai. At this meeting, closely watched by the agents of the local warlord and rival political organizations, the Communist party of China was born. In Paris a year earlier, *Zhou Enlai*, who like Mao was later to become one of the main communist leaders, and several other Chinese expatriate students had founded the Communist Youth Corps. In Paris and inside China itself, the development of communist organizations was supported by the advisors and funds of the Comintern, the international arm of the Bolshevik or Communist party of the Soviet Union. The Communist party was small, and at this time it was dogmatically fixed on a revolutionary program oriented to the small and scattered working class. But the communists at least offered a clear alternative to fill the ideological and institutional void left by the collapse of the Confucian order.

The Seizure of Power by the Guomindang, or Nationalist Party

While the communist movement in China was being put together by urban students and intellectuals, the *Guomindang,* or Nationalist party, which was to prove the communists' great rival for the mandate to rule in China, was struggling to survive in the south. Sun Yat-sen, the acknowledged head of the nationalist struggle from the 1911 revolution until his death in early 1925, had gone into exile in Japan in 1914, while warlords, such as Yuan Shikai, consolidated their regional power bases. After returning to China in 1919, Sun and his followers tried to unify the diverse political organizations struggling for political influence in China by reorganizing the revolutionary movement and naming it the Nationalist Party of China (the Guomindang).

The nationalists began the slow process of forging alliances with key social groups and building an army of their own, which they now saw as the only way to rid China of the warlord menace. Sun strove to enunciate a nationalist ideology that gave something to everyone. It stressed the need to unify China under a strong central government, to bring the imperialist intruders under control, and to introduce social reforms that would alleviate the poverty of the peasants and the oppressive working conditions of laborers in China's cities. Unfortunately for most Chinese people, for whom social reforms were the main concern, the Nationalist party leaders concentrated on political and international issues, such as relations with the Western powers and Japan. In part due to these priorities, they failed to implement most of the domestic programs they proposed, most especially land reform.

In this early stage, Sun and the Nationalist party built their power primarily on the support provided by urban businesspeople and merchants in coastal cities such as Canton. Although it received little publicity at the time, the Nationalist party also drew support from local warlords and the criminal underworld, especially the notorious Green Gang headquartered in Shanghai. After much factional infighting, Sun had secured control over the party, if not the warlords in the neighborhood of Canton. He forged an alliance with the communists that was proclaimed officially at the first Nationalist party conference in 1924. For the time being at least, the nationalist leaders were content to let the communists serve as their major link to the peasants and the urban workers.

Disappointed in their early hopes for assistance from the Europeans and the United States, Nationalist party leaders turned to Soviet Russia. Lenin and the Bolsheviks were eager to support a revolutionary movement in neighboring China. The Bolsheviks sent advisors and gave material assistance. They also encouraged the fledgling Communist party to join with the larger and richer Nationalist party in a common struggle to seize power.

In 1924, the *Whampoa Military Academy* was founded with Soviet help and partially staffed by Russian instructors. The academy gave the nationalists a critical military dimension to their political maneuvering. The first head of the academy was an ambitious young military officer named *Chiang Kai-shek*. The son of a poor salt merchant, Chiang had made his career in the military and by virtue of connections with powerful figures in the Shanghai underworld. He had received some military training in Japan and managed by the early 1920s to work his way into Sun Yat-sen's inner circle of advisors. Chiang was not happy with the communist alliance. But he was willing to bide his time until he had the military strength to deal with both the communists and the warlords, who remained the major obstacles to the nationalist seizure of power.

Absorbed by all these political machinations, Sun and other nationalist leaders had little time left for serious attention to the now severe deterioration of the Chinese economy or relief for the huge population whose sufferings mounted as a result. Urban laborers worked for pitiful wages and lived in appalling conditions. But the social condition of the peasantry, which made up nearly 90 percent of China's population, was perhaps the most pressing issue facing China's aspiring national leaders. Patterns of land ownership varied widely in different parts of China. But more than a century of corruption and weak Manchu rule, and then the Qing collapse in 1911 and the depredations of the warlords, had left the peasantry in many regions of China in misery. Big landlords and rich peasants amassed great landholdings, which they rented out at exorbitant rates that left the tenants who worked them little to feed and clothe their families. In times of flood and drought when the crops failed, tenants, landless laborers, and even small land owners could not make ends meet. Tenants and smallholders were turned off their lands, and landless laborers could not find crops to harvest. Famine and disease stalked China's heavily populated provinces, and its ancient irrigation systems fell into disrepair. Corrupt warlords and bureaucrats, including those allied to the Nationalist party, colluded with the landlords to extract taxes and labor from the peasantry.

As they had for millennia, dispossessed peasants took to banditry or vagabondage to survive. Many joined the hordes of beggars and unemployed in the towns; many more died, swept away by floods, famine, disease, or the local warlord's armies. Children were sold into slavery by their parents so that both might have a chance to survive. A growing number of cases of cannibalism were reported, which occurred after the bark and leaves had been stripped off all the trees to make the scarcely digestible "stew" that the peasants ate to put something in their bellies. Many peasants were too poor to perform the most basic social duties, such as burying their deceased parents, whose bodies often were left to be devoured by vultures and packs of wild dogs. Given the great reverence for family and parents that had been instilled for millennia by Confucian teachings, the psychological scars left by the nonperformance of such critical obligations must have been deep and lasting.

Although rural China cried out for strong leadership and far-reaching economic and social reform, China's leaders bickered and plotted but did little. Sun gave lip service to the need to deal with the peasant problem. But his ignorance of rural conditions was revealed by statements in which he denied that China had exploitive landlords and his refusal to recognize the conflict between the great mass of the peasantry and the land owners.

Mao and the Peasant Option

Though the son of a fairly prosperous peasant, Mao Zedong (Figure 41.3) rebelled early in his life against his father's exploitation of the tenants and laborers who worked the family fields. Receiving little assistance from his estranged father, Mao was forced to make his own way in the world. Through much of his youth and early adulthood, he struggled to educate himself in the history, philosophy, and economic theory that most other nationalist and revolutionary leaders mastered in private schools. Having moved to Beijing in the post–May Fourth era, Mao came under the influence of thinkers such as Li Dazhao, who emphasized solving the peasant problem as one of the keys to China's survival. As the following passage from Mao's early writings reveals, almost from the outset he was committed to revolutionary solutions that depended on peasant support:

> A revolution is an insurrection, an act of violence by which one class overthrows another. A rural revolution is a revolution by which the peasantry overthrows the power of the feudal landlord class. Without using the greatest force, the peasants cannot possibly overthrow the deep-rooted authority of the landlords which has lasted for thousands of years.

Figure 41.3 *Although he received no formal military training, Mao Zedong's adoption of a soldier's uniform reflected the importance of force in the highly militarized and deeply divided society that China had become by the early 20th century.*

Throughout most of the 1920s, however, Mao's vision of a rural revolution remained a minority and much repudiated position, even with the Communist party. Rivals such as Li Lisan, who favored a more orthodox Marxist strategy based on the urban working classes, dominated party policymaking. Ironically, the move by Chiang and the Nationalist party leaders to destroy all the communists in the late 1920s paved the way for Mao's rise to leadership in the party.

The Nationalist party's successful drive for national power began only after Sun Yat-sen's death in 1925, which opened the way for Chiang Kai-shek and his warlord allies to seize control of the party. After winning over or eliminating the military chiefs in the Canton area, Chiang marched north with his newly created armies. His first campaign culminated in the nationalists' seizure of the Yangtze River valley and Shanghai in early 1927 (see Map 41.1). Later his forces also captured the capital at Beijing and the rest of the Yellow River basin. The refusal of most of the warlords to end their feuding meant that Chiang could defeat them or buy them out, one by one. By the late 1920s, he was the master of China in name and international standing, if not in actual fact. He was, in reality, the head of a warlord hierarchy. But most political leaders within China and the outside world recognized him as the new president of China.

Because there were no elections, the people had no say in the matter. Nor had Chiang's political rivals, whom he ruthlessly purged even while he was still settling scores with the warlords. The most fateful of these purges came while Chiang's armies were occupying Shanghai in the spring of 1927. First the nationalists cleared the communists out of the Nationalist party's central committee, where they had been represented since 1924. Chiang then ordered his troops and gangster allies in Shanghai to round up the workers, despite the fact that their mass demonstrations had done so much to make possible the city's capture by the nationalist armies. In some of the most brutal scenes of an era when violence and human suffering were almost common (Figure 41.4), Chiang's soldiers and hired toughs machine-gunned

and beheaded communist supporters wherever they could be found throughout the city. Although the communists' Soviet advisors continued to insist that they cooperate with the nationalists, Chiang's extension of the bloody purge to other cities and into the countryside precipitated an open civil war between the two main branches of the nationalist movement. Despite temporary and half-hearted truces, this civil war ended only with the communist victory in 1949.

Reaction Versus Revolution and the Communist Victory

At the outset, all signs appeared to favor the Nationalist party in its violent contest with the communists for control of China. Despite the fact that Chiang did not fully control the more powerful regional warlords, as the heir of Sun Yat-sen and the architect of the victorious northern campaign he had the support of the richest and most powerful social groups in China. These included the urban businesspeople and merchants, most of the intellectuals, and a large por-

Figure 41.4 *The Guomindang's brutal suppression of the workers' organizations in Shanghai in 1927 was a turning point in the history of modern China. The Guomindang–Communist Party alliance was shattered, and Mao Zedong's call for a peasant-based revolution became imperative as the vulnerability of the small Chinese working class was exposed.*

tion of the university students, the rural landlords, and the military. Chiang could also count on the services of the bureaucrats and police throughout China, and he launched a calculated public relations campaign to win sympathy in the United States and the other Western democracies. The urban workers, who preferred the communists or other radical parties, had been beaten into submission. The peasants, who longed for stable government and state-sponsored relief, were willing, for the time being at least, to wait and see whether the nationalists would act to alleviate their distress.

Despite his ruthless betrayal of the communists, Chiang continued to receive assistance from the Soviet Union, where Stalin had emerged as the unchallenged dictator of a totalitarian state. Possibly because he preferred a weak China under the Nationalist party to a revolutionary one under the communists, Stalin gave little assistance to his alleged comrades and continued to push policies that left them at the mercy of Chiang and his henchmen. With what seemed to be insurmountable advantages, Chiang moved to eliminate his few remaining rivals for power, most especially the shattered remnants of the Communist party.

The smashing of the workers' movement in Shanghai and other urban centers greatly strengthened Mao's hand in his ongoing struggle with Li Lisan and other orthodox ideologues in the Communist party. Mao and much of what was left of the communist leadership retreated into the countryside and set to work carrying out land reform and improving life in China's tens of thousands of impoverished villages.

In the late 1920s, the center of communist operations came to be the south central province of Hunan (see Map 41.1), where the communists established soviets (named after the revolutionary workers' and soldiers' organizations in Russia) and "liberated" zones. This area became the main target of a succession of military campaigns that Chiang launched against the communists in the early 1930s. Although the communists successfully resisted the early campaigns, Chiang's reliance on German military advisors and his command of the rest of China eventually wore the communists down. By the autumn of 1934, it was clear that if the remaining communists did not break out of the nationalist encirclement and escape from Hunan, they would be eliminated. At the head of more than 90,000 party stalwarts, Mao set off on the *Long March* across thousands of miles of the most difficult terrain in China to Shaanxi in northwestern

China, where a smaller number of peasant soviets had been established earlier. At the end of the next year, Mao and only about 20,000 followers who had managed to survive fought their way into the rugged, sparsely populated terrain of Shaanxi. From that moment until the mid-1940s, Shaanxi with its capital at Yanan became the center of the communist movement in China.

By the end of the Long March, Mao was firmly established as the head of the Chinese Communist party. The heroic and successful struggle for survival in the Long March on the part of those who supported his peasant-based strategy of revolution greatly enhanced his stature and fired his followers with the conviction that whatever the odds, they could not be defeated. Chiang obviously did not agree. Soon after the communists were established in Shaanxi, he launched a new series of extermination campaigns. Again, the peasant supporters of the communists fought valiantly, but Chiang's armies were beginning to get the upper hand by early 1937.

Just as he was convinced that he was on the verge of victory, Chiang's anticommunist crusade was rudely interrupted by the Japanese invasion of the Chinese mainland. Obsessed with the communists, Chiang had done little to block the steady advance of Japanese forces in the early 1930s into Manchuria and the islands along China's coast. Even after the Japanese launched their assaults, aimed at conquering China, Chiang wanted to continue the struggle against the communists.

Forced by his military commanders to concentrate on the Japanese threat, Chiang grudgingly formed a military alliance with the communists. Although he did all he could to undermine the alliance and continue the anticommunist struggle by underhanded means, for the next seven years the war against Japan took priority over the civil war in the contest for control of China.

Although it brought more suffering to the Chinese people, the Japanese invasion was enormously advantageous for the Communist party. This turned out to be so vital to the ultimate communist victory that some writers have speculated that Mao chose Shaanxi in the northwest partly because it would put his forces in the probable path of the anticipated Japanese advance. Whatever his thinking, the war against the Japanese greatly strengthened his cause while weakening his nationalist rivals. The Japanese invaders captured much of the Chinese coast, where the cities were the centers of the business and mercantile backers of the Nationalists. Chiang's conventional military forces were pummeled by the superior air, land, and sea forces of the Japanese. The Nationalists' attempts to meet the Japanese in conventional battles led to disaster; their inability to defend the coastal provinces lowered their standing in the eyes of the Chinese people. Chiang's hasty and humiliating retreat to Chongqing (see Map 41.1), in the interior of China, further eroded his reputation as the savior of the nation and rendered him more dependent than ever on his military allies, the rural landlords, and—perhaps most humiliating—foreign powers such as the United States.

The guerrilla warfare the communists waged against the Japanese armies proved far more effective than Chiang's conventional approach. With the Nationalist extermination campaigns suspended, the communists used their anti-Japanese campaigns to extend their control over large areas of north China. By the end of World War II, the Nationalists controlled mainly the cities in the north; they had become (as Mao prescribed in his political writings) islands surrounded by a sea of revolutionary peasants. The communists' successes and their determination to fight the Japanese won them the support of most of China's intellectuals and many of the students who had earlier supported the Nationalists. By 1945, the balance of power within China was clearly shifting in the communists' favor. In the four-year civil war that followed, communist soldiers, who were well treated and fought for a cause, consistently routed the much-abused soldiers of the Nationalists, many of whom switched to the communist side. By 1949, it was over. Chiang and what was left of his armies fled to the island of Formosa (renamed Taiwan) off the China coast, and Mao proclaimed the establishment of *The People's Republic of China* in Beijing.

The Japanese invasion proved critical in the communist drive to victory. But equally important were the communists' social and economic reform programs, which eventually won the great majority of the peasantry, the students and intellectuals, and even many of the bureaucrats to their side. Whereas Chiang, whatever his intentions, was able to do little to improve the condition of the great mass of the people, Mao made uplifting the peasants the central element in his drive for power. Land reforms, access to education, and improved health care gave the peasantry a real stake in Mao's revolutionary movement

and good reason to defend their soviets against both the Nationalists and the Japanese. In contrast to Chiang's armies, whose arrival meant theft, rape, and murder to China's villagers, Mao's soldiers were indoctrinated with the need to protect the peasantry and win their support. Lest they forget, harsh penalties were levied, such as execution for stealing an egg.

As guerrilla fighters, Mao's soldiers had a much better chance to survive and advance in the ranks than did the forcibly conscripted, brutally treated footsoldiers of the Nationalists. Mao and the commanders around him, such as *Lin Biao,* who had been trained at Chiang's Whampoa Academy in the 1920s, proved far more gifted—even in conventional warfare—than the often corrupt and inept Nationalist generals. Thus, although the importance of the Japanese invasion cannot be discounted, the communists won the mandate to govern China because they offered solutions to China's fundamental social and economic problems. Even more critically, they actually put their programs into action in the areas that came under their control. In a situation in which revolutionary changes appeared to be essential, the communists alone convinced the Chinese people that they had the leaders and the program that could improve their lives.

MAO'S CHINA AND BEYOND

In assuming power in 1949, the communists faced the formidable task of governing a vast nation in ruins. But in contrast to the Bolsheviks, who seized power in 1917 in Russia quite easily but then had to face years of civil war and foreign aggression, the communists in China claimed a unified nation from which foreign aggressors had been expelled. Unlike the Bolsheviks, the communist leadership in China could move directly to the tasks of social reform and economic development that China so desperately needed. In so doing, they could build on the base they had established in the "liberated" zones during their long struggle for power. In these areas, land reforms had already been tested, mass literacy campaigns had been mounted, and young people, both male and female, had enjoyed opportunities to rise in the party ranks on the basis of hard work.

Although deep social divisions remained, the Chinese faced far less serious splits between different religious and ethnic groups than most other new nations of Africa and Asia. Millennia of common history and common cultural development had given the peoples of China a sense of identity and a tradition of political unity. The long struggle against foreign aggressors had strengthened these bonds and impressed upon the Chinese the importance of maintaining a united front against outsiders if they were to avoid future humiliations and exploitation.

The communists' long struggle for control had left the party with a strong political and military organization that was rooted in the *party cadres* and the *People's Liberation Army*. The continuing importance of the army was indicated by the fact that most of China was administered by military officials for five years after the communists came to power. But the army remained clearly subordinate to the party. Cadre advisors were attached to military contingents at all levels, and the central committees of the party were dominated by nonmilitary personnel

With this strong political framework in place, the communists moved quickly to assert China's traditional preeminence in east and much of southeast Asia. Potential secessionist movements were forcibly repressed in Inner Mongolia and Tibet, although resistance in the latter has erupted periodically and continues to the present day. In the early 1950s, the Chinese intervened militarily in the conflict between North and South Korea, an intervention that was critical in forcing the United States to settle for a stalemate and a lasting division of the peninsula. Refusing to accept a similar but far more lopsided two-nation outcome of the struggle in China itself, the communist leadership has periodically threatened to invade the Nationalists' refuge on Taiwan, often touching off international incidents. China also played an increasingly important role in the liberation struggle of the Vietnamese to the south, although that did not peak until the height of American involvement in the conflict in the 1960s.

By the late 1950s, the close collaboration between the Soviet Union and China that marked the early years of Mao's rule had broken down. Border disputes, focusing on territories the Russians had seized during the period of Qing decline, and the Chinese refusal to play second fiddle to Russia, especially after Stalin was succeeded by the less imposing Khrushchev, were key causes of the split. These causes of the breakdown in collaboration worsened the differences resulting from the meager economic assistance provided by the Soviet "comrades." They also fed Mao's sense that with the passing of Stalin, he was the chief theoretician and leader of the communist world. In the early 1960s, the Chinese flexed their military and technological muscle by defeating India in a brief war that resulted from a border dispute. More startling, however, was the Chinese success in exploding the first nuclear device developed by a nonindustrial nation.

Planning for Economic Growth and Social Justice

On the domestic front, the new leaders of China moved with equal vigor, though with a good deal less success. Their first priority was to complete the social revolution in the rural areas that had been carried through to some extent in communist-controlled areas during the wars against the Japanese and Guomindang. Between 1950 and 1952, the landlord class and the large landholders, most of whom had been spared in the earlier stages of the revolution, were dispossessed and purged. Village tribunals, overseen by party cadre members, gave tenants and laborers a chance to get even for decades of oppression. Perhaps as many as 3 million people who were denounced as members of the exploitive landlord class were executed. At the same time, the land taken from the landowning classes was distributed to peasants who had none or little. For a brief time at least, one of the central pledges of the communist revolutionaries was fulfilled: China became a land of peasant smallholders.

However, communist planners saw rapid industrialization, not peasant farmers, as the key to successful development. With the introduction of the first Stalinist-style five-year plan in 1953, the communist leaders turned away from the peasantry, which had brought them to power, to the urban workers as the hope for a new China. With little foreign assistance from either the West or the Soviet bloc, the state resorted to stringent measures to draw resources from the countryside to finance industrial growth. Some advances were made in industrialization, particularly in heavy industries such as steel. But the shift in direction had consequences that were increasingly unacceptable to Mao and his more radical supporters in the party. State planning and centralization were stressed, party bureaucrats greatly increased their power and influence, and an urban-based privileged class of technocrats began to develop.

These changes, and the external threat to China posed by the U.S. intervention in Korea and continuing U.S.–China friction, led Mao and his followers to force a change of strategies in the mid-1950s.

Mao had long nurtured a deep hostility toward elitism, which he associated with the discredited Confucian system. He had little use for Lenin's vision of revolution from above, led by a disciplined cadre of professional political activists. He distrusted intellectuals, disliked specialization, and clung to his faith in the peasants rather than the workers as the repository of basic virtue and the driving force of the revolution. Acting to stem the trend toward an elitist, urban–industrial focus, Mao and his supporters introduced the *Mass Line* approach, beginning with the formation of agricultural cooperatives in 1955. In the following year, cooperatives became farming collectives that soon accounted for more than 90 percent of China's peasant population. The peasants had enjoyed their own holdings for less than three years. As had occurred earlier in the Soviet Union, the leaders of the revolution, who had originally given the land over to the mass of the peasants, later took it away from them through collectivization.

In 1957 Mao struck at the intellectuals through what may have been a miscalculation or perhaps a clever ruse. Announcing that he wanted to "let a thousand flowers bloom," Mao encouraged professors, artists, and other intellectuals to speak out on the course of development under communist rule. His request stirred up a storm of angry protest and criticism of communist schemes. Having flushed the critics into the open (if the campaign was indeed a ruse) or having been shocked by the vehemence of the response, the party struck with demotions, prison sentences, and banishment to hard labor on the collectives. The flowers rapidly wilted in the face of this betrayal.

The Great Leap Backward

With political opposition within the party and army apparently in check (or in prison), Mao and his supporters launched the *Great Leap Forward* in 1958. The programs of the Great Leap were a further effort to revitalize the flagging revolution by restoring its mass, rural base. Rather than huge plants located in the cities, industrialization would be pushed through small-scale projects integrated into the peasant communes. Instead of the communes' surplus being siphoned off to build steel mills, industrial develop-

ment would be aimed at producing tractors, cement for irrigation projects, and other manufactures needed by the peasantry. Enormous publicity was given to efforts to produce steel in "backyard" furnaces (Figure 41.5) that relied on labor rather than machine-intensive techniques. Mao preached the benefits of backwardness and the joys of mass involvement, and he looked forward to the withering away of the meddling bureaucracy. Emphasis was placed on self-reliance within the peasant communes. All aspects of the lives of their members were regulated and regimented by the commune leaders and the heads of the local labor brigades.

Within months after it was launched, all indicators suggested that the Great Leap Forward and rapid collectivization were leading to economic disaster. Peasant resistance to collectivization, the abuses of commune leaders, and the dismal output of the backyard factories combined with drought to turn the Great Leap into a giant step backward. The worst famine of the communist era spread across China. For the first time since 1949 China had to import large amounts of grain to feed its people, and the numbers of Chinese to feed continued to grow at an alarming rate. Defiantly rejecting Western and United Nations proposals for family planning, Mao and like-thinking radicals charged that socialist China could care for its people, no matter how many they

Figure 41.5. *The famous backyard steel furnaces became a central symbol of China's failed drive for self-sufficiency during the Great Leap Forward in the late 1950s.*

were. Birth control was seen as a symptom of capitalist selfishness and inability to provide a decent living for all of the people.

Like those of India, China's birth rates were actually a good deal lower than those of many emerging nations. Also like India, however, the Chinese were adding people to a massive population base. At the time of the communist rise to power, China had approximately 550 million people. By 1965, this had risen to approximately 750 million. If that rate of growth had continued, some experts at the time predicted that China would have 1.8 billion people by the year 2000.

In the face of the environmental degradation and overcrowding that this leap in population produced, even the party ideologues came around to the view that something must be done to curb the birth rate. Beginning in the mid-1960s, the government launched a nationwide family planning campaign designed to limit urban couples to two children and those in rural areas to one. By the early 1970s, these targets had been revised to two children for either urban or rural couples. But by the 1980s, just one child per family was allowed. Although there is evidence of official excesses— undue pressure for women to have abortions, for example—these programs have greatly reduced the birth rate and have begun to slow China's overall population increase. But again, the base to which new births are added is already so large that China's population will not stabilize until well into the 21st century. By that time there will be far more people than now to educate, feed, house, and provide with productive work.

Advances made in the first decade of the new regime were lost through amateurish blunders, excesses of overzealous cadre leaders, and students' meddling. China's national productivity fell by as much as 25 percent. Population increase soon overwhelmed the stagnating productivity of the agricultural and industrial sectors. By 1960, it was clear that the Great Leap must be ended and a new course of development adopted. Mao lost his position as State Chairman (although he remained the head of the party's Central Committee). The *pragmatists,* including Mao's old ally Zhou Enlai, along with *Liu Shaoqui* and *Deng Xiaoping,* came to power determined to restore state direction and market incentives at the local level.

"Women Hold Up Half of the Heavens"

In Mao's struggles to renew the revolutionary fervor of the Chinese people, his wife, *Jiang Qing,* played an increasingly prominent role. Mao's reliance on her was consistent with the commitment to the liberation of Chinese women he had acted upon throughout his political career. As a young man he had been deeply moved by a newspaper story about a young girl who had committed suicide rather than be forced by her family to submit to the marriage they had arranged for her with a rich but very old man. From that point onward, women's issues and women's support for the communist movement became important parts of Mao's revolutionary strategy. Here he was drawing on a well-established revolutionary tradition, for women had been very active in the Taiping Rebellion of the mid-19th century, the Boxer revolt in 1900, and the 1911 revolution that had toppled the Manchu regime. One of the key causes taken up by the May Fourth intellectuals, who had a great impact on the youthful Mao Zedong, was women's rights. Their efforts put an end to foot-binding. They also did much to advance campaigns to end female seclusion, win legal rights for women, and open educational and career opportunities to them.

The attempts by the Nationalists in the late 1920s and 1930s to reverse many of the gains made by women in the early revolution brought many women into the communist camp. Led by Chiang's wife, Madam Chiang Kai-shek, the Nationalist counteroffensive (like comparable movements in the fascist countries of Europe at the time) tried to return Chinese women to the home and hearth. Madam Chiang proclaimed a special Good Mother's Day and declared that for women, "virtue was more important than learning." She taught that it was immoral for a wife to criticize her husband (an ethical precept she herself ignored regularly).

The nationalist campaign to restore Chinese women to their traditional domestic roles and dependence on men contrasted sharply with the communists' extensive employment of women to advance the revolutionary cause. Women served as teachers, nurses, spies, truck drivers, and laborers on projects ranging from growing food to building machine-gun bunkers. Although the party preferred to use them in these support roles, in moments of crisis women became soldiers on the front lines. Many won distinction for their bravery under fire. Some rose to become cadre leaders, and many were prominent in the antilandlord campaigns and agrarian reform. Their contribution to the victory of the revolutionary cause bore out Mao's early dictum that the energies and talents of women had to be harnessed to the national cause because "women hold up half of the heavens."

As was the case in many other African and Asian countries, the victory of the revolution brought

women legal equality with men—in itself a revolutionary development in a society such as China's. For example, women were given the right to choose their marriage partners without familial interference. But arranged marriages persist today, especially in rural areas, and the need to have party approval for all marriages is a new form of control. Since 1949, women have also been expected to work outside the home. Their opportunities for education and professional careers have improved greatly. As in other socialist states, however, openings for employment outside the home have proved to be a burden for Chinese

DOCUMENT

Women in the Revolutionary Struggle

Even more than in the nationalist movements in colonized areas such as India and Egypt, women were drawn in large numbers into revolutionary struggles in areas such as China and Vietnam. The breakdown of the political and social systems weakened the legal and family restrictions that had subordinated women and limited their career choices. The collapse of the Confucian order also ushered in decades of severe crisis and brutal conflict in which women's survival depended on their assumption of radically new roles and their active involvement in revolutionary activities. The following quotations are taken from Vietnamese and Chinese revolutionary writings and interviews with women involved in revolutionary movements in each country. They express the women's goals, their struggle to be taken seriously in the uncharacteristic political roles they had assumed, and some of the many ways women found self-respect and redress for their grievances as a result of the changes wrought by the spread of the new social order.

1. Women must first of all be masters of themselves. They must strive to become skilled workers ... and, at the same time, they must strictly observe family planning. Another major question is the responsibility of husbands to help their wives look after children and other housework.

2. We intellectuals had had little contact with the peasants and when we first walked through the village in our Chinese gowns or skirts the people would just stare at us and talk behind our backs. When the village head beat gongs to call out the women to the meeting we were holding for them, only men and old women came, but no young ones. Later

we found out that the landlords and rich peasants had spread slanders among the masses saying "They are a pack of wild women. Their words are not for young brides to hear."

3. Brave wives and daughters-in-law, untrammelled by the presence of their menfolk, could voice their own bitterness ... encourage their poor sisters to do likewise, and thus eventually bring to the village-wide gatherings the strength of "half of China" as the more enlightened women, very much in earnest, like to call themselves. By "speaking pains to recall pains," the women found that they had as many if not more grievances than the men, and that given a chance to speak in public, they were as good at it as their fathers and husbands.

4. In Chingtsun the work team found a woman whose husband thought her ugly and wanted to divorce her. She was very depressed until she learned that under the Draft Law [of the Communist party] she could have her own share of land. Then she cheered up immediately. "If he divorces me, never mind," she said. "I'll get my share and the children will get theirs. We can live a good life without him."

Questions: On the basis of these quotations, identify the traditional roles and attitudes toward women (explored in earlier chapters on China and Vietnam) that women engaged in revolutionary movements in China and Vietnam have rejected. What do they believe is essential if women are to gain equality with men? How do the demands of the women supporting these revolutionary movements compare with those of women's rights advocates in the United States?

women. Until the late 1970s, traditional attitudes toward child-rearing and home care prevailed. As a result, women were required not only to hold down a regular job but also to raise a family, cook meals, clean, and shop, all without the benefit of the modern appliances available in Western societies. Although many women held cadre posts at the middle and lower levels of the party and bureaucracy, the upper echelons of both were overwhelmingly controlled by men.

As in other developing societies, the short-lived but impressive power amassed by Mao's wife, Jiang Qing, in the early 1970s runs counter to the overall predominance of men in politics and the military. Like her counterparts elsewhere in Africa and Asia, Jiang Qing got to the top because she was married to Mao. She exercised power mainly in his name and was toppled soon after his death when she tried to rule in her own right. Women have come far in China, but—as is the case in most other societies in both the developed and developing worlds—they have not attained full equality with men in terms of career opportunities, social status, or political power.

Mao's Last Campaign and the Fall of the Gang of Four

Having lost his position as head of state but still the most powerful and popular leader in the Communist party, Mao worked throughout the early 1960s to establish grassroots support for yet another renewal of the revolutionary struggle. He fiercely opposed the efforts of *Deng Xiaoping* and his pragmatist allies to scale back the communes, promote peasant production on what were in effect private plots, and push economic growth over political orthodoxy. By late 1965, Mao was convinced that his support among the students, peasants, and military was strong enough to launch what would turn out to be his last campaign, the *Cultural Revolution*. With mass student demonstrations paving the way, he launched an all-out assault on the "capitalist-roaders" in the party.

Waving "little red books" of Mao's pronouncements on all manner of issues, the infamous *Red Guard* student brigades (Figure 41.6) publicly ridiculed and abused Mao's political rivals. Liu Shaoqui was killed, Deng Xiaoping was imprisoned, and Zhou Enlai was driven into seclusion. The aroused

students and the rank and file of the People's Liberation Army were used to pull down the bureaucrats from their positions of power and privilege. College professors, plant managers, and the children of the bureaucratic elite were berated and forced to confess publicly their many crimes against "the people." Those who were not imprisoned or, more rarely, killed were forced to do manual labor on rural communes to enable them to understand the hardships endured by China's peasantry. In cities such as Shanghai, workers seized control of the factories and local bureaucracy. As Mao had hoped, the centralized state and technocratic elites that had grown steadily since the first revolution won power in 1949 were being torn apart by the rage of the people.

However satisfying for advocates of continuing revolution such as Mao, it was soon clear that the Cultural Revolution threatened to return China to the chaos and vulnerability of the prerevolutionary era. The rank-and-file threat to the leaders of the People's Liberation Army eventually proved decisive in prompting countermeasures that forced Mao to call off the campaign by late 1968. The heads of the armed forces moved to bring the rank and file back into line; the student and worker movements were disbanded and in some cases forcibly repressed. By the early 1970s, Mao's old rivals had begun to surface again. For the next half decade, a hard-fought struggle was waged at the upper levels of the party and the army for control of the government. The reconciliation between China and the United States that was negotiated in the early 1970s suggested that, at least in foreign policy, the pragmatists were gaining the upper hand over the ideologues. Deng's growing role in policy formation from 1973 onward also represented a major setback for Jiang Qing, who led the notorious *Gang of Four* that increasingly contested power on behalf of the aging Mao.

The death in early 1976 of Zhou Enlai, who was second only to Mao in stature as a revolutionary hero and who had consistently backed the pragmatists, appeared to be a major blow to those whom the Gang of Four had marked out as "capitalist-roaders" and betrayers of the revolution. But Mao's death later in the same year cleared the way for an open clash between the rival factions. While the Gang of Four plotted to seize control of the government, the pragmatists acted in alliance with some of the more influ-

Figure 41.6. *In launching the Cultural Revolution in the mid-1960s, Mao Zedong and his allies tried to restore the revolutionary fervor of the 1930s and 1940s that they felt had been eroded by the growing bureaucratization of China. In this photo a crowd of Mao's zealous young supporters rally in Beijing. The vicious assaults on anyone branded as elitist or pro-Western by those in support of the Cultural Revolution led to killings, torture, and imprisonment on a scale that is not yet fully understood. As the movement degenerated into mindless radicalism for its own sake, many of the gains a more moderate approach had made in the preceding decade were lost.*

ential military leaders. The Gang of Four were arrested, and their supporters' attempts to foment popular insurrections were foiled easily. Later tried for their crimes against the people, Jiang Qing and the members of her clique were purged from the party and imprisoned for life after their death sentences were commuted.

In the late 20th century, the pragmatists have been ascendant, and leaders such as Deng Xiaoping have opened China to Western influences and capitalist development, if not yet democratic reform. Under Deng and his allies, the farming communes have been discontinued and private peasant production for the market has been encouraged. Private enterprise has also been promoted in the industrial sector, and experiments have been made with such capitalist institutions as a stock exchange and foreign hotel chains.

Although it has become fashionable to dismiss the development schemes of the communist states as misguided failures, the achievements of the communist regime in China in the late 20th century have been impressive. Despite severe economic setbacks, political turmoil, and a low level of foreign

assistance, the communists have managed a truly revolutionary redistribution of the wealth of the country. China's very large population remains poor, but in education, health care, housing, working conditions, and the availability of food, most of it is far better off than it was in the prerevolutionary era. The Chinese have managed to provide a decent standard of living for a higher proportion of their people than perhaps any other large developing country. They have also achieved higher rates of industrial and agricultural growth than neighboring India, with its mixed state–capitalist economy and its democratic polity. And the Chinese have done all of this without leaving up to half their people in misery, and with much less foreign assistance than most developing nations have had. If the pragmatists remain in power and the champions of the market economy are right, China's growth in the 21st century should be even more impressive. But the central challenge for China's leaders will be to nurture that growth and the improved living standards without a recurrence of the economic inequities and social injustice that brought about the revolution in the first place.

Visualizing THE PAST

Art and Revolutionary Propaganda

Artists and artistic expression of different kinds have long been enlisted in support of political regimes or institutionalized religion in varying civilizational centers. But the direct connections between art and politics have become more multifaceted and intense in the 20th century. In many ways, World War I was a watershed in this regard. The governments of the adversarial powers mobilized graphic artists and writers in diverse wartime activities ranging from camouflage techniques and posters advertising war bonds to propaganda campaigns to bolster the resolve of civilian populations or win over neutral powers.

In the decades of uncertainty and social tensions that followed the offical end of the war, art and artists continued to play key roles, especially in societies transformed by revolutionary upheavals, such as Mexico, Russia and China. In Russia, for example, the internationally acclaimed film director Sergei Eisenstein devoted his very considerable talents to dramatizing the fatal flaws of the old regime and the vision of hope offered by the Bolshevik revolutionaries in movies such as *The Battleship Potemkin* and *October*. The writer Maxim Gorky actually served as the head of the Soviet Propaganda bureau in the year after the Bolshevik seizure of power in 1917. In Germany, in these same years, both right and left drew on playwrights and

延 安 新 春

graphic artists to mobilize support for their efforts to denigrate and replace the fledgling Weimar democracy (see Chapter 35). After the Nazi seizure of power, art became a major focus of government propaganda. This trend was perhaps best exemplified by Leni Riefenstahl's mid-1930s films *Triumph of the Will* and *Olympiad*, and the architect Albert Speer's designs for Hitler's political rallies and the imperial capital that both envisioned would be built in Berlin.

As these examples illustrate, artists in widely varying fields were tapped for these political tasks. But until the advent of television in the decades after World War II, the film, paintings, massive sculptures and poster art were the preferred vehicles for tansmitting the state's designs to the mass of the people. The following paintings or posters from Mexico, Russia and China show some of the uses in which art was put in the service of revolutionary regimes over nearly half a century. Study each of the illustrations and compare it to the others. Then consider the questions about artistic expression in the service of the state that follow.

Questions: What social groups are the creators of each of these art/propaganda works seeking to link to the three revolutions? What sorts of efforts are the Mexican and Russian works seeking to inspire on the part of these groups? In the Chinese poster, how is Chairman Mao associated with the mass of the people? The future of China? What personal attributes does each of the art works seek to promote among the citizens of these revolutionary societies? Are there counterparts to this use of artists and art work to shape social values and mass behavior in non-revolutionary capitalist societies, such as those of the United States and Western Europe?

COLONIALISM AND REVOLUTION IN VIETNAM

Like most of the peoples of the former colonies in Africa and Asia, the Vietnamese, as well as their neighbors in Laos and Cambodia, were brought under European colonial rule in the second half of the 19th century. But because the Vietnamese had long modeled their polity on the Confucian system of their giant neighbor to the north and had borrowed heavily from China in the social and cultural spheres, their encounter with the expansive West had much in common with that of the Chinese. The Vietnamese were also shocked by the sudden and forcible intrusion of Western influences into their formerly sheltered world. As was the case in China, the failure of Vietnam's Confucian emperor and bureaucracy to repel the foreign French invaders discredited and eventually led to the complete collapse of the system around which the Vietnamese had organized civilized life for nearly two millennia. Just as in China, this collapse led to violent revolution against French colonial rule and a search for a viable social and political order.

French interest in Vietnam reached back as far as the 17th century. Driven from Japan by the founders of the Tokugawa Shogunate, French missionaries fell back on coastal Vietnam. Vietnam attracted them both because its Confucian elite seemed similar to that of the Japanese and because the continuing wars between rival dynastic houses in the Red River valley and central Vietnam gave the missionaries ample openings for their conversion efforts. From this time onward, French rulers, who considered themselves the protectors of the Catholic missions overseas, took an interest in Vietnamese affairs. As the numbers of converts grew into the tens of thousands and French merchants began to trade at Vietnamese ports, the French stake in the region increased.

By the late 18th century, French involvement had become distinctly political as a result of the power struggles that convulsed the whole region. In the south, a genuine peasant rebellion, the *Tayson Rebellion*, toppled the Nguyen dynasty in the late 1770s

(Map 41.2). In the years that followed, the Trinh dynasty, the northern rival of the Nguyen, was also dethroned. The Tayson controlled most of the country, eliminated the Trinh, and all but wiped out the Nguyen. Seeing a chance to win influence in the ruling house, the French head of the Vietnam mission, the Bishop of Adran, threw his support behind the one surviving prince of the southern house, *Nguyen Anh.*

Anh had fled into the Mekong wilderness with a handful of supporters, thus escaping death at the hands of the Tayson. With the arms and advice of the French, he rallied local support for the dynasty and soon fielded a large army. After driving the Tayson from the south, Nguyen Anh launched an invasion of Tayson strongholds in the north. His task of conquest was made easier by bitter quarrels between the Tayson leaders. By 1802, the Nguyen armies had prevailed, and Nguyen Anh had proclaimed himself the Gia Long emperor of Vietnam.

Gia Long made the old Nguyen capital at Hue in central Vietnam the imperial capital of a unified Vietnam. His French missionary allies were rewarded with a special place at court, and French traders were given greater access to the port of Saigon, which was rapidly emerging as the leading city of the Mekong River valley region in the south. The Nguyen dynasty was the first in centuries to rule all of Vietnam and the first to rule a Vietnamese kingdom that included both the Red River and Mekong deltas. In fact, the Mekong region had only begun to be settled extensively by Vietnamese in the century or so before Gia Long rose to power.

Gia Long and his successors proved to be archtraditionalists deeply committed to strengthening Confucianism in Vietnam. Their capital at Hue was intended to be a perfect miniature of the imperial palace at Beijing. The dynasty patronized Confucian schools and built its administration around scholar–bureaucrats who were well versed in Confucian learning. The second emperor, *Minh Mang* (1820–1841), prided himself on his knowledge of the Confucian classics and his mastery of the Chinese script. He even had the audacity to criticize the brushwork of the reigning Chinese emperor, who was not any more Chinese than Minh Mang but was descended from Manchu nomads. All of this proved deeply disappointing to the French missionaries, who hoped to baptize Gia Long and then carry out through the Vietnamese the sort of top-down conversion that the Jesuits had hoped for ever since their arrival in Asia.

Things actually got much worse. Gia Long's ultra-Confucian successor, Minh Mang, came to see the Catholics as a danger to the dynasty. His persecution of the Vietnamese Catholic community not only enraged the missionaries but also contributed to the growing political and military intervention of the French government in the region.

Pushed both by political pressures at home and military defeats in Europe, French adventurers and soldiers exploited quarrels with the Nguyen rulers to justify the piecemeal conquest of Vietnam and neighboring Cambodia and Laos, beginning in the late 1840s (Map 41.2). By the 1890s, the whole of the country was under French control, and the Nguyen dynasty had been reduced to the status of puppet princes. In the decades that followed, the French concentrated on drawing revenue and resources from Vietnam while providing very little in return.

The French determination to make Vietnam a colony that was profitable for the homeland worsened social and economic problems that were already severe under the Nguyen rulers. Most of the densely packed peasant population of the north lacked enough land for a subsistence livelihood. French taxes and the burden of obligatory purchases by each village of set amounts of government-sold opium and alcohol drove many peasants into labor in the mines.

Map 41.2 *Vietnam: Divisions in the Nguyen and French Periods*

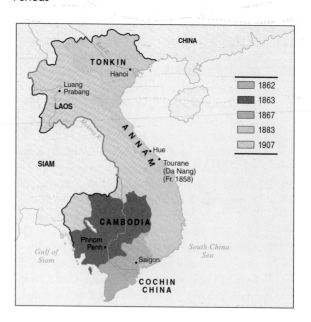

Even larger numbers left their ancestral villages and migrated to the Mekong region to work on the plantations established there by French and Chinese entrepreneurs. Other migrants chose to become tenants on the great estates that had been carved out of sparsely settled frontier regions by Vietnamese and Chinese landlords.

Migration brought little relief. Plantation workers were paid little and were treated much like slave laborers. The unchecked demands of the Mekong landlords left their tenants with scarcely enough of the crops they grew to feed, clothe, and house their families. The exploitive nature of French colonialism in Vietnam was graphically revealed by the statistics the French themselves collected. These showed a sharp drop in the food consumed by the peasantry in all parts of the colony between the early 1900s and the 1930s, a drop that occurred despite the fact that Vietnam became one of the world's major rice-exporting areas.

Vietnamese Nationalism: Bourgeois Dead Ends and Communist Survival

The failure of the Nguyen rulers after Minh Mang to rally the forces of resistance against the French did much to discredit the dynasty. But from the 1880s into the first decades of the 20th century, guerrilla warfare was waged in various parts of the country in support of the "Save the King" movement. Because this resistance was localized and small, the French were able to crush it on a piecemeal basis. In any case, French control over the puppet emperors who remained on the throne at Hue left the rebels with little cause worth fighting for. The failure of the Nguyen and the Confucian bureaucratic classes to defend Vietnam against the French did much to discredit the old order in the eyes of the new generations that came of age in the early decades of French rule. Perhaps because it was imported rather than home-grown, the Vietnamese were quicker than the Chinese to reject Confucianism once its failings were clear, and they did so with a good deal less trauma. But its demise left an ideological and institutional vacuum that the Vietnamese, again like the Chinese, would struggle for decades to fill.

In the early 20th century, a new Western-educated middle class, similar to that found in other colonial settings (see Chapters 30 and 39) was formed. It was made up mainly of the children of the traditional Confucian elite and the emerging landlord class in the Mekong region. Some, taking advantage of their parents' wealth, went to French schools and emerged speaking fluent French and with a taste for French fashions and frequent holiday jaunts to Paris and the French Riviera. Many of them went to work for the French as colonial administrators, bank managers, and even labor recruiters. Others pursued independent careers as lawyers, doctors, and journalists. Many who opted for French educations and French lifestyles were soon drawn into nationalist organizations. Like their counterparts elsewhere in the colonies, the members of these organizations initially concentrated on protesting French racism and discrimination, improving their wages, and gaining access to positions in the colonial government held by French people.

As in other colonies, nationalist newspapers and magazines proliferated. These became the focal point of an extended debate over the approach that should be taken toward winning freedom from French rule and, increasingly, what needed to be done to rebuild Vietnam as a whole. Because the French forcibly repressed all attempts to mount peaceful mass demonstrations or organize constitutional agitation, those who argued for violent resistance eventually gained the upper hand. In the early 1920s, the nationalist struggle was centered in the clandestine *Vietnamese Nationalist party* (Vietnamese Quoc Dan Dong, or VNQDD), which was committed to violent revolution against the French colonizers. Although the VNQDD made some attempt to organize urban laborers and peasant villagers, the party members were drawn overwhelmingly from the children of the landlord elite and urban professional classes. Their secret codes and elaborate rituals proved little protection against the dreaded Sûreté, or French secret police. A series of failed uprisings, culminating in a 1929 attempt to spark a general revolution with the assassination of a much-hated French official in charge of labor recruitment, decimated the party. It was particularly hard hit by the ensuing French campaign of repression, execution, and imprisonment. From that point onward, the bourgeois nationalists were never again the dominant force in the struggle for independence.

The demise of the VNQDD left its major rival, the *Communist Party of Vietnam,* as the main focus of nationalist resistance in Vietnam. As in China and Korea, the communist wing of the nationalist move-

...eveloped in Vietnam during the 1920s, ...e initiative of leaders in exile. By the late ...e party was dominated by the charismatic y... .guyen Ai Quoc, who would later be known as Ho Chi Minh. Ho had discovered Marxism while studying in France and Russia during and after World War I. Disillusioned by his failure to gain a hearing for his plea for the Vietnamese right to self-determination at the post–World War I Paris Peace Conference, Ho dedicated himself to a revolutionary struggle to drive the French from Indochina.

In the early 1930s, the Communist party still held to the rigid but unrealistic orthodox vision of a revolution based on the urban working classes. Because the workers in Vietnam made up as small a percentage of the population as they had in China, the orthodox strategy made little headway. A sudden shift in the early 1930s to a peasant emphasis, in part to take advantage of widespread but not communist–inspired peasant uprisings in central Vietnam, led to a disaster almost as great as that which had overtaken the VNQDD a year before. French repression smashed the Communist party hierarchy and drove most of the major communist leaders into exile. But the superior underground organization of the communists and the support they received from Comintern helped them survive the French onslaught.

Slowly, during the late 1930s, the discredited Ho reestablished his place in the party. The communists won growing peasant support because of their programs for land reform, higher wages for laborers, mass education, and health care. When the French were weakened by the Japanese invasion of Indochina in 1941, the communists were ready to use the colonizers' setbacks to advance the struggle for national liberation.

The War of Liberation Against the French

During World War II, operating out of bases in south China, the communist-dominated nationalist movement, known as the Viet Minh, established liberated areas throughout the northern Red River delta (see Map 41.2). The abrupt end of Japanese rule left a vacuum in Vietnam, which only the Viet Minh was prepared to fill. Its programs for land reform and mass education had wide appeal among the hard-pressed peasants of the north, where they had been propagated during the 1930s and especially during the war. The fact that the Viet Minh actually put their reform and community-building programs into effect in the areas they controlled won them very solid support among the rural population. The Viet Minh's efforts to provide assistance to the peasants during the terrible famine of 1944 and 1945 also convinced the much-abused Vietnamese people that here at last was a political organization genuinely committed to improving their lot.

Under the leadership of general Vo Nguyen Giap, the Viet Minh skillfully used guerrilla tactics similar to those devised by Mao in China. These offset the advantages that first the French and then the Japanese enjoyed in conventional firepower. With a strong base of support in much of the rural north and the hill regions, where they had won the support of key non-Vietnamese "tribal" peoples, the Viet Minh forces advanced triumphantly into the Red River delta as the Japanese withdrew. By August 1945, the Viet Minh were in control of Hanoi, where Ho Chi Minh proclaimed the establishment of the independent nation of Vietnam.

Although the Viet Minh had liberated much of the north, they had very little control in the south. In that part of Vietnam a variety of communist and bourgeois nationalist parties jostled for power. The French, eager to reclaim their colonial empire and put behind them their humiliations at the hands of the Nazis, were quick to exploit this turmoil. With British assistance, the French reoccupied Saigon and much of south and central Vietnam. In March 1946, they denounced the August declaration of Vietnamese independence and moved to reassert their colonial control over the whole of Vietnam and the rest of Indochina. An unsteady truce between the French and the Viet Minh quickly broke down. Soon Vietnam was consumed by a renewal of the Viet Minh's guerrilla war for liberation, as well as bloody infighting between the different factions of the Vietnamese. After nearly a decade of indecisive struggle, the Viet Minh had gained control of much of the Vietnamese countryside, and the French, with increasing American financial and military aid, clung to the fortified towns. In 1954, the Viet Minh decisively defeated the French at Dien Bien Phu in the mountain highlands hear the Laotian border. The victory won the Viet Minh control of the northern portions of Vietnam as a result of an international conference at Geneva in the same year. At Geneva, elections throughout Vietnam were promised within two years to decide who should govern a reunited north and the still politically fragmented south.

IN DEPTH

Decolonization With and Without Social Revolution

As we have seen, independence was won in most of the nonsettler colonized world with little violence and very limited changes in Africa and Asian economies and social hierarchies. Vietnam provides a sharp contrast to this dominant pattern, despite the fact that it had few French settlers and was colonized by the French in much the same way as the rest of Africa and Asia under European rule. The reasons for the divergent path to independence taken by the Vietnamese tell us much about the origins of revolutionary change as opposed to gradualist, reformist political transformations. They are rooted in the differences between Vietnam, China, Korea, and Cuba (see Chapter 38) and most of the rest of the postcolonial world. They are also tied to the exploitive and repressive nature of colonial rule under the French in Vietnam as well as the consequences of the brief period of Japanese control in the area.

Like the other peoples of east Asia, the Vietnamese already had a unified state, a common written and spoken language, and a strong sense of common identity long before the Europeans broke into their world. There were sharp cultural and political divisions between the lowland-dwelling, wet-rice–growing Vietnamese and the multitude of slash-and-burn cultivating peoples who lived in the hills. But the Vietnamese made up an overwhelming majority of the people who occupied the areas that eventually made up the nation of Vietnam. French rule promoted Vietnamese dominance over the hill peoples as well as over the lowland peoples of neighboring Laos and Cambodia. It also intensified the traditional Vietnamese sense of identity, both by providing a foreign target for them to resist and by enriching that sense of identity with the European concepts of the nation and patriotism. Like all peoples who had been deeply influenced by China's Confucian tradition, the Vietnamese found their political subjugation to the "barbarian" Europeans galling. Their own long tradition of violent resistance to political foreign domination, whether by the Chinese, the Mongols, or the Manchus, also fed the Vietnamese determination to fight against the French conquest.

In contrast to colonial India, Africa, and most of the rest of southeast Asia, from the outset Vietnamese cooperation with the French was branded by those who resisted French rule as a betrayal of the Vietnamese people and tradition. Also in contrast to other colonized areas, the Vietnamese continued to violently resist the imposition of French rule long after the initial wars of conquest and "pacification" had ended. There was to be no early colonial period of peace and submissiveness in Vietnam. From the outset, the Vietnamese fought the French encroachments into their country with fierce determination. This violent struggle continued through most of the period of French rule.

The crumbling of the Confucian order and the nature of French rule in Vietnam made it essential for those who tried to mobilize opposition to the French to promise far-reaching social and economic transformations. As in China and Korea, the failure of the Confucian elite in Vietnam to ward off the intrusions of the West led to the rejection of Confucian civilization as a whole. As a result and in contrast to the peoples of most of the rest of the Afro-Asian world, the Vietnamese were left without a tradition to defend and to revive as an alternative to European colonialism. Unlike Islam, Hinduism, and Buddhism elsewhere, the depoliticized, eclectic, and vague variant of Buddhism in Vietnam simply was not seen by the emerging nationalists of the country as a viable base on which to build a postcolonial order. Merely political responses were rendered insufficient by the fact that the breakdown of the Confucian system was paralleled by the worsening condition of the peasantry resulting from exploitive French policies. The substitution of French-educated, middle-class Vietnamese politicians for French colonial officials would do little to alleviate the misery of the peasant farmers of the north or the plantation workers in the south.

In any case, the middle class could make little headway against determined repression by the French, even in the political sphere. In contrast to the policies followed in most other nonsettler colonies, the French prohibited all but the most benign political organizations. The Vietnamese press was tightly controlled, even moderate political parties were smashed, and mass demonstrations of any kind were strictly prohibited. The French refused to negotiate seriously with, much less make any significant constitutional concessions to, the bourgeois nationalists, whose collaboration was a major prop of their continued domination in Indochina. Under these circumstances, the gradual transfer of power from the colonizers to the nationalists, which had been a key factor in peaceful decolonization in other areas, was out of the question. As a consequence, underground terrorist and guerrilla organizations such as the VNQDD and the Communist party dominated the struggle for independence by the 1920s.

Even the Japanese takeover in the 1940s, which proved so crucial in strengthening moderate, constitutional nationalist organizations in Burma, Indonesia, the Philippines, and other areas they occupied, had the reverse effect in Indochina. For most of the period of occupation, the Japanese were content to let French collaborators, linked to the Nazi-puppet Vichy regime then in power in France (see Chapter 34), continue to run the colony under their supervision. As a result, the policy of repressing nationalist organizations continued. Thus, any hopes for building a nonviolent, moderate party that could rival the communist-dominated Viet Minh were again crushed. The violent struggle against the Japanese, the French, and later the Americans only reinforced the revolutionary orientation of the Vietnamese Communist Party.

Questions: Compare the precolonial sense of identity and political unity in Vietnam with the situation found in most of the rest of the colonized world. How have the differences between the two made for very different paths of political development in Vietnam, as opposed to patterns of colonial dominance and nation-building in much of the rest of the postcolonial world? If the French had been more tolerant of moderate nationalist agitation, do you think that revolutionary parties such as the communists would have dominated the independence movement? Why or why not?

The War of Liberation Against the United States

The promise at Geneva that free elections would be held to determine who should govern a united Vietnam was never kept. Like the rest of east Asia, Vietnam had become entangled in the cold war maneuvers of the United States and the Soviet Union. Despite very amicable cooperation between the Viet Minh and United States armed forces during the war against Japan, U.S. support for the French in the First Indochina War and the growing fame of Ho Chi Minh as a communist leader drove the two further and further into opposition. The anticommunist hysteria in the United States in the early 1950s fed the perception of influential American leaders that South Vietnam, like South Korea, must be protected from communist takeover.

The search for a leader to build a government in the south that the United States could prop up with economic and military assistance led to *Ngo Dinh Diem.* Diem appeared to have impeccable nationalist credentials. In fact, he had gone into exile rather than give up the struggle against the French. His sojourn in the United States in the 1940s and the fact that he was Catholic also recommended him to American politicians and clergy. Unfortunately, these same attributes would alienate him from the great majority of the Vietnamese people.

With U.S. backing, Diem was installed as the president of Vietnam. He tried to legitimatize his status in the late 1950s by holding rigged elections in the south, in which the communists were not permitted to run. Diem also mounted a series of campaigns to eliminate by force all possible political rivals. Because the communists posed the biggest threat (and were of the greatest concern to Diem's American backers), the suppression campaign increasingly focused on the communist cadres that remained in the south after Vietnam had been divided at Geneva. By the mid-1950s, the *Viet Cong* (as the Diem regime dubbed the communist resistance) were threatened with extermination. In response to this threat, the communist regime in the north began to send weapons, advisors, and other resources to the southern cadres, which were reorganized as the National Liberation Front in 1958.

As guerrilla warfare spread and Diem's military responses expanded, both the United States and the North Vietnamese escalated their support for the warring parties. When Diem proved unable to stem the communist tide in the countryside, the United States authorized the military to overthrow him and take direct charge of the war. When the Vietnamese military could make little headway, the United States stepped up its military intervention.

From thousands of special advisors in the early 1950s, the United States commitment rose to nearly

500,000 men and women, who made up a massive force of occupation by 1968. But despite the loss of nearly 60,000 American lives and millions of Vietnamese casualties, the Americans could not defeat the communist movement. In part, their failure resulted from their very presence, which made it possible for the communists to convince the great majority of the Vietnamese people that they were fighting for their independence from yet another imperialist aggressor.

Although more explosives were dropped on tiny Vietnam, North and South, than in all of the theaters of World War II, and the United States resorted to chemical warfare against the very environment of the South Vietnamese they claimed to be trying to save, the communists would not yield. The Vietnamese emerged as the victors of the Second Indochina War. In the early 1970s, U.S. diplomats negotiated an end to direct American involvement in the conflict. Without that support, the unpopular military regime in the south fell apart by 1975 (Figure 41.7).

The communists united Vietnam under a single government for the first time since the late 1850s. But the nation they governed was shattered and impoverished by decades of civil war, revolution, and armed conflict with two major colonial powers and the most powerful nation of the second half of the 20th century.

After Victory: The Struggle to Rebuild Vietnam

In the years since 1975 and the end of what was, for the Vietnamese, decades of wars for liberation, communist efforts to complete the revolution by rebuilding Vietnamese society have failed. In part, this failure can be linked to Vietnam's isolation from much of the rest of the international community. This isolation resulted in part from pressures applied by a vengeful United States against relief from international agencies. It was increased by border clashes with China that were linked to ancient rivalries between the two countries. Deprived of assistance from abroad and faced with a shattered economy and a devastated environment at home, Vietnam's aging revolutionary leaders pushed hard-line Marxist–Leninist (and even Stalinist) political and economic agendas. Like their Chinese counterparts, they devoted their energies to persecuting old enemies (thus setting off mass migrations from what had been South Vietnam) and imposed a dictatorial regime that left little room for popular responses to government initiatives. In contrast to the Chinese in the past decade, however, the Vietnamese leadership also tried to maintain a highly centralized command economy. The rigid system that resulted stifled growth and, if anything, left the Vietnamese people almost as impoverished as they had been after a century of colonialism and decades of civil war.

By the late 1980s, the obvious failure of these approaches and the collapse of communist regimes throughout eastern Europe prompted measures aimed at liberalizing and expanding the market sector within the Vietnamese economy. The encouraging responses of Japanese and European corporations, eager to open

Figure 41.7 *After decades of struggle against foreign invaders, Vietnamese guerrillas march with the regular forces of the North Vietnamese army into Saigon in May 1975. The capture of the city marked the end of the long wars to free a unified Vietnam. It followed a return to conventional warfare by North Vietnamese and Viet Cong forces, which led to the rapid collapse of the South Vietnamese military and regime.*

Figure 41.8 *By the mid-1990s, the failed efforts of the United States to isolate Vietnam gave way to increasing economic and diplomatic contacts. One example of American corporate penetration is depicted in this street scene from Hanoi in 1993. The opening of Vietnam to foreign investment, assistance, and tourism accelerated through the 1990s. In this atmosphere it has been possible to begin to heal the deep wounds and animosities generated by decades of warfare waged by the Vietnamese people against advanced industrial nations such as Japan, France, and the United States.*

up Vietnamese markets, have done much to begin reviving the Vietnamese economy. Growing investments by their industrial rivals have placed increasing pressure on American firms to move into the Vietnamese market (see the photo in Figure 41.8). Combined with the genuine willingness shown by Vietnamese leaders in the past few years to work with U.S. officials to resolve questions about prisoners of war and soldiers missing in action from the Vietnam War, these economic incentives give promise of a new and much more constructive era in Vietnamese–United States relations in the 21st century.

Conclusion

Conclusion: Revolutions and Civilization in China and Vietnam

There can be little doubt that the ancient civilizations of both China and Vietnam have undergone revolutionary

transformations in the 20th century. Monarchies or autocratic colonial regimes have been replaced with Communist party cadres who seized power in the name of the peasants and workers. Whole social classes, such as the scholar–gentry and the landlords, have been eliminated. Education and writing systems developed by and centered on the elite have been replaced by mass-oriented schooling and simplified scripts designed to promote literacy. Women have greatly improved their legal status and position within the family, and a wide range of career opportunities, most of which would have been unthinkable under the prerevolutionary Confucian order, have opened to them. Marxist–Leninism, blended in recent years with experiments in Western-style capitalism, has replaced Confucianism as the state ideology and provided the philosophical basis for the new social order.

The breadth and depth of these changes might lead one to conclude that the patterns of civilized life nurtured by China and Vietnam for over two millennia disappeared as completely as Harappa vanished from the Indian landscape in the 2nd millennium B.C.E. But upon closer examination, it becomes clear that much more has been preserved than these gauges of radical change and the rhetoric of the ruling parties of China and Vietnam might lead one to believe. For example, both societies have retained deeply ingrained suspicions of the commercial and entrepreneurial classes. Both continue to stress that those who wield political power are obligated to rule in ways that promote the welfare of the mass of the people. Both China and Vietnam still adhere to ideological systems that stress secularism, social harmony, and life in this world rather than religious concerns and life hereafter. In both cases, these continuities between the prerevolutionary patterns and those of the postrevolutionary era exemplify important affinities between Marxist–Leninist and Confucian thought. They explain why Marxism had such a strong appeal to Chinese and Vietnamese intellectuals and revolutionary leaders.

These continuities caution us against overstating the extent to which the history of the 20th century marks a decisive break with the past. Just as the Bolsheviks in Russia drew on the political traditions of the Tsarist era and nationalists in India and Africa invoked the ancient symbols and beliefs of their societies, Chinese and Vietnamese revolutionaries struggled to build new societies that owed much to their Confucian past. These continuities also remind us of the resilience of ideas and patterns of civilized life that have been nurtured over centuries and, in the cases of China and Vietnam, over millennia. Civilizations weave dense and complex webs of human interaction. These patterns may be changed profoundly by the sort of revolutionary upheavals that have occurred in the 20th century. But more often than not, the changes are less sweeping, and much more is preserved than revolutionary leaders would like to admit.

Further Readings

Some of the best general studies on China in the 20th century include Lucian Bianco's *The Communist Revolution in China* (1967), C. P. Fitzgerald's *The Birth of Communist China* (1964), Wolfgang Franke's *A Century of Chinese Revolution* (1970), and Jonathan Spence's *The Search for Modern China* (1990). Maurice Meisner's *Li Ta-Chao and the Origins of Chinese Marxism* (1967) provides a detailed account of the transformations of Marxist thought in the Chinese revolutionary context. For firsthand accounts of conditions in the revolutionary era, see especially Graham Peck's *Two Kinds of Time* (1950), Edgar Snow's *Red Star Over China* (1938), and Theodore White and Analee Jacoby's *Thunder out of China* (1946). Mark Selden's *The Yenan Way to Revolution in China* (1971) provides the fullest account of the development of the communist movement after the Long March. Of the growing number of works on China after the communists came to power, Maurice Meisner's *Mao's China* (1977) and Michael Gasster's *China's Struggle to Modernize* (1987 ed.) are the most useful. Rodney Macfarquhar's two-volume study, *The Origins of the Cultural Revolution* (1974, 1983) is essential for an understanding of the last years of Mao's rule. Elisabeth Croll's *Feminism and Socialism in China* (1978) is by far the best single work on the position of women in revolutionary China.

There is a substantial literature on Vietnamese history during the Nguyen and French periods, as well as a large number of works on Vietnam during the Second Indochina War. Alexander Woodside's *Vietnam and the China Model* (1971) remains the place to start on the pre-French period, and Buttinger's *Political History of Vietnam* (1968) remains useful for general background. Woodside, Huynh Kim Khanh, David Marr, Milton Osborne, William Duiker, Pierre Brocheux, and Hue Tam Ho-Tai have all made important contributions to our knowledge of the rise of nationalism and communism in Vietnam. On U.S. intervention in the area, see the works by Marilyn Young, George Herring and Lloyd Gardner. On the conduct of the war, Jeffrey Race's *War Comes to Long An* (1972) and Malcolm Browne's *The New Face of War* (1965) are among the most insightful of many accounts.

On the Web

The voices of the leaders of the communist revolution in China can be heard at http://www4.cnd.org/fairbank/prc.html.

The story of the Red Guards and their songs can be explored at http://www.easc.indiana.edu/Pages/Easc/working_papers/NOFRAME_10b_song.htm.

The limits of the recent movement toward liberalization in China, and by extension, in the remaining communist nations, were tested during the student occupation of Tiananmen Square in 1989. A web site exploring this event (http://www.nmis.org/gate) offers film and music clips, a photo gallery and a transcript of Deng Xiaoping's June 9, 1989 speech declaring martial law.

A balanced survey of Vietnamese history encompassing the Vietnamese revolution and its aftermath in Vietnam can be found at http://www.viettouch.com/vietnam_history.html.

The Web is particularly rich in sites documenting the Vietnam War, including Vietnam's Declaration of Independence (http://.lbjlib.utexas.edu/shwv/doc/declar01.htm), the Viet Cong's Program of 1962 (http://www.fordham.edu/halsall/mod/1962vietcong1.html) and excerpts from a host of American documents on the war (http://depts.vassar.edu/~vietnam/).

Audio feed and visual images of Robert McNamara's speech on the instability of the Republic of Vietnam, President Johnson's announcement of his decision not to run for re-election and focus on a negotiated settlement of the war, the screams of students reacting to a National Guard unit's shooting of passers-by as well as antiwar demonstrators at Kent State University, and President Nixon's announcement that he had achieved peace with honor in Vietnam can all be found at http://www.historychannel.com/speeches/index.html.

Chapter 42

A 21st-Century World: Trends and Prospects

Midnight, December 31, 1999: Millenium celebration in Sydney, Australia.

Shortly before 1914, a major European banker, based in Vienna, tried to calculate the prospects for stability of the leading European countries so that he could invest wisely for the future. He assumed that past trends of political stability best predicted future performance, so he chose the three empires with the apparently strongest monarchies: Russia, Austria–Hungary, and Germany. France was an upstart republic, Britain filled with agitation, and Italy devoid of solid traditional credentials of any sort. By 1920, all his bets had failed, for his three choices were fully or partly dissolved. Morals: Don't predict too confidently, try to sort out short-term noise, as in the British case, and try to recognize change that has durable prospects for persistence (the French case). Another moral: Distrust even successful investment bankers if they're trying to calculate major world historical dynamics. Take a good history course instead.

We cannot know the future, but we can use history to develop a framework for evaluating it and partially anticipating it as it unfolds. We can know what factors to monitor. This chapter suggests several vantage points from which to relate past to present to future and presents several methods of approaching the future.

Since the formation of civilizations, the history of the world has involved rapid change, sometimes in directions already set, sometimes in new ones. This pattern continues as we enter the 21st century. Indeed, some people argue that the pace of change has sped up as new discoveries and new technologies press against older ideas and habits. In other words, world history offers no convenient stopping point at which one can lean back and say, "This is what it all means."

People in various civilizations have attempted to devise schemes to look beyond the present. From the time of the ancient river valley civilizations to the 21st century, some people have used astrology or other divinations to predict the future. More systematically, some scholars have assumed that time moves in cycles, so that one can count on repetition of basic patterns. This was a common assumption in Chinese historical thought and also among Muslim historians in the postclassical period. Others, including Christian thinkers and advocates of more secular faiths such as Marxism, have looked toward some great change in the future: the Last Judgment, for example, or the classless society toward which history is steadily working. The idea of a master plan guiding history, moving it in a steady direction and toward a purpose, runs deep in the thought of several cultures, including our own. Whatever the approach, the human impulse to know what we cannot definitely know seems inescapable.

Yet all the evidence suggests that our vision of the future remains cloudy at best. It has been calculated that more than 60 percent of all predictions or forecasts offered by serious social scientists in the United States since 1945—to sketch future business cycles, family trends, or political currents, for instance—have been wrong. How many observers just 60 years ago could have predicted such basic recent transformations as the end of Western empires; fundamental revolutions in China, Iran, and Cuba; the collapse of communist rule in Russia; the invention of computer and genetic engineering technologies; or the industrial breakthroughs of the Pacific Rim? Other developments that were confidently predicted have not come to pass: Americans normally do not ride about in helicopters rather than automobiles (an image of the 1940s), nor have families been replaced by promiscuous communes (a forecast of the 1960s). So we cannot know what is to come, but we can use history to speculate about the unknown.

OPTIMISM OR PESSIMISM

■■ *Value judgments about history are almost inevitable. Does history teach us to expect progress or deterioration?*

Many people believe that history has brought reasonably steady progress. Those who pin hopes on advancing technology can note more effective machines and better methods of preserving physical health. Those who point to progressive enlightenment can note new standards applied to the treatment of women and children, better formal education, and the abolition of slavery. Certainly improvements in life expectancy and scientific knowledge in the 20th century may easily sustain the history-as-progress theme. On this base, we might expect more to come.

But history, and certainly recent history, is also a record of tremendous cruelty and inhumanity. The 20th century has been one of unprecedented war and racial killings. Technologies have increased the carnage. Sixty million people were killed in World War

II alone; even small wars turn bloody, as with the 100,000 Iraqis killed by Western bombing in the Persian Gulf War of 1991. Armament sales by industrial nations such as the United States, Russia, France, and Israel heighten military competition in many parts of the world, and the ability to produce nuclear weapons continues to spread. Intolerance has risen in societies such as the Middle East and India, long known for religious harmony.

A compromise position makes most sense: Human history is a mixed record, and few major developments bring just hardship or just progress (although there may be a handful of exceptions). If so, we must be careful about undue optimism or pessimism in speculating about our future, unless it can be demonstrated that the future is about to become very different from the past.

A NEW PERIOD IN WORLD HISTORY

■■ *Understanding the 20th century as a new period in world history suggests that certain older trends are ending, but it does not specify what new trends will predominate.*

Using the Past to Assess the Future

What we know about 20th-century history both helps and hinders our use of the recent past to organize some sense of the future. It seems clear that in the 1920s and 1930s, a new phase in world history began to take shape. Decolonization, new international cultural exchanges, even new kinds of wars redirected global patterns on a variety of fronts.

Because this recent break in world history is so dramatic, some traditional patterns will not return. We need not expect a revival of Western colonial dominance, for example, or of monarchy or aristocracy as political and social forms. World contacts will continue to intensify. The necessary technology is increasingly available with international computer linkages and air delivery systems. Societies that tried to isolate themselves from larger world currents in the 20th century—the Soviet Union in the 1930s, to some extent, and China under Mao—have found it necessary to open up lest they lose the technological and economic benefits of contact.

The 20th century's entry into a major new period automatically limits more precise prediction. We may know that the West's dominance has declined, but we do not know whether it will continue to do so. Events in the 1990s, including the reunification of Germany, hopes for firmer west European unity, and Westernized leadership for many of the newly independent east European nations, point to a European revival well beyond what could have been foreseen just two decades ago. We do not know whether a new dominant civilization will emerge or whether the future will belong to a richer mixture of dynamic societies.

Other forecasts, based on recent trends, are also uncertain. The century has seen growing secularization of belief in otherwise varied societies. Trends are not uniform, given Islamic, Hindu, and Christian resurgences in various parts of the world, but the idea of a world without dominant religions is so strange to some observers that they predict a major religious revival, perhaps under some new doctrine, for the coming century. Who is to say they are wrong? The point is that a new period in world history inevitably produces doubt about the directions of the future precisely because old patterns are shaken up and emerging trends are hard to gauge.

Making Sense of Recent Developments

Events themselves establish uncertain directions. The biggest political development of the late 1980s–1990s involved explosions in the communist world. China experimented through the entire decade with a range of interactions with the capitalist world and with the introduction of more market devices into its own economy. Consumer interest grew in Chinese cities, and a number of peasant entrepreneurs amassed wealth by catering to market demand in their agricultural production. Gorbachev's ascent to leadership in the Soviet Union in 1985 triggered sharper change throughout eastern Europe.

This ferment was almost unprecedented. Most observers, including seasoned intelligence experts, were astounded at the events throughout the communist system, precisely because they overturned settled assumptions about Soviet power and the hold of what had been effective police states. Although it was essential to recast these assumptions, it was not clear how to predict subsequent patterns. We simply do not know whether Russia will stabilize, whether democracy will succeed.

In China, meanwhile, a massive student demonstration in 1989 in favor of greater democracy was repressed brutally. Would China remain an exception to trends in communism elsewhere, or was a seed of liberalization planted that must soon flower more fully?

Historical understanding helps us sort out the possibilities but only to a limited degree, simply because the future does not cleanly reproduce the past and the past offers various models. Some experts emphasize Russia's long authoritarian tradition and the more specific antecedents of Stalinist communism. In this view, democratic reform attempts will fail because they counter Russian officialdom's commitment to a strong state and a controlled social order. However, others have argued that reformers are reviving an important Russian tradition of looking to Western models. And who is to say that some new pattern might not emerge?

What about the end of the cold war? What historical models help predict the next international structure? Recall that the first initiative that briefly replaced Arab dominance in the 15th century—the Chinese surge in international trade—proved to be a false start. Perhaps the cold war, with its U.S.–Soviet international rivalry, can be seen as a similar episode, revealing the decline of the older west European dominance but providing no more than a temporary

Figure 42.1 *As part of the independence of the Baltic nation of Latvia, Soviet symbols are toppled. Here, in 1991, a crowd watches the dismantling of a giant statue of Lenin.*

alternative. This possibility does not predict what patterns may prove more durable, nor does it forecast the extent of Soviet decline or American constraint.

The decline of the cold war clearly encouraged realignments in troubled regions, now that superpower rivalry no longer served as a limitation. Iraq's ambitious leader, Saddam Hussein, judged the moment opportune for a more daring realignment in the Middle East. He invaded the small, oil-rich nation of Kuwait and may have hoped to use invasion to spearhead Muslim unity in the whole region, in the tradition of earlier conquerors such as the caliphs or the Ottomans. A U.S.-led coalition defeated Hussein, changing the balance of power in the area and making future arrangements extremely unpredictable. The victorious American president called for a "new world order" of stability, but the prospects for regional disruptions in the Middle East and elsewhere may have become more likely rather than less as various leaders probed the decline of superpower rivalry. The specter of nuclear armament by North Korea in 1994 highlighted another regional trouble spot that was breaking out of cold war constraints.

Key developments in the late 1990s raised additional questions. Other regional conflicts, mostly rooted in older enmities, took on more frightening contours. India and Pakistan, long enemies with disputed territory, tested new nuclear weapons in 1998. Tensions in the Balkans, Korea, the Indian subcontinent, and the Middle East heated up. Will one or more of these conflicts spill over into wider violence in a post–cold war age that seems to lack a clear framework for dispute and resolution? Also, the end of the 1990s saw a wave of banking and economic growth problems in east and southeast Asia, as well as in Russia. Were these temporary dislocations, or was the heralded rise of the Pacific Rim in jeopardy? Events offer more questions than answers.

EXTRAPOLATING TRENDS IN WORLD SOCIETIES

▪▪ *One forecasting mode attempts to cut through some of the problems of interpreting dramatic new developments by focusing on processes rather than events and by identifying strong current trends that may define the near future. Extrapolation can be applied to a whole range of issues, from politics to culture.*

Trend extrapolation can be quite precise. Within a particular society such as the West or Japan, for example, it is easy to predict an expansion of problems associated with retirement and old age costs in the near future, based on current patterns and the almost certain further results of low birth rates and growing longevity. The problems are present already, and they will increase. Only unforeseen changes, such as a spurt in the birth rate or new policies that deny medical care for older adults and so reduce longevity gains, can throw such short-term projections off.

Extrapolating vaguer trends, as well as adding an international basis, is obviously riskier. Nevertheless, several common questions or issues emerged in the late 20th century that provide a valid framework for anticipating ongoing opportunities or problems.

Political Issues

In the political sphere, the changing balance between democracy and other 20th-century government forms, notably communism and authoritarianism, provided the most obvious link between recent trends and future prospects.

Democratic parliamentarianism is now a well-established tradition in much of the West. Extremist movements still challenge it in some countries, and the memory of Nazi attacks on democratic trends scarcely half a century ago reminds us not to be too complacent. But although there are many problems with Western politics, the regimes do seem firmly rooted. They have withstood massive shocks, such as the loss of colonies. Indian and Japanese democracies are newer. Japanese democracy still combines somewhat uneasily with the tradition of upper-class dominance, whereas Indian democracy attempts to deal with the old tendency toward regional fragmentation plus new class and religious tensions. Here too, comparative stability has by now spanned several decades.

More generally, there is no question that a democratic impulse was spreading in the world by the late 1980s and 1990s. New currents in the former communist world suggested a clear link between democracy and economic reform, which resulted in

Figure 42.2 *Democracy in South Africa: Long lines of people wait to vote in the first open elections, 1994.*

widespread popular moves toward a democratic system. Successful attacks on authoritarianism in the Philippines and Korea in the 1980s raised new doubts about this system's future as well. In the 1990s, new democratic movements challenged authoritarianism in many African states and in Indonesia. By the 1990s, almost every Latin American nation had switched to democracy.

Buoyed by the trends, some observers argued that a form of liberal democracy would prove to be the only viable political style for modern nations because of the prestige it carried and because of the flexibility it allowed in responding to rapid social and economic change. But were the new democracies really firmly rooted? The year 2000, for example, saw challenge to democracy in Venezuela, Peru and Columbia, where a new authoritarianism or renewed chaos might develop. And what about China and much of the Middle East? It is hard to be confident about complex trends on an international scale.

Cultural Issues

Extrapolation of cultural trends obviously focuses on growing international contacts. Many people wonder or worry about the results of pressures for homogeneity, as the trappings of consumer culture, the popularity of Western fads, and the impact of the leading international artistic and architectural styles continue to spread. It is possible to travel to most of the world's cities today and stay in hotels, eat in restaurants, and buy goods that would scarcely differentiate downtown Chicago from downtown Istanbul. The dissemination of English as a world currency language for travel, business, and science adds to the impression of growing homogeneity. The popularity of Western-dominated cultural styles has raised issues for Japan, it has added to the confusions of growing up in modern African cities, and it has helped divide Islamic societies. To date, most civilizations have maintained their own tone, even as they selectively use international fads and products. But the further spread of global customs probably will intensify the friction between tradition and modernity while possibly undermining diversity around the world. It may also promote greater understanding. At their best, the modern Olympic games, based on an internationalization of key sports, have bridged some gaps that political leaders cannot close.

What are the trends in the arts, and how do they point to the future? Industrialization forces such a concentration on economic and technical needs and involves such an uprooting of established habits through emphasis on technical training that the arts may be pushed aside. The rise of science, spreading from the West, also challenges the importance of artistic expression. The resulting concern is phrased in various ways, depending on the civilization. Westerners worry that a rich popular cultural tradition has been replaced by commercialized, shallow entertainments designed to sell goods. The most creative artists may have become unusually remote from public taste. Non-Western intellectuals worry that their cultural traditions are being displaced by urban squalor or Westernization or that government controls bend culture to purposes of political obedience. Japanese intellectuals sometimes lament the materialism of their own culture, where traditional art survives but may play a less central role than in the past. Some dissident Russian intellectuals have expressed the same concern about their industrial society, whereas Africans worry that traditional art has degenerated into mass-produced trinkets for tourists.

How much will new technologies reshape beliefs and styles around the world? There are clear trends here, but their impact on major cultures is unclear. The question of the ongoing impact of new transmission technologies on popular culture as well as on intellectual creativity is a final open-ended issue for the world's cultural evolution at the end of the 20th century and beyond.

Economic Issues

Economic problems and prospects form the most familiar framework for discussing the future. Will the agricultural civilizations, such as those in Africa and Latin America, industrialize more fully? Can the environment withstand growing industrialization? Has Russian development, so vigorous earlier in the century, reached a plateau, and if so, what will the results be in terms of politics and diplomacy? Can the West, including the United States, withstand more global competition?

The economic divisions of the contemporary world are more subtle than the convenient dichotomy between industrial and developing nations suggests. Important differences divide nations struggling for agricultural subsistence from those involved in rapid economic transformation. Nations such as Brazil and China have developed strong industrial sectors amid many severe economic problems. Unequal levels of wealth in major civilizations are not new, but disparities in levels of development in such a tightly linked global economy are a novel combination. The stresses of trying to catch up in economic development and the resentments that can result on all sides—including those in wealthy nations trying to preserve their lead—are important but incalculable ingredients in the world's future.

Figure 42.3. *Change and continuity in rural India. New irrigation and electrification combine with traditional methods of tilling the soil as agricultural production rises.*

Economic imbalances also helped explain other important developments in the late 20th century for which no clear end was in sight. The international drug trade picked up steam from the 1920s onward. Supplies came largely from countries with poor peasantries and a desperate need for foreign exchange. Between the world wars, countries such as Turkey and China served as key suppliers; after World War II, as these countries moved toward greater economic development, areas such as northwestern Latin America moved toward center stage. Demand for the drugs resulted from tensions in several industrial societies as the burgeoning trade served as a link between very different kinds of economies in the interconnected world market.

The world's economic imbalances and the different rates of population growth also generated new pressures for immigration. Arabs and south Asians moved toward the oil-rich states of the Middle East. Growing minorities from Africa, Latin America, and Asia gravitated toward the United States and western Europe. Japan, though leery of immigrants, admitted laborers and prearranged brides from various Asian countries. The result of these movements has been a cross-civilization mixture of peoples unusual in world history and often associated with tension and confusion. Continued relocation pressures form vital issues for many societies, including those that depend on sending excess labor elsewhere. By 2000, most receiving societies were trying to set up new barriers to immigration, but results were complex.

Finally, population growth, though still a major problem, will continue to slow for two reasons. Here is a final trend, and it seems clear: First, the numbers of new children who will grow up to be parents already is decreasing; the trend has begun. Second, the causes of slower growth—government policies, world opinion, personal consumer expectations, and changes in children's roles—seem solid (although they could be reversed by some unexpected factors). Many observers believe that changes in women's education and awareness—another gradual, uneven, but definite trend—is the key factor. By 2050, the current extrapolations suggest, world population will stabilize.

Social Issues

Specific social trends continue to vary greatly with each civilization: India faces persistent, if informal, gaps between castes; peasant unrest continues in parts of Latin America; and the West worries about racial tensions surrounding new or traditional minorities. Even relations between the generations vary. Most industrial societies are gradually coming to terms with a growing old-age segment, and most agricultural civilizations are still focusing on problems of nurturing and educating the young.

A few fundamental questions apply to all societies. Industrialization has involved city growth, and urbanization in many cases races ahead of other eco-

nomic change. City life, in turn, poses some basic challenges, such as dealing with crowding, providing appropriate entertainment, and dealing with psychological stress stemming from the excitement and tension of city life. The impact of urbanization, both its promise and its difficulties, raises global questions for the present and the future.

Another trend involves social structure. Control of the land has become steadily less important as the basis for social position. Aristocracies and landlord classes loom less large in late 20th-century world history than at any time since the dawn of civilization. Urbanized societies tend to place emphasis on wealth, knowledge, and managerial control as the basis of social prestige. This has been the clear pattern in the West and in eastern Europe even under communism; the pattern seems to be emerging in Africa and Asia as well. Divisions between wealthy managerial classes and laboring groups with little or no property and inferior education form conflicts that cut across several different civilizations.

IN DEPTH

Evaluating the Conditions of Women

Judging women's conditions and predicting worldwide changes involves two analytical problems: determining current trends and assessing the ongoing diversities in civilizations.

Many Western feminists assume or hope for a modernization pattern in which women will continue to move toward greater equality in the West while their sisters elsewhere in the world push in the same direction. Several intercultural trends are encouraging. Women are gaining more education, though at very different levels depending on the wealth and traditions of each society. Voting rights are fairly common. Birth rates are falling (although in many areas they remain fairly high). These gains may foreshadow women's pressing for new jobs and new political positions, a trend visible not only in the West but in parts of Latin America and elsewhere.

But great inequalities may persist. Peasant women in India still live with a largely traditional patriarchy. The rise of Islamic fundamentalism has tightened constraints on women in parts of the Middle East. Furthermore, new developments can work against women. A more commercial economy in parts of Africa has reduced women's economic importance: As happened in the West in the 19th century, men got the new jobs. More effective governments can reduce women's informal political roles, even cutting into their family authority. Forecasting is difficult because of the complexity of current trends. It is not clear that these are worldwide patterns. Extrapolations can therefore be misleading.

Recently, women in some countries have also been arguing that judging their lives on the basis of Western standards is an ethnocentric distortion. They contend that there are different models for women's freedom. A magazine in India urges that women there not adopt the demanding Western standards of beauty, which force women to spend immense amounts of time prettying themselves. Some Muslim women argue that their traditions, though not Western, give them freedom. If they veil and dress according to custom, they will not be harassed by men, as in the urban West. Islamic law gives them vital rights in the family. A Nigerian woman states that in contrast to Western-style individualism, many African women work for tight family ties that unite mothers with daughters, even as they embrace more education and some birth control, and she says this modified traditionalism works well for women.

In sum, Western feminism has pushed hard for equality but according to some culturally conditioned ideas of what it is. These ideas make it easy to deplore women's lot in more traditional societies. But is this approach the best way to understanding? What is the balance between relativism and absolute standards in judging the validity of varied arrangements for women?

Questions: What reasons are there to believe that women's conditions may evolve in similar directions worldwide? What are the main problems with this approach? Why have some women had adverse reactions to Western feminist judgments? Can you think of any conditions for women—polygamy, for example—that should clearly be condemned in any society? Are women who argue that they are free under non-Western conditions deluding themselves?

FORECASTING BY A SINGLE CAUSAL FACTOR

Another common approach to the future involves identifying an overwhelming causal factor that will fundamentally alter the framework in which the societies of the world operate. The resulting dramatic forecast differs from careful trend extrapolation by seizing on one decisive ingredient and anticipating massive contrasts between future and present.

The Overcrowding Scenario

In the 1960s and early 1970s, gloomy "population bomb" predictions received growing attention. Experts correctly noted the unprecedented size and growth rates of world population and argued that, unchecked, the sheer number of people would outstrip available resources, produce unmanageable environmental degradation, and create rivalries for space that could usher in a series of bitter wars. Concern about world population trends, though still lively, had lessened by the 1990s, in part because growth rates had slowed. Some experts claimed that resources could expand with population growth and noted that historically, population expansion was often a major source of innovation and creativity. Population bomb forecasts had not been discounted entirely, and environmentalists picked up some of their concerns. As a tool for gauging the future, however, the bomb approach was yesterday's fad, although in the 1990s world population continued to grow at a rate of more than 200,000 new people per day.

A variant on the population bomb approach, though less widely publicized, played up the exhaustion of frontiers. By the late 20th century, some world historians argued, human societies had fully run out of room to expand, pending space travel. Each previous period of world history had featured expansions into empty or nearly empty spaces. Thus, the postclassical period saw movements into eastern Europe and western China as well as Bantu migrations southward in Africa, and the 19th century had climaxed the history of human frontiers with the fuller peopling of the Americas and Australia and with Russian settlement in Siberia. With frontiers gone by the late 20th century, organized societies bumped against each other far more than ever before, and immigration inevitably meant movement not into unsettled terrain but into highly populous, often suspicious host societies. The implications for potential conflict and environmental exhaustion are serious if this major factor is viewed as a basic distinction between society future and society past.

A Postindustrial World

Another effort to identify deterministic causation highlights a revolutionary wave of technological change. Here the spotlight is on computers, genetic engineering, robotics, and new devices for transmitting energy. According to some popular forecasters, late 20th-century society entered a postindustrial revolution as dramatic as the Industrial Revolution two centuries before or the Neolithic revolution 10,000 years before, with exactly the same potential for altering the framework of human existence. Postindustrial society will feature service occupations dealing with people and information exchange as both agriculture and industrial production are handled largely by machines. Social status will depend on technical knowledge, not money or land. Cities will change, becoming centers for meetings and recreation, not basic points of exchange and production. This change is dramatic, and some observers claim to find ample evidence of its accuracy in existing trends. The postindustrial vision usually is optimistic in assuming that key industrial problems will be resolved in the new order. For example, routine, repetitive work will be eliminated by automation, and computers will allow labor to become more varied and individualized.

Critics of the postindustrial vision raise several objections. They are not sure that the transformation discernible in the United States and western Europe is as fundamental as the analogies to the Industrial Revolution suggest. Change is occurring, to be sure, but it preserves management and labor structures similar to the patterns of industrial society. Computers usually make work more routine, not less, as rigorous supervision becomes automated. Corporate and government bureaucracies continue to expand. In other words, new technology does not necessarily change most basic trends, and technological determinism should not be pressed too far. Furthermore, if distinctive postindustrial societies are developing, they are concentrated in very few parts of the world,

such as the West and Japan. Postindustrialization mainly increases the economic inequalities between major areas that have already arisen as part of the world economy. How useful, then, is the concept for forecasting overall world history?

Dramatic forecasting of this sort—whether imbued with postindustrial optimism or population bomb gloom—relies heavily on a single basic casual factor: Technology or population determines all, and everything falls into place once this factor is established. Most historians reject this kind of determinism. Analysis of the past shows the power of continuity rather than single-minded transformation. Major changes do occur, but they result from the confluence of several factors, not a single cause. Although cataclysm is always possible, most historians assume that complexity will continue. Eye-catching forecasts can help organize our thinking about what makes history tick and how the present relates to the past, but there are other orientations toward the future as well.

WORLD HISTORY THEMES

Do changes and continuities in basic world history themes suggest probabilities for the future, either because of ongoing trends in the contemporary period or because of dramatic new factors?

A host of issues have described the human experience since the beginnings of human civilization (and sometimes before). Their content has changed, thanks to basic new developments in individual societies and around the globe, but as issues most of them persist. Only one major theme emphasized in this text, the importance of nomadic–civilization interactions, really ended with the decisive historical innovations in the early modern period.

Inequality clearly persists in contemporary society. Most societies no longer explicitly enforce inequalities by laws or by rigid frameworks such as slavery or caste. But remnants of these inequalities persist, as in discriminations against groups that once were low-caste in India, or the prejudice against people of African origins in the United States, in part because their ancestors were slaves. Gender inequality persists as well, as the In Depth section suggested, and interpreting its modern manifestations and variations is challenging. Literal enforcement of patriarchalism in law is rare (for example, most women can vote), but vivid power imbalances, including some new barriers to productive work in some changing economies, clearly survive and becloud the future.

However, by the end of the 20th century the most troubling case of growing inequality involved disparities in earnings and living standards between the wealthiest quarter of the world's population and the remaining three-quarters. Here, two developments created growing gaps in the 1990s. First, the long-standing gulf between rich industrial societies and other societies in which growing manufacturing had not generated a great leap into affluence continued the centuries-long pattern of international economic divisions. Second, within societies the increasing commitment to open economic competition and the decline of state regulation created new gaps between the minority of successful profit-takers

and others. For instance, from the 1970s onward most Americans saw little improvement in their standards of living, whereas the top tenth enjoyed soaring affluence. Other industrial countries were less divided, but here too disparities grew. A group of "new Russians," taking advantage of capitalism, soared above the hard-pressed majority in wealth. Industrial growth in Latin America and China also produced a wealthy minority (if somewhat smaller), playing against larger numbers trapped in mediocre living standards. This was the trend; what will it mean for the future? How does this pattern of inequality compare to earlier ones in world history, some of which were widely accepted and some of which generated bitter conflict?

Interactions between the environment and technology, another old issue in the human experience dating back at least to the beginning of agriculture, took an even more decisively new turn in the 20th century, with huge questions for the future. Levels of many types of pollution increased.

Figure 42.4 *Oil and the environment. A massive spill in the Persian Gulf, off the coast of Saudi Arabia, in 1991.*

The daily destruction of acres of natural vegetation in expanding societies, such as those of Latin America and Africa, hinders the natural production of oxygen through photosynthesis, and in other regions industrial plants lower air and water quality. The increased output of human wastes produces other environmental problems. Our ability to sustain growing populations may be jeopardized in the future, or the amenities to which many people have become accustomed may be reduced.

Major environmental accidents during the 1980s and 1990s indicated the severity of some of these problems. Many different societies were involved in these accidents. A Russian nuclear reactor at *Chernobyl* in the Ukraine experienced partial meltdown, devastating the immediate area and increasing radioactive levels in a wide area of Europe. An American chemical plant in Bhopal, India, suffered a huge explosion, killing hundreds of people and maiming many more. In 1989, a series of oceanic oil spills around the United States, including a particularly extensive accident in Alaska, severely damaged shorelines and marine life. The 1991 Persian Gulf War resulted in huge oil spills and oil fires. More general findings about the thinning of the ozone layer by chemical pollution and about widely anticipated global warming caused by the growing use of hydrocarbons demonstrated the international scope of environmental issues and the lag between policy controls and the acceleration of problems.

Yet new trends were not entirely unfavorable. Many industrial societies used part of their growing wealth to clean up polluted waterways, such as the Thames River in England. Japan, faced with choking air pollution in the 1970s, adopted new policies that applied novel technologies to control chemical emissions, with great success. By the 1990s, international discussion of pollution issues produced agreement on the need for discipline and control to attack threats such as global warming. It remained to be seen whether world societies, amid development efforts and intense competition, would choose to implement the controls agreed upon and whether the agreements themselves were adequate.

What of human agency? World history provides a mixed picture at all stages. Efforts by creative individuals have sometimes reshaped a culture, a stylistic movement, or a state. Ordinary people, even beset by massive impersonal forces such as industrialization, have often carved out some space for their own particular values. Yet even for the great and mighty, the leeway has often been slim. Changes caused by disease, war, technology, or cultural controls imposed by key power groups have often limited human agency. Judging the role of human agency in the past is tremendously complex, though always worth attention. And what of the present and future? Can individual leaders in places such as the Middle East push back the pressures of cultural and economic Westernization, or in the long run are the larger impersonal tides too strong? Have developments such as the growing size of organizations or the ability to manipulate people through consumer goods and symbols reduced individual power to shape history?

And what of that key tension in world history, perhaps related to issues of human agency: the tensions between separate regional identities and civilizations and the importance of contacts and crosscutting forces? We have already noted that the 20th century, like all major new periods in world history, redefined the tension somewhat. Some scholars argue that the redefinition, during the 21st century, may move beyond all precedent.

REGIONS, CIVILIZATIONS, AND WORLD FORCES

As we look to the future, what is the status of civilizations? Are we nearing the point when international forces override civilization characteristics in shaping our history?

Since the classical period, world history has involved a tension between the operations of individual civilizations and wider international forces that shape the way people think and behave across civilization boundaries around the world. At the beginning of the 21st century it is possible to predict a new splintering among civilizations, even a new selfish regionalism, with each area emphasizing its own flavor. There are also new homogenizing forces that may reduce variations between individual cultures in favor of more global trends.

The Quest for Separate Identities

Because the history of civilization began with widely separated communities, whether they were agricultural villages or hunting-and-gathering bands, patterns of aggregating and building larger units are an underlying theme in the larger world historical process. Yet aggregation into regions or whole civilizations has never been a constant. Empires and even cultural units become fragmented. The great multi-

national empires of the early modern period—the Mughal, Ottoman, and now Russian empires, for example—all split apart. Events in the 1980s and 1990s raised the prospect of new fragmentations to a surprising level. Peoples in small regions showed that old loyalties persisted fiercely. Thus, Slavic groups in eastern Europe, even in a single small nation such as Yugoslavia, turned on each other with demands for separation or at least autonomy. Central Asian peoples reasserted particularisms. Descendants of the French in Quebec, seeking greater independence, encountered hostility from their English-descended neighbors elsewhere in Canada.

Developments after 1950 continued to reflect civilization boundaries. Compare the struggles of China and India against high birth rates. The efforts of the Indian government have proved ineffective, given traditional resistance to state involvement, whereas Chinese efforts, though not completely successful, could build on earlier patterns of state intervention.

Regions and civilizations have not remained changeless, but they combine distinctive traditions, distinctive recent experiences, and a distinctive filter by which even common experiences are modified. This pattern survived in the late 20th century. Thus, the Indian interpretation of the problem of economic development differs from that of the Chinese, and the Chinese interpretation of the reform of communism turned out to differ from that of Russia. Moreover, despite important common themes, no overriding pattern of modernization has obliterated key boundaries between the major civilizations.

A basic theme of 20th-century history, almost certain to extend into the 21st century, thus involves an understanding of how each major civilization will interpret and adapt to the forces of modern politics and industrialization. Correspondingly, any common international process—for example, the modification of a patriarchal structure for women—must be evaluated specifically for each civilization. Generalizations about the whole world could easily misfire in light of separate traditions (such as the specific forms of patriarchy) and distinctive recent experiences.

A key result of decolonization and the growing challenge to Western dominance was a reassertion of the cultural independence of several civilizations. The end of the cold war enhanced the prospects for new regional separations. This was a strong ingredi-

Figure 42.5 *Civil war in Yugoslavia as the separate Slavic groups splinter. The Yugoslav army attacks the historic Croatian city of Dubrovnik, 1991.*

ent of the Iranian revolution, bent on guiding a reinvigoration of Islam more generally. It also infused Chinese communist reactions to the protest currents at the end of the 1980s, when renewed claims to China's superior devotion to order surfaced quickly. The same was true of rising Hindu nationalism in India in the 1990s.

Yet the emphasis on distinctive civilizations, increasingly conscious of their unique qualities, is not the only focus of world history as we approach the future. In the first place, there is little assurance that the civilization areas identifiable in the late 20th century will remain constant. Societies do collapse and merge, and they may split apart. Take Turkey as a borderline case. At the end of the 1980s Turkey applied for admission to the European Common Market. Without renouncing Islam but building on the special relationship Turks have long maintained with the West, Turkey asked to become part of the West. In western Europe, the application roused great anxieties and concern not only about Turkey's backwardness, despite recent industrial advance, but also about its strangeness. Possibly, the political boundary line between the Middle East and Europe was about to be redrawn yet again.

The most important question for the future, however, involves the civilization framework itself, as it has been elaborated over a 5000-year span. Civilizations, long functioning as forms that partially integrated more smaller regions, now may see a similar process pulling them closer on a global basis.

The Forces of International Integration

Previous crosscutting forces in world history, from agricultural technologies to the great world religions to new foodstuffs or inventions such as the printing press, all promoted transformation within the separate civilizations. Even the rise of Western-dominated world trade did not fuse the civilizations into a single basic pattern. Arab or Western dominance reduced the autonomy of most civilizations only modestly, except in special cases such as Latin America, where a prior civilization was largely destroyed. Even in Latin America, international contact brought sweeping change but not a full merger into Western cultural, political, or economic forms.

This balance—between separate regional and civilization identities and international pressure—may now be changing. The crosscutting forces of the past century or so have unquestionably increased the impact of international forces. One sign of this is the difficulty major societies have in trying to isolate themselves for ideological reasons. International movements of women, computer hackers, and soccer fans clearly override the boundaries of civilization, and they may gradually make those boundaries less distinct.

The internationalization of the world embraces several familiar features. The speed of modern transportation and communication brings societies closer together, as does the rising volume of world trade. International artistic styles, particularly in urban architecture, have more vitality than ever before. The popularity of Western fads and fashions, from clothes to television to sports, leads to cultural contact between ordinary people in daily activities. In this sense, the rise of the West continues to reverberate even as its dominance recedes. At the elite level, the spread of scientific training cuts across cultural boundaries as no world religion ever has.

Growing world contacts and a spreading array of global forces produced the understandable but erroneous attempt to simplify recent world history into a study of Westernization. Serious scholars assumed that the Western version of modernization, including industrialization, mass education, democratic parliamentary politics, low birth rate, a consumer society, and greater equality for women, would take hold around the world. Each civilization could thus be measured by the speed at which it adopted the standard modern (meaning Western) features. This analytical approach confused some undeniably common impulses, including the desire to replace traditional patterns, in the name of nationalism and economic development, with homogeneity. Moreover, it did not allow for the revived force of traditional values in societies such as Islam.

Still, if the simplest modernization or Westernization model has proved clearly inaccurate, as the world's civilizations continue to handle certain common impulses distinctively, the sense that a new simplifying framework may be right around the corner persists. Will one of the new technologies taking hold do the trick? This is a crucial aspect of any postindustrial argument applied at a global level. The spread of computer networks sometimes is believed to foreshadow new common patterns of organization, research, and thinking, bringing far greater similarities to the societies involved than the rhythms of the factory or the farm ever did. Some advocates even believe that agricultural societies can shift to a computer system for production and communication without going through a classic industrial phase. Technologies have cut across cultural divides before, and the power and speed of the computer revolution may have an even more sweeping impact.

Common cultures generate other forces through which specific international communities are obliterating civilization distinctions. Scientists and social scientists from almost every society can now meet and discuss common methods and common basic assumptions. Political or other divisions may complicate this harmony, but a fundamental international community exists with a shared frame of reference. At another level, soccer and a few other sports elicit very similar enthusiasms around much of the world, even though they also express competition among the societies fielding the teams.

International business is another integrating force. As Japanese and Korean firms join Americans and Europeans in setting up branches of production in almost every regional market, and as business leaders strive to imitate each other's organizational forms and labor policies, civilization boundaries retreat.

On several different fronts, then, the intensification of international networks, itself part of a long and varied process in world history, has proceeded to such a point that various scholars could seriously see in the late 20th century the beginning of the end of the civilization form. World diversities and inequalities obviously will persist amid new international communities, but coherent regional civilizations may gradually pull apart at the seams.

For the moment, separate civilizations are still very much alive. An equilibrium between distinct civilizations and unifying developments provides the most obvious interpretive basis for asking questions about the future. Increasingly rapid and intense contacts around the world have not created a single framework for world history. The pull of regional and civilization loyalties remains strong. The revival of divisive allegiances in many parts of the world in the early 1990s surely reflects a human need to counterbalance the large, impersonal forces stemming from international developments. The world, in some ways growing smaller, is becoming no less complex. Distinctive traditions continue to modify, and sometimes to reverse, seemingly powerful unifying forces, although these forces persist as well.

Conclusion

Asking Questions

Whatever the vantage point, questions easily outnumber answers as we contemplate the future. The international powers of industrial business, technology, and mass culture pose new challenges to particular civilizations. This is not a mere replay of earlier tensions between world currents and separate civilization traditions. Yet continuities from the past—the surge of religious sentiment in eastern Europe, for example—and possibly new needs for smaller-scale identities make predicting the triumph of a single world framework foolish. We know that tensions between international forces and needs, as well as the distinct reactions of individual societies, will shape the future. We know that the tensions have some new features. We know that the resulting interplay will be an important part of the future, for the tension between contacts and divisiveness has shaped world history for many centuries. However, we do not know what the precise results will be. We do not know whether most Muslims, neo-Confucians, or Westerners will emphasize what singles them out over the interests they share with the world as a whole.

But we do know a great deal about how world societies have behaved in the past. This involves more than just knowledge of ongoing traditions. It offers examples of past behaviors and the causes of change. It offers connections between the world's present and its past, and models of the kinds of questions we can ask about its future. We can count on the emerging world of the 21st century to challenge our understanding, but we can also learn to use a grasp of the world's past as a partial guide.

Further Readings

Several serious books (as well as many more simplistic, popularized efforts) attempt to sketch the world's or the West's future. On the postindustrial society concept, see Daniel Bell's *The Coming of Post-Industrial Society* (1974). For other projections, consult R. L. Heilbroner's *An Inquiry into the Human Prospect* (1974) and L. Stavrianos's *The Promise of the Coming Dark Age* (1976). An important, recent world order forecast is S. P. Huntington's *The Third Wave: Demoralization in the Late Twentieth Century* (1993).

On environment and resource issues, D. H. Meadows and D. L. Meadows's *The Limits of Growth* (1974) and L. Herbert's *Our Synthetic Environment* (1962) are worthwhile. M. ul Haq's *The Poverty Curtain: Choices for the Third World* (1976) and L. Solomon's *Multinational Corporations and the Emerging World Order* (1978) cover economic issues, in part from a non-Western perspective.

On military and diplomatic issues, A. Sakharov's *Progress, Coexistence and Intellectual Freedom*, rev. ed. (1970), is an important statement by a Russian dissident; other useful texts include S. Hoffman's *Primacy or World Order: American Foreign Policy Since the Cold War* (1978), S. Melman's *The Peace Race* (1961), and W. Epstein's *The Last Chance: Nuclear Proliferation and Arms Control* (1976).

On a leading social issue, see P. Hudson's *Third World Women Speak Out* (1979). A major interpretation of the 20th-century world is Theodore von Laue's *The World Revolution of Westernization* (1989). Two other recent assessments, both historically informed, are Richard Bulliet, ed., *The Columbia History of the 20th Century* (1998), and Andre Gunder Frank, *ReOrient: Global Economy in the Asian Age* (1998).

Glossary

Pronunciation guidance is supplied in square brackets, [ ], after difficult words. The symbols used for pronunciation are found in the table below. Syllables for primary stress are *italicized*.

a	act, bat, marry	j	just, tragic	u	sum, up
AY	age, rate	k	keep, coop	U	sue, blew, through
âr	air, dare	ng	sing	ûr	turn, urge, cur
ä	ah, part, calm			zh	vision, pleasure
ch	chief, beach	o	ox, hot	uh	*a*lone, syst*e*m, eas*i*ly, gall*o*p, circ*u*s
e	edge, set	O	hope, over		
EE	equal, seat, bee	ô	order, ball	A	as in French *a*mi
EER	here, ear	oi	oil, joint	KH	as in German a*ch*, i*ch*
g	give, trigger	oo	book, tour	N	as in French bo*n*
h	here	ou	plow, out	OE	as in French d*eux*
hw	which, when	sh	she, fashion	R	as in French *r*ouge
i	if, big	th	thin, ether	Y	as in German f*ü*hlen
I	bite, ice				

Abbas the Great Safavid ruler from 1587 to 1629; extended Safavid domain to greatest extent; created slave regiments based on captured Russians, who monopolized firearms within Safavid armies; incorporated Western military technology (p. 623)

Abdallahi, Khalifa [uh dool *ä* h*EE*] Successor of Muhammad Achmad as leader of Mahdists in Sudan; established state in Sudan; defeated by British General Kitchener in 1598. (p. 793)

Abduh, Muhammad Disciple of al-Afghani; Muslim thinker at end of 19th century; stressed need for adoption of Western scientific learning and technology, recognized importance of tradition of rational inquiry. (p. 791)

Abdul Hamid Ottoman sultan who attempted to return to despotic absolutism during reign from 1878 to 1908; nullified constitution and restricted civil liberties; deposed in coup in 1908. (p. 787)

absolute monarchy Concept of government developed during rise of nation-states in western Europe during the 17th century; featured monarchs who passed laws without parliaments, appointed professionalized armies and bureaucracies, established state churches, imposed state economic policies. (p. 532)

African National Congress Black political organization within South Africa; pressed for end to policies of apartheid; sought open democracy leading to black majority rule; until the 1990s declared illegal in South Africa. (p. 1015)

Afrikaner National party Emerged as the majority party in the all-white South African legislature after 1948; advocated complete independence from Britain; favored a rigid system of racial segregation called apartheid. (p. 986)

Akbar Son and successor of Humayan; oversaw building of military and administrative systems that became typical of Mughal rule in India; pursued policy of cooperation with Hindu princes; attempted to create new religion to bind Muslim and Hindu populations of India. (p. 628)

al-Afghani Muslim thinker at the end of the 19th century; stressed need for adoption of Western scientific learning and technology; recognized importance of tradition of rational inquiry. (p. 791)

Ali, Muhammad Won power struggle in Egypt following fall of Mamluks; established mastery of all of Egypt by 1811; introduced effective army based on Western tactics and supply and a variety of other reforms; by 1830s was able to challenge Ottoman government in Constantinople; died in 1848. (p. 791)

Allende, Salvador: [ä *yAHn* dAY, ä *yen* dEE] President of Chile; nationalized industries and banks; sponsored peasant and worker expropriations of lands and foreign-owned factories; overthrown in 1973 by revolt of Chilean military with the support of the United States. (p. 947)

Alliance for Progress   Begun in 1961 by the United States to develop Latin America as an alternative to radical political solutions; enjoyed only limited success; failure of development programs led to renewal of direct intervention. (p. 953)

Álvares Cabral, Pedro   Portuguese leader of an expedition to India; blown off course in 1500 and landed in Brazil. (p. 597)

Amaru, Tupac   Mestizo leader of Indian revolt in Peru; supported by many among lower social classes; revolt eventually failed because of Creole fears of real social revolution. (p. 606)

American Civil War   Fought from 1861 to 1865; first application of Industrial Revolution to warfare; resulted in abolition of slavery in the United States and reunification of North and South. (p. 712)

American exceptionalism   Historical argument that the development of the United States was largely distinctive; contact with Western Europe was incidental to the larger development of the United States on its own terms. (p. 721)

American Revolution   Rebellion of English American colonies along Atlantic seaboard between 1775 and 1783; resulted in independence for former British colonies and eventual formation of United States of America. (p. 699)

amigos del país   [uh *mEE* gOs, ä *mEE-*, del päEEs] Clubs and associations dedicated to improvements and reform in Spanish colonies; flourished during the 18th century; called for material improvements rather than political reform. (p. 602)

anarchists   Political groups that sought the abolition of all formal government; particularly prevalent in Russia; opposed tsarist autocracy; eventually became a terrorist movement responsible for assassination of Alexander II in 1881. (p. 815)

Anglican church   Form of Protestantism set up in England after 1534;

established by Henry VIII with himself as head at least in part to obtain a divorce from his first wife; became increasingly Protestant following Henry's death. (p. 526)

Anschluss   Hitler's union of Germany with the German-speaking population of Austria; took place in 1938, despite complaints of other European nations. (p. 852)

apartheid   Policy of strict racial segregation imposed in South Africa to permit the continued dominance of whites politically and economically. (p. 1015)

appeasement   Policy of Neville Chamberlain, British prime minister who hoped to preserve peace in the face of German aggression; particularly applied to Munich Conference agreements; failed when Hitler invaded Poland in 1939. (p. 853)

Aquino, Crazon   First president of the Philippines in the post-Marcos era of the late 1980s; Aquino, whose husband was assassinated by thugs in the pay of the Marcos regime, was one of the key leaders in the popular movement that toppled the dictattor. (p. 1002)

Arevalo, Juan José   Elected president of Guatemala in 1944; began series of Socialist reforms including land reform; Nationalist program directed against foreign-owned companies such as United Fruit Company. (p. 944)

Argentine Republic   Replaced state of Buenos Aires in 1862; result of compromise between centralists and federalists. (p. 758)

Asante Empire   [uh *san* tEE, uh *sän*] Established in Gold Coast among Akan people settled around Kumasi; dominated by Oyoko clan; many clans linked under Osei Tutu after 1650. (p. 642)

asantehene   [un san tAY hAY nAY] Title taken by ruler of Asante Empire; supreme civil and religious leader; authority symbolized by golden stool. (p. 647)

Asian sea trading network   Prior to intervention of Europeans, consisted of three zones: Arab zone based on glass, carpets, and tapestries; India based on cotton textiles; and China based on paper, porcelain, and silks. (p. 666)

Atlantic Charter of 1941   World War II alliance agreement between the United States and Britain; included a clause that recognized the right of all people to choose the form of government under which they live; indicated sympathy for decolonization. (p. 978)

Atlantic colonies   British colonies in North America; originally restricted to the coastline of the Atlantic Ocean from New England to Georgia. (p. 555)

audiencia   Royal court of appeals established in Spanish colonies of New World; there were ten in each viceroyalty; part of colonial administrative system; staffed by professional magistrates. (p. 596)

Aurangzeb   [*ôr* uhng zeb] Son and successor of Shah Jahan in Mughal India; determined to extend Mughal control over whole of subcontinent; wished to purify Islam of Hindu influences; incessant warfare exhausted empire despite military successes; died in 1707. (p. 631)

Babur   Founder of Mughal dynasty in India; descended from Turkic warriors; first led invasion of India in 1526; died in 1530. (p. 627)

Balboa, Vasco de   First Spanish captain to begin settlement on the mainland of Mesoamerica in 1509; initial settlement eventually led to conquest of Aztec and Inca empires by other captains. (p. 554)

Balfour Declaration   British minister's promise of support for the establishment of Jewish settlement in Palestine during World War I; issued in 1917. (p. 844)

Balkan nationalism   Movements to create independent nations within the Balkan possessions of the Ottoman Empire; provoked a series of crises within the European alliance system; eventually led to World War I. (p. 723)

Banana Republics   Term given to conservative governments supported or created by the United States in Latin America; believed to be either corrupt or subservient to U.S. interests. (p. 951)

Bangladesh   Founded as an independent nation in 1972; formerly East Pakistan. (p. 996)

banner armies   Eight armies of the Manchu tribes identified by separate flags; created by Nurhaci in early 17th century; utilized to defeat Ming emperor and establish Qing dynasty. (p. 794)

Batavia   Dutch fortress located after 1620 on the island of Java. (p. 659)

Batista, Fulgencio   Dictator of Cuba from 1934 to 1944; returned to presidency in 1952; ousted from government by revolution led by Fidel Castro. (p. 945)

Belgian Revolution of 1830   Produced Belgian independence from the

Dutch; established a liberal constitutional monarchy. (p. 703)

Benin A large and powerful kingdom of West Africa near the coast (in present-day Nigeria) which came into contact with the Portuguese in 1485 but remained relatively free of European influence; remained an important commercial and political entity until the 19th century. (p. 647)

Berlin Wall Built in 1961 to halt the flow of immigration from East Berlin to West Berlin; immigration was in response to lack of consumer goods and close Soviet control of economy and politics. Wall was torn down at end of Cold War in 1991. (p. 898)

Bhutto, Benazir Twice prime minister of Pakistan in the 1980s and 1990s; first ran for office to avenge her father's execution by the military clique then in power. (p. 1002)

Biafra Founded as an independent nation in eastern Nigeria, where the Ibo people were most numerous; suppressed as an independent state and reincorporated into Nigeria in 1970. (p. 997)

Bismarck, Otto von Conservative prime minister of Prussia; architect of German unification under Prussian king in 1870; utilized liberal reforms to attract support for conservative causes. (p. 711)

Blitzkrieg German term for lightning warfare; involved rapid movement of troops, tanks, and mechanized carriers; resulted in early German victories over Belgium, Holland, and France in World War II. (p. 854)

Boer republics Transvaal and Orange Free State in southern Africa; established to assert independence of Boers from British colonial government in Cape Colony in 1850s; discovery of diamonds and precious metals caused British migration into the Boer areas in 1860s. (p. 750)

Boer War Fought between 1899 and 1902 over the continued independence of Boer republics; resulted in British victory, but began the process of decolonization in South Africa. (p. 750)

Boers Dutch settlers in Cape Colony. (p. 560)

Bolívar, Simon Creole military officer in northern South America; won series of victories in Venezuela, Colombia, and Ecuador between 1817 and 1822; military success led to creation of independent state of Gran Colombia. (p. 757)

Bolshevik Revolution After initial revolution in March 1917 had set up a liberal regime in Russia, the well-organized Bolshevik faction of the communist party, under Lenin, seized power in November (October by the Russian calendar, hence often called the October Revolution); the Bolsheviks capitalized on worker strikes and widespread discontent with Russia's continued participation in World War I; quickly moved to set up a new political and social regime. (p. 819)

Bolsheviks Literally, the majority party; the most radical branch of the Russian Marxist movement; led by V.I. Lenin and dedicated to his concept of social revolution; actually a minority in the Russian Marxist political scheme until its triumph in the 1917 revolution. (p. 816)

Bonaparte, Napoleon Rose within the French army during the wars of the French Revolution; eventually became general; led a coup that ended the French Revolution and established the French Empire under his rule; defeated and deposed in 1815. (p. 702)

Boxer Rebellion Popular outburst in 1898 aimed at expelling foreigners from China; failed because of intervention of armies of Western powers in China; defeat of Chinese enhanced control by Europeans and the power of provincial officials. (p. 801)

Brest-Litovsk Treaty [*brest* li *tofsk*] Signed between the revolutionary government of Russia and Germany in March 1918; Russia withdrew from World War I and granted substantial territories to Germany in return for peace. (p. 844)

British East India Company Joint stock company that obtained government monopoly over trade in India; acted as virtually independent government in regions it claimed. (p. 548)

British Raj Government of the British East India Company; developed as a result of the rivalry between France and Britain in India. (p. 731)

Calcutta Headquarters of British East India Company in Bengal in Indian subcontinent; located on Ganges; captured in 1756 during early part of Seven Years' War; later became administrative center for all of Bengal. (p. 560)

Calvin, Jean French Protestant (16th century) who stressed doctrine of predestination; established center of his group at Swiss canton of Geneva; encouraged ideas of wider access to government, wider public education; Calvinism spread from Switzerland to northern Europe and North America. (p. 560)

candomble [kandom *blä*] African religious ideas and practices in Brazil, particularly among the Yoruba people. (p. 659)

Canton One of two port cities in which Europeans were permitted to trade in China during the Ming dynasty. (p. 679)

Cape Colony Dutch colony established at Cape of Good Hope in 1652 initially to provide a coastal station for the Dutch seaborne empire; by 1770 settlements had expanded sufficiently to come into conflict with Bantus. (p. 560)

Cape of Good Hope Southern tip of Africa; first circumnavigated in 1488 by Portuguese in search of direct route to India. (p. 545)

capitaincies Strips of land along Brazilian coast granted to minor Portuguese nobles for development; enjoyed limited success in developing the colony. (p. 597)

caravels Slender, long-hulled vessels utilized by Portuguese; highly maneuverable and able to sail against the wind; key to development of Portuguese trade empire in Asia. (p. 655)

Cárdenas, Lázaro President of Mexico from 1934 to 1940; responsible for redistribution of land, primarily to create ejidos, or communal farms; also began program of primary and rural education. (p. 938)

Caribbean First area of Spanish exploration and settlement; served as experimental region for nature of Spanish colonial experience; encomienda, system of colonial management, initiated here. (p. 583)

Casa de Contratación Spanish Board of Trade operated out of Seville; regularized commerce with New World; supplied colonial provisions (p. 595)

castas People of mixed origin in Spanish colonial society; relegated to secondary status in social system; constituted potentially revolutionary group. (p. 601)

Castro, Fidel Cuban revolutionary; overthrew dictator Fulgencio Batista in 1958; initiated series of reforms to establish Socialist reforms; came to depend almost exclusively on USSR. (p. 945)

Catherine the Great   German-born Russian tsarina in the 18th century; ruled after assassination of her husband; gave appearance of enlightened rule; accepted Western cultural influence; maintained nobility as service aristocracy by granting them new power over peasantry. (p. 571)

Catholic Reformation   Restatement of traditional Catholic beliefs in response to Protestant Reformation (16th century); established councils that revived Catholic doctrine and refuted Protestant beliefs. (p. 526)

caudillos   [kou *thEE* lyos, -*thEE* yos] Independent leaders who dominated local areas by force in defiance of national policies; sometimes seized national governments to impose their concept of rule; typical throughout newly independent countries of Latin America. (p. 760)

Cavour, Count Camillo di   [kä *voor*] Architect of Italian unification in 1858; formed an alliance with France to attack Austrian control of northern Italy; resulted in creation of constitutional monarchy under Piedmontese king. (p. 711)

centralists   Latin American politicians who wished to create strong, centralized national governments with broad powers; often supported by politicians who described themselves as conservatives. (p. 761))

Chaldiran   [chäl duh *rán*] Site of battle between Safavids and Ottomans in 1514; Safavids severely defeated by Ottomans; checked western advance of Safavid Empire. (p. 620)

Charles III   Spanish enlightened monarch; ruled from 1759 to 1788; instituted fiscal, administrative, and military reforms in Spain and its empire. (p. 603)

Chartist movement   Attempt by artisans and workers in Britain to gain the vote during the 1840s; demands for reform beyond the Reform Act of 1832 were incorporated into a series of petitions; movement failed. (p. 708)

Chernobyl   Massive meltdown in a Soviet nuclear reactor in 1986, causing widespread radiation damage. (p. 1042)

Chiang Ching-kuo   [jEE *äng ching gwO*] Son and successor of Chiang Kai-shek as ruler of Taiwanese government in 1978; continued authoritarian government; attempted to lessen gap between followers of his father and indigenous islanders. (p. 926)

Chiang Kai-shek   [chang kiy shek] A military officer who succeeded Sun Yat-sen as the leader of the Koumintang (Guomindung) or Nationalist Party in China in the mid-1920s; became the most powerful leader in China in the early 1930s, but his Nationalist forces were defeated and driven from China by the Com-munists after World War II. (p. 1025)

Chongzhen   [*choong juhn*] Last of the Ming emperors; committed suicide in 1644 in the face of a Jurchen invasion of the Forbidden City at Beijing. (p. 683)

Christian Democratic movement   Political movement common to many Western European nations after World War II; wedded to democratic institutions and moderate social reform. (p. 872)

Christian Fundamentalism, see Religious Revivalism

Churchill, Winston   British prime minister during World War II; responsible for British resistance to German air assaults. (p. 854)

cientificos   Advisors of government of Porfirio Díaz who were strongly influenced by positivist ideas; permitted government to project image of modernization. (p. 777)

Cixi   [*tsU shEE*] Ultraconservative dowager empress who dominated the last decades of the Qing dynasty; supported Boxer Rebellion in 1898 as a means of driving out Westerners. (p. 801)

Clive, Robert   Architect of British victory at Plassey; established foundations of British Raj in northern India (18th century). (p. 732)

cold war   The state of relations between the United States and its allies and the Soviet Union and its allies between the end of World War II to 1990; based on creation of political spheres of influence and a nuclear arms race rather than actual warfare. (p. 859)

collectivization   Creation of large, state-run farms rather than individual holdings; allowed more efficient control over peasants; part of Stalin's economic and political planning; often adopted in other Communist regimes. (p. 895)

Columbian exchange   Biological and ecological exchange that took place following Spanish establishment of colonies in New World; peoples of Europe and Africa came to New World; animals, plants, and diseases of two hemispheres were transferred. (p. 592)

Columbus, Christopher   Genoese captain in service of king and queen of Castile and Aragon; successfully sailed to New World and returned in 1492; initiated European discoveries in Americas. (p. 545)

Comintern   International office of communism under USSR dominance established to encourage the formation of Communist parties in Europe and elsewhere. (p. 892)

commercio libre   Policy established during reign of Charles III; opened trade in ports of Spain and Indies to all Spanish merchants; undercut monopoly of consulados. (p. 604)

Communist Party of Vietnam   Originally a wing of nationalist movement; became primary nationalist party after decline of VNQDD in 1929; led in late 1920s by Nguyen Ai Quoc, alias Ho Chi Minh. (p. 1039)

compradors   Wealthy new group of Chinese merchants under the Qing dynasty; specialized in the import-export trade on China's south coast; one of the major links between China and the outside world. (p. 797)

Comte, Auguste   [koNt] French philosopher (19th century); founder of positivism, a philosophy that stressed observation and scientific approaches to the problems of society. (p. 766)

Comunero Revolt   One of popular revolts against Spanish colonial rule in New Granada (Colombia) in 1781; suppressed as a result of divisions among rebels. (p. 605)

Congress of Soviets   Lenin's parliamentary institution based on the soviets and Bolshevik domination; replaced the initial parliament dominated by the Social Revolutionary party. (p. 891)

Congress of Vienna   Meeting in the aftermath of Napoleonic Wars (1815) to restore political stability in Europe and settle diplomatic disputes. (p. 702)

consulado   Merchant guild of Seville; enjoyed virtual monopoly rights over goods shipped to America and handled much of the silver received in return. (p. 595)

contested settler societies   Featured large-scale European settlement despite the existence of large, indigenous populations; generally resulted in clashes over land rights, resource control, social status, and differences in culture; typical of South Africa, New Zealand, Kenya, Algeria, and Hawaii. (p. 743)

Cook, Captain James   Made voyages to Hawaii from 1777 to 1779 resulting in opening of islands to the West; convinced Kamehameha to establish unified kingdom in the islands. (p. 751)

Copernicus   Polish monk and astronomer (16th century); disproved Hellenistic belief that the earth was at the center of the universe. (p. 530)

core nations   Nations, usually European, that enjoyed profit from world economy; controlled international banking and commercial services such as shipping; exported manufactured goods for raw materials. (p. 551)

Cornwallis, Lord Charles   Reformer of the East India Company administration of India in the 1790s; reduced power of local British administrators; checked widespread corruption. (p. 735)

Coronado, Francisco Vázquez de   Leader of Spanish expedition into northern frontier region of New Spain; entered what is now United States in search of mythical cities of gold. (p. 588)

corporatism   Political ideology that emphasized the organic nature of society and made the state a mediator, adjusting the interests of different social groups; appealed to conservative groups in European and Latin American societies and to the military. (p. 941)

Cortés, Hernán   Led expedition of 600 to coast of Mexico in 1519; conquistador responsible for defeat of Aztec Empire; captured Tenochtitlan. (p. 588)

cossacks   Peasants recruited to migrate to newly seized lands in Russia, particularly in south; combined agriculture with military conquests; spurred additional frontier conquests and settlements. (p. 567)

Council of People's Commissars   Government council composed of representatives from soviets across Russia and headed by Lenin; form of government initially established after November 1917. (p. 891)

Council of the Indies   Body within the Castilian government that issued all laws and advised king on all matters

dealing with the Spanish colonies of the New World. (p. 596)

Creole slaves   American-born descendants of "salt water" slaves; result of sexual exploitation of slave women or process of miscegenation. (p. 655)

Creoles   Whites born in the New World; dominated local Latin American economies; ranked just beneath peninsulares. (p. 601)

Crimean War   Fought between 1854 and 1856; began as Russian attempt to attack Ottoman Empire; opposed by France and Britain as well; resulted in Russian defeat in the face of Western industrial technology; led to Russian reforms under Tsar Alexander II. (p. 810)

Cristeros   Conservative peasant movement in Mexico during the 1920s; most active in central Mexico; attempted to halt slide toward secularism; movement resulted in armed violence. (p. 937)

Cromer, Lord   British adviser in khedival Egypt; pushed for economic reforms that reduced but failed to eliminate the debts of the khedival regime. (p. 966)

cubist movement   20th-century art style; best represented by Spanish artist Pablo Picasso; rendered familiar objects as geometrical shapes. (p. 884)

Cultural Revolution   Movement initiated in 1965 by Mao Zedong to restore his dominance over pragmatists; used mobs to ridicule Mao's political rivals; campaign was called off in 1968. (p. 1034)

da Gama, Vasco   Portuguese captain who first reached India in 1497; established early Portuguese dominance in Indian Ocean. (p. 545)

Dahomey   Kingdom developed among Fon or Aja peoples in 17th century; center at Abomey 70 miles from coast; under King Agaja expanded to control coastline and port of Whydah by 1727; accepted Western firearms and goods in return for African slaves. (p. 642)

Darwin, Charles   Biologist who developed theory of evolution of species (1859); argued that all living species evolved into their present form through the ability to adapt in a struggle for survival. (p. 715)

Decembrist uprising   Political revolt in Russia in 1825; led by middle-level

army officers who advocated reforms; put down by Tsar Nicholas I. (p. 809)

Declaration of the Rights of Man and the Citizen   Adopted during the liberal phase of the French Revolution (1789); stated the fundamental equality of all French citizens; later became a political source for other liberal movements. (p. 700)

Deism   Concept of God current during the scientific revolution; role of divinity was to set natural laws in motion, not to regulate once process was begun. (p. 531)

De Klerk, F. W.   White South African prime minister in the late 1980s and early 1990s. Working with Nelson Mandela and the African National Congress, De Klerk successfully dismantled the apartheid system and opened the way for a democratically elected government that represented all South Africans for the first time. (p. 1015)

de la Cruz, Sor Juana Inés   Author, poet, and musician of New Spain; eventually gave up secular concerns to concentrate on spiritual matters. (p. 597)

demographic transition   Shift to low birth rate, low infant death rate, stable population; first emerged in Western Europe and U.S. in late 19th century. (p. 710)

Deng Xiaoping   [Dung Shee-ow-ping] One of the more pragmatic, least ideological of the major Communist leaders of China; joined the party as a young man in the 1920s, survived the legendary Long March and persecution during the Cultural Revolution of the 1970s, and emerged as China's most influential leader in the early 1980s. (p. 1032)

dependency theory   Belief that development and underdevelopment were not stages but part of the same process; that development and growth of some areas such as Western Europe were achieved at the expense of underdevelopment of dependent regions such as Latin America. (p. 775)

Descartes, René   [dAY kärt] Established importance of skeptical review of all received wisdom (17th century); argued that human reason could then develop laws that would explain the fundamental workings of nature. (p. 530)

Deshima   Island port in Nagasaki Bay; only port open to non-Japanese after closure of the islands in the 1640s; only Chinese and Dutch ships were permitted to enter. (p. 687)

Díaz, Porfirio One of Juárez's generals; elected president of Mexico in 1876; dominated Mexican politics for 35 years; imposed strong central government. (p. 767)

Diem, Ngo Dinh Political leader of South Vietnam; established as president with United States support in the 1950s; opposed Communist government of North Vietnam; overthrown by military coup supported by United States. (p. 1042)

Dien Bien Phu Most significant victory of the Viet Minh over French colonial forces in 1954; gave the Viet Minh control of northern position of Vietnam. (p. 1040)

Diet Japanese parliament established as part of the new constitution of 1889; part of Meiji reforms; could pass laws and approve budgets; able to advise government, but not to control it. (p. 821)

Din-i-Ilahi [din i ilähee, dEEn] Religion initiated by Akbar in Mughal India; blended elements of the many faiths of the subcontinent; key to efforts to reconcile Hindus and Muslims in India, but failed. (p. 629)

Dinshawai incident [din shä wAY] Clash between British soldiers and Egyptian villagers in 1906; arose over hunting accident along Nile River where wife of prayer leader of mosque was accidentally shot by army officers hunting pigeons; led to Egyptian protest movement. (p. 967)

Disraeli, Benjamin Leading conservative political figure in Britain in the second half of the 19th century; took initiative of granting vote to working-class males in 1867; typical of conservative politician making use of popular politics. (p. 711)

Duarte, Eva Also known as Evita Perón; first wife of Juan Perón; became public spokesperson for Perón among the poor until her death in 1952. (p. 943)

duma National parliament created in Russia in the aftermath of the Revolution of 1905; progressively stripped of power during the reign of Tsar Nicholas II; failed to forestall further revolution. (p. 817)

Dutch East India Company Joint stock company that obtained government monopoly over trade in Asia; acted as virtually independent government in regions it claimed. (p. 547)

Dutch Studies Group of Japanese scholars interested in implications of Western science and technology beginning in the 18th century; urged freer exchange with West; based studies on few Dutch texts available in Japan. (p. 818)

Dutch trading empire Based on control of fortified towns and factories, warships on patrol, and monopoly control of limited number of products—particularly spices. (p. 669)

eastern bloc Nations favorable to the Soviet Union in Eastern Europe during the cold war—particularly Poland, Czechoslovakia, Bulgaria, Rumania, Hungary, and East Germany. (p. 859)

eastern front Most mobile of the fronts established during World War I; lacked trench warfare because of length of front extending from the Baltic to southern Russia; after early successes, military defeats led to downfall of the tsarist government in Russia. (p. 841)

edict of Nantes Grant of tolerance to Protestants in France in 1598; granted only after lengthy civil war between Catholic and Protestant factions. (p. 526)

Edo Tokugawa capital city; modern-day Tokyo; center of the Tokugawa shogunate. (p. 685)

effendi Class of prosperous business and professional urban families in khedival Egypt; as a class generally favored Egyptian independence. (p. 967)

Einstein, Albert Developed mathematical theories to explain the behavior of planetary motion and the movement of electrical particles; after 1900 issued theory of relativity. (p. 715)

El Mina Most important of early Portuguese trading factories in forest zone of Africa. (p. 638)

emancipation of the serfs Tsar Alexander II ended rigorous serfdom in Russia in 1861; serfs obtained no political rights; required to stay in villages until they could repay aristocracy for land. (p. 811)

encomendero [AYn kO mAYn dAU rO] Holder of an encomienda; able to use Indians as workers or to tax them. (p. 590)

encomienda Grants of Indian laborers made to Spanish conquerors and settlers in Mesoamerica and South America; basis for earliest forms of coerced labor in Spanish colonies. (p. 583)

English Civil War Conflict from 1640 to 1660; featured religious disputes mixed with constitutional issues concerning the powers of the monarchy; ended with restoration of the monarchy in 1660 following execution of previous king. (p. 527)

Enlightenment Intellectual movement centered in France during the 18th century; featured scientific advance, application of scientific methods to study of human society; belief that rational laws could describe social behavior. (p. 523)

European Economic Community The Common Market; an alliance of six European nations (Germany, France, Italy, Belgium, Luxembourg, and the Netherlands) set up to begin creation of a single economic entity across national boundaries in 1958; later joined by Britain, Ireland, Denmark, Greece, Spain, Portugal, Sweden, Austria, and Finland; during the early 1990s, the Community changed its name to the European Union and planned further economic integration. (p. 876)

factories Portuguese trading fortresses and compounds with resident merchants; utilized throughout Portuguese trading empire to assure secure landing places and commerce. (p. 657)

factory system Not to be confused with the fortified ports of the commercial revolution; intensification of processes of production at single sites during the Industrial Revolution; involved greater organization of labor and firmer discipline. (p. 704)

fascism Political philosophy that became predominant in Italy and then Germany during the 1920s and 1930s; attacked weakness of democracy, corruption of capitalism; promised vigorous foreign and military programs; undertook state control of economy to reduce social friction. (p. 870)

fazendas Coffee estates that spread within interior of Brazil between 1840 and 1860; created major export commodity for Brazilian trade; led to intensification of slavery in Brazil. (p. 770)

Federal Republic of Germany Eventual name of postwar West Germany; created by the merging of the zones of occupation held by France, Britain, and the United States. (p. 674)

federalists   Latin American politicians who wanted policies, especially fiscal and commercial regulation, to be set by regional governments rather than centralized national administrations; often supported by politicians who described themselves as liberals. (p. 761)

feminist movements   Sought various legal and economic gains for women, including equal access to professions and higher education; came to concentrate on right to vote; won support particularly from middle-class women; active in Western Europe at the end of the 19th century; revived in light of other issues in the 1960s. (p. 715)

Ferdinand of Aragon   Along with Isabella of Castile, monarch of largest Christian kingdoms in Iberia; marriage to Isabella created united Spain; responsible for reconquest of Granada, initiation of exploration of New World. (p. 582)

five-year plans   Stalin's plans to hasten industrialization of USSR; constructed massive factories in metallurgy, mining and electric power; led to massive state-planned industrialization at cost of availability of consumer products. (p. 895)

Francia, Dr. José Rodríguez de   Ruler of independent Paraguay; ruled country as dictator until 1840. (p. 760)

Francis I   King of France in the 16th century; regarded as Renaissance monarch; patron of arts; imposed new controls on Catholic church; ally of Ottoman sultan against holy Roman emperor. (p. 525)

Frederick the Great   Prussian king of the 18th century; attempted to introduce Enlightenment reforms into Germany; built on military and bureaucratic foundations of his predecessors; introduced freedom of religion; increased state control of economy. (p. 536)

Free Officers movement   Military nationalist movement in Egypt founded in the 1930s; often allied with the Muslim Brotherhood; led coup to seize Egyptian government from khedive in July 1952. (p. 1008)

French Revolution   Revolution in France between 1789 and 1800; resulted in overthrow of Bourbon monarchy and old regimes; ended with establishment of French Empire under Napoleon Bonaparte; source of many liberal movements and constitutions in Europe. (p. 700)

French Revolution of 1830   Second rebellion against Bourbon monarchy; essentially a liberal movement resulting in the creation of a bourgeois government under a moderate monarchy. (p. 703)

French Revolution of 1848   Overthrew the monarchy established in 1830; briefly established a democratic republic; failure of the republic led to the reestablishment of the French Empire under Napoleon III in 1850. (p. 708)

Freud, Sigmund   Viennese physician (19th-20th centuries); developed theories of the workings of the human unconscious; argued that behavior is determined by impulses. (p. 716)

Fulani   [*fU* lä nEE, foo *lä*-] Pastoral people of western Sudan; adopted purifying Sufi variant of Islam; under Usuman Dan Fodio in 1804, launched revolt against Hausa kingdoms; established state centered on Sokoto. (p. 650)

Galileo   Published Copernicus's findings (17th century); added own discoveries concerning laws of gravity and planetary motion; condemned by the Catholic church for his work. (p. 530)

galleons   Large, heavily armed ships used to carry silver from New World colonies to Spain; basis for convoy system utilized by Spain for transportation of bullion. (p. 595)

Gálvez, José de   Spanish minister of the Indies and chief architect of colonial reform; moved to eliminate Creoles from upper bureaucracy of the colonies; created intendants for local government. (p. 604)

Gandhi, Indira   Daughter of Jawaharlal Nehru (no relation to Mahatma Gandhi); installed as a figurehead prime minister by the Congress Party bosses in 1966; a strong-willed and astute politician, she soon became the central figure in India politics, a position she maintained through the 1970s and passed on to her sons. (p. 1002)

Gang of Four   Jiang Qing and four political allies who attempted to seize control of Communist government in China from the pragmatists; arrested and sentenced to life imprisonment in 1976 following Mao Zedong's death. (p. 1034)

gauchos   Bands of mounted rural workers in the region of the Rio de la Plata; aided local caudillos in splitting apart the United Provinces of the Rio de la Plata after 1816. (p. 762)

German Democratic Republic   Communist regime set up in the Soviet-occupied zone of Germany (East Germany) in 1949; became one of the most rigid members of the Soviet alliance system; regime collapsed from internal pressure in 1989, and was soon unified with West Germany (1990). (p. 861)

Gestapo   Secret police in Nazi Germany, known for brutal tactics. (p. 871)

Giap, General Vo Nguyen   Chief military commander of the Viet Minh; architect of the Vietnamese victory over the French at Dien Bien Phu in 1954. (p. 1040)

glasnost   Policy of political liberation in Soviet Union in the late 1980s. (p. 907)

Glorious Revolution   English overthrow of James II in 1688; resulted in affirmation of parliament as having basic sovereignty over the king. (p. 532)

Goa   Portuguese factory or fortified trade town located on western India coast, 16th century ff.; sites for forcible entry into Asian sea trade network. (p. 667)

Good Neighbor Policy   Established by Franklin D. Roosevelt for dealing with Latin America in 1933; intended to halt direct intervention in Latin American politics. (p. 952)

Gorbachev, Mikhail   USSR ruler after 1985; renewed attacks on Stalinism; urged reduction in nuclear armament; proclaimed policies of glasnost and perestroika. (p. 906)

Government of India Act of 1935   British agreed to retain control of the central administration in return for turning over the provincial governments to Indian leaders chosen by expanded electorate. (p. 972)

Gran Colombia   Independent state created in South America as a result of military successes of Simon Bolívar; existed only until 1830, at which time Colombia, Venezuela, and Ecuador became separate nations. (p. 757)

Great Depression   International economic crisis following the First World War; began with collapse of American stock market in 1929; actual causes included collapse of agricultural prices in 1920s; included collapse of banking houses in the United States and Western Europe, massive unemployment; contradicted optimistic assumptions of 19th century. (p. 847)

Great Leap Forward   Economic policy of Mao Zedong introduced in

1958; proposed industrialization of small-scale projects integrated into peasant communes; led to economic disaster; ended in 1960. (p. 1031)

Great Mahele [mä *hAY lAY* Hawaiian edict issued in 1848; imposed Western concept of property on Hawaiian land previously shared by Hawaiians; much of private property sold off to Western commercial interests by Hawaiian monarchy. (p. 753)

great trek Movement of Boer settlers in Cape Colony of southern Africa to escape influence of British colonial government in 1834; led to settlement of regions north of Orange River and Natal. (p. 651)

Greek Revolution Rebellion in Greece against the Ottoman Empire in 1820; key step in gradually dismantling the Ottoman Empire in the Balkans. (p. 703)

Green Revolution Introduction of improved seed strains, fertilizers, and irrigation as a means of producing higher yields in crops such as rice, wheat, and corn; particularly important in the densely populated countries of Asia, 1960s ff. (p. 1005)

guano Bird droppings utilized as fertilizer; exported from Peru as a major item of trade between 1850 and 1880; income from trade permitted end to Indian tribute and abolition of slavery. (p. 765)

Guevara, Ernesto "Che" Argentine revolutionary; aided Fidel Castro in overthrow of Fulgencio Batista; died while directing guerrilla movement in Bolivia in 1967. (p. 945)

guillotine [*gil* uh tEEn, *gEE* uh-, giluh *tEEn*, gEEuh-] Introduced as a method of humane execution; utilized to execute thousands during the most radical phase of the French Revolution known as the Reign of Terror. (p. 700)

Guomindang [*gwo min däng*] Chinese Nationalist party founded by Sun Yat-sen in 1919; drew support from local warlords and Chinese criminal underworld; initially forged alliance with Communists in 1924; dominated by Chiang Kai-shek after 1925. (p. 1024)

Gutenberg, Johannes Introduced movable type to western Europe in 15th century; credited with greatly expanded availability of printed books and pamphlets. (p. 525)

Habsburg, Archduke Maximilian von Proclaimed emperor of Mexico

following intervention of France in 1862; ruled until overthrow and execution by liberal revolutionaries under Benito Juárez in 1867. (p. 767)

haciendas Rural estates in Spanish colonies in New World; produced agricultural products for consumers in America; basis of wealth and power for local aristocracy. (p. 592)

Harvey, John English physician (17th century) who demonstrated circular movement of blood in animals, function of heart as pump. (p. 530)

Haya de la Torre, Victor Raul Peruvian politician; founder of APRA (American Popular Revolutionary Alliance) in 1924; aimed at establishing an international party throughout Western Hemisphere. (p. 941)

Henry the Navigator Portuguese prince responsible for direction of series of expeditions along the African coast in the 15th century; marked beginning of Western European expansion. (p. 545)

Herzl, Theodor [*hûrt* suhl, *hârt-*] Austrian journalist and Zionist; formed World Zionist Organization in 1897; promoted Jewish migration to Palestine and formation of a Jewish state. (p. 973)

Hidalgo, Father Miguel de Mexican priest who established independence movement among Indians and mestizos in 1810; despite early victories, was captured and executed. (p. 757)

Hideyoshi, Toyotomi [tO yO tO mAY] General under Nobunaga; succeeded as leading military power in central Japan; continued efforts to break power of daimyos; constructed a series of alliances that made him military master of Japan in 1590; died in 1598. (p. 684)

Hindu Fundamentalism, see Religious Revivalism

Hiroshima One of two Japanese cities on which the United States dropped atomic bombs in 1945; devastation of these cities caused Japanese surrender without invasion of home islands. (p. 856)

Hispaniola First island in Caribbean settled by Spaniards; settlement founded by Columbus on second voyage to New World; Spanish base of operations for further discoveries in New World. (p. 583)

Hitler, Adolf Nazi leader of fascist Germany from 1933 to his suicide in 1945; created a strongly centralized state in Germany; eliminated all rivals;

launched Germany on aggressive foreign policy leading to World War II; responsible for attempted genocide of European Jews. (p. 851)

Holocaust Term for Hitler's attempted genocide of European Jews during World War II; resulted in deaths of 6 million Jews. (p. 856)

Holy Alliance Alliance among Russia, Prussia, and Austria in defense of religion and the established order; formed at Congress of Vienna by most conservative monarchies of Europe. (p. 809)

homelands Under apartheid, areas in South Africa designated for ethnolinguistic groups within the black African population; such areas tend to be overpopulated and poverty-stricken. (p. 1015)

Hong Kong British colony on Chinese mainland; major commercial center; agreement reached between Britain and People's Republic of China returned colony to China in 1997. (p. 921)

Hong Xiuquan [*hoong* shEE *U* chY *än*] Leader of the Taiping rebellion; converted to specifically Chinese form of Christianity; attacked traditional Confucian teachings of Chinese elite. (p. 800)

Hongwu First Ming emperor in 1368; originally of peasant lineage; original name Zhu Yuanzhang; drove out Mongol influence; restored position of scholar-genty. (p. 674)

Huancavelica [wäng kuh vuh *IEE* kuh] Location of greatest deposit of mercury in South America; aided in American silver production; linked with Potosí. (p. 594)

Huerta, General Victoriano Attempted to reestablish centralized dictatorship in Mexico following the removal of Madero in 1913; forced from power in 1914 by Villa and Zapata. (p. 935)

human rights Certain universal rights many argue should be enjoyed by all people because they are justified by a moral standard that stands above the laws of any individual nation. (p. 953)

humanism Focus on humankind as center of intellectual and artistic endeavor; method of study that emphasized the superiority of classical forms over medieval styles, in particular the study of ancient languages. (p. 524)

Humayan Son and successor of Babur; expelled from India in 1540, but restored Mughal rule by 1556; died shortly thereafter. (p. 628)

Hussein, Saddam   Military ruler of Iraq; led Iraq in ten-year war with Iran; attempted to annex Kuwait to Iraq in 1990; defeated by coalition of American, European, and Arab forces in 1991 in Persian Gulf War. (p. 997)

Hyundai   Example of huge industrial groups that wield great power in modern Korea; virtually governed Korea's southeastern coast; vertical economic organization with ships, supertankers, factories, schools, and housing units. (p. 926)

Ieyasu, Tokugawa   [tO koog ä wä] Vassal of Toyotomi Hideyoshi; succeeded him as most powerful military figure in Japan; granted title of shogun in 1603 and established Tokugawa shogunate; established political unity in Japan. (p. 684)

imams   According to Shi'ism, rulers who could trace descent from Ali. (p. 624)

import substitution industrialization   Typical of Latin American economies; production of goods during the 20th century that had previously been imported; led to light industrialization. (p. 939)

Indian National Congress party   Grew out of regional associations of Western-educated Indians; originally centered in cities of Bombay, Poona, Calcutta, and Madras; became political party in 1885; focus of nationalist movement in India; governed through most of postcolonial period. (p. 963)

Indies piece   Term utilized within the complex exchange system established by the Spanish for African trade; referred to the value of an adult male slave. (p. 643)

Industrial Revolution   Series of changes in economy of Western Europe between 1740 and 20th century; stimulated by rapid population growth, increase in agricultural productivity, commercial revolution of 17th century, and development of new means of transportation; in essence involved technological change and the application of machines to the process of production. (p. 704)

intelligentsia   [in teli *jent* sEE uh, -*gent-*] Russian term denoting articulate intellectuals as a class; 19th century group bent on radical change in Russian political and social system; often

wished to maintain a Russian culture distinct from that of the West. (p. 815)

internationalization   Idea that peoples should unite across national boundaries; gained popularity during the mid-19th century; led to establishment of International Red Cross, Telegraphic Union, Postal Union, series of international fairs. (p. 838)

iron curtain   Phrase coined by Winston Churchill to describe the division between free and communist societies taking shape in Europe after 1946. (p. 659)

Isabella of Castile   Along with Ferdinand of Aragon, monarch of largest Christian kingdoms in Iberia; marriage to Ferdinand created united Spain; responsible for reconquest of Granada, initiation of exploration of New World. (p. 582)

Isandhlwana   [EE sän dl *wä* nuh] Location of battle fought in 1879 between the British and Zulu armies in South Africa; resulted in defeat of British; one of few victories of African forces over Western Europeans. (p. 742)

Isfahan   [isfuh *hän*] Safavid capital under Abbas the Great; planned city laid out according to shah's plan; example of Safavid architecture. (p. 624)

Islamic Fundamentalism, see Religious Revivalism

Ismâ'il   Sufi commander who conquered city of Tabriz in 1501; first Safavid to be proclaimed shah or emperor. (p. 621)

Isolationism   United States foreign policy after World War I, in which U.S. refused to join the League of Nations or engage in diplomatic alliances; lasted until U.S. entry into World War II. (p. 845)

Italian front   Front established in World War I; generally along Italian border with Austria-Hungary; also produced trench warfare; somewhat greater mobility than on western front. (p. 839)

Iturbide, Augustín de   Conservative Creole officer in Mexican army who signed agreement with insurgent forces of independence; combined forces entered Mexico City in 1821; later proclaimed emperor of Mexico until its collapse in 1824. (p. 757)

Ivan III   Also known as Ivan the Great; prince of Duchy of Moscow; claimed descent from Rurik; responsible for freeing Russia from Mongols

after 1462; took title of tsar or Caesar—equivalent of emperor. (p. 566)

Ivan IV   Also known as Ivan the Terrible; confirmed power of tsarist autocracy by attacking authority of boyars (aristocrats); continued policy of Russian expansion; established contacts with Western European commerce and culture. (p. 566)

Janissaries   Ottoman infantry divisions that dominated Ottoman armies; forcibly conscripted as boys in conquered areas of Balkans, legally slaves; translated military service into political influence, particularly after 15th century. (p. 615)

Jesuits   A new religious order founded during the Catholic Reformation; active in politics, education, and missionary work; sponsored missions to South America, North American and Asia. (p. 526)

Jewish Fundamentalism, see Religious Revivalism

Jiang Qing   [*jyäng ching*] Wife of Mao Zedong; one of Gang of Four; opposed pragmatists and supported Cultural Revolution of 1965; arrested and imprisoned for life in 1976. (p. 1032)

Jinnah, Muhammad Ali   Muslim nationalist in India; originally a member of the National Congress party; became leader of Muslim League; traded Muslim support for British during World War II for promises of a separate Muslim state after the war; first president of Pakistan. (p. 979)

João VI, Dom   Portuguese monarch who established seat of government in Brazil from 1808 to 1820 as a result of Napoleonic invasion of Iberian peninsula; made Brazil seat of empire with capital at Rio de Janeiro. (p. 759)

Juárez, Benito   Indian governor of state of Oaxcaca in Mexico; leader of liberal rebellion against Santa Anna; liberal government defeated by French intervention under Emperor Napoleon III of France and establishment of Mexican Empire under Maximilian; restored to power in 1867 until his death in 1872. (p. 767)

Kamehameha I   [kä *mAY* hä *mAY* hä, kuh *mAY* uh *mAY* uh] Fought series of wars backed by British weapons and advisors resulting in unified Hawaiian kingdom by 1810; as king he promoted economic change encouraging Western merchants to establish export trade in Hawaiian goods. (p. 751)

Kangxi [*käng shEE*] Confucian scholar and Manchu emperor of Qing dynasty from 1661 to 1722; established high degree of Sintification among the Manchus. (p. 795)

Kellogg-Briand Pact A treaty coauthored by American and French leaders in 1928; in principle outlawed war forever; ratified subsequently by other nations. (p. 868)

Kenyatta, Jomo Leader of the nonviolent nationalist party in Kenya; organized the Kenya Africa Union (KAU); failed to win concessions because of resistance of white settlers; came to power only after suppression of the Land Freedom Army, or Mau Mau. (p. 983)

Kerensky, Alexander Liberal revolutionary leader during the early stages of the Russian Revolution of 1917; sought development of parliamentary rule, religious freedom. (p. 890)

Keynes, John British economist who stressed importance of government spending to compensate for loss of purchasing power during a depression; played role in the policies of the American New Deal and European economic planning after World War II. (p. 884)

Khartoum River town that was administrative center of Egyptian authority in Sudan. (p. 793)

khedives [kuh *dEEv*] Descendants of Muhammad Ali in Egypt after 1867; formal rulers of Egypt despite French and English intervention until overthrown by military coup in 1952. (p. 791)

Khomeini, Ayatollah [KHO *mAY* nEE, kO-, äyuh *tO* luh] Religious ruler of Iran following revolution of 1979 to expel the Pahlavi shah of Iran; emphasized religious purification; tried to eliminate Western influences and establish purely Islamic government. (p. 1012)

Khrushchev, Nikita [*kroosh* chef, -chof, *krUsh*-] Stalin's successor as head of USSR; attacked Stalinism in 1956 for concentration of power and arbitrary dictatorship; failure of Siberian development program and antagonism of Stalinists led to downfall. (p. 905)

Korean War Fought from 1950 to 1953; North supported by USSR and later People's Republic of China; South supported by United States and small international United Nations force; ended in stalemate and continued division of Korea. (p. 920)

Korekiyo Takahashi [täk ä hä shEE] Minister of finance in Japan during the 1930s; increased government spending to provide jobs; created export boom and elimination of military purchasing. (p. 915)

kulaks Agricultural entrepreneurs who utilized the Stolypin and later NEP reforms to increase agricultural production and buy additional land. (p. 817)

L'Overture, Toussaint [lU veR *tYR*] Leader of slave rebellion on the French sugar island of St. Domingue in 1791; led to creation of independent republic of Haiti in 1804. (p. 756)

La Reforma The name given to the liberal rebellion of Benito Juárez against the forces of Santa Anna. (p. 767)

lançados Collection points for Portuguese trade in the interior of Africa; provided essential links between economies of African interior and factories on the coast. (p. 639)

Land Freedom Army Radical organization for independence in Kenya; frustrated by failure of nonviolent means, initiated campaign of terror in 1952; referred to by British as the Mau Mau. (p. 983)

Las Casas, Bartolomé de Dominican friar who supported peaceful conversion of the Native American population of the Spanish colonies; opposed forced labor and advocated Indian rights. (p. 587)

League of Nations International diplomatic and peace organization created in the Treaty of Versailles that ended World War I; one of the chief goals of President Woodrow Wilson of the United States in the peace negotiations; the United States was never a member. (p. 845)

Lee Kuan Yew Ruler of Singapore from independence in 1959 to present; established tightly controlled authoritarian government; ruled through People's Action party to suppress political diversity. (p. 926)

Lepanto Naval battle between the Spanish and the Ottoman Empire resulting in a Spanish victory in 1571; demonstrated European naval superiority over Muslims. (p. 551)

Lesotho Southern African state that survived mfecane; not based on Zulu model; less emphasis on military organization, less authoritarian government. (p. 652)

letrados University-trained lawyers from Spain in the New World; juridical core of Spanish colonial bureaucracy; exercised both legislative and administrative functions. (p. 596)

Li Dazhao [*lEE dä ja U*] Chinese intellectual who gave serious attention to Marxist philosophy; headed study circle at the University of Beijing; saw peasants as vanguard of revolutionary communism in China. (p. 1023)

liberal Political viewpoint with origins in Western Europe during the 19th century; stressed limited state interference in individual life, representation of propertied people in government; urged importance of constitutional rule and parliaments. (p. 702)

Liberal Democratic party Monopolized Japanese government from its formation in 1955 into the 1990s; largely responsible for the economic reconstruction of Japan. (p. 920)

liberation theology Combined Catholic theology and Socialist principles in effort to bring about improved conditions for the poor in Latin America (20th century). (p. 947)

Lin Zexu Distinguished Chinese official during the early 19th century; charged with stamping out the opium trade in southern China; ordered blockade of European trading areas in Canton and confiscation of opium; sent into exile following the Opium War. (p. 800)

Locke, John English philosopher during 17th century; argued that people could learn everything through senses; argued that power of government came from the people, not divine right of kings; offered possibility of revolution to overthrow tyrants. (p. 531)

Long March Communist escape from Hunan province during civil war with Guomindang in 1934; center of Communist power moved to Shaanxi province; firmly established Mao Zedong as head of the Communist party in China. (p. 1028)

Louis XIV French monarch of the late 17th century who personified absolute monarchy. (p. 532)

Louis XVI Bourbon monarch of France who was executed during the radical phase of the French Revolution (1792). (p. 700)

Luanda Portuguese factory established in 1520s south of Kongo; became basis for Portuguese colony of Angola. (p. 640)

Luddites Workers in Britain (1810–1820) who responded to replacement of human labor by machines during the Industrial Revolution by attempting to destroy the machines; named after a mythical leader, Ned Ludd. (p. 706)

Luo   Nilotic people who migrated from Upper Nile valley; established dynasty among existing Bantu population in lake region of central eastern Africa; center at Bunyoro. (p. 749)

Luther, Martin   German monk; initiated Protestant Reformation in 1517 by nailing 95 theses to door of Wittenberg church; emphasized primacy of faith over works stressed in Catholic church; accepted state control of Church. (p. 525)

Luzon   Northern island of Philippines; conquered by Spain during the 1560s; site of major Catholic missionary effort. (p. 671)

Macao   One of two ports in which Europeans were permitted to trade in China during the Ming dynasty. (p. 679)

MacArthur, General Douglas   American commander in Pacific campaign of World War II; headed American occupation government of Japan after the war; later commanded international forces during Korean War. (p. 917)

Machiavelli, Niccolo   [mak EE uh *vel* EE] Author of *The Prince* (16th century); emphasized realistic discussions of how to seize and maintain power; one of most influential authors of Italian Renaissance. (p. 524)

Madero, Francisco   Moderate democratic reformer in Mexico; proposed moderate reforms in 1910; arrested by Porfirio Díaz; initiated revolution against Díaz when released from prison; temporarily gained power, but removed and assassinated in 1913. (p. 935)

Magellan, Ferdinand   Spanish captain who in 1519 initiated first circumnavigation of the globe; died during the voyage; allowed Spain to claim Philippines. (p. 546)

Mahdi Muhammad Achmad   Head of a Sudanic Sufi brotherhood; claimed descent from Prophet; proclaimed both Egyptians and British as infidels; launched revolt to purge Islam of impurities; took Khartoum in 1883. (p. 793)

Mahmud II   Ottoman sultan; built a private, professional army; fomented revolution of Janissaries and crushed them with private army; destroyed power of Janissaries and their religious allies; initiated reform of Ottoman Empire on Western precedents. (p. 786)

Malacca   Portuguese factory or fortified trade town located on the tip of the Malayan peninsula; traditionally a center for trade among the southeastern Asian islands. (p. 667)

Manchus   Jurchen people from region to the northeast of the Chinese empire; seized power following collapse of Ming dynasty; established Qing dynasty, last of imperial houses. (p. 683)

mandates   Governments entrusted to European nations in the Middle East in the aftermath of World War I; Britain occupied mandates in Syria, Iraq, Lebanon, and Palestine after 1922. (p. 973)

Mandela, Nelson   Long-imprisoned leader of the African National Congress party; worked with the ANC leadership and F. W. De Klerk's supporters to dismantle the apartheid system from the mid-1980s onward; in 1994, became the first black prime minister of South Africa after the ANC won the first genuinely democratic elections in the country's history. (p. 1015)

manifest destiny   Belief of the government of the United States that it was destined to rule the continent from coast to coast; led to annexation of Texas and Mexican-American War. (p. 767)

Mao Zedong   Communist leader in revolutionary China; advocated rural reform and role of peasantry in Nationalist revolution; influenced by Li Dazhao; led Communist reaction against Guomindang purges in 1920s, culminating in Long March of 1934; seized control of all of mainland China by 1949; initiated Great Leap Forward in 1958. (p. 1026)

Marquis of Pombal   Prime minister of Portugal from 1755 to 1776; acted to strengthen royal authority in Brazil; expelled Jesuits; enacted fiscal reforms and established monopoly companies to stimulate the colonial economy. (p. 605)

Marshall Plan   Program of substantial loans initiated by the United States in 1947; designed to aid Western nations in rebuilding from the war's devastation; vehicle for American economic dominance. (p. 876)

Marx, Karl   German socialist of the mid-19th century; blasted earlier socialist movements as utopian; saw history as defined by class struggle between groups out of power and those controlling the means of production; preached necessity of social revolution to create proletarian dictatorship. (p. 713)

mask of Ferdinand   Term given to movements in Latin America allegedly loyal to the displaced Bourbon king of Spain, Ferdinand VII; actually Creole movements for independence. (p. 757)

mass leisure culture   An aspect of the later Industrial Revolution; based on newspapers, music halls, popular theater, vacation trips, and team sports. (p. 715)

Mass Line   Economic policy of Mao Zedong; led to formation of agricultural cooperatives in 1955; cooperatives became farming collectives in 1956. (p. 1031)

Mataram   Kingdom that controlled interior regions of Java in 17th century; Dutch East India Company paid tribute to the kingdom for rights of trade at Batavia; weakness of kingdom after 1670s allowed Dutch to exert control over all of Java. (p. 730)

May Fourth movement   Resistance to Japanese encroachments in China began on this date in 1919; spawned movement of intellectuals aimed at transforming China into a liberal democracy; rejected Confucianism. (p. 1022)

Mehmed II   [me *met*] Ottoman sultan called the "Conqueror"; responsible for conquest of Constantinople in 1453; destroyed what remained of Byzantine Empire. (p. 613)

mercantilism   Economic theory that stressed governments' promotion of limitation of imports from other nations and internal economies in order to improve tax revenues; popular during 17th and 18th centuries in Europe. (p. 532)

mestizos   People of mixed European and Indian ancestry in Mesoamerica and South America; particularly prevalent in areas colonized by Spain; often part of forced labor system. (p. 552)

Mexican Constitution of 1917   Promised land reform, limited foreign ownership of key resources, guaranteed the rights of workers, and placed restrictions on clerical education; marked formal end of Mexican Revolution. (p. 936)

Mexican Revolution   Fought over a period of almost ten years from 1910; resulted in ouster of Porfirio Díaz from power; opposition forces led by Pancho Villa and Emiliano Zapata. (p. 934)

Mexican-American War   Fought between Mexico and the United States from 1846 to 1848; led to devastating defeat of Mexican forces, loss of about one-half of Mexico's national territory to the United States. (p. 767)

Mexico City   Capital of New Spain; built on ruins of Aztec capital of Tenochtitlan. (p. 588)

mfecane   [um fuh *ka* nAY] Wars of 19th century in southern Africa; created by Zulu expansion under Shaka; revolutionized political organization of southern Africa. (p. 652)

Middle Passage   Slave voyage from Africa to the Americas (16th–18th centuries); generally a traumatic experience for black slaves, although it failed to strip Africans of their culture. (p. 654)

Minas Gerais   [*mEE* nuhs zhi *RIs*] Region of Brazil located in mountainous interior where gold strikes were discovered in 1695; became location for gold rush. (p. 599)

Mindanao   Southern island of Philippines; a Muslim kingdom that was able to successfully resist Spanish conquest. (p. 671)

Minh Mang   [min *mäng*] Second emperor of a united Vietnam; successor of Nguyen Anh; ruled from 1820 to 1841; sponsored emphasis of Confucianism; persecuted Catholics. (p. 1038)

miscegenation   [mi sejuh *nAY* shuhn, misi juh-] Practice of interracial marriage or sexual contact; found in virtually all colonial ventures. (p. 598)

mita   System of labor drafts that replaced encomienda system in Spanish colonies during the 16th century; particularly important in providing labor for mines. (p. 591)

Moctezuma II   [mokte *sU* mä] Last independent Aztec emperor; killed during Hernán Cortés' conquest of Tenochtitlan. (p. 588)

modernization theory   The belief that the more industrialized, urban, and modern a society became, the more social change and improvement were possible as traditional patterns and attitudes were abandoned or transformed; used as a blueprint for development in Latin America. (p. 774)

Monroe Doctrine   American declaration stated in 1823; established that any attempt of a European country to colonize in the Americas would be considered an unfriendly act by the United States; supported by Great Britain as a means of opening Latin American trade. (p. 764)

Montagu-Chelmsford reforms   Increased the powers of Indian legislators at the all-India level and placed much of the provincial administration of India under local ministries controlled by legislative bodies with substantial numbers of elected Indians; passed in 1919. (p. 971)

Morley-Minto reforms of 1909   Provided educated Indians with considerably expanded opportunities to elect and serve on local and all-Indian legislative councils. (p. 966)

Mughal Empire   Established by Babur in India in 1526; the name is taken from the supposed Mongol descent of Babur, but there is little indication of any Mongol influence in the dynasty; became weak after rule of Aurangzeb in first decades of 18th century. (p. 609)

Mullahs   Local mosque officials and prayer leaders within the Safavid Empire; agents of Safavid religious campaign to convert all of population to Shi'ism. (p. 624)

Multinational corporations   Powerful companies, mainly from the West or Pacific Rim, with production as well as distribution operations in many different countries. Multinationals surged in the decades after World War II. (p. 1055)

Munich Conference   Meeting concerning Germany's occupation of portions of Czechoslovakia in 1938; after receiving Hitler's assurances that he would take no more land, Western leaders agreed to the division of Czechoslovakia. (p. 852)

Murad   Head of the coalition of Mamluk households in Egypt; opposed Napoleonic invasion of Egypt and suffered devastating defeat; failure destroyed Mamluk government in Egypt and revealed vulnerability of Muslim core. (p. 789)

Muslim Brotherhood   Egyptian nationalist movement founded by Hasan al-Banna in 1928; committed to fundamentalist movement in Islam; fostered strikes and urban riots against the khedival government. (p. 1008)

Muslim League   Founded in 1906 to better support demands of Muslims for separate electorates and legislative seats in Hindu-dominated India; represented division within Indian nationalist movement. (p. 972)

Mussolini, Benito   Italian Fascist leader after World War I; created first fascist government based on aggressive foreign policy and new nationalist glories. (p. 851)

Mvemba, Nzinga   King of Kongo south of Zaire River from 1507 to 1543; converted to Christianity and took title of Alfonso I; under Portuguese influence attempted to Christianize all of kingdom. (p. 639)

nabobs   Name given to British representatives of the East India Company who went briefly to India to make fortunes through graft and exploitation. (p. 735)

Nadir Khan Afshar   Soldier-adventurer following fall of Safavid dynasty in 1722; proclaimed himself shah in 1736; established short-lived dynasty in reduced kingdom. (p. 626)

Nagasaki   Long a port open to Dutch traders; one of two Japanese cities on which the United States dropped atomic bombs in 1945; devastation of these cities caused Japanese surrender without invasion of home islands. (p. 856)

Nasser, Gamal Abdul   Took power in Egypt following a military coup in 1952; enacted land reforms and used state resources to reduce unemployment; ousted Britain from the Suez Canal zone in 1956. (p. 1007)

Natal   British colony in South Africa; developed after Boer trek north from Cape Colony; major commercial outpost at Durban. (p. 750)

National Liberation Front (FLN)   Radical nationalist movement in Algeria; launched sustained guerilla war against France in the 1950s; success of attacks led to independence of Algeria in 1958. (p. 984)

National Socialist party   Also known as the Nazi party; led by Adolf Hitler in Germany; picked up political support during the economic chaos of the Great Depression; advocated authoritarian state under a single leader, aggressive foreign policy to reverse humiliation of the Treaty of Versailles; took power in Germany in 1933. (p. 851)

nationalism   Political viewpoint with origins in Western Europe in the 19th century; often allied with one of other "isms"; urged importance of national unity; valued a collective identity based on culture, race, or ethnic origin. (p. 702)

négritude   Literary movement in Africa; attempted to combat racial stereotypes of African culture; celebrated the beauty of black skin and African physique; associated with origins of African nationalist movements. (p. 976)

Nehru, Jawaharlal [*nAΥ*rU, *nár* U] One of Gandhi's disciples; governed India after independence (1947); committed to program of social reform and economic development; preserved civil rights and democracy. (p. 1002)

neocolonial economy Economy that results from continued dominance of the first- and second-world nations of the world's economy; ability of the first- and second-world nations to maintain economic colonialism without political colonialism. (p. 1003)

New Deal President Franklin Roosevelt's precursor of the modern welfare state (1933–1939); programs to combat economic depression enacted a number of social insurance measures and used government spending to stimulate the economy; increased power of the state and the state's intervention in United States social and economic life. (p. 870)

New Economic Policy Initiated by Lenin in 1921; state continued to set basic economic policies, but efforts were now combined with individual initiative; policy allowed food production to recover. (p. 892)

new feminism New wave of women's rights agitation dating from 1949; emphasized more literal equality that would play down domestic roles and qualities for women; promoted specific reforms and redefinition of what it meant to be female. (p. 881)

New France French colonies in North America; extended from St. Lawrence River along Great Lakes and down Mississippi River valley system. (p. 555)

New Spain Spanish colonial possessions in Mesoamerica; included most of central Mexico; based on imperial system of Aztecs. (p. 588)

New Youth Marxist periodical in China; did much to spread the ideas of Marx and Lenin among the politically active youth of China's coastal cities. (p. 1024)

Newton, Isaac English scientist during the 17th century; author of *Principia;* drew the various astronomical and physical observations and wider theories together in a neat framework of natural laws; established principles of motion; defined forces of gravity. (p. 530)

Nguyen Anh [ngI *en, ngu yen än*] Last surviving member of Nguyen dynasty following Tayson Rebellion in Vietnam; with French support retook southern Vietnam; drove Tayson from northern Vietnam by 1802; proclaimed himself emperor with capital at Hue. (p. 1038)

Nkrumah, Kwame [uhn *krU* muh, uhng *krU-*] African nationalist during period of decolonization; responsible for creation of first independent, black African state of Ghana in 1957; established power through his own party, the Convention Peoples party (CPP). (p. 980)

Nobili, Robert di Italian Jesuit missionary; worked in India during the early 1600s; introduced strategy to convert elites first; strategy later widely adopted by Jesuits in various parts of Asia; mission eventually failed. (p. 672)

Nobunaga Japanese daimyo; first to make extensive use of firearms; in 1573 deposed last of Ashikaga shoguns; unified much of central Honshu under his command; killed in 1582. (p. 684)

Nonalignment Policies of countries like India, 1950s–1980s, that sought to avoid taking sides in the cold war. (p. 862)

North American Free Trade Agreement (NAFTA) Agreement that created an essentially free trade zone among Mexico, Canada, and the United States, in hopes of encouraging economic growth in all three nations; after difficult negotiations, went into effect January 1, 1994. (p. 937)

North Atlantic Treaty Organization (NATO) Created in 1949 under United States leadership to group most of the Western European powers plus Canada in a defensive alliance against possible Soviet aggression. (p. 861)

Northern Renaissance Cultural and intellectual movement of northern Europe; began later than Italian Renaissance c. 1450; centered in France, Low Countries, England, and Germany; featured greater emphasis on religion than Italian Renaissance. (p. 525)

Nur Jahan Wife of Jahangir; amassed power in court and created faction of male relatives who dominated Mughal empire during later years of Jahangir's reign. (p. 632)

Nurhaci Architect of Manchu unity; created distinctive Manchu banner armies; controlled most of Manchuria; adopted Chinese bureaucracy and court ceremonies in Manchuria; entered China and successfully captured Ming capital at Beijing. (p. 794)

obeah African religious ideas and practices in the English and French Caribbean islands. (p. xxxx)

Obregón, Alvaro Emerged as leader of the Mexican government in 1915; elected president in 1920. (p. 935)

obrok Labor obligations of Russian peasants to either their aristocratic landlords or to the state; typical of increased labor burdens placed on Russian peasantry during the 18th century. (p. 575)

old believers Russians who refused to accept the ecclesiastical reforms of Alexis Romanov (17th century); many exiled to Siberia or southern Russia, where they became part of Russian colonization. (p. 568)

Opium War Fought between the British and Qing China beginning in 1839; fought to protect British trade in opium; resulted in resounding British victory, opening of Hong Kong as British port of trade. (p. 799)

Orabi, Ahmad Student of Muhammad Abduh; led revolt in 1882 against Turkish influence in Egyptian army; forced khedive to call on British army for support. (p. 792)

Ormuz Portuguese factory or fortified trade town located at southern end of Persian Gulf; site for forcible entry into Asian sea trade network. (p. 657)

Orozco, José Clemente Mexican muralist of the period after the Mexican Revolution; like Rivera's, his work featured romantic images of the Indian past with Christian symbols and Marxist ideology. (p. 936)

Ottoman Society for Union and Progress Organization of political agitators in opposition to rule of Abdul Harmid; also called "Young Turks"; desired to restore 1876 constitution. (p. 787)

Ottomans Turkic people who advanced from strongholds in Asia Minor during 1350s; conquered large part of Balkans; unified under Mehmed I; captured Constantinople in 1453; established empire from Balkans that included most of Arab world. (p. 609)

Pacific Rim states Japan, South Korea, Singapore, Hong Kong, Taiwan; typified by rapid growth rates, expanding exports, and industrialization; either Chinese or strongly influenced by Confucian values; considerable reliance on government planning and direction, limitations on dissent and instability. (p. 913)

Palmares Kingdom of runaway slaves with a population of 8,000 to 10,000 people; located in Brazil during the 17th century; leadership was Angolan. (p. 659)

Panama Canal An aspect of American intervention in Latin America; resulted from United States support for a Panamanian independence movement in return for a grant to exclusive rights to a canal across the Panama isthmus; provided short route from Atlantic to Pacific Ocean; completed 1914. (p. 778)

Parliamentary monarchy Originated in England and Holland, 17th century, with kings partially checked by significantly legislative powers in parliaments. (p. 533)

partition of Poland Three separate divisions of Polish territory among Russia, Prussia, and Austria in 1772, 1793, and 1795; eliminated Poland as independent state; part of expansion of Russian influence in Eastern Europe. (p. 574)

Pasteur, Louis Discoverer of germs; discovery led to more conscientious sanitary regulation by the 1880s. (p. 710)

Paulistas Backwoodsmen from São Paulo in Brazil; penetrated Brazilian interior in search of precious metals during 17th century. (p. 599)

Pearl Harbor American naval base in Hawaii; attack by Japanese on this facility in December 1941 crippled American fleet in the Pacific and caused entry of United States into World War II. (p. 854)

Pedro I, Dom Son and successor of Dom João VI in Brazil; aided in the declaration of Brazilian independence from Portugal in 1822; became constitutional emperor of Brazil. (p. 759)

peninsulares People living in the New World Spanish colonies but born in Spain. (p. 601)

People's Democratic Republic of Korea Northern half of Korea dominated by USSR; long headed by Kim Il-Sung; attacked south in 1950 and initiated Korean War; retained independence as a Communist state after the war. (p. 920)

People's Liberation Army Chinese Communist army; administered much of country under People's Republic of China. (p. 1030)

People's Republic of China Communist government of mainland China; proclaimed in 1949 following military success of Mao Zedong over forces of Chiang Kai-shek and the Guomindang. (p. 1029)

perestroika [peruh *stroi* kuh] Policy of Mikhail Gorbachev calling for economic restructuring in the USSR in the late 1980s; more leeway for private ownership and decentralized control in industry and agriculture. (p. 907)

Perón, Juan D. Military leader in Argentina who became dominant political figure after military coup in 1943; used position as Minister of Labor to appeal to working groups and the poor; became president in 1946; forced into exile in 1955; returned and won presidency in 1973. (p. 941)

Perry, Matthew American commodore who visited Edo Bay with American fleet in 1853; insisted on opening ports to American trade on threat of naval bombardment; won rights for American trade with Japan in 1854. (p. 918)

Persian Gulf War 1991 war led by United States and various European and Middle Eastern allies, against Iraqi occupation of Kuwait. The war led to Iraqi withdrawal and a long confrontation with Iraq about armaments and political regime. (p. 1050)

Peter I Also known as Peter the Great; son of Alexis Romanov; ruled from 1689 to 1725; continued growth of absolutism and conquest; included more definite interest in changing selected aspects of economy and culture through imitation of Western European models. (p. 559)

Pinsker, Leon European Zionist who believed that Jewish assimilation into Christian European nations was impossible; argued for return to Middle Eastern Holy Land. (p. 973)

Pizarro, Francisco Led conquest of Inca Empire of Peru beginning in 1535; by 1540, most of Inca possessions fell to the Spanish. (p. 588)

Plassey Battle in 1757 between troops of the British East India Company and an Indian army under Sir àjud-daula, ruler of Bengal; British victory resulted in control of northern India. (p. 731)

Politburo Executive committee of the Soviet Communist party; 20 members. (p. 896)

Popular Front Combination of Socialist and Communist political parties in France; won election in 1936; unable to take strong measures of social reform because of continuing strength of conservatives; fell from power in 1938. (p. 870)

population revolution Huge growth in population in Western Europe beginning about 1730; prelude to Industrial Revolution; population of France increased 50 percent, England and Prussia 100 percent. (p. 698)

positivism French philosophy based on observation and scientific approach to problems of society; adopted by many Latin American liberals in the aftermath of independence. (p. 766)

Potosí Mine located in upper Peru (modern Bolivia); largest of New World silver mines; produced 80 percent of all Peruvian silver. (p. 594)

Potsdam Conference Meeting among leaders of the United States, Britain, and the Soviet Union just before the end of World War II in 1945; Allies agreed upon Soviet domination in Eastern Europe; Germany and Austria to be divided among victorious Allies. (p. 858)

pragmatists Chinese Communist politicians such as Zhou Enlai, Deng Xiaoping, and Liu Shaoqui; determined to restore state direction and market incentives at the local level; opposed Great Leap Forward. (p. 1032)

Presidencies Three districts that made up the bulk of the directly ruled British territories in India; capitals at Madras, Calcutta, and Bombay. (p. 733)

PRI Party of the Institutionalized Revolution; dominant political party in Mexico; developed during the 1920s and 1930s; incorporated labor, peasant, military, and middle-class sectors; controlled other political organizations in Mexico. (p. 937)

primary products Food or industrial crops for which there is a high demand in industrialized economies; prices of such products tend to fluctuate widely; typically the primary exports of Third World economies. (p. 1003)

Princely States Domains of Indian princes allied with the British Raj; agents of East India Company were stationed at the rulers' courts to ensure compliance; made up over one-third of the British Indian Empire. (p. 733)

proletariat   Class of working people without access to producing property; typically manufacturing workers, paid laborers in agricultural economy, or urban poor; in Europe, product of economic changes of 16th and 17th centuries. (p. 528)

Protestantism   General wave of religious dissent against Catholic church; generally held to have begun with Martin Luther's attack on Catholic beliefs in 1517; included many varieties of religious belief. (p. 526)

proto-industrialization   Preliminary shift away from agricultural economy in Europe; workers become full- or part-time producers of textile and metal products, working at home but in a capitalist system in which materials, work orders, and ultimate sales depended on urban merchants; prelude to Industrial Revolution. (p. 699)

Pugachev rebellion   During 1770s in reign of Catherine the Great; led by cossack Emelyan Pugachev, who claimed to be legitimate tsar; eventually crushed; typical of peasant unrest during the 18th century and thereafter. (p. 571)

Puyi   Last emperor of China; deposed as emperor while still a small boy in 1912. (p. 802)

radical   Political viewpoint with origins in Western Europe during the 19th century; advocated broader voting rights than liberals; in some cases advocated outright democracy; urged reforms in favor of the lower classes. (p. 703)

Rajput   [*räj* pUt] Regional princes in India following collapse of empire; emphasized military control of their regions. (p. xxxx)

Recopilación   [rAY kO pEEl ä sEE *On*] Body of laws collected in 1681 for Spanish possessions in New World; basis of law in the Indies. (p. 596)

Red Army   Military organization constructed under leadership of Leon Trotsky, Bolshevik follower of Lenin; made use of people of humble background. (p. 891)

Red Guard   Student brigades utilized by Mao Zedong and his political allies during the Cultural Revolution to discredit Mao's political enemies. (p. 1034)

Red Heads   Name given to Safavid followers because of their distinctive red headgear. (p. 620)

Reform Bill of 1832   Legislation passed in Great Britain that extended the vote to most members of the middle class; failed to produce democracy in Britain. (p. 703)

Religious Revivalism   An approach to religious belief and practice that stresses the literal interpretation of texts sacred to the religion in question and the application of their precepts to all aspects of social life; has been increasingly associated in the late 20th century with revivalist movements in a number of world religions, including Christianity, Islam, Judaism, and Hinduism. (p. 1002)

Republic of Korea   Southern half of Korea sponsored by United States following World War II; headed by nationalist Syngman Rhee; developed parliamentary institutions but maintained authoritarian government; defended by UN forces during Korean War; underwent industrialization and economic emergence after 1950s. (p. 920)

revisionism   Socialist movements that at least tacitly disavowed Marxist revolutionary doctrine; believed social success could be achieved gradually through political institutions. (p. 713)

Revolutions of 1848   Generally refers to those nationalist and liberal movements within France, Germany, and the Habsburg Empire, specifically in Italy, Austria, and Hungary; after temporary success, the revolutions failed. (p. 708)

Rhodes, Cecil   British entrepreneur in South Africa around 1900; manipulated political situation in South Africa to gain entry to resources of Boer republics; encouraged Boer War as means of destroying Boer independence. (p. 750)

Ricci, Matteo   [*rEEt* chEE] Along with Adam Schall, Jesuit scholar in court of Ming emperors; skilled scientist; corrected calendars, forged cannons, fixed clocks; won few converts to Christianity. (p. 683)

Rio de Janeiro   Brazilian port; close to mines of Minas Gerais; importance grew with gold strikes; became colonial capital in 1763. (p. 599)

Rivera, Diego   [ri *vär* uh] Mexican artist of the period after the Mexican Revolution; famous for murals painted on walls of public buildings; mixed romantic images of the Indian past

with Christian symbols and Marxist ideology. (p. 936)

Romanov, Alexis   Second Romanov tsar; abolished assemblies of nobles; gained new powers over Russian Orthodox church. (p. 568)

Romanov dynasty   Dynasty elected in 1613 at end of Time of Troubles; ruled Russia until 1917. (p. 568)

romanticism   Artistic and literary movement of the 19th century in Europe; held that emotion and impression, not reason, were the keys to the mysteries of human experience and nature; sought to portray passions, not calm reflection. (p. 717)

Rosas, Juan Manuel de   Strongman leader in Buenos Aires; took power in 1831; commanded loyalty of gauchos; restored local autonomy. (p. 761)

Rowlatt Act   Placed severe restrictions on key Indian civil rights such as freedom of the press; acted to offset the concessions granted under Montagu-Chelmsford reforms of 1919. (p. 971)

Royal African Company   Chartered in 1660s to establish a monopoly over the slave trade among British merchants; supplied African slaves to colonies in Barbados, Jamaica, and Virginia. (p. 642)

Russian Communist party   Bolshevik wing of the Social Democratic party in Russia in 1917; came to power under Lenin after the November expulsion of Kerensky's liberal government. (p. 890)

Russian Revolution of 1905   Consisted of strikes by urban workers and widespread insurrections among the peasantry; resulted in some temporary reforms such as the creation of the duma. (p. 816)

Russo-Japanese War   War between Japan and Russia over territory in Manchuria beginning in 1905; Japan defeated the Russians, largely because of its naval power; Japan annexed Korea in 1910 as a result of military dominance. (p. 808)

Sadat, Anwar   Successor to Gamal Abdul Nasser as ruler of Egypt; acted to dismantle costly state programs; accepted peace treaty with Israel in 1973; opened Egypt to investment by Western nations. (p. 1011)

Safavid dynasty   Originally a Turkic nomadic group; family originated in

Sufi mystic group; espoused Shi'ism; conquered territory and established kingdom in region equivalent to modern Iran; lasted until 1722. (p. 609)

Sail al-Din [sä EEl al din, dEEn] Early 14th century Sufi mystic; began campaign to purify Islam; first member of Safavid dynasty. (p. 620)

"salt water" slaves Slaves transported from Africa; almost invariably black. (p. 655)

San Martin, José de Leader of independence movement in Rio de la Plata; led to independence of the United Provinces of the Rio de la Plata by 1816; later led independence movement in Chile and Peru as well. (p. 757)

Sandinista party Nicaraguan Socialist movement named after Augusto Sandino; successfully carried out a Socialist revolution in Nicaragua during the 1980s. (p. 949)

Sandino, Augusto Led a guerrilla resistance movement against U.S. occupation forces in Nicaragua; assassinated by Nicaraguan National Guard in 1934; became national hero and symbol of resistance to U.S. influence in Central America. (p. 951)

Santa Anna, General Antonio López de Seized power in Mexico after collapse of empire of Mexico in 1824; after brief reign of liberals, seized power in 1835 as caudillo; defeated by Texans in war for independence in 1836; defeated by United States in Mexican-American War in 1848; unseated by liberal rebellion in 1854. (p. 761)

Santa Cruz, Andrés Mestizo general who established union of independent Peru and Bolivia between 1829 and 1839. (p. 760)

Sarmiento, Domingo F. Liberal politician and president of Argentine Republic; author of *Facundo*, a critique of caudillo politics; increased international trade, launched internal reforms in education and transportation. (p. 762)

satyagraha [*sut* yuh gruhuh, suht *yä* gruh-] Literally, "truth-force"; Gandhi's policy of nonviolent opposition to British colonialism. (p. 971)

Schall, Adam Along with Matteo Ricci, Jesuit scholar in court of Ming emperors; skilled scientist; corrected calendars, forged cannons, fixed clocks; won few converts to Christianity. (p. 683)

school of National Learning New ideology that laid emphasis on Japan's unique historical experience and the revival of indigenous culture at the expense of Chinese imports such as Confucianism; typical of Japan in 18th century. (p. 687)

scientific revolution Culminated in 17th century; period of empirical advances associated with the development of wider theoretical generalizations; resulted in change in traditional beliefs of Middle Ages. (p. 530)

Secret Army Organization (OAS) Organization of French settlers in Algeria; led guerrilla war following independence during the 1960s; assaults directed against Arabs, Berbers, and French who advocated independence. (p. 984)

Selim III Sultan who ruled Ottoman Empire from 1789 to 1807; aimed at improving administrative efficiency and building a new army and navy; toppled by Janissaries in 1807. (p. 786)

sepoys Troops that served the British East India Company; recruited from various warlike peoples of India. (p. 731)

settlement colonies Areas, such as North America and Australia, that were both conquered by European invaders and settled by large numbers of European migrants who made the colonized areas their permanent home and dispersed and decimated the indigenous inhabitants. (p. 742)

Seven Years' War Fought both in continental Europe and also in overseas colonies between 1756 and 1763; resulted in Prussian seizures of land from Austria, English seizures of colonies in India and North America. (p. 576)

Shaka Ruler and reformer of Nguni peoples after 1818; reformed loose forces into regiments organized by lineage and age; created Zulu chiefdom that began to absorb or destroy its neighbors in southern Africa. (p. 650)

siege of Stalingrad Turning point in Germany's assault on Soviet Union in 1942; despite massive losses, Russians successfully defended the city; over one-third of German army surrendered. (p. 855)

Simon Commission In 1927 considered future Indian colonial government responses to nationalist demands; served to unify nationalist politicians on

both right and left of independence movement and also to heal rift between Muslims and Hindus. (p. 972)

Singapore Originally held by British as part of colony of Malaya; largely Chinese population; British attempted to create invulnerable naval base; captured by Japanese during World War II; emerged after war as independent port. (p. 916)

Sino-Japanese War War fought between Japan and Qing China between 1894 and 1895; resulted in Japanese victory; frustrated Japanese imperial aims because of Western insistence that Japan withdraw from Liaotung peninsula. (p. 824)

Smith, Adam Established liberal economics (*Wealth of Nations*, 1776); argued that government should avoid regulation of economy in favor of the operation of market forces. (p. 536)

social question Issues relating to repressed classes in Western Europe during the Industrial Revolution, particularly workers and women; became more critical than constitutional issues after 1870. (p. 713)

Social Revolutionary party Winners of the parliamentary majority of the first Russian election held following the November 1917 Bolshevik seizure of power; emphasized peasant support and rural reform; expelled in favor of Bolsheviks. (p. 891)

socialism Political movement with origins in Western Europe during the 19th century; urged an attack on private property in the name of equality; wanted state control of means of production, end to capitalist exploitation of the working man. (p. 713)

socialism in one country Joseph Stalin's concept of Russian communism based solely on the Soviet Union rather than the Leninist concept of international revolution; by cutting off the Soviet Union from other economies, the USSR avoided worst consequences of the Great Depression. (p. 848)

Socialist realism Attempt within the USSR to relate formal culture to the masses in order to avoid the adoption of Western European cultural forms; begun under Joseph Stalin; fundamental method of Soviet fiction, art, and literary criticism. (p. 901)

Socialist Youth Corps Formed in 1920 in China; dedicated to recruiting urban working classes to the nationalist revolution in China. (p. 1024)

sociedad de castas American social system based on racial origins; Europeans or whites at top, black slaves or Indians at bottom, mixed races in middle. (p. xxx)

Solidarity Polish labor movement formed in 1970s under Lech Walesa; challenged USSR-dominated government of Poland. (p. 899)

Solzhenitsyn, Aleksandr [sOlzhuh nEEt sin, sol-] Russian author critical of the Soviet regime; published trilogy on the Siberian prison camps, *The Gulag Archipelago.* (p. 903)

soviet Council of workers formed to seize city government in Petrograd in 1917; basis for early political organization of Russian Revolution. (p. 890)

Spanish Civil War War pitting authoritarian and military leaders in Spain against republicans and leftists between 1936 and 1939; Germany and Italy supported the royalists; the Soviet Union supported the republicans; led to victory of the royalist forces. (p. 852)

Spanish-American War War fought between Spain and the United States beginning in 1898; centered on Cuba and Puerto Rico; permitted American intervention in Caribbean, annexation of Puerto Rico and the Philippines. (p. 778)

Sputnik First unmanned spacecraft in 1957; sent up during Khrushchev's government; initiated space race with the United States. (p. 905)

St. Petersburg New capital of Russia established during the reign of Peter the Great. (p. 570)

Stalin, Joseph Successor to Lenin as head of the USSR; strongly nationalist view of Communism; represented anti-Western strain of Russian tradition; crushed opposition to his rule; established series of five-year plans to replace New Economic Policy; fostered agricultural collectivization; led USSR through World War II; furthered cold war with Western Europe and the United States; died in 1953. (p. 892)

Stolypin reforms Reforms introduced by the Russian minister Stolypin intended to placate the peasantry in the aftermath of the Revolution of 1905; included reduction in redemption payments, attempt to create market-oriented peasantry. (p. 817)

submarine warfare Use of the relatively new sea weapon was a major aspect of the German naval effort against the Western Allies in World War I; unrestricted submarine warfare was major factor in bringing the United States into active participation. (p. 841)

Suez Canal Built across Isthmus of Suez to connect Mediterranean Sea with Red Sea in 1869; financed by European investors; with increasing indebtedness of khedives, permitted intervention of British into Egyptian politics to protect their investment. (p. 791)

Sun Yat-sen Head of Revolutionary Alliance, organization that led 1911 revolt against Qing dynasty in China; briefly elected president in 1911, but yielded in favor of Yuan Shikai in 1912; created Nationalist party of China (Guomindang) in 1919; died in 1925. (p. 802)

Supreme Soviet Parliament of Union of Soviet Socialist Republics; elected by universal suffrage; actually controlled by Communist party; served to ratify party decisions. (p. 892)

Suriname Formerly a Dutch plantation colony on the coast of South America; location of runaway slave kingdom in 18th century; able to retain independence despite attempts to crush guerrilla resistance. (p. 859)

Swazi New African state formed on model of Zulu chiefdom; survived mfecane. (p. 652)

syndicalism Economic and political system based on the organization of labor; imported in Latin America from European political movements; militant force in Latin American politics. (p. 939)

Taiping rebellion Broke out in south China in the 1850s and early 1860s; led by Hong Xiuquan, a semi-Christianized prophet; sought to overthrow Qing dynasty and Confucian basis of scholar-gentry. (p. 800)

Taiwan Island off Chinese mainland; became refuge for Nationalist Chinese regime under Chiang Kai-shek as Republic of China in 1948; successfully retained independence with aid of United States; rapidly industrialized after 1950s. (p. 917)

Taj Mahal Most famous architectural achievement of Mughal India; originally built as a mausoleum for the wife of Shah Jahan, Mumtaz Mahal. (p. 632)

Tanzimat reforms Series of reforms in Ottoman Empire between 1839 and 1876; established Westernstyle university, state postal system, railways, extensive legal reforms; resulted in creation of new constitution in 1876. (p. 786)

Tayson Rebellion Peasant revolution in southern Vietnam during the late 1770s; succeeded in toppling the Nguyen dynasty; subsequently unseated the Trinh dynasty of northern Vietnam. (p. 1037)

technocrat New type of bureaucrat; intensely trained in engineering or economics and devoted to the power of national planning; came to fore in offices of governments following World War II. (p. 875)

Teheran Conference Meeting among leaders of the United States, Britain, and the Soviet Union in 1943; agreed to the opening of a new front in France. (p. 858)

terakoya Commoner schools founded during the Tokugawa shogunate in Japan to teach reading, writing and the rudiments of Confucianism; resulted in high literacy rate, approaching 40 percent, of Japanese males. (p. 818)

Thatcher, Margaret Conservative British prime minister from 1979 to 1991; held that office longer than any other person; worked to cut welfare and housing expenses, promote free enterprise. (p. 876)

third Rome Russian claim to be successor state to Roman and Byzantine empires; based in part on continuity of Orthodox church in Russia following fall of Constantinople in 1453. (p. 566)

third world Nations outside the capitalist industrial nations of the first world and the industrialized Communist nations of the second world; generally less economically powerful, but with varied economies. (p. 933)

Thirty Years' War War within the Holy Roman Empire between German Protestants and their allies (Sweden, Denmark, France) and the emperor and his ally, Spain; ended in 1648 after great destruction with Treaty of Westphalia. (p. 526)

Tilak, B. G. Believed that nationalism in India should be based on appeals to Hindu religiosity; worked to promote the restoration and revival of ancient Hindu traditions; offended Muslims and other religious groups; first Populist leader in India. (p. 965)

Time of Troubles Followed death of Ivan IV without heir early in 17th century; boyars attempted to use vacuum of power to reestablish their authority; ended with selection of Michael Romanov as tsar in 1613. (p. 568)

Tojo Hideki Japanese general; put down attempted military coup in 1936; increasingly interfered with civilian cabinets to block appointment of liberal bureaucrats; helped create increasingly militaristic series of prime ministers after 1936. (p. 915)

total war Warfare of the 20th century; vast resources and emotional commitments of belligerent nations were marshaled to support military effort; resulted from impact of industrialization on the military effort reflecting technological innovation and organizational capacity. (p. 856)

totalitarian state A new kind of government in the 20th century that exercised massive, direct control over virtually all the activities of its subjects; existed in Germany, Italy, and the Soviet Union. (p. 870)

Tragic Week Occurred in Argentina in 1919; government response to general strike of labor forces led to brutal repression under guise of nationalism. (p. 939)

trans-Siberian railroad Constructed in 1870s to connect European Russia with the Pacific; completed by the end of the 1880s; brought Russia into a more active Asian role. (p. 813)

transformisimo Political system in late 19th century Italy that promoted alliance of conservatives and liberals; parliamentary deputies of all parties supported the status quo. (p. 712)

Treaty of Gijanti Signed in 1757; reduced remaining Javanese princes to vassals of Dutch East India Company; allowed Dutch to monopolize production of coffee on Java. (p. 671)

Treaty of Guadalupe-Hidalgo Agreement that ended the Mexican-American War; provided for loss of Texas and California to the United States; left legacy of distrust of the United States in Latin America. (p. 767)

Treaty of Paris Arranged in 1763 following Seven Years' War; granted New France to England in exchange for return of French sugar island in Caribbean. (p. 555)

Treaty of Tordesillas [torduh *sEEl* yäs, *-sEE-*] Signed in 1494 between Castile and Portugal; clarified spheres of influence and rights of possession in New World; reserved Brazil and all newly discovered lands east of Brazil to Portugal; granted all lands west of Brazil to Spain. (p. 596)

Treaty of Versailles [ver *sI*, vuhr-] Ended World War I (1919); provided for the League of Nations; also punished Germany with loss of territories and the payment of reparations as a result of their "war guilt"; Russia also lost territories with the reestablishment of Eastern European nations such as Poland. (p. 845)

Treaty of Westphalia Ended Thirty Years' War in 1648; granted right to individual rulers within the Holy Roman Empire to choose their own religion—either Protestant or Catholic. (p. 526)

triangular trade Commerce linking Africa, the New World colonies, and Europe; slaves carried to America for sugar and tobacco transported to Europe. (p. 644)

Tripartite Pact Alliance of Japan, Germany, and Italy signed in September 1940; created alliance system for World War II. (p. 852)

Triple Alliance Alliance among Germany, Austria-Hungary, and Italy at the end of the 19th century; part of European alliance system and balance of power prior to World War I. (p. 722)

Triple Entente Alliance among Britain, Russia, and France at the outset of the 20th century; part of European alliance system and balance of power prior to World War I. (p. 722)

Truman, Harry American president from 1945 to 1952; less eager for smooth relations with the Soviet Union than Franklin Roosevelt; authorized use of atomic bomb during World War II; architect of American diplomacy that initiated the cold war. (p. 856)

Tutu, Osei [*tU* tU] Member of Oyoko clan of Akan peoples in Gold Coast region of Africa; responsible for creating unified Asante Empire; utilized Western firearms. (p. 647)

Ulyanov, Vladimir Ilyich [Ul *yä* nuhf] Better known as Lenin; most active Russian Marxist leader; insisted on importance of disciplined revolutionary cells; leader of Bolshevik Revolution of 1917. (p. 816)

Union of Soviet Socialist Republics Federal system of socialist republics established in 1923 in various ethnic regions of Russia; firmly controlled by Communist party; diminished nationalities protest under Bolsheviks; dissolved 1991. (p. 892)

United Fruit Company Most important foreign economic concern in Guatemala during the 20th century; attempted land reform aimed at United Fruit caused U.S. intervention in Guatemalan politics leading to ouster of reform government in 1954. (p. 944)

United Nations International organization formed in the aftermath of World War II; included all of the victorious Allies; its primary mission was to provide a forum for negotiating disputes. (p. 857)

Valdivia, Pedro de Spanish conquistador; conquered Araucanian Indians of Chile and established city of Santiago in 1541. (p. 589)

Vargas, Getúlio [*vär* guhs] Elected president of Brazil in 1929; launched centralized political program by imposing federal administrators over state governments; held off coups by communists in 1935 and fascists in 1937; imposed a new constitution based on Mussolini's Italy; leaned to communists after 1949; committed suicide in 1954. (p. 942)

viceroyalties Two major divisions of Spanish colonies in New World; one based in Lima; the other in Mexico City; direct representatives of the King. (p. 596)

Vichy French collaborationist government established in 1940 in southern France following defeat of French armies by the Germans. (p. 854)

Viet Cong Name given by Diem regime to Communist guerrilla movement in southern Vietnam; reorganized with northern Vietnamese assistance as the National Liberation Front in 1958. (p. 1042)

Viet Minh Communist-dominated Vietnamese nationalist movement; operated out of base in southern China during World War II; employed guerrilla tactics similar to the Maoists in China. (p. 1040)

Vietnamese Nationalist party Also known as the Vietnamese Quoc Dan Dong or VNQDD; active in 1920s as revolutionary force committed to violent overthrow of French colonialism. (p. 1039)

Villa, Pancho [*vEE* uh] Mexican revolutionary and military commander in northern Mexico during the Mexican Revolution; succeeded along with Emiliano Zapata in removing Díaz from power; also participated in campaigns that removed Madero and Huerta. (p. 935)

vizier [vi *zEEr, viz* yuhr] Ottoman equivalent of the Abbasid wazir; head of the Ottoman bureaucracy; after 15th century often more powerful than sultan. (p. 615)

Vodun African religious ideas and practices among descendants of African slaves in Haiti. (p. 659)

Wafd party [wäft] Egyptian nationalist party that emerged after an Egyptian delegation was refused a hearing at the Versailles Treaty negotiations following World War I; led by Sa'd Zaghläl; negotiations eventually led to limited Egyptian independence beginning in 1922. (p. 974)

War of Spanish Succession Resulted from Bourbon family's succession to Spanish throne in 1701; ended by Treaty of Utrecht in 1713; resulted in recognition of Bourbons, loss of some lands, grants of commercial rights to English and French. (p. 603)

Water Margin, The; Monkey; and The Golden Lotus Novels written during the Ming period in China; recognized as classics in their own time; established standards for Chinese prose literature. (p. 679)

Watt, James Devised a steam engine in 1770s during the Industrial Revolution that could be used for production; steam engine was utilized in textile industries, mining, and railroads. (p. 704)

welfare state New activism of the West European state in economic policy and welfare issues after World War II; introduced programs to reduce the impact of economic inequality; typically included medical programs and economic planning. (p. 870)

western front Front established in World War I; generally along line from Belgium to Switzerland; featured trench warfare and horrendous casualties for all sides in the conflict. (p. 841)

Whampoa Military Academy Founded in 1924; military wing of the Guomindang; first head of the academy was Chiang Kai-shek. (p. 1025)

White Dominions Colonies in which European settlers made up the overwhelming majority of the population; small numbers of native inhabitants were typically reduced by disease and wars of conquest; typical of British holdings in North America and Australia with growing independence in the 19th century. (p. 743)

white racial supremacy Belief in the inherent mental, moral, and cultural superiority of whites; peaked in acceptance in decades before World War I; supported by social science doctrines of social Darwinists such as Herbert Spencer. (p. 746)

Wilberforce, William British statesman and reformer; leader of abolitionist movement in English parliament; led abolition of English slave trade in 1807. (p. 660)

witchcraft hysteria Reflected resentment against the poor, uncertainties about religious truth; resulted in death of over 100,000 Europeans between 1590 and 1650; particularly common in Protestant areas. (p. 530)

Witte, Count [*vit* uh] Russian minister of finance from 1892 to 1903; economic modernizer responsible for high tariffs, improved banking system; encouraged Western investors to build factories in Russia. (p. 813)

Wollstonecraft, Mary Enlightenment feminist thinker in England; argued that new political rights should extend to women. (p. 537)

World Court Developed during period of internationalization; permanent court of arbitration established at The Hague in 1899; intended to remove causes of war; failed to resolve problems of international conflict in 20th century. (p. 839)

world economy Established by Europeans by the late 16th century; based on control of seas including the Atlantic and Pacific; created an international exchange of foods, diseases, and manufactured products. (p. 550

World War I Fought from 1914 to 1918; involved almost all European nations and their respective colonies; arose over conflict in the Balkans; resulted in victory of allied countries of Britain, France, Italy, and the United States; ended with Treaty of Versailles. (p. 839)

World War II Fought from 1939 to 1945 on fronts including western Europe, northern Africa, the Middle East, Eurasia, southwestern Asia, China, and the Pacific; ended with defeat of Germany and Japan in 1945. (p. 849)

Xavier, Francis [*zAY* vEE uhr, *zav* EE-, *zAY* vyuhr] Spanish Jesuit missionary; worked in India in 1540s among the outcaste and lower caste groups; made little headway among elites. (p. 672)

Yalta Conference Meeting among leaders of the United States, Britain, and the Soviet Union in 1945; agreed to Soviet entry into the Pacific war in return for possessions in Manchuria, organization of the United Nations; disputed the division of political organization in the eastern European states to be reestablished after the war. (p. 858)

yellow peril Western term for perceived threat of Japanese imperialism around 1900; met by increased Western imperialism in region. (p. 826)

Yeltsin, Boris Began to move up the ladder of the Communist party in Soviet Union in 1968, becoming First Secretary of the Moscow City Party Committee in 1985; initially a loyal backer of Gorbachev but increasingly criticized him for unduly slow pace of reform; stood up to a coup attempt in 1991 but then managed to displace Gorbachev; in his position as president of the Russian Republic, sponsored several subsequent constitutional provisions and weathered battles with opponents in Parliament. (p. 909)

Yuan Shikai [yU *än shEE kI, yYän*] Warlord in northern China after fall of Qing dynasty; hoped to seize imperial throne; president of China after 1912; resigned in the face of Japanese invasion in 1916. (p. 1021)

zaibatsu [zI *bät* sU] Huge industrial combines created in Japan in the 1890s as part of the process of industrialization. (p. 823)

Zapata, Emilano Mexican revolutionary and military commander of peasant guerrilla movement after 1910 centered in Morelos; succeeded along with Pancho Villa in removing Díaz from power; also participated in campaigns that removed Madero and Huerta; demanded sweeping land reform. (p. 935)

zemstvoes [*zemst* vO, pl. -stvos] Local political councils created as part of reforms of Tsar Alexander II (1860s); gave some Russians, particularly middle-class professionals, some experience in government; councils had no impact on national policy. (p. 812)

Zhenghe expeditions [zang *g*EE] Series of seven overseas trade expeditions under third Ming emperor, Yunglo; led by court eunuch Zhenghe between 1405 and 1433; only Chinese attempt to create worldwide trade empire. (p. 680)

Zhou Enlai [*j*O en *lI*] After Mao Zedong, the most important leader of the Communist party in China from the 1930s until his death in 1976; premier of China from 1954; notable as perhaps the most cosmopolitan and moderate of the inner circle of Communist leaders. (p. 1024)

Zionism Movement originating in Eastern Europe during the 1860s and 1870s that argued that the Jews must return to a Middle Eastern Holy Land; eventually identified with the settlement of Palestine. (p. 973)

Credits

LITERARY CREDITS

PART IV

Chapter 24
Excerpt from *Imperial Russia: A Source Book, 1700-1917* by Basil Dmytryshyn. Copyright © 1999 by Academic International Press, Gulf Breeze, FL. Reprinted with the permission of the publisher.

Chapter 27
Excerpts from *Africa Remembered: Narratives by West Africans from the Era of the Slave Trade* by Philip Curtin. (Prospect Heights, IL; Waveland Press, Inc., 1967 [reissued 1997]. All rights reserved. Reprinted by permission of Waveland Press, Inc.

Chapter 28
From *Cultural Atlas of Japan* by Martin Collcutt, et al., 1988. Copyright © 1988. Reprinted by permission of Andromeda Oxford Ltd., Abington, UK.

PART V

Chapter 30
Map from *A Short History of Indonesia* by Ailsa Zainuíddin. Copyright © 1968 by Greenwood Publishing. Reprinted with permission of Greenwood Publishing Group, Inc., Westport, CT.

Chapter 32
From abridgment of "A People Made New (1902-1905)" by Liang Qichao, from *Sources of Chinese Tradition* by William T. DeBary, Tait Chan, and Burton Watson. Copyright © 1960 by Columbia University Press. Reprinted with permission of the publisher.

Chapter 33
From *Cultural Atlas of Japan* by Martin Collcutt, et al., 1988. Copyright © 1988. Reprinted by permission of Andromeda Oxford Ltd., Abington, UK.

PART VI

Chapter 36
Adaptation of Map, "The Civil War" from *The World Atlas of Revolutions* by Andrew Wheatcroft. Text copyright © 1983 Andrew Wheatcroft, cartography copyright © 1983 Hamish Hamilton Ltd. Reproduced by permission of Hamish Hamilton Ltd.

Chapter 36
Excerpts from *Readings in Russian Civilization, Vol. 3,* edited by Thomas Riha. Copyright © 1969 by The University of Chicago Press. Reprinted by permission of The University of Chicago Press.

Chapter 39
Excert (9 lines) from "Snow Upon Paris," from *Selected Poems* by Léopld Sédar Senghor, translated by John Reed and Clive Wake. Copyright © 1974 by Oxford University Press. Reprinted by permission of Oxford University Press.

Chapter 41
Adaptation of map, "The Development of the World Economy" from *The Times Atlas of World History*, edited by G. Barraclough. Copyright © 1984 by Times Books Ltd. Reprinted by permission.

Adaptation of map, "Industrialization Outsdie of Europe and North American" from *The Times Atlas of World History*, edited by G. Barraclough. Copyright © 1984 by Times Books Ltd. Reprinted by permission.

Adaptation of two maps, "The Northern Expedition" and "Warlord Groups" from *The Times Atlas of World History*, edited by G. Barraclough. Copyright © 1984 by Times Books Ltd. Reprinted by permission.

PHOTO CREDITS

PART IV

CHAPTER 22
Chapter Opener 22 Alinari /Art Resource, NY **Figure 22.02** On loan to the Scottish National Portrait Gallery, by permission of the Earl of Rosbery **22.03** Prints Division, The New York Public Library, Astor, Lenox and Tilden Foundations **22.04** Art Resource, NY

CHAPTER 23
Chapter Opener 23 The Asian Art Museum of San Francisco, The Avery Brundage Collection, B60 D78+ (detail) **Figure 23.01** North Wind Picture Archives **23.03** Bibliotecca Medices Laurenziana, Florence, Italy **23.04** Corbis **23.05** Library of Congress **23.06** The Granger Collection, New York **23.07** V&A Picture Library

CHAPTER 24
Chapter Opener 24 © Fotocommissie/Rijksmuseum Foundation, Amsterdam **Figure 24.01** SOVFOTO **24.03** By couresty of the Marjorie Merriweather Post Foundation of the District of Columbia **24.04** SOVFOTO **Visualizing the Past** SOVFOTO

CHAPTER 25
Chapter Opener 25 Bibliothèque Nationale de France, Paris **Figure 25.01** Bridgeman Art Library, London **25.02** Library of Congress **25.03** Courtesy of the Hispanic Society of America, New York
25.07 Arxiu, MAS **25.08** DeBry. America, 1585

CHAPTER 26
Chapter Opener 26 © British Museum **Figure 26.01** Bettmann/Corbis **26.02** Luigi Mayer/Bridgeman Art Library, London **26.03** National Maritime Museum, Greewich, Emgland **26.04** Dr. Laurence Lockhart, Cambridge, England **26.05** New

Index

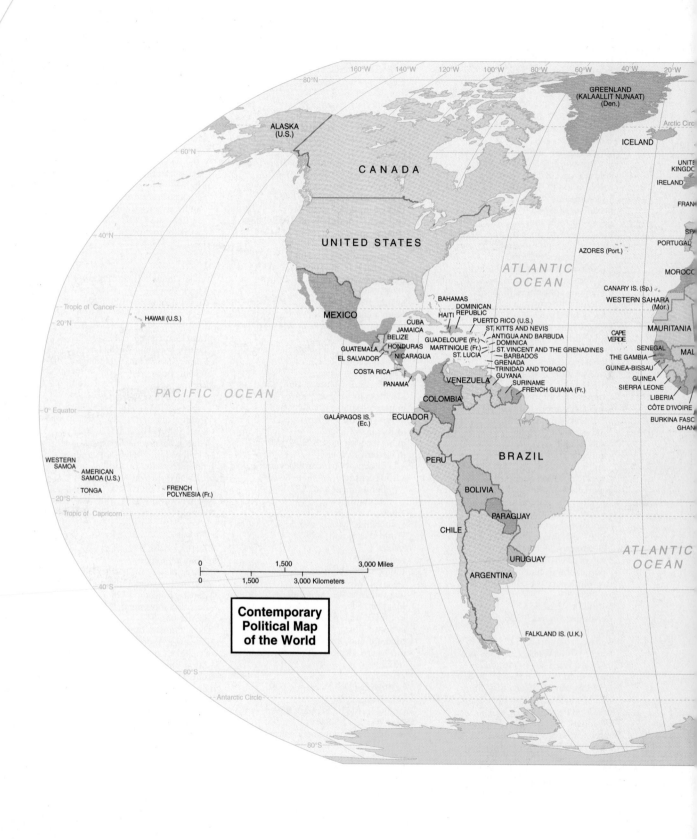

Contemporary
Political Map
of the World

20°E   40°E   60°E   80°E   100°E   120°E   140°E   160°E

ARCTIC OCEAN

NORWAY
SWEDEN
FINLAND
DENMARK
NETH.
GER.
BELG.
LUX.
CZ. REP.
AUS.
SWITZ.
SLOV.
CRO.
ITALY
B.-H.
YUGO.
ALB.
GREECE
MALTA
TUNISIA

LITH.
RUS.
LATVIA
ESTONIA
POLAND
BELARUS
UKRAINE
SLVK.
HUNG.
MOLDOVA
ROMANIA
BULGARIA
MAC.
GEORGIA
ARMENIA
AZERBAIJAN
TURKEY
CYPRUS
ISRAEL
LEB.
SYRIA
JORDAN

RUSSIA

KAZAKHSTAN

UZBEKISTAN
TURKMENISTAN
KYRGYZSTAN
TAJIKISTAN

MONGOLIA

CHINA

N. KOREA
S. KOREA
JAPAN

PACIFIC
OCEAN

ALGERIA
LIBYA
EGYPT

IRAQ
IRAN
KUWAIT
BAHRAIN
SAUDI ARABIA
QATAR
UNITED ARAB
EMIRATES
OMAN

AFGHANISTAN
PAKISTAN
NEPAL
BHUTAN
BANGLADESH

INDIA

MYANMAR
(BURMA)
LAOS
THAILAND
VIETNAM
CAMBODIA

Hong Kong
Macao (Port.)

TAIWAN

NORTHERN
MARIANA
IS. (U.S.)

GUAM (U.S.)

MARSHALL
IS.

NIGER
CHAD
SUDAN
YEMEN
ERITREA
DJIBOUTI

NIGERIA
BENIN
TOGO
CENTRAL
AFRICAN REP.
CAMEROON
EQ.
GUINEA
GABON
CONGO
SÃO TOMÉ
& PRINCIPE
CABINDA
(Ang.)

ETHIOPIA
SOMALIA

RWANDA
UGANDA
DEM. REP. OF
THE CONGO
BURUNDI
KENYA
TANZANIA

MALDIVES

SRI
LANKA

PHILIPPINES

BRUNEI

MALAYSIA

SINGAPORE

PALAU

FEDERATED STATES
OF MICRONESIA

NAURU

KIRIBATI

TUVALU

COMOROS
MAYOTTE (Fr.)
SEYCHELLES

INDONESIA

PAPUA
NEW
GUINEA

SOLOMON
IS.

ANGOLA
ZAMBIA
MALAWI
NAMIBIA
ZIMBABWE
BOTSWANA
MOZAMBIQUE
SOUTH
AFRICA
SWAZILAND
LESOTHO

MADAGASCAR
RÉUNION
(Fr.)
MAURITIUS

INDIAN
OCEAN

AUSTRALIA

VANUATU

FIJI

NEW
CALEDONIA
(Fr.)

NEW
ZEALAND

ANTARCTICA